INTRODUCTION TO
FINANCE

The Addison-Wesley Series in Finance

INTRODUCTION TO
FINANCE

LAWRENCE J. GITMAN
San Diego State University

JEFF MADURA
Florida Atlantic University

Addison
Wesley

Boston San Francisco New York
London Toronto Sydney Tokyo Singapore Madrid
Mexico City Munich Paris Cape Town Hong Kong Montreal

Executive Editor: Denise Clinton
Project Manager: Rebecca Ferris
Development Editor: Ann Torbert
Managing Editor: James Rigney
Production Supervisor: Nancy Fenton
Marketing Manager: Dara Lanier
Supplements Editor: Meredith Gertz
Media Producer: Jennifer Pelland
Editorial Assistant: Andrea Botticelli
Project Coordination, Text Design, Art Studio, and
    Electronic Page Makeup: Thompson Steele, Inc.
Design Manager: Regina Hagen
Cover Designer: Leslie Haimes
Cover Images: © PhotoDisk; William Taufic/Stock Market
Senior Manufacturing Buyer: Hugh Crawford
Printer and Binder: Quebecor World
Cover Printer: The Lehigh Press

Library of Congress Cataloging-in-Publication Data

Gitman, Lawrence J.
    Introduction to finance / Lawrence J. Gitman, Jeff Madura.—1st ed.
        p. cm.
    ISBN 0-201-63537-2
    1. Finance. I. Madura, Jeff. II. Title.

HG173.G58 2001
332—dc21   00-029966

ISBN 0-201-63537-2

2345678910—RNT—0403020100

*To our colleagues, whose
dedication to teaching finance
enriches students each day*

Brief Contents

Detailed Contents

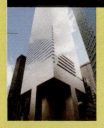

Chapter 3

**Corporate
Securities:
Bonds
and Stocks   51**

Chapter 4

**Interest Rate
Fundamentals   73**

Part 1

Part 2   Financial Tools for Firms and Investors   101

Chapter 5

Time Value of Money   102

Chapter 6

Return and Risk   147

Part 3   Financial Management   263

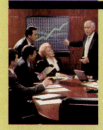

Chapter 9

The Firm and Its Financial Environment   264

Chapter 10

**Capital Budgeting:
Cash Flow
Principles   295**

Chapter 11

**Capital Budgeting
Techniques:
Certainty
and Risk   327**

Chapter 12

Cost of Capital   360

Chapter 13

Capital Structure and Dividends 388

Chapter 14

Financial Planning   423

Chapter 15

**Short-Term
Financial
Management   450**

Part 4   Investment Management   491

Chapter 16

Investment Information and Transactions   492

Chapter 17

How External Forces Affect Firm Value   524

Chapter 18

Investing in Stocks   551

Chapter 19

Investing in Bonds   581

Chapter 20

**Mutual Funds
and Asset
Allocation   613**

Chapter 21

**Derivative
Securities   637**

Part 5 How Investors Monitor and Control a Firm's Managers   665

Chapter 22

Corporate Control and Governance   666

PREFACE

The field of finance is broad and dynamic. Its breadth is both geographic, in that it is a global discipline, and functional, in that it involves transactions between suppliers and demanders of funds. Because of ongoing developments in technology, new legislation, and other innovations, the field is rapidly changing. Virtually everyone is directly impacted by the field of finance.

Rationale for This Text

For many years, the conventional wisdom in business schools and departments has been to focus the single required finance course on the role of the chief financial officer in a large corporation. This narrow view of finance as financial management made sense to most business faculty, who viewed the school's mission as preparing students to work in the treasury operations of the traditional corporation.

But times have certainly changed. Not only is an information and technology revolution changing the way firms are organized and the way they operate, but the financial marketplace is also undergoing a transformation. Today more financial professionals are involved in forming, managing, and "growing" firms. The emerging economy is being driven by new, rapidly growing businesses that are continuously accessing the expanding marketplace to obtain the financing they need to nurture great ideas into great businesses. In addition, the firm and its employees are much more active on the buy side of the market, managing company pension plans and self-directed investment/retirement programs.

Although finance has always encompassed three key areas—financial management, financial markets, and investments—there is now a greater need for students to be exposed to all three areas. This need exists for a number of reasons. First, finance is not just financial management. Second, today's financial managers and professionals are deeply involved in both sides of the financial marketplace: They issue as well as buy or sell securities. Third, many business students are required only to take a single finance course, so this course should expose them to the breadth of the field, rather than solely to financial management. Fourth, at some schools, non-business majors are eager to take a course that is broad enough to cover topics in which they have an interest (financial markets and, particularly, investments), even if they do not plan to pursue a career in financial management. And fifth, exposure to the entire field is consistent with the broadened responsibilities of all financial professionals—managers, intermediaries, and investors—in today's economy.

Objective and Primary Goals in This Text

Simply stated, this text's objective is to provide students with practical understanding of the scope, interrelationships, career opportunities, terminology, and key analytical and decision tools used by finance professionals in today's global environment. Achievement of the key aspects of the text's objective is tied to six **primary goals.**

Goal 1: Expose students to the breadth of finance. This goal differentiates this text from other introductory finance texts. The text provides functional breadth by covering the key aspects of financial management, financial markets, and investments—the three key areas of finance. Geographic breadth is provided by describing global aspects of the activities of financial professionals operating in each area of finance.

Goal 2: Provide an understanding of the interrelationships among the three areas of finance. This goal supports Goal 1 by making the dynamic interactions among the areas clear to the student. The student should understand how the global financial marketplace functions to allow firms (financial managers) and investors to achieve their investment and financing goals efficiently.

Goal 3: Make students aware of the many career opportunities in finance. As is consistent with the goal of most introductory business courses, the text makes clear the many career opportunities available in finance. Students will come away with an understanding of the numerous finance jobs in financial management, financial institutions, and investments. This insight should better prepare them to choose or redirect their planned career focus.

Goal 4: Acquaint students with the vocabulary of finance. The text clearly defines the key terms in all three areas of finance. A marginal glossary of all terms and the use of these terms in subsequent text discussions and Review Questions familiarize the student with the vocabulary of finance.

Goal 5: Expose students to the key tools used by financial managers and investors in analysis and decision making. Throughout the text, popular analytical and decision tools are introduced, demonstrated, and evaluated in light of the objectives of the financial manager or investor employing them. In addition to numerous examples demonstrating these tools, many applications of these tools are included in the end-of-chapter materials. Our intention is to provide students with useful insights into the concepts, tools, and techniques routinely used by finance professionals.

Goal 6: Keep all discussions practical. The student should understand how the financial world really works—that is, the activities and interactions between the three areas. All discussions, examples, pedagogical elements, and end-of-chapter materials have been crafted to emphasize the actual application and use of the concepts, tools, and techniques presented. The net result should give the student a real-world understanding of the fundamental aspects of finance.

Organization of the Text

This text was carefully designed to meet its objective and primary goals. It is divided into five parts and contains 22 chapters. The first chapter, which precedes Part 1, provides an overview of the financial environment that describes the basic roles and interactions among the three areas of finance—firms (financial managers), investors, and markets. The five part titles are:

Part 1: The Financial Marketplace
Part 2: Financial Tools for Firms and Investors
Part 3: Financial Management
Part 4: Investment Management
Part 5: How Investors Monitor and Control a Firm's Managers

Each of these parts is closely integrated with those that precede them. Rather than merely presenting the three areas of finance as separate topics, this text is integrative. The interrelatedness between financial management, financial markets, and investments that is established in Chapter 1 is continuously reinforced throughout the text, and its practical ramifications are summarized and strongly emphasized in Part 5. All text discussions recognize and reinforce the global aspects of the topics presented.

Part 1 includes three chapters that together describe the financial marketplace. The roles and interactions among financial institutions and markets, the key securities (bonds and stocks), and the fundamentals of interest rates are discussed. Part 2 presents the financial tools used by both firms and investors. It includes four chapters devoted to the time value of money, return and risk, valuation, and financial statements and analysis, respectively. These topics, which are routinely used by both financial managers and investors, are developed in such a way as to allow their straightforward application to the subsequent discussions. After covering Part 2, an instructor can proceed either to cover Part 3 on financial management or Part 4 on investments without losing continuity.

The seven chapters in Part 3 present the "traditional" financial management topics in a focused manner, but with enough detail to provide the student with the core coverage currently available in abbreviated editions of the leading financial management texts. The first chapter's description of the firm and environment is followed by capital budgeting (two chapters), cost of capital, capital structure and dividends, financial planning, and short-term financial management. The coverage of financial management was carefully determined on the basis of market research, reviewer feedback, and the experience we have gained from years of teaching. Our goal was to make sure that the text instills a core understanding of financial management. We strongly believe that the careful crafting of the material achieves our objective and that the transition from a traditional introduction to financial management course to the more enlightened approach will be seamless and add significant value to the students' first (and possibly only) exposure to finance.

Part 4 is devoted to investment management. Like Part 3 on financial management, this part builds on the basic financial tools presented in Part 2. It contains six chapters that together give the student a solid foundation in investments and an understanding of this area of the financial marketplace. Topics covered in this part include investment information and transactions, how external forces affect a firm's value, investing in stocks, investing in bonds, mutual funds and asset allocation, and derivative securities. Coverage of these topics was developed on the basis of market research, reviewer feedback, and our own experience. In addition, the discussions were carefully crafted for consistency with the goals cited earlier in this Preface.

The final part of the text, Part 5, presents a summarizing chapter that draws on modern finance theory to explain, in a simple and understandable fashion, how corporate control and governance provide the mechanisms through which investors effectively monitor and control a firm's managers. This chapter ties together the actions and activities of financial managers, financial markets, and investors in a way that fully reinforces the text's message that the three areas of finance exist in a dynamic, interactive environment.

How This Text Is Different

The preceding discussions make it clear that this text differs from both traditional financial management texts and existing introduction to finance texts. The key difference is its integrative focus. The three areas of finance are not presented as isolated topics but, rather, are developed in an interactive, dynamic, global framework that gives the reader a true introduction to the field of finance. Some of the key conceptual differences between this text and others are the following:

- The text explains how the investment decisions of financial managers require funding and how financial markets can facilitate the flow of funds from individual investors and institutional investors (financial institutions) to the firms.

- Financial management concepts are discussed with an emphasis on how they are related to financial markets and institutions, and to investors.

- The assessment and valuation of firms by investors is given much attention. Financial managers make investment decisions that are supposed to maximize the wealth of the shareholders who own the firm's stock. The text explains how investors monitor a firm's decisions to ensure that the firm's managers are acting in their best interest. Because investors do not have the same information about a firm as the firm's managers, they rely on a separate set of indicators to evaluate firms. The type of information that investors use to monitor firms is discussed, with emphasis on the sources that are available.

- When assessing or valuing a firm, investors consider not only the characteristics of the firm but also the impact of external forces. The potential impact of external forces on a firm's value is not emphasized in most introductory courses, yet it is one of the most popular topics in the financial news. This text identifies the external forces that influence a firm's performance and are therefore monitored by investors. It also explains how these forces affect a firm's value.

● Three of the most widely discussed investments topics are investing in mutual funds, asset allocation, and investing in derivative securities. The text discusses these topics, because many students will need to understand them for their own personal investing, even if they do not pursue careers related to these topics.

● In assessing various investment alternatives, investors sometimes take action in response to an investment that is not performing as well as it should. Investors not only provide funding for firms but may take actions to ensure that the firms are using the funds wisely. Thus financial management is implicitly controlled within constraints by investors who monitor and influence a firm's managers. These relationships are clearly explained in the text.

The Teaching/Learning System

Introduction to Finance's Teaching/Learning System is state-of-the-art. The system is driven by a set of carefully crafted learning goals that help guide and organize student reading and study. In addition, numerous other features facilitate teaching and reinforce student learning to promote achievement of the learning goals. Each of the system's key elements is described in the paragraphs that follow.

The Teaching/Learning System is anchored in a set of about six proven Learning Goals (LGs) per chapter. Marked by a special icon, which is shown here in the margin, the Learning Goals are listed at the start of each chapter, tied to major headings, reviewed point by point at the chapter's end, and noted in assignment material and supplements such as the Test Bank and Study Guide. These goals focus students' attention on what material they need to learn, where it can be found in the chapter, and whether they have mastered it by the end of the chapter. In addition, instructors can easily build lectures and assignments around the LGs.

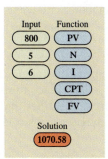

Example Method   The Example Method is an important component of the Teaching/Learning System, because it infuses practical demonstrations into the learning process. Seeing a financial concept or technique applied in a realistic example provides students with immediate reinforcement that helps cement their understanding of that concept or technique. Where applicable, the solution of each example shows the use of time lines, tables, and financial calculators. Calculator keystrokes of inputs, functions, and solutions are highlighted in discussions and examples of time value calculations in Chapter 5 and in the application of those techniques in subsequent chapters. Appendix A and the laminated table card included in all new books contain financial tables and note the basic calculator keystrokes for the most popular financial calculators.

NewsLine Boxes   Articles excerpted from financial news sources such as *The Wall Street Journal* appear in NewsLine boxes. The boxes encourage students to follow the financial news by introducing them to relevant news articles reported daily in the press. A short abstract focuses students' reading of each selection.

Key Equations   Key Equations are printed in color throughout the text to help students identify the most important mathematical relationships.

Marginal Glossary   Throughout the text, key terms and their definitions appear in the text margin when they are first introduced. In addition, these terms are printed in boldface type in the index so that the glossary entry is easy to find.

International Coverage   Discussions of the international dimensions of chapter topics are integrated throughout the book. Coverage of international events and topics is highlighted with an icon in the text margin and integrated into chapter learning goals and the end-of-chapter summary and exercises.

Review Questions   Review Questions appear at the end of each section of the chapter (positioned before the next first-level heading) and are marked with a special design element. As students progress through the chapter, they can test their understanding of each key concept, technique, and practice before moving on to the next section.

Tying It All Together   In keeping with the text's goal of providing an understanding of the interrelationships among the three areas of finance, each chapter concludes with Tying it All Together, a summary paragraph. The respective roles of financial managers, financial markets, and investors are then clearly outlined in an Integrative Table.

Summary   End-of-chapter Summaries are keyed to the learning goals, each of which is restated for reinforcement at the beginning of the appropriate paragraph in the Summary. The learning goal–driven Summary facilitates students' review of the key material that was presented to support mastery of the given goal.

Self-Test Exercises   At the end of most chapters, one or more Self-Test Exercises are included. Each exercise is keyed to the corresponding learning goal and software icons, as appropriate. Appendix B contains all answers and worked-out solutions to the self-test exercises in one location, marked with an easy-to-spot purple stripe on the edge of the page. These demonstration exercises and their answers and solutions help to strengthen students' understanding of the topics and techniques presented.

Chapter Exercises   A comprehensive set of exercises provides students with multiple self-testing opportunities and gives professors a wide choice to assign material. A short descriptor at the beginning of every exercise identifies the concept or technique that it has been designed to test. All exercises are keyed, via icons, to the learning goals and software resources.

Web Exercises   Web Exercises at the end of each chapter link the chapter topic to related sites on the Internet and require students to find information to answer various questions. These exercises will capture student interest in researching with the Internet, while educating them about finance-related sites. All the Web Exercises are available in up-to-date form on the text's Web site, www.awl.com/gitman_madura. In addition, an ongoing Fantasy Stock Market Game Web Exercise appears in Appendix C at the end of the book.

Continuing Case   At the end of each of the book's five parts is a Continuing Case that challenges students to use what they have learned in the several chapters. The case presents a financial dilemma for an Internet start-up company called exam-ace.net. Probing questions emphasize the small-business issues, communications challenges, team building, and ethical considerations that business people face.

Contemporary Design   A vibrant, contemporary design, with pedagogical use of colors in most charts and graphs, draws reader attention to features of the learning system. Bars of data are highlighted with color in tables and then graphed in the same color so that visual learners can immediately see relationships among the data.

First-Rate Supplements

The Teaching/Learning System includes a variety of useful supplements for teachers and for students.

Instructor's Manual   Prepared by Kurt R. Jesswein, Murray State University. This comprehensive resource pulls together a wide variety of teaching tools so that instructors can use the text easily and effectively in the classroom. Each chapter provides an overview of key topics, teaching tips, and detailed answers and solutions to all review questions and end-of-chapter exercises. Each part concludes with answers to the Continuing Case questions.

Test Bank   Authored by Curt Bacon, Southern Oregon University. The Test Bank contains 1,750 questions in short-essay and multiple-choice formats. For quick test selection and construction, each chapter features a handy chart for identifying each type of question, what learning goal it tests, and its level of difficulty.

Study Guide   Written by Kurt R. Jesswein, Murray State University. The Study Guide is an integral component of the Learning System. It offers many tools for studying finance. Each chapter contains the following features: chapter summary arranged in order of learning goals, chapter outline keyed to learning goals, key formulas list, and study tips. In addition, each chapter offers a wealth of practice exercises, including self-test exercises and true-false, multiple-choice, and essay questions. Finally, thumbnail printouts of the PowerPoint Lecture Presentation at the end of the guide facilitate classroom note taking.

Instructor's Resource Disk (IRD)

Fully compatible with Windows and Macintosh operating systems, this CD-ROM provides a number of resources.

PowerPoint Lecture Presentation   Created by Daniel Borgia, Florida Gulf Coast University. This presentation combines lecture notes with figures, tables, and equations selected from the textbook. The lecture presentations for each chapter can be viewed electronically in the classroom or can be printed as transparency masters.

Computerized Test Bank   The easy-to-use testing software (TestGen-EQ with QuizMaster-EQ for Windows and Macintosh) is a valuable test preparation tool that allows professors to view, edit, and add questions.

Instructor's Manual/Test Bank   For added convenience, the IRD also includes Microsoft Word files for the entire contents of the Instructor's Manual and Test Bank.

Companion Web Site

Available at www.awl.com/gitman_madura, the Web site provides online access to innovative teaching and learning tools.

Ten-question multiple-choice quizzes for each chapter allow students to gauge their grasp of concepts.

To enhance students' mastery of mathematically based concepts and techniques, we offer a number of **software resources**. All students who purchase a new copy of the text will receive an individualized coupon code that will allow them to download the software from the text's Web site at no additional cost. A system of icons in the end-of-chapter exercises alert students to corresponding software resources, which include the following:

Tutor   The Tutor helps students identify and solve various types of finance problems using Excel worksheets. Most important, Tutor provides an unlimited supply of problem types constructed via random-number generation so that students can get the practice necessary to master calculations.

Problem Solver   Many students are intimidated by the mathematics of finance and lose sight of the underlying concepts. Problem Solver addresses this issue by providing short, menu-driven Excel worksheets that are an efficient way to perform financial computations. Once the student inputs the data, Problem Solver performs the calculation. Page references are included for each computation.

Excel Spreadsheet Templates   Excel spreadsheets are universally accepted as powerful computational tools. Pre-programmed spreadsheet templates are provided for students to input data and solve problems.

An **Online Career Center** shows students career options in the finance field. Organized around job positions, the site features links to educational programs, information on certification requirements, career paths, and job-seeking advice.

An online syllabus builder enables instructors to create a calendar of assignments for each class and to track quiz grades with an electronic gradebook.

For students who use financial calculators, a guide called *Using Financial and Business Calculators* that supports Texas Instruments BA-35 and BAII Plus and Hewlett-Packard HP 12C, 17BII, and 19BII models is available in PDF format.

For added convenience, many of the instructor supplements are available for downloading from the site. Please contact your sales representative for the instructor resources password and information on obtaining Web content in WebCT and BlackBoard versions.

Acknowledgments

This project benefited immensely from feedback from colleagues, practitioners, and members of the publishing team. In particular, many mail survey respondents, focus group participants, and reviewers helped shape our vision. Addison Wesley Longman sought the advice of many excellent reviewers, all of whom strongly influenced various aspects of this book. The following individuals provided extremely useful evaluations:

Curt Bacon, Southern Oregon University
Daniel Borgia, Florida Gulf Coast University
Dallas Brozik, Marshall University
K.C. Chen, California State University, Fresno
Dean Drenk, Montana State University, Bozeman
Joe Fowler, Florida Community College at Jacksonville
Sharon Garrison, University of Arizona
Beverly Hadaway, University of Texas at Austin
William Handorf, George Washington University
John Helmuth, University of Michigan
Walter Hollingsworth, University of Mobile
Kenneth Huggins, Metropolitan State College
Peppi Kenny, Western Illinois University
Ed Krohn, Miami-Dade Community College, Kendall Campus
Lalatendu Misra, University of Texas at San Antonio
Oris Odom, University of Texas at Tyler
Mary L. Piotrowski, Northern Arizona University
Kean Song, Prairie View A&M University
James Tripp, Western Illinois University
David Upton, Virginia Commonwealth University
Chet Waters, Durham Technical College
Jill Wetmore, Saginaw Valley State University
Ray Whitmire, Texas A&M, Corpus Christi
Howard Whitney, Franklin University

Special acknowledgment is due to several members of our book team whose vision, creativity, and ongoing support are great assets: to Marlene Bellamy of Writeline Associates for excerpting the NewsLine boxes; to Bernard W. Weinrich of St. Louis Community College, Forest Park Campus, for preparing compelling Web exercises and for his accuracy-checking skills; to Mary L. Piotrowski of Northern Arizona University and Kean Song of Prairie View A&M University for their expert writing of end-of-chapter exercises; to Kurt R. Jesswein of Murray State University for authoring the Instructor's Manual and Study Guide; to Curt Bacon of Southern Oregon University for writing the Test Bank; to Daniel Borgia of Florida Gulf Coast University for crafting the PowerPoint Lecture Presentation; to Michael Griffin of KMT Software for developing the Excel-based software; and to Drew Windsor of the University of Central Florida for creating the innovative and effective structure used to prepare Chapter 15 on short-term financial management. All of your efforts are truly appreciated.

We wish to thank the publishing team assembled by Addison Wesley—including Denise Clinton, Andrea Botticelli, Gina Hagen, Nancy Fenton, Dara Lanier, Jennifer Pelland and others who worked on this book—for the inspiration and the perspiration that defines teamwork. Elinor Stapleton and all the people at Thompson Steele, Inc., deserve recognition. The outstanding work of Ann Torbert, whose development skills, creativity, expertise, and hard work have contributed to the book's standard of excellence is greatly appreciated. A special thanks is also due to Rebecca Ferris, who was involved in all phases of the production of this text. Finally, we thank the formidable sales force in finance, whose ongoing efforts keep the business fun!

We invite colleagues to share with us their classroom experiences using this book and its package, in care of the Acquisitions Editor in Finance, Addison Wesley Longman, One Jacob Way, Reading, Massachusetts 01867-3999. Your constructive criticism is much valued.

The Financial Environment: Firms, Investors, and Markets

LG1 Define the term *finance* and explain why finance is relevant to students.

LG2 Identify the components of the financial environment.

LG3 Explain how investors monitor managers to ensure that managerial decisions are in the best interests of the owners.

LG4 Describe how the financial environment has become internationalized.

LG1 What Is Finance?

Virtually all individuals and organizations earn or raise money and spend or invest money. **Finance** is the processes by which money is transferred (financing and investing) among businesses, individuals, and governments.

The activities involved in the field of finance are evident in the financial news that is reported on television shows such as *Money Line* and in business periodicals such as the *Wall Street Journal*. Every day, financial decisions made within firms result in financial actions, such as those listed here, which were taken from the financial news:

- Dell Computer expands its product line.
- The Gap builds additional stores.
- Nike closes a production plant in Asia.
- Du Pont restructures its chemicals business.
- Ford Motor Co. borrows $3 billion.
- Motorola acquires a company in Japan.
- Perot Systems issues stock valued at $3 billion.

Note that each action reflects a decision on either how to invest funds or how to obtain funds.

These financial actions are important not only to the firms involved but also to both existing and prospective investors in the firm. Financial decisions influence the value of the firm as reflected in its stock price, which affects how much investors earn on their investments in the firm. Thus many financial news headlines focus on the impact of a financial event on the firm's stock price:

- The stock price of Perot Systems rises by 50 percent within 2 days of its stock offering.
- Nike's stock price declines by 5 percent as a result of poor performance.
- Apple Computer's stock price declines by 12 percent as executives resign.
- The price of Comp USA stock increases by 30 percent on news that it is being acquired.

The field of finance also involves the conditions of the financial markets in which firms compete for investors and financing. Some of the more common types of financial news headlines are related to financial markets:

- The yields offered on bonds decline in response to a decision announced by the Federal Reserve.
- U.S. stock market prices decline as a result of concerns about the economy.
- U.S. interest rates rise in response to inflationary fears.
- The dollar's value declines against most major currencies as U.S. investors invest more money abroad.

The Relevance of Finance

The wide range of events just cited reflects the breadth of finance. This book discusses finance from two primary perspectives: the manager's perspective and the investor's perspective. It also illustrates how financial markets and institutions facilitate finance activities of both managers and investors. Thus this text is relevant to students who plan to pursue a career as a financial manager of a firm, at a financial institution, or at a business that deals with financial institutions and markets. It is also relevant to those who pursue nonfinancial positions but need to understand how finance is related to their job functions.

An understanding of finance not only prepares students for careers but also equips them to make decisions as investors. Regardless of how much you have to invest, finance can help you decide whether to invest your money, what type of financial instrument to invest in, how much money should be invested, and how invested funds should be allocated among different investments.

? Review Question

1–1   Why is finance relevant to you as a student?

LO2 Components of the Financial Environment

The financial environment is composed of three key components: (1) financial managers, (2) financial markets, and (3) investors (including creditors). This book discusses each of these components in detail and illustrates how they are integrated. This chapter introduces each component and briefly explains how the components are related. Thus this chapter provides an overview of the text.

Financial Managers

financial manager
A decision maker who invests funds to expand a business and obtains funds (financing) for the business.

Financial managers are responsible for deciding how to invest a company's funds to expand its business and how to obtain funds (financing). The actions taken by financial managers to make financial decisions for their respective firms are referred to as **financial management** (or **managerial finance**).

financial management (managerial finance)
The actions taken by financial managers to make financial decisions for a firm.

Financial managers are expected to make financial decisions that will maximize the firm's value and therefore maximize the value of the firm's stock price. They are usually compensated in a manner that encourages them to achieve this objective.

Some more common career opportunities for financial managers are shown in Table 1.1. This table summarizes the different types of duties that financial managers perform. When a firm is initially established, one person may perform all managerial finance duties. However, as the firm grows, financial managers are hired to specialize in particular managerial finance duties. In larger firms, financial managers direct and manage departments of staff analysts who do the day-to-day analysis.

chief financial officer
The officer who makes the key financial decisions of a firm.

In larger firms, financial managers fit within the firm's organizational structure as shown in Figure 1.1. The key financial decisions of a firm are commonly made by or under the supervision of the **chief financial officer (CFO)**, who typically reports directly to the chief executive officer (CEO). The lower portion of the organizational chart in Figure 1.1 shows the structure of the finance

TABLE 1.1 Career Opportunities in Financial Management

Position	Description
Financial analyst	Primarily prepares the firm's financial plans and budgets. Other duties include financial forecasting, performing financial comparisons, and working closely with accounting.
Capital expenditures manager	Evaluates and recommends proposed asset investments. May be involved in the financial aspects of implementing approved investments.
Project finance manager	In large firms, arranges financing for approved asset investments. Coordinates consultants, investment bankers, and legal counsel.
Cash manager	Maintains and controls the firm's daily cash balances. Frequently manages the firm's cash collection and disbursement activities and short-term investments and coordinates short-term borrowing and banking relationships.
Credit analyst/manager	Administers the firm's credit policy by evaluating credit applications, extending credit, and monitoring and collecting accounts receivable.
Pension fund manager	In large companies, oversees or manages the assets and liabilities of the employees' pension fund.
Foreign exchange manager	Manages specific foreign operations and the firm's exposure to exchange rate fluctuations.

treasurer
The officer responsible for the firm's financial activities.

controller
The officer responsible for the firm's accounting activities.

function in a typical medium-size to large firm, where the treasurer and the controller report to the CFO. The **treasurer** is commonly responsible for handling financial activities, such as obtaining funds, making capital expenditure decisions, and managing cash. The **controller** typically handles the accounting activities, such as corporate accounting, tax management, and financial and cost accounting.

Interaction Between Financial Management and Other Business Functions

Most firms required financing when they were first established, but the firm's finance function is not limited to this initial financing. Rather, the firm's finance function is conducted continuously and is integrated with other business functions, as illustrated in Figure 1.2. For larger firms, each function may be handled separately by a specific department.

Firms engage in a *production* function to produce products (including services), and they incur costs from the production function. They engage in a *marketing* function to forecast sales, promote the products, and distribute them. Because firms frequently incur costs from the production and marketing functions before receiving revenue for the products produced, they may also need to obtain financing. The amount of financing and the time period for which financing is needed depends on information drawn from the production and the marketing functions. Such information includes, for production, the amount of machinery and materials that must be purchased in the near future and, for marketing, the amount of expenses to be incurred from advertising.

Firms rely on *information systems* to ensure that information flows between the finance function and the other business functions. Firms perform an *account-*

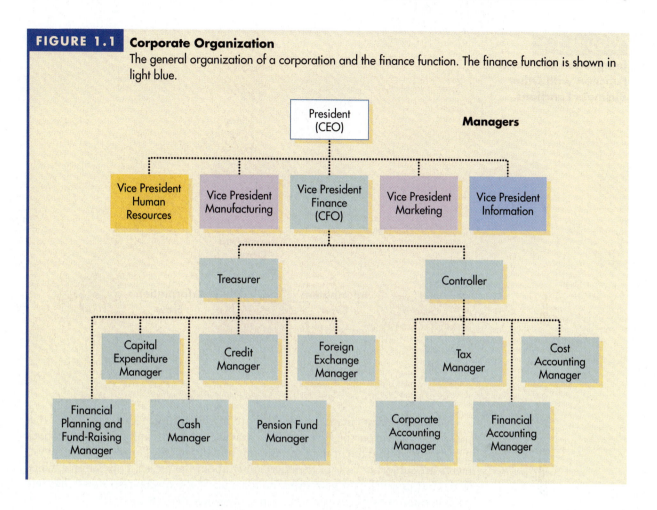

FIGURE 1.1　**Corporate Organization**

The general organization of a corporation and the finance function. The finance function is shown in light blue.

ing function that uses information to prepare financial statements on a periodic (such as quarterly) basis, to prepare and file tax returns, and to provide information and reports to other managers. The finance function analyzes these statements to assess the firm's past performance and to make financing and investing decisions consistent with the firm's plans and goals.

Investment Decisions by Financial Managers

Financial managers assess potential investment opportunities for the firm in order to determine whether to pursue those opportunities. The investment decisions of financial managers significantly affect the firm's degree of success, because they determine what types of businesses their respective firms engage in. Investment decisions determine the composition of assets found on the left-hand side of the balance sheet: The financial manager attempts to maintain optimal levels of each type of current asset, such as cash and inventory. The financial manager also decides which fixed assets (such as buildings or machinery) to invest in and when existing fixed assets need to be modified, replaced, or liquidated. These decisions are important because they affect the firm's success in achieving its goals.

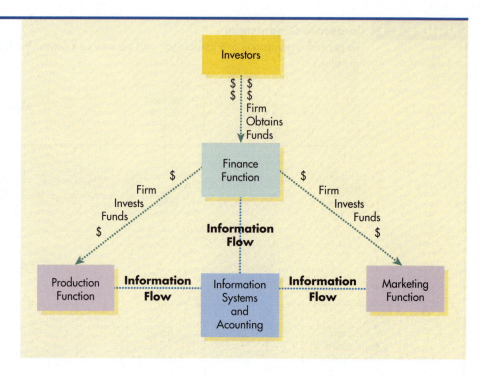

The investments made by the firm are intended to generate cash flows that provide a return on the investments. That is, the firm expects to receive back more from an investment than the amount initially put in. However, these investments are subject to risk, or the uncertainty about the return. For example, when Wal-Mart establishes a new store, its forecast of the future cash flows that will be generated may be overly optimistic, in which the return on the investment may be well below the forecast.

Financing Decisions by Financial Managers

When firms obtain funds, their financing can be classified as either debt financing or equity financing. In **debt financing,** *borrowed funds* are used to finance investments in projects. For example, firms can obtain loans or can issue **debt securities,** which are certificates representing credit provided to the firm by the security's purchaser. In **equity financing,** funds are obtained in exchange for *ownership* in the firm and used to finance investments in projects. Firms can obtain equity financing either by retaining some of their earnings or by issuing **equity securities** (stocks), which are certificates representing ownership interest in the issuing firm.

Financing decisions focus on the right-hand side of the firm's balance sheet and involve two major areas. First, levels of short-term and long-term financing must be established. A second and equally important concern is determining the optimal sources of financing at a given point in time. Many financing decisions are dictated by necessity, but some require in-depth analysis of the financing alternatives, their costs, and their long-run implications.

debt financing
The use of borrowed funds to finance investments.

debt securities
Certificates representing credit provided to the firm by the security's purchaser.

equity financing
The use of funds obtained in exchange for ownership in the firm to finance investments.

equity securities
Stocks; certificates representing ownership interest in a firm.

Investors

Investors are individuals or financial institutions that provide funds to firms, government agencies, or individuals who need funds. In this book, our focus regarding investors is on their provision of funds to firms. Individual investors commonly provide funds to firms by purchasing their securities (stocks and debt securities). The financial institutions that provide funds are referred to as **institutional investors.** Some of these institutions focus on providing loans, whereas others commonly purchase securities that are issued by firms.

Debt Financing Provided by Investors

Debt financing to firms is provided in various forms by individual and institutional investors. Financial institutions that provide *loans* employ loan officers, who evaluate the financial condition of potential borrowers to determine whether they are creditworthy. When the financial institutions provide loans, they receive periodic interest payments on the loans as compensation from borrowers. The debt has a specified maturity date at which the amount borrowed, which is called the **principal,** is repaid.

In another form of debt financing, individual investors and financial institutions purchase debt securities that are issued by firms and governments. They may be compensated by purchasing a debt security at a discount from its principal value, so that the principal they are repaid at maturity exceeds the amount they paid for the debt security. Alternatively, they may be compensated with periodic interest payments. If they desire, investors can sell to other investors most types of debt securities before their maturity, which transfers the loan to the other investors (lenders).

Equity Financing Provided by Investors

Equity financing is obtained when a firm sells shares of stock (ownership) to investors. Because a firm's ownership is represented by its stock, each investor who purchases stock becomes an owner of the firm. There is no maturity on stock; however, investors can sell the stock they own to other investors. The sale of stock results in the transfer of ownership. Investors who purchase a firm's stock expect to be compensated by the return on the stock, which results from dividends they receive and from any increase in the value (price) of the stock.

Return and Risk from Investing

Whether investors provide debt or equity financing, they expect to earn a return on their investment in exchange for allowing a firm to use their funds. In general, the **return** on any investment is the actual benefit (cash flow) that would be received if the investment were purchased at the start of a period and sold at the end of that period. The return to investors who provide funds to a firm can be highly dependent on decisions of the firm's financial managers. For example, if financial managers use funds received from investors to invest in very profitable projects, the firm earns a high return on its investments. Consequently, shareholders who invested in the firm's stock earn a high return on their investment in the firm. Conversely, bad investment decisions by a firm's financial managers result in poor returns on the firm's investments and, accordingly, poor returns to the shareholders who invested in the firm's stock. A return is sometimes measured as a percentage of the amount initially invested.

All investors are exposed to **risk,** or the uncertainty surrounding the return on their investments. They are **risk-averse,** which implies that they prefer less risk for a given expected return. When investors provide debt financing, there is *default risk,* or the possibility that the firm that borrowed funds will be unable to make scheduled interest payments or repay the principal on the loan. When investors provide equity financing, they are exposed to the risk that the return on their investment will be lower than expected. This may occur if the firm performs worse than expected and cannot pay out the expected dividends, or if its stock price does not rise to the level expected.

risk
The uncertainty surrounding the return on an investment

risk-averse
Preferring less risk for a given expected return.

Investor Use of Financial Services

When deciding how they should invest their funds, investors commonly utilize financial services (such as financial planning and insurance services provided by financial institutions). Thus financial services can affect the volume and the nature of the funds that flow from individual investors to financial institutions and therefore to firms that need financing.

Financial Markets

financial markets
Forums that facilitate the flow of funds among investors, firms, and government units.

Financial markets represent forums that facilitate the flow of funds among investors, firms, and government units and agencies. Each financial market is served by financial institutions that act as intermediaries. The *equity market* facilitates the sale of equity by firms to investors or between investors. Some financial institutions serve as intermediaries by executing transactions between willing buyers and sellers of stock at agreed-upon prices. The *debt markets* enable firms to obtain debt financing from institutional and individual investors or to transfer ownership of debt securities between investors. Some financial institutions serve as intermediaries by facilitating the exchange of funds in return for debt securities at an agreed-upon price. Thus it is quite common for one financial institution to act as the institutional investor while another financial institution serves as the intermediary by executing the transaction that transfers funds to a firm that needs financing. For example, Merrill Lynch (a financial institution) serves as an intermediary in an offering of new shares by Intel (a firm in need of financing) by selling these shares to investors, including the California Public Employees Retirement Fund (a financial institution).

Careers of Participants in Financial Markets

The career opportunities within the financial markets are summarized in Table 1.2. Most of these careers play a role in facilitating the flow of funds within the financial markets.

| TABLE 1.2 | Career Opportunities in Financial Markets |

Career	Career opportunities
Banking and related institutions	*Loan officers* evaluate and make recommendations on various types of loans. *Retail bank managers* run bank offices and supervise the programs offered by the bank. *Trust officers* administer trust funds for estates, foundations, and business firms.
Personal financial planning	*Financial planners* advise individuals on all aspects of their personal finances and help them develop comprehensive financial plans to meet their objectives.
Real estate	*Real estate agents/brokers* negotiate the sale or lease of residential and commercial property. *Appraisers* estimate the market values of all types of property. *Real estate lenders* analyze and make decisions with regard to loan applications. *Mortgage bankers* find and arrange financing for real estate projects. *Property managers* handle the day-to-day operations of properties to achieve maximum returns for their owners.
Insurance	*Insurance agents/brokers* sell insurance policies to meet clients' needs and assist in claims processing and settlement. *Underwriters* appraise and select the risks that their company will insure and set the associated premiums.
Investments	*Stockbrokers,* or account executives, assist clients in choosing, buying, and selling securities. *Securities analysts* study stocks and bonds and advise securities firms and insurance companies with regard to them. *Portfolio managers* build and manage portfolios of securities for firms and individuals. *Investment bankers* provide advice to security issuers and act as intermediaries between issuers and purchasers of newly issued stocks and bonds.

Integration of Components in the Financial Environment

The integration of components that exist within the financial environment will be explained throughout the text. Figure 1.3 offers a brief overview of that integration. When a firm's financial managers determine whether to use debt or equity financing, they rely on investors to supply those funds through the financial markets. For example, the investment decision by Dell Computer to expand its product line or by The Gap to establish additional stores that require external financing will result in the firm's obtaining funds from individual and institutional investors.

Financial managers and investors face similar types of investment decisions. They must decide what to invest in, how much to invest, and the length of the investment period. However, the typical types of investments made by financial managers are distinctly different from the types of investment decisions made by investors. The investment decisions of financial managers commonly focus on **real assets** such as buildings, machinery, and office equipment; the investment decisions of investors focus on **financial assets,** which include securities such as bonds and stocks.

Note in Figure 1.3 that the investment decisions of financial managers and investors are related. The investment decisions made by the firm's financial managers dictate how much funds the firm needs to invest in its businesses. That is, the investment decisions determine the amount of funds that the firm will obtain from investors. The firm issues financial assets (securities) in order to obtain funds, which are used by the firm's financial managers to invest in real assets.

real assets
Resources such as buildings, machinery, and office equipment.

financial assets
Resources such as bonds and stocks.

FIGURE 1.3

Integration of Components in the Financial Environment

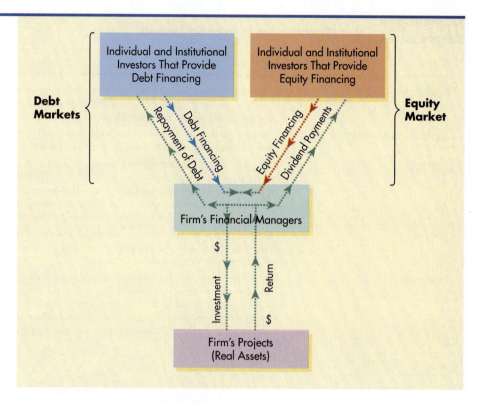

Debt Markets

Individual and Institutional Investors That Provide Debt Financing

Individual and Institutional Investors That Provide Equity Financing

Equity Market

Repayment of Debt

Debt Financing

Equity Financing

Dividend Payments

Firm's Financial Managers

$

Investment

Return

$

Firm's Projects (Real Assets)

? Review Questions

1–2 How is the finance function related to the marketing and production functions?

1–3 What is the difference between debt financing and equity financing?

1–4 How do investors benefit from investing in a firm?

LG3 Investor Monitoring of Firms

Like firms, investors attempt to make decisions that will enhance their stream of expected future cash flows. Investors' cash outflows result from purchases of stocks (and other investment vehicles), so they would like to purchase their investments at relatively low prices. Thus, if investors believe a firm's stock price may decline and later rise, they may wait until the price declines before buying the stock. Their cash inflows from owning stock result from dividends and from the proceeds from selling the stock. Thus they prefer to sell stock when share prices are high. To make decisions about when to buy and when to sell any investment, investors need information.

Using Information to Value the Firm

The value of a publicly traded stock changes every day in response to changes in the demand for and the supply of shares (for sale by investors who own the

*News*Line

STOP THE PRESS (RELEASES)! INTERNET FIRMS LOVE TO CHURN THEM OUT; INVESTORS GOBBLE THEM UP

Investors use information from a variety of sources, including the companies themselves, to decide whether to buy or sell stock. Their actions affect the firm's value, as the following article demonstrates. However, investors must be careful about overreacting to every piece of news they read.

It's an old investor axiom: Buy on the rumor, sell on the news. Here's a new one: "Buy on the press release, sell on the news."

Amazon.com provided the latest sign of Internet investor's ardor for press releases Monday when it announced that an announcement was coming the following day. The "preannouncement" sent the stock soaring 20%, adding $6 billion to its market value in a single stroke.

So what was the big news? Amazon said Tuesday it was entering four new markets and acquiring a tool catalog company. Whoah: That wasn't nearly as exciting as the runup. So the stock promptly sank 9.2%, closing Tuesday at $70.8125, down $7.1875, as investors focused again on the Internet e-commerce giant's lack of profits, rather than its marketing abilities.

The episode illustrates that Internet investors these days have come to regard press releases about new products, relationships, and strategies, among other things, as justification for sending a stock into orbit. With few Internet companies posting any earnings—and many more not expecting profits for years—investors have begun using the press releases—some of scanty substance—as a major tool for selecting Internet stocks.

Internet companies have been happy to oblige: Some churn out releases at a rate that might alarm environmentalists.... "It's the best marketed product or service that wins," says Jeff Brody, general partner with Redpoint Ventures in Menlo Park, Calif.

That couldn't be truer than with Internet stocks, which trade based on sky-high hopes of potential profits. Take Marimba.com, the Internet-based software company.... Though the company shows a mere $8 million in quarterly revenue and has yet to earn a profit, it has spit out 27 press releases in the past seven months alone, helping it to earn a market value in the neighborhood of $900 million....

Net2Phone—a long-distance Internet phone service that has developed a reputation among investors for its fondness for press releases—put out a string of them from Aug. 24 to Sept. 1, helping push its stock to a high of $92.625 on Sept. 1 from about $35 on Aug. 20.

Source: Susan Pulliam, "Stop the Press (Releases)! Internet Firms Love to Churn Them Out; Investors Gobble Them Up," Wall Street Journal, November 11, 1999, pp. C1, C2.

stock). Investors monitor the firms in which they are invested or plan to invest, so that they can properly "value" these firms to determine whether to buy or sell the firm's stock.

When favorable information about a particular firm's future cash flows (and therefore about its future performance) is disclosed to the market, investors value the firm more highly. The demand for the firm's stock at the prevailing price tends to increase, and the supply of the firm's stock for sale declines. At the prevailing stock price, the quantity of the shares demanded exceeds the quantity of the shares that investors are willing to sell. These forces result in a higher equilibrium price (at which the quantity demanded equals the quantity supplied) per share of the firm's stock.

Conversely, unfavorable information about a particular firm's future cash flows causes investors to revalue that firm downward. The demand for the firm's stock decreases, and the supply of the firm's stock for sale increases, resulting in a surplus of stock for sale at the prevailing price. These forces result in a lower equilibrium price per share of stock.

A firm's stock price can change continuously throughout the day, even though new information about the firm is not disclosed that frequently. Why?

Because the firm's value is influenced not only by firm-specific information but also by external information concerned with economic and political events that may affect the firm's cash flows.

How Investors Influence a Firm's Value

The return that investors earn on their equity investment in a firm depends on how the firm's value changes during the time they hold the stock. Because investors realize that managers make decisions that affect the firm's cash flows and therefore its value, they attempt to ensure that managers' actions will maximize the value of the firm. Three of the more common methods used by investors to influence management actions are (1) investor trading, (2) shareholder activism, and (3) threat of takeover.

Investor Trading

Investors rely on information to forecast the future cash flows (and therefore performance) of firms in which they invest. If the future performance is expected to be weak, investors may sell their shares of the firm's stock, which places downward pressure on the firm's stock price. In this way, investors penalize the firm for its behavior. Any managers of the firm whose compensation is tied to the firm's stock price will be directly penalized if the stock price declines. In addition, the board of directors, which is supposed to serve shareholders, may enact change if the firm's executives are not running the firm properly.

Conversely, if the future performance of a firm is expected to be strong as a result of managerial actions, some investors will attempt to buy more shares of the firm's stock, which places upward pressure on its price. In this way, investors reward the firm for its behavior. Those managers of the firm whose compensation is tied to the firm's stock price will be directly rewarded if the stock price increases.

Shareholder Activism

shareholder activism
Actions of stockholders to influence directly the decisions of the firms in which they are invested.

Alternatively, shareholders may attempt to influence the decisions of the firms in which they are invested, in order to align the firm's actions more closely with their financial interests. This effort is commonly referred to as **shareholder activism.** In particular, when institutional investors hold large blocks of the firm's outstanding shares, they can try to use their voting power to influence, and often change, the firm's management and/or board of directors. They may also sue the board of directors if they believe it is not acting in the shareholders' best interests.

In 1955, institutional investors held only about 10 percent of the total stocks (in terms of value) in the United States. Today, institutional investors hold more than 50 percent of the total. Thus institutional investors now have much more power to ensure that managers act in the interests of shareholders. The proportional increase in institutional ownership has significantly increased activism.

E x a m p l e ▼ Wilmington Inc. is a financial institution that presently holds 2 million shares of stock of Lexo Co. The portfolio managers of Wilmington Inc. believed that Lexo Co. had much potential when they purchased the stock 3 years ago, but Lexo has performed poorly over this period. Last year, the portfolio managers told Lexo's board of directors that unless Lexo's performance improved, Wilmington might sell all the Lexo stock it owns.

Lexo's board of directors responded by pressuring the executives of Lexo to implement changes that increased the firm's efficiency. These changes resulted in improved performance, and the stock price increased by $3 per share. Because Wilmington holds 2 million shares, it gained $6 million as a result of exerting its influence on Lexo Co. If Wilmington Inc. had held a much smaller number of shares (as most individual investors do), it would not have been able to influence

▲ Lexo's board of directors.

Threat of Takeover

If a firm's managers do not act to maximize the value of the firm, some investors may consider acquiring enough of the firm's stock to gain control of it. They then may restructure the firm in order to better achieve the shareholders' goal to maximize the share price. The incentive for such an effort is the potential reward from buying stock at a low price (when the firm is undervalued as a consequence of poor management) and then taking actions that cause the price to rise.

E x a m p l e ▼ Oregon Co. experienced poor performance in the last 3 years because of poor management, and its stock price declined from $40 to $15 per share over this period. Some institutional investors believed that the firm had excellent potential and that they could improve the firm if they could acquire enough shares to take control. These investors used some of their own money, along with borrowed funds, to acquire the needed shares. They then restructured the firm by firing the inefficient managers and replacing them. Once the better managers improve the firm's performance, the institutional investors could profit from selling some or all of their shares at a much higher price than the price they paid

▲ for them.

In many takeovers, some of the managers of the firm serve as the investors who take control of the firm. They have a vested interest in ensuring that the firm performs well once they become owners, because their investment is at stake. In other cases, managers may not be able to purchase underperforming firms, because the amount of funds needed to gain control of the firm is too large. Under these circumstances, another firm (perhaps a competitor) may serve as the investor and purchase a sufficient proportion of the firm's shares to gain control. Regardless of whether a firm might be acquired by some of its managers or by another firm, the threat of a takeover should give the firm's managers an incentive to perform well, because a takeover may result in the elimination of their jobs.

Effects of Asymmetric Information

Investors monitor firms by reviewing the financial statements that firms must provide to their shareholders on a periodic basis. They also rely on firm-specific information provided by various third-party information services (such as Moody's and Standard and Poor's) that have more experience in obtaining, summarizing, and analyzing the most relevant public information. They also may periodically meet with managers, and therefore have more detailed information about firms than other investors.

Monitoring the firm's actions can be difficult for investors, because the amount of information provided within financial statements is limited. A firm may experience problems that cannot be discerned in its published financial statements. This situation results from **asymmetric information,** whereby more information is available to the firm's managers than to its investors. Because a firm's stock price responds to new information, investors prefer that any asymmetric information be eliminated or reduced so that they can better monitor firms over time and make more informed investment decisions. Some firms are more willing than others to disclose relevant information to investors. Thus the degree of asymmetric information varies among firms.

asymmetric information
The imbalance of information that occurs when a firm's managers have more information than its investors.

Example ▼ Consider firms called Full-Info Co. and Limited-Info Co. that had the same historical and potential financial performance. Assume that Full-Info Co. discloses all information that its financial managers have about its future expansion plans. Conversely, Limited-Info Co. shares only the financial information that accounting standards require it to disclose. Limited-Info Co. therefore has a much higher degree of asymmetric information. Consequently, investors who monitor Limited-Info Co. are likely to develop less accurate expectations of its future performance. In general, the higher degree of asymmetric information results in **▲** greater uncertainty about the value of Limited-Info Co.'s stock.

Some institutional investors subscribe to proprietary services that provide assessments of firms, whereas other institutional investors have an in-house service. These services may reduce the degree of asymmetric information and therefore give institutional investors an advantage over individual investors. For this reason, some individual investors prefer to allow specific institutional investors (such as full-service brokers) to make their investment decisions for them. Yet even those individual investors should attempt to monitor the firms in which they have invested so that they can assess whether the investment advice they receive is reasonable. In essence, individual investors who pay for advice (in the form of higher commissions on transactions or in other ways) must ensure that their advisors are serving their best interests.

? Review Questions

1–5 Why do investors closely monitor a firm's financial decisions?
1–6 How does new information affect a firm's stock price?
1–7 How can shareholder activism influence management actions?
1–8 Why is there asymmetric information between a firm's managers and its investors?

The International Finance Environment

exporting
Shipping products to customers in other countries.

importing
Purchasing products from firms in other countries.

direct foreign investment
The investment of funds in production facilities in a foreign country in which a firm has substantial sales or from which it makes substantial purchases of materials.

In response to a lowering of various international barriers, financial managers and investors commonly pursue investment opportunities in foreign countries. For example, many firms pursue international business by **exporting,** in which they transport products to customers in other countries. They also engage in **importing,** in which they purchase supplies or materials from firms in other countries. Some firms with substantial sales of products in a particular foreign country invest funds to establish production facilities in that country. Such **direct foreign investment** is especially common in countries with low labor costs. Some U.S. firms, such as Coca-Cola and Exxon, now generate more than half of their total sales from foreign countries as a result of exports and direct foreign investment.

Risks of International Business

exchange rate risk
The risk that cash flows will be adversely affected by movements in the price of one currency in relation to another.

depreciation
The weakening of one currency relative to another.

appreciation
The strengthening of one currency relative to another.

Firms that pursue international business opportunities are exposed to additional forms of risk that are not normally considered when the focus is on domestic business. International businesses can be exposed to **exchange rate risk,** which represents the risk that their cash flows will be tracking adversely affected by movements in the price of one currency in relation to another (the exchange rate). If a U.S. firm receives a foreign currency that **depreciates** (weakens) against the U.S. dollar, the dollar cash inflows resulting from this business will be reduced. In addition, if the firm must make payment in a foreign currency that **appreciates** (strengthens) against the U.S. dollar by the time payment is due, it will be forced to increase its dollar cash outflows. Firms that conduct international business are exposed to other risks as well, such as the risk that the government of the foreign country will impose some restrictions that adversely affect the firm's cash flows.

International Finance by Investors

Just as U.S. firms can attempt to capitalize on foreign business opportunities by engaging in international business, U.S. investors can invest in securities issued by foreign firms. The Internet and other means of global communication are making it easier for investors to obtain information about firms in many other countries.

Some foreign securities are desirable because they may possibly offer a higher return to U.S. investors than any U.S. stocks, but they can cause exposure to exchange rate risk. For example, U.S. investors who invest in a Canadian stock receive dividends in Canadian dollars, which must be converted to U.S. dollars at the prevailing exchange rate. If the value of the Canadian dollar depreciates against the U.S. dollar over the investment horizon, the return to U.S. investors will be reduced. Conversely, these U.S. investors benefit from appreciation of the Canadian dollar.

? Review Questions

1–9   Why do firms engage in direct foreign investment?

1–10   How is a firm's cash flow exposed to exchange rate risk?

Using This Textbook

In this textbook we will focus on three key components of finance: financial managers, financial markets, and investors. As you've seen in this chapter, these components play critical roles in finance.

Financial managers: Obtain funds for their firms (arrange financing) and invest the firm's funds.

Financial markets: Facilitate the flow of funds between investors and firms.

Investors: Provide debt financing and equity financing to firms in pursuit of their own personal financial goals.

The activities of financial managers and investors, and the role of financial markets in channeling funds from investors to firms, are described in this book, which is divided into five parts:

Part 1   The Financial Marketplace

Part 2   Financial Tools for Firms and Investors

Part 3   Financial Management

Part 4   Investment Management

Part 5   How Investors Monitor and Control a Firm's Managers

Coverage of international events and topics is integrated into the discussions throughout the book.

As you study this book, you will observe that each chapter is organized and developed around a group of learning goals. The numbered learning goals listed at the beginning of each chapter are tied to text sections in the chapter and also to end-of-chapter materials (chapter summaries, questions, and problems). At periodic intervals in each chapter (usually before major section headings) review questions test your understanding of the material just presented. For best results in learning the text material, take a few moments to stop and consider the review questions. Think about what you've just read. (If you're shaky on any of the topics, be honest enough with yourself to go back and reread the material.) If you're able to answer the review questions, you'll be well on your way toward mastering the chapter's learning goals. Mastery of these goals will result in a broad understanding of the concepts, techniques, and practices of finance.

This chapter introduced financial managers, financial markets, and investors as the key components of the financial environment and explained how these components are related. The roles of financial managers, financial markets, and investors in the financial environment are summarized in the Integrative Table.

INTEGRATIVE TABLE
Participating in the Financial Environment

Role of **Financial Managers**	*Role of* **Financial Markets**	*Role of* **Investors**
Financial managers determine how to invest a firm's funds to capitalize on potential opportunities. They also determine how to obtain the funds needed to finance their respective firms' investments.	Financial markets facilitate the flow of funds from the suppliers of funds to firms or governments who need funds. Financial institutions serve as intermediaries by channeling the savings of individuals to firms that need funds.	Investors commonly finance the investments made by firms by purchasing debt securities or equity securities issued by those firms.

LG1 Define the term *finance* and explain why finance is relevant to students. Finance is the processes by which money is transferred among businesses, individuals, and governments. Virtually all individuals and organizations earn or raise money and spend or invest money.

An understanding of finance can prepare students for careers in managerial finance or in other areas of business, including work in financial institutions or in financial markets. It can also equip students to decide what types of investments to invest in, which securities to invest in, and how much to invest.

LG2 Identify the components of the financial environment. The components are (1) financial managers, who are responsible for investment decisions and financing decisions, (2) investors, who supply the funds to firms that need funding, and (3) financial markets, which facilitate the flow of funds from investors to financial managers.

LG3 Explain how investors monitor managers to ensure that managerial decisions are in the

best interests of the owners. Investors buy and sell the firm's stock, an activity that determines the equilibrium price of the stock. If the managers make poor decisions inconsistent with maximizing the value of the stock, the investors will sell the stock, placing downward pressure on its price. To the extent that managers' compensation levels are tied to the price of the stock, they are penalized when they do not focus on satisfying owners. In addition, investors can initiate various forms of shareholder activism. Some investors may even consider acquiring enough shares to take control of the firm.

LG4 Describe how the financial environment has become internationalized. The international financial environment provides additional investment opportunities for firms and investors, which may allow them to improve their stream of cash flows. However, the international environment can also cause future cash flows to be subject to more uncertainty because of currency exchange rate risk and other factors specific to foreign countries.

18

(Solutions in Appendix B)

 ST 1–1 What are the key components of the financial environment, and how are these components integrated in a business environment?

 ST 1–2 Discuss the three common methods used by investors to influence management to act in their interest.

EXERCISES

 1–1 Why is knowledge of finance important even to students in other business disciplines?

 1–2 Explain the role of the financial manager in the firm.

 1–3 Discuss the alternative sources of financing for a firm.

 1–4 How are investment decisions of financial managers different from those of individual investors?

 1–5 What factors can influence the equilibrium price of a firm's stock?

 1–6 How does favorable (or unfavorable) information relating to a firm's future cash flows affect the equilibrium price of its stock?

 1–7 Explain why investors would want to monitor the activities of managers in a corporation.

 1–8 What other methods do investors have to motivate management to act in their interest?

 1–9 **Agency issues** In each of the following examples, identify possible conflicts of interest between management and shareholders.
a. *Keirestus* in Japan are large groups of companies affiliated through (1) close business ties, (2) cross-holdings of shares between and among companies within the group, and (3) reliance on financing from each other or from a main partner in the group.
b. Nightlight Inc., a maker of security lights, is owned by Dan Druther, who has members of his own family in key positions in the company. All other management positions are held by employees who own no share in the company. Dan is involved in the day-to-day operations of the company and makes all important decisions, although he solicits input from trusted employees in the company.
c. Corporations in some developing countries are required to disclose only scant information on their operations and earnings once a year. Whether to make detailed disclosures is left to the discretion of each company. Members of the board are appointed by the company's chief executive officer.
d. Companies in Pandemonia are owned by thousands of shareholders all of whom own the same number of shares as a result of government policies to

"spread the wealth around." Further, government policies consider the takeover of companies as a capitalist tool, and members of the management team are appointed because they are firm supporters of government policies and are political members of the ruling party.

LG3 1–10 What is asymmetric information and how does it affect investors' ability to monitor the firm? Does the situation change in the presence of institutional investors?

LG3 1–11 Should managers in firms disclose all information to the investing public? Can you suggest a situation in which it is prudent for a manager to withhold some information from the public?

LG4 1–12 What is the primary source of risks for firms operating abroad? Can you identify other sources of risks?

LG4 1–13 Identify the benefits to an individual investor in a foreign country. What are the risks of such an investment?

web exercises   Search

For a listing of jobs in the financial industry, go to **www.monster.com**. From the monster.com home page, click on **Search Jobs**. On the Search Jobs screen, you can select the job location you want and then select the job category **Finance/Economics**. Click on the **Search Jobs** box. You can also post your résumé; research companies; tap into a career resource that offers help with interviewing, networking, and writing résumés; and chat online to share questions and concerns.

For other job sites, you can go to:

www.careermosaic.com
www.occ.treas.gov/
www.msn.com/

For additional practice with concepts from this chapter, visit
http://www.awl.com/gitman_madura

The Financial Marketplace

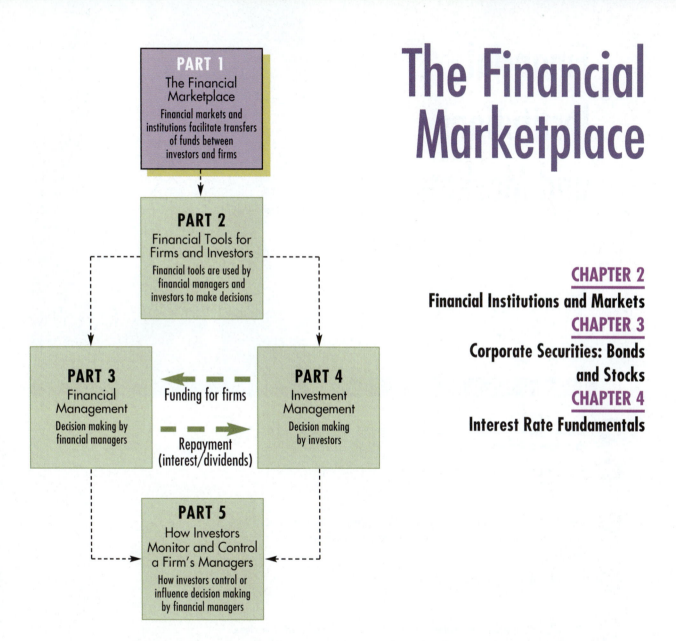

PART 1
The Financial Marketplace
Financial markets and institutions facilitate transfers of funds between investors and firms

PART 2
Financial Tools for Firms and Investors
Financial tools are used by financial managers and investors to make decisions

PART 3
Financial Management
Decision making by financial managers

Funding for firms

Repayment (interest/dividends)

PART 4
Investment Management
Decision making by investors

PART 5
How Investors Monitor and Control a Firm's Managers
How investors control or influence decision making by financial managers

Part 1 introduces the key financial components within the financial marketplace: financial managers, financial markets, and investors. It explains the roles of these three components, and describes how security prices and interest rates are determined in the financial marketplace. This background is necessary before we can focus on decision making, which is discussed throughout the rest of the text.

Financial Institutions and Markets

LEARNING GOALS

LG1 Explain how financial institutions serve as intermediaries between investors and firms.

LG2 Provide an overview of financial markets.

LG3 Explain how firms and investors trade money market and capital market securities in the financial markets in order to satisfy their needs.

LG4 Describe the major securities exchanges.

LG5 Describe derivative securities and explain why firms and investors use them.

LG6 Describe the foreign exchange market.

ⓛⓖ① Financial Institutions

financial institution
An intermediary that channels the savings of individuals, businesses, and governments into loans or investments.

Financial institutions serve as intermediaries by channeling the savings of individuals, businesses, and governments into loans or investments. They are major players in the financial marketplace, with more than $12 trillion of financial assets under their control. They often serve as the main source of funds for businesses and individuals. Some financial institutions accept customers' savings deposits and lend this money to other customers or to firms. In fact, many firms rely heavily on loans from institutions for their financial support. Financial institutions are required by the government to operate within established regulatory guidelines.

Key Customers of Financial Institutions

The key suppliers of funds to financial institutions and the key demanders of funds from financial institutions are individuals, businesses, and governments. The savings that individual consumers place in financial institutions provide these institutions with a large portion of their funds. Individuals not only supply funds to financial institutions but also demand funds from them in the form of loans. However, individuals as a group are the *net suppliers* for financial institutions: They save more money than they borrow.

Firms also deposit some of their funds in financial institutions, primarily in checking accounts with various commercial banks. Like individuals, firms also borrow funds from these institutions, but firms are *net demanders* of funds. They borrow more money than they save.

Governments maintain deposits of temporarily idle funds, certain tax payments, and Social Security payments in commercial banks. They do not borrow funds directly from financial institutions, although by selling their debt securities to various institutions, governments indirectly borrow from them. The government, like business firms, is typically a net demander of funds. It typically borrows more than it saves.

The different types of financial institutions are described in Table 2.1. The most important financial institutions that facilitate the flow of funds from investors to firms are commercial banks, mutual funds, security firms, insurance companies, and pension funds. Each of these financial institutions is discussed in more detail below.

Commercial Banks

commercial banks
Financial institutions that accumulate deposits from savers and provide credit to firms, individuals, and government agencies.

Commercial banks accumulate deposits from savers and use the proceeds to provide credit to firms, individuals, and government agencies. Thus they serve investors who wish to "invest" funds in the form of deposits. Commercial banks use the deposited funds to provide commercial loans to firms and personal loans to individuals and to purchase debt securities issued by firms or government agencies. They serve as a key source of credit to support expansion by firms. Historically, commercial banks were the dominant direct lender to firms. In recent years, however, other types of financial institutions have begun to provide more loans to firms.

TABLE 2.1	Major Financial Institutions
Institutions	**Description**
Commercial Bank	Accepts both demand (checking) and time (savings) deposits. Offers interest-earning savings accounts (NOW accounts) against which checks can be written. Offers money market deposit accounts, which pay interest at rates competitive with other short-term investment vehicles. Makes loans directly to borrowers or through the financial markets.
Mutual Fund	Pools funds of savers and makes them available to business and government demanders. Obtains funds through sales of shares and uses proceeds to acquire bonds and stocks. Creates a diversified and professionally managed portfolio of securities to achieve a specified investment objective. Thousands of funds, with a variety of investment objectives, exist. Money market mutual funds provide competitive returns with very high liquidity.
Securities Firm	Provides investment banking services by helping firms to obtain funds. Provides brokerage services to facilitate the sales of existing securities.
Insurance Company	The largest type of financial intermediary handling individual savings. Receives premium payments and places these funds in loans or investments to cover future benefit payments. Lends funds to individuals, businesses, and governments or channels them through the financial markets.
Pension Fund	Accumulates payments (contributions) from employees of firms or government units, and often from employers, in order to provide retirement income. Money is sometimes transferred directly to borrowers, but the majority is lent or invested via the financial markets.
Savings Institution	Similar to a commercial bank except that it may not hold demand (checking) deposits. Obtains funds from savings, NOW, and money market deposits. Also raises capital through the sale of securities in the financial markets. Lends funds primarily to individuals and businesses or real estate mortgage loans. Channels some funds into investments in the financial markets.
Savings Bank	Similar to a savings institution in that it holds savings, NOW, and money market deposit accounts. Makes residential real estate loans to individuals.
Finance Company	Obtains funds by issuing securities and lends funds to individuals and small businesses.
Credit Union	Deals primarily in transfer of funds between consumers. Membership is generally based on some common bond, such as working for a given employer. Accepts members' savings deposits, NOW account deposits, and money market accounts.

Like most other types of firms, commercial banks are created to generate earnings for their owners. In general, commercial banks generate earnings by receiving a higher return on their use of funds than the cost they incur from obtaining deposited funds. For example, a bank may pay an average annual interest rate of 4 percent on the deposits it obtains and may earn a return of 9 percent on the funds that it uses as loans or as investments in securities. Such banks can charge a higher interest rate on riskier loans, but they are then more exposed to the possibility that these loans will default.

Although the traditional function of accepting deposits and using funds for loans or to purchase debt securities is still important, banks now perform many other functions as well. In particular, banks generate fees by providing services such as travelers checks, foreign exchange, personal financial advising, insurance, and brokerage services. Thus commercial banks are able to offer customers "one-stop shopping."

Sources and Uses of Funds at Commercial Banks

Commercial banks obtain most of their funds by accepting deposits from investors. These investors are usually individuals, but some are firms and government agencies that have excess cash. Some deposits are held at banks for very short periods, such as a month or less. Commercial banks also attract deposits for longer time periods by offering certificates of deposit, which specify a minimum deposit level (such as $1,000) and a particular maturity (such as 1 year). Because most commercial banks offer certificates of deposit with many different maturities, they essentially diversify the times at which the deposits are withdrawn by investors.

Deposits at commercial banks are insured up to a maximum of $100,000 per account by the Federal Deposit Insurance Corporation (FDIC). Deposit insurance tends to reduce the concern of depositors about the possibility of a bank failure, and therefore it reduces the possibility that all depositors will try to withdraw their deposits from banks simultaneously. Thus the U.S. banking system efficiently facilitates the flow of funds from savers to borrowers.

Commercial banks use most of their funds either to provide loans or to purchase debt securities. In both cases they serve as creditors, providing credit to those borrowers who need funds. They provide commercial loans to firms, make personal loans to individuals, and purchase debt securities issued by firms or government agencies. Most firms rely heavily on commercial banks as a source of funds.

Some of the more popular means by which commercial banks extend credit to firms are term loans, lines of credit, and investment in debt securities issued by firms. **Term loans** are provided by banks for a medium-term period to finance a firm's investment in machinery or buildings. For example, consider a manufacturer of toys that plans to produce toys and sell them to retail stores. It will need funds to purchase the machinery for producing toys, to make lease payments on the manufacturing facilities, and to pay its employees. As time passes, it will generate cash flows that can be used to cover these expenses. However, there is a time lag between when it must cover these expenses (cash outflows) and when it receives revenue (cash inflows). The term loan can enable the firm to cover its expenses until a sufficient amount of revenue is generated.

The term loan typically lasts for a medium-term period, such as 4 to 8 years. The interest rate charged by the bank to the firm for this type of loan depends on the prevailing interest rates at the time the loan is provided. The interest rate changed on term loans is usually adjusted periodically (such as annually) to reflect movements in market interest rates.

Commercial banks can also provide credit to a firm by offering a **line of credit,** which allows the firm access to a specified amount of bank funds over a

term loans
Funds provided by commercial banks for a medium-term period.

line of credit
Access to a specified amount of bank funds over a specified period of time.

specified period of time. This form of bank credit is especially useful when the firm is not certain how much it will need to borrow over the period. For example, if the toy manufacturer in the previous example was not sure of what its expenses would be in the near future, it could obtain a line of credit and borrow only the amount that it needed. Once a line of credit is granted, it enables the firm to obtain funds quickly.

Commercial banks also invest in debt securities (bonds) that are issued by firms. When a commercial bank purchases securities, its arrangement with a firm is typically less personalized than when it extends a term loan or a line of credit. For example, it may be just one of thousands of investors who invest in a particular debt security the firm has issued. Nevertheless, recognize that a bank's credit provided to firms goes beyond the direct loans that it provides to firms, because it also includes all the securities purchased that were issued by firms.

Role of Commercial Banks as Financial Intermediaries

Commercial banks play several roles as financial intermediaries. First, they *repackage the deposits* received from investors into loans that are provided to firms. In this way, small deposits by individual investors can be consolidated and channeled in the form of large loans to firms. Individual investors would have difficulty achieving this by themselves because they do not have adequate information about the firms that need funds.

Second, commercial banks employ credit analysts who have the ability to *assess the creditworthiness* of firms that wish to borrow funds. Investors who deposit funds in commercial banks are not normally capable of performing this task and would prefer that the bank play this role.

Third, commercial banks have so much money to lend that they can *diversify loans* across several borrowers. In this way, the commercial banks increase their ability to absorb individual defaulted loans by reducing the risk that a substantial portion of the loan portfolio will default. As the lenders, they accept the risk of default. Many individual investors would not be able to absorb the loss of their own deposited funds, so they prefer to let the bank serve in this capacity. Even if a commercial bank were to close because of an excessive amount of defaulted loans, the deposits of each investor are insured up to $100,000 by the FDIC. Thus the commercial bank is a means by which funds can be channeled from small investors to firms without the investors having to play the role of lender.

Fourth, some commercial banks have recently been authorized (since the late 1980s) to *serve as financial intermediaries* by placing the securities that are issued by firms. Such banks may facilitate the flow of funds to firms by finding investors who are willing to purchase the debt securities issued by the firms. Thus they enable firms to obtain borrowed funds even though they do not provide the funds themselves.

Regulation of Commercial Banks

The banking system is regulated by the Federal Reserve System (the Fed), which serves as the central bank of the United States. The Fed is responsible for control-

NewsLine   CLINTON ENACTS GLASS–STEAGALL REPEAL

The repeal of the Glass–Steagall Act further deregulates the financial services industry. No longer will commercial banks be prohibited from engaging in investment banking and insurance activities, and vice versa.

The Glass–Steagall Act, the cornerstone of banking law for most of the 20th century, died Friday at the hands of marketplace changes and political compromise. It was 66 years old.

At 1:52 p.m. Eastern time, President William Jefferson Clinton carried out its death sentence, signing the Gramm–Leach–Bliley Act of 1999. In addition to eliminating the Depression-era law separating commercial and investment banking, it buried another key portion of banking law that had prevented banking organizations from underwriting insurance.

The demise of the longtime statutes that for years had dictated who can own banks and what they could do is expected to give birth to a new wave of financial conglomerates.

"It is true that the Glass–Steagall law is no longer appropriate to the economy in which we live," the President said. "It worked pretty well for the industrial economy...but the world is very different."

He said technology and other forces had demanded policy changes so that American firms can stay nimble and retain their dominance.

"Over the past seven years, we've tried to modernize the economy," the President said. "And today what we are doing is modernizing the financial services industry, tearing down these antiquated walls and granting banks significant new authority.... This is a very good day for the United States."

The President also said the legislation would benefit average Americans by saving consumers "billions of dollars a year," expanding the reach of the Community Reinvestment Act, and creating financial privacy protections "with teeth."...

"The world changes, and Congress and the laws have to change with it," Senate Banking Chairman Phil Gramm said. "When Glass–Steagall became law, it was believed that government was the answer. It was believed that stability and growth came from government overriding the functioning of free markets. We are here to repeal Glass–Steagall because we have learned government is not the answer. We have learned that freedom and competition are."

Source: Dean Anason, "Clinton Enacts Glass–Steagall Repeal," American Banker, November 15, 1999, p. 2.

ling the amount of money in the financial system. It also imposes regulations on activities of banks, thereby influencing the operations that banks conduct. Some commercial banks are members of the Federal Reserve and are therefore subject to additional regulations.

Commercial banks are regulated by various regulatory agencies. First, they are regulated by the Federal Deposit Insurance Corporation, the insurer for depositors. Because the FDIC is responsible for covering deposits of banks, it wants to ensure that banks do not take excessive risk that could result in failure. If several large banks failed, the FDIC would not be able to cover the deposits of all the depositors, which could result in a major banking crisis.

Those commercial banks that apply for a federal charter are referred to as national banks and are subject to regulations of the Comptroller of the Currency. They are also subject to Federal Reserve regulations, because all national banks are required to be members of the Federal Reserve. Alternatively, banks can apply for a state charter.

The general philosophy of regulators who monitor the banking system today is to promote competition among banks so that customers will be charged reasonable prices for the services that they obtain from banks. Regulators also attempt to limit the risk of banks in order to maintain the stability of the financial system.

Mutual Funds

Mutual funds sell shares to individuals, pool these funds, and use them to invest in securities.

Mutual funds are classified into three broad types. *Money market mutual funds* pool the proceeds received from individual investors to invest in money market (short-term) securities issued by firms and other financial institutions. *Bond mutual funds* pool the proceeds received from individual investors to invest in bonds, and *stock mutual funds* pool the proceeds received from investors to invest in stocks. Mutual funds are owned by investment companies. Many of these companies (such as Fidelity) have created several types of money market mutual funds, bond mutual funds, and stock mutual funds so that they can satisfy many different preferences of investors.

Role of Mutual Funds as Financial Intermediaries

When mutual funds use money from investors to invest in newly issued debt or equity securities, they finance new investment by firms. Conversely, when they invest in debt or equity securities already held by investors, they are transferring ownership of the securities among investors.

By pooling individual investors' small investments, mutual funds enable them to hold diversified portfolios (combinations) of debt securities and equity securities. They are also beneficial to individuals who prefer to let mutual funds make their investment decisions for them. The returns to investors who invest in mutual funds are tied to the returns earned by the mutual funds on their investments. Money market mutual funds and bond mutual funds determine which debt securities to purchase after conducting a credit analysis of the firms that have issued or will be issuing debt securities. Stock mutual funds invest in stocks that satisfy their specific investment objective (such as growth in value or high dividend income) and have potential for a high return, given the stock's level of risk.

Because mutual funds typically have billions of dollars to invest in securities, they use substantial resources to make their investment decisions. In particular, each mutual fund is managed by one or more portfolio managers, who purchase and sell securities in the fund's portfolio. These managers are armed with information about the firms that issue the securities in which they can invest.

After making an investment decision, mutual funds can always sell any securities that are not expected to perform well. However, if a mutual fund has made a large investment in a particular security, its portfolio managers may try to improve the performance of the security rather than sell it. For example, a given mutual fund may hold more than a million shares of a particular stock that has performed poorly. Rather than sell the stock, the mutual fund may attempt to influence the management of the firm that issued the security in order to boost the performance of the firm. These efforts should have a favorable effect on the firm's stock price.

Securities Firms

Securities firms include investment banks, investment companies, and brokerage firms. They serve as financial intermediaries in various ways. First, they play an investment banking role by placing securities (stocks and debt securities) issued by firms or government agencies. That is, they find investors who want to purchase these securities. Second, securities firms serve as investment companies by creating, marketing, and managing investment portfolios. A mutual fund is an example of an investment company. Finally, securities firms play a brokerage role by helping investors purchase securities or sell securities that they previously purchased. Securities firms are discussed in more detail in Chapter 3.

Insurance Companies

insurance companies
Financial institutions that provide various types of insurance (life, property, health) for their customers.

Insurance companies provide various types of insurance for their customers, including life insurance, property and liability insurance, and health insurance. They periodically receive payments (premiums) from their policyholders, pool the payments, and invest the proceeds until these funds are needed to pay off claims of policyholders. They commonly use the funds to invest in debt securities issued by firms or by government agencies. They also invest heavily in stocks issued by firms. Thus they help finance corporate expansion.

Insurance companies employ portfolio managers who invest the funds that result from pooling the premiums of their customers. An insurance company may have one or more bond portfolio managers to determine which bonds to purchase, and one or more stock portfolio managers to determine which stocks to purchase. The objective of the portfolio managers is to earn a relatively high return on the portfolios for a given level of risk. In this way, the return on the investments not only should cover future insurance payments to policyholders but also should generate a sufficient profit, which provides a return to the owners of insurance companies. The performance of insurance companies depends on the performance of their bond and stock portfolios.

Like mutual funds, insurance companies tend to purchase securities in large blocks, and they typically have a large stake in several firms. Thus they closely monitor the performance of these firms. They may attempt to influence the management of a firm to improve the firm's performance and therefore enhance the performance of the securities in which they have invested.

Pension Funds

pension funds
Financial institutions that receive payments from employees and invest the proceeds on their behalf.

Pension funds receive payments (called *contributions*) from employees, and/or their employers on behalf of the employees, and then invest the proceeds for the benefit of the employees. They typically invest in debt securities issued by firms or government agencies and in equity securities issued by firms.

Pension funds employ portfolio managers to invest funds that result from pooling the employee/employer contributions. They have bond portfolio managers who purchase bonds and stock portfolio managers who purchase stocks. Because of their large investments in debt securities or in stocks issued by firms, pension funds closely monitor the firms in which they invest. Like mutual funds and insurance companies, they may periodically attempt to influence the management of those firms to improve performance.

Other Financial Institutions

Other financial institutions also serve as important intermediaries. *Savings institutions* (also called thrift institutions or savings and loan associations) accept deposits from individuals and use the majority of the deposited funds to provide mortgage loans to individuals. Their participation is crucial in financing the purchases of homes by individuals. They also serve as intermediaries between investors and firms by lending these funds to firms.

Finance companies issue debt securities and lend the proceeds to individuals or firms in need of funds. Their lending to firms is focused on small businesses. When extending these loans, they incur a higher risk that borrowers will default on (will not pay) their loans than is typical for loans provided by commercial banks. Thus they charge a relatively high interest rate.

Comparison of the Key Financial Institutions

A comparison of the most important types of financial institutions that provide funding to firms appears in Figure 2.1. The financial institutions differ in the manner by which they obtain funds, but all provide credit to firms by purchasing debt securities the firms have issued. All of these financial institutions except commercial banks and savings institutions also provide equity investment by purchasing equity securities issued by firms.

FIGURE 2.1   How Financial Institutions Provide Financing for Firms

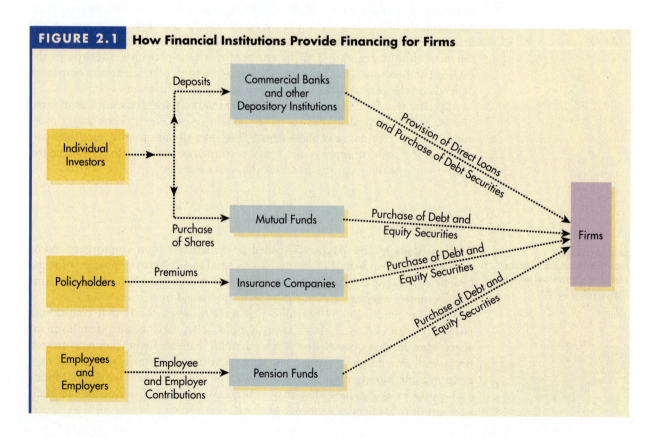

Securities firms are not shown in Figure 2.1 because they are not as important in actually providing the funds needed by firms. Yet they play a crucial role in facilitating the flow of funds from financial institutions to firms. In fact, each arrow representing a flow of funds from financial institutions to firms may have been facilitated by a securities firm that was hired by the business firm to sell its debt or equity securities. A securities firm also sells the debt and equity securities to individual investors, which results in some funds flowing directly from individuals to firms without first passing through a financial institution.

Consolidation of Financial Institutions

There has recently been a great deal of consolidation among financial institutions, and a single financial conglomerate may own every type of financial institution. Many financial conglomerates offer commercial banking services, investment banking services, brokerage services, mutual funds, and insurance services. They also have a pension fund and manage the pension funds of other companies. The most notable example of a financial conglomerate is Citigroup Inc., which offers commercial banking services through its Citibank unit, insurance services through its Travelers' insurance unit, and investment banking and brokerage services through its Salomon Smith Barney unit.

In recent years, many commercial banks have attempted to expand their offerings of financial services by acquiring other financial intermediaries that offer other financial services. Some banks even serve in advisory roles for firms that are considering the acquisition of other firms. Thus, much of the bank expansion is focused on services that were traditionally offered by securities firms. In general, the expansion of banks into these services is expected to increase the competition among financial intermediaries and therefore lower the price that individuals or firms pay for these services.

Globalization of Financial Institutions

Financial institutions not only have diversified their services in recent years but also have expanded internationally. This expansion was stimulated by various factors. First, the expansion of multinational corporations encouraged expansion of commercial banks to serve these foreign subsidiaries. Second, U.S. commercial banks had more flexibility to offer securities services and other financial services outside the United States, where fewer restrictions were imposed on commercial banks. Third, large commercial banks recognized that they could capitalize on their global image by establishing branches in foreign cities.

Financial institutions located in foreign countries facilitate the flow of funds between investors and the firms based in that country. During the 1997–1998 period, many Asian firms experienced poor performance and were cut off from funding by local banks and foreign banks. Before this time, some banks had been too willing to extend loans to Asian firms without determining whether the funding was really necessary and feasible. The crisis made some foreign banks realize that they should not extended credit to firms just because those firms had performed well during the mid-1990s. The crisis also caused Asian firms to realize how dependent they were on banks to run their businesses. As a result, Asian firms are expanding more cautiously, because they must now justify their request for additional funding from banks.

Review Questions

2–1 Distinguish between the role of a commercial bank and that of a mutual fund.

2–2 Which type of financial institution do you think is most critical for firms?

Overview of Financial Markets

Financial markets are crucial for firms and investors because they facilitate the transfer of funds between the investors who wish to invest and firms that need to obtain funds. Second, they can accommodate the needs of firms that temporarily have excess funds and wish to invest those funds. Third, they can accommodate the needs of investors who wish to liquidate their investments in order to spend the proceeds or invest them in alternative investments.

primary market
A financial market in which securities are initially issued; the only market in which the issuer is directly involved in the transaction.

initial public offering (IPO)
A firm's first offering of stock to the public.

secondary offering
Any offering of stock subsequent to an initial public offering.

secondary market
A financial market in which securities that are already owned (those that are not new issues) are traded.

Primary versus Secondary Markets

Debt and equity securities are issued by firms in the **primary market,** the market that facilitates the issuance of new securities. The first offering of stock to the public is referred to as an **initial public offering** (IPO). Any offering of stock by the firm after that point is referred to as a **secondary offering.** Once securities have been issued, they can be sold by investors to other investors in the so-called **secondary market,** the market that facilitates the trading of existing securities. The distinction between the primary market and the secondary market is illustrated in the following example.

Example ▼ Kenson Co. was established in Jacksonville, Florida, in July 1981. It enjoyed success as a privately held firm for more than 10 years, but it could not grow as much as desired because of a constraint on the amount of loans it could obtain from commercial banks. In order to expand its business throughout the southeastern United States, Kenson needed a large equity investment from other firms. On March 13, 1992, it engaged in an initial public offering. With the help of a securities firm, it was able to issue 2 million shares of stock on that day at an average price of $20 per share. Thus the company raised a total of $40 million. As investors in Kenson's stock later decided to sell it, they used the secondary market to sell the stock to other investors. The secondary market activity does not directly affect the amount of existing funds that Kenson has available to support its expansion. That is, Kenson gets no additional funds when investors sell their shares in the secondary market.

Kenson's expansion throughout the Southeast over the next several years was successful, and it decided to expand across the United States. By this time, its stock price was near $60 per share. On June 7, 2000, Kenson engaged in a sec-

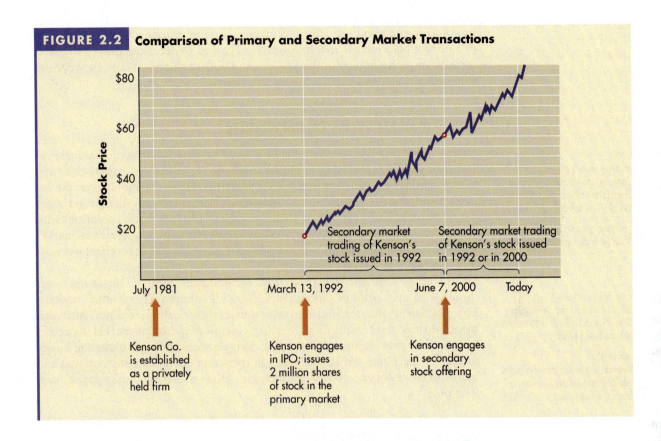

FIGURE 2.2 Comparison of Primary and Secondary Market Transactions

ondary stock offering by issuing another 1 million shares of stock. The new shares were sold at an average price of $60, thereby generating $60 million for Kenson to pursue its expansion plans. After that date, some of the new shares, as well as shares that resulted from the IPO, were traded in the secondary market. The evolution of Kenson's financing is shown in Figure 2.2.

Public Offering versus Private Placement

public offering
The nonexclusive sale of securities to the general public.

underwrite
To guarantee the dollar amount to be received by the issuing firm from a public offering of securities.

private placement
The sale of new securities directly to investors, rather than to the general public.

Most firms raise funds in the primary market by issuing securities through a **public offering,** which is the nonexclusive sale of securities to the general public. The IPO and the secondary offering by Kenson Co. in the previous example were public offerings. A public offering is normally conducted with the help of a securities firm that provides investment banking services. This firm may advise the issuing firm on the size of the offering and the price of the offering. It may also agree to place the offering with investors. It may even be willing to **underwrite** the offering, which means that it guarantees the dollar amount to be received by the issuing firm. In Chapters 3 and 16 we will discuss investment banking in more detail.

As an alternative to a public offering, firms may issue securities through a **private placement,** which is the sale of new securities directly to an investor or group of investors. Because a new offering of securities is often worth $40 to $100 million or more, only institutional investors (such as pension funds and insurance companies) can afford to invest in private placements. The advantage of a private placement is that it avoids fees charged by securities firms. However, some firms prefer to pay for the advising and underwriting services of a securities firm rather than conducting a private placement.

Money Markets versus Capital Markets

money markets
Financial markets that facilitate the flow of short-term funds (with maturities of 1 year or less).

money market securities
Securities traded in money markets.

Financial markets that facilitate the flow of *short-term funds* (with maturities of 1 year or less) are referred to as **money markets.** The securities that are traded in money markets are called **money market securities.** Firms commonly issue money market securities for purchase by investors in order to obtain funds for a short period of time. Firms may also consider purchasing money market securities with cash that is available temporarily. Likewise, investors purchase money market securities with funds that they may soon need for other (more profitable) investments in the near future.

capital markets
Financial markets that facilitate the flow of long-term funds (with maturities of more than 1 year).

securities
Financial instruments traded in capital markets; stock (equity securities) and bonds (debt securities).

In contrast, financial markets that facilitate the flow of *long-term funds* (funds with maturities of more than 1 year) are referred to as **capital markets.** The instruments that are traded in capital markets are called **securities.** Although stocks do not have maturities, they are classified as capital market securities because they provide long-term funding. Firms commonly issue stocks and bonds to finance their long-term investments in corporate operations. Institutional and individual investors purchase securities with funds that they wish to invest for a long time

International Capital Markets

Although U.S. capital markets are by far the world's largest, there are important debt and equity markets outside the United States. In the Eurobond market, which is the oldest and largest international bond market, corporations and governments typically issue bonds (Eurobonds) denominated in dollars and sell them to investors located outside the United States. A U.S. corporation might, for example, issue dollar-denominated bonds that would be purchased by investors in Belgium, Germany, or Switzerland. Issuing firms and governments appreciate the Eurobond market because it allows them to tap a much larger pool of investors than would generally be available in the local market.

foreign bond
A bond issued by a foreign corporation or government that is denominated in the investor's home currency and sold in the investor's home market.

The foreign bond market is another international market for long-term debt securities. A **foreign bond** is a bond issued by a foreign corporation or government that is denominated in the investor's home currency and sold in the investor's home market. A bond issued by a U.S. company that is denominated in Swiss francs and sold in Switzerland is an example of a foreign bond. Although the foreign bond market is much smaller than the Eurobond market, many issuers have found this to be an attractive way of tapping debt markets in Germany, Japan, Switzerland, and the United States.

Finally, a vibrant international equity market has emerged in the past decade. Many corporations have discovered that they can sell blocks of shares to investors in a number of different countries simultaneously. This market has enabled corporations to raise far larger amounts of capital than they could have raised in any single national market. International equity sales have also proved indispensable to governments that have sold state-owned companies to private investors in recent years, because the companies being privatized are often extremely large.

? Review Questions

2–3   Distinguish between the roles of primary and secondary markets.
2–4   Distinguish between money and capital markets.
2–5   How can corporations use international capital markets to raise funds?

LG3 Key Types of Securities

Securities are commonly classified as either money market securities or capital market securities.

Key Money Market Securities

liquidity
The ease with which securities can be converted into cash without a major loss in value.

Money market securities tend to have a high degree of **liquidity,** which means that they can be easily converted into cash without a major loss in their value. This is important to firms and investors who may need to sell the money market securities on a moment's notice in order to use their funds for other purposes. The money market securities most commonly used by firms and investors are Treasury bills, commercial paper, negotiable certificates of deposit, and foreign money market securities. These are described below.

Treasury Bills

Treasury bills
Short-term debt securities issued by the U.S. Treasury.

Treasury bills are short-term debt securities issued by the U.S. Treasury. Every Monday, Treasury bills are issued in two maturities, 13 weeks and 26 weeks; 1-year Treasury bills are issued once a month. The Treasury uses an auction process when issuing the securities. Competitive bids are submitted by 1:00 p.m. eastern time on Monday. Noncompetitive bids can also be submitted by firms and investors who are willing to pay the average accepted price paid by all competitive bidders. The Treasury has a plan for how much money it would like to raise every Monday. It accepts the highest competitive bids first and continues accepting bids until it has obtained the amount of funds desired.

The *par value* (principal to be paid at maturity) on Treasury bills is a minimum of $10,000, but those purchased by firms and institutional investors typically have a much higher par value. When Treasury bills are issued, they are sold at a discount from the par value; the par value is the amount received at maturity. The difference between the par value and the discount is the investor's return. Treasury bills do not pay coupon (interest) payments. Rather, they pay a yield equal to the percentage difference between the price at which they are sold and the price at which they were purchased.

Treasury bills are commonly purchased by firms and investors who wish to have quick access to funds if needed. They are very liquid because of an active secondary market in which previously issued Treasury bills are sold. Treasury bills are backed by the federal government and are therefore perceived as free from the risk of default. For this reason, the return that can be earned from investing in a Treasury bill (a risk-free security) and holding it until maturity is commonly referred to as a *risk-free rate*. Investors know the exact return they can earn by holding a Treasury bill until maturity.

Example ▼ San Marcos Co. purchased a 1-year Treasury bill with a par value of $100,000 and paid $94,000 for it. If it holds the Treasury bill until maturity, its return for the period will be

$$= \frac{\$100,000 - \$94,000}{\$94,000}$$

$$= 0.0638, \text{ or } 6.38\%$$

If San Marcos plans to hold the Treasury bill for 2 months (60 days) and then sell it in the secondary market, the return over this period is uncertain. The return will depend on the selling price of the Treasury bill in the secondary market 2 months from now. Assume that San Marcos expects to sell the Treasury bill for $95,000. Thus its expected return over this time period would be

$$= \frac{\$95,000 - \$94,000}{\$94,000}$$

$$= 0.01064, \text{ or } 1.064\%$$

Returns from investing in money market securities are commonly measured on an annualized basis by multiplying the return by 365 (days in a year) divided by the number of days the investment is held. In this example, the expected annualized return is

$$= \frac{(\$95,000 - \$94,000)}{\$94,000} \times \frac{365}{60}$$

$$= 0.0647, \text{ or } 6.47\%$$

In this example there is uncertainty because the firm is not planning to hold the Treasury bill until maturity. If San Marcos wished to take a risk-free position for the 2-month period, it could purchase a Treasury bill in the secondary market that had 2 months remaining until maturity. For example, assume that San Marcos could purchase a Treasury bill that had 2 months until maturity and had a par value of $100,000 and a price of $99,000. The annualized yield that would be earned on this investment is

$$= \frac{(\$100,000 - \$99,000)}{\$99,000} \times \frac{365}{60}$$

$$= 0.0614, \text{ or } 6.14\%$$

Commercial Paper

commercial paper
A short-term debt security issued by firms with a high credit standing.

Commercial paper is a short-term debt security issued by well-known, creditworthy firms. It serves the firm as an alternative to a short-term loan from a bank. Some firms issue their commercial paper directly to investors; others rely on financial institutions to place the commercial paper with investors. The minimum denomination is $100,000, although the more common denominations are in multiples of $1 million. Maturities are typically between 20 and 45 days but can be as long as 270 days.

Commercial paper is not so liquid as Treasury bills, because it does not have an active secondary market. Thus investors who purchase commercial paper normally plan to hold it until maturity. Like Treasury bills, commercial paper does not pay coupon (interest) payments and is issued at a discount. The return to investors is based solely on the difference between the selling price and the buying price. Because it is possible that the firm that issued commercial paper will default on its payment at maturity, investors require a slightly higher return on commercial paper than what they would receive from risk-free (Treasury) securities with a similar maturity.

Negotiable Certificates of Deposit

negotiable certificates of deposit (NCD)
Debt securities issued by financial institutions to obtain short-term funds.

A **negotiable certificate of deposit** (NCD) is a debt security issued by financial institutions to obtain short-term funds. The minimum denomination is typically $100,000, but the $1 million denomination is more common. Common maturities of NCDs are 10 days to 1 year. Unlike the other money market securities we have mentioned, NCDs do provide interest payments. There is a secondary market for NCDs, but it is not so active as the secondary market for Treasury bills. Because there is a slight risk that the financial institution issuing an NCD will default on its payment at maturity, investors require a return that is slightly above the return on Treasury bills with a similar maturity.

Foreign Money Market Securities

euro
The currency for 11 different European countries.

Firms and investors can also use foreign money markets to borrow or invest funds for short-term periods. Firms can issue short-term securities such as commercial paper in foreign markets, assuming that they are perceived as creditworthy in those markets. They may even attempt to borrow short-term funds in other currencies by issuing short-term securities denominated in foreign currencies. The most common reason for a firm to borrow in foreign money markets is to obtain funds in a currency that matches its cash flows. For example, IBM's European subsidiary may borrow **euros** (the currency for 11 different European countries) either from a bank or by issuing commercial paper to support its European operations, and it will use future cash inflows in euros to pay off this debt at maturity.

Investors may invest in foreign short-term securities because they have future cash outflows in those currencies. For example, say a firm has excess funds that it can invest for three months. If it needs Canadian dollars to purchase exports in 3 months, it may invest in a 3-month Canadian money market security (such as Canadian Treasury bills) and then use the proceeds at maturity to pay for its exports.

Alternatively, an investor may purchase a foreign money market security to capitalize on a high interest rate. Interest rates vary among countries, which causes some foreign money market securities to have a much higher interest rate than others. However, investors are subject to exchange rate risk when investing in securities denominated in a different currency from what they need once the investment period ends. If the currency denominating the investment weakens over the investment period, then the actual return that investors earn may be less than what they could have earned from domestic money market securities.

Key Capital Market Securities

The key capital market securities are bonds and stocks.

Bonds

bonds
Long-term securities issued by firms and governments to raise large amounts of long-term funds.

Treasury bonds
Bonds issued by the U.S. Treasury to obtain long-term (10 to 30 years) funds.

Bonds are long-term debt securities issued by firms and governments to raise large amounts of long-term funds. Bonds are differentiated by the issuer and can be classified as Treasury bonds, municipal bonds, or corporate bonds.

Treasury Bonds **Treasury bonds** are issued by the U.S. Treasury as a means of obtaining funds for a long-term period. They normally have maturities from 10 years to 30 years. (As noted previously, the Treasury issues short-term debt securities in the form of *Treasury bills*. It also issues medium-term debt securities in the form of *Treasury notes,* which have maturities between 1 and 10 years.) The minimum denomination of Treasury bonds is $1,000, but much larger denominations are more common. The federal government borrows most of its funds by issuing Treasury securities. An active secondary market for Treasury bonds exists, so investors can sell Treasury bonds at any time.

Treasury bonds pay interest (in the form of coupon payments) on a semiannual basis (every 6 months) to the investors who hold them. Investors earn a return from investing in Treasury bonds in the form of these coupon payments and also in the difference between the selling price and the purchase price of the bond.

A Treasury bond with a par value of $1,000,000 and an 8 percent coupon rate pays $80,000 per year, which is divided into $40,000 after the first 6-month period of the year and another $40,000 in the second 6-month period of the year. Interest payments on Treasury bonds received by investors are exempt from state and local income taxes.

Because Treasury bonds are backed by the federal government, the return to an investor who holds them until maturity is known with certainty. The coupon payments are known with certainty, and so is the payment at maturity (the par value). Accordingly, the return that could be earned on a Treasury bond is commonly referred to as a *long-term risk-free rate*. The annualized return promised on a 10-year bond today serves as the annualized risk-free rate of return over the next 10 years, and the annualized return that is promised on a 20-year Treasury bond serves as the annualized risk-free rate of return over the next 20 years. If investors want to earn a risk-free return over a period that is not available on newly issued Treasury bonds, they can purchase a Treasury bond in the secondary market with a time remaining until maturity that matches their desired investment period.

municipal bonds
Bonds issued by municipalities to support their expenditures.

general obligation bonds
Municipal bonds backed by the municipality's ability to tax.

revenue bonds
Municipal bonds that will be repaid with the funds generated from the project financed with the proceeds of the bond issue.

Municipal Bonds   **Municipal bonds** are bonds issued by municipalities to support their expenditures. They are typically classified into one of two categories. **General obligation bonds** provide investors with interest and principal payments that are backed by the municipality's ability to tax. Conversely, **revenue bonds** provide interest and principal payments to investors using funds generated from the project financed with the proceeds of the bond issue. For example, revenue bonds may be issued by a municipality to build a tollway. The proceeds received in the form of tolls would be used to make interest and principal payments to the investors who purchased these bonds. The minimum denomination is $5,000, but larger denominations are more common.

Municipal bonds pay interest on a semiannual basis. The interest paid on municipal bonds is normally exempt from federal income taxes and may even be exempt from state and local income taxes. This very attractive feature of municipal bonds enables municipalities to obtain funds at a lower cost. In other words, investors are willing to accept a lower pre-tax return on municipal bonds, because they tend to be more concerned with the after-tax return.

Municipal bonds have a secondary market, although that market is less active than the secondary market for Treasury bonds. Therefore, municipal bonds are less liquid than Treasury bonds that have a similar term to maturity.

corporate bonds
A debt instrument indicating that a corporation has borrowed a certain amount of money and promises to repay it in the future under clearly defined terms.

Corporate Bonds   **Corporate bonds** are bonds issued by corporations to finance their investment in long-term assets, such as buildings and machinery. Their standard denomination is $1,000, but other denominations are sometimes issued. The secondary market for corporate bonds is more active for those bonds that were issued in high volume. Because there is less secondary market activity for corporate bonds than there is for Treasury bonds, corporate bonds are less liquid than Treasury bonds with a similar term to maturity. Maturities of corporate bonds typically range between 10 and 30 years, but some recent corporate bond issues have maturities of 50 years or more. For example, both the Coca-Cola Company and Disney recently issued bonds with maturities of 100 years. A detailed discussion of corporate bonds is provided in Chapter 3.

Example ▼   MicroCircuit Industries, a major microprocessor manufacturer, has just issued a 20-year bond with 12% coupon interest rate and a $1,000 par value that pays interest semiannually. Investors who buy this bond receive the contractual right to (1) $120 annual interest (the 12% coupon interest rate × $1000 par value), distributed as $60 at the end of each 6 months (1/2 × $120) for 20 years, and (2) **▲** the $1,000 par value at the end of year 20.

International Bonds   Firms commonly issue bonds in the *Eurobond market,* which serves issuers and investors in bonds denominated in a variety of currencies. For example, General Motors may consider issuing a dollar-denominated bond to investors in the Eurobond market. Or it may consider issuing a bond denominated in Japanese yen to support its operations in Japan.

U.S. investors may use the Eurobond market to purchase bonds denominated in other currencies that are paying higher coupon rates than dollar-denominated bonds. However, they will be subject to exchange rate risk if they plan to convert the coupon and principal payments into dollars in the future.

Stocks

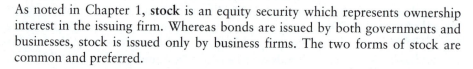

stock
An equity security that represents ownership interest in the issuing firm.

As noted in Chapter 1, **stock** is an equity security which represents ownership interest in the issuing firm. Whereas bonds are issued by both governments and businesses, stock is issued only by business firms. The two forms of stock are common and preferred.

common stock
Collectively, units of ownership interest, or equity, in a corporation.

preferred stock
A special form of ownership having a fixed periodic dividend that must be paid prior to payment of any common stock dividends.

Common and Preferred Stock   Shares of **common stock** are units of ownership interest, or equity, in a corporation. Common stockholders expect to earn a return by receiving dividends, by realizing gains through increases in share price, or both. **Preferred stock** is a special form of ownership that has features of both a bond and common stock. Preferred stockholders are promised a fixed periodic dividend that must be paid prior to payment of any dividends to the owners of common stock. In other words, preferred stock has priority over common stock when the firms dividends are disbursed. A detailed discussion of both common and preferred stock is provided in Chapter 3.

International Stocks   Many large U.S. firms issue stock in international equity markets. They may be able to sell all of their stock offering more easily by placing some of the stock in foreign markets, if there is not sufficient demand in the United States. In addition, they may be able to increase their global name recognition in countries where they conduct business by selling some of their newly issued stock in those foreign markets.

Investors commonly invest in stocks issued by foreign firms. They may believe that a particular foreign stock's price is undervalued in the foreign market. Alternatively, they may believe that a foreign country has much greater potential economic growth than can be found at home. Investors may also invest in foreign stocks to achieve international diversification. To the extent that most U.S. stocks are highly influenced by the U.S. economy, U.S. investors can reduce their exposure to potential weakness in the U.S. economy by investing in stocks of foreign firms whose performance is insulated from U.S. economic conditions.

Summary of Securities

A summary of the money market and capital market securities that we have described is provided in Table 2.2. All types of firms that need short-term funds issue commercial paper as a means of obtaining funds. They also invest in the other money market securities (such as Treasury bills) when they have temporary funds available.

Investors invest in all the kinds of securities disclosed in the table. In general, they tend to focus on the money market securities if they wish to invest their funds for a very short period of time and to choose capital market securities when they can invest their funds for long periods. The money market securities

TABLE 2.2	Summary of Money and Capital Market Securities		
	Issuer	Common Maturities	Secondary Market Activity
Money Market Securities			
Treasury bills	Federal government	13 weeks, 26 weeks, 1 year	High
Commercial paper	Firms	1 day to 270 days	Low
Negotiable CDs	Commercial banks	10 days to 1 year	Low
Capital Market Securities			
Treasury bonds	Federal government	10 to 30 years	High
Municipal bonds	State and local government	10 to 30 years	Moderate
Corporate bonds	Firms	10 to 30 years	Moderate
Stocks	Firms	No maturity	Moderate to high

provide a relatively low expected return, but offer some liquidity and generate a positive return until the investor determines a better use of funds.

The capital market securities offer more potential for higher returns, but their expected returns are subject to a higher degree of uncertainty (risk). Because the capital markets facilitate the exchange of long-term securities, they help to finance the long-term growth of government agencies and firms. Institutional investors play a major role in supplying funds in the capital markets. In particular, institutional investors such as commercial banks, insurance companies, pension funds, and bond mutual funds are major investors in the primary and secondary markets for bonds. Insurance companies, pension funds, and stock mutual funds are major investors in the primary and secondary markets for stocks.

? Review Questions

2–6   What is the meaning of the term *risk-free rate?*

2–7   Explain why firms that issue a corporate bond must promise investors a higher return than that available on a Treasury security that has the same maturity.

2–8   How does stock differ from bonds in terms of ownership privileges?

LG4 Major Securities Exchanges

securities exchanges
Organizations that provide the market-place in which firms can raise funds through the sale of new securities and in which purchasers can resell securities.

Securities exchanges provide the marketplace in which firms can raise funds through the sale of new securities and in which purchasers of securities can maintain liquidity by being able to resell them easily when necessary. Many people call securities exchanges "stock markets," but this label is somewhat misleading because bonds, common stock, preferred stock, and a variety of other investment vehicles are all traded on these exchanges. The two key types of securities exchanges are the organized exchange and the over-the-counter market.

Organized Securities Exchanges

Organized securities exchanges are tangible organizations that act as secondary markets in which outstanding securities are resold. Organized exchanges account for about 59 percent of the *total dollar volume* of domestic shares traded. The dominant organized exchanges are the New York Stock Exchange and the American Stock Exchange, both headquartered in New York City. There are also regional exchanges, such as the Chicago Stock Exchange and the Pacific Stock Exchange (co-located in Los Angeles and San Francisco).

The New York Stock Exchange

Most organized exchanges are modeled after the New York Stock Exchange (NYSE), which accounts for about 90 percent of the total annual dollar volume of shares traded on organized exchanges. To make transactions on the "floor" of the New York Stock Exchange, an individual or firm must own a "seat" on the exchange. There are a total of 1,366 seats on the NYSE, most of which are owned by brokerage firms. To be listed for trading on an organized exchange, a firm must file an application for listing and meet a number of requirements. For example, to be eligible for listing on the NYSE, a firm must have at least 2000 stockholders, each owning 100 or more shares, a minimum of 1.1 million shares of publicly held stock, a demonstrated earning power of $2.5 million before taxes at the time of listing and $2 million before taxes for each of the preceding 2 years, net tangible assets of $18 million, and a total of $18 million in market value of publicly traded shares. Clearly, only large, widely held firms are candidates for listing on the NYSE.

Trading is carried out on the floor of the exchange through an *auction process*. The goal of trading is to fill *buy orders* (orders to purchase securities) at the lowest price and to fill *sell orders* (orders to sell securities) at the highest price, thereby giving both purchasers and sellers the best possible deal. The general procedure for placing and executing an order can be described by a simple example.

Example ▼ Meredith Blake, who has an account with Merrill Lynch, wishes to purchase 200 shares of the IBM Corporation at the prevailing market price. Meredith calls her account executive,* Howard Kohn of Merrill Lynch, and places her order. Howard immediately has the order transmitted to the New York headquarters of Merrill Lynch, which immediately forwards the order to the Merrill Lynch clerk on the floor of the exchange. The clerk dispatches the order to one of the firm's seat holders, who goes to the appropriate trading post, executes the order at the best possible price, and returns to the clerk, who then wires the execution price and confirmation of the transaction back to the brokerage office. Howard is given the relevant information and passes it along to Meredith. Howard then ▲ does certain paperwork to complete the transaction.

*The title *account executive* or *financial consultant* is often used to refer to an individual who traditionally has been called a *stockbroker*. These titles are designed to change the image of the stockbroker from that of a salesperson to that of a personal financial manager who offers diversified financial services to clients.

*News*Line — NYSE GETS OFF THE FLOOR

Electronic communications networks (ECNs) can now register with the SEC as securities exchanges. Because the Internet-based ECNs allow institutional traders and some individuals to make direct transactions, without using brokers, they pose a threat to both the NYSE and Nasdaq.

The Big Board finally figures out it needs to have an Internet strategy to compete with ECNs—and to keep up with Nasdaq. The New York Stock Exchange finally has taken steps toward joining the rush of financial institutions moving online.

Richard Grasso, chairman of the NYSE, announced recently that the exchange plans to create an Internet-based order book, to be fully operational by mid-2000. The system will allow exchange members to directly execute orders of 1000 shares or less without having to go through a floor broker, as they do today. Also, members will have access to a "virtual" book, which will display all the orders as they are executed and will include data currently seen only by traders on the floor.

While the news from the NYSE may seem insignificant when compared to advancements others have made toward an electronic marketplace, it's indicative that the Big Board doesn't plan to miss the revolution.

"This is long overdue on the exchange's part," says Bernard Madoff, of market-making firm Bernard L. Madoff

Investment Securities, which trades both NYSE and Nasdaq stocks.

"They should have done this a year ago. This past year was crucial in terms of investments, partnerships, and advancements in technology. They probably waited too long, but that doesn't mean they can't play catch-up."

Indeed, it is difficult to imagine that at the turn of the century, the nation's largest exchange still operates with 1366 traders screaming orders on a paper-strewn floor at Broad and Wall Streets. Unlike Nasdaq, the NYSE has resisted moving toward an electronic platform, and it still treats its exclusive member base like an old boys' club.

Now that the Securities and Exchange Commission has given the green light to electronic communications networks to apply to become exchanges, the NYSE and Nasdaq need to open up access and improve execution practices, or risk losing market share to the upstarts....

Source: Megan Barnett, "NYSE Gets Off the Floor," The Industry Standard, November 15, 1999, downloaded from http://www.thestandard.com/article/display/0,1151,7607,00.html

Once placed, an order either to buy or to sell can be executed in seconds, thanks to sophisticated telecommunications devices. Information on the daily trading of securities is reported in various media, including financial publications such as the *Wall Street Journal*.

The American Stock Exchange

The American Stock Exchange (AMEX), now owned by the Nasdaq market, is also based in New York, but is smaller than the New York Stock Exchange. Its trading is also conducted on a trading floor.

The Over-the-Counter Exchange

over-the-counter (OTC) market
An intangible market (not an organization) for the purchase and sale of securities not listed by the organized exchanges.

The **over-the-counter (OTC) market** is not an organization but an intangible market for the purchase and sale of securities not listed by the organized exchanges. The market price of OTC securities results from a matching of the forces of supply and demand for securities by traders known as dealers. OTC dealers are linked with the purchasers and sellers of securities through the *National Association of Securities Dealers Automated Quotation (Nasdaq) System,* which is a sophisticated telecommunications network. In 1999 the

Nasdaq exchange merged with the American Stock Exchange to become Nasdaq–AMEX. This new entity continued to facilitate floor trading of stocks listed on the American Stock Exchange and computerized trading for stocks listed on Nasdaq.

Nasdaq provides current bid and ask prices on thousands of actively traded OTC securities. The *bid price* is the highest price offered by a dealer to purchase a given security, and the *ask price* is the lowest price at which the dealer is willing to sell the security. The dealer in effect adds securities to his or her inventory by purchasing them at the bid price and sells securities from his or her inventory at the ask price, hoping to profit from the spread between the bid and ask prices. Unlike the auction process on the organized securities exchanges, the prices at which securities are traded in the OTC market result from both competitive bids and negotiation.

In addition to creating a *secondary (resale) market* for outstanding securities, the OTC market, is also a *primary market* in which all new public issues are sold.

? Review Questions

2–9   How does the New York Stock Exchange facilitate the exchange of stocks?

2–10   How does the Nasdaq market differ from the New York Stock Exchange?

LG5 Derivative Securities Markets

derivative securities (derivatives)
Financial contracts whose values are derived from the value of underlying financial assets.

Derivative securities (also called derivatives) are financial contracts whose values are *derived from* the values of underlying financial assets (such as securities). Examples of derivative securities include stock options and financial futures contracts, which are discussed in detail in Chapter 21. Each derivative security's value tends to be related to the value of the underlying security in a manner that is understood by firms and investors. Consequently, derivative securities allow firms and investors to take positions in the securities on the basis of their expectations of movements in the underlying financial assets. In particular, investors commonly speculate on expected movements in the value of the underlying financial asset without having to purchase the financial asset. In many cases, a speculative investment in the derivative position can generate a much higher return than the same investment in the underlying financial asset. However, such an investment will also result in a much higher level of risk for the investors.

Derivative securities are used not only to take speculative positions but also to hedge, or reduce exposure to risk. For example, firms that are adversely affected by interest rate movements can take a particular position in derivative securities that can offset the effects of interest rate movements. By reducing a firm's exposure to some external force, derivative securities can reduce its risk.

Some investors use derivative securities to reduce the risk of their investment portfolio. For example, they can take a particular position in derivatives to insulate themselves against an expected temporary decline in the bonds or the stocks that they own.

Derivative securities are traded on special exchanges and through telecommunications systems. Financial institutions such as commercial banks and securities firms facilitate the trading of derivative securities by matching up buyers and sellers.

? Review Question

2–11 Why are derivative securities purchased by investors?

LG6 The Foreign Exchange Market

foreign exchange market
A market consisting of large international banks that purchase and sell currencies to facilitate international purchases of products, services, and securities.

The **foreign exchange market** allows for the purchase and sale of currencies to facilitate international purchases of products, services, and securities. The foreign exchange market is not based in one location; it is composed of large banks around the world that serve as intermediaries between those firms or investors who wish to purchase a specific currency and those that wish to sell it.

Spot Market for Foreign Exchange

spot market
A market that facilitates foreign exchange transactions that involve the immediate exchange of currencies.

spot exchange rate (spot rate)
The prevailing rate at which one currency can be immediately exchanged for another currency.

A key component of the foreign exchange market is the spot market. The **spot market** facilitates foreign exchange transactions that involve the immediate exchange of currencies. The prevailing exchange rate at which one currency can be immediately exchanged for another currency is referred to as the **spot exchange rate** (or **spot rate**). For example, the Canadian dollar's value has ranged between $0.60 and $0.80 in recent years. When U.S. firms purchase foreign supplies or acquire a firm in another country, and when U.S. investors invest in foreign securities, they commonly use the spot market to obtain the currency needed for the transaction.

During the so-called Bretton Woods era from 1944 to 1971, exchange rates were virtually fixed. They could change by only 1 percent from an initially established rate. Central banks of countries intervened by exchanging their currency on reserve for other currencies in the foreign exchange market to maintain stable exchange rates. By 1971 the boundaries of exchange rates were expanded to be 2.25 percent from the specified value, but this still restricted exchange rates from changing substantially over time.

In 1973 the boundaries were eliminated. This came as a result of pressure on some currencies to adjust their values because of large differences between the demand for a specific currency and the supply of that currency for sale. As the flow of trade and investing between the United States and a given country changes, so does the U.S. demand for that foreign currency and the supply of that foreign currency for sale (exchanged for dollars).

Because the demand and supply conditions for a given currency change continuously, so do the spot rates of most currencies. Thus most firms and investors that will need or receive foreign currencies in the future are exposed to exchange rate fluctuations.

Forward Market for Foreign Exchange

forward market
A market that facilitates foreign exchange transactions that involve the future exchange of currencies.

forward rate
The rate at which one currency can be exchanged for another currency on a specific future date.

forward contract
An agreement that specifies the amount of a specific currency that will be exchanged, the exchange rate, and the future date at which a currency exchange will occur.

The **forward market** facilitates foreign exchange transactions that involve the future exchange of currencies. The exchange rate at which one currency can be exchanged for another currency on a specific future date is referred to as the **forward rate.** The forward rate quote is usually close to the spot rate quote at a given point in time for most widely traded currency. Many of the commercial banks that participate in the spot market also participate in the forward market by accommodating requests of firms and investors. They provide quotes to firms or investors who wish to purchase or sell a specific foreign currency at a future time.

Firms or investors who use the forward market negotiate a **forward contract** with a commercial bank. This contract specifies the amount of a particular currency that will be exchanged, the exchange rate at which that currency will be exchanged (the forward rate), and the future date on which the exchange will occur. When a firm expects to need a foreign currency in the future, it can engage in a forward contract by "buying the currency forward." Conversely, if it expects to receive a foreign currency in the future, it can engage in a forward contract in which it "sells the currency forward."

Example ▼

Charlotte Co. expects to receive 100,000 euros from exporting products to a Dutch firm at the end of each of the next 3 months. The spot rate of the euro is $1.10. The forward rate of the euro for each of the next 3 months is also $1.10. Charlotte Co. expects that the euro will depreciate to $1.02 in 3 months.

If Charlotte Co. does not use a forward contract, it will convert the euros received into dollars at the spot rate that exists in 3 months. A comparison of the expected dollar cash flows that will occur in 3 months follows.

Choices	Exchange Rate	Expected $ Cash Inflows
1. Use the spot market.	The spot rate in 3 months is expected to be $1.02.	100,000 euros × $1.02 = $102,000
2. Use the forward market.	The 3-month forward rate is $1.10.	100,000 euros × $1.10 = $110,000

Thus Charlotte expects that its dollar cash inflows would be $8,000 higher as a result of hedging with a forward contract and decides to negotiate a forward contract to sell 100,000 euros forward. If Charlotte Co. were an investor instead of an exporter, and expected to receive euros in the future, it could have used a forward contract in the same manner. ▲

? Review Question

2–12 Distinguish between the *spot market* and *forward market* for foreign exchange.

TYING IT ALL TOGETHER

This chapter provided an overview of the financial institutions and markets that serve managers of firms and investors who invest in firms, and how those institutions and markets facilitate the flow of funds. The roles of financial managers, financial markets, and investors in channeling financial flows of funds are summarized in the Integrative Table.

INTEGRATIVE TABLE

Channeling Financial Flows of Funds

Role of **Financial Managers**	*Role of* **Financial Markets**	*Role of* **Investors**
Financial managers make financing decisions that require funding from investors in the financial markets.	The financial markets provide a forum in which firms can issue securities to obtain the funds that they need and in which investors can purchase securities to invest their funds.	Investors provide the funds that are to be used by financial managers to finance corporate growth.

LG1 **Explain how financial institutions serve as intermediaries between investors and firms.** Financial institutions channel the flow of funds between investors and firms. Individuals deposit funds at commercial banks, purchase shares of mutual funds, purchase insurance protection with insurance premiums, and make contributions to pension plans. All of these financial institutions provide credit to firms by purchasing debt securities. In addition, all of these financial institutions except commercial banks purchase stocks issued by firms.

LG2 **Provide an overview of financial markets.** Financial market transactions can be distinguished by whether they involve new or existing securities, whether the transaction of new securities reflects a public offering or a private placement, and whether the securities have short-term or long-term maturities. New securities are issued by firms in the primary market and purchased by investors. If investors desire to sell the securities they have previously purchased, they use the secondary market. The sale of new securities to the general public is referred to as a public offering; the sale of new securities to one investor or a group

of investors is referred to as a private placement. Securities with short-term maturities are called money market securities, and securities with long-term maturities are called capital market securities.

LG3 **Explain how firms and investors trade money market and capital market securities in the financial markets in order to satisfy their needs.** Firms obtain short-term funds by issuing commercial paper. Individual and institutional investors that wish to invest funds for a short-term period commonly purchase Treasury bills, commercial paper, and negotiable CDs. Firms that need long-term funds may issue bonds or stock. Institutional and individual investors invest funds for a long-term period by purchasing bonds or stock.

LG4 **Describe the major securities exchanges.** The major securities exchanges are the New York Stock Exchange and the Nasdaq–AMEX exchange. The stocks of the largest U.S. publicly traded firms are typically traded on the New York Stock Exchange, whereas stocks of smaller firms are traded on the Nasdaq–AMEX exchange.

LG5 Describe derivative securities and explain why they are used by firms and investors. Derivative securities are financial contracts whose values are derived from the values of underlying financial assets. They are commonly used by firms to reduce their exposure to a particular type of risk. Investors may use derivative securities to enhance their returns or reduce their exposure to some types of risk.

LG6 Describe the foreign exchange market. The foreign exchange market is composed of the spot market and the forward market. The spot market makes possible the immediate exchange of one currency for another at the prevailing exchange rate (spot rate). The forward market allows for the negotiation of contracts (forward contracts) that specify the exchange of an amount of one currency for another at a particular future date and a particular exchange rate (the forward rate).

SELF-TEST EXERCISES   (Solutions in Appendix B)

LG1 ST–1 Explain the process in which financial institutions channel funds from investors to firms.

LG3 ST–2 **Annualized return** You purchased a 180-day maturity, $100,000 par value Treasury bill for $96,800.
  a. Calculate your annualized return if you hold it until it matures.
  b. If you sell it for $98,100 after 90 days, what is your annualized return?
  c. What should the price be in part **b** in order for your annualized return to be the same as in part **a**?

EXERCISES

LG1 2–1 How is the role of the securities firms as intermediaries different from the roles of commercial banks and insurance companies?

LG1 2–2 Consolidation among financial institutions in recent years has changed the landscape of financial services offered to investors. How has consolidation affected the services offered?

LG1 2–3 Give three reasons why financial institutions have expanded globally in recent years.

LG2 2–4 Why are financial markets important to firms and investors?

LG2 2–5 Why are secondary markets important?

LG2 2–6 What are (a) initial public offerings and (b) secondary offerings?

LG2 2–7 Distinguish between public offering and private placement.

LG3   2–8   Describe the following money market securities: (a) Treasury bills, (b) commercial paper, and (c) negotiable certificates of deposit.

LG3   2–9   Money market securities, in general, provide lower returns than capital market securities. In the presence of the secondary market where capital securities are easily tradeable, why would anyone invest in money market securities instead of capital market securities?

LG3   2–10   Explain how foreign money market securities can be used for cash receipts or payments in the foreign currency.

LG4   2–11   Distinguish between a general obligation bond and a revenue bond.

LG4   2–12   What are the bid price and the ask price? Why are prices in the OTC market quoted in this way?

LG6   2–13   **Exchange rate transactions**   Suppose Charlotte Co. expects to pay out 100,000 euros to a Dutch exporter in 3 months' time. The current spot rate and forward rate remain at $1.10 per euro.
   a. If Charlotte Co. expects the euro to depreciate to $1.02, should Charlotte purchase euros forward?
   b. If Charlotte Co. expects the euro to appreciate to $1.18, should Charlotte purchase euros forward? Explain.

web exercises

Federal Reserve Bank of New York

Go to the New York Federal Reserve Bank web site **www.ny.frb.org/**.
a. Click on the **TreasuryDirect** box. On the next screen, click on **Treasury Bill Auction Results** for a list of Treasury bills that were auctioned weekly during the last 4 months. Information includes issue dates, maturity dates, discount rates, investment rates, and the price paid based on a $100 par value.

The discount rate is an annualized rate of return based on the par value of the bill. The investment rate, or equivalent coupon yield, is an annualized rate based on the purchase price of the bill and reflects the actual yield if the bill is held until maturity. Both rates are calculated on the basis of the actual number of days to maturity. The discount rate is calculated on a 360-day basis, the investment rate on a 365-day basis (or 366 days in a leap year).

Select one security and use its price to calculate the investment rate on the basis of the method given in this book. Compare your answer to that given in the table.

b. Go back to the home page and click on the **Statistics** box. On the next screen, click on the **FRED Federal Reserve Economic Database**. Under the **Database Categories**, click on **Monthly Interest Rates** and the **3-Month Treasury Bill Rate—Auction Average**. The table lists monthly T-bill rates since the 1940s and gives you some idea of the rates of return you would have earned over the years if you had invested in Treasury bills. You can also explore rates of return on other longer-term Treasury securities (such as notes and bonds).

For additional practice with concepts from this chapter, visit
http://www.awl.com/gitman_madura

Chapter

3

Corporate Securities: Bonds and Stocks

LEARNING GOALS

LG1 Describe the legal aspects of bond financing and bond cost.

LG2 Discuss the general features, ratings, popular types, and international issues of corporate bonds.

LG3 Differentiate between debt and equity capital.

LG4 Review the rights and features of common stock.

LG5 Discuss the rights and features of preferred stock.

LG6 Understand the role of the investment banker in securities offerings.

51

Corporate Bonds

corporate bond
A debt instrument indicating that a corporation has borrowed a certain amount of money and promises to repay it in the future under clearly defined terms.

A **corporate bond** is a debt instrument indicating that a corporation has borrowed a certain amount of money and promises to repay it in the future under clearly defined terms. Most bonds are issued with maturities of 10 to 30 years and with a par value, or face value, of $1,000. The **coupon interest rate** on a bond represents the percentage of the bond's par value that will be paid annually, typically in two equal semiannual payments, as interest. The bondholders, who are the lenders, are promised the semiannual interest payments and, at maturity, repayment of the principal amount.

coupon interest rate
The percentage of a bond's par value that will be paid annually, typically in two equal semiannual payments, as interest.

 Legal Aspects of Corporate Bonds

Certain legal arrangements are required to protect purchasers of bonds. Bondholders are protected primarily through the indenture and the trustee.

Bond Indenture

bond indenture
A legal document stating the conditions under which a bond has been issued.

A **bond indenture** is a legal document that specifies both the rights of the bondholders and the duties of the issuing corporation. Included in the indenture are the interest and principal payments, various standard and restrictive provisions, and (frequently) sinking-fund requirements and security interest provisions.

standard debt provisions
Provisions in a bond indenture specifying certain record keeping and general business practices that the bond issuer must follow; normally they do not place a burden on the financially sound business.

Standard Provisions   The **standard debt provisions** in the bond indenture specify certain record-keeping and general business practices that the bond issuer must follow. Standard debt provisions do not normally place a burden on a financially sound business.

The borrower commonly must (1) maintain satisfactory accounting records in accordance with generally accepted accounting principles (GAAP), (2) periodically supply audited financial statements, (3) pay taxes and other liabilities when due, and (4) maintain all facilities in good working order.

restrictive covenants
Contractual clauses in a bond indenture that place operating and financial constraints on the borrower.

Restrictive Provisions   Bond indentures also normally include certain **restrictive covenants,** which place operating and financial constraints on the borrower. These provisions help protect the bondholder against increases in borrower risk. Without them, the borrower could increase the firm's risk but not have to pay increased interest to compensate for the increased risk.

The most common restrictive covenants do the following:

1. Require a *minimum level of liquidity,* to ensure against loan default.
2. *Prohibit the sale of accounts receivable* to generate cash. Selling receivables could cause a long-run cash shortage if proceeds were used to meet current obligations.
3. Impose *fixed-asset restrictions.* The borrower must maintain a specified level of fixed assets to guarantee its ability to repay the bonds.
4. *Constrain subsequent borrowing.* Additional long-term debt may be prohibited, or additional borrowing may be subordinated to the original loan (subsequent creditors agree to wait until all claims of the senior debt are satisfied).

5. *Limit the firm's annual cash dividend payments* to a specified percentage or amount.

Other restrictive covenants are sometimes included in bond indentures.

The violation of any standard or restrictive provision by the borrower gives the bondholders the right to demand immediate repayment of the debt. Generally, bondholders will evaluate any violation to determine whether it jeopardizes the loan. They may then decide to demand immediate repayment, continue the loan, or alter the terms of the bond indenture.

sinking-fund requirement
A restrictive provision often included in a bond indenture, providing for the systematic retirement of bonds prior to their maturity.

Sinking-Fund Requirements   Another common restrictive provision is a **sinking-fund requirement.** Its objective is to provide for the systematic retirement of bonds prior to their maturity. To carry out this requirement, the corporation makes semiannual or annual payments that are used to retire bonds by purchasing them in the marketplace.

Security Interest   The bond indenture identifies any collateral pledged against the bond and specifies how it is to be maintained. The protection of bond collateral is crucial to guarantee the safety of a bond issue.

Trustee

trustee
A paid individual or organization that acts as the third party to a bond indenture and can take specified actions on behalf of the bondholders if the terms of the indenture are violated.

A **trustee** is a third party to a bond indenture. The trustee can be an individual, a corporation, or (most often) a commercial bank trust department. The trustee is paid to act as a "watchdog" on behalf of the bondholders and can take specified actions on behalf of the bondholders if the terms of the indenture are violated.

Cost of Bonds to the Issuer

The cost of bond financing is generally greater than the issuer would have to pay for short-term borrowing. The major factors that affect the cost, which is the rate of interest paid by the bond issuer, are the bond's maturity, the size of the offering, the issuer's risk, and the basic cost of money.

Impact of Bond Maturity on Bond Cost   Generally, long-term debt pays higher interest rates than short-term debt. In a practical sense, the longer the maturity of a bond, the less accuracy there is in predicting future interest rates, and therefore the greater the bondholders' risk of giving up an opportunity to lend money at a higher rate. In addition, the longer the term, the greater the chance that the issuer might default.

Impact of Offering Size on Bond Cost   The size of the bond offering also affects the interest cost of borrowing, but in an inverse manner: Bond flotation and administration costs per dollar borrowed are likely to decrease with increasing offering size. On the other hand, the risk to the bondholders may increase, because larger offerings result in greater risk of default.

Impact of Issuer's Risk   The greater the issuer's *default risk,* the higher the interest rate. Clearly, bondholders must be compensated with higher returns for taking greater risk. Frequently, bond buyers rely on bond ratings (discussed later) to determine the issuer's overall risk.

Impact of the Cost of Money   The cost of money in the capital market is the basis for determining a bond's coupon interest rate. Generally, the rate on U.S. Treasury securities of equal maturity is used as the lowest-risk cost of money. To that basic rate is added a *risk premium* that reflects the factors mentioned above (maturity, offering size, and issuer's risk).

 ## General Features of a Bond Issue

Three features often included in corporate bond issues are a conversion feature, a call feature, and stock purchase warrants. These features provide the issuer or the purchaser with certain opportunities for replacing or retiring the bond or supplementing it with some type of equity issue.

conversion feature (bond)
A feature of convertible bonds that allows bondholders to change each bond into a stated number of shares of common stock.

Convertible bonds offer a **conversion feature** that allows bondholders to change each bond into a stated number of shares of common stock. Bondholders will convert their bonds into stock only when the market price of the stock is such that the conversion will provide a profit for the bondholder. Inclusion of a conversion feature by the issuer lowers its interest cost and provides for automatic conversion of the bonds to stock if future stock prices appreciate noticeably.

call feature
A feature included in most corporate bond issues that gives the issuer the opportunity to repurchase bonds at a stated call price prior to maturity.

call price
The stated price at which a bond may be repurchased, by use of a call feature, prior to maturity.

call premium
The amount by which a bond's call price exceeds its par value.

The **call feature** is included in nearly all corporate bond issues. It gives the issuer the opportunity to repurchase bonds prior to maturity. The **call price** is the stated price at which bonds may be repurchased prior to maturity. Sometimes the call feature can be exercised only during a certain period. As a rule, the call price exceeds the par value of a bond by an amount equal to 1 year's interest. For example, a $1000 bond with a 10 percent coupon interest rate would be callable for around $1100 [$1,000 + (10% × $1,000)]. The amount by which the call price exceeds the bond's par value is commonly referred to as the **call premium**. This premium compensates bondholders for having the bond called away from them; to the issuer, it is the cost of calling the bonds.

The call feature enables an issuer to call an outstanding bond when interest rates fall and issue a new bond at a lower interest rate. When interest rates rise, the call privilege will not be exercised, except possibly to meet sinking-fund requirements. Of course, to sell a callable bond in the first place, the issuer must pay a higher interest rate than on noncallable bonds of equal risk, to compensate bondholders for the risk of having the bonds called away from them.

stock purchase warrants
Instruments that give their holders the right to purchase a certain number of shares of the issuer's common stock at a specified price over a certain period of time.

Bonds occasionally have stock purchase warrants attached as "sweeteners" to make them more attractive to prospective buyers. **Stock purchase warrants** are instruments that give their holders the right to purchase a certain number of shares of the issuer's common stock at a specified price over a certain period of time. This feature typically allows the issuer to pay a slightly lower coupon interest rate than would otherwise be required.

TABLE 3.1	Moody's and Standard & Poor's Bond Ratings[a]			
Moody's	Interpretation	Standard & Poor's	Interpretation	
Aaa	Prime quality	AAA	Bank investment quality	
Aa	High grade	AA		
A	Upper medium grade	A		
Baa	Medium grade	BBB		
Ba	Lower medium grade or speculative	BB	Speculative	
B	Speculative	B		
Caa	From very speculative to	CCC		
Ca	near or in default	CC		
C	Lowest grade	C	Income bond	
		D	In default	

[a]Some ratings may be modified to show relative standing within a major rating category; for example, Moody's uses numerical modifiers (1, 2, 3), whereas Standard & Poor's uses plus (+) and minus (−) signs.

Sources: Moody's Investor Services Inc. and Standard & Poor's Corporation.

Bond Ratings

Independent agencies such as Moody's and Standard & Poor's assess the riskiness of publicly traded bond issues. These agencies use financial ratio and cash flow analyses to assess the likely payment of bond interest and principal. Table 3.1 summarizes these ratings. Normally an inverse relationship exists between the quality of a bond and the rate of return that it must provide bondholders. High-quality (high-rated) bonds provide lower returns than lower-quality (low-rated) bonds. This reflects the lender's risk–return tradeoff. When considering bond financing, the financial manager must be concerned with the expected ratings of the bond issue, because these ratings affect salability and cost. The discussion of interest rates in Chapter 4 sheds further light on this relationship.

Popular Types of Bonds

Bonds can be classified in a variety of ways. Here we break them into traditional bonds (the basic types that have been around for years) and contemporary bonds (newer, more innovative types). The traditional types of bonds are summarized in terms of their key characteristics and priority of lender's claim in Table 3.2. Note that the first three types—**debentures, subordinated debentures,** and **income bonds**—are unsecured, whereas the last three—**mortgage bonds, collateral trust bonds,** and **equipment trust certificates**—are secured.

Table 3.3 describes the key characteristics of five contemporary types of bonds: **zero-coupon** or **low-coupon bonds, junk bonds, floating-rate bonds, extendible notes,** and **putable bonds.** These bonds can be either unsecured or secured. Changing capital market conditions and investor preferences have

debentures
See Table 3.2.

subordinated debentures
See Table 3.2.

income bonds
See Table 3.2.

mortgage bonds
See Table 3.2.

collateral trust bonds
See Table 3.2.

equipment trust certificates
See Table 3.2

zero- (or low-) coupon bonds
See Table 3.3.

junk bonds
See Table 3.3.

floating-rate bonds
See Table 3.3.

extendible notes
See Table 3.3.

putable bonds
See Table 3.3.

TABLE 3.2	Characteristics and Priority of Lender's Claim of Traditional Types of Bonds	
Bond type	**Characteristics**	**Priority of lender's claim**
Unsecured Bonds		
Debentures	Unsecured bonds that only creditworthy firms can issue. Convertible bonds are normally debentures.	Claims are the same as those of any general creditor. May have other unsecured bonds subordinated to them.
Subordinated debentures	Claims are not satisfied until those of the creditors holding certain (senior) debts have been fully satisfied.	Claim is that of a general creditor but not so good as a senior debt claim.
Income bonds	Payment of interest is required only when earnings are available. Commonly issued in reorganization of a failing firm.	Claim is that of a general creditor. Are not in default when interest payments are missed, because they are contingent only on earnings being available.
Secured Bonds		
Mortgage bonds	Secured by real estate or buildings.	Claim is on proceeds from sale of mortgaged assets; not fully satisfied, the lender becomes a general creditor. The *first-mortgage* claim must be fully satisfied before distribution of proceeds to *second-mortgage* holders, and so on. A number of mortgages can be issued against the same collateral.
Collateral trust bonds	Secured by stock and (or) bonds that are owned by the issuer. Collateral value is generally 25 to 35% greater than bond value.	Claim is on proceeds from stock and (or) bond collateral; if not fully satisfied, the lender becomes a general creditor.
Equipment trust certificates	Used to finance "rolling stock"—airplanes, trucks, boats, railroad cars. A trustee buys such an asset with funds raised through the sale of trust certificates and then leases it to the firm, which, after making the final scheduled lease payment, receives title to the asset. A type of leasing.	Claim is on proceeds from the sale of the asset; if proceeds do not satisfy outstanding debt, trust certificate lenders become general creditors.

spurred further innovations in bond financing in recent years and will probably continue to do so.

 ## International Bond Issues

Companies and governments borrow internationally by issuing bonds in two principal financial markets: the Eurobond market and the foreign bond market. Both give borrowers the opportunity to obtain large amounts of long-term debt financing quickly, in the currency of their choice and with flexible repayment terms.

A **Eurobond** is issued by an international borrower and sold to investors in countries with currencies other than the currency in which the bond is denominated. An example is a dollar-denominated bond issued by a U.S. corporation and sold to Belgian investors. From the founding of the Eurobond market in the 1960s until the mid-1980s, "blue-chip" U.S. corporations were the largest single class of Eurobond issuers. Some of these companies were able to borrow in this market at interest rates below those the U.S. government paid on Treasury bonds. As the market matured, issuers became able to choose the currency in

Eurobond
A bond issued by an international borrower and sold to investors in countries with currencies other than the currency in which the bond is denominated.

TABLE 3.3   Characteristics of Contemporary Types of Bonds

Bond type	Characteristics[a]
Zero- (or low-)-coupon bonds	Issued with no (zero) or a very low coupon (stated interest) rate and sold at a large discount from par. A significant portion (or all) of the investor's return comes from gain in value (i.e., par value minus purchase price). Generally callable at par value. Because the issuer can annually deduct the current year's interest accrual without having to pay the interest until the bond matures (or is called), its cash flow each year is increased by the amount of the tax shield provided by the interest deduction.
Junk bonds	Debt rated Ba or lower by Moody's or BB or lower by Standard & Poor's. Commonly used during the 1980s by rapidly growing firms to obtain growth capital, most often as a way to finance mergers and takeovers. High-risk bonds with high yields—typically yielding 3% more than the best quality corporate debt.
Floating-rate bonds	Stated interest rate is adjusted periodically within stated limits in response to changes in specified money market or capital market rates. Popular when future inflation and interest rates are uncertain. Tend to sell at close to par because of the automatic adjustment to changing market conditions. Some issues provide for annual redemption at par at the option of the bondholder.
Extendible notes	Short maturities, typically 1 to 5 years, that can be renewed for a similar period at the option of holders. Similar to a floating-rate bond. An issue might be a series of 3-year renewable notes over a period of 15 years; every 3 years, the notes could be extended for another 3 years, at a new rate competitive with market interest rates at the time of renewal.
Putable bonds	Bonds that can be redeemed at par (typically $1,000) at the option of their holder either at specific dates after the date of issue and every 1 to 5 years thereafter or when and if the firm takes specified actions such as being acquired, acquiring another company, or issuing a large amount of additional debt. In return for its conferring the right to "put the bond" at specified times or when the firm takes certain actions, the bond's yield is lower than that of a nonputable bond.

[a]The claims of lenders (i.e., bondholders) against issuers of each of these types of bonds vary, depending on their other features. Each of these bonds can be unsecured or secured.

which they borrowed, and European and Japanese borrowers rose to prominence. In more recent years, the Eurobond market has become much more balanced in terms of the mix of borrowers, total issue volume, and currency of denomination.

foreign bond
A bond issued in a host country's financial market, in the host country's currency, by a foreign borrower.

In contrast, a **foreign bond** is issued in a host country's financial market, in the host country's currency, by a foreign borrower. A pound-sterling-denominated bond issued in Great Britain by a U.S. company is an example of a foreign bond. The three largest foreign bond markets are Japan, Switzerland, and the United States.

Review Questions

3–1   What are typical maturities, denominations, and interest payments of a corporate bond? What mechanisms protect bondholders?
3–2   How are bonds rated, and why?
3–3   What major factors affect a bond's coupon interest rate?
3–4   Compare Eurobonds and foreign bonds.

 **BOND ISSUANCE IN EURO ZONE IS EXPLODING**

Bond financing is once again an attractive option for European companies, thanks to the introduction of the euro, a common currency unit for members of the European Union. Issuing bonds in euros, rather than in individual national currencies, improves the bonds' marketability and unifies the smaller national bond markets into a single, integrated whole.

The euro's slump to near parity with the dollar may wound the pride of European politicians and policy makers. But in one crucial place, the euro has outstripped even the most starry-eyed forecasts: the bond market.

While the new common currency was long expected to bring a major boost to the pan-European market for corporate bonds, few anticipated what actually happened: an astonishing explosion.

So far this year, the volume of bonds issued by corporations in the 11-country euro zone has already reached the equivalent of $131 billion, up from $52 billion last year, according to Capital Data Ltd. The European corporate bond market is still only about one-third the size of its U.S. counterpart. But it's growing so fast that Eden Riche, a managing director at Donaldson, Lufkin & Jenrette Inc. in London, expects it to approach the size of the U.S. market within five years—much quicker than expected.

This development marks a revolution of sorts in corporate finance. The role of corporate bonds in hostile takeovers has

been making headlines, of course: Olivette SpA probably could never have bought Telecom Italia SpA had it not had a subsidiary issue a 9.45-billion-euro bond, Europe's largest-ever corporate bond. But the story doesn't end there.

Routine corporate needs also are being financed with bonds, altering the way many midsize European companies raise capital. [Euro-denominated bonds] are helping corporate Europe to restructure, go global, and become a far more competitive force on the world stage.

...The euro changed everything, by binding a hodge-podge of national bond markets into a single, integrated whole, creating for companies a large critical mass, and for investors new opportunities and new risks. "The euro has made possible transactions that the Italian lira, German mark, and French franc markets couldn't handle themselves," notes Guido Pescione, Milan-based head of corporate client management for Chase Manhattan Bank in Italy.

Source: Michael R. Sesit, "Bond Issuance in Euro Zone Is Exploding," Wall Street Journal, December 1, 1999, pp. C1, C23.

Differences Between Debt and Equity Capital

capital
The long-term funds of a firm.

debt capital
All long-term borrowing incurred by a firm, including bonds.

equity capital
The long-term funds provided by the firm's owners, the stockholders.

The term **capital** denotes the long-term funds of a firm. **Debt capital** includes all long-term borrowing incurred by a firm, including bonds. **Equity capital** consists of long-term funds provided by the firm's owners, the stockholders. A firm can obtain equity capital either *internally*, by retaining earnings rather than paying them out as dividends to its stockholders, or *externally*, by selling common or preferred stock. The key differences between debt and equity capital are summarized in Table 3.4 and discussed below.

Voice in Management

Unlike creditors (lenders), holders of equity capital (common and preferred stockholders) are owners of the firm. Holders of common stock have voting rights that permit them to select the firm's directors and to vote on special issues. In contrast, debtholders and preferred stockholders may receive voting privileges only when the firm has violated its stated contractual obligations to them.

TABLE 3.4	Key Differences Between Debt and Equity Capital	
	Type of capital	
Characteristic	Debt	Equity
Voice in management[a]	No	Yes
Claims on income and assets	Senior to equity	Subordinate to debt
Maturity	Stated	None
Tax treatment	Interest deduction	No deduction

[a]In the event that the issuer violates its stated contractual obligations to them, debtholders and preferred stockholders *may* receive a voice in management; otherwise, only common stockholders have voting rights.

Claims on Income and Assets

Holders of equity have claims on both income and assets that are secondary to the claims of creditors. Their *claims on income* cannot be paid until the claims of all creditors (including both interest and scheduled principal payments) have been satisfied. After satisfying them, the firm's board of directors decides whether to distribute dividends to the owners.

The equity holders' *claims on assets* also are secondary to the claims of creditors. If the firm fails, its assets are sold, and the proceeds are distributed in this order: employees and customers, the government, creditors, and (finally) equity holders. Because equity holders are the last to receive any distribution of assets, they expect greater returns from dividends and/or increases in stock price.

As is explained in Chapter 12, the costs of equity financing are generally higher than debt costs. One reason is that the suppliers of equity capital take more risk because of their subordinate claims on income and assets. Despite being more costly, equity capital is necessary for a firm to grow. All corporations must initially be financed with some common stock equity.

Maturity

Unlike debt, equity capital is a permanent form of financing for the firm. It does not "mature" and so repayment is not required. Because equity is liquidated only during bankruptcy proceedings, stockholders must recognize that although a ready market may exist for their shares, the price that can be realized may fluctuate. This fluctuation of the market price of equity makes the overall returns to a firm's stockholders even more risky.

Tax Treatment

Interest payments to debtholders are treated as tax-deductible expenses by the issuing firm, whereas dividend payments to a firm's common and preferred stockholders are not tax-deductible. The tax deductibility of interest lowers the cost of debt financing, further causing it to be lower than the cost of equity financing.

Review Question

3–5   What are the key differences between debt capital and equity capital?

  Common Stock

A firm can obtain equity, or ownership, capital by selling either common or preferred stock. The true owners of business firms are the common stockholders. Common stockholders are sometimes referred to as *residual owners* because they receive what is left—the residual—after all other claims on the firm's income and assets have been satisfied. They are assured of only one thing: that they cannot lose any more than they have invested in the firm. As a result of this generally uncertain position, common stockholders expect to be compensated with adequate dividends and, ultimately, capital gains.

All corporations initially issue common stock to raise equity capital. Some of these firms later issue either additional common stock or preferred stock to raise more equity capital. Although both common and preferred stock are forms of equity capital, preferred stock has some similarities to debt capital that significantly differentiate it from common stock. We consider the fundamental aspects of common stock in this section and of preferred stock in the next section.

Ownership

privately owned (stock)
All common stock of a firm owned by a single individual.

closely owned (stock)
All common stock of a firm owned by a small group of investors.

publicly owned (stock)
Common stock of a firm owned by a broad group of unrelated individual or institutional investors.

The common stock of a firm can be **privately owned** by a single individual, **closely owned** by a small group of investors (such as a family), or **publicly owned** by a broad group of unrelated individual or institutional investors. Typically, small corporations are privately or closely owned; if their shares are traded, this occurs infrequently and in small amounts. Large corporations, which are emphasized in the following discussions, are publicly owned, and their shares are generally actively traded on the major securities exchanges described in Chapter 2.

Par Value

par value
A relatively useless value for a stock, established for legal purposes in the firm's corporate charter.

Unlike bonds, which always have a par value, common stock may be sold with or without a par value. The **par value** of a common stock is a relatively useless value, established for legal purposes in the firm's corporate charter. It is generally quite low, about $1.

Firms often issue stock with no par value, in which case they may assign the stock a value or record it on the books at the price at which it is sold. A low par value may be advantageous in states where certain corporate taxes are based on the par value of stock; if a stock has no par value, the tax may be based on an arbitrarily determined per-share figure.

Preemptive Rights

preemptive right
Allows common stockholders to maintain their *proportionate* ownership when new shares are issued.

dilution of ownership
Occurs when a new stock issue results in each present shareholder having a claim on a *smaller* part of the firm's earnings than previously.

rights
Financial instruments that permit stockholders to purchase additional shares at a price below the market price, in direct proportion to their number of owned shares.

The **preemptive right** allows common stockholders to maintain their *proportionate* ownership in the corporation when new shares are issued. It allows existing shareholders to maintain voting control and protects them against the dilution of their ownership. **Dilution of ownership** usually results in the dilution of earnings, because each present shareholder has a claim on a *smaller* part of the firm's earnings than previously.

In a rights offering, the firm grants **rights** to its shareholders. These financial instruments permit stockholders to purchase additional shares at a price below the market price, in direct proportion to their number of owned shares. Rights are used primarily by smaller corporations whose shares are either closely owned or publicly owned and not actively traded. In these situations, rights are an important financing tool without which shareholders would run the risk of losing their proportionate control of the corporation. From the firm's viewpoint, the use of rights offerings to raise new equity capital may be less costly and generate more interest than a public offering of stock.

Authorized, Outstanding, and Issued Shares

authorized shares
The number of shares of common stock that a firm's corporate charter allows it to issue.

outstanding shares
The number of shares of common stock held by the public.

treasury stock
The number of shares of outstanding stock that have been repurchased by the firm.

issued shares
The number of shares of common stock that have been put into circulation; the sum of outstanding shares and treasury stock.

A firm's corporate charter indicates how many **authorized shares** it can issue. The firm cannot sell more shares than the charter authorizes without obtaining approval through a shareholder vote. To avoid later having to amend the charter, firms generally attempt to authorize more shares than they initially plan to issue.

Authorized shares become **outstanding shares** when they are held by the public. If the firm repurchases any of its outstanding shares, these shares are recorded as **treasury stock** and are no longer considered to be outstanding shares. **Issued shares** are the shares of common stock that have been put into circulation; they represent the sum of outstanding shares and treasury stock.

Voting Rights

supervoting shares
Stock that carries with it multiple votes per share rather than the single vote per share typically given on regular shares of common stock.

nonvoting common stock
Common stock that carries no voting rights; issued when the firm wishes to raise capital through the sale of common stock but does not want to give up its voting control.

Generally, each share of common stock entitles its holder to one vote in the election of directors and on special issues. Votes are generally assignable and may be cast at the annual stockholders' meeting.

In recent years, many firms have issued two or more classes of common stock; they differ mainly in having unequal voting rights. A firm can use different classes of stock as a defense against a hostile takeover in which an outside group, without management support, tries to gain voting control of the firm by buying its shares in the marketplace. **Supervoting shares** of stock give each owner multiple votes. When supervoting shares are issued to "insiders," an outside group whose shares have only one vote each typically cannot obtain enough votes to gain control of the firm. At other times, a class of **nonvoting common stock** is issued when the firm wishes to raise capital through the sale of common stock but does not want to give up its voting control.

When different classes of common stock are issued on the basis of unequal voting rights, class A common is typically—but not universally—designated as nonvoting, and class B common has voting rights. Generally, higher classes of shares (class A, for example) are given preference in the distribution of earnings (dividends) and assets; lower-class shares, in exchange, receive voting rights. Treasury stock, which is held within the corporation, generally does not have voting rights, does not earn dividends, and does not have a claim on assets in liquidation.

Because most small stockholders do not attend the annual meeting to vote, they may sign a **proxy statement** giving their votes to another party. The solicitation of proxies from shareholders is closely controlled by the Securities and Exchange Commission to ensure that proxies are not solicited on the basis of misleading information. Existing management generally receives the stockholders' proxies, because it is able to solicit them at company expense.

Occasionally, when a firm is widely owned, outsiders may wage a **proxy battle** to unseat the existing management and gain control. To win a corporate election, votes from a majority of the shares voted are required. However, the odds of a nonmanagement group winning a proxy battle are generally slim.

Dividends

The payment of dividends to the firm's shareholders is at the discretion of the corporation's board of directors. Most corporations pay dividends quarterly. Dividends may be paid in cash, stock, or merchandise. Cash dividends are the most common, merchandise dividends the least.

Common stockholders are not promised a dividend, but they come to expect certain payments on the basis of the historical dividend pattern of the firm. Before dividends are paid to common stockholders, the claims of the government, all creditors, and preferred stockholders must be satisfied. Because of the importance of the dividend decision to the growth and valuation of the firm, dividends are discussed in greater detail in Chapter 13.

International Stock Issues

Although the international market for common stock is not so large as the international market for bonds, cross-border issuance and trading of common stock have increased dramatically in the past 20 years.

Some corporations issue stock in foreign markets. For example, the stock of General Electric trades in Frankfurt, London, Paris, and Tokyo; the stocks of AOL and Microsoft trade in Frankfurt; and the stock of McDonald's trades in Frankfurt and Paris. The London, Frankfurt, and Tokyo markets are the most popular. Issuing stock internationally broadens the ownership base and also helps a company to integrate itself into the local business scene. A listing on a foreign stock exchange both increases local business press coverage and serves as effective corporate advertising. Having locally traded stock can also facilitate corporate acquisitions, because shares can be used as an acceptable method of payment.

Foreign corporations have also discovered the benefits of trading their stock in the United States. The disclosure and reporting requirements mandated by the U.S. Securities and Exchange Commission have historically discouraged all but the largest foreign firms from directly listing their shares on the New York Stock Exchange or the American Stock Exchanges. For example, in 1993, Daimler-Benz (now DaimlerChrysler) became the first large German company to be listed on the NYSE.

American depository receipts (ADRs)
Claims issued by U.S. banks representing ownership of shares of a foreign company's stock held on deposit by the U.S. bank in the foreign market and issued in dollars to U.S. investors.

Alternatively, most foreign companies tap the U.S. market through **American depository receipts (ADRs).** These are claims issued by U.S. banks representing ownership of shares of a foreign company's stock held on deposit by the U.S. bank in the foreign market. Because ADRs are issued, in dollars, by a U.S. bank to U.S. investors, they are subject to U.S. securities laws. Yet they still give investors the opportunity to diversify their portfolios internationally.

? Review Questions

3–6   What risks do common stockholders take that other suppliers of long-term capital do not?

3–7   Explain the relationships among authorized shares, outstanding shares, treasury stock, and issued shares.

Preferred Stock

Preferred stock gives its holders certain privileges that make them senior to common stockholders. Preferred stockholders are promised a fixed periodic dividend, which is stated either as a percentage or as a dollar amount. How the dividend is specified depends on whether the preferred stock has a *par value,* which, as in common stock, is a relatively useless stated value established for legal purposes. **Par-value preferred stock** has a stated face value, and its annual dividend is specified as a percentage of this value. **No-par preferred stock** has no stated face value, but its annual dividend is stated in dollars. Preferred stock is most often issued by public utilities, by acquiring firms in merger transactions, or by firms that are experiencing losses and need additional financing.

par-value preferred stock
Preferred stock with a stated face value that is used with the specified dividend percentage to determine the annual dollar dividend.

no-par preferred stock
Preferred stock with no stated face value but with a stated annual dollar dividend.

Basic Rights of Preferred Stockholders

The basic rights of preferred stockholders are somewhat more favorable than the rights of common stockholders. Preferred stock is often considered *quasi-debt* because, much like interest on debt, it specifies a fixed periodic payment (dividend). Of course, as ownership, preferred stock is unlike debt in that it has no maturity date. Because they have a fixed claim on the firm's income that takes precedence over the claim of common stockholders, preferred stockholders are exposed to less risk. They are consequently not normally given a voting right.

Preferred stockholders have preference over common stockholders in the distribution of earnings. If the stated preferred stock dividend is "passed" (not paid) by the board of directors, the payment of dividends to common stockholders is prohibited. It is this preference in dividend distribution that makes common stockholders the true risk takers. Preferred stockholders are also usually given preference over common stockholders in the liquidation of assets in a legally bankrupt firm, although they must "stand in line" behind creditors. The amount of the claim of preferred stockholders in liquidation is normally equal to the par or stated value of the preferred stock.

Features of Preferred Stock

A number of features are generally included as part of a preferred stock issue. These features, along with the stock's par value, the amount of dividend payments, the dividend payment dates, and any restrictive covenants, are specified in an agreement similar to a *bond indenture*.

Restrictive Covenants

The restrictive covenants in a preferred stock issue are aimed at ensuring the firm's continued existence and regular payment of the dividend. These covenants include provisions about passing dividends, the sale of senior securities, mergers, sales of assets, minimum liquidity requirements, and common stock repurchases. The violation of preferred stock covenants usually permits preferred stockholders either to obtain representation on the firm's board of directors or to force the retirement of their stock at or above its par or stated value.

Cumulation

cumulative preferred stock
Preferred stock for which all passed (unpaid) dividends in arrears must be paid, along with the current dividend, prior to payment of dividends to common stockholders.

noncumulative preferred stock
Preferred stock for which passed (unpaid) dividends do not accumulate.

Most preferred stock is **cumulative** with respect to any dividends passed. That is, all dividends in arrears, along with the current dividend, must be paid before dividends can be paid to common stockholders. If preferred stock is **noncumulative**, passed (unpaid) dividends do not accumulate. In this case, only the current dividend must be paid before dividends can be paid to common stockholders. Because the common stockholders can receive dividends only after the dividend claims of preferred stockholders have been satisfied, it is in the firm's best interest to pay preferred dividends when they are due.

Other Features

conversion feature (preferred stock)
A feature of convertible preferred stock that allows holders to change each share into a stated number of shares of common stock.

Preferred stock is generally *callable*—the issuer can retire outstanding stock within a certain period of time at a specified price. The call option generally cannot be exercised until a specified date. The call price is normally set above the initial issuance price, but it may decrease as time passes. Making preferred stock callable provides the issuer with a way to bring the fixed-payment commitment of the preferred issue to an end if conditions in the financial markets make it desirable to do so.

Preferred stock quite often contains a **conversion feature** that allows holders of convertible preferred stock to change each share into a stated number of shares of common stock. Sometimes the number of shares of common stock that the preferred stock can be exchanged for changes according to a prespecified formula.

? Review Questions

3–8   What claims do preferred stockholders have with respect to the distribution of earnings (dividends) and assets?

3–9   Explain the cumulative feature of preferred stock. What is the purposes of a call feature in a preferred stock issue?

The Role of the Investment Banker

public offering
The sale of either bonds or stocks to the general public.

Corporations can raise long-term funds through a **public offering,** which is the sale of either bonds or stocks to the general public. As noted in Chapter 2, the initial public sale of bonds or stock occurs in the *primary market,* typically the *over-the-counter (OTC) exchange.* Once issued, these securities trade on one of the securities exchanges.

Today the Internet is expanding the options for selling new securities to the public. Acceptable new procedures are being established and tested by issuers and regulators. Because use of the Internet in public offerings is still evolving, here we focus on the traditional role of the investment banker in the initial sale of securities by the issuer.

Investment banking helps firms raise long-term financing—both debt and equity—in the capital markets by finding buyers for new security issues. The term *investment bankers* is not really accurate: These days, investment bankers are neither investors nor bankers; they do not make long-term investments, nor do they warehouse ("bank") the savings of others. Instead, acting as an intermediary between the issuer and the buyers of new security issues, **investment bankers** purchase securities from corporate and government issuers and resell them to the general public. Investment bankers typically are investment banking *firms,* which operate in other areas as well. They may be securities brokerage firms, selling securities to the public. They may also perform an advisory function by giving firms advice on mergers, acquisitions, and refinancing decisions.

investment banker
A financial intermediary that purchases securities from corporate and government issuers and resells them to the general public.

Underwriting

underwriting
The process in which an investment banker buys a security issue from the issuing firm at a discount from the planned resale price, guaranteeing the issuer a specified amount from the issue and assuming the risk of price changes between purchase and sale.

An investment banker often guarantees the issuing firm that it will receive a specified amount from the issue. This guarantee is called **underwriting.** The banker buys the securities at a discount from the planned resale price, expecting to profit from the discount, which is commonly called the **spread.** The investment banker therefore bears the risk of price changes or a market collapse between the time of purchase and the time of sale of securities. For example, an investment banking firm might agree to purchase an issue of new stock for $48 million. To recoup that amount, it must attempt to sell the stock for net proceeds of at least $48 million. If it can sell the stock for $50 million, it will earn a $2 million commission. Of course, it will instead lose part of the $48 million if it fails to sell the stock for that amount.

spread
The discount from a security's sale price in the market reflected in the price the investment banker paid for it.

In some public offerings, the investment banker may not underwrite the issue but may instead sell the securities on a **best-efforts basis.** In this case, the banker does not take on the financial risk associated with underwriting, and compensation is based on the number of securities sold.

best-efforts basis
A public offering in which the investment banker uses its resources to sell the security issue without taking on the risk of underwriting and is compensated on the basis of the number of securities sold.

Organization of Investment Banking Activity

competitive bidding
A method of choosing an investment banker in which the highest bidder for a security issue is awarded the issue.

A firm that needs to raise additional financing through the capital markets initiates the fund-raising process by selecting an investment banker. The selection might be made through **competitive bidding,** in which the investment banker or group of bankers that bids the highest price is awarded the issue. If the investment banker is hired by the issuing firm through a process of contract negotiation, the security issue is called a **negotiated offering.** Once selected, the investment banker helps the firm determine how much capital should be raised and in what form—debt or equity.

negotiated offering
A security issue for which the investment banker is hired through a process of contract negotiation.

Syndicating the Underwriting

Because of the size of many new security issues, it is often necessary for the originating investment banker to form an **underwriting syndicate.** This is a group of investment banking firms that combine to underwrite the issue. The use of an underwriting syndicate reduces the risk of loss to any single firm. Each underwriter in the syndicate must sell its portion of the issue. This is likely to result in a wider distribution of the new securities.

underwriting syndicate
A group of investment banking firms, each of which will underwrite a portion of a security issue, thus reducing the risk of loss to any single firm.

The originating underwriter and the syndicate members put together a **selling group,** which distributes the new issue to the investing public. The selling group is normally made up of a large number of brokerage firms, each of which agrees to sell a certain portion of the issue. Members of the selling group, like underwriters, expect to make a profit on the spread between the price at which they buy and that at which they sell the securities. But unlike underwriters, they are not at risk for unsold shares. Figure 3.1 depicts the selling process for a new security issue.

selling group
A group of brokerage firms, each of which agrees to sell a portion of a security issue (without assuming risk for unsold shares) and expects to make a profit on the spread between the price at which it buys and sells the securities.

Fulfilling Legal Requirements

Through the Securities and Exchange Commission (SEC), the federal government regulates the initial and subsequent trading of publicly owned securities. The issuer of a new security must obtain the approval of the SEC by filing a registration statement, which must be on file for at least 20 days before approval is granted. The sale of the new security cannot begin until the registration statement is approved.

One portion of the registration statement is the **prospectus;** it details the firm's operating and financial position. The prospectus may be issued to potential buyers during the pre-approval waiting period if a **red herring**—a statement indicating the tentative nature of the offering—is printed in red ink on the prospectus. Once the registration statement has been approved, the new security can be offered for sale if the prospectus is made available to all interested parties.

prospectus
A portion of a security registration statement filed with the SEC that details the firm's operating and financial position; it must be made available to all interested parties.

red herring
On a prospectus, a statement printed in red ink, indicating the tentative nature of a security offering while it is being reviewed by the SEC.

Investors should realize what approval of the registration statement by the SEC signifies. *It indicates only that the facts presented in the statement accurately reflect the firm's operating and financial position.* It does not guarantee that the security is a good investment.

As an alternative to filing a lengthy registration statement, firms with more than $150 million in outstanding common stock can use a procedure known as **shelf registration.** This procedure allows a firm to file a master registration statement, which is a single document summarizing planned financing for a 2-year period. At any time during these 2 years, the firm can file a "short statement" and then sell securities that have already been approved under the master statement. Under this procedure, the approved securities are effectively warehoused and kept "on the shelf" until the need exists or market conditions are appropriate. Shelf registration is popular with large firms that frequently need access to the capital markets.

shelf registration
An SEC procedure that allows large firms to file a "master registration statement" that in effect pre-approves the sale of securities for a 2-year period.

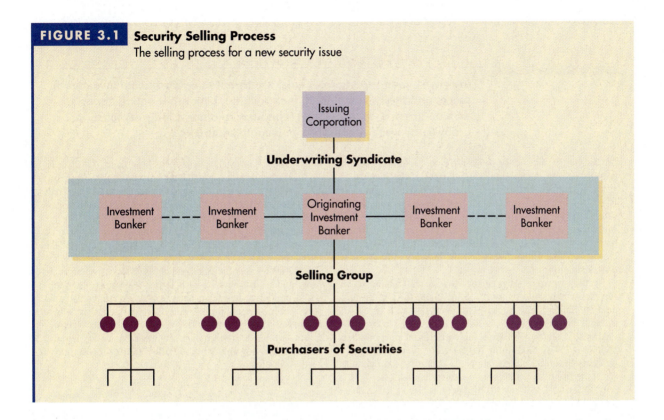

FIGURE 3.1 **Security Selling Process**
The selling process for a new security issue

Underwriting syndicates generally wait until the end of the registration period to price securities. The pricing decision affects the ease with which the issue can be sold and also the issuer's proceeds. The investment banker's "feel" for the mood of the market should result in a price that achieves the optimal mix of marketability and financial return.

Cost of Investment Banking Services

The overall cost of a security issue (the *flotation* cost) has two basic components: underwriting cost and administrative cost. The underwriting cost is the spread (the discount given the investment banker). The issuer also pays the administrative costs associated with the security issue, which include the SEC registration fee, printing costs, and accounting and legal fees. Generally, the larger the issue, the lower the overall cost in percentage terms. It is also generally true that common stock has highest overall flotation cost, followed by preferred stock and bonds in that order. Flotation costs can range from about 1.5 percent of the total proceeds on a large bond issue (more than $500 million) to 15 percent or more on a small common stock issue (around $6 million).

Private Placement

private placement
The direct sale of a new security issue to one or more purchasers.

As an alternative to a public offering, a firm can sometimes *negotiate private* (or *direct*) *placement* of a security issue. **Private placement** occurs when an investment banker arranges for the direct sale of a new security issue to one or more

 **WILL THE WEB EAT WALL STREET?**

Internet-based investment banks are threatening traditional investment banks and their profitable market position. Like other online financial service firms, they are using technology to change long-established procedures and reduce costs of issuing securities.

[W]hat the Web has done to Wall Street's retail business it could do to its institutional side as well....Particularly at risk is investment banking,...with its lofty (and suspiciously uniform) fees, its sports-star-sized compensation, and its often outrageous profit margins. Critics of the Street—including some of the biggest customers in...Silicon Valley—say the business is an anachronism, sustained only by a cartel-like clubbishness and the bankers' stranglehold on information.

In other words, it's precisely the sort of business the Internet was born to overturn. [S]ays Sanford C. Bernstein analyst Sallie Krawcheck, "The Web is a real threat to inflated fees."...

[Fees] are almost always the same from one bank to another—7% on deals up to $100 million, declining to 4% on deals in the $2 billion range....[This may soon change with] the rise of new Internet investment banks....

E*Offering—25% owned by discount broker E*Trade—just held an $84 million secondary offering for an Internet bank called First Sierra, with zero help from Wall Street. Part of the deal is traditional investment banking: E*Offering's salespeople and analysts are marketing half the issue to institutions. But the firm is selling the other half to E*Trade's retail customers directly over the Net. Surfers click into a prospectus and listen to the CEO's presentation online, then type in the amount they want to pay and the number of shares.

E*Offering sets the price, much as Wall Street firms do now, and it also sets its own fee. But because the Web-based brokerage has fewer costs—it doesn't have to pay a sales force, for example—E*Offering is charging First Sierra just 5%. Executives at E*Offering and other electronic banks dismiss traditional investment banks as "legacy" firms, borrowing the Silicon Valley snub for yesterday's rusty technology....

Source: Shawn Tully, "Will the Web Eat Wall Street?" Fortune, August 2, 1999, pp. 112–118.

purchasers. For example, a firm may be able to place an issue with a large pension fund. The investment banker is paid a commission for acting as an intermediary in the transaction.

Private placement usually reduces administrative and issuance costs and provides flexibility, because the issuing firm need not file registration statements and is not required to obtain SEC approval. In addition, the issuer has more flexibility in tailoring terms and in renegotiating them later, should the need arise, than it does with a public offering. On the other hand, private placement poses a disadvantage to the *buyer* who at some future date may wish to sell the securities on the open market. SEC registration and approval would be required prior to public sale.

The trend in recent years is toward increasing use of public offerings and diminished use of private placements. Private placements are used primarily for bonds and preferred stock. Some large firms have in-house services for private placement of their short- and long-term debt. Common stock is sometimes directly placed when the firm believes that the existing shareholders might purchase the issue through a rights offering, which was described earlier.

? Review Questions

3–10   What functions does an investment banker perform? Explain the sequence of events in the issuing of a new security.

3–11   How are underwriting costs affected by the size and type of an issue?

TYING IT ALL TOGETHER

This chapter described the key aspects of the two basic corporate securities, bonds and stocks. By issuing these securities, firms are able to raise long-term funds with which to expand their business. The roles of financial managers, financial markets, and investors in issuing corporate securities and making transactions in them are summarized in the Integrative Table that follows.

INTEGRATIVE TABLE

Making Corporate Securities Transactions

Role of **Financial Managers**	*Role of* **Financial Markets**	*Role of* **Investors**
Financial managers raise long-term financing of the right type at the right time, and at a low cost. The manager must decide whether to issue bonds, common stock, or preferred stock; what features to include; and how best to market, distribute, and price the corporate security.	The financial markets provide the forum in which corporate security issuers and investors make transactions. Corporate securities are the products that are available for purchase by investors in the primary market and that can later be sold in secondary markets. Investment bankers act as the distributors of new corporate issues into the market.	Investors in corporate securities need to understand the issuer's obligations and the security's features. Thus they can better assess the inherent risk and return behaviors of various corporate securities.

 Describe the legal aspects of bond financing and bond cost. Corporate bonds are debt instruments indicating that a corporation has borrowed a certain amount that it promises to repay in the future. Most bonds are issued with maturities of 10 to 30 years and a par value of $1,000. The bond indenture, enforced by a trustee, states all conditions of the bond issue. It contains both standard debt provisions and restrictive covenants, which may include a sinking-fund requirement. The interest rate on a bond depends on its maturity, the offering size, the issuer risk, and the basic cost of money.

Discuss the general features, ratings, popular types, and international issues of corporate bonds. A bond issue may include a conversion feature, a call feature, or stock purchase warrants. Bond ratings by independent agencies indicate the risk of a bond issue. A variety of tradi-

tional and contemporary types of bonds, some unsecured and others secured, are available. Eurobonds and foreign bonds enable established, creditworthy companies and governments to borrow large amounts internationally.

Differentiate between debt and equity capital. Holders of equity capital (common and preferred stock) are owners of the firm. Typically, only common stockholders have a voice in management through their voting rights. Equity holders have claims on income and assets that are secondary to the claims of creditors, there is no maturity date, and the firm does not benefit from tax deductibility of dividends paid to stockholders, as is the case for interest paid to debtholders.

 Review the rights and features of common stock. A common stockholder is a residual owner who receives what is left after all other claims have been satisfied. The common stock of a firm can be privately owned, closely owned, or publicly owned. It can be sold with or without a par value. Preemptive rights allow common stockholders to avoid dilution of ownership when new shares are issued. Not all shares authorized in the corporate charter are outstanding. If a firm has treasury stock, it will have issued more shares than are outstanding. Some firms have two or more classes of common stock that differ mainly in having unequal voting rights. Proxies transfer voting rights from one party to another. Dividend distributions to common stockholders are made at the discretion of the firm's board of directors. Firms can issue stock in foreign markets. The stock of many foreign corporations is traded in the form of American depository receipts (ADRs) in U.S. markets.

 Discuss the rights and features of preferred stock. Preferred stockholders have preference over common stockholders with respect to the distribution of earnings and assets and so are normally not given voting privileges. Preferred stock issues may have certain restrictive covenants, cumulative dividends, a call feature, and a conversion feature.

 Understand the role of the investment banker in securities offerings. Corporations can raise long-term funds through a public offering, the sale of either bonds or stock to the general public. Investment bankers purchase securities from corporate and government issuers and resell them to the general public. Their primary function is underwriting, which guarantees the issuer a specified amount from the issue. Some public offerings are instead sold on a best-efforts basis. The investment banker, which may syndicate the underwriting, forms a selling group, fulfills legal requirements, and prices and distributes the issue. An alternative to public offerings is private placement of securities.

SELF-TEST EXERCISES

(Solutions in Appendix B)

ST 3–1   What are the key differences between bonds, common stock, and preferred stock?

ST 3–2   Why can an investment banker be viewed as an intermediary between the firm and investors?

EXERCISES

 3–1   **Bond interest payments**   Charter Corp. has issued 2,500 debentures with a total principal value of $2,500,000. The bonds have a coupon rate of 7%.
   a. What dollar amount of interest per bond can an investor expect to receive each year from Charter Corp.?
   b. What is Charter's total interest expense per year associated with this bond issue?

 3–2   **Authorized and available shares**   Aspin Corporation's charter authorizes issuance of 2,000,000 shares of common stock. Currently, 1,400,000 shares are outstanding and 100,000 shares are being held as treasury stock. The firm wishes to raise $48,000,000 for a plant expansion. Discussions with its investment bankers indicate that the sale of new common stock will net the firm $60 per share.

a. What is the maximum number of new shares of common stock the firm can sell without receiving further authorization from shareholders?
b. Based on the data given and your finding in part **a,** will the firm be able to raise the needed funds without receiving further authorization?
c. What must the firm do to obtain authorization to issue more than the number of shares found in part **a?**

LG5 **3–3** **Preferred dividends** Slater Lamp Manufacturing has an outstanding issue of preferred stock with an $80 par value and an 11% annual dividend.
a. What is the annual dollar dividend? If it is paid quarterly, how much will be paid each quarter?
b. If the preferred stock is *noncumulative* and the board of directors has passed the preferred dividend for the last 3 years, how much must be paid to preferred stockholders before dividends are paid to common stockholders?
c. If the preferred stock is *cumulative* and the board of directors has passed the preferred dividend for the last 3 years, how much must be paid to preferred stockholders before dividends are paid to common stockholders?

LG5 **3–4** **Preferred dividends** In each case in the following table, how many dollars of preferred dividends per share must be paid to preferred stockholders before common stock dividends are paid?

Case	Type	Par value	Dividend per share per period	Periods of dividends passed
A	Cumulative	$ 80	$5	2
B	Noncumulative	110	8%	3
C	Noncumulative	100	$11	1
D	Cumulative	60	8.5%	4
E	Cumulative	90	9%	0

LG6 **3–5** **Underwriting spread** Hildreth Recycling is interested in selling common stock to raise capital for plant expansion. The firm has hired First Atlanta Company, a large investment banking firm, to serve as underwriter. First Atlanta believes that the stock can be sold for $80 per share, that its administrative costs will be 2% of the sale price, and that its selling costs will be 1.5% of the sale price. If First Atlanta requires a profit equal to 1% of the sale price, how much will the *spread* have to be, *in dollars,* to cover its costs and profits?

LG6 **3–6** **Bond underwriting analysis** RM International wishes to sell $100 million of bonds whose net proceeds will be used in the acquisition of Little Books. The company has estimated that the net proceeds, after paying the underwriting costs, should provide an amount sufficient to make the acquisition. The underwriter believes that the 100,000 bonds can be sold to the public at their $1,000 par value and estimates that its administrative costs will be $3.5 million. It also must sell the bonds at a 0.75% discount from their par value to members of the selling group. The underwriting commission (in addition to recovery of its administrative costs) is 1% of the par value of the offering.
a. Calculate the per-bond *spread* required by the underwriter to cover its costs.

b. How much will RM International net from the issue?

c. How much will the selling group receive? How much will the underwriter receive?

d. Assuming that this is a public offering, describe the nature of the underwriter's risk.

web exercises | Search

InvestingBonds.com

Go to **www.investinginbonds.com.** Click on **Information for Investors.** Under BOND PRICES, click on **CORPORATE BONDS.** In the right column choose Sector "All Market Sectors" and Sort by "Credit Rating." Click on **SEARCH,** and then click on **RATINGS.**

1. Who are the major rating services? What is each of their symbols for the following *credit risks:* Prime, Upper Medium, and Speculative?

Close the window and return to the chart.

2. Give the following data for the first three bonds on the chart: Issue, Rating, Coupon, Maturity, Yield, and Price.

Issue	Rating	Coupon	Maturity	Yield	Price
1.					
2.					
3.					

In the left column under Investor's Guide Click on **Corporate Bonds.** Click on **How Big is the Market and Who Buys?**

3. What is the total value of bonds outstanding? Where are the two markets for bonds? Who are the buyers of bonds?

StockMaster.com

Go to **www.stockmaster.com.** Enter LUV into the **Quote & Chart** space.

4. Which company uses the symbol LUV? What is the price of the last shares of LUV sold?

5. What is the 52-week range of LUV? How many shares have been sold on this date?

6. What are its price/earnings ratio, earnings per share (EPS), and yield?

At the top of the page Click On Earnings History.

7. What was LUV's EPS for each of the last eight quarters? In which quarter did they have the highest EPS?

For additional practice with concepts from this chapter, visit
http://www.awl.com/gitman_madura

Interest Rate Fundamentals

L EARNING G OALS

LG1 Discuss the components that comprise the interest rate at a given point in time.

LG2 Explain why the risk-free interest rate changes over time.

LG3 Explain why the risk-free rate of interest varies among possible maturities (investment horizons).

LG4 Explain the relationship between risk and the nominal interest rate on a debt security.

LG5 Explain why the returns required on risky assets change over time.

Interest Rate Fundamentals

interest rate
The compensation paid by the borrower of funds to the lender; from the borrower's point of view, the cost of borrowing funds.

The **interest rate** represents the cost of borrowing money. It is the level of compensation that a demander of funds must pay the supplier of funds. Business borrowers must attempt to use the funds in a manner that will generate sufficient cash flows (after covering expenses) to make the interest payments and have some earnings left over.

Risk-Free versus Real Rate of Return

risk-free rate of interest, R_F
The required return on a risk-free asset, typically a 3-month U.S. Treasury bill.

U.S. Treasury bills (T-bills)
Short-term IOUs issued by the U.S. Treasury; considered the risk-free asset.

The **risk-free rate of interest, R_F,** is defined as the required return on a risk-free asset. **U.S. Treasury bills (T-bills),** which are short-term IOUs issued by the U.S. Treasury, are commonly considered the risk-free asset. When the Treasury borrows funds, it pays the risk-free rate. Other borrowers (such as firms or individuals) must pay a premium above the prevailing risk-free rate. This premium reflects their risk of default on the loan, in addition to other characteristics. The following example demonstrates the practical distinction between *nominal* (stated) and real rates of interest.

Example ▼   Debbie Sompels has $10,000 that she can spend on furniture costing $10,000. The nominal rate of interest on a 1-year certificate of deposit is currently 7%, and the expected rate of inflation over the coming year is 4%. If instead of buying the furniture today, Debbie invested the $10,000 in a 1-year CD now, at the end of 1 year she would have $10,700. She would have earned interest of $700 ($0.07 \times \$10,000$) on her $10,000 deposit.

Over the 1-year period the 4% inflation rate would increase the cost of the furniture by 4%, to $10,400. As a result, at the end of the 1-year period Debbie would be able to buy the same furniture and would have $300 left over, which she could use to buy additional furniture. The increase in the amount of money available to Debbie at the end of 1 year is the nominal (quoted) rate of return (7%), which must be reduced by the rate of inflation (4%) during the period to determine her real (inflation-adjusted) rate of return of 3% (7% − 4%). Debbie's increased buying power therefore equals her 3% **▲** real rate of return.

Figure 4.1 illustrates the annual rate of inflation and changes in the annual risk-free rate of interest over time. Note that the two rates generally move in a similar fashion. Between 1978 and the early 1980s, inflation (based on an index of product prices) and interest rates were quite high, peaking in the early 1980s. Since then, these rates have declined to levels generally below those in the early 1980s. The data clearly illustrate the significant impact of inflation on the risk-free interest rate.

? Review Question

4–1   What is the real rate of return? How does it differ from the nominal rate of interest?

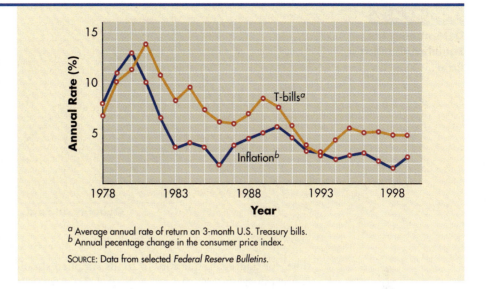

FIGURE 4.1

Impact of Inflation
Relationship between annual rate of inflation and 3-month U.S. Treasury bill average annual returns 1978–1999

[a] Average annual rate of return on 3-month U.S. Treasury bills.
[b] Annual pecentage change in the consumer price index.

SOURCE: Data from selected *Federal Reserve Bulletins*.

LG2 Explaining Changes in the Risk-Free Interest Rate

We've seen that the required return on assets is dependent on the prevailing risk-free interest rate. As the risk-free interest rate changes, so do the rate of return required by investors who provide debt or equity financing for firms and the rate of return required by financial managers when investing in projects for their firms. Thus, a change in the risk-free interest rate can affect the feasibility of possible investments by investors, as well as the feasibility of investment in possible projects by financial managers.

If borrowers anticipate changes in interest rates, they may be able to time their borrowing of funds when interest rates are relatively low and thereby reduce their financing costs. If investors anticipate changes in interest rates, they may be able to time their investment in a debt security when interest rates are higher and thus increase their return.

How the Equilibrium Interest Rate Is Determined

The nominal risk-free interest rate on borrowed funds is determined by the total (or aggregate) supply of funds provided by all investors and the total (or aggregate) demand for funds by all borrowers. This can be most easily understood by assuming that there is a single commercial bank that accepts deposits from any investors who have funds they wish to invest and that channels the funds as loans to all borrowers who need funds. Assume for now that all borrowers can borrow at the risk-free rate. This assumption is relaxed later in the chapter.

Aggregate Supply of Funds

The aggregate supply of funds at a given time depends on the interest rate offered to investors, as shown in Figure 4.2. If the interest rate is very low at a given

FIGURE 4.2

Determining the Equilibrium Interest Rate

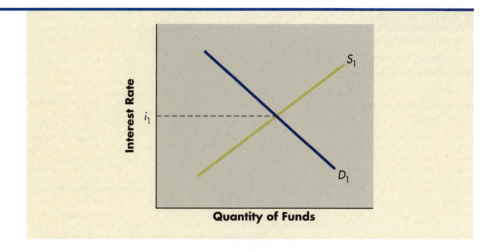

time, the aggregate quantity of funds supplied should also be low, because there is not much of a reward to investors. However, if the interest rate were 2 percentage points higher at that time, the aggregate supply of funds would be higher, because the reward to investors would be higher. For higher interest rate levels, the aggregate quantity of funds supplied would be even higher. The supply curve (labeled S_1) in Figure 4.2 illustrates that the aggregate supply of funds provided by investors is positively related to the interest rate offered to investors who are willing to supply the funds at a given time.

Aggregate Demand for Funds

Likewise, the aggregate demand for funds depends on the prevailing interest rate, as shown in Figure 4.2. If the nominal interest rate is very low at a given time, the aggregate demand for funds should be very high, because the cost of obtaining funds would be low. However, if the nominal interest rate were 2 percentage points higher at that time, the aggregate demand for funds would be lower, because firms would be less willing to invest in some projects if they had to incur a higher cost of funds. For higher levels of interest rates, the aggregate demand for funds would be even lower. The demand curve (labeled D_1) in Figure 4.2 illustrates that the aggregate demand for funds provided by investors is inversely related to the interest rate that would have to be offered to obtain the funds at a given time.

Combining Supply and Demand

The intersection between the supply curve and the demand curve for funds results in an equilibrium interest rate, in which the quantity of funds supplied is equal to the quantity of funds demanded. At an interest rate above this equilibrium point, labeled i_1 on Figure 4.2, the quantity of funds supplied would exceed the quantity of funds demanded at that time. There would be a surplus of funds, so some of the funds would not be used. Conversely, at an interest rate below i_1 in Figure 4.2, the quantity of funds supplied would not be sufficient to accommodate the demand for funds. The nominal interest rate at a given time should be the rate that equates the aggregate supply and the aggregate demand for funds.

How Shifts in the Supply of Funds Affect Interest Rates

Any factors that cause a change in the supply of funds available will shift the supply curve and, therefore, affect the equilibrium interest rate. The two most important factors that affect the aggregate supply of funds are (1) a shift in savings by investors, and (2) monetary policy.

Shift in Savings by Investors

Because investors supply funds, any change in their saving behavior will affect the aggregate supply of funds available and, therefore, the interest rate. For example, if investors receive a tax break and have more disposable income, they may increase their deposits in financial institutions. This increase in deposits reflects a willingness to provide a larger supply of savings for any interest rate level that may exist, as illustrated by the shift from S_1 to S_2 in Figure 4.3. This shift results in a surplus of funds at the original equilibrium interest rate and places downward pressure on the interest rate. The new equilibrium interest rate will fall to i_2, where the new supply curve (S_2) intersects the demand curve.

A shift in savings by foreign investors can also affect the interest rate in the United States. For example, if foreign investors invest more funds as deposits in the United States, there will be an increase in the supply of savings in the United States. This will result in downward pressure on the interest rate in the United States.

Shift in Monetary Policy

money supply
The total amount of specific types of deposits at financial institutions, plus currency held by the public.

Money supply represents the total amount of specific types of deposits at financial institutions, plus currency held by the public. The money supply is commonly used as an indicator of the amount of funds that financial institutions can provide to consumers or businesses as loans. There are various measures of

FIGURE 4.3

Effect of an Increase in Savings

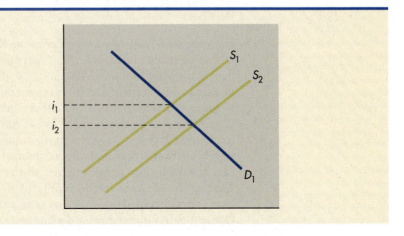

money supply, the most popular of which are M1, M2, and M3. *M1* represents the total amount of funds in checking accounts, plus currency held by the public. *M2* is composed of M1 plus savings accounts and small time-deposits. *M3* is composed of M2 plus large time-deposits.

The U.S. money supply is controlled by the Federal Reserve System ("the Fed"), which is the central bank of the United States. Because measures of money supply can be used as an indicator of the supply of funds available to borrowers, the Fed tries to control each of these measures within a range, in order to influence interest rates. The act of controlling the money supply is referred to as **monetary policy.** Whether the Fed can continuously control interest rates over a long period of time by implementing a specific monetary policy is subject to debate. However, the Fed can definitely push interest rates to a specific desired level over a short-term period. Thus, by influencing interest rate movements, the Fed can affect the cost of financing and therefore the value of firms.

Open Market Operations   The Federal Reserve bank maintains funds that are not deposited in any commercial bank or other financial institution. The method by which the Fed most commonly uses monetary policy to affect the money supply is through **open market operations:** the Fed's buying and selling of Treasury securities. The Fed can either use some of its funds to buy Treasury securities in the secondary market or sell to investors some of the Treasury securities that it previously purchased in the secondary market. These transactions affect the account balances maintained by investors, and therefore they affect the level of the money supply.

Discount Rate   An alternative monetary policy tool is the **discount rate,** the interest rate at which the Fed lends to depository institutions. If the Fed wants to increase the money supply, it may reduce the discount rate, encouraging depository banks to borrow funds from it. When depository institutions borrow from the Fed, there is an infusion of funds into the banking system. A change in the discount rate does not have a major impact on the money supply, but the Fed's change in the discount rate may signal that it is planning to push other interest rates in that same direction (through open market operations). Therefore, firms and investors closely monitor changes in the Fed's discount rate when attempting to anticipate changes in the Fed's monetary policy.

How the Fed Uses Monetary Policy to Reduce Interest Rates   When the Fed wishes to reduce interest rates, it increases the amount of funds at commercial banks by using some of its funds to purchase Treasury securities held by investors. The transaction involves sending checks to individual or institutional investors, who deposit the checks in their accounts at commercial banks. Consequently, the commercial banks have more funds in the accounts of customers, and therefore have more funds to lend. Given the increase in the supply of funds that commercial banks have, these banks lower the interest rate at which they provide loans so that they can attract enough borrowers. That is, the increase in the supply of funds available places downward pressure on the equilibrium interest rate, as was shown in Figure 4.3. Consequently, interest rates decline in response to the Fed's monetary policy.

monetary policy
The Federal Reserve's policy for controlling the U.S. money supply.

open market operations
Operations of monetary policy, in which the Fed buys and sells Treasury securities in the secondary market.

discount rate
The interest rate at which the Fed lends to depository institutions; an aspect of monetary policy, because the Fed raises or lowers the discount rate to decrease or increase the money supply.

NewsLine   UNSUNG OFFICIALS GET THE CREDIT FOR SAVVY BOND SALES

Corporate financial executives must project changes in the risk-free interest rate when making financing decisions. Those that issued bonds in early 1999, before the Federal Reserve raised interest rates, saved their companies many millions of dollars in interest costs.

...The bond market has been as tough on the nerves as a fourth cup of coffee, and executives who guessed right and sold a ton of bonds at just the right time saved their companies hundreds of millions of dollars.

Consider AT&T Corp.'s decision in March 1999 to sell $8 billion of bonds, shattering the record for the biggest bond deal on record. Some on Wall Street questioned the wisdom of raising so much money then, after interest rates had already moved higher. But rates have continued to climb, and the move now looks like a savvy one: If AT&T were to sell the same amount of bonds today it would have to pay $86 million a year more in interest payments over

the next 30 years, a whopping $680 million in today's dollars.

The Fed proceeded to raise interest rates three times this year [1999] and bond investors have gone through periods in which they fled from all kinds of bonds. So what should companies eager to raise money do now? Head for the bond market, say top financing executives. The economy shows few signs of slowing and the Fed may have to raise rates several times next year to keep inflation under wraps.

Source: Excerpted from Gregory Zuckerman, "Unsung Officials Get the Credit for Savvy Bond Sales," Wall Street Journal, December 14, 1999, pp. C1, C30.

How the Fed Uses Monetary Policy to Increase Interest Rates When the Fed wishes to increase interest rates, it reduces the amount of funds at commercial banks by selling to investors some of the Treasury securities that it had previously purchased in the secondary market. These transactions require payments from investors to the Fed, and the checking account balances of the investors are reduced. Therefore, the commercial banks have less funds to lend. The reduction in the supply of funds available at commercial banks places upward pressure on the equilibrium interest rate, as shown in Figure 4.4. Commercial banks have less funds than businesses or households wish to borrow.

FIGURE 4.4

Effect of the Fed's Reduction in the Money Supply

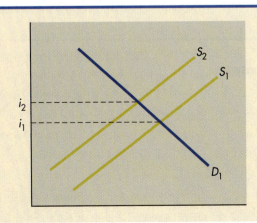

How Shifts in the Demand for Funds Affect Interest Rates

Any factors that cause a change in the demand for funds will shift the demand curve and therefore affect the equilibrium interest rate. The key factors that affect the aggregate demand for funds are (1) shifts in government demand for funds, (2) shifts in business demand for funds, and (3) shifts in the household demand for funds.

Shift in the Government Demand for Funds

The U.S. government frequently borrows substantial amounts of money. Thus any shift in the government's borrowing behavior can affect the aggregate demand for funds and therefore the equilibrium interest rate. For example, assume the U.S. government suddenly needs to borrow more than it normally borrows. In that case the quantity of funds demanded will be larger at any interest rate level, as illustrated by the shift in the demand curve from D_1 to D_2 in Figure 4.5. This shift results in a shortage of funds at the original equilibrium interest rate and places upward pressure on the interest rate. The new equilibrium interest rate is i_2, where the new demand curve intersects the supply curve.

   If the government had reduced the amount it borrows, the opposite effects would have occurred. The demand curve would have shifted inward (that is, to the left), resulting in a surplus of funds at the original interest rate, and therefore would have resulted in a lower interest rate.

Shift in the Business Demand for Funds

Firms also borrow often. When economic conditions change, businesses adjust their spending plans and therefore their demand for funds. During a period in which businesses are optimistic about the economy, they are more willing to expand. Thus they borrow more funds in periods of high economic growth. This reflects an increase in the aggregate demand for funds (an outward shift in the demand curve), similar to the effect of increased government borrowing. The shift results in a higher equilibrium interest rate. During a weak economy, firms tend to reduce their spending on new projects and therefore borrow less. This reflects a reduction in the aggregate demand for funds (an inward shift in the demand curve) and results in a lower equilibrium interest rate.

FIGURE 4.5

Effect of an Increase in the Government Demand for Funds

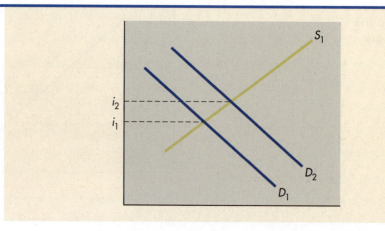

A shift in the business demand for funds in the United States can be triggered by a change in the behavior of foreign firms. For example, if foreign firms increase their demand for dollar-denominated loans, they can cause an upward shift in the U.S. interest rate in the same manner as if U.S. firms increased their demand for dollar-denominated loans.

Shift in the Household Demand for Funds

Similarly, in periods when households are more optimistic about the future stability of their income, they may be more willing to borrow funds to purchase new homes, automobiles, or other products. This reflects an increase in the aggregate demand for funds, which results in a higher equilibrium interest rate. In periods when households fear the possible loss of jobs, they tend to borrow less, which is reflected in an inward shift in the demand curve and a lower equilibrium interest rate.

Combining Shifts in Supply and Demand

Some economic conditions can affect more than one factor. For example, an increase in expected inflation can reduce the aggregate supply of saving because it encourages savers to spend now before prices increase further. It can also increase the demand for funds by borrowers (firms or individuals) who decide to make more purchases now, before prices rise further. In this case, both factors place upward pressure on the equilibrium interest rate.

Factors sometimes change in ways that bring opposing forces to bear on the equilibrium interest rate. For example, the government may need to borrow additional funds (which places upward pressure on interest rates) while the Fed increases the money supply (which can place downward pressure on interest rates). The ultimate effect on the equilibrium interest rate depends on the relative degrees of impact.

Review Questions

4–2   Explain how the Fed can change the money supply.
4–3   When the Fed reduces the money supply, how is the supply of funds affected? How are interest rates affected?

LG3 Term Structure of Interest Rates

The previous discussion of interest rates was not focused on any particular investment horizon. Yet there are unique demand and supply conditions for each possible investment horizon, and these conditions influence the interest rate. Therefore, at any time there is a unique risk-free interest rate for each possible investment horizon. For example, the 3-month Treasury bill rate is the risk-free rate for a 3-month investment horizon, whereas the 10-year Treasury bond is the risk-free rate for a 10-year investment horizon. For any class of similar-risk

term structure of interest rates
The relationship between the interest rate or rate of return and the time to maturity.

securities, the **term structure of interest rates** relates the interest rate or rate of return to the time to maturity. For convenience we will continue to use Treasury securities as an example, but other classes could include securities that have similar overall quality or risk. The riskless nature of Treasury securities also provides a laboratory in which to develop the term structure.

Yield Curves

yield to maturity
The annual rate of interest earned on a debt security purchased on a given day and held to maturity.

yield curve
A graph of the relationship between a debt security's yield to maturity (*y* axis) and the time to maturity (*x* axis); it shows the pattern of annualized returns on debt securities of equal quality and different maturities.

A debt security's **yield to maturity** (discussed in Chapter 7) represents the annualized rate of return earned on a security purchased on a given day and held to maturity. The relationship between the debt security's remaining time to maturity and its yield to maturity is represented by the **yield curve.** In other words, the yield curve shows the yields to maturity for debt securities of equal quality and different maturities; it is a graphical depiction of the term structure of interest rates. Figure 4.6 shows three yield curves for all U.S. Treasury securities: one at May 22, 1981, a second at September 29, 1989, and a third at January 26, 2000. Note that both the position and the shape of the yield curves change over time. The yield curve of January 26, 2000, indicates that short-term borrowing costs at that time were slightly below long-term borrowing costs. Such *upward-sloping* yield curves occur most frequently. Sometimes, a *flat yield curve,* similar to that of September 29, 1989, exists. It reflects relatively similar borrowing costs for both short- and longer-term loans. The May 22, 1981, curve indicates high short-term interest rates and lower longer-term rates. This curve is described as *downward-sloping,* reflecting generally cheaper long-term borrowing costs than short-term borrowing costs. The *downward-sloping* yield curve exists occasionally but is not common.

FIGURE 4.6

Treasury Yield Curves
Yield curves for U.S. Treasury securities on three different dates

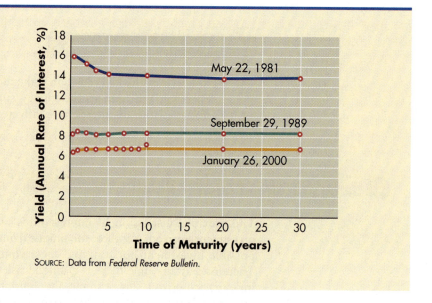

SOURCE: Data from *Federal Reserve Bulletin.*

Theories of Term Structure

Three theories are frequently cited to explain the general shape of the yield curve. They are the expectations theory, liquidity preference theory, and market segmentation theory.

Expectations Theory

expectations theory
The theory that the yield curve reflects investor expectations about future interest rates; expectation of higher interest rates results in an upward-sloping yield curve, and an expectation of lower interest rates results in a downward-sloping yield curve.

One theory of the term structure of interest rates, the **expectations theory,** suggests that the yield curve reflects investor expectations about future interest rates and inflation.

If interest rates were expected to increase, investors would prefer to invest in short-term funds, so that they could reinvest the money once interest rates rise. Conversely, borrowers who expect interest rates to rise would prefer to borrow long-term funds to lock in today's rate for a long time. There would be a relatively large amount of short-term funds supplied to the market, compared with the demand for short-term funds, which would result in a relatively low short-term interest rate. Conversely, there would also be a relatively large demand for long-term funds relative to the amount of funds supplied, which would result in a relatively high long-term interest rate. Therefore, the yield curve should be upward-sloping (because the long-term interest rates exceed short-term interest rates) when interest rates are expected to rise.

If interest rates were expected to decline, the opposite forces would prevail. Most investors would prefer to invest their funds long-term in order to lock in the interest rate for an extended period. Many borrowers would prefer to borrow for just a short time so that they could borrow funds again once interest rates declined. Overall, the demand for short-term funds would be relatively high compared with the supply of short-term funds available in short-term debt markets, whereas the demand for long-term funds would be relatively low compared to the supply of long-term funds available. This would result in a relatively high short-term interest rate, a relatively low long-term interest rate, and an inverted yield curve.

Liquidity Preference Theory

liquidity preference theory
The theory that for any given issuer, long-term interest rates tend to be higher than short-term rates because of the lower liquidity and higher responsiveness to general interest rate movements of longer-term securities; causes the yield curve to be upward-sloping.

According to the **liquidity preference theory,** investors perceive less risk in short-term securities than in longer-term securities and are therefore willing to accept lower yields on them. The reason is that shorter-term securities are more *liquid.* They can be converted into cash quickly with little or no loss in value, because their values are less responsive to general interest rate movements.

In addition, borrowers are generally willing to pay a higher rate for long-term than for short-term financing. The reason is that they can lock in funds for a longer period of time and eliminate the potential adverse consequences of having to roll over short-term debt at unknown costs in order to obtain needed long-term financing.

In a sense, investors (lenders) tend to require a premium for tying up funds for longer periods, whereas borrowers are generally willing to pay a premium to obtain longer-term financing. Given these preferences, the yield curve tends to be upward-sloping, reflecting a general liquidity preference from the lender's viewpoint.

U.S. CREDIT OUTLOOK—CURVE FLATTENING AHEAD?

News services such as Reuters Business Report provide articles like this one to many web sites and newspapers. This story discusses how the Federal Reserve's actions affect bond yields. (The Federal Reserve raised interest rates the following day.)

The U.S. bond yield curve will probably flatten if the Federal Reserve raises interest rates Tuesday [1999], traders and analysts said.

Rates and yields on short maturities could rise to reflect the higher [costs] imposed by a Federal funds rate targeted at 5½ percent instead of 5¼ percent, they said. But long maturities could rally, if moderately, on the perception that the central bank is "ahead of the curve" with regard to fighting inflation.

If the Fed raises rates Tuesday and adopts a neutral policy directive, "the curve would probably flatten and the long end would do somewhat better," said Vincent Verterano, head trader at Nomura Securities International.

"We think this is going to be more of a situation of where the curve will change, rather than creating a big change in rates," Verterano said. "The economy is strong, but people are getting used to that."

William Sullivan, senior vice president and chief money market economist at Morgan Stanley Dean Witter, said...that prices of short-term maturities would be vulner-

able if the Federal Reserve raises interest rates.... "But it would be a yield curve flattening phenomenon we'd deal with if they raise rates and change the directive to neutral," he added. "The long-dated assets could prosper." Long-dated notes and bonds could benefit from a Fed rate hike if investors conclude that the Fed is standing firm against potential inflation....

One thing a Fed rate hike could do for the bond market is inoculate it somewhat against the possibility of an unfriendly October Consumer Price Index (CPI) report Wednesday, analysts said.... Jeffrey Palma, U.S. economist at Warburg Dillon Read, said even if the CPI reading Wednesday is not that friendly for bonds, a rate hike the preceding day would let people figure that the Fed "has gotten way ahead of the inflation curve and that inflation risks are certainly going to be diminished" next year.

Source: Ellen Freilich, "U.S. Credit Outlook—Curve Flattening Ahead?" Reuters Business Report, November 15, 1999, downloaded from Electric Library Business Edition, business.elibrary.com.

Market Segmentation Theory

market segmentation theory
The theory that the market for loans is segmented on the basis of maturity and that the sources of supply and demand for loans within each segment determine its prevailing interest rate; the slope of the yield curve is determined by the general relationship between the prevailing rates in each segment.

Another often-cited theory, **market segmentation theory,** suggests that the market for loans is segmented on the basis of maturity and that the sources of supply of and demand for funds within each maturity segment determine its prevailing interest rate. In other words, the equilibrium between suppliers (lenders) and demanders (borrowers) of short-term funds would determine prevailing short-term interest rates, and the equilibrium between suppliers and demanders of long-term funds would determine prevailing long-term interest rates.

Assume the supply of short-term funds is large relative to the demand for short-term funds while the supply of long-term funds is low relative to the demand for long-term funds. Based on these assumptions, the short-term interest rate will be relatively low and the long-term rate relatively high. An upward-sloping yield curve will result. If supply and demand conditions were opposite of what was just assumed, an inverted yield curve would exist. The shape of the yield curve is derived from the supply and demand conditions in each maturity segment.

Consolidating the Theories of Term Structure

All three theories of term structure have merit. From them we can conclude that at any time, the slope of the yield curve is affected by (1) interest rate expectations, (2) liquidity preferences, and (3) the general maturity preferences by investors and borrowers. At any time, the interaction of these three forces will determine the prevailing slope of the yield curve.

Review Questions

4–4   What is the *term structure of interest rates*, and how is it related to the yield curve?

4–5   Assuming that an upward-sloping yield curve exists because of interest rate expectations, what does it indicate about the direction of future interest rates?

4–6   Briefly describe the three theories cited to explain the general shape of the yield curve.

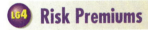 **Risk Premiums**

So far we have considered only the risk-free interest rate. At this point we reintroduce the concept of the risk premium, which exists whenever firms or individuals attempt to obtain funds.

Risk Premiums on Debt Securities

The nominal rate of interest for a debt security with a specific maturity (k_1) is equal to the risk-free rate (R_F) for that same maturity, plus the risk premium (RP_1):

$$k_1 = R_F + RP_1 \tag{4.1}$$

risk premium
The additional amount required by investors to compensate them for uncertainty surrounding the return on a security.

default risk
The possibility that the issuer of a security will default on its payments to investors who hold the security.

The **risk premium** represents the additional amount required by investors to compensate them for uncertainty surrounding the return on the security. It varies with the risk of the borrower and can cause debt securities with similar maturities to have different interest rates.

One of the most important reasons for the existence of a risk premium on some debt securities is **default risk,** or the possibility that the issuer of the security will default on its payments to the investors who hold debt securities. The firms that issue debt securities are thoroughly examined by investors to determine whether they will be able to cover the payments on debt securities they issued.

Many investors rely on rating agencies such as Moody's Investors Service and Standard & Poor's to rate the debt securities issued by firms (as explained in Chapter 3). These agencies consider characteristics specific to each firm as well as economic conditions to grade a firm's ability to cover its future debt payments. (The rating classifications used by each of these agencies were shown in Table 3.1, page 55). If the returns for all debt securities were more or less equal, investors would of course prefer the higher-rated securities. However, debt securities that are perceived to have more risk (and therefore have lower ratings) offer a higher yield to compensate investors. Thus investors must weigh the higher potential return against the higher default risk of risky debt securities.

E x a m p l e ▼ On February 1, 2000, the nominal interest rates on various types of long-term securities were as follows:

Security	Nominal interest (%)
U.S. Treasury bonds (average)	6.60
Corporate bonds (by rating):	
Aaa	7.85
Aa	8.03
A	8.24
Baa	8.39

The U.S. Treasury bond represents the risk-free long-term security. We can calculate the risk premium associated with the other securities listed by subtracting the risk-free rate of the T-bond, 6.60 percent, from each nominal rate (yield):

Security	Risk premium (%)
Corporate bonds (by rating):	
Aaa	$7.85 - 6.60 = 1.25$
Aa	$8.03 - 6.60 = 1.43$
A	$8.24 - 6.60 = 1.64$
Baa	$8.39 - 6.60 = 1.79$

These risk premiums reflect differing issuer and issue risks. The lower-rated corporate issues (A and Baa) have higher risk premiums than the higher-rated corporates (Aaa and Aa). ▲

The risk premium consists of a number of issuer- and issue-related components, including default risk, liquidity risk, contractual provisions, and tax risk. Each of these components is described briefly in Table 4.1. In general, the highest risk premiums and therefore the highest nominal returns are to be found in debt securities that are issued by firms with a high risk of default, are issued in long maturities that are traded in thin markets, have unfavorable contractual provisions, and are not tax-exempt.

Risk Premiums on Equity Securities

Like debt securities, equity securities also have risk premiums. The risk premium on equity securities is not so observable as it is on debt securities because equity securities do not have an interest rate or a yield to maturity that indicates the return to investors. Because investors are risk-averse, however, they will invest in an equity security only if the expected return exceeds the risk-free rate they could earn by simply purchasing Treasury securities.

E x a m p l e ▼ Stephanie Daniels plans to invest in the stock of the Coca Cola Company over a 10-year period. She recognizes the uncertainty surrounding the return from this investment. She can avoid the uncertainty by simply purchasing 10-year Treasury bonds, so the only way it is worthwhile for Stephanie to invest in Coca-Cola Company stock instead is if she expects a sufficiently high return to compensate her for the risk (uncertainty) surrounding the return that she will earn from investing in the stock. Stephanie decides that she will invest in Coca-Cola only if the annualized return on Coca-Cola stock is at least 5% above the annualized return she could earn on a risk-free basis by purchasing a 10-year Treasury bond. That is, when the prevailing rate on a 10-year Treasury bond is 7%, she will invest in Coca-Cola Company stock only if it is expected to provide a return of at least 12%.

Stephanie also considers investing in Amazon.com, a company that has much potential but has a limited track record. She decides that she will invest in Amazon.com only if she thinks it will provide a return of at least 16%, which reflects a 9% risk premium above the risk-free (Treasury bond) rate of 7%. Her annualized risk premium on Amazon.com is 4% above that of the Coca-Cola Company because of the higher degree of risk that investing in Amazon.com entails.

TABLE 4.1   Issuer- and Issue-Related Risk Components

Component	Description
Default Risk	The possibility that the issuer of debt will not pay the contractual interest or principal as scheduled. The greater the uncertainty as to the borrower's ability to meet these payments, the greater the risk premium. High bond ratings reflect the low default risk, and low bond ratings reflect high default risk.
Maturity Risk (also called *interest rate risk*)	The fact that the longer the maturity, the more the value of a debt security will change in response to a given change in interest rates. If interest rates on otherwise similar-risk securities suddenly rise because of a change in the money supply, the prices of long-term debt securities will decline by more than the prices of debt securities, and vice versa.[a]
Liquidity Risk	The ease with which debt securities can be converted into cash without experiencing a loss in value. Generally, securities that are actively traded on major exchanges and over the counter have low liquidity risk. Less actively traded securities that have a "thin" market have high liquidity risk.
Contractual Provisions	Conditions that are often included in a debt agreement of a stock issue. Some of these reduce risk, whereas others may increase risk. For example, a provision allowing a bond issuer to retire its bonds prior to maturity would increase the bond's risk.
Tax Risk	The chance that Congress will make unfavorable changes in tax laws. The greater the potential impact of a change in tax law on the return of a given debt security, the greater its tax risk. Generally, long-term securities are subject to greater tax risk than those that are closer to their maturity dates.

[a]A detailed discussion of the effects of interest rates on the price or value of bonds and other fixed-income securities is presented in Chapter 7.

Investors will not necessary agree on the exact risk premium that is required for every stock. This explains why some investors are willing to purchase a particular stock at a given time (because the expected return is sufficient to cover their risk premium), whereas others are not. Although investors do not agree on the exact risk premium, they would agree that all stocks must have a risk premium. They also would normally agree that the risk premiums on well-known stocks with stable historical performance levels should be less than those of stocks that have been less stable. They may still prefer the more risky stocks, as long as they believe that the riskier stocks offer a sufficiently high return to compensate for the higher degree of risk.

Risk and Return

A positive relationship exists between the risk and the expected return of a security. After assessing the risk of a given security, investors tend to purchase those securities that are expected to provide a return corresponding to the perceived risk. The actual return earned on the security will affect investors' subsequent decisions to sell, hold, or buy additional securities. In addition, most investors look to certain types of securities that can be classified in a specific risk category.

risk–return tradeoff
The expectation that for accepting greater risk, investors must be compensated with greater returns.

A **risk–return tradeoff** exists: Investors must be compensated for accepting greater risk with the expectation of greater returns. Figure 4.7 illustrates the typical relationship between risk and return for a number of popular securities. Securities that have a higher degree of risk offer a higher expected return to investors, which also implies a higher cost to the issuers. Financial managers must consider the risks and costs associated with each financing alternative. Their financing decisions will ultimately rest on an analysis of the impact of risk and return on share price. Similarly, investors compare the expected return and risk of securities when making their investment decisions.

Note that equity securities (stocks) are included in Figure 4.7 along with debt securities. The equity securities tend to have a higher expected return than debt securities, because the owners of equity securities share the earnings of the firm.

FIGURE 4.7

Risk–Return Tradeoff
Risk–return profile for popular securities

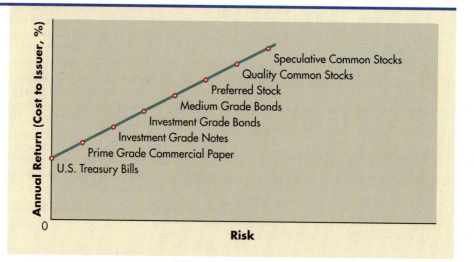

However, these securities are also more risky than debt securities, because they have a much higher probability of experiencing a substantial decline in value. Firms must cover all debt payments that are due before determining whether any earnings can be distributed to stockholders as dividends or reinvested in the business.

? Review Questions

4–7   Describe the components contained in the risk premium of a risky debt security.

4–8   What is the risk–return tradeoff?

LG5 Explaining Shifts in the Required Returns on Risky Securities

As the required return of investors changes, so does the demand for securities, and therefore the price. Thus any factors that affect the return required by investors will also affect security prices. First let's look at the factors that cause a shift in the required returns of debt securities.

Explaining Shifts in the Required Returns on Debt Securities

Recall that the required rate of return on risky debt and equity securities is equal to the risk-free rate plus a risk premium. A change in either of these components will cause a change in the expected return of a risky debt security.

Shift in the Risk-Free Rate

When the risk-free rate changes, so does the required rate of return on these securities, even if the risk premium has not changed. This relationship can be explained intuitively, as in the following example.

Example ▼   Last month, investors who purchased a 10-year Treasury bond required a return of 7% on the 10-year Treasury (risk-free) bond. At the same time, the required return on a 10-year medium-grade corporate bond was 9%. The risk premium on the medium-grade corporate bond is 2%.

In the last few weeks, the Fed decreased the money supply substantially, increasing the risk-free rate on a 10-year Treasury bond to 8%. However, the Fed's actions did not affect the general risk perception of firms. Because the risk premium on corporate bonds has not changed, the prevailing required return by investors who purchase the corporate bonds has increased by the amount of the increase in the risk-free rate, as shown here:

	Last Month	Today
Risk-free rate	7%	8%
Risk premium on medium-grade bond	2%	2%
Required return on medium-grade bonds	9%	10%

Shift in the Risk Premium on Debt Securities

Even if the risk-free rate does not change, the risk premium may change and therefore affect the nominal interest rate on risky debt securities. Recall that an interest rate charged on debt reflects the risk-free rate plus a risk premium. As the market's perception of default risk changes, so does the default risk premium.

Example ▼ Reconsider the previous example in which the initial 10-year risk-free rate was 7% and the risk premium was 2%. If new information suggests a higher degree of uncertainty about the future cash inflows of firms, investors who invest in those firms may require a higher risk premium on debt issued by those firms to compensate for the higher risk. If the risk premium is increased to 3%, investors will now require a return of 10% on debt issued by the firms. If the new information is about the economy, it may affect the default risk premium of most firms. If the information is about a particular industry, then only those firms in that industry may experience a higher default risk premium. ▲

FIGURE 4.8

How the Required Return on a Risky Asset Can Change

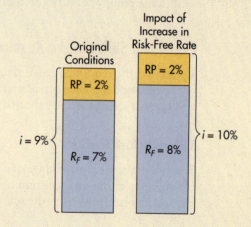

Impact of a Shift in Risk-Free Rate on Required Return of Medium-Grade Corporate Bond

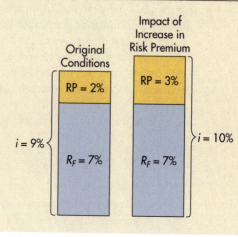

Impact of a Shift in Risk Premium on Required Return of Medium-Grade Corporate Bond

Figure 4.8 compares the impact of a shift in the risk-free rate to the impact of a shift in the risk premium.

Actual Shifts in Risk Premiums Over Time

Changes in the actual risk premium can be measured by comparing the interest rate offered on a risky debt security with the risk-free rate. Figure 4.9 shows the risk premium on medium-grade corporate bonds over time. Note that the risk premium was higher during the early 1980s, when there was a major recession in the United States, and more uncertainty about whether firms could repay their debt.

Risk premiums do not change to the same degree as the risk-free rate, as Figure 4.9 shows. Thus, a change in the rate of return required by investors who invest in firms or by financial managers who invest in projects is largely attributable to a change in the risk-free rate, but it can also be attributed to a change in the risk premium.

Explaining Shifts in Required Returns on Equity Securities

Just as the required return on a debt security can change, so can the required return on a equity security. The required return from investing in a stock can change in response to a change in the risk-free rate or to a change in the risk premium required by investors who invest in the stock.

Shift in the Risk-Free Rate

If the risk-free rate changes and the risk premium on a stock does not change, investors will adjust their required return on a stock by the amount of a change in the risk-free rate. The change can be understood more intuitively by considering the following example.

FIGURE 4.9

Risk Premium on Medium-Grade Corporate Bonds

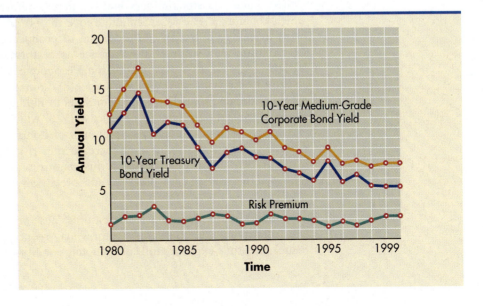

Example ▼ Recall the earlier example in which Stephanie Daniels required a return of 16% to invest in Amazon.com. At that time, the risk-free rate was 7%, and the risk premium necessary to invest in the stock was 9%. Assume that before Stephanie completes the analysis necessary to make her investment decision, the risk-free rate rises to 8%, while the risk premium remains unchanged. Now Stephanie will consider investing in Amazon.com only if she expects to receive a return of at least 17% on Amazon.com. If she expected that the investment would provide a return of 16%, this return's premium of 8% over the prevailing risk-free rate would be less than the 9% risk premium necessary to compensate her for the risk (uncertainty) involved. Under these conditions, Stephanie would prefer either to invest in Treasury securities and earn the risk-free rate or to invest in some other stock—one with an expected return that is high enough to cover the risk

▲ premium.

Shift in the Risk Premium on Equity Securities

Even if the risk-free rate remains unchanged, the required rate of return on a stock could change in response to a change in the risk premium on the stock. For example, information about new technology may increase the degree of confidence that investors have in specific Internet companies and thus reduce uncertainty about the future return from investing in these stocks. Less uncertainty about future returns could reduce the risk premium that investors require to consider investing in these stocks.

How a Stock's Risk Premium Can Be Affected by Its International Ventures
Firms that pursue international business ventures can affect the uncertainty surrounding their future cash flows and therefore affect the return required by investors who invest in the firm, as the following example demonstrates.

Example ▼ Lomax Co. is a U.S. firm that has historically focused most of its business in the United States. Its stockholders had required a return of 11% on the equity, which contains a 4% risk premium above the prevailing risk-free rate. Lomax plans to build a subsidiary in Indonesia to produce and sell its product there. This venture may substantially enhance its performance over time. However, Indonesia has recently experienced some economic and political problems that could adversely affect the performance of Lomax Co. Consequently, some investors decided that they would continue to hold Lomax stock only if it was expected to generate a return of at least 17%, which reflects a premium of 10 percentage points. Thus the risk premium of Lomax stock had increased by 6 percentage points as a result of an increase in its risk. Consequently, its financial managers would consider pursuing this venture only if they expected that the
▲ return on this investment would exceed its relatively high cost of funds.

Not all international business ventures cause an increase in the risk premium. In fact, some international ventures may reduce the firm's risk if they can reduce the firm's exposure to U.S. economic conditions.

? Review Questions

4–9   Explain how the required return on debt securities is affected by an increase in the risk-free rate.

4–10   Explain how the required return on equity securities is affected by an increase in the risk premium.

TYING IT ALL TOGETHER

This chapter explained why interest rates vary over time and why interest rates vary among debt securities at a given time. The variation in interest rates over time and in debt securities at a particular time is largely attributable to the rates of return that a firm's managers and its investors require. Like debt securities, equity securities also have risk premium, meaning that investors will only invest in them if the expected return compensates for the risk. Financial managers, financial markets, and investors affect the required return on funds, and therefore cause variation in interest rates over time. The role of financial managers, financial markets, and investors in affecting the required rate of return is summarized in the following Integrative Table.

INTEGRATIVE TABLE
Determining the Required Return

Role of Financial Managers	Role of Financial Markets	Role of Investors
Financial managers of firms invest in projects only if the expected rate of return on those projects will satisfy the investors who provide funds to the firms.	Investors use the financial markets to purchase those securities whose return is sufficient to cover the risk premium. They also use the financial markets to sell previously purchased securities that are no longer expected to provide a return sufficient to cover the risk premium.	Investors invest in firms by purchasing debt and equity securities that are issued by firms. Investors will be willing to invest funds in these securities only if the expected return exceeds the risk-free rate by an amount that is sufficient to cover the risk premium.

LG1 **Discuss the components that comprise the interest rate at a given point in time.** The interest rate of a risk-free debt security is composed of the real rate of interest and the expected rate of inflation. Thus, the stated interest rate exceeds the expected rate of inflation by an amount that reflects the real rate of interest that investors expect to earn.

The real rate of interest is the return investors expect to earn after accounting for inflation.

LG2 **Explain why the risk-free interest rate changes over time.** The risk-free interest rate changes over time in response to changes in the supply of funds available and in the demand for funds. An increase in the supply of funds or a decrease in the demand for funds places downward pressure on the risk-free interest rate, and therefore on interest rates of all other debt securities. Conversely, a decrease in the supply of funds or an increase in the demand for funds places upward pressure on the risk-free interest rate and therefore on interest rates of all other debt securities. The key factors that affect the aggregate supply of funds are shifts in savings by investors and shifts in monetary policy. The key factors that affect the aggregate demand for funds are shifts in the government demand for funds, in business demand for funds, and in household demand for funds.

 Explain why the risk-free rate of interest varies among possible maturities (investment horizons). At a given time, the risk-free rate of interest varies among maturities. This can be observed by reviewing the term structure of interest rates, which shows the annualized yields of Treasury securities for various maturities. The risk-free (Treasury) securities with different maturities offer different annualized yields at a given time because of differences in (1) liquidity levels of the securities for each investment horizon, (2) interest rate expectations, and (3) the demand and supply of funds for each investment horizon.

 Explain the relationship between risk and the nominal interest rate on a debt security. The nominal interest rate of a risky debt security is composed of its nominal risk-free interest rate and the risk premium. Because the risk-free component is the same for all risky debt securities at a given time, the difference in nominal interest rates among the debt securities is attributed to the risk premium. The nominal interest rates are higher for debt securities that entail more risk because investors require a higher risk premium to invest in those securities.

 Explain why the returns required on risky assets change over time. The returns required on risky assets change in response to changes in the risk-free rate or in the risk premium required by investors. As the risk-free rate changes, the required return on a security changes by the same amount and in the same direction, assuming that there is no change in the risk premium. When the risk of a security increases, there is an increase in the return that investors require to invest in the security.

SELF-TEST EXERCISES   (Solutions in Appendix B)

 ST 4–1   Real rate of return   Refer to the example in the text (page 74) in which Debbie Sompels has $10,000 with which to buy furniture today or invest in a certificate of deposit for 1 year and then purchase the furniture after that.
  a. Suppose the nominal rate of interest remains at 7% but the expected rate of inflation is 7%. Will Debbie expect to benefit from her investment in the certificate of deposit that pays 7%?
  b. If the rate on the certificate of deposit is 10% when the expected inflation is 7%, what is her expected benefit?
  c. From your answers in parts a and b, what can you say about the real rate of return?

 ST 4–2   Yields; risk premiums   The following are average annualized yields on Treasury and corporate securities.

Security	Yield
Expected inflation rate	3.10%
30-day T-bill	6.60%
10-year T-bond	7.10%
10-year Aaa corporate bond	8.00%
5-year Ba corporate bond	8.60%
10-year Ba corporate bond	8.85%
15-year Ba corporate bond	9.10%
10-year B corporate bond	10.04%
30-year Baa corporate bond	8.55%
Corporate stocks (S&P 500)	13.50%

a. On the basis of the above data, determine the premium paid on 10-year Treasury bonds as a result of the longer term to maturity.

b. What is the real rate of return on Treasury bills?

c. What is the risk premium on the highest-grade corporate bonds? On the lowest-grade corporate bonds?

d. If you are working for a financial institution bound by regulations to invest only in investment grade bonds (bonds graded Baa and higher), what is the highest return you can receive on your investment?

EXERCISES

LG1   4–1   Why is it important for borrowers and lenders to understand how the risk-free interest rate changes?

LG1   4–2   **Rate of return**   Debbie Sompels invested $10,000 in a certificate of deposit with a stated rate of return of 7% when the expected inflation is 4%, and she buys the furniture 1 year later with the money from this investment. The current cost of the furniture is $10,000. As it turns out, the actual rate of inflation is not 4% but 6%. What is Debbie's real rate of return in this situation?

LG2   4–3   How is the equilibrium interest rate determined?

LG2   4–4   What are the factors that will cause a shift in the supply of funds?

LG2   4–5   What are the factors that affect aggregate demand for funds?

LG3   4–6   How does the liquidity preference theory explain why short-term securities give lower yields than long-term securities?

LG3   4–7   Can the liquidity preference theory provide an explanation for the downward-sloping yield curve?

LG4   4–8   a. What is the risk premium?
        b. Rank the following stocks in order from the lowest return to the highest return, and explain your choice.

(1) General Electric Company (GE), an established conglomerate in many
lines of business
(2) E-Bay, a newly established company engaged in auction over the Internet
(3) Merck, a pharmaceuticals company developing new drugs

  4–9   **Term structure of interest rates**   The following are yields on Treasury securities
with different maturities.

Security	Maturity	Yield
T-bill	3 months	4.80%
T-bill	12 months	4.95%
T-note	5 years	5.35%
T-note	10 years	5.70%
T-bond	15 years	6.00%
T-bond	20 years	6.27%

Plot a graph of yield against maturity. What does this graph
indicate?

 4–10   What are the factors that can affect the risk premium of a bond?

 4–11   Explain how risk premiums on bonds change with economic conditions and
suggest an explanation for this.

  4–12   **Expected rate of return**   The risk-free rate on long-term capital is 5.80%. Rates
of return on A grade corporate bonds average 7.80%, and the average return on
the S&P 500 (a basket of stocks consisting of 500 of the largest companies in
different industries) is 12.60%.
  a. If inflation is expected to increase by another 1.10%, what will be the
  expected return on the A grade corporate bond? On the S&P 500? What can
  you say about the new expected returns on both groups of securities?
  b. Suppose investors expect the economy to deteriorate. The new rate of return
  on A grade corporate bonds is averaging 8.60%. Do you expect the rate of
  return on the S&P 500 to increase too?
  Explain.

 4–13   Why are stocks considered more risky than bonds in general?

 4–14   **Changes in the risk-free rate and risk premium**   State how each of the following
examples will affect the risk-free rate and how it will affect the risk premium of
the outstanding stock and bond. State whether there is an increase, decrease, or
no change.

Situations	Risk-Free Rate	Premium on Bond	Premium on Stock
a. Consumers are saving less as the result of a tax increase.			
b. The price of oil increases, and this increase will be borne by consumers. (Assume that the firm's business is not affected by this price increase.)			
c. The firm operates a subsidiary in a foreign country that is in turmoil.			
d. The firm is acquired, and the new company is overfinanced with debt.			
e. The industry is facing phenomenal growth, and the firm is well positioned to capture this growth.			

web exercises   Search

Bloomberg.com

Go to the Bloomberg web site, www.bloomberg.com/. Under **Markets**, click on **U.S. Treasuries**. You will see the latest information on coupon payments, maturity dates, and yields on Treasury securities of various maturities. A plot of the yield curve, based on the information given, is also shown.

1. Under **Rates & Bonds**, click on **International Bonds**. This screen gives yields on government bonds from Canada, France, Germany, Italy, Japan, and the United Kingdom. Compare this yield with the U.S. Treasury yields of equivalent maturities. Plot the yield curves for each of the countries. Do they all look alike?

2. Now click on **Muni Bond Yield** under **Rates & Bonds** to obtain municipal bond yields for different maturities. Plot this yield and compare it with the yield curve for U.S. Treasuries. Unlike U.S. Treasury securities, municipal securities are not default-free. Why are their yields less than those quoted for U.S. Treasuries?

web exercises   Search

Bureau of Labor Statistics

Go to the Bureau of Labor Statistics web site, stats.bls.gov/cpihome.htm. Under News Release, click on Consumer Price Index. Then, in the Table of Contents, click on Consumer Price Index Summary. Assuming that the CPI data computed for the current year up to the most recent month is the average for this year, calculate the real rate of return if you invest in a Treasury bill.

**For additional practice with concepts from this chapter, visit
http://www.awl.com/gitman_madura**

Creating and Financing the Business at exam-ace.net

Business Idea

Tom Turner graduated with a business major and decided to start his own business called exam-ace.net. This service provides online practice tests for college students who are preparing to take an exam in any of various business courses. On Tom's web site, there is a menu of courses from which students can select those topics (arranged by common chapter titles) in which they will be tested. When students order the practice test for a particular topic, they are charged $1 per chapter, and they use a credit card to make payment. The service provides the practice exam (in multiple-choice format) online to the student right after the order is placed. The correct answers to the practice exam are also provided. Tom's general business objective is to provide an online testing service to customers who are seeking a degree or a license. At this point, his business is focused on college students, but he also plans to provide practice tests for accountants, lawyers, brokers, or other professionals some time in the future.

Expenses

Tom hired instructors on a part-time basis to create the practice tests. He incurred expenses to develop the web site and the system for providing practice tests online. He also incurred expenses as a result of marketing his service in student newspapers at many colleges.

Financing the Business

Tom invested $20,000 of his own savings in the business. However, the business relied mostly on investors and financial markets for financing. He approached a wealthy friend, Dan Atkinson, to obtain funding for this business. Dan liked the business idea, because he knew of no other firm that was providing students with this type of service. Dan provided financing for the business in the form of a $80,000 (nonvoting) equity investment in shares of the business for a period of 5 years. Tom agreed to pay Dan a dividend of $12,000 per year, which reflects a 15% return on the $80,000 equity investment. In addition, Tom agreed that he would purchase Dan's shares back at that same price in 5 years and that he would pay a premium for those shares that would be based on the performance of the firm over this period.

Tom also obtained funding within the financial markets by borrowing $100,000 from a financial institution. The financing was provided for a 5-year term. The payments on the loan would take priority over any return to the equity investors. The financial institution offered Tom two alternatives: (1) a fixed-rate loan with an annual interest rate of 10%, or (2) a floating interest rate that would be adjusted annually, set at 4 percentage points above the prevailing 1-year Treasury bill rate at the beginning of each year. The 1-year Treasury bill rate was presently 5%. Tom chose the fixed-rate arrangement. Thus, Tom owed the financial institution $10,000 in interest each year for the next 5 years and would also have to pay back the principal in 5 years.

These financing arrangements gave Tom funding for the next 5 years. During this time, Tom hopes to establish consistently high performance so that he can more easily tap the financial markets for additional (and lower-cost) funding in the future.

Exercises

CC1-1 Explain why Tom selected the fixed interest rate for the loan from the financial institution, even though he could have selected a floating-rate loan that would have had a lower initial interest rate. What economic factors would Tom have considered when attempting to determine the interest rate that he would have to pay in the future on the floating-rate loan?

CC1–2 Tom was unaware that an existing local retail store had just borrowed from a financial institution for a 3-year period at a fixed interest rate of a 9%. Why do you think Tom was charged a higher interest rate?

CC1–3 Why would the financial institution impose a requirement that it would provide a loan only if exam-ace.net obtained at least half of its funds in equity?

CC1–4 Note that the firm's cost of equity financing is higher that the cost of borrowing from the financial institution. Why must the firm be willing to pay the equity investor (Dan Atkinson) more than it pays the financial institution?

CC1–5 Communication Tom's ability to obtain funding from a commercial bank would depend on the bank's assessment of Tom's business and the likelihood that the loan would be repaid on time. Put yourself in Tom's position and outline your arguments to the bank as to why it could trust that your business would be able to repay this loan on time, even though there is some uncertainty regarding the future performance of this business.

CC1–6 Teamwork Create a team of three students in which one student serves as Tom (manager and owner), another serves as Dan Atkinson (investor), and the third serves as the lender. Explain your major concerns about the financing relationship from the perspective of the role you are assigned to play. How can Tom attempt to satisfy all stakeholders (investors and lenders)?

CC1–7 Ethics Tom recognizes that there is some risk to anyone who invests equity in his firm. He believes that it is not his responsibility to identify the possible risks that could prevent his firm from meeting obligations to investors. Does Tom have a responsibility to any equity investors? To any creditors? Explain.

CC1–8 Ethics A friend advised Tom that he could reduce his expenses by simply using multiple-choice questions that were provided as self-tests in various textbooks. Tom decided to hire instructors to make up questions rather than to pull questions from textbooks. Should Tom have followed his friend's advice? Why or why not?

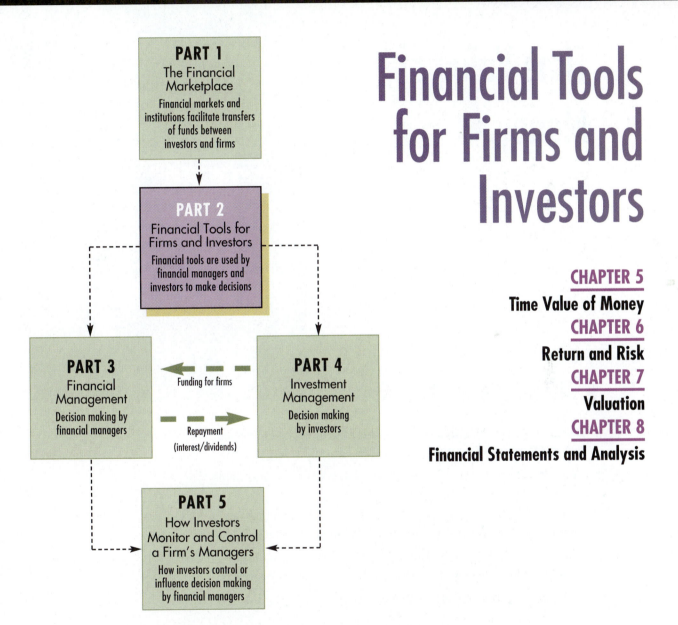

Financial Tools for Firms and Investors

Managers and investors use the common financial tools presented in this part to make forward-looking decisions consistent with their common objective of maximizing value—firm value for managers and investment value for investors. They also must understand the tools of financial analysis in order to monitor the firm's progress. The financial tools presented in this part are of fundamental importance to successful financial and investment management.

Time Value of Money

LG1 Discuss the role of time value in finance and the use of computational aids to simplify its application.

LG2 Understand the concept of future value and its calculation for a single amount.

LG3 Understand the concept of present value, its calculation for a single amount, and the relationship of present value to future value.

LG4 Find the future value and present value of an ordinary annuity, the future value of an annuity due, and the present value of a perpetuity.

LG5 Calculate the present value of a mixed stream of cash flows.

LG6 Understand the effect that compounding more frequently than annually has on future value and the effective annual rate of interest.

LG7 Describe the procedures involved in (1) determining deposits to accumulate a future sum, (2) loan amortization, and (3) finding interest or growth rates.

LG1 The Role of Time Value in Finance

Financial managers and investors are always confronted with opportunities to earn positive rates of return on their funds, whether through investment in attractive projects or in interest-bearing securities or deposits. Therefore, the timing of cash outflows and inflows has important economic consequences, which financial managers explicitly recognize as the *time value of money*. We begin our study of time value in finance by considering the two views of time value—future value and present value—and the computational aids used to streamline time value calculations.

Future Value versus Present Value

Financial values and decisions can be assessed by using either future value or present value techniques. Although these techniques will result in the same decisions, they view the decision differently. Future value techniques typically measure cash flows at the *end* of a project's life. Present value techniques measure cash flows at the *start* of a project's life (time zero). *Future value* is cash you will receive at a given future date, and *present value* is just like cash in hand today.

time line
A horizontal line on which time zero appears at the leftmost end and future periods are marked from left to right; can be used to depict investment cash flows.

A **time line** can be used to depict the cash flows associated with a given investment. It is a horizontal line on which time zero appears at the leftmost end and future periods are marked from left to right. A line covering five periods (in this case, years) is given in Figure 5.1. The cash flow occurring at time zero and that at the end of each year are shown above the line; the negative values represent cash outflows ($10,000 at time zero) and the positive values represent cash inflows ($3,000 inflow at the end of year 1, $5,000 inflow at the end of year 2, and so on).

Because money has a time value, all of the cash flows associated with an investment, such as those in Figure 5.1, must be measured at the same point in time. Typically, that point is either the end or the beginning of the investment's life. The future value technique uses *compounding* to find the *future value* of each cash flow at the end of the investment's life and then sums these values to find the investment's future value. This approach is depicted above the time line in Figure 5.2. The figure shows that the future value of each cash flow is measured at the end of the investment's 5-year life. Alternatively, the present value technique uses *discounting* to find the *present value* of each cash flow at time

FIGURE 5.1

Time Line
Time line depicting an investment's cash flows

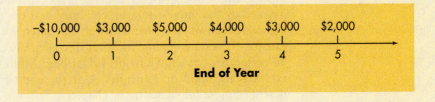

FIGURE 5.2

Compounding and Discounting
Time line showing compounding to find future value and discounting to find present value

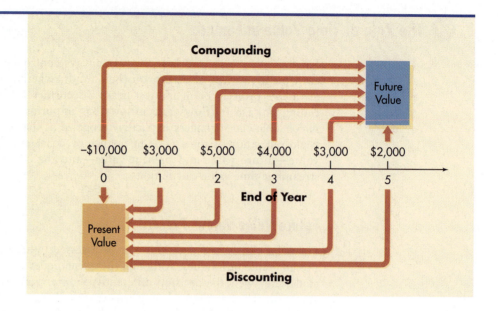

zero and then sums these values to find the investment's value today. Application of this approach is depicted below the time line in Figure 5.2.

The meaning and mechanics of compounding to find future value and of discounting to find present value are covered in this chapter. Although future value and present value result in the same decisions, both financial managers and investors—because they make decisions at time zero—tend to rely primarily on present value techniques.

Computational Aids

Time-consuming calculations are often involved in finding future and present values. Although your goal should be to understand the concepts and mathematics underlying these calculations, the application of time value techniques can be streamlined. We focus on the use of financial tables and hand-held financial calculators as computational aids. Personal computers can also be used to simplify time value calculations, using spreadsheets.

Financial Tables

Financial tables include various future and present value interest factors that simplify time value calculations. The values shown in these tables are easily developed from formulas, with various degrees of rounding. The tables are typically indexed by the interest rate (in columns) and the number of periods (in rows). Figure 5.3 shows this general layout. The interest factor at a 20 percent interest rate for 10 years would be found at the intersection of the 20% column and the 10-period row, as shown by the bright box. A full set of the four basic financial tables is included in Appendix A at the end of the book. These tables are described more fully later in the chapter.

FIGURE 5.3

Financial Tables
Layout and use of a financial table

Period	\multicolumn{8}{c}{Interest Rate ↓}
	1%	2%	⋯	10%	⋯	**20%**	⋯	50%
1			⋯		⋯	⋮	⋯	
2			⋯		⋯	⋮	⋯	
3			⋯		⋯	⋮	⋯	
⋮	⋮	⋮	⋯	⋮	⋯	⋮	⋯	⋮
→ 10	⋯	⋯	⋯	⋯	⋯	**X.XXX**	⋯	⋯
⋮	⋮	⋮	⋯	⋮	⋯	⋮	⋯	⋮
20			⋯		⋯	⋮	⋯	
⋮	⋮	⋮	⋯	⋮	⋯	⋮	⋯	⋮
50			⋯		⋯	⋮	⋯	

Financial Calculators

Financial calculators also can be used for time value computations. Generally, *financial calculators* include numerous preprogrammed financial routines. This chapter and those that follow show the keystrokes for calculating interest factors and making other financial computations. For convenience, we use the important financial keys, labeled in a fashion consistent with most major financial calculators.

We focus primarily on the keys pictured and defined in Figure 5.4. We typically use four of the five keys in the left column, along with the compute (CPT) key. One of the four keys represents the unknown value being calculated. (Occasionally, all five of the keys are used, with one representing the unknown value.) The keystrokes on some of the more sophisticated calculators are menu-driven: After you select the appropriate routine, the calculator prompts you to input each value; on these calculators, a compute key is not

FIGURE 5.4

Calculator Keys
Important financial keys on the typical calculator

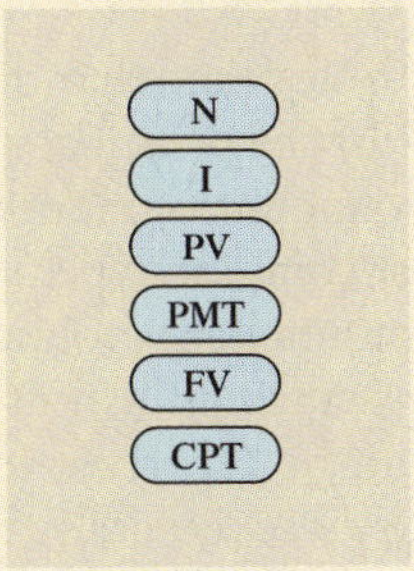

N	— Number of periods
I	— Interest rate per period
PV	— Present value
PMT	— Amount of payment (used only for annuities)
FV	— Future value
CPT	— Compute key used to initiate financial calculation once all values are input

needed to obtain a solution. Regardless, any calculator with the basic future and present value functions can be used in lieu of financial tables. The keystrokes for other financial calculators are explained in the reference guides that accompany them.

Once you understand the basic underlying concepts, you probably will want to use a calculator to streamline routine financial calculations. With a little practice, you can increase both the speed and the accuracy of your financial computations. Note that because of a calculator's greater precision, slight differences are likely to exist between values calculated by using financial tables and those found with a financial calculator. Remember that *conceptual understanding of the material is the objective*. An ability to solve problems with the aid of a calculator does not necessarily reflect such an understanding, so don't just settle for answers. Work with the material until you are sure you also understand the concepts.

Review Question

5–1   What is the difference between *future value and present value?* Which approach is generally preferred by financial managers and investors? Why?

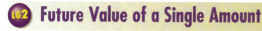

Future Value of a Single Amount

Imagine that at age 25 you began making annual purchases of $2,000 of an investment that earns a guaranteed 5 percent annually. At the end of 40 years, at age 65, you would have invested a total of $80,000 (40 years × $2,000 per year). Assuming that all funds remain invested, how much would you have accumulated at the end of the fortieth year? $100,000? $150,000? $200,000? No, your $80,000 would have grown to $242,000! Why? Because the time value of money allowed your investments to generate returns that built on each other over the 40 years.

The Concept of Future Value

compound interest
Interest earned on a given deposit that has become part of the principal at the end of a specified period.

principal
The amount of money on which interest is paid.

future value
The value of a present amount at a future date, found by applying *compound interest* over a specified period of time.

We speak of **compound interest** to indicate that the amount of interest earned on a given deposit has become part of the principal at the end of a specified period. The term **principal** refers to the amount of money on which the interest is paid. Annual compounding is the most common type.

The **future value** of a present amount is found by applying *compound interest* over a specified period of time. Savings institutions advertise compound interest returns at a rate of x percent, or x percent interest, compounded annually, semiannually, quarterly, monthly, weekly, daily, or even continuously. The concept of future value with annual compounding can be illustrated by a simple example.

Example ▼ If Fred Vanek places $100 in a savings account paying 8% interest compounded annually, at the end of 1 year he will have $108 in the account—the initial principal of $100 plus 8% ($8) in interest. The future value at the end of the first year is calculated by using Equation 5.1:

$$\text{Future value at end of year 1} = \$100 \times (1 + 0.08) = \$108 \qquad (5.1)$$

If Fred were to leave this money in the account for another year, he would be paid interest at the rate of 8% on the new principal of $108. At the end of this second year there would be $116.64 in the account. This amount would represent the principal at the beginning of year 2 ($108) plus 8% of the $108 ($8.64) in interest. The future value at the end of the second year is calculated by using Equation 5.2:

$$\text{Future value at end of year 2} = \$108 \times (1 + 0.08) \qquad (5.2)$$
$$= \$116.64$$

Substituting the expression between the equals signs in Equation 5.1 for the $108 figure in Equation 5.2 gives us Equation 5.3:

$$\text{Future value at end of year 2} = \$100 \times (1 + 0.08) \times (1 + 0.08) \qquad (5.3)$$
$$= \$100 \times (1 + 0.08)^2$$
$$= \$116.64$$

The equations in the preceding example lead to a more general formula for calculating future value.

The Equation for Future Value

The basic relationship in Equation 5.3 can be generalized to find the future value after any number of periods. We use the following notation for the various inputs:

FV_n = future value at the end of period n
PV = initial principal, or present value
i = annual rate of interest paid. (*Note:* On financial calculators, **I** is typically used to represent this rate.)
n = number of periods (typically years) that the money is left on deposit

The general equation for the future value at the end of period n is

$$FV_n = PV \times (1 + i)^n \qquad (5.4)$$

A simple example will illustrate how to apply Equation 5.4.

Example ▼ Val Fuentes places $800 in a savings account paying 6% interest compounded annually, and wants to know how much money will be in the account at the end of 5 years. Substituting $PV = \$800$, $i = 0.06$, and $n = 5$ into Equation 5.4 gives the amount at the end of year 5:

$$FV_5 = \$800 \times (1 + 0.06)^5 = \$800 \times (1.338) = \$1{,}070.40$$

This analysis can be depicted on a time line as follows:

Time line for future value of a single amount ($800 initial principal, earning 6%, at the end of 5 years)

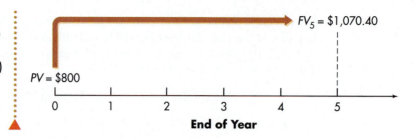

$PV = \$800$

$FV_5 = \$1,070.40$

0   1   2   3   4   5

End of Year

Using Tables and Calculators to Find Future Value

Solving the equation in the preceding example involves raising 1.06 to the fifth power. Using a future value interest table or a financial calculator greatly simplifies the calculation. A table that provides values for $(1 + i)^n$ in Equation 5.4 is included near the back of the book in Appendix Table A-1. The value in each cell of the table is called the **future value interest factor**. This factor is the multiplier used to calculate, at a specified interest rate, the future value of a present amount as of a given time. The future value interest factor for an initial principal of $1 compounded at i percent for n periods is referred to as $FVIF_{i,n}$:

future value interest factor
The multiplier used to calculate, at a specified interest rate, the future value of a present amount as of a given time.

$$\text{Future value interest factor} = FVIF_{i,n} = (1 + i)^n \tag{5.5}$$

By finding the intersection of the annual interest rate, i, and the appropriate periods, n, you will find the future value interest factor that is relevant to a particular problem. Using $FVIF_{i,n}$ as the appropriate factor, we can rewrite the general equation for future value (Equation 5.4) as follows:

$$FV_n = PV \times (FVIF_{i,n}) \tag{5.6}$$

This expression indicates that to find the future value at the end of period n of an initial deposit, we have merely to multiply the initial deposit, PV, by the appropriate future value interest factor.

Example ▼ In the preceding example, Val Fuentes placed $800 in her savings account at 6% interest compounded annually and wishes to find out how much will be in the account at the end of 5 years.

Table Use   The future value interest factor for an initial principal of $1 on deposit for 5 years at 6% interest compounded annually, $FVIF_{6\%, 5\text{yrs}}$, found in Table A-1, is 1.338. Using Equation 5.6, $\$800 \times 1.338 = \$1,070.40$. Therefore, the future value of Val's deposit at the end of year 5 will be $1,070.40.

Calculator Use[1]   The financial calculator can be used to calculate the future value directly.[2] First punch in $800 and depress **PV**; next punch in 5 and depress **N**; then punch in 6 and depress **I** (which is equivalent to "i" in our notation[3];

---

[1]Many calculators allow the user to set the number of payments per year. Most of these calculators are preset for monthly payments—12 payments per year. Because we work primarily with annual payments—one payment per year—it is important to be sure that your calculator is set for one payment per year. And although most calculators are preset to recognize that all payments occur at the end of the period, it is important to make sure that your calculator is correctly set on the END mode. Consult the reference guide that accompanies your calculator for instructions for setting these values.

[2]To avoid including previous data in current calculations, *always* clear all registers of your calculator before inputting values and making each computation.

[3]The known values *can be punched into the calculator in any order*; the order specified in this as well as other demonstrations of calculator use included in this text merely reflects convenience and personal preference.

finally, to calculate the future value, depress **CPT** and then **FV.** The future value of $1,070.58 should appear on the calculator display as shown at the left below. On many calculators, this value will be preceded by a minus sign ($-1{,}070.58$). *If a minus sign appears on your calculator, ignore it here as well as in all other "Calculator Use" illustrations in this text.*[4]

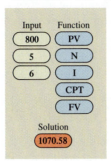

Input	Function
800	PV
5	N
6	I
	CPT
	FV

Solution
1070.58

Because the calculator is more accurate than the future value factors, which have been rounded to the nearest 0.001, a slight difference—in this case, $0.18—will frequently exist between the values found by these alternative methods. Clearly, the improved accuracy and ease of calculation tend to favor the use of the calculator. (*Note:* In future examples of calculator use, we will use only a display similar to that shown at the left. If you need a reminder of the procedures involved, go back and review the preceding paragraph.)

A Graphical View of Future Value

Remember that we measure future value at the *end* of the given period. Figure 5.5 illustrates the relationship among various interest rates, the number of periods interest is earned, and the future value of one dollar. The figure shows that (1) the higher the interest rate, the higher the future value, and (2) the longer the period of time, the higher the future value. Note that for an interest rate of 0 percent, the future value always equals the present value ($1.00). But for any interest rate greater than zero, the future value is greater than the present value of $1.00.

FIGURE 5.5

Future Value Relationship

Interest rates, time periods, and future value of one dollar

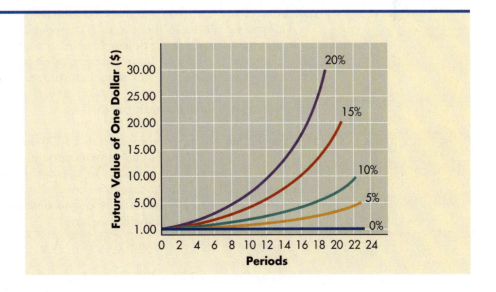

---

[4]The calculator differentiates inflows from outflows by preceding the outflows with a negative sign. For example, in the problem just demonstrated, the $800 present value (PV), because it was keyed as a positive number (800), is considered an inflow or deposit. Therefore, the calculated future value (FV) of $-1{,}070.58$ is preceded by a minus sign to show that it is the resulting outflow or withdrawal. Had the $800 present value been keyed in as a negative number (-800), the future value of $1,070.58 would have been displayed as a positive number (1,070.58). Simply stated, *the cash flows—present value* (PV) *and future value* (FV)—*will have opposite signs.*

? Review Questions

5–2   How is the *compounding process* related to the payment of interest on savings? What is the general equation for future value?

5–3   What effect would a *decrease* in the interest rate have on the future value of a deposit? What effect would an *increase* in the holding period have on future value?

Present Value of a Single Amount

present value
The current dollar value of a future amount; the amount of money that would have to be invested today at a given interest rate over a specified period to equal the future amount.

It is often useful to determine the value today of a future amount of money. For example, how much would I have to deposit today into an account paying 7 percent annual interest in order to accumulate $3,000 at the end of 5 years? **Present value** is the current dollar value of a future amount—the amount of money that would have to be invested today at a given interest rate over a specified period to equal the future amount. Present value depends largely on the investment opportunities and the point in time at which the amount is to be received. This section explores the present value of a single amount.

The Concept of Present Value

discounting cash flows
The process of finding present values; the inverse of compounding interest.

The process of finding present values is often referred to as **discounting cash flows.** It is concerned with answering the following question: "If I can earn *i* percent on my money, what is the most I would be willing to pay now for an opportunity to receive FV_n dollars *n* periods from today?"

This process is actually the inverse of compounding interest. Instead of finding the future value of present dollars invested at a given rate, discounting determines the present value of a future amount, assuming an opportunity to earn a certain return on the money. This annual rate of return is variously referred to as the *discount rate, required return, cost of capital,* and *opportunity cost.* These terms will be used interchangeably in this text.

Example ▼   Pete Vaughn has an opportunity to receive $300 one year from now. If he can earn 6% on his investments in the normal course of events, what is the most he should pay now for this opportunity? To answer this question, Pete must determine how many dollars would have to be invested at 6% today to have $300 one year from now. Letting *PV* equal this unknown amount and using the same notation as in the future value discussion, we have

$$PV \times (1 + 0.06) = \$300 \qquad (5.7)$$

Solving Equation 5.7 for *PV* gives us Equation 5.8:

$$PV = \frac{\$300}{(1 + 0.06)} \qquad (5.8)$$
$$= \$283.02$$

The value today ("present value") of $300 received one year from today, given an opportunity cost of 6%, is $283.02. That is, investing $283.02 today at the 6% opportunity cost would result in $300 at the end of one year.

The Equation for Present Value

The present value of a future amount can be found mathematically by solving Equation 5.4 for PV. In other words, the present value, PV, of some future amount, FV_n, to be received n periods from now, assuming an opportunity cost of i, is calculated as follows:

$$PV = \frac{FV_n}{(1+i)^n} = \frac{FV_n \times 1}{(1+i)^n} \qquad (5.9)$$

Note the similarity between this general equation for present value and the equation in the preceding example (Equation 5.8). Let's use this equation in an example.

Example ▼ Pearle Vincente wishes to find the present value of $1,700 that will be received 8 years from now. Pearl's opportunity cost is 8%. Substituting $FV_8 = \$1,700$, $n = 8$, and $i = 0.08$ into Equation 5.9 yields Equation 5.10:

$$PV = \frac{\$1,700}{(1+0.08)^8} = \frac{\$1,700}{1.851} = \$918.42 \qquad (5.10)$$

The following time line shows this analysis.

Time line for present value of a single amount ($1,700 future amount, discounted at 8%, from the end of 8 years)

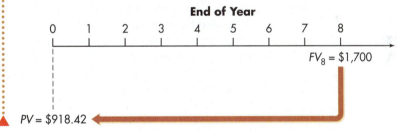

Using Tables and Calculators to Find Present Value

present value interest factor
The multiplier used to calculate, at a specified discount rate, the present value of an amount to be received in a future period.

The present value calculation can be simplified by using a **present value interest factor**. This factor is the multiplier used to calculate, at a specified discount rate, the present value of an amount to be received in a future period. The present value interest factor for the present value of $1 discounted at i percent for n periods is referred to as $PVIF_{i,n}$:

$$\text{Present value interest factor} = PVIF_{i,n} = \frac{1}{(1+i)^n} \qquad (5.11)$$

Appendix Table A-2 presents present value interest factors for $1. By letting $PVIF_{i,n}$ represent the appropriate factor, we can rewrite the general equation for present value (Equation 5.9) as follows:

$$PV = FV_n \times (PVIF_{i,n}) \qquad (5.12)$$

This expression indicates that to find the present value of an amount to be received in a future period, *n*, we have merely to multiply the future amount, FV_n, by the appropriate present value interest factor.

E x a m p l e ▼ As noted, Pearle Vincente wishes to find the present value of $1,700 to be received 8 years from now, assuming an 8% opportunity cost.

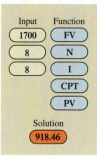

Input	Function
1700	FV
8	N
8	I
	CPT
	PV

Solution
918.46

Table Use   The present value interest factor for 8% and 8 years, $PVIF_{8\%,\ 8\ yrs}$, found in Table A-2, is .540. Using Equation 5.12, $1,700 \times 0.540 = \$918$. The present value of the amount Pearle expects to receive in 8 years is $918.

Calculator Use   Using the calculator's financial functions and the inputs shown at the left, you should find the present value to be $918.46. The value obtained with the calculator is more accurate than the values found using the equation or the table, although for the purposes of this text, these differences are insignificant.

A Graphical View of Present Value

Remember that present value calculations assume that the future values are measured at the *end* of the given period. The relationships among the factors in a present value calculation are illustrated in Figure 5.6. The figure clearly shows that, everything else being equal, (1) the higher the discount rate, the lower the present value, and (2) the longer the period of time, the lower the present value. Also note that given a discount rate of 0 percent, the present value always equals the future value ($1.00). But for any discount rate greater than zero, the present value is less than the future value of $1.00.

FIGURE 5.6

Present Value Relationship
Discount rates, time periods, and present value of one dollar

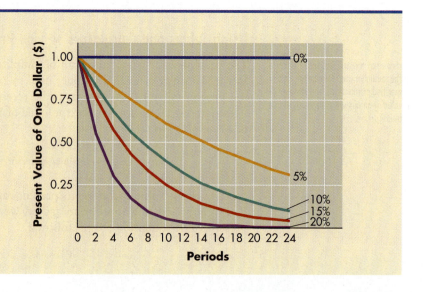

*News*Line   LOTTO WINNER KNOWS THE TIME VALUE OF MONEY

By taking the time value of money into account, a California Super Lotto grand-prize winner decides to take his prize in a lump sum rather than installments over 25 years. He recognizes that $100 received a year from now will almost always buy less than $100 received today.

If you had to choose between receiving $33 million or $16.1 million, which would you pick? Tony Vetromile, a senior at Santa Clara University, chose $16.1 million when he won the California Super Lotto grand prize.... That's the right choice from a financial standpoint, as long as he invests his money prudently.

Vetromile will get the entire $16.1 million in the next few weeks [March 1999]. If he had opted for the $33 million, he would have received annual checks ranging from $825,000 to $1.7 million for 25 years. Vetromile's dilemma brings to mind something that most of us often forget: the time value of money....

Most of us often think in terms of the dollars we expect to receive, rather than their present value [which reflects our opportunity to earn a return on the money we receive]. Professors of economics and psychology call this phenomenon the "money illusion."...

The California Lottery takes advantage of the money illusion when it advertises a $33 million value for a prize that costs it only $16.1 million. Here's how the lottery would have paid $33 million had Vetromile opted to receive his prize in installments:

First, the lottery would have made an $825,000 payment to Vetromile in the next few weeks. Then it would have purchased 25 ... U.S. Treasury bonds worth a total of $32,175,000 ($33 million minus $825,000) at maturity.

One of the bonds would have matured every February 24 (the anniversary of the date on which Vetromile's ticket was drawn) for 25 years. The first, worth $891,000 at maturity in 2000, would have cost $850,000, says Cathy Doyle Johnston, a spokeswoman for the lottery. The last, worth $1,683,000 at maturity in 2024, would have cost only $385,000.

Interest rates on these bonds would have ranged from 4.91 percent, for the bond that matures next year, to 5.99 percent for the bond that matures in 2024, Johnston says.

And those low rates are the reason... Vetromile made the right choice.... He can earn a safe, but higher, rate of return by putting the money in a combination of stocks and bonds, as long as he does so sensibly and invests for the long term. Doing this, the total value of his winnings will be well in excess of the $33 million.

Source: James J. Mitchell, "Lotto Winner Knows the Time Value of Money." San Jose Mercury News, March 7, 1999, downloaded from Dow Jones Interactive Publications Library.

Comparing Present Value and Future Value

We will close this section with some important observations about present values. One is that the expression for the present value interest factor for i percent and n periods, $1/(1 + i)^n$, is the *inverse* of the future value interest factor for i percent and n periods, $(1 + i)^n$. You can confirm this very simply: divide a present value interest factor for i percent and n periods, $PVIF_{i,n}$, given in Table A-2, into 1.0, and compare the resulting value to the future value interest factor given in Table A-1 for i percent and n periods, $FVIF_{i,n}$. The two values should be equivalent.

Second, because of the relationship between present value interest factors and future value interest factors, we can find the present value interest factors given a table of future value interest factors, and vice versa. For example, the future value interest factor (from Table A-1) for 10 percent and 5 periods is 1.611. Dividing this value into 1.0 yields .621, which is the present value interest factor (given in Table A-2) for 10 percent and 5 periods.

? Review Questions

5–4   What is meant by "the present value of a future amount"? What is the general equation for present value?

5–5   What effect does *increasing* the required return have on the present value of a future amount? Why?

5–6   How are present value and future value calculations related?

Annuities

annuity
A stream of equal periodic cash flows, over a specified time period. These cash flows can be *inflows* of returns earned on investments or *outflows* of funds invested to earn future returns.

ordinary annuity
An annuity for which the cash flow occurs at the *end* of each period.

annuity due
An annuity for which the cash flow occurs at the *beginning* of each period.

How much would you pay today, given you can earn 7 percent on low-risk investments, to receive a guaranteed $3,000 at the end of *each* of the next 20 years? How much will you have at the end of 5 years if your employer withholds and invests $1,000 of your year-end bonus at the end of *each* of the next 5 years, guaranteeing you a 9 percent annual rate of return? To answer each of these questions, you need to understand the application of the time value of money to *annuities*. An **annuity** is a stream of equal periodic cash flows, over a specified time period. These cash flows are usually annual but can occur at other intervals, such as monthly (rent, car payments). The cash flows in an annuity can be *inflows* (the $3,000 received at the end of each of the next 20 years) or *outflows* (the $1,000 invested at the end of each of the next 5 years). There are two basic types of annuities.

Types of Annuities

There are two basic types of annuities. For an **ordinary annuity,** the cash flow occurs at the *end* of each period. For an **annuity due,** the cash flow occurs at the *beginning* of each period.

E x a m p l e ▼

Frank Adams is choosing which of two annuities to receive. Both are 5-year, $1,000 annuities; annuity A is an ordinary annuity, and annuity B is an annuity due. To better understand the difference between these annuities, he has listed their cash flows in Table 5.1. Note that the amount of each annuity totals $5,000. The two annuities differ in the timing of their cash flows: The cash flows are received sooner with the annuity due than with the ordinary annuity.

▲

Although the cash flows of both annuities in Table 5.1 total $5,000, the annuity due would have a higher future value than the ordinary annuity, because each of its five annual cash flows can earn interest for one year more than each of the ordinary annuity's cash flows. In general, as will be demonstrated later in this chapter, *the future value of an annuity due is always greater than the future value of an otherwise identical ordinary annuity.*

Because ordinary annuities are more frequently used in finance, *unless otherwise specified, the term* annuity *is used throughout this book to refer to ordinary annuities.*

Finding the Future Value of an Ordinary Annuity

The calculations required to find the future value of an ordinary annuity are illustrated in the following example.

TABLE 5.1	Comparison of Ordinary Annuity and Annuity Due Cash Flows ($1,000, 5 Years)

	Annual cash flows	
End of year[a]	Annuity A (*ordinary*)	Annuity B (*annuity due*)
0	$ 0	$1,000
1	1,000	1,000
2	1,000	1,000
3	1,000	1,000
4	1,000	1,000
5	1,000	0
Totals	$5,000	$5,000

[a]The ends of years 0, 1, 2, 3, 4, and 5 are equivalent to the beginnings of years 1, 2, 3, 4, 5, and 6, respectively.

Example ▼

Frank Adams wishes to determine how much money he will have at the end of 5 years if he chooses annuity A, the ordinary annuity. It represents deposits of $1,000 annually, at the end of each of the next 5 years, into a savings account paying 7% annual interest. This situation is depicted on the following time line:

Time line for future value of an ordinary annuity ($1,000 end-of-year deposit, earning 7%, at the end of 5 years)

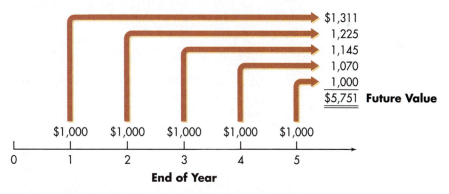

As the figure shows, at the end of year 5, Frank will have $5,751 in his account. Note that because the deposits are made at the end of the year, the first deposit will earn interest for 4 years, the second for 3 years, and so on.

Using Tables and Calculators to Find the Future Value of an Ordinary Annuity

Annuity calculations can be simplified by using an interest table or a financial calculator. A table for the future value of a $1 *annuity* is given in Appendix Table A-3. The factors in the table are derived by summing the future value interest factors for the appropriate number of years. For example, the factor for the annuity in the preceding example is the sum of the factors for the five years (years 4 through 0): 1.311 + 1.225 + 1.145 + 1.070 + 1.000 = 5.751. Because the deposits occur at the end of each year, they will earn interest from the end of the year in which each occurs to the end of year 5. Therefore, the first deposit earns

future value interest factor for an annuity
The multiplier used to calculate the future value of an *ordinary annuity* at a specified interest rate over a given period of time.

interest for 4 years (end of year 1 through end of year 5), and the last deposit earns interest for zero years. The future value interest factor for zero years at any interest rate, $FVIF_{i,0}$, is 1.00, as we have noted. The formula for the **future value interest factor for an annuity** when interest is compounded annually at i percent for n periods, $FVIF_{i,n}$, is

$$FVIFA_{i,n} = \sum_{t=1}^{n} (1+i)^{t-1} \tag{5.13}$$

This factor is the multiplier used to calculate the future value of an *ordinary annuity* at a specified interest rate over a given period of time.[5]

Using FVA_n for the future value of an n-year annuity, PMT for the amount to be deposited annually at the end of each year, and $FVIFA_{i,n}$ for the appropriate *future value interest factor for a one-dollar annuity compounded at* i *percent for* n *years,* we can express the relationship among these variables alternatively as:

$$FVA_n = PMT \times (FVIFA_{i,n}) \tag{5.14}$$

The following example illustrates this calculation using both a table and a financial calculator.

Example ▼

As noted earlier, Frank Adams wishes to find the future value (FVA_n) at the end of 5 years (n) of an annual end-of-year deposit of $1,000 ($PMT$) into an account paying 7% annual interest (i) during the next 5 years.

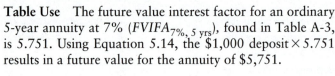

Input	Function
1000	PMT
5	N
7	I
	CPT
	FV

Solution
5750.74

Table Use   The future value interest factor for an ordinary 5-year annuity at 7% ($FVIFA_{7\%, 5 \text{ yrs}}$), found in Table A-3, is 5.751. Using Equation 5.14, the $1,000 deposit $\times$ 5.751 results in a future value for the annuity of $5,751.

Calculator Use   Using the calculator inputs shown at the left, you will find the future value of the ordinary annuity to be $5,750.74, a slightly more precise answer than that found using the table.

Finding the Present Value of an Ordinary Annuity

Quite often in finance, there is a need to find the present value of a *stream* of cash flows to be received in future periods. An annuity is, of course, a pattern of equal cash flows. (We'll explore the case of unequal periodic cash flows in a later section.) The method for finding the present value of an ordinary annuity is similar to the method just discussed. There are long and short methods for this calculation.

---

[5]A mathematical expression that can be applied to calculate the future value interest factor for an ordinary annuity more efficiently is

$$FVIFA_{i,n} = \frac{1}{i} \times [(1+i)^n - 1] \tag{5.13a}$$

The use of this expression is especially attractive in the absence of the appropriate financial tables and of any financial calculator or personal computer.

TABLE 5.2	The Long Method for Finding the Present Value of an Ordinary Annuity

Year (n)	Cash flow (1)	$PVIF_{8\%,n}$[a] (2)	Present value [(1) × (2)] (3)
1	$700	0.926	$ 648.20
2	700	0.857	599.90
3	700	0.794	555.80
4	700	0.735	514.50
5	700	0.681	476.70
		Present value of annuity	$2,795.10

[a]Present value interest factors at 8% are from Table A-2.

Example ▼ Lenk Company, a small producer of plastic toys, wants to determine the most it should pay to purchase a particular ordinary annuity. The annuity consists of cash flows of $700 at the end of each year for 5 years. The firm requires the annuity to provide a minimum return of 8%. This situation is depicted on the following time line:

Time line for present value of an annuity ($700 end-of-year cash flows, discounted at 8%, over 5 years)

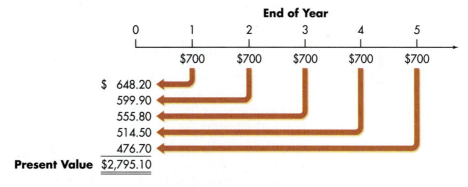

Table 5.2 shows the long method for finding the present value of the annuity. This method involves finding the present value of each payment and summing them. This procedure yields a present value of $2,795.10.

Using Tables and Calculators to Find the Present Value of an Ordinary Annuity

Annuity calculations can be simplified by using a short method—an interest table for the present value of an annuity or a financial calculator. The values for the present value of a $1 annuity are given in Appendix Table A-4. The factors in the table are derived by summing the present value interest factors (in Table A-2) for the appropriate number of years at the given discount rate. The formula for the **present value interest factor for an annuity** with end-of-year cash flows that are discounted at i percent for n periods, $PVIFA_{i,n}$, is:

present value interest factor for an annuity
The multiplier used to calculate the present value of an *ordinary annuity* at a specified discount rate over a given period of time.

$$PVIFA_{i,n} = \sum_{t=1}^{n} \frac{1}{(1+i)^t} \qquad (5.15)$$

This factor is the multiplier used to calculate the present value of an *ordinary annuity* at a specified discount rate over a given period of time.[6]

By letting PVA_n equal the present value of an *n*-year annuity, letting PMT equal the amount to be received annually at the end of each year, and letting $PVIFA_{i,n}$ represent the appropriate *present value interest factor for a one-dollar annuity discounted at* i *percent for* n *years*, we can express the relationship among these variables as

$$PVA_n = PMT \times (PVIFA_{i,n}) \tag{5.16}$$

The following example illustrates this calculation for both a table and a financial calculator.

Example ▼

Input	Function
700	PMT
5	N
8	I
	CPT
	PV

Solution
2794.90

Lenk Company, as we have noted, wants to find the present value of a 5-year annuity of $700, assuming an 8% opportunity cost.

Table Use The present value interest factor for an annuity at 8% for 5 years ($PVIFA_{8\%, \, 5yrs}$) found in Table A-4, is 3.993. Using Equation 5.16, $700 annuity $\times$ 3.993 results in a present value of $2,795.10.

Calculator Use Using the calculator's inputs shown at the left, you will find the present value of the annuity to be $2,794.90. The value obtained with the calculator is more accurate than those found using the equation or the table.

Finding the Future Value of an Annuity Due

We now turn the attention to annuities due. Remember that the cash flows of an annuity due occur at the start of the period. A simple conversion is applied when we want to use the future value interest factors for an ordinary annuity (in Table A-3) with annuities due. Equation 5.17 presents this conversion:

$$FVIFA_{i,n} \, (\text{annuity due}) = FVIFA_{i,n} \times (1 + i) \tag{5.17}$$

This equation says that the future value interest factor for an annuity due can be found merely by multiplying the future value interest factor for an ordinary annuity at the same percent and length of time by $(1 + i)$. Why is this adjustment necessary? Because each cash flow of an annuity due earns interest for one year more than an ordinary annuity (from the start to the end of the year). Multiplying $FVIFA_{i,n}$ by $(1 + i)$ simply adds an additional year's interest to *each* annuity cash flow. The following example demonstrates how to find the future value of an annuity due.

---

[6]A mathematical expression that can be applied to calculate the present value interest factor for an ordinary annuity more efficiently is

$$PVIFA_{i,n} = \frac{1}{i} \times \left[1 - \frac{1}{(1+i)^n} \right] \tag{5.15a}$$

The use of this expression is especially attractive in the absence of the appropriate financial tables and of any financial calculator or personal computer.

Example ▼ Remember from an earlier example that Frank Adams wanted to choose between an ordinary annuity and an annuity due, both offering similar terms except for the timing of cash flows. We calculated the future value of the ordinary annuity in the example on page 116. We now will calculate the future value of the annuity due, using the cash flows represented by annuity B in Table 5.1 (page 115).

Table Use Substituting $i = 7\%$ and $n = 5$ years into Equation 5.17, with the aid of the appropriate interest factor from Table A-3, we get:

$$FVIFA_{7\%, \, 5 \, yrs}(\text{annuity due}) = FVIFA_{7\%, \, 5 \, yrs} \times (1 + 0.07)$$
$$= 5.751 \times 1.07 = 6.154$$

Then, substituting $PMT = \$1,000$ and $FVIFA_{7\%, \, 5 \, yrs}$ (annuity due) = 6.154 into Equation 5.14, we get a future value for the annuity due:

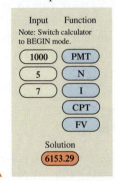

$$FVA_5 = \$1,000 \times 6.154 = \$6,154$$

Calculator Use Before using your calculator to find the future value of an annuity due, depending on the specific calculator, you must either switch it to BEGIN mode or use the DUE key. Then, using the inputs shown at the left, you will find the future value of the annuity due to be $6,153.29. (*Note:* Because we nearly always assume end-of-period cash flows, *be sure to switch your calculator back to* END *mode when you have completed your annuity due calculations.*)

Comparison of an Annuity Due with an Ordinary Annuity

The future value of an annuity due is *always greater* than the future value of an otherwise identical ordinary annuity. We saw this in comparing the future values at the end of year 5 of Frank Adams's two annuities:

Ordinary annuity = $5,751   Annuity due = $6,154

Because the cash flow of the annuity due occurs at the beginning of the period rather than at the end, its future value is greater. In the example, Frank would earn about $400 more with the annuity due.

Finding the Present Value of a Perpetuity

perpetuity
An annuity with an infinite life, providing continual annual cash flow.

A **perpetuity** is an annuity with an infinite life—in other words, an annuity that never stops providing its holder with a cash flow at the end of each year (for example, the right to receive $500 at the end of each year forever).

It is sometimes necessary to find the present value of a perpetuity. The present value interest factor for a perpetuity discounted at the rate i is:

$$PVIFA_{i,\infty} = \frac{1}{i} \qquad (5.18)$$

As the equation shows, the appropriate factor, $PVIFA_{i, \, \infty}$, is found simply by dividing the discount rate, i (stated as a decimal), into 1. The validity of this method can be seen by looking at the factors in Table A-4 for 8, 10, 20, and 40 percent: As the number of periods (typically years) approaches 50, these factors approach the values calculated using Equation 5.18: $1 \div 0.08 = 12.50$; $1 \div 0.10 = 10.00$; $1 \div 0.20 = 5.00$; and $1 \div 0.40 = 2.50$.

Example ▼

Mary See wishes to endow a chair in finance at her alma mater. The university indicated that it requires $200,000 per year to support the chair, and the endowment would earn 10% per year. To determine the amount Mary must give the university to fund the chair, we must determine the present value of a $200,000 perpetuity discounted at 10%. The appropriate present value interest factor can be found by dividing 1 by 0.10, as noted in Equation 5.18. Substituting the resulting factor, 10, and the amount of the perpetuity, $PMT = \$200,000$, into Equation 5.16 results in a present value of $2,000,000 for the perpetuity. In other words, to generate $200,000 every year for an indefinite period requires $2,000,000 today if Mary See's alma mater can earn 10% on its investments. If the university earns 10% interest annually on the $2,000,000, it could withdraw $200,000 a year indefinitely without touching the initial $2,000,000, which would never be drawn upon. **▲**

? Review Questions

5–7   What is the difference between an *ordinary annuity* and an *annuity due?* Which always has greater future value for identical annuities and interest rates? Why?

5–8   What are the most efficient ways to calculate the present value of an ordinary annuity? What is the relationship between the *PVIF* and *PVIFA* interest factors given in Tables A-2 and A-4, respectively?

5–9   How can the future value interest factors for an ordinary annuity be modified to find the future value of an annuity due?

5–10   What is a *perpetuity?* How can the present value interest factor for such a stream of cash flows be determined?

LG5 Mixed Streams

mixed stream
A stream of unequal periodic cash flows that reflect no particular pattern.

Two basic types of cash flow streams are possible: the annuity and the mixed stream. Whereas an *annuity* is a pattern of equal periodic cash flows, a **mixed stream** is a stream of unequal periodic cash flows that reflect no particular pattern. Both financial managers and investors frequently need to evaluate opportunities that are expected to provide mixed streams of cash flows.

Present Value of a Mixed Stream

Finding the present value of a mixed stream of cash flows is straightforward. We determine the present value of each future amount and then add all the individual present values together to find the total present value.

Example ▼ Quam Company, a shoe manufacturer, has been offered an opportunity to receive the following mixed stream of cash flows over the next 5 years:

Year	Cash flow
1	$400
2	800
3	500
4	400
5	300

If the firm must earn at least 9% on its investments, what is the most it should pay for this opportunity? This situation is depicted on the following time line:

Time line for present value of a mixed stream (end-of-year cash flows, discounted at 9%, over the corresponding number of years)

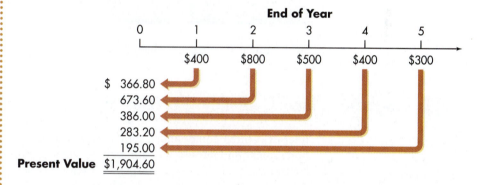

Table Use   To solve this problem, determine the present value of each cash flow discounted at 9% for the appropriate number of years. The sum of these individual values is the present value of the total stream. The present value interest factors required are those shown in Table A-2. Table 5.3 presents the calculations

TABLE 5.3	The Present Value of a Mixed Stream of Cash Flows

Year (n)	Cash flow (1)	$PVIF_{9\%,n}{}^{a}$ (2)	Present value [(1) × (2)] (3)
1	$400	0.917	$ 366.80
2	800	0.842	673.60
3	500	0.772	386.00
4	400	0.708	283.20
5	300	0.650	195.00
		Present value of mixed stream	$1,904.60

[a]Present value interest factors at 9% are from Table A-2.

needed to find the present value of the cash flow stream, which turns out to be $1,904.60.

Calculator Use   You can use a calculator to find the present value of each individual cash flow, as demonstrated earlier (page 112), and then sum the present values, to get the present value of the stream. However, most financial calculators have a function that allows you to punch in *all cash flows,* specify the discount rate, and then directly calculate the present value of the entire cash flow stream. Because calculators provide solutions more precise than those based on rounded table factors, the present value of Quam Company's cash flow stream found using a calculator will be close, but not precisely equal, to the $1,904.60 value calculated before.

Paying $1,904.60 would provide exactly a 9% return. Quam should pay no more than that amount for the opportunity to receive these cash flows.

? Review Question

5–11 How is the present value of a mixed stream of cash flows calculated?

LG6 Compounding More Frequently Than Annually

Interest is often compounded more frequently than once a year. Savings institutions compound interest semiannually, quarterly, monthly, weekly, daily, or even continuously. This section discusses various issues and techniques related to these more frequent compounding intervals.

Semiannual Compounding

semiannual compounding
Compounding of interest over two periods within the year.

Semiannual compounding of interest involves two compounding periods within the year. Instead of the stated interest rate being paid once a year, one-half of the stated interest rate is paid twice a year.

Example ▼ Freda Morgan has decided to invest $100 in a savings account paying 8% interest *compounded semiannually*. If she leaves her money in the account for 24 months (2 years), she will be paid 4% interest compounded over four periods, each of which is 6 months long. Table 5.4 uses interest factors to show that at the end of 12 months (1 year) with 8% semiannual compounding, Freda will have $108.16; at the end of 24 months (2 years), she will have $116.99.

Quarterly Compounding

quarterly compounding
Compounding of interest over four periods within the year.

Quarterly compounding of interest involves four compounding periods within the year. One-fourth of the stated interest rate is paid four times a year.

Example ▼ Freda Morgan has found an institution that will pay her 8% interest *compounded quarterly*. If she leaves her money in this account for 24 months (2 years), she will be paid 2% interest compounded over eight periods, each of which is 3

TABLE 5.4	The Future Value from Investing $100 at 8% Interest Compounded Semiannually Over 24 Months (2 Years)		
Period	Beginning principal (1)	Future value interest factor (2)	Future value at end of period [(1) × (2)] (3)
6 months	$100.00	1.04	$104.00
12 months	104.00	1.04	108.16
18 months	108.16	1.04	112.49
24 months	112.49	1.04	116.99

TABLE 5.5	The Future Value from Investing $100 at 8% Interest Compounded Quarterly Over 24 Months (2 Years)		
Period	Beginning principal (1)	Future value interest factor (2)	Future value at end of period [(1) × (2)] (3)
3 months	$100.00	1.02	$102.00
6 months	102.00	1.02	104.04
9 months	104.04	1.02	106.12
12 months	106.12	1.02	108.24
15 months	108.24	1.02	110.40
18 months	110.40	1.02	112.61
21 months	112.61	1.02	114.86
24 months	114.86	1.02	117.16

months long. Table 5.5 uses interest factors to show the amount Freda will have at the end of each period. At the end of 12 months (1 year), with 8% quarterly compounding, Freda will have $108.24; at the end of 24 months (2 years), she will have $117.16.

Table 5.6 compares values for Freda Morgan's $100 at the end of years 1 and 2 given annual, semiannual, and quarterly compounding periods at the 8 percent rate. As shown, *the more frequently interest is compounded, the greater the amount of money accumulated*. This is true for *any interest rate* for *any period of time*.

A General Equation for Compounding More Frequently Than Annually

The formula for annual compounding (Equation 5.4) can be rewritten for use when compounding takes place more frequently. If *m* equals the number of times per year interest is compounded, the formula for annual compounding can be rewritten as

$$FV_n = PV \times \left(1 + \frac{i}{m}\right)^{m \times n} \tag{5.19}$$

TABLE 5.6	The Future Value at the End of Years 1 and 2 from Investing $100 at 8% Interest Given Various Compounding Periods		

	Compounding period		
End of year	Annual	Semiannual	Quarterly
1	$108.00	$108.16	$108.24
2	116.64	116.99	117.16

If $m = 1$, Equation 5.19 reduces to Equation 5.4. Thus, if interest is compounded annually (once a year), Equation 5.19 will provide the same result as Equation 5.4. The general use of Equation 5.19 can be illustrated with a simple example.

Example ▼ The preceding examples calculated the amount that Freda Morgan would have at the end of 2 years if she deposited $100 at 8% interest compounded semiannually and compounded quarterly. For semiannual compounding, m would equal 2 in Equation 5.19; for quarterly compounding, m would equal 4. Substituting the appropriate values for semiannual and quarterly compounding into Equation 5.19, we find that

1. *For semiannual compounding:*

$$FV_2 = \$100 \times \left(1 + \frac{0.08}{2}\right)^{2 \times 2} = \$100 \times (1 + 0.04)^4 = \$116.99$$

2. *For quarterly compounding:*

$$FV_2 = \$100 \times \left(1 + \frac{0.08}{4}\right)^{4 \times 2} = \$100 \times (1 + 0.02)^8 = \$117.16$$

▲ These results agree with the values for FV_2 in Tables 5.4 and 5.5.

If the interest were compounded monthly, weekly, or daily, m would equal 12, 52, or 365, respectively.

Using Tables and Calculators for More-Frequent-than-Annual Compounding

We can use the future value interest factors for one dollar, given in Table A-1, when interest is compounded m times each year. Instead of indexing the table for i percent and n years, as we do when interest is compounded annually, we index it for $(i \div m)$ percent and $(m \times n)$ periods. However, the table is less useful, because it includes only selected rates for a limited number of periods. Instead, a financial calculator or personal computer is typically required.

Example ▼ Freda Morgan wished to find the future value of $100 invested at 8% compounded both semiannually and quarterly for 2 years. The number of compounding periods, m, the interest rate, and the number of periods used in each case, along with the future value interest factor, are as follows:

Compounding period	m	Interest rate $(i \div m)$	Periods $(m \times n)$	Future value interest factor from Table A–1
Semiannual	2	8% ÷ 2 = 4%	2 × 2 = 4	1.170
Quarterly	4	8% ÷ 4 = 2%	4 × 2 = 8	1.172

Table Use Multiplying each of the future value interest factors by the initial $100 deposit results in a value of $117.00 (1.170 × $100) for semiannual compounding and a value of $117.20 (1.172 × $100) for quarterly compounding.

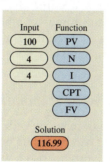

Calculator Use If the calculator were used for the semiannual compounding calculation, the number of periods would be 4 and the interest rate would be 4%. The future value of $116.99 will appear on the calculator display as shown at the left.

For the quarterly compounding case, the number of periods would be 8 and the interest rate would be 2%. The future value of $117.17 will appear on the calculator display as shown at the right.

Comparing the calculator and table values, we can see that the calculator values agree generally with the values in Table 5.6 but are more precise because the table factors have been rounded.

▲

Continuous Compounding

continuous compounding
Compounding of interest an infinite number of times per year at intervals of microseconds.

In the extreme case, interest can be compounded continuously. **Continuous compounding** involves compounding over every microsecond—the smallest time period imaginable. In this case, m in Equation 5.19 would approach infinity. Through the use of calculus we know that as m approaches infinity, the equation becomes

$$FV_n \text{ (continuous compounding)} = PV \times (e^{i \times n}) \qquad (5.20)$$

where e is the exponential function[7], which has a value of 2.7183. The future value interest factor for continuous compounding is therefore

$$FVIF_{i,n} \text{ (continuous compounding)} = e^{i \times n} \qquad (5.21)$$

---

[7]Most calculators have the exponential function, typically noted by e^x, built into them. The use of this key is especially helpful in calculating future value when interest is compounded continuously.

Example ▼ To find the value at the end of 2 years ($n = 2$) of Freda Morgan's $100 deposit ($PV = \$100$) in an account paying 8% annual interest ($i = 0.08$) compounded continuously, we can substitute into Equation 5.20:

$$PV_2 \text{ (continuous compounding)} = \$100 \times e^{0.08 \times 2}$$
$$= \$100 \times 2.7183^{0.16}$$
$$= \$100 \times 1.1735 = \$117.35$$

Calculator Use To find this value using the calculator, you need first to find the value of $e^{0.16}$ by punching in .16 and then pressing **2nd** and then e^x to get 1.1735. Next multiply this value by $100 to get the future value of $117.35 as shown at the left. (*Note:* On some calculators, you may not have to press **2nd** before pressing e^x.)

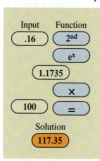

The future value with continuous compounding therefore equals $117.35. As expected, the continuously compounded value is larger than the future value of interest compounded semiannually ($116.99) or quarterly ($117.16). Continuous compounding offers the largest amount that would result from compounding interest more frequently than annually.

Nominal and Effective Annual Rates of Interest

Both businesses and investors need to make objective comparisons of loan costs or investment returns over different compounding periods. In order to put interest rates on a common basis, to allow comparison, we distinguish between nominal and effective annual rates. The **nominal,** or **stated, annual rate** is the contractual annual rate charged by a lender or promised by a borrower. The **effective,** or **true, annual rate** (**EAR**) is the annual rate of interest actually paid or earned. The effective annual rate reflects the impact of compounding frequency, whereas the nominal annual rate does not.

nominal (stated) annual rate
Contractual annual rate of interest charged by a lender or promised by a borrower.

effective (true) annual rate (EAR)
The annual rate of interest actually paid or earned.

Using the notation introduced earlier, we can calculate the effective annual rate, EAR, by substituting values for the nominal annual rate, i, and the compounding frequency, m, into Equation 5.22:

$$EAR = \left(1 + \frac{i}{m}\right)^m - 1 \tag{5.22}$$

We can apply this equation using data from preceding examples.

Example ▼ Freda Morgan wishes to find the effective annual rate associated with an 8% nominal annual rate ($i = 0.08$) when interest is compounded (1) annually ($m = 1$); (2) semiannually ($m = 2$); and (3) quarterly ($m = 4$). Substituting these values into Equation 5.22, we get

1. *For annual compounding:*

$$EAR = \left(1 + \frac{0.08}{1}\right)^1 - 1 = (1 + 0.08)^1 - 1 = 1 + 0.08 - 1 = 0.08 = 8\%$$

2. *For semiannual compounding:*

$$EAR = \left(1 + \frac{0.08}{2}\right)^2 - 1 = (1 + 0.04)^2 - 1 = 1.0816 - 1 = 0.0816 = 8.16\%$$

3. *For quarterly compounding:*

$$EAR = \left(1 + \frac{0.08}{4}\right)^4 - 1 = (1 + 0.02)^4 - 1 = 1.0824 - 1 = 0.0824 = 8.24\%$$

These values demonstrate two important points: The first is that nominal and effective annual rates are equivalent for annual compounding. The second is that the effective annual rate increases with increasing compounding frequency, up to a limit that occurs with *continuous compounding.*

At the consumer level, "truth-in-lending laws" require disclosure on credit card and loan agreements of the **annual percentage rate** (**APR**). The APR is the *nominal annual rate* found by multiplying the periodic rate by the number of periods in one year. For example, a bank credit card that charges 1 1/2 percent per month (the periodic rate) would have an APR of 18% (1.5% per month × 12 months per year).

"Truth-in-savings laws," on the other hand, require banks to quote the **annual percentage yield** (**APY**). The APY is the *effective annual rate* a savings product pays. For example, a savings account that pays 0.5 percent per month would have an APY of 6.17 percent [$(1.005)^{12} - 1$].

Quoting loan interest rates at their lower nominal annual rate (the APR) and savings interest rates at the higher effective annual rate (the APY) offers two advantages: It tends to standardize disclosure to consumers, and it allows financial institutions to quote the most attractive interest rates: low loan rates and high savings rates.

annual percentage rate (APR)
The *nominal annual rate* of interest, found by multiplying the periodic rate by the number of periods in 1 year, that must be disclosed to consumers on credit cards and loans as a result of "truth-in-lending laws."

annual percentage yield (APY)
The *effective annual rate* of interest that must be disclosed to consumers by banks on their savings products as a result of "truth-in-savings laws."

? Review Questions

5–12 What effect does compounding interest more frequently than annually have on (**a**) future value and (**b**) the effective annual rate (EAR)? Why?

5–13 How does the future value of a deposit subject to continuous compounding compare to the value obtained by annual compounding?

5–14 Differentiate between a *nominal annual rate* and an *effective annual rate (EAR)*. Define *annual percentage rate (APR)* and *annual percentage yield (APY)*.

 Special Applications of Time Value

Future value and present value techniques have a number of important applications in finance. We'll study three of them in this section: (1) deposits needed to accumulate a future sum, (2) loan amortization, and (3) interest or growth rates.

Deposits Needed to Accumulate a Future Sum

Suppose you want to buy a house 5 years from now, and you estimate that an initial down payment of $20,000 will be required at that time. You wish to make equal annual end-of-year deposits into an account paying annual interest of 6 percent. The solution to this problem is closely related to the process of finding the future value of an annuity. You must determine what size annuity will result in a lump sum equal to $20,000 at the end of year 5.

Earlier in the chapter, we found the future value of an *n*-year annuity, FVA_n by multiplying the annual deposit, *PMT,* by the appropriate interest factor, $FVIFA_{i,n}$. The relationship of the three variables was defined by Equation 5.14, which is repeated here as Equation 5.23:

$$FVA_n = PMT \times (FVIFA_{i,n}) \tag{5.23}$$

We can find the annual deposit required to accumulate FVA_n dollars by solving Equation 5.23 for *PMT.* Isolating *PMT* on the left side of the equation gives us

$$PMT = \frac{FVA_n}{FVIFA_{i,n}} \tag{5.24}$$

Once this is done, we have only to substitute the known values of FVA_n and $FVIFA_{i,n}$ into the right side of the equation to find the annual deposit required.

Example ▼

As just stated, you want to determine the equal annual end-of-year deposits required to accumulate $20,000 at the end of 5 years given an interest rate of 6%.

Table Use Table A-3 indicates that the future value interest factor for an annuity at 6% for 5 years ($FVIFA_{6\%, \text{5yrs}}$) is 5.637. Substituting $FVA_5 = \$20,000$ and $FVIFA_{6\%, \text{5yrs}} = 5.637$ into Equation 5.24 yields an annual required deposit, *PMT,* of $3,547.99. Thus, if $3,547.99 is deposited at the end of each year for 5 years at 6% interest, there will be $20,000 in the account at the end of the 5 years.

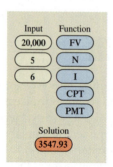

Input	Function
20,000	FV
5	N
6	I
	CPT
	PMT
Solution	
3547.93	

Calculator Use Using the calculator inputs shown at the left, you will find the annual deposit amount to be $3,547.93. Note that this value, except for a slight rounding difference, agrees with the value found by using Table A-3.

Loan Amortization

loan amortization
The determination of the equal periodic loan payments necessary to provide a lender with a specified interest return and to repay the loan principal over a specified period.

loan amortization schedule
A schedule of equal payments to repay a loan. It shows the allocation of each loan payment to interest and principal.

The term **loan amortization** refers to the computation of equal periodic loan payments. These payments provide a lender with a specified interest return and repay the loan principal over a specified period. The loan amortization process involves finding the future payments, over the term of the loan, whose present value at the loan interest rate equals the amount of initial principal borrowed. Lenders use a **loan amortization schedule** to determine these payment amounts and the allocation of each payment to interest and principal. In the case of home mortgages, these tables are used to find the equal *monthly* payments necessary to *amortize,* or pay off, the mortgage at a specified interest rate over a 15- to 30-year period.

Amortizing a loan actually involves creating an annuity out of a present amount. For example, say you borrow $6,000 at 10 percent and agree to make equal annual end-of-year payments over 4 years. To find the size of the pay-

*News*Line   **BORROWING TROUBLE**

Borrowing from your long-term savings plan may sound like a good idea until you consider the long-range effect. By tapping into the principal, you lose the considerable rewards of compound interest.

For Gregg Simmons, the decision was a no-brainer. Mr. Simmons, vice president of franchise administration for Metromedia Restaurant Group in Dallas, borrowed about $20,000 in 1988 from his 401(k) retirement savings plan at his former job to pay off bills. He had about $40,000 in his nest egg, and it seemed like a good idea at the time.

"It just made more sense mathematically to borrow against my 401(k) and pay myself 8 percent vs. paying someone else 12 percent." he said. Many people think along the same lines as Mr. Simmons. But financial planners frown on 401(k) loans, saying that tapping that sacred money would be to mortgage a person's future....

One attraction [of 401(k) plans] is that money in the account grows, taxes deferred, until the employee withdraws it at retirement. If the employer matches an employee's contribution, it bolsters the argument for participation. Many 401(k) nest eggs have swollen to the point where they're an employee's largest asset....

In a rising stock market, the most damaging consequence of taking out a 401(k) loan is slowing the compounding growth of money—a concept financial planners call the "time value of money." "When you borrow from a 401(k), you're losing that momentum toward your retirement goal," said Anne Marie Guerriero, investor education specialist at the Financial Literacy Center in Kalamazoo, Michigan....

The time value of money has taken on more importance with the stock market's seemingly endless upward trajectory. What's more, the tax-deferred status of 401(k) money makes the benefits of compounding more valuable....

Like Mr. Simmons, many people feel that it's better to borrow from their 401(k), and pay themselves back with interest, than to repay someone else.

But financial planners say people miss a key point. "You can't equate the cost of borrowing from someone else with what you would be paying yourself in the 401(k)," Mr. Gill said. "Those numbers are not the critical point in this. The critical point is the loss of tax-deferred compounding."

Source: Pamela Yip, "Borrowing Trouble," The Dallas Morning News, *August 9, 1999, p. 1D.*

ments, the lender determines the amount of a 4-year annuity discounted at 10 percent that has a present value of $6,000. This process is actually the inverse of finding the present value of an annuity.

Earlier in the chapter, we found the present value, PVA_n, of an n-year annuity by multiplying the annual amount, PMT, by the present value interest factor for an annuity, $PVIFA_{i,n}$. This relationship, which was originally expressed as Equation 5.16, is repeated here as Equation 5.25:

$$PVA_n = PMT \times (PVIFA_{i,n}) \tag{5.25}$$

To find the equal annual payment required to pay off, or amortize, the loan, PVA_n, over a certain number of years at a specified interest rate, we need to solve Equation 5.25 for PMT. Isolating PMT on the left side of the equation gives:

$$PMT = \frac{PVA_n}{PVIFA_{i,n}} \tag{5.26}$$

Once this is done, we have only to substitute the known values into the right side of the equation to find the annual payment required.

Example ▼   As just stated, you want to determine the equal annual end-of-year payments necessary to amortize fully a $6,000, 10% loan over 4 years.

Table Use   Table A-4 indicates that the present value interest factor for an annuity corresponding to 10% and 4 years ($PVIFA_{10\%, 4yrs}$) is 3.170.

TABLE 5.7	Loan Amortization Schedule ($6,000 Principal, 10% Interest, 4-Year Repayment Period)				
End of year	Beginning-of-year principal (1)	Loan payment (2)	Payments Interest [0.10 × (2)] (3)	Principal [(1) − (3)] (4)	End-of-year principal [(2) − (4)] (5)
1	$6,000.00	$1,892.74	$600.00	$1,292.74	$4,707.26
2	4,707.26	1,892.74	470.73	1,422.01	3,285.25
3	3,285.25	1,892.74	328.53	1,564.21	1,721.04
4	1,721.04	1,892.74	172.10	1,720.64	—[a]

[a]Because of rounding, a slight difference ($0.40) exists between the beginning-of-year-4 principal (in column 1) and the year-4 principal payment (in column 4).

Substituting $PVA_4 = \$6,000$ and $PVIFA_{10\%, 4yrs} = 3.170$ into Equation 5.26 and solving for PMT yields an annual loan payment of $1,892.74. Thus, to repay the interest and principal on a $6,000, 10%, 4-year loan, equal annual end-of-year payments of $1,892.74 are necessary.

Calculator Use   Using the calculator inputs shown at the left, you will find the annual payment amount to be $1,892.82. Except for a slight rounding difference, this value agrees with the table solution.

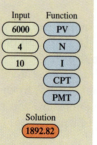

The allocation of each loan payment to interest and principal can be seen in columns 3 and 4 of the *loan amortization schedule* in Table 5.7. The portion of each payment representing interest (column 3) declines over the repayment period, and the portion going to principal repayment (column 4) increases. This pattern is typical of amortized loans; as the principal is reduced, the interest component declines, leaving a larger portion of each subsequent loan payment to repay principal.

Interest or Growth Rates

It is often necessary to calculate the compound annual interest or *growth rate* (that is, the annual rate of change in values) of a series of cash flows. Examples include finding the interest rate on a loan, the rate of growth in sales, or the rate of growth in earnings. In doing this, we can use either future value or present value interest factors. The use of present value interest factors is described in this section. The simplest situation is one in which a person wishes to find the rate of interest or growth in a *series of cash flows*.

Example ▼   Al Taylor wishes to find the rate of interest or growth reflected in the stream of cash flows he received from a real estate investment over the period 1997 through 2001. The following table lists those cash flows:

Year	Cash flow
2001	$1,520 ⎫4
2000	1,440 ⎬3
1999	1,370 ⎬2
1998	1,300 ⎬1
1997	1,250 ⎭

By using the first year (1997) as a base year, we see that interest has been earned (or growth experienced) for 4 years.

Table Use   The first step in finding the interest or growth rate is to divide the amount received in the earliest year (PV) by the amount received in the latest year (FV_n). Looking back at Equation 5.12, this results in the present value interest factor for a *single amount* for 4 years, $PVIF_{i,\ 4\text{yrs}}$, which is 0.822 ($\$1{,}250 \div \$1{,}520$). The interest rate in Table A-2 associated with the factor closest to 0.822 for 4 years is the interest or growth rate of Al's cash flows. In the row for year 4 in Table A-2, the factor for 5 percent is .823—almost exactly the 0.822 value. Therefore, the interest or growth rate of the given cash flows is approximately (to the nearest whole percent) 5%.

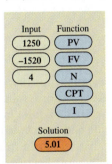

Input	Function
1250	PV
–1520	FV
4	N
	CPT
	I
Solution	
5.01	

Calculator Use   Using the calculator, we treat the earliest value as a present value, PV, and the latest value as a future value, FV_n. (*Note:* Most calculators require *either* the PV or the FV value to be input as a negative number to calculate an unknown interest or growth rate. That approach is used here.) Using the inputs shown at the left, you will find the interest or growth rate to be 5.01%, which is consistent with, but more precise than, the value found using Table A-2.

Another type of interest-rate problem involves finding the interest rate associated with an *annuity*, or equal-payment loan.

Example ▼   Rana Hong can borrow $2,000 to be repaid in equal annual end-of-year amounts of $514.14 for the next 5 years. She wants to find the interest rate on this loan.

Table Use   Substituting $PVA_5 = \$2{,}000$ and $PMT = \$514.14$ into Equation 5.25 and rearranging the equation to solve for $PVIFA_{i,\ 5\text{yrs}}$, we get

Input	Function
514.14	PMT
–2000	PV
5	N
	CPT
	I
Solution	
9.00	

$$PVIFA_{i,\ 5\ yrs} = \frac{PVA_5}{PMT} = \frac{\$2{,}000}{\$514.14} = 3.890 \qquad (5.27)$$

The interest rate for 5 years associated with the annuity factor closest to 3.890 in Table A-4 is 9%. Therefore, the interest rate on the loan is approximately (to the nearest whole percent) 9%.

Calculator Use   (*Note:* Most calculators require either the PMT or the PV value to be input as a negative number in order to calculate an unknown interest rate on an equal-payment loan. That approach is used here.) Using the inputs shown at the left on the bottom of page 131, you will find the interest rate to be 9.00%, which is consistent with the value found using Table A-4.

? Review Questions

5–15 How can you determine the size of the equal end-of-period deposits necessary to accumulate a certain future sum at the end of a specified future period?

5–16 Describe the procedure used to amortize a loan into a series of equal periodic payments.

5–17 Which present value interest factors would be used to find (a) the growth rate associated with a series of cash flows and (b) the interest rate associated with an equal-payment loan?

TYING IT ALL TOGETHER

This chapter presented the key conceptual and computational aspects of the time value of money. It differentiated between future value and present value and demonstrated computations of the key techniques: future value and present value of a single amount, future value and present value of annuities, present value of perpetuities, and present values of mixed streams of cash flows. It discussed procedures for finding nominal and effective annual rates of interest at various compounding frequencies and demonstrated various applications of time value techniques. These techniques are the backbone of finance. The importance of time value of money from the viewpoints of financial managers, financial markets, and investors are summarized in the Integrative Table that follows.

INTEGRATIVE TABLE

Applying Time Value of Money Techniques

Role of **Financial Managers**	*Role of* **Financial Markets**	*Role of* **Investors**
Financial managers use time value of money techniques to make asset investment decisions. The techniques allow them to equate cash flows occurring at different points in time and to value assets, regardless of whether they are being bought or sold.	The activities between financial managers and investors, coupled with economic factors, affect the interest rates and required returns used by the financial managers and investors to value investments and to estimate acceptable returns on them.	Investors use time value of money techniques to make security investment decisions. The techniques allow them to equate cash flows occurring at different points in time from bond or stock investments in order to estimate their values and potential returns.

LG1 **Discuss the role of time value in finance and the use of computational aids to simplify its application.** Financial managers and investors use time value of money techniques when assessing the value of the expected cash flow streams associated with investment alternatives. Alternatives can be assessed by either compounding to find future value or discounting to find present value. Because they are at time zero when making decisions, financial managers and investors rely primarily on present value techniques. Both financial tables and financial calculators can streamline the application of time value techniques.

LG2 **Understand the concept of future value and its calculation for a single amount.** Future value relies on compound interest to measure future amounts: The initial principal or deposit in one period, along with the interest earned on it, becomes the beginning principal of the following period. The interest factor formula and basic equation for the future value of a single amount with annual compounding are given in Table 5.8.

LG3 **Understand the concept of present value, its calculation for a single amount, and the relationship of present value to future value.** Present value is the inverse of future value. The present value of a future amount is the amount of money today that is equivalent to the given future amount, considering the return that can be earned on the current money. The interest factor formula and basic equation for the present value of a single amount are given in Table 5.8.

LG4 **Find the future value and present value of an ordinary annuity, the future value of an annuity due, and the present value of a perpetuity.** An annuity is a pattern of equal periodic cash flows. For an ordinary annuity, the cash flows occur at the end of the period. For an annuity due, cash flows occur at the beginning of the period. The future value of an ordinary annuity can be found by using the future value interest factor for an annuity; the present value of an ordinary annuity can be found by using the present value interest factor for an annuity. A simple conversion can be applied to use the future value interest factors for

an ordinary annuity to find the future value of an annuity due. The present value of a perpetuity—an infinite-lived annuity—is found using 1 divided by the discount rate to represent the present value interest factor. The interest factor formulas and basic equations for the future value and present value of an ordinary annuity, the future value of an annuity due, and the present value of a perpetuity are given in Table 5.8.

LG5 **Calculate the present value of a mixed stream of cash flows.** A mixed stream of cash flows is a stream of unequal periodic cash flows that reflect no particular pattern. The present value of a mixed stream of cash flows is the sum of the present values of each individual cash flow.

LG6 **Understand the effect that compounding more frequently than annually has on future value and the effective annual rate of interest.** Interest can be compounded at intervals ranging from annually to daily, and even continuously. The more frequently interest is compounded, the larger the future amount that will be accumulated, and the higher the effective, or true, annual rate (EAR). The annual percentage rate (APR)—a nominal annual rate—is quoted on credit cards and loans. The annual percentage yield (APY)—an effective annual rate—is quoted on savings products. The interest factor formulas for compounding more frequently than annually are given in Table 5.8.

LG7 **Describe the procedures involved in (1) determining deposits to accumulate a future sum, (2) loan amortization, and (3) finding interest or growth rates.** The periodic deposit to accumulate a given future sum can be found by solving the equation for the future value of an annuity for the annual payment. A loan can be amortized into equal periodic payments by solving the equation for the present value of an annuity for the periodic payment. Interest or growth rates can be estimated by finding the unknown interest rate in the equation for the present value of a single amount or an annuity.

TABLE 5.8	Summary of Key Definitions, Formulas, and Equations for Time Value of Money

Variable definitions

e = exponential function = 2.7183
EAR = effective annual rate
FV_n = future value or amount at the end of period n
FVA_n = future value of an n-year annuity
i = annual rate of interest
m = number of times per year interest is compounded
n = number of periods—typically years—over which money earns a return
PMT = amount deposited or received annually at the end of each year
PV = initial principal or present value
PVA_n = present value of an n-year annuity
t = period number index

Interest factor formulas

Future value of a single amount with annual compounding:

$$FVIF_{i,n} = (1 + i)^n \qquad \text{[Eq. 5.5; factors in Table A-1]}$$

Present value of a single amount:

$$PVIF_{i,n} = \frac{1}{(1 + i)^n} \qquad \text{[Eq. 5.11; factors in Table A-2]}$$

Future value of an ordinary annuity:

$$FVIFA_{i,n} = \sum_{t=1}^{n} (1 + i)^{t-1} \qquad \text{[Eq. 5.13; factors in Table A-3]}$$

Present value of an ordinary annuity:

$$PVIFA_{i,n} = \sum_{t=1}^{n} \frac{1}{(1 + i)^t} \qquad \text{[Eq. 5.15; factors in Table A-4]}$$

Future value of an annuity due:

$$FVIFA_{i,n} \text{ (annuity due)} = FVIFA_{i,n} \times (1 + i) \qquad \text{[Eq. 5.17]}$$

Present value of a perpetuity:

$$PVIFA_{i,\infty} = \frac{1}{i} \qquad \text{[Eq. 5.18]}$$

Future value with compounding more frequently than annually:

$$FVIF_{i,n} = \left(1 + \frac{i}{m}\right)^{m \times n} \qquad \text{[Eq. 5.19]}$$

for continuous compounding, $m = \infty$:

$$FVIF_{i,n} \text{ (continuous compounding)} = e^{i \times n} \qquad \text{[Eq. 5.21]}$$

to find the effective annual rate:

$$EAR = \left(1 + \frac{i}{m}\right)^m - 1 \qquad \text{[Eq. 5.22]}$$

Basic equations

Future value (single amount):	$FV_n = PV \times (FVIF_{i,n})$	[Eq. 5.6]
Present value (single amount):	$PV = FV_n \times (PVIF_{i,n})$	[Eq. 5.12]
Future value (annuity):	$FVA_n = PMT \times (FVIFA_{i,n})$	[Eq. 5.14]
Present value (annuity):	$PVA_n = PMT \times (PVIFA_{i,n})$	[Eq. 5.16]

SELF-TEST EXERCISES   (Solutions in Appendix B)

  ST 5–1   Future values for various compounding frequencies   Debra Martinez has $10,000 that she can deposit in any of three savings accounts for a 3-year period. Bank A compounds interest on an annual basis, bank B compounds interest twice each year, and bank C compounds interest each quarter. All three banks have a stated annual interest rate of 4%.

    a. What amount would Ms. Martinez have at the end of the third year, leaving all interest paid on deposit, in each bank?

    b. What effective annual rate (EAR) would she earn in each of the banks?

    c. On the basis of your findings in parts **a** and **b,** which bank should Ms. Martinez deal with? Why?

    d. If a fourth bank (Bank D), also with a 4% stated interest rate, compounds interest continuously, how much would Ms. Martinez have at the end of the third year? Does this alternative change your recommendation in part **c**? Explain why or why not.

 ST 5–2   Future values of annuities   Ran Aggarwal wishes to choose the better of two equally costly cash flow streams: annuity X and annuity Y. X is an *annuity due* with a cash inflow of $9,000 for each of 6 years. Y is an *ordinary annuity* with a cash inflow of $10,000 for each of 6 years. Assume that Ran can earn 15% on his investments.

    a. On a purely subjective basis, which annuity do you think is more attractive? Why?

    b. Find the future value at the end of year 6, FVA_6, for both annuity X and annuity Y.

    c. Use your finding in part **b** to indicate which annuity is more attractive. Why? Compare your finding to your subjective response in **a.**

   ST 5–3   Present values of lump sums and streams   You have a choice of accepting either of two 5-year cash flow streams or lump-sum amounts. One cash flow stream is an annuity, and the other is a mixed stream. You may accept alternative A or B—either as a cash flow stream or as a lump sum. Given the cash flow stream and lump-sum amounts associated with each (at top of next page), and assuming a 9% opportunity cost, which alternative (A or B) and in which form (cash flow stream or lump-sum amount) would you prefer?

	Cash flow stream	
End of year	Alternative A	Alternative B
1	$700	$1,100
2	700	900
3	700	700
4	700	500
5	700	300
	Lump-sum amount	
At time zero	$2,825	$2,800

LG7 **ST 5–4** **Deposits needed to accumulate a future sum**   Judy Janson wishes to accumulate $8,000 by the end of 5 years by making equal annual end-of-year deposits over the next 5 years. If Judy can earn 7% on her investments, how much must she deposit at the *end of each year* to meet this goal?

EXERCISES

LG1 **5–1** **Using a time line**   The financial manager at Stockholm Industries is considering an investment that requires an initial outlay of $25,000 and is expected to result in cash inflows of $3,000 at the end of year 1, $6,000 at the end of years 2 and 3, $10,000 at the end of year 4, $8,000 at the end of year 5, and $7,000 at the end of year 6.

   a. Draw and label a time line depicting the cash flows associated with Stockholm Industries' proposed investment.
   b. Use arrows to demonstrate, on the time line in part **a,** how compounding to find future value can be used to measure all cash flows at the end of year 6.
   c. Use arrows to demonstrate, on the time line in part **b,** how discounting to find present value can be used to measure all cash flows at time zero.
   d. Which of the approaches—future value or present value—do financial managers rely on most often for decision making? Why?

LG2 **5–2** **Future value calculation**   *Without referring to tables or to the preprogrammed function on your financial calculator,* use the basic formula for future value along with the given interest rate, i, and number of periods, n, to calculate the future value interest factor in each of the cases shown in the following table. Compare the calculated value to the table value in Appendix Table A-1.

Case	Interest rate, i	Number of periods, n
A	12%	2
B	6	3
C	9	2
D	3	4

5–3   **Future values**   For each of the cases shown in the table below, calculate the future value of the single cash flow deposited today that will be available at the end of the deposit period if the interest is compounded annually at the rate specified over the given period.

Case	Single cash flow	Interest rate	Deposit period (years)
A	$ 200	5%	20
B	4,500	8	7
C	10,000	9	10
D	25,000	10	12
E	37,000	11	5
F	40,000	12	9

5–4   **Future value**   You have $1,500 to invest today at 7% interest compounded annually.
   a. Find how much you will have accumulated in the account at the end of (1) 3 years, (2) 6 years, and (3) 9 years.
   b. Use your findings in part **a** to calculate the amount of interest earned in (1) the first 3 years (years 1 to 3), (2) the second 3 years (years 4 to 6), and (3) the third 3 years (years 7 to 9).
   c. Compare and contrast your findings in **b.** Explain why the amount of interest earned increases in each succeeding 3-year period.

5–5   **Inflation and future value**   As part of your financial planning, you wish to purchase a new car exactly 5 years from today. The car you wish to purchase costs $14,000 today, and your research indicates that its price will increase by 2% to 4% per year over the next 5 years.
   a. Estimate the price of the car at the end of 5 years if inflation is (1) 2% per year, and (2) 4% per year.
   b. How much more expensive will the car be if the rate of inflation is 4% rather than 2%?

5–6   **Future value and time**   You can deposit $10,000 into an account paying 9% annual interest either today or exactly 10 years from today. How much better off will you be at the end of 40 years if you decide to make the initial deposit today rather than 10 years from today?

5–7   **Single-payment loan repayment**   A person borrows $200 to be repaid in 8 years with 14% annually compounded interest. The loan may be repaid at the end of any earlier year with no prepayment penalty.
   a. What amount will be due if the loan is repaid at the end of year 1?
   b. What is the repayment at the end of year 4?
   c. What amount is due at the end of the eighth year?

5–8   **Present value calculation**   *Without referring to tables or to the preprogrammed function on your financial calculator,* use the basic formula for present value, along with the given opportunity cost, i, and number of periods, n, to calculate the present value interest factor in each of the cases shown in the table at the top of the following page. Compare the calculated value to the table value.

Case	Opportunity cost, i	Number of periods, n
A	2%	4
B	10	2
C	5	3
D	13	2

5–9   Present values   For each of the cases shown in the following table, calculate the present value of the cash flow, discounting at the rate given and assuming that the cash flow is received at the end of the period noted.

Case	Single cash flow	Discount rate	End of period (years)
A	$ 7,000	12%	4
B	28,000	8	20
C	10,000	14	12
D	150,000	11	6
E	45,000	20	8

5–10   Present value concept   Answer each of the following questions.
a. What single investment made today, earning 12% annual interest, will be worth $6,000 at the end of 6 years?
b. What is the present value of $6,000 to be received at the end of 6 years if the discount rate is 12%?
c. What is the most you would pay today for a promise to repay you $6,000 at the end of 6 years if your opportunity cost is 12%?
d. Compare, contrast, and discuss your findings in parts a through c.

5–11   Present value and discount rates   You just won a lottery that promises to pay you $1,000,000 exactly 10 years from today. Because the $1,000,000 payment is guaranteed by the state in which you live, opportunities exist to sell the claim today for an immediate lump-sum cash payment.
a. What is the least you will sell your claim for if you can earn the following rates of return on similar-risk investments during the 10-year period? (1) 6%, (2) 9%, (3) 12%.
b. Rework part a under the assumption that the $1,000,000 payment will be received in 15 rather than 10 years.
c. On the basis of your findings in parts a and b, discuss the effect of both the size of the rate of return and the time until receipt of payment on the present value of a future sum.

5–12 Future value of an annuity For each of the following cases.

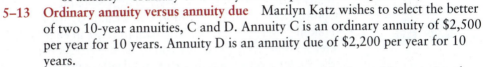

Case	Amount of annuity	Interest rate	Deposit period (years)
A	$ 2,500	8%	10
B	500	12	6
C	30,000	20	5
D	11,500	9	8
E	6,000	14	30

a. Calculate the future value of the annuity assuming that it is an
   (1) ordinary annuity
   (2) annuity due.
b. Compare your findings in **a**(1) and **a**(2). All else being identical, which type of annuity—ordinary or annuity due—is preferable? Explain why.

5–13 Ordinary annuity versus annuity due Marilyn Katz wishes to select the better of two 10-year annuities, C and D. Annuity C is an ordinary annuity of $2,500 per year for 10 years. Annuity D is an annuity due of $2,200 per year for 10 years.

a. Find the future value of both annuities at the end of year 10, assuming that Marilyn can earn (1) 10% annual interest and (2) 20% annual interest.
b. Use your findings in part **a** to indicate which annuity has the greater future value at the end of year 10 for both the (1) 10% and (2) 20% interest rates.
c. Briefly compare, contrast, and explain any differences between your findings using the 10% and 20% interest rates in part **b**.

5–14 Future value of a retirement annuity Calvin Twan, a 25-year-old college graduate, wishes to retire at age 65. To supplement other sources of retirement income, he can deposit $2,000 each year into a tax-deferred individual retirement arrangement (IRA). The IRA will be invested to earn an annual return of 10%, which is assumed to be attainable over the next 40 years.

a. If Calvin makes annual end-of-year $2,000 deposits into the IRA, how much will he have accumulated by the end of his 65th year?
b. If Calvin decides to wait until age 35 to begin making annual end-of-year $2,000 deposits into the IRA, how much will he have accumulated by the end of his 65th year?
c. Using your findings in parts **a** and **b**, discuss the impact of delaying making deposits into the IRA for 10 years (age 25 to age 35) on the amount accumulated by the end of Calvin's 65th year.
d. Rework parts **a, b,** and **c,** assuming that Calvin makes all deposits at the beginning, rather than the end, of each year. Discuss the effect of beginning-of-year deposits on the future value accumulated by the end of Calvin's 65th year.

5–15   Present value of an annuity   For each of the cases shown in the following table, calculate the present value of the annuity, assuming that the annuity cash flows occur at the end of each year.

Case	Amount of annuity	Interest rate	Period (years)
A	$ 12,000	7%	3
B	55,000	12	15
C	700	20	9
D	140,000	5	7
E	22,500	10	5

5–16   Present value of a retirement annuity   An insurance agent is trying to sell you an immediate retirement annuity, which for a lump-sum fee paid today will provide you with $12,000 at the end of each year for the next 25 years. You currently earn 9% on low-risk investments comparable to the retirement annuity. Ignoring taxes, what is the most you would pay for this annuity?

5–17   Funding your retirement   You plan to retire in exactly 20 years. Your goal is to create a fund that will allow you to receive $20,000 at the end of each year for the 30 years between retirement and death (a psychic told you would die after 30 years). You know that you will be able to earn 11% per year during the 30-year retirement period.

a. How large a fund will you need *when you retire* in 20 years to provide the 30-year, $20,000 retirement annuity?

b. How much would you need *today* as a lump sum to provide the amount calculated in part **a** if you earn only 9% per year during the 20 years preceding retirement?

c. What effect would an increase in the rate you can earn both during and prior to retirement have on the values found in parts **a** and **b**? Explain.

5–18   Perpetuities   Given the data in the following table, determine, for each of the perpetuities:

Perpetuity	Annual amount	Discount rate
A	$ 20,000	8%
B	100,000	10
C	3,000	6
D	60,000	5

a. The appropriate present value interest factor.

b. The present value.

5–19   Creating an endowment   Upon completion of her introductory finance course, Molly Link was so pleased with the amount of useful and interesting knowledge she gained that she convinced her parents, who were wealthy alums of the university she was attending, to create an endowment. The endowment is to allow three needy students to take the introductory finance course each year into perpetuity. The guaranteed annual cost of tuition and books for the course is $600 per student. The endowment will be created by making a lump-sum payment to the university. The university expects to earn exactly 6% per year on these funds.

a. How large an initial lump-sum payment must Molly's parents make to the university to fund the endowment?

b. What amount would be needed to fund the endowment if the university could earn 9% rather than 6% per year on the funds?

   5–20 **Present value—Mixed streams**   Consider the mixed streams of cash flows shown in the following table.

Year	Cash flow stream	
	A	B
1	$ 50,000	$ 10,000
2	40,000	20,000
3	30,000	30,000
4	20,000	40,000
5	10,000	50,000
Totals	$150,000	$150,000

a. Find the present value of each stream using a 15% discount rate.

b. Compare the calculated present values and discuss them in light of the fact that the undiscounted cash flows total $150,000 in each case.

  5–21 **Funding budget shortfalls**   As part of your personal budgeting process, you have determined that in each of the next 5 years you will have budget shortfalls. In other words, you will need the amounts shown in the following table at the end of the given year to balance your budget—that is, to make inflows equal outflows. You expect to be able to earn 8% on your investments during the next 5 years and wish to fund the budget shortfalls over the next 5 years with a single lump sum.

End of year	Budget shortfall
1	$ 5,000
2	4,000
3	6,000
4	10,000
5	3,000

a. How large must the lump-sum deposit today into an account paying 8% annual interest be to provide for full coverage of the anticipated budget shortfalls?

b. What effect would an increase in your earnings rate have on the amount calculated in part **a**? Explain.

5–22   Changing compounding frequency   Using annual, semiannual, and quarterly compounding periods, for each of the following: (1) Calculate the future value if $5,000 is initially deposited, and (2) determine the effective annual rate (EAR).
  a. At 12% annual interest for 5 years.
  b. At 16% annual interest for 6 years.
  c. At 20% annual interest for 10 years.

5–23   Compounding frequency, future value, and effective annual rates   For each of the cases in the following table:

Case	Amount of initial deposit	Nominal annual rate, i	Compounding frequency, m (times/year)	Deposit period (years)
A	$ 2,500	6%	2	5
B	50,000	12	6	3
C	1,000	5	1	10
D	20,000	16	4	6

  a. Calculate the future value at the end of the specified deposit period.
  b. Determine the effective annual rate, EAR.
  c. Compare the nominal annual rate, i, to the effective annual rate, EAR. What relationship exists between compounding frequency and the nominal and effective annual rates?

5–24   Continuous compounding   For each of the cases in the following table, find the future value at the end of the deposit period, assuming that interest is compounded continuously at the given nominal annual rate.

Case	Amount of initial deposit	Nominal annual rate, i	Deposit period (years), n
A	$1,000	9%	2
B	600	10	10
C	4,000	8	7
D	2,500	12	4

5–25   Compounding frequency and future value   You plan to invest $2,000 in an individual retirement arrangement (IRA) today at a *nominal annual rate* of 8%, which is expected to apply to all future years.
  a. How much will you have in the account at the end of 10 years if interest is compounded (1) annually? (2) semiannually? (3) daily (assume a 360-day year)? (4) continuously?
  b. What is the *effective annual rate, EAR,* for each compounding period in part **a**?
  c. How much greater will your IRA account balance be at the end of 10 years if interest is compounded continuously rather than annually?
  d. How does the compounding frequency affect the future value and effective annual rate for a given deposit? Explain in terms of your findings in parts **a** through **c**.

5–26   Deposits to accumulate future sums   For each of the cases shown in the following table, determine the amount of the equal annual end-of-year deposits required to accumulate the given sum at the end of the specified period, assuming the stated annual interest rate.

Case	Sum to be accumulated	Accumulation period (years)	Interest rate
A	$ 5,000	3	12%
B	100,000	20	7
C	30,000	8	10
D	15,000	12	8

5–27   Creating a retirement fund   To supplement your planned retirement in exactly 42 years, you estimate that you need to accumulate $220,000 by the end of 42 years from today. You plan to make equal annual end-of-year deposits into an account paying 8% annual interest.
  a. How large must the annual deposits be to create the $220,000 fund by the end of 42 years?
  b. If you can afford to deposit only $600 per year into the account, how much will you have accumulated by the end of the 42nd year?

5–28   Loan amortization   Determine the equal annual end-of-year payment required each year over the life of the loans shown in the following table to repay them fully during the stated term of the loan.

Loan	Principal	Interest rate	Term of loan (years)
A	$12,000	8%	3
B	60,000	12	10
C	75,000	10	30
D	4,000	15	5

5–29   Loan interest deductions   Laura Redden just closed a $10,000 business loan that is to be repaid in three equal annual end-of-year payments. The interest rate on the loan is 13%. As part of her firm's detailed financial planning, Laura wishes to determine the annual interest deduction attributable to the loan. (Because it is a business loan, the interest portion of each loan payment is tax-deductible to the business.)
  a. Determine the firm's annual loan payment.
  b. Prepare an amortization schedule for the loan.
  c. How much interest expense will Laura's firm have in *each* of the next 3 years as a result of this loan?

5–30 Growth rates You are given the series of cash flows shown in the following table.

	Cash flows		
Year	A	B	C
1	$500	$1,500	$2,500
2	560	1,550	2,600
3	640	1,610	2,650
4	720	1,680	2,650
5	800	1,760	2,800
6		1,850	2,850
7		1,950	2,900
8		2,060	
9		2,170	
10		2,280	

a. Calculate the compound annual growth rate associated with each cash flow stream.
b. If year-1 values represent initial deposits in a savings account paying annual interest, what is the annual rate of interest earned on each account?
c. Compare and discuss the growth rate and interest rate found in parts **a** and **b**, respectively.

  5–31 Rate of return and investment choice Connie Jaxon has $5,000 to invest. Because she is only 25 years old, she is not concerned about the length of the investment's life. What she is sensitive to is the rate of return she will earn on the investment. With the help of her financial advisor, Connie has isolated the four equally risky investments, each providing a lump-sum return, shown in the following table. All of the investments require an initial $5,000 payment.

Investment	Lump-sum return	Investment life (years)
A	$ 8,400	6
B	15,900	15
C	7,600	4
D	13,000	10

a. Calculate, to the nearest 1%, the rate of return on each of the four investments available to Connie.
b. Which investment would you recommend to Connie, given her goal of maximizing the rate of return?

  5–32 Rate of return—Annuity What is the rate of return on an investment of $10,606 if the company expects to receive $2,000 each year for the next 10 years?

5–33   Loan rates of interest   Don Porter has been shopping for a loan to finance the purchase of a used car. He has found three possibilities that seem attractive and wishes to select the one with the lowest interest rate. The information available with respect to each of the three $5,000 loans is shown in the following table.

Loan	Principal	Annual payment	Term (years)
A	$5,000	$1,352.81	5
B	5,000	1,543.21	4
C	5,000	2,010.45	3

a. Determine the interest rate associated with each of the loans.
b. Which loan should Mr. Porter take?

web exercises   Search

www.arachnoid.com

Go to web site **www.arachnoid.com/**. Type in "Financial Calculator" and click **Search**. Then click on **Financial Calculator**.
1. To determine the future value of a fixed amount, enter the following:
Into **PV**, enter −10000; into **np**, enter 1; into **pmt**, enter 0; and, into **ir**, enter 8.
Decimal format should be *U.S.* and Payment should be at *End*.
Now click on the **Calculate FV**, and 10800.00 should appear in the FV window.
2. Determine the future value for each of the following compounding periods by changing *only* the following:
    a. **np** to 2, and **ir** to 8/2
    b. **np** to 12, and **ir** to 8/12
    c. **np** to 52, and **ir** to 8/52
3. To determine the present value of a fixed amount, enter the following:
Into **FV**, 1080; into **np**, 1; into **pmt**, 0; and into **ir**, 8.
Now click **Calculate PV**. What is the present value?
4. To determine the future value of an annuity, enter the following:
Into **PV**, 0; into **FV**, 0; into **np**, 12; into **pmt**, 1000; and into **ir**, 8.
Now click **Calculate FV**. What is the future value?
5. To determine the present value of an annuity, change only the FV setting to 0 and keep the other entries the same as in 4.
    a. Click **Calculate PV**. What is the present value?
    b. Change Payment to *Beginning*. Click on **Calculate PV**. What is the present value?
6. Check your answers in Exercises 4 and 5 by using the techniques discussed in this chapter.

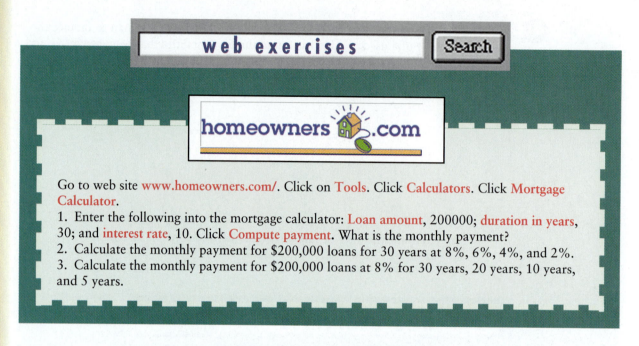

Go to web site **www.homeowners.com/**. Click on **Tools**. Click **Calculators**. Click **Mortgage Calculator**.

1. Enter the following into the mortgage calculator: **Loan amount**, 200000; **duration in years**, 30; and **interest rate**, 10. Click **Compute payment**. What is the monthly payment?

2. Calculate the monthly payment for $200,000 loans for 30 years at 8%, 6%, 4%, and 2%.

3. Calculate the monthly payment for $200,000 loans at 8% for 30 years, 20 years, 10 years, and 5 years.

For additional practice with concepts from this chapter, visit
http://www.awl.com/gitman_madura

Return and Risk

LEARNING GOALS

LG1 Understand the meaning and fundamentals of return, risk, and risk aversion.

LG2 Describe procedures for assessing the risk of a single asset.

LG3 Discuss risk measurement for a single asset using the standard deviation and coefficient of variation.

LG4 Understand the return and risk characteristics of a portfolio in terms of correlation and diversification, and the impact of international assets on a portfolio.

LG5 Review the two types of risk and the derivation and role of beta in measuring the relevant risk of both an individual security and a portfolio.

LG6 Explain the capital asset pricing model (CAPM) and its relationship to the security market line (SML).

Fundamental Concepts About Return and Risk

To maximize stock and investment values, financial managers and investors must learn to assess two key determinants: return and risk. Each financial or investment decision presents certain return and risk characteristics, and the unique combination of these characteristics has an impact on stock and investment values. Here we begin by discussing the fundamentals of return, risk, and risk aversion.

Fundamentals of Return

The key variable used by financial managers and investors to compare actual and expected gains of the firm overall or of specific investments is the return. The **return** is the total gain or loss experienced on an investment over a given period of time. As we'll learn in Chapter 7, it is the combined impact of return and risk that determines the value of a firm or an investment. But first we need to understand the concepts of return and risk in their own right.

There are two possible forms of return. The most common is the cash flow received from an investment during a given period. This cash flow is the **current income** received in the form of profits, dividends, or interest. To be considered income, it must be received in the form of cash or be readily convertible into cash.

The second form of return is the change in the value of the investment. A positive change in value during a given period is commonly called a **capital gain.** A negative change in value is a **capital loss.** Clearly, capital gains increase return and capital losses decrease return. The total return during a given period is the sum of the current income and the capital gain or loss. Therefore, a negative return can occur when an investment suffers a capital loss in excess of the amount of current income.

return
The total gain or loss experienced on an investment over a given period of time; calculated by dividing the investment's *current income* plus its *capital gain (or loss)* during the period by its beginning-of-period investment value.

current income
Cash flow received from an investment during a given period.

capital gain
Positive change in the value of an investment over a given period.

capital loss
Negative change in the value of an investment over a given period.

Calculating the Rate of Return

The return on an investment is typically measured in percentage terms as a *rate of return* rather than as the dollar amount of gain or loss. It is calculated by expressing the sum of the current income and capital gain (or loss) as a percentage of the beginning-of-period investment value. The expression for calculating the rate of return earned on any investment over period t, k_t, is commonly defined as follows:

$$k_t = \frac{C_t + P_t - P_{t-1}}{P_{t-1}} \tag{6.1}$$

where

k_t = rate of return during period t

C_t = current income (cash flow) received from the investment in the time period $t-1$ to t

P_t = price (value) of investment at time t

P_{t-1} = price (value) of investment at time $t-1$

Equation 6.1 is used to determine the rate of return over a time period as short as 1 day or as long as 10 years or more. However, in most cases t is equal to 1 year, and k therefore represents an annual rate of return.

Example ▼

Bobbie's Gameroom, a video arcade, wishes to determine the return on two of its video machines, Commando and Dagger. Commando was purchased 1 year ago for $20,000 and currently has a market value of $21,500. During the year, it generated $800 of current income. Dagger was purchased 4 years ago; its market value in the past year declined from $12,000 to $11,800. During the year, it generated $1,700 of current income. Substituting into Equation 6.1, we can calculate the annual rate of return, k, for each video machine.

Commando(C):

$$k_C = \frac{\$800 + \$21,500 - \$20,000}{\$20,000} = \frac{\$2,300}{\$20,000} = \underline{\underline{11.5\%}}$$

Dagger(D):

$$k_D = \frac{\$1,700 + \$11,800 - \$12,000}{\$12,000} = \frac{\$1,500}{\$12,000} = \underline{\underline{12.5\%}}$$

Although the market value of Dagger declined during the year, its current income caused it to earn a higher rate of return than Commando earned during the same period. Clearly, the combined impact of current income and changes in value, measured by the rate of return, is important.

▲

Fundamentals of Risk

risk
The chance that the actual return will be different from the return that is expected.

The other side of the coin, so to speak, is risk. Risk can be viewed in the context of either a single asset or a group of assets. In the most basic sense, **risk** is the chance that the actual return will be different from the return that is expected. In this sense, risk is used interchangeably with *uncertainty* to refer to the variability of returns. A $1,000 government bond that guarantees its holder $100 interest after 30 days has no risk, because there is no variability associated with the return. A $1,000 investment in a firm's common stock, which over the same period may earn anywhere from $0 to $200, is very risky because of the high variability of its return. The more nearly certain the return from an asset, the less variability and therefore the less risk.

Sources of Risk

The sources of risk for a given firm or investment vary. Some risks directly affect both financial managers and investors, although their specific effects may differ. Table 6.1 briefly describes the common sources of risk affecting firms and investors. As you can see from the table, business and financial risk are more firm-specific and therefore of greatest interest to financial managers; interest rate, liquidity, and market risks are more investor-specific and therefore of greatest interest to investors; and event, exchange rate, purchasing-power, and tax risk directly affect both firms and investors. Many of these risks are discussed in

TABLE 6.1	Popular Sources of Risk Affecting Financial Managers and Investors
Source of risk	**Description**
Firm-Specific Risks	
Business risk	The chance that the firm will be unable to cover its operating costs. Level is driven by the firm's revenue stability and the structure of its operating costs (fixed vs. variable).
Financial risk	The chance that the firm will be unable to cover its financial obligations. Level is driven by the predictability of the firm's operating cash flows and its fixed-cost financial obligations.
Investor-Specific Risks	
Interest rate risk	The chance that changes in interest rates will adversely affect the value of an investment. Most investments lose value when the interest rate rises, and increase in value when it falls.
Liquidity risk	The chance that an investment cannot be easily liquidated at a reasonable price. Liquidity is significantly affected by the size and depth of the market in which an investment is customarily traded.
Market risk	The chance that the value of an investment will decline because of market factors that are independent of the investment (such as economic, political, and social events). In general, the more a given investment's value responds to the market, the greater its risk, and the less it responds, the less its risk.
Firm and Investor Risks	
Event risk	The chance that a totally unexpected event occurs that has a significant effect on the value of the firm or a specific investment. These infrequent events, such as government-mandated withdrawal of a popular prescription drug, typically affect only a small group of firms or investments.
Exchange rate risk	The exposure of future expected cash flows to currency exchange rate fluctuations. The greater the chance of undesirable exchange rate fluctuations, the greater the risk of the cash flows and therefore the lower the value of the firm or investment.
Purchasing-power risk	The chance that changing price levels caused by inflation or deflation in the economy will adversely affect the firm's or investment's cash flows and value. Typically, firms or investments with cash flows that move with general price levels have a low purchasing-power risk, and those with cash flows that do not move with general price levels have high purchasing-power risk.
Tax risk	The chance that unfavorable tax law changes will occur. Firms and investments with values that are sensitive to tax law changes are more risky.

greater detail later in this text. Clearly, both financial managers and investors must assess these and other risks in order to make good decisions consistent with their goals.

Risk Aversion

risk-averse
Requiring an increased return to compensate for an increase in risk.

Financial managers and investors generally are **risk-averse:** Given two choices with similar expected returns, they prefer the less risky one. Both managers and investors generally tend to be conservative rather than aggressive when accepting risk. When they accept increased risk, they require an increase in return. Accordingly, risk-averse financial managers and investors, requiring higher returns for greater risk, are assumed throughout this text.

Review Questions

6–1   Define *return,* and describe how to find the rate of return on an investment.

*News*Line   THE FINEST IN FINANCE

CFO magazine recently awarded Microsoft's former CFO Gregory Maffei its "Finest in Finance" honor in the category of information/knowledge management and risk management. Mr. Maffei oversaw the company-wide assessment program at the software giant. The following excerpt describes several of that program's components.

Microsoft is a pioneer of the enterprise approach to risk management, dating back to the creation of the Microsoft Risk Management Group in fiscal 1997....[T]he group [of finance executives] conducted a thorough risk assessment of the entire company. Today, the group watches no fewer than 144 separate risks, from market share and pricing wars to industrial espionage and workforce skill-sets.

One result of the assessment was an umbrella insurance policy, crafted in fiscal 1998 to cover a variety of risks. But perhaps more important was the promotion of a heightened awareness of risk throughout the company. Microsoft wants managers in every function to understand the risk embodied in every decision they make. And to help them do that, the company developed a Web-based knowledge tool in 1997 called RISKS (Risk Information System for Knowledge Sharing).

Residing on the intranet, RISKS has eight major components, including a menu of risks organized by type; contacts for internal experts on risk subjects; anecdotes of lessons learned from dealing with risks; and best practices for minimizing risk in the design of business processes. Before launching any new projects, managers are encouraged to consult the system.

Meanwhile, to manage financial risk, treasury has pioneered hedging techniques [strategies to protect against risk of adverse price movements] and improved on existing ones....

Maffei also pushed Microsoft to take a systematic approach to foreign-exchange hedging. Starting in 1997, the company began matching the time horizons of hedges with the horizons of exposures. Treasury staffers run...simulations to determine probability distributions of future exchange rates; the distributions are used to compare the effectiveness of different hedges with their costs....

There's no speculation afoot, though. "The vast majority of programs are straight hedges," says Maffei. "I expect that they will continue to make money, but we don't run [hedging] as a profit center."

Source: Edward Teach, "The Finest in Finance: Gregory B. Maffei—Microsoft Corp.," CFO, October 1999, downloaded from www.cfonet.com/html/Articles/CFO/1999/99Ocmaff.html.

6–2   What is *risk* in the context of financial decision making?

6–3   Describe the attitude toward risk of a *risk-averse* financial manager or investor.

Risk of a Single Asset

To make optimal decisions, financial managers and investors seek to quantify the effects of risk on return. Expected return behaviors can be used to assess risk, and statistics can be used to measure it.

Risk Assessment

Sensitivity analysis and probability distributions can be used to assess the general level of risk embodied in a given asset.

sensitivity analysis
An approach to assessing risk that uses several possible return estimates to obtain a sense of the variability among outcomes.

Sensitivity Analysis

Sensitivity analysis uses several possible return estimates to obtain a sense of the variability among outcomes. One common method involves estimating the

range
A measure of an asset's risk, which is found by subtracting the pessimistic (worst) outcome from the optimistic (best) outcome.

pessimistic (worst), the most likely (expected), and the optimistic (best) returns associated with a given asset. In this case, the asset's risk can be measured by the range of the returns. The **range** is found by subtracting the pessimistic outcome from the optimistic outcome. The greater the range, the more variability, or risk, the asset is said to have.

Example ▼

PlusFours Company, a custom golf equipment manufacturer, wants to choose the better of two investments, Birdie and Eagle. Each requires an initial outlay of $10,000, and each has a *most likely* annual rate of return of 15%. Management has made *pessimistic* and *optimistic* estimates of the returns associated with each. The three estimates for each asset, along with its range, are given in Table 6.2. Birdie appears to be less risky than Eagle; its range of 4% (17%–13%) is less than the range of 16% (23%–7%) for Eagle. The risk-averse decision maker would prefer Birdie over Eagle, because Birdie offers the same most likely return as Eagle (15%) but with lower risk (smaller range). **▲**

Although the use of sensitivity analysis and the range is rather crude, it does give the decision maker a feel for the behavior of returns, which can be used to estimate the risk involved.

Probability Distributions

Probability distributions provide a more quantitative insight into an asset's risk. The **probability** of a given outcome is its *chance* of occurring. An outcome with an 80 percent probability of occurrence would be expected to occur 8 out of 10 times. An outcome with a probability of 100 percent is certain to occur. Outcomes with a probability of zero will never occur.

probability
The *chance* that a given outcome will occur.

Example ▼

PlusFours Company's past estimates indicate that the probabilities of the pessimistic, most likely, and optimistic outcomes are 25%, 50%, and 25%, respectively. Note that the sum of these probabilities must equal 100%; that is, they must be based on all the alternatives considered. **▲**

probability distribution
A model that relates probabilities to the associated outcomes.

A **probability distribution** is a model that relates probabilities to the associated outcomes. The simplest type of probability distribution is the **bar chart,**

TABLE 6.2	Range of Returns for Birdie and Eagle	
	Birdie	Eagle
Initial investment	$10,000	$10,000
Annual rate of return		
Pessimistic	13%	7%
Most likely	15%	15%
Optimistic	17%	23%
Range	4%	16%

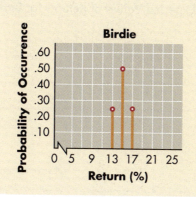 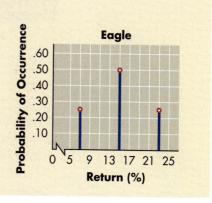

FIGURE 6.1

Bar Charts

Bar charts for Birdie's and Eagle's returns

which shows only a limited number of outcome–probability coordinates. The bar charts for PlusFours Company's Birdie and Eagle investments are shown in Figure 6.1. Although both assets have the same most likely return, the range of return is much more dispersed for Eagle than for Birdie—16 percent versus 4 percent.

bar chart
The simplest type of probability distribution; shows only a limited number of outcomes and associated probabilities for a given event.

continuous probability distribution
A probability distribution showing all the possible outcomes and associated probabilities for a given event.

If we knew all the possible outcomes and associated probabilities, we could develop a **continuous probability distribution.** This type of distribution can be thought of as a bar chart for a very large number of outcomes. Figure 6.2 presents continuous probability distributions for Birdie and Eagle. Note that although Birdie and Eagle have the same most likely return (15 percent), the distribution of returns for Eagle has much greater *dispersion* than the distribution for Birdie. Clearly, Eagle is more risky than asset Birdie.

 Risk Measurement

In addition to its range, the risk of an asset can be measured quantitatively by using statistics. Here we consider two statistics—the standard deviation and the coefficient of variation—that can be used to measure the variability of asset returns.

FIGURE 6.2

Continuous Probability Distributions

Continuous probability distributions for Birdie's and Eagle's returns

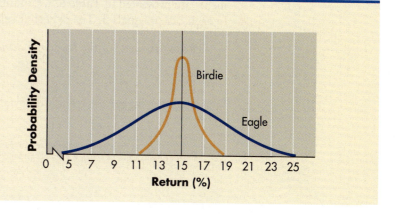

TABLE 6.3	Expected Values of Returns for Birdie and Eagle		
Possible outcomes	Probability (1)	Returns (2)	Weighted value [(1) × (2)] (3)
Birdie			
Pessimistic	0.25	13%	3.25%
Most likely	0.50	15	7.50
Optimistic	0.25	17	4.25
Total	1.00	Expected return	15.00%
Eagle			
Pessimistic	0.25	7%	1.75%
Most likely	0.50	15	7.50
Optimistic	0.25	23	5.75
Total	1.00	Expected return	15.00%

standard deviation (σ_k)
The most common statistical indicator of an asset's risk; it measures the dispersion around the *expected value*.

expected value of a return ($\bar{k}$)
The most likely return on a given asset.

Standard Deviation

The most common statistical indicator of an asset's risk is the **standard deviation,** σ_k, which measures the dispersion around the *expected* value. The **expected value of a return,** $\bar{k}$, is the most likely return on an asset. It is calculated as follows[1]:

$$\bar{k} = \sum_{j=1}^{n} k_j \times Pr_j \qquad (6.2)$$

where

k_j = return for the *j*th outcome

Pr_j = probability of occurrence of the *j*th outcome

n = number of outcomes considered

Example ▼

The expected values of returns for PlusFours Company's Birdie and Eagle investments are presented in Table 6.3. Column 1 gives the Pr_j's and column 2 the k_j's. In each case *n* equals 3. The expected value for each asset's return is 15%.

The expression for the *standard deviation of returns,* σ_k, is[2]

$$\sigma_k = \sqrt{\sum_{j=1}^{n} (k_j - \bar{k})^2 \times Pr_j} \qquad (6.3)$$

In general, the higher the standard deviation, the greater the risk.

---

[1]The formula for finding the expected value of return, $\bar{k}$, when all of the outcomes, k_j, are known *and* their related probabilities are assumed to be equal, is a simple arithmetic average:

$$\bar{k} = \frac{\sum_{j=1}^{n} k_j}{n} \qquad (6.2a)$$

where *n* is the number of observations. Equation 6.2 is emphasized in this chapter because returns and related probabilities are often available.

TABLE 6.4	The Calculation of the Standard Deviation of the Returns for Birdie and Eagle[a]

Birdie

j	k_j	$\bar{k}$	$k_j - \bar{k}$	$(k_j - \bar{k})^2$	Pr_j	$(k_j - \bar{k})^2 \times Pr_j$
1	13%	15%	−2%	4%	.25	1%
2	15	15	0	0	.50	0
3	17	15	2	4	.25	1

$$\sum_{j=1}^{3} (k_j - \bar{k})^2 \times Pr_j = 2\%$$

$$\sigma_{k_A} = \sqrt{\sum_{j=1}^{3} (k_j - \bar{k})^2 \times Pr_j} = \sqrt{2}\% = \underline{1.41\%}$$

Eagle

j	k_j	$\bar{k}$	$k_j - \bar{k}$	$(k_j - \bar{k})^2$	Pr_j	$(k_j - \bar{k})^2 \times Pr_j$
1	7%	15%	−8%	64%	.25	16%
2	15	15	0	0	.50	0
3	23	15	8	64	.25	16

$$\sum_{j=1}^{3} (k_j - \bar{k})^2 \times Pr_j = 32\%$$

$$\sigma_{k_B} = \sqrt{\sum_{j=1}^{3} (k_j - \bar{k})^2 \times Pr_j} = \sqrt{32}\% = \underline{5.66\%}$$

[a]Calculations in this table are made in percentage form rather than decimal form—e.g., 13% rather than .13. As a result, some of the intermediate computations may appear to be inconsistent with those that would result from using decimal form. Regardless, the resulting standard deviations are correct and identical to those that would result from using decimal rather than percentage form.

Example ▼

Table 6.4 presents the standard deviations for PlusFours Company's Birdie and Eagle, based on the earlier data. The standard deviation for Birdie is 1.41%, and the standard deviation for Eagle is 5.66%. The higher risk of Eagle is clearly reflected in its higher standard deviation.

Coefficient of Variation

coefficient of variation (CV)
A measure of relative dispersion that is useful in comparing the risk of assets with differing expected returns.

The **coefficient of variation, *CV*,** is a measure of relative dispersion that is useful in comparing the risk of assets with differing expected returns. Equation 6.4 gives the expression for the coefficient of variation:

$$CV = \frac{\sigma_k}{\bar{k}} \tag{6.4}$$

The higher the coefficient of variation, the greater the risk.

---

[2]The formula that is commonly used to find the standard deviation of returns, σ_k, in a situation in which *all* outcomes are known *and* their related probabilities are assumed equal, is

$$\sigma_k = \sqrt{\frac{\sum_{j=1}^{n} (k_j - \bar{k})^2}{n - 1}} \tag{6.3a}$$

where n is the number of observations. Equation 6.3 is emphasized in this chapter because returns and related probabilities are often available.

Example ▼   When the standard deviation (in Table 6.4) and the expected returns (in Table 6.3) for Birdie and Eagle are substituted into Equation 6.4, the coefficients of variation for Birdie and Eagle are 0.094 (1.41% ÷ 15%) and 0.377 (5.66% ÷ 15%), respectively. Eagle has the higher coefficient of variation and is therefore more risky than Birdie—which we already know from the standard deviation. (Because both assets have the same expected return, the coefficient of variation has not provided any new information.)
▲

The real utility of the coefficient of variation comes in comparing the risks of assets that have *different* expected returns.

Example ▼   A firm wants to select the less risky of two alternative assets, This and That. The expected return, standard deviation, and coefficient of variation for each of these assets' returns are

Statistics	This	That
(1) Expected return	12%	20%
(2) Standard deviation	9%[a]	10%
(3) Coefficient of variation [(2) ÷ (1)]	.75	.50[a]

[a]Preferred asset using the given risk measure.

Judging solely on the basis of their standard deviations, the firm would prefer asset This, which has a lower standard deviation than asset That (9% versus 10%). However, management would be making a serious error in choosing asset This over asset That, because the relative dispersion—the risk—of the assets, as reflected in the coefficient of variation, is lower for That (0.50) than for This (0.75). Clearly, the use of the coefficient of variation to compare asset risk is effective because it also considers the relative size, or expected return, of the assets.
▲

? Review Questions

6–4   Describe the role of the *range* in sensitivity analysis.

6–5   What does a plot of the *probability distribution* of outcomes show a decision maker about an asset's risk?

6–6   What relationship exists between the size of the standard deviation and the degree of asset risk?

6–7   When is the *coefficient of variation* preferred over the standard deviation for comparing asset risk?

LG4 Risk of a Portfolio

In real-world situations, the risk of any single investment would not be viewed independently of other assets. (We did so for teaching purposes.) New investments must be considered in light of their impact on the risk and return of the entire collection or group of assets—the **portfolio** of assets. The goal of both

portfolio
An entire collection or group of assets.

efficient portfolio
A portfolio that maximizes return for a given level of risk or minimizes risk for a given level of return.

financial managers and investors is to create an **efficient portfolio,** one that maximizes return for a given level of risk or minimizes risk for a given level of return. The statistical concept of correlation underlies the development of an efficient portfolio.

Correlation

correlation
A statistical measure of the relationship between any two series of numbers representing data of any kind.

positively correlated
Descriptive of two series that move in the same direction.

negatively correlated
Descriptive of two series that move in opposite directions.

Correlation is a statistical measure of the relationship between any two series of numbers. The numbers may represent data of any kind, from investment returns to test scores. If two series move in the same direction, they are **positively correlated.** If the series move in opposite directions, they are **negatively correlated.**

The degree of correlation is measured by the **correlation coefficient,** which ranges from $+1$ for **perfectly positively correlated** series to -1 for **perfectly negatively correlated** series. These two extremes are depicted for series M and N in Figure 6.3. The perfectly positively correlated series move exactly together; the perfectly negatively correlated series move in exactly opposite directions.

correlation coefficient
A measure of the degree of correlation between two series.

perfectly positively correlated
Describes two *positively correlated* series that have a *correlation coefficient* of $+1$.

perfectly negatively correlated
Described two *negatively correlated* series that have a *correlation coefficient* of -1.

uncorrelated
Describes two series that lack any interaction and therefore have a *correlation coefficient* close to zero.

Diversification

The concept of correlation is essential to developing an efficient portfolio. To reduce overall risk, it is best to combine, or add to the portfolio, assets that have a negative (or a low positive) correlation. Combining negatively correlated assets can reduce the overall variability of returns. Figure 6.4 shows that a portfolio containing the negatively correlated assets Yin and Yang, both of which have the same expected return, $\bar{k}$, also has that same return $\bar{k}$ but has less risk (variability) than either of the individual assets. Even if assets are not negatively correlated, the lower the positive correlation between them, the lower the resulting risk.

Some assets are **uncorrelated**—that is, there is no interaction between their returns. Combining uncorrelated assets can reduce risk, though not so effectively as combining negatively correlated assets. The correlation coefficient for uncorrelated assets is close to zero and acts as the midpoint between perfect positive and perfect negative correlation.

The creation of a portfolio that combines two assets with perfectly positively correlated returns results in overall portfolio risk that at a minimum equals that of the least risky asset and at a maximum equals that of the most risky asset. However, a portfolio combining two assets with less than perfectly positive

FIGURE 6.3

Correlations
The correlation between series M and N

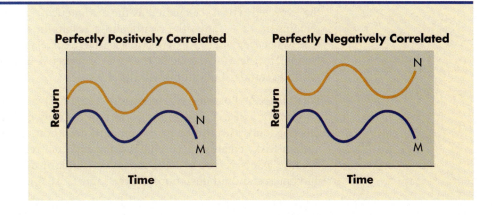

FIGURE 6.4

Diversification
Combining negatively correlated assets to diversify risk

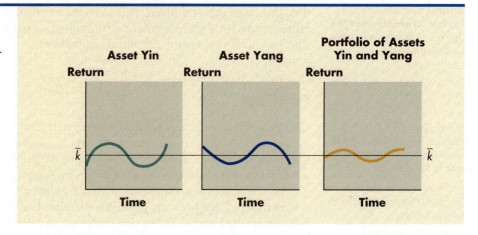

correlation *can* reduce total risk to a level below that of either of the components. For example, assume that you manufacture machine tools. The business is very *cyclical,* with high sales when the economy is expanding and low sales during a recession. If you acquired another machine-tool company, with sales positively correlated with those of your firm, the combined sales would still be cyclical and risk would remain the same. Alternatively, however, you could acquire a sewing machine manufacturer, whose sales are *countercyclical.* It typically has low sales during economic expansion and high sales during recession (when consumers are more likely to make their own clothes). Combination with the sewing machine manufacturer, which has negatively correlated sales, should reduce risk.

Example ▼

Table 6.5 presents the forecasted returns from three different assets—X, Y, and Z—over the next 5 years, along with their expected values and standard deviations. Each of the assets has an expected value of return of 12% and a standard deviation of 3.16%. The assets therefore have equal return and equal risk. The return patterns of assets X and Y are perfectly negatively correlated: They move in exactly opposite directions over time. The returns of assets X and Z are perfectly positively correlated: They move in precisely the same direction. (*Note:* The returns for X and Z are identical.)

Portfolio XY   Portfolio XY (shown in Table 6.5) is created by combining equal portions of assets X and Y, the perfectly negatively correlated assets. The risk in this portfolio, as reflected by its standard deviation, is reduced to 0%, whereas the expected return (calculated as the arithmetic average of the 5 years' returns) remains at 12%. Thus the combination results in the complete elimination of risk. Whenever assets are perfectly negatively correlated, an optimal combination (similar to the 50–50 mix in the case of assets X and Y) exists for which the resulting standard deviation will equal 0.

Portfolio XZ   Portfolio XZ (shown in Table 6.5) is created by combining equal portions of assets X and Z, the perfectly positively correlated assets. The risk in this portfolio, as reflected by its standard deviation, is unaffected by this combination: Risk remains at 3.16%, and the expected return value remains at 12%. Because assets X and Z have the same standard deviation, the minimum and maximum standard deviations are the same (3.16%).

▲

TABLE 6.5 Forecasted Returns, Expected Values, and Standard Deviations for Assets X, Y, and Z and Portfolios XY and XZ

	Assets			Portfolios	
Year	X	Y	Z	XY[a] (50%X + 50%Y)	XZ[b] (50%X + 50%Z)
2002	8%	16%	8%	12%	8%
2003	10	14	10	12	10
2004	12	12	12	12	12
2005	14	10	14	12	14
2006	16	8	16	12	16
Statistics:					
Expected value[c]	12%	12%	12%	12%	12%
Standard deviation[d]	3.16%	3.16%	3.16%	0%	3.16%

[a]Portfolio XY, which consists of 50% of asset X and 50% of asset Y, illustrates *perfect negative correlation* because these two return streams behave in completely opposite fashion over the 5-year period. Its return values are calculated as shown in the following table.

	Forecasted Return			
Year	Asset X (1)	Asset Y (2)	Portfolio Return Calculation (3)	Expected Portfolio Return, $\bar{k}_p$ (4)
2002	8%	16%	$(0.50 \times 8\%) + (0.50 \times 16\%) =$	12%
2003	10	14	$(0.50 \times 10) + (0.50 \times 14) =$	12
2004	12	12	$(0.50 \times 12) + (0.50 \times 12) =$	12
2005	14	10	$(0.50 \times 14) + (0.50 \times 10) =$	12
2006	16	8	$(0.50 \times 16) + (0.50 \times 8) =$	12

[b]Portfolio XZ, which consists of 50% of asset X and 50% of asset Z, illustrates *perfect positive correlation* because these two return streams behave identically over the 5-year period. Its return values are calculated using the same method demonstrated in the note above for portfolio XY.

[c]Because the probabilities associated with the returns are not given, the general equation, Equation 6.2a in footnote 1 on page 154, is used to calculate the expected values as demonstrated below for portfolio XY.

$$k_{xy} = \frac{12\% + 12\% + 12\% + 12\% + 12\%}{5} = \frac{60\%}{5} = \underline{\underline{12\%}}$$

The same formula is applied to find the expected value of return for assets X, Y, and Z and portfolio XZ.

[d]Because the probabilities associated with the returns are not given, the general equation, Equation 6.3a in footnote 2 on page 155, is used to calculate the standard deviations as demonstrated below for portfolio XY.

$$\sigma_{k_{xy}} = \sqrt{\frac{(12\% - 12\%)^2 + (12\% - 12\%)^2 + (12\% - 12\%)^2 + (12\% - 12\%)^2 + (12\% - 12\%)^2}{5 - 1}}$$

$$= \sqrt{\frac{0\% + 0\% + 0\% + 0\% + 0\%}{4}} = \sqrt{\frac{0}{4}}\% = \underline{\underline{0\%}}$$

The same formula is applied to find the standard deviation of returns for assets X, Y, and Z and portfolio XZ.

BEWARE THE EXTREMES OF DIVERSIFICATION

Diversification is a strategy to reduce the overall risk of a portfolio. But what is the "right" number of stocks in a diversified portfolio? Here is one opinion from The Motley Fool, a source of investment information found both online and in many newspapers as a weekly syndicated feature.

When learning about investing, you'll often read about the importance of diversification. Well, true, it's important. But almost as bad as being underdiversified is being overdiversified.

Let's look at some examples to see how this works. Imagine that your portfolio consists of just two stocks, A and B. You have $5,000 tied up in each, for a total of $10,000. If A suddenly drops in half, your portfolio's value sinks to $7,500. It falls by 25 percent, just because of one stock's move. That's exposing yourself to quite a bit of risk.

At the other extreme, let's say that you hold 25 stocks, with about $2,000 in each, for a portfolio total of $50,000. Each stock represents 4 percent of the portfolio's value. Imagine that one of your holdings triples! It's now worth $6,000. But since it was such a small part of your portfolio, its amazing 200 percent surge will boost your portfolio by only 8 percent. If you hold only 10 stocks (in equal measure) and one of them triples in value, your portfolio will gain 20 percent. See the difference?

Overdiversification is one of the problems with most mutual funds. When they own 100 or more different securities, it's hard for their home runs to make much of a difference on their bottom line.

There's no absolute best number of stocks to own. Different numbers work for different people. If you have 20 and you're confident that they're all strong performers, you could do well. But if you think that only 15 are truly outstanding companies with great growth potential, you should consider trimming your holdings to just those 15.

The idea is to invest your money in your best ideas. By concentrating your portfolio this way, you set it up to grow more quickly.

A final consideration is that to be a solid...investor, you'll need to follow your companies' progress at least once a quarter, reading news reports, financial statements, and annual reports. If you own stock in 30 companies, this can be very hard or even impossible to do. Most people find that between 8 and 15 companies is a manageable number.

Source: The Motley Fool, "Beware the Extremes of Diversification," The San Diego Union-Tribune, December 19, 1999, p. I–5.

The important point about the behaviors illustrated in Table 6.5 is that assets can be combined so that the resulting portfolio has less risk than either of the assets independently—and this can be achieved without any loss of return. Portfolio XY illustrates such behavior. The more negative (or less positive) the correlation between asset returns, the greater the risk-reducing benefits of diversification. In no case does creating portfolios of assets result in greater risk than that of the riskiest asset included in the portfolio. These relationships also apply when one is considering the addition of an asset to an existing portfolio.

International Diversification

The ultimate example of portfolio diversification involves including foreign assets in a portfolio. The inclusion of assets from countries with business cycles that are not highly correlated with the U.S. business cycle reduces the portfolio's responsiveness to market movements.

Returns from International Diversification

Over long periods, returns from internationally diversified portfolios tend to be superior to those of purely domestic ones. This is particularly so if the U.S. economy is performing relatively poorly and the dollar is depreciating in value against most foreign currencies. At such times, the dollar returns to U.S. investors on a portfolio of foreign assets can be very attractive. However, over any single short or intermediate period, international diversification can yield subpar returns, particularly during periods when the dollar is appreciating in value relative to other currencies.

The logic of international portfolio diversification assumes that these fluctuations in currency values and relative performance will average out over long periods. Compared to similar, purely domestic portfolios, an internationally diversified portfolio will tend to yield a comparable return at a lower level of risk.

Risks of International Diversification

political risk
Risk that arises from the possibility that a host government might take actions harmful to foreign investors or that political turmoil in a country might endanger investments there.

U.S. investors should also be aware of the potential dangers of international investing. In addition to the risk induced by currency fluctuations, several other financial risks are unique to international investing. Most important is **political risk,** which arises from the possibility that a host government might take actions harmful to foreign investors or that political turmoil in a country might endanger investments there. Political risks are particularly acute in developing countries. An example of political risk was the heightened concern after Desert Storm in the early 1990s that Saudi Arabian fundamentalists would take over and nationalize the U.S. oil facilities located there.

Even where governments do not impose exchange controls or seize assets, international investors may suffer if a shortage of hard currency prevents payment of dividends or interest to foreigners. When governments are forced to allocate scarce foreign exchange, they rarely give top priority to the interests of foreign investors. Instead, hard currency reserves are typically used to pay for necessary imports such as food, medicine, and industrial materials and to pay interest on the government's debt. Because most of the debt of developing countries is held by banks rather than individuals, foreign investors are often badly harmed when a country experiences political or economic problems.

? **Review Questions**

6–8   What is an *efficient portfolio?*
6–9   Why is the *correlation* between asset returns important?
6–10 When might international diversification result in subpar returns?

Return and Risk: The Capital Asset Pricing Model (CAPM)

capital asset pricing model (CAPM)
The basic theory that links return and risk for all assets.

The most important aspect of risk is the *overall risk* of the firm as viewed by investors in the marketplace. Overall risk significantly affects investment opportunities and—even more important—the owners' wealth. The basic theory that links return and risk for all assets is the **capital asset pricing model (CAPM).** We will use the CAPM to understand the basic risk–return tradeoffs involved in all types of financial decisions.

FIGURE 6.5
Risk Reduction
Portfolio risk and diversification

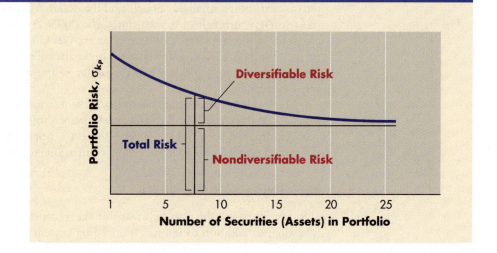

Types of Risk

To understand the basic types of risk, consider what happens to the risk of a portfolio that consists of a single security (asset), to which we add securities randomly selected from, say, the population of all actively traded securities. Using the standard deviation of return, σ_{kp}, to measure the total portfolio risk, Figure 6.5 depicts the behavior of the total portfolio risk (*y* axis) as more securities are added (*x* axis). With the addition of securities, the total portfolio risk declines, as a result of the effects of diversification, and it tends to approach a lower limit. Research has shown that, on average, most of the risk-reduction benefits of diversification can be gained by forming portfolios containing 15 to 20 randomly selected securities.

The **total risk** of a security can be viewed as consisting of two parts:

total risk
The combination of a security's nondiversifiable and diversifiable risk.

$$\text{Total security risk} = \text{Nondiversifiable risk} + \text{Diversifiable risk} \qquad (6.5)$$

diversifiable risk
The portion of an asset's risk that is attributable to firm-specific, random causes; can be eliminated through diversification.

Diversifiable risk (sometimes called *unsystematic risk*) represents the portion of an asset's risk that is associated with random causes that can be eliminated through diversification. It is attributable to firm-specific events, such as strikes, lawsuits, regulatory actions, and loss of a key account. **Nondiversifiable risk** (also called *systematic risk*) is attributable to market factors that affect all firms; it cannot be eliminated through diversification. (It is the investor-specific *market risk* described in Table 6.1.) Factors such as war, inflation, international incidents, and political events account for nondiversifiable risk.

nondiversifiable risk
The relevant portion of an asset's risk attributable to market factors that affect all firms; cannot be eliminated through diversification.

Because any investor can create a portfolio of assets that will eliminate virtually all diversifiable risk, *the only relevant risk is nondiversifiable risk.* Any firm or investor therefore must be concerned solely with nondiversifiable risk.

The Model: CAPM

The capital asset pricing model (CAPM) links return and nondiversifiable risk for all assets. We will discuss the model in four sections. The first deals with the beta coefficient, which is a measure of nondiversifiable risk. The second section presents an equation of the model itself, and the third graphically describes the relationship between return and risk. The final section offers some comments on the CAPM.

The Beta Coefficient

beta coefficient (*b*)
A relative measure of nondiversifiable risk. An index of the degree of movement of an asset's return in response to a change in the *market return*.

market return
The return on the market portfolio of all traded securities.

The **beta coefficient,** *b,* is a relative measure of nondiversifiable risk. It is an index of the degree of movement of an asset's return in response to a change in the *market return.* The **market return** is the return on the market portfolio of all traded securities. The *Standard & Poor's 500 Stock Composite Index* or some similar stock index is commonly used as the market return. Betas for actively traded stocks can be obtained from a variety of sources, but you should understand how they are derived and interpreted and how they are applied to portfolios.

Deriving Beta from Return Data   An asset's historical returns are used in finding the asset's beta coefficient. Figure 6.6 plots the relationship between the returns of two assets—R and S—and the market return. Note that the horizontal (*x*) axis measures the historical market returns and the vertical (*y*) axis measures the individual asset's historical returns. The first step in deriving beta involves plotting the coordinates for the market return and asset returns from various points in time. Such annual "market return–asset return" coordinates are shown

---

FIGURE 6.6

Beta Derivation[a]
Graphical derivation of beta for assets R and S

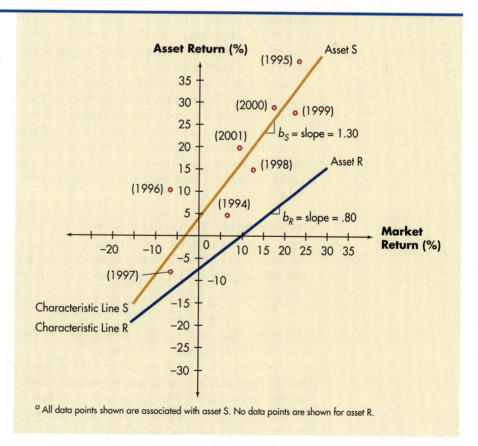

[a] All data points shown are associated with asset S. No data points are shown for asset R.

TABLE 6.6	Selected Beta Coefficients and Their Interpretations	
Beta	**Comment**	**Interpretation**
2.0	⎫	Twice as responsive as the market
1.0	⎬ Move in same direction as market	Same response as the market
.5	⎭	Only half as responsive as the market
0		Unaffected by market movement
− .5	⎫	Only half as responsive as the market
−1.0	⎬ Move in opposite direction to market	Same response as the market
−2.0	⎭	Twice as responsive as the market

for asset S only for the years 1994 through 2001. For example, in 2001, asset S's return was 20 percent when the market return was 10 percent. By use of statistical techniques, the "characteristic line" that best explains the relationship between the asset return and the market return coordinates is fit to the data points. The slope of this line is *beta*. The beta for asset R is about .80, and that for asset S is about 1.30. Asset S's higher beta (steeper characteristic line slope) indicates that its return is more responsive to changing market returns. *Therefore asset S it is more risky than asset R.*

Interpreting Betas   The beta coefficient for the market is considered to be equal to 1.0. All other betas are viewed in relation to this value. Asset betas may be positive or negative, but positive betas are the norm. The majority of beta coefficients fall between .5 and 2.0. The return of a stock that is half as responsive as the market ($b = .5$) is expected to change by $\frac{1}{2}$ percent for each 1 percent change in the return of the market portfolio. A stock that is twice as responsive as the market ($b = 2.0$) is expected to experience a 2 percent change in its return for each 1 percent change in the return of the market portfolio. Table 6.6 provides various beta values and their interpretations. Beta coefficients for actively traded stocks can be obtained from published sources, such as *Value Line Investment Survey,* or through brokerage firms. Betas for some selected stocks are given in Table 6.7.

Portfolio Betas   The beta of a portfolio can be easily estimated by using the betas of the individual assets it includes. Letting w_j represent the proportion of the portfolio's total dollar value represented by asset j, and letting b_j equal the beta of asset j, we can use Equation 6.6 to find the portfolio beta, b_p:

$$b_p = (w_1 \times b_1) + (w_2 \times b_2) + \cdots + (w_n \times b_n) = \sum_{j=1}^{n} w_j \times b_j \qquad (6.6)$$

Of course, $\sum_{j=1}^{n} w_j = 1$, which means that 100 percent of the portfolio's assets must be included in this computation.

Portfolio betas are interpreted in the same way as the betas of individual assets. They indicate the degree of responsiveness of the *portfolio's* return to changes in the market return. For example, when the market return increases by 10 percent, a portfolio with a beta of .75 will experience a 7.5 percent increase in its return (.75 × 10%); a portfolio with a beta of 1.25 will experience a 12.5 per-

---

TABLE 6.7 **Beta Coefficients for Selected Stocks (April 7, 2000)**

Stock	Beta	Stock	Beta
Amazon.com	1.55	McDonalds Corp.	.85
Anheuser-Busch	.70	Merrill Lynch & Company	1.90
Cisco Systems	1.45	Microsoft Corp.	1.05
Coca-Cola	1.10	NIKE Inc.	.95
Exxon Mobil Corp.	.80	Procter & Gamble	.90
Gap (The) Inc.	1.45	Quicksilver Inc.	1.15
General Motors	1.05	Sempra Energy	.55
Harley-Davidson	1.15	Sony Corporation	.90
Intel Corp.	1.05	Southwest Airlines	1.25
IBM	1.00	Yahoo! Inc.	1.65

Source: Value Line Investment Survey (New York: Value Line Publishing, April 7, 2000).

---

cent increase in its return $(1.25 \times 10\%)$. Clearly, a portfolio containing mostly low-beta assets will have a low beta, and one containing mostly high-beta assets will have a high beta.

Example ▼ The Russell Fund, a large investment company, wishes to assess the risk of two portfolios it is considering assembling—V and W. Both portfolios contain five assets, with the proportions and betas shown in Table 6.8 on page 166. The betas for the two portfolios, b_v and b_w, can be calculated by substituting data from the table into Equation 6.6:

$$b_v = (.10 \times 1.65) + (.30 \times 1.00) + (.20 \times 1.30) + (.20 \times 1.10) + (.20 \times 1.25)$$

$$= .165 + .300 + .260 + .220 + .250 = 1.195 \approx \underline{\underline{1.20}}$$

$$b_w = (.10 \times .80) + (.10 \times 1.00) + (.20 \times .65) + (.10 \times .75) + (.50 \times 1.05)$$

$$= .080 + .100 + .130 + .075 + .525 = \underline{\underline{.91}}$$

Portfolio V's beta is 1.20, and portfolio W's is .91. These values make sense, because portfolio V contains relatively high-beta assets, and portfolio W contains relatively low-beta assets. Clearly, portfolio V's returns are more responsive to changes in market returns and are therefore more risky than portfolio W's.

The Equation

Using the beta coefficient to measure nondiversifiable risk, the *capital asset pricing model (CAPM)* is given in Equation 6.7.

$$k_j = R_F + [b_j \times (k_m - R_F)] \tag{6.7}$$

where

k_j = required return on asset j

TABLE 6.8	Russell Fund's Portfolios V and W				
	Portfolio V			Portfolio W	
Asset	Proportion	Beta		Proportion	Beta
1	.10	1.65		.10	.80
2	.30	1.00		.10	1.00
3	.20	1.30		.20	.65
4	.20	1.10		.10	.75
5	.20	1.25		.50	1.05
Totals	1.00			1.00	

R_F = risk-free rate of return, commonly measured by the return on a U.S. Treasury bill

b_j = beta coefficient or index of nondiversifiable risk for asset j

k_m = market return; return on the market portfolio of assets

The CAPM can be divided into two parts: (1) the *risk-free rate,* and (2) the *risk premium.* These are, respectively, the two elements on either side of the plus sign in Equation 6.7. The $(k_m - R_F)$ portion of the risk premium is called the *market risk premium,* because it represents the premium the investor must receive for taking the average amount of risk associated with holding the market portfolio of assets.

Example ▼ Hanover Corporation, a growing computer software developer, wishes to determine the required return on its ZWare subsidiary, which has a beta of 1.5. The risk-free rate of return is 7%; the return on the market portfolio of assets is 11%. Substituting $b_{ZWare} = 1.5$, $R_F = 7\%$, and $k_m = 11\%$ into the capital asset pricing model given in Equation 6.7 yields a required return of

$$k_{ZWare} = 7\% + [1.5 \times (11\% - 7\%)] = 7\% + 6\% = \underline{13\%}$$

The market risk premium of 4% (11% − 7%), when adjusted for ZWare's index of risk (beta) of 1.5, results in a risk premium of 6% (1.5 × 4%). That risk premium, when added to the 7% risk-free rate, results in a 13% required return. ▲

Other things being equal, the higher the beta, the higher the required return, and the lower the beta, the lower the required return.

The Graph: The Security Market Line (SML)

security market line (SML)
The depiction of the *capital asset pricing model (CAPM)* as a graph that refelects the required return in the marketplace for each level of nondiversifiable risk (beta).

When the capital asset pricing model (Equation 6.7) is depicted graphically, it is called the **security market line (SML).** The SML will, in fact, be a straight line. It reflects the required return in the marketplace for each level of nondiversifiable risk (beta). In the graph, risk as measured by beta is plotted on the x axis, and required returns are plotted on the y axis. The risk–return tradeoff is clearly represented by the SML.

FIGURE 6.7

Security Market Line
Security market line (SML)
with Hanover Corporation's
ZWare data shown

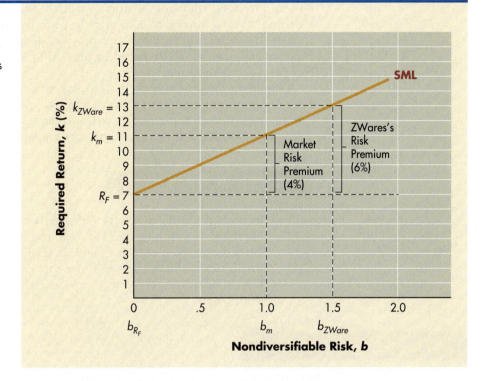

Example ▼ In the preceding example for Hanover Corporation, the risk-free rate, R_F, was 7%, and the market return, k_m, was 11%. The SML can be plotted by using the two sets of coordinates for the betas associated with R_F and k_m, b_{R_F} and b_m (that is, $b_{R_F} = 0$, $R_F = 7\%$; and $b_m = 1.0$, $k_m = 11\%$). Figure 6.7 presents the resulting security market line. As traditionally shown, the security market line in Figure 6.7 presents the required return associated with all positive betas. The market risk premium of 4% (k_m of 11% − R_F of 7%) has been highlighted. For a beta for ZWare, b_{ZWare}, of 1.5, its corresponding required return, k_{ZWare}, is 13%. Also shown in the figure is ZWare's risk premium of 6% (k_{ZWare} of 13% − R_F of 7%). It should be clear that for assets with betas greater than 1, the risk premium is greater than that for the market; for assets with betas less than 1, the risk premium is less than that for the market.

Some Comments on the CAPM

The capital asset pricing model generally relies on historical data. The betas may or may not actually reflect the *future* variability of returns. Therefore, the required returns specified by the model can be viewed only as rough approximations. Users of betas commonly make subjective adjustments to the historically determined betas to reflect their expectations of the future.

The CAPM was developed to explain the behavior of security prices and provide a mechanism whereby investors could assess the impact of a proposed security investment on their portfolio's overall return and risk. It is based on an assumed **efficient market** with the following characteristics: many small investors, each having the same information and expectations with respect to securities; no restrictions on investment, no taxes, and no transaction costs; and

efficient market
A market with the following characteristics: many small investors, each having the same information and expectations with respect to securities; no restrictions on investment, no taxes, and no transaction costs; and rational investors, who view securities similarly and are risk-averse, preferring higher returns and lower risk.

rational investors, who view securities similarly and are risk-averse, preferring higher returns and lower risk. Although the perfect world of the efficient market appears to be unrealistic, studies have provided support for the existence of the expectational relationship described by the CAPM in active markets such as the New York Stock Exchange.

Despite the limitations of the CAPM, it provides a useful conceptual framework for evaluating and linking return and risk. An awareness of this tradeoff and an attempt to consider risk as well as return in financial decision making should help financial managers and investors achieve their goals.

? Review Questions

6–11 Why is nondiversifiable risk the only *relevant risk?*

6–12 What risk does *beta* measure? How can you find the beta of a portfolio?

6–13 Explain the meaning of each variable in the CAPM equation.

6–14 Why do financial managers and investors have some difficulty applying CAPM in financial decision making? Generally, what benefit does CAPM provide them?

TYING IT ALL TOGETHER

This chapter described the key aspects of return and risk and demonstrated techniques for assessing the risk of a single asset and of a portfolio of assets. It introduced the capital asset pricing model (CAPM) as a quantitative way to link return and risk using the beta coefficient. The importance of return and risk from viewpoints of financial managers, financial markets, and investors is summarized in the Integrative Table that follows.

INTEGRATIVE TABLE
Assessing Return and Risk

Role of **Financial Managers**	*Role of* **Financial Markets**	*Role of* **Investors**
Financial managers assess the return and risk of all major decisions to make sure that the best return is being earned for a given level of risk, or that risk is being minimized for a given level of return. Managers determine whether a proposed action positively contributes to the firm's goal of maximizing owner wealth. Return and risk are the key inputs to financial decisions.	The financial markets provide the forum in which competition takes place among financial managers and investors for assets and investments that provide the highest returns for a given level of risk or the minimum risk for a given level of return. The markets through their competitive structure create opportunities to find assets and investments consistent with efficient portfolios.	Investors assess the return and risk behaviors of proposed investments to find those that provide the best returns for a given level of risk or that minimize risk for a given level of return, and that are consistent with their risk disposition. They want to find investments that, for their chosen level of risk, provide competitive returns in order to improve the value of their portfolios.

LG1 **Understand the meaning and fundamentals of return, risk, and risk aversion.** Return is the current income plus any capital gain or loss during the period, expressed as a percentage of the beginning-of-period investment value. The equation for the rate of return is given in Table 6.9. Risk is the chance that the actual return will differ from what is expected. Both firms and investors face risk. Firm-specific risks include business and financial risk; investor-specific risks include interest rate, liquidity, and market risks; and firms and investors face event, exchange rate, purchasing-power, and tax risks. Most managers and investors are risk-averse: They generally prefer less risky alternatives, and they require higher expected returns as compensation for taking greater risk.

LG2 **Describe procedures for assessing the risk of a single asset.** Sensitivity analysis and probability distributions can be used to assess risk. Sensitivity analysis uses several possible return estimates to assess the variability of outcomes. Probability distributions, both bar charts and continuous distributions, provide a more quantitative insight into an asset's risk.

LG3 **Discuss risk measurement for a single asset using the standard deviation and coefficient of variation.** In addition to the range, which is the optimistic (best) outcome minus the pessimistic (worst) outcome, the standard deviation and the coefficient of variation can be used to quantify risk. The standard deviation measures the dispersion around an asset's expected value. The coefficient of variation uses the standard deviation to measure dispersion on a relative basis. The key equations for the expected value of a return, the standard deviation of a return, and the coefficient of variation are summarized in Table 6.9.

LG4 **Understand the return and risk characteristics of a portfolio in terms of correlation and diversification, and the impact of international assets on a portfolio.** The financial manager's goal for the firm and the investor's goal are to create an efficient portfolio, one that maximizes return for a given level of risk or minimizes risk for a given level of return. The risk of a portfolio of assets may be reduced through diversification. New investments must be considered in light of their effect on the return and risk of the portfolio. Correlation, which is the statistical measure of the relationship between any two series of numbers, affects diversification: The more negative (or less positive) the correlation between asset returns, the greater the risk-reducing benefits of diversification. International diversification can be used to reduce a portfolio's risk further. With foreign assets come the risk of currency fluctuation and political risks.

LG5 **Review the two types of risk and the derivation and role of beta in measuring the relevant risk of both an individual security and a portfolio.** The total risk of a security consists of nondiversifiable and diversifiable risk. Nondiversifiable risk is the only relevant risk; diversifiable risk can be eliminated through diversification. Nondiversifiable risk is measured by the beta coefficient, which is a relative measure of the relationship between an asset's return and the market return. Beta is derived by finding the slope of the "characteristic line" that best explains the historical relationship between the asset's return and the market return. The beta of a portfolio is a weighted average of the betas of the individual assets that it includes. The equations for total risk and the portfolio beta are given in Table 6.9.

LG6 **Explain the capital asset pricing model (CAPM) and its relationship to the security market line (SML).** The capital asset pricing model (CAPM) uses beta to relate an asset's risk relative to the market to the asset's required return. The equation for the CAPM is given in Table 6.9. The graphical depiction of CAPM is the security market line (SML). Although it has some shortcomings, CAPM provides a useful conceptual framework for evaluating and linking return and risk.

TABLE 6.9	Summary of Key Definitions and Formulas for Return and Risk

Variable definitions

b_j = beta coefficient or index of nondiversifiable risk for asset j

b_p = portfolio beta

C_t = current income (cash flow) received from the investment in the time period $t-1$ to t

CV = coefficient of variation

$\bar{k}$ = expected value of a return

k_j = return for the jth outcome

k_j = required return on asset j

k_m = market return; the return on the market portfolio of assets

k_t = actual, expected, or required rate of return during period t

n = number of outcomes considered

P_t = price (value) of investment at time t

P_{t-1} = price (value) of investment at time $t-1$

Pr_j = probability of occurrence of the jth outcome

R_F = risk-free rate of return

σ_k = standard deviation of returns

w_j = proportion of total portfolio dollar value represented by asset j

Return and Risk formulas

Rate of return during period t:

$$k_t = \frac{C_t + P_t - P_{t-1}}{P_{t-1}}$$ [Eq. 6.1]

general formula,

$$\sigma_k = \sqrt{\frac{\sum_{j=1}^{n}(k_j - \bar{k})^2}{n-1}}$$ [Eq. 6.3a]

Expected value of a return: for probabilistic data,

$$\bar{k} = \sum_{j=1}^{n} k_j \times Pr_j$$ [Eq. 6.2]

Coefficient of variation:

$$CV = \frac{\sigma_k}{\bar{k}}$$ [Eq. 6.4]

general formula,

$$\bar{k} = \frac{\sum_{j=1}^{n} k_j}{n}$$ [Eq. 6.2a]

Total security risk = Nondiversifiable risk + Diversifiable risk [Eq. 6.5]

Portfolio beta:

$$b_p = \sum_{j=1}^{n} w_j \times b_j$$ [Eq. 6.6]

Standard deviation of return: for probabilistic data,

$$\sigma_k = \sqrt{\sum_{j=1}^{3}(k_j - \bar{k})^2 \times Pr_j}$$ [Eq. 6.3]

Capital asset pricing model (CAPM):

$$k_j = R_F + [b_j \times (k_m - R_F)]$$ [Eq. 6.7]

ST 6–1 Portfolio analysis You have been asked for your advice in selecting a portfolio of assets and have been given the following data:

	Expected return		
Year	Asset A	Asset B	Asset C
2002	12%	16%	12%
2003	14	14	14
2004	16	12	16

No probabilities have been supplied. You have been told that you can create two portfolios—one consisting of assets A and B and the other consisting of assets A and C—by investing equal proportions (50%) in each of the two component assets.

a. What is the expected return for each asset over the 3-year period?

b. What is the standard deviation for each asset's return?

c. What is the expected return for each of the two portfolios?

d. How would you characterize the correlations of returns of the two assets making up each of the two portfolios, identified in part **c**?

e. What is the standard deviation for each portfolio?

f. Which portfolio do you recommend? Why?

  ST 6–2 Beta and CAPM Currently under consideration is a project with a beta, b, of 1.50. At this time, the risk-free rate of return, R_F, is 7%, and the return on the market portfolio of assets, k_m, is 10%. The project is actually expected to earn an annual rate of return of 11%.

a. If the return on the market portfolio were to increase by 10%, what would you expect to happen to the project's *required return*? What if the market return were to decline by 10%?

b. Use the capital asset pricing model (CAPM) to find the *required return* on this investment.

c. On the basis of your calculation in part **b**, would you recommend this investment? Why or why not?

d. Assume that as a result of investors becoming less risk-averse, the market return drops by 1% to 9%. What impact would this change have on your responses in parts **b** and **c**?

EXERCISES

 6–1 Rate of return Darren Kahn, a financial analyst for Oberlin Industries, wishes to estimate the rate of return for two similar-risk investments, X and Y. Kahn's research indicates that the immediate past returns will serve as reasonable estimates of future returns. A year earlier, investment X had a market value of

$20,000, investment Y of $55,000. During the year, investment X generated cash flow of $1,500, and investment Y generated cash flow of $6,800. The current market values of investments X and Y are $21,000 and $55,000, respectively.

a. Calculate the expected rate of return on investments X and Y using the most recent year's data.

b. Assuming that the two investments are equally risky, which one should Kahn recommend? Why?

LG1   **6–2   Return calculations**   For each of the investments shown in the following table, calculate the rate of return earned over the unspecified time period.

Investment	Cash flow during period	Beginning-of-period value	End-of-period value
A	$ −100	$ 800	$ 1,100
B	15,000	120,000	118,000
C	7,000	45,000	48,000
D	80	600	500
E	1,500	12,500	12,400

LG1   **6–3   Risk aversion**   Pearl Watson, the financial manager for Kool Enterprises, wishes to evaluate three prospective investments: X, Y, and Z. Currently, the firm earns 12% on its investments, which have a risk index of 6%. The three investments under consideration are profiled in the following table in terms of expected return and expected risk. If Pearl Watson is risk-averse, which investment, if any, will she select? Explain why.

Investment	Expected return	Expected risk index
X	14%	7%
Y	12	8
Z	10	9

LG2   **6–4   Risk analysis**   Bulton Products is considering an investment in an expanded product line. Two possible types of expansion are being considered. After investigating the possible outcomes, the company made the estimates shown in the following table.

	Expansion A	Expansion B
Initial investment	$12,000	$12,000
Annual rate of return		
Pessimistic	16%	10%
Most likely	20%	20%
Optimistic	24%	30%

a. Determine the *range* of the rates of return for each of the two projects.
b. Which project is less risky? Why?
c. If you were making the investment decision, which one would you choose? Why? What does this imply about your feelings toward risk?
d. Assume that expansion B's most likely outcome is 21% per year and that all other facts remain the same. Does this change your answer to part c? Why?

 6–5 **Risk and probability**   Art Book Publishers is considering the purchase of one of two microfilm cameras, R and S. Both should provide benefits over a 10-year period, and each requires an initial investment of $4,000. Management has constructed the following table of estimates of rates of return and probabilities for pessimistic, most likely, and optimistic results.

	Camera R		Camera S	
	Amount	Probability	Amount	Probability
Initial investment	$4,000	1.00	$4,000	1.00
Annual rate of return				
Pessimistic	20%	.25	15%	.20
Most likely	25%	.50	25%	.55
Optimistic	30%	.25	35%	.25

a. Determine the *range* for the rate of return for each of the two cameras.
b. Determine the *expected value* of return for each camera.
c. Purchase of which camera is riskier? Why?

6–6 **Bar charts and risk**   Denny's Sportswear is considering bringing out a line of designer jeans. Currently, it is negotiating with two different well-known designers. Because of the highly competitive nature of the industry, the two lines of jeans have been given code names. After market research, the firm has established the expectations shown in the following table about the annual rates of return.

		Annual rate of return	
Market acceptance	Probability	Line J	Line K
Very poor	.05	.0075	.010
Poor	.15	.0125	.025
Average	.60	.0850	.080
Good	.15	.1475	.135
Excellent	.05	.1625	.150

Use the table to
a. Construct a bar chart for each line's annual rate of return.
b. Calculate the *expected value* of return for each line.
c. Evaluate the relative riskiness for each jean line's rate of return using the bar charts.

6–7   Coefficient of variation   Steel Manufacturing has isolated four alternatives for meeting its need for increased production capacity. The data gathered relative to each of these alternatives is summarized in the following table.

Alternative	Expected return	Standard deviation of return
A	20%	7.0%
B	22	9.5
C	19	6.0
D	16	5.5

a. Calculate the *coefficient of variation* for each alternative.
b. If the firm wishes to minimize risk, which alternative do you recommend? Why?

6–8   Integrative—Expected return, standard deviation, and coefficient of variation   Three assets—F, G, and H—are currently being considered by Blane Manufacturing. The probability distributions of expected returns for these assets are shown in the following table.

	Asset F		Asset G		Asset H	
j	Pr_j	Return, k_j	Pr_j	Return, k_j	Pr_j	Return, k_j
1	.10	40%	.40	35%	.10	40%
2	.20	10	.30	10	.20	20
3	.40	0	.30	−20	.40	10
4	.20	−5			.20	0
5	.10	−10			.10	−20

a. Calculate the expected value of return, $\bar{k}$, for each of the three assets. Which provides the greatest expected return?
b. Calculate the standard deviation, σ_k, for each of the three assets' returns. Which appears to have the greatest risk?
c. Calculate the coefficient of variation, CV, for each of the three assets. Which appears to have the greatest *relative* risk?

6–9   Portfolio return and standard deviation   Jane Warren is considering building a portfolio containing two assets, L and M. Asset L will represent 40% of the dollar value of the portfolio, and asset M will account for the other 60%. The expected returns over the next 6 years, 2002–2007, for each of these assets, are shown in the following table.

	Expected return	
Year	Asset L	Asset M
2002	14%	20%
2003	14	18
2004	16	16
2005	17	14
2006	17	12
2007	19	10

a. Calculate the expected portfolio return, $\bar{k}_p$, for *each* of the 6 years.
b. Calculate the expected value of portfolio returns, $\bar{k}_p$, over the 6-year period.
c. Calculate the standard deviation of expected portfolio returns, σ_{k_p}, over the 6-year period.
d. How would you characterize the correlation of returns of the two assets L and M?
e. Discuss any benefits of diversification achieved through creation of the portfolio.

 6–10 Portfolio analysis   You have been given the return data shown in the first table on three assets—F, G, and H—over the period 2002–2005.

	Expected return		
Year	Asset F	Asset G	Asset H
2002	16%	17%	14%
2003	17	16	15
2004	18	15	16
2005	19	14	17

Using these assets, you have isolated the three investment alternatives shown in the following table.

Alternative	Investment
1	100% of asset F
2	50% of asset F and 50% of asset G
3	50% of asset F and 50% of asset H

a. Calculate the expected return over the 4-year period for each of the three alternatives.
b. Calculate the standard deviation of returns over the 4-year period for each of the three alternatives.

c. Use your findings in parts **a** and **b** to calculate the coefficient of variation for each of the three alternatives.

d. On the basis of your findings, which of the three investment alternatives do you recommend? Why?

 6–11 Correlation, risk, and return   Pete Masters wishes to evaluate the return and risk behaviors associated with various combinations of assets V and W under three assumed degrees of correlation: perfect positive, uncorrelated, and perfect negative. The expected return and risk values calculated for each of the assets are shown in the following table.

Asset	Expected return, $\bar{k}$	Risk (standard deviation), σ_k
V	8%	5%
W	13	10

a. If the returns of assets V and W are *perfectly positively correlated* (correlation coefficient = +1), describe the *range* of (1) expected return and (2) risk associated with all possible portfolio combinations.

b. If the returns of assets V and W are *uncorrelated* (correlation coefficient = 0), describe the *approximate range* of (1) expected return and (2) risk associated with all possible portfolio combinations.

c. If the returns of assets V and W are *perfectly negatively correlated* (correlation coefficient = −1), describe the *range* of (1) expected return and (2) risk associated with all possible portfolio combinations.

 6–12 Total, nondiversifiable, and diversifiable risk   Frank Allen randomly selected securities from all those listed on the New York Stock Exchange for his portfolio. He began with one security and added securities one by one until a total of 20 securities were held in the portfolio. After each security was added, Frank calculated the portfolio standard deviation, σ_{k_p}. The calculated values are shown in the following table.

Number of securities	Portfolio risk, σ_{k_p}	Number of securities	Portfolio risk, σ_{k_p}
1	14.50%	11	7.00%
2	13.30	12	6.80
3	12.20	13	6.70
4	11.20	14	6.65
5	10.30	15	6.60
6	9.50	16	6.56
7	8.80	17	6.52
8	8.20	18	6.50
9	7.70	19	6.48
10	7.30	20	6.57

a. On a set of "number of securities in portfolio (*x* axis)–portfolio risk (*y* axis)" axes, plot the portfolio risk data given in the preceding table.

b. Divide the total portfolio risk in the graph into its *nondiversifiable* and *diversifiable* risk components and label each of these on the graph.

c. Describe which of the two risk components is the *relevant risk,* and explain why it is relevant. How much of this risk exists in Frank Allen's portfolio?

 6–13   **Graphic derivation of beta**   A firm wishes to estimate graphically the betas for two assets, A and B. It has gathered the return data shown in the following table for the market portfolio and for both assets over the last 10 years, 1992–2001.

| | Actual return | | |
Year	Market portfolio	Asset A	Asset B
1992	6%	11%	16%
1993	2	8	11
1994	−13	−4	−10
1995	−4	3	3
1996	−8	0	−3
1997	16	19	30
1998	10	14	22
1999	15	18	29
2000	8	12	19
2001	13	17	26

a. On a single set of "market return (*x* axis)–asset return (*y* axis)" axes, use the data given to draw the characteristic line for asset A and for asset B.

b. Use the characteristic lines from part **a** to estimate the betas for assets A and B.

c. Use the betas found in part **b** to comment on the relative risks of assets A and B.

6–14   **Interpreting beta**   A firm wishes to assess the impact of changes in the market return on an asset that has a beta of 1.20.

a. If the market return increased by 15%, what impact would this change be expected to have on the asset's return?

b. If the market return decreased by 8%, what impact would this change be expected to have on the asset's return?

c. If the market return did not change, what impact, if any, would be expected on the asset's return?

d. Would this asset be considered more or less risky than the market? Explain.

6–15   **Betas**   Answer the following questions for assets A to D shown in the accompanying table.

Asset	Beta
A	.50
B	1.60
C	−.20
D	.90

a. What impact would a 10% increase in the market return be expected to have on each asset's return?
b. What impact would a 10% decrease in the market return be expected to have on each asset's return?
c. If you were certain that the market return would increase in the near future, which asset would you prefer? Why?
d. If you were certain that the market return would decrease in the near future, which asset would you prefer? Why?

LG5 **6–16** **Portfolio betas** Betty Rose is attempting to evaluate two possible portfolios, both consisting of the same five assets held in different proportions. She is particularly interested in using beta to compare the risks of the portfolios, so she has gathered the data shown in the following table.

Asset	Asset beta	Portfolio weights	
		Portfolio A	Portfolio B
1	1.30	10%	30%
2	.70	30	10
3	1.25	10	20
4	1.10	10	20
5	.90	40	20
Totals		100%	100%

a. Calculate the betas for portfolios A and B.
b. Compare the risk of each portfolio to the market as well as to each other. Which portfolio is more risky?

LG6 **6–17** **Capital asset pricing model (CAPM)** For each of the cases shown in the following table, use the capital asset pricing model to find the required return.

Case	Risk-free rate, R_F	Market return, k_m	Beta, b
A	5%	8%	1.30
B	8	13	.90
C	9	12	−.20
D	10	15	1.00
E	6	10	.60

LG6 **6–18** **Manipulating CAPM**   Use the basic equation for the capital asset pricing model (CAPM) to work each of the following problems.

    a. Find the *required return* for an asset with a beta of .90 when the risk-free rate and the market return are 8% and 12%, respectively.

    b. Find the *risk-free rate* for a firm with a required return of 15% and a beta of 1.25 when the market return is 14%.

    c. Find the *market return* for an asset with a required return of 16% and a beta of 1.10 when the risk-free rate is 9%.

    d. Find the *beta* for an asset with a required return of 15% when the risk-free rate and the market return are 10% and 12.5%, respectively.

 LG6 **6–19** **Security market line, SML**   Assume that the risk-free rate, R_F, is currently 9% and that the market return, k_m, is currently 13%.

    a. Draw the security market line (SML) on a set of "nondiversifiable risk (*x* axis)–required return (*y* axis)" axes.

    b. Calculate and label the *market risk premium* on the axes in part **a**.

    c. Given the previous data, calculate the required return on asset A having a beta of .80 and asset B having a beta of 1.30.

    d. Draw in the betas and required returns from part **c** for assets A and B on the axes in part **a**. Label the *risk premium* associated with each of these assets, and discuss them.

LG6 **6–20** **Integrative—Risk, return, and CAPM**   Septor Company must consider several investment projects, A through E, using the capital asset pricing model (CAPM) and its graphical representation, the security market line (SML). Relevant information is presented in the following table.

Item	Rate of return	Beta, b
Risk-free asset	9%	0
Market portfolio	14	1.00
Project A	—	1.50
Project B	—	.75
Project C	—	2.00
Project D	—	0
Project E	—	−.50

    a. Calculate the required rate of return and risk premium for each project, given its level of nondiversifiable risk.

    b. Use your findings in part **a** to draw the security market line (required return relative to nondiversifiable risk).

    c. Discuss the relative nondiversifiable risk of projects A through E.

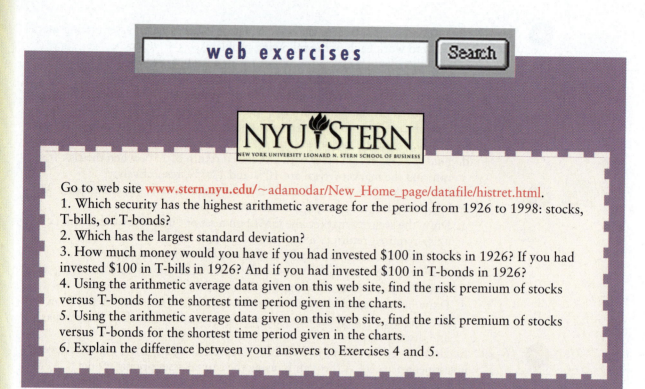

Go to web site **www.stern.nyu.edu/~adamodar/New_Home_page/datafile/histret.html**.

1. Which security has the highest arithmetic average for the period from 1926 to 1998: stocks, T-bills, or T-bonds?

2. Which has the largest standard deviation?

3. How much money would you have if you had invested $100 in stocks in 1926? If you had invested $100 in T-bills in 1926? And if you had invested $100 in T-bonds in 1926?

4. Using the arithmetic average data given on this web site, find the risk premium of stocks versus T-bonds for the shortest time period given in the charts.

5. Using the arithmetic average data given on this web site, find the risk premium of stocks versus T-bonds for the shortest time period given in the charts.

6. Explain the difference between your answers to Exercises 4 and 5.

For additional practice with concepts from this chapter, visit
http://www.awl.com/gitman_madura

Valuation

LEARNING GOALS

LG1 Describe the key inputs and basic model used in the valuation process.

LG2 Review the basic bond valuation model.

LG3 Discuss bond value behavior, particularly the impact that required return and time to maturity have on bond value.

LG4 Explain yield to maturity and the procedure used to value bonds that pay interest semiannually.

LG5 Perform basic common stock valuation using each of three models: zero-growth, constant-growth, and variable-growth.

LG6 Understand the relationships among financial decisions, return, risk, and stock value.

Valuation Fundamentals

valuation
The process that links return and risk to determine the worth of an asset.

Valuation is the process that links return and risk to determine the worth of an asset. It is a relatively simple process that can be applied to *expected* streams of benefits from any real or financial assets. To determine an asset's worth at a given point in time, a financial manager or investor uses time-value-of-money techniques presented in Chapter 5 and the concepts of return and risk developed in Chapter 6.

Key Inputs

There are three key inputs to the valuation process: (1) cash flows (returns), (2) timing, and (3) a measure of risk, which determines the required return. Each is described below.

Cash Flows (Returns)

The value of any asset depends on the cash flow(s) it is expected to provide over the ownership period. To have value, an asset does not have to provide an annual cash flow; it can provide an intermittent cash flow or even a single cash flow over the period.

Example ▼ Nina Diaz, financial analyst for King Industries, a diversified holding company, wishes to estimate the value of three of its assets: common stock in Unitech, an interest in an oil well, and an original painting by a well-known artist. Her cash flow estimates for each are as follows.

Stock in Unitech *Expect* to receive cash dividends of $300 per year indefinitely.

Oil Well *Expect* to receive cash flow of $2,000 at the end of 1 year, $4,000 at the end of 2 years, and $10,000 at the end of 4 years, when the well is to be sold.

Original Painting *Expect* to be able to sell the painting in 5 years for $85,000.

▲ With these cash flow estimates, Nina has taken the first step toward placing a value on each of the assets.

Timing

In addition to making cash flow estimates, we must know the timing of the cash flows. For example, Nina expects the cash flows of $2,000, $4,000, and $10,000 for the oil well to occur at the end of years 1, 2, and 4, respectively. The combination of the cash flow and its timing fully defines the return expected from the asset.

Risk and the Required Return

The level of risk associated with a given cash flow can significantly affect its value. In general, the greater the risk of (or the less certain) a cash flow, the lower its value. Greater risk can be incorporated into a valuation analysis by using a higher required return or discount rate. As in the previous chapter, the higher the risk, the greater the required return, and the lower the risk, the less the required return.

Example ▼ Let's return to Nina Diaz's task of placing a value on King Industries' original painting and consider two scenarios:

Scenario 1—Certainty A major art gallery has contracted to buy the painting for $85,000 at the end of 5 years. Because this is considered a certain situation, Nina views this asset as "money in the bank." She thus would use the prevailing risk-free rate of 9% as the required return when calculating the value of the painting.

Scenario 2—High Risk The values of original paintings by this artist have fluctuated widely over the past 10 years. Although Nina expects to be able to get $85,000 for the painting, she realizes that its sale price in 5 years could range between $30,000 and $140,000. Because of the high uncertainty surrounding the painting's value, Nina believes that a 15% required return is appropriate.

These two estimates of the appropriate required return illustrate how this rate captures risk. The often subjective nature of such estimates is also clear.

The Basic Valuation Model

Simply stated, the value of any asset is *the present value of all future cash flows it is expected to provide over the relevant time period*. The time period can be any length, even infinity. The value of an asset is therefore determined by discounting

TABLE 7.1   Valuation of King Industries' Assets

Asset	Cash flow, CF	Appropriate required return	Valuation[a]
Unitech stock[b]	$300/year indefinitely	12%	$V_0 = \$300 \times (PVIFA_{12\%,\infty})$ $= \$300 \times \dfrac{1}{.12} = \$2,500$
Oil well[c]	Year (t) CF_t 1 $ 2,000 2 4,000 3 0 4 10,000	20%	$V_0 = [\$2,000 \times (PVIF_{20\%,1})]$ $+ [\$4,000 \times (PVIF_{20\%,2})]$ $+ [\$0 \times (PVIF_{20\%,3})]$ $+ [\$10,000 \times (PVIF_{20\%,4})]$ $= [\$2,000 \times (.833)]$ $+ [\$4,000 \times (.694)]$ $+ [\$0 \times (.579)]$ $+ [\$10,000 \times (.482)]$ $= \$1,666 + \$2,776$ $+ \$0 + \$4,820$ $= \$9,262$
Original painting[d]	$85,000 at end of year 5	15%	$V_0 = \$85,000 \times (PVIF_{15\%,5})$ $= \$85,000 \times (.497)$ $= \$42,245$

[a]Based on *PVIF* interest factors from Table A-2. Using a calculator, the values of the oil well and original painting would have been $9,266.98 and $42,260.03, respectively.

[b]This is a perpetuity (infinite-lived annuity), and therefore the present value interest factor given in Equation 5.18 is applied.

[c]This is a mixed stream of cash flows and therefore requires a number of *PVIFs*, as noted.

[d]This is a lump-sum cash flow and therefore requires a single *PVIF*.

the expected cash flows back to their present value. Utilizing the present value techniques presented in Chapter 5, we can express the value of any asset at time zero, V_0, as

$$V_0 = \frac{CF_1}{(1+k)^1} + \frac{CF_2}{(1+k)^2} + \cdots + \frac{CF_n}{(1+k)^n} \tag{7.1}$$

where

V_0 = value of the asset at time zero
CF_t = cash flow expected at the end of year t
k = appropriate required return (discount rate)
n = relevant time period

Using present value interest factor notation, $PVIF_{k,n}$ from Chapter 5, Equation 7.1 can be rewritten as follows:[1]

$$V_0 = [CF_1 \times (PVIF_{k,1})] + [CF_2 \times (PVIF_{k,2})] + \cdots + [CF_n \times (PVIF_{k,n})] \tag{7.2}$$

We can use Equation 7.2, to determine the value of any asset.

Example ▼ Nina Diaz used Equation 7.2 to calculate the value of each asset (using present value interest factors from Table A-2), as shown in Table 7.1. Unitech stock has a value of $2,500, the oil well's value is $9,262, and the original painting has a value of $42,245. Note that regardless of the pattern of the expected cash flow from an asset, the basic valuation equation can be used to determine its value. ▲

? Review Questions

7–1   Why is it important for financial managers and investors to understand the valuation process?

7–2   What are the three key inputs to the valuation process?

7–3   Does the valuation process apply only to assets that provide an annual cash flow? Explain.

Bond Valuation

The basic valuation equation can be customized for use in valuing specific financial securities: bonds, preferred stock, and common stock. Bonds and preferred stock are similar, because they have stated contractual interest and dividend cash flows. The dividends on common stock, on the other hand, are not known in advance. Bond valuation is described in this section, and valuing common stock and preferred stock is discussed in following sections.

 ### Bond Fundamentals

As discussed in Chapter 3, *bonds* are long-term debt instruments used by business and government to raise large sums of money, typically from a diverse group of lenders. Most corporate bonds pay interest *semiannually* (every 6 months) at a stated *coupon interest rate,* have an initial *maturity* of 10 to 30 years, and have a *par value,* or *face value,* of $1,000 that must be repaid at maturity.

Example ▼ Northern Company, a large defense contractor, on January 1, 2002, issued a 10% coupon interest rate, 10-year bond with a $1,000 par value that pays interest semiannually. Investors who buy this bond receive the contractual right to two cash flows: (1) $100 annual interest (10% coupon interest rate × $1,000 par value) distributed as $50 (1/2 × $100) at the end of each 6 months, and (2) the $1,000 par value at the end of the tenth year. ▲

We will use data for Northern's bond issue to look at basic bond valuation.

---

[1]As is customary, k is used to represent required returns and is therefore substituted for i, the annual interest rate, in formulas and financial factor notation throughout this text. The use of this notation in no way changes computational procedures, including calculator keystrokes where the I key input would often be the required return, k.

Basic Bond Valuation

The value of a bond is the present value of the payments its issuer is contractually obligated to make, from the current time until it matures. The basic model for the value, B_0, of a bond is given by Equation 7.3:

$$B_0 = I \times \left[\sum_{t=1}^{n} \frac{1}{(1+k_d)^t} \right] + M \times \left[\frac{1}{(1+k_d)^n} \right] \tag{7.3}$$

$$= I \times (PVIFA_{k_d,n}) + M \times (PVIF_{k_d,n}) \tag{7.3a}$$

where

B_0 = value of the bond at time zero
I = *annual* interest paid in dollars[2]
n = number of years to maturity
M = par value in dollars
k_d = required return on a bond

We can calculate bond value using Equation 7.3a and the appropriate financial tables (Tables A-2 and A-4) or by using a financial calculator.

Example ▼ *Assuming that interest on the Northern Company bond issue is paid annually and that the required return is equal to the bond's coupon interest rate, $I = \$100$, $k_d = 10\%$, $M = \$1,000$, and $n = 10$ years.*

Table Use   Substituting the values noted above into Equation 7.3a yields

B_0 = $\$100 \times (PVIFA_{10\%,10yrs}) + \$1,000 \times (PVIF_{10\%,10yrs})$

   = $\$100 \times (6.145) + \$1,000 \times (.386)$

   = $\$614.50 + \$386.00 = \underline{\$1,000.50}$

The bond therefore has a value of approximately $1,000.

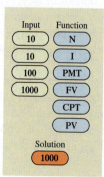

Calculator Use   Using the Northern Company's inputs shown at the left, you should find the bond value to be exactly $1,000. Note that *the calculated bond value is equal to its par value; this will always be the case when the required return is equal to the coupon interest rate.*

The computations involved in finding the bond value are depicted graphically on the following time line.

---

[2]The payment of annual rather than semiannual bond interest is assumed throughout the following discussion. This assumption simplifies the calculations involved, while maintaining the conceptual accuracy of the valuation procedures presented.

Graphical depiction of bond valuation (Northern Company's 10% coupon interest rate, 10-year maturity, $1,000 par, January 1, 2002, issue paying annual interest; required return = 10%)

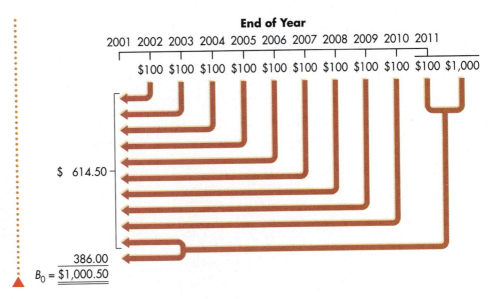

 Bond Value Behavior

In practice, the value of a bond in the marketplace is rarely equal to its par value. In bond quotations (discussed in Chapter 19), the closing prices of bonds often differ from their par values of 100 (100 percent of par). Some bonds are valued below par (quoted below 100), and others are valued above par (quoted above 100). A variety of forces in the economy, as well as the passage of time, tend to affect value. Although these external forces are in no way controlled by bond issuers or investors, it is useful to understand the impact that required return and time to maturity have on bond value.

Required Returns and Bond Values

Whenever the required return on a bond differs from the bond's coupon interest rate, the bond's value will differ from its par value. The required return is likely to differ from the coupon interest rate because either (1) economic conditions have changed, causing a shift in the basic cost of long-term funds, or (2) the firm's risk has changed. Increases in the basic cost of long-term funds or in risk will raise the required return; decreases in the cost of funds or in risk will lower the required return.

Regardless of the exact cause, what is important is the relationship between the required return and the coupon interest rate: When the required return is greater than the coupon interest rate, the bond value, B_0, will be less than its par value, M. In this case, the bond is said to sell at a **discount**, which will equal $M - B_0$. When the required return falls below the coupon interest rate, the bond value will be greater than par. In this situation, the bond is said to sell at a **premium**, which will equal $B_0 - M$.

discount
The amount by which a bond sells at a value that is less than its par value.

premium
The amount by which a bond sells at a value that is greater than its par value.

Example ▼ The preceding example showed that when the required return equaled the coupon interest rate, the bond's value equaled its $1,000 par value. If for the same bond the required return were to rise or fall, its value would be found as follows (using Equation 7.3a):

Table Use

Required Return = 12%   Required Return = 8%

$$B_0 = \$100 \times (PVIFA_{12\%,\ 10\ yrs}) + \$1,000 \qquad B_0 = \$100 \times (PVIFA_{8\%,\ 10\ yrs}) + \$1,000$$

$$\times (PVIF_{12\%,\ 10yrs}) = \underline{\$887.00} \qquad\qquad \times (PVIF_{8\%,\ 10yrs}) = \underline{\$1,134.00}$$

Calculator Use Using the inputs shown below for the two different required returns, you will find the value of the bond to be below or above par.

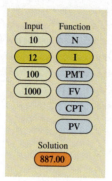 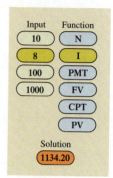

At a 12% required return, the bond would sell at a *discount* of $113.00 ($1,000 par value − $887.00 value). At the 8% required return, the bond would sell for a *premium* of about $134.00 ($1,134.00 value − $1,000 par value). The results of this and earlier calculations for Northern Company's bond values are graphically depicted in Figure 7.1. The inverse relationship between bond value and required return is clearly shown in the figure.

Time to Maturity and Bond Values

Whenever the required return is different from the coupon interest rate, the amount of time to maturity affects bond value. An additional factor is whether required returns are constant or changing over the life of the bond.

Constant Required Returns When the required return is different from the coupon interest rate and is assumed to be *constant until maturity,* the value of the bond will approach its par value as the passage of time moves the bond's value closer to maturity. (Of course, when the required return equals the coupon interest rate, the bond's value will remain at par until it matures.)

Example ▼ Figure 7.2 depicts the behavior of the bond values calculated earlier for Northern Company's 10% coupon interest rate bond paying annual interest and having 10 years to maturity. Each of the three required returns—12%, 10%, and 8%—is assumed to remain constant over the 10 years to the bond's maturity. The bond's value at both 12% and 8% approaches and ultimately equals the bond's $1,000 par value at its maturity, as the discount (at 12%) or premium (at 8%) declines with the passage of time. ▲

Changing Required Returns The chance that interest rates will change and thereby change the required return and bond value is called **interest rate risk,** (This was described as an investor-specific risk in Chapter 6, Table 6.1.)

FIGURE 7.1

Bond Values and Required Returns

Bond values and required returns (Northern Company's 10% coupon interest rate, 10-year maturity, $1,000 par, January 1, 2002, issue paying annual interest)

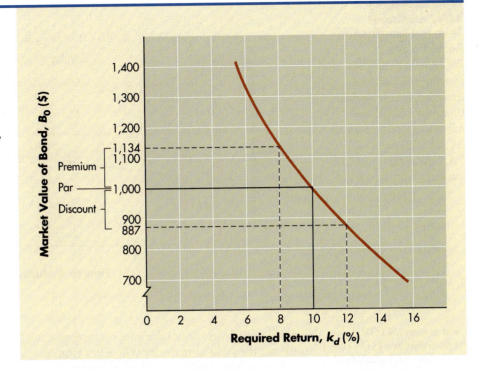

interest rate risk
The chance that interest rates will change and thereby change the required return and bond value. Rising rates, which result in decreasing bond values, are of greatest concern.

Bondholders are typically more concerned with rising interest rates because a rise in interest rates, and therefore in the required return, causes a decrease in bond value. The shorter the amount of time until a bond's maturity, the less responsive is its market value to a given change in the required return. In other words, short maturities have less interest rate risk than long maturities when all other features (coupon interest rate, par value, and interest payment frequency) are the same. This is because of the mathematics of time value; the present values of short-term cash flows change far less that the present values of longer-term cash flows in response to a given change in the discount rate (required return).

Example The effect of changing required returns on bonds of differing maturity can be illustrated by using Northern Company's bond and Figure 7.2. If the required return rises from 10% to 12% (see the dashed line at 8 years), the bond's value decreases from $1,000 to $901—a 9.9% decrease. If the same change in required return had occurred with only 3 years to maturity (see the dashed line at 3 years), the bond's value would have dropped to just $952—only a 4.8% decrease. Similar types of responses can be seen for the change in bond value associated with decreases in required returns. The shorter the time to maturity, the smaller the impact on bond value caused by a given change in the required return.

Yield to Maturity (YTM)

When investors evaluate bonds, they commonly consider **yield to maturity (YTM).** This is the rate of return that investors earn if they buy the bond at a specific price and hold it until maturity. (The measure assumes, of course, that the issuer makes all scheduled interest and principal payments as promised.) The yield to maturity on a bond with a current price equal to its par value (that is,

FIGURE 7.2

Time to Maturity and Bond Values

Relationship among time to maturity, required returns, and bond values (Northern Company's 10% coupon interest rate, 10-year maturity, $1,000 par, January 1, 2002, issue paying annual interest)

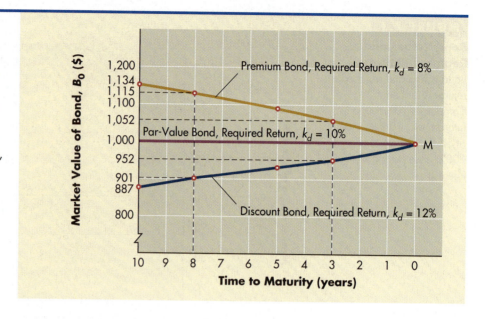

yield to maturity (YTM)
The rate of return investors earn if they buy a bond at a specific price and hold it until maturity. (Assumes that the issuer makes all scheduled interest and principal payments as promised.)

$B_0 = M$) will always equal the coupon interest rate. When the bond value differs from par, the yield to maturity will differ from the coupon interest rate.

Assuming that interest is paid annually, the yield to maturity on a bond can be found by solving Equation 7.3 for k_d. In other words, the current value, the annual interest, the par value, and the years to maturity are known, and the required return must be found. The required return is the bond's yield to maturity. The YTM can be found with minimum effort by using a financial calculator.[3]

Example ▼

The Northern Company bond, which currently sells for $1,080, has a 10% coupon interest rate and $1,000 par value, pays interest annually, and has 10 years to maturity. Because $B_0 = \$1,080$, $I = \$100$ ($0.10 \times \$1,000$), $M = \$1,000$, and $n = 10$ years, substituting into Equation 7.3, we get

$$\$1,080 = \$100 \times \left[\sum_{t=1}^{10} \frac{1}{(1+k_d)^t} \right] + \$1,000 \times \left[\frac{1}{(1+k_d)^{10}} \right]$$

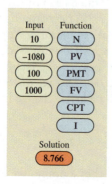

Our objective is to solve the equation for k_d, the YTM.

Calculator Use   [*Note:* Most calculators require *either* the present value (B_0 in this case) or the future values (I and M in this case) to be input as negative numbers to calculate yield to maturity. That approach is employed here.] Using the inputs shown at the left, you should find the YTM to be 8.766%.

----

[3]The YTM can also be found by a trial-and-error method. For those interested in this method, see the book's web site at: **http://www.awl.com/gitman_madura**.

Semiannual Interest and Bond Values

The procedure used to value bonds paying interest semiannually is similar to that shown in Chapter 5 for compounding interest more frequently than annually, except that here we need to find present value instead of future value. It involves

1. Converting annual interest, I, to semiannual interest by dividing I by 2.
2. Converting the number of years to maturity, n, to the number of 6-month periods to maturity by multiplying n by 2.
3. Converting the required return for similar-risk bonds that also pay semiannual interest from an annual rate, k_d, to a semiannual rate by dividing k_d by 2.[4]

Substituting these three changes into Equation 7.3 yields

$$B_0 = \frac{I}{2} \times \left[\sum_{i=1}^{2n} \frac{1}{\left(1 + \frac{k_d}{2}\right)^t} \right] + M \times \left[\frac{1}{\left(1 + \frac{k_d}{2}\right)^{2n}} \right] \tag{7.4}$$

$$= \frac{I}{2} \times \left(PVIFA_{\frac{k_d}{2},2n}\right) + M \times \left(PVIF_{\frac{k_d}{2},2n}\right) \tag{7.4a}$$

E x a m p l e ▼ Assuming that the Northern Company bond pays interest semiannually and that the required return, k_d, is 12% for similar-risk bonds that also pay semiannual interest, substituting these values into Equation 7.4a yields

$$B_0 = \frac{\$100}{2} \times \left(PVIFA_{\frac{12\%}{2},2 \times 10\text{yrs}}\right) + \$1,000 \times \left(PVIF_{\frac{12\%}{2},2 \times 10\text{yrs}}\right)$$

Table Use

$$B_0 = \$50 \times (PVIFA_{6\%,20 \text{ periods}}) + \$1,000 \times (PVIF_{6\%,20 \text{ periods}})$$
$$= \$50 \times (11.470) + \$1,000 \times (.312) = \underline{\$885.50}$$

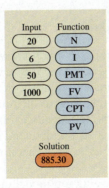

Input	Function
20	N
6	I
50	PMT
1000	FV
	CPT
	PV

Solution
885.30

Calculator Use In using a calculator to find bond value when interest is paid semiannually, we must double the number of periods and divide both the required return and the annual interest by 2. For the Northern Company bond, we would use 20 periods (2 × 10 years), a required return of 6% (12% ÷ 2), and an interest payment of $50 ($100 ÷ 2). Using those inputs, you should find the bond value with semiannual interest to be $885.30 as shown at the left. Note that this value is more precise than the value calculated using the rounded financial table factors.

---

[4]This methodology is based on specification of the nominal required return, k_d, rather than an effective required return where

$$\text{Effective required return} = \left(1 + \frac{\text{nominal required return}}{2}\right)^2 - 1.$$

To simplify the discussion, we do not specify the effective required return.

Comparing this result with the $887.00 value found earlier for annual compounding, we can see that the bond's value is lower when semiannual interest is paid. *This will always occur when the bond sells at a discount.* For bonds selling at a premium, the opposite will occur: The value with semiannual interest will be greater than that with annual interest.

Review Questions

7–4   What relationship between the required return and the coupon interest rate will cause a bond to sell at a *discount?* at a *premium?* and at its *par value?*

7–5   If the required return on a bond differs from its coupon interest rate, describe the behavior of the bond value over time as the bond moves toward maturity.

7–6   As a risk-averse investor, would you prefer bonds with short or long periods until maturity? Why?

7–7   What is a bond's *yield to maturity (YTM)?*

7–8   What procedure is used to value bonds that pay interest *semiannually?*

Common Stock Valuation

Common stockholders expect to be rewarded through periodic cash dividends and an increasing—or at least nondeclining—share value. Like current owners, prospective owners and security analysts frequently estimate the firm's value. Investors purchase the stock when they believe it is *undervalued*—when its true value is greater than its market price. They sell the stock when they feel it is *overvalued*—when its market price is greater than its true value. Here we consider some popular stock valuation techniques.

The Basic Stock Valuation Equation

Like the value of a bond, the *value of a share of common stock is equal to the present value of all future benefits (dividends) it is expected to provide.* Although a stockholder can earn capital gains by selling stock at a price above that originally paid, what is really sold is the right to all future dividends. What about stocks that are not expected to pay dividends in the foreseeable future? Such stocks have a value attributable to a distant dividend expected to result from sale of the company or liquidation of its assets. Therefore, *from a valuation viewpoint, only dividends are relevant.*

By redefining terms, the basic valuation model in Equation 7.1 can be specified for common stock, as given in Equation 7.5.

$$P_0 = \frac{D_1}{(1+k_s)^1} + \frac{D_2}{(1+k_s)^2} + \cdots + \frac{D_\infty}{(1+k_s)^\infty}$$ (7.5)

where

P_0 = value of common stock
D_t = per-share dividend expected at the end of year t
k_s = required return on common stock

The equation can be simplified somewhat by redefining each year's dividend, D_t, in terms of anticipated growth. We will consider three models here: zero-growth, constant-growth, and variable-growth.

Zero-Growth Model

zero-growth model
An approach to dividend valuation that assumes a constant, nongrowing dividend stream.

The simplest approach to dividend valuation, the **zero-growth model,** assumes a constant, nongrowing dividend stream. In terms of the notation already introduced,

$$D_1 = D_2 = \cdots = D_\infty$$

When we let D_1 represent the amount of the annual dividend, Equation 7.5 under zero growth reduces to

$$P_0 = D_1 \times \sum_{t=1}^{\infty} \frac{1}{(1+k_s)^t} = D_1 \times (PVIFA_{k_s,\infty}) = D_1 \times \frac{1}{k_s} = \frac{D_1}{k_s} \qquad (7.6)$$

The equation shows that with zero growth, the value of a share of stock would equal the present value of a perpetuity of D_1 dollars discounted at a rate k_s. (Perpetuities were introduced in Chapter 5; see Equation 5.18 and the related discussion.)

Example ▼

The dividend of Wesley Company, an established textile producer, is expected to remain constant at $3 per share indefinitely. If the required return on its stock is 15%, the stock's value is $20 ($3 ÷ 0.15) per share. **▲**

Preferred Stock Valuation

Because preferred stock typically provides its holders with a fixed annual dividend over its assumed infinite life, Equation 7.6 can be used to find the value of preferred stock. The value of preferred stock can be estimated by substituting the stated dividend on the preferred stock for D_1 and the required return for k_s in Equation 7.6. For example, a preferred stock paying a $5 stated annual dividend and having a required return of 13 percent would have a value of $38.46 ($5 ÷ 0.13) per share. Detailed discussion of preferred stock was included in Chapter 3.

Constant-Growth Model

constant-growth model
A widely cited dividend valuation approach that assumes that dividends will grow at a constant rate, but a rate that is less than the required return.

The most widely cited dividend valuation approach, the **constant-growth model,** assumes that dividends will grow at a constant rate, but a rate that is less than the required return. (The assumption that the constant rate of growth, g, is less than the required return, k_s, is a necessary mathematical condition for deriving this model.) By letting D_0 represent the most recent dividend, we can rewrite Equation 7.5 as follows:

$$P_0 = \frac{D_0 \times (1+g)^1}{(1+k_s)^1} + \frac{D_0 \times (1+g)^2}{(1+k_s)^2} + \cdots + \frac{D_0 \times (1+g)^\infty}{(1+k_s)^\infty} \qquad (7.7)$$

If we simplify Equation 7.7, it can be rewritten as:

$$P_0 = \frac{D_1}{k_s - g} \qquad (7.8)$$

Gordon model
A common name for the *constant-growth model* that is widely cited in dividend valuation.

The constant-growth model in Equation 7.8 is commonly called the **Gordon model.** An example will show how it works.

E x a m p l e ▼ Hotnet Company, a small net-based cosmetics company, from 1996 through 2001 paid the following per-share dividends:

Year	Dividend per share
2001	$1.40
2000	1.29
1999	1.20
1998	1.12
1997	1.05
1996	1.00

We assume that the historical compound annual growth rate of dividends is an accurate estimate of the future constant annual rate of dividend growth, *g*. Using Appendix Table A-2 or a financial calculator, we find that the historical compound annual growth rate of Hotnet Company dividends equals 7%.[5] The company estimates that its dividend in 2002, D_1, will equal $1.50. The required return, k_s, is assumed to be 15 percent. By substituting these values into Equation 7.8, we find the value of the stock to be

$$P_0 = \frac{\$1.50}{0.15 - 0.07} = \frac{\$1.50}{0.08} = \underline{\$18.75}$$

------

[5]The technique involves solving the following equation for *g*:

$$D_{2001} = D_{1996} \times (1+g)^5$$

$$\frac{D_{1996}}{D_{2001}} = \frac{1}{(1+g)^5} = PVIF_{g,5}$$

To do so, we can use financial tables or a financial calculator.

Two basic steps can be followed using the present value table. First, dividing the earliest dividend ($D_{1996} = \$1.00$) by the most recent dividend ($D_{2001} = \$1.40$) yields a factor for the present value of one dollar, *PVIF*, of .714 ($1.00 ÷ $1.40). Although six dividends are shown, *they reflect only 5 years of growth*. (The number of years of growth can also be found by subtracting the earliest year from the most recent year—that is, 2001 – 1996 = 5 years of growth. By looking across Appendix Table A-2 at the *PVIF* for 5 years, we find that the factor closest to .714 occurs at 7 percent (.713). Therefore, the growth rate of the dividends, rounded to the nearest whole percent, is 7 percent.

Alternatively, a financial calculator can be used. (*Note:* Most calculators require either the *PV* or *FV* value to be input as a negative number to calculate an unknown interest or growth rate. That approach is used here.) Using the inputs shown at the right, you should find the growth rate to be 6.96%, which we round to 7%.

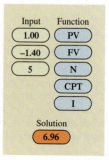

Input	Function
1.00	PV
−1.40	FV
5	N
	CPT
	I

Solution
6.96

:
▲ Assuming that the values of D_1, k_s, and g are accurately estimated, Hotnet Company's stock value is \$18.75 per share.

Variable-Growth Model

variable-growth model
A dividend valuation approach that allows for a change in the dividend growth rate.

The zero- and constant-growth common stock models do not allow for any shift in expected growth rates. Because future growth rates might shift up or down because of changing expectations, it is useful to consider a **variable-growth model** that allows for a change in the dividend growth rate. We will assume that a single shift in growth rates occurs at the end of year N, and we will use g_1 to represent the initial growth rate and g_2 for the growth rate after the shift. To determine the value of a share of stock in the case of variable growth, we use a four-step procedure.

Step 1 Find the value of the cash dividends at the end of each year, D_t, during the initial growth period, years 1 through N. This step may require adjusting the most recent dividend, D_0, using the initial growth rate, g_1, to calculate the dividend amount for each year. Therefore, for the first N years,

$$D_t = D_0 \times (1 + g_1)^t = D_0 \times FVIF_{g_1,t}$$

Step 2 Find the present value of the dividends expected during the initial growth period. Using the notation presented earlier, we can give this value as

$$\sum_{t=1}^{N} \frac{D_0 \times (1+g_1)^t}{(1+k_s)^t} = \sum_{t=1}^{N} \frac{D_t}{(1+k_s)^t} = \sum_{t=1}^{N} (D_t \times PVIF_{k_s,t})$$

Step 3 Find the value of the stock *at the end of the initial growth period*, $P_N = (D_{N+1})/(k_s - g_2)$, which is the present value of all dividends expected from year $N+1$ to infinity, assuming a constant dividend growth rate, g_2. This value is found by applying the constant-growth model (Equation 7.8) to the dividends expected from year $N+1$ to infinity. The present value of P_N would represent the value *today* of all dividends that are expected to be received from year $N+1$ to infinity. This value can be represented by

$$\frac{1}{(1+k_s)^N} \times \frac{D_{N+1}}{k_s - g_2} = PVIF_{k_s,N} \times P_N$$

Step 4 Add the present value components found in Steps 2 and 3 to find the value of the stock, P_0, given in Equation 7.9:

$$P_0 = \underbrace{\sum_{t=1}^{N} \frac{D_0 \times (1+g_1)^t}{(1+k_s)^t}}_{\substack{\text{Present value} \\ \text{of dividends} \\ \text{during initial} \\ \text{growth period}}} + \underbrace{\left[\frac{1}{(1+k_s)^N} \times \frac{D_{N+1}}{k_s - g_2} \right]}_{\substack{\text{Present value of} \\ \text{price of stock at} \\ \text{end of initial} \\ \text{growth period}}} \tag{7.9}$$

The following example illustrates the application of these steps to a variable-growth situation with only one growth rate change.

Example ▼   The most recent (2001) annual dividend payment of Wycraft Industries, a rapidly growing boat manufacturer, was $1.50 per share. The firm's financial manager expects that these dividends will increase at a 10% annual rate, g_1, over the next 3 years (2002, 2003, and 2004) because of the introduction of a hot new boat. At the end of the 3 years (the end of 2004), the firm's mature product line is expected to result in a slowing of the dividend growth rate to 5% per year, g_2, for the foreseeable future. The firm's required return, k_s, is 15%. To estimate the current (end-of-2001) value of Wycraft's common stock, $P_0 = P_{2001}$, the four-step procedure must be applied to these data.

Step 1   The value of the cash dividends in each of the next 3 years is calculated in columns 1, 2, and 3 of Table 7.2. The 2002, 2003, and 2004 dividends are $1.65, $1.82, and $2.00, respectively.

Step 2   The present value of the three dividends expected during the 2002–2004 initial growth period is calculated in columns 3, 4, and 5 of Table 7.2. The sum of the present values of the three dividends is $4.14—the total of the column 5 values.

Step 3   The value of the stock at the end of the initial growth period ($N = 2004$) can be found by first calculating $D_{N+1} = D_{2005}$.

$$D_{2005} = D_{2004} \times (1 + .05) = \$2.00 \times (1.05) = \$2.10$$

By using $D_{2005} = \$2.10$, a 15% required return, and a 5% dividend growth rate, we can calculate the value of the stock at the end of 2004 as follows:

$$P_{2004} = \frac{D_{2005}}{k_s - g_2} = \frac{\$2.10}{0.15 - 0.05} = \frac{\$2.10}{0.10} = \$21.00$$

Finally, in Step 3, the share value of $21 at the end of 2004 must be converted into a present (end-of-2001) value. Using the 15% required return, we get

$$PVIF_{k_s,N} \times P_N = PVIF_{15\%,3yrs} \times P_{2004} = .658 \times \$21.00 = \$13.82$$

TABLE 7.2   Calculation of Present Value of Wycraft Industries' Dividends (2002–2004)

t	End of year	$D_0 = D_{2001}$ (1)	$FVIF_{10\%,t}$ (2)	D_t [(1) × (2)] (3)	$PVIF_{15\%,t}$ (4)	Present value of dividends [(3) × (4)] (5)
1	2002	$1.50	1.100	$1.65	.870	$1.44
2	2003	1.50	1.210	1.82	.756	1.38
3	2004	1.50	1.331	2.00	.658	1.32

$$\text{Sum of present value of dividends} = \sum_{t=1}^{3} \frac{D_0 \times (1 + g_1)^t}{(1 + k_s)^t} = \$4.14$$

Step 4   Adding the present value of the initial dividend stream (found in Step 2) to the present value of the stock at the end of the initial growth period (found in Step 3) as specified in Equation 7.9, we get the current (end-of-2001) value of Wycraft Industries' stock:

$$P_{2001} = \$4.14 + \$13.82 = \underline{\$17.96}$$

The stock is currently worth $17.96 per share. The calculation of this value is summarized diagrammatically as follows:

Finding Wycraft Industries' current (end-of-2001) value with variable growth

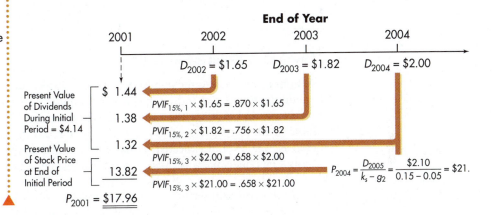

The zero-, constant-, and variable-growth valuation models provide useful frameworks for estimating stock value. Clearly, the estimates produced cannot be very precise, given that the forecasts of future growth and discount rates are themselves necessarily approximate. Looked at another way, a great deal of measurement error can be introduced into the stock price estimate as a result of the imprecise and rounded growth and discount rate estimates used as inputs. When applying valuation models, it is therefore advisable to estimate these rates carefully and round them conservatively, probably to the nearest tenth of a percent.

? Review Questions

7–9   Compare the following common stock valuation models: the zero-growth model, the constant-growth model, and the variable-growth model.

7–10   Which common stock valuation model can be used to find the value of *preferred stock?*

LG6 Decision Making and Common Stock Value

Valuation equations measure the stock value at a point in time based on expected return and risk. Any decisions of the financial manager that affect these variables can cause the value of the firm to change. Figure 7.3 depicts the relationship among financial decisions, return, risk, and stock value.

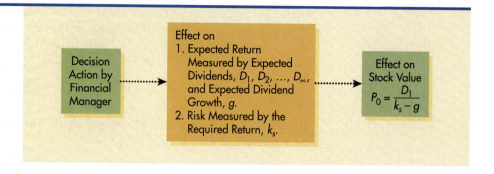

FIGURE 7.3

Decision Making and Stock Value
Financial decisions, return, risk, and stock value

Changes in Expected Return

Assuming that economic conditions remain stable, any management action that would cause current and prospective stockholders to raise their dividend expectations should increase the firm's value. In Equation 7.8, we can see that P_0 will increase for any increase in D_1 or g. Any action of the financial manager that will increase the level of expected returns without changing risk (the required return) should be undertaken, because it will positively affect owners' wealth.

Example ▼
Using the constant-growth model, we found Hotnet Company to have a share value of $18.75. On the following day, the firm announced a major technological breakthrough that would revolutionize its industry. Current and prospective stockholders would not be expected to adjust their required return of 15%, but they would expect that future dividends will increase. Specifically, they expect that although the dividend next year, D_1, will remain at $1.50, the expected rate of growth thereafter will increase from 7% to 9%. If we substitute $D_1 = 1.50, $k_s = 0.15$, and $g = 0.09$ into Equation 7.8, the resulting value is $25 [$1.50 \div (0.15 - 0.09)]$. The increased value therefore resulted from the higher expected future dividends reflected in the increase in the growth rate.
▲

Changes in Risk

Although k_s is defined as the required return, we know from Chapter 6 that it is directly related to the nondiversifiable risk, which can be measured by beta. The *capital asset pricing model (CAPM)* given in Equation 6.7 is restated here as Equation 7.10:

$$k_s = R_F + [b \times (k_m - R_F)] \tag{7.10}$$

With the risk-free rate, R_F, and the market return, k_m, held constant, the required return, k_s, depends directly on beta. Any action taken by the financial manager that increases risk (beta) will also increase the required return. In Equation 7.8 we can see that with everything else constant, an increase in the required return, k_s, will reduce share value, P_0. Likewise, a decrease in the required return will increase share value. Thus any action of the financial manag-

 **BUSINESS FOR SALE: BUSINESS-TO-BUSINESS WEB**

How do you value a small, privately held business, where "standard" stock-based measures don't apply? Check out the "Business for Sale" column in *Inc.*, a magazine focused on small emerging businesses. Each month the magazine presents a business for sale and describes the operations, financial situation, industry outlook, price rationale, and pros and cons of the small business offered for sale. Here is part of a recent offering.

The Business

Looking to link up to your own Internet deal? Consider this already-profitable three-year-old commercial Web site with a focus on the international import–export market, plenty of electronic traffic (currently about 350,000 hits each month), and all kinds of business-to-business growth opportunities. About 80% of its revenues come from corporate subscribers, who pay annual fees ranging from $244 to $324 for unlimited access to postings...about international-trade opportunities, financing options, and the like....
Price: $229,000

Outlook

As we move into the new global economy, this company's prospects could be nearly as limitless as, well, cyberspace. After all, a new growth-oriented owner could push the "on" button by hiring a sales force to woo new business customers (or, better still, to add big-name advertisers to the current roster of three). Other options include boosting the company's activities as a reseller of international-trade software, which currently provides 2% of sales. The site faces competition, which makes raising fees for its subscribers a no-no. But a new owner can count on great Web-site-name recognition; a fairly robust base of 2,000 active subscribers; and an information-swapping relationship with an international-trade publication, which provides valuable publicity at no cost.

Price Rationale

In a market this hot, anyone who claims there are rational rules of thumb is probably just keeping his or her fingers crossed. Everyone is on the prowl for established Web sites—especially the small handful that, like this one, have a proven record of actually making money. So even though this company has no assets worth mentioning except the owner's computer and a subscriber list, prospective buyers should be prepared to ante up, especially if a bidding war develops. At about three times recast earnings, the current price is well within the recent sales pattern for companies of this size and geographical base....

Source: Jill Andresky Fraser, "Business for Sale: Business-to-Business Web," Inc., October, 1999, p. 116.

---

er that increases risk contributes to a reduction in value, and any action that decreases risk contributes to an increase in value.

Example ▼ Assume that Hotnet Company's 15% required return resulted from a risk-free rate of 9%, a market return of 13%, and a beta of 1.50. Substituting into the capital asset pricing model, Equation 7.10, we get a required return, k_s, of 15%:

$$k_s = 9\% + [1.50 \times (13\% - 9\%)] = \underline{15\%}$$

With this return, the value of the firm was calculated in the example above to be $18.75.

Now imagine that the financial manager makes a decision that, without changing expected dividends, causes the firm's beta to increase to 1.75. Assuming that R_F and k_m remain at 9% and 13%, respectively, the required return will increase to 16% $\{9\% + [1.75 \times (13\% - 9\%)]\}$ to compensate stockholders for the increased risk. Substituting $D_1 = \$1.50$, $k_s = 0.16$, and $g = 0.07$ into the valuation equation, Equation 7.8, results in a share value of $16.67 [$1.50 ÷ (0.16 − 0.07)].

As expected, raising the required return, without any corresponding increase in expected return, causes the firm's stock value to decline. Clearly, the financial manager's action was not in the owners' best interest.

Combined Effect

A financial decision rarely affects return and risk independently; most decisions affect both factors. In terms of the measures presented, with an increase in risk (b), one would expect an increase in return (D_1 or g, or both), assuming that R_F and k_m remain unchanged. The net effect on value depends on the size of the changes in these variables.

Example ▼ If we assume that the two changes illustrated for Hotnet Company in the preceding examples occur simultaneously, key variable values would be $D_1 = \$1.50$, $k_s = 0.16$, and $g = 0.09$. Substituting into the valuation model, we obtain a share price of $21.43 [\$1.50 \div (0.16 - 0.09)]$. The net result of the decision, which increased return (g, from 7% to 9%) as well as risk (b, from 1.50 to 1.75 and therefore k_s from 15% to 16%), is positive: The share price increased from $18.75 to $21.43. The decision appears to be in the best interest of the firm's owners, because it increases their wealth.

Review Questions

7–11 Explain the linkages among financial decisions, return, risk, and stock value.

7–12 Assuming that all other variables remain unchanged, what impact would each of the following have on stock price? (a) The firm's beta increases. (b) The firm's required return decreases. (c) The dividend expected next year decreases. (d) The rate of growth in dividends is expected to increase.

TYING IT ALL TOGETHER

This chapter presented the key conceptual and computational procedures for use in valuation—determining the worth, or value, of an asset. Returns, timing, and risk are the three key inputs to the basic valuation model, which can be customized to value specific securities (bonds, preferred stock, and common stock). The importance of valuation to financial managers, financial markets, and investors is summarized in the Integrative Table that follows.

INTEGRATIVE TABLE

Valuing Bonds and Stocks

Role of **Financial Managers**	*Role of* **Financial Markets**	*Role of* **Investors**
Financial managers can make decisions that create value through the proper balancing of expected return and risk. They apply valuation techniques to long-term decisions such as asset acquisition, and to certain types of financing actions. Managers should take only those actions that will increase share price.	The interactions of buyers and sellers of bonds and stocks in the financial markets result in their market prices. Investors buy and sell bonds and stocks on the basis of assessments of their value using valuation techniques, and comparison of that value to the market price. The markets balance changes in supply and demand to create the equilibrium prices that investors use with their valuations to make decisions.	Investors use valuation techniques to assess the true worth of bond and stock investments in order to find attractive investment opportunities. Investors who believe a stock or bond is worth more than its market price buy it. Those who feel that the true value of a stock or bond is less than its market price sell it. Ability to estimate the true worth of an investment is critical to making good decisions.

LG1 **Describe the key inputs and basic model used in the valuation process.** Key inputs to the valuation process include cash flows (returns), timing, and risk and the required return. The value of any asset is equal to the present value of all future cash flows it is *expected* to provide over the relevant time period. The key variable definitions and the basic valuation model for any asset are summarized in Table 7.3.

LG2 **Review the basic bond valuation model.** The value of a bond is the present value of its interest payments plus the present value of its par value. The basic valuation model for a bond is summarized in Table 7.3.

LG3 **Discuss bond value behavior, particularly the impact that required return and time to maturity have on bond value.** The discount rate used to determine bond value is the required return, which may differ from the bond's coupon interest rate. A bond can sell at a discount, at par, or at a premium. The amount of time to maturity affects bond values. Even if required return remains constant, the value of a bond will approach its par value as the bond moves closer to maturity. The chance that interest rates will change and thereby change the required return and bond value is called interest rate

risk. The shorter the amount of time until a bond's maturity, the less responsive is its market value to a given change in the required return.

LG4 **Explain yield to maturity and the procedure used to value bonds that pay interest semiannually.** Yield to maturity (YTM) is the rate of return investors earn if they buy a bond at a specific price and hold it until maturity. Bonds that pay interest semiannually are valued by using the same procedure used to value bonds paying annual interest except that the interest payments are one-half of the annual interest payments, the number of periods is twice the number of years to maturity, and the required return is one-half of the stated annual required return on similar-risk bonds.

LG5 **Perform basic common stock valuation using each of three models: zero-growth, constant-growth, and variable-growth.** The value of a share of common stock is the present value of all future dividends it is expected to provide. Zero-growth, constant-growth, and variable-growth models of dividend growth can be considered in common stock valuation. These models are summarized in Table 7.3. The most widely cited model is the constant-growth (Gordon) model.

TABLE 7.3	Summary of Key Valuation Definitions and Models

Variable definitions

B_0 = bond value
CF_t = cash flow *expected* at the end of year t
D_0 = most recent per-share dividend
D_t = per-share dividend expected at the end of year t
g = constant rate of growth in dividends
g_1 = initial dividend growth rate (in variable-growth model)
g_2 = subsequent dividend growth rate (in variable-growth model)
I = annual interest on a bond
k = appropriate required return (discount rate)
k_d = required return on a bond
k_s = required return on common stock
M = par value of a bond
n = relevant time period, or number of years to maturity
N = last year of initial growth period (in variable-growth model)
P_0 = value of common stock
V_0 = value of the asset at time zero

Valuation models

Value of any asset:

$$V_0 = \frac{CF_1}{(1+k)^1} + \frac{CF_2}{(1+k)^2} + \cdots + \frac{CF_n}{(1+k)^n}$$ [Eq. 7.1]

$$= [CF_1 \times (PVIF_{k,1}) + [CF_2 \times (PVIF_{k,2})] + \cdots + [CF_n \times (PVIF_{k,n})]$$ [Eq. 7.2]

Bond value:

$$B_0 = I \times \left[\sum_{t=1}^{n} \frac{1}{(1+k_d)^n} \right] + M \times \left[\frac{1}{(1+k_d)^n} \right]$$ [Eq. 7.3]

$$= I \times (PVIFA_{k_d,n}) + M \times (PVIF_{k_d,n})$$ [Eq. 7.3a]

Common stock value:

Zero-model growth: $P_0 = \dfrac{D_1}{k_s}$ (also used to value preferred stock)   [Eq. 7.6]

Constant-growth model: $P_0 = \dfrac{D_1}{k_s - g}$ [Eq. 7.8]

Variable-growth model: $P_0 = \sum_{t=1}^{N} \dfrac{D_0 \times (1+g_1)^t}{(1+k_s)^t} + \left[\dfrac{1}{(1+k_s)^N} \times \dfrac{D_{N+1}}{k_s - g_2} \right]$ [Eq. 7.9]

LG6 **Understand the relationships among financial decisions, return, risk, and stock value.**
In a stable economy, any action of the financial manager that increases the level of expected return without changing risk should increase share value, and any action that reduces the level of expected return without changing risk should reduce share value. Similarly, any action that increases risk (required return) will reduce share value, and any action that reduces risk will increase share value. Because most financial decisions affect both return and risk, an assessment of their combined effect on stock value must be part of the financial decision-making process.

SELF-TEST EXERCISES   **(Solutions in Appendix B)**

  ST 7–1 Bond valuation   Haley Industries has outstanding a $1,000 par-value bond with an 8% coupon interest rate. The bond has 12 years remaining to its maturity date.
  a. If interest is paid *annually*, find the value of the bond when the required return is (1) 7%, (2) 8%, and (3) 10%.
  b. Indicate for each case in part **a** whether the bond is selling at a discount, at a premium, or at its par value.
  c. Using the 10% required return, find the bond's value when interest is paid *semiannually*.

 ST 7–2 Yield to maturity   Encast Enterprises bonds currently sell for $1,150, have an 11% coupon interest rate and a $1,000 par value, pay interest *annually*, and have 18 years to maturity.
  a. Calculate the bonds' yield to maturity (YTM).
  b. Compare the YTM calculated in part **a** to the bonds' coupon interest rate, and use a comparison of the bonds' current price and their par value to explain this difference.

ST 7–3 Common stock valuation   Regent Motors' common stock currently pays an annual dividend of $1.80 per share. The required return on the common stock is 12%. Estimate the value of the common stock under each of the following assumptions about the dividend growth rate.
  a. Dividends are expected to grow at an annual rate of 0% to infinity.
  b. Dividends are expected to grow at a constant annual rate of 5% to infinity.
  c. Dividends are expected to grow at an annual rate of 5% for each of the next 3 years, followed by a constant annual growth rate of 4% in years 4 to infinity.

EXERCISES

 7–1 Valuation fundamentals   Imagine that you are trying to evaluate the economics of purchasing an automobile. You expect the car to provide annual after-tax cash benefits at the end of each year of $1,200 and assume that you can sell the car for after-tax proceeds of $5,000 at the end of the planned 5-year ownership period. All funds for purchasing the car will be drawn from your savings, which are currently earning 6% after taxes.
  a. Identify the cash flows, their timing, and the required return applicable to valuing the car.
  b. What is the maximum price you would be willing to pay to acquire the car? Explain.

 7–2 Valuation of assets   Using the information provided in the table at the top of the following page, find the value of each asset.

Asset	End of year	Amount	Appropriate required return
A	1	$ 5,000	18%
	2	5,000	
	3	5,000	
B	1 through ∞	$ 300	15%
C	1	$ 0	16%
	2	0	
	3	0	
	4	0	
	5	35,000	
D	1 through 5	$ 1,500	12%
	6	8,500	
E	1	$ 2,000	14%
	2	3,000	
	3	5,000	
	4	7,000	
	5	4,000	
	6	1,000	

The table has a spanning header "Cash flow" over the "End of year" and "Amount" columns.

7–3   Asset valuation and risk   Haley Dobbs wishes to estimate the value of an asset expected to provide cash inflows of $3,000 per year at the end of years 1 through 4 and $15,000 at the end of year 5. His research indicates that he must earn 10% on low-risk assets, 15% on average-risk assets, and 22% on high-risk assets.

  a. Determine what is the most Haley should pay for the asset if it is classified as (1) low-risk, (2) average-risk, and (3) high-risk.

  b. Say Haley is unable to assess the risk of the asset and wants to be certain he's making a good deal. On the basis of your findings in part **a,** what is the most he should pay? Why?

  c. All else being the same, what effect does increasing risk have on the value of an asset? Explain in light of your findings in part **a.**

7–4   Basic bond valuation   Steck Industries has an outstanding issue of $1,000-par-value bonds with a 12% coupon interest rate. The issue pays interest *annually* and has 16 years remaining to its maturity date.

  a. If bonds of similar risk are currently earning a 10% rate of return, how much should the Steck Industries bond sell for today?

  b. Describe the *two* possible reasons why similar-risk bonds are currently earning a return below the coupon interest rate on the Steck Industries bond.

  c. If the required return were at 12% instead of 10%, what would the current value of Steck's bond be? Contrast this finding with your findings in part **a** and discuss.

7–5 Bond valuation—Annual interest   Calculate the value of each of the bonds shown in the following table, all of which pay interest annually.

Bond	Par value	Coupon interest rate	Years to maturity	Required return
A	$1,000	14%	20	12%
B	1,000	8	16	8
C	100	10	8	13
D	500	16	13	18
E	1,000	12	10	10

7–6 Bond value and changing required returns   Culbert National has outstanding a bond issue that will mature to its $1,000 par value in 12 years. The bond has a coupon interest rate of 11% and pays interest *annually*.
a. Find the value of the bond if the required return is (1) 11%, (2) 15%, and (3) 8%.
b. Plot your findings in part **a** on a set of "required return (*x* axis)–market value of bond (*y* axis)" axes.
c. Use your findings in parts **a** and **b** to discuss the relationship between the coupon interest rate on a bond and the required return and the market value of the bond relative to its par value.
d. For what *two* reasons is the required return different from the coupon interest rate?

7–7 Bond value and time—Constant required returns   Rost Manufacturing has just issued a 15-year, 12% coupon interest rate, $1,000-par bond that pays interest *annually*. The required return is currently 14%, and the company is certain it will remain at 14% until the bond matures in 15 years.
a. Assuming that the required return does remain at 14% until maturity, find the value of the bond with (1) 15 years, (2) 12 years, (3) 9 years, (4) 6 years, (5) 3 years, and (6) 1 year to maturity.
b. Plot your findings on a set of "time to maturity (*x* axis)–market value of bond (*y* axis)" axes constructed similarly to Figure 7.2.
c. All else remaining the same, when the required return differs from the coupon interest rate and is assumed to be constant to maturity, what happens to the bond value as time moves toward maturity? Explain in light of the graph in part **b**.

7–8 Bond value and time—Changing required returns   Pat Lynn is considering investing in either of two outstanding bonds. The bonds both have $1,000 par values and 11% coupon interest rates and pay *annual* interest. Bond A has exactly 5 years to maturity, and bond B has 15 years to maturity.
a. Calculate the value of bond A if the required return is (1) 8%, (2) 11%, and (3) 14%.
b. Calculate the value of bond B if the required return is (1) 8%, (2) 11%, and (3) 14%.
c. From your findings in parts **a** and **b**, complete the table at the top of the following page, and discuss the relationship between time to maturity and changing required returns.

Required return	Value of bond A	Value of bond B
8%	?	?
11	?	?
14	?	?

d. If Pat wanted to minimize *interest rate risk*, which bond should she purchase? Why?

 7–9 Yield to maturity   Each of the bonds shown in the following table pays interest *annually*.

Bond	Par value	Coupon interest rate	Years to maturity	Current value
A	$1,000	9%	8	$ 820
B	1,000	12	16	1,000
C	500	12	12	560
D	1,000	15	10	1,120
E	1,000	5	3	900

a. Calculate the yield to maturity (YTM) for each bond.
b. What relationship exists between the coupon interest rate and yield to maturity and the par value and market value of a bond? Explain.

 7–10 Bond valuation—Semiannual interest   Calculate the value of each of the bonds shown in the following table, all of which pay interest *semiannually*.

Bond	Par value	Coupon interest rate	Years to maturity	Required return
A	$1,000	10%	12%	8%
B	1,000	12	20	12
C	500	12	5	14
D	1,000	14	10	10
E	100	6	4	14

 7–11 Common stock valuation—Zero-growth model   Connect Enterprises is a mature firm in the machine tool component industry. The firm's most recent common stock dividend was $2.40 per share. Because of its maturity as well as its stable sales and earnings, the firm's management feels that dividends will remain at the current level for the foreseeable future.
a. If the required return is 12%, what will be the value of Connect Enterprises' common stock?

   b. If the firm's risk as perceived by market participants suddenly increases, causing the required return to rise to 20%, what will be the common stock value?

   c. On the basis of your findings in parts **a** and **b,** what impact does risk have on value? Explain.

7–12 Preferred stock   Katlop Stamping wishes to estimate the value of its outstanding preferred stock. The preferred issue has an $80 par value and pays an annual dividend of $6.40 per share. Similar-risk preferred stocks are currently earning a 9.3% annual rate of return.

   a. What is the market value of the outstanding preferred stock?

   b. If an investor purchases the preferred stock at the value calculated in part **a,** how much does she gain or lose per share if she sells the stock when the required return on similar-risk preferreds has risen to 10.5%? Explain.

7–13 Common stock value—Constant-growth model   Use the constant-growth model (Gordon model) to find the value of each firm in the following table.

Firm	Dividend expected next year	Dividend growth rate	Required return
A	$1.20	8%	13%
B	4.00	5	15
C	.65	10	14
D	6.00	8	9
E	2.25	8	20

7–14 Common stock value—Constant-growth model   Lafayette Boiler Company has paid the dividends shown in the following table over the past 6 years.

Year	Dividend per share
2001	$2.87
2000	2.76
1999	2.60
1998	2.46
1997	2.37
1996	2.25

The firm's dividend per share next year is expected to be $3.02.

   a. If you can earn 13% on similar-risk investments, what is the most you would be willing to pay per share for this firm?

   b. If you can earn only 10% on similar-risk investments, what is the most you would be willing to pay per share?

   c. Compare and contrast your findings in parts **a** and **b,** and discuss the impact of changing risk on share value.

7–15   Common stock value—Variable-growth model   Florence Industries' most recent annual dividend was $1.80 per share ($D_0 = \$1.80$), and the firm's required return is 11%. Find the market value of Florence's shares when:

a. Dividends are expected to grow at 8% annually for 3 years, followed by a 5% constant annual growth rate in years 4 to infinity.

b. Dividends are expected to grow at 8% annually for 3 years, followed by 0% constant annual growth rate in years 4 to infinity.

c. Dividends are expected to grow at 8% annually for 3 years, followed by a 10% constant annual growth rate in years 4 to infinity.

7–16   Common stock value—All growth models   You are evaluating the potential purchase of a small business currently generating $42,500 of after-tax cash flow ($D_0 = \$42,500$). On the basis of a review of similar-risk investment opportunities, you must earn an 18% rate of return on the proposed purchase. Because you are relatively uncertain about future cash flows, you decide to estimate the firm's value using several possible assumptions about the growth rate of cash flows.

a. What is the firm's value if cash flows are expected to grow at an annual rate of 0% from now to infinity?

b. What is the firm's value if cash flows are expected to grow at a constant annual rate of 7% from now to infinity?

c. What is the firm's value if cash flows are expected to grow at an annual rate of 12% for the first 2 years, followed by a constant annual rate of 7% in years 3 from now to infinity?

7–17   Management action and stock value   Jezak Enterprises' most recent dividend was $3 per share, its expected annual rate of dividend growth is 5%, and the required return is now 15%. A variety of proposals are being considered by management to redirect the firm's activities. Determine the impact on share price for each of the following proposed actions, and indicate the best alternative.

a. Do nothing, which will leave the key financial variables unchanged.

b. Invest in a new machine that will increase the dividend growth rate to 6% and lower the required return to 14%.

c. Eliminate an unprofitable product line, which will increase the dividend growth rate to 7% and raise the required return to 17%.

d. Merge with another firm, which will reduce the growth rate to 4% and raise the required return to 16%.

e. Acquire a subsidiary operation from another manufacturer. The acquisition should increase the dividend growth rate to 8% and increase the required return to 17%.

7–18   Integrative—Valuation and CAPM formulas   Given the following information for the stock of Deeter Company, calculate its beta.

Current price per share of common	$50.00
Expected dividend per share next year	$ 3.00
Constant annual dividend growth rate	9%
Risk-free rate of return	7%
Return on market portfolio	10%

7–19 **Integrative—Valuation and CAPM**   Japan Steel Company wishes to determine the value of Del Mar Foundry, a firm that it is considering acquiring for cash. Japan wishes to use the capital asset pricing model (CAPM) to determine the applicable discount rate to use as an input to the constant-growth valuation model. Del Mar's stock is not publicly traded. After studying the betas of firms similar to Del Mar that are publicly traded, Japan believes that an appropriate beta for Del Mar's stock would be 1.25. The risk-free rate is currently 9%, and the market return is 13%. Del Mar's historical dividend per share for each of the past 6 years is shown in the following table.

Year	Dividend per share
2001	$3.44
2000	3.28
1999	3.15
1998	2.90
1997	2.75
1996	2.45

a. Given that Del Mar is expected to pay a dividend of $3.68 next year, determine the maximum cash price that Japan should pay for each share of Del Mar.

b. Discuss the use of the CAPM for estimating the value of common stock, and describe the effect on the resulting value of Del Mar of:
   (1) A decrease in its dividend growth rate of 2% from that exhibited over the 1996–2001 period.
   (2) A decrease in its beta to 1.

web exercises   Search

Go to www.marketguide.com. Click on **Research**. Enter YUM in the symbol box. Click on **Price Charts**.
1. What was the highest price for Tricon Global Restaurants in this 12-month period? What was its lowest price? Has its price been stable or dynamic? Increasing or decreasing? Click on **Performance**.
2. What has been the Actual Price Performance YTD for Tricon Global Restaurants? For the S&P 500?

web exercises   Search

Go to web site www.smartmoney.com. Click Bond. Next click on Bond Investing. Then click on Bond Calculator (located under the column "Understanding Bonds"). Read the instructions on how to use the bond calculator.

Using the bond calculator, do the following:

1. Calculate the yield to maturity (YTM) for a bond whose coupon rate is 8.0% with a maturity date of July 31, 2025, which you bought for 110.5.
2. What is the YTM of the above bond if you bought it for 105? For 100?
3. Change the yield % box to 8.5. What would be the price of this bond?
4. Change the yield % box to 6.5. What is the bond's price?
5. Change the maturity date to 2003 and reset yield % to 6.5. What is the price of this bond?
6. Why is the price of the bond in Exercise 5 lower than the price of the bond in Exercise 4?

For additional practice with concepts from this chapter, visit
http://www.awl.com/gitman_madura

Financial Statements and Analysis

LEARNING GOALS

LG1 Review the contents of the stockholders' report and the procedures for consolidating international financial statements.

LG2 Understand who uses financial ratios, and how.

LG3 Use ratios to analyze a firm's liquidity and activity

LG4 Discuss the relationship between debt and financial leverage and the ratios used to analyze a firm's debt.

LG5 Use ratios to analyze a firm's profitability and its market value.

LG6 Use a summary of financial ratios and the DuPont system of analysis to perform a complete ratio analysis.

The Stockholders' Report

generally accepted accounting principles (GAAP)
The practice and procedure guidelines used to prepare and maintain financial records and reports; authorized by the *Financial Accounting Standards Board (FASB)*.

Financial Accounting Standards Board (FASB)
The accounting profession's rule-setting body, which authorizes *generally accepted accounting principles (GAAP)*.

Securities and Exchange Commission (SEC)
The federal regulatory body that governs the sale and listing of securities.

stockholders' report
Annual report that publicly owned corporations must provide to stockholders; it summarizes and documents the firm's financial activities during the past year.

letter to stockholders
Typically, the first element of the annual stockholders' report and the primary communication from management.

income statement
Provides a financial summary of the firm's operating results during a specified period.

Every corporation has many and varied uses for the standardized records and reports of its financial activities. Periodically, reports must be prepared for regulators, creditors (lenders), owners, and management. The guidelines used to prepare and maintain financial records and reports are known as **generally accepted accounting principles (GAAP)**. These accounting practices and procedures are authorized by the accounting profession's rule-setting body, the **Financial Accounting Standards Board (FASB)**.

Publicly owned corporations with more than $5 million in assets and 500 or more stockholders are required by the **Securities and Exchange Commission (SEC)**—the federal regulatory body that governs the sale and listing of securities—to provide their stockholders with an annual **stockholders' report**. The annual report summarizes and documents the firm's financial activities during the past year. It begins with a letter to the stockholders from the firm's president and/or chairman of the board.

The Letter to Stockholders

The **letter to stockholders** is the primary communication from management. It describes the events that are considered to have had the greatest impact on the firm during the year. It also generally discusses management philosophy, strategies, and actions, as well as plans for the coming year. Links at this book's web site (**http://www.awl.com/gitman_madura**) will take you to some representative letters to stockholders.

The Four Key Financial Statements

The four key financial statements required by the Securities and Exchange Commission (SEC) for reporting to shareholders are (1) the income statement, (2) the balance sheet, (3) the statement of retained earnings, and (4) the statement of cash flows. The financial statements from the 2001 stockholders' report of Daton Company, a small manufacturer of wicker furniture, are presented and briefly discussed.

Income Statement

The **income statement** provides a financial summary of the firm's operating results during a specified period. Most common are income statements covering a 1-year period ending at a specified date, ordinarily December 31 of the calendar year. Many large firms, however, operate on a 12-month financial cycle, or *fiscal year,* that ends at a time other than December 31. In addition, monthly income statements are typically prepared for use by management, and quarterly statements must be made available to the stockholders of publicly owned corporations.

Table 8.1 presents Daton Company's income statements for the years ended December 31, 2001 and 2000. The 2001 statement begins with sales revenue—the total dollar amount of sales during the period—from which the cost of goods sold is deducted. The resulting gross profits of $986,000 represent the amount

TABLE 8.1	Daton Company Income Statements ($000)

	For the years ended December 31	
	2001	2000
Sales revenue	$3,074	$2,567
Less: Cost of goods sold	2,088	1,711
Gross profits	$ 986	$ 856
Less: Operating expenses		
Selling expense	$ 100	$ 108
General and administrative expenses	194	187
Lease expense[a]	35	35
Depreciation expense	239	223
Total operating expense	$ 568	$ 553
Operating profits	$ 418	$ 303
Less: Interest expense	93	91
Net profits before taxes	$ 325	$ 212
Less: Taxes (rate = 29%)[b]	94	64
Net profits after taxes	$ 231	$ 148
Less: Preferred stock dividends	10	10
Earnings available for common stockholders	$ 221	$ 138
Earnings per share (EPS)[c]	$ 2.90	$ 1.81
Dividend per share (DPS)[d]	$ 1.29	$ .75

[a]Lease expense is shown here as a separate item rather than being included as interest expense and amortization, as specified by the FASB for financial-reporting purposes. The approach used here is consistent with tax-reporting rather than financial-reporting procedures.

[b]The 29% tax rate for 2001 results because the firm has certain special tax write-offs that do not show up directly on its income statement.

[c]Calculated by dividing the earnings available for common stockholders by the number of shares of common stock outstanding—76,262 in 2001 and 76,244 in 2000. Earnings per share in 2001: $221,000 ÷ 76,262 = $2.90; in 2000: $138,000 ÷ 76,244 = $1.81.

[d]Calculated by dividing the dollar amount of dividends paid to common stockholders by the number of shares of common stock outstanding. Dividends per share in 2001: $98,000 ÷ 76,262 = $1.29; in 2000: $57,183 ÷ 76,244 = $.75.

remaining to satisfy operating, financial, and tax costs. Next, *operating expenses,* which include selling expense, general and administrative expense, lease expense, and depreciation expense, are deducted from gross profits. The resulting *operating profits* of $418,000 represent the profits earned from producing and selling products; this amount does not consider financial and tax costs. (Operating profit is often called *earnings before interest and taxes,* or *EBIT.*) Next, the financial cost—*interest expense*—is subtracted from operating profits to find *net profits* (or *earnings) before taxes.* After subtracting $93,000 in 2001 interest, Daton Company had $325,000 of net profits before taxes.

Next, taxes are calculated at the appropriate tax rates and deducted to determine *net profits* (or *earnings) after taxes.* Daton Company's net profits after taxes for 2001 were $231,000. Any preferred stock dividends must be subtracted from net profits after taxes to arrive at *earnings available for common stockholders*. This is the amount earned by the firm on behalf of the common stockholders during the period.

Dividing earnings available for common stockholders by the number of shares of common stock outstanding results in **earnings per share (EPS)**. EPS represents the number of dollars earned during the period on behalf of each outstanding share of common stock. In 2001, Daton Company earned $221,000 for its common stockholders, which represents $2.90 for each outstanding share. The actual cash **dividend per share (DPS),** which is the dollar amount of cash distributed during the period on behalf of each outstanding share of common stock, paid in 2001 was $1.29.

earnings per share (EPS)
The number of dollars earned during the period on behalf of each outstanding share of common stock.

dividend per share (DPS)
The dollar amount of cash distributed during the period on behalf of each outstanding share of common stock.

Balance Sheet

balance sheet
Summary statement of the firm's financial position at a given point in time.

The **balance sheet** presents a summary statement of the firm's financial position at a given point in time. The statement balances the firm's *assets* (what it owns) against its financing, which can be either *debt* (what it owes) or *equity* (what was provided by owners). Daton Company's balance sheet as of December 31, 2001, is presented in Table 8.2, along with values from the previous year for comparison. The balance sheets show a variety of asset, liability (debt), and equity accounts.

current assets
Short-term assets, expected to be converted into cash within 1 year or less.

current liabilities
Short-term liabilities, expected to be paid within 1 year or less.

An important distinction is made between short-term and long-term assets and liabilities. The **current assets** and **current liabilities** are *short-term* assets and liabilities, which are expected to be converted into cash (current assets) or paid (current liabilities) within 1 year. All other assets and liabilities, along with stockholders' equity, which is assumed to have an infinite life, are considered *long-term,* or *fixed,* because they are expected to remain on the firm's books for 1 year or more.

As is customary, the assets are listed from the most liquid—*cash*—down to the least liquid. *Marketable securities* are very liquid short-term investments, such as U.S. Treasury bills or certificates of deposit, held by the firm. Because they are highly liquid, marketable securities are viewed as a form of cash ("near cash"). *Accounts receivable* represent the total monies owed the firm by its customers on credit sales made to them. *Inventories* include raw materials, work in process (partially finished goods), and finished goods held by the firm. The entry for *gross fixed assets* is the original cost of all fixed (long-term) assets owned by the firm. *Net fixed assets* represent the difference between gross fixed assets and *accumulated depreciation*—the total expense recorded for the depreciation of fixed assets. (The net value of fixed assets is called their *book value.*)

long-term debt
Debts for which payment is not due in the current year.

Like assets, the liabilities and equity accounts are listed from short-term to long-term. Current liabilities include *accounts payable,* amounts owed for credit purchases by the firm; *notes payable,* outstanding short-term loans; and *accruals,* amounts owed for services for which a bill may not or will not be received. (Examples of accruals include taxes due the government and wages due employees.) **Long-term debt** represents debt for which payment is not due in the current year. *Stockholders' equity* represents the owners' claims on the firm. The *preferred stock* entry shows the historical proceeds from the sale of preferred stock to investors ($200,000 for Daton Company).

Next, the amount paid by the original purchasers of common stock is shown by two entries: common stock and paid-in capital in excess of par on common

TABLE 8.2	Daton Company Balance Sheets ($000)

	December 31	
Assets	2001	2000
Current assets		
Cash	$ 363	$ 288
Marketable securities	68	51
Accounts receivable	503	365
Inventories	289	300
Total current assets	$1,223	$1,004
Gross fixed assets (at cost)[a]		
Land and buildings	$2,072	$1,903
Machinery and equipment	1,866	1,693
Furniture and fixtures	358	316
Vehicles	275	314
Other (includes financial leases)	98	96
Total gross fixed assets (at cost)	$4,669	$4,322
Less: Accumulated depreciation	2,295	2,056
Net fixed assets	$2,374	$2,266
Total assets	$3,597	$3,270
Liabilities and stockholders' equity		
Current liabilities		
Accounts payable	$ 382	$ 270
Notes payable	79	99
Accruals	159	114
Total current liabilities	$ 620	$ 483
Long-term debt (includes financial leases)[b]	$1,023	$ 967
Total liabilities	$1,643	$1,450
Stockholders' equity		
Preferred stock—cumulative 5%, $100 par, 2,000 shares authorized and issued[c]	$ 200	$ 200
Common stock—$2.50 par, 100,000 shares authorized, shares issued and outstanding in 2001: 76,262; in 2000: 76,244	191	190
Paid-in capital in excess of par on common stock	428	418
Retained earnings	1,135	1,012
Total stockholders' equity	$1,954	$1,820
Total liabilities and stockholders' equity	$3,597	$3,270

[a] In 2001, the firm has a 6-year financial lease requiring annual beginning-of-year payments of $35,000. Four years of the lease have yet to run.

[b] Annual principal repayments on a portion of the firm's total outstanding debt amount to $71,000.

[c] The annual preferred stock dividend would be $5 per share (5% × $100 par), or a total of $10,000 annually ($5 per share × 2,000 shares).

paid-in capital in excess of par
The amount of proceeds in excess of the par value received from the original sale of common stock.

retained earnings
The cumulative total of all earnings, net of dividends, that have been retained and reinvested in the firm since its inception.

stock. The *common stock* entry is the *par value* of common stock. **Paid-in capital in excess of par** represents the amount of proceeds in excess of the par value received from the original sale of common stock. The sum of the common stock and paid-in capital accounts divided by the number of shares outstanding represents the original price per share received by the firm on a single issue of common stock. Daton Company therefore received about $8.12 per share [($191,000 par + $428,000 paid-in capital in excess of par) ÷ 76,262 shares] from the sale of its common stock. Finally, **retained earnings** represent the cumulative total of all earnings, net of dividends, that have been retained and reinvested in the firm since its inception. It is important to recognize that retained earnings *are not cash* but rather have been utilized to finance the firm's assets.

Daton Company's balance sheets in Table 8.2 show that the firm's total assets increased from $3,270,000 in 2000 to $3,597,000 in 2001. The $327,000 increase was due primarily to the $219,000 increase in current assets. The asset increase in turn appears to have been financed primarily by an increase of $193,000 in total liabilities. Better insight into these changes can be derived from the statement of cash flows, which we will discuss shortly.

Statement of Retained Earnings

statement of retained earnings
Reconciles the net income earned during a given year, and any cash dividends paid, with the change in retained earnings between the start and the end of that year.

The **statement of retained earnings** reconciles the net income earned during a given year, and any cash dividends paid, with the change in retained earnings between the start and the end of that year. Table 8.3 presents this statement for Daton Company for the year ended December 31, 2001. The statement shows that the company began the year with $1,012,000 in retained earnings and had net profits after taxes of $231,000, from which it paid a total of $108,000 in dividends, resulting in year-end retained earnings of $1,135,000. Thus the net increase for Daton Company was $123,000 ($231,000 net profits after taxes minus $108,000 in dividends) during 2001.

Statement of Cash Flows

statement of cash flows
Provides a summary of the firm's operating, investment, and financing cash flows and reconciles them with changes in its cash and marketable securities during the period.

The **statement of cash flows** is a summary of the cash flows over the period of concern. The statement provides insight into the firm's operating, investment, and financing cash flows and reconciles them with changes in its cash and marketable securities during the period. Daton Company's statement of cash flows for the year ended December 31, 2001, is presented in Table 8.4. Further insight into this statement is included in the cash flow discussion in Chapter 9.

TABLE 8.3	Daton Company Statement of Retained Earnings ($000) for the Year Ended December 31, 2001		
Retained earnings balance (January 1, 2001)			$1,012
Plus: Net profits after taxes (for 2001)			231
Less: Cash dividends (paid during 2001)			
Preferred stock		($10)	
Common stock		(98)	
Total dividends paid			(108)
Retained earnings balance (December 31, 2001)			$1,135

TABLE 8.4	Daton Company Statement of Cash Flows ($000) for the Year Ended December 31, 2001

Cash Flow from Operating Activities	
Net profits after taxes	$ 231
Depreciation	239
Increase in accounts receivable	(138)[a]
Decrease in inventories	11
Increase in accounts payable	112
Increase in accruals	45
Cash provided by operating activities	$ 500
Cash Flow from Investment Activities	
Increase in gross fixed assets	($347)
Change in business interests	0
Cash provided by investment activities	(347)
Cash Flow from Financing Activities	
Decrease in notes payable	($20)
Increase in long-term debts	56
Changes in stockholders' equity[b]	11
Dividends paid	($108)
Cash provided by financing activities	(61)
Net increase in cash and marketable securities	$ 92

[a]As is customary, parentheses are used to denote a negative number, which in this case is a cash outflow.

[b]Retained earnings are excluded here, because their change is actually reflected in the combination of the "net profits after taxes" and "dividends paid" entries.

Notes to Financial Statements

notes to financial statements
Footnotes detailing information on the accounting policies, procedures, calculations, and transactions underlying entries in the financial statements.

Included with published financial statements are explanatory notes keyed to the relevant accounts in the statements. These **notes to financial statements** provide detailed information on the accounting policies, procedures, calculations, and transactions underlying entries in the financial statements. Common issues addressed by these notes include revenue recognition, income taxes, breakdowns of fixed asset accounts, debt and lease terms, and contingencies. Professional securities analysts use the data in the statements and notes to develop estimates of the value of securities that the firm issues, which influence the actions of investors and therefore the firm's share value.

Consolidating International Financial Statements

So far, we've discussed financial statements involving only one currency, the U.S. dollar. The issue of how to consolidate a company's foreign and domestic financial statements has bedeviled the accounting profession for many years. The current policy is described in **Financial Accounting Standards Board (FASB)**

Standard No. 52, which mandates that U.S.-based companies translate their foreign-currency-denominated assets and liabilities into dollars, for consolidation
with the parent company's financial statements. This is done by using a technique called the **current rate (translation) method,** under which all of a U.S.
parent company's foreign-currency-denominated assets and liabilities are converted into dollar values using the exchange rate prevailing at the fiscal year
ending date (the current rate). Income statement items are treated similarly.
Equity accounts, on the other hand, are translated into dollars by using the
exchange rate that prevailed when the parent's equity investment was made (the
historical rate). Retained earnings are adjusted to reflect each year's operating
profits or losses. Further details on this procedure can be found at the book's
web site at **http://www.awl.com/gitman_madura** or in an intermediate accounting text.

? Review Questions

8–1   Describe the purpose of each of the four major financial statements
8–2   Why are the notes to financial statements important to professional secu-
       rities analysts?

Using Financial Ratios

ratio analysis
Involves methods of calculating and
interpreting financial ratios to analyze
and monitor the firm's performance.

The information contained in the four basic financial statements is of major significance to various interested parties who regularly need relative measures of the
company's operating efficiency. *Relative* is the key word here, because the analysis of financial statements is based on the use of *ratios* or *relative values.* **Ratio
analysis** involves methods of calculating and interpreting financial ratios to analyze and monitor the firm's performance. The basic inputs to ratio analysis are
the firm's income statement and balance sheet.

Interested Parties

Ratio analysis is of interest to shareholders, creditors, and the firm's own management. Both present and prospective shareholders are interested in the firm's
current and future level of risk and return, which directly affect share price. The
firm's creditors are interested primarily in the short-term liquidity of the company and its ability to make interest and principal payments. A secondary concern
of creditors is the firm's profitability; they want assurance that the business is
healthy. Management, like stockholders, is concerned with all aspects of the
firm's financial situation, and it attempts to produce financial ratios that will be
considered favorable by both owners and creditors. In addition, management
uses ratios to monitor the firm's performance from period to period.

Types of Ratio Comparisons

Ratio analysis is not merely the calculation of a given ratio. More important is
the *interpretation* of the ratio value. A meaningful basis for comparison is needed

BENCHMARK YOUR BUSINESS

Comparing company performance, as measured by financial ratios, to the performance of other firms in the same industry can identify problem spots. This benchmarking allows managers to determine where to make improvements in order to compete more effectively.

Benchmarking is growing quickly among small companies as it becomes easier to do....Huge amounts of data have become accessible, on software and through the Web, that allow owners to find out how rival companies are doing—and how they do it.

Benchmarking falls into two major categories. The first is a simple comparison of common financial measures....to the norms for a particular industry. But these ratios tell you only that something is wrong. Finding the problem and fixing it requires a second kind of benchmarking, a more qualitative but still systematic search to identify the best practices in your industry.

The financial snapshot is an important first step, though. The idea is to focus on key business ratios to see if you're way out of sync with similar companies. For example, if you're carrying more debt than most rivals, you might have trouble weathering a recession or price war. Other criteria to focus on include inventory turnover, return on investment, selling, general and administrative expenses as a percentage of revenue, and liquidity measures, such as current and

quick ratios, which tell you whether you have enough cash on hand to pay routine bills. "Often, businesses think their performance is pretty good and are shocked to see how they compare to others," says Samuel W. Bookhart, a benchmarking consultant in Chadds Ford, Pa....

Rountree Transport & Rigging Inc., a specialized long-distance trucking company based in Jacksonville, Fla....used Dun & Bradstreet's BusinesScope database to see how its accounts receivable and payable stacked up against its rivals. It discovered that its receivables went uncollected for an average of 48 days, versus an average 33 days for the industry....

The problem...was that Rountree drivers waited until they returned to the home terminal to turn in invoices. Now, invoices are turned in immediately....This simple change cut billing time in half, from 12 days to 6 days, and outstanding receivables dropped to 28.5 days, well below the industry average.

Source: Toddi Gutner, "Better Your Business: Benchmark It," Business Week Online/Frontier, *April 27, 1998, downloaded from* www.businessweek.com/smallbiz/news/columns/98-17/e3575051.htm.

to answer such questions as, "Is it too high or too low?" and "Is it good or bad?" Two types of ratio comparisons can be made: cross-sectional and time-series.

Cross-Sectional Analysis

cross-sectional analysis
Comparison of different firms' financial ratios at the same point in time; involves comparing the firm's ratios to those of other firms in its industry or to industry averages.

benchmarking
A type of *cross-sectional analysis* in which the firm's ratio values are compared to those of a key competitor or group of competitors that it wishes to emulate.

Cross-sectional analysis involves the comparison of different firms' financial ratios at the same point in time. Analysts are often interested in how well a firm has performed in relation to other firms in its industry. Frequently, a firm will compare its ratio values to those of a key competitor or group of competitors that it wishes to emulate. This type of cross-sectional analysis, called **benchmarking,** has become very popular.

Comparison to industry averages is also popular. These figures can be found in the *Almanac of Business and Industrial Financial Ratios, Dun & Bradstreet's Industry Norms and Key Business Ratios, Business Month, FTC Quarterly Reports, Robert Morris Associates Statement Studies,* and industry sources.

Many people mistakenly believe that as long as the firm being analyzed has a value "better than" the industry average, it can be viewed favorably. However, this "better than average" viewpoint can be misleading. Quite often a ratio value that is far better than the norm can indicate problems that, on more careful analysis, may be more severe than had the ratio been worse than the industry average. It is therefore important to investigate significant deviations *to either side* of the industry standard.

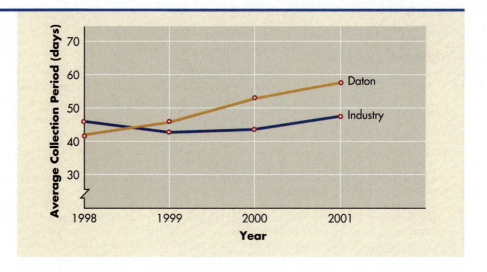

FIGURE 8.1

Combined Analysis
Combined cross-sectional and time-series view of Daton Company's average collection period, 1998–2001

Time-Series Analysis

time-series analysis
Evaluation of the firm's financial performance over time using financial ratio analysis.

Time-series analysis evaluates performance over time. Comparison of current to past performance, using ratios, allows analysts to assess the firm's progress. Developing trends can be seen by using multiyear comparisons. As in cross-sectional analysis, any significant year-to-year changes may be symptomatic of a major problem.

Combined Analysis

The most informative approach to ratio analysis is one that combines cross-sectional and time-series analyses. A combined view makes it possible to assess the trend in the behavior of the ratio in relation to the trend for the industry. Figure 8.1 depicts this type of approach using the average collection period ratio of Daton Company, over the years 1998–2001. This ratio reflects the average amount of time it takes the firm to collect bills, and lower values of this ratio generally are preferred. The figure quickly discloses that (1) Daton's effectiveness in collecting its receivables is poor in comparison to the industry, and (2) Daton's trend is toward longer collection periods. Clearly, Daton needs to shorten its collection period.

Cautions About Ratio Analysis

Before discussing specific ratios, we should consider the following cautions:

1. Ratios with large deviations from the norm only indicate *symptoms* of a problem. Additional analysis is typically needed to isolate the causes of the problem. The fundamental point is this: Ratio analysis merely directs attention to potential areas of concern; it does not provide conclusive evidence as to the existence of a problem.
2. A single ratio does not generally provide sufficient information from which to judge the *overall* performance of the firm. Only when a group of ratios is used can reasonable judgments be made. However, if an analysis is con-

cerned only with certain *specific* aspects of a firm's financial position, one or two ratios may be sufficient.

3. The ratios being compared should be calculated using financial statements dated at the same point in time during the year. If they are not, the effects of *seasonality* may produce erroneous conclusions and decisions. For example, comparison of the inventory turnover of a toy manufacturer at the end of June with its end-of-December value can be misleading. Clearly, the seasonal impact of the December holiday selling season would skew any comparison of the firm's inventory management.

4. It is preferable to use *audited financial statements* for ratio analysis. If the statements have not been audited, the data contained in them may not reflect the firm's true financial condition.

5. The financial data being compared should have been developed in the same way. The use of differing accounting treatments—especially relative to inventory and depreciation—can distort the results of ratio analysis, regardless of whether cross-sectional or time-series analysis is used.

6. Results can be distorted by *inflation,* which can cause the book values of inventory and depreciable assets to differ greatly from their true (replacement) values. Additionally, inventory costs and depreciation write-offs can differ from their true values, thereby distorting profits. Without adjustment, inflation tends to cause older firms (older assets) to appear more efficient and profitable than newer firms (newer assets). Clearly, care must be taken in using ratios to compare older to newer firms or a firm to itself over a long period of time.

Categories of Financial Ratios

Financial ratios can be divided for convenience into five basic categories: liquidity, activity, debt, profitability, and market ratios. Liquidity, activity, and debt ratios primarily measure risk. Profitability ratios measure return. Market ratios capture both return and risk.

As a rule, the inputs necessary to an effective financial analysis include, at a minimum, the income statement and the balance sheet. We will use the 2001 and 2000 income statements and balance sheets for Daton Company, presented earlier in Tables 8.1 and 8.2, to demonstrate ratio calculations. Note, however, that the ratios presented in the remainder of this chapter can be applied to almost any company. Of course, many companies in different industries use ratios that focus on aspects peculiar to their industry.

Review Questions

8–3   With regard to financial ratio analyses, how do the viewpoints held by the firm's present and prospective shareholders, creditors, and management differ?

8–4   What is the difference between cross-sectional and time-series ratio analysis?

8–5   Why is it preferable to compare ratios calculated using financial statements that are dated at the same point in time during the year?

Liquidity Ratios

liquidity
A firm's ability to satisfy its short-term obligations as they come due.

The **liquidity** of a firm is measured by its ability to satisfy its short-term obligations as they come due. Liquidity refers to the solvency of the firm's *overall* financial position—the ease with which it can pay its bills. Because a common precursor to financial distress and bankruptcy is low or declining liquidity, these ratios are viewed as good leading indicators of cash flow problems. The two basic measures of liquidity are the current ratio and the quick (acid-test) ratio.

Current Ratio

current ratio
A measure of liquidity calculated by dividing the firm's current assets by its current liabilities.

The **current ratio,** one of the most commonly cited financial ratios, measures the firm's ability to meet its short-term obligations. It is expressed as follows:

$$\text{Current ratio} = \frac{\text{Current assets}}{\text{Current liabilities}}$$

The current ratio for Daton Company in 2001 is

$$\frac{\$1,223,000}{\$620,000} = 1.97$$

A current ratio of 2.0 is occasionally cited as acceptable, but a value's acceptability depends on the industry in which the firm operates. For example, a current ratio of 1.0 would be considered acceptable for a public utility but might be unacceptable for a manufacturing firm. The more predictable a firm's cash flows, the lower the acceptable current ratio. Because Daton Company is in a business with a relatively predictable annual cash flow, its current ratio of 1.97 should be quite acceptable.

Quick (Acid-Test) Ratio

quick (acid-test) ratio
A measure of liquidity calculated by dividing the firm's current assets minus inventory by current liabilities.

The **quick (acid-test) ratio** is similar to the current ratio except that it excludes inventory, which is generally the least liquid current asset. The quick ratio is calculated as follows:

$$\text{Quick ratio} = \frac{\text{Current assets} - \text{Inventory}}{\text{Current liabilities}}$$

The quick ratio for Daton Company in 2001 is

$$\frac{\$1,223,000 - \$289,000}{\$620,000} = \frac{\$934,000}{\$620,000} = 1.51$$

A quick ratio of 1.0 or greater is occasionally recommended, but as with the current ratio, what value is acceptable depends largely on the industry. The quick ratio provides a better measure of overall liquidity only when a firm's inventory cannot be easily converted into cash. If inventory is liquid, the current ratio is a preferred measure of overall liquidity.

? Review Question

8–6   Under what circumstances would the current ratio be the preferred measure of overall firm liquidity? Under what circumstances would the quick ratio be preferred?

LG3 Activity Ratios

activity ratios
Measure the speed with which various accounts are converted into sales or cash—inflows or outflows.

Activity ratios measure the speed with which various accounts are converted into sales or cash—inflows or outflows. With regard to current accounts, measures of liquidity are generally inadequate because differences in the *composition* of a firm's current assets and current liabilities can significantly affect its "true" liquidity. It is therefore important to look beyond measures of overall liquidity and to assess the activity (liquidity) of specific current accounts. A number of ratios are available for measuring the activity of the most important current accounts, which include inventory, accounts receivable, and accounts payable. The efficiency with which total assets are used can also be assessed.

Inventory Turnover

inventory turnover
Measures the activity, or liquidity, of a firm's inventory.

Inventory turnover commonly measures the activity, or liquidity, of a firm's inventory. It is calculated as follows:

$$\text{Inventory turnover} = \frac{\text{Cost of goods sold}}{\text{Inventory}}$$

Applying this relationship to Daton Company in 2001 yields

$$\text{Inventory turnover} = \frac{\$2,088,000}{\$289,000} = 7.2$$

The resulting turnover is meaningful only when it is compared with that of other firms in the same industry or to the firm's past inventory turnover. An inventory turnover of 20.0 would not be unusual for a grocery store, whereas a common inventory turnover for an aircraft manufacturer would be 4.0.

average age of inventory
Average number of days' sales in inventory.

Inventory turnover can be easily converted into an **average age of inventory** by dividing it into 360—the assumed number of days in a year. For Daton Company, the average age of inventory in 2001 is 50.0 days ($360 \div 7.2$). This value can also be viewed as the average number of days' sales in inventory.

Average Collection Period

average collection period
The average amount of time needed to collect accounts receivable.

The **average collection period,** or average age of accounts receivable, is useful in evaluating credit and collection policies. It is arrived at by dividing the average daily sales into the accounts receivable balance:

$$\text{Average collection period} = \frac{\text{Accounts receivable}}{\text{Average sales per day}}$$

$$= \frac{\text{Accounts receivable}}{\dfrac{\text{Annual sales}}{360}}$$

The average collection period for Daton Company in 2001 is

$$\frac{\$503,000}{\dfrac{\$3,074,000}{360}} = \frac{\$503,000}{\$8,539} = 58.9 \text{ days}$$

On the average, it takes the firm 58.9 days to collect an account receivable.

The average collection period is meaningful only in relation to the firm's credit terms. If Daton Company extends 30-day credit terms to customers, an average collection period of 58.9 days may indicate a poorly managed credit or collection department, or both. It is also possible that the lengthened collection period resulted from an intentional relaxation of credit-term enforcement in response to competitive pressures. If the firm had extended 60-day credit terms, the 58.9-day average collection period would be quite acceptable. Clearly, additional information is needed to evaluate the effectiveness of the firm's credit and collection policies.

Average Payment Period

average payment period
The average amount of time needed to pay accounts payable.

The **average payment period,** or average age of accounts payable, is calculated in the same manner as the average collection period:

$$\text{Average payment period} = \frac{\text{Accounts payable}}{\text{Average purchases per day}}$$

$$= \frac{\text{Accounts payable}}{\dfrac{\text{Annual purchases}}{360}}$$

The difficulty in calculating this ratio stems from the need to find annual purchases, a value not available in published financial statements. Ordinarily, purchases are estimated as a given percentage of cost of goods sold. If we assume that Daton Company's purchases equaled 70 percent of its cost of goods sold in 2001, its average payment period is

$$\frac{\$382,000}{\dfrac{0.70 \times \$2,088,000}{360}} = \frac{\$382,000}{\$4,060} = 94.1 \text{ days}$$

This figure is meaningful only in relation to the average credit terms extended to the firm. If Daton Company's suppliers have extended, on average, 30-day credit terms, an analyst would give Daton a low credit rating. Prospective lenders and suppliers of trade credit are most interested in the average payment period because it provides insight into the firm's bill-paying patterns.

Total Asset Turnover

total asset turnover
Indicates the efficiency with which the firm uses its assets to generate sales.

The **total asset turnover** indicates the efficiency with which the firm uses its assets to generate sales. Total asset turnover is calculated as follows:

$$\text{Total asset turnover} = \frac{\text{Sales}}{\text{Total assets}}$$

The value of Daton Company's total asset turnover in 2001 is

$$\frac{\$3,074,000}{\$3,597,000} = 0.85$$

This means the company turns over its assets 0.85 times a year.

Generally, the higher a firm's total asset turnover, the more efficiently its assets have been used. This measure is probably of greatest interest to management, because it indicates whether the firm's operations have been financially efficient.

? Review Question

8–7   To assess the firm's average collection period ratio, what additional information is needed, and why?

Debt Ratios

The *debt position* of a firm indicates the amount of other people's money being used to generate profits. In general, the financial analyst is most concerned with long-term debts, because these commit the firm to a stream of payments over the long run. Because creditors' claims must be satisfied before the earnings can be distributed to shareholders, present and prospective shareholders pay close attention to the firm's ability to repay debts. Lenders are also concerned about the degree of indebtedness. Management obviously must be concerned with indebtedness.

financial leverage
The magnification of return and risk introduced through the use of fixed-cost financing, such as debt and preferred stock.

In general, the more debt a firm uses in relation to its total assets, the greater its *financial leverage*. **Financial leverage** is the magnification of return and risk introduced through the use of fixed-cost financing, such as debt and preferred stock. The more fixed-cost debt a firm uses, the greater will be its expected return and risk.

Example ▼

Patty Akers is in the process of incorporating her new business. After much analysis she determined that an initial investment of $50,000—$20,000 in current assets and $30,000 in fixed assets—is necessary. These funds can be obtained in either of two ways. The first is the *no-debt plan,* under which she would invest the full $50,000 without borrowing. The other alternative, the *debt plan,* involves investing $25,000 and borrowing the balance of $25,000 at 12% annual interest.

Regardless of which alternative she chooses, Patty expects sales to average $30,000, costs and operating expenses to average $18,000, and earnings to be taxed at a 40% rate. Projected balance sheets and income statements associated with the two plans are summarized in Table 8.5. The no-debt plan results in after-

| TABLE 8.5 | Financial Statements Associated with Patty's Alternatives |

Balance Sheets	No-debt plan	Debt plan
Current assets	$20,000	$20,000
Fixed assets	30,000	30,000
Total assets	$50,000	$50,000
Debt (12% interest)	$ 0	$25,000
(1) Equity	50,000	25,000
Total liabilities and equity	$50,000	$50,000

Income Statements		
Sales	$30,000	$30,000
Less: Costs and operating expenses	18,000	18,000
Operating profits	$12,000	$12,000
Less: Interest expense	0 $.12 \times \$25,000 =$	3,000
Net profit before taxes	$12,000	$ 9,000
Less: Taxes (rate = 40%)	4,800	3,600
(2) Net profit after taxes	$ 7,200	$ 5,400
Return on equity [(2) ÷ (1)]	$\dfrac{\$7,200}{\$50,000} = 14.4\%$	$\dfrac{\$5,400}{\$25,000} = 21.6\%$

tax profits of $7,200, which represent a 14.4% rate of return on Patty's $50,000 investment. The debt plan results in $5,400 of after-tax profits, which represent a 21.6% rate of return on Patty's investment of $25,000. The debt plan provides Patty with a higher rate of return, but the risk of this plan is also greater, because the annual $3,000 of interest must be paid before receipt of earnings.

The example demonstrates that *with increased debt comes higher potential return as well as greater risk.* Therefore, the greater the financial leverage, the greater the potential return and risk. A detailed discussion of the impact of debt on the firm's return, risk, and value is included in Chapter 13. Here, we emphasize the use of financial debt ratios to assess externally a firm's debt position.

There are two general types of debt measures: measures of the degree of indebtedness and measures of the ability to service debts. The **degree of indebtedness** measures the amount of debt relative to other significant balance sheet amounts. A popular measure of the degree of indebtedness is the debt ratio.

The second type of debt measure, the **ability to service debts,** reflects a firm's ability to make the payments required on a scheduled basis over the life of a debt. The firm's ability to pay certain fixed charges is measured using **coverage ratios.** Typically, higher coverage ratios are preferred, but too high a ratio (above industry norms) may result in unnecessarily low return and risk. In general, the lower the firm's coverage ratios, the less certain it is to be able to pay fixed obligations. If a firm is unable to pay these obligations, its creditors may seek immediate repayment, which in most instances would force a firm into bankruptcy. Two popular coverage ratios are the times interest earned ratio and the fixed-payment coverage ratio.

degree of indebtedness
Measures the amount of debt relative to other significant balance sheet amounts.

ability to service debts
The ability of a firm to make the payments required on a scheduled basis over the life of a debt.

coverage ratios
Ratios that measure the firm's ability to pay certain fixed charges.

Debt Ratio

debt ratio
Measures the proportion of total assets financed by the firm's creditors.

The **debt ratio** measures the proportion of total assets financed by the firm's creditors. The higher this ratio, the greater the amount of other people's money being used to generate profits. The ratio is calculated as follows:

$$\text{Debt ratio} = \frac{\text{Total liabilities}}{\text{Total assets}}$$

The debt ratio for Daton Company in 2001 is

$$\frac{\$1,643,000}{\$3,597,000} = 0.457 = 45.7\%$$

This value indicates that the company has financed close to half of its assets with debt. The higher this ratio, the greater the firm's degree of indebtedness and the more financial leverage it has.

Times Interest Earned Ratio

times interest earned ratio
Measures the firm's ability to make contractual interest payments.

The **times interest earned ratio** measures the firm's ability to make contractual interest payments. The higher its value, the better able the firm is to fulfill its interest obligations. The times interest earned ratio is calculated as follows:

$$\text{Times interest earned ratio} = \frac{\text{Earnings before interest and taxes}}{\text{Interest}}$$

The figure for *earnings before interest and taxes* is the same as that for *operating profits* shown in the income statement. Applying this ratio to Daton Company yields the following 2001 value:

$$\text{Times interest earned ratio} = \frac{\$418,000}{\$93,000} = 4.5$$

The times interest earned ratio for Daton Company seems acceptable. A value of at least 3.0—and preferably closer to 5.0—is often suggested. The firm's earnings before interest and taxes could shrink by as much as 78 percent $[(4.5 - 1.0) \div 4.5]$, and the firm would still be able to pay the $93,000 in interest it owes. Thus it has a good margin of safety.

Fixed-Payment Coverage Ratio

fixed-payment coverage ratio
Measures the firm's ability to meet all fixed-payment obligations.

The **fixed-payment coverage ratio** measures the firm's ability to meet all fixed-payment obligations, such as loan interest and principal, lease payments, and preferred stock dividends. As is true of the times interest earned ratio, the higher this value, the better. The formula for the fixed-payment coverage ratio is

$$\begin{array}{l}\text{Fixed-payment} \\ \text{coverage} \\ \text{ratio}\end{array} = \frac{\text{Earnings before interest and taxes + Lease payments}}{\text{Interest + Lease payments + \{(Principal payments + Preferred stock dividends)} \times [1/(1 - T)]\}}$$

where T is the corporate tax rate applicable to the firm's income. The term $1/(1 - T)$ is included to adjust the after-tax principal and preferred stock dividend payments back to a before-tax equivalent that is consistent with the before-tax values of all other terms. Applying the formula to Daton Company's 2001 data yields

$$\text{Fixed-payment coverage ratio} = \frac{\$418,000 + \$35,000}{\$93,000 + \$35,000 + \{(\$71,000 + \$10,000) \times [1/(1 - 0.29)]\}}$$

$$= \frac{\$453,000}{\$242,000} = 1.9$$

Because the earnings available are nearly twice as large as its fixed-payment obligations, the firm appears safely able to meet the latter.

Like the times interest earned ratio, the fixed-payment coverage ratio measures risk. The lower the ratio, the greater the risk to both lenders and owners; the greater the ratio, the lower the risk. This ratio allows interested parties to assess the firm's ability to meet additional fixed-payment obligations without being driven into bankruptcy.

? Review Questions

8–8   What is *financial leverage?*
8–9   What ratio measures the firm's degree of indebtedness? What ratios assess the firm's ability to service debts?

LG5 Profitability Ratios

There are many measures of profitability. As a group, these measures allow the analyst to evaluate the firm's profits with respect to a given level of sales, a certain level of assets, or the owners' investment. Without profits, a firm could not attract outside capital. Owners, creditors, and management pay close attention to boosting profits because of the great importance placed on earnings in the marketplace.

Common-Size Income Statements

common-size income statement
An income statement in which each item is expressed as a percentage of sales.

A popular tool for evaluating profitability in relation to sales is the **common-size income statement.** Each item on this statement is expressed as a percentage of sales. Common-size income statements are especially useful in comparing performance across years. Three frequently cited ratios of profitability that can be read directly from the common-size income statement are (1) the gross profit margin, (2) the operating profit margin, and (3) the net profit margin.

Common-size income statements for 2001 and 2000 for Daton Company are presented and evaluated in Table 8.6. These statements reveal that the firm's cost of goods sold increased from 66.7 percent of sales in 2000 to 67.9 percent in 2001, resulting in a worsening gross profit margin. However, thanks to a decrease in total operating expenses, the firm's net profit margin rose from 5.4 percent of sales in 2000 to 7.2 percent in 2001. The decrease in expenses more than compensated for the increase in the cost of goods sold. A decrease in the firm's 2001 interest expense (3.0 percent of sales versus 3.5 percent in 2000) added to the increase in 2001 profits.

Gross Profit Margin

gross profit margin
Measures the percentage of each sales dollar remaining after the firm has paid for its goods.

The **gross profit margin** measures the percentage of each sales dollar remaining after the firm has paid for its goods. The higher the gross profit margin, the better (that is, the lower the relative cost of merchandise sold). The gross profit margin is calculated as follows:

$$\text{Gross profit margin} = \frac{\text{Sales} - \text{Cost of goods sold}}{\text{Sales}} = \frac{\text{Gross profits}}{\text{Sales}}$$

Daton Company's gross profit margin for 2001 is

$$\frac{\$3,074,000 - \$2,088,000}{\$3,074,000} = \frac{\$986,00}{\$3,074,000} = 32.1\%$$

This value is labeled (1) on the common-size income statement in Table 8.6.

TABLE 8.6	Daton Company Common-Size Income Statements		
	For the years ended December 31		Evaluation[a]
	2001	2000	2000–2001
Sales revenue	100.0%	100.0%	same
Less: Cost of goods sold	67.9	66.7	worse
(1) Gross profit margin	32.1%	33.3%	worse
Less: Operating expenses			
Selling expense	3.3%	4.2%	better
General and administrative expenses	6.8	6.7	better
Lease expense	1.1	1.3	better
Depreciation expense	7.3	9.3	better
Total operating expense	18.5%	21.5%	better
(2) Operating profit margin	13.6%	11.8%	better
Less: Interest expense	3.0	3.5	better
Net profits before taxes	10.6%	8.3%	better
Less: Taxes	3.1	2.5	worse[b]
Net profits after taxes	7.5%	5.8%	better
Less: Preferred stock dividends	.3	.4	better
(3) Net profit margin	7.2%	5.4%	better

[a]Subjective assessments based on data provided.
[b]Taxes as a percent of sales increased noticeably between 2000 and 2001 due to differing costs and expenses, whereas the average tax rates (taxes ÷ net profits before taxes) for 2000 and 2001 remained about the same—30% and 29%, respectively.

Operating Profit Margin

operating profit margin
Measures the percentage of each sales dollar remaining after all costs and expenses *other than* interest, taxes, and preferred stock dividends are deducted; the "pure profits" earned on each sales dollar.

The **operating profit margin** measures the percentage of each sales dollar remaining after all costs and expenses *other than* interest, taxes, and preferred stock dividends are deducted. It represents the "pure profits" earned on each sales dollar. Operating profits are "pure" because they measure only the profits earned on operations and ignore interest, taxes, and preferred stock dividends. A high operating profit margin is preferred. The operating profit margin is calculated as follows:

$$\text{Operating profit margin} = \frac{\text{Operating profits}}{\text{Sales}}$$

Daton Company's operating profit margin for 2001 is

$$\frac{\$418,000}{\$3,074,000} = 13.6\%$$

This value is labeled (2) on the common-size income statement in Table 8.6.

Net Profit Margin

net profit margin
Measures the percentage of each sales dollar remaining after all costs and expenses, *including* interest, taxes, and preferred stock dividends, have been deducted.

The **net profit margin** measures the percentage of each sales dollar remaining after all costs and expenses, *including* interest, taxes, and preferred stock dividends, have been deducted. The higher the firm's net profit margin, the better. The net profit margin is calculated as follows:

$$\text{Net profit margin} = \frac{\text{Earnings available for common stockholders}}{\text{Sales}}$$

Daton Company's net profit margin for 2001 is

$$\frac{\$221,000}{\$3,074,000} = 7.2\%$$

This value is labeled (3) on the common-size income statement in Table 8.6.

The net profit margin is a commonly cited measure of the firm's success with respect to earnings on sales. "Good" net profit margins differ considerably across industries. A net profit margin of 1 percent or less would not be unusual for a grocery store, whereas a net profit margin of 10 percent would be low for a retail jewelry store.

Earnings per Share (EPS)

The firm's *earnings per share (EPS)* is generally of interest to present or prospective stockholders and management. As we noted earlier, EPS represents the number of dollars earned during the period on behalf of each outstanding share of common stock. Earnings per share is calculated as follows:

$$\text{Earnings per share} = \frac{\text{Earnings available for common stockholders}}{\text{Number of shares of common stock outstanding}}$$

Daton Company's earnings per share in 2001 is

$$\frac{\$221,000}{76,262} = \$2.90$$

This figure represents the dollar amount earned on behalf of each share. The dollar amount of cash *actually distributed* to each shareholder is the *dividend per share (DPS)*, which, as noted in Daton Company's income statement (Table 8.1), rose to $1.29 in 2001 from $0.75 in 2000. EPS is closely watched by the investing public and is considered an important indicator of corporate success.

Return on Total Assets (ROA)

return on total assets (ROA)
Measures the overall effectiveness of management in generating profits with its available assets; also called the *return on investment (ROI)*.

The **return on total assets (ROA)**, often called the *return on investment (ROI)*, measures the overall effectiveness of management in generating profits with its available assets. The higher the firm's return on total assets, the better. The return on total assets is calculated as follows:

$$\text{Return on total assets} = \frac{\text{Earnings available for common stockholders}}{\text{Total assets}}$$

Daton Company's return on total assets in 2001 is

$$\frac{\$221,000}{\$3,597,000} = 6.1\%$$

This value indicates that the firm earned 6.1 cents on each dollar of asset investment.

Return on Common Equity (ROE)

return on common equity (ROE)
Measures the return earned on the common stockholders' investment in the firm.

The **return on common equity (ROE)** measures the return earned on the common stockholders' investment in the firm. Generally, the higher this return, the better off are the owners. Return on common equity is calculated as follows:

$$\text{Return on common equity} = \frac{\text{Earnings available for common stockholders}}{\text{Common stock equity}}$$

This ratio for Daton Company in 2001 is

$$\frac{\$221,00}{\$1,754,000} = 12.6\%$$

Note that the value for common stock equity ($1,754,000) was found by subtracting the $200,000 of preferred stock equity from the total stockholders' equity of $1,954,000 (see Daton Company's 2001 balance sheet in Table 8.2). The calculated ROE of 12.6 percent indicates that during 2001 Daton earned 12.6 cents on each dollar of common stock equity.

? Review Questions

8–10 What three ratios of profitability are found on a common-size income statement?

8–11   What would explain a firm's having a high gross profit margin and a low net profit margin?

8–12   Which measure of profitability is probably of greatest interest to the investing public? Why?

 ## Market Ratios

market ratios
Relate a firm's market value, as measured by its current share price, to certain accounting values.

Market ratios relate the firm's market value, as measured by its current share price, to certain accounting values. These ratios give insight into how well investors in the marketplace feel the firm is doing in terms of return and risk. They tend to reflect, on a relative basis, the common stockholders' assessment of all aspects of the firm's past and expected future performance. Here we consider two popular market ratios, one that focuses on earnings and another that considers book value.

Price/Earnings (P/E) Ratio

price/earnings (P/E) ratio
Measures the amount that investors are willing to pay for each dollar of a firm's earnings; the higher the P/E ratio, the greater is investor confidence.

The **price/earnings (P/E) ratio** is commonly used to assess the owners' appraisal of share value. The P/E ratio measures the amount that investors are willing to pay for each dollar of a firm's earnings. The level of the price/earnings ratio indicates the degree of confidence that investors have in the firm's future performance. The higher the P/E ratio, the greater is investor confidence. The P/E ratio is calculated as follows:

$$\text{Price/earnings (P/E) ratio} = \frac{\text{Market price per share of common stock}}{\text{Earnings per share}}$$

If Daton Company's common stock at the end of 2001 was selling at 32 1/4 (that is, $32.25), using the EPS of $2.90, the P/E ratio at year-end 2001 is

$$\frac{\$32.25}{\$2.90} = 11.1$$

This figure indicates that investors were paying $11.10 for each $1.00 of earnings. The P/E ratio is most informative when applied in cross-sectional analysis using an industry average P/E ratio or the P/E ratio of a benchmark firm.

Market/Book (M/B) Ratio

market/book (M/B) ratio
Provides an assessment of how investors view the firm's performance. Firms expected to earn high returns relative to their risk typically sell at higher M/B multiples.

The **market/book (M/B) ratio** provides an assessment of how investors view the firm's performance. It relates the market value of the firm's shares to their book—strict accounting—value. To calculate the firm's M/B ratio, we first need to find the book value per share of common stock:

$$\text{Book value per share of common stock} = \frac{\text{Common stock equity}}{\text{Number of shares of common stock outstanding}}$$

Substituting the appropriate values for Daton Company from its 2001 balance sheet, we get

$$\text{Book value per share of common stock} = \frac{\$1,754,000}{76,262} = \$23.00$$

The formula for the market/book ratio is

$$\text{Market/book (M/B) ratio} = \frac{\text{Market price per share of common stock}}{\text{Book value per share of common stock}}$$

Substituting Daton Company's end of 2001 common stock price of $32.25 and its $23.00 book value per share of common stock (calculated above) into the M/B ratio formula, we get

$$\text{Market/book (M/B) ratio} = \frac{\$32.25}{\$23.00} = 1.40$$

This M/B ratio means that investors are currently paying $1.40 for each $1.00 of book value of Daton Company's stock.

The stocks of firms that are expected to perform well—improve profits, increase their market share, or launch successful products—typically sell at higher M/B ratios than firms with less attractive outlooks. Simply stated, firms expected to earn high returns relative to their risk typically sell at higher M/B multiples. Clearly, Daton's future prospects are being viewed favorably by investors, who are willing to pay more than its book value for the firm's shares. Like P/E ratios, M/B ratios are typically assessed cross-sectionally, to get a feel for the firm's return and risk compared to peer firms.

? Review Question

8–13   How do the price/earnings (P/E) ratio and the market/book (M/B) ratio provide a feel for the firm's return and risk?

LG6 A Complete Ratio Analysis

Analysts frequently wish to take an overall look at the firm's financial performance and status. Here we consider two popular approaches to a complete ratio analysis: (1) summarizing all ratios and (2) the DuPont system of analysis. The summary analysis approach tends to view *all aspects* of the firm's financial activities to isolate key areas of responsibility. The DuPont system acts as a search technique aimed at finding the *key areas* responsible for the firm's financial condition.

Summarizing All Ratios

We can use Daton Company's ratios to perform a complete ratio analysis using both cross-sectional and time-series analysis approaches. The 2001 ratio values calculated earlier and the ratio values calculated for 1999 and 2000 for Daton Company, along with the industry average ratios for 2001, are summarized in Table 8.7, which also shows the formula used to calculate each ratio. Using these data, we can discuss the five key aspects of Daton's performance—liquidity, activity, debt, profitability, and market.

TABLE 8.7   Summary of Daton Company Ratios (1999–2001, Including 2001 Industry Averages)

Ratio	Formula	Year			Industry average 2001[c]	Evaluation[d]		
		1999[a]	2000[b]	2001[b]		Cross-sectional 2001	Time-series 1999–2001	Overall
Liquidity								
Current ratio	$\dfrac{\text{Current assets}}{\text{Current liabilities}}$	2.04	2.08	1.97	2.05	OK	OK	OK
Quick (acid-test) ratio	$\dfrac{\text{Current assets} - \text{Inventory}}{\text{Current liabilities}}$	1.32	1.46	1.51	1.43	OK	good	good
Activity								
Inventory turnover	$\dfrac{\text{Cost of goods sold}}{\text{Inventory}}$	5.1	5.7	7.2	6.6	good	good	good
Average collection period	$\dfrac{\text{Accounts receivable}}{\text{Average sales per day}}$	43.9 days	51.2 days	58.9 days	44.3 days	poor	poor	poor
Average payment period	$\dfrac{\text{Accounts payable}}{\text{Average purchases per day}}$	75.8 days	81.2 days	94.1 days	66.5 days	poor	poor	poor
Total asset turnover	$\dfrac{\text{Sales}}{\text{Total assets}}$	0.94	0.79	0.85	0.75	OK	OK	OK
Debt								
Debt ratio	$\dfrac{\text{Total liabilities}}{\text{Total assets}}$	36.8%	44.3%	45.7%	40.0%	OK	OK	OK
Times interest earned ratio	$\dfrac{\text{Earnings before interest and taxes}}{\text{Interest}}$	5.6	3.3	4.5	4.3	good	OK	OK
Fixed-payment coverage ratio	$\dfrac{\text{Earnings before interest and taxes} + \text{Lease payments}}{\text{Int.} + \text{Lease pay.} + \{(\text{Prin.} + \text{Pref. div.}) \times [1/(1-T)]\}}$	2.4	1.4	1.9	1.5	good	OK	good

Ratio	Formula	Year 1999[a]	Year 2000[b]	Year 2001[b]	Industry average 2001[c]	Evaluation[d] Cross-sectional 2001	Evaluation[d] Time-series 1999–2001	Evaluation[d] Overall
Profitability								
Gross profit margin	$\dfrac{\text{Gross profits}}{\text{Sales}}$	31.4%	33.3%	32.1%	30.0%	OK	OK	OK
Operating profit margin	$\dfrac{\text{Operating profits}}{\text{Sales}}$	14.6%	11.8%	13.6%	11.0%	good	OK	good
Net profit margin	$\dfrac{\text{Earnings available for common stockholders}}{\text{Sales}}$	8.2%	5.4%	7.2%	6.2%	good	OK	good
Earnings per share (EPS)	$\dfrac{\text{Earnings available for common stockholders}}{\text{Number of shares of common stock outstanding}}$	$3.26	$1.81	$2.90	$2.26	good	OK	good
Return on total assets (ROA)	$\dfrac{\text{Earnings available for common stockholders}}{\text{Total assets}}$	7.8%	4.2%	6.1%	4.6%	good	OK	good
Return on common equity (ROE)	$\dfrac{\text{Earnings available for common stockholders}}{\text{Common stock equity}}$	13.7%	8.5%	12.6%	8.5%	good	OK	good
Market								
Price/earnings (P/E) ratio	$\dfrac{\text{Market price per share of common stock}}{\text{Earnings per share}}$	10.5	10.0[e]	11.1	12.5	OK	OK	OK
Market/book (M/B) ratio	$\dfrac{\text{Market price per share of common stock}}{\text{Book value per share of common stock}}$	1.25	0.85[e]	1.40	1.30	OK	OK	OK

[a]Calculated from data not included in the chapter.
[b]Calculated by using the financial statements presented in Tables 8.1 and 8.2.
[c]Obtained from sources not included in this chapter.
[d]Subjective assessments based on data provided.
[e]The market price per share at the end of 2000 was $18.06.

Liquidity

The overall liquidity of the firm seems to exhibit a reasonably stable trend, having been maintained at a level that is relatively consistent with the industry average in 2001. The firm's liquidity seems to be good.

Activity

Daton Company's inventory appears to be in good shape. Its inventory management seems to have improved, and in 2001 it performed at a level above that of the industry. The firm may be experiencing some problems with accounts receivable. The average collection period seems to have crept up above that of the industry. Daton also appears to be slow in paying its bills; it pays nearly 30 days slower than the industry average. This could adversely affect the firm's credit standing. Although overall liquidity appears to be good, the management of receivables and payables should be examined. Daton's total asset turnover reflects a decline in the efficiency of total asset utilization between 1999 and 2000. Although in 2001 it rose to a level considerably above the industry average, it appears that the pre-2000 level of efficiency has not yet been achieved.

Debt

Daton Company's indebtedness increased over the 1999–2001 period and is currently above the industry average. Although this increase in the debt ratio could be cause for alarm, the firm's ability to meet interest and fixed-payment obligations improved from 2000 to 2001 to a level that outperforms the industry. The firm's increased indebtedness in 2000 apparently caused a deterioration in its ability to pay debt adequately. However, Daton has evidently improved its income in 2001 so that it is able to meet its interest and fixed-payment obligations consistent with the average in the industry. In summary, it appears that although 2000 was an off year, the company's ability to pay debts in 2001 compensates for its increased degree of indebtedness.

Profitability

Daton's profitability relative to sales in 2001 was better than the average company in the industry, although it did not match the firm's 1999 performance. Although the gross profit margin in 2000 and 2001 was better than in 1999, higher levels of operating and interest expenses in 2000 and 2001 appear to have caused the 2001 net profit margin to fall below that of 1999. However, Daton Company's 2001 net profit margin is quite favorable when compared to the industry average.

The firm's earnings per share, return on total assets, and return on common equity behaved much as its net profit margin did over the 1999–2001 period. Daton appears to have experienced either a sizable drop in sales between 1999 and 2000 or a rapid expansion in assets during that period. The exceptionally high 2001 level of return on common equity suggests that the firm is performing quite well. The firm's above-average returns—net profit margin, EPS, ROA, and ROE—may be attributable to the fact that it is more risky than average. A look at market ratios is helpful in assessing risk.

Market

Investors have greater confidence in the firm in 2001 than in the prior two years, as reflected in the price/earnings (P/E) ratio of 11.1. However, this ratio is below the industry average. The P/E ratio suggests that the firm's risk has declined but remains above that of the average firm in its industry. The firm's market/book (M/B) ratio has increased over the 1999–2001 period, and in 2001 it exceeds the industry average. This implies that investors are optimistic about the firm's future performance. The P/E and M/B ratios reflect the firm's increased profitability over the 1999–2001 period: Investors expect to earn high future returns as compensation for the firm's above-average risk.

In summary, the firm appears to be growing and has recently undergone an expansion in assets, financed primarily through the use of debt. The 2000–2001 period seems to reflect a phase of adjustment and recovery from the rapid growth in assets. Daton's sales, profits, and other performance factors seem to be growing with the increase in the size of the operation. In addition, the market response to these accomplishments appears to have been positive. In short, the firm appears to have done well in 2001.

DuPont System of Analysis

DuPont system of analysis
System used to dissect the firm's financial statements and to assess its financial condition.

The **DuPont system of analysis** is used to dissect the firm's financial statements and to assess its financial condition. It merges the income statement and balance sheet into two summary measures of profitability: return on total assets (ROA) and return on common equity (ROE). Figure 8.2 depicts the basic DuPont system with Daton Company's 2001 monetary and ratio values. The upper portion of the chart summarizes the income statement activities; the lower portion summarizes the balance sheet activities.

The DuPont system first brings together the *net profit margin,* which measures the firm's profitability on sales, with its *total asset turnover,* which indicates how efficiently the firm has used its assets to generate sales. In the **DuPont formula,** the product of these two ratios results in the *return on total assets (ROA)*:

DuPont formula
Multiplies the firm's *net profit margin* by its *total asset turnover* to calculate the firm's *return on total assets (ROA).*

$$\text{ROA} = \text{Net profit margin} \times \text{Total asset turnover}$$

Substituting the appropriate formulas into the equation and simplifying results in the formula given earlier,

$$\text{ROA} = \frac{\text{Earnings available for common stockholders}}{\text{Sales}} \times \frac{\text{Sales}}{\text{Total assets}} = \frac{\text{Earnings available for common stockholders}}{\text{Total assets}}$$

When the 2001 values of the net profit margin and total asset turnover for Daton Company, calculated earlier, are substituted into the DuPont formula, the result is

$$\text{ROA} = 7.2\% \times 0.85 = 6.1\%$$

This value is the same as that calculated directly in an earlier section (page 231). The DuPont formula allows the firm to break down its return into profit-on-sales and efficiency-of-asset-use components. Typically, a firm with a low net profit margin has a high total asset turnover, which results in a reasonably good return on total assets. Often, the opposite situation exists.

FIGURE 8.2   DuPont System of Analysis

The DuPont system of analysis with application to Daton Company (2001)

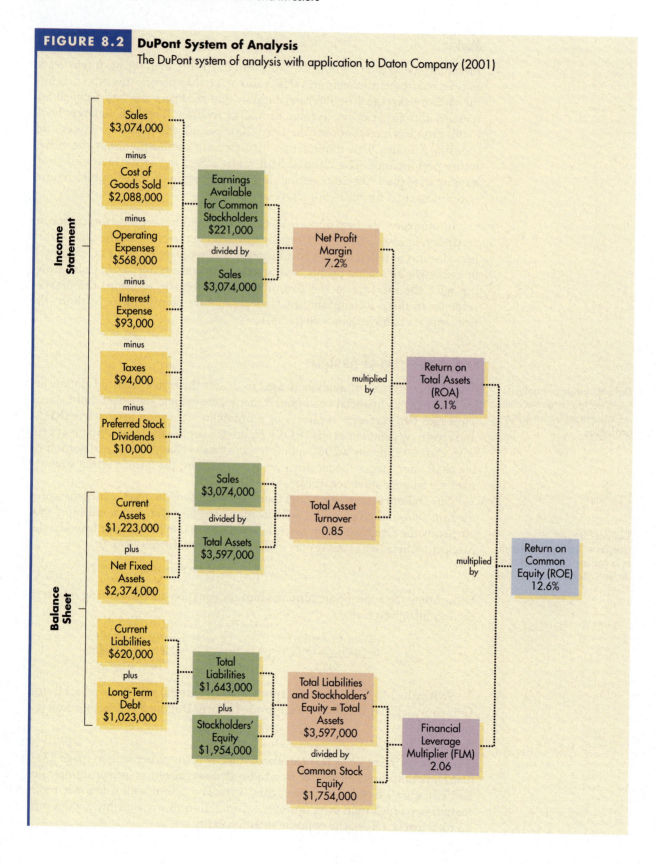

modified DuPont formula
Relates the firm's *return on total assets (ROA)* to its *return on common equity (ROE)* using the *financial leverage multiplier (FLM)*.

financial leverage multiplier (FLM)
The ratio of the firm's total assets to its common stock equity.

The second step in the DuPont system employs the **modified DuPont formula.** This formula relates the firm's return on total assets (ROA) to its return on common equity (ROE). The latter is calculated by multiplying the return on total assets (ROA) by the **financial leverage multiplier (FLM),** which is the ratio of total assets to common stock equity:

$$ROE = ROA \times FLM$$

Substituting the appropriate formulas into the equation and simplifying results in the formula given earlier,

$$ROE = \frac{\text{Earnings available for common stockholders}}{\text{Total assets}} \times \frac{\text{Total assets}}{\text{Common stock equity}} = \frac{\text{Earnings available for common stockholders}}{\text{Common stock equity}}$$

Use of the financial leverage multiplier (FLM) to convert the ROA into the ROE reflects the impact of financial leverage on owners' return. Substituting the values for Daton Company's ROA of 6.1 percent, calculated earlier, and Daton's FLM of 2.06 ($3,597,000 total assets ÷ $1,754,000 common stock equity) into the modified DuPont formula yields

$$ROE = 6.1\% \times 2.06 = 12.6\%$$

The 12.6 percent ROE calculated by using the modified DuPont formula is the same as that calculated directly (page 231).

The advantage of the DuPont system is that it allows the firm to break its return on equity into a profit-on-sales component (net profit margin), an efficiency-of-asset-use component (total asset turnover), and a use-of-financial-leverage component (financial leverage multiplier). The total return to owners therefore can be analyzed in these important dimensions.

The use of the DuPont system of analysis as a diagnostic tool is best explained using Figure 8.1. Beginning with the rightmost value—the ROE—the financial analyst moves to the left, dissecting and analyzing the inputs to the formula in order to isolate the probable cause of the resulting above-average (or below-average) value. For the sake of discussion, let's assume that Daton's ROE of 12.6% is actually below the industry average. Moving to the left, we would examine the inputs to the ROE—the ROA and the FLM—relative to the industry averages. Let's assume that the FLM is in line with the industry average, but the ROA is below the industry average. Moving farther to the left, we examine the two inputs to the ROA—the net profit margin and total asset turnover. Assume that the net profit margin is in line with the industry average, but the total asset turnover is below the industry average. Moving still farther to the left, we find that whereas the firm's sales are consistent with the industry value Daton's total assets have grown significantly during the past year. Looking farther to the left, we would review the firm's activity ratios for current assets. Let's say that whereas the firm's inventory turnover is in line with the industry average, its average collection period is well above the industry average.

Clearly, we can trace the possible problem back to its cause: Daton's low ROE is primarily the consequence of slow collections of accounts receivable, which resulted in high levels of receivables and therefore high levels of total assets. The high total assets slowed Daton's total asset turnover, driving down its ROA, which then drove down its ROE. By using the DuPont system of analysis to dissect Daton's overall returns as measured by its ROE, we found that slow collections of receivables caused the below-industry-average ROE. Clearly, the firm needs to manage its credit operations better.

? Review Questions

8–14   Describe how you would use a large number of ratios to perform a complete ratio analysis of the firm.

8–15   What three areas of analysis are combined in the *modified DuPont formula*? Explain how the *DuPont system of analysis* is used to dissect the firm's results and isolate their causes.

TYING IT ALL TOGETHER

This chapter reviewed the annual stockholders' report with special emphasis on the four key financial statements and described the calculation and interrelationships of the most popular financial ratios. The importance of financial statements and ratio analysis of them from the viewpoints of financial managers, financial markets, and investors are summarized in the Integrative Table that follows.

INTEGRATIVE TABLE

Understanding and Analyzing Financial Statements

Role of **Financial Managers**	*Role of* **Financial Markets**	*Role of* **Investors**
Financial managers rely on financial statements to accurately summarize the firm's activities and financial position. They use financial statement data to monitor the firm's progress toward its strategic goals. To monitor specific accounts the manager relies on financial ratios, which provide for standardized comparisons both on cross-sectional and time-series bases. Ratios alert financial managers to symptoms of possible problems.	Financial markets through the Securities and Exchange Commission dictate all aspects of financial reporting by public companies. They assure investors that accurate financial information will be available for use in assessing the financial performance and condition of public companies. Financial statements provide information that investors can use to assess firms whose securities can be bought and sold in financial markets.	Investors use financial statements to understand the firm's financial activities and to assess whether to purchase or sell the firm's bonds or stocks. Investors can use data in financial statements to calculate financial ratios that give insight into a firm's financial performance. Investors use ratio analysis to better understand the return and risk behavior of the firm—both of which have direct bearing on the firm's value in the marketplace.

LG1 **Review the contents of the stockholders' report and the procedures for consolidating international financial statements.** The annual stockholders' report, which publicly owned corporations are required to provide to stockholders, documents the firm's financial activities during the past year. It includes the letter to stockholders and various subjective and factual information plus four key financial statements: the income statement, the balance sheet, the statement of retained earnings, and the statement of cash flows. Notes describing the technical aspects of the financial statements follow them. Financial statements of companies that have operations whose cash flows are denominated in one or more foreign currencies must be translated into dollars in accordance with *FASB Standard No. 52.*

LG2 **Understand who uses financial ratios, and how.** Ratio analysis allows present and prospective stockholders and lenders and the firm's management to evaluate the firm's financial performance. It can be performed on a cross-sectional or a time-series basis. Benchmarking is a popular type of cross-sectional analysis. Key cautions for applying financial ratios are: (1) Ratios with large deviations from the norm only indicate symptoms of a problem. (2) A single ratio does not generally provide sufficient information. (3) The ratios being compared should be calculated using financial statements dated at the same point in time during the year. (4) Audited financial statements should be used. (5) Data should be checked for consistency of accounting treatment. (6) Inflation and different asset ages can distort ratio comparisons.

LG3 **Use ratios to analyze a firm's liquidity and activity.** Liquidity, or ability of the firm to pay its bills as they come due, can be measured by the current ratio and the quick (acid-test) ratio. Activity ratios measure the speed with which accounts are converted into sales or cash—inflows or outflows. The activity of inventory can be measured by its turnover; that of accounts receivable by the average collection period; and that of accounts payable by the average payment period. Total asset turnover measures the efficiency with which the firm uses its assets to generate sales. Formulas for these liquidity and activity ratios are summarized in Table 8.7.

LG4 **Discuss the relationship between debt and financial leverage and the ratios used to analyze a firm's debt.** The more debt a firm uses, the greater its financial leverage, which magnifies both return and risk. Financial debt ratios measure both the degree of indebtedness and the ability to service debts. A common measure of indebtedness is the debt ratio. The ability to pay fixed charges can be measured by times interest earned and fixed-payment coverage ratios. Formulas for these debt ratios are summarized in Table 8.7.

 Use ratios to analyze a firm's profitability and its market value. The common-size income statement, which shows all items as a percentage of sales, can be used to determine gross profit margin, operating profit margin, and net profit margin. Other measures of profitability include earnings per share, return on total assets, and return on common equity. Market ratios include the price/earnings ratio and the market/book ratio. Formulas for these profitability

and market ratios are summarized in Table 8.7.

 Use a summary of financial ratios and the DuPont system of analysis to perform a complete ratio analysis. A summary of all ratios—liquidity, activity, debt, profitability, and market—as shown in Table 8.7 can be used to perform a complete ratio analysis using cross-sectional and time-series analysis approaches. The DuPont system of analysis is a diagnostic tool used to find the key areas responsible for the firm's financial performance. It allows the firm to break the return on common equity into three components: profit on sales, efficiency of asset use, and use of leverage. The DuPont system of analysis makes it possible to assess all aspects of the firm's activities in order to isolate key areas of responsibility.

SELF-TEST EXERCISES   (Solutions in Appendix B)

   ST 8–1   Ratio formulas and interpretations   Without referring to the text, indicate for each of the following ratios the formula for its calculation and the kinds of problems, if any, the firm is likely to have if these ratios are too high relative to the industry average. What if they are too low relative to the industry? Create a table similar to the one that follows and fill in the empty blocks.

Ratio	Too high	Too low
Current ratio =		
Inventory turnover =		
Times interest earned =		
Gross profit margin =		
Return on total assets =		

   ST 8–2   Balance sheet completion using ratios   Complete the 2001 balance sheet for Orphan Industries using the information that follows it.

Balance Sheet
Orphan Industries
December 31, 2001

Cash	$ 30,000	Accounts payable	$120,000
Marketable securities	25,000	Notes payable	
Accounts receivable	_____	Accruals	20,000
Inventories	_____	Total current liabilities	_____
Total current assets	_____	Long-term debt	
Net fixed assets	_____	Stockholders' equity	$600,000
Total assets	========	Total liabilities and stockholders' equity	========

The following financial data for 2001 are also available:
(1) Sales totaled $1,800,000.
(2) The gross profit margin was 25%.
(3) Inventory turnover was 6.0.
(4) There are 360 days in the year.
(5) The average collection period was 40 days.
(6) The current ratio was 1.60.
(7) The total asset turnover ratio was 1.20.
(8) The debt ratio was 60%.

EXERCISES

 8–1   Reviewing basic financial statements   The income statement for the year ended December 31, 2001, the balance sheets for December 31, 2001 and 2000, and the statement of retained earnings for the year ended December 31, 2001, for Networld, Inc., are given on this and the following page. Briefly discuss the form and informational content of each of these statements.

Income Statement
Networld, Inc.
for the year ended December 31, 2001

Sales revenue		$600,000
Less: Cost of goods sold		460,000
Gross profits		$140,000
Less: Operating expenses		
General and administrative expense	$30,000	
Depreciation expense	30,000	
Total operating expense		60,000
Operating profits		$ 80,000
Less: Interest expense		10,000
Net profits before taxes		$ 70,000
Less: Taxes		27,100
Earnings available for common stockholders		$ 42,900
Earnings per share (EPS)		$2.15

Balance Sheets
Networld, Inc.

Assets	December 31 2001	December 31 2000
Cash	$ 15,000	$ 16,000
Marketable securities	7,200	8,000
Accounts receivable	34,100	42,200
Inventories	82,000	50,000
Total current assets	$138,300	$116,200
Land and buildings	$150,000	$150,000
Machinery and equipment	200,000	190,000
Furniture and fixtures	54,000	50,000
Other	11,000	10,000
Total gross fixed assets	$415,000	$400,000
Less: Accumulated depreciation	145,000	115,000
Net fixed assets	$270,000	$285,000
Total assets	$408,300	$401,200

Liabilities and stockholders' equity

	2001	2000
Accounts payable	$ 57,000	$ 49,000
Notes payable	13,000	16,000
Accruals	5,000	6,000
Total current liabilities	$ 75,000	$ 71,000
Long-term debt	$150,000	$160,000
Stockholders' equity		
Common stock equity (shares outstanding: 19,500 in 2001 and 20,000 in 2000)	$110,200	$120,000
Retained earnings	73,100	50,200
Total stockholders' equity	$183,300	$170,200
Total liabilities and stockholders' equity	$408,300	$401,200

Statement of Retained Earnings
Networld, Inc.
for the year ended December 31, 2001

Retained earnings balance (January 1, 2001)	$50,200
Plus: Net profits after taxes (for 2001)	42,900
Less: Cash dividends (paid during 2001)	(20,000)
Retained earnings balance (December 31, 2001)	$73,100

8–2   Financial statement account identification   Mark each of the accounts listed in the following table as follows:

   a. In column (1), indicate in which statement—income statement (IS) or balance sheet (BS)—the account belongs.

   b. In column (2), indicate whether the account is a current asset (CA), current liability (CL), expense (E), fixed asset (FA), long-term debt (LTD), revenue (R), or stockholders' equity (SE).

Account name	(1) Statement	(2) Type of account
Accounts payable	——	——
Accounts receivable	——	——
Accruals	——	——
Accumulated depreciation	——	——
Administrative expense	——	——
Buildings	——	——
Cash	——	——
Common stock (at par)	——	——
Cost of goods sold	——	——
Depreciation	——	——
Equipment	——	——
General expense	——	——
Interest expense	——	——
Inventories	——	——
Land	——	——
Long-term debts	——	——
Machinery	——	——
Marketable securities	——	——
Notes payable	——	——
Operating expense	——	——
Paid-in capital in excess of par	——	——
Preferred stock	——	——
Preferred stock dividends	——	——
Retained earnings	——	——
Sales revenue	——	——
Selling expense	——	——
Taxes	——	——
Vehicles	——	——

8–3   Income statement preparation   On December 31, 2001, Rachel Liu, a self-employed certified public accountant (CPA), completed her first full year in business. During the year, she billed $180,000 for her accounting services. She had two employees: a bookkeeper and a clerical assistant. In addition to her *monthly* salary of $4,000, Ms. Liu paid *annual* salaries of $24,000 and $18,000 to the bookkeeper and the clerical assistant, respectively. Employment taxes and benefit costs for Ms. Liu and her employees totaled $17,300 for the year. Expenses for office supplies, including postage, totaled $5,200 for the year. In addition, Ms. Liu spent $8,500 during the year on tax-deductible travel and entertainment associated with client visits and new business development. Lease payments for the office space rented (a tax-deductible expense) were $1,350 *per month*.

Depreciation expense on the office furniture and fixtures was $7,800 for the year. During the year, Ms. Liu paid interest of $7,500 on the $60,000 borrowed to start the business. She paid an average tax rate of 30 percent during 2001.

a. Prepare an income statement for Rachel Liu, CPA, for the year ended December 31, 2001.

b. Evaluate her 2001 financial performance.

8–4   Calculation of EPS and retained earnings   Gemtel, Inc., ended 2001 with net profit *before* taxes of $218,000. The company is subject to a 40% tax rate and must pay $32,000 in preferred stock dividends before distributing any earnings on the 85,000 shares of common stock currently outstanding.

a. Calculate Gemtel's 2001 earnings per share (EPS).

b. If the firm paid common stock dividends of $.80 per share, how many dollars would go to retained earnings?

8–5   Balance sheet preparation   Use the *appropriate items* from the following list to prepare in good form Dave Owens Company's balance sheet at December 31, 2001.

Item	Value ($000) at December 31, 2001
Accounts payable	$ 220
Accounts receivable	450
Accruals	55
Accumulated depreciation	265
Buildings	225
Cash	215
Common stock (at par)	90
Cost of goods sold	2,500
Depreciation expense	45
Equipment	140
Furniture and fixtures	170
General expense	320
Inventories	375
Land	100
Long-term debts	420
Machinery	420
Marketable securities	75
Notes payable	475
Paid-in capital in excess of par	360
Preferred stock	100
Retained earnings	210
Sales revenue	3,600
Vehicles	25

8–6   Impact of net income on a firm's balance sheet   Charter Air, Inc., reported net income of $1,365,000 for the year ended December 31, 2001. Show the effect of these funds on the firm's balance sheet (given on the following page for the previous year) in each of the scenarios following the balance sheet.

Balance Sheet
Charter Air, Inc.
as of December 31, 2000

Assets		Liabilities and Stockholders' Equity	
Cash	$ 120,000	Accounts payable	$ 70,000
Marketable securities	35,000	Short-term notes	55,000
Accounts receivable	45,000	Current liabilities	$ 125,000
Inventories	130,000	Long-term debt	$2,700,000
Current assets	$ 330,000	Total liabilities	$2,825,000
Equipment	$2,970,000	Common stock	$ 500,000
Buildings	1,600,000	Retained earnings	1,575,000
Fixed assets	$4,570,000	Stockholders' equity	$2,075,000
Total assets	$4,900,000	Total liabilities and equity	$4,900,000

a. Charter paid no dividends during the year and invested the funds in marketable securities.
b. Charter paid dividends totaling $500,000 and used the balance of the net income to retire (pay off) long-term debt.
c. Charter paid dividends totaling $500,000 and invested the balance of the net income in building a new hangar.
d. Charter paid out all $1,365,000 as dividends to its stockholders.

LG1 8–7 **Initial sale price of common stock**   Kleck Corporation has one issue of preferred stock and one issue of common stock outstanding. Given Kleck's stockholders' equity account that follows, determine the original price per share at which the firm sold its single issue of common stock.

Stockholders' equity ($000)	
Preferred stock	$ 125
Common stock ($.75 par, 300,000 shares outstanding)	225
Paid-in capital in excess of par on common stock	2,625
Retained earnings	900
Total stockholders' equity	$3,875

  LG1 8–8 **Statement of retained earnings**   Saylor Enterprises began 2001 with a retained earnings balance of $928,000. During 2001, the firm earned $377,000 after taxes. From this amount, preferred stockholders were paid $47,000 in dividends. At year-end 2001, the firm's retained earnings totaled $1,048,000. The firm had 140,000 shares of common stock outstanding during 2001.
a. Prepare a statement of retained earnings for the year ended December 31, 2001, for Saylor Enterprises. (*Note:* Be sure to calculate and include the amount of cash dividends paid in 2001.)
b. Calculate the firm's 2001 earnings per share (EPS).

c. How large a per-share cash dividend did the firm pay on common stock during 2001?

 8–9 **Changes in stockholders' equity**   Listed are the equity sections of balance sheets for years 2000 and 2001 as reported by Resort World, Inc. The overall value of stockholders' equity has risen from $2,000,000 to $7,500,000. Use the statements to discover how and why this happened.

Resort World Inc.		
	2000	**2001**
Stockholders' equity		
Common stock ($1.00 par)		
Authorized—5,000,000 shares		
Outstanding—1,500,000 shares 2001		
— 500,000 shares 2000	$ 500,000	$1,500,000
Paid-in capital in excess of par	500,000	4,500,000
Retained earnings	1,000,000	1,500,000
Total stockholders' equity	$2,000,000	$7,500,000

The company paid total dividends of $200,000 during fiscal 2001.
a. What was Resort World's net income for fiscal 2001?
b. How many new shares did the corporation issue and sell during the year?
c. At what average price per share did the new stock sold during 2001 sell?
d. At what price per share did Resort World's original 500,000 shares sell?

   8–10 **Ratio comparisons**   Arnold Roberts recently inherited a stock portfolio from his uncle. Wishing to learn more about the companies that he is now invested in, Arnold performs a ratio analysis on each one and decides to compare them to each other. Some of his ratios are listed below.

	Atlantic Electric Utility	Mighty Burger	Think Software	Rauch Motors
Current ratio	1.10	1.3	6.8	4.5
Quick ratio	0.90	0.82	5.2	3.7
Debt ratio	0.68	0.46	0	0.35
Net profit margin	6.2%	14.3%	28.5%	8.4%

Assuming that his uncle was a wise investor who assembled the portfolio with care, Arnold finds the wide differences in these ratios confusing. Help him out.
a. What problems might Arnold encounter in comparing these companies to one another on the basis of their ratios?
b. Why might the current and quick ratios for the electric utility and the fast-food stock be so much lower than the same ratios for the other companies?
c. Why might it be all right for the electric utility to carry a large amount of debt, but the same is not true for the software company?

d. Why wouldn't investors invest all of their money in software companies instead of less profitable companies? (Focus on return and risk.)

 **8–11 Liquidity management** Beacon Company's total current assets, total current liabilities, and inventory for each of the past 4 years follow:

Item	1998	1999	2000	2001
Total current assets	$16,950	$21,900	$22,500	$27,000
Total current liabilities	9,000	12,600	12,600	17,400
Inventory	6,000	6,900	6,900	7,200

a. Calculate the firm's current and quick ratios for each year. Compare the resulting time series of these measures of liquidity.
b. Comment on the firm's liquidity over the 1998-2001 period.
c. If you were told that Beacon Company's inventory turnover for each year in the 1998–2001 period and the industry averages were as follows, would this support or conflict with your evaluation in part **b**? Why?

Inventory turnover	1998	1999	2000	2001
Beacon Company	6.3	6.8	7.0	6.4
Industry average	10.6	11.2	10.8	11.0

 8–12 Inventory management Parsons Manufacturing has sales of $4 million and a gross profit margin of 40%. Its *end-of-quarter inventories* are as follows:

Quarter	Inventory
1	$ 400,000
2	800,000
3	1,200,000
4	200,000

a. Find the average quarterly inventory and use it to calculate the firm's inventory turnover and the average age of inventory.
b. Assuming that the company is in an industry with an average inventory turnover of 2.0, how would you evaluate the activity of Parsons' inventory?

 8–13 Accounts receivable management An evaluation of the books of Mayer Supply, shown in the table at the top of the following page, gives the end-of-year accounts receivable balance, which is believed to consist of amounts originating in the months indicated. The company had annual sales of $2.4 million. The firm extends 30-day credit terms.

Month of origin	Amounts receivable
July	$ 3,875
August	2,000
September	34,025
October	15,100
November	52,000
December	193,000
Year-end accounts receivable	$300,000

    a. Use the year-end total to evaluate the firm's collection system.

    b. If 70% of the firm's sales occur between July and December, would this affect the validity of your conclusion in part **a**? Explain.

 8–14 **Interpreting liquidity and activity ratios** The new owners of Celestial Natural Foods, Inc., have hired you to help them diagnose and cure problems that the company has had in maintaining adequate liquidity. As a first step, you perform a liquidity analysis. You then do an analysis of the company's short-term activity ratios. Your calculations and appropriate industry norms are listed.

	Celestial	Industry norm
Current ratio	4.5	4.0
Quick ratio	2.0	3.1
Inventory turnover	6.0	10.4
Average collection period	73 days	52 days
Average payment period	31 days	40 days

    a. What recommendations relative to the amount and the handling of inventory could you make to the new owners?

    b. What recommendations relative to amount and handling of accounts receivable could you make to the new owners?

    c. What recommendations relative to amount and handling of accounts payable could you make to the new owners?

    d. What results, overall, would you hope your recommendations would achieve? Why might your recommendations not be effective?

  8–15 **Debt analysis** Zenia Bank is evaluating Rock Enterprises, which has requested a $4,000,000 loan, to assess the firm's financial leverage and financial risk. On the basis of the debt ratios for Rock, along with the industry averages and Rock's recent financial statements (which appear on the following pages), evaluate and recommend appropriate action on the loan request.

Income Statement
Rock Enterprises
for the year ended December 31, 2001

Sales revenue		$30,000,000
Less: Cost of goods sold		21,000,000
Gross profits		$ 9,000,000
Less: Operating expenses		
Selling expense	$3,000,000	
General and administrative expenses	1,800,000	
Lease expense	200,000	
Depreciation expense	1,000,000	
Total operating expense		6,000,000
Operating profits		$ 3,000,000
Less: Interest expense		1,000,000
Net profits before taxes		$ 2,000,000
Less: Taxes (rate = 40%)		800,000
Net profits after taxes		$ 1,200,000
Less: Preferred stock dividends		100,000
Earnings available for common stockholders		$ 1,100,000

Balance Sheet
Rock Enterprises
December 31, 2001

Assets		Liabilities and stockholders' equity	
Current assets		Current liabilities	
Cash	$ 1,000,000	Accounts payable	$ 8,000,000
Marketable securities	3,000,000	Notes payable	8,000,000
Accounts receivable	12,000,000	Accruals	500,000
Inventories	7,500,000	Total current liabilities	$16,500,000
Total current assets	$23,500,000	Long-term debt (includes financial leases)[b]	$20,000,000
Gross fixed assets (at cost)[a]		Stockholders' equity	
Land and buildings	$11,000,000	Preferred stock (25,000 shares,	
Machinery and equipment	20,500,000	$4 dividend)	$ 2,500,000
Furniture and fixtures	8,000,000	Common stock (1 million shares at $5 par)	5,000,000
Gross fixed assets	$39,500,000	Paid-in capital in excess of par value	4,000,000
Less: Accumulated depreciation	13,000,000	Retained earnings	2,000,000
Net fixed assets	$26,500,000	Total stockholders' equity	$13,500,000
Total assets	$50,000,000	Total liabilities and stockholders' equity	$50,000,000

[a]The firm has a 4-year financial lease requiring annual beginning-of-year payments of $200,000. Three years of the lease have yet to run.

[b]Required annual principal payments are $800,000.

Note: Industry averages appear at the top of the following page.

Industry averages	
Debt ratio	0.51
Times interest earned ratio	7.30
Fixed-payment coverage ratio	1.85

 8–16 Common-size statement analysis A common-size income statement for Rock Enterprises' 2000 operations follows. Using the firm's 2001 income statement presented in Problem 8-15, develop the 2001 common-size income statement and compare it to the 2000 statement. Which areas require further analysis and investigation?

Common-size Income Statement Rock Enterprises for the year ended December 31, 2000		
Sales revenue ($35,000,000)		100.0%
Less: Cost of goods sold		65.9
Gross profits		34.1%
Less: Operating expenses		
Selling expense	12.7%	
General and administrative expenses	6.3	
Lease expense	0.6	
Depreciation expense	3.6	
Total operating expense		23.2
Operating profits		10.9%
Less: Interest expense		1.5
Net profits before taxes		9.4%
Less: Taxes (rate = 40%)		3.8
Net profits after taxes		5.6%
Less: Preferred stock dividends		0.1
Earnings available for common stockholders		5.5%

    8–17 The relationship between financial leverage and profitability Winner Paper, Inc., and Oregon Forest, Inc., are rivals in the manufacture of craft papers. Some financial statement values for each company are listed at the top of the following page. Use them in a ratio analysis that compares their financial leverage and profitability.

	Winner Paper, Inc.	Oregon Forest, Inc.
Total assets	$10,000,000	$10,000,000
Total equity (all common)	9,000,000	5,000,000
Total debt	1,000,000	5,000,000
Annual interest	100,000	500,000
Total sales	$25,000,000	$25,000,000
EBIT	6,250,000	6,250,000
Net income	3,690,000	3,450,000

a. Calculate the following debt and coverage ratios for the two companies. Discuss their financial risk and ability to cover the costs in relation to each other.
   (1) Debt ratio
   (2) Times interest earned ratio
b. Calculate the following profitability ratios for the two companies. Discuss their profitability relative to each other.
   (1) Operating profit margin
   (2) Net profit margin
   (3) Return on total assets
   (4) Return on common equity
c. In what way has the larger debt of Oregon Forest made it more profitable than Winner Paper? What are the risks that Oregon's investors undertake when they choose to purchase its stock instead of Winner's?

 8–18 **Ratio proficiency**   Solana Printing, Inc., had sales totaling $40,000,000 in fiscal year 2001. Some ratios for the company are listed below. Use this information to determine the dollar values of various income statement and balance sheet accounts as requested.

Solana Printing, Inc. year ended December 31, 2001	
Sales	$40,000,000
Gross profit margin	80%
Operating profit margin	35%
Net profit margin	8%
Return on total assets	16%
Return on common equity	20%
Total asset turnover	2
Average collection period	62.2 days

Calculate values for the following:
a. Gross profits
b. Cost of goods sold
c. Operating profits

    d. Operating expenses

    e. Earnings available for common stockholders

    f. Total assets

    g. Total common stock equity

    h. Accounts receivable

8–19   **Dupont system of analysis**   Use the following ratio information for Besseli International and the industry averages for Besseli's line of business to:

    a. Construct the DuPont system of analysis for both Besseli and the industry.

    b. Evaluate Besseli (and the industry) over the 3-year period.

    c. In which areas does Besseli require further analysis? Why?

Besseli	1999	2000	2001
Financial leverage multiplier	1.75	1.75	1.85
Net profit margin	0.059	0.058	0.049
Total asset turnover	2.11	2.18	2.34
Industry averages			
Financial leverage multiplier	1.67	1.69	1.64
Net profit margin	0.054	0.047	0.041
Total asset turnover	2.05	2.13	2.15

8–20   **Cross-sectional ratio analysis**   Use the following financial statements for Mark Manufacturing Company for the year ended December 31, 2001, along with the industry average ratios also given in what follows, to:

    a. Prepare and interpret a complete ratio analysis of the firm's 2001 operations.

    b. Summarize your findings and make recommendations.

Income Statement
Mark Manufacturing Company
for the year ended December 31, 2001

Sales revenue		$600,000
Less: Cost of goods sold		460,000
Gross profits		$140,000
Less: Operating expenses		
General and administrative expenses	$30,000	
Depreciation expense	30,000	
Total operating expense		60,000
Operating profits		$ 80,000
Less: Interest expense		10,000
Net profits before taxes		$ 70,000
Less: Taxes		27,100
Net profits after taxes (earnings available for common stockholders)		$ 42,900
Earnings per share (EPS)		$ 2.15

Balance Sheet
Mark Manufacturing Company
December 31, 2001

Assets

Cash	$ 15,000
Marketable securities	7,200
Accounts receivable	34,100
Inventories	82,000
Total current assets	$138,300
Net fixed assets	$270,000
Total assets	$408,300

Liabilities and stockholders' equity

Accounts payable	$ 57,000
Notes payable	13,000
Accruals	5,000
Total current liabilities	$ 75,000
Long-term debt	$150,000
Stockholders' equity	
Common stock equity (20,000 shares outstanding)	$110,200
Retained earnings	73,100
Total stockholders' equity	$183,300
Total liabilities and stockholders' equity	$408,300

Ratio	Industry average, 2001
Current ratio	2.35
Quick ratio	0.87
Inventory turnover[a]	4.55
Average collection period[a]	35.3 days
Total asset turnover	1.09
Debt ratio	0.300
Times interest earned ratio	12.3
Gross profit margin	0.202
Operating profit margin	0.135
Net profit margin	0.091
Return on total assets (ROA)	0.099
Return on common equity (ROE)	0.167
Earnings per share (EPS)	$3.10

[a]Based on a 360-day year and on end-of-year figures.

  8–21   Financial statement analysis   The financial statements of Jessica Industries for the year ended December 31, 2001, appear on the following page.

Income Statement
Jessica Industries
for the year ended December 31, 2001

Sales revenue	$160,000
Less: Cost of goods sold	106,000
Gross profits	$ 54,000
Less: Operating expenses	
Selling expense	$ 16,000
General and administrative expenses	10,000
Lease expense	1,000
Depreciation expense	10,000
Total operating expense	$ 37,000
Operating profits	$ 17,000
Less: Interest expense	6,100
Net profits before taxes	$ 10,900
Less: Taxes	4,360
Net profits after taxes	$ 6,540

Balance Sheet
Jessica Industries
December 31, 2001

Assets

Cash	$ 500
Marketable securities	1,000
Accounts receivable	25,000
Inventories	45,500
Total current assets	$ 72,000
Land	$ 26,000
Buildings and equipment	90,000
Less: Accumulated depreciation	38,000
Net fixed assets	$ 78,000
Total assets	$150,000

Liabilities and stockholders' equity

Accounts payable	$ 22,000
Notes payable	47,000
Total current liabilities	$ 69,000
Long-term debt	$ 22,950
Common stock[a]	$ 31,500
Retained earnings	$ 26,550
Total liabilities and stockholders' equity	$150,000

[a]The firm's 3,000 outstanding shares of common stock closed 2001 at a price of $25 per share.

a. Use the preceding financial statements to complete the following table. Assume that the industry averages given in the table are applicable for both 2000 and 2001.

Ratio	Industry average	Actual 2000	Actual 2001
Current ratio	1.80	1.84	_____
Quick ratio	0.70	0.78	_____
Inventory turnover^a	2.50	2.59	_____
Average collection period^a	37 days	36 days	_____
Debt ratio	65%	67%	_____
Times interest earned ratio	3.8	4.0	_____
Gross profit margin	38%	40%	_____
Net profit margin	3.5%	3.6%	_____
Return on total assets	4.0%	4.0%	_____
Return on common equity	9.5%	8.0%	_____
Market/book ratio	1.1	1.2	_____

^{a}Based on a 360-day year and on end-of-year figures.

b. Analyze Jessica Industries' financial condition as it relates to (1) liquidity, (2) activity, (3) debt, (4) profitability, and (5) market. Summarize the company's overall financial condition.

 8–22 **Integrative—Complete ratio analysis**   Given the following financial statements, historical ratios, and industry averages, calculate the Glinst Company's financial ratios for the most recent year. Analyze its overall financial situation from both a cross-sectional and a time-series viewpoint. Break your analysis into an evaluation of the firm's liquidity, activity, debt, profitability, and market.

Income Statement Glinst Company for the year ended December 31, 2001		
Sales revenue		$10,000,000
Less: Cost of goods sold		7,500,000
Gross profits		$ 2,500,000
Less: Operating expenses		
Selling expense	$300,000	
General and administrative expenses	650,000	
Lease expense	50,000	
Depreciation expense	200,000	
Total operating expense		1,200,000
Operating profits		$ 1,300,000
Less: Interest expense		200,000
Net profits before taxes		$ 1,100,000
Less: Taxes (rate = 40%)		440,000
Net profits after taxes		$ 660,000
Less: Preferred stock dividends		50,000
Earnings available for common stockholders		$ 610,000
Earnings per share (EPS)		$3.05

Balance Sheet
Glinst Company
December 31, 2001

Assets		Liabilities and stockholders' equity	
Current assets		**Current liabilities**	
Cash	$ 200,000	Accounts payable[b]	$ 900,000
Marketable securities	50,000	Notes payable	200,000
Accounts receivable	800,000	Accruals	100,000
Inventories	950,000	Total current liabilities	$ 1,200,000
Total current assets	$ 2,000,000	Long-term debt (includes financial leases)[c]	$ 3,000,000
Gross fixed assets (at cost)[a] $12,000,000		Stockholders' equity	
Less: Accumulated depreciation 3,000,000		Preferred stock (25,000 shares, $2 dividend)	$ 1,000,000
Net fixed assets	$ 9,000,000	Common stock (200,000 shares at $3 par)[d]	600,000
Other assets	$ 1,000,000	Paid-in capital in excess of par value	5,200,000
Total assets	$12,000,000	Retained earnings	1,000,000
		Total stockholders' equity	$ 7,800,000
		Total liabilities and stockholders' equity	$12,000,000

[a]The firm has an 8-year financial lease requiring annual beginning-of-year payments of $50,000. Five years of the lease have yet to run.
[b]Annual credit purchases of $6,200,000 were made during the year.
[c]The annual principal payment on the long-term debt is $100,000.
[d]On December 31, 2001, the firm's common stock closed at 39 ½ (i.e., $39.50).

Historical and Industry Average Ratios for Glinst Company

Ratio	Actual 1999	Actual 2000	Industry average, 2001
Current ratio	1.40	1.55	1.85
Quick ratio	1.00	.92	1.05
Inventory turnover	9.52	9.21	8.60
Average collection period	45.0 days	36.4 days	35.0 days
Average payment period	58.5 days	60.8 days	45.8 days
Total asset turnover	0.74	0.80	0.74
Debt ratio	0.20	0.20	0.30
Times interest earned ratio	8.2	7.3	8.0
Fixed-payment coverage ratio	4.5	4.2	4.2
Gross profit margin	0.30	0.27	0.25
Operating profit margin	0.12	0.12	0.10
Net profit margin	0.062	0.062	0.053
Return on total assets (ROA)	0.045	0.050	0.040
Return on common equity (ROE)	0.061	0.067	0.066
Earnings per share (EPS)	$1.75	$2.20	$1.50
Price/earnings (P/E) ratio	12.0	10.5	11.2
Market/book (M/B) ratio	1.20	1.05	1.10

web exercises   Search

Go to web site **www.Yahoo.com**. On the Yahoo home page screen click **Business & Economy**. On the next screen click **Y! Finance**. Enter the stock symbol YUM in the **Quotes** box.

1. Which of the financial ratios that were covered in this chapter are given for Tricon Global Restaurants?
2. How much is the annual dividend of Tricon Global Restaurants?

Click on **Ratio comparisons**.

3. What are the three groups of standards to which Tricon Global Restaurants ratios are compared?
4. Which of the financial ratios that were covered in this chapter are given for Tricon Global Restaurants Companies, Inc.?
5. When compared to the industry standards, which two ratios does Tricon Global Restaurants seem to be doing very well? Which two ratios does Tricon Global Restaurants seem to be doing *not* so well?
6. Where does YUM rank in its industry in total market capitalization?

Go to web site **www.hoovers.com**. In the toolbox, click **Ticker Symbol**. Enter YUM into the search box and then click **GO>>**.

7. Who are the top competitors to Tricon Global Restaurants?
8. Who is the CFO of Tricon Global Restaurants?

Click **Financials**.

9. For which two financial statements are data given for Tricon Global Restaurants?
10. How many years of data are given here?

For additional practice with concepts from this chapter, visit
http://www.awl.com/gitman_madura

Part 2

exam-ace.net

Assessing exam-ace.net's Financial Condition

After one year of being in business, Tom Turner, owner of exam-ace.net, decided to assess the firm's financial condition. Its income statement is shown in Exhibit 1, and its balance sheet is shown in Exhibit 2. The firm's cost of goods sold was zero because all of its expenses (such as those for developing the web site, hiring instructors to write practice exam questions, and marketing) were classified as operating expenses.

EXHIBIT 1
exam-ace.net
Income Statement

Sales revenue	$130,000
Less: Cost of goods sold	0
Gross profit	$130,000
Less: Operating expenses	90,000
Operating profit	$ 40,000
Less: Interest expenses	10,000
Net profits before taxes	$ 30,000
Less: Taxes	10,000
Net profits after taxes	$ 20,000

EXHIBIT 2
exam-ace.net
Balance Sheet

Assets		
Current assets		
Cash	$ 20,000	
Accounts receivable	0	
Marketable securities	120,000	
Inventories	0	
Total current assets		$140,000
Gross fixed assets	$ 80,000	
Less: Accumulated depreciation	20,000	
Net fixed assets		60,000
Total assets		$200,000
Liabilities and Stockholders' Equity		
Current liabilities		
Accounts payable	$ 0	
Total current liabilities		$ 0
Long-term debt		100,000
Total liabilities		$100,000
Stockholders' equity		
Common stock		$100,000
Retained earnings		0
Total liabilities and stockholders' equity		$200,000

Note: The firm paid out a total of $20,000 in dividends last year to its two owners. Because net profits are $20,000 and dividends of $20,000 were paid, the firm's retained earnings are zero after 1 year.

Exercises

CC2-1 Tom Turner compared his Internet testing service to other types of firms that sell practice testing materials through retail book stores. Tom noticed that the financial statements for exam-ace.net (as shown in Exhibits 1 and 2) looked much different for his firm, because his cost of goods sold, accounts receivable, and inventories were zero.

a. On the income statement, why do you think the cost of goods sold for exam-ace.net is zero? Does this suggest that exam-ace.net is more efficient than other firms?

b. On the balance sheet, why do you think the accounts receivable for exam-ace.net are zero? Is this a problem for exam-ace.net?

c. On the balance sheet, why do you think the inventories for exam-ace.net are zero? Does this suggest that exam-ace.net is more efficient than other firms?

d. Explain why the gross profits of exam-ace.net seem unusually high compared to its net profits.

CC2-2 After a year in business, Tom Turner decided to determine the value of his business. During the year, the firm paid out total of $20,000 in dividends to himself and the other investor, Dan Atkinson. Tom first created a conservative estimate in which he expected that he would be able to continue that dividend for the next 10 years, at which time the business would be terminated (once many other competitors entered this market). He also created a more optimistic estimate in which the dividends would grow at a rate of 2% per year and would continue forever. For each estimate, Tom plans to use a required rate of return of 14%.

a. Determine the value of the firm on the basis of the more conservative estimate.

b. Determine the value of the firm on the basis of the more optimistic estimate.

c. What might cause the risk of the firm to change in a manner that would make the actual required rate of return higher than 14%?

d. Redo the valuations based on the conservative estimate and the more optimistic estimate using a required rate of return of 18%. Explain how the valuations changed.

e. Offer some reasons why the risk of the firm could change in a manner that would cause the actual required rate of return to be less than 14%.

f. Redo the valuations on the basis of a required rate of return of 10%. Explain how the valuations changed.

CC2-3 Communication Tom wants to hire you as a consultant to conduct a financial analysis of his business. He wants you to compare the financial ratios to assess efficiency of his business relative to those of the traditional testing services. Communicate to Tom, through a memo that you would e-mail to him, why such an analysis will lead to distorted results. Explain to Tom which parts of the financial analysis may offer some insight.

CC2-4 Teamwork Create a team of three students in which one student serves as Tom (manager and owner), another serves as Dan Atkinson (investor), and the third serves as the lender. What financial ratios would you focus on, given the role you are assigned? Identify where there are differences among roles. Explain what causes the differences among roles.

CC2–5 Ethics Tom is aware that investors and creditors look closely at earnings when determining whether to invest in a firm. He knows that he may need additional financing in the future and wonders whether he could make his earnings look better. For example, although he did not do so, he had considered asking some of the instructors who created questions for him to bill him after the end of the year so that the cost would not show up in the current year's income statement. Thus the earnings for the year would be more favorable. Should Tom have made such a request?

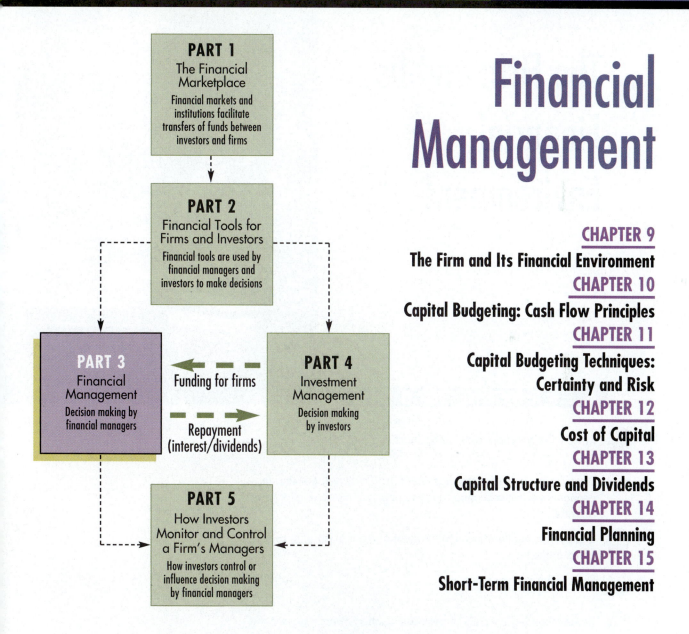

PART 1
The Financial Marketplace
Financial markets and institutions facilitate transfers of funds between investors and firms

PART 2
Financial Tools for Firms and Investors
Financial tools are used by financial managers and investors to make decisions

PART 3
Financial Management
Decision making by financial managers

Funding for firms

Repayment (interest/dividends)

PART 4
Investment Management
Decision making by investors

PART 5
How Investors Monitor and Control a Firm's Managers
How investors control or influence decision making by financial managers

Financial Management

The topic of this part is the role of the financial manager in guiding the business firm. It covers important aspects of the firm's environment, investment decisions, financial costs and structure, dividends, financial planning, and short-term financial management. An understanding of these activities of the financial manager provides insight into how economically rational firms create value for their shareholders.

The Firm and Its Financial Environment

LEARNING GOALS

LG1 Review the common forms of business organization.

LG2 Describe the financial management function, its relationship to economics and accounting, and the financial manager's primary activities.

LG3 Explain the wealth maximization goal of the firm and the role of ethics in the firm.

LG4 Discuss the agency issue.

LG5 Review the fundamentals of business taxation of ordinary income and capital gains.

LG6 Understand the effect of depreciation on the firm's cash flows, the depreciable value of an asset, its depreciable life, and tax depreciation methods.

LG7 Discuss the firm's cash flows, particularly the statement of cash flows.

Common Forms of Business Organization

The three most common legal forms of business organization are the *sole proprietorship*, the *partnership*, and the *corporation*. Sole proprietorships are the most numerous.

Sole Proprietorships

sole proprietorship
A business owned by one person who operates it for his or her own profit.

A **sole proprietorship** is a business owned by one person who operates it for his or her own profit. About 75 percent of all business firms are sole proprietorships. Typically, the proprietor, along with a few employees, runs the business. He or she normally raises capital from personal resources or by borrowing and is responsible for all business decisions. The sole proprietor has **unlimited liability:** His or her total wealth, not merely the amount originally invested, can be taken to satisfy business debts. The majority of sole proprietorships operate in the wholesale, retail, service, and construction industries. The key strengths and weaknesses of sole proprietorships are summarized in Table 9.1.

unlimited liability
The condition of a sole proprietorship (and general partnership) allowing the owner's total wealth to be taken to satisfy business debts.

Partnerships

partnership
A business owned by two or more people and operated for profit.

A **partnership** consists of two or more owners doing business together for profit. Partnerships account for about 10 percent of all businesses. Finance, insurance, and real estate firms are the most common types of partnerships. Public accounting and stock brokerage partnerships often have large numbers of partners.

articles of partnership
The written contract used to establish a business partnership formally.

Most partnerships are established by a written contract known as **articles of partnership.** In a *general* (or *regular*) *partnership*, all partners have unlimited liability, and each partner is legally liable for all of the debts of the partnership. The strengths and weaknesses of partnerships are summarized in Table 9.1.

Corporations

corporation
An intangible business entity created by law (often called a "legal entity").

A **corporation** is an intangible business entity created by law. Often called a "legal entity," a corporation has the powers of an individual in that it can sue and be sued, make and be party to contracts, and acquire property in its own name. Although only about 15 percent of all businesses are incorporated, the corporation accounts for nearly 90 percent of business receipts and 80 percent of net profits. Corporations are involved in all types of business, but manufacturing corporations account for the largest portion of corporate business receipts and net profits. The key strengths and weaknesses of large corporations are summarized in Table 9.1.

It is important to recognize that there are many small private corporations in addition to the large corporations emphasized throughout this text. For many small corporations there is limited access to financing, and the frequent requirement that the owner co-sign a loan eliminates limited liability.

stockholders
The owners of a corporation, whose ownership, or "equity," is evidenced by either common stock or preferred stock.

The owners of a corporation are its **stockholders,** whose ownership, or "equity," is evidenced by either common stock or preferred stock. Stockholders expect to earn a return by receiving dividends and by realizing gains through

TABLE 9.1	Strengths and Weaknesses of the Basic Legal Forms of Business Organization

	Legal form		
	Sole proprietorship	Partnership	Corporation
Strengths	• Owner receives all profits • Low organizational costs • Income included and taxed on proprietor's personal tax return • Independence • Secrecy • Ease of dissolution	• Can raise more funds than sole proprietorships • Borrowing power enhanced by more owners • More available brain power and managerial skill • Income included and taxed on partners' personal tax returns	• Owners have *limited liability*, which guarantees that they cannot lose more than they invest • Can achieve large size via sale of stock • Ownership (stock) is readily transferable • Long life of firm • Can hire professional managers • Has better access to financing • Receives certain tax advantages
Weaknesses	• Owner has *unlimited liability*—total wealth can be taken to satisfy debts • Limited fund-raising power tends to inhibit growth • Proprietor must be "jack of all trades" • Difficult to give employees long-run career opportunities • Lacks continuity when proprietor dies	• Owners have *unlimited liability* and may have to cover debts of other partners • Partnership is dissolved when a partner dies • Difficult to liquidate or transfer partnership	• Taxes generally higher, because corporate income is taxed and dividends paid to owners are also taxed • More expensive to organize than other business forms • Subject to greater government regulation • Lacks secrecy, because stockholders must receive financial reports

increases in share price. As noted in Figure 9.1, the stockholders vote periodically to elect the members of the board of directors and to amend the firm's corporate charter.

The **board of directors** has the ultimate authority in guiding corporate affairs and in making general policy. The directors include key corporate personnel as well as outside individuals who usually are successful businesspeople. Outside directors for major corporations are typically paid an annual fee of $15,000 to $30,000 or more and are frequently granted options to buy a specified number of shares of the firm's stock at a stated (and often attractive) price.

The **president** or **chief executive officer (CEO)** is responsible for managing day-to-day operations and carrying out the policies established by the board of directors. Vice presidents, including the *vice president of finance*, or **chief financial officer (CFO)**, typically report to the CEO. The CFO is responsible for managing the firms financial activities. The CEO is required to report periodically to the firm's directors. It is important to note the division between owners and managers in a large corporation, as shown by the dashed horizontal line in Figure 9.1. We will address this separation and some of the issues surrounding it when we discuss the *agency issue* later in this chapter.

board of directors
Group that is elected by the firm's stockholders and has ultimate authority to guide corporate affairs and make general policy.

president or chief executive officer (CEO)
Corporate official responsible for managing the firm's day-to-day operations and carrying out the policies established by the board of directors.

chief financial officer (CFO)
Corporate official who typically reports to the *CEO* and is responsible for managing the firm's financial activities. Often called the vice president of finance.

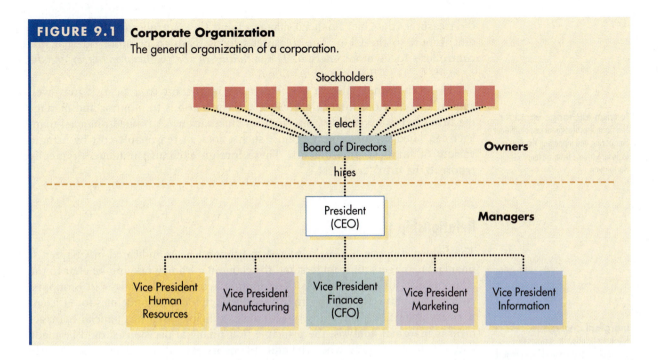

FIGURE 9.1 **Corporate Organization**
The general organization of a corporation.

FIGURE 9.1

Corporate Organization
The general organization of a corporation.

Stockholders

elect

Board of Directors   **Owners**

hires

President
(CEO)   **Managers**

Vice President Human Resources | Vice President Manufacturing | Vice President Finance (CFO) | Vice President Marketing | Vice President Information

Review Questions

9–1   Which form of business organization is most common? Which form is dominant in terms of business receipts and net profits?

9–2   Describe the roles of, and the basic relationship among, the major parties in a corporation: stockholders, board of directors, and president.

LG2 The Financial Management Function

People in all areas of responsibility within the firm must interact with finance personnel and procedures to get their jobs done. For financial personnel to make useful forecasts and decisions, they must be willing and able to talk to individuals in other areas of the firm. The managerial finance function can be broadly described by considering its role within the organization, its relationship to economics and accounting, and the primary activities of the financial manager.

Organization of the Finance Function

The size and importance of the managerial finance function depend on the size of the firm. In small firms, the finance function is generally performed by the accounting department. As a firm grows, the finance function typically evolves into a separate department linked directly to the company president or CEO through the chief financial officer (CFO). As noted in Chapter 1 (see Figure 1.1), the treasurer (the chief financial manager) and the controller (the chief accountant) report to the CFO. The treasurer's focus tends to be more external, the controller's focus more internal. *The activities of the financial manager are the primary focus of this part of the book.*

If international sales or purchases are important to a firm, it may well employ one or more finance professionals whose job is to monitor and manage the firm's exposure to loss from currency fluctuations. A trained financial manager can "hedge," or protect against such a loss, at reasonable cost by using a variety of financial instruments. These **foreign exchange managers** typically report to the firm's treasurer.

foreign exchange manager
The finance professional responsible for monitoring and managing the firm's exposure to loss from currency fluctuations.

Relationship to Economics

The field of finance is closely related to economics. As indicated in Chapter 4, financial managers must understand the economic framework and be alert to the consequences of varying levels of economic activity and changes in economic policy. They must also be able to use economic theories as guidelines for efficient business operation. The primary economic principle used in financial management is **marginal analysis,** the principle that financial decisions should be made and actions taken only when the added benefits exceed the added costs. Nearly all financial decisions ultimately come down to an assessment of their marginal benefits and marginal costs.

marginal analysis
Economic principle that states that financial decisions should be made and actions taken only when the added benefits exceed the added costs.

E x a m p l e ▼   Alice Conklin is a financial manager for Doth Department Stores, a large chain of upscale department stores operating primarily in the western United States. She is currently trying to decide whether to replace one of the firm's computers with a new, more sophisticated model that would both speed processing time and handle a larger volume of transactions. The new computer would require a cash outlay of $80,000, and the old computer could be sold to net $28,000. The total benefits from the new computer (measured in today's dollars) would be $100,000, and the benefits over a similar time period from the old computer (measured in today's dollars) would be $35,000. Doing a marginal analysis of these data, Alice organizes this information as follows:

Benefits with new computer	$100,000	
Less: Benefits with old computer	35,000	
(1) Marginal (added) benefits		$65,000
Cost of new computer	$ 80,000	
Less: Proceeds from sale of old computer	28,000	
(2) Marginal (added) costs		52,000
Net benefit [(1) − (2)]		$13,000

Because the marginal (added) benefits of $65,000 exceed the marginal (added) costs of $52,000, Alice recommends that the firm purchase the new computer to replace the old one. The firm will experience a net benefit of $13,000 as a result ▲ of this action.

Relationship to Accounting

The firm's finance and accounting activities are closely related and generally overlap. Indeed, financial management and accounting are often not easily distinguishable. In small firms the controller often carries out the financial function, and in large firms many accountants are closely involved in various finance activities. However, there are two basic differences between finance and accounting; one is related to the emphasis on cash flows and the other to decision making.

Emphasis on Cash Flows

The accountant's primary function is to develop and provide data for measuring the performance of the firm, assessing its financial position, and paying taxes. Using generally accepted accounting principles, the accountant prepares financial statements that recognize revenue at the time of sale (whether payment has been received or not) and recognize expenses when they are incurred. This approach is referred to as the **accrual basis.**

accrual basis
In preparation of financial statements, recognizes revenue at the time of sale and recognizes expenses when they are incurred.

cash basis
Recognizes revenues and expenses only with respect to actual inflows and outflows of cash.

The financial manager, on the other hand, places primary emphasis on *cash flows,* the intake and outgo of cash. He or she maintains the firm's solvency by planning the cash flows necessary to satisfy its obligations and to acquire assets needed to achieve the firm's goals. The financial manager uses this **cash basis** to recognize the revenues and expenses only with respect to actual inflows and outflows of cash. Regardless of its profit or loss, a firm must have a sufficient flow of cash to meet its obligations as they come due.

Example ▼

Coastal Yachts, a small yacht dealer, sold one yacht for $100,000 in the calendar year just ended. The yacht was purchased during the year at a total cost of $80,000. Although the firm paid in full for the yacht during the year, at year end it has yet to collect the $100,000 from the customer. The accounting view and the financial view of the firm's performance during the year are given by the following income and cash flow statements, respectively.

Accounting view (accrual basis)		Financial view (cash basis)	
Income Statement Coastal Yachts for the year ended 12/31		Cash Flow Statement Coastal Yachts for the year ended 12/31	
Sales revenue	$100,000	Cash inflow	$ 0
Less: Costs	80,000	Less: Cash outflow	80,000
Net profit	$ 20,000	Net cash flow	($80,000)

In an accounting sense Coastal Yachts is profitable, but in terms of actual cash flow it is a financial failure. Without adequate cash inflows to meet its obligations, the firm will not survive, regardless of its level of profits.

As the example shows, accrual accounting data do not fully describe the circumstances of a firm. Thus the financial manager must look beyond financial

FIGURE 9.2

Financial Activities
Primary activities of the
financial manager

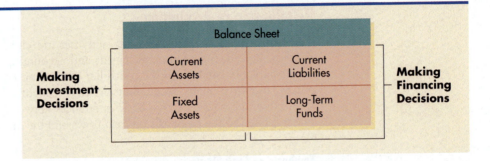

statements to obtain insight into existing or developing problems. Of course, accountants are well aware of the importance of cash flows, and financial managers use and understand accrual-based financial statements. Nevertheless, the primary emphasis of accountants is on accrual methods, and the primary emphasis of financial managers is on cash flow methods.

Decision Making

The second major difference between finance and accounting has to do with decision making. Accountants devote most of their attention to the *collection and presentation of financial data.* Financial managers evaluate the accounting statements, develop additional data, and *make decisions* on the basis of their assessment of the associated returns and risks. Of course, this does not mean that accountants never make decisions or that financial managers never gather data. Rather, the primary focuses of accounting and finance are distinctly different.

Primary Activities of the Financial Manager

In addition to ongoing involvement in financial analysis and planning, the financial manager's primary activities are making investment decisions and making financing decisions. Investment decisions determine both the mix and type of assets held by the firm. Financing decisions determine both the mix and type of financing used by the firm. These sorts of decisions can be conveniently viewed in terms of the firm's balance sheet, as shown in Figure 9.2. However, the decisions are actually made on the basis of their cash flow effects on the overall value of the firm.

Review Questions

9–3   How do the financial activities of the treasurer, or financial manager, differ from those of the controller?

9–4   What is the primary economic principle used in managerial finance?

9–5   What are the major differences between accounting and finance with respect to emphasis on cash flows and decision making?

9–6   How are the two key activities of the financial manager related to the firm's balance sheet?

(LG3) Goal of the Firm

As noted earlier, the owners of a corporation are normally distinct from its managers. Actions of the financial manager should be taken to achieve the objectives of the firm's owners, its stockholders. In most cases, if financial managers are successful in this endeavor, they will also achieve their own financial and professional objectives. Thus financial managers need to know what the objectives of the firm's owners are.

Maximize Profit?

Some people believe that the firm's objective is always to maximize profits. To achieve this goal, the financial manager would take only those actions that were expected to make a major contribution to the firm's overall profits. For each alternative being considered, the financial manager would select the one expected to result in the highest monetary return, commonly measured in terms of *earnings per share (EPS)*.

Example ▼ Brett Kramer, the financial manager of Ramona Industries, a manufacturer of fishing gear, is choosing between two investments, Sinker and Float. The following table shows the EPS that each investment is expected to have over its 3-year life.

Investment	Year 1	Year 2	Year 3	Total for years 1, 2, and 3
			Earnings per share (EPS)	
Sinker	$1.40	$1.00	$ .40	$2.80
Float	60	1.00	1.40	3.00

In terms of the profit maximization goal, Float would be preferred over Sinker, because it results in higher total earnings per share over the 3-year period ($3.00 EPS for Float compared with $2.80 EPS for Sinker).

▲

But is profit maximization a reasonable goal? No, it fails for several reasons. First, *it ignores the timing of returns*. Because of the time value of money, *the receipt of funds sooner rather than later is preferred*. In the preceding example, Sinker provides much greater earnings per share in the first year. The larger first-year returns could be reinvested to provide greater future earnings.

Second, profit maximization *ignores cash flows available to stockholders*. Profits do not necessarily represent cash flows available to the stockholders. Owners receive cash flow in the form of either cash dividends paid to them or the proceeds from selling their shares for a higher price than initially paid. A greater EPS does not necessarily mean that a firm's board of directors will vote to increase dividend payments. Nor does a higher EPS necessarily translate into a higher stock price. As explained in Chapter 7, only when earnings increases are accompanied by the expectation of increased future cash flows would a higher stock price be expected.

Finally, *profit maximization disregards risk.* As noted in Chapters 6 and 7, a tradeoff exists between return (cash flow) and risk. *Return and risk are, in fact, the key determinants of share price.* Cash flow and risk affect share price differently: Higher cash flow is generally associated with a higher share price. But higher risk tends to result in a lower share price, because the stockholder must be compensated for the greater risk.

Because profit maximization does not achieve the objectives of the firm's owners, it should *not* be the goal of the financial manager.

Maximize Shareholder Wealth

The goal of the firm, and therefore of all managers and employees, is *to maximize the wealth of the owners for whom it is being operated.* The wealth of corporate owners is measured by the share price of the stock, which in turn is based on the timing of returns (cash flows), their magnitude, and their risk. When considering each financial decision alternative in terms of its impact on the share price of the firm's stock, *financial managers should accept only those actions that are expected to increase share price.* (Figure 7.3 on page 199 depicts this process.) Because share price represents the owners' wealth in the firm, maximizing share price will maximize owner wealth. Note that *return (cash flows) and risk are the key decision variables* in *maximizing owner wealth.*

Two important issues related to share price maximization are economic value added (EVA) and the focus on stakeholders.

Economic Value Added (EVA)

economic value added (EVA)
A measure used by many firms to determine whether an investment—proposed or existing—contributes positively to the owners' wealth; calculated by subtracting the cost of funds used to finance an investment from its after-tax operating profits.

Economic value added (EVA) is a measure used by many firms to determine whether an investment—proposed or existing—contributes positively to the owners' wealth. EVA is calculated by subtracting the cost of funds used to finance an investment from its after-tax operating profits. Investments with positive EVAs increase shareholder value; those with negative EVAs reduce shareholder value. Clearly, only those investments with positive EVAs are desirable. For example, the EVA of an investment with after-tax operating profits of $410,000 and associated financing costs of $375,000 would be $35,000 ($410,000 − $375,000). Because this EVA is positive, the investment is expected to increase owner wealth and is therefore acceptable. Of course, in practice numerous accounting and financial issues would be involved in making these estimates.

Although there is no denying the current popularity of EVA, it is simply a repackaged application of a standard investment decision-making technique called *net present value (NPV),* which is described in detail in Chapter 11. What's important at this point is to recognize that useful tools, such as EVA, are available for measuring the contributions of proposed actions to the owners' wealth maximization goal, particularly when one is making investment decisions.

What About Stakeholders?

Although maximizing shareholder wealth is the primary goal, many firms broaden their focus to include the interests of *stakeholders* as well as sharehold-

stakeholders
Groups such as employees, customers, suppliers, creditors, and owners who have a direct economic link to the firm.

ers. **Stakeholders** are groups such as employees, customers, suppliers, creditors, and owners who have a direct economic link to the firm. A firm with a stakeholder focus consciously avoids actions that would prove detrimental to stakeholders. Such a view is often considered part of the firm's "social responsibility." It is expected to provide long-run benefit to shareholders by maintaining positive stakeholder relationships that minimize turnover, conflicts, and litigation. Clearly, the firm can better achieve its goal of shareholder wealth maximization with the cooperation of its other stakeholders, rather than conflict with them.

The Role of Ethics

In recent years the actions taken by certain businesses have received major media attention. Examples include Liggett & Meyers' early 1999 agreement to fund the payment of more than $1 billion in smoking-related health claims; the late 1995 withdrawal, in response to intense public pressure, of the Calvin Klein advertising campaign that many believed bordered on child pornography; and Salomon Brothers' 1992 agreement to pay $122 million to the U.S. Treasury, create a $100 million restitution fund, and be temporarily banned from bidding in government security auctions as a consequence of having made illegal bids in U.S. Treasury auctions. Clearly, these and similar actions have raised the question of **ethics**—standards of conduct or moral judgment. Today, the business community in general and the financial community in particular are developing and enforcing ethical standards. The goal of these standards is to motivate business and market participants to adhere to both the letter and the spirit of laws and regulations concerned with business and professional practice. Most business leaders believe businesses actually strengthen their competitive positions by maintaining high ethical standards.

ethics
Standards of conduct or moral judgment.

Considering Ethics

Robert A. Cooke, a noted ethicist, suggests that the following questions be used to assess the ethical viability of a proposed action.

1. Is the action arbitrary or capricious? Does it unfairly single out an individual or group?
2. Does the action violate the moral or legal rights of any individual or group?
3. Does the action conform to accepted moral standards?
4. Are there alternative courses of action that are less likely to cause actual or potential harm?

Clearly, considering such questions before taking an action can help to ensure its ethical viability.

Today, more and more firms are directly addressing the issue of ethics by establishing corporate ethics policies and requiring employee compliance with them. Frequently, employees are required to sign a formal pledge to uphold the firm's ethics policies. Such policies typically apply to employee actions in dealing with all corporate stakeholders, including the public. Many companies also require employees to participate in ethics seminars and training programs.

*News*Line   BEING GREEN DOESN'T MEAN A RED BOTTOM LINE

Companies that implement socially responsible business practices, such as protecting the environment and providing good working conditions and employee benefits, are finding that customers and investors approve of these actions.

[A] number of companies, large and small, say corporate profitability isn't sacrificed—and indeed may even be enhanced—by exhibiting a social conscience.

"There's no question companies can be responsible on the environmental front and be responsive to worker rights and still be competitive," says David Shilling, director of the Interfaith Center on Corporate Responsibility in New York. "A number of companies are helping set the standard and raising the bar for others."

Among the names that he cites are Mattel, Inc., El Segundo, Calif.; Levi Strauss & Co., San Francisco; Reebok International Ltd., Stoughton, Mass.; Gap Inc., San Francisco; and Liz Claiborne Inc., New York....

Toy maker Mattel created global manufacturing principles two year ago, specifying working conditions that must be satisfied in 20 foreign facilities it owns, as well as in 300 factories that rely on Mattel for at least 40% of their business. Among these criteria: one toilet per 35 workers; no workers under 16 years of age; a 40-hour workweek; and the right to form unions.

"We hope our stand will improve profitability by making customers feel more comfortable buying our products," a Mattel spokesman says. About 15 primary contractors, he adds, have been dismissed "because they couldn't live up to our code."...

For some, the environment is a focus. Fetzer Vineyards Corp., of Hopland, Calif., converted to all-organic farming five years ago on the 1,000 acres it owns. Organic practices also are followed on 3,000 of the 8,000 acres owned by the company's grape suppliers....It's "a societal contribution," says Mr. Dolan, who notes Fetzer's profit and revenue have grown at a 15% annual compounded rate during the past six years.

As the number of companies adhering to social principles grows, investors have taken notice. In fact, some mutual funds have experienced explosive growth on the premise that companies that go the extra mile on such matters often make superior investment vehicles....

Source: Jim Carlton, Rodney Ho, and Rebecca Smith, "Some Companies Say Being Green Doesn't Mean a Red Bottom Line," Wall Street Journal, *December 3, 1999, p. A6.*

Ethics and Share Price

An effective ethics program is believed to enhance corporate value. An ethics program can produce positive benefits: It can reduce potential litigation and judgment costs; maintain a positive corporate image; build shareholder confidence; and gain the loyalty, commitment, and respect of the firm's stakeholders. Such actions, by maintaining and enhancing cash flow and reducing perceived risk, can positively affect the firm's share price. Ethical behavior is therefore viewed as necessary for achieving the firm's goal of owner wealth maximization.

? Review Questions

9–7   List three reasons why profit maximization is not consistent with wealth maximization.

9–8   What is the goal of the firm and therefore of its managers and employees, and how is achievement of this goal measured?

9–9   Who are a firm's *stakeholders?*

9–10   Discuss the relationship between ethics and share price.

🟣 **The Agency Issue**

We have seen that the goal of the financial manager should be to maximize the wealth of the firm's owners. Thus managers can be viewed as agents of the owners who have hired them and given them decision-making authority to manage the firm. Technically, any manager who owns less than 100 percent of the firm is to some degree an agent of the other owners. This separation of owners and managers is shown by the dashed horizontal line in Figure 9.1 (page 267).

In theory, most financial managers would agree with the goal of owner wealth maximization. In practice, however, managers are also concerned with their personal wealth, job security, and fringe benefits. Such concerns may make managers reluctant or unwilling to take more than moderate risk if they perceive that taking too much risk might jeopardize their job or reduce their personal wealth. The result is a less-than-maximum return and a potential loss of wealth for the owners.

The Agency Problem

agency problem
The likelihood that managers may place personal goals ahead of corporate goals.

From this conflict of owner and personal goals arises what has been called the **agency problem,** the likelihood that managers may place personal goals ahead of corporate goals. Two factors—market forces and agency costs—serve to prevent or minimize agency problems.

Market Forces

One market force is *major shareholders,* particularly large institutional investors, such as mutual funds, life insurance companies, and pension funds. These holders of large blocks of a firm's stock exert pressure on management to perform. When necessary they exercise their voting rights as stockholders to replace underperforming management.

Another market force is the *threat of takeover* by another firm that believes it can enhance the firm's value by restructuring its management, operations, and financing. The constant threat of takeover tends to motivate management to act in the best interests of the firm's owners.

Agency Costs

agency costs
The costs borne by stockholders to minimize agency problems.

To minimize agency problems and contribute to the maximization of owners' wealth, stockholders incur **agency costs.** These are the costs of monitoring management behavior, ensuring against dishonest acts of management, and giving managers the financial incentive to maximize share price.

stock options
An incentive allowing management to purchase stock at the market price set at the time of the grant.

The most popular, powerful, and expensive approach is to *structure management compensation* to correspond with share price maximization. The objective is to give managers incentives to act in the best interests of the owners. *Incentive plans* tend to tie management compensation to share price. The most popular incentive plan is the granting of **stock options** to management. These options allow managers to purchase stock at the market price set at the time of the grant.

If the market price subsequently rises, managers will be rewarded by being able to resell the shares at the higher market price. More firms also are offering *performance plans,* which tie management compensation to measures such as earnings per share (EPS), growth in EPS, or other ratios of return. Use of incentive and performance plans appears to motivate managers to operate in a manner reasonably consistent with stock price maximization. In addition, well-structured compensation packages allow firms to hire the best managers available.

The Current View of Management Compensation

The execution of many management compensation plans has been closely scrutinized in recent years. Both individual and institutional stockholders, as well as the Securities and Exchange Commission (SEC), have publicly questioned the appropriateness of the multimillion-dollar compensation packages that many corporate executives receive. For example, the three highest-paid CEOs in 1999 were (1) Charles Wang, of Computer Associates International, who earned $655.4 million; (2) L. Dennis Kozlowski, of Tyco International, who earned $170.0 million; and (3) David Pottruck, of Charles Schwab, who earned $127.9 million. Tenth on the same list was Reuben Mark, of Colgate-Palmolive, who earned $85.3 million. During 1999, the compensation of the average CEO of a major U.S. corporation rose by about 17 percent over 1998. CEOs of 362 of the largest U.S. companies surveyed by *Business Week,* using data from Standard & Poor's Institutional Market Services, earned an average of $12.4 million in total compensation (including salary, bonus, and long-term compensation). The average for the 20 highest paid CEOs was $112.9 million.

Recent studies have failed to find a strong relationship between CEO compensation and share price. Publicity surrounding these large compensation packages (without corresponding share price performance) is expected to drive down executive compensation in the future. Contributing to this publicity is the relatively recent SEC requirement that publicly traded companies disclose to shareholders and others both the amount of compensation to their highest paid executives and the method used to determine it. Unconstrained, managers may have other goals in addition to share price maximization, but much of the evidence suggests that share price maximization—the focus of the financial manager—is the primary goal of most firms.

? Review Question

9–11 Explain how market forces and agency costs act to prevent or minimize the agency problem.

Business Taxation

Businesses, like individuals, must pay taxes on income. The income of sole proprietorships and partnerships is taxed as the income of the individual owners; corporate income is subject to corporate taxes. Regardless of their legal form, all

TABLE 9.2	Corporate Tax Rate Schedule			
		Tax calculation		
Range of taxable income	**Base tax**	**+**	**(Marginal rate × Amount over base bracket)**	
$ 0 to $ 50,000	$ 0	+	(15% × amount over $ 0)	
50,000 to 75,000	7,500	+	(25 × amount over 50,000)	
75,000 to 100,000	13,750	+	(34 × amount over 75,000)	
100,000 to 335,000	22,250	+	(39 × amount over 100,000)	
335,000 to 10,000,000	113,900	+	(34 × amount over 335,000)	
Over $10,000,000	3,400,000	+	(35 × amount over 10,000,000)	

businesses can earn two types of income: ordinary income and capital gains. Under current law, these two types of income are treated differently in the taxation of individuals; they are not treated differently for entities subject to corporate taxes. Frequent amendments in the tax code make it likely that these rates will change before the next edition of this text is published. Emphasis here is given to *corporate taxation*.

Ordinary Income

ordinary income
Income earned through the sale of goods or services.

The **ordinary income** of a corporation is income earned through the sale of goods or services. Ordinary income is currently taxed subject to the rates depicted in the corporate tax rate schedule in Table 9.2.

Example ▼

DB Manufacturing, Inc., a small manufacturer of office products, has before-tax earnings of $250,000. The tax on these earnings can be found by using the tax rate schedule in Table 9.2:

$$\text{Total taxes due} = \$22,250 + [0.39 \times (\$250,000 - \$100,000)]$$
$$= \$22,250 + (0.39 \times \$150,000)$$
$$= \$22,250 + \$58,500 = \underline{\underline{\$80,750}}$$

▲

From a financial point of view, it is important to understand the difference between average and marginal tax rates, the treatment of interest and dividend income, and the effects of tax deductibility.

Average versus Marginal Tax Rates

average tax rate
A firm's taxes divided by its taxable income.

The **average tax rate** paid on the firm's ordinary income can be calculated by dividing its taxes by its taxable income. The average tax rate paid by DB Manufacturing, Inc., in the preceding example was 32.3 percent ($80,750 ÷ $250,000). As a corporation's taxable income increases, its average tax rate approaches and finally reaches 34 percent. It remains at that level up to $10,000,000 of taxable income, beyond which it rises toward but never reaches 35 percent.

marginal tax rate
The rate at which *additional income* is taxed.

The **marginal tax rate** represents the rate at which *additional income* is taxed. In the current corporate tax structure, the marginal tax rate on income up to $50,000 is 15 percent; from $50,000 to $75,000 it is 25 percent; and so on, as shown in Table 9.2. DB Manufacturing's marginal tax rate is currently 39 percent because its next dollar of taxable income (bringing before-tax earnings to $250,001) would be taxed at that rate. To simplify calculations in the text, *a fixed 40 percent tax rate is assumed to be applicable to ordinary corporate income.* Given our focus on financial decision making, this rate is assumed to represent the firm's marginal tax rate.

Interest and Dividend Income

double taxation
Occurs when the already once-taxed earnings of a corporation are distributed as cash dividends to stockholders, who must pay taxes on them.

intercorporate dividends
Dividends received by one corporation on common and preferred stock held in other corporations.

In the process of determining taxable income, any interest received by the corporation is included as ordinary income. Dividends, on the other hand, are treated differently as a result of **double taxation,** which occurs when the already once-taxed earnings of a corporation are distributed as cash dividends to stockholders, who must pay taxes on them. Therefore, dividends the firm receives on common and preferred stock held in other corporations, and representing less than 20 percent ownership in them, are subject to a 70 percent exclusion for tax purposes.[1] Because of the dividend exclusion, only 30 percent of these **intercorporate dividends** are included as ordinary income. The tax law provides this exclusion to avoid *triple taxation.* Triple taxation would occur if the first and second corporations were taxed on income before the second corporation pays dividends to its shareholders, who must then include the dividend in their taxable income. The dividend exclusion in effect eliminates most of the potential tax liability from the dividend received by the second and any subsequent corporations.

Example ▼   Syntex Industries, a major manufacturer of plastic resins, during the year just ended received $100,000 in interest on bonds it held and $100,000 in dividends on common stock it owned in other corporations. The firm is subject to a 40 percent marginal tax rate and is eligible for a 70 percent exclusion on its intercorporate dividend receipts. The after-tax income realized by Syntex from each of these sources of investment income is found as follows:

	Interest income		Dividend income
(1) Before-tax amount	$100,000		$100,000
Less: Applicable exclusion	0	(.70 × $100,000) =	70,000
Taxable amount	$100,000		$ 30,000
(2) Tax (40%)	40,000		12,000
After-tax amount [(1) − (2)]	$ 60,000		$ 88,000

---

[1]The exclusion is 80 percent if the corporation owns between 20 and 80 percent of the stock in the corporation paying it dividends; 100 percent of the dividends received are excluded if it owns more than 80 percent of the corporation paying it dividends. For convenience, we are assuming here that the ownership interest in the dividend-paying corporation is less than 20 percent.

As a result of the 70 percent dividend exclusion, the after-tax amount is greater for the dividend income than for the interest income. Clearly, the dividend exclusion enhances the attractiveness of stock investments relative to bond investments made by one corporation in another.

Tax-Deductible Expenses

In calculating their taxes, corporations are allowed to deduct operating expenses, as well as interest expense. The tax deductibility of these expenses reduces their after-tax cost. The following example illustrates the benefit of tax deductibility.

Example ▼ Two companies, Debt Co. and NoDebt Co., both expect in the coming year to have earnings before interest and taxes of $200,000. Debt Co. during the year will have to pay $30,000 in interest; NoDebt Co. has no debt and therefore will have no interest expense. Calculation of the earnings after taxes for these two firms is as follows:

	Debt Co.	NoDebt Co.
Earnings before interest and taxes	$200,000	$200,000
Less: Interest expense	30,000	0
Earnings before taxes	$170,000	$200,000
Less: Taxes (40%)	68,000	80,000
Earnings after taxes	$102,000	$120,000
Difference in earnings after taxes		$18,000

Whereas Debt Co. had $30,000 more interest expense than NoDebt Co., Debt Co.'s earnings after taxes are only $18,000 less than those of NoDebt Co. ($102,000 versus $120,000). This difference is attributable to the fact that Debt Co.'s $30,000 interest expense deduction provided a tax savings of $12,000 (taxes paid were $68,000 for Debt Co. versus $80,000 for NoDebt Co.). This amount can be calculated directly by multiplying the tax rate by the amount of interest expense ($0.40 \times \$30,000 = \$12,000$).

The tax deductibility of certain expenses reduces their actual (after-tax) cost to the profitable firm. Note that for both accounting and tax purposes *interest is a tax-deductible expense, whereas dividends are not.* Because dividends are not tax-deductible, their after-tax cost is equal to the amount of the dividend. Thus a $30,000 cash dividend has an after-tax cost of $30,000.

Capital Gains

capital gain
The amount by which the sale price of an asset exceeds the asset's initial purchase price.

If a firm sells a capital asset (such as stock held as an investment) for more than its initial purchase price, the difference between the sale price and the purchase price is called a **capital gain.** For corporations, capital gains are added to

NewsLine   **A TAXING CHALLENGE**

Understanding business taxation is the first step toward managing taxes. Today's financial managers are paying increased attention to tax efficiency as a way to improve earnings and increase value.

For profitable companies, it sometimes seems that the only certainty is taxes. Within that framework, however, adroit management can make a profound difference. And finance departments across America are seeing that, even beyond the welcome boost to earnings, sustainable tax efficiency in a highly valued stock market can add to market capital....

Were pretax income to govern incentives, then employees with bonuses on their minds would pay far less attention to favorable tax implications, notes Colgate-Palmolive Co. CFO Stephen Patrick. But because incentive compensation reflects after-tax earnings at the $9.5 billion consumer-products company, in New York, managers are rewarded when taxes are lowered. "It's a very high priority. Managing taxes is a job for everyone at Colgate," he says, noting that each year, tax executives set specific tax-rate targets as part of the budget-planning process. And, within legal and regulatory guidelines, Colgate managers routinely watch for ways to time remittances from overseas, maximize research and development tax credits, and ensure assets are written up to

maximum levels for purposes of depreciation. The payoff? Collectively, Colgate...has lowered its effective tax rate each year since 1992.

At many companies these days, there's a similar refrain, as top executives elevate the status of tax management from an afterthought to a part of advanced planning. "Our people think it's a competitive advantage," insists Lester Ezrati, vice president of tax, licensing, and customs at Hewlett-Packard Co., the $47 billion computer company in Palo Alto, California. "It's just like managing any other expense, so long as you do it legitimately." Carol Garnant, vice president of taxes at Sears, Roebuck and Co., in Hoffman Estates, Illinois, who also chairs the corporate tax management committee for the Tax Executives Institute, in Washington, D.C., observes that "there is more attention being placed on driving effective tax rates as low as possible—obviously within legal constraints."...

Source: Steven L. Mintz, "A Taxing Challenge," CFO, November 1999, downloaded from www.cfonet.com/html/Articles/CFO/1999/99NOatax.html.

ordinary corporate income and taxed at the regular corporate rates, with a maximum marginal tax rate of 39 percent. To simplify the computations presented in the text, as for ordinary income, *a fixed 40 percent tax rate is assumed to be applicable to corporate capital gains.*

Example ▼ The Walt Company, a manufacturer of heart monitors, has pre-tax operating earnings of $500,000 and has just sold for $40,000 an asset that was purchased 2 years ago for $36,000. Because the asset was sold for more than its initial purchase price, there is a capital gain of $4,000 ($40,000 sale price − $36,000 initial purchase price). The corporation's taxable income will total $504,000 ($500,000 ordinary income plus $4,000 capital gain). Because this total is above $335,000, the capital gain will be taxed at the 34% rate (see Table 9.2), resulting in a tax of $1,360 (0.34 × $4,000). ▲

? Review Questions

9–12 Describe the tax treatments of ordinary corporate income and capital gains. What is the difference between the average tax rate and the marginal tax rate?

9–13 Why might the intercorporate dividend exclusion make corporate stock investments by one corporation in another more attractive than bond investments?

9–14 What benefit results from the tax deductibility of certain corporate expenses?

Ⓛ6 Depreciation

depreciation
The systematic charging of a portion of the costs of fixed assets against annual revenues over time.

Business firms are permitted to charge a portion of the costs of fixed assets systematically against annual revenues. This allocation of historical cost over time is called **depreciation.** For tax purposes, the depreciation of business assets is regulated by the Internal Revenue Code. Because the objectives of financial reporting are sometimes different from those of tax legislation, firms often use different depreciation methods for financial reporting from those required for tax purposes. Tax laws are used to accomplish economic goals such as providing incentives for business investment in certain types of assets, whereas the objectives of financial reporting are of course quite different. Keeping two different sets of records for these two different purposes is legal.

modified accelerated cost recovery system (MACRS)
System used to determine the depreciation of assets for tax purposes.

Depreciation for tax purposes is determined by using the **modified accelerated cost recovery system (MACRS);** a variety of depreciation methods are available for financial reporting purposes. Before we discuss the methods of depreciating an asset, you must understand the relationship among depreciation and cash flows, the depreciable value of an asset, and the depreciable life of an asset.

Depreciation and Cash Flows

noncash charges
Expenses deducted on the income statement that do not involve an actual outlay of cash during the period.

The financial manager is concerned with *cash flows* rather than net profits as reported on the income statement. To adjust the income statement to estimate cash flow from operations, all noncash charges must be added back to the firm's net profits after taxes. **Noncash charges** are expenses that are deducted on the income statement but do not involve an actual outlay of cash during the period. Depreciation, amortization, and depletion allowances are examples. Because depreciation expenses are the most common noncash charges, we shall demonstrate their treatment. Amortization and depletion charges are treated in a similar fashion.

The general rule for adjusting net profits after taxes by adding back all noncash charges is expressed as follows:

$$\text{Cash flow from operations} = \text{Net profits after taxes} + \text{Noncash charges} \qquad (9.1)$$

For example, applying Equation 9.1 to the 2001 income statement for Nolte Corporation, presented under the heading "Accrual Basis" in Table 9.3, yields the following cash flow from operations:

Net profits after taxes	$180,000
Plus: Depreciation expense	100,000
Cash flow from operations	$280,000

Depreciation and other noncash charges shield the firm from taxes by lowering taxable income. Some people do not define depreciation as a source of funds; however, in financial analysis it is a source of funds in the sense that it represents a "nonuse" of funds. Table 9.3 also shows Nolte Corporation's income statement prepared on a *cash basis* (under the heading "Cash Flow Basis") to illustrate how depreciation shields income and frees up funds that would otherwise be paid as taxes. It shows that by ignoring depreciation (except in determining

TABLE 9.3	Nolte Corporation Income Statement Calculated on Both Accrual and Cash Bases ($000) for the Year Ended December 31, 2001		
		Accrual Basis	**Cash Flow Basis**
Sales revenue		$1,700	$1,700
Less: Cost of goods sold		1,000	1,000
Gross profits		$ 700	$ 700
Less: Operating expenses			
Selling expense	$ 80		$ 80
General and administrative expense	150		150
Depreciation expense (noncash charge)	100		0
Total operating expense		330	230
Operating profits		$ 370	$ 470
Less: Interest expense		70	70
Net profits before taxes		$ 300	$ 400
Less: Taxes		120	120
Net profits after taxes		$ 180	
Cash flow from operations			$ 280

the firm's taxes), we get cash flow from operations of $280,000—the value obtained before. Adjustment of the firm's net profits after taxes by adding back depreciation is used to estimate cash flow in a number of contexts in finance.

Depreciable Value of an Asset

Under the basic MACRS procedures, the depreciable value of an asset (the amount to be depreciated) is its *full* cost, including outlays for installation. No adjustment is required for expected salvage value.

Example  Nolte Corporation acquired a new machine at a cost of $38,000, with installation costs of $2,000. Regardless of its expected salvage value, the depreciable value of the machine is $40,000: $38,000 cost + $2,000 installation cost.

Depreciable Life of an Asset

depreciable life
Time period over which an asset is depreciated.

The time period over which an asset is depreciated—its **depreciable life**—can significantly affect the pattern of cash flows. The shorter the depreciable life, the more quickly the cash flow created by the depreciation write-off will be received. Given the financial manager's preference for faster receipt of cash flows, a shorter depreciable life is preferred to a longer one. However, the firm must abide by certain Internal Revenue Service (IRS) requirements for determining depreciable life. These MACRS standards, which apply to both new and used assets, require the taxpayer to use as an asset's depreciable life the appropriate MACRS **recovery period**. There are six MACRS recovery periods—3, 5, 7, 10, 15, and 20

recovery period
The appropriate depreciable life of a particular asset as determined by MACRS.

TABLE 9.6 The Sources and Uses of Cash

Sources	Uses
Decrease in any asset	Increase in any asset
Increase in any liability	Decrease in any liability
Net profits after taxes	Net loss
Depreciation and other noncash charges	Dividends paid
Sale of stock	Repurchase or retirement of stock

Developing the Statement of Cash Flows

The statement of cash flows for a given period is developed using the income statement for the period, along with the beginning- and end-of-period balance sheets. The statement of cash flows for the year ended December 31, 2001, for Nolte Corporation is presented in Table 9.7. Note that all sources as well as net profits after taxes and depreciation are treated as positive values—cash

TABLE 9.7 Nolte Corporation Statement of Cash Flows ($000) for the Year Ended December 31, 2001

Cash Flow from Operating Activities		
Net profits after taxes	$180	
Depreciation	100	
Decrease in accounts receivable	100	
Decrease in inventories	300	
Increase in accounts payable	200	
Decrease in accruals	(100)[a]	
Cash provided by operating activities		$780
Cash Flow from Investment Activities		
Increase in gross fixed assets	($300)	
Changes in business interests	0	
Cash provided by investment activities		(300)
Cash Flow from Financing Activities		
Decrease in notes payable	($100)	
Increase in long-term debts	200	
Changes in stockholders' equity[b]	0	
Dividends paid	(80)	
Cash provided by financing activities		20
Net increase in cash and marketable securities		$500

[a]As is customary, parentheses are used to denote a negative number, which in this case is a cash outflow.

[b]Retained earnings are excluded here, because their change is actually reflected in the combination of the "Net profits after taxes" and "Dividends paid" entries.

inflows. All uses, any losses, and dividends paid are treated as negative values—cash outflows. The items in each category—operating, investment, and financing—are totaled, and the three totals are added to get the "Net increase (decrease) in cash and marketable securities" for the period. As a check, this value should reconcile with the actual change in cash and marketable securities for the year, which is obtained from the beginning- and end-of-period balance sheets.

Interpreting the Statement

The statement of cash flows allows the financial manager and other interested parties to analyze the firm's cash flow. The manager should pay special attention both to the major categories of cash flow and to the individual items of cash inflow and outflow, to assess whether any developments have occurred that are contrary to the company's financial policies. In addition, the statement can be used to evaluate progress toward projected goals or to isolate inefficiencies. For example, increases in accounts receivable or inventories resulting in major cash outflows may signal credit or inventory problems, respectively. The financial manager also can prepare a statement of cash flows developed from projected financial statements. This approach can be used to determine whether planned actions are desirable in view of the resulting cash flows.

An understanding of the basic financial principles presented throughout Part 3 of this text is absolutely essential to the effective interpretation of the statement of cash flows.

Review Questions

9–17 Describe the overall cash flow through the firm in terms of operating flows, investment flows, and financing flows.

9–18 Discuss why a decrease in cash is a source and an increase in cash is a use.

9–19 How are cash inflows differentiated from cash outflows on the statement of cash flows?

TYING IT ALL TOGETHER

This chapter has described some of the key financial aspects of business firms and the environment in which they operate. Specific attention has been given to the common forms of business organization, the financial management function, the goal of the firm, the agency issue, business taxation, depreciation, and cash flow. The importance of the firm and its financial environment from the viewpoints of financial managers, financial markets, and investors are summarized in the Integrative Table that follows.

INTEGRATIVE TABLE

Interacting with the Firm and Its Financial Environment

Role of **Financial Managers**	*Role of* **Financial Markets**	*Role of* **Investors**
Financial managers must understand their roles in the firm and the legal and operational effects of the firm's organizational form on their activities. Most important, they must understand the shareholder wealth maximization goal and the ethical and agency issues related to achievement of that goal. They also need to understand business taxation, depreciation, and cash flow issues in order to create value for shareholders.	The financial markets provide the forum in which firms obtain needed financing and disseminate information to investors. They serve as a pricing mechanism that provides continuous assessments of the firm's value and allows financial managers and investors to determine how well the goal of maximizing owner wealth is being achieved. The markets also recognize the impact of taxes and cash flow on the firm's value. And they serve as a forum in which investors respond to the actions of financial managers, sometimes positively, sometimes negatively.	Investors need to understand the implications of the corporate form of organization for their rights and opportunities as suppliers of debt and equity capital. They need to understand how financial managers carry out their activities to maximize shareholder wealth. They also need to recognize the importance of ethical practices by the firm and its need to incur agency costs. Finally, the impact of taxes, depreciation, and cash flow on the value of the firm is important.

LG1 **Review the common forms of business organization.** The common forms of business organization are the sole proprietorship, the partnership, and the corporation. The corporation is dominant in terms of business receipts and net profits. The owners of a corporation are its stockholders, those who hold either common stock or preferred stock. Stockholders expect to earn a return by receiving dividends or by realizing gains through increases in share price. The key strengths and weaknesses of each form of business organization are summarized in Table 9.1.

LG2 **Describe the financial management function, its relationship to economics and accounting, and the financial manager's primary activities.** All areas of responsibility within a firm interact with finance personnel and processes. In large firms, the financial management function may be handled by a separate department headed by the vice president of finance (CFO), to whom the treasurer and controller report; in small firms the finance function is generally performed by the accounting department. The financial manager must understand the economic environment and relies heavily on the economic principle of marginal analysis when making decisions. Financial managers use accounting data but concentrate on cash flows and decision making. In addition to her or his ongoing involvement in financial analysis and planning, the primary activities of the financial manager are making investment decisions and making financing decisions.

LG3 **Explain the wealth maximization goal of the firm and the role of ethics in the firm.** The goal of the financial manager is to maximize the owners' wealth, as evidenced by stock price, rather than profits. Profit maximization ignores the timing of returns, does not directly consider cash flows, and ignores risk, so it is an inappropriate goal. Both return and risk must be assessed by the financial manager when evaluating decision alternatives. The wealth-maximizing actions of financial managers should also consider the interests of stakeholders, groups who have a direct economic link to the firm. Positive ethical practices by the firm and its managers are believed to be necessary for achieving the firm's goal of maximizing owner wealth.

LG4 **Discuss the agency issue.** An agency problem results when managers, as agents for owners, place personal goals ahead of corporate goals. Market forces, in the form of shareholder activism and the threat of takeover, tend to prevent or minimize agency problems. In addition, firms incur agency costs to monitor management behavior and provide incentives to management to act in the best interest of owners. Stock options and performance plans are examples of such agency costs.

LG5 **Review the fundamentals of business taxation of ordinary income and capital gains.** Corporate income is subject to corporate taxes. Corporate tax rates are applicable to both ordinary income (after deduction of allowable expenses) and capital gains. The average tax rate paid by a corporation ranges from 15 to nearly 35 percent. (For convenience, we assume a 40 percent marginal tax rate in this book.) Certain provisions in the tax code, such as intercorporate dividend exclusions and tax-deductible expenses, provide corporate taxpayers with opportunities to reduce their taxes.

LG6 **Understand the effect of depreciation on the firm's cash flows, the depreciable value of**

an asset, its depreciable life, and tax depreciation methods. Depreciation, the allocation of historical cost, is the most common type of noncash expenditure. To estimate cash flow from operations, depreciation and any other noncash charges are added back to net profits after taxes. Because they lower taxable income without an actual outflow of cash, noncash charges act as a source of funds to the firm. The depreciable value of an asset and its depreciable life are determined by using the modified accelerated cost recovery system (MACRS) standards of the federal tax code. MACRS groups assets into six property classes based on length of recovery period and can be applied using a schedule of yearly depreciation percentages for each period.

LG7 **Discuss the firm's cash flows, particularly the statement of cash flows.** The statement of cash flows is divided into operating, investment, and financing flows. It can be developed using the income statement for the period, along with beginning- and end-of-period balance sheets. The statement reconciles changes in the firm's cash flows with changes in cash and marketable securities for the period. Interpreting the statement of cash flows requires an understanding of basic financial principles and involves both the major categories of cash flow and the individual items of cash inflow and outflow.

SELF-TEST EXERCISES   (Solutions in Appendix B)

 ST 9–1   **Corporate taxes**   Rivera Enterprises, Inc., had operating earnings of $280,000 for the year just ended. During the year the firm sold stock that it held in another company for $180,000, which was $30,000 above its original purchase price of $150,000, paid 1 year earlier.

a. What is the amount, if any, of capital gains realized during the year?
b. How much total taxable income did the firm earn during the year?
c. Use the corporate tax rate schedule given in Table 9.2 on page 277 to calculate the firm's total taxes due.
d. Calculate both the *average tax rate* and the *marginal tax rate* on the basis of your findings.

LG6   **ST 9–2   Depreciation and cash flow.**   A firm expects to have earnings before depreciation and taxes (EBDT) of $160,000 in each of the next 6 years. It is considering the purchase of an asset that costs $140,000, requires $10,000 in installation costs, and has a recovery period of 5 years.

a. Calculate the annual depreciation for the asset purchase, using the MACRS depreciation percentages in Table 9.5 on page 284.

b. Calculate the annual operating cash flows for each of the 6 years. Assume that the new asset is the firm's only depreciable asset and that it is subject to a 40% ordinary tax rate.

c. Compare and discuss your findings in parts **a** and **b**.

EXERCISES

LG1   **9–1   Liability comparisons**   Beth Phillips has invested $25,000 in Technology Development Company. The firm has recently declared bankruptcy and has $60,000 in unpaid debts. Explain the nature of payments, if any, by Ms. Phillips in each of the following situations.

a. Technology Development Company is a sole proprietorship owned by Ms. Phillips.

b. Technology Development Company is a 50-50 partnership of Ms. Phillips and Ted Bachelor.

c. Technology Development Company is a corporation.

LG2   **9–2   Accrual income versus cash flow**   Ellis Book Sales, Inc., supplies textbooks to college and university bookstores. The books are shipped with a proviso that they must be paid for within 30 days but can be returned for a full refund credit within 90 days. Ellis shipped and billed book titles totaling $760,000. Collections net of return credits during the year totaled $690,000. The company spent $300,000 acquiring the books that it shipped.

a. Using accrual-basis accounting and the figures above, show the firm's income for the past year.

b. Using cash-basis accounting and the figures above, show the firm's cash flow for the past year.

c. Which of these statements is more useful to the financial manager? Why?

LG4   **9–3   Identifying agency problems and costs**   Explain why each of the following situations is an agency problem and what costs to the firm might result from it. Suggest how the problem might be dealt with short of firing the individual(s) involved.

a. The front desk receptionist routinely takes an extra 20 minutes of lunch time to take care of her personal errands.

b. Division managers are padding cost estimates in order to show short-term efficiency gains when the costs come in lower than the estimates.

c. The firm's chief executive officer has secret talks with a competitor about the possibility of a merger in which he or she would become the CEO of the combined firms.

d. A branch manager lays off experienced full-time employees and staffs customer service positions with part-time or temporary workers to lower employment costs and raise this year's branch profit. The manager's bonus is based on profitability.

9–4   Corporate taxes   Tenacity Supply, Inc., is a small corporation acting as the exclusive distributor of a major line of sporting goods. During 2001 the firm earned $92,500 before taxes.

a. Calculate the firm's tax liability using the corporate tax rate schedule given in Table 9.2 on page 277.

b. How much is Tenacity Supply's 2001 after-tax earnings?

c. What was the firm's *average tax rate,* based on your findings in part a?

d. What is the firm's *marginal tax rate,* based on your findings in part a?

9–5   Average corporate tax rates   Refer to the corporate tax rate schedule given in Table 9.2 on page 277.

a. Calculate the tax liability, after-tax earnings, and average tax rates for the following levels of corporate earnings before taxes: $10,000; $80,000; $300,000; $500,000; $1.5 million; $10 million; and $15 million.

b. Plot the average tax rates (measured on the *y* axis) against the pre-tax income levels (measured on the *x* axis). What generalization can be made about the relationship between these variables?

9-6   Marginal corporate tax rates   Refer to the corporate tax rate schedule given in Table 9.2 on page 277.

a. Find the marginal tax rate for the following levels of corporate earnings before taxes: $15,000; $60,000; $90,000; $200,000; $400,000; $1 million; and $20 million.

b. Plot the marginal tax rates (measured on the *y* axis) against the pre-tax income levels (measured on the *x* axis). Explain the relationship between these variables.

9–7   Interest versus dividend income   During the year just ended, Oceanic Distributors, Inc., had pre-tax earnings from operations of $490,000. In addition, during the year it received $20,000 in income from interest on bonds it held in Peg Manufacturing and received $20,000 in income from dividends on its 5% common stock holding in Stone Industries, Inc. Oceanic is in the 40% tax bracket and is eligible for a 70% dividend exclusion on its Stone Industries stock.

a. Calculate the firm's tax on its operating earnings only.

b. Find the tax and after-tax amount attributable to the interest income from Peg Manufacturing bonds.

c. Find the tax and after-tax amount attributable to the dividend income from the Stone Industries, Inc., common stock.

d. Compare, contrast, and discuss the after-tax amounts resulting from the interest income and dividend income calculated in parts b and c.

e. What is the firm's total tax liability for the year?

9–8   Interest versus dividend expense   Mina Corporation expects earnings before interest and taxes to be $40,000 for this period. Assuming an ordinary tax rate of 40%, compute the firm's earnings after taxes and earnings available for common stockholders (earnings after taxes and preferred stock dividends, if any) under the following conditions:

a. The firm pays $10,000 in interest.

b. The firm pays $10,000 in preferred stock dividends.

9–9   Capital gains taxes   Premium Manufacturing is considering the sale of two nondepreciable assets, X and Y. Asset X was purchased for $2,000 and will be sold today for $2,250. Asset Y was purchased for $30,000 and will be sold today for $35,000. The firm is subject to a 40% tax rate on capital gains.

a. Calculate the amount of capital gain, if any, realized on each of the assets.

b. Calculate the tax on the sale of each asset.

LG6 9–10 **Cash flow**   A firm had earnings after taxes of $50,000 in 2001. Depreciation charges were $28,000, and a $2,000 charge for amortization of a bond discount was incurred. What was the firm's cash flow from operations during 2001?

LG6 9–11 **Depreciation**   On January 1, 2001, Spectra Systems acquired two new assets. Asset A was research equipment costing $17,000 and having a 3-year recovery period. Asset B was duplicating equipment having an installed cost of $45,000 and a 5-year recovery period. Using the MACRS depreciation percentages in Table 9.5 on page 284, prepare a depreciation schedule for each of these assets.

LG6 9–12 **Depreciation and cash flow**   A firm in the third year of depreciating its only asset, which originally cost $180,000 and has a 5-year MACRS recovery period, has gathered the following data relative to the current year's operations.

Accruals	$ 15,000
Current assets	120,000
Interest expense	15,000
Sales revenue	400,000
Inventory	70,000
Total costs before depreciation, interest, and taxes	290,000
Tax rate on ordinary income	40%

a. Use the relevant data to determine the cash flow from operations for the current year.

b. Explain the impact that depreciation, as well as any other noncash charges, has on a firm's cash flows.

LG7 9–13 **Classifying sources and uses**   Classify each of the following items as a source of funds (S), a use of funds (U), or neither (N).

Item	Change ($)	Item	Change ($)
Cash	+100	Accounts receivable	−700
Accounts payable	−1,000	Net profits	+600
Notes payable	+500	Depreciation	+100
Long-term debt	−2,000	Repurchase of stock	+600
Inventory	+200	Cash dividends	+800
Fixed assets	+400	Sale of stock	+1,000

web exercises   `Search`

Go to web site **www.aflcio.org/paywatch/tooclose.htm**.
1. According to this CEO Pay Watch group, what are the four methods used by CEOs to "rig" their own pay?
Click on **Some Recommendations for Cleaning Up Boards**.
2. What are the recommendations for cleaning up boards?

Go to web site **www.amcity.com/journals/demographics/reports/27/**.
Click on **Corporate Income** in the Corporate Income Taxes section.
3. Which state(s) has the lowest corporate income tax per capita? How much is it?
Which state(s) has the highest corporate income tax per capita? How much is it?
What is the average corporate income tax per capita?

Go to web site **www.corpreform.org**. Click on **The Declaration**.
4. What is STARC? What is its mission?
5. According to STARC, what is the reason for its struggle?

For additional practice with concepts from this chapter, visit
http://www.awl.com/gitman_madura

Chapter

10

Capital Budgeting:
Cash Flow
Principles

LEARNING GOALS

LG1 Understand the key capital expenditure motives and the steps in the capital budgeting process.

LG2 Define basic capital budgeting terminology.

LG3 Discuss the major components of relevant cash flows, expansion versus replacement cash flows, and international capital budgeting and long-term investments.

LG4 Calculate the initial investment associated with a proposed capital expenditure.

LG5 Determine relevant operating cash inflows using the income statement format.

LG6 Find the terminal cash flow.

The Capital Budgeting Decision Process

capital budgeting
The process of evaluating and selecting long-term investments that are consistent with the firm's goal of maximizing owner wealth.

Long-term investments represent sizable outlays of funds that commit a firm to some course of action. Consequently, the firm needs procedures to analyze and properly select its long-term investments. It must be able to measure cash flows and apply appropriate decision techniques. As time passes, fixed assets may become obsolete or may require an overhaul; at these points, too, financial decisions may be required. **Capital budgeting** is the process of evaluating and selecting long-term investments that are consistent with the firm's goal of maximizing owner wealth.

Firms typically make a variety of long-term investments, but the most common for the manufacturing firm is in *fixed assets,* which include property (land), plant, and equipment. These assets, often referred to as *earning assets,* generally provide the basis for the firm's earning power and value. Because firms treat capital budgeting (investment) and financing decisions *separately,* both this chapter and the next concentrate on fixed-asset acquisition without regard to the specific method of financing used. We begin by discussing the motives for capital expenditure.

Motives for Capital Expenditure

capital expenditure
An outlay of funds by the firm that is expected to produce benefits over a period of time *greater than* 1 year.

operating expenditure
An outlay of funds by the firm resulting in benefits received *within* 1 year.

A **capital expenditure** is an outlay of funds by the firm that is expected to produce benefits over a period of time *greater than* 1 year. An **operating expenditure** is an outlay resulting in benefits received *within* 1 year. Fixed-asset outlays are capital expenditures, but not all capital expenditures are classified as fixed assets. A $60,000 outlay for a new machine with a usable life of 15 years is a capital expenditure that would appear as a fixed asset on the firm's balance sheet. A $60,000 outlay for advertising that produces benefits over a long period is also a capital expenditure but would rarely be shown as a fixed asset.

Capital expenditures are made for many reasons. The basic motives for capital expenditures are to expand, replace, or renew fixed assets or to obtain some other, less tangible benefit over a long period. Details with regard to those motives can be found on the book's web site at www.awl.com/gitman_madura.

Steps in the Process

capital budgeting process
Five distinct but interrelated steps: proposal generation, review and analysis, decision making, implementation, and follow-up.

The **capital budgeting process** consists of five distinct but interrelated steps.

1. *Proposal generation.* Proposals are made at all levels within a business organization and are reviewed at a high level. Proposals that require large outlays are more carefully scrutinized than less costly ones.
2. *Review and analysis.* Formal review and analysis assesses the appropriateness of proposals and evaluates their economic viability. Once the analysis is complete, a summary report is submitted to decision makers.
3. *Decision making.* Firms typically delegate capital expenditure decision making on the basis of dollar limits. Generally, the board of directors must authorize expenditures beyond a certain amount. Often plant managers are

 **Coor's New Brew**

Capital spending at Coors Brewing Co. lacked a key ingredient: financial discipline. CFO Tim Wolf implemented capital budgeting procedures that controlled spending and required managers to justify projects and quantify returns.

Until [CFO Tim] Wolf came to Coors,... the company always went "the Cadillac route" when it came to deciding what kind of equipment to invest in. Sometimes these projects went forward even with unattractive ROI prospects; other times they were far down the road before they were scrapped.

In April 1996, Wolf's new capital disciplines were put to the test, when Coors began to plan construction of a new bottle-wash facility. The facility, which washes and sanitizes returnable bottles for reuse, represented one of the largest capital outlays Coors would make in several years. There was no question of the need to replace the outdated equipment at the Golden brewery, but there was also a new willingness to step back and take a hard look at all the options for replacing this asset....

The project team looked at six different operating scenarios and ran a sensitivity analysis around each before determining that it made the most sense to construct a new facility in the Shenandoah Valley, in Virginia. It then became necessary to investigate the effect of this move on everything from transportation costs to waste-treatment costs, because fewer bottles would be washed in Golden and more in Shenandoah.

"The process promoted a lot of brainstorming," says director of business analysis Mike Gannon.... Eventually, every department that would be affected by the new facility signed agreements stating that the expected cost differences were realistic.

The same kind of dialogue also took place around the design and operational costs of the new facility.... In mid-1996, once the viability of the business case was set, the project team made a presentation to Wolf. The CFO started asking questions—and kept doing so for the next six months.... Over the course of the relentless analysis, Coors was able to knock investment cost down by 25 percent....

"I think the extra time was well spent," says Wolf. "If you can reduce your capital costs, leverage the benefits, and get them faster, that's the way you want to run your capital process...."

Source: Stephen Barr, "Coor's New Brew," CFO, March 1998, downloaded from www.cfonet.com.

given authority to make decisions necessary to keep the production line moving.

4. *Implementation*. Following approval, expenditures are made and projects implemented. Often expenditures for a large project occur in phases.
5. *Follow-up*. Results are monitored, and actual costs and benefits are compared with those that were expected. Action may be required if actual outcomes differ from projected ones.

Each step in the process is important. Review and analysis and decision making (Steps 2 and 3) consume the majority of time and effort, however. Follow-up (Step 5) is an important, but often ignored step aimed at allowing the firm to keep improving the accuracy of its cash flow estimates.

Because of their fundamental importance, this and the following chapter give primary attention to review and analysis and decision making.

 ## Basic Terminology

Before we develop the concepts, techniques, and practices related to the capital budgeting process, we need to explain some basic terminology. In addition, we will present some key assumptions that are used to simplify the discussion in the remainder of this chapter and in Chapter 11.

Independent versus Mutually Exclusive Projects

independent projects
Projects whose cash flows are unrelated or independent of one another; the acceptance of one *does not eliminate* the others from further consideration.

mutually exclusive projects
Projects that compete with one another, so that the acceptance of one *eliminates* from further consideration all other projects that serve a similar function.

The two most common project types are (1) independent projects and (2) mutually exclusive projects. **Independent projects** are those whose cash flows are unrelated or independent of one another; the acceptance of one *does not eliminate* the others from further consideration. **Mutually exclusive projects** are those that have the same function and therefore compete with one another. The acceptance of one *eliminates* from further consideration all other projects that serve a similar function. For example, a firm in need of increased production capacity could obtain it by (1) expanding its plant, (2) acquiring another company, or (3) contracting with another company for production. Clearly, the acceptance of any one option eliminates the need for either of the others.

Unlimited Funds versus Capital Rationing

unlimited funds
The financial situation in which a firm is able to accept all independent projects that provide an acceptable return.

capital rationing
The financial situation in which a firm has only a fixed number of dollars available for capital expenditures, and numerous projects compete for these dollars.

The availability of funds for capital expenditures affects the firm's decisions. If a firm has **unlimited funds** for investment, making capital budgeting decisions is quite simple: All independent projects that will provide an acceptable return can be accepted. Typically, though, firms operate under **capital rationing** instead. This means that they have only a fixed number of dollars available for capital expenditures and that numerous projects will compete for these dollars. The discussions here and in the following chapter assume unlimited funds.

Accept–Reject versus Ranking Approaches

accept–reject approach
The evaluation of capital expenditure proposals to determine whether they meet the firm's minimum acceptance criterion.

ranking approach
The ranking of capital expenditure projects on the basis of some predetermined measure, such as the rate of return.

Two basic approaches to capital budgeting decisions are available. The **accept–reject approach** involves evaluating capital expenditure proposals to determine whether they meet the firm's minimum acceptance criterion. The second method, the **ranking approach,** involves ranking projects on the basis of some predetermined measure, such as the rate of return. The project with the highest return is ranked first, and the project with the lowest return is ranked last. Only acceptable projects should be ranked.

Conventional versus Nonconventional Cash Flow Patterns

conventional cash flow pattern
An initial outflow followed only by a series of inflows.

nonconventional cash flow pattern
An initial outflow followed by a series of inflows *and* outflows.

Cash flow patterns associated with capital investment projects can be classified as *conventional* or *nonconventional*. A **conventional cash flow pattern** consists of an initial outflow followed only by a series of inflows. For example, a firm may spend $10,000 today and as a result expect to receive equal annual cash inflows (an annuity) of $2,000 each year for the next 8 years, as depicted on the time line in Figure 10.1. A **nonconventional cash flow pattern** is one in which an initial outflow is followed by a series of inflows *and* outflows. A nonconventional pattern is illustrated on the time line in Figure 10.2. Difficulties often arise in evaluating projects with nonconventional patterns of cash flow. *The discussions in the remainder of this chapter and in the following chapter are therefore limited to the evaluation of conventional cash flow patterns.*

? Review Questions

10–1   Do all capital expenditures involve fixed assets? Explain.

FIGURE 10.1

Conventional Cash Flow

Time line for a conventional cash flow pattern

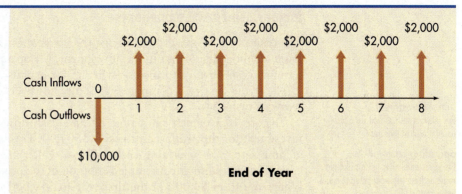

Note: Arrows rather than plus or minus signs are frequently used on time lines to distinguish between cash inflows and cash outflows. Upward-pointing arrows represent cash inflows (positive cash flows), and downward-pointing arrows represent cash outflows (negative cash flows).

FIGURE 10.2

Nonconventional Cash Flow

Time line for a nonconventional cash flow pattern

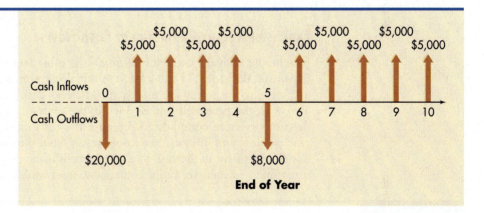

10–2   What are the five steps involved in the capital budgeting process?

10–3   Differentiate between the members of each of the following sets of capital budgeting terms: independent versus mutually exclusive projects; unlimited funds versus capital rationing; accept–reject versus ranking approaches; and conventional versus nonconventional cash flow patterns.

LG3 The Relevant Cash Flows

relevant cash flows
The incremental cash outflow (investment) and resulting subsequent inflows associated with a proposed capital expenditure.

incremental cash flows
The additional cash flows—outflows or inflows—expected to result from a proposed capital expenditure.

To evaluate capital expenditure alternatives, the firm must determine the **relevant cash flows.** These are the incremental cash outflow (investment) and resulting subsequent inflows. The **incremental cash flows** represent the additional cash flows—outflows or inflows—expected to result from a proposed capital expenditure. As noted in Chapter 9, cash flows rather than accounting figures are used, because cash flows directly affect the firm's ability to pay bills and purchase assets. The remainder of this chapter is devoted to the procedures for measuring the relevant cash flows associated with proposed capital expenditures.

Major Cash Flow Components

The cash flows of any project having the *conventional pattern* can include three basic components: (1) an initial investment, (2) operating cash inflows, and (3) terminal cash flow. All projects—whether for expansion, replacement, or renewal—have the first two components. Some, however, lack the final component, terminal cash flow.

Figure 10.3 depicts on a time line the cash flows for a project. The **initial investment** for the proposed project is $50,000. This is the relevant cash outflow at time zero. The **operating cash inflows,** which are the incremental after-tax cash inflows resulting from implementation of the project during its life, gradually increase from $4,000 in the first year to $10,000 in its tenth and final year. The **terminal cash flow** is the after-tax nonoperating cash flow occurring in the final year of the project. It is usually attributable to liquidation of the project. In this case it is $25,000, received at the end of the project's 10-year life. Note that the terminal cash flow does not include the $10,000 operating cash inflow for year 10.

initial investment
The relevant cash outflow for a proposed project at time zero.

operating cash inflows
The incremental after-tax cash inflows resulting from implementation of a project during its life.

terminal cash flow
The after-tax nonoperating cash flow occurring in the final year of a project. It is usually attributable to liquidation of the project.

Expansion versus Replacement Cash Flows

Developing relevant cash flow estimates is most straightforward in the case of expansion decisions. In this case, the initial investment, operating cash inflows, and terminal cash flow are merely the after-tax cash outflow and inflows associated with the proposed outlay. Identifying relevant cash flows for replacement decisions is more complicated, because the firm must identify the *incremental* cash outflow and inflows that would result from the proposed replacement. The initial investment in the case of a replacement is the difference between the initial investment needed to acquire the new asset and any after-tax cash inflows

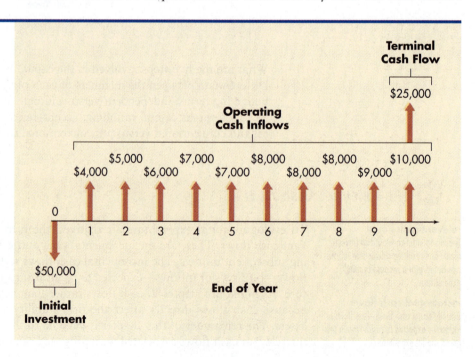

FIGURE 10.3

Cash Flow Components
Time line for major cash flow components

Relevant Cash Flows for Replacement Decisions
Calculation of the three components of relevant cash flow for a replacement decision

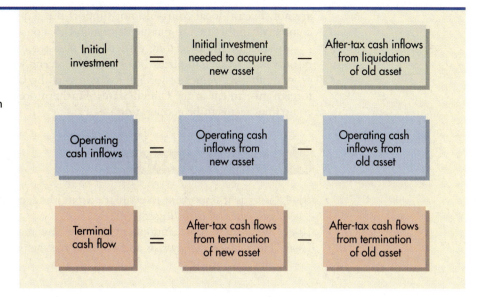

expected from liquidation of the old asset. The operating cash inflows are the difference between the operating cash inflows from the new asset and those from the old asset. The terminal cash flow is the difference between the after-tax cash flows expected upon termination of the new and the old assets. These relationships are shown in Figure 10.4. This chapter focuses primarily on replacement decisions.

International Capital Budgeting and Long-Term Investments

Although the same basic capital budgeting principles are used for domestic and international projects, several additional factors must be addressed in evaluating foreign investment opportunities. International capital budgeting differs from the domestic version because (1) cash outflows and inflows occur in a foreign currency, and (2) foreign investments entail potentially significant political risk. Both of these risks can be minimized through careful planning.

Companies face long-term and short-term *currency risks* related to both the invested capital and the cash flows resulting from it. Long-term currency risk can be minimized by financing the foreign investment at least partly in the local capital markets rather than with dollar-denominated capital from the parent company. This step ensures that the project's revenues, operating costs, and financing costs will be in the local currency. Likewise, the dollar value of short-term, local-currency cash flows can be protected by using special securities and strategies such as futures, forwards, and options market instruments.

Political risks can be minimized by using both operating and financial strategies. For example, by structuring the investment as a joint venture and selecting a well-connected local partner, the U.S. company can minimize the risk of its operations being seized or harassed. Companies also can protect themselves from having their investment returns blocked by local governments by structuring the financing of such investments as debt rather than as equity. Debt-service payments are legally enforceable claims, whereas equity returns (such as dividends) are not. Even if local courts do not support the claims of the U.S. company, the company can threaten to pursue its case in U.S. courts.

In spite of the preceding difficulties, investment of capital and managerial resources in other countries has surged in recent years. This is evident in the growing market values of foreign assets owned by U.S.-based companies and of foreign investment in the United States. Furthermore, foreign investment by U.S. companies seems to be accelerating.

? Review Questions

10–4   Why is it important to evaluate capital budgeting projects on the basis of *incremental cash flows*?

10–5   What three basic components of cash flow may exist for a given project?

10–6   How can *currency risk* and *political risk* be minimized when making foreign investments?

Finding the Initial Investment

The term *initial investment* as used here refers to the relevant cash outflows to be considered when evaluating a prospective capital expenditure. Because our discussion of capital budgeting is concerned only with investments that exhibit conventional cash flows, the initial investment occurs at *time zero*—the time at which the expenditure is made. The initial investment is calculated by subtracting all cash inflows occurring at time zero from all cash outflows occurring at time zero.

The basic format for determining the initial investment is given in Table 10.1. The cash flows that must be considered when determining the initial investment associated with a capital expenditure are the installed cost of the new asset, the after-tax proceeds (if any) from the sale of an old asset, and the change (if any) in net working capital. Note that if there are no installation costs and the firm is not replacing an existing asset, then the purchase price of the asset, adjusted for any change in net working capital, is equal to the initial investment.

Installed Cost of New Asset

cost of new asset
The net outflow necessary to acquire a new asset.

As shown in Table 10.1, the installed cost of the new asset is found by adding the cost of the new asset to its installation costs. The **cost of new asset** is the net outflow that its acquisition requires. Usually, we are concerned with the acquisition of a fixed asset for which a definite purchase price is paid. **Installation costs** are

installation costs
Any added costs that are necessary to place an asset into operation.

any added costs that are necessary to place an asset into operation. The Internal Revenue Service (IRS) requires the firm to add installation costs to the purchase price of an asset to determine its depreciable value, which is expensed over a period of years. The **installed cost of new asset,** calculated by adding the cost of the asset to its installation costs, equals its depreciable value.

installed cost of new asset
The cost of the asset plus its installation costs; equals the asset's depreciable value.

TABLE 10.1	**The Basic Format for Determining Initial Investment**

Installed cost of new asset =
   Cost of new asset
   + Installation costs
− After-tax proceeds from sale of old asset =
   Proceeds from sale of old asset
   +Tax on sale of old asset
± Change in net working capital
─────────────────────────
Initial investment

After-Tax Proceeds from Sale of Old Asset

after-tax proceeds from sale of old asset
The difference between the old asset's sale proceeds and any applicable taxes or tax refunds related to its sale.

proceeds from sale of old asset
The cash inflows, net of any removal or cleanup costs, resulting from the sale of an existing asset.

tax on sale of old asset
Tax that depends on the relationship among the old asset's sale price, initial purchase price, and book value, and on existing government tax rules.

book value
The strict accounting value of an asset, calculated by subtracting its accumulated depreciation from its installed cost.

Table 10.1 shows that the **after-tax proceeds from sale of old asset** decrease the firm's initial investment in the new asset. These proceeds are the difference between the old asset's sale proceeds and any applicable taxes or tax refunds related to its sale. The **proceeds from sale of old asset** are the net cash inflows it provides. This amount is net of any costs incurred in the process of removing the asset. Included in these removal costs are cleanup costs, such as those related to the removal and disposal of chemical and nuclear wastes. These costs may not be trivial.

The proceeds from the sale of an old asset are normally subject to some type of tax. The **tax on sale of old asset** depends on the relationship among its sale price, initial purchase price, and book value, and on existing government tax rules.

Book Value

The **book value** of an asset is its strict accounting value. It can be calculated by using the following equation:

$$\text{Book value} = \text{Installed cost of asset} - \text{Accumulated depreciation} \qquad (10.1)$$

Example ▼ Klanger Industries, a small electronics company, 2 years ago acquired a machine tool with an installed cost of $100,000. The asset was being depreciated under MACRS using a 5-year recovery period.[1] Table 9.5 (page 284) shows that under MACRS for a 5-year recovery period, 20 and 32 percent of the installed cost would be depreciated in years 1 and 2, respectively. In other words, 52% (20% + 32%) of the $100,000 cost, or $52,000 (0.52 × $100,000), would represent the accumulated depreciation at the end of year 2. Substituting into Equation 10.1, we get

$$\text{Book value} = \$100,000 - \$52,000 = \$48,000$$

▲ The book value of Klanger's asset at the end of year 2 is therefore $48,000.

[1]For a review of MACRS, see Chapter 9. Under current tax law, most manufacturing equipment has a 7-year recovery period, as noted in Table 9.4. Using this recovery period results in 8 years of depreciation, which unnecessarily complicates examples and exercises. To simplify, manufacturing equipment is treated as a 5-year asset in this and the following chapters.

TABLE 10.2	Tax Treatment on Sales of Assets		
Form of taxable income	Definition	Tax treatment	Assumed tax rate
Capital gain	Portion of the sale price that is in excess of the initial purchase price.	Regardless of how long the asset has been held, the total capital gain is taxed as ordinary income.	40%
Recaptured depreciation	Portion of the sale price that is in excess of book value and represents a recovery of previously taken depreciation.	All recaptured depreciation is taxed as ordinary income.	40%
Loss on sale of asset	Amount by which sale price is *less than* book value.	If asset is depreciable and used in business, loss is deducted from ordinary income.	40% of loss is a tax savings
		If asset is *not* depreciable or is *not* used in business, loss is deductible only against capital gains.	40% of loss is a tax savings

Basic Tax Rules

Four potential tax situations can occur when an asset is sold. These situations depend on the relationship among the asset's sale price, its initial purchase price, and its book value. The three key forms of taxable income and their associated tax treatments are defined and summarized in Table 10.2. The assumed tax rates used throughout this text are noted in the final column. There are four possible tax situations, which result in one or more forms of taxable income: The asset may be sold (1) for more than its initial purchase price, (2) for more than its book value but less than its initial purchase price, (3) for its book value, or (4) for less than its book value. An example will illustrate.

Example ▼ The old asset purchased 2 years ago for $100,000 by Klanger Industries has a current book value of $48,000. What will happen if the firm now decides to sell the asset and replace it? The tax consequences depend on the sale price. Figure 10.5 depicts the taxable income resulting from four possible sale prices in light of the asset's initial purchase price of $100,000 and its current book value of $48,000. The taxable consequence of each of these sale prices is described below.

FIGURE 10.5	Taxable Income from Sale of Asset

Taxable income from sale of asset at various sale prices for Klanger Industries

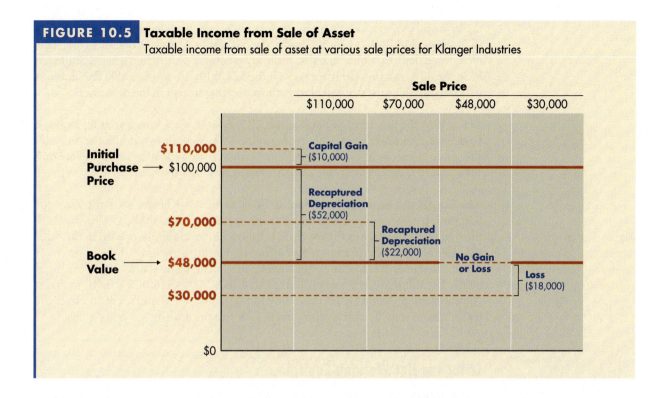

The sale of the asset for more than its initial purchase price   If Klanger sells the old asset for $110,000, it realizes a capital gain of $10,000, which is taxed as ordinary income. The firm also experiences ordinary income in the form of **recaptured depreciation,** which is the portion of the sale price that is above book value and below the initial purchase price. In this case there is recaptured depreciation of $52,000 ($100,000 − $48,000). Both the $10,000 capital gain and the $52,000 recaptured depreciation are shown under the $110,000 sale price in Figure 10.5. The taxes on the total gain of $62,000 are calculated as follows:

recaptured depreciation
The portion of an asset's sale price that is above its book value and below its initial purchase price.

	Amount (1)	Rate (2)	Tax [(1) × (2)] (3)
Capital gain	$10,000	.40	$ 4,000
Recaptured depreciation	52,000	.40	20,800
Total	$62,000		$24,800

These taxes should be used in calculating the initial investment in the new asset, using the format in Table 10.1. In effect, the taxes raise the amount of the firm's initial investment in the new asset by reducing the proceeds from the sale of the old asset.

The sale of the asset for more than its book value but less than its initial purchase price   If Klanger sells the old asset for $70,000, there is no capital gain. However, the firm still experiences a gain in the form of recaptured depreciation of $22,000 ($70,000 − $48,000), as shown under the $70,000 sale price in Figure 10.5. This recaptured depreciation is taxed as ordinary income. Because the firm is assumed to be in the 40% tax bracket, the taxes on the $22,000 gain are $8,800. This amount in taxes should be used in calculating the initial investment in the new asset.

The sale of the asset for its book value If the asset is sold for $48,000, its book value, the firm breaks even. There is no gain or loss, as shown under the $48,000 sale price in Figure 10.5. Because *no tax results from selling an asset for its book value*, there is no effect on the initial investment in the new asset.

The sale of the asset for less than its book value If Klanger sells the asset for $30,000, it experiences a loss of $18,000 ($48,000 − $30,000), as shown under the $30,000 sale price in Figure 10.5. If this is a depreciable asset used in the business, the loss may be used to offset ordinary operating income. If the asset is *not* depreciable or is *not* used in the business, the loss can be used only to offset capital gains. In either case, the loss will save the firm $7,200 ($18,000 × 0.40) in taxes. And, if current operating earnings or capital gains are not sufficient to offset the loss, the firm may be able to apply these losses to prior or future years' taxes.

Change in Net Working Capital

net working capital
The amount by which a firm's current assets exceed its current liabilities.

Net working capital is the amount by which a firm's current assets exceed its current liabilities. This topic is more fully discussed in Chapter 15, but at this point it is important to note that changes in net working capital often accompany capital expenditure decisions. If a firm acquires new machinery to expand its level of operations, it will experience an increase in levels of cash, accounts receivable, inventories, accounts payable, and accruals. These increases result from the need for more cash to support expanded operations, more accounts receivable and inventories to support increased sales, and more accounts payable and accruals to support increased outlays made to meet expanded product demand. As noted in Chapter 9, increases in cash, accounts receivable, and inventories are *uses of cash*, whereas increases in accounts payable and accruals are *sources of cash*.

change in net working capital
The difference between a change in current assets and a change in current liabilities.

The difference between the change in current assets and the change in current liabilities is the **change in net working capital**. Generally, current assets increase by more than current liabilities, resulting in an increased investment in net working capital. This increased investment is treated as an initial outflow. If the change in net working capital were negative, it would be shown as an initial inflow. The change in net working capital—regardless of whether it is an increase or a decrease—is *not taxable* because it merely involves a net buildup or reduction of current accounts.

Example ▼ Pearson Company, a metal products manufacturer, is contemplating expanding its operations. Financial analysts expect that the changes in current accounts summarized in Table 10.3 will occur and will be maintained over the life of the expansion. Current assets are expected to increase by $22,000, and current liabilities are expected to increase by $9,000, resulting in a $13,000 increase in net working capital. In this case, the increase will represent an increased net working capital investment and will be treated as a cash outflow in calculating the initial investment. ▲

NewsLine

WHAT ARE THE RELEVANT CASH FLOWS FOR INFORMATION TECHNOLOGY INVESTMENTS?

Businesses know that investments in information technology usually improve operations and produce positive cash flows. Banks, in particular, are these days installing data warehouses (collections of databases that are analyzed to support management decisions) to improve marketing efforts. However, quantifying the relevant cash flows, particularly the initial investment, for this technology investment in order to perform a capital budgeting analysis is no easy task.

No one seems to dispute the importance and value of data warehousing. Knowing its costs is another matter....

KeyCorp of Cleveland, for one, is using this capability to expand relationships with its most profitable customers and improve the unprofitable ones' results....KeyCorp chairman and chief executive officer Robert W. Gillespie said, "I couldn't tell you" how much the database effort has cost.

Joseph W. Saunders, chairman and chief executive officer of Fleet Card Services, said he would be "hard-pressed to put an actual number" on the technology investments his organization has made....The endless investing is necessary, he added. Organizations that do it can transform a raw list of names into a successful, national mailing solicitation that earns superior response rates and leads to lower losses, he said.

Randall B. Grossman, senior vice president for customer data management and analysis at Fleet Financial Group, knew exactly how much his bank spent on its data warehouse, which was completed last year: $28.1 million....That was about $10 million under budget, he

said. Fleet never proceeded with a planned second phase of the project, after determining its goals had been met with the first, larger phase. Fleet's secret was fixed-price contracts, he said. "There's nothing like the discipline of a fixed budget to force you to compromise and manage scope."...

Making the multimillion-dollar investment pay off is Boston-based Fleet's next project. Mr. Grossman estimates that by 2001 the company will be generating $100 million a year from its data warehouse. "The warehouse itself doesn't make money," he said. "It's the decisions that the warehouse helps you make that make the money." At least 12 projects under way in Fleet's retail bank are using information from the warehouse, he said. One benefit is lowering the cost of mailing solicitations to certificate-of-deposit customers by 60%, without affecting response rates. The value of the warehouse will keep rising, as it used to guide an increasing number of decisions in more departments throughout the bank, he said.

Source: Chris Costanzo, "On Data Warehouses: Their Value Is Clear, But Cost Is Another Matter," American Banker, March 5, 1999, p. 13.

| TABLE 10.3 | Calculation of Change in Net Working Capital for Pearson Company |

Current account	Change in balance	
Cash	+ $ 4,000	
Accounts receivable	+ 10,000	
Inventories	+ 8,000	
(1) Current assets		+ $22,000
Accounts payable	+ $ 7,000	
Accruals	+ 2,000	
(2) Current liabilities		+ 9,000
Change in net working capital [(1) − (2)]		+ $13,000

Calculating the Initial Investment

A variety of tax and other considerations enter into the initial investment calculation. The following example illustrates the calculation of the initial investment according to the format in Table 10.1.

Example ▼   Morton Company, a large diversified manufacturer of electronics components, is trying to determine the initial investment required to replace an old machine with a new, more sophisticated model. The machine's purchase price is $380,000, and an additional $20,000 will be necessary to install it. It will be depreciated under MACRS using a 5-year recovery period. The present (old) machine was purchased 3 years ago at a cost of $240,000 and was being depreciated under MACRS using a 5-year recovery period. The firm has found a buyer willing to pay $280,000 for the present machine and to remove it at the buyer's expense. The firm expects that a $35,000 increase in current assets and an $18,000 increase in current liabilities will accompany the replacement; these changes will result in a $17,000 ($35,000 − $18,000) *increase* in net working capital. Both ordinary income and capital gains are taxed at a rate of 40%.

The only component of the initial investment calculation that is difficult to obtain is taxes. Because the firm is planning to sell the present machine for $40,000 more than its initial purchase price, it will realize a *capital gain* of $40,000. The book value of the present machine can be found by using the depreciation percentages from Table 9.5 (page 284) of 20, 32, and 19% for years 1, 2, and 3, respectively. The resulting book value is $69,600 ($240,000 − [(0.20 + 0.32 + 0.19) × $240,000]). An *ordinary gain* of $170,400 ($240,000 − $69,600) in recaptured depreciation is also realized on the sale. The total taxes on the gain are $84,160 [($40,000 + $170,400) × 0.40]. Substituting these amounts into the format in Table 10.1 results in an initial investment of $221,160, which represents the net cash outflow required at time zero:

Installed cost of proposed machine		
Cost of proposed machine	$380,000	
+ Installation costs	20,000	
Total installed cost—proposed (depreciable value)		$400,000
− **After-tax proceeds from sale of present machine**		
Proceeds from sale of present machine	$280,000	
− Tax on sale of present machine	84,160	
Total after-tax proceeds—present		195,840
+ **Change in net working capital**		17,000
Initial investment		$221,160

❓ Review Questions

10–7 Explain how each of the following inputs is used to calculate the *initial investment*: (a) cost of new asset, (b) installation costs, (c) proceeds from sale of old asset, (d) tax on sale of old asset, and (e) change in net working capital.

10–8 What are the three key forms of taxable income?

10–9 What four tax situations may result from the sale of an asset that is being replaced?

LG5 Finding the Operating Cash Inflows

The benefits expected from a capital expenditure are measured by its *operating cash inflows,* which are *incremental after-tax cash inflows.* In this section we use the income statement format to develop clear definitions of the terms *after-tax, cash inflows,* and *incremental.*

Interpreting the Term *After-Tax*

Benefits expected to result from proposed capital expenditures must be measured on an *after-tax basis,* because the firm will not have the use of any benefits until it has satisfied the government's tax claims. These claims depend on the firm's taxable income, so deducting taxes before making comparisons between proposed investments is necessary for consistency when evaluating capital expenditure alternatives.

Interpreting the Term *Cash Inflows*

All benefits expected from a proposed project must be measured on a *cash flow basis.* Cash inflows represent dollars that can be spent, not merely "accounting profits." A simple technique for converting after-tax net profits into operating cash inflows was illustrated in Chapter 9. The basic calculation requires adding back to net profits after taxes any *noncash charges* deducted as expenses on the firm's income statement. Depreciation, the most common noncash charge found on income statements, is the only noncash charge that will be considered in this section. The following example calculates after-tax operating cash inflows for a proposed and a present project.

Example ▼ Morton Company's estimates of its revenue and expenses (excluding depreciation), with and without the proposed new machine described in the preceding example, are given in Table 10.4. Note that both the expected usable life of the proposed machine and the remaining usable life of the present machine are 5 years. The amount to be depreciated with the proposed machine is calculated by

TABLE 10.4 Morton Company's Revenue and Expenses (Excluding Depreciation) for Proposed and Present Machines

With proposed machine			With present machine		
Year	Revenue (1)	Expenses (excl. depr.) (2)	Year	Revenue (1)	Expenses (excl. depr.) (2)
1	$2,520,000	$2,300,000	1	$2,200,000	$1,990,000
2	2,520,000	2,300,000	2	2,300,000	2,110,000
3	2,520,000	2,300,000	3	2,400,000	2,230,000
4	2,520,000	2,300,000	4	2,400,000	2,250,000
5	2,520,000	2,300,000	5	2,250,000	2,120,000

TABLE 10.5	Depreciation Expense for Proposed and Present Machines for Morton Company

Year	Cost (1)	Applicable MACRS depreciation percentages (from Table 9.5) (2)	Depreciation [(1) × (2)] (3)
With proposed machine			
1	$400,000	20%	$ 80,000
2	400,000	32	128,000
3	400,000	19	76,000
4	400,000	12	48,000
5	400,000	12	48,000
6	400,000	5	20,000
Totals		100%	$400,000
With present machine			
1	$240,000	12% (year-4 depreciation)	$28,800
2	240,000	12 (year-5 depreciation)	28,800
3	240,000	5 (year-6 depreciation)	12,000
4	} Because the present machine is at the end of the third year of its cost		0
5	} recovery at the time the analysis is performed, it has only the final		0
6	} 3 years of depreciation (as noted above) yet applicable.		0
Total			$69,600[a]

[a]The total $69,600 represents the book value of the present machine at the end of the third year, as calculated in the preceding example.

summing the purchase price of $380,000 and the installation costs of $20,000. The proposed machine is to be depreciated under MACRS using a 5-year recovery period. The resulting depreciation on this machine for each of the 6 years, as well as the remaining 3 years of depreciation (years 4, 5, 6) on the present machine, are calculated in Table 10.5.[2]

The operating cash inflows in each year can be calculated using the income statement format shown in Table 10.6. Substituting the data from Tables 10.4 and 10.5 into this format and assuming a 40 percent tax rate, we get Table 10.7. It demonstrates the calculation of operating cash inflows for each year for both the proposed and the present machine. Because the proposed machine is depreciated over 6 years, the analysis must be performed over the 6-year period to capture fully the tax effect of its year-6 depreciation. The resulting operating cash inflows are shown in the final row of Table 10.7 for each machine. The $8,000 year-6 cash inflow for the proposed machine results solely from the tax benefit of its year-6 depreciation deduction.

[2]It is important to recognize that although both machines will provide 5 years of use, the proposed new machine will be depreciated over the 6-year period, whereas the present machine, as noted in the preceding example, has been depreciated over 3 years and therefore has remaining only its final 3 years (years 4, 5 and 6) of depreciation (12, 12, and 5 percent, respectively, under MACRS).

TABLE 10.6	Calculation of Operating Cash Inflows Using the Income Statement Format

Revenue

− Expenses (excluding depreciation)

Profits before depreciation and taxes

− Depreciation

Net profits before taxes

− Taxes

Net profits after taxes

+ Depreciation

Operating cash inflows

TABLE 10.7	Calculation of Operating Cash Inflows for Morton Company's Proposed and Present Machines

	Year					
	1	2	3	4	5	6
With proposed machine						
Revenue[a]	$2,520,000	$2,520,000	$2,520,000	$2,520,000	$2,520,000	$ 0
− Expenses (excl. depr.)[b]	2,300,000	2,300,000	2,300,000	2,300,000	2,300,000	0
Profits before depr. and taxes	$ 220,000	$ 220,000	$ 220,000	$ 220,000	$ 220,000	$ 0
− Depreciation[c]	80,000	128,000	76,000	48,000	48,000	20,000
Net profits before taxes	$ 140,000	$ 92,000	$ 144,000	$ 172,000	$ 172,000	−$20,000
− Taxes (rate = 40%)	56,000	36,800	57,600	68,800	68,800	− 8,000
Net profits after taxes	$ 84,000	$ 55,200	$ 86,400	$ 103,200	$ 103,200	−$12,000
+ Depreciation[c]	80,000	128,000	76,000	48,000	48,000	20,000
Operating cash inflows	$ 164,000	$ 183,200	$ 162,400	$ 151,200	$ 151,200	$ 8,000
With present machine						
Revenue[a]	$2,200,000	$2,300,000	$2,400,000	$2,400,000	$2,250,000	$ 0
− Expenses (excl. depr.)[b]	1,990,000	2,110,000	2,230,000	2,250,000	2,120,000	0
Profits before depr. and taxes	$ 210,000	$ 190,000	$ 170,000	$ 150,000	$ 130,000	$ 0
− Depreciation[c]	28,800	28,800	12,000	0	0	0
Net profits before taxes	$ 181,200	$ 161,200	$ 158,000	$ 150,000	$ 130,000	$ 0
− Taxes (rate = 40%)	72,480	64,480	63,200	60,000	52,000	0
Net profits after taxes	$ 108,720	$ 96,720	$ 94,800	$ 90,000	$ 78,000	$ 0
+ Depreciation[c]	28,800	28,800	12,000	0	0	0
Operating cash inflows	$ 137,520	$ 125,520	$ 106,800	$ 90,000	$ 78,000	$ 0

[a]From column 1 of Table 10.4.

[b]From column 2 of Table 10.4.

[c]From column 3 of Table 10.5.

	Operating cash inflows		
Year	Proposed machine[a] (1)	Present machine[a] (2)	Incremental (relevant) [(1) − (2)] (3)
1	$164,000	$137,520	$26,480
2	183,200	125,520	57,680
3	162,400	106,800	55,600
4	151,200	90,000	61,200
5	151,200	78,000	73,200
6	8,000	0	8,000

TABLE 10.8 Incremental (Relevant) Operating Cash Inflows for Morton Company

[a]From final row for respective machine in Table 10.7.

Interpreting the Term *Incremental*

The final step in estimating the operating cash inflows for a proposed project is to calculate the *incremental (relevant)* cash inflows. Incremental operating cash inflows are needed, because our concern is *only* with the change in operating cash flows as a result of the proposed project.

Example ▼ Table 10.8 demonstrates the calculation of Morton Company's incremental (relevant) operating cash inflows for each year. The estimates of operating cash inflows developed in Table 10.7 are given in columns 1 and 2. Column 2 values represent the amount of operating cash inflows that Morton Company will receive if it does not replace the present machine. If the proposed machine replaces the present machine, the firm's operating cash inflows for each year will be those shown in column 1. Subtracting the present machine's operating cash inflows from the proposed machine's operating cash inflows, we get the incremental operating cash inflows for each year, shown in column 3. These cash flows represent the amounts by which each respective year's cash inflows will increase as a result of the replacement. For example, in year 1, Morton Company's cash inflows would increase by $26,480 if the proposed project were undertaken. ▲

Review Questions

10–10 How does depreciation enter into the calculation of operating cash inflow?

10–11 How are the incremental (relevant) *operating cash inflows* associated with a replacement decision calculated?

Finding the Terminal Cash Flow

Terminal cash flow is the cash flow resulting from termination and liquidation of a project at the end of its economic life. It represents the after-tax cash flow, exclusive of operating cash inflows, occurring in the final year of the project. When it applies, this flow can significantly affect the capital expenditure decision. Terminal cash flow can be calculated for replacement projects by using the basic format presented in Table 10.9.

Proceeds from Sale of Assets

The proceeds from sale of the new and old asset, often called "salvage value," represent the amount *net of any removal or cleanup costs* expected upon termination of the project. For replacement projects, proceeds from both the new asset and the old asset must be considered. For expansion and renewal types of capital expenditures, the proceeds from the old asset would be zero. Of course, it is not unusual for the value of an asset to be zero at the termination of a project.

Taxes on Sale of Assets

Earlier we calculated the tax on sale of old assets (as part of finding the initial investment). Similarly, taxes must be considered on the terminal sale of both the new and the old asset for replacement projects and on only the new asset in other cases. The tax calculations apply whenever an asset is sold for a value different from its book value. If the net proceeds from the sale are expected to exceed book value, a tax payment shown as an *outflow* (deduction from sale proceeds) will occur. When the net proceeds from the sale are less than book value, a tax rebate shown as a cash *inflow* (addition to sale proceeds) will result. For assets sold to net exactly book value, no taxes will be due.

TABLE 10.9	The Basic Format for Determining Terminal Cash Flow

> After-tax proceeds from sale of new asset =
>   Proceeds from sale of new asset
>   ∓ Tax on sale of new asset
> − After-tax proceeds from sale of old asset =
>   Proceeds from sale of old asset
>   ∓ Tax on sale of old asset
> ± Change in net working capital
>
> Terminal cash flow

Change in Net Working Capital

When we calculated the initial investment, we took into account any change in net working capital that is attributable to the new asset. Now, when we calculate the terminal cash flow, the change in net working capital represents the reversion of any initial net working capital investment. Most often, this will show up as a cash inflow due to the reduction in net working capital; with termination of the project, the need for the increased net working capital investment is assumed to end. Because the net working capital investment is in no way consumed, the amount recovered at termination will equal the amount shown in the calculation of the initial investment. Tax considerations are not involved.

The terminal cash flow calculation involves the same procedures as those used to find the initial investment. In the following example, the terminal cash flow is calculated for a replacement decision.

Example ▼ Continuing with the Morton Company example, assume that the firm expects to be able to liquidate the new machine at the end of its 5-year usable life to net $50,000 after paying removal and cleanup costs. The old machine can be liquidated at the end of the 5 years to net $0 because it will then be completely obsolete. The firm expects to recover its $17,000 net working capital investment upon termination of the project. Both ordinary income and capital gains are taxed at a rate of 40%.

From the analysis of the operating cash inflows presented earlier, we can see that the proposed (new) machine will have a book value of $20,000 (equal to the year-6 depreciation) at the end of 5 years. The present (old) machine will be fully depreciated and therefore have a book value of zero at the end of the 5 years. Because the sale price of $50,000 for the proposed (new) machine is below its initial installed cost of $400,000 but greater than its book value of $20,000, taxes will have to be paid only on the recaptured depreciation of $30,000 ($50,000 sale proceeds − $20,000 book value). Applying the ordinary tax rate of 40% to this $30,000 results in a tax of $12,000 (0.40 × $30,000) on the sale of the proposed machine. Its after-tax sale proceeds would therefore equal $38,000 ($50,000 sale proceeds − $12,000 taxes). Because the present machine would net $0 at termination and its book value would be $0, no tax would be due on its sale. Its after-tax sale proceeds would therefore equal $0. Substituting the appropriate values into the format in Table 10.9 results in the terminal cash inflow value of $55,000

After-tax proceeds from sale of proposed machine			
	Proceeds from sale of proposed machine	$50,000	
−	Tax on sale of proposed machine	12,000	
	Total after-tax proceeds—proposed		$38,000
−	**After-tax proceeds from sale of present machine**		
	Proceeds from sale of present machine	$ 0	
∓	Tax on sale of present machine	0	
	Total after-tax proceeds—present		0
+	**Change in net working capital**		17,000
	Terminal cash flow		$55,000

? Review Question

10–12 Explain how the value of the *terminal cash flow* is calculated for replacement projects.

  ## LG4 Summarizing the Relevant Cash Flows

The initial investment, operating cash inflows, and terminal cash flow together represent a project's *relevant cash flows*. These cash flows can be viewed as the incremental after-tax cash flows attributable to the proposed project. They represent, in a cash flow sense, how much better or worse off the firm will be if it chooses to implement the proposal.

Example ▼   The relevant cash flows for Morton Company's proposed replacement expenditure can now be shown graphically, on a time line. Note that because the new asset is assumed to be sold at the end of its 5-year usable life, the year-6 incremental operating cash inflow calculated in Table 10.8 has no relevance; the terminal cash flow effectively replaces this value in the analysis. As the time line shows, the relevant cash flows follow a *conventional cash flow pattern*.

Morton Company's relevant cash flows with the proposed machine

Techniques for analyzing conventional cash flow patterns to determine whether to undertake a proposed capital investment are discussed in Chapter 11.

? Review Question

10–13 Diagram and describe the three components of the *relevant cash flows* for a capital budgeting project.

TYING IT ALL TOGETHER

This chapter described the capital budgeting decision process and the procedures used to estimate the relevant cash flows associated with a proposed capital expenditure. Specific attention was given to the three components of a proposed project's cash flows: the initial investment, the operating cash inflows, and the terminal cash flow. The importance of capital budgeting cash flow principles from the viewpoints of financial managers, financial markets, and investors is summarized in the Integrative Table that follows.

INTEGRATIVE TABLE

Measuring Cash Flow in Capital Budgeting

Role of **Financial Managers**	*Role of* **Financial Markets**	*Role of* **Investors**
Financial managers must understand the capital budgeting process and must know how to estimate relevant cash flows associated with all types of proposed capital expenditures. The financial manager must prepare realistic estimates of the cash flows associated with estimated costs and benefits of proposed long-term investments. Good cash flow estimates are a prerequisite to good decisions that contribute to the maximization of owner wealth.	Financial markets are not directly involved in the firm's capital budgeting and cash flow estimation process. But they do provide a forum where information on the investment activities of firms can be disseminated and evaluated by investors eager to assess the value-creating prospects of those actions. The voice of investors reacting to the capital budgeting decisions of firms will determine the market price of the firm's shares and therefore affect the wealth of those who them.	Investors pay close attention to the quality of the firm's investment decisions, which should result from the development of good cash flow estimates in the firm's capital budgeting decision process. Investors will invest in firms that make good capital budgeting decisions and will divest themselves of ownership in those that make poor decisions. Investor assessment of the quality of the firm's capital budgeting activities thus affects share value and owner wealth.

LG1 **Understand the key capital expenditure motives and the steps in the capital budgeting process.** Capital budgeting is the process used to evaluate and select capital expenditures consistent with the firm's goal of maximizing owner wealth. Capital expenditures are long-term investments made to expand, replace, or renew fixed assets or to obtain some less tangible benefit. The capital budgeting process includes five distinct but interrelated steps: proposal generation, review and analysis, decision making, implementation, and follow-up.

LG2 **Define basic capital budgeting terminology.** Capital expenditure proposals may be independent or mutually exclusive. Typically, firms have only limited funds for capital invest-

ments and must ration them among carefully selected projects. The two basic approaches to capital budgeting decisions are the accept–reject approach and the ranking approach. Conventional cash flow patterns consist of an initial outflow followed by a series of inflows; any other pattern is nonconventional.

LG3 **Discuss the major components of relevant cash flows, expansion versus replacement cash flows, and international capital budgeting and long-term investments.** The relevant cash flows for capital budgeting decisions are the initial investment, the operating cash inflows, and the terminal cash flow. For replacement decisions, these flows are found by determining the difference between the cash flows of the new asset and the old asset. In international capital budgeting, currency risks and political risks can be minimized through careful planning.

 Calculate the initial investment associated with a proposed capital expenditure. The initial investment is the initial outflow required, taking into account the installed cost of the new asset, the after-tax proceeds from the sale of the old asset, and any change in net working capital. Finding the after-tax proceeds from sale of the old asset, which reduces the initial investment, involves cost, depreciation, and tax data. The book value of an asset is its accounting value, which is used to determine what taxes are owed as a result of its sale. Any of three forms of taxable income—capital gain, recaptured depreciation, or a loss—can result from sale of an asset. The form of taxable income that applies depends on whether the asset is sold for (1) more than its initial purchase price, (2) more than book value but less than what was initially paid, (3) book value, or (4) less than book value. The change in net working capital is the difference between the change in current assets and the change in current liabilities expected to accompany a given capital expenditure.

 Determine relevant operating cash inflows using the income statement format. The operating cash inflows are the incremental after-tax cash inflows expected to result from a project. The income statement format involves adding depreciation back to net profits after taxes and gives the operating cash inflows associated with the proposed and present projects. The relevant (incremental) cash inflows are the difference between the operating cash inflows of the proposed project and those of the present project.

 Find the terminal cash flow. The terminal cash flow represents the after-tax cash flow, exclusive of operating cash inflows, that is expected from liquidation of a project. It is calculated by finding the difference between the after-tax proceeds from sale of the new and the old asset at project termination and then adjusting this difference for any change in net working capital. Sale price and depreciation data are used to find the taxes and the after-tax sale proceeds on the new and old assets. The change in net working capital typically represents the reversion of any initial net working capital investment.

SELF-TEST EXERCISES

(Solutions in Appendix B)

 ST 10–1   Book value, taxes, and initial investment   Siebert Enterprises is considering the purchase of a new piece of equipment to replace the current equipment. The new equipment costs $75,000 and requires $5,000 in installation costs. It will be depreciated under MACRS using a 5-year recovery period. The old piece of equipment was purchased for an installed cost of $50,000 4 years ago; it was being depreciated under MACRS using a 5-year recovery period. The old equipment can be sold today for $55,000 net of any removal and cleanup costs. As a result of the proposed replacement, the firm's investment in net working capital is expected to increase by $15,000. The firm pays taxes at a rate of 40% on both ordinary income and capital gains. (Table 9.5 on page 284 contains the applicable MACRS depreciation percentages.)

a. Calculate the book value of the old piece of equipment.

b. Determine the taxes, if any, attributable to the sale of the old equipment.

c. Find the initial investment associated with the proposed equipment replacement.

ST 10–2   Determining relevant cash flows   A machine currently in use was originally purchased 2 years ago for $40,000. The machine is being depreciated under MACRS using a 5-year recovery period; it has 3 years of usable life remaining. The current machine can be sold today to net $42,000 after removal and cleanup costs. A new machine, using a 3-year MACRS recovery period, can be purchased at a price of $140,000. It requires $10,000 to install and has a 3-year usable life. If the new machine is acquired, the investment in accounts receivable will be expected to rise by $10,000, the inventory investment will increase by $25,000, and accounts payable will increase by $15,000. *Profits before depreciation and taxes* are expected to be $70,000 for each of the next 3 years with the old machine and to be $120,000 in the first year and $130,000 in the second and third years with the new machine. At the end of 3 years, the market value of the old machine will equal zero, but the new machine could be sold to net $35,000 before taxes. Both ordinary corporate income and capital gains are subject to a 40% tax. (Table 9.5 on page 284 contains the applicable MACRS depreciation percentages.)

a. Determine the initial investment associated with the proposed replacement decision.

b. Calculate the incremental operating cash inflows for years 1 to 4 associated with the proposed replacement. (*Note:* Only depreciation cash flows must be considered in year 4.)

c. Calculate the terminal cash flow associated with the proposed replacement decision. (*Note:* This is at the end of year 3.)

d. Depict on a time line the relevant cash flows found in parts **a, b,** and **c** that are associated with the proposed replacement decision, assuming that it is terminated at the end of year 3.

EXERCISES

10–1   Classification of expenditures   Given the following list of outlays, indicate whether each is normally considered a *capital* or an *operating* expenditure. Explain your answers.

a. An initial lease payment of $5,000 for electronic point-of-sale cash register systems.

b. An outlay of $20,000 to purchase patent rights from an inventor.

c. An outlay of $80,000 for a major research and development program.

d. An $80,000 investment in a portfolio of marketable securities.

e. A $300 outlay for an office machine.

f. An outlay of $2,000 for a new machine tool.

g. An outlay of $240,000 for a new building.

h. An outlay of $1,000 for a marketing research report.

10–2   Basic terminology   A firm is considering the following three separate situations.
Situation A   Build either a small office building or a convenience store on a parcel of land located in a high-traffic area. Adequate funding is available, and both projects are known to be acceptable. The office building requires an initial investment of $620,000 and is expected to provide operating cash inflows of $40,000 per year for 20 years. The convenience store is expected to cost $500,000 and to provide a growing stream of operating cash inflows over its

20-year life. The initial operating cash inflow is $20,000, and it will increase by 5% each year.

Situation B   Replace a machine with a new one that requires a $60,000 initial investment and will provide operating cash inflows of $10,000 per year for the first 5 years. At the end of year 5, a machine overhaul costing $20,000 will be required. After it is completed, expected operating cash inflows will be $10,000 in year 6; $7,000 in year 7; $4,000 in year 8; and $1,000 in year 9, at the end of which the machine will be scrapped.

Situation C   Invest in any or all of the four machines whose relevant cash flows are given in the following table. The firm has $500,000 budgeted to fund these machines, all of which are known to be acceptable. Initial investment for each machine is $250,000.

	Operating cash inflows			
Year	Machine 1	Machine 2	Machine 3	Machine 4
1	$ 50,000	$70,000	$65,000	$90,000
2	70,000	70,000	65,000	80,000
3	90,000	70,000	80,000	70,000
4	−30,000	70,000	80,000	60,000
5	100,000	70,000	−20,000	50,000

For each situation, indicate

a. Whether the projects involved are independent or mutually exclusive.

b. Whether the availability of funds is unlimited or capital rationing exists.

c. Whether accept–reject or ranking decisions are required.

d. Whether each project's cash flows are conventional or nonconventional.

LG3   10–3   Relevant cash flow pattern fundamentals   For each of the following projects, determine the relevant cash flows, classify the cash flow pattern, and depict the cash flows on a time line.

a. A project that requires an initial investment of $120,000 and will generate annual operating cash inflows of $25,000 for the next 18 years. In each of the 18 years, maintenance of the project will require a $5,000 cash outflow.

b. A new machine with an installed cost of $85,000. Sale of the old machine will yield $30,000 after taxes. Operating cash inflows generated by the replacement will exceed the operating cash inflows of the old machine by $20,000 in each year of a 6-year period. At the end of year 6, liquidation of the new machine will yield $20,000 after taxes, which is $10,000 greater than the after-tax proceeds expected from the old machine had it been retained and liquidated at the end of year 6.

c. An asset that requires an initial investment of $2 million and will yield annual operating cash inflows of $300,000 for each of the next 10 years. Operating cash outlays will be $20,000 for each year except year 6, when an overhaul requiring an additional cash outlay of $500,000 will be required. The asset's liquidation value at the end of year 10 is expected to be $0.

LG3   10–4   Expansion versus replacement cash flows   Stan Nichols, Inc. has estimated the cash flows over the 5-year lives for two projects, A and B. These cash flows are summarized in the table at the top of page 320.

	Project A	Project B
Initial investment	$40,000	$12,000ᵃ
Year	Operating cash inflows	
1	$10,000	$6,000
2	12,000	6,000
3	14,000	6,000
4	16,000	6,000
5	10,000	6,000

ᵃAfter-tax cash inflow expected from liquidation.

If project A were actually a *replacement* for project B and if the $12,000 initial investment shown for project B were the after-tax cash inflow expected from liquidating it, what would be the relevant cash flows for this replacement decision?

 10–5 Book value Find the book value for each of the assets shown in the following table, assuming that MACRS depreciation is being used. (*Note:* See Table 9.5 on page 284 for the applicable depreciation percentages.)

Asset	Installed cost	Recovery period	Elapsed time since purchase
A	$ 950,000	5 years	3 years
B	40,000	3 years	1 year
C	96,000	5 years	4 years
D	350,000	5 years	1 year
E	1,500,000	7 years	5 years

10–6 Book value and taxes on sale of assets Actual Manufacturing purchased a new machine 3 years ago for $80,000. It is being depreciated under MACRS with a 5-year recovery period using the percentages given in Table 9.5 on page 284. Assume 40% ordinary and capital gains tax rates.
a. What is the book value of the machine?
b. Calculate the firm's tax liability if it sold the machine for each of the following amounts: $100,000; $56,000; $23,200; and $15,000.

10–7 Tax calculations For each of the following cases, describe the various taxable components of the funds received through sale of the asset, and determine the total taxes resulting from the transaction. Assume 40% ordinary and capital gains tax rates. The asset was purchased 2 years ago for $200,000 and is being depreciated under MACRS using a 5-year recovery period. (See Table 9.5 on page 284 for the applicable depreciation percentages.)
a. The asset is sold for $220,000.
b. The asset is sold for $150,000.
c. The asset is sold for $96,000.
d. The asset is sold for $80,000.

LG4 **10–8** **Change in net working capital calculation**   Ultegra Manufacturing is considering the purchase of a new machine to replace one they feel is obsolete. The firm has total current assets of $920,000 and total current liabilities of $640,000. As a result of the proposed replacement, the following changes are anticipated in the levels of the current asset and current liability accounts noted.

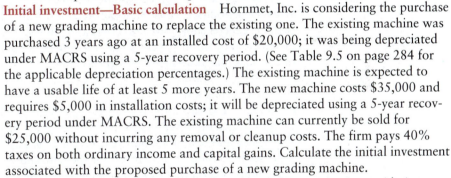

Account	Change
Accruals	+ $ 40,000
Marketable securities	0
Inventories	− 10,000
Accounts payable	+ 90,000
Notes payable	0
Accounts receivable	+ 150,000
Cash	+ 15,000

a. Using the information given, calculate the change, if any, in net working capital that is expected to result from the proposed replacement action.
b. Explain why a change in these current accounts would be relevant in determining the initial investment for the proposed capital expenditure.
c. Would the change in net working capital enter into any of the other cash flow components that make up the relevant cash flows? Explain.

   LG4 **10–9** **Initial investment—Basic calculation**   Hornmet, Inc. is considering the purchase of a new grading machine to replace the existing one. The existing machine was purchased 3 years ago at an installed cost of $20,000; it was being depreciated under MACRS using a 5-year recovery period. (See Table 9.5 on page 284 for the applicable depreciation percentages.) The existing machine is expected to have a usable life of at least 5 more years. The new machine costs $35,000 and requires $5,000 in installation costs; it will be depreciated using a 5-year recovery period under MACRS. The existing machine can currently be sold for $25,000 without incurring any removal or cleanup costs. The firm pays 40% taxes on both ordinary income and capital gains. Calculate the initial investment associated with the proposed purchase of a new grading machine.

  LG4 **10–10** **Initial investment at various sale prices**   Boston Corporation is considering replacing one machine with another. The old machine was purchased 3 years ago for an installed cost of $10,000. The firm is depreciating the machine under MACRS, using a 5-year recovery period. (See Table 9.5 on page 284 for the applicable depreciation percentages.) The new machine costs $24,000 and requires $2,000 in installation costs. The firm is subject to a 40% tax rate on both ordinary income and capital gains. In each of the following cases, calculate the initial investment for the replacement.
a. Boston Corporation (BC) sells the old machine for $11,000.
b. BC sells the old machine for $7,000.
c. BC sells the old machine for $2,900.
d. BC sells the old machine for $1,500.

LG5   **10-11**   **Depreciation**   A firm is evaluating the acquisition of an asset that costs $64,000 and requires $4,000 in installation costs. If the firm depreciates the asset under MACRS using a 5-year recovery period (see Table 9.5 on page 284 for the applicable depreciation percentages), determine the depreciation charge for each year.

     10-12   **Incremental operating cash inflows**   A firm is considering renewing its equipment to meet increased demand for its product. The cost of equipment modifications is $1.9 million plus $100,000 in installation costs. The firm will depreciate the equipment modifications under MACRS, using a 5-year recovery period. (See Table 9.5 on page 284 for the applicable depreciation percentages.) Additional sales revenue from the renewal should amount to $1.2 million per year, and additional operating expenses and other costs (excluding depreciation) will amount to 40% of the additional sales. The firm has an ordinary tax rate of 40%. (*Note:* Answer the following questions for each of the next 6 years.)

a. What incremental earnings before depreciation and taxes will result from the renewal?

b. What incremental earnings after taxes will result from the renewal?

c. What incremental operating cash inflows will result from the renewal?

LG5   **10-13**   **Incremental operating cash inflows—Expense reduction**   Tongas Corporation is considering replacing a machine. The replacement will reduce operating expenses (that is, increase revenues) by $16,000 per year for each of the 5 years the new machine is expected to last. Although the old machine has zero book value, it can be used for 5 more years. The depreciable value of the new machine is $48,000. The firm will depreciate the machine under MACRS using a 5-year recovery period (see Table 9.5 on page 284 for the applicable depreciation percentages) and is subject to a 40% tax rate on ordinary income. Estimate the incremental operating cash inflows generated by the replacement. (*Note:* Be sure to consider the depreciation in year 6.)

LG5   **10-14**   **Incremental operating cash inflows**   Earlham Tool Company has been considering purchasing a new lathe to replace a fully depreciated lathe that will last 5 more years. The new lathe is expected to have a 5-year life and depreciation charges of $2,000 in year 1; $3,200 in year 2; $1,900 in year 3; $1,200 in both year 4 and year 5; and $500 in year 6. The firm estimates the revenues and expenses (excluding depreciation) for the new and the old lathes to be as shown in the following table. The firm is subject to a 40% tax rate on ordinary income.

	New lathe		Old lathe	
Year	Revenue	Expenses (excl. depr.)	Revenue	Expenses (excl. depr.)
1	$40,000	$30,000	$35,000	$25,000
2	41,000	30,000	35,000	25,000
3	42,000	30,000	35,000	25,000
4	43,000	30,000	35,000	25,000
5	44,000	30,000	35,000	25,000

a. Calculate the operating cash inflows associated with each lathe. (*Note:* Be sure to consider the depreciation in year 6.)

b. Calculate the incremental (relevant) operating cash inflows resulting from the proposed lathe replacement.

c. Depict on a time line the incremental operating cash inflows calculated in part **b**.

10–15 Terminal cash flows—Various lives and sale prices Freight Industries is currently analyzing the purchase of a new machine that costs $160,000 and requires $20,000 in installation costs. Purchase of this machine is expected to result in an increase in net working capital of $30,000 to support the expanded level of operations. The firm plans to depreciate the asset under MACRS using a 5-year recovery period (see Table 9.5 on page 284 for the applicable depreciation percentages) and expects to sell the machine to net $10,000 before taxes at the end of its usable life. The firm is subject to a 40% tax rate on both ordinary and capital gains income.

a. Calculate the terminal cash flow for a usable life of (1) 3 years, (2) 5 years, and (3) 7 years.

b. Discuss the effect of usable life on terminal cash flows using your findings in part **a**.

c. Assuming a 5-year usable life, calculate the terminal cash flow if the machine were sold to net (1) $9,000 or (2) $170,000 (before taxes) at the end of 5 years.

d. Discuss the effect of sale price on terminal cash flows using your findings in part **c**.

10–16 Terminal cash flow—Replacement decision Ridell Industries is considering replacing a fully depreciated machine that has a remaining useful life of 10 years with a newer, more sophisticated machine. The new machine will cost $200,000 and will require $30,000 in installation costs. It will be depreciated under MACRS using a 5-year recovery period (see Table 9.5 on page 284 for the applicable depreciation percentages). A $25,000 increase in net working capital will be required to support the new machine. The firm's managers plan to evaluate the potential replacement over a 4-year period. They estimate that the old machine could be sold at the end of 4 years to net $15,000 before taxes; the new machine at the end of 4 years will be worth $75,000 before taxes. Calculate the terminal cash flow at the end of year 4 that is relevant to the proposed purchase of the new machine. The firm is subject to a 40% tax rate on both ordinary and capital gains income.

10–17 Relevant cash flows for a marketing campaign Calter Tube, a manufacturer of high-quality aluminum tubing, has maintained stable sales and profits over the past 10 years. Although the market for aluminum tubing has been expanding by 3% per year, Calter has been unsuccessful in sharing this growth. To increase its sales, the firm is considering an aggressive marketing campaign that centers on regularly running ads in all relevant trade journals and exhibiting products at all major regional and national trade shows. This campaign is expected to require an *annual* tax-deductible expenditure of $150,000 over the next 5 years. Sales revenue, as shown in the income statement for 2001 (at the top of page 324), totaled $20,000,000. If the proposed marketing campaign is not initiated, sales are expected to remain at this level in each of the next 5 years, 2002–2006. With the marketing campaign, sales are expected to rise to the levels shown in the second table (on page 324) for each of the next 5 years; cost of goods sold is expected to remain at 80% of sales; general and administrative expense (exclusive of any marketing campaign outlays) is expected to remain at 10% of sales;

and annual depreciation expense is expected to remain at $500,000. Assuming a 40% tax rate, find the relevant cash flows over the next 5 years associated with the proposed marketing campaign.

Income Statement Calter Tube for the year ended December 31, 2001		
Sales revenue		$20,000,000
Less: Cost of goods sold (80%)		16,000,000
Gross profits		$ 4,000,000
Less: Operating expenses		
General and administrative expense (10%)	$2,000,000	
Depreciation expense	500,000	
Total operating expense		2,500,000
Net profits before taxes		$ 1,500,000
Less: Taxes (rate = 40%)		600,000
Net profits after taxes		$ 900,000

Sales Forecast Calter Tube	
Year	Sales revenue
2002	$20,500,000
2003	21,000,000
2004	21,500,000
2005	22,500,000
2006	23,500,000

  10–18   Relevant cash flows—No terminal value   Statt Company is considering replacing an existing piece of machinery with a more sophisticated machine. The old machine was purchased 3 years ago at a cost of $50,000, and this amount was being depreciated under MACRS using a 5-year recovery period. The machine has 5 years of usable life remaining. The new machine that is being considered costs $76,000 and requires $4,000 in installation costs. The new machine would be depreciated under MACRS using a 5-year recovery period. The firm can currently sell the old machine for $55,000 without incurring any removal or cleanup costs. The firm pays a tax rate of 40% on both ordinary income and capital gains. The revenues and expenses (excluding depreciation) associated with the new and the old machine for the next 5 years are given in the table at the top of page 325. (Table 9.5 on page 284 contains the applicable MACRS depreciation percentages.)

a. Calculate the initial investment associated with replacement of the old machine by the new one.

b. Determine the incremental operating cash inflows associated with the proposed replacement. (*Note:* Be sure to consider the depreciation in year 6.)

	New machine		Old machine	
Year	Revenue	Expenses (excl. depr.)	Revenue	Expenses (excl. depr.)
1	$750,000	$720,000	$674,000	$660,000
2	750,000	720,000	676,000	660,000
3	750,000	720,000	680,000	660,000
4	750,000	720,000	678,000	660,000
5	750,000	720,000	674,000	660,000

c. Depict on a time line the relevant cash flows found in parts **a** and **b** associated with the proposed replacement decision.

10–19   Integrative—Determining relevant cash flows   Brooke Company is contemplating the purchase of a new high-speed widget grinder to replace the existing grinder. The existing grinder was purchased 2 years ago at an installed cost of $60,000; it was being depreciated under MACRS using a 5-year recovery period. The existing grinder is expected to have a usable life of 5 more years. The new grinder costs $105,000 and requires $5,000 in installation costs; it has a 5-year usable life and would be depreciated under MACRS using a 5-year recovery period. The existing grinder can currently be sold for $70,000 without incurring any removal or cleanup costs. To support the increased business resulting from purchase of the new grinder, accounts receivable would increase by $40,000, inventories by $30,000, and accounts payable by $58,000. At the end of 5 years, the existing grinder is expected to have a market value of zero; the new grinder would be sold to net $29,000 after removal and cleanup costs and before taxes. The firm pays taxes at the rate of 40% on both ordinary income and capital gains. The estimated *profits before depreciation and taxes* over the 5 years for both the new and the existing grinder are shown in the accompanying table. (Table 9.5 on page 284 contains the applicable MACRS depreciation percentages.)

	Profits before depreciation and taxes	
Year	New grinder	Existing grinder
1	$43,000	$26,000
2	43,000	24,000
3	43,000	22,000
4	43,000	20,000
5	43,000	18,000

a. Calculate the initial investment associated with the replacement of the existing grinder by the new one.

    b. Determine the incremental operating cash inflows associated with the proposed grinder replacement. (*Note:* Be sure to consider the depreciation in year 6.)

    c. Determine the terminal cash flow expected at the end of year 5 from the proposed grinder replacement.

    d. Depict on a time line the relevant cash flows associated with the proposed grinder replacement decision.

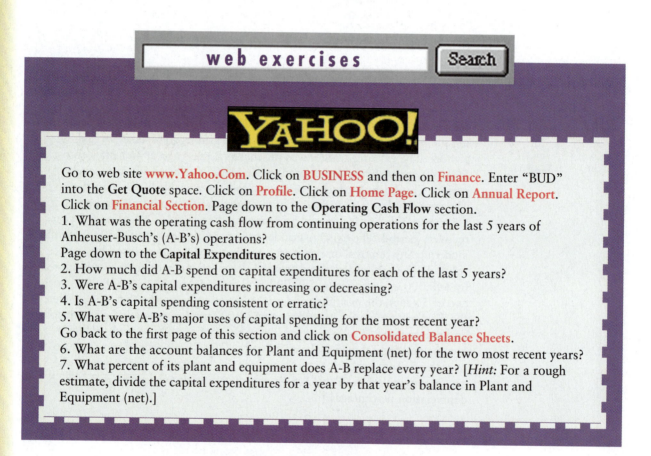

web exercises

Go to web site **www.Yahoo.Com**. Click on **BUSINESS** and then on **Finance**. Enter "BUD" into the **Get Quote** space. Click on **Profile**. Click on **Home Page**. Click on **Annual Report**. Click on **Financial Section**. Page down to the **Operating Cash Flow** section.

1. What was the operating cash flow from continuing operations for the last 5 years of Anheuser-Busch's (A-B's) operations?

Page down to the **Capital Expenditures** section.

2. How much did A-B spend on capital expenditures for each of the last 5 years?

3. Were A-B's capital expenditures increasing or decreasing?

4. Is A-B's capital spending consistent or erratic?

5. What were A-B's major uses of capital spending for the most recent year?

Go back to the first page of this section and click on **Consolidated Balance Sheets**.

6. What are the account balances for Plant and Equipment (net) for the two most recent years?

7. What percent of its plant and equipment does A-B replace every year? [*Hint:* For a rough estimate, divide the capital expenditures for a year by that year's balance in Plant and Equipment (net).]

For additional practice with concepts from this chapter, visit
http://www.awl.com/gitman_madura

Capital Budgeting Techniques: Certainty and Risk

Capital Budgeting Techniques

When firms have developed relevant cash flows, as demonstrated in Chapter 10, they analyze them to assess whether a project is acceptable or to rank projects. A number of techniques are available for performing such analyses. The preferred approaches integrate time value procedures, return and risk considerations, and valuation concepts to select capital expenditures that are consistent with the firm's goal of maximizing owners' wealth. This section and the following one focus on the use of these techniques in an environment of certainty. Later in the chapter, we will look at capital budgeting under risk.

We will use one basic problem to illustrate all the techniques described in this chapter. The problem concerns Onlab Company, a medium-sized metal fabricator that is currently contemplating two projects: Project A requires an initial investment of $42,000, project B an initial investment of $45,000. The projected relevant operating cash inflows for the two projects are presented in Table 11.1 and depicted on the time line in Figure 11.1.[1] The projects exhibit *conventional cash flow patterns,* which are assumed throughout the text. In addition, we initially assume that all projects' cash flows have the same level of risk, that projects being compared have equal usable lives, and that the firm has unlimited funds. (The risk assumption will be relaxed later in this chapter.) We begin with a look at the three most popular capital budgeting techniques: payback period, net present value, and internal rate of return.

TABLE 11.1	Capital Expenditure Data for Onlab Company	
	Project A	**Project B**
Initial investment	$42,000	$45,000
Year	**Operating cash inflows**	
1	$14,000	$28,000
2	14,000	12,000
3	14,000	10,000
4	14,000	10,000
5	14,000	10,000
Average	$14,000	$14,000

[1]For simplification, these 5-year-lived projects with 5 years of cash inflows are used throughout this chapter. Projects with usable lives equal to the number of years of cash inflows are also included in the end-of-chapter exercises. Recall from Chapter 10 that under current tax law, MACRS depreciation results in $n + 1$ years of depreciation for an n-year asset. This means that projects will commonly have at least 1 year of cash flow beyond their recovery period. In actual practice, the usable lives of projects (and the associated cash inflows) may differ significantly from their depreciable lives. Generally, under MACRS, usable lives are longer than depreciable lives.

Onlab Company's Projects A and B
Time lines depicting the conventional cash flows of Projects A and B

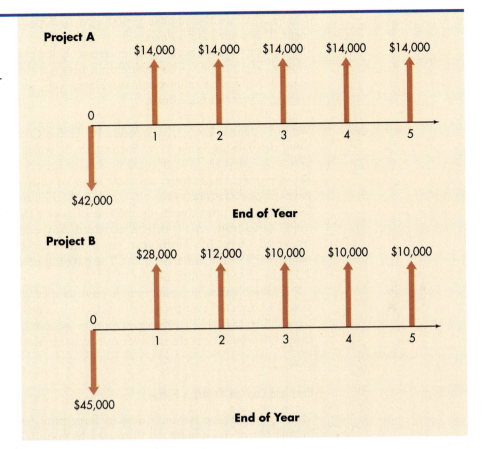

Payback Period

Payback periods are commonly used to evaluate proposed investments. The **payback period** is the amount of time required for the firm to recover its initial investment in a project, as calculated from cash inflows. In the case of an annuity, the payback period can be found by dividing the initial investment by the annual cash inflow. For a mixed stream of cash inflows, the yearly cash inflows must be accumulated until the initial investment is recovered. Although popular, the payback period is generally viewed as an *unsophisticated capital budgeting technique,* because it does not explicitly consider the time value of money.

payback period
The amount of time required for a firm to recover its initial investment in a project, as calculated from cash inflows.

The Decision Criteria

When the payback period is used to make accept–reject decisions, the decision criteria are as follows:

- If the payback period is *less than* the maximum acceptable payback period, *accept* the project.
- If the payback period is *greater than* the maximum acceptable payback period, *reject* the project.

The length of the maximum acceptable payback period is determined by management. This value is set *subjectively* on the basis of a number of factors, including the type of project (expansion, replacement, renewal), the perceived risk of the project, and the perceived relationship between the payback period and share value. It is simply a value that management feels, on average, will result in value-creating investment decisions.

E x a m p l e ▼   We can calculate the payback period for Onlab Company's projects A and B by using the data in Table 11.1. For project A, which is an annuity, the payback period is 3.0 years ($42,000 initial investment ÷ $14,000 annual cash inflow). Because project B generates a mixed stream of cash inflows, the calculation of its payback period is not so clear-cut. In year 1, the firm will recover $28,000 of its $45,000 initial investment. By the end of year 2, $40,000 ($28,000 from year 1 + $12,000 from year 2) will be recovered. At the end of year 3, $50,000 will be recovered. Only 50% of the year 3 cash inflow of $10,000 is needed to complete the payback of the initial $45,000. The payback period for project B is therefore 2.5 years (2 years + 50% of year 3).

If Onlab's maximum acceptable payback period were 2.75 years, project A would be rejected and project B would be accepted. If the maximum payback were 2.25 years, both projects would be rejected. If the projects were being ranked, B would be preferred over A, because it has a shorter payback period. ▲

Pros and Cons of Payback Periods

The payback period is widely used by large firms to evaluate small projects and by small firms to evaluate most projects. Its popularity results from its computational simplicity and intuitive appeal. It is also appealing in that it considers cash flows rather than accounting profits. By measuring how quickly the firm recovers its initial investment, the payback period also gives *implicit* consideration to the timing of cash flows and therefore to the time value of money. Because it can be viewed as a measure of *risk exposure*, many firms use the payback period as a decision criterion or as a supplement to other decision techniques.

The major weakness of the payback period is that the appropriate payback period is merely a subjectively determined number. It does not link the payback period to the wealth maximization goal. A second weakness is that this approach fails to take *fully* into account the time factor in the value of money. A third weakness is the failure to recognize cash flows that occur *after* the payback period. This weakness can be illustrated by an example.

E x a m p l e ▼   Rincon Company, a software developer, has two investment opportunities, X and Y. Data for X and Y are given in Table 11.2. The payback period for project X is 2 years; for project Y it is 3 years. Strict adherence to the payback approach suggests that project X is preferable to project Y. However, if we look beyond the payback period, we see that project X returns only an additional $1,200 ($1,000 in year 3 + $100 in year 4 + $100 in year 5), whereas project Y returns an additional $7,000 ($4,000 in year 4 + $3,000 in year 5). On the basis of this information, project Y appears preferable to X. The payback approach ignored the cash inflows occurring after the end of the payback period. ▲

TABLE 11.2	Calculation of the Payback Period for Rincon Company's Two Alternative Investment Projects	
	Project X	Project Y
Initial investment	$10,000	$10,000
Year	Cash inflows	
1	$5,000	$3,000
2	5,000	4,000
3	1,000	3,000
4	100	4,000
5	100	3,000
Payback period	2 years	3 years

 ## Net Present Value (NPV)

Because *net present value (NPV)* gives explicit consideration to the time value of money, it is considered a *sophisticated capital budgeting technique*. All such techniques in one way or another discount the firm's cash flows at a specified rate. This rate—called the *discount rate, required return, cost of capital,* or *opportunity cost*—is the minimum return that must be earned on a project to leave the firm's market value unchanged. In this chapter, we take this rate as a "given." In Chapter 12 we will explore how it is calculated.

net present value (NPV)
A sophisticated capital budgeting technique; found by subtracting a project's initial investment from the present value of its cash inflows discounted at a rate equal to the firm's cost of capital.

The **net present value** (**NPV**) is found by subtracting a project's initial investment (CF_0) from the present value of its cash inflows (CF_t) discounted at a rate equal to the firm's cost of capital (k).

$$\text{NPV} = \text{Present value of cash inflows} - \text{Initial investment}$$

$$\text{NPV} = \sum_{t=1}^{n} \frac{CF_t}{(1+k)^t} - CF_0 \qquad (11.1)$$

When NPV is used, both inflows and outflows are measured in terms of present dollars.

The Decision Criteria

When NPV is used to make accept–reject decisions, the decision criteria are as follows:

- If the NPV is *greater than* $0, *accept* the project.
- If the NPV is *less than* $0, *reject* the project.

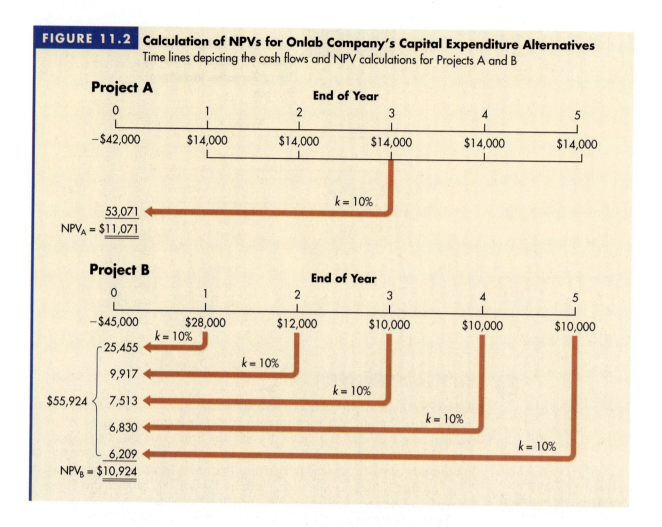

FIGURE 11.2   Calculation of NPVs for Onlab Company's Capital Expenditure Alternatives
Time lines depicting the cash flows and NPV calculations for Projects A and B

If the NPV is greater than $0, the firm will earn a return greater than its cost of capital. Such action should enhance the market value of the firm and therefore the wealth of its owners.

Example ▼   We can illustrate the net present value (NPV) approach using Onlab Company data presented in Table 11.1. If the firm has a 10% cost of capital, the net present values for projects A (an annuity) and B (a mixed stream) can be calculated as shown on the time lines in Figure 11.2. These calculations result in net present values for projects A and B of $11,071 and $10,924, respectively. Both projects are acceptable, because the net present value of each is greater than $0. If the projects were being ranked, however, project A would be considered superior to B, because it has a higher net present value than that of B ($11,071 versus $10,924).

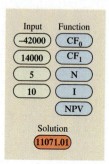

Calculator Use   The preprogrammed NPV function in a financial calculator can be used to simplify the NPV calculation. The keystrokes for project A—the annuity—typically are as shown at the left. Note that because project A is an

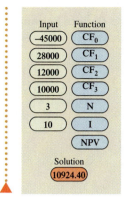

Input	Function
−45000	CF_0
28000	CF_1
12000	CF_2
10000	CF_3
3	N
10	I
	NPV

Solution
10924.40

annuity, only its first cash inflow, $CF_1 = 14000$, is input, followed by its frequency, $N = 5$.

The keystrokes for project B—the mixed stream—are as shown at the left. Note that because the last three cash inflows for project B are the same ($CF_3 = CF_4 = CF_5 = 10000$), after inputting the first of these cash inflows, CF_3, we merely input its frequency, $N = 3$.

The calculated NPVs for projects A and B of $11,071 and $10,924, respectively, agree with the NPVs cited above.

Internal Rate of Return (IRR)

The *internal rate of return (IRR)* is probably the most widely used *sophisticated capital budgeting technique*. However, it is considerably more difficult than NPV to calculate by hand. The **internal rate of return (IRR)** is the discount rate that equates the NPV of an investment opportunity with $0 (because the present value of cash inflows equals the initial investment). It is the compound annual rate of return that the firm will earn if it invests in the project and receives the given cash inflows. Mathematically, the IRR is the value of k in Equation 11.1 that causes NPV to equal $0:

internal rate of return (IRR)
A sophisticated capital budgeting technique; the discount rate that equates the NPV of an investment opportunity with $0 (because the present value of cash inflows equals the initial investment).

$$\$0 = \sum_{t=1}^{n} \frac{CF_t}{(1+IRR)^t} - CF_0 \tag{11.2}$$

$$\sum_{t=1}^{n} \frac{CF_t}{(1+IRR)^t} = CF_0 \tag{11.2a}$$

The Decision Criteria

When IRR is used to make accept–reject decisions, the decision criteria are as follows:

- If the IRR is *greater than* the cost of capital, *accept* the project.
- If the IRR is *less than* the cost of capital, *reject* the project.

These criteria guarantee that the firm earns at least its required return. Such an outcome should enhance the market value of the firm and therefore the wealth of its owners.

Calculating the IRR

The actual calculation by hand of the IRR from Equation 11.2a is no easy chore. It involves a complex trial-and-error technique that is described and demonstrated on this text's web site: http://www.awl.com/gitman_madura. Fortunately, many financial calculators have a preprogrammed IRR function that can be used to simplify the IRR calculation. With these calculators, you merely punch in all cash flows as is done to calculate NPV, and then depress IRR to find the internal rate of return. Computer software, including spreadsheets, is also available for simplifying these calculations. All IRR and NPV values presented in this and subse-

FIGURE 11.3   Calculation of IRRs for Onlab Company's Capital Expenditure Alternatives
Time lines depicting the cash flows and IRR calculations for Projects A and B

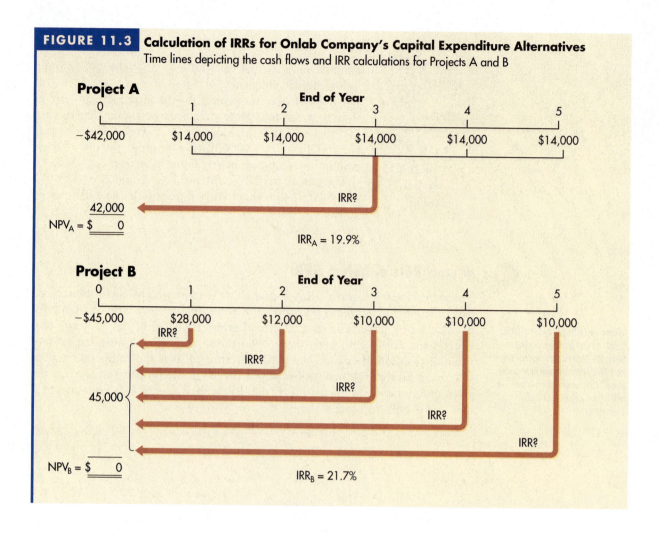

quent chapters are obtained by using these functions on a popular financial calculator.

Example ▼ We can demonstrate the internal rate of return (IRR) approach using Onlab Company data presented in Table 11.1. Figure 11.3 uses time lines to depict the framework for finding the IRRs for Onlab's projects A and B, both of which have conventional cash flow patterns. It can be seen in the figure that the IRR is the unknown discount rate that causes the NPV just to equal 0.

Calculator Use   To find the IRR using the preprogrammed function in a financial calculator, the keystrokes for each project would be the same as those shown earlier for the NPV calculation, except that the last two NPV keystrokes (punching **I** and then **NPV**) would be replaced by a single **IRR** keystroke.

Comparing the IRRs of projects A and B given in Figure 11.3 to Onlab Company's 10% cost of capital, we can see that both are acceptable because

$$IRR_A = 19.9\% > 10.0\% \text{ cost of capital}$$

$$IRR_B = 21.7\% > 10.0\% \text{ cost of capital}$$

Comparing the two project's IRRs, we would prefer project B over project A because $IRR_B = 21.7\% > IRR_A = 19.9\%$. If these projects are mutually exclusive, the IRR decision technique would recommend implementation of project B.

It is interesting to note in the preceding example that the IRR suggests that project B, which has an IRR of 21.7%, is preferable to project A, which has an IRR of 19.9%. This conflicts with the NPV rankings obtained in an earlier example. Such conflicts are not unusual. There is no guarantee that NPV and IRR will rank projects in the same order. However, both methods should reach the same conclusion about the acceptability or nonacceptability of projects.

? Review Questions

11–1   How is the payback period calculated? What are its weaknesses?
11–2   What is the acceptance criterion for net present value (NPV)? How is it related to the firm's market value?
11–3   What is the acceptance criterion for internal rate of return (IRR)? How is it related to the firm's market value?
11–4   Do NPV and IRR always agree with respect to accept–reject decisions? With respect to ranking decisions? Explain.

LG3 Comparing NPV and IRR Techniques

To understand the differences and preferences surrounding the NPV and IRR techniques, we need to look at net present value profiles, conflicting rankings, and the question of which approach is better.

Net Present Value Profiles

net present value profile
Graph that depicts projects' NPVs for various discount rates.

Projects can be compared graphically by constructing **net present value profiles** that depict projects' NPVs for various discount rates. These profiles are useful in evaluating and comparing projects, especially when conflicting rankings exist. They are best demonstrated via an example.

Example ▼   To prepare net present value profiles for Onlab Company's two projects, A and B, the first step is to develop a number of "discount rate–net present value" coordinates. Three coordinates can be easily obtained for each project, at discount rates of 0%, 10% (the cost of capital, k), and the IRR. The net present value at a 0% discount rate is found by merely adding all the cash inflows and subtracting the initial investment. Using the data in Table 11.1 and Figure 11.1, we get

For project A:
$$(\$14,000 + \$14,000 + \$14,000 + \$14,000 + \$14,000) - \$42,000 = \$28,000$$

TABLE 11.3	Discount-Rate–NPV Coordinates for Projects A and B	
Discount rate	Net present value	
	Project A	Project B
0%	$28,000	$25,000
10	11,071	10,924
19.9	0	—
21.7	—	0

For project B:

$$(\$28,000 + \$12,000 + \$10,000 + \$10,000 + \$10,000) - \$45,000 = \$25,000$$

The net present values for projects A and B at the 10% cost of capital are $11,071 and $10,924, respectively (from Figure 11.2). Because the IRR is the discount rate for which net present value equals zero, the IRRs of 19.9% for project A and 21.7% for project B result in $0 NPVs. The three sets of coordinates for each of the projects are summarized in Table 11.3.

Plotting the data from Table 11.3 results in the net present value profiles for projects A and B shown in Figure 11.4. The figure indicates that for any discount rate less than approximately 10.7%, the NPV for project A is greater than the NPV for project B. Beyond this point, the NPV for project B is greater. Because the net present value profiles for projects A and B cross at a positive NPV, the IRRs for the projects cause conflicting rankings whenever they are compared to NPVs calculated at discount rates below 10.7%.

Conflicting Rankings

Ranking is an important consideration when projects are mutually exclusive or when capital rationing is necessary. When projects are mutually exclusive, rank-

FIGURE 11.4

NPV Profiles
Net present value profiles for Onlab Company's projects A and B

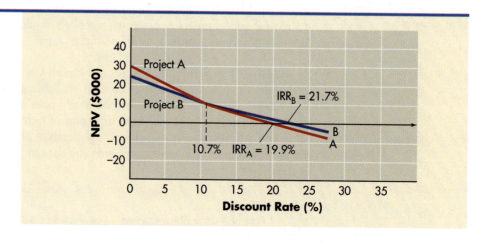

TABLE 11.4	Preferences Associated with Extreme Discount Rates and Dissimilar Cash Inflow Patterns	
	Cash inflow pattern	
Discount rate	Lower early-year cash inflows	Higher early-year cash inflows
Low	Preferred	Not preferred
High	Not preferred	Preferred

conflicting rankings
Conflicts in the ranking given a project by NPV and IRR, resulting from *differences in the magnitude and timing of cash flows.*

intermediate cash inflows
Cash inflows received prior to the termination of a project.

ing enables the firm to determine which project is best from a financial viewpoint. When capital rationing is necessary, ranking projects will provide a logical starting point for determining what group of projects to accept. As we'll see, **conflicting rankings** using NPV and IRR result from *differences in the magnitude and timing of cash flows.*

The underlying cause of conflicting rankings is the implicit assumption concerning the reinvestment of **intermediate cash inflows**—cash inflows received prior to the termination of a project. NPV assumes that intermediate cash inflows are reinvested at the cost of capital, whereas IRR assumes that intermediate cash inflows are invested at a rate equal to the project's IRR.

In general, projects with similar-sized investments and lower cash inflows in the early years tend to be preferred at lower discount rates. Projects that have higher cash inflows in the early years tend to be preferred at higher discount rates. Why? Because at high discount rates, later-year cash inflows tend to be severely penalized in present value terms. For example, at a high discount rate, say 20 percent, the present value of $1 received at the end of 5 years is about 40 cents, whereas for $1 received at the end of 15 years it is less than 7 cents. Clearly, at high discount rates a project's early-year cash inflows count most in terms of its NPV. Table 11.4 summarizes the preferences associated with extreme discount rates and dissimilar cash inflow patterns.

Example ▼

Onlab's projects A and B were found to have conflicting rankings at the firm's 10% cost of capital (as depicted in Figure 11.4). If we review each project's cash inflow pattern as presented in Table 11.1 and Figure 11.1, we see that although the projects require similar initial investments, they have dissimilar cash inflow patterns. Table 11.4 indicates that project B, which has higher early year cash inflows than project A, would be preferred over project A at higher discount rates. Figure 11.4 shows that this is in fact the case. At any discount rate in excess of 10.7%, project B's NPV is above that of project A. Clearly, the magnitude and timing of the projects' cash inflows do affect their rankings. ▲

Which Approach Is Better?

It is difficult to choose one approach over the other, because the theoretical and practical strengths of the approaches differ. It is therefore wise to view both NPV and IRR techniques in each of those dimensions.

Theoretical View

On a purely theoretical basis, NPV is the better approach to capital budgeting as a result of several factors. Most important is that the use of NPV implicitly assumes that any intermediate cash inflows generated by an investment are *reinvested at the firm's cost of capital.* The use of IRR assumes *reinvestment at the often high rate specified by the IRR.* Because the cost of capital tends to be a reasonable estimate of the rate at which the firm could *actually reinvest* intermediate cash inflows, the use of NPV, with its more conservative and realistic reinvestment rate, is in theory preferable.

In addition, certain mathematical properties may cause a project with a nonconventional cash flow pattern to have zero or more than one *real* IRR; this problem does not occur with the NPV approach.

Practical View

Evidence suggests that in spite of the theoretical superiority of NPV, *financial managers prefer to use IRR.* The preference for IRR is due to the general disposition of businesspeople toward rates of return rather than actual dollar returns. Because interest rates, profitability, and so on are most often expressed as annual rates of return, the use of IRR makes sense to financial decision makers. They tend to find NPV less intuitive, because it does not measure benefits *relative to the amount invested.* Because a variety of techniques are available for avoiding the pitfalls of the IRR, its widespread use does not imply a lack of sophistication on the part of financial decision makers.

? Review Questions

11–5 What causes conflicts in the ranking of projects via net present value and internal rate of return?

11–6 Does the assumption concerning the reinvestment of intermediate cash inflow tend to favor NPV or IRR? In practice, which technique is preferred and why?

Behavioral Approaches for Dealing with Risk

risk (in capital budgeting)
The chance that a project will prove unacceptable or, more formally, the degree of variability of cash flows.

In the discussion of capital budgeting, **risk** refers to the chance that a project will prove unacceptable—that is, NPV < $0 or IRR < cost of capital. More formally, risk in capital budgeting refers to the degree of variability of cash flows. Projects with a small chance of acceptability and a broad range of expected cash flows are more risky than projects with a high chance of acceptability and a narrow range of expected cash flows.

In the conventional capital budgeting projects assumed here, risk stems almost entirely from *cash inflows,* because the initial investment is generally known with relative certainty. These inflows, of course, derive from a number of variables related to revenues, expenditures, and taxes. Examples include the level of sales, the cost of raw materials, labor rates, utility costs, and tax rates. We will concentrate on the risk in the cash inflows, but remember that this risk actually results from the interaction of these underlying variables. Using the basic risk concepts presented in Chapter 6, here we present a few behavioral approaches for dealing with risk in capital budgeting: sensitivity and scenario analysis and simulation. In addition, some international risk considerations are discussed.

Sensitivity and Scenario Analysis

Two approaches for dealing with project risk to capture the variability of cash inflows and NPVs are sensitivity analysis and scenario analysis. As noted in Chapter 6, *sensitivity analysis* is a behavioral approach that uses multiple possible values for a given variable, such as cash inflows, to assess its impact on the firm's return, measured here by NPV. This technique is often useful in getting a feel for the variability of return in response to changes in a key variable. In capital budgeting, one of the most common sensitivity approaches is to estimate the NPVs associated with pessimistic (worst), most likely (expected), and optimistic (best) estimates of cash inflow. The *range* can be determined by subtracting the pessimistic-outcome NPV from the optimistic-outcome NPV.

Example ▼   Bigpaw Tire Company, a tire retailer with a 10% cost of capital, is considering investing in either of two mutually exclusive projects, A or B. Each requires a $10,000 initial investment, and both are expected to provide equal annual cash inflows over their 15-year lives. The firm's financial manager made pessimistic, most likely, and optimistic estimates of the cash inflows for each project. The cash inflow estimates and resulting NPVs in each case are summarized in Table 11.5. Comparing the ranges of cash inflows ($1,000 for project A and $4,000 for B) and, more important, the ranges of NPVs ($7,606 for project A and $30,424 for B) makes it clear that project A is less risky than project B. Given that both projects have the same most likely NPV of $5,212, the assumed risk-averse decision maker will take project A because it has less risk and no possibil-**▲** ity of loss.

scenario analysis
A behavioral approach that evaluates the impact on the firm's return of simultaneous changes in a *number of variables.*

Scenario analysis is a behavioral approach similar to sensitivity analysis but broader in scope. It evaluates the impact on the firm's return of simultaneous changes in a *number of variables,* such as cash inflows, cash outflows, and the cost of capital. For example, the firm could evaluate the impact of both high inflation (scenario 1) and low inflation (scenario 2) on a project's NPV. Each scenario will affect the firm's cash inflows, cash outflows, and cost of capital, thereby resulting in different levels of NPV. The decision maker can use these NPV estimates to estimate the risk involved with respect to the level of inflation. The widespread availability of computer-based spreadsheet programs has greatly enhanced the use of both scenario and sensitivity analysis.

Simulation

simulation
A statistically based behavioral approach that applies predetermined probability distributions and random numbers to estimate risky outcomes.

Simulation is a statistically based behavioral approach that applies predetermined probability distributions and random numbers to estimate risky outcomes. By tying the various cash flow components together in a mathematical model and repeating the process numerous times, the financial manager can develop a probability distribution of project returns. Figure 11.5 on page 341 presents a flowchart of the simulation of the net present value of a project.

Source: Bill Birchard, "Intangible Assets Plus Hard Numbers Equals Soft Finance," Fast Company, *October 1999, p. 316.*

NewsLine — PUTTING HARD NUMBERS ON INTANGIBLE ASSETS

Instead of plant and equipment, companies today compete on ideas and relationships. To analyze projects, financial managers need new techniques to assign a dollar value to these intangible assets—patents, knowledge, and people.

Betsey Nelson, CFO of software maker Macromedia, knows all about intangible value. Among Nelson's biggest leadership challenges: assessing the value of projects like the New Way, an internal-investment strategy aimed at shifting much of Macromedia's business onto the Web....

Nelson sorts the components of any deal or investment into four "buckets": market, product and technology, team, and financial. And to evaluate those components, she reaches back to a trusted tool in the CFO tool kit: discounted cash flow, a standard technique for projecting annual cash flow into the future and then discounting its value back to the present, taking into account the time value of money.

Nelson still reduces every idea to revenue streams: How much will come in and when? And she uses her cash-flow projections to calculate present value with a discount factor that shrinks the value of future cash flows in proportion to increased risk. But that's where the similarities end. At Macromedia, Nelson uses this very traditional tool in very nontraditional ways, adapting DCF to the intangibles of the new economy.

Nelson takes the vagaries of intangible assets into account by conducting sensitivity, or "what if," analyses. After carefully and systematically running the DCF numbers for Plan A, Nelson runs dozens of scenarios, generating alternatives, asking questions based on a broad set of changing assumptions, and poking holes in those assumptions.

[To discover what the New Way is worth,] Nelson...measures the value of the project in three ways: marketing return on investment, the cost of sales, and share of customer loyalty...."What's the value of a customer relationship?" asks Nelson. "You don't have a lot of hard data. You have to draw on a lot of gut in order to come up with the numbers that correspond to the market, the technology, and the ability of the team."

TABLE 11.5 Sensitivity Analysis of Bigpaw's Projects A and B

	Project A	Project B
Initial investment	$10,000	$10,000
Annual cash inflows		
Outcome		
Pessimistic	$ 1,500	$ 0
Most likely	2,000	2,000
Optimistic	2,500	4,000
Range	$ 1,000	$ 4,000
Net present values[a]		
Outcome		
Pessimistic	$ 1,409	−$10,000
Most likely	5,212	5,212
Optimistic	9,015	20,424
Range	$ 7,606	$30,424

[a]These values were calculated by using the corresponding annual cash inflows. A 10% cost of capital and a 15-year life for the annual cash inflows were used.

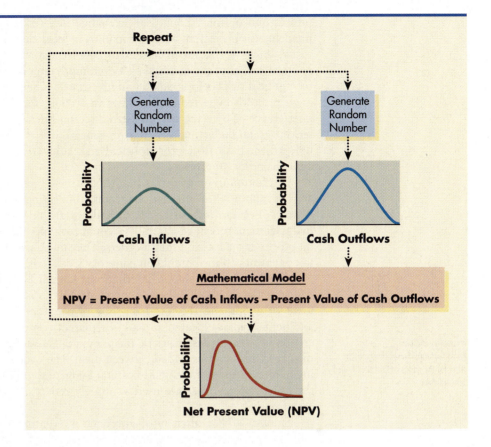

FIGURE 11.5

NPV Simulation
Flowchart of a net present value simulation

Although only gross cash inflows and outflows are simulated in Figure 11.5, more sophisticated simulations using individual inflow and outflow components, such as sales volume, sale price, raw material cost, labor cost, maintenance expense, and so on, are quite common. From the distribution of returns, the decision maker can determine not only the expected value of the return but also the probability of achieving or surpassing a given return. The use of computers has made the simulation approach feasible. The output of simulation provides an excellent basis for decision making, because it allows the decision maker to view a continuum of risk–return tradeoffs rather than a single-point estimate.

International Risk Considerations

Although the basic techniques of capital budgeting are the same for purely domestic firms as for multinational companies (MNCs), firms that operate in several countries face risks that are unique to the international arena. Two types of risk are particularly important: exchange rate risk and political risk.

As indicated in Chapter 1, **exchange rate risk** refers to the danger that an unexpected change in the exchange rate between the dollar and the currency in which a project's cash flows are denominated will reduce the market value of that project's cash flow. The dollar value of future cash inflows can be dramatically altered if the local currency depreciates against the dollar. In the short term, specific cash flows can be hedged by using financial instruments such as currency

exchange rate risk
The danger that an unexpected change in the exchange rate between the dollar and the currency in which a project's cash flows are denominated will reduce the market value of that project's cash flow.

futures and options. Long-term exchange rate risk can best be minimized by financing the project, in whole or in part, in local currency.

Political risk is much harder to protect against. The inability to manage political risk after the fact makes it even more important that managers account for political risks before making an investment. They can do so either by adjusting a project's expected cash inflows to account for the probability of political interference or by using risk-adjusted discount rates (discussed later in this chapter) in capital budgeting formulas. In general, it is much better to adjust individual project cash flows for political risk subjectively than to use a blanket adjustment for all projects.

In addition to unique risks that MNCs must face, several other special issues are relevant only for international capital budgeting. One of these special issues is *taxes*. Because only after-tax cash flows are relevant for capital budgeting, financial managers must carefully account for taxes paid to foreign governments on profits earned within their borders. They must also assess the impact of these tax payments on the parent company's U.S. tax liability.

Another special issue in international capital budgeting is *transfer pricing*. Much of the international trade involving MNCs is, in reality, simply the shipment of goods and services from one of a parent company's subsidiaries to another subsidiary located abroad. The parent company therefore has great discretion in setting **transfer prices,** the prices that subsidiaries charge each other for the goods and services traded between them. The widespread use of transfer pricing in international trade makes capital budgeting in MNCs very difficult unless the transfer prices that are used accurately reflect actual costs and incremental cash flows.

Finally, MNCs often must approach international capital projects from a *strategic point of view,* rather than from a strictly financial perspective. For example, an MNC may feel compelled to invest in a country to ensure continued access, even if the project itself may not have a positive net present value. This motivation was important for Japanese automakers who set up assembly plants in the United States in the early 1980s. For much the same reason, U.S. investment in Europe surged during the years before the market integration of the European Community in 1992. MNCs often invest in production facilities in the home country of major rivals to deny these competitors an uncontested home market. MNCs also may feel compelled to invest in certain industries or countries to achieve a broad corporate objective, such as diversifying raw material sources, even when the project's cash flows may not be sufficiently profitable.

transfer prices
Prices that subsidiaries charge each other for the goods and services traded between them.

? Review Questions

11–7 Describe how each of the following behavioral approaches can be used to deal with project risk: sensitivity analysis, scenario analysis, and simulation.

11–8 Briefly explain how the following items affect the capital budgeting decisions of multinational companies: exchange rate risk, political risk, tax law differences, transfer pricing, and a strategic rather than a strict financial viewpoint.

LG6 Risk-Adjusted Discount Rates

The approaches for dealing with risk that have been presented so far allow the financial manager to get a "feel" for project risk. Unfortunately, they do not provide a quantitative basis for evaluating risky projects. We will now illustrate the most popular risk-adjustment technique that employs the net present value (NPV) decision method. The NPV decision rule of accepting only those projects with NPVs>$0 will continue to hold. Close examination of the basic equation for NPV, Equation 11.1, should make it clear that because the initial investment (CF_0) is known with certainty, a project's risk is embodied in the present value of its cash inflows:

$$\sum_{t=1}^{n} \frac{CF_t}{(1+k)^t}$$

Two opportunities to adjust the present value of cash inflows for risk exist: (1) The cash inflows (CF_t) can be adjusted, or (2) the discount rate (k) can be adjusted. Adjusting cash flows is highly subjective, so here we describe the more popular process of adjusting discount rates. In addition, we consider the practical aspects of risk-adjusted discount rates.

Determining Risk-Adjusted Discount Rates (RADRs)

A popular approach for risk adjustment involves the use of *risk-adjusted discount rates (RADRs)*. This approach uses Equation 11.1 but employs a risk-adjusted discount rate, as noted in the following expression:

$$NPV = \sum_{t=1}^{n} \frac{CF_t}{(1+RADR)^t} - CF_0 \tag{11.3}$$

risk-adjusted discount rate (RADR)
The rate of return that must be earned on a given project to compensate the firm's owners adequately—that is, to maintain or improve the firm's share price.

The **risk-adjusted discount rate (RADR)** is the rate of return that must be earned on a given project to compensate the firm's owners adequately—that is, to maintain or improve the firm's share price. The higher the risk of a project, the higher the RADR, and therefore the lower the net present value for a given stream of cash inflows.

The logic underlying the use of RADRs is closely linked to the capital asset pricing model (CAPM) developed in Chapter 6. Because the CAPM is based on an assumed *efficient market*, which does *not* exist for real corporate (nonfinancial) assets such as plant and equipment, the CAPM is not directly applicable in making capital budgeting decisions. Financial managers therefore assess the *total risk* of a project and use it to determine the risk-adjusted discount rate (RADR), which can be used in Equation 11.3 to find the NPV.

In order not to damage its market value, the firm must use the correct discount rate to evaluate a project. If a firm discounts a risky project's cash inflows at too low a rate and accepts the project, the firm's market price may drop as investors recognize that the firm itself has become more risky. On the other hand, if the firm discounts a project's cash inflows at too high a rate, it will reject acceptable projects. Eventually the firm's market price may drop, because investors who believe that the firm is being overly conservative will sell their stock, putting downward pressure on the firm's market value.

Unfortunately, there is no formal mechanism for linking total project risk to the level of required return. As a result, most firms subjectively determine the RADR by adjusting their existing required return. They adjust it up or down depending on whether the proposed project is more or less risky, respectively, than the average risk of the firm. This CAPM-type of approach provides a "rough estimate" of project risk and required return because both the project risk measure and the linkage between risk and required return are estimates.

Example ▼ Onlab Company wishes to use the risk-adjusted discount rate approach to determine, according to NPV, whether to implement project A or project B. In addition to the data presented earlier, Onlab's management after much analysis assigned a "risk index" of 1.6 to project A and 1.0 to project B. The risk index is merely a numerical scale used to classify project risk: Higher index values are assigned to higher-risk projects, and vice versa. The CAPM-type relationship used by the firm to link risk (measured by the risk index) and the required return (RADR) is shown in the following table:

	Risk index	Required return (RADR)
	0.0	6% (risk-free rate, R_F)
	0.2	7
	0.4	8
	0.6	9
	0.8	10
Project B →	1.0	11
	1.2	12
	1.4	13
Project A →	1.6	14
	1.8	16
	2.0	18

Because project A is riskier than project B, its RADR of 14% is greater than project B's 11%. The net present value of each project, using its RADR, is calculated as shown on the time lines in Figure 11.6. The results clearly show that project B is preferable, because its risk-adjusted NPV of $9,798 is greater than the $6,063 risk-adjusted NPV for project A. As reflected by the NPVs in Figure 11.2, if the discount rates were not adjusted for risk, project A would be preferred to project B.

Input	Function
−42000	CF₀
14000	CF₁
5	N
14	I
	NPV

Solution
6063.13

Calculator Use We can again use the preprogrammed NPV function in a financial calculator to simplify the NPV calculation. The keystrokes for project A—the annuity—typically are as shown at the left. The keystrokes for project B—the mixed stream—are as shown at the right. It can be seen that the calculated NPVs for projects A and B of $6,063 and $9,798, respectively, agree with those shown in Figure 11.6.

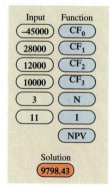

Input	Function
−45000	CF₀
28000	CF₁
12000	CF₂
10000	CF₃
3	N
11	I
	NPV

Solution
9798.43

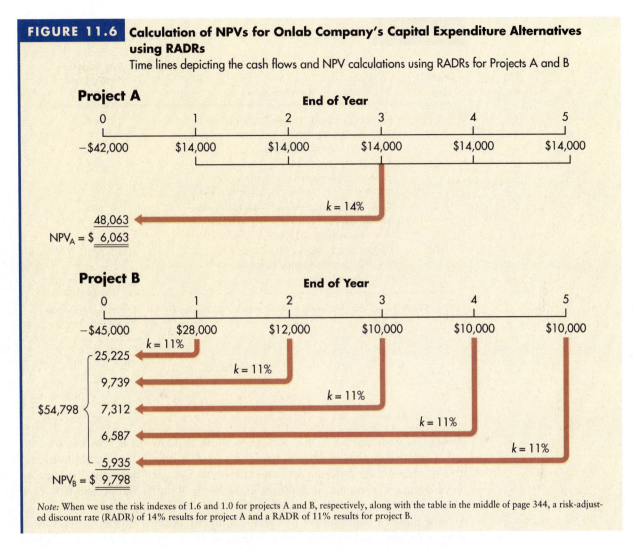

FIGURE 11.6 **Calculation of NPVs for Onlab Company's Capital Expenditure Alternatives using RADRs**
Time lines depicting the cash flows and NPV calculations using RADRs for Projects A and B

Note: When we use the risk indexes of 1.6 and 1.0 for projects A and B, respectively, along with the table in the middle of page 344, a risk-adjusted discount rate (RADR) of 14% results for project A and a RADR of 11% results for project B.

The usefulness of risk-adjusted discount rates should now be clear. The real difficulty lies in estimating project risk and linking it to the required return (RADR).

RADRs in Practice

RADRs are often used in practice. Their popularity stems from two facts: (1) They are consistent with the general disposition of financial decision makers toward rates of return, and (2) they are easily estimated and applied. The first reason is clearly a matter of personal preference, but the second is based on the computational convenience and well-developed procedures involved in the use of RADRs.

In practice, firms often establish a number of *risk classes*, with an RADR assigned to each. Each project is then subjectively placed in the appropriate risk class, and the corresponding RADR is used to evaluate it. This is sometimes done on a division-by-division basis, in which case each division has its own set of risk

TABLE 11.6	Onlab Company's Risk Classes and RADRs	
Risk class	Description	Risk-adjusted discount rate, RADR
I	*Below-average risk:* Projects with low risk. Typically involve routine replacement without renewal of existing activities.	8%
II	*Average risk:* Projects similar to those currently implemented. Typically involve replacement or renewal of existing activities.	10%[a]
III	*Above-average risk:* Projects with higher than normal, but not excessive, risk. Typically involve expansion of existing or similar activities.	14%
IV	*Highest risk:* Projects with very high risk. Typically involve expansion into new or unfamiliar activities.	20%

[a]This RADR is actually the firm's cost of capital, which is discussed in detail in Chapter 12. It represents the firm's required return on its existing portfolio of projects, which is assumed unchanged with acceptance of the "average-risk" project.

classes and associated RADRs, similar to those in Table 11.6. The use of *divisional costs of capital* and associated risk classes allows a large multidivisional firm to incorporate differing levels of divisional risk into the capital budgeting process and still recognize differences in the levels of individual project risk.

Example ▼

Assume that the management of Onlab Company decided to use risk classes to analyze projects and so placed each project in one of four risk classes according to its perceived risk. The classes were ranged from I for the lowest-risk projects to IV for the highest-risk projects. Associated with each class was an RADR appropriate to the level of risk of projects in the class, as given in Table 11.6. Onlab classified as lower-risk those projects that tend to involve routine replacement or renewal activities; higher-risk projects involve expansion, often into new or unfamiliar activities.

The financial manager of Onlab has assigned project A to Class III and project B to Class II. The cash flows for project A would be evaluated using a 14% RADR, and project B's would be evaluated by using a 10 percent RADR. The NPV of project A at 14% was calculated in Figure 11.6 to be $6,063, and the NPV for project B at a 10% RADR was calculated in Figure 11.2 to be $10,924. Clearly, with RADRs based on the use of risk classes, project B is preferred over project A. As noted earlier, this result is contrary to the preferences shown in Figure 11.2, where the differing risks of projects A and B were not taken into account.

▲

 GETTING REAL

This excerpt from an article on real options analysis, a new modeling technique used to analyze uncertainty in investment decisions, discusses the limitations of using net present value analysis.

Net present value ultimately boils down to one of two decisions: go or no-go. When the net present value of expected cash flows is positive, companies usually proceed. As a practical consequence, managers concentrate on prospects for favorable outcomes. Prospects for unfavorable outcomes get short shrift. In this analysis, certainty enjoys a premium—and that's a narrow path. . . .

"Unfortunately, discounted cash flow collapses to a single path," says [Soussan] Faiz [manager of global valuation services at oil giant Texaco Inc.]. . . . In the oil business, oil prices don't remain low for the life of a project; they bounce back. "The likelihood of prices being low for the rest of the project [is] zero or nearly zero," says Faiz. But even if prices do remain stagnant, defying the odds, managers don't snooze the whole time. They wake up and react. Net present value, however, treats investments as if outcomes are cast in stone.

"Net present value makes a lot of heroic assumptions," warns Tom Copeland, chief corporate finance officer of Monitor, a strategy consultancy in Cambridge, Massachusetts. Typically, a multiyear project is plotted along a single trajectory worth pursuing only if the net present value exceeds zero or some hurdle rate. This type of reasoning may satisfy requirements for a midterm exam, said Copeland, but situations in the real world change constantly as new information surfaces. Most managers realize that flexibility ought to be included in valuations, Copeland says. "The bridge they have to cross is understanding the methodology to capture the value" of flexibility.

Source: S. L. Mintz, "Getting Real," CFO, November 1999, downloaded from www.cfonet.com.

 Review Questions

11–9   How is the risk-adjusted discount rate (RADR) approach related to the capital asset pricing model (CAPM)?

11–10   How are risk classes often used to apply RADRs?

TYING IT ALL TOGETHER

This chapter presented the three most popular capital budgeting techniques—the payback period, net present value (NPV), and internal rate of return (IRR)—first assuming certainty and then considering risk. Each has specific strengths and weaknesses. The behavioral approaches for dealing with risk—sensitivity and scenario analysis and simulation—were described and demonstrated, and a detailed discussion of the risk-adjusted discount rate (RADR) was presented. Important aspects of capital budgeting techniques under both certainty and risk from the viewpoints of financial managers, financial markets, and investors are summarized in the Integrative Table that follows.

INTEGRATIVE TABLE

Using Capital Budgeting Techniques Under Both Certainty and Risk

Role of **Financial Managers**	*Role of* **Financial Markets**	*Role of* **Investors**
Financial managers must understand the major capital budgeting techniques, their strengths and weaknesses, and their use in both certain and risky situations. These techniques—particularly NPV and IRR—are widely used by financial managers to make investment decisions that can affect the firm's success in creating value for owners. An ability to incorporate project risk into the analysis is also important in selecting projects that will add to owners' wealth.	The financial markets create the forum in which firms can disseminate and investors can gather information on the firm's capital budgeting activities. In that forum the price or value of the firm is determined. By allowing the free flow of information, the markets create an environment where investors can research and analyze the firm's actions and, through their purchase and sale reactions, affect the owners' wealth.	Investors monitor the firm's capital budgeting decisions in order to make sure that they are consistent with maximization of owner wealth. Their assessment of the quality of the capital budgeting decisions often determines whether or not they invest in the firm. Firms that effectively apply capital budgeting techniques and correctly capture risk in their analyses are more likely to attract investors, thereby driving up share prices and increasing the owners' wealth.

LG1 **Calculate, interpret, and evaluate the payback period.** The payback period is the amount of time required for the firm to recover its initial investment, as calculated from cash inflows. The formula and decision criterion for the payback period are summarized in Table 11.7. Shorter payback periods are preferred. The payback period's strengths include ease of calculation, simple intuitive appeal, consideration of cash flows, the implicit consideration given to timing, and its ability to measure risk exposure. Its weaknesses include its lack of linkage to the wealth maximization goal, its failure to consider time value explicitly, and the fact that it ignores cash flows that occur after the payback period.

LG2 **Apply net present value (NPV) and internal rate of return (IRR) to relevant cash flows to choose acceptable capital expenditures.** Sophisticated capital budgeting techniques use the cost of capital to consider the time factor in the value of money. Two such techniques are net present value (NPV) and internal rate of return (IRR). The key formulas and decision criteria for them are summarized in Table 11.7. Both NPV and IRR yield the same accept–reject decisions but often provide conflicting ranks.

LG3 **Use net present value profiles to compare NPV and IRR techniques in light of conflicting rankings.** Net present value profiles are useful in comparing projects, especially when conflicting rankings exist between NPV and IRR. On a purely theoretical basis, NPV is preferred over IRR, because NPV assumes reinvestment of intermediate cash inflows at the cost of capital and does not exhibit the mathematical problems that often occur when IRRs are calculated for nonconventional cash flows. In practice, however, the IRR is more commonly used because it is consistent with the general preference toward rates of return.

LG4 **Recognize sensitivity and scenario analysis and simulation as behavioral approaches for dealing with project risk.** Risk in capital budgeting is the chance that a project will prove unacceptable or, more formally, the degree of variability of cash flows. Sensitivity analysis and scenario analysis are two behavioral approaches for dealing with project risk to capture the variability of cash inflows and NPVs. Simulation is a statistically based behavioral approach that results in a probability distribution of project returns. It usually requires a computer and allows the decision maker

| TABLE 11.7 | Summary of Key Formulas/Definitions and Decision Criteria for Capital Budgeting Techniques | |

Technique	Formula/Definition	Decision criteria
Payback period[a]	*For annuity:* $$\frac{\text{initial investment}}{\text{annual cash inflow}}$$ *For mixed stream:* Calculate cumulative cash inflows on year-to-year basis until the initial investment is recovered.	*Accept* if < maximum acceptable payback period. *Reject* if > maximum acceptable payback period.
Net present value (NPV)[b]	Present value of cash inflows − initial investment.	*Accept* if > $0. *Reject* if < $0.
Internal rate of return (IRR)[b]	The discount rate that causes NPV = $0 (present value of cash inflows equals the initial investment).	*Accept* if > the cost of capital. *Reject* if < the cost of capital.

[a]Unsophisticated technique, because it does not give explicit consideration to the time value of money.

[b]Sophisticated technique, because it gives explicit consideration to the time value of money.

to understand the risk–return tradeoffs involved in a proposed investment.

 Discuss the unique risks that multinational companies face. Although the basic capital budgeting techniques are the same for purely domestic and multinational companies, firms that operate in several countries must also deal with both exchange rate and political risks, tax law differences, transfer pricing, and a strategic rather than a strict financial viewpoint.

 Understand how to determine and use risk-adjusted discount rates (RADRs). Risk-adjusted discount rates (RADR) are a popular risk-adjustment technique that uses a market-based adjustment of the discount rate to calculate the NPV. The logic underlying the RADR is closely linked to the capital asset pricing model (CAPM). Most firms subjectively adjust the RADR up or down depending on whether the proposed project is more or less risky than the average risk of the firm. RADRs are commonly used in practice, because decision makers prefer rates of return and find them easier to estimate and apply.

SELF-TEST EXERCISES (Solutions in Appendix B)

  ST 11–1 All techniques with NPV profile—Mutually exclusive projects Falcon Industries is in the process of choosing the better of two equal-risk, mutually exclusive capital expenditure projects—M and N. The relevant cash flows for each project are shown in the table at the top of page 350. The firm's cost of capital is 14%.

	Project M	Project N
Initial investment (CF_0)	$28,500	$27,000
Year (t)	Cash inflows (CF_t)	
1	$10,000	$11,000
2	10,000	10,000
3	10,000	9,000
4	10,000	8,000

a. Calculate each project's payback period.
b. Calculate the net present value (NPV) for each project.
c. Calculate the internal rate of return (IRR) for each project.
d. Summarize the preferences dictated by each measure calculated above, and indicate which project you would recommend. Explain why.
e. Draw the net present value profiles for these projects on the same set of axes, and explain the circumstances under which a conflict in rankings might exist.

 ST 11–2   Risk-adjusted discount rates (RADRs)   Coba Company is considering two mutually exclusive projects—A and B. The CAPM-type relationship between a risk index and required return (RADR) applicable to Coba Company is shown in the following table.

Risk index	Required return (RADR)
0.0	7.0% (risk-free rate, R_F)
0.2	8.0
0.4	9.0
0.6	10.0
0.8	11.0
1.0	12.0
1.2	13.0
1.4	14.0
1.6	15.0
1.8	16.0
2.0	17.0

Project data are as follows:

	Project A	Project B
Initial investment (CF_0)	$15,000	$20,000
Project life	3 years	3 years
Annual cash inflow (CF_t)	$ 7,000	$10,000
Risk index	0.4	1.8

a. Ignoring any differences in risk, and assuming that the firm's cost of capital is 10%, calculate the net present value (NPV) of each project.
b. Use NPV to evaluate the projects, using *risk-adjusted discount rates* (*RADRs*) to account for risk.
c. Compare, contrast, and explain your findings in parts **a** and **b**.

EXERCISES

11–1   Payback comparisons   Slater Tool has a 5-year maximum acceptable payback period. The firm is considering the purchase of a new machine and must choose between two alternative ones. The first machine requires an initial investment of $14,000 and generates annual after-tax cash inflows of $3,000 for each of the next 7 years. The second machine requires an initial investment of $21,000 and provides an annual cash inflow after taxes of $4,000 for 20 years.
a. Determine the payback period for each machine.
b. Comment on the acceptability of the machines, assuming that they are independent projects.
c. Which machine should the firm accept? Why?
d. Do the machines in this problem illustrate any of the weaknesses of using payback? Discuss.

11–2   NPV for varying costs of capital   Merle's Hearing Aids is evaluating a new demonstration/display device. The device requires an initial investment of $24,000 and will generate after-tax cash inflows of $5,000 per year for 8 years. For each of the costs of capital listed, (1) calculate the net present value (NPV), (2) indicate whether to accept or reject the device, and (3) explain your decision.
a. The cost of capital is 10%.
b. The cost of capital is 12%.
c. The cost of capital is 14%.

11–3   Net present value—Independent projects   Using a 14% cost of capital, calculate the net present value for each of the independent projects shown in the table at the top of page 352, and indicate whether each is acceptable.

	Project A	Project B	Project C	Project D	Project E
Initial investment (CF_0)	$26,000	$500,000	$170,000	$950,000	$80,000
Year (t)			Cash inflows (CF_t)		
1	$4,000	$100,000	$20,000	$230,000	$70,000
2	4,000	120,000	19,000	230,000	0
3	4,000	140,000	18,000	230,000	0
4	4,000	160,000	17,000	230,000	20,000
5	4,000	180,000	16,000	230,000	30,000
6	4,000	200,000	15,000	230,000	0
7	4,000		14,000	230,000	50,000
8	4,000		13,000	230,000	60,000
9	4,000		12,000		70,000
10	4,000		11,000		

11–4 NPV—Mutually exclusive projects   Leap Enterprises is considering the replacement of one of its old drill presses. Three alternative replacement presses are under consideration. The relevant cash flows associated with each are shown in the following table. The firm's cost of capital is 15%.

	Press A	Press B	Press C
Initial investment (CF_0)	$85,000	$60,000	$130,000
Year (t)		Cash inflows (CF_t)	
1	$18,000	$12,000	$50,000
2	18,000	14,000	30,000
3	18,000	16,000	20,000
4	18,000	18,000	20,000
5	18,000	20,000	20,000
6	18,000	25,000	30,000
7	18,000	—	40,000
8	18,000	—	50,000

a. Calculate the net present value (NPV) of each press.
b. Using NPV, evaluate the acceptability of each press.
c. Rank the presses from best to worst using NPV.

11–5 **Payback and NPV**   Allison Products has three projects under consideration. The cash flows for each of them are shown in the following table. The firm has a 16% cost of capital.

	Project A	Project B	Project C
Initial investment (CF_0)	$40,000	$40,000	$40,000
Year (t)	**Cash inflows (CF_t)**		
1	$13,000	$ 7,000	$19,000
2	13,000	10,000	16,000
3	13,000	13,000	13,000
4	13,000	16,000	10,000
5	13,000	19,000	7,000

a. Calculate each project's payback period. Which project is preferred according to this method?
b. Calculate each project's net present value (NPV). Which project is preferred according to this method?
c. Comment on your findings in parts **a** and **b,** and recommend the best project. Explain your recommendation.

11–6 **Internal rate of return**   For each of the projects shown in the following table, calculate the internal rate of return (IRR). Then indicate, for each project, the maximum cost of capital that the firm could have and still find the IRR acceptable.

	Project A	Project B	Project C	Project D
Initial investment (CF_0)	$90,000	$490,000	$20,000	$240,000
Year (t)	**Cash inflows (CF_t)**			
1	$20,000	$150,000	$7,500	$120,000
2	25,000	150,000	7,500	100,000
3	30,000	150,000	7,500	80,000
4	35,000	150,000	7,500	60,000
5	40,000	—	7,500	—

11–7 **IRR—Mutually exclusive projects**   Saltus Corporation is attempting to choose the better of two mutually exclusive projects for expanding the firm's warehouse capacity. The relevant cash flows for the projects are shown in the table at the top of page 354. The firm's cost of capital is 15%.

	Project X	Project Y
Initial investment (CF_0)	$500,000	$325,000
Year (t)	Cash inflows (CF_t)	
1	$100,000	$140,000
2	120,000	120,000
3	150,000	95,000
4	190,000	70,000
5	250,000	50,000

a. Calculate the IRR to the nearest whole percent for each of the projects.
b. Assess the acceptability of each project on the basis of the IRRs found in part a.
c. Which project, on this basis, is preferred?

 **11–8 NPV and IRR** Tampa Manufacturing Enterprises has prepared the following estimates for a long-term project it is considering. The initial investment is $18,250, and the project is expected to yield after-tax cash inflows of $4,000 per year for 7 years. The firm has a 10% cost of capital.
a. Determine the net present value (NPV) for the project.
b. Determine the internal rate of return (IRR) for the project.
c. Would you recommend that the firm accept or reject the project? Explain your answer.

 11–9 NPV, IRR, and NPV profiles Fox Enterprises is considering two mutually exclusive projects. The firm, which has a 12% cost of capital, has estimated its cash flows as shown in the following table.

	Project A	Project B
Initial investment (CF_0)	$130,000	$85,000
Year (t)	Cash inflows (CF_t)	
1	$25,000	$40,000
2	35,000	35,000
3	45,000	30,000
4	50,000	10,000
5	55,000	5,000

a. Calculate the NPV of each project, and assess its acceptability.
b. Calculate the IRR for each project, and assess its acceptability.
c. Draw the NPV profiles for both projects on the same set of axes.
d. Evaluate and discuss the rankings of the two projects on the basis of your findings in parts a, b, and c.
e. Explain your findings in part d in light of the pattern of cash inflows associated with each project.

11–10 **All techniques—Mutually exclusive investment decision**   Next Company is attempting to select the best of three mutually exclusive projects. The initial investment and after-tax cash inflows associated with each project are shown in the following table.

Cash flows	Project A	Project B	Project C
Initial investment (CF_0)	$60,000	$100,000	$110,000
Cash inflows (CF_t), years 1–5	$20,000	$ 31,500	$ 32,500

a. Calculate the payback period for each project.
b. Calculate the net present value (NPV) of each project, assuming that the firm has a cost of capital equal to 13%.
c. Calculate the internal rate of return (IRR) for each project.
d. Draw the net present value profiles for both projects on the same set of axes, and discuss any conflict in ranking that may exist between NPV and IRR.
e. Summarize the preferences dictated by each measure, and indicate which project you would recommend. Explain why.

   11–11 **All techniques with NPV profile—Mutually exclusive projects**   Projects A and B, of equal risk, are alternatives for expanding a firm's capacity. The firm's cost of capital is 13%. The cash flows for each project are shown in the following table.

	Project A	Project B
Initial investment (CF_0)	$80,000	$50,000
Year (t)	Cash inflows (CF_t)	
1	$15,000	$15,000
2	20,000	15,000
3	25,000	15,000
4	30,000	15,000
5	35,000	15,000

a. Calculate each project's payback period.
b. Calculate the net present value (NPV) for each project.
c. Calculate the internal rate of return (IRR) for each project.
d. Draw the net present value profiles for both projects on the same set of axes, and discuss any conflict in ranking that may exist between NPV and IRR.
e. Summarize the preferences dictated by each measure, and indicate which project you would recommend. Explain why.

    11–12 **Integrative—Complete investment decision**   Quick Press is considering the purchase of a new printing press. The total installed cost of the press is $2.2 million. This outlay would be partially offset by the sale of an existing press. The old press has zero book value, cost $1 million 10 years ago, and can be sold currently for $1.2 million before taxes. As a result of the new press, sales in each of the next 5 years are expected to increase by $1.6 million, but product costs (excluding depreciation) will represent 50% of sales. The new press will not affect the firm's net working capital requirements. The new press will be depreciated under MACRS using a 5-year recovery period (see Table 9.5 on page 284). The firm is subject to a 40% tax rate on both ordinary income and capital gains. Quick Press's cost of capital is 11%. (*Note:* Assume that both the old and the new press will have terminal value of $0 at the end of year 6.)

a. Determine the initial investment required by the new press.
b. Determine the operating cash inflows attributable to the new press. (*Note:* Be sure to consider the depreciation in year 6.)
c. Determine the payback period.
d. Determine the net present value (NPV) and the internal rate of return (IRR) related to the proposed new press.
e. Make a recommendation to accept or reject the new press, and justify your answer.

 **LG4** **11–13** **Sensitivity analysis** Diagnostic Pharmaceutical is in the process of evaluating two mutually exclusive additions to their processing capacity. The firm's financial analysts have developed pessimistic, most likely, and optimistic estimates of the annual cash inflows associated with each project. These estimates are shown in the following table.

	Project A	Project B
Initial investment (CF_0)	$8,000	$8,000
Outcome	Annual cash inflows (CF_t)	
Pessimistic	$ 200	$ 900
Most likely	1,000	1,000
Optimistic	1,800	1,100

a. Determine the range of annual cash inflows for each of the two projects.
b. Assume that the firm's cost of capital is 10% and that both projects have 20-year lives. Construct a table similar to that above for the NPVs for each project. Include the range of NPVs for each project.
c. Do parts a and b provide consistent views of the two projects? Explain.
d. Which project do you recommend? Why?

LG4 **11–14** **Simulation** Sellall Castings has compiled the following information on a capital expenditure proposal:
(1) The projected cash inflows are normally distributed with a mean of $36,000 and a standard deviation of $9,000.
(2) The projected cash outflows are normally distributed with a mean of $30,000 and a standard deviation of $6,000.
(3) The firm has an 11% cost of capital.
(4) The probability distributions of cash inflows and cash outflows are not expected to change over the project's 10-year life.

a. Describe how the preceding data can be used to develop a simulation model for finding the net present value of the project.
b. Discuss the advantages of using a simulation to evaluate the proposed project.

11–15   Risk-adjusted discount rates—Equation   Omar, Inc., is considering investing in one of three mutually exclusive projects, E, F, and G. The firm's cost of capital, k, is 15%, and the risk-free rate, R_F, is 10%. The firm has gathered the following basic cash flow and risk index data for each project.

	Project (j)		
	E	F	G
Initial investment (CF_0)	$15,000	$11,000	$19,000
Year (t)	Cash inflows (CF_t)		
1	$ 6,000	$ 6,000	$ 4,000
2	6,000	4,000	6,000
3	6,000	5,000	8,000
4	6,000	2,000	12,000
Risk index (RI_j)	1.80	1.00	0.60

a. Find the net present value (NPV) of each project using the firm's cost of capital. Which project is preferred in this situation?

b. The firm uses the following equation to determine the risk-adjusted discount rate, $RADR_j$, for each project j:

$$RADR_j = R_F + [RI_j \times (k - R_F)]$$

where

R_F = risk-free rate
RI_j = risk index for project j
k = cost of capital

Substitute each project's risk index into this equation to determine its RADR.

c. Use the RADR for each project to determine its risk-adjusted NPV. Which project is preferable in this situation?

d. Compare and discuss your findings in parts **a** and **c**. Which project do you recommend that the firm accept?

   11–16   Risk-adjusted discount rates—Tabular   After a careful evaluation of investment alternatives and opportunities, Koel Company has developed a CAPM-type relationship linking a risk index to the required return (RADR), as shown in the table at the top of page 358.

Risk index	Required return (RADR)
0.0	7.0% (risk-free rate, R_F)
0.2	8.0
0.4	9.0
0.6	10.0
0.8	11.0
1.0	12.0
1.2	13.0
1.4	14.0
1.6	15.0
1.8	16.0
2.0	17.0

The firm is considering two mutually exclusive projects, A and B. The following are the data the firm has been able to gather about the projects.

	Project A	Project B
Initial investment (CF_0)	$20,000	$30,000
Project life	5 years	5 years
Annual cash inflow (CF_t)	$ 7,000	$10,000
Risk index	0.2	1.4

All the firm's cash inflows have already been adjusted for taxes.

a. Evaluate the projects using risk-adjusted discount rates.

b. Discuss your findings in part **a,** and recommend the preferred project.

  11–17   Risk classes and RADRs   Umbert Industries is attempting to select the best of three mutually exclusive projects, X, Y, and Z. Though all the projects have 5-year lives, they possess differing degrees of risk. Project X is in Class V, the highest-risk class; project Y is in Class II, the below-average-risk class; and project Z is in Class III, the average-risk class. The basic cash flow data for each project and the risk classes and risk-adjusted discount rates (RADRs) used by the firm are shown in the following tables.

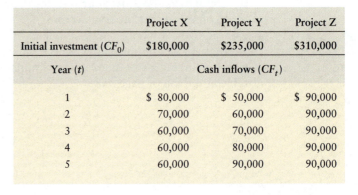

	Project X	Project Y	Project Z
Initial investment (CF_0)	$180,000	$235,000	$310,000
Year (t)		Cash inflows (CF_t)	
1	$ 80,000	$ 50,000	$ 90,000
2	70,000	60,000	90,000
3	60,000	70,000	90,000
4	60,000	80,000	90,000
5	60,000	90,000	90,000

Risk Classes and RADRs

Risk class	Description	Risk-adjusted discount rate (RADR)
I	Lowest risk	10%
II	Below-average risk	13
III	Average risk	15
IV	Above-average risk	19
V	Highest risk	22

a. Find the risk-adjusted NPV for each project.
b. Which, if any, project would you recommend that the firm undertake?

web exercises

www.arachnoid.com

Go to web site **www.arachnoid.com/lutusp/finance.html**. Page down to the portion that contains the financial calculator.

1. To determine the internal rate of return (IRR) of a project for which the initial investment was $5,000 and the cash flows are $1,000/year for the next 10 years, perform the steps outlined below. By entering various interest rates, you will eventually get a present value of −$5,000. When this happens, you have determined the IRR of the project.

To get started, into **PV** enter 0; into **FV** enter 0; into **np** enter 1000; into **pmt** enter 10; and into **ir** enter 8. Click **Calculate PV**. This gives you a number much greater than $5,000. Now change **ir** to 20 and then click **Calculate PV**. Keep changing the **ir** until **PV** = −$5,000, the same as the initial investment.

2. Try another problem. The initial investment is $10,000. The time period for the cash flows is 6 years, and the cash flow per year is $2,500. What is its IRR?

3. To calculate the IRR of an investment of $3,000 with a single cash flow of $4,800 in 3 years from the initial investment, do the following: Into **FV** enter 4800; into **np** enter 3; into **pmt** enter 0; and into **ir** enter 8. Click **Calculate PV**. As above, keep changing **ir** until the PV is equal to the initial investment of $3,000. What is this investment's IRR?

For additional practice with concepts from this chapter, visit
http://www.awl.com/gitman_madura

Cost of Capital

LG1 Understand the basic concept of cost of capital and the specific sources of capital that it includes.

LG2 Determine the cost of long-term debt and the cost of preferred stock.

LG3 Calculate the cost of common stock equity and convert it into the cost of retained earnings and the cost of new issues of common stock.

LG4 Find the weighted average cost of capital.

LG5 Describe the procedures used to determine break points and the weighted marginal cost of capital.

LG6 Explain how the weighted marginal cost of capital can be used with the investment opportunities schedule to make the firm's financing/investment decisions.

An Overview of the Cost of Capital

cost of capital
The rate of return that a firm must earn
on the projects in which it invests to
maintain its market value and attract
funds.

The **cost of capital** is the rate of return that a firm must earn on the projects in which it invests to maintain the market value of its stock. It can also be thought of as the rate of return required by the market suppliers of capital to attract their funds to the firm. If risk is held constant, projects with a rate of return above the cost of capital will increase the value of the firm, and projects with a rate of return below the cost of capital will decrease the value of the firm.

The cost of capital is an extremely important financial concept. It acts as a major link between the firm's long-term investment decisions (discussed in Chapters 10 and 11) and the wealth of the owners as determined by investors in the marketplace. It is in effect the "magic number" that is used to decide whether a proposed corporate investment will increase or decrease the firm's stock price. Clearly, only those investments that are expected to increase stock price (NPV>$0, or IRR>cost of capital) would be recommended. Because of its key role in financial decision making, the importance of the cost of capital cannot be overemphasized.

The Basic Concept

target capital structure
The desired optimal mix of debt and
equity financing that most firms
attempt to maintain.

The cost of capital is estimated at a given point in time. It reflects the expected average future cost of funds over the long run. Although firms typically raise money in lumps, the cost of capital should reflect the interrelatedness of financing activities. For example, if a firm raises funds with debt (borrowing) today, it is likely that some form of equity, such as common stock, will have to be used the next time it needs funds. Most firms attempt to maintain a desired, optimal mix of debt and equity financing. This mix is commonly called a **target capital structure**—a topic that will be addressed in Chapter 13. Here, it is sufficient to say that although firms raise money in lumps, they tend toward some desired *mix of financing*.

To capture the interrelatedness of financing assuming the presence of a target capital structure, we need to look at the *overall cost of capital* rather than the cost of the specific source of funds used to finance a given expenditure. A simple example will illustrate.

Example ▼ A firm is currently faced with an investment opportunity. Assume the following:

Best project available today

   Cost = $100,000
   Life = 20 years
   IRR = 7%

Cost of least-cost financing source available

   Debt = 6%

Because it can earn 7% on the investment of funds costing only 6%, the firm undertakes the opportunity. Imagine that 1 week later a new investment opportunity is available:

Best project available 1 week later

  Cost = $100,000
  Life = 20 years
  IRR = 12%

Cost of least-cost financing source available

  Equity = 14%

In this instance, the firm rejects the opportunity, because the 14% financing cost is greater than the 12% expected return.

Were the firm's actions in the best interests of its owners? No; it accepted a project yielding a 7% return and rejected one with a 12% return. Clearly, there should be a better way, and there is: The firm can use a combined cost, which over the long run would provide for better decisions. By weighting the cost of each source of financing by its *target proportion* in the firm's capital structure, the firm can obtain a *weighted average cost* that reflects the interrelationship of financing decisions. Assuming that a 50–50 mix of debt and equity is targeted, the weighted average cost here would be 10% [(0.50 × 6% debt) + (0.50 × 14% equity)]. With this cost, the first opportunity would have been rejected (7% IRR<10% weighted average cost), and the second would have been accepted (12% IRR>10% weighted average cost). Such an outcome would clearly be more desirable.

The Cost of Specific Sources of Capital

This chapter focuses on finding the costs of specific sources of capital and combining them to determine the weighted average cost of capital. Our concern is only with the *long-term* sources of funds available to a business firm, because these sources supply the permanent financing. Long-term financing supports the firm's fixed-asset investments. We assume throughout the chapter that such investments are selected using appropriate capital budgeting techniques.

There are four basic sources of long-term funds for the business firm: long-term debt, preferred stock, common stock, and retained earnings. The right-hand side of a balance sheet can be used to illustrate these sources:

Although not every firm will use all of these methods of financing, each firm is expected to have funds from some of these sources in its capital structure.

The *specific cost* of each source of financing is the *after-tax* cost of obtaining the financing today, not the historically based cost reflected by the existing financing on the firm's books. Techniques for determining the specific cost of each source of long-term funds are presented on the following pages. Although these techniques tend to develop precisely calculated values, the resulting values are at best *rough approximations* because of the numerous assumptions and forecasts that underlie them. Although we round calculated costs to the nearest 0.1 percent throughout this chapter, it is not unusual for practicing financial managers to use costs rounded to the nearest 1 percent because these values are merely estimates.

? Review Questions

12–1 What role does the cost of capital play in long-term investment decisions? Why is use of a weighted average cost rather than the specific cost recommended?

12–2 You have just been told, "Because we are going to finance this project with debt, its required rate of return must exceed the cost of debt." Do you agree or disagree? Explain.

12–3 Why is the cost of capital most appropriately measured on an after-tax basis?

The Cost of Long-Term Debt

cost of long-term debt, k_i
The after-tax cost today of raising long-term funds through borrowing.

net proceeds
Funds actually received from the sale of a security.

flotation costs
The total costs of issuing and selling a security.

The **cost of long-term debt, k_i**, is the after-tax cost today of raising long-term funds through borrowing. For convenience, we typically assume that the funds are raised through the sale of bonds. In addition, as we did in Chapter 7, we assume that the bonds pay *annual* (rather than semiannual) interest.

Net Proceeds

Most corporate long-term debts are incurred through the sale of bonds. The **net proceeds** from the sale of a bond, or any security, are the funds that are actually received from the sale. **Flotation costs**—the total costs of issuing and selling a security—reduce the net proceeds from the sale.

Example ▼ Procyber Company, a major computer manufacturer, is contemplating selling $10 million worth of 20-year, 9% coupon (stated annual interest rate) bonds, each with a par value of $1,000. Because similar-risk bonds earn returns greater than 9%, the firm must sell the bonds for $980 to compensate for the lower coupon interest rate. The flotation costs are 2% of the par value of the bond (0.02 × $1,000), or $20. The net proceeds to the firm from the sale of each bond **▲** are therefore $960 ($980 – $20).

Before-Tax Cost of Debt

The before-tax cost of debt, k_d, for a bond can be obtained in any of three ways: quotation, calculation, or approximation.

Using Cost Quotations

When the net proceeds from the sale of a bond equal its par value, the before-tax cost just equals the coupon interest rate. For example, a bond with a 10% coupon interest rate that nets proceeds equal to the bond's $1,000 par value would have a before-tax cost, k_d, of 10%.

A second quotation that is sometimes used is the *yield to maturity (YTM)* on a similar-risk bond (see Chapter 7). For example, if a similar-risk bond has a YTM of 9.7%, this value can be used as the before-tax cost of debt, k_d.

Calculating the Cost

This approach finds the before-tax cost of debt by calculating the internal rate of return (IRR) on the bond cash flows. From the issuer's point of view, this value is the *cost to maturity* of the cash flows associated with the debt. The cost to maturity can be calculated by using either a trial-and-error technique[1] or a financial calculator. It represents the annual before-tax percentage cost of the debt.

Example ▼   In the preceding example, the net proceeds of a $1,000, 9% coupon interest rate, 20-year bond were found to be $960. The calculation of the annual cost is quite simple. The cash flow pattern is exactly the opposite of a conventional pattern; it consists of an initial inflow (the net proceeds) followed by a series of annual outlays (the interest payments). In the final year, when the debt is retired, an outlay representing repayment of the principal also occurs. The cash flows associated with Procyber Company's bond issue are as follows:

End of year(s)	Cash flow
0	$ 960
1–20	−$ 90
20	−$1,000

The initial $960 inflow is followed by annual interest outflows of $90 (9% coupon interest rate × $1,000 par value) over the 20-year life of the bond. In year 20, an outflow of $1,000 (the repayment of the principal) occurs. We can determine the cost of debt by finding the IRR, which is the discount rate that equates the present value of the outflows to the initial inflow.

---

[1] The trial-and-error technique is presented at the book's web site, http://www.awl.com/gitman_madura.

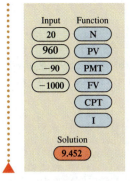

Calculator Use [*Note:* Most calculators require either the present (net proceeds) or the future (annual interest payments and repayment of principal) values to be input as negative numbers when we calculate cost to maturity. That approach is used here.] Using the calculator and the inputs shown at the left, you should find the before-tax cost (cost to maturity) to be 9.452%.

Approximating the Cost

The before-tax cost of debt, k_d, for a bond with a $1,000 par value can be approximated by using the equation

$$k_d = \frac{I + \frac{\$1,000 - N_d}{n}}{\frac{N_d + \$1,000}{2}} \tag{12.1}$$

where

I = annual interest in dollars
N_d = net proceeds from the sale of debt (bond)
n = number of years to the bond's maturity

Example ▼ Substituting the appropriate values from the Procyber Company example into the approximation formula given in Equation 12.1, we get

$$k_d = \frac{\$90 + \frac{\$1,000 - \$960}{20}}{\frac{\$960 + \$1,000}{2}} = \frac{\$90 + \$2}{\$980}$$

$$= \frac{\$92}{\$980} = \underline{\underline{9.4\%}}$$

This approximate before-tax cost of debt is close to the 9.452% value calculated precisely in the preceding example.

After-Tax Cost of Debt

However, as indicated earlier, the specific cost of financing must be stated on an after-tax basis. Because interest on debt is tax deductible, it reduces the firm's taxable income. The after-tax cost of debt, k_i, can be found by multiplying the before-tax cost, k_d, by 1 minus the tax rate, T, as stated in the following equation:

$$k_i = k_d \times (1 - T) \tag{12.2}$$

 **CHOOSING THE RIGHT MIXTURE**

Company treasurers must consider the cost of capital in relation to the changing economic environment. Lower inflation and possible deflation call for new strategies.

For decades, conventional wisdom has told finance directors that they can lower their companies' cost of capital by borrowing more, because debt is cheaper than equity. But that was during the long inflation. These days, prices in many countries and industries are falling, or at least threatening to do so. Treasurers fear that debt...could just become a burden. "In a deflationary environment, you want to have less debt and more equity," declares Anthony Stern, treasurer of Bass, a British brewer.

Today, companies in industries that have been hit hardest by deflationary pressures, such as manufacturing, chemicals, or oil and gas, are thinking once again about restructuring their balance sheets....."The tide is turning" in favour of a higher proportion of equity, says Reg Hinkley of BP Amoco, an oil multinational.

This has an appealing logic. Debt is the promise to pay money back in the future. While inflation erodes that sum's real value, deflation increases it. Moreover, as prices fall, so do returns on assets financed with borrowed money. Companies are stuck with repaying the same amounts out of declining profits....

The only good answer to the dilemma, therefore, seems to be to raise equity capital. Companies are not compelled to pay it back and, if profits and cash flow really do head south, they can stop paying dividends....

Unfortunately, says Paul Gibbs, an analyst at J.P. Morgan,...treasurers...tend to mistake the hard numbers of interest and dividend payments for the actual cost of capital. Properly defined, that cost includes all future returns (income and capital gains) that investors expect when they accept a company's risk. This cost—rather than merely the size of current dividend payments—determines the value of a firm and its share price....

Source: "Choosing the Right Mixture," The Economist, *February 27, 1999, downloaded from Electric Library Business Edition, business.elibrary.com.*

Example ▼ Procyber Company has a 40% tax rate. Using the 9.4% before-tax debt cost calculated above, and applying Equation 12.2, we find an after-tax cost of debt of 5.6% [9.4% × (1 − 0.40)]. Typically, the explicit cost of long-term debt is less than the explicit cost of any of the alternative forms of long-term financing, primarily because of the tax deductibility of interest. ▲

? Review Questions

12–4   What are the *net proceeds* from the sale of a bond?

12–5   What three methods can be used to find the before-tax cost of debt?

12–6   How is the before-tax cost of debt converted into the after-tax cost?

LG2 The Cost of Preferred Stock

Preferred stock represents a special type of ownership interest in the firm. It gives preferred stockholders the right to receive their stated dividends before any earnings can be distributed to common stockholders. Because preferred stock is a form of ownership, the proceeds from its sale are expected to be held for an infinite period of time. The key characteristics of preferred stock were described in Chapter 3. However, the one aspect of preferred stock that requires review is dividends.

Preferred Stock Dividends

Most preferred stock dividends are stated as a *dollar amount:* "x dollars per year." When dividends are stated this way, the stock is often referred to as "*x*-dollar preferred stock." Thus a "$4 preferred stock" is expected to pay preferred stockholders $4 in dividends each year on each share of preferred stock owned.

Sometimes preferred stock dividends are stated as an *annual percentage rate.* This rate represents the percentage of the stock's par value, or face value, that equals the annual dividend. For instance, an 8% preferred stock with a $50 par value would be expected to pay an annual dividend of $4 a share ($0.08 \times \$50$ par = $4). Before the cost of preferred stock is calculated, any dividends stated as percentages should be converted to annual dollar dividends.

Calculating the Cost of Preferred Stock

cost of preferred stock, k_p
The ratio of the preferred stock dividend to the firm's net proceeds from the sale of preferred stock; calculated by dividing the annual dividend, D_p, by the net proceeds from the sale of the preferred stock, N_p.

The **cost of preferred stock, k_p,** is the ratio of the preferred stock dividend to the firm's net proceeds from the sale of the preferred stock. The net proceeds represents the amount of money to be received minus any flotation costs. Equation 12.3 gives the cost of preferred stock, k_p, in terms of the annual dollar dividend, D_p, and the net proceeds from the sale of the stock, N_p:

$$k_p = \frac{D_p}{N_p} \tag{12.3}$$

Because preferred stock dividends are paid out of the firm's *after-tax* cash flows, a tax adjustment is not required.

Example ▼

Procyber Company is contemplating issuance of a 10% preferred stock that is expected to sell for its $87-per-share par value. The cost of issuing and selling the stock is expected to be $5 per share. The first step in finding the cost of the stock is to calculate the dollar amount of the annual preferred dividend, which is $8.70 ($0.10 \times \$87$). The net proceeds per share from the proposed sale of stock equals the sale price minus the flotation costs ($87 - $5 = $82). Substituting the annual dividend, D_p, of $8.70 and the net proceeds, N_p, of $82 into Equation 12.3 gives the cost of preferred stock, 10.6% ($8.70 ÷ $82).

The cost of Procyber's preferred stock (10.6%) is much greater than the cost of its long-term debt (5.6%). This difference exists primarily because the cost of long-term debt (the interest) is tax deductible.

? Review Question

12–7   How would you calculate the cost of preferred stock?

 The Cost of Common Stock

The cost of common stock is the return required on the stock by investors in the marketplace. There are two forms of common stock financing: (1) retained earnings and (2) new issues of common stock. As a first step in finding each of these costs, we must estimate the cost of common stock equity.

Finding the Cost of Common Stock Equity

cost of common stock equity, k_s
The rate at which investors discount the expected dividends of the firm to determine its share value.

The **cost of common stock equity, k_s,** is the rate at which investors discount the expected dividends of the firm to determine its share value. Two techniques are used to measure the cost of common stock equity. One relies on the constant-growth valuation model, the other on the capital asset pricing model (CAPM).

Using the Constant-Growth Valuation (Gordon) Model

constant-growth valuation (Gordon) model
Defines the value of a share of stock as equal to the present value of all future dividends which are assumed to grow at a constant annual rate over an infinite time horizon.

In Chapter 7 we found the value of a share of stock to be equal to the present value of all future dividends, which in one model were assumed to grow at a constant annual rate over an infinite time horizon. This is the **constant-growth valuation model,** also known as the **Gordon model.** The key expression for this model was presented as Equation 7.8 and is restated here:

$$P_0 = \frac{D_1}{k_s - g} \tag{12.4}$$

where

P_0 = value of common stock
D_1 = per-share dividend expected at the end of year 1
k_s = required return on common stock
g = constant rate of growth in dividends

Solving Equation 12.4 for k_s results in the following expression for the *cost of common stock equity:*

$$k_s = \frac{D_1}{P_0} + g \tag{12.5}$$

Equation 12.5 indicates that the cost of common stock equity can be found by dividing the dividend expected at the end of year 1 by the current price of the stock and adding the expected growth rate. Because common stock dividends are paid from *after-tax* income, no tax adjustment is required.

Example ▼ Procyber Company wishes to determine its cost of common stock equity, k_s. The market price, P_0, of its common stock is $50 per share. The firm expects to pay a dividend, D_1, of $4 at the end of the coming year, 2002. The dividends paid on the outstanding stock over the past 6 years (1996–2001) were as follows:

Year	Dividend
2001	$3.80
2000	3.62
1999	3.47
1998	3.33
1997	3.12
1996	2.97

Using the table for the present value interest factors, *PVIF* (Table A-2), or a financial calculator in conjunction with the technique described for finding growth rates in Chapter 5, we can calculate the annual growth rate of dividends, g. It turns out to be approximately 5% (more precisely, 5.05%). Substituting $D_1 = \$4$, $P_0 = \$50$, and $g = 5\%$ into Equation 12.5 results in the cost of common stock equity:

$$k_s = \frac{\$4}{\$50} + 0.05 = 0.08 + 0.05 = 0.130, \text{ or } \underline{\underline{13.0\%}}$$

The 13.0% cost of common stock equity represents the return required by *existing* shareholders on their investment. If the actual return is less than that, shareholders are likely to begin selling their stock.

Using The Capital Asset Pricing Model (CAPM)

capital asset pricing model (CAPM)
Describes the relationship between the required return, k_s, and the nondiversifiable risk of the firm as measured by the beta coefficient, b.

Recall from Chapter 6 that the **capital asset pricing model (CAPM)** describes the relationship between the required return, k_s, and the nondiversifiable risk of the firm as measured by the beta coefficient, b. The basic CAPM is

$$k_s = R_F + [b \times (k_m - R_F)] \tag{12.6}$$

where

R_F = risk-free rate of return
k_m = market return; return on the market portfolio of assets

The CAPM indicates that the cost of common stock equity is the return required by investors as compensation for the firm's nondiversifiable risk, measured by beta.

Example ▼ Procyber Company now wishes to calculate its cost of common stock equity, k_s, by using the capital asset pricing model. The firm's investment advisers and its own analyses indicate that the risk-free rate, R_F, equals 7%; the firm's beta, b, equals 1.5; and the market return, k_m, equals 11%. Substituting these values into Equation 12.6, the company estimates the cost of common stock equity, k_s, to be

$$k_s = 7.0\% + [1.5 \times (11.0\% - 7.0\%)] = 7.0\% + 6.0\% = \underline{\underline{13.0\%}}$$

The 13.0% cost of common stock equity represents the required return of investors in Procyber Company common stock. It is the same as that found by using the constant-growth valuation model. ▲

The Cost of Retained Earnings

As you know, dividends are paid out of a firm's earnings. Their payment, made in cash to common stockholders, reduces the firm's retained earnings. Let's say a firm needs common stock equity financing of a certain amount; it has two choices that relate to retained earnings: It can issue additional common stock in that

*News*Line

THE FINEST IN FINANCE: ANDREW S. FASTOW, ENRON CORPORATION

Innovative financing strategies developed by Enron Corporation CFO Andrew S. Fastow helped the company grow from a heavily regulated domestic natural-gas pipeline business to a fully integrated global energy company. Enron raised the huge amounts of capital it needed without raising its cost of capital, which earned Fastow *CFO* magazines's "Finest in Finance" award in the category of capital structure management.

Enron's challenge in entering multiple deregulating energy markets has been to secure the necessary capital without sacrificing its credit rating....[T]o launch an energy trading operation required a reservoir of capital just to get started. And therein lay the rub: Conventional financing techniques would jeopardize its BBB+ rating from Standard & Poor's and other agencies, raising the cost of capital.

"We couldn't just issue equity and dilute shareholders in the near term," [Andrew S. Fastow, CFO of Enron Corp.] says. "On the other hand, we couldn't jeopardize our rating by issuing debt, which would raise the cost of capital and hinder our energy trading operations." Plus, he says, "there was a one-to-three-year lag time" before Enron would receive any cash flow from its investments....

To solve the dilemma, Fastow first decided to capture the attention of the rating agencies, sending a message that Enron placed a high importance on its credit rating. The way he would do that, he planned, was to issue equity....Subsequently, Enron issued...more than $800 million in equity, its first significant public offering of common stock in five years, with no share-price dilution. The rating agencies responded enthusiastically....

The second part of the action plan was the sale of assets....In 1998, Enron reduced its portfolio by a third, selling more than $1 billion of assets...with no negative earnings impact....

He then turned his attention to new [innovative] forms of capital raising...to achieve an incredibly low cost of capital, while allowing 100 percent debt financing [of certain acquisitions] with no negative credit impact....

Despite the traditional rules of financing, Fastow reduced the balance-sheet debt, maintained the credit rating, and reduced the cost of capital while simultaneously growing the balance sheet...."He has successfully financed billions of dollars in a manner that has held credit quality," says S&P's Barone....

Source: Russ Banham, *"The Finest in Finance: Andrew S. Fastow, Enron Corp.—Category: Capital Structure Management,"* CFO, *October 1999, downloaded from www.cfonet.com/html/Articles/CFO/1999/99OCfast.html.*

cost of retained earnings, k_r
The same as the cost of an *equivalent fully subscribed issue of additional common stock,* which is equal to the cost of common stock equity, k_s.

amount and still pay dividends to stockholders out of retained earnings. Or it can increase common stock equity by retaining the earnings (not paying the cash dividends) in the needed amount. In a strict accounting sense, the retention of earnings increases common stock equity in the same way that the sale of additional shares of common stock does. Thus, the **cost of retained earnings, k_r,** to the firm is the same as the cost of an *equivalent fully subscribed issue of additional common stock.* Stockholders find the firm's retention of earnings acceptable only if they expect that it will earn at least their required return on the reinvested funds.

Viewing retained earnings as a fully subscribed issue of additional common stock, we can set the firm's cost of retained earnings, k_r, equal to the cost of common stock equity as given by Equations 12.5 and 12.6.

$$k_r = k_s \tag{12.7}$$

It is not necessary to adjust the cost of retained earnings for flotation costs, because by retaining earnings, the firm "raises" equity capital without incurring these costs.

Example ▼ The cost of retained earnings for Procyber Company was actually calculated in the preceding example: It is equal to the cost of common stock equity. Thus k_r equals 13.0%. As we will show in the next section, the cost of retained earnings is always lower than the cost of a new issue of common stock, because of the absence of flotation costs. ▲

The Cost of New Issues of Common Stock

cost of a new issue of common stock, k_n
The cost of common stock, net of underpricing and associated flotation costs.

underpriced
Stock sold at a price below its current market price, P_0.

Our purpose in finding the firm's overall cost of capital is to determine the after-tax cost of *new* funds required for financing projects. The **cost of a new issue of common stock, k_n,** is determined by calculating the cost of common stock, net of underpricing and associated flotation costs. Normally, to sell a new issue, it will have to be **underpriced**—sold at a price below its current market price, P_0. In addition, flotation costs paid for issuing and selling the new issue will further reduce proceeds.

We can use the constant-growth valuation model expression for the cost of existing common stock, k_s, as a starting point. If we let N_n represent the net proceeds from the sale of new common stock after subtracting underpricing and flotation costs, the cost of the new issue, k_n, can be expressed as follows:

$$k_n = \frac{D_1}{N_n} + g \tag{12.8}$$

The net proceeds from sale of new common stock, N_n, will be less than the current market price, P_0. Therefore the cost of new issues, k_n, will always be greater than the cost of existing issues, k_s, which is equal to the cost of retained earnings, k_r. *The cost of new common stock is normally greater than any other long-term financing cost.* Because common stock dividends are paid from after-tax cash flows, no tax adjustment is required.

Example ▼ In the constant-growth valuation example, we found Procyber Company's cost of common stock equity, k_s, to be 13%, using the following values: an expected dividend, D_1, of $4; a current market price, P_0, of $50; and an expected growth rate of dividends, g, of 5%.

To determine its cost of *new* common stock, k_n, Procyber Company has estimated that on average, new shares can be sold for $47. The $3-per-share underpricing is due to the competitive nature of the market. A second cost associated with a new issue is flotation costs of $2.50 per share that would be paid to issue and sell the new shares. The total underpricing and flotation costs per share are therefore expected to be $5.50.

Subtracting the $5.50 per share underpricing and flotation cost from the current $50 share price results in expected net proceeds of $44.50 per share ($50.00 − $5.50). Substituting $D_1 = $4, $N_n = $44.50, and $g = 5\%$ into Equation 12.8 results in a cost of new common stock, k_n, as follows:

$$k_n = \frac{\$4.00}{\$44.50} + 0.05 = 0.09 + 0.05 = 0.140, \text{ or } \underline{\underline{14.0\%}}$$

Procyber Company's cost of new common stock is therefore 14.0%. This is the value to be used in subsequent calculations of the firm's overall cost of capital. ▲

? Review Questions

12–8 What premise about share value underlies the constant-growth valuation (Gordon) model that is used to measure the cost of common stock equity, k_s?

12–9 Why is the cost of financing a project with retained earnings less than the cost of financing it with a new issue of common stock?

LG4 The Weighted Average Cost of Capital

weighted average cost of capital (WACC), k_a
Reflects the expected average future cost of funds over the long run; found by weighting the cost of each specific type of capital by its proportion in the firm's capital structure.

Now that we have calculated the cost of specific sources of financing, we can determine the overall cost of capital. As noted earlier, the **weighted average cost of capital (WACC)**, k_a, reflects the expected average future cost of funds over the long run. It is found by weighting the cost of each specific type of capital by its proportion in the firm's capital structure.

Calculating the weighted average cost of capital (WACC) is straightforward: Multiply the specific cost of each form of financing by its proportion in the firm's capital structure and sum the weighted values. As an equation, the weighted average cost of capital, k_a, can be specified as follows:

$$k_a = (w_i \times k_i) + (w_p \times k_p) + (w_s \times k_{r \text{ or } n}) \tag{12.9}$$

where

w_i = proportion of long-term debt in capital structure
w_p = proportion of preferred stock in capital structure
w_s = proportion of common stock equity in capital structure
$w_i + w_p + w_s = 1.0$

Three important points should be noted with respect to Equation 12.9.

1. For computational convenience, it is best to convert the weights into decimal form and leave the specific costs in percentage terms.
2. *The sum of weights must equal 1.0.* Simply stated, all capital structure components must be accounted for.
3. The firm's common stock equity weight, w_s, is multiplied by either the cost of retained earnings, k_r, or the cost of new common stock, k_n. Which cost is used depends on whether the firm's common stock equity will be financed using retained earnings, k_r, or new common stock, k_n.

Example ▼ In earlier examples, we found the costs of the various types of capital for Procyber Company to be as follows:

Cost of debt, k_i = 5.6%
Cost of preferred stock, k_p = 10.6%
Cost of retained earnings, k_r = 13.0%
Cost of new common stock, k_n = 14.0%

TABLE 12.1   Calculation of the Weighted Average Cost of Capital for Procyber Company

Source of capital	Weight (1)	Cost (2)	Weighted cost [(1) × (2)] (3)
Long-term debt	0.40	5.6%	2.2%
Preferred stock	0.10	10.6	1.1
Common stock equity	0.50	13.0	6.5
Totals	1.00		9.8%

Weighted average cost of capital = 9.8%

The company uses the following weights in calculating its weighted average cost of capital:

Source of capital	Weight
Long-term debt	40%
Preferred stock	10
Common stock equity	50
Total	100%

Because the firm expects to have a sizable amount of retained earnings available ($300,000), it plans to use its cost of retained earnings, k_r, as the cost of common stock equity. Procyber Company's weighted average cost of capital is calculated in Table 12.1. The resulting weighted average cost of capital for Procyber is 9.8%. Assuming an unchanged risk level, the firm should accept all projects that will earn a return greater than 9.8%.

? Review Question

12–10   What is the weighted average cost of capital (WACC), and how is it calculated?

The Marginal Cost and Investment Decisions

The firm's weighted average cost of capital is a key input to the investment decision-making process. As demonstrated earlier in the chapter, the firm should make only those investments for which the expected return is greater than the weighted average cost of capital. Of course, at any given time, the firm's financing costs and investment returns will be affected by the volume of financing and investment undertaken. The *weighted marginal cost of capital* and the *investment opportunities schedule* are mechanisms whereby financing and investment decisions can be made simultaneously.

 ## The Weighted Marginal Cost of Capital

weighted marginal cost of capital (WMCC)
The firm's weighted average cost of capital (WACC) associated with its *next dollar* of total new financing.

The weighted average cost of capital may vary over time, depending on the volume of financing that the firm plans to raise. *As the volume of financing increases, the costs of the various types of financing will increase, raising the firm's weighted average cost of capital.* Therefore, it is useful to calculate the **weighted marginal cost of capital (WMCC),** which is simply the firm's weighted average cost of capital associated with its *next dollar* of total new financing. This marginal cost is relevant to current decisions.

The costs of the financing components (debt, preferred stock, and common stock) rise as larger amounts are raised. Suppliers of funds require greater returns in the form of interest, dividends, or growth as compensation for the increased risk introduced by larger volumes of *new* financing. The WMCC is therefore an increasing function of the level of total new financing.

Another factor that causes the weighted average cost of capital to increase is the use of common stock equity financing. New financing provided by common stock equity will be taken from available retained earnings until this supply is exhausted and then will be obtained through new common stock financing. Because retained earnings are a less expensive form of common stock equity financing than the sale of new common stock, the weighted average cost of capital will rise with the addition of new common stock.

Finding Break Points

break point
The level of *total* new financing at which the cost of one of the financing components rises, thereby causing an upward shift in the weighted marginal cost of capital (WMCC).

To calculate the WMCC, we must calculate **break points,** which reflect the level of *total* new financing at which the cost of one of the financing components rises. The following general equation can be used to find break points:

$$BP_j = \frac{AF_j}{w_j} \qquad (12.10)$$

where

BP_j = break point for financing source j
AF_j = amount of funds available from financing source j at a given cost
w_j = capital structure weight (stated in decimal form) for financing source j

Example ▼ When Procyber Company exhausts its $300,000 of available retained earnings (at $k_r = 13.0\%$), it must use the more expensive new common stock financing (at $k_n = 14.0\%$) to meet its common stock equity needs. In addition, the firm expects that it can borrow only $400,000 of debt at the 5.6% cost; additional debt will have an after-tax cost (k_i) of 8.4%. Two break points therefore exist: (1) when the $300,000 of retained earnings costing 13.0% is exhausted, and (2) when the $400,000 of long-term debt costing 5.6% is exhausted.

The break points can be found by substituting these values and the corresponding capital structure weights given earlier into Equation 12.10. We get the dollar amounts of *total* new financing at which the costs of the given financing sources rise:

$$BP_{\text{common equity}} = \frac{\$300{,}000}{0.50} = \$600{,}000$$

$$BP_{\text{long-term debt}} = \frac{\$400{,}000}{0.40} = \$1{,}000{,}000$$

Calculating the WMCC

Once the break points have been determined, the next step is to calculate the weighted average cost of capital over the range of total new financing between break points. First, we find the WACC for a level of total new financing between zero and the first break point. Next, we find the WACC for a level of total new financing between the first and second break points, and so on. By definition, for each of the ranges of total new financing between break points, certain component capital costs (such as debt or common equity) will increase. This will cause the weighted average cost of capital to increase to a higher level than that over the preceding range.

weighted marginal cost of capital (WMCC) schedule
Graph that relates the firm's weighted average cost of capital to the level of total new financing.

Together, these data can be used to prepare a **weighted marginal cost of capital (WMCC) schedule**. This is a graph that relates the firm's weighted average cost of capital to the level of total new financing.

Example ▼

Table 12.2 on page 376 summarizes the calculation of the WACC for Procyber Company over the three ranges of total new financing created by the two break points—$600,000 and $1,000,000. Comparing the costs in column 3 of the table for each of the three ranges, we can see that the costs in the first range ($0 to $600,000) are those calculated in earlier examples and used in Table 12.1. The second range ($600,000 to $1,000,000) reflects the increase in the common stock equity cost to 14.0%. In the final range, the increase in the long-term debt cost to 8.4% is introduced.

The weighted average costs of capital for the three ranges are summarized in the table shown at the bottom of Figure 12.1 on page 376. These data describe the weighted marginal cost of capital, which increases as levels of total new financing increase. Figure 12.1 presents the WMCC schedule. Again, it is clear that the WMCC is an increasing function of the amount of total new financing raised. **▲**

The Investment Opportunities Schedule

At any given time, a firm has certain investment opportunities available to it. These opportunities differ with respect to the size of investment, return, and risk.[2] The firm's **investment opportunities schedule (IOS)** is a ranking of investment possibilities from best (highest return) to worst (lowest return). Generally, the first project selected will have the highest return, the next project the second highest, and so on. The return on investments will *decrease* as the firm accepts additional projects.

investment opportunities schedule (IOS)
A ranking of investment possibilities from best (highest return) to worst (lowest return).

_____

[2]Because the calculated weighted average cost of capital does not apply to risk-changing investments, we assume that all opportunities have equal risk similar to the firm's risk.

TABLE 12.2   Weighted Average Cost of Capital for Ranges of Total New Financing for Procyber Company

Range of total new financing	Source of capital (1)	Weight (2)	Cost (3)	Weighted cost [(2) × (3)] (4)
$0 to $600,000	Debt	0.40	5.6%	2.2%
	Preferred	0.10	10.6	1.1
	Common	0.50	13.0	6.5
		Weighted average cost of capital		9.8%
$600,000 to $1,000,000	Debt	0.40	5.6%	2.2%
	Preferred	0.10	10.6	1.1
	Common	0.50	14.0	7.0
		Weighted average cost of capital		10.3%
$1,000,000 and above	Debt	0.40	8.4%	3.4%
	Preferred	0.10	10.6	1.1
	Common	0.50	14.0	7.0
		Weighted average cost of capital		11.5%

FIGURE 12.1

WMCC Schedule
Weighted marginal cost of capital (WMCC) schedule for Procyber Company

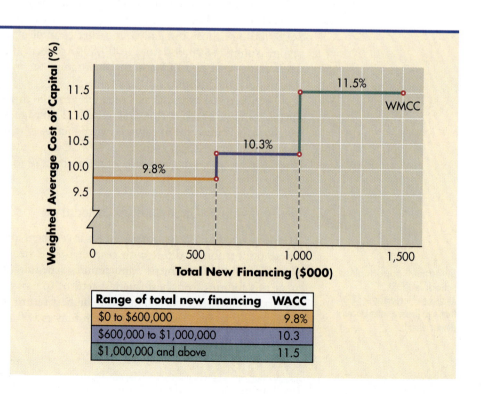

Range of total new financing	WACC
$0 to $600,000	9.8%
$600,000 to $1,000,000	10.3
$1,000,000 and above	11.5

TABLE 12.3	Investment Opportunities Schedule (IOS) for Procyber Company		
Investment opportunity	Internal rate of return (IRR) (1)	Initial investment (2)	Cumulative investment[a] (3)
A	15.0%	$100,000	$ 100,000
B	14.5	200,000	300,000
C	14.0	400,000	700,000
D	13.0	100,000	800,000
E	12.0	300,000	1,100,000
F	11.0	200,000	1,300,000
G	10.0	100,000	1,400,000

[a]The cumulative investment represents the total amount invested in projects with higher returns plus the investment required for the corresponding investment opportunity.

Example ▼

Column 1 of Table 12.3 shows Procyber Company's current investment opportunities schedule (IOS) listing the investment possibilities from best (highest return) to worst (lowest return). Column 2 of the table shows the initial investment required by each project. Column 3 shows the cumulative total invested funds required to finance all projects better than and including the corresponding investment opportunity. Plotting the project returns against the cumulative investment (column 1 against column 3) results in the firm's investment opportunities schedule (IOS). A graph of the IOS for Procyber Company is given in **▲** Figure 12.2 on page 378.

Using the WMCC and IOS to Make Financing/Investment Decisions

As long as a project's internal rate of return is greater than the weighted marginal cost of new financing, the firm should accept the project. The return will decrease with the acceptance of more projects, and the weighted marginal cost of capital will increase because greater amounts of financing will be required. The decision rule therefore would be: *Accept projects up to the point at which the marginal return on an investment equals its weighted marginal cost of capital.* Beyond that point, its investment return will be less than its capital cost.

This approach is consistent with the maximization of net present value (NPV) for conventional projects for two reasons: (1) The NPV is positive as long as the IRR exceeds the weighted average cost of capital, k_a. (2) The larger the difference between the IRR and k_a, the larger the resulting NPV. Therefore, the acceptance of projects beginning with those that have the greatest positive difference between IRR and k_a, down to the point at which IRR just equals k_a, should result in the maximum total NPV for all independent projects accepted. Such an outcome is completely consistent with the firm's goal of maximizing owner wealth.

FIGURE 12.2

IOS and WMCC Schedules for Procyber Company

Using the IOS and WMCC to select projects

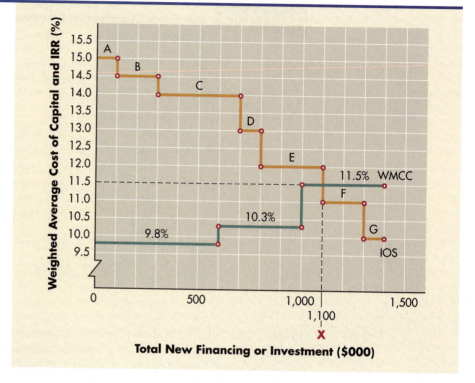

Total New Financing or Investment ($000)

Example ▼ Figure 12.2 shows Procyber Company's WMCC schedule and IOS on the same set of axes. By raising $1.1 million of new financing and investing these funds in projects A, B, C, D, and E, the firm should maximize the wealth of its owners, because these projects result in the maximum total net present value. Note that the 12.0% return on the last dollar invested (in project E) *exceeds* its 11.5% weighted average cost. Investment in project F is not feasible, because its 11.0% ▲ return is *less than* the 11.5% cost of funds available for investment.

The firm's optimal capital budget of $1,100,000 is marked with an **X** in Figure 12.2. At that the point, the IRR equals the weighted average cost of capital, and the firm's size as well as its shareholder value will be optimized. In a sense, the size of the firm is determined by the market—the availability of and returns on investment opportunities, and the availability and cost of financing.

In practice, most firms operate under *capital rationing*. That is, management imposes constraints that keep the capital expenditure budget below optimal (where IRR $= k_a$). Because of this, a gap frequently exists between the theoretically optimal capital budget and the firm's actual level of financing/investment.

? Review Questions

12–11 Why does the weighted marginal cost of capital schedule increase?

12–12 Is the investment opportunities schedule typically depicted as an increasing or a decreasing function? Why?

12–13 How can the WMCC schedule and the IOS be used to find the level of financing/investment that maximizes owner wealth? Why do many firms finance/invest at a level below this optimum?

TYING IT ALL TOGETHER

This chapter focused on the concepts and procedures related to estimation of a firm's cost of capital. We found that we needed the costs of long-term debt, preferred stock, and common stock (both retained earnings and new common stock) in order to find the firm's weighted average cost of capital. The WACC was used to develop the weighted marginal cost of capital (WMCC), which was then used in combination with the investment opportunities schedule (IOS) to determine the firm's optimal capital budget. The importance of the cost of capital from the viewpoints of financial managers, financial markets, and investors are summarized in the Integrative Table that follows.

INTEGRATIVE TABLE
Estimating the Cost of Capital

Role of **Financial Managers**	*Role of* **Financial Markets**	*Role of* **Investors**
Because of cost of capital's pivotal role in the firm's investment decision process, financial managers need to understand the procedures for estimating the firm's cost of capital. Applying a realistic cost of capital improves the chance that the firm's capital budgeting decisions will create value for the firm and its owners. A poorly developed cost of capital can result in accepting bad investments or rejecting good ones.	The financial markets, through the actions of investors, help to determine the firm's cost of capital by pricing the debt and equity securities of various issuers. Financial managers study the returns and risk of their own and comparable companies' securities to develop realistic estimates of long-term financing costs. Incorporating these estimates in its cost of capital should result in a realistic value that will help ensure that the firm's investment decisions are consistent with its goal of maximizing owner wealth.	By requiring certain returns from the firm's debt and equity securities, investors affect the firm's cost of capital. In addition, by monitoring and responding to the firm's investment actions, investors further influence the valuation of the firm's stock in the financial markets. If investors feel the firm's actions are value-creating, they will bid up the stock, thereby reducing its equity cost and creating wealth for owners. If investors are dissatisfied with the firm's investments, they will sell shares, bringing the price down and raising the firm's cost of capital.

LG1 **Understand the basic concept of cost of capital and the specific sources of capital that it includes.** The cost of capital is the rate of return that a firm must earn on its investments to maintain its market value and attract needed funds. To capture the interrelatedness of financing, a weighted average cost of capital should be used to find the expected average future cost of funds over the long run. The specific costs of the basic sources of capital (long-term debt, preferred stock, retained earnings, and common stock) can be calculated individually.

TABLE 12.4   **Summary of Key Definitions and Formulas for Cost of Capital**

Definitions of variables

AF_j = amount of funds available from financing source j at a given cost

b = beta coefficient or measure of nondiversifiable risk

BP_j = break point for financing source j

D_1 = per share dividend expected at the end of year 1

D_p = annual preferred stock dividend (in dollars)

g = constant rate of growth in dividends

I = annual interest in dollars

k_a = weighted average cost of capital

k_d = before-tax cost of debt

k_i = after-tax cost of debt

k_m = required return on the market portfolio

k_n = cost of a new issue of common stock

k_p = cost of preferred stock

k_r = cost of retained earnings

k_s = required return on common stock

n = number of years to the bond's maturity

N_d = net proceeds from the sale of debt (bond)

N_n = net proceeds from the sale of new common stock

N_p = net proceeds from the sale of preferred stock

P_0 = value of common stock

R_F = risk-free rate of return

T = firm's tax rate

w_i = proportion of long-term debt in capital structure

w_j = capital structure proportion (stated in decimal form) for financing source j

w_p = proportion of preferred stock in capital structure

w_s = proportion of common stock equity in capital structure

Formulas for cost of capital

Before-tax cost of debt (approximation):

$$k_d = \frac{I + \frac{\$1{,}000 - N_d}{n}}{\frac{N_d + \$1{,}000}{2}} \qquad \text{[Eq. 12.1]}$$

After-tax cost of debt:

$$k_i = k_d \times (1 - T) \qquad \text{[Eq. 12.2]}$$

Cost of preferred stock:

$$k_p = \frac{D_p}{N_p} \qquad \text{[Eq. 12.3]}$$

Cost of common stock equity:

Using constant-growth valuation model:

$$k_s = \frac{D_1}{P_0} + g \qquad \text{[Eq. 12.5]}$$

Using CAPM:

$$k_s = R_F + [b \times (k_m - R_F)] \qquad \text{[Eq. 12.6]}$$

Cost of retained earnings:

$$k_r = k_s \qquad \text{[Eq. 12.7]}$$

Cost of new issues of common stock:

$$k_n = \frac{D_1}{N_n} + g \qquad \text{[Eq. 12.8]}$$

Weighted average cost of capital (WACC):

$$k_a = (w_i \times k_i) + (w_p \times k_p) + (w_s \times k_{r \text{ or } n}) \qquad \text{[Eq. 12.9]}$$

Break point:

$$BP_j = \frac{AF_j}{w_j} \qquad \text{[Eq. 12.10]}$$

LG2 Determine the cost of long-term debt and the cost of preferred stock. The cost of long-term debt is the after-tax cost today of raising long-term funds through borrowing. Cost quotations, calculation (using either a trial-and-error technique or a financial calculator), or an approximation can be used to find the before-tax cost of debt, which must then be tax-adjusted. The cost of preferred stock is the ratio of the preferred stock dividend to the firm's net proceeds from the sale of preferred stock. The key formulas for the before- and after-tax cost of debt and the cost of preferred stock are given in Table 12.4.

LG3 Calculate the cost of common stock equity and convert it into the cost of retained earnings and the cost of new issues of common stock. The cost of common stock equity can be calculated by using the constant-growth valuation (Gordon) model or the CAPM. The cost of retained earnings is equal to the cost of common stock equity. An adjustment in the cost of common stock equity to reflect underpricing and flotation costs is required to find the cost of new issues of common stock. The key formulas for the cost of common stock equity, the cost of retained earnings, and the cost of new issues of common stock are given in Table 12.4.

LG4 Find the weighted average cost of capital. The firm's weighted average cost of capital (WACC) reflects the expected average future cost of funds over the long run. It can be determined by combining the costs of specific types of capital after weighting each of them by its proportion in the firm's capital structure. The key formula for WACC is given in Table 12.4.

LG5 Describe the procedures used to determine break points and the weighted marginal cost of capital. As the volume of total new financing increases, the costs of the various types of financing will increase, raising the firm's WACC. The weighted marginal cost of capital (WMCC) is the firm's WACC associated with its next dollar of total new financing. Break points represent the level of total new financing at which the cost of one of the financing components rises, causing an upward shift in the WMCC. The general formula for break points is given in Table 12.4.. The WMCC schedule relates the WACC to each level of total new financing.

LG6 Explain how the weighted marginal cost of capital can be used with the investment opportunities schedule to make the firm's financing/investment decisions. The investment opportunities schedule (IOS) presents a ranking of currently available investments from best (highest return) to worst (lowest return). It is used in combination with the WMCC to find the level of financing/investment that maximizes owner wealth. The firm accepts projects up to the point at which the marginal return on an investment equals its weighted marginal cost of capital.

SELF-TEST EXERCISE   (Solution in Appendix B)

ST 12–1   Specific costs, WACC, WMCC, and IOS   Glock Manufacturing is interested in measuring its overall cost of capital. The firm is in the 40% tax bracket. Current investigation has gathered the following data.

Debt   The firm can raise an unlimited amount of debt by selling $1,000-par-value, 10% coupon interest rate, 10-year bonds on which *annual interest* payments will be made. To sell the issue, an average discount of $30 per bond must be given. The firm must also pay flotation costs of $20 per bond.

Preferred stock   The firm can sell 11% (annual dividend) preferred stock at its $100-per-share par value. The cost of issuing and selling the preferred stock is expected to be $4 per share. An unlimited amount of preferred stock can be sold under these terms.

Common stock The firm's common stock is currently selling for $80 per share. The firm expects to pay cash dividends of $6 per share next year. The firm's dividends have been growing at an annual rate of 6%, and this rate is expected to continue in the future. The stock will have to be underpriced by $4 per share, and flotation costs are expected to amount to $4 per share. The firm can sell an unlimited amount of new common stock under these terms.

Retained earnings The firm expects to have $225,000 of retained earnings available in the coming year. Once these retained earnings are exhausted, the firm will use new common stock as the form of common stock equity financing.

a. Calculate the specific cost of each source of financing. (Round to the nearest 0.1%.)

b. The firm uses the weights shown in the following table to calculate its weighted average cost of capital. (Round to the nearest 0.1%.)

Source of capital	Weight
Long-term debt	40%
Preferred stock	15
Common stock equity	45
Total	100%

(1) Calculate the single break point associated with the firm's financial situation. (*Hint:* This point results from the exhaustion of the firm's retained earnings.)

(2) Calculate the weighted average cost of capital associated with total new financing below the break point calculated in part (1).

(3) Calculate the weighted average cost of capital associated with total new financing above the break point calculated in part (1).

c. Using the results of part **b** along with the information shown in the following table on the available investment opportunities, draw the firm's weighted marginal cost of capital (WMCC) schedule and investment opportunities schedule (IOS) on the same set axes (total new financing or investment on the x axis and weighted average cost of capital and IRR on the y axis).

Investment opportunity	Internal rate of return (IRR)	Initial investment
A	11.2%	$100,000
B	9.7	500,000
C	12.9	150,000
D	16.5	200,000
E	11.8	450,000
F	10.1	600,000
G	10.5	300,000

d. Which, if any, of the available investments do you recommend that the firm accept? Explain your answer. How much total new financing is required?

EXERCISES

 12–1   Concept of cost of capital   Rooney Manufacturing is in the process of analyzing its investment decision-making procedures. The two projects evaluated by the firm during the past month were projects 263 and 264. The basic variables surrounding each project analysis, using the IRR decision technique and the resulting decision actions, are summarized in the following table.

Basic variables	Project 263	Project 264
Cost	$64,000	$58,000
Life	15 years	15 years
IRR	8%	15%
Least-cost financing		
Source	Debt	Equity
Cost (after-tax)	7%	16%
Decision		
Action	Accept	Reject
Reason	8% IRR > 7% cost	15% IRR < 16% cost

a. Evaluate the firm's decision-making procedures, and explain why the acceptance of project 263 and rejection of project 264 may not be in the owners' best interest.
b. If the firm maintains a capital structure containing 40% debt and 60% equity, find its weighted average cost using the data in the table.
c. Had the firm used the weighted average cost calculated in part **b**, what actions would have been indicated relative to projects 263 and 264?
d. Compare and contrast the firm's actions with your findings in part **c**. Which decision method seems more appropriate? Explain why.

 12–2   Cost of debt using both methods   Currently, Knott and Company can sell 15-year, $1,000-par-value bonds paying *annual interest* at a 12% coupon rate. As a result of current interest rates, the bonds can be sold for $1,010 each; flotation costs of $30 per bond will be incurred in this process. The firm is in the 40% tax bracket.
a. Find the net proceeds from sale of the bond, N_d.
b. Show the cash flows from the firm's point of view over the maturity of the bond.
c. Use the *IRR approach* to calculate the before-tax and after-tax cost of debt.
d. Use the *approximation formula* to estimate the before-tax and after-tax cost of debt.
e. Compare and contrast the costs of debt calculated in parts **c** and **d**. Which approach do you prefer? Why?

12–3   Cost of preferred stock   Tremain Systems has just issued preferred stock. The stock has a 12% annual dividend and a $100 par value and was sold at $97.50 per share. In addition, flotation costs of $2.50 per share must be paid.
a. Calculate the cost of the preferred stock.

b. If the firm sells the preferred stock with a 10% annual dividend and nets $90.00 after flotation costs, what is its cost?

12–4 **Cost of common stock equity—CAPM** AMJ Corporation common stock has a beta, *b*, of 1.2. The risk-free rate is 6%, and the market return is 11%.

a. Determine the risk premium on AMJ common stock.
b. Determine the required return that AMJ common stock should provide.
c. Determine AMJ's cost of common stock equity using the CAPM.

12–5 **Cost of common stock equity** Delish Meat Packing wishes to measure its cost of common stock equity. The firm's stock is currently selling for $57.50. The firm expects to pay a $3.40 dividend at the end of the year (2002). The dividends for the past 5 years are shown in the following table.

Year	Dividend
2001	$3.10
2000	2.92
1999	2.60
1998	2.30
1997	2.12

After underpricing and flotation costs, the firm expects to net $52 per share on a new issue.

a. Determine the growth rate of dividends.
b. Determine the net proceeds, N_n, that the firm actually receives.
c. Using the constant-growth valuation model, determine the cost of retained earnings, k_r.
d. Using the constant-growth valuation model, determine the cost of new common stock, k_n.

12–6 **WACC** After careful analysis, Extine Company has determined that its optimal capital structure is composed of the sources and weights shown in the following table.

Source of capital	Weight
Long-term debt	30%
Preferred stock	15
Common stock equity	55
Total	100%

The cost of debt is estimated to be 7.2%; the cost of preferred stock is estimated to be 13.5%; the cost of retained earnings is estimated to be 16.0%; and the cost of new common stock is estimated to be 18.0%. All of these are after-tax rates. The company expects to have a significant amount of retained earnings available and does not expect to sell any new common stock. Calculate the weighted average cost of capital using the data provided.

12–7   **Calculation of specific costs, WACC, and WMCC**   Otago Pump has asked its financial manager to measure the cost of each specific type of capital as well as the weighted average cost of capital. The weighted average cost is to be measured by using the following weights: 40% long-term debt, 10% preferred stock, and 50% common stock equity (retained earnings, new common stock, or both). The firm's tax rate is 40%.

Debt   The firm can sell for $980 a 10-year, $1,000-par-value bond paying *annual interest* at a 10% coupon rate. A flotation cost of 3% of the par value is required in addition to the discount of $20 per bond.

Preferred stock   Eight percent (annual dividend) preferred stock having a par value of $100 can be sold for $65. An additional fee of $2 per share must be paid to the underwriters.

Common stock   The firm's common stock is currently selling for $50 per share. The dividend expected to be paid at the end of the coming year (2002) is $4. Its dividend payments, which have been approximately 60% of earnings per share in each of the past 5 years, were as shown in the following table.

Year	Dividend
2001	$3.75
2000	3.50
1999	3.30
1998	3.15
1997	2.85

It is expected that in order to sell, new common stock must be underpriced $5 per share, and the firm must also pay $3 per share in flotation costs. Dividend payments are expected to continue at 60% of earnings.

a. Calculate the specific cost of each source of financing. (Assume that $k_r = k_s$.)

b. If earnings available to common shareholders are expected to be $7 million, what is the break point associated with the exhaustion of retained earnings?

c. Determine the weighted average cost of capital between zero and the break point calculated in part **b**.

d. Determine the weighted average cost of capital just beyond the break point calculated in part **b**.

12–8   **Integrative—WACC, WMCC, and IOS**   Horane Company has compiled the data shown in the following table for the current costs of its three basic sources of capital—long-term debt, preferred stock, and common stock equity—for various ranges of new financing.

Source of capital	Range of new financing	After-tax cost
Long-term debt	$0 to $320,000	6%
	$320,000 and above	8
Preferred stock	$0 and above	17%
Common stock equity	$0 to $200,000	20%
	$200,000 and above	24

The company's capital structure weights used in calculating its weighted average cost of capital are shown in the following table.

Source of capital	Weight
Long-term debt	40%
Preferred stock	20
Common stock equity	40
Total	100%

a. Determine the break points and ranges of *total* new financing associated with each source of capital.
b. Using the data developed in part **a,** determine the break points (levels of *total* new financing) at which the firm's weighted average cost of capital will change.
c. Calculate the weighted average cost of capital for each range of total new financing found in part **b.** (*Hint:* There are three ranges.)
d. Using the results of part **c,** along with the following information on the available investment opportunities, draw the firm's weighted marginal cost of capital (WMCC) schedule and investment opportunities schedule (IOS) on the same set of axes (total new financing or investment on the *x* axis and weighted average cost of capital and IRR on the *y* axis).

Investment opportunity	Internal rate of return (IRR)	Initial investment
A	19%	$200,000
B	15	300,000
C	22	100,000
D	14	600,000
E	23	200,000
F	13	100,000
G	21	300,000
H	17	100,000
I	16	400,000

e. Which, if any, of the available investments do you recommend that the firm accept? Explain your answer.

web exercises   Search

FEDERAL RESERVE BANK *of St. Louis*

Go to web site **www.stls.frb.org**. Click on **Economic Research**; click on **FRED**; click on **Monthly Interest Rates**; and then click on **Bank Prime Loan Rate Changes—Historic Dates of Changes and Rates—1929**.

1. What was the prime interest rate in 1934?
2. What was the highest the prime interest rate has been? When was that?
3. What was the highest prime interest rate since you've been born?
4. What is the present prime interest rate?
5. Between the years of 1987 and the present, what was the lowest prime interest rate? The highest prime interest rate?

Now go to web site **www.stern.nyu.edu/~adamodar/New_Home_Page/ datafile/histret.html**.
6. What was the arithmetic average for stock returns during the same time period as in Question 5? How does this return compare to your answers to Question 5?

Now go to web site **www.yahoo.com**. Click on **Business & Economy**. Click on **Y!Finance**. Enter MSFT into the "GET QUOTES" space. Click on **GET QUOTES**. Click on **Profile**. Click on **Financials**.
7. What is the amount of Long Term Debt, Preferred Stock, and Common Stockholder's Equity for Microsoft Corporation?
8. How much is the total Capital of Microsoft Corporation? What is the percentage of each of its components?
Repeat Questions 7 and 8 for the following symbols: LG, BUD, DIS, and SBC. Just enter the symbol into the "GET FINANCIALS" space and then click on **GET FINANCIALS**.
9. How do the component percentages compare among these five corporations? Why?

For additional practice with concepts from this chapter, visit
http://www.awl.com/gitman_madura

Capital Structure and Dividends

LEARNING GOALS

LG1 Describe the basic types of capital, external assessment of capital structure, the capital structure of non-U.S. firms, and the optimal capital structure.

LG2 Discuss the EBIT–EPS approach to capital structure.

LG3 Review the return and risk of alternative capital structures, their relationship to market value, and other important capital structure considerations.

LG4 Explain cash dividend payment procedures, dividend reinvestment plans, the residual theory of dividends, and the key arguments with regard to dividend irrelevance or relevance.

LG5 Understand the key factors involved in formulating a dividend policy and the three basic types of dividend policies.

LG6 Evaluate the key aspects of stock dividends, stock splits, and stock repurchases.

The Firm's Capital Structure

capital structure
The mix of long-term debt and equity maintained by a firm.

Capital structure, the mix of long-term debt and equity maintained by the firm, is one of the most complex areas of financial decision making because of its interrelationship with other financial decision variables. Poor capital structure decisions can result in a high cost of capital, thereby lowering the NPVs of projects and making more of them unacceptable. Effective capital structure decisions can lower the cost of capital, resulting in higher NPVs and more acceptable projects—and thereby increasing the value of the firm. This topic links together many of the concepts presented in Chapters 5, 6, 7, and 12.

Types of Capital

All of the items on the right-hand side of the firm's balance sheet, excluding current liabilities, are sources of capital. The following simplified balance sheet illustrates the basic breakdown of total capital into its two components, debt capital and equity capital.

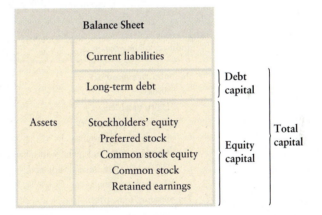

Corporate bonds are the major source of *debt capital.* The cost of debt is lower than the cost of other forms of financing. Lenders demand relatively lower returns because they take the least risk of any long-term contributors of capital: (1) They have a higher priority of claim against any earnings or assets available for payment. (2) They can exert far greater legal pressure against the company to make payment than can holders of preferred or common stock. (3) The tax deductibility of interest payments lowers the debt cost to the firm substantially.

Unlike debt capital, which must be repaid at some future date, *equity capital* is expected to remain in the firm for an indefinite period of time. The two basic sources of equity capital are (1) preferred stock equity and (2) common stock equity, which includes common stock and retained earnings. Common stock is typically the most expensive form of equity, followed by retained earnings and then preferred stock. Our concern here is the relationship between debt and equity capital: Because of its secondary position relative to debt, suppliers of equity capital take greater risk than suppliers of debt capital and therefore must be compensated with higher expected returns.

External Assessment of Capital Structure

In Chapter 8 it was shown that *financial leverage* results from the use of fixed-cost financing, such as debt and preferred stock, to magnify return and risk. The amount of leverage in the firm's capital structure can affect its value by affecting return and risk. A rough assessment of capital structure can be made by those outside the firm by using measures found in the firm's financial statements. For example, a direct measure of the degree of indebtedness is the *debt ratio*. The higher this ratio, the greater the relative amount of debt (or financial leverage) in the firm's capital structure. A measure of the firm's ability to meet contractual payments associated with debt is the *times-interest-earned ratio*. This ratio provides indirect information on financial leverage. Generally, the smaller it is, the greater the firm's financial leverage and the less able it is to meet payments as they come due.

A level of debt (financial leverage) that is acceptable for one industry or line of business can be highly risky in another, as a consequence of differing operating characteristics between industries or lines of business. Table 13.1 presents

TABLE 13.1	Debt Ratios for Selected Industries and Lines of Business (1998–1999)		
Industry or line business		Debt ratio	Times interest earned ratio
Manufacturing industries			
Books		61.0%	3.2
Dairy products		85.1	4.1
Electronic computers		65.8	4.3
Iron and steel forgings		56.8	4.0
Machine tools and metalworking equipment		63.6	4.1
Wines, distilled liquors, liqueurs		67.7	3.2
Women's dresses		55.8	2.4
Wholesaling industries			
Furniture		68.1	3.6
General groceries		73.2	2.6
Men's and boys' clothing		63.1	2.4
Retailing industries			
Autos, new and used		72.5	2.8
Department stores		60.0	3.3
Restaurants		89.7	2.6
Service industries			
Accounting, auditing, bookkeeping		73.5	5.0
Advertising agencies		79.3	5.0
Auto repair—general		61.1	4.0
Insurance agents and brokers		99.4	3.5

Source: RMA Annual Statement Studies, 1999–2000 (fiscal years ended 4/1/98 through 3/31/99. (Philadelphia: Robert Morris Associates, 1999). Copyright © 1999 by Robert Morris Associates.)

Note: Robert Morris Associates recommends that these ratios be regarded only as general guidelines and not as absolute industry norms. No claim is made as to the representativeness of their figures.

*News*Line   IS THE U.S. BUILDING A DEBT BOMB?

Corporations are adding debt to their capital structure at what some see as an alarming rate. Some analysts worry that the increased debt burden could lead to cutbacks in capital spending and, if economic activity slows, to an increase in defaults.

The most alarming sign of trouble ahead may be what's happening to corporate balance sheets. Despite the huge gains in the stock market, there is a pronounced tilt in corporate financing toward debt and away from equity. Even at today's prices, companies are buying back far more stock than they are issuing....even with the IPO boom, nearly $500 billion in equities have been taken off the market since 1997. Making the situation even worse, some companies are borrowing to finance [stock] buybacks....

At the same time, companies have been issuing more and more debt to finance acquisitions and expansion. DuPont, for example, sold $2 billion in bonds on October 13 [1999] to replenish its coffers after spending $7.7 billion to purchase Pioneer High-Bred International Inc. earlier in the month. And Williams Communication Group Inc. raised $2 billion in debt—an amount that about tripled the proceeds from its October 1 IPO—to expand its fiber-optic networks.

High-tech companies justify their accelerated borrowing by pointing to prospects for exceptional growth. Software maker Computer Associates International Inc. went from $50 million in long-term debt in 1995 to almost $5 billion in the latest quarter, but revenues rose as well, from $2.6 billion to a $5.6 billion rate today. "Our customers can see value beyond just saving on costs," says CEO Charles B. Wang, whose company just reported a 32% increase in revenues in the latest quarter. Still, what happens if sales don't continue to grow?

The belief in growth prospects is strongest in the telecom industry, where deregulation, new technology, and intense competition have unleashed massive spending. AT&T, MCI WorldCom, and Bell Atlantic alone have piled on more than $30 billion in long-term debt over the past two years....

Problem is, not all these bets pay off. The most notorious dud to date is satellite-phone service Iridium LLC. With too few customers willing to pay for its pricey service, Iridium couldn't meet interest payments on its huge loans used to buy satellites. The company is now in bankruptcy, owing billions to banks and bondholders....

Source: Michael J. Mandell, "Is the U.S. Building a Debt Bomb?" Business Week, November 1, 1999, pp. 40–42.

debt ratios for selected industries and lines of business. Significant industry differences can be seen in these data. Differences in debt positions are also likely to exist *within* an industry or line of business.

Comparing Capital Structures of U.S. and Non-U.S. Firms

In general, non-U.S. companies have much higher degrees of indebtedness than their U.S. counterparts. Most of the reasons for this are related to the fact that U.S. capital markets are much more developed than those elsewhere and have played a greater role in corporate financing than has been the case in other countries. In most European countries and especially in Japan and other Pacific Rim nations, large commercial banks are more actively involved in the financing of corporate activity than has been true in the United States. Furthermore, in many of these countries, banks are allowed to make large equity investments in nonfinancial corporations—a practice that is prohibited for U.S. banks. Finally, share ownership tends to be more tightly controlled among founding-family, institutional, and even public investors in Europe and Asia than it is for most large U.S. corporations. Tight ownership enables owners to understand the firm's financial condition better, resulting in their willingness to tolerate a higher degree of indebtedness.

On the other hand, similarities do exist between U.S. corporations and corporations in other countries. First, the same industry patterns of capital structure tend to be found all around the world. For example, in nearly all countries, pharmaceutical and other high-growth industrial firms tend to have lower debt ratios than do steel companies, airlines, and electric utility companies. Second, the capital structures of the largest U.S.-based multinational companies, which have access to many different capital markets around the world, typically resemble the capital structures of multinational companies from other countries more than they resemble those of smaller U.S. companies. Finally, the worldwide trend is away from reliance on banks for corporate financing and toward greater reliance on security issuance. Over time the differences in the capital structures of U.S. and non-U.S. firms will probably lessen.

The Optimal Capital Structure

A firm's capital structure is closely related to its cost of capital. Many debates over whether an "optimal" capital structure exists are found in the financial literature. Although the theoretical controversy over this point that began in the 1950s continues today, most financial managers behave as though they believe an optimal capital structure exists.

To provide some insight into what is meant by an optimal capital structure, we examine some basic financial relationships. It is generally believed that *the value of the firm is maximized when the cost of capital is minimized.* By using a modification of the simple zero-growth valuation model (see Equation 7.6 in Chapter 7), we can define the value of the firm, *V*, by Equation 13.1:

$$V = \frac{\text{EBIT} \times (1 - T)}{k_a} \tag{13.1}$$

where

$$
\begin{aligned}
\text{EBIT} &= \text{earnings before interest and taxes} \\
T &= \text{tax rate} \\
\text{EBIT} \times (1 - T) &= \text{the after-tax operating earnings available to the debt and} \\
&\quad \text{equity holders} \\
k_a &= \text{the weighted average cost of capital}
\end{aligned}
$$

Clearly, if we assume that EBIT is constant, the value of the firm, *V*, is maximized by minimizing the weighted average cost of capital, k_a.

Cost Functions

Figure 13.1(a) plots three cost functions—the cost of debt, the cost of equity, and the weighted average cost of capital (WACC)—as a function of financial leverage measured by the debt ratio (debt to total assets). The cost of debt remains low because of the tax shield, but it slowly increases as leverage increases, to compensate lenders for increasing risk. The cost of equity is above the cost of debt. It increases as financial leverage increases, but it generally increases more rapidly than the cost of debt. The cost of equity rises because the stockholders require a higher return as leverage increases, to compensate for the higher degree of financial risk.

FIGURE 13.1

Cost Functions and Value

Capital costs and the optimal capital structure

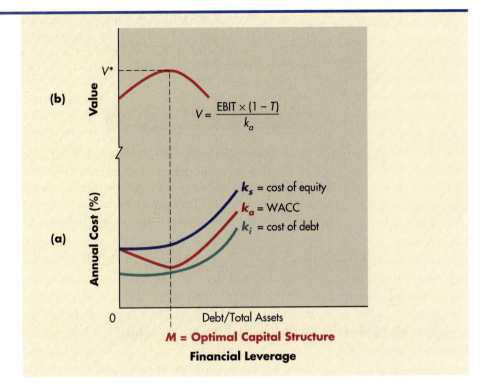

(b) Value

$$V = \frac{EBIT \times (1 - T)}{k_a}$$

k_s = cost of equity
k_a = WACC
k_i = cost of debt

(a) Annual Cost (%)

0   Debt/Total Assets

M = Optimal Capital Structure

Financial Leverage

The *weighted average cost of capital(WACC)* results from a weighted average of the firm's debt and equity capital costs. At a debt ratio of zero, the firm is 100 percent equity-financed. As debt is substituted for equity and as the debt ratio increases, the WACC declines because the debt cost is less than the equity cost ($k_i < k_s$). As the debt ratio continues to increase, the increased debt and equity costs eventually cause the WACC to rise (after point M in Figure 13.1). This behavior results in a U-shaped, or saucer-shaped, weighted average cost of capital function, k_a.

A Graphical View of the Optimal Capital Structure

optimal capital structure
The capital structure at which the weighted average cost of capital is minimized, thereby maximizing the firm's value.

Because the maximization of value, V, is achieved when the overall cost of capital, k_a, is at a minimum (see Equation 13.1), the **optimal capital structure** is that at which the weighted average cost of capital, k_a, is minimized. In Figure 13.1(a), point M represents the *minimum weighted average cost of capital*—the point of optimal financial leverage and hence of optimal capital structure for the firm. Figure 13.1(b) plots the value of the firm that results from substitution of k_a in Figure 13.1(a) for various levels of financial leverage into the zero-growth valuation model in Equation 13.1. As shown in Figure 13.1(b), at the optimal capital structure, point M, the value of the firm is maximized at V^*.

Generally, the lower the firm's weighted average cost of capital, the greater the difference between the return on a project and the WACC, and therefore the greater the owners' return. Simply stated, minimizing the weighted average cost of capital allows management to undertake a larger number of profitable projects, thereby further increasing the value of the firm.

As a practical matter, there is no way to calculate the optimal capital structure implied by Figure 13.1. Because it is impossible either to know or to remain at the precise optimal capital structure, firms generally try to operate in a *range* that places them near what they believe to be the optimal capital structure.

? Review Questions

13–1   What is a firm's *capital structure?* What ratios assess the degree of financial leverage in a firm's capital structure?

13–2   In what ways are the capital structures of U.S. and non-U.S. firms different? How are they similar?

13–3   What is the major benefit of debt financing? How does it affect the firm's cost of debt?

13–4   Where is the *optimal capital structure?* What is its relationship to the firm's value at that point?

The EBIT–EPS Approach to Capital Structure

EBIT–EPS approach
An approach for selecting the capital structure that maximizes earnings per share (EPS) over the expected range of earnings before interest and taxes (EBIT).

One of the key variables affecting the market value of the firm's shares is its returns to owners, as reflected by the firm's earnings. Therefore, earnings per share (EPS) can be conveniently used to analyze alternative capital structures. The **EBIT–EPS approach** to capital structure involves selecting the capital structure that maximizes EPS over the expected range of earnings before interest and taxes (EBIT).

Presenting a Financing Plan Graphically

To graph a financing plan, we need to know at least two EBIT–EPS coordinates. The approach for obtaining coordinates can be illustrated by the following example.

Example ▼   The current capital structure of Buzz Company, a soft-drink manufacturer, is as shown in the table below.

Current capital structure	
Long-term debt	$ 0
Common stock equity (25,000 shares at $20)	500,000
Total capital (assets)	$500,000

Note that Buzz's capital structure currently contains only common stock equity; the firm has no debt or preferred stock. If for convenience we assume that the firm has no current liabilities, its debt ratio is currently 0% ($0 ÷ $500,000); it therefore has *zero* financial leverage. Assume the firm is in the 40% tax bracket.

EBIT–EPS coordinates for Buzz's current capital structure can be found by assuming two EBIT values and calculating the EPS associated with them. Because the EBIT–EPS graph is a straight line, any two EBIT values can be used to find coordinates. Here we arbitrarily use values of $100,000 and $200,000.

	$100,000	$200,000
EBIT (assumed)	$100,000	$200,000
− Interest (rate × $0 debt)	0	0
Net profits before taxes	$100,000	$200,000
− Taxes (T = 0.40)	40,000	80,000
Net profits after taxes	$ 60,000	$120,000
EPS	$\dfrac{\$60,000}{25,000 \text{ sh.}} = \$2.40$	$\dfrac{\$120,000}{25,000 \text{ sh.}} = \$4.80$

The two EBIT–EPS coordinates resulting from these calculations are (1) $100,000 EBIT and $2.40 EPS and (2) $200,000 EBIT and $4.80 EPS.

The two EBIT–EPS coordinates developed for Buzz Company's current zero-leverage (debt ratio = 0%) situation can now be plotted on a set of EBIT–EPS axes, as shown in Figure 13.2. The figure shows the level of EPS expected for each level of EBIT. For levels of EBIT below the *x* intercept (the point where the line touches the *x* axis), a loss (negative EPS) would result. The *x* intercept is the **financial breakeven point,** the level of EBIT necessary to just cover all *fixed financial costs* (EPS = $0). As noted in Figure 13.2, Buzz's zero-leverage financing plan has a financial breakeven point of $0 EBIT, because it has no fixed financial cost (interest = $0).

financial breakeven point
The level of EBIT necessary to just cover all *fixed financial costs;* the level of EBIT for which EPS = $0.

FIGURE 13.2

Graphical Presentation of a Financing Plan
Buzz Company's zero-leverage financing plan

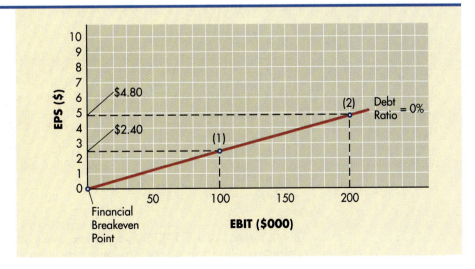

TABLE 13.2	Basic Information on Buzz Company's Current and Alternative Capital Structures

Capital structure debt ratio (1)	Total assets^a (2)	Debt $[(1) \times (2)]$ (3)	Equity $[(2) - (3)]$ (4)	Interest rate on debt^b (5)	Annual interest $[(3) \times (5)]$ (6)	Shares of common stock outstanding $[(4) \div \$20]^c$ (7)
0% (current)	$500,000	$ 0	$500,000	0 %	$ 0	25,000
30	500,000	150,000	350,000	10	15,000	17,500
60	500,000	300,000	200,000	16.5	49,500	10,000

^{a}Because for convenience the firm is assumed to have no current liabilities, total assets equals total capital of $500,000.
^{b}The interest rate on all debt increases with increases in the debt ratio because of the greater leverage and risk associated with higher debt ratios.
^{c}The $20 value represents the book value of common stock equity.

Comparing Alternative Capital Structures

We can compare alternative capital structures by graphing financing plans, much as shown in Figure 13.2.

Example ▼ Buzz Company is contemplating shifting its capital structure from its current zero leverage to either of two leveraged positions. To maintain its $500,000 of total capital, Buzz will shift to greater leverage by issuing debt and using the proceeds to retire an equivalent amount of common stock. The two alternative capital structures under consideration result in debt ratios of 30% and 60%, respectively. The basic information on the current and two alternative capital structures is summarized in Table 13.2.

   Using the data in Table 13.2, we can calculate the coordinates needed to plot the capital structures for 30% and 60% debt. Using, for convenience, the same $100,000 and $200,000 EBIT values used to plot the current capital structure, we get the information in the following table.

	Capital structure			
	30% Debt ratio		60% Debt ratio	
EBIT (assumed)	$100,000	$200,000	$100,000	$200,000
− Interest (Table 13.2)	15,000	15,000	49,500	49,500
Net profits before taxes	$ 85,000	$185,000	$ 50,500	$150,500
− Taxes ($T = 0.40$)	34,000	74,000	20,200	60,200
Net profits after taxes	$ 51,000	$111,000	$ 30,300	$ 90,300
EPS	$\dfrac{\$51,000}{17,500 \text{ sh.}} = \$2.91$	$\dfrac{\$111,000}{17,500 \text{ sh.}} = \$6.34$	$\dfrac{\$30,300}{10,000 \text{ sh.}} = \$3.03$	$\dfrac{\$90,300}{10,000 \text{ sh.}} = \$9.03$

These two sets of EBIT–EPS coordinates, along with those developed for the current zero-leverage capital structure, are plotted on the EBIT–EPS axes in Figure 13.3.

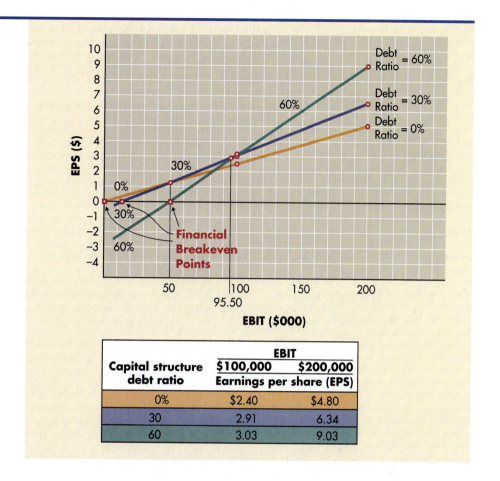

FIGURE 13.3

EBIT–EPS Approach
A comparison of selected capital structures for Buzz Company

Capital structure debt ratio	EBIT	
	$100,000	**$200,000**
	Earnings per share (EPS)	
0%	$2.40	$4.80
30	2.91	6.34
60	3.03	9.03

This figure shows that *each* capital structure is superior to the others in terms of maximizing EPS over certain ranges of EBIT: The zero-leverage capital structure (debt ratio = 0%) is superior to either of the other capital structures for levels of EBIT between $0 and $50,000. Between $50,000 and $95,500 of EBIT, the capital structure associated with a debt ratio of 30% is preferred. And at a level of EBIT above $95,500, the 60% debt ratio capital structure provides the highest earnings per share.

Considering Risk in EBIT–EPS Analysis

When interpreting EBIT–EPS analysis, it is important to consider the risk of each capital structure alternative. Graphically, the risk of each capital structure can be viewed in light of two measures: (1) the *financial breakeven point* (EBIT-axis intercept) and (2) the *degree of financial leverage* reflected in the slope of the capital structure line. The higher the financial breakeven point and the steeper the slope of the capital structure line, the greater the financial risk.

Further assessment of risk can be performed by using ratios. As financial leverage (measured by the debt ratio) increases, we expect a corresponding decline in the firm's ability to make scheduled interest payments (measured by the times-interest-earned ratio).

Example ▼

Reviewing the three capital structures plotted for Buzz Company in Figure 13.3, we can see that as the debt ratio increases, so does the financial risk of each alternative. Both the financial breakeven point and the slope of the capital structure lines increase with increasing debt ratios. If we use the $100,000 EBIT value, for example, the times-interest-earned ratio (EBIT ÷ interest) for the zero-leverage capital structure is infinity ($100,000 ÷ $0); for the 30% debt case, it is 6.67 ($100,000 ÷ $15,000); and for the 60% debt case, it is 2.02 ($100,000 ÷ $49,500). Because lower times interest earned ratios reflect higher risk, these ratios support the conclusion that the risk of the capital structures increases with increasing financial leverage. The capital structure for a debt ratio of 60% is riskier than that for a debt ratio of 30%, which in turn is riskier than the capital structure for a debt ratio of 0%.

▲

Basic Shortcoming of EBIT–EPS Analysis

EBIT–EPS analysis is basically descriptive in that it can identify capital structures of greater or less risk. But it is not prescriptive in the sense of being able to help the firm choose a particular capital structure that will optimize the firm's value. The reason is that although the EBIT–EPS analysis shows the amount of risk, the decision variable—EPS—does not capture risk. Therefore, the choice of a capital structure that maximizes EPS generally ignores risk. If investors did not require risk premiums (additional returns) as the firm increased the proportion of debt in its capital structure, a strategy involving maximizing EPS would also maximize owner wealth. But because risk premiums increase with increases in financial leverage, the maximization of EPS *does not* ensure owner wealth maximization. To select the best capital structure, both return (EPS) and risk (via the required return, k_s) must be integrated into a valuation framework consistent with the model presented earlier in Equation 13.1.

? Review Question

13–5 Explain the EBIT–EPS approach to capital structure. Include in your explanation a graph indicating the *financial breakeven point*; label the axes.

LG3 Choosing the Optimal Capital Structure

A wealth maximization framework for use in making capital structure decisions should include the two key factors of return and risk. This section describes the procedures for linking to market value the return and risk associated with alternative capital structures.

Linkage

To determine the firm's value under alternative capital structures, the firm must find the level of return that must be earned to compensate owners for the risk

TABLE 13.3	Calculation of Share Value Estimates Associated with Alternative Capital Structures for Buzz Company			
Capital structure debt ratio	Estimated expected EPS (1)	Estimated coefficient of variation of EPS (2)	Estimated required return, k_s (3)	Estimated share value [(1) ÷ (3)] (4)
0%	$2.40	0.71	0.115	$20.87
10	2.55	0.74	0.117	21.79
20	2.72	0.78	0.121	22.48
30	2.91	0.83	0.125	23.28
40	3.12	0.91	0.140	22.29
50	3.18	1.07	0.165	19.27
60	3.03	1.40	0.190	15.95

being incurred. Such a framework is consistent with the overall valuation framework developed in Chapter 7 and applied to capital budgeting decisions in Chapter 11.

The required return associated with a given level of financial risk can be estimated in a number of ways. Theoretically, the preferred approach would be first to estimate the beta associated with each alternative capital structure and then to use the CAPM framework presented in Equation 6.7 to calculate the required return, k_s. A more operational approach involves linking the financial risk associated with each capital structure alternative directly to the required return. Such an approach is similar to the CAPM-type approach demonstrated in Chapter 11 for linking project required return (RADR) and risk. Here it involves estimating the required return associated with each level of financial risk, as measured by a statistic such as the coefficient of variation of EPS. Regardless of the approach used, one would expect that the required return would increase as the financial risk increases.

Example ▼

Expanding the Buzz Company example, we assume that the firm is attempting to choose the best of seven alternative capital structures—debt ratios of 0%, 10%, 20%, 30%, 40%, 50%, and 60%. For each of these structures, the firm estimated (1) the expected EPS, (2) the coefficient of variation of EPS, and (3) the required return, k_s. These values are shown in columns 1 through 3 of Table 13.3. Note that expected EPS (in column 1) is maximized at a 50% debt ratio, whereas the risk of EPS measured by its coefficient of variation (in column 2) is constantly increasing. As expected, the estimated required return of owners, k_s (in column 3), increases with increasing risk. Simply stated, for higher debt ratios (higher financial leverage) owners require higher rates of return. ▲

Estimating Value

The value of the firm associated with alternative capital structures can be estimated by using one of the standard valuation models. If, for simplicity, we assume that all earnings are paid out as dividends, we can use a zero-growth

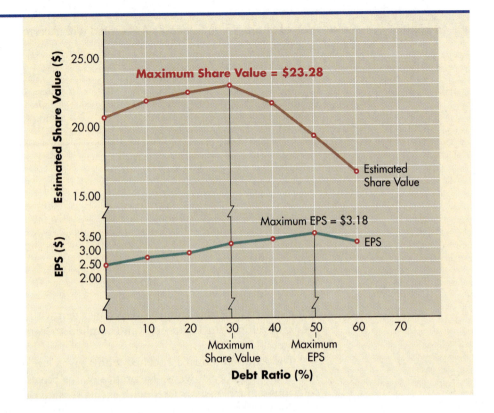

FIGURE 13.4

Estimating Value
Estimated share value and EPS for alternative capital structures for Buzz Company

valuation model such as that developed in Chapter 7. The model, originally stated in Equation 7.6, is restated here with EPS substituted for dividends (because in each year the dividends would equal EPS):

$$P_0 = \frac{\text{EPS}}{k_s} \tag{13.2}$$

By substituting the expected level of EPS and the associated required return, k_s, into Equation 13.2, we can estimate the per-share value of the firm.

Example ▼ We can now estimate the value of Buzz Company's stock under each of the alternative capital structures. Substituting the expected EPS (column 1 of Table 13.3) and the required returns, k_s (column 3), into Equation 13.2 for each of the capital structures, we obtain the share values given in column 4. Plotting the resulting share values against the associated debt ratios, as shown in Figure 13.4, clearly illustrates that the maximum share value occurs at the capital structure associated with a debt ratio of 30%. **▲**

Maximizing Value versus Maximizing EPS

Throughout this part of the text, the goal of the financial manager has been specified as maximizing owner wealth, not profit. Although there is some relation-

TABLE 13.4	Important Factors to Consider in Making Capital Structure Decisions
Factor	**Description**
Revenue stability	Firms that have stable and predictable revenues can more safely undertake highly leveraged capital structures than can firms with volatile patterns of sales revenue. Firms with growing sales tend to benefit from added debt because they can reap the positive benefits of financial leverage, which magnifies the effect of these increases.
Cash flow	When considering a new capital structure, the firm must focus on its ability to generate the cash flows necessary to meet obligations. Cash forecasts reflecting an ability to service debts (and preferred stock) must support any shift in capital structure.
Contractual obligations	A firm may be contractually constrained with respect to the type of funds that it can raise. For example, a firm might be prohibited from selling additional debt except when the claims of holders of such debt are made subordinate to the existing debt. Contractual constraints on the sale of additional stock, as well as on the ability to distribute dividends on stock, might also exist.
Management preferences	Occasionally, a firm will impose an internal constraint on the use of debt to limit its risk exposure to a level deemed acceptable to management. In other words, because of risk aversion, the firm's management constrains the firm's capital structure at a level that may or may not be the true optimum.
Control	A management concerned about control may prefer to issue debt rather than (voting) common stock. Under favorable market conditions, a firm that wanted to sell equity could make a *preemptive offering* or issue *nonvoting shares* (see Chapter 3), allowing each shareholder to maintain proportionate ownership. Generally, only in closely held firms or firms threatened by takeover does control become a major concern in the capital structure decision.
External risk assessment	The firm's ability to raise funds quickly and at favorable rates depends on the external risk assessments of lenders and bond raters. The firm must therefore consider the impact of capital structure decisions both on share value and on published financial statements from which lenders and raters assess the firm's risk.
Timing	At times when the general level of interest rates is low, debt financing might be more attractive; when interest rates are high, the sale of stock may be more appealing. Sometimes both debt and equity capital become unavailable at what would be viewed as reasonable terms. General economic conditions—especially those of the capital market—can thus significantly affect capital structure decisions.

ship between expected profit and value, there is no reason to believe that profit-maximizing strategies necessarily result in wealth maximization. It is therefore the wealth of the owners as reflected in the estimated share value that should serve as the criterion for selecting the best capital structure. A final look at Buzz Company will highlight this point.

Example ▼ Further analysis of Figure 13.4 clearly shows that although the firm's profits (EPS) are maximized at a debt ratio of 50%, share value is maximized at a 30% debt ratio. Therefore, the preferred capital structure would be the 30% debt ratio. The two approaches provide different calculations because EPS maximization does not consider risk. ▲

Some Other Important Considerations

Because there is really no practical way to calculate the optimal capital structure, any quantitative analysis of capital structure must be tempered with other important considerations. Some of the more important additional factors involved in capital structure decisions are summarized in Table 13.4.

13–6 Why do maximizing EPS and maximizing value not necessarily lead to the same conclusion about the optimal capital structure?

13–7 What important factors in addition to quantitative considerations should a firm consider when it is making a capital structure decision?

Dividend Fundamentals

retained earnings
Earnings not distributed as dividends; a form of *internal* equity financing.

We've seen that the firm's capital structure is the mix of long-term financing—debt and common or preferred stock that it maintains. In addition to raising debt and equity capital *externally,* the firm can obtain *internal* equity financing from **retained earnings,** earnings not distributed to owners as dividends. Therefore, the firm's dividend decision can significantly affect its external financing requirements. In addition, dividends are important because they are the key return variable from which owners and investors determine share value. Expected cash dividends represent a source of cash flow to stockholders and provide information about the firm's current and future performance. Therefore, we now turn our attention to dividends. The first thing to know about cash dividends is the procedures for paying them.

Cash Dividend Payment Procedures

The payment of cash dividends to corporate stockholders is decided by the firm's board of directors at quarterly or semiannual meetings. The past period's financial performance and future outlook, as well as recent dividends paid, are key inputs to the dividend decision. The payment date of the cash dividend, if one is declared, must also be established.

Amount of Dividends

Whether dividends should be paid, and if so, in what amount, are important decisions that depend primarily on the firm's dividend policy. Most firms have a set policy with respect to the periodic dividend, but the firm's directors can change this amount, largely on the basis of significant increases or decreases in earnings.

Relevant Dates

If the directors of the firm declare a dividend, they also typically issue a statement indicating the dividend decision, the record date, and the payment date. This statement is generally quoted in the *Wall Street Journal* and other financial news media.

date of record (dividends)
Set by the firm's directors, the date on which all persons whose names are recorded as stockholders receive a declared dividend at a specified future time.

Record Date   All persons whose names are recorded as stockholders on the **date of record** set by the directors receive a declared dividend at a specified future time. These stockholders are often referred to *as holders of record.*

ex dividend
Period beginning *two business days* prior to the date of record during which a stock is sold without the right to receive the current dividend.

Because of the time needed to make bookkeeping entries when a stock is traded, the stock begins selling **ex dividend** *two business days* prior to the date of record. Purchasers of a stock selling ex dividend do not receive the current dividend. A simple way to determine the first day on which the stock sells ex dividend is to subtract two days from the date of record; if a weekend intervenes, subtract four days. Ignoring general market fluctuations, the stock's price is expected to drop by the amount of the declared dividend on the ex dividend date.

payment date
Set by the firm's directors, the actual date on which the firm mails the dividend payment to the holders of record.

Payment Date   The **payment date,** also set by the directors, is the actual date on which the firm mails the dividend payment to the holders of record. It is generally a few weeks after the record date. An example will clarify the various dates and the accounting effects.

Example ▼

At the quarterly dividend meeting of Jillian Company, a distributor of office products, held on June 10, the directors declared an $.80-per-share cash dividend for holders of record on Monday, July 1. The firm had 100,000 shares of common stock outstanding. The payment date for the dividend was August 1. Before the dividend was declared, the key accounts of the firm were as follows:

Cash	$200,000	Dividends payable	$ 0
		Retained earnings	1,000,000

When the dividend was announced by the directors, $80,000 of the retained earnings ($.80 per share × 100,000 shares) was transferred to the dividends payable account. The key accounts thus became

Cash	$200,000	Dividends payable	$ 80,000
		Retained earnings	920,000

Jillian Company's stock began selling ex dividend two business days prior to the date of record, which was June 27. This date was found by subtracting 4 days (a weekend intervened) from the July 1 date of record. Purchasers of Jillian's stock on June 26 or earlier received the rights to the dividends; those who purchased the stock on or after June 27 did not. Assuming a stable market, Jillian's stock price was expected to drop by approximately $.80 per share when it began selling ex dividend on June 27. On August 1 the firm mailed dividend checks to the holders of record as of July 1. This produced the following balances in the key accounts of the firm:

Cash	$120,000	Dividends payable	$ 0
		Retained earnings	920,000

▲

The net effect of declaring and paying the dividend was to reduce the firm's total assets (and stockholders' equity) by $80,000.

dividend reinvestment plans (DRIPs)
Plans that enable stockholders to use dividends received on the firm's stock to acquire additional shares—even fractional shares—at little or no transaction cost.

Dividend Reinvestment Plans

Today many firms offer **dividend reinvestment plans (DRIPs),** which enable stockholders to use dividends received on the firm's stock to acquire additional shares—even fractional shares—at little or no transaction cost. Some companies even allow investors to make their *initial purchases* of the firm's stock directly from the company without going through a broker. With DRIPs, plan participants typically can acquire shares at about 5 percent below the prevailing market price. From its point of view, the firm can issue new shares to participants more economically, avoiding the underpricing and flotation costs that would accompany the public sale of new shares. Clearly, the existence of a DRIP may enhance the market appeal of a firm's shares.

The Residual Theory of Dividends

Numerous theories and studies of dividend policy exist. They ask several key questions: Does dividend policy matter? What effect does dividend policy have on share price? Is there a model that can be used to evaluate alternative dividend policies in view of share value? A backdrop for consideration of these questions is the residual theory of dividends.

residual theory of dividends
A school of thought that suggests that the dividend paid by a firm should be viewed as a *residual*—the amount left over after all acceptable investment opportunities have been undertaken.

The **residual theory of dividends** is a school of thought that suggests that the dividend paid by a firm should be viewed as a *residual*—the amount left over after all acceptable investment opportunities have been undertaken. According to this approach, as long as the firm's equity need exceeds the amount of retained earnings, no cash dividend is paid. If an excess of retained earnings exists, then the residual amount is distributed as dividends. The argument for this approach is that it is sound management to be certain that the company has the money it needs to compete effectively. This view of dividends suggests that the required return of investors, k_s, is *not* influenced by the firm's dividend policy—a premise that in turn implies that dividend policy is irrelevant.

Dividend Irrelevance Arguments

The residual theory of dividends implies that if the firm cannot invest its earnings to earn a return (IRR) that is in excess of cost (WMCC), it should distribute the earnings by paying dividends to stockholders. This approach suggests that dividends represent an earnings residual rather than an active decision variable that affects the firm's value. Such a view is consistent with the **dividend irrelevance theory** put forth by Merton H. Miller and Franco Modigliani (M and M). They argue that the firm's value is determined solely by the earning power and risk of its assets (investments) and that the manner in which it splits its earnings stream between dividends and internally retained (and reinvested) funds does not affect this value. M and M's theory suggests that in a perfect world (certainty, no taxes, no transactions costs, and no other market imperfections), the value of the firm is unaffected by the distribution of dividends.

dividend irrelevance theory
Miller and Modigliani's theory that, in a perfect world, the firm's value is determined solely by the earning power and risk of its assets (investments) and that the manner in which it splits its earnings stream between dividends and internally retained (and reinvested) funds does not affect this value.

However, studies have shown that large changes in dividends do affect share price. Increases in dividends result in increased share price, and decreases in dividends result in decreased share price. In response, M and M argue that these effects are attributable not to the dividend itself but rather to the **informational content** of dividends with respect to future earnings. In other words, say M and M, it is not the preference of shareholders for current dividends (rather than future capital gains) that is responsible for this behavior. Instead, investors view a change in dividends, up or down, as a *signal* that management expects future earnings to change in the same direction. An increase in dividends is viewed as a

informational content
The information provided by the dividends of a firm with respect to future earnings, which causes owners to bid up or down the price of the firm's stock.

positive signal, and investors bid up the share price; a decrease in dividends is a *negative signal* that causes a decrease in share price as investors sell their shares.

clientele effect
The argument that a firm attracts shareholders whose preferences for the payment and stability of dividends correspond to the payment pattern and stability of the firm itself.

M and M further argue that a **clientele effect** exists: A firm attracts shareholders whose preferences for the payment and stability of dividends correspond to the payment pattern and stability of the firm itself. Investors who desire stable dividends as a source of income hold the stock of firms that pay about the same dividend amount each period. Investors who prefer to earn capital gains are more attracted to growing firms that reinvest a large portion of their earnings, favoring growth over a stable pattern of dividends. Because the shareholders get what they expect, M and M argue, the value of their firm's stock is unaffected by dividend policy.

In summary, M and M and other proponents of dividend irrelevance argue that, all else being equal, an investor's required return—and therefore the value of the firm—is unaffected by dividend policy for three reasons:

1. The firm's value is determined solely by the earning power and risk of its assets.
2. If dividends do affect value, they do so solely because of their informational content, which signals management's earnings expectations.
3. A clientele effect exists that causes a firm's shareholders to receive the dividends they expect.

These views of M and M with respect to dividend irrelevance are consistent with the residual theory, which focuses on making the best investment decisions to maximize share value. The proponents of dividend irrelevance conclude that because dividends are irrelevant to a firm's value, the firm does not need to have a dividend policy. Although many research studies have been performed to validate or refute the dividend irrelevance theory, none has been successful in providing irrefutable evidence.

Dividend Relevance Arguments

dividend relevance theory
The theory, advanced by Gordon and Lintner, that there is a direct relationship between a firm's dividend policy and its market value.

The key argument in support of **dividend relevance theory** is attributed to Myron J. Gordon and John Lintner, who suggest that there is, in fact, a direct relationship between the firm's dividend policy and its market value. Fundamental to this proposition is their **bird-in-the-hand argument,** which suggests that investors see current dividends as less risky than future dividends or capital gains. "A bird in the hand is worth two in the bush." Gordon and Lintner argue that current dividend payments reduce investor uncertainty, causing investors to discount the firm's earnings at a lower rate and, all else being equal, to place a higher value on the firm's stock. Conversely, if dividends are reduced or are not paid, investor uncertainty will increase, raising the required return and lowering the stock's value.

bird-in-the-hand argument
The belief, in support of *dividend relevance theory,* that investors see current dividend's as less risky than future dividends or capital gains.

Although many other arguments related to dividend relevance have been put forward, *empirical studies fail to provide conclusive evidence in support of the intuitively appealing dividend relevance argument.* In practice, however, the actions of both financial managers and stockholders tend to support the belief that dividend policy does affect stock value.[1] Because we focus on the day-to-day behavior of firms, the remainder of this chapter is consistent with the belief that

---

[1]A common exception is small firms, because they frequently treat dividends as a residual remaining after all acceptable investments have been initiated. Small firms follow this course of action because they usually do not have ready access to capital markets. The use of retained earnings therefore is a key source of financing for growth, which is generally an important goal of a small firm.

dividends are relevant—that each firm must develop a dividend policy that fulfills the goals of its owners and maximizes their wealth as reflected in the firm's share price.

? Review Questions

13–8   Who are holders of record? When does a stock sell ex dividend?

13–9   What benefit is available to participants in a dividend reinvestment plan? How might the firm benefit?

13–10   Does following the residual theory of dividends lead to a stable dividend? Is this approach consistent with dividend relevance?

13–11   Contrast the basic arguments about dividend policy advanced by Miller and Modigliani (M and M) and by Gordon and Lintner.

Dividend Policy

dividend policy
The firm's plan of action to be followed whenever a dividend decision is made.

The firm's **dividend policy** represents a plan of action to be followed whenever the dividend decision is made. Firms develop policies consistent with their goals. Before we review some of the most popular types of dividend policies, we discuss the factors that are considered in establishing a dividend policy.

Factors That Affect Dividend Policy

Most firms consider a variety of factors when formulating dividend policy. These include legal constraints, contractual constraints, internal constraints, the firm's growth prospects, owner considerations, and market considerations.

Legal Constraints

Most states prohibit corporations from paying out as cash dividends any portion of the firm's "legal capital," which is typically measured by the par value of common stock. These *capital impairment restrictions* are generally established to provide a sufficient equity base to protect creditors' claims.

An earnings requirement limiting the amount of dividends is sometimes imposed. With this restriction, the firm cannot pay more in cash dividends than the sum of its most recent and past retained earnings. However, *the firm is not prohibited from paying more in dividends than its current earnings.*

excess earnings accumulation tax
The tax the IRS levies on retained earnings above $250,000 when it determines that the firm has accumulated an excess of earnings to allow owners to delay paying ordinary income taxes on dividends received.

If a firm has overdue liabilities or is legally insolvent or bankrupt, most states prohibit its payment of cash dividends. In addition, the Internal Revenue Service prohibits firms from accumulating earnings to reduce the owners' taxes. If the IRS can determine that a firm has accumulated an excess of earnings to allow owners to delay paying ordinary income taxes on dividends received, it may levy an **excess earnings accumulation tax** on any retained earnings above $250,000.

Contractual Constraints

Often the firm's ability to pay cash dividends is constrained by restrictive provisions in a loan agreement. Generally, these constraints prohibit the payment of cash dividends until a certain level of earnings has been achieved, or they may limit dividends to a certain dollar amount or percentage of earnings. Constraints on dividends help to protect creditors from losses due to the firm's insolvency.

Internal Constraints

The firm's ability to pay cash dividends is generally constrained by the amount of liquid assets (cash and marketable securities) available. Although it is possible for a firm to borrow funds to pay dividends, lenders are generally reluctant to make such loans because they produce no tangible or operating benefits that will help the firm repay the loan.

Growth Prospects

The firm's financial requirements are directly related to how much it expects to grow and what assets it will need to acquire. It must evaluate its profitability and risk to develop insight into its ability to raise capital externally. In addition, the firm must determine the cost and speed with which it can obtain financing. Generally, a large, mature firm has adequate access to new capital, whereas a rapidly growing firm may not have sufficient funds available to support its acceptable projects. A growth firm is likely to have to depend heavily on internal financing through retained earnings, and so it is likely to pay out only a very small percentage of its earnings as dividends. A more established firm is in a better position to pay out a large proportion of its earnings, particularly if it has ready sources of financing.

Owner Considerations

The firm must establish a dividend policy that has a favorable effect on the wealth of the *majority* of owners. One consideration is the *tax status of a firm's owners*. If a firm has a large percentage of wealthy stockholders who are in a high tax bracket, it may decide to pay out a lower percentage of its earnings to allow the owners to delay the payment of taxes until they sell the stock. Of course, lower-income shareholders, who need dividend income, will prefer a higher payout of earnings.

A second consideration is the *owners' investment opportunities*. A firm should not retain funds for investment in projects yielding lower returns than the owners could obtain from external investments of equal risk. If it appears that the owners have better opportunities externally, the firm should pay out a higher percentage of its earnings. If the firm's investment opportunities are at least as good as similar-risk external investments, a lower payout is justifiable.

A final consideration is the *potential dilution of ownership*. If a firm pays out a high percentage of earnings, new equity capital will have to be raised with common stock. The result of a new stock issue may be dilution of both control and earnings for the existing owners. By paying out a low percentage of its earnings, the firm can minimize the possibility of such dilution.

Market Considerations

An awareness of the market's probable response to certain types of policies is also helpful in formulating dividend policy. Stockholders are believed to value *a fixed or increasing level of dividends* as opposed to a fluctuating pattern of dividends.

In addition, stockholders are believed to value a policy of *continuous dividend payment*. Because regularly paying a fixed or increasing dividend eliminates uncertainty about the frequency and magnitude of dividends, the returns of the firm are likely to be discounted at a lower rate. This should result in an increase in the market value of the stock and therefore an increase in owners' wealth.

A final market consideration is *informational content*. As noted earlier, shareholders often view a dividend payment as a *signal* of the firm's future success. A stable and continuous dividend is a *positive signal*, conveying the firm's good financial health. Shareholders are likely to interpret a passed dividend payment due to a loss or to very low earnings as a *negative signal*. The nonpayment of the dividend creates uncertainty about the future, which is likely to result in lower stock value. Owners and investors generally construe a dividend payment during a period of losses as an indication that the loss is merely temporary.

Types of Dividend Policies

The firm's dividend policy must be formulated with two basic objectives in mind: providing for sufficient financing and maximizing the wealth of the firm's owners. Three of the more commonly used dividend policies are described in the following sections. A particular firm's cash dividend policy may incorporate elements of each.

Constant-Payout-Ratio Dividend Policy

dividend payout ratio
Indicates the percentage of each dollar earned that is distributed to the owners in the form of cash. It is calculated by dividing the firm's cash dividend per share by its earnings per share.

constant-payout-ratio dividend policy
A dividend policy based on the payment of a certain percentage of earnings to owners in each dividend period.

One type of dividend policy is the use of a constant payout ratio. The **dividend payout ratio** indicates the percentage of each dollar earned that is distributed to the owners in the form of cash. It is calculated by dividing the firm's cash dividend per share by its earnings per share. With a **constant-payout-ratio dividend policy**, the firm establishes that a certain percentage of earnings is paid to owners in each dividend period.

The problem with this policy is that if the firm's earnings drop or if a loss occurs in a given period, the dividends may be low or even nonexistent. Because dividends are often considered an indicator of the firm's future condition and status, the firm's stock price may thus be adversely affected.

Example ▼ Matoon Industries, a miner of potassium, has a policy of paying out 40% of earnings in cash dividends. In periods when a loss occurs, the firm's policy is to pay no cash dividends. Data on Matoon's earnings, dividends, and average stock prices for the past 6 years are as follows:

Year	Earnings/share	Dividends/share	Average price/share
2001	−$ .50	$ .00	$42.00
2000	3.00	1.20	52.00
1999	1.75	.70	48.00
1998	− 1.50	.00	38.00
1997	2.00	.80	46.00
1996	4.50	1.80	50.00

Dividends increased in 1999 and in 2000 but decreased in the other years. In years of decreasing dividends, the firm's stock price dropped; when dividends increased, the price of the stock increased. Matoon's sporadic dividend payments appear to make its owners uncertain about the returns they can expect.

Although some firms use a constant-payout-ratio dividend policy, it is not recommended.

Regular Dividend Policy

regular dividend policy
A dividend policy based on the payment of a fixed-dollar dividend in each period.

The **regular dividend policy** is based on the payment of a fixed-dollar dividend in each period. This policy provides the owners with generally positive information, thereby minimizing their uncertainty. Often, firms that use this policy increase the regular dividend once a *proven* increase in earnings has occurred. Under this policy, dividends are almost never decreased.

Example ▼ The dividend policy of Actum Laboratories, a producer of a popular artificial sweetener, is to pay annual dividends of $1.00 per share until per-share earnings have exceeded $4.00 for three consecutive years. At that point the annual dividend is raised to $1.50 per share, and a new earnings plateau is established. The firm does not anticipate decreasing its dividend unless its liquidity is in jeopardy. Data for Actum's earnings, dividends, and average stock prices for the past 12 years are as follows:

Year	Earnings/share	Dividends/share	Average price/share
2001	$4.50	$1.50	$47.50
2000	3.90	1.50	46.50
1999	4.60	1.50	45.00
1998	4.20	1.00	43.00
1997	5.00	1.00	42.00
1996	2.00	1.00	38.50
1995	6.00	1.00	38.00
1994	3.00	1.00	36.00
1993	.75	1.00	33.00
1992	.50	1.00	33.00
1991	2.70	1.00	33.50
1990	2.85	1.00	35.00

target dividend-payout ratio
A dividend policy under which the firm attempts to pay out a certain *percentage* of earnings as a stated dollar dividend and adjusts that dividend toward a target payout as proven earnings increases occur.

Whatever the level of earnings, Actum Laboratories paid dividends of $1.00 per share through 1998. In 1999, the dividend increased to $1.50 per share because earnings in excess of $4.00 per share had been achieved for 3 years. In 1999, the firm also had to establish a new earnings plateau for further dividend increases. Actum Laboratories' average price per share exhibited a stable, increasing behavior in spite of a somewhat volatile pattern of earnings. ▲

Often, a regular dividend policy is built around a **target dividend-payout ratio.** Under this policy, the firm attempts to pay out a certain *percentage* of earnings, but rather than let dividends fluctuate, it pays a stated dollar dividend and adjusts that dividend toward the target payout as proven earnings increases occur. For instance, Actum Laboratories appears to have a target payout ratio of around 35 percent. The payout was about 35 percent ($1.00 ÷ $2.85) when the dividend policy was set in 1990, and when the dividend was raised to $1.50 in 1999, the payout ratio was about 33 percent ($1.50 ÷ $4.60).

Low-Regular-and-Extra Dividend Policy

**low-regular-and-extra divi-
dend policy**
A dividend policy based on paying a low
regular dividend, supplemented by an
additional dividend when earnings are
higher than normal in a given period.

extra dividend
An additional dividend optionally paid
by the firm if earnings are higher than
normal in a given period.

Some firms establish a **low-regular-and-extra dividend policy,** paying a low regular dividend, supplemented by an additional dividend when earnings are higher than normal in a given period. By calling the additional dividend an **extra dividend,** the firm avoids giving shareholders false hopes. This policy is especially common among companies that experience cyclical shifts in earnings.

By establishing a low regular dividend that is paid each period, the firm gives investors the stable income necessary to build confidence in the firm, and the extra dividend permits them to share in the earnings from an especially good period. Firms using this policy must raise the level of the regular dividend once proven increases in earnings have been achieved. The extra dividend should not be a regular event; otherwise, it becomes meaningless. The use of a target dividend-payout ratio in establishing the regular dividend level is advisable.

? Review Questions

13–12 What are the six factors that affect dividend policy?
13–13 Describe a constant-payout-ratio dividend policy, a regular dividend policy, and a low-regular-and-extra dividend policy. What are the effects of these policies?

LG6 Other Forms of Dividends

Dividends can be paid in forms other than cash. Here we discuss two other methods of paying dividends—stock dividends and stock repurchases—as well as a closely related topic, stock splits.

Stock Dividends

stock dividend
The payment, to existing owners, of a
dividend in the form of stock.

A **stock dividend** is the payment, to existing owners, of a dividend in the form of stock. Often, firms pay stock dividends as a replacement for or a supplement to cash dividends. Although stock dividends do not have a real value, stockholders may perceive them to represent something they did not have before.

Accounting Aspects

In an accounting sense, the payment of a stock dividend is a shifting of funds between stockholders' equity accounts rather than a use of funds. When a firm

small (ordinary) stock dividend
A stock dividend representing less than 20 to 25 percent of the common stock outstanding when the dividend is declared.

declares a stock dividend, the procedures for announcement and distribution are the same as those described earlier for a cash dividend. The accounting entries associated with the payment of a stock dividend vary depending on its size. A **small (ordinary) stock dividend** is a stock dividend representing less than 20 to 25 percent of the common stock outstanding when the dividend is declared. Small stock dividends are most common.

E x a m p l e ▼   The current stockholders' equity on the balance sheet of Trimline Corporation, a distributor of prefabricated cabinets, is as shown in the following accounts.

Preferred stock	$ 300,000
Common stock (100,000 shares at $4 par)	400,000
Paid-in capital in excess of par	600,000
Retained earnings	700,000
Total stockholders' equity	$2,000,000

Trimline, which has 100,000 shares outstanding, declares a 10% stock dividend when the market price of its stock is $15 per share. Because 10,000 new shares (10% of 100,000) have been issued at the prevailing market price of $15 per share, $150,000 ($15 per share × 10,000 shares) is shifted from retained earnings to the common stock and paid-in capital accounts. A total of $40,000 ($4 par × 10,000 shares) is added to common stock, and the remaining $110,000 [($15 − $4) × 10,000 shares] is added to the paid-in capital in excess of par. The resulting account balances are as follows:

Preferred stock	$ 300,000
Common stock (110,000 shares at $4 par)	440,000
Paid-in capital in excess of par	710,000
Retained earnings	550,000
Total stockholders' equity	$2,000,000

▲ The firm's total stockholders' equity has not changed; funds have only been *shifted* among stockholders' equity accounts.

The Shareholder's Viewpoint

The shareholder receiving a stock dividend typically receives nothing of value. After the dividend is paid, the per-share value of the shareholder's stock decreases in proportion to the dividend in such a way that the market value of his or her total holdings in the firm remains unchanged. The shareholder's proportion of ownership in the firm also remains the same, and *as long as the firm's earnings remain unchanged,* so does his or her share of total earnings. (However, if the firm's earnings and cash dividends increase when the stock dividend is issued, an increase in share value is likely to result.)

The Company's Viewpoint

Stock dividends are more costly to issue than cash dividends, but certain advantages may outweigh these costs. Firms find the stock dividend a way to give owners something without having to use cash. Generally, when a firm needs to preserve cash to finance rapid growth, a stock dividend is used. When the stockholders recognize that the firm is reinvesting the cash flow so as to maximize future earnings, the market value of the firm should at least remain unchanged. However, if the stock dividend is paid so that cash can be retained to satisfy past-due bills, a decline in market value may result.

Stock Splits

stock split
A method commonly used to lower the market price of a firm's stock by increasing the number of shares belonging to each shareholder.

Although not a type of dividend, *stock splits* have an effect on a firm's share price similar to that of stock dividends. A **stock split** is a method commonly used to lower the market price of a firm's stock by increasing the number of shares belonging to each shareholder. In a 2-for-1 split, for example, two new shares are exchanged for each old share, with each new share worth half the value of each old share. A stock split has no effect on the firm's capital structure.

Quite often, a firm believes that its stock is priced too high and that lowering the market price will enhance trading activity. Stock splits are often made prior to issuing additional stock to enhance that stock's marketability and stimulate market activity. It is not unusual for a stock split to cause a slight increase in the market value of the stock, attributable to its informational content.

reverse stock split
A method used to raise the market price of a firm's stock by exchanging a certain number of outstanding shares for one new share.

Stock can be split in any way desired. Sometimes a **reverse stock split** is made: A certain number of outstanding shares are exchanged for one new share. For example, in a 1-for-3 split, one new share is exchanged for three old shares. Reverse stock splits are initiated to raise the market price of a firm's stock when it is selling at too low a price to appear respectable.

Stock Repurchases

stock repurchase
The repurchase by the firm of outstanding common stock in the marketplace; desired effects of stock repurchases are an increase in earnings per share and (therefore) in the market price per share.

In recent years firms have increased their repurchasing of outstanding common stock in the marketplace. The practical motives for **stock repurchases** include obtaining shares to be used in acquisitions, having shares available for employee stock option plans, and retiring shares. Here we focus on retiring shares through repurchase, because this motive for repurchase is similar to the payment of cash dividends.

Stock Repurchases Viewed as a Cash Dividend

When common stock is repurchased for retirement, the underlying motive is to distribute excess cash to the owners. Generally, as long as earnings remain constant, the repurchase reduces the number of outstanding shares, raising the earnings per share and therefore the market price per share. The repurchase of common stock results in a type of *reverse dilution,* because the EPS and the market price are increased by reducing the number of shares outstanding. The net effect of the repurchase is similar to the payment of a cash dividend.

E x a m p l e ▼   Badd Company, a national sportswear chain, has released the following financial data:

NewsLine   STOCKS SPLITTING AMID SOARING MARKETS

Stock splits are on the rise, thanks to sharp run-ups in share prices, particularly in the technology sector. Investors have reacted favorably to these stock divisions, even though the moves themselves add no tangible value.

From trusty blue chips to red-hot tech issues, U.S. companies in record numbers are capitalizing on market euphoria by splitting their shares like Yule logs bound for the holiday hearth. Investors have responded positively, bidding share prices up even further, and stoking the eye-popping run-up seen on the U.S. stock markets in the last two months....

Although stock splits add zero liquidity or additional tangible value to investors, they nonetheless broadcast a bullish message that resonates powerfully with investors, experts say. A stock split lowers the price of a company's shares and usually makes them more attractive to more investors because more people are more likely to buy a $25 stock than one trading at $100 a share....

[I]t is not easy to dispel the seeming magic of stock splits. Wireless phone company Qualcomm Inc. announced a 2-for-1 split on May 10 [1999] and a 4-for-1 split three weeks ago. The company's stock closed Thursday at $466.50 a share, up more than 1,500% this year.

General Electric Co.'s 3-for-1 split on December 17 [1999] sent its share price up $3.50 to a then-record close at $151....

Not all stocks climb post-split. Shares of IBM Corp. surged...on January 26 [1999], the day that Big Blue announced a 2-for-1 split. By February 9, IBM's stock had fallen...on investors' concerns that technology shares were overpriced.

Rick Escherich, a managing director at J.P. Morgan & Co.,...said that institutional investors, still the force behind the market, do not care about the price of a single share because they think in dollars.... "An institutional investor won't say 'I want 500,000 shares.' They'll say, 'I want a million dollars' worth of stock,'" Escherich said.

"I would hope that companies are doing this [splitting] because they are optimistic about the long term, and that investors are bidding up shares because of attractive fundamentals," Escherich said. But he added that there is a lot of "psychology" in the market, and that can lead to dangerous investment strategies....

Source: Elizabeth Smith, "Stocks Splitting Amid Soaring Markets," Los Angeles Times, December 25, 1999, p. C-1.

Earnings available for common stockholders	$1,000,000
Number of shares of common stock outstanding	400,000
Earnings per share ($1,000,000 ÷ 400,000)	$2.50
Market price per share	$50
Price/earnings (P/E) ratio ($50 ÷ $2.50)	20

The firm wants to use $800,000 of its earnings either to pay cash dividends or to repurchase shares. If the firm pays cash dividends, the amount of the dividend would be $2 per share ($800,000 ÷ 400,000 shares). If the firm pays $52 per share to repurchase stock, it could repurchase approximately 15,385 shares ($800,000 ÷ $52 per share). As a result of this repurchase, 384,615 shares (400,000 shares − 15,385 shares) of common stock would remain outstanding. Earnings per share (EPS) would rise to $2.60 ($1,000,000 ÷ 384,615). If the stock still sold at 20 times earnings (P/E = 20), its market price could be estimated by multiplying the new EPS by this P/E ratio. The price would therefore rise to $52 per share ($2.60 × 20). In both cases, the stockholders would receive $2 per share: a $2 cash dividend in the dividend case or a $2 increase in share price ($50 per share to $52 per share) in the repurchase case.

Besides the advantage of an increase in per-share earnings, certain owner tax benefits also result. If the cash dividend were paid, the owners would have to pay ordinary income taxes on it, whereas the $2 increase in the market value of the stock that resulted from the repurchase would not be taxed until the owner sold the stock. Of course, when the stock is sold, the capital gain is taxed, but possibly at a more favorable rate than the one applied to ordinary income.

Accounting Entries

The accounting entries that result when common stock is repurchased are a reduction in cash and the establishment of a contra capital account called "treasury stock," which is shown as a deduction from stockholders' equity. The label *treasury stock* is used on the balance sheet to indicate the presence of repurchased shares.

The Repurchase Process

When a company intends to repurchase a block of outstanding shares, it should make shareholders aware of its intentions. Specifically, it should advise them of the purpose of the repurchase (acquisition, stock options, retirement) and the disposition (if any) planned for the repurchased shares (traded for shares of another firm, distribution to executives, or held in the treasury).

Review Questions

13–14 Why do firms issue *stock dividends*? Comment on the following statement: "I have a stock that promises to pay a 20% stock dividend every year, and therefore it guarantees that I will break even in 5 years."

13–15 Compare a *stock split* with a stock dividend.

13–16 What is the logic behind repurchasing shares of common stock to distribute excess cash to the firm's owners?

TYING IT ALL TOGETHER

This chapter described the key aspects of a firm's capital structure and its dividend policy. The discussion of capital structure centered on the EBIT–EPS approach to capital structure and some procedures for selecting the value-maximizing rather than EPS-maximizing capital structure. Dividend fundamentals included the residual theory of dividends and dividend irrelevance/relevance arguments, dividend policy, and forms of dividends other than cash. The importance of capital structure and dividends from the viewpoints of financial managers, financial markets, and investors are summarized in the Integrative Table that follows.

INTEGRATIVE TABLE

Making Capital Structure and Dividend Decisions

Role of **Financial Managers**	*Role of* **Financial Markets**	*Role of* **Investors**
Financial managers must understand the firm's cash flows, market responses to changing financial risks, and the associated rates of return in order to develop and recommend both the best capital structure and the best dividend policy. The effectiveness of these decisions will significantly influence the firm's cost of capital, capital budgeting decisions, and stock price, which should be maximized to achieve the firm's goal.	The financial markets serve as the forum in which investors respond to the firm's capital structure and dividend actions. If the investors' general view is unfavorable because they feel the firm's returns are below a competitive level given the accompanying risk, their actions in the market will drive share price down; favorable responses will raise share price. The financial markets allow capital structure and dividend information to be incorporated into share price.	Investors in the financial marketplace pay close attention to both the firm's capital structure and its dividend policy. They assess the firm's financial risk using ratios to evaluate capital structure, and they evaluate dividend policy to determine whether the firm's actions are consistent with its opportunities and their cash flow needs. The responses of investors to the firm's capital structure and dividend policy will cause them to buy or sell shares, which will directly affect share price. Positive responses that increase share price are the goal.

 Describe the basic types of capital, external assessment of capital structure, the capital structure of non-U.S. firms, and the optimal capital structure. Two basic types of capital—debt capital and equity capital—make up a firm's capital structure. Capital structure can be externally assessed by using the debt ratio and the times-interest-earned ratio. Non-U.S. companies tend to have much higher degrees of indebtedness than their U.S. counterparts, primarily because U.S. capital markets are much better developed.

The zero-growth valuation model can be used to define the firm's value as its after-tax EBIT divided by its weighted average cost of capital. Assuming that EBIT is constant, the value of the firm is maximized by minimizing its weighted average cost of capital (WACC). The optimal capital structure is the one that minimizes the WACC. Graphically, the firm's WACC exhibits a U-shape, whose minimum value defines the optimal capital structure that maximizes owner wealth.

LG2 Discuss the EBIT–EPS approach to capital structure. The EBIT–EPS approach evaluates capital structures in light of the returns they provide the firm's owners and their degree of financial risk. Under the EBIT–EPS approach, the preferred capital structure is the one that is expected to provide maximum EPS over the firm's expected range of EBIT. Graphically, this approach reflects risk in terms of the financial breakeven point and the slope of the capital structure line. The major shortcoming of EBIT–EPS analysis is that it concentrates on maximizing earnings rather than owners' wealth.

LG3 Review the return and risk of alternative capital structures, their relationship to market value, and other important capital structure considerations. The best capital structure can be selected by using a valuation model to link return and risk factors. The preferred capital structure is the one that results in the highest estimated share value, not the highest EPS. Other important nonquantitative factors, such as revenue stability, cash flow, contractual obligations, management preferences, control, external risk assessment, and timing, must also be considered when making capital structure decisions.

Explain cash dividend payment procedures, dividend reinvestment plans, the residual theory of dividends, and the key arguments with regard to dividend irrelevance or relevance. The cash dividend decision is normally made by the board of directors, which establishes the record and payment dates. Generally, the larger the dividend charged to retained earnings and paid in cash, the greater the amount of financing that must be raised externally. Some firms offer dividend reinvestment plans that allow stockholders to acquire shares in lieu of cash dividends.

The residual theory suggests that dividends should be viewed as the earnings left after all acceptable investment opportunities have been undertaken. Miller and Modigliani argue in favor of dividend irrelevance, using a perfect world wherein information content and clientele effects exist. Gordon and Lintner advance the theory of dividend relevance, basing their argument on the uncertainty-reducing effect of dividends, supported by their bird-in-the-hand argument. The actions of financial managers and stockholders tend to support the belief that dividend policy does affect stock value.

Understand the key factors involved in formulating a dividend policy and the three basic types of dividend policies. A firm's dividend policy should provide for sufficient financing and maximize the wealth of the firm's owners. Dividend policy is affected by certain legal, contractual, and internal constraints, as well as by growth prospects, owner considerations, and market considerations.

With a constant-payout-ratio dividend policy, the firm pays a fixed percentage of earnings to the owners each period; dividends move up and down with earnings, and no dividend is paid when a loss occurs. Under a regular dividend policy, the firm pays a fixed-dollar dividend each period; it increases the amount of dividends only after a proven increase in earnings has occurred. The low-regular-and-extra dividend policy is similar to the regular dividend policy, except that it pays an "extra dividend" in periods when the firm's earnings are higher than normal. The regular and the low-regular-and-extra dividend policies are generally preferred because their stable patterns of dividends reduce uncertainty.

Evaluate the key aspects of stock dividends, stock splits, and stock repurchases. The payment of stock dividends involves a shifting of funds between capital accounts rather than a use of funds. Shareholders receiving stock dividends receive nothing of value; the market value of their holdings, their proportion of ownership, and their share of total earnings remain unchanged. However, the firm may use stock dividends to satisfy owners and preserve its market value without having to use cash.

Stock splits are used to enhance trading activity of a firm's shares by lowering or raising the market price. A stock split merely involves accounting adjustments; it has no effect on the firm's cash or on its capital structure. Stock repurchases can be made in lieu of cash dividend payments to retire outstanding shares. They reduce the number of outstanding shares and thereby increase earnings per share and the market price per share. They also delay the tax burden of shareholders.

SELF-TEST EXERCISES   (Solutions in Appendix B)

ST 13–1 **EBIT–EPS analysis** Nesbitt Electronics is considering additional financing of $10,000. It currently has $50,000 of 12% (annual interest) bonds and 10,000 shares of common stock outstanding. The firm can obtain the financing through a 12% (annual interest) bond issue or through the sale of 1,000 shares of common stock. The firm has a 40% tax rate.
   a. Calculate two EBIT–EPS coordinates for each plan by selecting any two EBIT values and finding their associated EPS values.
   b. Plot the two financing plans on a set of EBIT–EPS axes.
   c. On the basis of your graph in part **b**, at what level of EBIT does the bond plan become superior to the stock plan?

ST 13–2 **Optimal capital structure**   Kona Macadamia Nut Company has collected the following data with respect to its capital structure, expected earnings per share, and required return.

Capital structure debt ratio	Expected earnings per share	Required return, k_s
0%	$3.12	13%
10	3.90	15
20	4.80	16
30	5.44	17
40	5.51	19
50	5.00	20
60	4.40	22

a. Compute the estimated share value associated with each of the capital structures, using the simplified method described in this chapter (see Equation 13.2).
b. Determine the optimal capital structure based on (1) maximization of expected earnings per share and (2) maximization of share value.
c. Which capital structure do you recommend? Why?

 ST 13–3 **Stock repurchase**   The Rigid Steel Company has earnings available for common stockholders of $2 million and 500,000 shares of common stock outstanding at $60 per share. The firm is currently contemplating the payment of $2 per share in cash dividends.
a. Calculate the firm's current earnings per share (EPS) and price/earnings (P/E) ratio.
b. If the firm can repurchase stock at $62 per share, how many shares can be purchased in lieu of making the proposed cash dividend payment?
c. How much will the EPS be after the proposed repurchase? Why?
d. If the stock sells at the old P/E ratio, what will the market price be after repurchase?
e. Compare and contrast the earnings per share before and after the proposed repurchase.
f. Compare and contrast the stockholders' position under the dividend and repurchase alternatives.

EXERCISES

 13–1 **Various capital structures**   Ultegra Corporation currently has $1 million in total assets and is totally equity-financed. It is contemplating a change in capital structure. Compute the amount of debt and equity that would be outstanding if the firm were to shift to each of the following debt ratios: 10%, 20%, 30%, 40%, 50%, 60%, and 90%. (*Note:* The amount of total assets would not change.) Is there a limit to the debt ratio's value?

13–2 EBIT–EPS and capital structure Williams Petroleum is considering two capital structures. The key information is shown in the following table. Assume a 40% tax rate.

Source of capital	Structure A	Structure B
Long-term debt	$100,000 at 16% coupon rate	$200,000 at 17% coupon rate
Common stock	4,000 shares	2,000 shares

a. Calculate two EBIT–EPS coordinates for each of the structures by selecting any two EBIT values and finding their associated EPS values.
b. Plot the two capital structures on a set of EBIT–EPS axes.
c. Indicate over what EBIT range, if any, each structure is preferred.
d. Discuss the leverage and risk aspects of each structure.
e. If the firm is fairly certain that its EBIT will exceed $75,000, which structure would you recommend? Why?

13–3 EBIT–EPS and preferred stock Paxton Diaper is considering two possible capital structures, A and B, shown in the following table. Assume a 40% tax rate.

Source of capital	Structure A	Structure B
Long-term debt	$75,000 at a 16% coupon rate	$50,000 at a 15% coupon rate
Preferred stock	$10,000 with an 18% annual dividend	$15,000 with an 18% annual dividend
Common stock	8,000 shares	10,000 shares

a. Calculate two EBIT–EPS coordinates for each of the structures by selecting any two EBIT values and finding their associated EPS values.
b. Graph the two capital structures on the same set of EBIT–EPS axes.
c. Discuss the leverage and risk associated with each of the structures.
d. Over what range of EBIT is each structure preferred?
e. Which structure do you recommend if the firm expects its EBIT to be $35,000? Explain.

13–4 Optimal capital structure Anson Corporation has collected the following data associated with four possible capital structures.

Capital structure debt ratio	Expected EPS	Estimated coefficient of variation of EPS
0%	$1.92	0.4743
20	2.25	0.5060
40	2.72	0.5581
60	3.54	0.6432

The firm's research indicates that the marketplace assigns the following required returns to risky earnings per share.

Coefficient of variation of EPS	Estimated required return, k_s
0.43	15%
0.47	16
0.51	17
0.56	18
0.60	22
0.64	24

a. Find the required return associated with each of the four capital structures.
b. Compute the estimated share value associated with each of the four capital structures, using the simplified method described in this chapter (see Equation 13.2).
c. Determine the optimal capital structure on the basis of (1) maximization of expected EPS and (2) maximization of share value.
d. Construct a graph (similar to Figure 13.4) showing the relationships in part c.
e. Which capital structure do you recommend? Why?

LG2 LG3   13–5   Integrative—Optimal capital structure   Trisport Corporation wishes to analyze five possible capital structures—0%, 15%, 30%, 45%, and 60% debt ratios. The firm's total assets of $1 million are assumed to be constant. Its common stock has a book value of $25 per share, and the firm is in the 40% tax bracket. The following additional data have been gathered for use in analyzing the five capital structures under consideration.

Capital structure debt ratio	Interest rate on debt, k_d	Expected EPS	Required return, k_s
0%	0.0%	$3.60	10.0%
15	8.0	4.03	10.5
30	10.0	4.50	11.6
45	13.0	4.95	14.0
60	17.0	5.18	20.0

a. Calculate the amount of debt, the amount of equity, and the number of shares of common stock outstanding for each of the capital structures being considered.
b. Calculate the annual interest on the debt under each of the capital structures being considered. (*Note:* The interest rate given is applicable to all debt associated with the corresponding debt ratio.)
c. Calculate the EPS associated with $150,000 and $250,000 of EBIT for each of the five capital structures being considered.

d. Using the EBIT–EPS data developed in part **c,** plot the capital structures on the same set of EBIT–EPS axes, and discuss the ranges over which each is preferred. What is the major problem with the use of this approach?

e. Using the valuation model given in Equation 13.2 and the appropriate data, estimate the share value for each of the capital structures being considered.

f. Construct a graph similar to Figure 13.4, showing the relationships between the debt ratio (*x* axis) and expected EPS (*y* axis) and share value (*y* axis).

g. Referring to the graph in part **f:** Which structure is preferred if the goal is to maximize EPS? Which structure is preferred if the goal is to maximize share value? Which capital structure do you recommend? Explain.

13–6 **Dividend payment procedures**   At the quarterly dividend meeting, Philadelphia Foundry declared a cash dividend of $1.10 per share for holders of record on Monday, July 10. The firm has 300,000 shares of common stock outstanding and has set a payment date of July 31. Prior to the dividend declaration, the firm's key accounts were as follows:

Cash	$500,000	Dividends payable	$ 0
		Retained earnings	2,500,000

a. Show the entries after the meeting adjourned.

b. When is the ex dividend date?

c. What values will the key accounts have after the July 31 payment date?

d. What effect, if any, will the dividend have on the firm's total assets?

e. Ignoring general market fluctuations, what effect, if any, will the dividend have on the firm's stock price on the ex dividend date?

13–7 **Alternative dividend policies**   Over the last 10 years, a firm has had the earnings per share shown in the following table.

Year	Earnings per share
2001	$4.00
2000	3.80
1999	3.20
1998	2.80
1997	3.20
1996	2.40
1995	1.20
1994	1.80
1993	– .50
1992	.25

a. If the firm's dividend policy were based on a constant payout ratio of 40% for all years with positive earnings and 0% otherwise, what would be the annual dividend for each year?

b. If the firm had a dividend payout of $1.00 per share, increasing by $.10 per share whenever the dividend payout fell below 50% for two consecutive years, what annual dividend would the firm pay each year?

c. If the firm's policy were to pay $.50 per share each period except when earnings per share exceed $3.00, when an extra dividend equal to 80% of earnings beyond $3.00 would be paid, what annual dividend would the firm pay each year?

d. Discuss the pros and cons of each dividend policy described in **a** through **c.**

   13–8   Cash versus stock dividend   American Steel has the stockholders' equity account given below. The firm's common stock currently sells for $4 per share.

Preferred stock	$ 100,000
Common stock (400,000 shares at $1 par)	400,000
Paid-in capital in excess of par	200,000
Retained earnings	320,000
Total stockholders' equity	$1,020,000

a. Show the effects on the firm of a cash dividend of $.01, $.05, $.10, and $.20 per share.

b. Show the effects on the firm of a 1%, 5%, 10%, and 20% stock dividend.

c. Compare the effects in parts **a** and **b.** What are the significant differences between the two methods of paying dividends?

13–9   Stock repurchase   The following financial data on the Growth Stock Company are available:

Earnings available for common stockholders	$800,000
Number of shares of common stock outstanding	400,000
Earnings per share ($800,000 ÷ 400,000)	$2
Market price per share	$20
Price/earnings (P/E) ratio ($20 ÷ $2)	10

The firm is currently contemplating using $400,000 of its earnings to pay cash dividends of $1 per share or repurchase stock at $21 per share.

a. Approximately how many shares of stock can the firm repurchase at the $21-per-share price, using the funds that would have gone to pay the cash dividend?

b. Calculate the EPS after the repurchase. Explain your calculations.

c. If the stock still sells at 10 times earnings, what will the market price be after the repurchase?

d. Compare the pre- and post-repurchase earnings per share.

e. Compare and contrast the stockholders' positions under the dividend and repurchase alternatives. What are the tax implications under each alternative?

web exercises   Search

Go to web site **www.smartmoney.com**. In the column on the right under **Quotes & Research**, enter the symbol DIS; click **Stock Snapshot**; and then click **Go**.
1. What is the market value of Walt Disney Co.?
Click on **Financials**
2. Under Annual Financials, what is Disney's most recent revenues? Under Financial Trends, what is its operating margin percentage?
3. Calculate its EBIT by multiplying its revenues by its operating margin percentage.
4. Assuming a tax rate (T) of 40% and by using equation 13.1 on page 392, calculate the value of Disney using a weighted average cost of capital (k_a) of 5%.
5. Prepare a table with the following column headings. Symbol; Company Name; Market Value; Revenues; Operating Margin %; EBIT; and Value. Enter into the table the information you found in Questions 1 through 4.
At the bottom of the screen under Stock Search, enter the next stock symbol from the list below, click Submit. After you find the name of each company and the Market Value, click Financials. Enter into your table the Symbol; Company Name; Market Value; Revenues; and Operating Margin % for each of the listed companies. Complete the table by answering questions 3 and 4.

Symbol
AIT   MRK   LG   LUV   IBM   GE   BUD   PFE   INTC

6. Now rank these companies by their Market Value. Then, rank them by the Value you calculated. Generally what conclusion can you come to about the relationship between Market Value and the Value you calculated? Can you give possible explanations to the exceptions?

Go to web site **www.smartmoney.com**. In the column on the right under **Quotes & Research**, enter the symbol DIS; click **Stock Snapshot**; and then click **Go**.
7. What is the name of the company?
8. What is its dividend amount? Its dividend frequency? Its dividend yield?
9. Prepare a table with the following column headings: Symbol; Company Name; Dividend Amount ($): Dividend Frequency; Dividend Yield(%). Enter into the table the information you found in Questions 7 and 8.
   Enter the next stock symbol from the list below, click **Stock Snapshot**, and then click **Go**. Enter into your table the company name and the dividend information for each of the listed companies.

Symbol
AIT   MRK   LG   LUV   IBM   GE   BUD   PFE   INTC

10. Which companies have the lowest dividend yields?
11. Which companies have the highest dividend yields?

For additional practice with concepts from this chapter, visit
http://www.awl.com/gitman_madura

Financial Planning

LEARNING GOALS

LG1 Understand the financial planning process, including long-term (strategic) financial plans and short-term (operating) financial plans.

LG2 Discuss cash planning, sales forecasts, and the procedures for preparing the cash budget.

LG3 Describe how the cash budget is evaluated and the procedures for coping with uncertainty in the cash budget.

LG4 Prepare a pro forma income statement using both the percent-of-sales method and a breakdown of costs and expenses into their fixed and variable components.

LG5 Explain the procedures used to develop a pro forma balance sheet using the judgmental approach and an "external financing required" figure.

LG6 Cite the weaknesses of the simplified approaches to pro forma preparation and the common uses of pro forma financial statements.

The Financial Planning Process

Financial planning is an important aspect of the firm's operations, because it provides road maps for guiding, coordinating, and controlling the firm's actions to achieve its objectives. Two key aspects of the financial planning process are *cash planning* and *profit planning*. Cash planning involves preparation of the firm's cash budget; profit planning involves preparation of pro forma financial statements. Both the cash budget and the pro forma statements are useful for internal financial planning; they also are routinely required by existing and prospective lenders.

The **financial planning process** begins with long-term, or *strategic,* financial plans. These in turn guide the formulation of short-term, or *operating,* plans and budgets. Generally, the short-term plans and budgets implement the firm's long-term strategic objectives. Although the major emphasis in this chapter is on preparing short-term financial plans and budgets, we begin with a few comments on long-term financial plans.

financial planning process
Planning that begins with long-term, or *strategic,* financial plans that in turn guide the formulation of short-term, or *operating,* plans and budgets.

Long-Term (Strategic) Financial Plans

Long-term (strategic) financial plans lay out a company's planned financial actions and the anticipated impact of those actions over periods ranging from 2 to 10 years. Five-year strategic plans, which are revised as significant new information becomes available, are common. Generally, firms that are subject to high degrees of operating uncertainty, relatively short production cycles, or both, tend to use shorter planning horizons. Long-term financial plans are part of an integrated strategy that, along with production and marketing plans, guides the firm toward achievement of strategic goals. Such plans tend to be supported by a series of annual budgets and profit plans.

long-term (strategic) financial plans
Lay out a company's planned financial actions and the anticipated impact of those actions over periods ranging from 2 to 10 years.

Short-Term (Operating) Financial Plans

Short-term (operating) financial plans specify short-term financial actions and the anticipated impact of those actions. These plans most often cover a 1- to 2-year period. Key inputs include the sales forecast and various forms of operating and financial data. Key outputs include a number of operating budgets, the cash budget, and pro forma financial statements. The entire short-term financial planning process is outlined in Figure 14.1.

Short-term financial planning begins with the sales forecast. From it, production plans are developed that take into account lead (preparation) times and include estimates of the required raw materials. Using the production plans, the firm can estimate direct labor requirements, factory overhead outlays, and operating expenses. Once these estimates have been made, the firm's pro forma income statement and cash budget can be prepared. With the basic inputs (pro forma income statement, cash budget, fixed asset outlay plan, long-term financing plan, and current-period balance sheet), the pro forma balance sheet can finally be developed.

Throughout the remainder of this chapter, we will concentrate on the key outputs of the short-term financial planning process: the cash budget, the pro

short-term (operating) financial plans
Specify short-term financial actions and the anticipated impact of those actions.

FIGURE 14.1   **Short-Term Financial Planning**
The short-term (operating) financial planning process.

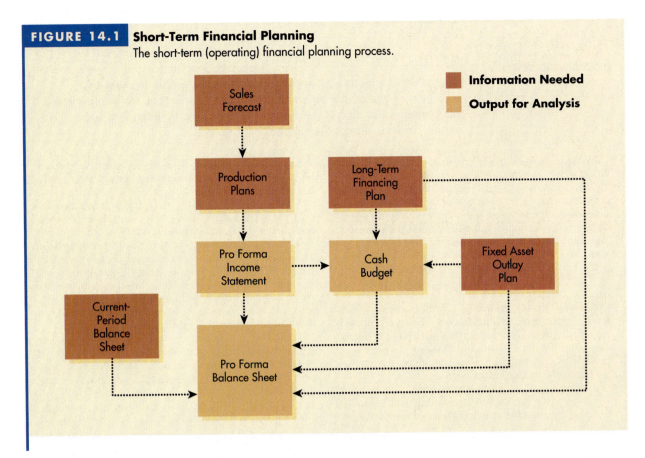

forma income statement, and the pro forma balance sheet. Although they are not specifically discussed in this chapter, electronic spreadsheets are widely used to streamline the process of preparing and evaluating these short-term financial planning statements.

? Review Questions

14–1   Contrast long-term (strategic) financial plans and short-term (operating) financial plans.

14–2   Which three statements result as part of the short-term (operating) financial planning process?

Cash Planning: Cash Budgets

cash budget (cash forecast)
A statement of the firm's planned inflows and outflows of cash that is used by the firm to estimate its short-term cash requirements.

The **cash budget,** or **cash forecast,** is a statement of the firm's planned inflows and outflows of cash. It is used by the firm to estimate its short-term cash requirements, with particular attention to planning for surplus cash and for cash shortages.

Typically, the cash budget is designed to cover a 1-year period, divided into smaller time intervals. The number and type of intervals depend on the nature of

REVOLUTION IN PLANNING

Like other disciplines, financial planning must evolve to meet the changing needs of a company's business environment. Re-engineering the planning function is a lot more difficult, time-consuming, and expensive than companies expect.

[M]arket pressures dictate that businesses plan better. At Nortel Networks Corp., a Toronto-based global telecommunications equipment supplier with $17.6 billion in 1998 revenues, "we have short windows of opportunity and short time frames to market," explains Peter Browne, vice president, business planning and analysis. Yet the company's traditional process "reflected where we were five years ago, when we could take as much time as needed to perfect a product. Today, customers want the product immediately; we had to change the planning processes to satisfy that need."…

Two years ago, in an effort to stop the madness, Nortel's finance group reviewed the process. The team…quickly realized that the current process involved a series of discrete events that did not respond to its changing customer needs and market opportunities. "They were financial exercises, not business exercises," Mackinnon says.…

In Nortel's old planning environment, the company would prepare profit-and-loss statements with up to 100 line-item details. After examining the numbers [that] man-

agement mainly relied on to run the business, the company whittled it down to 8, including cost of sales and research and development.

Tying those targets into the strategic plan is now a continuous process that starts when a senior management group at headquarters defines the business objectives and communicates them to the presidents of Nortel's two operating lines. The dialogue continues on down through the five presidents within the operating divisions, to the general managers, department heads, and so on. Then, says Browne, "we take the strategic objectives and turn them into tactical objectives, and at the same time come up with a plan that meets the financial performance expectations."

The result has been a newfound nimbleness. "Our culture is predicated on action now," says Browne. "By linking our planning process to an ongoing validation of strategic directions and near-term financial dynamics, we can adjust direction to drive growth."

Source: Russ Banham, "Revolution in Planning," CFO, August 1999, downloaded from http://www.cfonet.com/html/Articles/CFO/1999/99AUrevo.html.

the business. The more seasonal and uncertain a firm's cash flows, the greater the number of intervals. Because many firms are confronted with a seasonal cash flow pattern, the cash budget is quite often presented on a monthly basis. Firms with stable patterns of cash flow may use quarterly or annual time intervals.

 ## The Sales Forecast

sales forecast
The prediction of the firm's sales over a given period on the basis of external and/or internal data; used as the key input to the short-term financial planning process.

The key input to the short-term financial planning process is the **sales forecast.** This prediction of the firm's sales over a given period is prepared by the marketing department. On the basis of the sales forecast, the financial manager estimates the monthly cash flows that will result from projected sales receipts and from outlays related to production, inventory, and sales. The manager also determines the level of fixed assets required and the amount of financing, if any, needed to support the forecast level of sales and production. In practice, obtaining good data is the most difficult aspect of forecasting.

The sales forecast may be based on an analysis of *external data* by using the relationships observed between the firm's sales and certain key external economic indicators such as the gross domestic product (GDP), new housing starts, and disposable personal income. Alternatively, *internal data* could be used to develop a sales forecast based on a buildup of sales forecasts obtained through the firm's own sales channels. Firms generally use a combination of external and internal

TABLE 14.1	The General Format of the Cash Budget					
	Jan.	Feb.	...	Nov.	Dec.
Cash receipts	$XXX	$XXG		$XXM	$XXT
Less: Cash disbursements	XXA	XXH	...	XXN	XXU
Net cash flow	$XXB	$XXI		$XXO	$XXV
Add: Beginning cash	XXC	XXD	XXJ	XXP	XXQ
Ending cash	$XXD	$XXJ		$XXQ	$XXW
Less: Minimum cash balance	XXE	XXK	...	XXR	XXY
Required total financing		$XXL		$XXS	
Excess cash balance	$XXF				$XXZ

forecast data to make the final sales forecast. The internal data provide insight into sales expectations, and the external data are used to adjust these expectations to account for general economic factors.

Preparing the Cash Budget

The general format of the cash budget is presented in Table 14.1. We will discuss each of its components individually.

Cash Receipts

cash receipts
All of a firm's inflows of cash in a given financial period.

Cash receipts include all of a firm's inflows of cash in a given financial period. The most common components of cash receipts are cash sales, collections of accounts receivable, and other cash receipts.

Example ▼ Intercon Company, a small defense subcontractor, is developing a cash budget for October, November, and December. Intercon's sales in August and September were $100,000 and $200,000, respectively. Sales of $400,000, $300,000, and $200,000 have been forecast for October, November, and December. Historically, 20% of the firm's sales have been for cash, 50% have generated accounts receivable collected after 1 month, and the remaining 30% have generated accounts receivable collected after 2 months. Bad debt expenses (uncollectible accounts) have been negligible. In December, the firm will receive a $30,000 dividend from stock in a subsidiary. The schedule of expected cash receipts for the company is presented in Table 14.2 on page 428. It contains the following items.

Forecast sales   This initial entry is merely informational. It is provided as an aid in calculating other sales-related items.

Cash sales   The cash sales shown for each month represent 20% of the total sales forecast for that month.

Collections of A/R   These entries represent the collection of accounts receivable (A/R) resulting from sales in earlier months.

TABLE 14.2	A Schedule of Projected Cash Receipts for Intercon Company ($000)				
	Aug.	Sept.	Oct.	Nov.	Dec.
Forecast sales	$100	$200	$400	$300	$200
Cash sales (0.20)	$ 20	$ 40	$ 80	$ 60	$ 40
Collections of A/R:					
Lagged 1 month (0.50)		50	100	200	150
Lagged 2 months (0.30)			30	60	120
Other cash receipts					30
Total cash receipts			$210	$320	$340

Lagged 1 month   These figures represent sales made in the preceding month that generated accounts receivable collected in the current month. Because 50% of the current month's sales are collected 1 month later, the collections of A/R with a 1-month lag shown for September represent 50% of the sales in August, collections for October represent 50% of September sales, and so on.

Lagged 2 months   These figures represent sales made 2 months earlier that generated accounts receivable collected in the current month. Because 30% of sales are collected 2 months later, the collections with a 2-month lag shown for October represent 30% of the sales in August, and so on.

Other cash receipts   These are cash receipts expected from sources other than sales. Interest received, dividends received, proceeds from the sale of equipment, stock and bond sale proceeds, and lease receipts may show up here. For Intercon Company, the only other cash receipt is the $30,000 dividend due in December.

Total cash receipts   This figure represents the total of all the cash receipts listed for each month. For Intercon Company, we are concerned only with October, November, and December, as shown in Table 14.2.

Cash Disbursements

cash disbursements
All outlays of cash by the firm during a given financial period.

Cash disbursements include all outlays of cash by the firm during a given financial period. The most common cash disbursements are

Cash purchases	Fixed asset outlays
Payments of accounts payable	Interest payments
Rent (and lease) payments	Cash dividend payments
Wages and salaries	Principal payments (loans)
Tax payments	Repurchases or retirements of stock

It is important to recognize that depreciation and other noncash charges are *not* included in the cash budget, because they merely represent a scheduled write-off of an earlier cash outflow. The impact of depreciation, as noted in Chapter 9, is reflected in the reduced cash outflow for tax payments.

Example ▼ Intercon Company has gathered the following data needed for the preparation of a cash disbursements schedule for October, November, and December.

Purchases   The firm's purchases represent 70% of sales. Of this amount, 10% is paid in cash, 70% is paid in the month immediately following the month of purchase, and the remaining 20% is paid 2 months following the month of purchase.

Rent payments   Rent of $5,000 will be paid each month.

Wages and salaries   Fixed salary cost for the year is $96,000, or $8,000 per month. In addition, wages are estimated as 10% of monthly sales.

Tax payments   Taxes of $25,000 must be paid in December.

Fixed asset outlays   New machinery costing $130,000 will be purchased and paid for in November.

Interest payments   An interest payment of $10,000 is due in December.

Cash dividend payments   Cash dividends of $20,000 will be paid in October.

Principal payments (loans)   A $20,000 principal payment is due in December.

Repurchases or retirements of stock   No repurchase or retirement of stock is expected between October and December.

The firm's cash disbursements schedule, using the preceding data, is shown in Table 14.3 on page 430. Some items in the table are explained in greater detail below.

Purchases   This entry is merely informational. The figures represent 70% of the forecast sales for each month. They have been included to facilitate calculation of the cash purchases and related payments.

Cash purchases   The cash purchases for each month represent 10% of the month's purchases.

Payments of A/P   These entries represent the payment of accounts payable (A/P) resulting from purchases in earlier months.

Lagged 1 month   These figures represent purchases made in the preceding month that are paid for in the current month. Because 70% of the firm's purchases are paid for 1 month later, the payments with a 1-month lag shown for September represent 70% of the August purchases, payments for October represent 70% of the September purchases, and so on.

Lagged 2 months   These figures represent purchases made 2 months earlier that are paid for in the current month. Because 20% of the firm's purchases are paid for 2 months later, the payments with a 2-month lag for October represent 20% of the August purchases, and so on.

Wages and salaries   These amounts were obtained by adding $8,000 to 10% of the sales in each month. The $8,000 represents the fixed salary component; the rest represents wages.

▲ The remaining items on the cash disbursements schedule are self-explanatory.

TABLE 14.3	A Schedule of Projected Cash Disbursements for Intercon Company ($000)				
Purchases (0.70 × sales)	Aug. $70	Sept. $140	Oct. $280	Nov. $210	Dec. $140
Cash purchases (0.10)	$ 7	$ 14	$ 28	$ 21	$ 14
Payments of A/P:					
Lagged 1 month (0.70)		49	98	196	147
Lagged 2 months (0.20)			14	28	56
Rent payments			5	5	5
Wages and salaries			48	38	28
Tax payments					25
Fixed asset outlays				130	
Interest payments					10
Cash dividend payments			20		
Principal payments					20
Total cash disbursements			$213	$418	$305

net cash flow
The mathematical difference between the firm's cash receipts and its cash disbursements in each period.

ending cash
The sum of the firm's beginning cash and its net cash flow for the period.

required total financing
Amount of funds needed by the firm if the ending cash for the period is less than the desired minimum cash balance; typically represented by notes payable.

excess cash balance
The (excess) amount available for investment by the firm if the period's ending cash is greater than the desired minimum cash balance; assumed to be invested in marketable securities.

Net Cash Flow, Ending Cash, Financing, and Excess Cash

Look back at the general-format cash budget in Table 14.1. We have inputs for the first two entries, and we now continue calculating the firm's cash needs. The firm's **net cash flow** is found by subtracting the cash disbursements from cash receipts in each period. Then, we add beginning cash to the firm's net cash flow to determine the **ending cash** for each period. Finally, we subtract the desired minimum cash balance from ending cash to find either the **required total financing** or the **excess cash balance.** If the ending cash is less than the minimum cash balance, *financing* is required. Such financing is typically viewed as short-term and therefore represented by notes payable. If the ending cash is greater than the minimum cash balance, *excess cash* exists. Any excess cash is assumed to be invested in a liquid, short-term, interest-paying vehicle—that is, in marketable securities.

Example ▼

Table 14.4 presents Intercon Company's cash budget, based on the data already developed. At the end of September, Intercon's cash balance was $50,000, and its notes payable and marketable securities equaled $0. The company wishes to maintain, as a reserve for unexpected needs, a minimum cash balance of $25,000.

For Intercon Company to maintain its required $25,000 ending cash balance, it will need total borrowing of $76,000 in November and $41,000 in December. In October, the firm will have an excess cash balance of $22,000, which can be held in an interest-earning marketable security. The required total financing figures in the cash budget refer to *how much will be owed at the end of the month;* they do *not* represent the monthly changes in borrowing.

The monthly changes in borrowing and in excess cash can be found by further analyzing the cash budget. In October, the $50,000 beginning cash, which becomes $47,000 after the $3,000 net cash outflow, results in a $22,000 excess cash balance once the $25,000 minimum cash is deducted. In November, the $76,000 of required total financing resulted from the $98,000 net cash outflow less the $22,000 of excess cash from October. The $41,000 of required total

TABLE 14.4   **A Cash Budget for Intercon Company ($000)**

	Oct.	Nov.	Dec.
Total cash receipts[a]	$210	$320	$340
Less: Total cash disbursements[b]	213	418	305
Net cash flow	$ (3)	$ (98)	$ 35
Add: Beginning cash	50	47	(51)
Ending cash	$ 47	$ (51)	$ (16)
Less: Minimum cash balance	25	25	25
Required total financing (notes payable)[c]	—	$ 76	$ 41
Excess cash balance (marketable securities)[d]	$ 22	—	—

[a]From Table 14.2.
[b]From Table 14.3.
[c]Values are placed in this line when the ending cash is less than the desired minimum cash balance. These amounts are typically financed short-term and therefore are represented by notes payable.
[d]Values are placed in this line when the ending cash is greater than the desired minimum cash balance. These amounts are typically assumed to be invested short-term and therefore are represented by marketable securities.

financing in December resulted from reducing November's $76,000 of required total financing by the $35,000 of net cash inflow during December. Summarizing, the financial activities for each month were as follows:

October: Invest the $22,000 excess cash balance in marketable securities.

November: Liquidate the $22,000 of marketable securities and borrow $76,000 (notes payable).

December: Repay $35,000 of notes payable, to leave $41,000 of outstanding required total financing.

Evaluating the Cash Budget

The cash budget indicates whether a cash shortage or surplus is expected in each of the months covered by the forecast. Each month's figure is based on the internally imposed requirement of a minimum cash balance and *represents the total balance at the end of the month*.

At the end of each of the 3 months, Intercon Company expects the following balances in cash, marketable securities, and notes payable:

Account	End-of-month balance ($000)		
	Oct.	Nov.	Dec.
Cash	$25	$25	$25
Marketable securities	22	0	0
Notes payable	0	76	41

 **THE CASH FORECASTER'S ALMANAC**

Eliminating unnecessary detail from its sales forecasting procedures has reduced the time it takes Alcan Aluminum to prepare forecasts. Alcan's risk manager applies qualitative judgment to quantitive data to develop meaningful and accurate forecasts.

Linda A. Lepore is risk manager at $8-billion (in U.S. dollars) Alcan Aluminum Ltd., Montreal.... Alcan has streamlined its forecasting process and reduced the time spent preparing it.

"We've stopped asking for detail that doesn't add value," she explains. "We ask for summary forecasts and compare them to actual results. Only when we find a problem do we ask ... for detail."

Alcan ... builds its corporate forecast by compiling the forecasts of its divisions. Sales forecasts are used to project revenue; raw materials forecasts are used to project expenses. The forecast is based on prospective, not historical, business....

"I take the information the divisions give me, look at the total, compare the forecast to historic actuals and decide that some of the numbers don't make sense," she explains. "So I start looking for reasons. Usually someone has forgotten to include capital expenditures. Based on what I learn, and sometimes on my gut feeling, I make adjustments to the forecast." She uses actual data to see where the forecasts break down....

She uses a simple spreadsheet for forecasting because she finds that commercially available forecasting software is too detailed. "Most of the systems I've seen analyze the transactions to death. They go through the portfolios supplier by supplier and customer by customer, looking at how much you have to pay or collect from each on which days. We don't care who the suppliers and customers are; we just need to know the total," she says....

Alcan forecasts primarily to minimize its borrowing. "We don't like to borrow, and we certainly don't like to have borrowed money invested for several days," she explains. Alcan's liquidity cushion is a $100 million pool of cash invested in short-term instruments. "We keep that float for ourselves and can draw down on it any day we need cash," she says. "History tells us that at our size and in our line of business, $100 million is the right amount."

Source: Richard H. Gamble, "The Cash Forecaster's Almanac," Controller (now called Business Finance), May 1998, downloaded from www.businessfinancemag.com/archives/main.cfm.

Note that the firm is assumed first to liquidate its marketable securities to meet deficits and then to borrow with notes payable if additional financing is needed. As a result, it will not have marketable securities and notes payable on its books at the same time.

Because it may be necessary to borrow up to $76,000 for the 3-month period, the financial manager should be certain that some arrangement is made to ensure the availability of these funds. The manager will usually seek to borrow more than the maximum financing indicated in the cash budget, because of the uncertainty of the ending cash values.

 ## Coping with Uncertainty in the Cash Budget

Aside from careful estimation of cash budget inputs, there are two ways of coping with the uncertainty of the cash budget. One is to prepare several cash budgets—based on pessimistic, most likely, and optimistic forecasts. From this range of cash flows, the financial manager can determine the amount of financing necessary to cover the most adverse situation. The use of several cash budgets, based on differing assumptions, also should give the financial manager a sense of the riskiness of various alternatives. This *sensitivity analysis*, or "what

TABLE 14.5 A Sensitivity Analysis of Intercon Company's Cash Budget ($000)

	October			November			December		
	Pessi-mistic	Most likely	Opti-mistic	Pessi-mistic	Most likely	Opti-mistic	Pessi-mistic	Most likely	Opti-mistic
Total cash receipts	$160	$210	$285	$210	$320	$410	$275	$340	$422
Less: Total cash disbursements	200	213	248	380	418	467	280	305	320
Net cash flow	$(40)	$(3)	$37	$(170)	$(98)	$(57)	$(5)	$35	$102
Add: Beginning cash	50	50	50	10	47	87	(160)	(51)	30
Ending cash	$10	$47	$87	$(160)	$(51)	$30	$(165)	$(16)	$132
Less: Minimum cash balance	25	25	25	25	25	25	25	25	25
Required total financing	$15	—	—	$185	$76	—	$190	$41	—
Excess cash balance	—	$22	$62	—	—	$5	—	—	$107

if" approach, is often used to analyze cash flows under a variety of circumstances. Computers and electronic spreadsheets simplify the process of performing sensitivity analysis.

Example ▼ Table 14.5 presents the summary of Intercon Company's cash budget prepared for each month of concern using pessimistic, most likely, and optimistic estimates of total cash receipts and disbursements. The most likely estimate is based on the expected outcomes presented earlier.

During October, Intercon will, at worst, need a maximum of $15,000 of financing and will, at best, have a $62,000 excess cash balance. During November, its financing requirement will be between $0 and $185,000, or it could experience an excess cash balance of $5,000. The December projections show maximum borrowing of $190,000 with a possible excess cash balance of $107,000. By considering the extreme values in the pessimistic and optimistic outcomes, Intercon Company should be better able to plan its cash requirements. For the 3-month period, the peak borrowing requirement under the worst circumstances would be $190,000, which happens to be considerably greater than the most likely estimate of $76,000 for this period.

A second and more sophisticated way of coping with uncertainty in the cash budget is *simulation* (discussed in Chapter 11). By simulating the occurrence of sales and other uncertain events, the firm can develop a probability distribution of its ending cash flows for each month. The financial decision maker can then use the probability distribution to determine the amount of financing needed to protect the firm adequately against a cash shortage.

Review Questions

14–3 What is the purpose of the cash budget? What role does the sales forecast play in its preparation?

14–4 Briefly describe the basic format of the cash budget.

14–5 How can the two "bottom lines" of the cash budget be used to determine the firm's short-term borrowing and investment requirements?

14–6 What is the cause of uncertainty in the cash budget, and what two techniques can be used to cope with this uncertainty?

LG4 Profit Planning: Pro Forma Statement Fundamentals

pro forma statements
Projected, or forecast, income statements and balance sheets.

Whereas cash planning focuses on forecasting cash flows, profit planning centers on the preparation of **pro forma statements,** which are projected, or forecast, income statements and balance sheets. The basic steps in this process were shown in Figure 14.1. Various approaches for estimating the pro forma statements are based on the belief that the financial relationships reflected in the firm's past financial statements will not change in the coming period. The commonly used approaches are presented in subsequent discussions.

Two key inputs are required for preparing pro forma statements: (1) financial statements for the preceding year and (2) the sales forecast for the coming year. A variety of assumptions must also be made. The company that we will use

TABLE 14.6	An Income Statement for Carson Manufacturing Company for the Year Ended December 31, 2001

Sales revenue		
Model X (1,000 units at $20/unit)	$20,000	
Model Y (2,000 units at $40/unit)	80,000	
Total sales		$100,000
Less: Cost of goods sold		
Labor	$28,500	
Material A	8,000	
Material B	5,500	
Overhead	38,000	
Total cost of goods sold		80,000
Gross profits		$ 20,000
Less: Operating expenses		10,000
Operating profits		$ 10,000
Less: Interest expense		1,000
Net profits before taxes		$ 9,000
Less: Taxes (0.15 × $9,000)		1,350
Net profits after taxes		$ 7,650
Less: Common stock dividends		4,000
To retained earnings		$ 3,650

TABLE 14.7	A Balance Sheet for Carson Manufacturing Company (December 31, 2001)

Assets		Liabilities and equities	
Cash	$ 6,000	Accounts payable	$ 7,000
Marketable securities	4,000	Taxes payable	300
Accounts receivable	13,000	Notes payable	8,300
Inventories	16,000	Other current liabilities	3,400
Total current assets	$39,000	Total current liabilities	$19,000
Net fixed assets	$51,000	Long-term debt	$18,000
Total assets	$90,000	Stockholders' equity	
		Common stock	$30,000
		Retained earnings	$23,000
		Total liabilities and stockholders' equity	$90,000

TABLE 14.8	2002 Sales Forecast for Carson Manufacturing Company

Unit sales	
Model X	1,500
Model Y	1,950
Dollar sales	
Model X ($25/unit)	$ 37,500
Model Y ($50/unit)	97,500
Total	$135,000

to illustrate the simplified approaches to pro forma preparation is Carson Manufacturing Company, which manufactures and sells one product. It has two basic product models—X and Y—which are produced by the same process but require different amounts of raw material and labor.

Preceding Year's Financial Statements

The income statement for the firm's 2001 operations is given in Table 14.6. It indicates that Carson had sales of $100,000, total cost of goods sold of $80,000, net profits before taxes of $9,000, and net profits after taxes of $7,650. The firm paid $4,000 in cash dividends, leaving $3,650 to be transferred to retained earnings. The firm's balance sheet for 2001 is given in Table 14.7.

Sales Forecast

Just as for the cash budget, the key input for pro forma statements is the sales forecast. The sales forecast for the coming year, based on both external and internal data, is presented in Table 14.8. The unit sale prices of the products reflect an increase from $20 to $25 for model X and from $40 to $50 for model Y. These increases are required to cover anticipated increases in costs.

Review Question

14–7 What two key inputs are required for preparing pro forma statements using the simplified approaches?

Preparing the Pro Forma Income Statement

percent-of-sales method
A simple method for developing the pro forma income statement; it forecasts sales and then expresses the various income statement items as percentages of projected sales.

A simple method for developing a pro forma income statement is the **percent-of-sales method.** It forecasts sales and then expresses the various income statement items as percentages of projected sales. The percentages used are likely to be the percentages of sales for these items in the previous year. By using dollar values taken from Carson's 2001 income statement (Table 14.6), we find that these percentages are

$$\frac{\text{Cost of goods sold}}{\text{Sales}} = \frac{\$80,000}{\$100,000} = 80.0\%$$

$$\frac{\text{Operating expenses}}{\text{Sales}} = \frac{\$10,000}{\$100,000} = 10.0\%$$

$$\frac{\text{Interest expense}}{\text{Sales}} = \frac{\$1,000}{\$100,000} = 1.0\%$$

Applying these percentages to the firm's forecast sales of $135,000 (developed in Table 14.8), we get the 2002 pro forma income statement in Table 14.9. We have assumed that Carson will pay $4,000 in common stock dividends, so the expected contribution to retained earnings is $6,327. This represents a considerable increase over $3,650 in the preceding year (Table 14.6).

Considering Types of Costs and Expenses

The technique used to prepare the pro forma income statement in Table 14.9 assumed that all the firm's costs and expenses are variable. That is, we assumed that for a given percentage increase in sales, the same percentage increase in cost of goods sold, operating expenses, and interest expense to sales would result. For example, as Carson's sales increased by 35 percent (from $100,000 in 2001 to $135,000 projected for 2002), we assumed that its cost of goods sold also increased by 35 percent (from $80,000 in 2001 to $108,000 projected for 2002). On the basis of this assumption, the firm's net profits before taxes also increased by 35 percent.

This approach implies that the firm will not receive the benefits that result from fixed costs when sales are increasing. Clearly, though, if the firm has fixed costs, these costs do not change when sales increase; the result is increased profits. By remaining unchanged when sales decline, these costs tend to lower profits.

TABLE 14.9	A Pro Forma Income Statement, Using the Percent-of-Sales Method, for Carson Manufacturing Company for the Year Ended December 31, 2002

Sales revenue	$135,000
Less: Cost of goods sold (0.80)	108,000
Gross profits	$ 27,000
Less: Operating expenses (0.10)	13,500
Operating profits	$ 13,500
Less: Interest expense (0.01)	1,350
Net profits before taxes	$ 12,150
Less: Taxes (0.15 × $12,150)	1,823
Net profits after taxes	$ 10,327
Less: Common stock dividends	4,000
To retained earnings	$ 6,327

Therefore, the use of past cost and expense ratios generally *tends to understate profits when sales are increasing.* (Likewise, it *tends to overstate profits when sales are decreasing.*) The best way to adjust for the presence of fixed costs when preparing a pro forma income statement is to break the firm's historical costs and expenses into *fixed* and *variable components.*

Example ▼ Carson Manufacturing Company's 2001 actual and 2002 pro forma income statements, broken into fixed and variable cost components, follow:

Income Statements
Carson Manufacturing Company

	2001 Actual	2002 Pro forma
Sales revenue	$100,000	$135,000
Less: Cost of good sold		
Fixed cost	40,000	40,000
Variable cost (0.40 × sales)	40,000	54,000
Gross profits	$ 20,000	$ 41,000
Less: Operating expenses		
Fixed expense	5,000	5,000
Variable expense (0.05 × sales)	5,000	6,750
Operating profits	$ 10,000	$ 29,250
Less: Interest expense (all fixed)	1,000	1,000
Net profits before taxes	$ 9,000	$ 28,250
Less: Taxes (0.15 × net profits before taxes)	1,350	4,238
Net profits after taxes	$ 7,650	$ 24,012

Breaking Carson's costs and expenses into fixed and variable components provides a more accurate projection of its pro forma profit. By assuming that *all* costs are variable (as shown in Table 14.9), we find that projected net profits before taxes would have been $12,150 (0.09 × $135,000 projected sales) instead of the $28,250 obtained by using the firm's fixed cost–variable cost breakdown.

Clearly, when using a simplified approach to pro forma income statement preparation, we should break down costs and expenses into fixed and variable components.

? Review Questions

14–8 How is the percent-of-sales method used to prepare pro forma income statements?

14–9 Why does the presence of fixed costs cause the percent-of-sales method of pro forma income statement preparation to fail? What's a better method?

🔵 Preparing the Pro Forma Balance Sheet

judgmental approach
A simplified approach for preparing the pro forma balance sheet under which the values of certain balance sheet accounts are estimated and the firm's external financing is used as a balancing, or "plug," figure.

A number of simplified approaches are available for preparing the pro forma balance sheet. Probably the best and most popular is the **judgmental approach,** under which the values of certain balance sheet accounts are estimated and the firm's external financing is used as a balancing, or "plug," figure. To apply the judgmental approach to prepare Carson Manufacturing Company's 2002 pro forma balance sheet, a number of assumptions must be made about levels of various balance sheet accounts:

1. A minimum cash balance of $6,000 is desired.
2. Marketable securities are assumed to remain unchanged from their current level of $4,000.
3. Accounts receivable on average represents 45 days of sales. Because Carson's annual sales are projected to be $135,000, accounts receivable should average $16,875 (1/8 × $135,000). (Forty-five days expressed fractionally is one-eighth of a year: 45/360 = 1/8.)
4. The ending inventory should remain at a level of about $16,000, of which 25 percent (approximately $4,000) should be raw materials and the remaining 75 percent (approximately $12,000) should consist of finished goods.
5. A new machine costing $20,000 will be purchased. Total depreciation for the year is $8,000. Adding the $20,000 acquisition to the existing net fixed assets of $51,000 and subtracting the depreciation of $8,000 yields net fixed assets of $63,000.
6. Purchases are expected to represent approximately 30 percent of annual sales, which in this case is approximately $40,500 (0.30 × $135,000). The firm estimates that it can take 72 days on average to satisfy its accounts payable. Thus accounts payable should equal one-fifth (72 days ÷ 360 days) of the firm's purchases, or $8,100 (1/5 × $40,500).
7. Taxes payable are expected to equal one-fourth of the current year's tax liability, which equals $455 (one-fourth of the tax liability of $1,823 shown in the pro forma income statement presented in Table 14.9).

8. Notes payable are assumed to remain unchanged from their current level of $8,300.
9. No change in other current liabilities is expected. They remain at the level of the previous year: $3,400.
10. The firm's long-term debt and its common stock are expected to remain unchanged at $18,000 and $30,000, respectively; no issues, retirements, or repurchases of bonds or stocks are planned.
11. Retained earnings will increase from the beginning level of $23,000 (from the balance sheet dated December 31, 2001, in Table 14.7) to $29,327. The increase of $6,327 represents the amount of retained earnings calculated in the year-end 2002 pro forma income statement in Table 14.9.

external financing required ("plug" figure)
Under the judgmental approach for developing a pro forma balance sheet, the amount of external financing needed to bring the statement into balance.

A 2002 pro forma balance sheet for Carson Manufacturing Company based on these assumptions is presented in Table 14.10. A **"plug" figure**—called the **external financing required**— of $8,293 is needed to bring the statement into balance. This means that the firm will have to obtain about $8,293 of additional external financing to support the increased sales level of $135,000 for 2002.

A *positive* value for "external financing required," like that shown in Table 14.10, means that to support the forecast level of operation, the firm must raise funds externally by using debt and/or equity financing or by reducing dividends. Once the form of financing is determined, the pro forma balance sheet is modified to replace "external financing required" with the planned increases in the debt and/or equity accounts.

A *negative* value for "external financing required" indicates that the firm's forecast financing is in excess of its needs. In this case, funds are available for use in repaying debt, repurchasing stock, or increasing dividends. Once the specific actions are determined, "external financing required" is replaced in the pro

---

TABLE 14.10   **A Pro Forma Balance Sheet, Using the Judgmental Approach, for Carson Manufacturing Company (December 31, 2002)**

Assets			Liabilities and equities	
Cash		$ 6,000	Accounts payable	$ 8,100
Marketable securities		4,000	Taxes payable	455
Accounts receivable		16,875	Notes payable	8,300
Inventories			Other current liabilities	3,400
Raw materials	$4,000		Total current liabilities	$ 20,255
Finished goods	12,000		Long-term debt	$ 18,000
Total inventory		16,000	Stockholders' equity	
Total current assets		$ 42,875	Common stock	$ 30,000
Net fixed assets		$ 63,000	Retained earnings	$ 29,327
Total assets		$ 105,875	Total	$ 97,582
			External financing required[a]	$ 8,293
			Total liabilities and stockholders' equity	$105,875

[a]The amount of external financing needed to force the firm's balance sheet to balance. Because of the nature of the judgmental approach, the balance sheet is not expected to balance without some type of adjustment.

forma balance sheet with the planned reductions in the debt and/or equity accounts. Obviously, besides being used to prepare the pro forma balance sheet, the judgmental approach is also frequently used specifically to estimate the firm's financing requirements.

? Review Questions

14–10 Describe the judgmental approach for simplified preparation of the pro forma balance sheet.

14–11 What is the significance of the "plug" figure called *external financing required?* Differentiate between the strategies associated with positive and negative values for external financing required.

LG6 Evaluation of Pro Forma Statements

It is difficult to forecast the many variables involved in pro forma statement preparation. As a result, investors, lenders, and managers frequently use the techniques presented in this chapter to make rough estimates of pro forma financial statements. However, it is important to recognize the basic weaknesses of these simplified pro forma approaches. The weaknesses lie in two assumptions: (1) that the firm's past financial condition is an accurate indicator of its future, and (2) that certain variables (such as cash, accounts receivable, and inventories) can be forced to take on certain "desired" values. These assumptions cannot be justified solely on the basis of their ability to simplify the calculations involved. However, despite their weaknesses, the simplified approaches to pro forma preparation are likely to remain popular because of their relative simplicity. Eventually, the use of computers to streamline financial planning will become the norm.

However pro forma statements are prepared, analysts must understand how to use them to make financial decisions. Both financial managers and lenders can use pro forma statements to analyze the firm's expected sources and uses of cash, as well as its liquidity, activity, debt, profitability, and market value. Various ratios can be calculated form the pro forma income statement and balance sheet to evaluate performance. Sources and uses can be evaluated by preparing a pro forma statement of cash flows. After analyzing the pro forma statements, the financial manager can take steps to adjust planned operations to achieve short-term financial goals. For example, if projected profits on the pro forma income statement are too low, a variety of pricing or cost-cutting actions, or both, might be initiated. If the projected level of accounts receivable on the pro forma balance sheet is too high, changes in credit or collection policy may be called for. Pro forma statements are therefore of key importance in solidifying the firm's financial plans for the coming year.

? Review Questions

14–12 What are the two key weaknesses of the simplified approaches to preparing pro forma statements?

14–13 What is the financial manager's objective in evaluating pro forma statements?

TYING IT ALL TOGETHER

The key aspects of financial planning were described in this chapter. The financial planning process begins with long-term (strategic) planning that guides short-term (operating) plans and budgets. Cash planning focuses primarily on preparation and evaluation of cash budgets. Profit planning, with particular emphasis on the preparation and interpretation of pro forma income statements and balance sheets, is an important aspect of financial planning. The importance of financial planning from the viewpoints of financial managers, financial markets, and investors is summarized in the Integrative Table that follows.

INTEGRATIVE TABLE

Planning Short-Term Cash Flows and Profits

Role of **Financial Managers**	*Role of* **Financial Markets**	*Role of* **Investors**
Financial managers must actively participate in the firm's long-term financial planning and must typically manage the firm's short-term financial planning. Their effectiveness in financial planning directly affects the firm's success in establishing and attaining realistic goals that allow the firm to remain competitive, grow markets and market share, and ultimately create value for the shareholders.	The financial markets serve as the locus of information exchange where financial managers can carefully disseminate information with regard to the firm's broad future plans and investors can gather and evaluate this information. Investor assessment of the firm's plans will affect the firm's share price, thereby providing market feedback to managers.	Investors monitor the firm' success in establishing and achieving its goals by focusing on the firm's competitive position, market share, and growth. Although investors will not be privy to the firm's detailed financial plans, they are aware of new initiatives and strategies, and they assess the firm's future success and value on the basis of their evaluation of this information.

 Understand the financial planning process, including long-term (strategic) financial plans and short-term (operating) financial plans. The two key aspects of the financial planning process are cash planning and profit planning. Cash planning involves the cash budget or cash forecast. Profit planning relies on the pro forma income statement and balance sheet. Long-term (strategic) financial plans act as a guide for preparing short-term (operating) financial plans. Long-term plans tend to cover periods ranging from 2 to 10 years. Short-term plans most often cover a 1- to 2-year period.

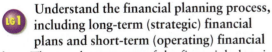 **Discuss cash planning, sales forecasts, and the procedures for preparing the cash budget.** The cash planning process uses the cash budget, based on a sales forecast, to estimate short-term cash surpluses and shortages. The sales forecast may be based on external or internal data or on a combination of the two. The cash budget is typically prepared for a 1-year period divided into months. It nets cash receipts and disbursements for each period to calculate net cash flow. Ending cash is estimated by adding beginning cash to the net cash flow. By subtracting the desired minimum cash balance from the ending cash, the financial manager can determine the required total financing (typically notes payable) or the excess cash balance (typically held as marketable securities).

LG3 Describe how the cash budget is evaluated and the procedures for coping with uncertainty in the cash budget. The cash budget indicates whether the firm is likely to have cash surpluses and allows the firm to arrange for adequate borrowing to meet forecast cash shortages. To cope with uncertainty in the cash budget, sensitivity analysis (preparation of several cash budgets) or simulation can be used.

LG4 Prepare a pro forma income statement using both the percent-of-sales method and a breakdown of costs and expenses into their fixed and variable components. A pro forma income statement can be developed by calculating past percentage relationships between certain cost and expense items and the firm's sales and then applying these percentages to forecast sales. Because this approach implies that all costs and expenses are variable, it tends to understate profits when sales are increasing and to overstate profits when sales are decreasing. This problem can be avoided by breaking down costs and expenses into fixed and variable components. In this case, only the variable costs and expenses are forecast on a percent-of-sales basis.

LG5 Explain the procedures used to develop a pro forma balance sheet using the judgmental approach and an "external financing required" figure. Under the judgmental approach, the values of certain balance sheet accounts are estimated, frequently on the basis of their relationship to sales, and the firm's external financing is used as a balancing, or "plug," figure. A positive value for "external financing required" means that the firm must raise funds externally, by using debt and/or equity financing or by reducing dividends; a negative value indicates that funds are available for use in repaying debt, repurchasing stock, or increasing dividends.

LG6 Cite the weaknesses of the simplified approaches to pro forma preparation and the common uses of pro forma financial statements. Simplified approaches for pro forma statement preparation, although popular, can be criticized for assuming that the firm's past financial condition is an accurate indicator of its future and that certain variables can be forced to take on certain "desired" values. Pro forma statements are commonly used to forecast and analyze the firm's level of profitability and overall financial performance so that adjustments can be made to planned operations in order to achieve short-term financial goals.

SELF-TEST EXERCISES   (Solutions in Appendix B)

  ST 14–1   Cash budget and pro forma balance sheet inputs Jane Madson, a financial analyst for Caldera Company, has prepared the following sales and cash disbursement estimates for the period February–June of the current year.

Month	Sales	Cash disbursements
February	$500	$400
March	600	300
April	400	600
May	200	500
June	200	200

Ms. Madson notes that historically, 30% of sales have been for cash. Of *credit sales,* 70% are collected 1 month after the sale, and the remaining 30% are collected 2 months after the sale. The firm wishes to maintain a minimum ending balance in its cash account of $25. Balances above this amount would be invested in short-term government securities (marketable securities), whereas any deficits would be financed through short-term bank borrowing (notes payable). The beginning cash balance at April 1 is $115.

a. Prepare a cash budget for April, May, and June.

b. How much financing, if any, at a maximum would Caldera Company need to meet its obligations during this 3-month period?

c. A pro forma balance sheet dated at the end of June is to be prepared from the information presented. Give the size of each of the following: cash, notes payable, marketable securities, and accounts receivable.

 ST 14–2   Pro forma income statement   Digital Designs, Inc., expects sales during 2002 to rise from the 2001 level of $3.5 million to $3.9 million. Because of a scheduled large loan payment, the interest expense in 2002 is expected to drop to $325,000. The firm plans to increase its cash dividend payments during 2002 to $320,000. The company's year-end 2001 income statement follows.

Income Statement Digital Designs, Inc. for the year ended December 31, 2001	
Sales revenue	$3,500,000
Less: Cost of goods sold	1,925,000
Gross profits	$1,575,000
Less: Operating expenses	420,000
Operating profits	$1,155,000
Less: Interest expense	400,000
Net profits before taxes	$ 755,000
Less: Taxes (rate = 40%)	302,000
Net profits after taxes	$ 453,000
Less: Cash dividends	250,000
To retained earnings	$ 203,000

a. Use the percent-of-sales method to prepare a 2002 pro forma income statement for Digital Designs, Inc.

b. Explain why the statement may underestimate the company's actual 2002 pro forma income.

EXERCISES

  14–1   Cash receipts   A firm has actual sales of $65,000 in April and $60,000 in May. It expects sales of $70,000 in June and $100,000 in July and in August. Assuming that sales are the only source of cash inflows and that half of these are for cash and the remainder are collected evenly over the following 2 months, what are the firm's expected cash receipts for June, July, and August?

14–2   Cash budget—Basic   Quality Digital Company had sales of $50,000 in March and $60,000 in April. Forecast sales for May, June, and July are $70,000, $80,000, and $100,000, respectively. The firm has a cash balance of $5,000 on May 1 and wishes to maintain a minimum cash balance of $5,000. Given the following data, prepare and interpret a cash budget for the months of May, June, and July.

(1) The firm makes 20% of its sales for cash, 60% are collected in the next month, and the remaining 20% are collected in the second month following sale.

(2) The firm receives other income of $2,000 per month.

(3) The firm's actual or expected purchases, all made for cash, are $50,000, $70,000, and $80,000 for the months of May through July, respectively.

(4) Rent is $3,000 per month.

(5) Wages and salaries are 10% of the previous month's sales.

(6) Cash dividends of $3,000 will be paid in June.

(7) Payment of principal and interest of $4,000 is due in June.

(8) A cash purchase of equipment costing $6,000 is scheduled in July.

(9) Taxes of $6,000 are due in June.

14–3   Cash budget—Advanced   The actual sales and purchases for Tiffany Furniture Company for September and October 2001, along with its forecast sales and purchases for the period November 2001 through April 2002, follow.

Year	Month	Sales	Purchases
2001	September	$210,000	$120,000
2001	October	250,000	150,000
2001	November	170,000	140,000
2001	December	160,000	100,000
2002	January	140,000	80,000
2002	February	180,000	110,000
2002	March	200,000	100,000
2002	April	250,000	90,000

The firm makes 20% of all sales for cash and collects on 40% of its sales in each of the 2 months following the sale. Other cash inflows are expected to be $12,000 in September and April, $15,000 in January and March, and $27,000 in February. The firm pays cash for 10% of its purchases. It pays for 50% of its purchases in the following month and for 40% of its purchases 2 months later.

Wages and salaries amount to 20% of the preceding month's sales. Rent of $20,000 per month must be paid. Interest payments of $10,000 are due in January and April. A principal payment of $30,000 is also due in April. The firm expects to pay cash dividends of $20,000 in January and April. Taxes of $80,000 are due in April. The firm also intends to make a $25,000 cash purchase of fixed assets in December.

a. Assuming that the firm has a cash balance of $22,000 at the beginning of November, determine the end-of-month cash balances for each month, November through April.

     b. Assuming that the firm wishes to maintain a $15,000 minimum cash balance, determine the required total financing or excess cash balance for each month, November through April.

     c. If the firm were requesting a line of credit to cover needed financing for the period November to April, how large would this line have to be? Explain your answer.

 14–4   Cash flow concepts   The following represent financial transactions that Baltex Company will be undertaking in the next planning period. For each transaction, check the statement or statements that will be affected immediately.

	Statement		
Transaction	**Cash budget**	**Pro forma income statement**	**Pro forma balance sheet**
Cash sale			
Credit sale			
Accounts receivable are collected			
Asset with 5-year life is purchased			
Depreciation is taken			
Amortization of goodwill is taken			
Sale of common stock			
Retirement of outstanding bonds			
Fire insurance premium is paid for the next 3 years			

  14–5   Multiple cash budgets—Sensitivity analysis   Weprin's Parts Store expects sales of $100,000 during each of the next 3 months. It will make monthly purchases of $60,000 during this time. Wages and salaries are $10,000 per month plus 5% of sales. Weprin's expects to make a tax payment of $20,000 in the next month and a $15,000 purchase of fixed assets in the second month and to receive $8,000 in cash from the sale of an asset in the third month. All sales and purchases are for cash. Beginning cash and the minimum cash balance are assumed to be zero.

     a. Construct a cash budget for the next 3 months.

     b. Weprin's is unsure of the sales levels, but all other figures are certain. If the most pessimistic sales figure is $80,000 per month and the most optimistic is $120,000 per month, what are the monthly minimum and maximum ending cash balances that the firm can expect for each of the 1-month periods?

     c. Briefly discuss how the financial manager can use the data in parts **a** and **b** to plan for Weprin's financing needs.

 14–6   Pro forma income statement   The marketing department of Harnet Manufacturing estimates that its sales in 2002 will be $1.5 million. Interest expense is expected to remain unchanged at $35,000, and the firm plans to pay $70,000 in cash dividends during 2002. Harnet Manufacturing's income statement for the year ended December 31, 2001, is given at the top of page 446, followed by a breakdown of the firm's cost of goods sold and operating expenses into their fixed and variable components.

**Income Statement
Harnet Manufacturing
for the year ended December 31, 2001**

Sales revenue	$1,400,000
Less: Cost of goods sold	910,000
Gross profits	$ 490,000
Less: Operating expenses	120,000
Operating profits	$ 370,000
Less: Interest expense	35,000
Net profits before taxes	$ 335,000
Less: Taxes (rate = 40%)	134,000
Net profits after taxes	$ 201,000
Less: Cash dividends	66,000
To retained earnings	$ 135,000

**Fixed and Variable Cost Breakdown
Harnet Manufacturing
for the year ended December 31, 2001**

Cost of goods sold	
Fixed cost	$210,000
Variable cost	700,000
Total cost	$910,000
Operating expenses	
Fixed expenses	$ 36,000
Variable expenses	84,000
Total expenses	$120,000

a. Use the percent-of-sales method to prepare a pro forma income statement for the year ended December 31, 2002.

b. Use fixed and variable cost data to develop a pro forma income statement for the year ended December 31, 2002.

c. Compare and contrast the statements developed in parts **a** and **b.** Which statement will probably provide the better estimates of 2002 income? Explain why.

LG5   14–7   **Pro forma balance sheet**   Klear Cosmetics wishes to prepare a pro forma balance sheet for December 31, 2002. The firm expects 2002 sales to total $3,000,000. The following information has been gathered.

(1) A minimum cash balance of $50,000 is desired.

(2) Marketable securities are expected to remain unchanged.

(3) Accounts receivable represent 10% of sales.

(4) Inventories represent 12% of sales.

(5) A new machine costing $90,000 will be acquired during 2002. Total depreciation for the year will be $32,000.

(6) Accounts payable represent 14% of sales.

(7) Accruals, other current liabilities, long-term debt, and common stock are expected to remain unchanged.

(8) The firm's net profit margin is 4%, and it expects to pay out $70,000 in cash dividends during 2002.

(9) The December 31, 2001, balance sheet follows.

Balance Sheet Klear Cosmetics December 31, 2001			
Assets		**Liabilities and equities**	
Cash	$ 45,000	Accounts payable	$ 395,000
Marketable securities	15,000	Accruals	60,000
Accounts receivable	255,000	Other current liabilities	30,000
Inventories	340,000	Total current liabilities	$ 485,000
Total current assets	$ 655,000	Long-term debt	$ 350,000
Net fixed assets	$ 600,000	Common stock	$ 200,000
Total assets	$1,255,000	Retained earnings	$ 220,000
		Total liabilities and stockholders' equity	$1,255,000

a. Use the judgmental approach to prepare a pro forma balance sheet dated December 31, 2002, for Klear Cosmetics.

b. How much, if any, additional financing will Klear Cosmetics require in 2002? Discuss.

c. Could Klear Cosmetics adjust its planned 2002 dividend to avoid the situation described in part b? Explain how.

      14–8   **Integrative—Pro forma statements**   Columb Daughters Corporation wishes to prepare financial plans. Use the financial statements and the other information provided in what follows and on page 448 to prepare the financial plans.

Income Statement Columb Daughters Corporation for the year ended December 31, 2001	
Sales revenue	$800,000
Less: Cost of goods sold	600,000
Gross profits	$200,000
Less: Operating expenses	100,000
Net profits before taxes	$100,000
Less: Taxes (rate = 40%)	40,000
Net profits after taxes	$ 60,000
Less: Cash dividends	20,000
To retained earnings	$ 40,000

Balance Sheet
Columb Daughters Corporation
December 31, 2001

Assets		Liabilities and equities	
Cash	$ 32,000	Accounts payable	$100,000
Marketable securities	18,000	Taxes payable	20,000
Accounts receivable	150,000	Other current liabilities	5,000
Inventories	100,000	Total current liabilities	$125,000
Total current assets	$300,000	Long-term debt	$200,000
Net fixed assets	$350,000	Common stock	$150,000
Total assets	$650,000	Retained earnings	$175,000
		Total liabilities and stockholders' equity	$650,000

The following financial data are also available:
(1) The firm has estimated that its sales for 2002 will be $900,000.
(2) The firm expects to pay $35,000 in cash dividends in 2002.
(3) The firm wishes to maintain a minimum cash balance of $30,000.
(4) Accounts receivable represent approximately 18% of annual sales.
(5) The firm's ending inventory will change directly with changes in sales in 2002.
(6) A new machine costing $42,000 will be purchased in 2002. Total depreciation for 2002 will be $17,000.
(7) Accounts payable will change directly in response to changes in sales in 2002.
(8) Taxes payable will equal one-fourth of the tax liability on the pro forma income statement.
(9) Marketable securities, other current liabilities, long-term debt, and common stock will remain unchanged.

a. Prepare a pro forma income statement for the year ended December 31, 2002, using the percent-of-sales method.
b. Prepare a pro forma balance sheet dated December 31, 2002, using the judgmental approach.
c. Analyze these statements, and discuss the resulting external financing required.

web exercises   Search

Go to web site metalab.unc.edu/reference/moss/usbus. Under **Industry Research,** click on **Key Industry Overviews**.
1. What are the printed sources of Multi-Industry Overviews?
2. What are the related Internet links listed on this screen?

Go to web site **www.edgeonline.com**.
3. What tools are available in the Interactive Toolbox?
Select **Profit and Loss Statement** from the menu in the Interactive Toolbox.
4. Enter the following account balances into the Profit and Loss Statement.

Net Sales	$10,000,000
Salaries and wages	4,000,000
Rent	2,000,000
Light, heat, and power	900,000
Other expenses	200,000
Provision for income tax	200,000
In all other blanks, enter:	0

Click **Calculate**. What is the net profit after income tax?

Go to web site **www.census.gov** to find information useful for sales forecasting.
5. What is the U.S. population?
Select the state in which you live or go to school. Click **Get State Profile**. On the state map, double-click on the county in which your home or school is located. Click on the **19xx/20xx Economic Census**. (Choose the latest available year.)
6. Which is the largest city in the county you have chosen? What is its population?
7. In that county, how many manufacturing establishments are there?
8. From the state data, how many manufacturing establishments are there in the state?
9. From the data for the entire United States, how many manufacturing establishments are there?

For additional practice with concepts from this chapter, visit
http://www.awl.com/gitman_madura

Short-Term Financial Management

LEARNING GOALS

LG1 Describe the scope of short-term financial management and the cash conversion cycle.

LG2 Explain the funding requirements of the cash conversion cycle and strategies for minimizing negotiated liabilities.

LG3 Understand inventory management: differing views, common techniques, and international concerns.

LG4 Explain the key aspects of accounts receivable management, including credit selection and standards, credit terms, and credit monitoring.

LG5 Review the management of receipts and disbursements, including float, speeding collections, slowing payments, cash concentration, and zero-balance accounts.

LG6 Discuss current liability management, including spontaneous liabilities, unsecured short-term financing, and secured short-term financing.

Managing the Cash Conversion Cycle

short-term financial management
Management of current assets and current liabilities.

Important components of the firm's financial structure include the level of investment in current assets and the extent of current liability financing. In U.S. manufacturing firms, current assets presently account for about 40% of total assets; current liabilities represent about 26% of total financing. Therefore, it should not be surprising to learn that **short-term financial management**—managing current assets and current liabilities—is one of the financial manager's most important and time-consuming activities. The goal of short-term financial management is to manage each of the firm's current assets (inventory, accounts receivable, cash, and marketable securities) and current liabilities (accruals, accounts payable, and notes payable) to achieve a balance between profitability and risk that contributes positively to the firm's value. Central to short-term financial management is an understanding of the firm's *cash conversion cycle*.

Cash Conversion Cycle

operating cycle (OC)
The time from the beginning of the production process to the point in time when cash is collected from the sale of the finished product.

A firm's **operating cycle (OC)** is the time from the beginning of the production process to the point in time when cash is collected from the sale of the finished product. The operating cycle encompasses two major short-term asset categories: inventory and accounts receivable. It is measured in elapsed time by summing the *average age of inventory (AAI)* and the *average collection period (ACP)*.

$$OC = AAI + ACP \qquad (15.1)$$

cash conversion cycle (CCC)
The amount of time a firm's resources are tied up; calculated by subtracting the average payment period from the operating cycle.

However, the process of producing and selling a product also includes the purchase of production inputs (raw materials) on account, which results in accounts payable. Accounts payable reduce the number of days a firm's resources are tied up in the operating cycle. The time it takes to pay the accounts payable, measured in days, is the *average payment period (APP)*. The operating cycle less the average payment period is referred to as the **cash conversion cycle (CCC)**. It represents the amount of time the firm's resources are tied up. The formula for the cash conversion cycle is

$$CCC = OC - APP \qquad (15.2)$$

Substituting the relationship in Equation 15.1 into Equation 15.2, we can see that the cash conversion cycle has three main components, as shown in Equation 15.3: (1) average age of the inventory, (2) average collection period, and (3) average payment period.

$$CCC = AAI + ACP - APP \qquad (15.3)$$

Clearly, if a firm changes any of these time periods, it changes the amount of resources tied up in the day-to-day operation of the firm.

Example ▼
Justin Industries, an electronic equipment manufacturer, has annual sales of $10 million, a cost of goods sold of 75% of sales, and purchases that are 65% of cost of goods sold. Justin has an average age of inventory (AAI) of 60 days, an average

FIGURE 15.1

Time Line for Justin Industries' Cash Conversion Cycle
Justin Industries' operating cycle is 100 days and its cash conversion cycle is 65 days

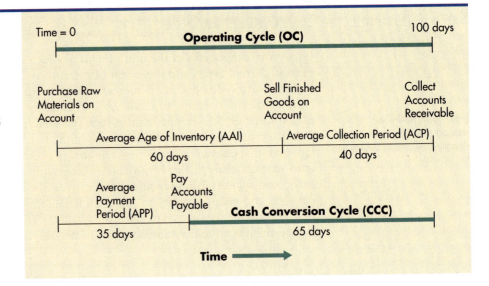

collection period (ACP) of 40 days, and an average payment period (APP) of 35 days. Thus the cash conversion cycle for Justin is 65 days $(60 + 40 - 35)$. Figure 15.1 presents Justin Industries' cash conversion cycle as a time line.

The resources Justin has invested in this cash conversion cycle (assuming a 360-day year) are

$$
\begin{array}{lll}
\text{Inventory} = (\$10{,}000{,}000 \times 0.75) \times (60/360) & = \$1{,}250{,}000 \\
+ \ \text{Accounts receivable} = (\ 10{,}000{,}000 \times 40/360) & = \ 1{,}111{,}111 \\
- \ \text{Accounts payable} = (\ 10{,}000{,}000 \times 0.75 \times 0.65) \times (35/360) & = \ \underline{\ 473{,}958} \\
= \ \text{Resources invested} & = \underline{\$1{,}887{,}153}
\end{array}
$$

Changes in any of the time periods will change the resources tied up in operations. For example, if Justin could reduce the average collection period on its accounts receivable by 5 days, it would shorten the cash conversion time line and thus reduce the amount of resources Justin has invested in operations. For Justin, a 5-day reduction in the average collection period would reduce the resources invested in the cash conversion cycle by $138,889 $[\$10{,}000{,}000 \times (5/360)]$.

 ## Funding Requirements of the Cash Conversion Cycle

We can use the cash conversion cycle as a basis for discussing how the firm funds its required investment in operating assets. We first differentiate between permanent and seasonal funding needs and then describe aggressive and conservative seasonal funding strategies.

Permanent versus Seasonal Funding Needs

permanent funding requirement
A constant investment in operating assets resulting from constant sales over time

seasonal funding requirement
An investment in operating assets that varies over time as a result of cyclical sales.

If the firm's sales are constant, then its investment in operating assets should also be constant, and the firm will have only a **permanent funding requirement.** If the firm's sales are cyclical, then its investment in operating assets will vary over time

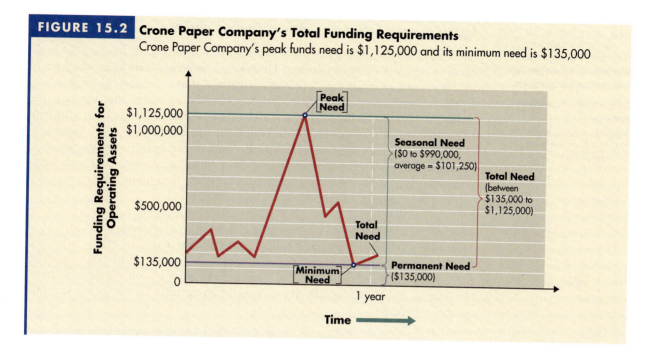

FIGURE 15.2   Crone Paper Company's Total Funding Requirements
Crone Paper Company's peak funds need is $1,125,000 and its minimum need is $135,000

with its sales cycles, and the firm will have **seasonal funding requirements** in addition to the permanent funding required for its minimum investment in operating assets.

Example ▼   Hutter Barry Enterprises holds, on average, $50,000 in cash and marketable securities, $1,250,000 in inventory, and $750,000 in accounts receivable. Hutter Barry's business is very stable over time, so its operating assets can be viewed as permanent. In addition, Hutter Barry's accounts payable of $425,000 are stable over time. Thus Hutter Barry has a permanent investment in operating assets of $1,625,000 ($50,000 + $1,250,0000 + $750,000 − $425,000). That amount would also equal its permanent funding requirement.

In contrast, Crone Paper Company, which produces notebook paper, has seasonal funding needs. Crone has seasonal sales, with its peak sales driven by the back-to-school purchases of paper. Crone holds, at minimum, $25,000 in cash and market securities, $100,000 in inventory, and $60,000 in accounts receivable. At peak times, Crone's inventory increases to $750,000, and its accounts receivable increase to $400,000. To capture production efficiencies, Crone produces paper at a constant rate throughout the year. Thus accounts payable remain at $50,000 throughout the year. Accordingly, Crone has a permanent funding requirement for its minimum level of operating assets of $135,000 ($25,000 + $100,000 + $60,000 − $50,000) and peak seasonal funding requirements (in excess of its permanent need) of $990,000 [($25,000 + $750,000 + $400,000 − $50,000) − $135,000]. Crone's total funding requirements for operating assets vary from a minimum of $135,000 (permanent) to a seasonal peak of $1,125,000 ($135,000 + $990,000). Figure 15.2 ▲ depicts these needs over time.

aggressive funding strategy
A funding strategy under which the firm funds its seasonal requirements with short-term debt and its permanent requirements with long-term debt.

conservative funding strategy
A funding strategy under which the firm funds both its seasonal and its permanent requirements with long-term debt.

Aggressive versus Conservative Seasonal Funding Strategies

Short-term funds are typically less expensive than long-term funds. (The yield curve is typically upward sloping.) However, long-term funds allow the firm to lock in its cost of funds over a period of time and thus avoid the risk of increases in short-term interest rates. Also, long-term funding ensures that the required funds are available to the firm when needed. Short-term funding exposes the firm to the risk that it may not be able to obtain the funds needed to cover its seasonal peaks. Under an **aggressive funding strategy** the firm funds its seasonal requirements with short-term debt and its permanent requirements with long-term debt. Under a **conservative funding strategy** the firm funds both its seasonal and its permanent requirements with long-term debt.

Example ▼

Crone Paper Company has a permanent funding requirement of $135,000 in operating assets and seasonal funding requirements that vary between $0 and $990,000 and average $101,250. If Crone can borrow short-term funds at 6.25% and long-term funds at 8%, and if it can earn 5% on the investment of any surplus balances, then the annual cost of an aggressive strategy for seasonal funding would be

	Cost of short-term financing	$= 0.0625 \times \$101,250$	$=$	$ 6,328.13
+	Cost of long-term financing	$= 0.0800 \times 135,000$	$=$	10,800.00
−	Earnings on surplus balances[1]	$= 0.0500 \times 0$	$=$	0
	Total cost of aggressive strategy			$17,128.13

Alternatively, Crone can choose a conservative strategy, under which surplus cash balances are fully invested. (In Figure 15.2, this surplus would be the difference between the peak need of $1,125,000 and the total need, which varies between $135,000 and $1,125,000 during the year.) The cost of the conservative strategy would be

	Cost of short-term financing	$= 0.0625 \times \$0$	$=$	$ 0
+	Cost of long-term financing	$= 0.0800 \times 1,125,000$	$=$	90,000.00
−	Earnings on surplus balances[2]	$= 0.0500 \times 888,750$	$=$	44,437.50
	Total cost of conservative strategy			$45,562.50

It is clear from these calculations that for Crone, the aggressive strategy is far less expensive than the conservative strategy. However, it is equally clear that Crone has substantial peak-season operating-asset needs and that it must have adequate funding available to meet the peak needs and ensure ongoing operations.

▲

Clearly, the aggressive strategy's heavy reliance on short-term financing makes it riskier than the conservative strategy because of interest rate swings and possible difficulties in obtaining needed short-term financing quickly when seasonal peaks occur. The conservative strategy avoids these risks through the

---

[1] Because under this strategy the amount of financing exactly equals the estimated funding need, no surplus balances exist.

[2] The average surplus balance would be calculated by subtracting the sum of the permanent need ($135,000) and the average seasonal need ($101,250) from the seasonal peak need ($1,125,000) to get $888,750 ($1,125,000 − $135,000 − $101,250). This represents the surplus amount of financing that on average could be invested in short-term vehicles that earn a 5% annual return.

locked-in interest rate and long-term financing, but is more costly because of the negative spread between the earnings rate on surplus funds (5% in the example) and the cost of the long-term funds that create the surplus (8% in the example). Where the firm operates, between the extremes of the aggressive and conservative seasonal funding strategies, depends on management's disposition toward risk and the strength of its banking relationships.

Strategies for Managing the Cash Conversion Cycle

A positive cash conversion cycle, as we saw for Justin Industries in the earlier example, means the firm must use negotiated liabilities (such as bank loans) to support its operating assets. Negotiated liabilities carry an explicit cost, so the firm benefits by minimizing their use in supporting operating assets. Minimum negotiated liabilities can be realized through application of the following strategies:

1. *Turn over inventory as quickly as possible* without stockouts that result in lost sales.
2. *Collect accounts receivable as quickly as possible* without losing sales from high-pressure collection techniques.
3. *Manage mail, processing, and clearing time* to reduce them when collecting from customers and to increase them when paying suppliers.
4. *Pay accounts payable as slowly as possible* without damaging the firm's credit rating.

Techniques for implementing these four strategies are the focus of the remainder of this chapter.

Review Questions

15–1   What is the difference between the firm's operating cycle and its cash conversion cycle?
15–2   Why is it helpful to divide the funding needs of a seasonal business into its permanent and seasonal funding requirements when developing a funding strategy?
15–3   What are the benefits, costs, and risks of an aggressive funding strategy and of a conservative funding strategy? Under which strategy is the borrowing often in excess of the actual need?
15–4   Why is it important for a firm to minimize the length of its cash conversion cycle?

Inventory Management

The first component of the cash conversion cycle is the average age of inventory. The objective for managing inventory, as noted above, is to turn over inventory as quickly as possible without losing sales from stockouts. The financial manager tends to act as an advisor or "watchdog" in matters concerning inventory; he or she does not have direct control over inventory but does provide input to the inventory management process.

 **THE RIGHT AMOUNT OF SUPPLY CAN BE CRUCIAL**

Efficient inventory management—how much is needed, when to buy it, and where to keep it—is crucial to business success. What appears to be the right amount may in fact be too little. This small business learned the hard way the payoff of keeping extra supplies on hand.

Smithereens nearly blew its big break.

QVC [the cable TV consumer marketplace] had agreed to feature the company's hand-painted glasses on its home shopping show before hundreds of thousands of impulse buyers. But its supplier was two weeks late delivering blank wine goblets for the company to paint. When the truck finally arrived, the glasses were flawed, and Smithereens had no other ones on hand.

Founder Vikki Smith had to dip into her children's education fund to pay for an express shipment from another supplier. With the help of Smith's mother, housekeeper, and other recruits, Smithereens did two weeks of glass painting in 72 hours. "We were blowing on glasses to dry as we were putting them in boxes to ship," Smith said. "We knew we had one shot or we'd never hear from them [QVC] again."...

After the QVC debacle, Smithereens co-founder Linda Brannen found such a great deal on a few popular styles of glasses [that] she bought several years' supply. She also decided that keeping some European glassware on hand was worth the storage cost because it's a high-margin item that can be difficult to get.

Smithereens, which has grown from an artist's garage five years ago to a $1.4 million business occupying 6,000 square feet in southwest Houston, is an inventory and production obstacle course. It manufactures glassware using 40 kinds of glasses, plates, and decorative housewares, with 40 different designs in four different colors.

Behind these creations are the sponges, brushes, paint, X-acto knives, Styrofoam peanuts, bubblewrap, and cardboard boxes that are the artists' and shippers' tools. In glassware alone, Smithereens has eight suppliers. Some can deliver overnight; others take six to eight weeks to ship glasses from Europe.

Smithereens has installed a computer accounting system with an inventory function. Painters count their progress daily, and the art and shipping departments make weekly supply tallies to feed the computer.

Every Wednesday Brannen holds a meeting to reconcile supply counts, glassware production, and sales orders....

Source: Rebecca Mowbray, "Having the Right Amount of Supply Can Be Crucial to a Company's Success," Houston Chronicle, *April 11, 1999, downloaded from Dow Jones Interactive Publication Library, nrstg1s.djnr.com.*

Differing Viewpoints About Inventory Level

Differing viewpoints about appropriate inventory levels commonly exist among a firm's finance, marketing, manufacturing, and purchasing managers. Each views inventory levels in light of his or her own objectives. The *financial manager's* general disposition toward inventory levels is to keep them low, to ensure that the firm's money is not being unwisely invested in excess resources. The *marketing manager,* on the other hand, would like to have large inventories of the firm's finished products. This would ensure that all orders could be filled quickly, eliminating the need for backorders due to stockouts.

The *manufacturing manager's* major responsibility is to implement the production plan so that it results in the desired amount of finished goods of acceptable quality at a low cost. In fulfilling this role, the manufacturing manager would keep raw materials inventories high to avoid production delays. He or she also would favor large production runs for the sake of lower unit production costs, which would result in high finished goods inventories.

The *purchasing manager* is concerned solely with the raw materials inventories. He or she must have on hand, in the correct quantities at the desired times and at a favorable price, whatever raw materials are required by production. Without proper control, the purchasing manager may purchase larger quantities of resources than are actually needed to get quantity discounts or in anticipation of rising prices or a shortage of certain materials.

Common Techniques for Managing Inventory

Numerous techniques are available for effectively managing the firm's inventory. Here we briefly consider four commonly used techniques.

The ABC System

ABC inventory system
Inventory management technique that divides inventory into three groups—A, B, and C, in descending order of importance and levels of monitoring, on the basis of the dollar investment in each.

A firm using the **ABC inventory system** divides its inventory into three groups, A, B, and C. The A group includes those items with the largest dollar investment. Typically, this group consists of 20 percent of the firm's inventory items but 80 percent of its investment in inventory. The B group consists of items that account for the next largest investment in inventory. The C group consists of a large number of items that require a relatively small investment. The inventory group of each item determines the item's level of monitoring. The A group items receive the most intense monitoring because of the high dollar investment. Typically, A group items are tracked on a perpetual inventory system that allows daily verification of each item's inventory level. B group items are frequently controlled through periodic, perhaps weekly, checking of their levels. C group items are monitored with unsophisticated techniques, such as the two-bin method. With the **two-bin method,** the item is stored in two bins. As an item is needed, inventory is removed from the first bin. When that bin is empty, an order is placed to refill the first bin while inventory is drawn from the second bin. The second bin is used until empty, and so on.

two-bin method
Unsophisticated inventory-monitoring technique that is typically applied to C group items and involves reordering inventory when one of two bins is empty.

The large dollar investment in A and B group items suggests the need for a better method of inventory management than the ABC system. The EOQ model, discussed next, is an appropriate model for the management of A and B group items.

The Economic Order Quantity (EOQ) Model

economic order quantity (EOQ) model
Inventory management technique for determining an item's optimal order size, which is the size that minimizes the total of its order costs and carrying costs.

One of the most common techniques for determining the optimal order size for inventory items is the **economic order quantity (EOQ) model.** The EOQ model considers various costs of inventory and then determines what order size minimizes total inventory cost.

EOQ assumes that the relevant costs of inventory can be divided into *order costs* and *carrying costs*. (The model excludes the actual cost of the inventory item.) Each of them has certain key components and characteristics. **Order costs** include the fixed clerical costs of placing and receiving orders: the cost of writing a purchase order, of processing the resulting paperwork, and of receiving an order and checking it against the invoice. Order costs are stated in dollars per order. **Carrying costs** are the variable costs per unit of holding an item of inventory for a specific period of time. Carrying costs include storage costs, insurance costs, the costs of deterioration and obsolescence, and the opportunity or financial cost of having funds invested in inventory. These costs are stated in dollars per unit per period.

order costs
The fixed clerical costs of placing and receiving an inventory order.

carrying costs
The variable costs per unit of holding an item in inventory for a specific period of time.

Order costs decrease as the size of the order increases. Carrying costs, however, increase with increases in the order size. The EOQ model analyzes the tradeoff between order costs and carrying costs to determine the *order quantity that minimizes the total inventory cost.*

Mathematical Development of EOQ   A formula can be developed for determining the firm's EOQ for a given inventory item, where

$$S = \text{usage in units per period}$$
$$O = \text{order cost per order}$$
$$C = \text{carrying cost per unit per period}$$
$$Q = \text{order quantity in units}$$

The first step is to derive the cost functions for order cost and for carrying cost. The order cost can be expressed as the product of the cost per order and the number of orders. Because the number of orders equals the usage during the period divided by the order quantity (S/Q), the order cost can be expressed as follows:

$$\text{Order cost} = O \times S/Q \qquad (15.4)$$

The carrying cost is defined as the cost of carrying a unit of inventory per period multiplied by the firm's average inventory. The average inventory is the order quantity divided by 2 ($Q/2$), because inventory is assumed to be depleted at a constant rate. Thus carrying cost can be expressed as follows:

$$\text{Carrying cost} = C \times Q/2 \qquad (15.5)$$

total cost of inventory
The sum of order costs and carrying costs of inventory.

The firm's **total cost of inventory** is found by summing the order cost and the carrying cost. Thus the total cost function is

$$\text{Total cost} = (O \times S/Q) + (C \times Q/2) \qquad (15.6)$$

Because the EOQ is defined as the order quantity that minimizes the total cost function, we must solve the total cost function for the EOQ. The resulting equation follows.

$$\text{EOQ} = \sqrt{\frac{2 \times S \times O}{C}} \qquad (15.7)$$

Although the EOQ model has weaknesses, it is certainly better than subjective decision making. Despite the fact that the use of the EOQ model is outside the control of the financial manager, the financial manager must be aware of its utility and must provide certain inputs, specifically with respect to inventory carrying costs.

reorder point
The point at which to reorder inventory, expressed as days of lead time × daily usage.

Reorder Point   Once the firm has determined its economic order quantity, it must determine when to place an order. The **reorder point** reflects the firm's daily usage of the inventory item and the number of days needed to place and receive an order. Assuming that inventory is used at a constant rate, the formula for the reorder point is

$$\text{Reorder point} = \text{Days of lead time} \times \text{Daily usage} \qquad (15.8)$$

For example, if a firm knows it takes 3 days to place and receive an order, and if it uses 15 units per day of the inventory item, then the reorder point is 45 units of inventory (3 days × 15 units/day). Thus, as soon as the item's inventory level falls to the reorder point (45 units, in this case) an order will be placed at the item's EOQ. If the estimates of lead time and usage are correct, then the order will arrive exactly as the inventory level reaches zero. However, lead times and usage rates are not precise, so most firms hold **safety stock** (extra inventory) to prevent stockouts of important items.

safety stock
Extra inventory that is held to prevent stockouts of important items.

Example ▼ Justin Industries has an A group inventory item that is vital to the production process. This item costs $1,500, and Justin uses 1,100 units of the item per year. Justin wants to determine its optimal order strategy for the item. To calculate the EOQ, we need the following inputs:

Order cost per order = $150
Carrying cost per unit per year = $200

Substituting into Equation 15.7, we get

$$\text{EOQ} = \sqrt{\frac{2 \times 1,100 \times \$150}{\$200}} \approx \underline{\underline{40 \text{ units}}}$$

The reorder point for Justin depends on the number of days Justin operates per year. Assuming that Justin operates 250 days per year and uses 1,100 units of this item, its daily usage is 4.4 units ($1,100 \div 250$). If its lead time is 2 days and Justin wants to maintain a safety stock of 4 units, the reorder point for this item is 12.8 units [$(2 \times 4.4) + 4$]. However, orders are made only in whole units, so ▲ the order is placed when the inventory falls to 13 units.

The firm's goal for inventory is to turn over the inventory as quickly as possible without stockouts. Inventory turnover is best calculated by dividing cost of goods sold by average inventory. The EOQ model determines the optimal order size and, indirectly, through the assumption of constant usage, the average inventory. Thus the EOQ model determines the firm's optimal inventory turnover rate given the firm's specific costs of inventory.

Just-in-Time (JIT) System

just-in-time (JIT) system
Inventory management technique that minimizes inventory investment by having materials arrive at exactly the time they are needed for production.

The **just-in-time (JIT) system** is used to minimize inventory investment. The philosophy is that materials should arrive at exactly the time they are needed for production. Ideally, the firm would have only work-in-progress inventory. Because its objective is to minimize inventory investment, a JIT system uses no, or very little, safety stock. Extensive coordination must exist between the firm, its suppliers, and shipping companies to ensure that material inputs arrive on time. Failure of materials to arrive on time results in a shutdown of the production line until the materials arrive. Likewise, a JIT system requires high-quality parts from suppliers. When quality problems arise, production must be stopped until the problems are resolved.

The goal of the JIT system is manufacturing efficiency. It uses inventory as a tool for attaining efficiency by emphasizing quality of the materials used and their timely delivery. When JIT is working properly, it forces process inefficiencies to surface. A JIT system requires cooperation among all parties involved in the process—suppliers, shipping companies, and the firm's employees.

Materials Requirement Planning (MRP) System

materials requirement planning (MRP) system
Inventory management technique that applies EOQ concepts and a computer to compare production needs to available inventory balances and determine when orders should be placed for various items on a product's *bill of materials*.

Many companies use a **materials requirement planning (MRP) system** to determine what materials to order and when to order them. MRP applies EOQ concepts to determine how much to order. By means of a computer, it simulates each product's bill of materials, inventory status, and manufacturing process. *The bill of materials* is simply a list of every part or material that goes into making the finished product. For a given production plan, the computer simulates materials requirements by comparing production needs to available inventory balances. On the basis of the time it takes for a product that is in process to move through the various production stages and the lead time required to get materials, the MRP system determines when orders should be placed for the various items on the bill of materials.

The advantage of the MRP system is that it forces the firm to consider its inventory needs more carefully. The objective is to lower the firm's inventory investment without impairing production. If the firm's opportunity cost of capital for investments of equal risk is 15 percent, every dollar of investment released from inventory increases before-tax profits by $0.15.

International Inventory Management

International inventory management is typically much more complicated for exporters in general, and for multinational companies in particular, than for purely domestic firms. The production and manufacturing economies of scale that might be expected from selling products globally may prove elusive if products must be tailored for individual local markets, as very frequently happens, or if actual production takes place in factories around the world. When raw materials, intermediate goods, or finished products must be transported long distances—particularly by ocean shipping—there will inevitably be more delays, confusion, damage, theft, and other difficulties than occur in a one-country operation. The international inventory manager therefore puts a premium on flexibility. He or she is usually less concerned about ordering the economically optimal quantity of inventory than about making sure that sufficient quantities of inventory are delivered where they are needed, when they are needed, and in a condition to be used as planned.

? Review Questions

15–5   What are likely to be the viewpoints of each of the following managers about the levels of the various types of inventory: finance, marketing, manufacturing, and purchasing?

15–6   Briefly describe each of the following techniques for managing inventory: ABC system, economic order quantity (EOQ) model, just-in-time (JIT) system, and materials requirement planning (MRP) system.

15–7   What factors make managing inventory more difficult for exporters and multinational companies?

LG4 Accounts Receivable Management

The second component of the cash conversion cycle is the average collection period. This period is the average length of time from a sale on credit until the payment becomes usable funds for the firm. The average collection period has two parts. The first part is the time from the sale until the customer mails the payment. The second part is the time from when the payment is mailed until the firm has the collected funds in its bank account. The first part of the average collection period involves managing the credit available to the firm's customers, and the second part involves collecting and processing payments. This section of the chapter discusses the firm's accounts receivable credit management.

The objective for managing accounts receivable is to collect accounts receivable as quickly as possible without losing sales from high-pressure collection techniques. Accomplishing this goal encompasses three topics: (1) credit selection and standards, (2) credit terms, and (3) credit monitoring.

Credit Selection and Standards

credit standards
The firm's minimum requirements for extending credit to a customer.

Credit selection involves application of techniques for determining which customers should receive credit. This process involves evaluating the customer's creditworthiness and comparing it to the firm's **credit standards,** its minimum requirements for extending credit to a customer.

Five C's of Credit

Five C's of Credit
The five key dimensions—character, capacity, capital, collateral, and conditions—used by credit analysts to provide a framework for in-depth credit analysis.

One popular credit selection technique is the **Five C's of Credit,** which provides a framework for in-depth credit analysis. Because of the time and expense involved, this credit selection method is used for large-dollar credit requests. The Five C's are

1. *Character:* The applicant's record of meeting past obligations.
2. *Capacity:* The applicant's ability to repay the requested credit, as judged in terms of financial statement analysis focused on cash flows available to service debt obligations.
3. *Capital:* The applicant's debt relative to equity.
4. *Collateral:* The amount of assets the applicant has available for use in securing the credit. The larger the amount of available assets, the greater the chance that a firm will recover funds if the applicant defaults.
5. *Conditions:* Current general and industry-specific economic conditions, and any unique conditions surrounding a specific transaction.

Analysis via the Five C's of Credit does not yield a specific accept/reject decision, so its use requires an analyst experienced in reviewing and granting credit requests. Application of this framework tends to assure the firm that its credit customers will pay, without being pressured, within the stated credit terms.

Credit Scoring

credit scoring
A credit selection method commonly used with high-volume/small-dollar credit requests; relies on a credit score determined by applying statistically derived weights to a credit applicant's scores on key financial and credit characteristics.

Credit scoring is a method of credit selection that is commonly used with high-volume/small-dollar credit requests. **Credit scoring** applies statistically derived

COLLECT FROM THE WORST

Because most of its clients are new companies with no financial track record, this high-tech public relations firm relies largely on qualitative measures to determine whether to extend credit.

It's a problem as old as business itself: How can you make sure your new customers will be reliable payers? For HighTech Connect, a $1-million PR firm in Pleasanton, California, the problem has been especially severe: 50% of its clients are start-ups. Still, those start-ups represent the company's meal ticket because of its location near Silicon Valley and its specialty in publicizing high-tech products.

So president René Siegel devised a method for screening rookie companies. First she judges them by the credibility of their financial backers—and the amount of backing provided. The *San Jose Mercury News* prints a quarterly venture-capital survey that details what companies were funded by which venture firms and for how much. "You don't worry if it's an established firm...," says Siegel. "Having private investors doesn't mean the start-ups are unreliable, but [having a big-name investor] helps if we're doubtful."

A little gossiping helps, too. After scrutinizing the bios of a start-up's executives, Siegel drops the execs' names with members of her two business organizations, the Forum for Women Entrepreneurs and GraceNet, to check whether they

have any inside knowledge of the management team of her prospective client. Siegel also runs names by clients she's come to trust, and she relies on referrals whenever she can....

Siegel has learned to avoid customers who don't cherish her service—those who, for example, challenge her prices or expect two-week marketing miracles. Some casual questioning, usually during a first or second conversation with the prospect, tells her all she needs to know. "I'm looking for answers that show they have a realistic understanding of marketing costs, expectations, and results. If they're an order of magnitude off, no matter what I do they're not going to be happy and are more likely not to pay on time," she says. Like any other company, Siegel admits, HighTech Connect has made mistakes in choosing customers, but her diligence in screening has helped keep them from greatly affecting her bottom line....

Source: Ilan Mochari, "Collect from the Worst," Inc., September 1999, p. 101.

weights for key financial and credit characteristics to predict whether or not a credit applicant will pay the requested credit in a timely fashion. Simply stated, the procedure results in a score that measures the applicant's overall credit strength, and the score is used to make the accept/reject decision for granting the applicant credit. Credit scoring is most commonly used by large credit card operations, such as those of banks, oil companies, and department stores. The purpose of credit scoring is to make a relatively informed credit decision quickly and inexpensively, recognizing that the cost of a single bad scoring decision is small. However, if bad debts from scoring decisions increase, then the scoring system must be re-evaluated.

Changing Credit Standards

The firm sometimes will contemplate changing its credit standards in order to improve its returns and create greater value for its owners. To demonstrate, consider the following changes and effects on profits expected to result from the *relaxation* of credit standards.

Effects of Relaxation of Credit Standards		
Variable	Direction of change	Effect on profits
Sales volume	Increase	Positive
Investment in accounts receivable	Increase	Negative
Bad debt expenses	Increase	Negative

If credit standards were tightened, the opposite effects would be expected.

Example ▼   Orbit Tool, a manufacturer of lathe tools, is currently selling a product for $10 per unit. Sales (all on credit) for last year were 60,000 units. The variable cost per unit is $6. The firm's total fixed costs are $120,000.

The firm is currently contemplating a *relaxation of credit standards* that is expected to result in the following: a 5% increase in unit sales to 63,000 units; an increase in the average collection period from 30 days (its current level) to 45 days; an increase in bad-debt expenses from 1% of sales (the current level) to 2%. The firm's required return on equal-risk investments, which is the opportunity cost of tying up funds in accounts receivable, is 15%.

To determine whether to relax its credit standards, Orbit Tool must calculate the effect on the firm's additional profit contribution from sales, the cost of the marginal investment in accounts receivable, and the cost of marginal bad debts.

Additional Profit Contribution from Sales   Because fixed costs are "sunk" and therefore are unaffected by a change in the sales level, the only cost relevant to a change in sales is variable costs. Sales are expected to increase by 5%, or 3,000 units. The profit contribution per unit will equal the difference between the sale price per unit ($10) and the variable cost per unit ($6). The profit contribution per unit therefore will be $4. The total additional profit contribution from sales will be $12,000 (3,000 units × $4 per unit).

Cost of the Marginal Investment in Accounts Receivable   To determine the cost of the marginal investment in accounts receivable, Orbit must find the difference between the cost of carrying receivables under the two credit standards. Because its concern is only with the out-of-pocket costs, *the relevant cost is the variable cost.* The average investment in accounts receivable can be calculated by using the following formula:

$$\frac{\text{Average investment}}{\text{in accounts receivable}} = \frac{\text{Total variable cost of annual sales}}{\text{Turnover of accounts receivable}} \qquad (15.9)$$

where

$$\text{Turnover of accounts receivable} = \frac{360}{\text{Average collection period}}$$

The total variable cost of annual sales under the present and proposed plans can be found as follows, using the variable cost per unit of $6.

Total variable cost of annual sales

Under present plan: ($6 × 60,000 units) = $360,000
Under proposed plan: ($6 × 63,000 units) = $378,000

The turnover of accounts receivable refers to the number of times each year that the firm's accounts receivable are actually turned into cash. It is found by dividing the average collection period into 360 (the number of days assumed in a year).

Turnover of accounts receivable

$$\text{Under present plan: } \frac{360}{30} = 12$$

$$\text{Under proposed plan: } \frac{360}{45} = 8$$

By substituting the cost and turnover data just calculated into Equation 15.9 for each case, we get the following average investments in accounts receivable:

Average investment in accounts receivable

$$\text{Under present plan: } \frac{\$360,000}{12} = \$30,000$$

$$\text{Under proposed plan: } \frac{\$378,000}{8} = \$47,250$$

The marginal investment in accounts receivable and its cost are calculated as follows:

Cost of marginal investment in accounts receivable

Average investment under proposed plan	$47,250
− Average investment under present plan	30,000
Marginal investment in accounts receivable	$17,250
× Required return on investment	0.15
Cost of marginal investment in A/R	$ 2,588

The resulting value of $2,588 is considered a cost because it represents the maximum amount that could have been earned on the $17,250 had it been placed in the best equal-risk investment alternative available at the firm's required return on investment of 15%.

Cost of Marginal Bad Debts   The cost of marginal bad debts is found by taking the difference between the levels of bad debts before and after the proposed relaxation of credit standards.

Cost of marginal bad debts

Under proposed plan: (0.02 × $10/unit × 63,000 units)	=	$12,600
Under present plan: (0.01 × $10/unit × 60,000 units)	=	6,000
Cost of marginal bad debts		$ 6,600

Note that the bad-debt costs are calculated by using the sale price per unit ($10) to back out not just the true loss of variable cost ($6) that results when a customer fails to pay its account, but also the profit contribution per unit (in this case $4) that is included in the "additional profit contribution from sales." Thus the resulting cost of marginal bad debts is $6,600.

Making the Credit Standard Decision   To decide whether to relax its credit standards, the firm must compare the additional profit contribution from sales to

TABLE 15.1	The Effects on Orbit Tool of a Relaxation of Credit Standards	
Additional profit contribution from sales [3,000 units × ($10 − $6)]		$12,000
Cost of marginal investment in A/R[a]		
Average investment under proposed plan: $\dfrac{\$6 \times 63,000}{8} = \dfrac{\$378,000}{8}$	$47,250	
Average investment under present plan: $\dfrac{\$6 \times 60,000}{12} = \dfrac{\$360,000}{12}$	30,000	
Marginal investment in A/R	$17,250	
Cost of marginal investment in A/R (0.15 × $17,250)		($ 2,588)
Cost of marginal bad debts		
Bad debts under proposed plan (0.02 × $10 × 63,000)	$12,600	
Bad debts under present plan (0.01 × $10 × 60,000)	6,000	
Cost of marginal bad debts		($ 6,600)
Net profit from implementation of proposed plan		$ 2,812

[a]The denominators 8 and 12 in the calculation of the average investment in accounts receivable under the proposed and present plans are the accounts receivable turnovers for each of these plans (360/45 = 8 and 360/30 = 12).

the added costs of the marginal investment in accounts receivable and marginal bad debts. If the additional profit contribution is greater than marginal costs, credit standards should be relaxed.

Example ▼
The results and key calculations relating to Orbit Tool's decision to relax its credit standards are summarized in Table 15.1. The net addition to total profits resulting from such an action will be $2,812 per year. Therefore, the firm *should* relax its credits standards as proposed. **▲**

The procedure described here for evaluating a proposed change in credit standards is also commonly used to evaluate other changes in the management of accounts receivable. If Orbit Tool had been contemplating tightening its credit standards, for example, the cost would have been a reduction in the profit contribution from sales, and the return would have been from reductions in the cost of the investment in accounts receivable and in the cost of bad debts. Another application of this procedure is demonstrated later in the chapter.

Managing International Credit

Whereas credit management is difficult enough for managers of purely domestic companies, these tasks become much more complex for companies that operate internationally. This is partly because (as we have seen before) international operations typically expose a firm to *exchange rate risk*. It is also due to the dangers and delays involved in shipping goods long distances and having to cross at least two international borders.

Exports of finished goods are usually priced in the currency of the importer's local market; most commodities, on the other hand, are priced in dollars.

Therefore, a U.S. company that sells a product in France, for example, would have to price that product in French francs and extend credit to a French wholesaler in the local currency (francs). If the franc *depreciates* against the dollar before the U.S. exporter collects on its account receivable, the U.S. company experiences an exchange rate loss; the francs collected are worth fewer dollars than expected at the time the sale was made. Of course, the dollar could just as easily depreciate against the franc, yielding an exchange rate gain to the U.S. exporter. Most companies fear the loss more than they welcome the gain.

For a major currency such as the French franc, the exporter can *hedge* against this risk by using the currency futures, forward, or options markets, but it is costly to do so, particularly for relatively small amounts. If the exporter is selling to a customer in a developing country—where 40 percent of U.S. exports are now sold—there will probably be no effective instrument available for protecting against exchange rate risk at any price. This risk may be further magnified because credit standards (and acceptable collection techniques) may be much lower in developing countries than in the United States. Although it may seem tempting to just "not bother" with exporting, U.S. companies no longer can concede foreign markets to international rivals. These export sales, if carefully monitored and, where possible, effectively hedged against exchange rate risk, often prove to be very profitable.

Credit Terms

credit terms
The terms of sale for customers who have been extended credit by the firm.

cash discount
A percentage deduction from the purchase price; available to the credit customer who pays its account within a specified time.

Credit terms are the terms of sale for customers who have been extended credit by the firm. Terms of *net 30* mean the customer has 30 days from the beginning of the credit period (typically *end of month* or *date of invoice*) to pay the full invoice amount. Some firms offer **cash discounts**, percentage deductions from the purchase price for paying within a specified time. For example, terms of *2/10 net 30* mean the customer can take a 2 percent discount from the invoice amount if the payment is made within 10 days of the beginning of the credit period or can pay the full amount of the invoice within 30 days.

A firm's regular credit terms are strongly influenced by the firm's business. For example, a firm selling perishable items will have very short credit terms, because its items have little long-term collateral value; a firm in a seasonal business may tailor its terms to fit the industry cycles. A firm wants its regular credit terms to conform to its industry's standards. If its terms are more restrictive than its competitors', it will lose business; if its terms are less restrictive than its competitors', it will attract poor-quality customers that probably could not pay under the standard industry terms. The bottom line is that a firm should compete based on the quality and price of its product and service offerings, not its credit terms. Accordingly, the firm's regular credit terms should match the industry standards, but individual customer terms should reflect the riskiness of the customer.

Cash Discounts

Including a cash discount in the credit terms is a popular way to achieve the goal of speeding up collections without putting pressure on customers. The cash discount provides an incentive for customers to pay sooner. By speeding collections, the discount decreases the firm's investment in accounts receivable (which is the objective), but it also decreases the per-unit profit. Additionally, initiating a cash

---

TABLE 15.2   **Analysis of a Cash Discount for Justin Industries**

Additional profits from increased sales
  [50 units × ($3,000 − $2,300)] $35,000

Cost of marginal investment in accounts receibable[a]

  Current average investment in accounts receivable:

  $$\frac{\$2,300 \times 1,100 \text{ units}}{9} = \frac{\$2,530,000}{9}$$ $281,111

  New average investment in accounts receivable[b]:

  $$\frac{\$2,300 \times 1,156 \text{ units}}{14.4} = \frac{\$2,645,000}{14.4}$$ <u>183,681</u>

  Reduction in accounts receivable investment $ 97,430

   Cost savings from reduced investments in
   accounts receivable (0.14 × $97,430)[c] $13,640

Cost of cash discount (0.02 × 0.80 × $1,150 × 3,000)   ($55,200)

Net profit from proposed cash discount   <u>($ 6,560)</u>

---

[a]In analyzing the investment in accounts receivable, we use the cost of the product sold ($1,500 raw materials cost + $800 production cost = $2,300 unit cost) instead of the sale price, because the cost is a better indicator of the firm's investment.

[b]The new investment in accounts receivable is estimated to be tied up for an average of 25 days instead of the 40 days under the original terms.

[c]Justin's opportunity cost of funds is 14%.

---

discount should reduce bad debts because customers will pay sooner, and it should increase sales volume because customers who take the discount pay a lower price for the product. Accordingly, firms considering offering a cash discount must perform a cost/benefit analysis to determine whether extending a cash discount is profitable.

Example ▼ Justin Industries has an average collection period of 40 days (turnover $= \frac{360}{40} = 9$). In accordance with the firm's credit terms of net 30, this period is divided into 32 days until the customers place their payments in the mail (not everyone pays within 30 days) and 8 days to receive, process, and collect payments once they are mailed. Justin is considering changing its credit terms from net 30 to 2/10 net 30. The firm expects this change to reduce the amount of time until the payments are placed in the mail, resulting in an average collection period of 25 days (turnover $= \frac{360}{25} = 14.4$).

 As noted earlier in the EOQ example (page 459), Justin has a raw material with current annual usage of 1,100 units. Each finished product produced requires 1 unit of this raw material at a cost of $1,500 per unit, incurs another $800 of cost in the production process, and sells for $3,000 on terms of net 30. Justin estimates that 80% of its customers will take the 2% discount and that offering the discount will increase sales of the finished product by 50 units (from 1,100 to 1,150 units) per year but will not alter its bad-debt percentage. Justin's opportunity cost of funds invested in accounts receivable is 14%. Should Justin offer the proposed cash discount? An analysis similar to that demonstrated earlier for the credit standard decision, presented in Table 15.2, shows a net loss from the cash discount of $6,560. Thus *Justin should not implement the proposed*
▲ *cash discount.* However, other discounts may be advantageous.

Credit Monitoring

credit monitoring
The ongoing review of a firm's accounts receivable to determine whether customers are paying according to the stated credit terms.

The final issue a firm should consider in its accounts receivable management is credit monitoring. **Credit monitoring** is an ongoing review of the firm's accounts receivable to determine whether customers are paying according to the stated credit terms. If they are not paying accordingly, credit monitoring will alert the firm to the problem. Slow payments are costly to a firm because they lengthen the average collection period and thus increase the firm's investment in accounts receivable. Two frequently cited techniques for credit monitoring are average collection period and aging of accounts receivable. In addition, a number of popular collection techniques are used by firms.

Average Collection Period

The *average collection period* is the second component of the cash conversion cycle. As noted in Chapter 8, it is the average number of days that credit sales are outstanding. The average collection period has two components: (1) the time from sale until the customer places the payment in the mail and (2) the time to receive, process, and collect the payment once it has been mailed by the customer. The formula for finding the average collection period is

$$\text{Average collection period} = \frac{\text{Accounts receivable}}{\text{Average sales per day}} \quad (15.10)$$

Assuming receipt, processing, and collection time is constant, the average collection period tells the firm, on average, when its customers pay their accounts.

The average collection period allows the firm to determine whether there is a general problem with accounts receivable. For example, a firm that has credit terms of net 30 would expect its average collection period (minus receipt, processing, and collection time) to equal about 30 days. If the actual collection period is significantly greater than 30 days, the firm has reason to review its credit operations. If the firm's average collection period is increasing over time, it has reason for concern about its accounts receivable management. A first step in analyzing an accounts receivable problem is to "age" the accounts receivable. By this process the firm can determine whether the problem exists in its accounts receivable in general or is attributable to a few specific accounts.

Aging of Accounts Receivable

aging of accounts receivable
A credit-monitoring technique that uses a schedule that indicates the percentages of the total accounts receivable balance that have been outstanding for specified periods of time.

The **aging of accounts receivable** requires the firm's accounts receivable to be broken down into groups on the basis of the time of origin. The breakdown is typically made on a month-by-month basis, going back 3 or 4 months. The result is a schedule that indicates the percentages of the total accounts receivable balance that have been outstanding for specified periods of time. Its purpose is to allow the firm to pinpoint problems.

If a firm with terms of net 30 has an average collection period (minus receipt, processing, and collection time) of 50 days, the firm will want to age its accounts receivable. If the majority of accounts are 2 months old, then the firm has a general problem and should review its accounts receivable operations. If the aging shows that most accounts are collected in about 35 days and a few accounts are way past due, then the firm should analyze and pursue collection of those specific past-due accounts.

TABLE 15.3	Popular Collection Techniques
Technique[a]	**Brief description**
Letters	After a certain number of days, the firm sends a polite letter reminding the customer of the overdue account. If the account is not paid within a certain period after this letter has been sent, a second, more demanding letter is sent.
Telephone calls	If letters prove unsuccessful, a telephone call may be made to the customer to request immediate payment. If the customer has a reasonable excuse, arrangements may be made to extend the payment period. A call from the seller's attorney may be used.
Personal visits	This technique is much more common at the consumer credit level, but it may also be effectively employed by industrial suppliers. Sending a local salesperson or a collection person to confront the customer can be very effective. Payment may be made on the spot.
Collection agencies	A firm can turn uncollectible accounts over to a collection agency or an attorney for collection. The fees for this service are typically quite high; the firm may receive less than 50 cents on the dollar from accounts collected in this way.
Legal action	Legal action is the most stringent step, an alternative to the use of a collection agency. Not only is direct legal action expensive, but it may force the debtor into bankruptcy, without guaranteeing the ultimate receipt of the overdue amount.

[a]Techniques are listed in the order in which they are typically followed in the collection process.

Popular Collection Techniques

A number of collection techniques, ranging from letters to legal action, are employed. As an account becomes more and more overdue, the collection effort becomes more personal and more intense. In Table 15.3 the popular collection techniques are listed, and briefly described, in the order typically followed in the collection process.

❓ Review Questions

15–8   What is the role of the *Five C's of Credit* in the credit selection activity?

15–9   Explain why credit scoring is typically applied to consumer credit decisions rather than to mercantile credit decisions.

15–10   What are the basic tradeoffs in a *tightening* of credit standards?

15–11   Why are the risks involved in international credit management more complex than those associated with purely domestic credit sales?

15–12   Why do a firm's regular credit terms typically conform to those of its industry?

15–13   Why should a firm actively monitor the accounts receivable of its credit customers? How do the *average collection period* and *aging of accounts receivable* work?

Management of Receipts and Disbursements

As discussed in the previous section, the average collection period (the second component of the cash conversion cycle) has two parts: (1) the time from sale until the customer mails the payment and (2) the receipt, processing, and collection time. The third component of the cash conversion cycle, the average payment period, also has two parts: (1) the time from purchase of goods on account until the firm mails its payment and (2) the receipt, processing, and collection time required by the firm's suppliers. The receipt, processing, and collection time for the firm both from its customers and to its suppliers is the focus of receipts and disbursements management.

Float

float
Funds that have been sent by the payer but are not yet usable funds to the payee.

mail float
The time delay between when payment is placed in the mail and when it is received.

processing float
The time between receipt of a payment and its deposit into the firm's account.

clearing float
The time between deposit of a payment and when spendable funds become available to the firm.

Float refers to funds that have been sent by the payer but are not yet usable funds to the payee. Float is important in the cash conversion cycle because its presence lengthens both the firm's average collection period and its average payment period. However, the goal of the firm should be to shorten its average collection period and lengthen its average payment period. Both can be accomplished by managing float.

Float has three component parts:

1. **Mail float** is the time delay between when payment is placed in the mail and when it is received.
2. **Processing float** is the time between receipt of the payment and its deposit into the firm's account.
3. **Clearing float** is the time between deposit of the payment and when spendable funds become available to the firm. This component of float is attributable to the time required for a check to clear the banking system.

Some popular techniques for managing the component parts of float to speed up collections and slow down payments are described here.

Speeding Up Collections

lockbox system
A collection procedure in which customers mail payments to a post office box that is emptied regularly by the firm's bank, who processes the payments and deposits them in the firm's account. Speeds up collection time by reducing processing time as well as mail and clearing time.

Speeding up collections reduces customer *collection float* time and thus reduces the firm's average collection period, which reduces the investment the firm must make in its cash conversion cycle. In our earlier examples, Justin Industries had annual sales of $10 million and 8 days of total collection float (receipt, processing, and collection time). If Justin can reduce its float time to 5 days, it will reduce its investment in the cash conversion cycle by $83,333 ([$10,000,000 / 360 days] × 3 days).

A popular technique for speeding up collections is a lockbox system. A **lockbox system** works as follows: Instead of mailing payments to the company, customers mail payments to a post office box. The firm's bank empties the post office box regularly, processes each payment, and deposits the payments in the firm's account. Deposit slips, along with payment enclosures, are sent (or transmitted electronically) to the firm by the bank so that the firm can properly credit customers' accounts. Lockboxes are geographically dispersed to match the locations of the firm's customers. A lockbox system affects all three components of float. Lockboxes reduce mail time and often clearing time by being near the firm's customers. Lockboxes reduce processing time to nearly zero because the bank deposits payments before the firm processes them. Obviously a lockbox system reduces collection float time, but not without a cost; therefore, a firm must perform an economic analysis to determine whether to implement a lockbox system.

Lockbox systems are commonly used by large firms whose customers are geographically dispersed. However, a firm does not have to be large to benefit from a lockbox. Smaller firms can also benefit from a lockbox system. The benefit to small firms often comes primarily from transferring the processing of payments to the bank.

Slowing Down Payments

controlled disbursing
The strategic use of mailing points and bank accounts to lengthen mail float and clearing float, respectively.

Float is also a component of the firm's average payment period. In this case, the float is in the favor of the firm. The firm may benefit by increasing all three of the components of its *payment float*. One popular technique for increasing payment float is **controlled disbursing**, which involves the strategic use of mailing points and bank accounts to lengthen mail float and clearing float, respectively. This approach should be used carefully, though, because longer payment periods may strain supplier relations.

In summary, a reasonable overall policy for float management is (1) to collect payments as quickly as possible, because once the payment is in the mail, the funds belong to the firm, and (2) to delay making payment to suppliers, because once the payment is mailed, the funds belong to the supplier.

Cash Concentration

cash concentration
The process used by the firm to bring lockbox and other deposits together into one bank, often called the *concentration bank.*

Cash concentration is the process used by the firm to bring lockbox and other deposits together into one bank, often called the *concentration bank*. Cash concentration has three main advantages. First, it creates a large pool of funds for use in making short-term cash investments. Because there is a fixed-cost component in the transaction cost associated with such investments, investing a single pool of funds reduces the firm's transaction costs. The larger investment pool also allows the firm to choose from a larger variety of short-term investment vehicles. Second, concentrating the firm's cash in one account improves the tracking and internal control of the firm's cash. Third, having one concentration bank allows the firm to implement payment strategies that reduce idle cash balances.

depository transfer check (DTC)
An unsigned check drawn on one of a firm's bank accounts and deposited in another.

There are a variety of mechanisms for transferring cash from the lockbox bank and other collecting banks to the concentration bank. One mechanism is a **depository transfer check (DTC)**, which is an unsigned check drawn on one of the firm's bank accounts and deposited in another. For cash concentration, a DTC is drawn on each lockbox or other collecting bank account and deposited in the concentration bank account. Once the DTC has cleared the bank on which it is drawn (which may take several days), the transfer of funds is completed. Most firms currently provide deposit information by telephone to the concentration bank, which then prepares and deposits into its account the DTC drawn on the lockbox or other collecting bank account.

ACH (automated clearing-house) transfer
Preauthorized electronic withdrawal from the payer's account and deposit into the payee's account via a settlement among banks by the *automated clearinghouse*, or *ACH*.

A second mechanism is an **ACH (automated clearinghouse) transfer,** which is a preauthorized electronic withdrawal from the payer's account. A computerized clearing facility (called the *automated clearinghouse*, or *ACH*) makes a paperless transfer of funds between the payer and payee banks. An ACH settles accounts among participating banks. Individual accounts are settled by respective bank balance adjustments. ACH transfers clear in one day. For cash concentration, an ACH transfer is made from each lockbox bank or other collecting bank to the concentration bank. An ACH transfer can be thought of as an electronic DTC, but because the ACH transfer clears in one day, it provides benefits over a DTC; however, both banks in the ACH transfer must be members of the clearinghouse.

wire transfer
An electronic communication that, via bookkeeping entries, removes funds from the payer's bank and deposits them in the payee's bank.

A third cash concentration mechanism is a **wire transfer.** A wire transfer is an electronic communication that, via bookkeeping entries, removes funds from the payer's bank and deposits them in the payee's bank. Wire transfers can eliminate mail and clearing float and may reduce processing float as well. For cash concentration, the firm moves funds using a wire transfer from each lockbox or other collecting account to its concentration account. Wire transfers are a substitute for DTC and ACH transfers, but are more expensive.

It is clear that the firm must balance the costs and benefits of concentrating cash to determine the type and timing of transfers from its lockbox and other collecting accounts to its concentration account. The transfer mechanism selected should be the one that is most profitable. (The profit per period of any transfer mechanism equals earnings on the increased funds availability minus the cost of the transfer system.)

Zero-Balance Accounts

zero-balance account (ZBA)
A disbursement account that always has an end-of-day balance of zero because the firm deposits money to cover checks drawn on the account only as they are presented for payment each day.

Zero-balance accounts (ZBAs) are disbursement accounts that always have an end-of-day balance of zero. The purpose is to eliminate nonearning cash balances in corporate checking accounts. A ZBA works well as a disbursement account under a cash concentration system.

ZBAs work as follows: Once all of a given day's checks are presented for payment from the firm's ZBA, the bank notifies the firm of the total amount of checks, and the firm transfers funds into the account to cover the amount of that day's checks. This leaves an end-of-day balance of $0 (zero dollars). The ZBA allows the firm to keep all of its operating cash in an interest-earning account, thereby eliminating idle cash balances. Thus a firm that uses a ZBA in conjunction with a cash concentration system would need two accounts. The firm would concentrate its cash from the lockboxes and other collecting banks into an interest-earning account and would write checks against its ZBA. The firm would cover the exact dollar amount of checks presented against the ZBA with transfers from the interest-earning account, leaving the end-of-day balance in the ZBA at $0.

A ZBA is a disbursement management tool. As we discussed earlier, the firm would prefer to maximize its payment float. However, some cash managers feel that actively attempting to increase float time on payments is unethical. A ZBA allows the firm to maximize the use of float on each check without altering the float time of payments to its suppliers. Keeping all the firm's cash in an interest-earning account allows the firm to maximize earnings on its cash balances by capturing the full float time on each check it writes.

❓ **Review Questions**

15–14   What is *float* and what are its three components?

15–15   What are the firm's objectives with regard to collection float and to payment float?

15–16   What are the three main advantages of cash concentration?

15–17   What are three mechanisms of cash concentration? What is the objective of using a zero-balance account (ZBA) in a cash concentration system?

Current Liability Management

spontaneous liabilities
Liabilities that arise in the normal course of business operations; the two major short-term sources of such liabilities are accruals and accounts payable.

unsecured short-term financing
Short-term financing (loans) obtained without pledging specific assets as collateral.

secured short-term financing
Short-term financing (loans) that has specific assets pledged as collateral.

accruals
Spontaneous liabilities, typically wages and taxes that are owed but for which payment is not yet due.

The short-term financing of the firm is represented on its balance sheet by its current liabilities. Both *accruals* and *accounts payable* are considered **spontaneous liabilities** because they arise in the normal course of business operations. *Notes payable*, on the other hand, reflect negotiated sources of short-term financing (loans). Some of them are **unsecured short-term financing**—short-term financing obtained without pledging specific assets as collateral. Other notes payable are **secured short-term financing**—short-term financing that has specific assets pledged as collateral. We'll first discuss spontaneous liabilities.

Spontaneous Liabilities

The two most significant spontaneous liabilities are accruals and accounts payable. **Accruals** are typically wages and taxes that are owed but for which payment is not yet due. Accruals should not be actively managed as a source of funds and therefore are not discussed as a funding source in the cash conversion cycle. On the other hand, accounts payable is a major source of short-term financing and is a key component of the cash conversion cycle. This section focuses on the management of accounts payable and addresses the final goal in managing the cash conversion cycle, which is to pay accounts payable as slowly as possible without damaging the firm's credit rating.

Accounts Payable Management

accounts payable management
Management by the firm of the time that elapses between the purchase of raw materials and its mailing payment to the supplier.

The final component of the cash conversion cycle is the *average payment period*. The average payment period has two parts: (1) the time from the purchase of raw materials until the firm mails the payment and (2) payment float time (the time it takes after the firm mails its payment until the supplier has withdrawn spendable funds from the firm's account). In the preceding section, we discussed issues related to payment float time. In this section, we discuss the management by the firm of the time that elapses between the purchase of raw materials and its mailing payment to the supplier. This activity is **accounts payable management.**

The firm's goal is to pay as slowly as possible without damaging its credit rating. This means that accounts should be paid on the last day possible given the supplier's stated credit terms. For example, if the terms are net 30, then the account should be paid 30 days from the *beginning of the credit period*, which is typically either the *date of invoice* and the *end of the month (EOM)* in which the purchase was made. This allows for the maximum use of an interest-free loan from the supplier and will not damage the firm's credit rating (because the account is paid within the stated credit terms).

Example ▼ In the earlier demonstration of the cash conversion cycle, Justin Industries has an average payment period of 35 days (consisting of 30 days until payment is mailed and 5 days of payment float), which results in average accounts payable of $473,958. Thus the daily accounts payable generated by Justin is $13,542 ($473,958/35). If Justin were to mail its payments in 35 days instead of 30, its accounts payable would increase by $67,710 ($13,542 × 5). As a result, Justin's cash conversion cycle would decrease by 5 days and the firm would reduce its investment in operations by $67,710. Clearly, if this action did not damage Justin's credit rating, it would be in its best interest.

Cash Discounts

When the firm's suppliers offer *cash discounts* to encourage it to pay before the end of the credit period, it may not be in the firm's best financial interest to pay on the last day of the credit period. Taking the discount is at the discretion of the purchaser. Here we discuss when the firm should take advantage of a cash discount that has been offered.

When the firm is offered credit terms that include a cash discount, it has two options: (1) pay the full invoice amount at the end of the credit period, or (2) pay the invoice amount less the cash discount at the end of the cash discount period. In either case, the firm purchases the same goods. Thus the difference between the payment amount without and with the cash discount is in effect an interest payment made by the firm to its supplier. The firm in need of short-term funds must therefore compare the interest rate charged by its supplier to the best rates charged by the other sources of short-term financing, and choose the lowest-cost option. This comparison is important, because if the firm takes the cash discount, it will shorten its average payment period and thus increase the amount of resources it has invested in operating assets, which will require additional non-spontaneous short-term financing.

The formula for calculating the interest rate associated with *not taking* the cash discount but paying at the end of the credit period when cash discount terms are offered is

$$k_{discount} = \frac{d}{(1-d)} \times \frac{360}{(CP - DP)} \tag{15.11}$$

where

$k_{discount}$ = annual interest cost of not taking a cash discount
d = percent discount (in decimal form)
CP = credit period
DP = cash discount period

Example ▼ Assume a supplier of Justin Industries has changed its terms from *net 30* to *2/10 net 30*. Justin needs short-term financing and has a bank line of credit with a current interest rate of 10.0%. Should Justin take the cash discount or continue to use 30 days of credit from its supplier? The interest rate effectively charged by the supplier is calculated using Equation 15.11.

$$k_{\text{discount}} = \frac{0.02}{(1 - 0.02)} \times \frac{360}{(30 - 10)} = 0.367 = \underline{\underline{36.7\%}}$$

Thus the annualized rate charged by the supplier for *not taking* the cash discount is 36.7%, whereas the bank charges 10.0% for use of funds. Justin should *take the cash discount* and obtain needed short-term financing by drawing on its bank line of credit.

Unsecured Short-Term Financing

Businesses obtain unsecured short-term loans from two major sources, banks and commercial paper. Unlike the spontaneous sources of unsecured short-term financing, bank loans and commercial paper are negotiated and result from actions taken by the firm's financial manager. Bank loans are more popular because they are available to firms of all sizes; commercial paper tends to be available only to large firms. In addition, international loans can be used to finance international transactions.

Bank Loans

short-term, self-liquidating loan
An unsecured short-term loan in which the use to which the borrowed money is put provides the mechanism through which the loan is repaid.

Banks are a major source of unsecured short-term loans to businesses. The major type of loan made by banks to businesses is the **short-term, self-liquidating loan.** These loans are intended merely to carry the firm through seasonal peaks in financing needs that are due primarily to buildups of accounts receivable and inventory. As receivables and inventories are converted into cash, the funds needed to retire these loans are generated. In other words, the use to which the borrowed money is put provides the mechanism through which the loan is repaid—hence the term *self-liquidating.* Banks lend unsecured, short-term funds in three basic ways: through single-payment notes, lines of credit, and revolving credit agreements. The cost of these types of loans is related to the prime rate of interest.

prime rate of interest (prime rate)
The lowest rate of interest charged by leading banks on business loans to their most important business borrowers.

Prime Rate of Interest   The interest rate on a bank loan is typically based on the **prime rate of interest (prime rate),** which is the lowest rate of interest charged by leading banks on business loans to their most important business borrowers. The prime rate fluctuates with changing supply-and-demand relationships for short-term funds. Banks generally determine the rate to be charged to various borrowers by adding a premium to the prime rate to adjust it for the borrower's "riskiness." The premium may amount to 4 percent or more, although most unsecured short-term loans carry premiums of less than 2 percent. Recently, the prime rate has been between 9 and 10 percent.

single-payment note
A short-term, one-time loan made to a borrower who needs funds for a specific purpose for a short period.

Single-Payment Notes   A **single-payment note** can be obtained from a commercial bank by a creditworthy business borrower. This type of loan is usually a one-time loan made to a borrower who needs funds for a specific purpose for a short period. The resulting instrument is a *note,* signed by the borrower, that states the terms of the loan, including the length of the loan and the interest rate. This type of short-term note generally has a maturity of 30 days to 9 months or more. The interest charged is generally tied in some way to the prime rate of interest.

line of credit
An agreement between a commercial bank and a business specifying the amount of unsecured short-term borrowing the bank will make available to the firm over a given period of time.

operating change restrictions
Restrictions that a bank may impose on a firm's financial condition or operations as part of a line-of-credit agreement.

compensating balance
A required checking account balance equal to a certain percentage of the amount borrowed from a bank under a line-of-credit or revolving credit agreement.

annual cleanup
The requirement that for a certain number of days during the year borrowers under a line of credit carry a zero loan balance (that is, they owe the bank nothing).

revolving credit agreement
A line of credit *guaranteed* to a borrower by a commercial bank regardless of the scarcity of money.

commitment fee
The fee that is normally charged on a *revolving credit agreement*; it often applies to the average unused balance of the borrower's credit line.

commercial paper
A form of financing consisting of short-term, unsecured promissory notes issued by firms with a high credit standing.

Lines of Credit A **line of credit** is an agreement between a commercial bank and a business specifying the amount of unsecured short-term borrowing the bank will make available to the firm over a given period of time. It is similar to the agreement under which issuers of bank credit cards, such as MasterCard, Visa, and Discover, extend preapproved credit to cardholders. A line of credit agreement is typically made for a period of one year and often places certain constraints on the borrower. It is *not a guaranteed loan* but indicates that if the bank has sufficient funds available, it will allow the borrower to owe it up to a certain amount of money. The amount of a line of credit is the *maximum amount the firm can owe the bank* at any point in time. The interest rate on a line of credit is normally tied to the prime rate.

The bank may impose **operating change restrictions,** which give it the right to revoke the line if any major changes occur in the firm's financial condition or operations. The firm is usually required to submit up-to-date financial statements for periodic review.

To ensure that the borrower will be a good customer, many short-term unsecured bank loans often require the borrower to maintain, in a checking account, a **compensating balance** equal to a certain percentage of the amount borrowed. Compensating balances of 10 to 20 percent are frequently required. A compensating balance not only forces the borrower to be a good customer of the bank but may also raise the interest cost to the borrower.

To ensure that money lent under a line-of-credit agreement is actually being used to finance seasonal needs, many banks require an **annual cleanup.** This means that the borrower must have a loan balance of zero—that is, owe the bank nothing—for a certain number of days during the year. Insisting that the borrower carry a zero loan balance for a certain period ensures that short-term loans do not turn into long-term loans.

All the characteristics of a line-of-credit agreement are negotiable to some extent. Today, banks bid competitively to attract large, well-known firms. A prospective borrower should attempt to negotiate a line of credit with the most favorable interest rate, for an optimal amount of funds, and with a minimum of restrictions. The lender attempts to get a good return with maximum safety. Negotiations should produce a line of credit that is suitable to both borrower and lender.

Revolving Credit Agreements A **revolving credit agreement** is nothing more than a *guaranteed line of credit.* It is guaranteed in the sense that the commercial bank assures the borrower that a specified amount of funds will be made available regardless of the scarcity of money. The interest rate and other requirements are similar to those for a line of credit. Because the bank guarantees the availability of funds, a **commitment fee** is normally charged on a revolving credit agreement. This fee often applies to the average unused balance of the borrower's credit line. It is normally about 0.5 percent of the *average unused portion* of the line.

Commercial Paper

Commercial paper, as noted in Chapter 2, is a form of financing that consists of short-term, unsecured promissory notes issued by firms with a high credit standing. Generally, only quite large firms of unquestionable financial soundness are able to issue commercial paper. Most commercial paper has maturities ranging from 3 to 270 days. Although there is no set denomination, it is generally issued in multiples of $100,000 or more. A large portion of the commercial paper today is issued by finance companies; manufacturing firms account for a smaller portion of this type of financing. Businesses often purchase commercial paper, which they hold as marketable securities, to provide an interest-earning reserve of liquidity.

An interesting characteristic of commercial paper is that its interest cost is *normally* 2 to 4 percent below the prime rate. In other words, firms are able to raise funds more cheaply through the sale of commercial paper than by borrowing from a commercial bank. The reason is that many suppliers of short-term funds do not have the option, as banks do, of making low-risk business loans at the prime rate. They can invest safely only in marketable securities such as Treasury bills and commercial paper.

International Loans

In some ways, arranging short-term financing for international trade is no different from financing purely domestic operations. In both cases, producers must finance production and inventory and then continue to finance accounts receivable before collecting any cash payments from sales. In other ways, however, the short-term financing of international sales and purchases is fundamentally different from strictly domestic trade.

International Transactions   The important difference between international and domestic transactions is that payments are often made or received in a foreign currency. Not only must a U.S. company pay the costs of doing business in the foreign exchange market, but it also is exposed to *exchange rate risk*. A U.S.-based company that exports goods and has accounts receivable denominated in a foreign currency faces the risk that the U.S. dollar will appreciate in value relative to the foreign currency. The risk to a U.S. importer with foreign-currency-denominated accounts payable is that the dollar will depreciate. Typical international transactions are large in size and have long maturity dates. Therefore, companies that are involved in international trade generally have to finance larger dollar amounts for longer time periods than companies who operate domestically.

Financing International Trade   Several specialized techniques have evolved for financing international trade. Perhaps the most important financing vehicle is the **letter of credit**, a letter written by a company's bank to the company's foreign supplier, stating that the bank guarantees payment of an invoiced amount if all the underlying agreements are met. The letter of credit essentially substitutes the bank's reputation and creditworthiness for that of its commercial customer. A U.S. exporter is more willing to sell goods to a foreign buyer if the transaction is covered by a letter of credit issued by a well-known bank in the buyer's home country.

Firms that do business in foreign countries on an ongoing basis often finance their operations, at least in part, in the local market. A company that has an assembly plant in Mexico, for example, might choose to finance its purchases of Mexican goods and services with peso funds borrowed from a Mexican bank.

letter of credit
A letter written by a company's bank to the company's foreign supplier, stating that the bank guarantees payment of an invoiced amount if all the underlying agreements are met.

This not only minimizes exchange rate risk but also improves the company's business ties to the host community. Multinational companies, however, sometimes finance their international transactions through dollar-denominated loans from international banks. The *Eurocurrency loan markets* allow creditworthy borrowers to obtain financing on very attractive terms.

Transactions Between Subsidiaries   Much international trade involves transactions between corporate subsidiaries. A U.S. company might, for example, manufacture one part in an Asian plant and another part in the United States, assemble the product in Brazil, and sell it in Europe. The shipment of goods back and forth between subsidiaries creates accounts receivable and accounts payable, but the parent company has considerable discretion about how and when payments are made. In particular, the parent can minimize foreign exchange fees and other transaction costs by "netting" what affiliates owe each other and paying only the net amount due, rather than having both subsidiaries pay each other the gross amounts due.

Secured Short-Term Financing

When a firm has exhausted its unsecured sources of short-term financing, it may be able to obtain additional short-term loans on a secured basis. Secured short-term financing has specific assets pledged as collateral. The *collateral* commonly takes the form of an asset, such as accounts receivable or inventory. The lender obtains a security interest in the collateral through the execution of a **security agreement** with the borrower that specifies the collateral held against the loan.

security agreement
The agreement between the borrower and the lender that specifies the collateral held against a secured loan.

Characteristics of Secured Short-Term Loans

Although many people believe that holding collateral as security reduces the risk of a loan, lenders do not usually view loans in this way. Lenders recognize that holding collateral can reduce losses if the borrower defaults, but *the presence of collateral has no impact on the risk of default*. A lender requires collateral to ensure recovery of some portion of the loan in the event of default. What the lender wants above all, however, is to be repaid as scheduled. In general, lenders prefer to make less risky loans at lower rates of interest than to be in a position in which they must liquidate collateral. Lenders of secured short-term funds prefer current assets—accounts receivable and inventory—as short-term loan collateral, because they can normally be converted into cash much sooner than fixed assets.

percentage advance
The percent of the book value of the collateral that constitutes the principal of a secured loan.

Typically, the lender determines the desirable **percentage advance** to make against the collateral. This percentage advance constitutes the principal of the secured loan and is normally between 30 and 100 percent of the book value of the collateral. The interest rate that is charged on secured short-term loans is typically *higher* than the rate on unsecured short-term loans. Lenders do not normally consider secured loans less risky than unsecured loans. In addition, negotiating and administering secured loans is more troublesome for the lender than negotiating and administering unsecured loans.

The Use of Accounts Receivable as Collateral

Two commonly used means of obtaining short-term financing with accounts receivable are *pledging accounts receivable* and *factoring accounts receivable*. A **pledge of accounts receivable** is often used as collateral to secure a short-term loan. Because accounts receivable are normally quite liquid, they are an attractive form of collateral. Both commercial banks and commercial finance companies (institutions that make *only* secured loans) extend loans against pledges of accounts receivable.

Factoring accounts receivable involves selling them outright, at a discount, to a financial institution. A **factor** is a financial institution that specializes in purchasing accounts receivable from businesses. Some commercial banks and commercial finance companies also factor accounts receivable. Although it is not the same as obtaining a short-term loan, factoring accounts receivable is similar to borrowing with accounts receivable as collateral.

The Use of Inventory as Collateral

Inventory is generally second to accounts receivable in desirability as short-term loan collateral. A lender securing a loan with inventory will probably be able to sell that inventory for at least its book value if the borrower defaults on its obligations. When evaluating inventory as possible loan collateral, the lender looks for items with very stable market prices that have ready markets and that lack undesirable physical properties.

A **floating inventory lien,** which is a claim on inventory in general, is used when the firm has a stable level of inventory that consists of a diversified group of relatively inexpensive merchandise. Because it is difficult for a lender to verify the presence of the inventory, the lender generally advances less than 50 percent of the book value of the average inventory.

A **trust receipt inventory loan** often can be made against relatively expensive automotive, consumer durable, and industrial goods that can be identified by serial number. Under this agreement, the borrower keeps the inventory and the lender may advance 80 to 100 percent of its cost. The borrower is free to sell the merchandise but is trusted to remit the amount lent, along with accrued interest, to the lender immediately after the sale. Trust receipt loans are often made by manufacturers' wholly owned financing subsidiaries, known as *captive finance companies*, to their customers.

A **warehouse receipt loan** is an arrangement whereby the lender receives control of the pledged inventory collateral, which is stored by a designated agent on the lender's behalf. After selecting acceptable collateral, the lender hires a warehousing company to act as its agent and take possession of the inventory. Only on written approval of the lender can any portion of the secured inventory be released by the warehousing company. As in the case of other secured loans, the lender accepts only collateral that is believed to be readily marketable and advances only a portion—generally 75 to 90 percent—of the collateral's value. The specific costs of warehouse receipt loans are generally higher than those of any other secured lending arrangements because of the need to hire and pay a warehousing company to guard and supervise the collateral.

---

pledge of accounts receivable
The use of a firm's accounts receivable as collateral to secure a short-term loan.

factoring accounts receivable
The outright sale of accounts receivable at a discount to a *factor* or other financial institution.

factor
A financial institution that specializes in purchasing accounts receivable from businesses.

floating inventory lien
A secured short-term loan against inventory under which the lender's claim is on the borrower's inventory in general.

trust receipt inventory loan
A secured short-term loan against inventory under which the lender advances 80 to 100 percent of the cost of the borrower's relatively expensive inventory items in exchange for the borrower's promise to repay the lender, with accrued interest, immediately after the sale of each item of collateral.

warehouse receipt loan
A secured short-term loan against inventory under which the lender receives control of the pledged inventory collateral, which is stored by a designated warehousing company on the lender's behalf.

? Review Questions

15–18   Is there a cost of *not taking* a cash discount offered on accounts payable? How do short-term borrowing costs affect the cash discount decision?

15–19   How is the prime rate of interest relevant to short-term financing costs?

15–20   Briefly describe each of the following forms of unsecured, short-term bank loans: single-payment notes, lines of credit, and revolving credit agreements.

15–21   How do firms use commercial paper to raise short-term funds?

15–22   Are secured short-term loans viewed as more or less risky than unsecured short-term loans? Why?

15–23   What is the difference between *pledging accounts receivable* and *factoring accounts receivable*? Describe the following methods of using inventory as short-term loan collateral: floating inventory lien, trust receipt inventory loan, and warehouse receipt loan.

TYING IT ALL TOGETHER

This chapter focused on the most important topics related to short-term financial management. The cash conversion cycle provides a framework for linking the key aspects of short-term financial management—inventory, receivables, float, and payables—to the goal of minimizing the firm's reliance on negotiated liabilities. The short-term financing of the firm is represented by its current liabilities, both spontaneous and negotiated. The importance of short-term financial management from the viewpoints of financial managers, financial markets, and investors are summarized in the Integrative Table that follows.

INTEGRATIVE TABLE

Managing Current Assets and Current Liabilities

Role of **Financial Managers**	*Role of* **Financial Markets**	*Role of* **Investors**
Financial managers actively manage the firm's current assets and current liabilities, with the goal of minimizing inventory and accounts receivable and using accruals, accounts payable, and notes payable to obtain short-term financing at minimum cost. They actively manage cash receipts and disbursements to use float to their advantage. The benefits of effective short-term financial management should be larger net cash inflows, reduced negotiated financing, and increased share value.	The financial markets act as the forum in which firms' short-term financial management actions are analyzed and reacted to by investors. Financial markets will respond favorably by buying shares of firms whose short-term financial management activities are deemed efficient and cost-effective. The aggregate responses of investors in the financial marketplace to the financial manager's short-term actions will affect the firm's share price—and therefore owners' wealth.	Investors, often with the aid of financial ratios, attempt to evaluate how well the firm is managing inventory, accounts receivable, cash receipts, cash disbursements, accounts payable, and short-term financing. Good short-term financial management is reflected in minimum reliance on negotiated forms of financing. The net results should be lower costs, greater cash flows, and higher valuations, which should result in increased share values.

LG1 **Describe the scope of short-term financial management and the cash conversion cycle.** Short-term financial management is focused on managing each of the firm's current assets (inventory, accounts receivable, cash, and marketable securities) and current liabilities (accruals, accounts payable, and notes payable) in a manner that positively contributes to the firm's value. The cash conversion cycle represents the amount of time a firm's resources are tied up. It has three components: (1) average age of inventory, (2) average collection period, and (3) average payment period. The length of the cash conversion cycle determines the amount of time resources are tied up in the firm's day-to-day operations.

LG2 **Explain the funding requirements of the cash conversion cycle and strategies for minimizing negotiated liabilities.** The firm's investment in short-term assets often consists of both permanent and seasonal funding requirements. Cyclical or seasonal firms have operating peaks and valleys that cause their level of operating assets to fluctuate and that therefore create seasonal funding requirements. These seasonal requirements can be financed using either a low-cost, high-risk, aggressive financing strategy or a high-cost, low-risk, conservative financing strategy. The firm's funding decision for its cash conversion cycle ultimately depends on management's disposition toward risk and the strength of the firm's banking relationships. To minimize its reliance on negotiated liabilities, the financial manager seeks to (1) turn over inventory as quickly as possible, (2) collect accounts receivable as quickly as possible, (3) manage mail, processing, and clearing time, and (4) pay accounts payable as slowly as possible. Use of these strategies should minimize the cash conversion cycle.

LG3 **Understand inventory management: differing views, common techniques, and international concerns.** The viewpoints of marketing, manufacturing, and purchasing managers about the appropriate levels of inventory tend to cause higher inventories than those deemed appropriate by the financial manager. Four commonly used techniques for effectively managing inventory to keep its level low are (1) the ABC system, (2) the economic order quantity (EOQ) model, (3) the just-in-time (JIT) system, and (4) the materials requirement planning (MRP) system. International inventory managers place greater emphasis on making sure that sufficient quantities of inventory are delivered where they are needed, when they are needed, and in the right condition, than on ordering the economically optimal quantities.

LG4 **Explain the key aspects of accounts receivable management, including credit selection and standards, credit terms, and credit monitoring.** Credit selection and standards are concerned with applying techniques for determining which customers' creditworthiness is consistent with the firm's credit standards. Two popular credit selection techniques are the Five C's of Credit and credit scoring. Changes in credit standards can be evaluated mathematically by assessing the effects of a proposed change on profits on sales, the cost of accounts receivable investment, and bad-debt costs. Changes in credit terms (particularly the initiation of, or a change in, the cash discount) can be quantified in a way similar to that for changes in credit standards. Credit monitoring, the ongoing review of customer payment of accounts receivable, frequently involves use of the average collection period and the aging of accounts receivable. A number of popular collection techniques are used by firms.

LG5 **Review the management of receipts and disbursements, including float, speeding collections, slowing payments, cash concentration, and zero-balance accounts.** Float is the amount of time that elapses between when a payment is mailed by the payer and when the payee has spendable funds. The components of float are mail time, processing time, and clearing time. Float occurs in both the average collection period and the average payment period. One technique for speeding up collections to reduce collection float is a lockbox system. A popular technique for slowing payments to increase payment float is controlled disbursing, which involves strategic use of mailing points and bank accounts. The goal for managing operating cash is to balance the opportunity cost of nonearning balances against the transaction cost of temporary investments. Firms commonly use depository transfer checks (DTCs), ACH transfers, and wire transfers to transfer lockbox receipts to their concentration banks quickly. Zero-balance accounts (ZBAs) can be used to eliminate nonearning cash balances in corporate checking accounts.

 Discuss current liability management, including spontaneous liabilities, unsecured short-term financing, and secured short-term financing. Spontaneous liabilities include accruals and accounts payable. The objective of accounts payable management is to pay accounts as slowly as possible without damaging the firm's credit rating. This is accomplished by paying on the last day of the credit period. If a supplier offers a cash discount, the firm in need of short-term funds must compare the cost of not availing itself of the discount to its least-cost alternative financing source in order to decide whether to decline the discount or take it and borrow elsewhere.

Unsecured short-term financing can be obtained from a bank at a rate tied to the prime rate of interest by using a single-payment note, a line of credit, or a revolving credit agreement. Large firms with high credit standing may issue commercial paper to obtain unsecured short-term financing. International transactions that expose the firm to exchange rate risk can be financed using a letter of credit, by borrowing in the local market, or through dollar-denominated loans from international banks.

Secured short-term financing requires collateral—typically accounts receivable or inventory—and is more costly because the collateral does not reduce the risk of default. Both pledging and factoring accounts receivable can be used to obtain needed short-term funds. Inventory can be used as short-term loan collateral under a floating lien, a trust receipt loan, or a warehouse receipt loan.

SELF-TEST EXERCISES   (Solutions in Appendix B)

LG1 **ST 15–1** **Cash conversion cycle**   Hicks Manufacturing Company pays accounts payable on the tenth day after purchase. The average collection period is 30 days, and the average age of inventory is 40 days. The firm currently spends about $18 million on operating cycle investments. The firm is considering a plan that would stretch its accounts payable by 20 days. If the firm pays 12% per year for its financing, what annual savings can it realize by this plan? Assume no discount for early payment of accounts payable and a 360-day year.

LG3 **ST 15–2** **EOQ analysis**   Frazer Paint Company uses 60,000 gallons of pigment per year. The cost of ordering pigment is $200 per order, and the cost of carrying the pigment in inventory is $1 per gallon per year. The firm uses pigment at a constant rate every day throughout the year.
  a. Calculate the EOQ.
  b. Assuming that it takes 20 days to receive an order once it has been placed, determine the reorder point in terms of gallons of pigment. *(Note:* Use a 360-day year.)

LG4 **ST 15–3** **Relaxing credit standards**   Zoldan Rug Repair Company is trying to decide whether it should relax its credit standards. The firm repairs 72,000 rugs per year at an average price of $32 each. Bad-debt expenses are 1% of sales, the average collection period is 40 days, and the variable cost per unit is $28. If it does relax its credit standards, Zoldan expects that bad debts will increase to 1½% of sales and that the average collection period will increase to 48 days. Sales will increase by 4,000 repairs per year. If the firm has a required rate of return on equal-risk investments of 14%, what recommendation would you give the firm? Use your analysis to justify your answer.

 ST 15–4   Cash discount decisions   The credit terms for each of three suppliers are shown in the following table.

Supplier	Credit terms
X	1/10 net 55 EOM
Y	2/10 net 30 EOM
Z	2/20 net 60 EOM

a. Determine the annual interest cost of *not taking* the cash discount from each supplier.
b. Assuming that the firm needs short-term financing, recommend whether it would be better not to take the cash discount or to take the discount and borrow from a bank at 15% annual interest. Evaluate each supplier separately, using your findings in part **a**.

EXERCISES

  15–1   Cash conversion cycle   Wannemaker Products is concerned about managing cash efficiently. On the average, inventories have an age of 90 days, and accounts receivable are collected in 60 days. Accounts payable are paid approximately 30 days after they arise. The firm spends $30 million on operating cycle investments each year, at a constant rate. Assume a 360-day year.

a. Calculate the firm's operating cycle.
b. Calculate the firm's cash conversion cycle.
c. Calculate the amount of negotiated financing required to support the firm's cash conversion cycle.
d. Discuss how management might be able to reduce the cash conversion cycle.

 15–2   Changing cash conversion cycle   Bonham Industries turns over its inventory 8 times each year, has an average payment period of 35 days, and has an average collection period of 60 days. The firm's total annual outlays for operating cycle investments are $3.5 million. Assume a 360-day year.
a. Calculate the firm's operating and cash conversion cycles.
b. Calculate the firm's daily cash operating expenditure. How much negotiated financing is required to support its cash conversion cycle?
c. If the firm pays 14% for its financing, by how much would it increase its annual profits by *favorably* changing its current cash conversion cycle by 20 days?

  15–3   Multiple changes in cash conversion cycle   Orbell Corporation turns over its inventory six times each year; it has an average collection period of 45 days and an average payment period of 30 days. The firm's annual operating cycle investment is $3 million. Assume a 360-day year.

a. Calculate the firm's cash conversion cycle, its daily cash operating expenditure, and the amount of negotiated financing required to support its cash conversion cycle.

b. Find the firm's cash conversion cycle and negotiated financing requirement if it makes the following changes simultaneously.
   (1) Shortens the average age of inventory by 5 days.
   (2) Speeds the collection of accounts receivable by an average of 10 days.
   (3) Extends the average payment period by 10 days.

c. If the firm pays 13% for its negotiated financing, by how much, if anything, could it increase its annual profit as a result of the changes in part **b**?

d. If the annual cost of achieving the profit in part **c** is $35,000, what action would you recommend to the firm? Why?

 15–4 **Aggressive versus conservative seasonal funding strategy**   Dyster Tool has forecast its total funds requirements for the coming year as shown in the following table.

Month	Amount	Month	Amount
January	$2,000,000	July	$12,000,000
February	2,000,000	August	14,000,000
March	2,000,000	September	9,000,000
April	4,000,000	October	5,000,000
May	6,000,000	November	4,000,000
June	9,000,000	December	3,000,000

a. Divide the firm's monthly funds requirement into (1) a permanent component and (2) a seasonal component, and find the monthly average for each of these components.

b. Describe the amount of long-term and short-term financing used to meet the total funds requirement under (1) an *aggressive funding strategy* and (2) a *conservative funding strategy*. Assume that under the aggressive strategy, long-term funds finance permanent needs and short-term funds are used to finance seasonal needs.

c. Assuming that short-term funds cost 12% annually and that the cost of long-term funds is 17% annually, use the averages found in part **a** to calculate the total cost of each of the strategies described in part **b**.

d. Discuss the profitability–risk tradeoffs associated with the aggressive strategy and those associated with the conservative strategy.

 15–5 **EOQ analysis**   Lauras Electronics purchases 1,200,000 units per year of one component. The fixed cost per order is $25. The annual carrying cost of the item is 27% of its $2 cost.

a. Determine the EOQ under the following conditions: (1) no changes, (2) order cost of zero, and (3) carrying cost of zero.

b. What do your answers illustrate about the EOQ model? Explain.

 15–6 **EOQ, reorder point, and safety stock**   Scala Company uses 800 units of a product per year on a continuous basis. The product has a fixed cost of $50 per order, and its carrying cost is $2 per unit per year. It takes 5 days to receive a shipment after an order is placed, and the firm wishes to hold 10 days' usage in inventory as a safety stock.

a. Calculate the EOQ.

b. Determine the average level of inventory. *(Note: Use a 360-day year to calculate daily usage.)*

c. Determine the reorder point.

d. Indicate which of the following variables change if the firm does not hold the safety stock: (1) order cost, (2) carrying cost, (3) total inventory cost, (4) reorder point, (5) economic order quantity. Explain.

LG4 **15–7** **Accounts receivable changes without bad debts**   Stahl Appliance currently has credit sales of $360 million per year and an average collection period of 60 days. Assume that the price of Stahl's products is $60 per unit and that the variable costs are $55 per unit. The firm is considering an accounts receivable change that will result in a 20% increase in sales and a 20% increase in the average collection period. No change in bad debts is expected. The firm's equal-risk opportunity cost on its investment in accounts receivable is 14%.

a. Calculate the additional profit contribution from new sales that the firm will realize if it makes the proposed change.

b. What marginal investment in accounts receivable will result?

c. Calculate the cost of the marginal investment in accounts receivable.

d. Should the firm implement the proposed change? What other information would be helpful in your analysis?

LG4 **15–8** **Accounts receivable changes with bad debts**   A firm is evaluating an accounts receivable change that would increase bad debts from 2% to 4% of sales. Sales are currently 50,000 units, the selling price is $20 per unit, and the variable cost per unit is $15. As a result of the proposed change, sales are forecast to increase to 60,000 units.

a. What are bad debts in dollars currently and under the proposed change?

b. Calculate the cost of the marginal bad debts to the firm.

c. Ignoring the additional profit contribution from increased sales, if the proposed change saves $3,500 and causes no change in the average investment in accounts receivable, would you recommend it? Explain.

d. Considering *all* changes in costs and benefits, would you recommend the proposed change? Explain.

e. Compare and discuss your answers in parts c and d.

LG4 **15–9** **Relaxation of credit standards**   Aboud Industries is considering relaxing its credit standards to increase its currently sagging sales. As a result of the proposed relaxation, sales are expected to increase by 10% from 10,000 to 11,000 units, during the coming year; the average collection period is expected to increase from 45 to 60 days; and bad debts are expected to increase from 1% to 3% of sales. The sale price per unit is $40, and the variable cost per unit is $31. The firm's required return on equal-risk investments is 25%. Evaluate the proposed relaxation, and make a recommendation to the firm.

LG4 **15–10** **Initiating a cash discount**   Preston Products currently makes all sales on credit and offers no cash discount. The firm is considering offering a 2% cash discount for payment within 15 days. The firm's current average collection period is 60 days, sales are 40,000 units, selling price is $45 per unit, and variable cost per unit is $36. The firm expects that the change in credit terms will result in an increase in sales to 42,000 units, that 70% of the sales will take the discount, and that the average collection period will fall to 30 days. If the firm's required rate of return on equal-risk investments is 25%, should the proposed discount be offered?

LG5 **15–11** **Float**   Ensor Industries has daily cash receipts of $65,000. A recent analysis of its collections indicated that customers' payments were in the mail an average of 2.5 days. Once received, the payments are processed in 1.5 days. After payments are deposited, it takes an average of 3 days for these receipts to clear the banking system.

a. How much collection float (in days) does the firm currently have?

b. If the firm's opportunity cost is 11%, would it be economically advisable for the firm to pay an annual fee of $16,500 to reduce collection float by 3 days? Explain why or why not.

LG5   15–12   Lockbox system   Asian Oil feels that a lockbox system can shorten its accounts receivable collection period by 3 days. Credit sales are $3,240,000 per year, billed on a continuous basis. The firm has other equally risky investments with a return of 15%. The cost of the lockbox system is $9,000 per year.

a. What amount of cash will be made available for other uses under the lockbox system?

b. What net benefit (cost) will the firm realize if it adopts the lockbox system? Should it adopt the proposed lockbox system?

LG5   15–13   Zero-balance account   Duong Industries is considering establishment of a zero-balance account. The firm currently maintains an average balance of $420,000 in its disbursement account. As compensation to the bank for maintaining the zero-balance account, the firm will have to pay a monthly fee of $1,000 and maintain a $300,000 non–interest-earning deposit in the bank. The firm currently has no other deposits in the bank. Evaluate the proposed zero-balance account, and make a recommendation to the firm, assuming that it has a 12% opportunity cost.

LG6   15–14   Cost of not taking cash discounts   Determine the cost of *not taking* cash discounts under each of the following terms of sale.

a. 2/10 net 30   **e.** 1/10 net 60

b. 1/10 net 30   **f.** 3/10 net 30

c. 2/10 net 45   **g.** 4/10 net 180

d. 3/10 net 45

LG6   15–15   Cash discount versus loan   Dan Andrews works in an accounts payable department. He has attempted to convince his boss to take the discount on the 3/10 net 45 credit terms most suppliers offer, but his boss argues that giving up the 3% discount is less costly than a short-term loan at 14%. Prove that either Dan or his boss is incorrect.

LG6   15–16   Cash discount decisions   Renly Manufacturing has four possible suppliers, each offering different credit terms. Except for the differences in credit terms, their products and services are virtually identical. The credit terms offered by each supplier are shown in the following table.

Supplier	Credit terms
Q	1/10 net 30 EOM
R	2/20 net 80 EOM
S	1/20 net 60 EOM
T	3/10 net 55 EOM

a. Calculate the cost of *not taking* the cash discount from each supplier.

b. If the firm needs short-term funds, which are currently available from its commercial bank at 16%, and if each of the suppliers is viewed *separately*, which, if any, of the suppliers' cash discounts should the firm not take? Explain why.

c. What impact, if any, would the fact that the firm could stretch its accounts payable (net period only) by 30 days from supplier T have on your answer in part **b** relative to this supplier?

web exercises   Search

Go to web site **www.firstar.com**. Click **BUSINESS SERVICES**.
1. What are the business services offered for Small Business Banking?
Click **TREASURY MANAGEMENT SERVICES**.
2. What are the services available to Speed Up Collections? To Control Cash Flow?
Click **RETAIL LOCKBOX SERVICE**.
3. What companies could use this service?

Go to web site **www.national-city.com**. Click on **Business Banking**.
4. Under the **More Info** menu, what are the services available for Treasury Management?
5. Under the **More Info** menu, what are the services available for International Services?

Go to web site **www.firstmerchants.com**. Click on **FIRST MERCHANTS BANK—Hamilton County**. Next, click on **COMMERCIAL BANKING SERVICES**.
6. What are the services available to businesses?

Go to web site **www.citgroup.com**. On the menu under **Business Financing Solutions,** scroll down to "I want to know more info about."
7. What options are available?
On that same menu, select **Factoring Services** and then click **Go**.
8. What is the complete financial package of factoring?
At the end of that screen, click **"Why do companies use factoring?"**
9. Why use factoring?
On the **Business Financing Solutions** menu, select **Receivables Outstanding Service** and then click **Go**.
10. What are the commercial services options available?

For additional practice with concepts from this chapter, visit
http://www.awl.com/gitman_madura

exam-ace.net

Assessing the Feasibility of exam-ace.net's Expansion Idea

The investment decisions of exam-ace.net will determine how the business grows. Tom Turner, the owner, considers investing funds to offer a "practice test" service for professional license examinations for accountants. Although there are many accounting testing services, these services have not taken advantage of the Internet to provide tests in the way Tom plans (although they have the ability to do so). Tom has already obtained bids on the work that needs to be done for this project, and he realizes that he would need more funds to pursue this project. Tom himself would provide a small amount of the investment for this new project. He plans to invite the other investor, Dan Atkinson, to provide most of the funding and hopes to obtain partial funding (another loan) from the same financial institution from which the firm already borrowed funds.

Tom developed the following cash flow estimates for the proposed new service:

- Hire consultants immediately to develop a tailor-made web site and computer system to receive orders online, accept payment online (credit card), and provide practice tests online. Initial outlay = $75,000 (after considering tax effects).

- Hire instructors immediately to develop practice tests and to improve the questions over time. Cost = $20,000 at the end of each year.

- Advertise in numerous accounting magazines and in college newspapers. Cost = $40,000, with payments made at the end of this year.

Tom also developed estimates of the revenue he would generate as a result of providing the new service. He expects to generate the following revenue over time:

End of year	Revenue
1	$ 60,000
2	70,000
3	70,000
4	80,000
5	90,000
6	$100,000

The company pays its expenses as they occur (there are no accounts payable). The revenue is received immediately (there are no accounts receivable). Tom expects to pay 30% taxes on any earnings from this project. Tom is planning to sell this business at the end of the sixth year. He expects that he will be able to sell the business at that time for $90,000 (after considering taxes).

Exercises

CC3–1 Tom requires a return of 20% on the new project; if the project is expected to generate a return less than 20%, Tom will not pursue it. Given the data outlined above, will Tom pursue the project?

CC3–2 Assume that although the estimated sale price of $90,000 (after paying any capital gains taxes) in 6 years was Tom's best guess (60% probability), Tom thought there was a 40% probability that the estimated sale price would be $70,000. Should Tom pursue this project given this information?

CC3–3 Consider that just before Tom conducts his analysis, he hears a rumor that an existing

Internet firm is planning to pursue the same type of project. How might Tom revise his analysis on the basis of this information? Why might his decision of whether to accept or reject the project change?

CC3-4 Tom's initial capital budgeting analysis was based on his plan to obtain mostly equity financing from an investor (such as Dan Atkinson). Explain in general terms how the analysis would change if Tom obtained two-thirds of the funds by borrowing from a commercial bank at an interest rate of 13%. What is a disadvantage of using a large amount of debt instead of equity to finance this project?

CC3-5 Up to this point, this specific project has been assessed independently of the existing business conducted by exam-ace.net. Is there any reason to think that the cash flows of this project might be affected because the project would be managed by ExamAce.net?

CC3-6 Communication Tom asks you to offer your opinion of whether the new ideas will work and of the risk involved. Communicate to Tom, with an email memo, your opinion of whether the new idea will work and of the risk involved.

CC3-7 Teamwork Create a team of three students, in which one student plays the role of Tom; one student plays the role of the investor, Dan; and one student plays the role of the lender. Assume that all three students agree that Tom's original estimates are reasonable as a best guess. Is the student who plays the role of the investor willing to invest in this firm? Is the student who plays the role of the lender willing to lend more to the firm? How can Tom attempt to convince the investor and the lender to provide financing for this project?

CC3-8 Ethics Tom sincerely believes in this new project. However, he is concerned that an investor will not see the value of this project and therefore will not provide the funding that is needed. Therefore, he considers adjusting the analysis to make the NPV look higher than what he really expects. Should Tom adjust the analysis?

Investment Management

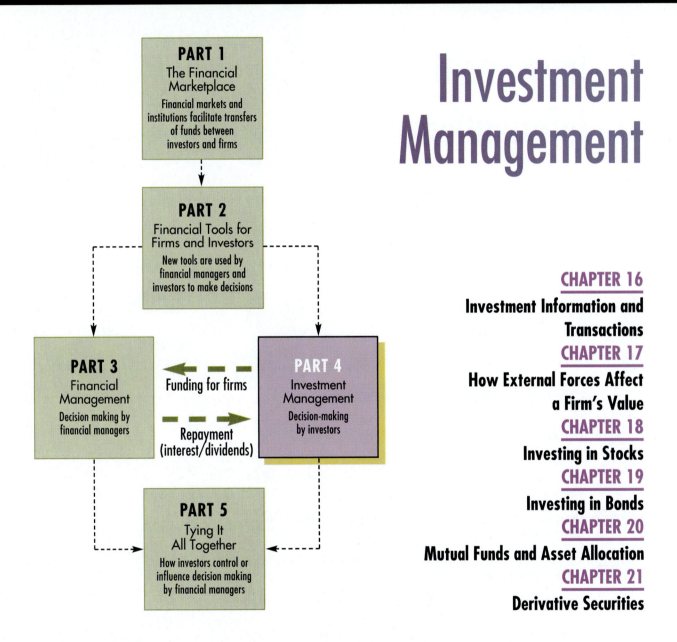

PART 1
The Financial Marketplace
Financial markets and institutions facilitate transfers of funds between investors and firms

PART 2
Financial Tools for Firms and Investors
New tools are used by financial managers and investors to make decisions

PART 3
Financial Management
Decision making by financial managers

Funding for firms

Repayment (interest/dividends)

PART 4
Investment Management
Decision-making by investors

PART 5
Tying It All Together
How investors control or influence decision making by financial managers

Up to this point, we have addressed the topics covered in this text from the financial manager's perspective. At this point, the focus shifts to the investor's perspective. Part 4 addresses the topic of investment management. It shows how investors can assess and value the financial performance of firms, and it explores various investment alternatives for individual investors.

Investment Information and Transactions

LEARNING GOALS

LG1 Review background material on investing.

LG2 Describe the economic, industry, global, and market information sources used to make investment decisions.

LG3 Describe the firm-specific information services used to make investment decisions.

LG4 Identify the main U.S. and foreign securities exchanges in the U.S. that facilitate the investing process.

LG5 Describe the types of securities transactions requested by investors, and explain how these transactions are accommodated by brokerage firms.

Background on Investing

Investors can be classified as *individual* investors or *institutional* investors. Most individual investors focus on investing a portion of the funds that they earned from their regular jobs. When they sell securities that they have held for 12 months or longer, gains are subject to a *long-term capital gains tax*. The capital gains tax is dependent on one's income but has a maximum limit of 20 percent. By contrast, the *short-term capital gains* (on investments held for less than 12 months) is treated as ordinary income.

day traders
Individuals who make investments and close out their positions in the same day.

Some individual investors, called **day traders,** make investments and close out those positions in the same day. They hope to capitalize on very short-term movements in security prices. In many cases, their investments may last for only a few minutes or a few hours. Many day traders conduct their investing as a career. That is, they rely on their returns from investing as their main source of income. Because day traders generate short-term capital gains they incur high taxes on their gains (assuming that they are in a high ordinary income tax bracket).

Institutional investors are employed by firms (especially financial institutions) to invest funds on behalf of their employers or the clients they are serving. They are commonly referred to as **portfolio managers** because they manage a portfolio of securities. Some commercial bank portfolio managers manage a portfolio of bonds, mortgages, or money market securities for their respective banks. Portfolio managers at savings institutions play a similar role. Insurance company portfolio managers invest the proceeds received from insurance premiums in bond or stock portfolios. The portfolios are intended to increase in value until the funds are needed to pay insurance claims.

portfolio managers
Employees of financial institutions who are responsible for managing a portfolio of securities.

Mutual fund portfolio managers use the proceeds received from shareholders (who invest in mutual funds) to invest in securities (mostly stocks or bonds). *Pension fund portfolio managers* invest the proceeds received from retirement contributions in bond or stock portfolios. The portfolios are intended to increase in value until the funds are needed to make payments to participants after retirement. In the aggregate, institutional investors have a major influence on market prices because of the large volume of their investments.

Impact of Investment Decisions on Wealth

Institutional and individual investors recognize that their future wealth is dependent on their investment decisions. If an individual investor invests $50,000 today in a stock that appreciates 5 percent annually, the stock will be worth $132,665 in 20 years. But if the investor can select a stock that appreciates 8 percent annually, the investment will accumulate to $233,050. Thus the extra 3 percentage points in the return reflects an additional $100,385 in wealth. If the investor could earn 12 percent annually, the investment would accumulate to $482,315 in 20 years. Thus the extra 4 percentage points in return (relative to the 8 percent return) generate an additional $249,265 in wealth in 20 years. An investor's investment decisions will determine the annual return and, therefore, the accumulated wealth resulting from those investments.

Similarly, the decisions of institutional investors determine the wealth of the security portfolios they are managing. For example, a pension fund portfolio that

FIGURE 16.1

FIGURE 16.1

Dollar Value of a $10,000 Investment in 20 Years, Based on Various Annualized Returns

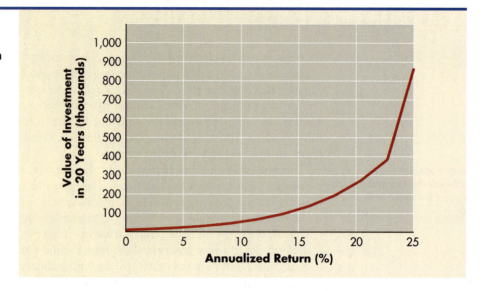

is worth $10,000 today will be worth $26,533 in 20 years if it earns a 5 percent return (assuming returns are reinvested), $46,610 if it earns an 8 percent return, or $96,463 if it earns a 12 percent return. Thus the wealth accumulated in 20 years with a 12 percent return is about $50,000 more than the wealth accumulated with an 8 percent return, and about $70,000 more than the wealth accumulated with a 5 percent return.

Given that earning an extra few percentage points of annual return yields such large differences in the accumulated portfolio value, some investors spend much time assessing investment information, which may enable them to achieve higher returns. Figure 16.1 illustrates the value in 20 years resulting from a $10,000 investment today under different assumptions about the annualized return. This figure reinforces the notion that a slight difference in annualized return can have a large impact on the future dollar value of an investment over time.

Just as financial managers face a return and risk tradeoff when making investment decisions for a firm, individual and institutional investors face such a tradeoff when making their investment decisions. They can select investments that are subject to little or no uncertainty (risk) but will earn a relatively low return. At the other extreme, they can select investments that have the potential to earn more than 50 percent in a single year (or even within a single month), but there is much risk associated with these investments. There are many other investments available that are in between these two extremes. Investors who decide to pursue investments that have much higher potential returns must be willing to accept the higher risk associated with these investments. Investors rely on information to determine the types of securities that may satisfy their desired return from investing and not exceed their degree of risk tolerance.

Some of the more common investment decisions are how much to invest in securities, how to allocate funds between different types of securities (such as stocks and bonds), and which specific securities to purchase as investments. Before deciding which securities to purchase, investors consider their anticipated income and expenses. Investors with large anticipated incomes relative to their expenses have more flexibility to invest in risky securities. When making their investment decisions, investors must understand the securities exchanges that exist and how they function. Investors must also be aware of the sources from which they can obtain information before making investment decisions. We turn our attention next to a description of securities-related information that is available to investors. Later in the chapter, we will discuss securities exchanges.

? Review Question

16–1 Why might an investor prefer to invest in a bank deposit that offers only a 5 percent annual return rather than in a stock that some investors expect to earn a return of 40 percent over the next year?

General Information Used to Make Investment Decisions

Recall that the value of securities issued by firms is equal to the present value of their future cash flows. When investors value securities that they own or consider purchasing, they use any information that can affect either the expected cash flows generated by the security or the required rate of return used to discount cash flows. Information can be segmented according to whether it pertains to economic conditions, industry conditions, global conditions, market conditions, or the issuer's financial condition. All of these types of information may be important. For example, the valuation of a stock or bond requires an assessment of external forces (including economic, industry, and global conditions), the firm's financial condition, and the firm's sensitivity to external forces.

Economic Information

A substantial amount of economic information is provided by the federal government and by the private sector. This information includes trends of interest rates, inflation rates, and economic growth. The main sources of economic information are listed in Table 16.1.

Industry Information

The most popular sources of industry information are provided by the private sector. Useful information about industry conditions includes industry ratios, forecasts of growth in each industry, and commentaries about competition within each industry. Sources of industry information are identified in Table 16.2.

Global Information

Some publications provide economic and industry information on a global basis. This type of information is especially relevant for investors who are assessing firms with foreign subsidiaries. Economic conditions can vary substantially across countries. In addition, political conditions of foreign countries must be considered, and some publications disclose political information for various countries. A summary of sources of global information appears in Table 16.3.

Market Information

Market conditions indicate how investors in general are valuing firms and how investors are responding to economic, industry, and global conditions. Market conditions include not only price quotations of securities but also opinions about specific firms or industries. A summary of market information sources is given in Table 16.4.

? Review Questions

16–2 Explain why investors should monitor economic conditions.
16–3 Explain why investors should monitor industry conditions.

TABLE 16.1	Sources of Economic Information
Published Sources	
Federal Reserve Bulletin	Provides data on economic conditions, including interest rates, unemployment rates, inflation rates, and money supply. Also provides information about activity in the stock market, bond market, and money markets. Published monthly.
Survey of Current Business	Issued monthly by the Department of Commerce. Provides data on national income and production levels, and employment levels. It also discloses various economic indicators.
Economic Report of the President	Reports the economic conditions over the last year, and provides an economic outlook. Published each January.
Quarterly Financial Report (QFR)	Issued by the Federal Trade Commission. Provides financial statement data for manufacturing companies, including income statements, balance sheets, and various financial ratios.
Federal Reserve Bank publication	Reports on national and regional economic conditions, economic statistics, research reports on specific banking issues, and reports on other economic issues.
Reports by securities firms	Provide economic summaries and outlooks as a service to existing and potential clients.
Online Sources	
Bloomberg	(www.bloomberg.com) Provides economic reports.
Yahoo!	(www.yahoo.com) Provides information about U.S. economic conditions.
Moody's	(www.moodys.com) Provides an economic commentary.
Federal Reserve System	(www.bog.frb.fed.us/) Provides press releases related to the economy and offers economic research.
Investorlinks	(www.investorlinks.com/charts/index.html) Provides an outlook for U.S. gross domestic product, unemployment, inflation, payrolls, and the federal budget deficit.
U.S. Census Bureau	(www.census.gov/econ/www/toc.html) Provides an overview of the U.S. economy.

TABLE 16.2   Sources of Industry Information

Published Sources

Value Line Survey	Provides background on the performance of various industries and offers an industry outlook. Also provides detailed information about various industries, including mean financial statistics among firms in each industry over time. Provides a table with comparative data that corresponds to its analysis of individual firms to facilitate comparison analysis to industry norms.
Standard and Poor's Industry Survey	Provides a detailed summary of several different industries. The summary includes a historical assessment of each industry, as well as statistics, and an outlook for investors who consider investing in that industry.
Standard and Poor's Analysts Handbook	Provides detailed information about various industries, including mean financial statistics (such as some financial ratios) among the firms in each industry over time. This provides investors with an industry norm to which any individual firm's statistics can be compared.
Reports by securities firms	Provide information on the outlook for specific industries to existing and potential clients.
Industry-specific periodicals	Focused on a single industry for those investors or analysts who concentrate their efforts in one industry.

Online Sources

Investorlinks	(www.investorlinks.com) Contains news articles related to specific industries.
The U.S. Census Bureau	(www.census.gov/econ/www/toc.html) Provides an overview of several broad industry sectors, including construction, mining, retail, and wholesale sectors.
Yahoo!	(www.yahoo.com) Provides stock indexes for various industry sectors.
CNBC	(www.cnbc.com/tickerguide/indices.html) Provides stock indexes for various industry sectors.
Bloomberg	(www.bloomberg.com) Identifies industry movers that, as measured by industry stock indexes, experienced substantial change recently.

TABLE 16.3   Sources of Global Information

Published Sources

International Financial Statistics	Published by the International Monetary Fund. Provides data on exchange rates, interest rates, national income levels, and employment levels for each country.
Financial Times	Provides information about global economic conditions around the world. Published on weekdays in London.
Asian Wall Street Journal	Provides information about economic conditions in Asia. Published weekly.
European Wall Street Journal	Provides information about economic conditions in Europe. Published weekly.
Survey of Current Business	Issued monthly by the Department of Commerce. Provides data on direct foreign investment in the United States and by U.S. firms in foreign countries.
Reports by securities firms	Provide summaries of economic conditions in foreign countries and offers global outlooks to clients.

Online Sources

The Federal Reserve	(www.bog.frb.fed.us/) Provides information on international economic conditions.
Investorlinks	(investorlinks.com/global.html) Provides economic statistics and economic indicators for various countries.
Bloomberg	(www.bloomberg.com) Provides information about international interest rates, exchange rates, and financial markets.
Yahoo!	(www.yahoo.com) Contains news about exchange rate movements and international economic conditions.

TABLE 16.4	Sources of Market Information
Published Sources	
The Wall Street Journal	Provides stock market quotations, bond market quotations, money market quotations, and quotations for various derivative securities markets. Includes information about securities markets around the world. Also provides articles that explain recent market conditions. Published on weekdays.
Investor's Business Daily	Provides price quotations on securities and also offers much information about market activity. Published on weekdays.
Barron's	Provides stock market quotations, bond market quotations, money market quotations, and quotations for various derivative security markets. Includes information about securities markets around the world. Also provides articles that explain recent market conditions. Barron's has more information about the markets than the *Wall Street Journal* and is less focused on general news about corporations. Published weekly.
Financial Times	Offers corporate news and investing news from around the world. Provides quotations for various securities markets and derivative securities markets. Published on weekdays in London.
Asian Wall Street Journal	Provides information about economic conditions and securities markets in Asia. Published weekly.
European Wall Street Journal	Provides information about economic conditions and securities markets in Europe. Published weekly.
Reports by securities firms	Provide clients with summaries of existing market conditions and forecasts of future market conditions.
Online Services	
Investorlinks	(www.investorlinks.com) Provides a summary of U.S. market conditions and important related news and highlights. A particular Investorlinks web site link (www.investorlinks.com/commentary/index.html) provides market commentary articles related to stock and bond markets.
Bloomberg	(www.bloomberg.com) Provides quotations and commentaries on various markets.
Yahoo!	(www.yahoo.com) Provides quotations for numerous market indexes.

LG3 Firm-Specific Information

Just as financial managers continuously assess the firm that they manage, investors continuously assess firms in which they have invested or may invest. As new information about a firm becomes available, they revalue the firm by incorporating that information.

However, the assessment of a firm by investors is different from the assessment of a firm by its financial managers. Financial managers have access to much more information about the firm. For example, the financial managers may know what the forecasted cash flows are for various projects, the various types of businesses that the firm may pursue in the future, and the projects that the firm is presently considering or will be implementing in the future. The investors are at a disadvantage because of this *asymmetric information,* or the difference in the amount of relevant information about a firm that its financial managers have and the amount of relevant information available to investors. Nevertheless, there is some publicly available information about firms that may be useful when making investment decisions, which is identified next.

TABLE 16.5	How Investors Use Balance Sheet and Income Statement Information
Assessment of liquidity	Investors assess a firm's liquidity by estimating various liquidity measures, such as *net working capital,* the *current ratio,* and the *quick ratio.* These measures attempt to measure a firm's ability to cover short-term obligations as they come due. If a firm has difficulty covering its short-term obligations, it may need either to borrow more funds or to sell some of its existing assets to obtain cash. Higher values relative to an industry norm reflect higher degrees of liquidity.
Assessment of efficiency	Investors assess a firm's efficiency by considering various activity ratios that measure the speed at which assets can generate cash. The *inventory turnover* measures the activity of a firm's inventory—how many times a year the inventory "turns over" (is sold). The *average collection period* measures the average age of accounts receivable. The *total asset turnover* measures the efficiency with which a firm uses its assets to generate revenues. Higher values relative to an industry norm reflect higher degrees of efficiency.
Assessment of financial leverage	Investors assess a firm's ability to repay debt by considering its degree of financial leverage. A common measure of financial leverage is the *debt ratio,* which measures the proportion of total assets financed by creditors. A high debt ratio relative to an industry norm reflects a high degree of financial leverage and a high risk of default on future debt payments. An alternative measure of a firm's ability to repay its debt is the *times-interest-earned ratio,* which is the ratio of the firm's earnings before interest and taxes to its interest payments. A higher times-interest-earned ratio relative to an industry norm reflects a greater ability to cover future interest payments.
Profitability	Investors assess a firm's profitability by considering profitability ratios. Some profitability margins are measured as a percentage of sales over a specific period. The *gross profit margin* measures gross profits as a percentage of sales; the *operating profit margin* measures the operating profit as a percentage of sales; and the *net profit margin* measures net profit as a percentage of sales. Other profitability margins are measured as a percentage of balance sheet items. The *return on assets* measures net profit as a percentage of total assets, and the *return on equity* measures net profit as a percentage of the owners' investment in the firm (stockholders' equity). A higher value for all of the profitability measures identified here, relative to an industry norm, reflect high profitability.

Annual Report

As explained in Chapter 8, publicly traded firms are required to file with the Securities and Exchange Commission (SEC) an annual report, which includes financial statements in a standardized format. The three financial statements most important to investors are the balance sheet, income statement, and statement of cash flows.

Balance Sheet

Investors use the balance sheet of a firm to determine how it has obtained funds (liabilities and stockholder's equity) and how it has invested funds (assets) as of a particular point in time. The balance sheet identifies the proportion of funds obtained in the form of debt and therefore is used to measure financial leverage to assess the firm's financial risk.

Income Statement

Investors use the income statement of a firm to determine the firm's flow of revenues, expenses, and earnings over a particular period of time (such as a quarter or a year). Most investors rely on information from the balance sheet and income statement to assess the firm's liquidity, efficiency in managing its assets, ability to repay debt, and profitability. How investors assess these characteristics was discussed in detail in Chapter 8 and is summarized in Table 16.5.

GOSSIPING AROUND THE ELECTRONIC WATER COOLER

The wealth of investment information available online has made some people more aggressive investors. However, investors need to be careful how they interpret and use that information, and they must continue to do basic research and planning, as this reading suggests. The web site at which the reading originated, MSN MoneyCentral, is a comprehensive investment site that includes articles on investing as well as current stock information.

The Web has democratized investing. When I started as a financial reporter on the business desk of the *Kansas City Star* 25 years ago, information belonged to the wealthy, to the insiders, to those who had the right stockbroker. Those who had the information could arbitrage it, making a profit from those of us who didn't.

Today, the information belongs to all of us. The Web has given us access not just to data but to the analytics we need to help us make investment decisions....I can research a stock or mutual fund's investment performance or financial health, read the latest news, or see what analysts think with just a click of a mouse in the stock or fund research areas.

So today we are much better able to invest on our own. That's the good news. Here's the bad news: You still need to come up with a strategy and a plan, set goals, and do your research. Just because the medium has changed doesn't mean the investing basics have.

The same people who used to pick up tips at the office water cooler are now coming online and mistaking stock touts and gossip for real information....

This technologically enhanced form of stock gossip has produced a new type of speculation in the financial markets. Floyd Norris, one of the most influential reporters on Wall Street, wrote an interesting column...[on] "the one-day wonder," which he defined as a "long-dormant stock that leaps from a low price to a very high one in the course of a single day, or at most two."...Norris mentioned a company called V-ONE (VONE), which went public at $5 in 1996 and has steadily lost money. Early this month, V-ONE announced it was ready to ship an Internet-related product. That is the type of information that travels like lightning on the Web. V-ONE's shares leapt from less than $4 to $15.50 in just a day. Two days later, they were back under $8.

Source: Mary Rowland, "How the Web Helps You 'Grow' As an Investor," MSN MoneyCentral, December 15, 1999, downloaded from moneycentral.msn.com/articles/invest/careful/4889.asp?ID=4889.

Statement of Cash Flows

Investors estimate future cash flows of firms by using their recent statement of cash flows as a base. When estimating cash flows in future years, investors must distinguish between those cash flows reported in the most recent year that are likely to occur in following years, and one-time cash flows that are not likely to occur again. For example, it would be a mistake to use last year's cash flow of $500 million as a forecast of cash flows in future years if $200 million of the $500 million is attributed to the firm's sale of one of its divisions. First, the $200 million is a one-time cash inflow that will not occur again. Second, if that division were responsible for generating cash flow in the past, investors must avoid counting that cash flow when estimating future estimated cash flows.

Other Financial Reports

Publicly traded firms also file an *8-K form* monthly with the SEC; this form discloses any significant changes in the firm's capital structure, asset structure, or ownership structure that could affect the firm's value. They file a *9-K form* every six months; it primarily discloses income statement information. They also file a *10-K form*, which has a more detailed income statement and other information that is not provided in the 9-K form or in the annual report. Firms make the 10-K form available to investors upon request, and many investors prefer to use this form for analyzing firms. These reports are available online at the Electronic Data Gathering, Analysis, and Retrieval (EDGAR) web site (www.sec.gov/index.html), which is a filing database of the Securities and Exchange Commission.

Security Prospectus

prospectus
Documents submitted by a firm to the SEC that summarize the firm's financial condition.

A firm that plans to issue new securities is required to file a **prospectus** with the Securities and Exchange Commission. The prospectus is especially useful for investors who are considering investing in the new securities issued by the firm. Because it contains very detailed financial information, it is also useful for investors who are monitoring the firm for other reasons.

Firm-Specific Information Provided by Publications

In addition to firm-specific information provided by the firm itself, various publications and online information are provided by other investment services. Some of these key sources of firm-specific information are listed in Table 16.6.

Close-up of Value Line Information

One of the most commonly used sources of firm-specific information (included in Table 16.6) is the *Value Line Investment Survey*. An example of the type of information provided by Value Line is shown in Figure 16.2. Because this type of analysis is very useful for investors who assess individual stocks, we will describe it here in detail. Each segment of the figure is marked to correspond with the following discussion.

In Figure 16.2, first notice the name of the stock in the top left corner (marked 1). Second, the recent stock price and the price/earnings (P/E) ratio (based on expected earnings), the relative P/E ratio (the firm's P/E ratio divided by the average P/E ratio of comparable firms in the industry), and the firm's dividend yield (annual dividends/price per share) are shown along the top line (marked 2).

The trend in the firm's stock price over the last several years is shown at the top of the page and is adjusted for stock splits (marked 3). Trading volume information is shown at the bottom of the stock price trend.

The spreadsheet shown just below the stock price trend (near the middle of the page, marked 4) provides the trend of various financial statement items, which are identified in the right margin. Some of the items (such as revenues, cash flow, capital spending, and book value) are standardized on a per-share basis, which allows for comparison to corresponding items of other firms in the same industry.

The time series of the P/E ratio, relative P/E ratio, and dividend yield is shown in that spreadsheet. Various profitability ratios are also disclosed, including the net profit margin and the net income earned as a percent of net worth ("% Earned Net Worth"), which represents the return on shareholders' equity.

Just to the left of the bottom part of the spreadsheet is the firm's capital structure (marked 5). Just below is information used to assess the firm's liquidity. Below that are historical data on revenues, earnings, and dividends (marked 6).

TABLE 16.6	Sources of Firm-Specific Information
Published Sources	
Standard & Poor's Corporate Records	Provides detailed financial information about each corporation, including selected income statement and balance sheet items, capital structure information, and the history of securities issuances by the corporation.
Standard & Poor's Stock Reports	Provide historical stock price information, balance sheet and income statement information, financial ratios, and an outlook for the future. The summaries of all firms are categorized according to the stock exchange on which their stock is traded.
Standard & Poor's Stock Guide	Provides financial information focused on the stock of a firm, including the proportion of the firm's stock that is held by institutional investors and the range of the stock price.
Standard & Poor's Bond Guide	A monthly publication offering financial information related to bonds that have been issued.
The Outlook	Provides information about existing market and future market conditions. Provides stock index quotations for numerous industries, so that investors can monitor the stock performance of any particular industry or compare an individual firm to a specific industry index. Published weekly by Standard & Poor's Corporation.
Moody's Industrial Manual	Provides detailed financial information about each corporation, including selected income statement and balance sheet items and capital structure information for each firm.
Moody's OTC Manual	Provides detailed financial information for each firm that is traded on the over-the-counter market.
Moody's Bank and Finance Manual	Provides information on firms in financial industries such as banking and insurance.
Value Line Investment Survey	Provides detailed information pulled from financial statements, along with projections of earnings for the future. It also discloses growth rates and measures of the firm's risk.
Reports by securities firms	Provide clients with reports on individual companies that the securities firms monitor.
Online Sources	
Many firms provide their annual reports on their web sites.	
Report Gallery	(www.reportgallery.com) Provides annual reports for many firms.
Yahoo!	(www.yahoo.com) Provides a stock screener that allows investors to identify stocks that have particular financial characteristics.

A general description of the firm's business appears just below the right portion of the spreadsheet (marked 7). Just below that description is Value Line's assessment of the firm's value (marked 8). This description commonly offers useful insights not immediately apparent from the financial data.

Near the upper left corner of the page (marked 9), Value Line rates the firm according to timeliness (to purchase shares of the stock) and safety and also discloses the firm's beta (measurement of its risk). Just below that information, Value Line reports its stock price projections for the firm over the next few years (marked 10). Value Line also provides information on trading by insiders (marked 11) and trading activity by institutional investors (marked 12).

Insider Trading by the Firm's Financial Managers

inside information
Relevant information for investment decisions, known by a firm's financial managers but not known by its investors.

The relevant information known by a firm's financial managers, but not known by its investors is referred to as **inside information.** Financial managers are commonly referred to as *insiders* because they have access to the inside information.

FIGURE 16.2 **Example of Firm-Specific Information Provided by** *Value Line Investment Survey*

Source: Value Line Investment Survey, December 17, 1999.

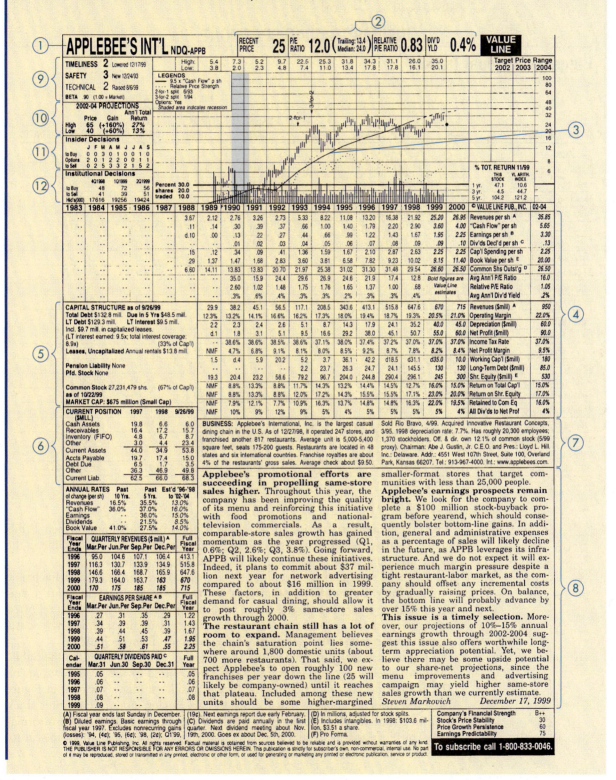

FIGURE 16.3   **Insider Trading**
Biggest individual trades by insiders, reported by the *Wall Street Journal*.

Source: *Wall Street Journal*, February 2, 2000, p. C17.

INSIDER TRADING SPOTLIGHT

Biggest Individual Trades
(Based on reports filed with regulators last week)

COMANY NAME	EXCH.	INSIDER'S NAME	TITLE	$ VALUE (000)	NO. OF SHRS. IN TRANS. (000)	% OF HLDNG. EXCLD. OPTNS.	TRANSACTION DATES
BUYERS							
American Financial Grp	N	C. H. Lindner x	CB	4,816	187.0	2.00	12/06-30/99
Oakley	N	J. Jannard	CB	1,112	200.0	0.50	12/08/99
Hewlett-Packard	N	P. C. Dunn	D	541	5.0	133.00	12/09/99
Meadowbrook Insur Grp	N	L. F. Swider x	D	310	55.0	17.00	12/02-17/99
Hearx Ltd	A	T. W. Archibald s	D	260	65.6	285.00	12/02-31/99
LTC Properties	N	A. C. Dimitriadis	CB	145	17.7	2.00	12/14-15/99
American Sfty Insur Grp	N	F. C. Treadway	D	131	19.2	21.00	12/02-10/99
Sholodge	O	E. H. Sadler	D	115	24.4	14.00	12/17-29/99
Indymac Mrtg Hldgs	N	M. Nelson	VP	106	10.0	n	12/02/99
Eagle Bancshares	O	R. J. Burrell	D	100	6.7	15.00	12/16-17/99
SELLERS							
24 / 7 Media	O	D. J. Moore	P	5,788	110.5	11.00	12/03-09/99
24 / 7 Media	O	J. L. Friessel	VP	5,298	100.0	16.00	12/03-09/99
Hewlett-Packard	N	W. B. Hewlett	D	4,210	40.0	25.00	12/07/99
Adobe Systems	O	G. K. Freeman	O	4,374	66.5	98.00	12/28-31/99 r
Hewlett-Packard	N	W. B. Hewlett	D	4,210	40.0	25.00	12/07/99
Hewlett-Packard	N	L. E. Platt	CB	4,132	40.0	13.00	12/02-03/99 r
Digital Lightwave	O	S. Grant	VP	2,195	65.0	86.00	12/02/99 r
Computer Network Tech	O	T. G. Hudson	P	1,739	80.0	69.00	12/08-14/99 r
Hewlett-Packard	N	R. P. Wayman	VP	1,556	15.0	9.00	12/14/99 r
Cell Genesys	O	D. Carter	D	1,438	105.0	95.00	12/29-30/99 r

When these managers decide to sell some of their own holdings of their firm's stock, this may suggest that they believe the firm's stock price will decline in the future (although it may simply reflect a need to obtain cash).

Financial managers are required to disclose to the Securities and Exchange Commission their monthly transactions in their own firm's stock. Board members are also required to disclose their monthly transactions. With this reported information, the SEC attempts to ensure that insiders are not trading on the basis of inside information that is presently being withheld from the public.

The transactions disclosed to the SEC are disclosed by the SEC to the public about six weeks later. Insider transactions are reported by financial newspapers. The *Wall Street Journal* discloses the biggest insider trades, as shown in Figure 16.3. Investors may believe that the insiders are buying more of the firm's stock or selling some of their holdings of the firm's stock because of inside information. Thus investors may interpret these transactions as a signal about the future movement in the value of the stock.

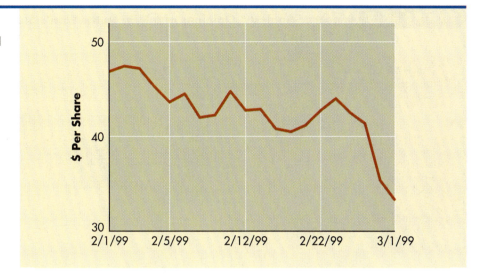

FIGURE 16.4

Stock Price of Compaq Computer Following Sales of Shares by Insiders

Example ▼   During the period from February 1 to February 24, 1999, 11 executives of Compaq Computer Corp. sold more than 1 million shares of Compaq stock. The selling price for these trades ranged from about $41 to $48 per share. Just after this period, Compaq announced that portable computer sales were less than what has been expected. Within the next week, Compaq's stock price sank to $32, which was at least 20 percent less than even the lowest stock price received by the 11 executives. The stock price trend of Compaq is illustrated in Figure 16.4. If investors who were holding Compaq stock had been aware of what Compaq's insiders had done, they would have been able to sell their stock before **▲** the price declined substantially.

Just as investors may interpret insider selling as an unfavorable signal, they may interpret insider buying as a favorable signal. If one or more insiders purchase a substantial amount of the firm's stock, investors may assume that insiders know some favorable inside information. Thus investors may act on that signal and purchase additional shares themselves.

Information Provided by Insider Communication to Analysts

Many firms frequently communicate information to analysts employed by securities firms. The analysts use this information when conducting their own valuation of a particular set of firms (such as those within one industry). Analysts develop recommendations (buy, sell, or hold) about the corresponding stocks of those firms for potential customers of the securities firm. Firms realize that the recommendations of analysts can affect the demand for their stock, so they try to develop positive relationships with analysts.

The means by which communication from the firm to analysts can affect a firm's stock price is illustrated in Figure 16.5. The communication from firms to analysts is not illegal, but it puts smaller investors at a disadvantage in some

FIGURE 16.5 Impact of Analysts' Opinions of a Firm on the Firm's Stock Price

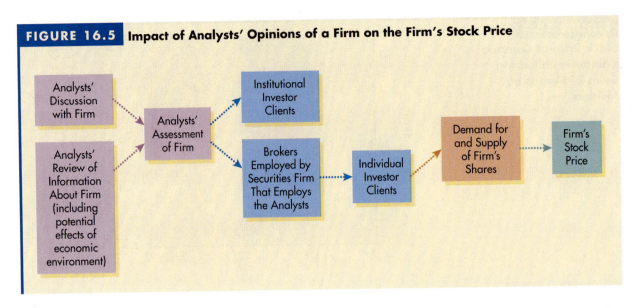

instances. Consequently, some investors may monitor analysts' recommendations as a source of information, because analysts are sometimes acting on information about firms that has not yet been disclosed to the public. However, by the time an analyst's recommendation is made public, any useful information about the firm may have been disclosed anyway. Thus it is the larger investor clients who receive information from analysts before the analysts publicize their revised recommendation that are most likely to benefit from the privileged information.

Information Signaled Through a Firm's Financial Decisions

Investors recognize that a financial decision by a firm that affects the firm's investing or financing policies may affect the value of the firm. They attempt to anticipate a decision by the firm in advance of its actual public announcement so that they can act on the information before the market responds.

There are some generalizations that can be made about how financial decisions affect value, but the results can vary among firms. The typical impacts of some of the most popular financial decisions on the value of a firm are summarized here.

Dividend Policy

A change in a firm's dividend policy may signal information about the firm's expectations of its future cash flows. An increase in dividends may signal that the firm expects its future cash flows to increase and, therefore, can afford to distribute more cash to its investors.

There is evidence that announcements by firms of plans to increase their dividends result in an immediate (on the same day) increase in the stock price of those firms, on average. This implies that the announcement resulted in an increase in the demand for the stock and therefore was interpreted by investors as favorable information. By the time many investors respond to this information, the stock price may have already increased. Thus, the evidence does not imply that the market is inefficient but, rather, that an increase in dividends is interpreted as a positive signal by investors.

A decline or omission of dividends may signal that a firm is expecting a reduction in cash flows and can no longer afford to continue its dividend payments at the prevailing level. There is strong evidence that the stock prices of firms decline immediately, on average after they report a decline or omission of dividends. This observation confirms that investors view the information as a *negative signal* about the firm's future cash flows.

Earnings Surprises

Investors commonly use the reported earnings of a firm as a base from which to derive forecasts of future cash flows. When a firm reports a higher level of earnings than was expected, it may signal favorable information about the firm's future earnings and about future cash flows. There is substantial evidence that these so-called *positive earnings surprises* result in an immediate increase in the stock prices of those firms, on average.

When a firm reports a lower level of earnings than was expected, it may signal unfavorable information about the firm's future earnings and about future cash flows. There is substantial evidence that these so-called *negative (or unfavorable) earnings surprises* result in an immediate decrease in the stock prices of those firms, on average.

Acquisitions

When a firm attempts to acquire another firm (called the target), it has to offer the target's shareholders a price that is high enough to obtain their shares. This can place upward pressure on the stock price of the target firm's shares. There is strong evidence that the shares of target firms experience a major increase in price (often between 20 and 40 percent) when an acquisition is announced. Some investors recognize how this financial decision can affect the target's shares and, consequently, attempt to invest in firms that they expect will be acquired.

The stock prices of acquirer firms tend to decline slightly, on average, which may suggest that investors do not anticipate the same benefits from the acquisition as the financial managers of the acquirer firm who make the acquisition decision. Alternatively, the investors may believe that the acquirer is paying too much to acquire the target, so that any potential benefits of the acquisition are more than offset by the high cost of acquiring the target.

Secondary Stock Offerings

When a publicly traded firm issues new stock, it may be interpreted as a signal that the stock is overvalued. The argument is that financial managers are more willing to raise funds with a stock offering if they believe that the prevailing stock price is relatively high. If they expected the price to increase in the near future, they would wait until that time to issue the stock, because they would receive more funds for issuing the same amount of shares. Thus, by issuing stock now, they may be signaling that the stock price is not expected to rise in the near future. In addition, issuing new stock may cause an excessive supply of stock for sale (dilution), which places downward pressure on the stock price.

There is strong evidence that the stock prices of firms decline (by about 3 percent), on average, in response to announcements that they will issue new stock. Thus the evidence suggests that stock offerings are generally perceived as a *negative signal* about the issuing firm's value. Yet there are many exceptions, because some firms issue stock to finance new investment opportunities that will be beneficial to shareholders.

Stock Repurchases

When a firm repurchases some of its outstanding stock, it may be interpreted as a signal that the firm's management believes its stock is undervalued. The argument is that financial managers repurchase shares of the firm when they believe that they can buy them back at a relatively low price.

Several studies have found that the stock prices of firms that repurchase stock increase, on average. Thus the evidence suggests that stock repurchases are generally perceived as a *positive signal* about the firm's value.

Information Leakages

information leakages
The sharing of useful information about a firm before the information is publicly announced.

Investors recognize that financial information can influence the stock price of a firm but that it is difficult to benefit from public news if the stock price adjusts immediately upon the arrival of new information. Thus, some investors attempt to take positions before the news is publicly announced. They search for so-called **information leakages,** in which useful information about a particular firm occurs before the information is publicly announced. For example, an information leakage occurs when individual investors who are employed as salespeople in the computer industry may recognize a reduction in industry sales before the change in sales and earnings are reported by various computer firms. Because information that can affect a firm's value leaks out before it is publicly

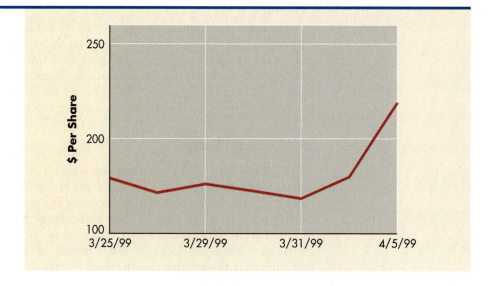

FIGURE 16.6

Response of Yahoo! Stock Price to a Favorable Earnings Surprise

announced, it may not necessarily have a large impact on the stock price at the time of the public announcement. The market may have already responded to the leakages before the public announcement, resulting in an adjustment to the stock price prior to the announcement.

To illustrate the concept of news leakages, consider the example in which the reported earnings during the first quarter of 1999 for Yahoo! were higher than expected. The stock price of Yahoo! increased by about 4 percent on April 7 just after the earnings announcement. However, investors had anticipated that the earnings announcement was going to be favorable and increased their demand for Yahoo! shares in the previous week. Figure 16.6 shows that the price of Yahoo! increased to about $219 per share over the week before the earnings announcement.

Review Questions

16–4   Why might managers make more appropriate decisions for the firm when they own some of the firm's stock?
16–5   Why might investors perceive a firm's increase in dividends as a favorable signal?

Securities Exchanges

When investors consider buying or selling securities, they need to know what securities are available and at what price at which they can be purchased or sold. They also need a mechanism that allows their trades to be executed quickly and at low cost. Securities exchanges provide these services and thus facilitate the trading of securities by investors. As we noted in Chapter 2, the main organized exchanges are the New York Stock Exchange (NYSE) and the American Stock Exchange (AMEX). There are also regional stock exchanges. Transactions are executed by individuals who own "seats" on the trading floor.

Recall that in addition to organized exchanges, the over-the-counter (OTC) market is an intangible market for the purchase and sale of securities not listed by the organized exchanges. The OTC facilitates primary- and secondary-market transactions, whereas the organized exchanges facilitate only secondary-market transactions. So-called dealers facilitate the execution of transactions on the OTC.

The Electronics Communication Network (ECN) is now commonly used within the OTC market, which allows some stocks to be traded electronically without dealers. Many online brokerage firms give their investors a choice of whether to use dealers or the ECN. The ECN can avoid the cost of the spread between the bid and ask prices that results from using a dealer.

Merger Between the American Stock Exchange and Nasdaq

In March 1998 the Nasdaq and Amex merged, and the Philadelphia Stock Exchange plans to merge with them in the future. The Amex was historically an auction market like the New York Stock Exchange, while the Nasdaq used dealers who communicated across a computerized system to make markets in various stocks. The merger between the American Stock Exchange and Nasdaq is likely to increase the use of electronic orders.

Foreign Securities Exchanges

Foreign securities exchanges facilitate investment in foreign securities. U.S. investors can purchase foreign stocks listed on foreign stock exchanges. Investors can benefit by diversifying internationally.

The stocks of most firms are highly influenced by the country in which those firms reside (although some firms are more vulnerable to economic conditions than others). Because stock markets partially reflect the current and/or forecasted state of their countries' economies, and because their economies do not move in tandem, particular stocks of the various markets are not expected to be highly correlated.

American depository receipts (ADRs)
Certificates representing shares of foreign stocks.

U.S. investors also invest in foreign stocks by purchasing **American depository receipts (ADRs),** which are certificates representing shares of foreign stocks. There are more than 1,000 ADRs available in the United States, representing foreign firms from a wide variety of countries. Most ADRs are traded on the OTC exchange. ADRs may be purchased for such well-known firms as Fuji Photo, Japan Airlines, Kirin Beer, Nissan, Sanyo, and Toyota.

world equity benchmark shares (WEBS)
Indexes that reflect composites of stocks for particular countries and whose shares can be traded by investors.

Alternatively, U.S. investors can invest in composites of foreign stocks representing a particular country. This is partially due to the creation of **world equity benchmark shares (WEBS),** which are indexes that reflect composites of stocks for particular countries. Shares of the index are traded by investors who wish to take or sell a position in a composite of stocks representing a specific country.

Foreign markets are attracting investors because of the increased availability of information about foreign securities and foreign market conditions. The Internet affords investors access to much information about foreign stocks, so that they can make more informed decisions without having to purchase information about these stocks. Differences in accounting rules may still limit the degree to which financial data about foreign companies can be interpreted or compared to firms in other countries, but there is some momentum toward making accounting standards uniform across some countries.

Market Price Quotations

Price quotations are readily available for actively traded bonds and stocks, as well as for stock mutual funds and bond mutual funds. The most up-to-date "quotes" can be obtained electronically, via a personal computer. Price information is available from stockbrokers and is widely published in news media—both financial and nonfinancial. Popular sources of daily security price quotations are financial newspapers, such as the *Wall Street Journal* and *Investor's Business Daily,* and the business sections of daily general newspapers published in most major cities. Quotations are also available on financial news television networks such as the Cable News Network (CNN).

? Review Questions

16–6   Why might investors consider investing in American depository receipts (ADRs)?

16–7   Why might investors consider investing in world equity benchmark shares (WEBS)?

LG5 Investor Transactions

The market for a security is created from the flow of orders from investors to buy or sell each stock. The orders to buy a security are matched with orders to sell that security at a price agreeable to both parties in each transaction.

Market and Limit Orders

market order
An order to buy or sell a stock at the prevailing market price.

limit order
An order to buy a stock at or below a specified price, or to sell a stock at or above a specified price.

Investors communicate their order to stock brokers by specifying (1) the name of the stock, (2) whether to buy or sell that stock, (3) the number of shares to be bought or sold, and (4) whether it is a market or a limit order. When investors place a **market order** to buy or sell a stock, the transaction will be executed at the prevailing market price. When investors place a **limit order,** they impose a maximum limit on the price at which they will be willing to buy a stock.

Conversely, sellers of a stock use limit orders to place a minimum limit on the price at which they will be willing to sell the stock. A limit order can be *for the day, good until canceled,* or *open* (in effect for six months). Investors who request limit orders specify whether they are willing to accept a portion of the shares desired (normally in lots of 100) or whether they want the transaction only if it can accommodate the entire amount of shares requested.

Example ▼ Three students met after the stock market closed on November 5 to discuss a possible investment in an Internet stock called wild.com, which had been issued through an IPO three months before. Its closing price was $18 per share. On the next morning, before the market opened, Kate placed a market order to purchase the stock, Matt placed a limit order at $17 for the day, and Tom placed a limit order at $16 for the day. Each order was for 100 shares. When the market opened, the opening market price was $19, so Kate's market order was fulfilled at that price. The price declined to $16.50 in the afternoon, before rising to $18.50 by the end of the day. When the stock price declined to a level of $17, Matt's limit order was filled. The price on November 6 did not decline to $16, so **▲** Tom's order expired without being filled.

This example shows the advantages and disadvantages of a limit order. The advantage is that a limit order may be filled at a more favorable price than the prevailing market price. Matt paid $17 per share, or $1,700, using a limit order, whereas Kate paid $19 per share, or $1,900, using a market order. Thus Matt saved $200 by choosing to use a limit order.

The disadvantage of the limit order is that an investor's order may not be fulfilled if the market price does not reach the limit price specified in the limit order.

*News*Line   HOW TO BE A BETTER ONLINE INVESTOR

Investors who choose to trade stocks online should be aware of how online transactions are made. Some adjustments in trading practices may be in order.

When you trade stocks online, it's easy to imagine that the instant you click the mouse, your order is zapped directly to the exchange floor.... What really happens can be much clunkier: Your order wends its way through a series of brokers and electronic-trading venues, and ends up with someone who is supposed to get you the best price around, known as the "national best bid or offer," or NBBO. All of these layers can add delay, confusion, and, worst of all, cost to your order. If you're smart, however, you can learn what really goes on with your trades and avoid some of the pitfalls. Here's how:

Keep Two Accounts: Technological glitches are among the most common pitfalls of online trading, frustrating investors by blocking access to their online accounts. In about 15% of cases, traders can't get to the trading page in a reasonable amount of time (defined as 12 seconds per Web page you have to click through to get there).... A way to avoid being locked out of a stock you want to buy when you can't access your account: Keep accounts with two different brokerages.

Speed Is Not Everything: If you are a day trader, speed is all-important. But if you're an investor, a slightly slower trade is not always a bad thing. The compensation for less than instant execution can be "price improvement"—getting a price better than the NBBO....If your trade takes longer than a few seconds, it doesn't necessarily mean that you got a bad deal.

Beware the Nighthawks: [In] real after-hours trading,... hard-core buyers and sellers come together to trade after dark on electronic communications networks, or ECNs. Most brokers treat this kind of trading as a separate and treacherous universe....After hours, each ECN is in its own world. The electronic links that allow market participants to compare prices shut off.

...To protect investors, brokers allow only limited orders at night....It's still possible to enter an idiotic limit order—day or night—though, so keep track of the closing price and watch the relatively liquid Island ECN (www.isld.com) so that you don't end up paying more than you should....

Source: Carol Vinzant, "How to Be a Better Online Investor," Fortune, December 12, 1999, pp. 106–108.

Because the stock price of wild.com was always higher than $16, Tom's order expired without being filled. Tom could place the limit order for longer than one day, but if the price of wild.com stock continued to rise after this day, the order still would not be filled.

Use of Technology to Place and Execute Orders

Once placed, an order to buy or sell a security can be executed in seconds, especially for those orders that are completely handled by sophisticated telecommunications devices. Technology has increased the speed at which orders are placed and executed. Internet brokerage firms, such as Ameritrade and E*Trade, are available to execute orders. There are more than 5 million online brokerage accounts maintained by individual investors. The typical trading commission for many Internet brokerage services is between $8 and $20. This is substantially less than what many traditional brokerage firms have historically charged. In response, many traditional brokerage firms now also offer online services. Some full-service brokerage firms have reduced their commissions for investors who use their online services instead of the more costly personalized services.

When the placing of an online order is combined with the Electronic Communications Network (ECN) that executes trades electronically, the entire process of ordering and execution of trades can be handled electronically. The popularity of electronic orders and electronic execution of trades is growing.

Stop Orders

stop order
An order to execute a transaction when the stock price reaches a specified level.

Stop orders are orders to execute a transaction when the stock price reaches a specified level. A *buy stop order* represents an order for the brokerage firm to buy a stock for the investor if the price reaches a specified level (above the prevailing price). Some investors may believe that if a stock rises to a specific price, it is likely to continue rising. Thus, the buy stop order allows them to buy the stock only if it reaches the price they specify.

Conversely, a *sell stop order* is an order for the brokerage firm to sell a stock if the price reaches a specified level (below the prevailing price). This is intended to trigger the sale of their stock when the price is declining and reaches a specified level.

Buying Stock on Margin

buying on margin
Using borrowed funds to finance a portion of a stock investment.

Investors are allowed to make stock investments **on margin,** meaning that they can use borrowed funds to finance a portion of their investment. When investors invest on margin, they take a position similar to financial managers who use financial leverage. By financing a portion of their investment with debt, they can magnify the return on their invested funds. However, the use of debt financing also magnifies the potential loss on an investment.

margin requirements
Regulations imposed by the Federal Reserve on the proportion of invested funds that must be paid in cash and how much can be in the form of debt.

The Federal Reserve regulates the trading of stocks by imposing on investors **margin requirements,** which specify the proportion of invested funds that must be paid in cash. The present requirement is that at least 50 percent of the invested funds must be in cash. Margin requirements are intended to ensure that investors can cover their position if the value of their investment declines over time. With margin requirements in place, a major decline in stock prices is less likely to cause defaults on loans from brokers and therefore will be less damaging to the financial system. If investors purchase stock on margin, and the stock's market value declines, investors may receive a so-called **margin call** from their broker, requesting that they put additional funds (called a maintenance margin) in the margined account.

margin call
A call from an investor's broker, requesting that more funds be added to a margined account.

How Investing on Margin Affects Returns

To recognize how investing on margin affects the return (R), first consider the return from investing in a stock:

$$R = \frac{(SP - II + D - LP)}{II}$$

(16.1)

where

R = the return from investing in a stock

SP = the proceeds from selling the stock at the end of the investment period

II = the initial investment of equity funds made by the investor at the beginning of the investment period

D = the dividends received over the investment period

LP = the loan payoff made to the broker after the stock is sold at the end of the investment period.

The numerator represents the proceeds earned from the investment after any loans used to make the investment are paid off. The denominator represents the initial amount of equity funds invested by the investor. If an investor does not use any borrowed funds, *LP* is zero and *II* is the total amount of funds paid for the investment. If an investor invests on margin instead of using entirely equity funds, the numerator is affected because there will be a loan payoff at the end of the period, and the denominator is affected because the initial amount of equity funds invested by the investor is less.

Example ▼ Stan Adams determines that a new Internet stock called Rocket.com is undervalued at its prevailing price of $10 per share. The stock is not expected to pay any dividend. Stan considers using his own cash to purchase the 100 shares of the stock. Alternatively, he considers financing a portion of his investment with a loan from the broker, which charges 10% interest. Stan plans to sell the stock in 1 year.

Stan wants to determine his expected return when paying for his entire investment (1) using 100% of his own funds, (2) borrowing 30% of the investment ($700 of his own funds(his equity) and $300 of borrowed funds), and (3) borrowing 50% of the investment ($500 of his own funds (his equity) and $500 of borrowed funds). He estimates the return on the basis of two possible outcomes: (1) He expects that the stock will rise to $14 in 1 year or, alternatively, (2) there is a slight chance of adverse conditions that would cause the stock to decline to $6 in 1 year.

The estimated proceeds from selling the stock is the expected price per share times 100 shares. The loan payment is the repayment of the amount of funds borrowed plus an interest payment; the interest payment is equal to the amount of funds borrowed times the interest rate over the investment period.

Stan estimates the returns as follows:

Results If Share Price = $14 at the End of 1 Year:

	Using 100% of Own Funds (Margin = 100%)	Using 30% Borrowed Funds (Margin = 70%)	Using 50% Borrowed Funds (Margin = 50%)
SP	100 shares × $14 = $1,400	100 shares × $14 = $1,400	$100 shares × $14 = $1,400
II	$1,000	$700	$500
LP	$0	$300 + ($300 × 0.10) = $330	$500 + ($500 × 0.10) = $550
R	($1,400 − $1,000)/$1,000	($1,400 − $700 − $330)/$700	($1,400 − $500 − $55)/$500
	= 40.00%	= 52.86%	= 70%

Results If Share Price = $6 at the End of 1 Year:

SP	100 shares × 6 = $600	100 shares × $6 = $600	100 shares × $6 = $600
II	$1,000	$700	$500
LP	$0	$300 + ($300 × 0.10) = $330	$500 + ($500 × 0.10) = $550
R	($600 − $1,000)/$1,000	($600 − $700 − $330)/$700	($600 − $500 − $550)/$500
	= −40.00%	= −61.42%	= −90.00%

The results show that by investing on margin, Stan can magnify his returns if the stock price rises over his investment period. However, if the stock price decreases, his percentage loss is much higher when investing on margin. The potential return from investing on margin can be magnified to a greater degree when a larger proportion of funds are borrowed. Notice that investing with a 50% margin results in higher gains and higher losses. Since Stan is concerned about the possibility that the stock price could decline, he decides to use all cash for his investment, but other investors who are more willing to accept the risk may have decided to invest on margin.

The distribution of possible percentage gains or losses on the equity investment is more dispersed when the investor invests on margin, and the degree of dispersion is greater the larger the portion of borrowed funds used.

Short Sales

short sale
The sale of a stock by an investor who does not own stock.

A **short sale** represents the sale of a stock by an investor who does not own the stock. Investors may desire to sell a stock short (or "short the stock") when they believe that the stock is overvalued. To short a stock, they borrow it from another investor and will have to buy that stock in the market and return it to the investor at some point in the future. Investors who sell a stock short earn the difference between what they initially sold the stock for and what they later paid to buy the stock. They must reimburse the investor from whom the stock was borrowed for any dividend payments that the investor would have received during the period in which the short position was held.

Example ▼   On March 5, Bob Blake calls his broker and places an order to sell 100 shares of Cyber stock short. The broker notices that one of its other clients, Lisa Lynch, owns 100 shares of Cyber stock. The broker takes the 100 shares of Cyber stock owned by Lisa and sells the shares in the secondary market at the prevailing price of $80 per share. Bob receives $8,000 ($80 × 100 shares) as a result of this sale. On April 20, Cyber pays its shareholders a dividend of $1 per share. Because Lisa's shares were sold, she will not receive a dividend directly from Cyber. The broker will request that Bob provide a payment to cover the dividend that Lisa would have received if she had still owned the stock. This same process is repeated for every dividend payment that occurs while Bob maintains his short position in Cyber stock.

By May 4, the stock price of Cyber has declined to $73 per share. Bob decides to purchase Cyber stock at that time because he does not expect the price to decrease any further. He calls his broker and places an order to purchase 100 shares of Cyber and to "close out" his short position. The broker executes the order by purchasing 100 shares of Cyber in the secondary market at the prevailing market price of $73 per share, and returns the stock to Lisa's account. Bob paid the broker $7,300 ($73 × 100 shares) for this transaction. Lisa was not affected as a result of lending her stock in the short sale and, in fact, was probably not aware that her stock had been lent to someone else. Bob earned a $7 gain per share from the difference between the price at which he bought Cyber stock ($73) and the price at which he sold the stock short ($80). However, he incurred an expense of $1 per share as a result of providing the payment to cover dividends owed to the lender (Lisa) of the stock he borrowed. Thus, his gain after considering that expense was $6 per share, or $600 for 100 shares.

Largest Short Positions

Rank		Jan. 14	Dec. 15	Change
	NYSE			
1	At&T	74,321,531	79,641,975	−5,320,444
2	Vodafone (Ads)	68,596,385	71,809,300	−3,212,915
3	America Online	64,305,968	60,868,701	3,437,267
4	Walt Disney-hldg	61,897,330	61,068,546	828,784
5	Qwest Comm Intl	52,059,751	0	52,059,752
6	Sprint (Pcs)	43,591,236	36,361,743	7,229,493
7	Kmart	38,078,039	36,690,178	1,387,861
8	Lucent Technologies	38,028,314	38,858,872	−830,558
9	Wal-Mart Stores	36,955,964	40,812,511	−3,856-647
10	Time Wrner (Hldg)	36,631,438	38,997,033	−2,365,595
11	Nortel Networks	32,418,727	29,063,486	3,35,241
12	Columbia/HCA	31,602,801	31,990,328	−387,527
13	EMC	31,474,660	33,079,296	−1,604,636
14	BP Amoco P.L.C.	25,743,988	37,332,256	−11,588,268
15	Kroger	24,878,572	24,210,701	667,871
16	Citigroup	23,792,557	25,614,424	−1,821,867
17	Compaq Computer	23,631,238	22,769,674	861,564
18	Clear Channel Cms	23,560,660	21,790,898	1,769,762
19	At&T-Liberty (CIA)	23,507,627	25,817,744	−2,310,117
20	Bell Atlantic	21,911,215	20,801,439	1,109,776
	AMEX			
1	Nasdaq-100 Trust	23,047,608	27,458,403	−4,410,795
2	Standard&Poors Dp	15,357,657	19,187,459	−3,829,802
3	Trans World Cmn	13,071,545	14,839,305	−1,767,760
4	Organogenesis	5,620,804	5,977,627	−356,823
5	Echo Bay Mines Ltd.	5,208,390	4,774,197	434,193

The risk of a short sale is the possibility that the stock price will increase over time, forcing Bob to pay a higher price on the stock than the price at which he initially sold the stock. If the price of Cyber stock had increased rather than decreased over this period, Bob would have incurred a loss on the short position. For example, if the price had increased to $88 on May 4, when Bob closed out his short position, he would have incurred a loss of $8 per share, in addition to the $1 per share dividend payment to the investor (Lisa) from whom he borrowed the stock.

Bob is not forced to close out his position at any specific date, so he could wait until the stock price declines before purchasing the stock to close out his position. However, if the stock price continues to rise, the loss when closing out the short position would be even greater. In addition, Bob would need to make the payments to cover the dividends that would normally have been received by the investor whose stock was borrowed.

short-interest ratio
A measure of the level of short sales in the market, measured as the number of shares sold short divided by the average daily trading volume.

Financial publications measure the level of short sales for stocks with the **short-interest ratio,** which is the number of shares sold short divided by the average daily trading volume over a recent period. A higher short-interest ratio reflects a high level of short sales. A short-interest ratio of 3.0 for a particular stock, for example, would imply that the number of shares that are presently sold short is three times the number of shares traded per day, on average. Stocks with a short-interest ratio of 10 or more have an unusually high level of short sales, which means there is some sentiment that these stocks are priced too high. The short-interest ratio for the overall stock market is a useful indicator of the general perception of stock market prices. When the market's short-interest ratio is high, this suggests sentiment that the stock market is overvalued.

The largest short positions are periodically reported in the *Wall Street Journal*, as shown in Figure 16.7. For each firm for which there is a large short position, the number of shares sold short is disclosed (second column) and compared to the corresponding number a month earlier (third column). The change in the overall short position by investors from the previous month is provided in the fourth column.

? Review Questions

16–8   What is an advantage of using a limit order instead of a market order to purchase a stock? What is a disadvantage of doing so?

16–9   What is an advantage of buying stock on margin? What is a disadvantage of doing so?

TYING IT ALL TOGETHER

This chapter described the type of information that investors use to make investments, how financial markets facilitate investment transactions, and the types of transactions requested by investors. The roles of managers, financial markets, and investors in assessing investment information and executing investment transactions are summarized in the Integrative Table that follows.

INTEGRATIVE TABLE

Assessing the Value of Securities and Executing Securities Transactions

Role of **Financial Managers**	*Role of* **Financial Markets**	*Role of* **Investors**
Financial managers compile information about their respective firms in an annual report and other financial reports and make these reports available to investors.	Securities exchanges facilitate transactions desired by investors. Brokerage firms serve as intermediaries between the investors and the exchanges; they execute the specific orders (market, limit, stop orders) requested by the investors, and they also execute purchases on margin and short sales.	Investors rely on information provided by firms, government sources, investment service companies, and securities firms to conduct economic analyses, industry analyses, global analyses, market analyses, and firm-specific analyses. They use this information to make their investment decisions.

Review background material on investing. Investments are made by individual and institutional investors. The investment decisions made by investors will determine the annual return on investment portfolios and, therefore, the accumulated value of those portfolios.

Describe the economic, industry, global, and market information sources used to make investment decisions. Investors rely on information sources such as the Federal Reserve and Bloomberg to conduct economic analyses; Standard and Poor's, Moody's, and Value Line to conduct industry analyses; and the International Financial Statistics and international financial newspapers to conduct global analyses.

Describe the firm-specific information sources used to make relevant investment decisions. For firm-specific information, investors rely on the annual report or other financial reports provided by the firm, as well as information provided by investment service companies such as Moody's, Standard and Poor's, and Value Line.

Identify the main U.S. and foreign securities exchanges in the U.S. that facilitate the investing process. The main securities exchanges are the organized exchanges (including the New York Stock Exchange and the American Stock Exchange) and the over-the-counter market. Organized exchanges act as secondary markets for securities. The over-the-counter market facilitates trading of securities in the secondary market and of new issues in the primary market.

   Describe the types of securities transactions requested by investors, and explain how these transactions are accommodated by brokerage firms. Investors can place a market order, a limit order, or a stop order. A market order is executed at the prevailing market price. A limit order imposes a limit on the price at which investors are willing to buy or sell a stock. Stop orders are orders to execute a transaction when the stock price reaches a specified level. A buy stop order represents an order for the brokerage firm to buy a stock for the investor when the price reaches a specified level (above the prevailing price). Conversely, a sell stop order is an order for the brokerage firm to sell a stock when the price reaches a specified level (below the prevailing price).

Investors can also purchase stocks on margin, financing part of the investment with borrowed funds. Buying stocks on margin results in a higher potential return on investment, but it also results in higher risk. Investors can also make short-sale transactions, in which they borrow a stock that they sell in the market. They hope to purchase that stock in the market in the future (when they will return the stock to the investor from whom it was borrowed) at a lower price than the price at which they sold it. They consider short sale transactions for stocks that they expect will experience a decline in price.

SELF-TEST EXERCISES   (Solutions in Appendix B)

ST 16–1   Mike Price has researched Ray Catcher, Inc., a retail sporting goods chain. He believes that the stock is significantly undervalued and hopes to profit by a rise in the price. His analysis has led him to believe that 1 year from now, the worst-case scenario would result in a price of $18.00 per share, whereas his expected price would be $30.00. The stock is selling for $22.00 per share today. It pays no dividend. Mike would like to purchase 100 shares at $22.00. He is trying to decide whether to make this investment entirely with his own money or to engage in a margin transaction by borrowing a portion of the purchase price from his brokerage firm. The firm charges 8% on such loans.

a. Estimate Mike's 1-year return if he makes the investment with 100% of his own funds and (1) sells for $30 per share; (2) sells for $18 per share.

    b. Estimate Mike's 1-year return if he makes the investment using $1,540 of his own cash and $660 of borrowed funds at 8% if he (1) sells at $30 per share; (2) sells at $18 per share.

    c. Estimate Mike's 1-year return if he makes the investment using $1,100 of his own cash and $1,100 of borrowed funds at 8% if he (1) sells at $30 per share; (2) sells at $18 per share.

LG5 ST 16–2 Frank, Carmen, Tim, Kris, and Anna make up the Fabulous Five Investment Club. They meet for supper once a week to discuss investment issues and their portfolio. For the past 2 weeks they have been discussing the pros and cons of limit orders. They have decided to conduct an experiment in purchasing a stock they are interested in, Unity Communications, which closed that afternoon at $21 per share. They have decided to enter three orders for 100 shares each when the market opens in the morning. One order would be to buy 100 shares at market; the second would be a limit order to buy 100 shares at $20 per share; and the last order would be a limit order to buy 100 shares at $19 per share.

    a. Which orders would have filled, and at what total cost, if the stock opened at $21.50 and its range for the day was $20 on the low side and $22 on the high side?

    b. Which orders would have filled, and at what total cost, if the stock opened at $20 and its range for the day was $18 on the low side and $20 on the high side?

    c. Which orders would have filled, and at what total cost, if the stock had opened at $22 and its range for the day was $22 on the low side and $24 on the high side?

    d. In each case, what advantages or disadvantages would result from using limit orders?

LG1 16–1 Taxation of gains Jillian Foster has $25,000.00 in capital gains to report this year. She is in a 32% marginal personal income tax bracket.
    a. Calculate the taxes due if the gains are classified as short-term.
    b. Calculate the maximum taxes due if the gains are classified as long-term.

LG1 16–2 Long-term investing Joel Collins recently inherited $5,000, which he plans to use to establish a college fund for his 2-year-old son. He is looking at three different mutual funds. His research indicates the long-term results listed below:

Fund	10-year annualized return
Maple Tree Fund	12%
Shepherd Growth Fund	14
Capital Conservation Fund	9

    a. Assuming that future results are the same as those listed, calculate, for each of the three alternatives, the value of the college fund in 16 years when his son is ready to go to college.

b. If Joel can invest $6,000 now, how much will the funds be worth in 16 years?

c. If Joel chooses the Shepherd Growth Fund and invests $5,000, but his actual results average out to 13% per year, how far short of his expected value will the fund be when his son is ready for college?

 16–3 **Using online information** Using the URL listed in Table 16.1, explore the Federal Reserve's web site.

a. Locate and print out the daily update of selected interest rates.

b. Using the "Treasury constant maturities" rates for the most recent day, create a yield curve graph by placing the yields on the vertical axis and the maturities on the horizontal axis. (Refer to Figure 4.6 for an example.)

c. Compare your curve to those in Figure 4.6. Is its shape *upward-sloping, flat, or downward-sloping?*

d. Make an interest rate prediction based on the shape of your curve and what you learned in Chapter 4 about the expectations hypothesis and the use of yield curves.

 16–4 **Using online information** Use the URL for the U.S. Census Bureau to get an overview of the U.S. economy.

a. Move into the "Economic Briefing Room" section of the "Economy Page" selection. List all of the current and previous statistics, and beside each pair, comment on whether the current figure is an improvement or a deterioration.

b. Print out charts for median income and poverty. Comment on any relationships that you see between the charts.

16–5 **Using published industry data** *Standard and Poor's Industry Surveys* is kept as a reference in most university and many public libraries. Obtain the most recent "Current Analysis" of Textiles, Apparel & Home Furnishings. Read through it and answer the following questions.

a. What key economic statistics from government sources are important to this industry group?

b. Within the Apparel group, what industry-specific statistics (the names) are cited and/or graphed?

c. From your reading, assess the general outlook for this industry group. What are some of the factors that support your answer?

d. On the basis of your reading, would you purchase stock in this industry?

 16–6 **Global rates online** Use the URL provided in Table 16.3 to access Bloomberg. The functions used in this exercise are international bonds, cross-currency rates, and the currency calculator.

a. Access the international bonds function of the web site. Look up and compare the yield on 5-year government bonds from the United States, Italy, Canada, Great Britain, and Japan.

b. Access the cross-currency rates chart and list the currency per $1.00 US for the Euro, Canadian dollar, British pound, and Japanese yen. Which currencies are closest in value to the U.S. dollar? Which are most different?

c. Access the currency calculator and translate $500.00 in U.S. dollars to Dronning Mauland Krone.

 16–7 **Analysis of data from the annual report** The CanyonLands Corp. annual report contains the following information:

Income Statement		
	Year ended	
	July 1, 2000	**July 1, 1999**
Sales	$4,354,000	$4,247,000
Net income	431,000	429,000

Balance Sheet		
	As of	
	July 1, 2000	**July 1, 1999**
Total assets	$2,360,000	$2,300,000
Total liabilities	1,300,000	1,270,000
Total equity	1,060,000	1,030,000
Total shares outstanding	247,500	260,000

a. Assess this firm's profitability year-to-year using net profit margin, return on assets, and return on equity.

b. Calculate earnings per share for each of the 2 years. Explain how emphasis on the per-share measure may mask a profitability trend in the company.

c. Calculate book value per share for each of the 2 years. Explain how this and the earnings-per-share figures calculated in part **b** may help to support the price of shares in the market place.

16–8   Using *Value Line*   Sally Roberts has the most recent *Value Line* report on Jelly Pops, Inc. Sally has not used *Value Line* before, so some of the information contained in the sheet is mysterious to her. She has asked you to help her understand it.

a. Jelly Pops is ranked "2" for timeliness. Describe the ranking system to Sally, and explain what the ranking of 2 may mean to her as an investor.

b. Sally has noticed that the average annual P/E ratio in the spreadsheet section of the report is different from the P/E ratio that is listed at the top of the page. How are each of the P/E ratios calculated? Why does *Value Line* use the method it does for the P/E at the top of the page? Explain the relative P/E ratio.

c. Sally's grandmother, a long-time investor in Jelly Pops, bought 100 shares at $30.00 per share in 1993. You see from the price trend graph that the stock split 2-for-1 in 1996 and 3-for-2 in 1999. How many shares does Sally's grandmother have now?

16–9   Dividend policy and stock price   Redmond Motors, a well-established maker of quality replacement parts for automobiles, has had a rough year, complicated by a labor strike and raw materials price increases that could not be completely offset in finished goods pricing. As a result, net income is significantly diminished. Although the labor problems are not likely to recur, the cost/pricing problem will persist for the foreseeable future. The company's board of directors has met to discuss whether they should continue paying dividends at the current level.

a. What argument can be made for continuing to pay at the current level, even in the absence of net income to support the payment this year?

b. What are the possible consequences of an announcement that the dividend will be reduced or eliminated?

  16–10   Investing on margin   Juan Martinez wants to invest in Catalyst Solutions, Inc. common stock, currently priced at $40.00. He has $4,000 of his own money but wishes to borrow an additional $4,000 from his brokerage firm in order to purchase 200 shares total. His broker has explained to Juan that he must put up a 50% initial margin (his $4,000) and that at no time can his ownership portion (maintenance margin) fall below 30% of the total value of the position. Ignore commission and interest charges that may be involved in this transaction. This stock pays no dividend.

a. Assume that Juan goes ahead with the margin purchase of 200 shares at $40.00 each. If the stock price increases to $50.00 per share, what are the values of Juan's ownership portion and his loan, respectively?

b. If Juan were to sell the entire position at a price of $50.00 per share, what would his return be? (Use Equation 16.1.)

c. If Juan bought the 200 shares as he planned at $40.00 and the stock price declined to $30.00 per share, what are the values of Juan's ownership portion and his loan, respectively?

d. If Juan were to sell the entire position at a price of $30.00 per share, what would his return be? (Use Equation 16.1.)

e. At what price per share would Juan's ownership position be 30% of the total value of the position (thus placing him in danger of getting a margin call)?

16–11   Investing on margin with interest   Mollie Lund purchased 500 shares of Caroline Corp. at $35.00 per share in her margin account. She invested $10,500 of her own money as margin and borrowed the balance of the purchase amount from her brokerage firm at 10% interest. She held the shares for 1 year, during which time she received dividends of $1.20 per share. Ignore commission and interest charges that may be involved in these transactions and use Equation 16.1 to figure her return under the following two alternative outcomes:

a. She sold the shares for $50.00 per share.

b. She sold the shares for $20.00 per share.

 16–12   Short selling   James Mason short sold 300 shares of Spitzer Corp. at $45.00 per share. He kept the position open for 3 months, during which time the stock paid a dividend of $.35 per share.

a. Calculate his dollar profit if he closed out the position by purchasing Spitzer shares at $38.00 per share.

b. Calculate his dollar loss if he closed out the position by purchasing Spitzer shares at $52.00 per share.

16–13   Margin investing with interest charges   Henry Tucker's brokerage firm lent him 50% of the purchase price when he bought 400 shares of Denton Textiles common stock at $26.00 per share. Margin interest is charged at 9% per year. During the year that Henry held the stock, it paid dividends of $1.64 per share. Use Equation 16.1 to calculate Henry's return. Ignore any commission costs that may be involved in these transactions.

a. Calculate his return if Henry sold the shares at $38.00 per share after holding them for 1 year.

b. Calculate his return if Henry sold the shares at $23.00 per share after holding them for 1 year.

c. Explain the effect that the interest charges had on return in both of the foregoing calculations.

d. Estimate the annualized holding period return for parts **a** and **b** as if Henry held the shares for only 6 months before selling them. Again use Equation 16.1.

web exercises   [Search]

Go to web site finance.yahoo.com. Enter "INTC" into the Get Quotes space. Click on Profile. Click Top Inst./M.Fund Holders.

1. Which institution holds the most shares of Intel Corporation? Which mutual fund?

2. What is the total number of Intel shares held by the top institutions and the top ten mutual funds?

Click Profile. Click Homepage. Under Company Info, click Investor Relations. Click Annual Reports. Click on the most recent Annual Report. Click on Annual Report; click on Financial Information; then click on Consolidated Balance Sheet.

3. How many outstanding shares of Intel Corporation are there? What percentage of these outstanding shares do the number of shares in Question 2 represent?

Go to web site www.intel.com. Under **Company Info,** click Investor Relations. Under **Broker/Analyst Info,** click Earnings Estimate.

4. Which quarter is generally Intel's best quarter?

5. What is the EPS estimate for this year? In percentage terms, how does this compare to last year's actual EPS?

6. What is Intel's consensus 5-year growth rate?

7. How many analysts were involved in the estimate for this year?

For additional practice with concepts from this chapter, visit
http://www.awl.com/gitman_madura

How External Forces Affect a Firm's Value

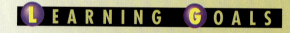

L EARNING **G** OALS

LG1 Identify economic conditions that affect a firm's value, and explain how those conditions can affect firm value.

LG2 Identify government policies that affect a firm's value, and explain how those policies can do so.

LG3 Identify industry conditions that affect a firm's value, and explain how those conditions can do so.

LG4 Identify global conditions that affect a firm's value, and explain how those conditions can do so.

LG1 Economic Factors and a Firm's Value

Recall that a firm's value is the present value of its expected cash flows, based on investor's required rate of return. Firms conduct business in an economic environment in which they are exposed to external forces for which they have no control. Any forces that affect either the firm's cash flows or the required rate of return will affect the firm's value. The financial managers of firms must recognize the potential impact of these forces on their firms, because their future financial decisions may be affected by these forces. Likewise, investors who invest in firms must recognize the potential impact of these forces so that they can assess how the values of firms may be affected by expected conditions in the economic environment.

The cash flows of a firm, and therefore the value of a firm, can be affected by conditions in the economic environment. Financial managers need to understand how their firms can be affected so that they may be able to prepare for the economic effects or even insulate their businesses from adverse economic conditions. Investors who continuously monitor firms to make investment decisions must recognize how expected economic conditions may affect firms so that they can decide which firms they should invest in.

The economic factors that have the largest impact on the value of the firm are economic growth, interest rates, and inflation. We will discuss each of these economic factors.

Economic Growth

economic growth
The change in the level of economic activity over a particular period, commonly measured in the United States by the change in gross domestic product.

gross domestic product (GDP)
Measure of the level of U.S. economic activity, calculated as the total market value of all final products and services produced.

Economic growth represents the change in the level of economic activity over a particular period. It is commonly measured in the United States as the percentage change in the **gross domestic product (GDP)**, which reflects the total market value of all final products and services produced in the United States. The production level of products and services tends to rise in response to a high aggregate demand by consumers so that there is sufficient inventory to accommodate the purchases by consumers. Conversely, when consumers reduce their aggregate demand, inventory levels rise, and production is reduced because firms are not selling their existing inventory. The aggregate demand by consumers depends on the level of their disposable income (income after taxes). Similarly, the income levels of consumers are dependent on the aggregate demand, because the higher the demand, the more people firms employ to achieve the production level that will satisfy the demand.

Some firms are more exposed to changes in economic conditions than others. For example, the performance levels of automobile manufacturers are sensitive to economic conditions, because consumers reduce their spending for new automobiles when their income is reduced. Conversely, the value of other firms (such as producers of bread or other necessities) is not affected as much by economic conditions.

Impact on a Firm's Cash Flows

When financial managers anticipate a change in economic growth, they determine how their cash flows will be affected. There is a direct effect on the cash inflows. When economic growth is expected to decline, financial managers reduce their investment in production used to build inventory because they expect demand for their products to decline. They also reduce their investment in their new projects, because some of these proposed projects will not be feasible if economic conditions are unfavorable. For example, the expected demand for a new product that the firm plans to create may be weak. This implies that the cash flows resulting from that project would be relatively small and would not generate a sufficient return to the firm (and to the firm's owners). Given the reduction in investment by a firm when economic growth slows, the amount of financing required by the firm is also reduced. Financial managers reduce their financing in accordance with the reduction in investment.

The reduction in cash flows from existing business and the lack of growth in new business can cause a firm's value to decline when the economy is weak. Investors attempt to measure the effects of changing economic conditions on each firm in which they may invest. During a weak economy, investors tend to shift their investment to those firms that are more insulated from changes in economic conditions.

Interest Rates

Interest rate movements can affect a firm's value by influencing its cash flows, thereby encouraging financial managers and investors to monitor interest rate movements closely. Specifically, changes in interest rates affect consumers' purchases with borrowed funds and the firm's cost of financing.

Impact on a Firm's Cash Flows Due to Purchases with Borrowed Funds

First, the firm's cash inflows are driven by the demand for its products, which may be influenced by interest rate movements. For example, the demand for new automobiles is dependent on interest rates, because a lower interest rate allows for a lower monthly payment for consumers who use credit. Thus a lower interest rate results in a higher level of sales by the automobile manufacturer. Conversely, a higher interest rate may cause the monthly payments by consumers to be too high and discourage purchases of new automobiles. Therefore, the cash flows of automobile manufacturers should be higher when interest rates are lower, other factors being equal.

The firms whose cash flows are most sensitive to interest rate movements are those that commonly sell products on credit. Such firms include not only automobile manufacturers but also home builders and appliance manufacturers. Many other firms that provide supplies in these industries that generate credit sales are also affected by interest rate movements, as illustrated next.

Example ▼ Detroit Co. produces custom-designed windows that are commonly purchased and inserted into new automobiles by automobile manufacturers. It also produces windows that are purchased by construction companies to use in the construction of new homes. Interest rates in the United States increased by 2 percentage points in the last 6 months, which caused a reduction in the demand for new automobiles and new homes, because many consumers who had planned to make purchases could no longer afford the monthly payments. The automobile manufacturers reduced the production of automobiles in response to the decline in demand, so they also reduced their orders of windows from Detroit Co. In addition, the construction companies reduced their orders of windows from Detroit Co. in response to the decline in the demand for new homes.

The impact of the interest rates does not end at Detroit Co., because it relies on other companies for glass and other materials. As the demand for its products declines, Detroit reduces its orders of supplies from its supplier firms. Thus *their* cash flows are also reduced by the increase in interest rates, even if their sales are in cash.

Other types of firms that sell supplies or products to automobile manufacturers or construction companies would also be adversely affected by an increase in interest rates. Some tire companies, auto part companies, and steel companies rely on sales to automobile manufacturers and would be sensitive to interest rate movements. Some brick companies, roof material companies, wood paneling companies, and faucet companies rely on sales to construction companies.

interest rate sensitive
Changing more than the norm in response to changes in interest rates.

Firms whose values are more sensitive to the influence of interest rate movements are referred to as **interest-rate sensitive.** Most of these firms are unfavorably affected by upward movements in interest rates, and are favorably affected by downward movements in interest rates, for reasons stated earlier. Financial managers of these firms closely assess possible interest rate movements and try to make decisions that may capitalize on the favorable interest rate movements, while insulating against unfavorable interest rate movements. Investors closely assess possible interest rate movements when deciding whether to purchase or sell stocks of these firms, because they recognize that any interest rate movements will affect the value of these stocks.

Impact on a Firm's Cost of Financing

floating interest rates
Interest rates that adjust periodically to changes in market interest rates.

Interest rates can also affect the firm's value by affecting its cost of financing. Some firms obtain loans from financial institutions that have **floating interest rates,** which means that the interest rate on the loans adjusts periodically (such as every 6 months) to changes in market interest rates. Therefore, any change in market interest rates affects the interest rate charged to the firm. When interest rates are low, firms can borrow funds at a lower cost. However, when interest rates rise, the firm's cost of borrowing funds also rises. Many large firms such as IBM have more than $20 billion dollars in debt at any time. Thus a change in the interest rate by just 1 percentage point can change the annual interest payments on debt by $200 million. For many smaller firms that have debt of at least $100 million, a change in the interest rate by 1 percentage point can change the annual interest payments on debt by at least $1 million. Thus, higher interest rates may have an adverse effect on firms not only because of the potential reduction in cash flows but also because of the potential increase in financing costs.

A change in the interest rate affects the cost of equity as well as the cost of debt. Thus, firms experience a higher cost of capital in response to higher interest rates. This may force them to reassess the feasibility of some projects that were previously approved but not yet implemented, because the projects may no longer be feasible at the higher cost of capital.

Impact on the Return Required by Investors

When interest rates rise, investors use a higher required rate of return to assess the value of a firm. A higher interest rate means that there is a higher opportunity cost of investing in the firm as opposed to a risk-free asset. Investors, then, will be willing to invest in the risk-free asset only if the expected return is sufficiently above the prevailing risk-free rate to make the investment worthwhile. Thus, investors not only may reduce their estimates of a firm's cash flows in response to a higher interest rate (for reasons stated earlier) but also will use a higher discount rate when determining the present value of the cash flows. This results in a lower valuation of the firm.

Inflation

inflation
Increase in the general price level of products and services.

consumer price index (CPI)
An index that reflects the prices of consumer products (such as bread and gasoline).

producer price index (PPI)
An index that reflects the prices of materials (such as steel) that are used to produce other products.

A firm's value can also be affected by **inflation,** or the increase in the general level of prices of products and services. One of the most common measures of inflation is the change in the **consumer price index (CPI),** which reflects the prices of various consumer products, such as grocery products, household products, housing, and gasoline. An alternative measure of inflation is the change in the **producer price index (PPI),** which reflects the prices of various producer products, such as coal, lumber, and metals, that are used to produce other products. Inflation can directly affect the cash flows (and therefore the value) of a firm by affecting its expenses or its cost of capital.

Impact on a Firm's Cash Flows

Inflation can force the firm to have higher cash outflows (in order to pay expenses) as the cost of purchasing supplies or hiring labor rises during periods of high inflation. It can also result in higher cash inflows if the firm is able to increase the price of its products. Whether the favorable effects on cash inflows outweigh the unfavorable effects on cash outflows may vary with the characteristics of the firm.

Impact on a Firm's Cost of Financing

Inflation can affect the value of the firm through its influence on interest rate movements. A high level of inflation tends to cause a high level of interest rates. As inflation rises, savers tend to reduce the amount of funds that they save, because they prefer to purchase products with their funds now, before the prices of products rise further. In addition, borrowers tend to borrow larger amounts of funds in periods of rising inflation, because they prefer to purchase the products now (with borrowed funds) before the prices of products rise further. To the extent that higher expected inflation can cause interest rates to rise, it can increase the firm's cost of financing. In addition, it will also increase the rate of return that investors require, which reduces the present value of the firm's expected cash flows from the investor's perspective.

Comparison of Economic Effects on a Firm's Value

Figure 17.1 offers a comparison of the economic effects on a firm's value. Economic conditions can affect the firm's cash flows or the rate of return required by investors who invest in the firm. One economic factor can also

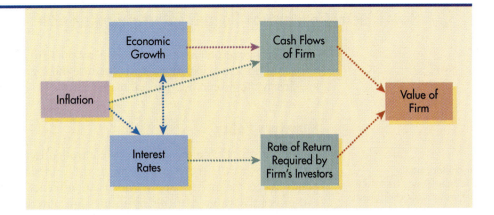

FIGURE 17.1

How Economic Conditions Affect a Firm's Value

affect other economic conditions and therefore have indirect effects on a firm's value.

Economic Indicators

Table 17.1 summarizes the popular economic indicators that financial managers and investors monitor. Which indicators are most closely monitored may vary with the firm. An indicator such as gasoline prices may be critical for a trucking company, whereas the volume of new housing may be critical for a financial institution that provides mortgage loans.

? Review Questions

17–1 Explain how changes in economic growth can affect a firm's cash flows.

17–2 Explain how changes in interest rates can affect the rate of return required by investors who consider investing in a firm.

TABLE 17.1   Popular Economic Growth Indicators

Indicators of Economic Growth	Indicators of Inflation	Indicators of Interest Rates
Steel production	Consumer price index (CPI)	Volume of new housing or office buildings
Coal production	Producer price index (PPI)	Money supply movements
Electric power usage	Gasoline prices	
Oil production	Steel prices	
Lumber production	Lumber prices	
Inventories of manufactured products	Housing prices	
Inventories of retail stores		

How Federal Government Policies Affect a Firm's Value

The federal government affects the value of the firm by enacting monetary policy and fiscal policy, as explained next. Because these policies affect firm value, they are closely monitored by financial managers and investors.

Monetary Policy

monetary policy
The Federal Reserve's control of the U.S. money supply, which influences market interest rates.

Recall that the U.S. money supply is controlled by the Federal Reserve System (the Fed), which is the central bank of the United States. The Fed's **monetary policy** affects the money supply, which can influence interest rates. Thus, the Fed can affect the value of firms by influencing interest rate movements. Before explaining how the Fed can influence interest rate movements, we will briefly consider the structure of the Fed.

The Fed's Structure for Conducting Monetary Policy

The Fed has a *Federal Open Market Committee (FOMC),* which is composed of 12 voting members. The members of the FOMC attempt to conduct a monetary policy that achieves low inflation and low unemployment. Seven of those members are appointed by the president and confirmed by the Senate, and they make up the so-called *Board of Governors.* These 7 members serve 14-year nonrenewable terms, which are staggered so that one member is replaced every 2 years. In this way, there tends to be more diversity in the member's views about monetary policy than if they were all elected during one presidential term. The nonrenewable 14-year term is also intended to ensure that monetary policy decisions are made without political motivation. That is, decisions may focus on what is best for the U.S. economy in the long run, rather than on self-centered reasons (such as trying to achieve optimal economic conditions in the short run in order to get reelected).

The other 5 voting members are presidents of the Federal Reserve district banks. Each president of a district bank was elected by its respective directors. There are 12 Federal Reserve district banks, so the presidents of 5 of those 12 banks serve as voting members at any one time. The voting privilege is rotated among the 12 banks over time, except for the district bank in New York, the president of which is always a voting member.

When the 12 voting members consider whether U.S. interest rates should be adjusted, they assess the existing economic conditions. In general, if the Fed believes that the economy is too weak, it attempts to stimulate the economy by lowering interest rates. Conversely, if the Fed is concerned that inflation is too high, it attempts to slow down economic growth by raising interest rates.

How the Fed Adjusts Interest Rate Levels

When the Fed wishes to reduce interest rates, it increases the amount of funds at commercial banks by using some of its reserves to purchase Treasury securities (debt securities that were issued by the Treasury) held by investors. This results in an increase in the supply of funds available and places downward pressure on the equilibrium interest rate. The lower interest rate tends to increase the values of firms.

FIGURE 17.2

Money Supply Information

Data on the money supply, reported by the *Wall Street Journal*.

Source: Wall Street Journal, January 21, 2000, p. C19.

FEDERAL RESERVE DATA

MONETARY AGGREGATES
(daily average in billions)

	One week ended:	
	Jan. 10	Jan. 3
Money supply (M1) sa	1123.7	1149.8
Money supply (M1) nsa	1134.9	1198.7
Money supply (M2) sa	4685.2	4690.2
Money supply (M2) nsa	4711.0	4709.8
Money supply (M3) sa	6504.6	6561.5
Money supply (M3) nsa	6537.1	6543.4
	Four weeks ended:	
	Jan. 10	Dec. 13
Money supply (M1) sa	1133.3	1111.9
Money supply (M1) nsa	1162.9	1119.7
Money supply (M2) sa	4682.7	4640.0
Money supply (M2) nsa	4696.5	4645.1
Money supply (M3) sa	6524.3	6418.6
Money supply (M3) nsa	6527.8	6436.8
	Month	
	Dec.	Nov.
Money supply (M1) sa	1125.4	1108.4
Money supply (M2) sa	4662.6	4627.4
Money supply (M3) sa	6484.7	6384.6

nsa-Not seasonally adjusted.   sa-Seasonally adjusted.

MEMBER BANK RESERVE CHANGES

Changes in weekly averages of reserves and related items during the week and year ended January 19, 2000 were as follows (in millions of dollars)

When the Fed wishes to increase interest rates, it sells to investors some of the Treasury securities that it had previously purchased in the secondary market. This reduces the supply of funds available at commercial banks and places upward pressure on the equilibrium interest rate. A higher interest rate tends to decrease the values of firms.

Levels of money supply are reported in financial newspapers. An example of the information disclosed by the *Wall Street Journal* is provided in Figure 17.2. Note that the levels are reported for three different money supply levels on a "seasonally adjusted" (sa) basis and a "not seasonally adjusted" (nsa) basis. M1 is the most narrow measure. Other information about the amount of money in the financial system is also provided.

How Firms and Investors Respond to Expected Monetary Policies

Because interest rate movements can have a major impact on the firm's value and the Fed influences interest rate movements, firms and investors monitor the Fed closely. They try to anticipate how the Fed will adjust monetary policy so that they will be in a position to benefit from a change in interest rates. For example, if firms expect that the Fed will lower interest rates, they may defer long-term financing until interest rates are reduced. Conversely, if they expect that the Fed will increase interest rates, they may attempt to lock in the prevailing long-term interest rate before it increases.

NewsLine   COUNTERACTING INTEREST RATE CREEP

Corporate financial managers carefully monitor the Federal Reserve System's decisions on interest rate levels. The following article demonstrates how financial managers' reactions vary, depending on the individual company's situation and its industry sector.

In late August [1999], the Fed weighed in with its second rate hike of the summer. . . . The rate bumps signaled to corporations, bankers, and their economists that the Fed means business in its efforts to forestall inflation and rein in unrealistic expectations of continuous economic growth. . . .

Corporate executives have a practical view of the effects of interest-rate creep and how best to play it. Rate hikes can be a double-edged sword—enhancing bottom lines for cash-rich companies that can put excess funds to work at higher returns, but squeezing the bottom lines of companies with heavy borrowing requirements. The impact, of course, can vary greatly according to a company's size, financing strategy, and industry sector. But it appears that most CFOs and treasurers today are on heightened alert—though not seriously worrying. They believe that rates will creep, rather than gallop, upwards.

Active short-term borrowers, to be sure, cannot remain entirely passive. "In response to the rise in interest rates, we have reduced the amount of our floating-rate portfolio in favor of the fixed-rate percentage of our portfolio," says Michael J. Gapinsky, treasurer at Dayton, Ohio–based Reynolds and Reynolds Co. ($1.5 billion sales), which sells integrated information management systems and services. . . .

Safeco Corp., an insurance heavyweight based in Seattle, views rate increases from a different perspective than most nonfinancial companies. "Higher interest rates are good for our insurance operations," says its CFO, Rod Pierson. "Lots of [our] products stand to perform better with high interest rates. Even though we have both short-term and long-term debt on our books, on balance we prefer rising interest rates.". . .

Barry Donnell, chairman of the $615 million Addison, Alabama–based Cavalier Homes, Inc., says his company has tracked interest rates back to 1950 and has found no coorelation between rates and the number of manufactured home units it shipped. . . . "The recent quarter-point rise will have essentially no impact on operations or sales at this point, other than our having to pay a bit more on our variable-rate credit lines," he said in early September. "We are not changing our capital expenditure or financing plans."

Source: Richard Maturi, "Counteracting Interest Rate Creep," Treasury & Risk Management, October 1999, downloaded from www.cfonet.com/html/Articles/TRM/1999/99OCcoun.html.

Investors attempt to anticipate how the Fed will adjust monetary policy because the values of many of the securities they invest in are sensitive to interest rate movements. In particular, bond prices are very sensitive to interest rate movements. If investors expect that the Fed will raise interest rates, they try to sell their bond holdings now, because they recognize that bond prices will decline once interest rates rise. Conversely, investors commonly purchase more bonds when they anticipate that the Fed will lower interest rates, because they can obtain the bonds at a relatively low price before bond prices rise (once the Fed reduces interest rates).

Because the Fed does not normally announce its monetary policy in advance, some firms and investors will not necessarily predict the Fed's monetary policy. Nevertheless, they pay close attention to any statement made by officials of the Fed and to articles in the financial press about the Fed. The attention given to the Fed's actions is well deserved because of the impact that those actions can have on the values of firms managed by financial managers and by security portfolios managed by investors.

Fiscal Policy

fiscal policy
The government's program of taxation and public spending.

Fiscal policy is the means by which the federal government imposes taxes and allocates funds to the public. Because fiscal policy can affect the cash flows of a firm, it can affect the value of the firm. Some of the more important components of fiscal policy are discussed next.

Effect of Changes in Personal Income Taxes on a Firm's Value

The federal government imposes taxes on personal income earned by households. When the federal government changes personal income tax rates, it changes the level of disposable income of consumers. Some consumer purchases are influenced by the purchaser's level of disposable income, so the demand for products and services that are produced by firms is affected by personal income tax rates.

Effect of Reduced Personal Tax Rates   The federal government can attempt to stimulate the economy by reducing personal tax rates, which increases disposable income and increases the consumer demand for products and services. Thus, some firms should experience an increase in the demand for their products and services, which results in additional cash flows (and therefore a higher value of the firm).

Effect of Increased Personal Tax Rates   Conversely, if the federal government increases tax rates, it reduces the disposable income of consumers and reduces the consumer demand for products and services. Thus, firms should experience a reduction in the demand for their products and services, which results in a reduction in cash flows and therefore a lower firm value.

Effect of Changes in Corporate Tax Rates on a Firm's Value

The earnings generated by corporations are subject to a corporate tax, and the federal government periodically changes the corporate tax rates.

Effect of Reduced Corporate Tax Rates   When the federal government reduces corporate tax rates, this reduces the cash outflows of the corporation. For example, a reduction in the corporate tax rate from 34 percent to 30 percent on annual before-tax earnings of $100 million would reduce taxes from $34 million to $30 million. Consequently, the corporation's cash flows would increase by $4 million in that year.

Effects of Increased Corporate Tax Rates   When the federal government increases corporate tax rates, this increases the cash outflows of the corporation. For example, an increase in the corporate tax rate from 34 percent to 37 percent on annual before-tax earnings of $100 million would increase taxes from $34 million to $37 million. Consequently, the corporation's cash flows would decrease by $3 million in that year.

Excise Taxes

excise taxes
Taxes imposed by the federal government on specific products and services.

Excise taxes are taxes imposed by the federal government on specific products or services. Their effects are generally limited to those firms that are subject to excise taxes, such as cigarette and gasoline manufacturers. If the excise tax imposed on a firm's products is increased, the firm incurs higher taxes and experiences an increase in cash outflows. The firm may attempt to pass on the higher tax by raising prices (which could increase cash inflows), but this strategy might not be effective because it could reduce the demand for the firm's products or services. Thus, a higher excise tax is normally expected to reduce a firm's cash flows, whereas a lower excise tax is expected to increase the firm's cash flows.

Effect of Changes in Government Expenditures on a Firm's Value

The fiscal policy also specifies how the federal government will spend funds. The allocation of the spending can have a major impact on the cash flows of some firms. A new fiscal policy that increases the amount of funds allocated for military equipment may boost the expected cash inflows for those firms that will produce the equipment the federal government will purchase. Conversely, a reduction in the allocation for that type of equipment would reduce the expected cash flows for those firms. Similarly, health care companies are affected by the spending decisions by the government, which determine what types of health care are covered by insurance and therefore will be requested more frequently by customers. The greater the health care coverage by the government, the higher will be the cash flows for most health care companies.

Effect of the Federal Government Debt Level on a Firm's Value

crowding-out effect
The inability of some households or firms to borrow at the higher interest rate that results from the government's need to borrow large amounts of funds.

The federal government has a large amount of debt outstanding. When it increases the debt level substantially by spending more funds than it received from taxes, it may place upward pressure on interest rates, because the demand for loanable funds exceeds the amount of funds that is supplied by savers. In essence, the government's need for an abnormally large amount of funds in a given period can result in a rise in interest rates, such that some firms or households cannot afford to borrow at the higher interest rate. This is referred to as the **crowding-out effect,** because it crowds out some potential borrowers. To the extent that a change in the government debt level can affect U.S. interest rates, it can affect a firm's value, because that value is sensitive to interest rate movements, as we saw earlier.

Comparison of Government Effects

A comparison of how monetary and fiscal policies affect a firm's value is shown in Figure 17.3. The effect of monetary policy is due to changes in interest rates, whereas the effect of fiscal policy is due to tax rates imposed on firms or on the income of consumers. However, fiscal policy actions can also affect interest rates because of their effect on the amount of borrowing by the federal government to support its expenditures. The Fed and the presidential administration frequently disagree on the proper policies to be enacted. The administration commonly argues that the Fed should allow lower interest rates, and the Fed counters that interest rates would be lower if the administration had not enacted policies that required so much debt.

FIGURE 17.3   **How Government Policies Affect a Firm's Value**

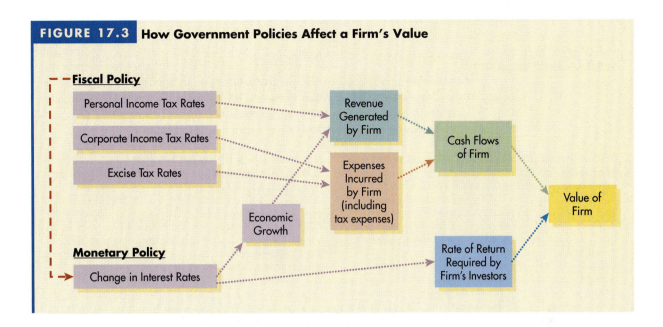

Review Questions

17–3   How can the Fed's monetary policy affect the value of a firm?
17–4   How can fiscal policies affect the value of a firm?

LG3   How Industry Conditions Affect a Firm's Value

A firm's value can change in response to changes in the industry conditions surrounding the firm. It is necessary to assess an industry, even after assessing general economic conditions, because industry performance levels vary over a particular period. Some of the more relevant industry factors that can affect a firm's value are industry demand, industry competition, industry labor conditions, and industry regulatory conditions. We will discuss each of these industry factors.

Industry Demand

The total demand for products or services within an industry can change abruptly in response to consumer preferences. For example, in response to increased awareness of health and fitness, the demand for health foods, fitness videos, barbells, and aerobics steps in the United States increased. The firms that produce these types of products should experience an increase in cash flows and an increase in value as a result of the increased demand within each of these industries (assuming that new competitors do not attract all the additional demand).

ON THE LOOKOUT FOR TRENDS

Companies and investors should track changes in specific sectors. Each January *Business Week* presents its Industry Outlook for 21 major industry groupings. The following excerpt on the metals industry discusses trends that could affect performance in the year 2000

With Washington's help, the U.S. steel industry has beaten back a devastating flood of cheap foreign imports. A robust economy, led by extraordinary demand for autos, has also helped bring prices and earnings back to healthy levels. This year [2000], the industry is poised to build on 1999's gains. But Big Steel's big question still looms: Will it finally bite the bullet and undergo a long-overdue consolidation, just as aluminum did?

The good news is that a strong economy should keep demand robust, even though some analysts expect revenue growth to slow slightly in 2000. Imports will retreat from a record high of 23% of total consumption this year to about 21% as antidumping duties and the Asian economic recov-

ery do their work. "Prices are being restored," says Curtis H. Barnette, chairman and chief executive of Bethlehem Steel Corp.

One pleasant surprise in 1999 was the big surge in auto production, to nearly 17 million units. That kept mills rolling out high-quality product. Demand for sport-utility vehicles, in particular has been so strong that some mills are working at better than 100% of normal capacity. But that adds expenses in maintenance and overtime that have actually eaten into profits.

Source: Peter Galuszka, "Industry Outlook 2000—Manufacturing: Metals," Business Week, January 10, 2000, p. 24.

Conversely, the demand for cigarettes in the United States declined in response to increased awareness of health, which should reduce the cash flows of the U.S. cigarette manufacturers. Clearly, demand within each industry does not automatically move in line with the economy.

Industry Competition

The degree of competition within each industry changes over time. As competition increases, firms can be adversely affected for two reasons. First, they may have to reduce their prices just to maintain their market share, which is measured by the ratio of the firm's revenues to total revenues in the industry. Alternatively, they may lose consumers to competitors. The first reason represents a reduction in expected revenues because of a reduction in price at the same sales volume. The second reason represents a reduction in expected revenues because of a reduction in market share and therefore sales volume. In each case, the firm experiences a reduction of expected cash flows (and its value will therefore decline) as a result of more intense competition.

Impact of Technology on Industry Competition

Improvements in technology have intensified the competition in many industries. Many firms are now selling their products over the Internet and fulfill orders by delivery. This can reduce marketing expenses and allow those firms to provide products without maintaining retail or wholesale outlets. Consequently, these firms may be able to offer their products at lower prices than other firms in the industry that have not capitalized on new technology.

Industry Labor Conditions

The labor conditions in each industry also change over time. When an industry becomes unionized, the firms in the industry are likely to experience substantially higher cash outflows as they pay higher wages to unionized workers. Unless the firms in this industry are able to pass the increased expenses on to consumers in the form of higher prices on products, they will experience a reduction in expected cash flows—and therefore a decline in value.

If one firm's workers go on strike as a result of a breakdown in labor negotiations, that firm's cash flows will obviously be reduced, at least in the short run. In addition, this labor condition will force customers to switch to competitors, which will increase the cash flows of the competitor firms. Thus, labor conditions can cause some firms to benefit at the expense of others.

Industry Regulatory Conditions

Some industries are subject to more government regulation than others. For example, the banking industry in the United States is subject to rules imposed by government regulators. Consequently, the future cash flows that can be generated by a specific bank are influenced by the government regulations.

Comparison of Industry Effects

A comparison of industry effects on firm value is shown in Figure 17.4. Depending on the specific industry condition, the firm may be exposed to either a decline in cash inflows or an increase in cash outflows. In either case, the value of the firm is reduced. Financial managers may be able to take actions that insulate the firm against adverse industry effects if they can anticipate them in advance.

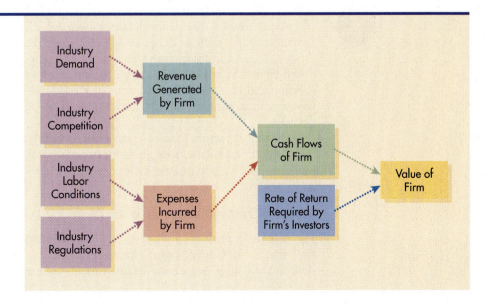

FIGURE 17.4

How Industry Conditions Affect a Firm's Value

Indicators of Industry Conditions

Information about the main firms in any industry is commonly available on various financial web sites. In addition, many magazines focus on a specific industry, such as chemicals, real estate, or computers. The publication *Standard & Poor's Industry Survey* provides an assessment of several industries. It describes historical trends and gives an outlook for each industry. Another useful reference for industry data is the *Value Line Industry Survey,* which provides financial statistics that can be used to measure the performance of each industry and offers an outlook on each industry. It also compares the main firms within each industry, including a comparison of their financial strength.

There are numerous stock indexes that reflect a particular industry. These allow financial managers to compare any particular firm's stock movements over a recent period with the stock movements of the respective industry. The industries that have experienced either very high or very low performance in a recent period are identified in the *Wall Street Journal.* A firm's stock performance may best be compared with the industry by considering competitive firms that are similar in size to the firm itself. Nevertheless, comparing the firm to the overall industry will still offer useful insight on how the firm is performing.

Review Questions

17–5 How can a change in industry demand affect a firm's cash flows?
17–6 How can a change in industry competition affect a firm's cash flows?

 ## How Global Conditions Affect a Firm's Value

 A firm with a successful business in the United States will not necessarily be successful outside the United States because of conditions specific to the foreign country, such as the economy, exchange rate fluctuations, political conditions, labor conditions, and the views of customers toward products produced by a U.S. firm. Just as the performance of a business in the United States is influenced by economic conditions in the United States, the performance of a business in a foreign country is influenced by economic conditions in that country.

The global factors that have the greatest influence on a firm's value are foreign economic growth, foreign interest rates, exchange rate fluctuations, and political risk. We will discuss each of these global factors.

Impact of Foreign Economic Growth

The economic growth in a specific foreign country can be distinctly different from that in the United States. Therefore, a firm that produces a specific product both in the United States and in one foreign country could experience different demand patterns for its product simply because of differences in the economic conditions in the two countries.

One potential benefit from conducting business in a foreign country is that the firm's cash flows are not completely influenced by U.S. economic conditions. If the economic growth in the United States during a particular period is weak, the cash flows from the firm's business may be adversely affected. However, if the economic growth in the foreign country is strong during that period, the firm's foreign business may have performed well, partially offsetting the adverse effects on the U.S. business. However, there will also be some periods in which the U.S. economic growth is higher than the foreign country's economic growth, so that the firm's overall performance may be weaker because it diversified its business across two countries instead of focusing its business in the United States.

recession
A decline in business activity, measured by at least two consecutive quarters of a decline in country's gross domestic product.

Most countries periodically experience a **recession,** defined as at least two consecutive quarters of a decline in the gross domestic product. Firms typically experience a significant decline in demand for their products in countries that are undergoing a recession. For example, U.S.-based multinational corporations, such as Nike, 3M Co., IBM, and DuPont, experienced a decline in sales in response to recessions in Asian countries during the 1997–1998 period (the period of the so-called *Asian crisis*).

For any type of foreign condition to which the firm is exposed, the potential impact on the firm depends on the type of country in which it conducts business. Developed countries tend to be more predictable than less developed countries, so the expected cash flows to be generated from business in the developed countries are generally subject to less risk.

Diversification to Reduce Exposure

The exposure of a firm's degree to the economic conditions of a foreign country is dependent on how much business the firm has in that country. A firm that has 40 percent of its business in one country is much more exposed to a specific condition than a firm that has only 10 percent of its business in each of four different countries. Firms that diversify their foreign business across countries may be less exposed to conditions in any particular foreign country. However, diversification does not always reduce the exposure. For example, U.S. firms that diversified businesses throughout Asia during the Asian crisis were adversely affected by conditions in all the Asian countries.

Impact of Foreign Interest Rates

A change in the foreign interest rates can affect the cash flows and the cost of financing of a U.S. firm.

Impact on a Firm's Cash Flows

Just as U.S. interest rates affect the level of borrowing by U.S. consumers who finance some of their purchases, the interest rate in a foreign country affects the level of borrowing by consumers in that country who finance some of their purchases. Therefore, the performance of a U.S. firm that sells products in a foreign country that are purchased on credit will be influenced by interest rate movements in that country. In particular, U.S. automobile manufacturers are affected by foreign interest rate movements, because they have foreign subsidiaries that produce and sell automobiles in several countries. A higher foreign interest rate will normally cause a reduction in the demand for new automobiles, which will reduce the cash inflows to the U.S. automobile companies.

A change in the demand for a foreign product that is due to a change in the foreign interest rate will affect the demand for supplies or materials used to make that product. Thus a U.S. auto parts firm that sells products in foreign countries will be adversely affected by a rise in foreign interest rates. Conversely, a decline in foreign interest rates should have a favorable effect on these companies.

To illustrate the potential impact of a change in foreign interest rates, consider the action taken by the European Central Bank to reduce interest rates in Europe in March 1999. The stock prices of many U.S. firms that have some operations in Europe increased immediately in response to this news, as investors sensed that the lower interest rates would increase borrowing by consumers and stimulate the European economy.

Impact on a Firm's Cost of Financing

When foreign interest rates rise, U.S. firms that obtain funds in foreign countries may experience an increase in financing costs. Conversely, a reduction in foreign interest rates can reduce the financing costs of these firms and may enhance their value.

Impact of Exchange Rate Fluctuations

One of the main concerns of a firm when it considers engaging in international business is the **exchange rate risk,** or exposure of its future cash flows to exchange rate fluctuations. As exchange rates change, they can affect the cash inflows or outflows of firms that make transactions in those currencies—and therefore can affect firm value.

Exposure of Importing and Exporting Firms

U.S. firms that export products denominated in foreign currencies are exposed to exchange rate risk because they will convert their receivables to dollars in the future. The U.S. firms will experience a reduction in dollar cash flows if the foreign currency depreciates shortly before the receivables are converted.

U.S. firms that import products denominated in foreign currencies are exposed to exchange rate risk because they will need to convert dollars to the foreign currency in the future. U.S. firms will experience an increase in cash outflows if the foreign currency appreciates shortly before the payables are converted.

Exposure of a U.S. Exporter   When the payments made to U.S. exporters are converted to dollars, the U.S.-dollar cash inflows are dependent on the exchange rate at the time.

E x a m p l e ▼   Seattle Co. exports products to Canada and expects to receive C$1,000,000 at the end of the year.

Assume that Seattle Co. expects that the Canadian dollar will remain close to its prevailing exchange rate of $.70 at the time it receives payment. The dollar cash inflows resulting from this payment are expected to be $700,000 (computed as C$1,000,000 × $.70). If the Canadian dollar depreciates (weakens) by the time Seattle Co. receives payment, the U.S.-dollar cash flows will be less than what was expected. At an exchange rate of $.60, the payments would convert to $600,000 (computed as C$1,000,000 × $.60), which is $100,000 less than what was expected. In this situation, Seattle Co. may not even generate a sufficient amount of cash inflows to cover the costs of producing the exported products.

Conversely, if the Canadian dollar had appreciated (strengthened in value) before the end of the year, Seattle Co. would have received a larger amount of U.S.-dollar cash inflows than expected. Thus the value of a U.S. firm that heavily relies on exporting tends to rise in response to expectations that the foreign currencies will strengthen against the dollar, and it tends to decline in response to expectations that the foreign currencies will weaken against the dollar. ▲

Exposure of a U.S. Importer   A firm that is engaged in importing products is also affected by exchange rate risk, but in the opposite manner.

E x a m p l e ▼   Duluth Inc. will pay 1 million Canadian dollars for imports at the end of the year. If the Canadian dollar was expected to be worth $.70 at the end of the year but is actually worth only $.60, Duluth Inc. will need only $600,000 instead of $700,000. Thus it "saved" $100,000 as a result of the depreciation of the Canadian dollar. ▲

Exposure of U.S. Firms That Engage in Direct Foreign Investment

subsidiary
A company whose stock ownership is controlled by another company.

parent company
The company that has ownership control of another company.

The cash flows of U.S. firms that engage in direct foreign investment are also affected by exchange rate fluctuations. Many of their businesses in foreign countries (referred to as **subsidiaries**) periodically send a portion of their earnings to the headquarters (or **parent company**) in the United States. The payments are denominated in a foreign currency and are converted by the U.S. parent into dollars. If the foreign currency depreciates over time, a given amount of earnings sent to the parent will convert to a smaller number of dollars. Conversely, if the foreign currency appreciates over time, a given amount of earnings will convert to a larger number of dollar cash flows.

During the Asian crisis, the currencies of many Asian currencies depreciated by more than 50 percent against the dollar. Under these conditions, the earnings remitted by the Asian subsidiaries converted to less than half the dollars that they would have converted to if their currencies had been stable.

Exposure of Purely Domestic Firms to Exchange Rate Risk

Even U.S. firms that have no international business can be exposed to exchange rate fluctuations if they face foreign competition in the United States. As exchange rates change, the prices paid by U.S. consumers for the foreign products change. This can cause consumers to shift their purchases to the foreign firms.

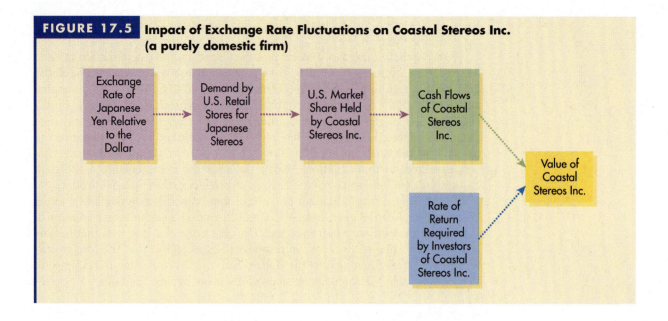

FIGURE 17.5 Impact of Exchange Rate Fluctuations on Coastal Stereos Inc. (a purely domestic firm)

Example ▼ Coastal Stereos Inc. is a U.S. firm that produces stereos and sells them to large retail stores in the United States. These retail stores commonly purchase stereos from Japan as well. The Japanese stereos sell for 40,000 Japanese yen (JY). Because the yen's exchange rate has recently been about $.01, the cost to the retail stores is JY40,000 × $.01 = $400.

If the Japanese yen depreciates until it is worth $.009, the retail stores can obtain the stereos produced in Japan for

$$JY40,000 \times \$.009 = \$360$$

The retail stores may pass that lower cost on to their customers in the form of lower prices. When consumers can obtain the Japanese stereos at a lower price, the purchases of stereos produced by Coastal decline. Therefore, Coastal's cash flows have been reduced in response to the Japanese yen's depreciation against the dollar, even though Coastal has no business in Japan. This effect is summarized in Figure 17.5.

If the Japanese yen appreciates against the dollar, the opposite effects may occur. The retail stores will have to pay more for the stereos imported from Japan (unless the Japanese producers lower the price of the stereos to offset the exchange rate effect), and they may pass the higher cost on to consumers. ▲

Impact of Political Risk

political risk
The risk that the host country's political actions will adversely affect the firm's performance.

Firms that are engaged in international business are typically exposed to **political risk,** or the risk that the host country's political actions will adversely affect the firm's performance. Some of the more common forms that political risk can take are the attitude of consumers in the host country, taxes imposed by the host government, host government restrictions on fund transfers, and bureaucracy. We will discuss each of these forms of political risk.

Attitude of Consumers in the Host Country

Consumers in some countries may want to purchase products produced by firms in their own country because of an allegiance to their country or because they believe the quality of products is better.

Alternatively, consumers may make their purchase decisions on the basis of the relationship between their country and other countries. For example, consumers in a country may avoid buying products produced by U.S. firms in a period of poor relations between their country's government and the U.S. government. Consequently, a U.S. firm may experience weak cash flows from business in this country during this period.

Taxes Imposed by Host Government

A host government may offer a U.S. firm special incentives if it wishes to attract direct foreign investment from the U.S. A common way to attract direct foreign investment is to offer a tax break on income earned by the firm in that country. The foreign subsidiary will have higher cash flows as a result of this incentive, and the parent will generate higher cash flows once the funds of the subsidiary are sent to the parent.

In some cases, a host government offers more favorable treatment to its locally owned firms by imposing higher taxes on foreign subsidiaries located there. Under these conditions, the cash flows of the firm that established the foreign subsidiary will be reduced once the higher taxes are imposed.

Host Government Restrictions on Fund Transfers

A host government may temporarily force local firms to spend or invest their funds within that country. Thus it can prevent the subsidiary from sending earnings to its parent. This delays the time at which the parent can generate cash flows from its investment in the foreign subsidiary. Alternatively, the host government may impose a tax on any funds that are remitted by the subsidiary to the parent. In either case, the U.S. firm's cash flows are adversely affected.

Bureaucracy

Some countries have a massive bureaucracy, which can significantly reduce the cash flows of firms that do business there. One of the most common forms of bureaucracy is that the host government may take several months to approve a request for the establishment of a business in its country. The delay may be intentional or it may be due to inefficiency. Some of the less developed countries tend to have huge bureaucracies.

Comparison of Global Effects on a Firm's Value

A comparison of the global effects on firm value is shown in Figure 17.6. The specific exposure of any firm to global conditions is dependent on the type of international business conducted by the firm. U.S. firms that focus on international trade are primarily exposed to exchange rate risk and to possible effects from foreign economic conditions. Firms engaged in direct foreign investment

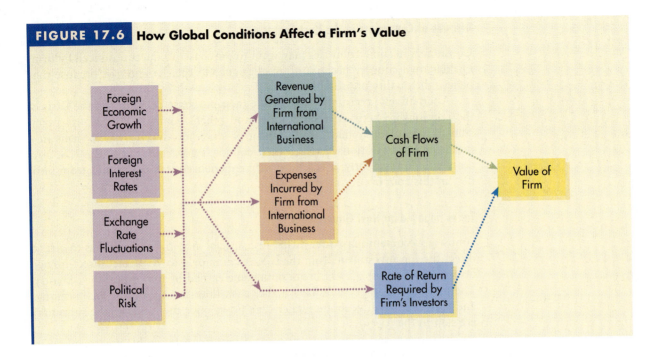

FIGURE 17.6   **How Global Conditions Affect a Firm's Value**

are exposed to these effects, as well as to political conditions in foreign countries where they have subsidiaries. The primary effects of political risk and exchange rate risk are on the cash flows of a firm, but the required rate of return may also increase for a firm that is highly exposed to these risks.

Indicators of Global Conditions

Financial managers and investors in the United States have easy access to information about foreign countries from foreign financial newspapers and from web sites. For example, web sites such as www.bloomberg.com provide information on foreign stock market indexes, foreign interest rates, and other international data. There are publications that forecast exchange rates of currencies and those that offer an assessment of the political risk level in every country.

? Review Questions

17–7   How can foreign economic growth affect a U.S. firm's cash flows?

17–8   How can the appreciation of the Japanese yen affect the cash flows of a U.S. firm that imports Japanese supplies?

TYING IT ALL TOGETHER

This chapter explained how a firm's cash flows and required rate of return (and therefore its value) can be affected by economic conditions. The impact of economic factors, government policies, industry conditions, and global conditions were discussed. Managers and investors may be able to anticipate changes in the firm's value by monitoring changes in economic conditions over time. The roles of managers, financial markets, and investors in monitoring economic conditions are summarized in the Integrative Table that follows.

INTEGRATIVE TABLE

Assessing and Responding to Changes in the External Forces

Role of **Financial Managers**	*Role of* **Financial Markets**	*Role of* **Investors**
Financial managers assess external forces so that they can make proper investment and financing decisions for their firms. Because the outcomes of these decisions are influenced by external forces, they must monitor the environment and consider the impact of changes in external forces on their business operations.	When external forces change, and investors revalue the firms on the basis of these changes, they purchase or sell stocks in the stock markets. These actions by all investors result in a new equilibrium stock price for every firm that is perceived to be affected by the change in external forces. Thus, the financial markets facilitate the change in the market value of the firm in response to changes in external forces.	Investors assess external forces to determine how the values of firms in which they may invest will be affected. As the external forces change, investors again estimate each firm's expected cash flows and may change the return that they require to invest in any firm. This results in the revaluation of firms.

LG1 Identify economic conditions that affect a firm's value, and explain how those conditions can do so. The main economic conditions that affect a firm's value are economic growth, interest rates, and inflation. Economic growth can affect the demand for a firm's products and therefore affect its cash flows. Interest rate movements can affect the volume of purchases of particular products that are supported by credit and therefore affect the cash flows of firms that sell these types of products. They can also affect a firm's cash inflows indirectly by affecting the general level of economic growth. Interest rate movements also affect the rate of return required by investors who invest in firms. Inflation can affect a

firm's cash outflows through its impact on the firm's cost of labor and materials used to produce products. It may also affect the firm's cash inflows if the firm changes the prices it charges for its products. In general, high economic growth, low interest rates, and low inflation have a favorable impact on a firm's value. In some periods, one or more economic conditions exert a favorable effect on firm value, while others exert an unfavorable impact.

LG2 Identify government policies that affect a firm's value, and explain how those policies can do so. The main government policies that affect a firm's value are monetary policy and fiscal policy. Monetary policy can affect firm value by affecting interest rates, which influence the cash flows of firms, and the rate of return required by investors who invest in firms. Low interest rates tend to enhance the expected cash flows and to lower the rate of return required by investors, which increases a firm's value. Higher interest rates tend to reduce expected cash flows, to increase the rate of return required by investors, and therefore to reduce a firm's value.

 Identify industry conditions that affect a firm's value, and explain how those conditions can do so. A firm's value can be affected by demand in its industry, as some industries experience shifts in demand over time in response to consumer behavior. Firms generally benefit from such an increase in their industry demand. An increase in competition within an industry tends to reduce a firm's value, as firms lose market share or need to reduce their prices (resulting in lower cash

inflows) to maintain market share. Firms can be adversely affected by industry labor conditions such as strikes and by government regulations.

 Identify global conditions that affect a firm's value, and explain how those conditions can do so. Global conditions can affect a firm with international business. Exporters and importers are affected by foreign economic conditions and exchange rates. Strong economic growth normally has a favorable effect on the firm's cash flows. Appreciation of a foreign currency tends to increase the demand for a U.S. exporter's products (and therefore increases its cash flows); depreciation of a foreign currency has the opposite effect. Firms with direct foreign investment are affected by these conditions, as well as by political risk. An increase in political risk in a foreign country can result in a reduction in dollar cash flows to the U.S. firm.

SELF-TEST EXERCISES   (Solutions in Appendix B)

 ST 17–1   Savannah Carpets, Inc. makes a variety of carpets used in homes, businesses, cars, and airplanes. It also produces a line of industrial upholstery used in vehicles of all sorts.

    a. What impacts on which of Savannah's product lines would you expect from a rise in interest rates?

    b. What kinds of suppliers to Savannah might be affected by changes in the demand for Savannah's product lines?

    c. What other types of firms that also sell to Savannah's customers might be affected by the rise in rates?

 ST 17–2   Allman's Jewelry Stores, Inc. sells a full line of men's and ladies' watches. Although it buys quite a few watches from domestic manufacturers, still others are imported from Europe and Japan. Allman's best-selling Japanese watch costs 32,000 yen wholesale and retails for $450.00. Its best-selling European watch costs 320 euro and also retails for $450.

    a. At an exchange rate of $.01 US per yen, what is Allman's dollar cost per unit for the Japanese watch? What is its percentage retail mark-up?

    b. If the exchange rate for the yen changed to $.012 US per yen, what would Allman's cost be? If the company wished to maintain the same percentage retail mark-up, what would the new retail price be?

    c. At an exchange rate of $1.00 US per euro, what is Allman's dollar cost per unit for the European watch? What is its percentage retail mark-up?

    d. If the exchange rate for the euro changed to $.98 US per euro, what would Allman's cost be? If the company wished to maintain the same percentage retail mark-up, what would the new retail price be?

    e. Why might Allman's not want to change the retail price for its watches in response to changes in exchange rates? What consequences would holding the retail price for both watches at $450 have for Allman's?

EXERCISES

 17–1   Economic growth and the firm   For an investor, changes in gross domestic product (GDP)-related statistics have special significance. Certain types of firms will benefit from rising GDP; others will do well when GDP is slowing or declining; still others are not particularly sensitive to changes in GDP.

    a. Use your common sense and experience to classify each type of firm in the list below as either more sensitive or less sensitive to changes in GDP. Give a one- or two-word reason for your answer.

        (1) Electric utilities

        (2) Furniture makers

        (3) Cruise lines

        (4) Food producers

        (5) Drug companies

        (6) Tire manufacturers

        (7) Home improvement stores

    b. For each of the companies that you classified as "more sensitive," state whether you think they would benefit from a rising GDP or a slowing/falling GDP. For each, give a short reason for your choice.

17–2   Interest rates and the firm   Many companies are interest-rate-sensitive because changes in rates affect their cost of borrowing, or because changes in rates affect their sales, or both. Explain what effect an increase in rates will have on the following types of companies.

    (1) Home builders

    (2) Consumer finance companies

    (3) Automobile manufacturers

17–3   Inflation and the firm   Inflation is defined as a generalized rise in the prices of products and service. Firms may be affected positively or negatively by inflation, depending on their ability to pass through increased costs in the form of higher prices.

    a. List at least four categories of costs to the firm affected by inflation.

    b. How does inflation affect borrowing behavior?

    c. What effect might inflation have on interest rates? Why?

 17–4   Monetary policy and the firm   In his semiannual report to the U.S. Congress on July 28, 1999, Federal Reserve Chairman Alan Greenspan said, "The already shrunken pool of job-seekers and considerable strength of aggregate demand suggest that the Federal Reserve will need to be especially alert to inflation risks."

    a. Reading that statement, and knowing that the Federal Reserve may engage in monetary policy actions to control any inflationary threat, what expectation for the probable direction of interest rates do you think would be reasonable?

b. If you were in management at a corporation, what long-term financing actions might you engage in? Why?

c. If you were an investor, what adjustments might you make to your portfolio? Why?

d. Go to the Federal Reserve's web site, www.frb.bog.fed.us/, and look up the most recent Humphrey–Hawkins testimony before Congress. What hints does it give you for the current Federal Reserve policy toward inflation? On the basis of your reading, in what direction do you think interest rates are likely to go?

LG2 17–5 Fiscal policy spending and the firm   The Department of Transportation has announced a major new mass transportation initiative with large federal grants to cities for the replacement and upgrading of older fuel-inefficient bus fleets. Name at least three types of businesses that might benefit from such a program. Give reasons for your choices.

LG2 17–6 Taxation and the firm   Changes in taxation of income or various excise taxes have a ripple effect on the profitability and value of many companies.

a. If a change in personal income taxation resulted in an average reduction of $100 per household for 50 million households, how much disposable income would be created?

b. What impact would that have on consumer demand for products and services?

c. How might that affect a firm's cash flows and value?

d. What are some of the ways in which firms handle excise taxes imposed on their products or services? With what consequences?

LG3 17–7 Industry conditions and the firm   Two widely available services provide useful information on industry conditions, as well as appraisals of individual companies. Both publications are carried by university and public libraries. Use them to investigate conditions in the Paper and Forest Products industry group.

a. Consult *Standard and Poor's Industry Survey* to get a detailed check of demand, competition, labor, and regulatory conditions within the industry. State the current conditions and the outlook for each type of condition.

b. Check in *Value Line Investment Survey* for the industry summary page at the beginning of the Paper & Forest Products section. Do these comments confirm what you found in *Standard and Poor's?* What companies within the group does *Value Line* believe are especially well positioned with regard to current conditions?

c. What other resources do financial managers use to compare the performance of their firm to that of others in the same industry?

LG4 17–8 Pricing and foreign exchange rates   Legacy Communications, Inc., a maker of telecommunications switching systems, has a cost basis of $3,400,000 in equipment that the company has contracted to sell to the city of Churchill, New Zealand. Legacy priced the equipment at cost plus 40%. The currency exchange rate as of the July 1 contract date was 2.04 New Zealand dollars per $1 US.

a. Calculate the selling price in U.S. dollars.

b. Because the contract specifies payment in New Zealand dollars, translate the U.S. dollar price into New Zealand dollars.

c. Assuming that the price calculated in part **b** is written into the contract, if the exchange rate changes to 1.95 New Zealand dollars per $1 US by the delivery date, what U.S. dollar equivalent will Legacy receive for the equipment? What percentage over cost will the company make?

   d. At what exchange rate would Legacy just break even on the cost basis of the equipment?

   e. The Currency Calculator feature of www.bloomberg.com can be a big help when one is dealing with real-world currency problems. Try part **b** of this problem at today's exchange rate between the U.S. dollar and the New Zealand dollar, using Bloomberg's Currency Calculator.

 17–9   **Doing business in foreign markets**   Walker Stores, Inc., a large U.S.-based general retailer, has a joint venture with El Dia, a Mexican general retailer. As a result of the joint venture, 30% of Walker's revenues stem from Mexican sales. Walker now is considering two different new joint-venture proposals. One is an additional joint venture in Mexico; the other is a joint venture in Canada.

   a. Discuss the advantages and disadvantages of pursuing the new joint venture in Mexico.

   b. Discuss the advantages and disadvantages of pursuing the new joint venture in Canada.

 17–10 **Exchange rates and competitive pricing**   Borstadt, Inc. makes one of the best remote control race cars on the market. It retails for $350. Borstadt's chief competition is a car made by Fiji Racing, Inc., a Japanese manufacturer. Fiji's car is priced at $350, also. Fiji's sales are translated back into yen before that company can pay its expenses and calculate net income. At an exchange rate of 110 yen/$1 US, the sale price of each car translates into 38,500 yen.

   a. Assuming that Fiji wishes to maintain a price of 38,500 yen, if the exchange rate changes to 118 yen/$1 US, what price will Fiji charge in U.S. dollars for its car?

   b. What would that price change probably do to Fiji's market share relative to Borstadt's?

   c. If the exchange rate changed to 103 yen/$1 US, what U.S. dollar price would Fiji charge for its 38,500-yen car?

   d. What would that price change probably do to Fiji's market share relative to Borstadt's?

  17–11 **Multiple facets of doing business overseas**   A number of U.S.-based companies moved to open the markets of eastern Europe after the breakup of the former Soviet Union. After the first 5 or 6 years, many of these same companies terminated their ventures into countries with regret, saying that they were losing money at a tremendous rate.

   How could a well-known U.S. fast-food company, which had customers lined up around the block to visit its Moscow franchises, have lost money on the venture? Use your imagination and what you know about general problems that any company may encounter overseas. Touch on politics, legal considerations, cultural norms, and exchange rates in your answer.

 17–12 **Government incentives and restrictions on foreign direct investments**   Ruby Red, Inc. is talking with the government of a West African nation about opening a manufacturing division there. Because of the employment potential, the country is willing to offer Ruby Red a significant tax break for the first 5 years that it is operating there. However, the government has imposed a restriction on taking profits out of the country that will require Ruby Red to reinvest, in its local operation, 60% of locally generated cash flow.

a. What effect would the tax break have on the cash flows of the proposed division relative to the parent company?

b. What positive results may come from the requirement to reinvest in the local division? What disadvantages may result from this restriction?

c. What exchange rate risks does the proposed set of incentives and restrictions impose on Ruby Red?

web exercises   Search

Bureau of Labor Statistics

Go to web site www.bls.gov. Click on Economy at a Glance.

1. What has been the unemployment rate for each of the most recent 6 months of data reported?

2. What has happened to productivity for the last 4 quarters reported?

3. What has happened to the CPI for the last 4 months reported? To the PPI?

Click on Consumer Price Index. Click on Most Requested Data. Click on All Urban Consumers (Current Series). Click on the first item on this list, and then click Retrieve Data.

4. What is the CPI for the latest month reported? What was it a year ago that same month? At this same web site, from the **Most Requested Data** screen, click on International Price Index.

5. What items are included in the International Price Index? (*Hint:* What items are listed below the International Price Index?)

6. What was the International Price Index for the last month reported? What was it a year ago that same month?

The World Bank Group
Our Dream is a World Free of Poverty
IBRD · IDA · IFC · MIGA · ICSID

Go to web site www.worldbank.org. Click on Research; click on Data; click on Data by Topic; click on Macroeconomics & Growth; and click on GDP per capita (year) table Atlas method and PPP.

7. Using the Atlas method data, determine which five nations have the highest GDP per capita? Which five have the lowest?

8. Using the Atlas method data, how many U.S. dollars is considered low income? Middle income? High income?

For additional practice with concepts from this chapter, visit
http://www.awl.com/gitman_madura

Investing in Stocks

LG1 Explain how stocks can be valued using valuation models that are alternatives to the dividend discount model.

LG2 Explain the valuation of the stock market.

LG3 Describe the valuation and performance of initial public offering (IPO) stocks.

LG4 Identify benchmarks commonly used for assessing investment performance.

LG5 Describe the forms of stock market efficiency.

LG6 Describe the valuation, performance measurement, and efficiency of foreign stocks.

Alternative Stock Valuation Models

As indicated in the previous chapter, a stock's price changes during any particular investment period in response to the economic environment, which reflects economic conditions, industry conditions, and global conditions. The economic environment affects the firm's cash flows and the rate of return required by investors. In addition, the stock return is affected by the decisions of those who manage the firm. Investors attempt to value a firm by using economic information about the firm itself. They consider investing in stocks whose valuations exceed their respective market prices. In addition, they consider selling stocks whose valuations are below their respective market prices.

The basic stock valuation method (also referred to as the dividend discount model) was explained in Chapter 7 as a way for financial managers to value the stock of their respective firms. Recall that this method takes as the value of a share of stock the present value of all future dividends the stock is expected to provide. Expressed as an equation, the dividend discount model values a share of stock as

$$V_0 = \frac{CF_1}{(1+k)^1} + \frac{CF_2}{(1+k)^2} + \cdots + \frac{CF_n}{(1+k)^n} \tag{18.1}$$

where

V_0 = value of the stock at time zero
CF_t = cash flow *expected* at the end of year t
k = appropriate required return (discount rate)
n = relevant time period

Dividends contribute to the immediate return received by investors, but they reduce the amount of earnings that are reinvested by the firm, which may limit the potential growth of the firm. Firms that pay a relatively high level of dividends tend to have more stable growth but less chance for very quick growth. Those firms are normally perceived to have lower risk than firms that pay no dividends and reinvest all earnings to support a high level of growth.

The dividend discount model is not directly applicable to valuing firms that have low or zero dividends. Therefore, investors commonly use various alternative valuation methods in addition to the dividend discount model. The most popular of these use other measures—price/earnings multiples, book value multiples, or revenue multiples—to value a share of common stock.

P/E Multiples

P/E method
Method used to value firms, in which a firm's earnings is multiplied by the industry P/E ratio.

A popular method used by investors to value firms is based on a multiple of the firm's earnings because many investors believe that earnings are a reasonable measure of a firm's cash flows. A direct measure of an earnings multiple is the firm's price-earnings (P/E) ratio. The **P/E method** applies the mean price/earnings (P/E) ratio of publicly traded competitors in the same industry to a specific firm's earnings for the next year to value that firm's stock. The P/E method can use the recently reported earnings of a firm (called *trailing earnings*) or the expected earnings in the next period (called *forward earnings*). For example, if the firm were expected to generate earnings of $4 per share this year, and the mean ratio of share price to expected earnings of competitor firms in the same industry were 12, then the valuation of the firm's shares would be

$$\text{Firm's stock price per share} = (\text{Expected earnings of firm per share}) \times (\text{Mean industry P/E ratio}) \quad (18.2)$$
$$= \$4 \times 12$$
$$= \$48$$

The logic of this method is that forward earnings are an important determinant of a firm's value. Although earnings beyond the next year are also relevant, this method implicitly assumes that the earnings growth potential in future years and the risk will be similar to those of the industry. If the actual stock price is less than the valuation, the stock is viewed as undervalued, and the investor conducting the valuation would consider investing in that stock. Conversely, if the actual stock price exceeds the valuation, the stock is viewed as overvalued, and the investor would not invest in that stock or possibly would sell any holdings of that stock.

Forecasting Earnings

In the application of the P/E method, a firm's stock valuation is highly influenced by its level of future earnings. Therefore, investors allocate much time to predicting a firm's future earnings.

Relying on Sources for Forecasted Earnings   Some investors rely on outside sources for earnings estimates. For example, Value Line, the Institutional Brokerage Estimate System (IBES), First Call, and many other investment service companies publicly disclose their forecasts of earnings for each firm. In addition, securities analysts employed by securities firms commonly develop earnings forecasts for the firms in the industries they monitor.

However, earnings forecasts by investment service companies commonly are off by 20 to 40 percent of the earnings estimate, and they are especially subject to error for firms that experience volatile earnings patterns.

Forecasting Earnings with the Pro Forma Income Statement Method   One of the most popular ways to estimate a firm's future earnings is to develop a pro forma income statement for the firm. In general, this involves a sales forecast and expense forecasts over the time period for which earnings estimates are needed.

Example ▼   Bob Duever wants to estimate earnings for Stream Inc. and apply a price/earnings ratio to those estimates to derive a value for Stream's stock. The stock is presently trading for $41 per share. Its latest income statement figures are shown in the second column of Table 18.1. Bob conducts an economic and industry analysis and believes that the industry will experience sales growth of 7% next year. He expects Stream to be positioned to benefit more from this growth than its competitors, and he expects that Stream's sales revenue will increase by 10%.

Bob applies this year's cost of goods sold as a percent of revenue to next year's forecasted revenue so that he can forecast the future cost of goods sold. On the basis of his industry analysis and the growth in sales revenue, he believes that the operating expenses will rise by 4%. He expects no changes in the interest expense, and uses a 30% tax rate to estimate taxes.

TABLE 18.1	Income Statement for Stream Inc. Example (in thousands)		
	This Year	Next Year	Explanation
Sales revenue	$6,000	$6,600	10% growth
Less: Cost of goods sold	3,000	3,300	50% of sales revenue
Gross profits	3,000	3,300	
Less: Operating expenses	2,000	2,080	4% increase
Operating profits	1,000	1,220	
Less: Interest expense	300	300	No change
Net profits before taxes	700	920	
Less: Taxes	210	276	30% tax rate
Net profits after taxes	490	644	

His pro forma income statement for Stream Inc. is given in the third column of Table 18.1, with an explanation of each item in the fourth column. He estimates that next year's earnings will be $644 million. Given that the firm has 280 million shares outstanding, his estimate for earnings per share is

$$\text{Forecasted EPS} = \frac{\text{Forecasted earnings}}{\text{Number of shares outstanding}} \qquad (18.3)$$

$$= \frac{644,000,000}{280,000,000}$$

$$= \$2.30$$

Bob's next task is to apply an industry P/E ratio to the forecasted EPS to derive an estimate of the appropriate stock price for Stream Inc. He notices that most of the firms in the industry have a P/E ratio between 18 and 22. He decides to apply a P/E ratio of 20 to Stream's forecasted EPS:

$$\text{Value of Stream's stock} = \text{Forecasted EPS} \times \text{Mean industry P/E ratio} \qquad (18.4)$$

$$= \$2.30 \times 20$$

$$= \$46.00$$

This valuation convinces Bob that Stream's stock, presently priced at $41, is overvalued.

Relationship Between the P/E Ratio and the Dividend Discount Model

The P/E method is useful as a complement to or substitute for the dividend discount model. Some investors are more confident when estimating the P/E multiple of comparable firms and the firm's earnings than when estimating the firm's future cash flows. The P/E method and the dividend discount model are related, however, because their valuations are influenced by industry conditions. The P/E multiple is influenced by the required rate of return on stocks of competitors and by the expected growth rate of competitor firms, as explained next.

When investors use the P/E ratio for valuation, they are assuming that the required rate of return and the growth rate for the firm being valued is similar to those of the other firms in the industry that they use to derive a mean P/E ratio. If competitors have a high degree of risk, the return investors require is high, and the P/E multiple for the industry is relatively low. In addition, a low growth rate of these firms will also result in a low P/E multiple. Thus, investors consider risk and the growth rate when using the P/E method.

Limitations of Applying P/E Multiples

Several limitations of the P/E method can result in different valuations.

Uncertainty Surrounding the Proper Earnings Forecast   Investors may use different forecasts for the firm's earnings or the mean industry earnings over the next year. The previous year's earnings are often used as a base for forecasting future earnings, but the recent year's earnings do not always provide an accurate forecast of the future. Thus, even if the valuation uses a proper P/E multiple, it is subject to error if the earnings forecast is inaccurate.

Uncertainty Surrounding the Proper P/E Multiple   The price/earnings method requires investors to determine which firms to include within the respective industry. The P/E multiple is dependent on whether one uses a broad industry composite or a narrow industry composite made up of firms that have operations very similar to those of the firm being valued. The valuation is subject to error if the P/E multiple that is applied does not properly reflect the firm being valued.

Example ▼   Consider the information in Table 18.2, which provides P/E ratios of computer firms as of March 2000. The P/E ratios range from 16.53 to 125.25 and have a mean of 64.02. Investors may vary in deciding which firms to use when applying the P/E multiple and how to weight each computer firm. Some computer firms may be more similar to the firm being valued than others. The mean P/E ratio of these firms was 19.33 one year earlier. This illustrates how the P/E multiple can change over time. ▲

The P/E ratio method typically values a particular firm at the same multiple (on average) as its competitors, yet there may be some firm-specific characteristics that distinguish the firm from its competitors. For example, if a firm is expected to grow faster than its competitors, and other characteristics are similar, a higher multiple should be applied to its expected earnings per share. Using the P/E method without any adjustments would undervalue that firm.

P/E Multiple Is Not Applicable to Firms with Negative Earnings   The P/E method cannot be applied to firms with an expected EPS that is negative. Thus the earnings of comparable firms with negative earnings may not be included in a composite used to derive a P/E ratio. To ignore any comparable firms that have negative earnings can cause an upward bias in the P/E ratio that is applied, because only the comparable firms with positive earnings are considered.

Valuing the Internet firms via the P/E method is difficult because many of them had negative earnings in their initial years. Those Internet firms with any amount of positive earnings typically have very high P/E ratios because of their potential. For example, Yahoo! had a P/E ratio of more than 1,200 in recent years, which is attributed to its tremendous growth potential. It would be

TABLE 18.2 P/E Ratios and Other Information About Large Firms in the Computer Industry (as of March 2000)

Firm	Price Per Share	Reported EPS	P/E Ratio	Dividend Yield (Annual Dividend ÷ Stock Price)
Apple Computer	$122.38	$3.69	33.16	0%
Compaq Computer	28.12	.32	87.88	.36%
Dell Computer	46.00	.61	75.40	0
Hewlett-Packard	146.44	3.19	45.90	.64
Sun Microsystems	96.44	.77	125.25	0
Unisys	26.94	1.63	16.53	0

dangerous to apply a P/E multiple of this size to any firm in a business similar to that of Yahoo!, because other such Internet firms are probably not positioned to grow and prosper as well as Yahoo!

Book Value Multiples

book value multiple
The market value of a firm's equity as a multiple of the firm's book value of equity; can be used to calculate a firm's value by multiplying the mean market/book ratio for the industry in which the firm operates by the firm's book value per share.

market/book (M/B) ratio
A popular book value multiple, calculated as the market price per share of common stock divided by the book value per share.

Some investors use book value multiples to estimate the value of a firm. A **book value multiple** is the market value of the firm's common stock in relation to (as a multiple of) the book value of the firm's common stock. (Book value represents the accounting value of the firm's stock, as shown in its financial statements.) The most popular book value multiple is the **market/book (M/B) ratio,** which was introduced in Chapter 8. It is the market price per share of common stock divided by the book value per share. Investors can use the mean market/book ratio for the industry in which a firm operates to value the firm's stock price per share. For example, say a firm has a book value of $10 per share, and the mean ratio of share price to book value in its particular industry is 5.0. The value of this firm is estimated to be

Firm's stock price
per share = (Book value of firm per share) × (Mean industry M/B ratio)   (18.5)
= ($10) × (5.0)
= $50

Limitations of Applying Market-to-Book Multiples

The use of a market-to-book multiple is subject to error if an improper M/B multiple is applied. An improper M/B multiple would be one that included other firms in the industry that have much different business operations. Another limiting factor is that the book value of a firm does not reflect relevant information such as the firm's potential for growth. Investors may adjust the multiple when applying it to a firm whose financial characteristics are different from those of the comparable firms. However, this type of adjustment is also subject to error, so the valuation is subject to error.

TABLE 18.3	Comparison of Multiples Used to Value Stocks	
Method	**Information Needed for Firm Being Valued**	**Information Needed for Comparable Firms**
Price/earnings multiple	Forecast of annual earnings per share	Mean ratio of the stock price relative to annual earnings per share
Book value multiple	Book value	Mean ratio of the stock price relative to book value per share
Revenue multiple	Revenue	Mean ratio of the stock price relative to the annual revenue per share

Revenue Multiples

revenue multiple
The market value of a firm's equity as a multiple of the firm's revenue per share; can be used to calculate a firm's value by multiplying the mean P/R ratio for the industry in which the firm operates by the firm's expected revenues per share.

price/revenue (P/R) ratio
The ratio of a firm's share price to its revenue per share.

An alternative method that can be used to value a firm is a **revenue multiple.** One of the most common revenue multiples is the **price/revenue (P/R) ratio,** which is the ratio of the share price to a stock's revenue per share. The revenue per share is simply total revenues divided by number of shares. Investors may use trailing revenue if they expect them to serve as an accurate forecast. Alternatively, they could use a public forecast of the firm's revenue in the next period, or they could forecast it themselves. They could value the firm by applying the mean ratio of share price to revenue per share in the respective industry to the firm's revenue per share. For example, assume that a firm has expected revenue of $40 per share and that the mean ratio of price to revenue in its industry is 2.0. The value of the firm is estimated to be

Firm's stock price
per share = (Expected revenue of firm per share) × (Mean industry P/R ratio)   (18.6)
= ($40) × (2.0)
= $80

The revenue-multiple method is compared to the earnings-multiple and market/book-multiple methods in Table 18.3.

Limitations of Applying Revenue Multiples

The use of a revenue multiple is subject to error because an improper P/R ratio may be applied if it includes firms in the same industry that have much different business operations. In addition, the revenue of a firm does not reflect relevant information such as the firm's potential for growth, so investors who use the P/R multiple may need to consider growth potential as an additional input when valuing a stock by this method.

 **Review Questions**

18–1   Explain in general terms how the P/E method is used to value a firm's stock.

18–2 Explain in general terms how a book value multiple is used to value a firm's stock.

18–3 Explain in general terms how a revenue multiple is used to value a firm's stock.

LG2 Valuing the Stock Market

Valuation models are applicable not only to individual firms but also to the market in general. Investors commonly value the market in the aggregate to determine whether they should invest more funds in the market or liquidate some of their existing investments. Because any particular stock market represents a group of stocks, the valuation of the market should be high when conditions are favorable to most firms.

Valuation During the Recent Market Run-up

During the middle and late 1990s, the U.S. stock market performed extremely well. In fact, the stock valuations appeared to exceed the operating performance of firms. In particular, the P/E ratios of firms were unusually high. This prompted a question about stock valuations that was continually asked during this bullish market run. How can the fundamental stock valuation models be used to justify such high valuations? Let's look at two possible explanations.

Explanation Based on the Dividend Discount Model

When we use a dividend discount model, a high valuation is the result of either improved cash flow estimates or a reduction in the required rate of return, or both. Therefore, one possible explanation is that the required rate of return was reduced during that period, because the risk-free interest rate had declined. However, this is not by itself sufficient to explain such high valuations.

Strong economic conditions could have caused improved estimates of growth in cash flows, but there is some question whether the cash flows would improve to the degree reflected by the valuations. The expected growth in cash flows could also have improved because improvements in technology allowed for more efficient production or new ways to generate revenues.

Explanation Based on Speculative-Bubble Theory

speculative bubble
High stock prices due to irrational speculation.

An alternative explanation for the high valuations is simply that stock prices are exceeding their proper values. That is, the market is overvalued. This implies that investors are overly optimistic, which is creating a **speculative bubble** (high stock prices due to irrational speculation) that will burst someday. A speculative bubble could occur if the demand for stocks was influenced by the recognition of how well stocks performed recently and the investors' assumption that past performance is indicative of future performance.

It has been argued that investors have been blindly investing on the basis of recent performance without conducting proper valuations of stocks. Although it

*News*Line   *HITTING THE BULL'S-EYE*

When securities analysts announce an unusually high stock-price target, investors flock to buy that company's stock, pushing the share price closer to the target. However, investors should understand the analyst's justification for arriving at the target before placing a buy order.

Investors are making prophets of analysts by driving stocks up to what the seers say they're worth.

It isn't hard to create a lengthy list of 1999's market excesses. The top spot would go to the stunning 86% run-up in the tech-heavy Nasdaq composite index—the largest one-year gain in history for a major index. Also somewhere high on the list would be the practically indecent $1,000 price target one analyst set for Qualcomm (QCOM) on December 29. That call set off a one-day rally in the stock of 156 points, or 31%. Qualcomm, which has a central role in developing digital wireless technology, ended the year up more than 2,600%, the top-performing stock in the S&P 500 in 1999.

Analysts are sure to make many other seemingly ridiculous calls in 2000. In fact, the Qualcomm price target is part of a growing trend on Wall Street, where investors have begun making prophets of analysts by driving stocks up to whatever the supposed seers say they're worth.

On January 3, for instance, a handful of Internet stocks scored double-digit gains based on triple-digit price targets,

sparking a dramatic run in the sector. Morgan Stanley Dean Witter initiated coverage of DoubleClick(DCLK) with a $300 price target (the stock rose more than 14, to 268), and First Union Securities issued a $600 price target on Yahoo! (YHOO), which rose more than 42, to 475....

In the current, momentum-driven stock market, high price targets set by popular analysts quickly become self-fulfilling prophecies—and investors know it, says Arthur Hogan, chief market analyst at Jefferies & Co. He points out that in Qualcomm's case, the huge one-day run-up was fueled by the analyst's call and by an impending four-for-one stock split, which took place on December 30. "Keep in mind, nothing changed at Qualcomm," he says. Still, the stock closed on January 3 at 179 5/16 (717.25 pre-split), which puts it well on its way to Paine Webber analyst Walter Piecyk's $1,000 call. Six days earlier, the stock was at $522.

Source: Amey Stone, "How Stock-Price Targets Create a Bull's-Eye—Then Hit It," Business Week Online, January 4, 2000, downloaded from www.businessweek.com/bwdaily/dnflash/jan2000/sw00104.htm.

is true that many individual investors do not try to value stocks, institutional investors tend to use more sophisticated valuation techniques. However, even sophisticated valuation techniques are subject to error.

When abrupt declines in the stock prices in the market or specific sectors are not triggered by any fundamental changes in the economic environment, this reflects a correction to a perceived speculative bubble. For example, on April 19, 1999, stocks traded on the Nasdaq market declined by 5.57 percent on average. The Internet stocks whose prices increased substantially over the previous weeks experienced the largest decline on this day. The stock price of amazon.com declined by 16.3 percent on this day; America Online's stock price declined by 17.1 percent, and the stock price of Ameritrade (an Internet discount brokerage firm) declined by 30.3 percent. Some investors referred to this day as the "burst in the speculative Internet bubble."

The burst of the bubble does not imply that the firms are worthless but merely that the run-up in prices exceeded the level that may have been appropriate. For example, Ameritrade's price increased by more than 800 percent over the 12 months prior to this day in which its stock price declined. However, over the next two days, prices of stocks on the Nasdaq increased substantially, completely offsetting the one-day loss on average. Thus some investors viewed the correction as a mistake and purchased shares whose prices had declined.

The uncertainty surrounding the value of a stock is not restricted to Internet firms or other small publicly traded firms. Even large, well-known stocks are subject to high degrees of volatility. For example, Intel was priced at $85 on October 27, 1997. It declined to $69 by the next day and then climbed back to $85 on the following day. One of the reasons for the high degree of volatility is that some investors commonly rely on momentum and rumors because there simply is not a continuous flow of fundamental information available about a stock. Momentum and rumors can push a stock far away from its fundamental value before there is an adjustment by the market.

Review Question

18–4   Why might stocks be overvalued in some periods when applying the dividend discount model?

 ## Valuation and Performance of IPO Stocks

Recall from Chapter 3 that an *initial public offering (IPO)* represents the first offering of stock to the public by a particular firm. A firm is not valued by the market before its IPO, because investors do not have easy access to investment in the firm. Many investors want to purchase shares during an IPO because they anticipate that the firm has much potential to grow. They expect that their investment may experience high appreciation of the share price over time.

Valuation

To value an IPO, investors can use the discounted cash flow method or various multiples for valuing newly issued stock. However, one obvious difference between valuing the stock from an IPO and valuing other stock is that there is no history of valuations by the market. Thus, investors do not have a market price as a basis of comparison when determining their own value. They can only guess at the market's valuation of the stock at the time of an IPO.

Performance

If investors had purchased shares during the IPO of a firm such as amazon.com, they would have earned very large returns. The stock price of amazon.com increased by 10,000 percent within 2 years of its IPO. Thus, investors who recognized that it was undervalued at the time of the IPO would have been able to benefit. If an investor had invested $100,000 in amazon.com at its initial offer price during the IPO, the investment would have been worth more than $10 million within 2 years. On January 15, 1999, an IPO by another Internet stock called MarketWatch.com had an initial price of $17 per share and increased to $130 per share within the first 2 *hours* of trading. Even when considering the decline in price to $97.50 per share by the end of the day, the one-day return for investors who purchased shares at the initial price was about 474 percent. Thus anyone who invested $100,000 at the initial price of $17 and sold their shares at the end of the first day would have accumulated $574,000.

FIGURE 18.1

Stock-Price Movements Following Prodigy's IPO on February 12, 1999

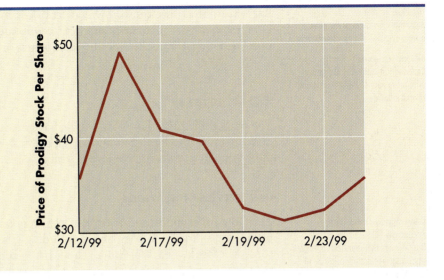

In 1998 Internet stocks, on average, increased by 84 percent on the first trading day following their IPOs. This caught the attention of many investors who wanted a piece of the action. Many investors had not earned a return of 84 percent over an entire decade. Brokerage firms such as E*Trade, Fidelity, and Schwab now attempt to obtain portions of the IPO shares from the investment bankers underwriting the IPOs so that they can sell IPO shares online to their individual investors. They have received only a small portion, though, and therefore cannot satisfy many individual investors who would like to purchase shares of firms engaging in an IPO.

The potential gains from investing in an IPO are well publicized, but there is also much downside risk. Figure 18.1 shows how volatile the price of Prodigy's stock was around the time of its February 1999 IPO, which confirms the high degree of uncertainty regarding the stock's value.

After the first day, IPOs tend to perform poorly on average (when compared to general market movements) over a period of several months. This suggests that many IPOs may be overvalued on the first day following the offering.

Review Question

18–5   Describe the performance of firms in general following their initial public offerings (IPOs).

 Stock Performance Benchmarks for Investors

Investors commonly measure the performance of their investments by comparison to various benchmarks. Stock *indexes* are useful benchmarks, because they reflect the general movements in the entire stock market or in specific segments of the stock market. Investors monitor specific indexes during the day or for longer

market indexes
Benchmark measures of the general price movement of a particular market.

sector indexes
Benchmark measures of the general price movement of a particular group of related industries.

intervals so that they know how market prices changed in general. **Market indexes** represent a particular stock market; **sector indexes** represent a particular group of related industries, such as utility companies or transportation companies.

Market Indexes

The market measure that most people have heard of, because it is reported daily in many radio and television newscasts, is the Dow Jones Industrial Average. The most popular market indexes are described next.

Dow Jones Industrial Average

Dow Jones Industrial Average (DJIA)
Market index that represents a weighted average of the stock prices of 30 large U.S. firms.

The **Dow Jones Industrial Average (DJIA)** represents a weighted average of stock prices of 30 large U.S. companies, including Chevron, Disney, General Electric, IBM, Microsoft, and Wal-Mart. The DJIA is commonly monitored by investors as an indicator of the price movement of large, well-known ("blue chip") stocks. However, it does not serve as a useful indicator for smaller stocks.

Standard & Poor's 500

Standard & Poor's (S&P) 500
Market index that represents a weighted average of the stock prices of 500 large U.S. firms.

The **Standard & Poor's (S&P) 500** index is a weighted average of stocks representing 500 large U.S. firms. Although it represents more stocks than the DJIA, its focus is also entirely on large U.S. stocks. The S&P 500 index and the DJIA tend to move closely in tandem over time.

New York Stock Exchange Index

New York Stock Exchange (NYSE) Composite
Market index that represents the average price of all stocks traded on the NYSE.

The **New York Stock Exchange (NYSE) Composite** represents the average price of all stocks traded on the NYSE (some 2,800 stocks). This index represents many more stocks than the S&P 500 or the DJIA.

Nasdaq Composite

Nasdaq Composite
Market index that represents the price of stocks traded in the Nasdaq market.

The **Nasdaq Composite** represents the stocks that are traded in the Nasdaq market. Because the stocks traded in the Nasdaq tend to be smaller, this index is more representative of smaller publicly traded stocks.

Sector Indexes

There are NYSE indexes for industrial, transportation, utility, and financial sectors. Each sector's performance can be driven by unique forces, so sector indexes are useful for distinguishing among sector performance levels. The sector indexes are more appropriate than the general market indexes as benchmarks when assessing a firm that is represented by a sector. For example, a utility company's stock-price performance should be compared to a utility index rather than to a broad market index, because the difference between the utility company performance and the broad market performance may be attributed to factors specific to utility companies in general, not to the utility company of concern.

*News*Line   **WEALTHIER, BUT NOT NECESSARILY WISER**

Many investors, blinded by the phenomenal bull market in recent years, are forgetting that stock prices can fall as well as rise and that diversification is still a valid strategy.

As the curtain closed on the 1990s, most investors were undoubtedly feeling pretty smart....But despite the extraordinary success investors have had, many advisers say that investment IQs haven't improved much since the 1980s....

Thanks to the phenomenal returns of U.S. large-capitalization stocks, many people now believe that "stocks only go up, diversification makes no sense, and they should buy individual stocks instead of funds," says Harold Evensky, a financial planner in Coral Gables, Florida.

While the 1980s were also strong years—the average annual return of the Standard & Poor's 500-stock index was 17.4%—investors maintained a reasonable grasp on the risks associated with stock-market investing, thanks to the 1987 crash. The '80s also taught investors the merits of diversifying because no single asset class was the clear winner.

Not so in the '90s. U.S. large-cap stocks left other investments in the dust, prompting investors to ask, "Why diversify?"

Even worse, many investors now have dangerously inflated expectations....Just try telling...investors who got into the market for the first time during the '90s they should be happy with 11% [the average annual stock market return since 1926 based on the S&P 500]! After all, the S&P 500's average annual return was about 19% for the past decade, and 30.6% for the past four years. Gains in some high-flying tech stocks have been simply mind-boggling: America Online Inc. soared 590% last year; Yahoo! Inc. turned in a 511% return in 1997.

Such phenomenal gains have all but blinded many individual investors to risk and to the merits of a diversified portfolio....Moreover, the onslaught of investment information in the media...has inflated investors' confidence to dangerous levels.

"This overconfidence makes people believe they can beat the market, so they abandon a buy-and-hold strategy and trade more actively," says Terrance Odean, a finance professor at the University of California at Davis....

Source: Karen Hube, "Investors Will Greet New Decade Wealthier, But Many Won't Necessarily Be All That Wiser," Wall Street Journal, *December 15, 1999, C1, C20.*

There are also Dow Jones sector indexes, including a Dow Jones Internet index. Nasdaq sector indexes include insurance, banking, computer, and telecommunications sectors. These are most appropriate for monitoring the relatively small firms within a specific sector. Performance levels can vary because of the size of the firm, so investors who assess a small firm in a particular sector are more likely to use the Nasdaq sector indexes for a comparison, whereas investors who assess a large firm in a particular sector use NYSE sector indexes.

Stock-Price Quotations

Investors monitor stock quotations to determine changes in the valuation of stocks that they consider trading. Quotations are available for individual stocks, for market and sector indexes, and for publicly traded stock indexes.

Quotations for Individual Stocks

Figure 18.2 includes an excerpt from the NYSE stock quotations, reported in the January 21, 2000, *Wall Street Journal* for transactions through the close of trading on Thursday, January 20, 2000. We'll look at both the common stock and the preferred stock quotations for IBM, highlighted in Figure 18.2. The quotations show that stock prices are quoted in sixteenths of a dollar, with the fractions

FIGURE 18.2

Stock Quotations

Selected stock quotations, reported by the *Wall Street Journal.*

Source: Wall Street Journal, January 21, 2000, p. C4.

	52 Weeks Hi	52 Weeks Lo	Stock	Sym	Div	Yld %	PE	Vol 100s	Hi	Lo	Close	Net Chg
	41 1/2	**23 11/16**	**InfntyBrd A**	**INF**		**...**	**84**	**10256**	**37 3/4**	**34 1/4**	**34 3/8**	**– 1 15/16**
n▲	**30**	**19**	**InfontSvcs B**	**IN**		**...**	**...**	**43586**	**31 3/8**	**24 3/4**	**29 7/8**	**+ 5 3/4**
	29 3/4	15 3/4	InfoHldg	IHI		...	73	94	29 11/16	29	29	– 1/4
	73 13/16	**44 7/8**	**IngRnd**	**IR**	**.68**	**1.4**	**14**	**10687**	**52 1/2**	**49 3/16**	**49 5/16**	**– 2 11/16**
	31	20 5/16	IngRndGrth PRIDES		.20	.9	...	.9	23	22 3/4	22 3/4	– 1/2
	33 5/8	22 1/4	IngRndInco PRIDES		1.69	6.9	...	40	25	24	24 3/8	– 3/8
	33 5/16	**10**	**IngramMicro A**	**IM**	1.121	**...**	**10**	**3855**	**12 3/16**	**11 3/8**	**11 7/16**	**– 5/8**
	11 3/4	7 5/8	Innkeepers	KPA		4.0	10	1662	8	7 13/16	8	+ 1/8
	9	4 1/4	InpOutpt	IO		...	dd	1048	6 1/16	5 13/16	5 7/8	– 1/8
	15 1/8	**7 1/4**	**InsigniaFnl**	**IFS**		**...**	**44**	**661**	**9 7/8**	**9 1/8**	**9 11/16**	**+ 9/16**
	9 7/8	5 3/8	InsteelInd	III	.24	3.1	7	15	7 7/8	7 13/16	7 13/16	– 1/16
	14 3/8	11 5/16	InsrdMuniFd	PIF	.77	6.7	...	221	11 7/16	11 3/8	11 7/16	...
	21 11/16	8 1/8	♣ IntgElec	IEE		...	6	239	8 15/16	8 11/16	8 11/16	– 1/16
	24 13/16	13 3/4	InterimSvc	IS		...	17	2622	22 5/8	21 1/2	22 1/16	– 5/8
	6 3/4	2 11/16	IntlCer ADR	ICM		...	...	4	6 3/8	6 5/16	6 5/16	– 1/16
	30 5/8	22 5/8	♣ IntAlum	IAL	1.20	5.2	11	20	22 15/16	22 7/8	22 7/8	...
s	**139 3/16**	**80 7/8**	**IBM**	**IBM**	**.48**	**.4**	**30**	**176994**	**124 3/4**	**120 5/16**	**121 9/16**	**+ 6 1/16**
	27 1/2	25 1/8	IBM pf		1.88	7.3	...	28	25 11/16	25 7/16	25 11/16	+ 3/16
	48 1/2	33 5/8	IntFlavor	IFF	1.52	4.1	24	2362	37 1/16	36 9/16	36 13/16	+ 1/8
▲	22 1/4	14 1/8	IntGameTch	IGT	.12	.5	14	6059	22 9/16	21 3/8	22 7/16	+ 1
	20 11/16	13 11/16	IntHomeFood	IHF		...	13	2659	16 9/16	16 3/16	16 5/16	– 1/8
	25	11 5/8	IntMultfood	IMC	.80	6.2	86	283	12 15/16	12 5/8	12 7/8	+ 1/8
	26	20 1/2	IntPapCapIII	IPP	1.97	9.0	...	377	22	21 13/16	21 15/16	+ 1/16
	60	39 1/2	IntPaper	IP	1.00	2.0	94	28242	53 3/8	50 5/16	50 11/16	– 1 13/16
▲	27 7/8	6 1/4	IntRectifr	IRF		...	71	7271	27 15/16	26 11/16	27 7/8	+ 1 1/8
	16 5/16	9 15/16	IntShiphld	ISH	.25	2.5	4	208	10 1/2	10 1/16	10 1/16	– 7/16
	11 11/16	7	IntSpcPdt	ISP		...	18	825	7 13/16	7 11/16	7 3/4	+ 1/16
	16	**6 7/8**	**♣ Interpool**	**IPX**	**.15**	**2.1**	**6**	**822**	**7 7/8**	**7**	**7**	**– 7/8**
s	58 3/8	34 13/32	IntpubGp	IPG	.34	.6	43	6455	55 9/16	53 3/16	53 5/16	– 2 1/4
▼	26 1/16	16 3/16	IntsBaker	IBC	.28	1.7	10	2493	16 1/8	16 1/16	16 3/16	– 5/16
s	19 7/16	4 3/16	IntertanInc	ITN		...	dd	2119	15 3/16	14 5/8	15 3/16	+ 3/16
	33 3/8	23 9/16	♣ IntrtapPly g	ITP	.16q	...	...	239	25 1/2	24 7/8	25 3/16	+ 1/8
	52 3/8	32 5/8	IntimrBrnd A	IBI	.56b	1.7	21	4702	34 1/2	33 1/8	33 7/16	– 5/16
▼	17 7/8	14 9/16	Intrawest g	IDR	.16g	...	...	383	15	14 3/16	14 3/8	– 1/2
	26 15/16	17 7/16	Invacare	IVC	.05	.3	12	1435	19 5/16	18 9/16	19 5/16	+ 11/16
	20	13 5/16	♣ InvcoGlbl	GHS	2.39e	14.8	...	1647	16 3/8	15 7/8	16 3/16	+ 3/16
	16 3/16	12 11/16	InvGrdMuni	PPM	.30a	2.3	...	74	12 15/16	12 13/16	12 13/16	– 1/8
s	**48 1/2**	**17 13/16**	**♣ InvTchGp**	**ITG**	**4.00e**	**11.3**	**21**	**11426**	**36**	**31**	**35 1/4**	**+ 4 3/8**
	10	**2 7/8**	**Iomega**	**IOM**		**...**	**dd**	**56067**	**5 1/2**	**5 3/16**	**5 7/16**	**+ 3/8**
▲	**36 15/16**	**24 7/8**	**Ionics**	**ION**		**...**	**30**	**980**	**37 11/16**	**35**	**37 5/8**	**+ 3 1/2**
s	26 7/16	15 5/8	IpalcoEnt	IPL	.60	3.3	13	1899	18 1/8	17 3/4	18 1/8	+ 3/8
	24 1/8	15 5/8	Ipsco g	IPS	.50g	...	...	44	20 1/8	19 13/16	19 13/16	– 11/16
	21 9/16	14 1/2	IrishInvFd	IRL	1.73e	11.1	...	594	15 13/16	15 1/2	15 5/8	...
	39 1/2	25 1/8	IronMtn	IRM		...	dd	569	33 5/8	32 5/8	33 1/2	+ 13/16
s	17 3/8	11 7/8	Italy Fd	ITA	1.25	7.5	...	120	16 13/16	16 11/16	16 3/4	+ 1/16
	22 11/16	6 7/8	IvexPckgng	IXX		...	...	353	10 1/8	9 13/16	9 15/16	– 1/4

J-J-J

reduced to their lowest common denominator. Quotations may be shown in decimals rather than fractions. The first two columns, labeled "Hi" and "Lo," contain the highest price and the lowest price at which a share of stock sold during the preceding 52 weeks. IBM common stock, for example, traded between 139 3/16 ($139.19) and 80 7/8 ($80.87) during the 52-week period ending January 20, 2000.

Listed to the right of the company's abbreviated name is its stock symbol—"IBM." Stock symbols are used by securities industry professionals and traders to identify specific companies. The number listed right after the stock symbol under "Div" is the annual cash dividend paid on each share of stock. The dividend for IBM was $0.48 per share. The next item, labeled "Yld%," is the dividend yield, which is found by dividing the stated dividend by the closing share price. The dividend yield for IBM is 0.4 percent (0.48 ÷ 121 9/16 = (0.48 ÷ 121.5625) = 0.004 = 0.4%.

The price/earnings (P/E) ratio, labeled "PE," is next. It is calculated by dividing the closing market price by the firm's most recent annual earnings per share (EPS). The price/earnings (P/E) ratio measures the amount that investors are willing to pay for each dollar of the firm's earnings. It is believed to reflect investor expectations concerning the firm's future prospects: Higher P/E ratios reflect investor optimism and confidence; lower P/E ratios reflect investor pessimism and concern. IBM's P/E ratio was 30, which means that the stock was trading at 30 times its earnings.

The daily volume, labeled "Vol 100s," follows the P/E ratio. Here the day's sales are quoted in lots of 100 shares. The value 176994 for IBM indicates that 17,699,400 shares of its common stock were traded on January 20, 2000. The "Hi," "Lo," and "Close" columns contain the highest, lowest, and closing (last) price, respectively, at which the stock sold on the given day. These values for IBM were a high of $124.75, a low of $120.3125, and a closing price of $121.5625. The final column, "Net Chg," indicates the change in the closing price from that on the prior trading day. IBM closed up 6 1/16 ($6.0625) from January 19, 2000, which means the closing price on that day was $115.50 (115 1/2).

Note that preferred stocks are listed with common stocks. For example, following IBM's common stock in quotes in Figure 18.2 is its preferred stock, which is identified by the letters "pf." The quotation for preferred stock is nearly identical to that for common stock except that the value for the P/E ratio is left blank because it is not applicable.

Similar quotation systems are used for common and preferred stocks that trade on other exchanges, such as the American Stock Exchange (AMEX) and the over-the-counter exchange's National Association of Securities Dealers Automated Quotation (Nasdaq) national market issues. Also note that when a bond or stock issue is not traded on a given day, it generally is not quoted in the financial and business press.

Price quotations for some of the American depository receipts (ADRs) most widely traded on the Nasdaq exchange are published daily in the *Wall Street Journal,* as shown in Figure 18.3. The second column indicates the number of shares outstanding that are traded, the third column gives the price per ADR, and the fourth column cites the change in the price from the previous day.

Quotations for Market and Sector Indexes

Quotations of index levels for market and sector indexes are published in financial newspapers. The *Wall Street Journal* provides a daily "Stock Market Data Bank," as shown in Figure 18.4. The high, low, and closing index levels are shown for the previous day. The net and percentage changes in each index are measured over the previous day, the last 12 months, and since the start of the calendar year. The *Wall Street Journal* also identifies specific industry groups that have experienced unusually strong or weak performance.

Quotations for Publicly Traded Stock Indexes

Investors not only use stock indexes as performance benchmarks but also invest directly in indexes. The American Stock Exchange created various composite indexes that can be traded on its exchange. One of the most popular is the **Standard & Poor's Depository Receipt** (**SPDR**, also called **Spider**), which is a

Standard & Poor's Depository Receipt (SPDR, or Spider)
A composite index that represents a basket of stocks matched to the S&P 500 index, shares of which investors can buy and sell (instead of trading shares of individual stocks).

FIGURE 18.3

ADR Quotations

ADR quotations, reported by the *Wall Street Journal.*

Source: Wall Street Journal, January 20, 2000, p. C12.

ADRs

Wednesday, Jan. 19, 2000

AngloAmr .42e	437	67 3/8	+	1 5/16
CSK .11e	7	114	–	2
CnPacMin	240	7 1/4	+	1/4
DBeer .79e	1408	28 11/16	–	3/16
DigitTel	14	6 1/2		. . .
Euro909	8544	28 1/2	+	1 5/8
Euro909 wt	526	22 1/8	+	1 3/16
FujiPh .19e	481	40 3/4		. . .
Ftrmdia	2502	1 7/32	–	1/32
GoldFLtd. .05e	1053	5	+	9/32
GoldFd .48i	44	2 1/2		. . .
Highvld .11e	1	4 1/16	+	3/16
IncmAG n	238	2	+	1/16
InstruCp .32e	2	18 1/2	+	1 1/4
JapnAr .05e	27	6 1/8	+	1/16
KirinBr .96e	5	115 5/8	–	1 3/8
LundnOil .08e	543	3 3/8	+	3/8
NewTel .01e	1812	18 15/16	+	11/16
Nissan	244	9 1/2	+	1/4
RankGrp .60e	61	6 3/8	–	5/16
RealaxS	320	5 7/8	–	3/16
Santos .64e	32	11 1/4	–	1/4
Sanyo .22e	33	24 1/2		. . .
Sasol .25e	46	8 5/8		. . .
Senetek	9484	2 1/8	+	7/16
SoPacPet	103	3 7/16	+	5/16
TeleMex .09e	4290	5 11/16	–	3/16
TrnGlbl	6	1 13/32	–	3/32
TrnBio	1543	2 9/32	+	1/32
Wacoal .55e	26	43	–	1/8

basket of stocks matched to the S&P 500 index. It enables investors to take positions in the index by purchasing shares. Thus investors who anticipate that the stock market as represented by the S&P 500 will perform well may consider purchasing shares of Spiders, especially when their expectations reflect the composite as a whole rather than any individual stock within the composite. Spiders trade at one-tenth the S&P 500 value, so if the S&P 500 is valued at 1400, a Spider is valued at $140. Thus the percentage change in the price of the shares over time is equivalent to the percentage change in the value of the S&P 500 index. Spiders pay dividends in the form of additional shares to the investors. The exchange charges investors a small annual fee against the dividends owed to shareholders.

Several other composites also have been created for trading purposes. For example, *Diamonds* are shares of the Dow Jones Industrial Average (DJIA) and are measured as 1 one-hundredth of the DJIA value. *Mid-cap Spiders* are shares that represent the S&P 400 Midcap Index. There are also *Sector Spiders,* which are intended to match a specific sector index. For example, a *Technology Spider* is a fund representing 79 technology stocks from the S&P 500 composite.

? Review Question

18–6 If you were attempting to assess the performance of a small stock, would the S&P 500 or Nasdaq be a more appropriate benchmark? Explain.

FIGURE 18.4

Stock Market Data Bank

Data on the stock market, reported by the *Wall Street Journal.*

Source: Wall Street Journal, January 21, 2000, p. C2.

STOCK MARKET DATA BANK   1/20/00

Major Indexes

12-MO HIGH	12-MO LOW		DAILY HIGH	DAILY LOW	CLOSE	NET CHG%	CHG	12-MO CHG	%CHG	FROM 12/31	%CHG
DOW JONES AVERAGES											
11722.98	9120.67	30 Industrials	11558.70	11274.98	1135.30	− 138.06	− 1.20	+ 2087.22	+ 22.53	− 145.82	− 1.27
3783.50	2784.31	20 Transportation	2845.76	2768.32	2784.31	− 53.73	− 1.89	− 310.50	− 10.03	− 192.89	− 6.48
333.45	269.20	15 Utilities	308.95	300.14	308.82	+ 7.28	+ 2.41	+ 1.83	+ 0.60	+ 25.46	+ 8.99
3366.13	2832.10	65 Composite	3229.94	3166.90	3193.64	− 23.30	− 0.72	+ 326.06	+ 11.37	− 20.74	− 0.65
1390.32	1154.51	DJ Global-US	1391.24	1366.22	1373.65	− 8.31	− 0.60	+ 200.37	+ 17.08	− 16.67	− 1.20
NEW YORK STOCK EXCHANGE											
663.12	576.17	Composite	647.68	637.50	640.51	− 4.86	− 0.75	+ 52.48	+ 8.92	− 9.79	− 1.51
836.88	722.97	Industrials	837.28	822.74	826.66	− 7.41	− 0.89	+ 96.88	+ 13.28	− 1.55	− 0.19
518.74	426.40	Utilities	487.64	480.05	487.64	+ 7.27	+ 1.51	+ 33.81	+ 7.45	− 23.51	− 4.60
560.33	428.31	Transportation	467.91	455.95	457.59	− 8.08	− 1.74	− 10.83	− 2.31	− 9.11	− 1.95
584.22	457.63	Finance	503.56	493.69	493.89	− 8.53	− 1.70	− 22.77	− 4.41	− 22.72	− 4.40
STANDARD & POOR'S INDEXES											
1469.25	1216.14	500 Index	1465.56	1438.56	1445.57	− 10.33	− 0.71	+ 210.41	+ 17.04	− 23.68	− 1.61
1841.92	1466.86	Indistrials	1844.02	1810.09	1818.81	− 11.11	− 0.61	+ 329.00	+ 22.08	− 23.11	− 1.25
269.98	215.62	Utilities	246.65	238.05	246.65	+ 8.06	+ 3.38	− 5.12	− 2.03	+ 19.43	+ 8.55
452.16	353.14	400 MidCap	454.23	448.34	452.16	+ 0.18	+ 0.04	+ 74.80	+ 19.82	+ 7.49	+ 1.68
205.12	154.83	600 SmallCap	205.83	203.39	205.12	+ 1.73	+ 0.85	+ 31.08	+ 17.86	+ 7.33	+ 3.71
308.89	255.39	1500 Index	308.48	303.48	305.05	− 1.88	− 0.61	+ 44.83	+ 17.23	− 3.84	− 1.24
NASDAQ STOCK MARKET											
4189.51	2248.91	Composite	4227.35	4143.61	4189.51	+ 38.22	+ 0.92	+ 1844.79	+ 78.68	+ 120.20	+ 2.95
3841.74	1888.66	Nasdaq 100	3877.43	3782.43	3841.74	+ 50.85	+ 1.34	+ 1879.98	+ 95.83	+ 133.91	+ 3.61
2334.16	1294.40	Industrials	2352.43	2306.29	2334.16	+ 22.29	+ 0.96	+ 976.22	+ 71.89	+ 95.19	+ 4.25
2372.33	1702.46	Insurance	1843.59	1808.72	1809.58	− 34.09	− 1.85	+ 53.00	+ 3.02	− 86.70	− 4.57
1898.49	1549.74	Banks	1581.30	1549.14	1549.74	− 28.72	− 1.82	− 242.79	− 13.54	− 141.55	− 8.37
2370.99	1164.77	Computer	2397.94	2341.52	2365.65	+ 14.42	+ 0.61	+ 1113.37	+ 88.91	+ 40.25	+ 1.73
1050.57	542.90	Telecommunications	1054.15	1036.24	1050.57	+ 20.45	+ 1.99	+ 507.67	+ 93.51	+ 35.17	+ 3.46
OTHERS											
899.61	688.65	Amex Composite	902.22	890.34	899.61	+ 9.04	+ 1.02	+ 194.62	+ 27.61	+ 22.64	+ 2.58
769.96	632.53	Russell 1000	772.07	758.16	762.48	− .30	− 0.56	+ 117.97	+ 18.30	− 5.49	− 0.71
527.28	383.37	Russell 2000	528.23	520.02	527.28	+ 7.26	+ 1.40	+ 103.23	+ 24.34	+ 22.53	+ 4.46
795.53	652.13	Russell 3000	799.56	785.77	790.50	− 3.34	− 0.42	+ 124.40	+ 18.68	− 2.81	− 0.35
472.95	398.58	Value-Line(geom.)	431.49	426.73	428.17	− 2.55	− 0.59	− 5.20	− 1.20	− 2.87	− 0.67
13812.67	11146.59	Wilshire 5000	...	...	13773.95	− 33.62	− 0.24	+ 2405.11	+ 1.16	− 3 8.72	− 0.28

†-Based on comparable trading day in preceding year.

Stock Market Efficiency

Given that investors continuously search for pricing discrepancies, the equilibrium price of stock should continuously reflect the aggregate consensus of all investors in the market. The stock price of the firm responds to the shift in market conditions that was triggered by new information. The response of a stock price to new information is almost instantaneous in many cases, as some investors make trades immediately following announcements about a firm or economic conditions.

Periodically, changes in economic conditions or changes in a firm's management or financial condition affect the firm's future prospects. As new information about these changes is released to the market, investors respond. Favorable information about a firm causes investors to increase their demand for the firm's shares; unfavorable information causes investors to reduce their demand for the firm's shares. The stock price of the firm responds to the shift in market conditions that was triggered by new information.

efficient market
A stock market in which stock prices fully reflect all information that is available to investors.

inefficient market
A stock market in which stock prices do not reflect all information that is available to investors and in which undervalued stocks can therefore be found.

If the stock prices fully reflect information that is available to investors, the stock market is referred to as **efficient.** Conversely, if stock prices do not reflect all information, the stock market is referred to as **inefficient.** Investors search for inefficiencies in the stock market, because this would allow them to capitalize when pricing discrepancies occur. For example, if stock prices of firms always increased for firms that announced that their earnings increased in the most recent quarter, this would allow some investors to capitalize on the market inefficiency by purchasing shares of those firms at the time of the announcement. Information about the firm such as favorable earnings reports or changes in economic conditions can have a major impact on stock prices, but it is difficult to take positions in the stocks based on that information before the stock prices have adjusted.

Forms of Efficiency

Three forms of efficiency are commonly used to determine whether the prices of stocks properly reflect their appropriate values: weak-form, semistrong-form, and strong-form market efficiency.

Weak-Form Efficiency

weak-form efficiency
Form of market efficiency in which stock prices fully reflect market-related information, including historical price movement and the trading volume of a stock.

Weak-form efficiency means that the stock prices fully reflect *market-related information,* including historical stock-price movements and the trading volume of any particular stock. Thus an investment strategy such as buying a stock if its price increased for four consecutive days or if its trading volume increased should not generate abnormal risk-adjusted returns if the stock market is weak-form efficient.

Several studies have tested the theory of weak-form market efficiency. For example, studies have tested whether a particular trend in a stock's prices over previous days or weeks predicts the future pattern of that stock's prices. If there were a persistent pattern, it would enable investors to earn abnormal risk-adjusted returns by purchasing stocks whenever a recent pattern indicated that the stock prices would rise substantially in the future. This procedure was applied to many different stocks over several different time horizons. In general, the studies found that the use of previous stock-price patterns *does not* enable investors to achieve abnormal risk-adjusted returns.

Semistrong-Form Efficiency

semistrong-form efficiency
Form of market efficiency in which stock prices fully reflect all information that is publicly available.

Semistrong-form efficiency means that stock prices fully reflect *all information that is publicly available.* In addition to market-related information that is public (such as historical price movements and trading volume), there is other publicly available information, such as news about economic conditions, public forecasts of stock prices by institutional investors, and public comments made by Federal Reserve officials.

If it was determined that investors could use public information such as publicly announced forecasts of stock prices by a particular institutional investor to earn abnormally high returns, the theory of semistrong-form efficiency would be refuted. However, because this type of information is not about market-related

TABLE 18.4	Comparison of Forms of Efficiency	
Form of Efficiency	Description	Type of Information Used to Test Whether Efficiency Exists
Weak-form	Stock prices reflect all market-related information.	Historical stock-price movements, and trading volume.
Semistrong-form	Stock prices reflect all publicly available information.	Analyst recommendations and other public information.
Strong-form	Stock prices reflect all information.	Any public information and inside information.

data (such as historical stock prices or trading volume), weak-form efficiency could still exist even if semistrong-form efficiency were refuted.

There is some evidence that refutes the theory of semistrong-form market efficiency. For example, studies have provided evidence that stock prices of firms that acquire unrelated targets experience abnormally weak returns, on average, over time. Thus it appears that investors may have overvalued the acquirer's stock at the time of the acquisition, which means that they did not fully incorporate the existing information when valuing the acquirer's stock.

Strong-Form Efficiency

strong-form efficiency
Form of market efficiency in which stock prices fully reflect all public information as well as all private information.

Strong-form efficiency means that stock prices fully reflect *all public information as well as all private information.* Private information includes information that is known by financial managers who work for a firm and by board members. If financial managers could use private (inside) information about their own firm to earn abnormal risk-adjusted returns when investing in the stock of their firm (which, by law, they cannot), this would refute the theory of strong-form market efficiency. Strong-form efficiency is compared to weak-form and semistrong-form efficiency in Table 18.4.

There is limited research that tests strong-form market efficiency, because private information is not available to test whether it could be used to achieve abnormal risk-adjusted returns. Some studies have found that if investors could have used recommendations by well-known stock portfolio managers or analysts before the recommendations became public, they would have earned abnormal risk-adjusted returns.

Evidence of Inefficiencies

Despite the evidence generally in favor of market efficiency, many investors continue to believe in market inefficiencies. Indeed, there is some evidence of market inefficiencies, as described here.

January Effect

Investors commonly sell stocks whose prices have declined before the end of the year so that, to reduce their taxes, they can apply the losses to offset some gains earned on other stocks that were sold in that year. This pattern of year-end sales

January effect
Evidence of market inefficiency in which stocks, especially small ones, decline in value in November and December and rebound in January.

places downward pressure on stock prices in November and December. In the following January, investors either repurchase those stocks or purchase others, which exerts upward pressure on stock prices. This **January effect** is especially pronounced for small stocks.

Monday and Weekend Effects

Monday effect
Evidence of market inefficiency in which stock market returns are lower on Mondays than on other days of the week.

weekend effect
Evidence of market inefficiency in which stock prices open lower on Monday than the price at which they closed on Friday.

Studies have found that stock returns (percentage changes in stock prices) vary on average with the day of the week. Specifically, there is evidence that the return on Mondays is lower, on average, than the return during other days in the week; this is referred to as the **Monday effect.** However, it appears that some stocks do not necessarily weaken during Monday's trading hours but, rather, do so when the market opens on Monday. The opening price on Monday is lower than the Friday closing price. In other words, the view of the market during nontrading hours over the weekend is dampened by Monday morning. This **weekend effect** is especially felt by very large stocks. Other stocks experience lower returns on Monday because of a lower opening price and a weakening of the price during the day, on average. That is, prices of these stocks tend to weaken because of a weekend effect *and* a Monday effect.

Size Effect

size effect
Evidence of market inefficiency in which smaller firms tend to have larger risk-adjusted returns over the long term than do larger firms.

Some studies have found that stocks of different size classifications have different mean risk-adjusted returns over a particular long-term period. This discrepancy is often called the **size effect.** Specifically, smaller firms (as measured by the total market value of the their stock) tend to have larger risk-adjusted returns than larger firms. However, during the large market run-up in the late 1990s, larger firms outperformed smaller firms. The relationship between size and relative performance has changed over time.

Price/Earnings (P/E) Effect

P/E effect
Evidence of market inefficiency in which stocks with low price-earnings (P/E) ratios have outperformed stocks with high P/E ratios.

Studies have found a so-called **price/earnings (P/E) effect,** which means that stocks with low price/earnings (P/E) ratios have outperformed stocks with high P/E ratios. This may imply that investors are overly optimistic when they value a stock high relative to its recent earnings, whereas they are overly pessimistic when they value a stock low relative to its recent earnings. Even after controlling for size classifications and the industry, low-P/E stocks have outperformed high-P/E stocks.

Limitations of Capitalizing on Price Discrepancies

Although specific relationships between firm-specific characteristics and risk-adjusted returns have been identified, it is difficult for investors to exploit these apparent discrepancies, for the following reasons.

Trading Commissions

The commissions that investors incur from trading stocks can offset any abnormal gains achieved by taking advantage of discrepancies. For example, assume that investors try to capitalize on a discrepancy by purchasing stocks that have the lowest P/E ratios every quarter and selling them at the end of that quarter. Stocks with lower P/E ratios indeed have historically outperformed high P/E stocks, but the difference in performance may not be sufficient to cover the trading commissions such investors pay.

Tax Effects

When investors use frequent trading to capitalize on perceived stock-pricing discrepancies, they may be subject to *short-term capital gains*, which are taxed at the investor's ordinary income tax rate. This rate is typically higher than the tax on long-term capital gains. For example, investors who are subject to a marginal federal income tax of 39.6 percent would have to pay this tax rate on short-term capital gains. They would pay a maximum of only 20 percent on long-term capital gains. Thus, even if their attempt to capitalize on discrepancies results in larger before-tax gains than would an alternative passive buy-and-hold investing strategy, their after-tax gains may be lower.

Relationships Are Not Applicable to All Firms

The relationships between risk-adjusted returns and time or firm-specific characteristics are not applicable to all firms. Investors who decide to purchase a stock of a firm just because it has a low P/E ratio or a low market/book ratio are not guaranteed high performance. The relationships determined in studies are generalized after assessing hundreds or thousands of stocks and do not represent every stock.

Review Questions

18–7   What is the key difference between weak-form efficiency and semistrong-form efficiency?

18–8   What is the key difference between semistrong-form efficiency and strong-form efficiency?

 ## Foreign Stock Valuation, Performance, and Efficiency

 U.S. investors have become increasingly interested in foreign investing, so it is important to understand the valuation, performance, and efficiency of foreign stocks.

Valuation of Foreign Stocks

Foreign stocks can be valued by using the dividend discount model or the price/earnings model, with an adjustment to reflect international conditions.

Dividend Discount Model

The dividend discount model values foreign stocks by discounting the stream of expected dividends denominated in dollars. To do so requires conversion of the foreign dividend amount to a dollar amount, estimated as the dividend denominated in the foreign currency multiplied by the value of that foreign currency in dollars. If the foreign currency denominating the foreign stock appreciates, the expected dollar amount of dividends increases. U.S. investors must recognize that there is uncertainty associated with their valuation even if they could perfectly forecast foreign dividends, because of the uncertainty surrounding future exchange rate movements.

Price/Earnings (P/E) Method

The P/E method values foreign stocks by applying the price/earnings ratio for the particular industry in the foreign country to determine the appropriate price of the firm's stock. However, accounting standards vary across countries, which makes it difficult to assess earnings in a foreign country. The P/E method would generate a value of the foreign firm that is influenced by the firm's accounting guidelines and tax laws. Thus, the application of the P/E method to foreign stocks is very limited.

Foreign Stock Performance Benchmarks

When U.S. portfolio managers invest in foreign stocks, they are typically assigned a specific country or region of the world. Their performance should be compared to the performance of a market index in that country. The comparison should convert both the foreign stock values and the index into dollars. Thus the performance measurement controls for general market movements and exchange rate movement in the country of concern.

This type of performance evaluation captures market and exchange rate conditions that are not under the control of investors who purchase foreign stocks. For example, if investors invest in Japanese stocks, they can compare the performance of their portfolios to that of the Japanese index. Note that their performance is measured relative to an index that requires no portfolio management. It is to be hoped that portfolio managers provide benefits to their financial institutions by outperforming the respective country index where they invest. Otherwise, the financial institution could simply invest in the index and earn the same return without compensating portfolio managers.

Foreign Stock Market Efficiency

The potential to find inefficiencies in a market depends on how quickly and thoroughly investors respond to information. However, there may be more potential for inefficiencies in other markets that are monitored by fewer investors. For this reason, some U.S. investors allocate much of their time to assessing foreign stock prices.

There is some evidence of inefficiencies in foreign stock markets. For example, there is evidence of a relatively slow stock market response (a few days), on average, to changes in earnings reported by firms. This implies that an investor could purchase stocks for which there is favorable earnings news before the stock price completely adjusts to the favorable information. However, any abnormal risk-adjusted return from such inefficiencies may be offset by the high trading commissions associated with the purchases of foreign stocks. In addition, as many U.S. investors have attempted to capitalize on inefficiencies in foreign markets, their trading behavior has caused a quicker response of foreign stock prices to new information. Consequently, the recent increase in international investing has made it more difficult to identify inefficiencies in foreign markets.

? Review Questions

18–9   What is the key adjustment that is incorporated when applying the dividend discount model to value a foreign stock, but not when applying it to value a U.S. stock?

18–10   What would be an appropriate benchmark for assessing the performance of an Australian stock?

TYING IT ALL TOGETHER

This chapter explained how a firm's stock can be valued, how a stock's performance can be evaluated, and the meaning of market efficiency as related to valuation. The roles of managers, financial markets, and investors in the stock valuation process are summarized in the Integrative Table that follows.

INTEGRATIVE TABLE

Valuing Stocks and Executing Stock Transactions

Role of **Financial Managers**	*Role of* **Financial Markets**	*Role of* **Investors**
Financial managers make decisions that affect the expected future cash flows of the firm—and therefore the value of the firm. Financial managers can attempt to obtain funds by issuing more shares of their firm's stock.	The financial markets establish a market price for each stock that is traded. When investors use their own valuation methods, they commonly derive a value that differs from the prevailing market price of the stock. Investors commonly respond to large differences by purchasing the stocks that they perceive as undervalued by the market and selling stocks they perceive as overvalued by the market.	Investors monitor the decisions made by a firm's financial managers, along with other conditions, when valuing a firm. Because they do not have the same detailed information as the firm's financial managers, they may use multiples to value the firm.

LG1 **Explain how stocks can be valued using valuation models that are alternatives to the dividend discount model.** The P/E method estimates the price as the product of the respective industry P/E ratio and the firm's expected annual earnings. The industry P/E ratio is based on a composite of comparable firms with characteristics similar to those of the firm being valued. The P/E method is subject to error because of the possibility of using an improper mix of comparable firms or using a poor forecast of the firm's earnings.

The market-book (M/B) ratio is the market price per share of common stock divided by the book value per share. The industry M/B ratio is based on the composite of comparable firms. The price/revenue (P/R) value method estimates the firm's stock price as the product of the respective industry price/revenue ratio and the annual revenue of the firm. The use of these types of multiples to value firms is subject to error because of the possibility of using an improper mix of comparable firms to derive the multiple.

LG2 **Explain the valuation of the stock market.** The stock market valuation is the weighted sum of the values of firms within that market. Therefore, any factors that influence the firms that constitute the market will affect the general stock market conditions. Very favorable stock market conditions in the mid- and late 1990s were attributed to strong economic growth (which increased the expected growth of firms), advances in technology (which increase efficiency), and a reduction in interest rates (which reduced the rate of return required by investors). It has also been argued that these favorable stock market conditions cannot be completely explained and that they partially reflect a speculative bubble that will burst someday.

LG3 **Describe the valuation and performance of initial public offering (IPO) stocks.** Stocks can be valued at the time of an IPO by applying multiples, such as the price/earnings multiple, the market/book ratio, and the price/revenue ratio. Some IPO stocks have experienced very high performance during the first day of trading but gen-

erally have not performed well over periods of 1 year or longer. They are normally subject to more uncertainty than other stocks because they have not been valued by the market in the past.

LG4 **Identify benchmarks commonly used for assessing investment performance.** Stock market indexes are commonly used to assess investment performance. Each index reflects a specific market or sector. If investors are effective at selecting investments, their performance should exceed that of a corresponding index in the same sector. Stock price quotations are used to assess investment performance of individual firms.

LG5 **Describe the forms of stock market efficiency.** Stock market efficiency takes three forms. Weak-form efficiency suggests that stock prices fully reflect historical price, volume, and other market-related information. Semistrong-form efficiency suggests that stock prices fully reflect all publicly available information, including market-related information and other information about the firm. Strong-form efficiency suggests that stock prices fully reflect all information, including information that is not publicly available. Evidence generally supports weak-form and semistrong-form efficiency. However, there are some exceptions including a size effect and a P/E effect in some periods. There is also evidence that refutes the notion of strong-form efficiency.

LG6 **Describe the valuation, performance measurement, and efficiency of foreign stocks.** Foreign stock values are commonly measured by using the price/earnings multiple, or the dividend discount model. The dividend discount model is used by the investors to derive cash flow estimates. U.S. investors who use this method are most concerned with the dividends from a U.S. perspective. Thus they must convert the dividends into dollars, on the basis of forecasted exchange rates in the future periods, and this creates an additional source of uncertainty. The price/earnings multiple is usually based on a composite of comparable foreign firms in the same country, because each country's P/E ratios can be affected by country-specific accounting rules.

ST 18–1 Cognitive Designs, Inc., a maker of electronic equipment, is a young company that has been growing rapidly. Its common stock pays no dividend. The company just reported earnings per share of $2.45 for last year. Analysts expect earnings per share for the coming year to grow at 40%. Jen Selvey is considering the purchase of this stock, which is currently priced at $75 per share. Her research indicates that the average price/earnings ratio for companies in this industry is 21.

a. On the basis of the just-reported earnings, calculate Cognitive Design's trailing price per share.

b. On the basis of an anticipated 40% growth in earnings per share, calculate the company's expected earnings per share for next year. Calculate its forward price per share.

c. Discuss which of the two price-per-share calculations is appropriate for Jen to base her investment decision on.

d. Should Jen buy this stock? Why?

 ST 18–2 David Allen wants to estimate the earnings per share for Atkinson, Inc. His analysis of the industry resulted in an estimate of 5% sales growth for next year. Because Atkinson's market niche is growing faster than those of its competitors, he estimates 8% sales growth for the company.

a. Use a percent-of-sales method and assumptions of 8% sales growth, unchanged interest expense, and a 30% tax rate to create Atkinson's pro forma income statement for next year. The most recent reported income statement follows.

Atkinson, Inc.	
Reported Income Statement	
	(000s)
Sales	$10,000
Less:	
Cost of goods sold	6,000
Gross profit	4,000
Less:	
Operating expenses	2,800
Operating earnings	1,200
Less:	
Interest expense	250
Earnings before tax	950
Less:	
Taxes at 30%	285
Net income	$ 665

b. Atkinson has 150,000 shares outstanding. Calculate the firm's current earnings per share.

c. Assuming that the number of shares remains constant in the coming year, calculate the firm's expected earnings per share.

d. Judging on the basis of David Allen's research, a price/earnings ratio of 10 is appropriate for this company. Use it to calculate both a trailing and a forward price per share for Cognitive Designs, Inc. common stock.

EXERCISES

 18–1 **Valuation with price/earnings ratios** Penstamen Corp., a maker of outdoor furniture, reported earnings of $3.60 per share for the last year and is expected to earn $4.40 per share in the coming year. The average P/E of the company's publicly traded competitors is 8.

a. Using trailing earnings, calculate a price per share for Penstamen stock.

b. Using forward earnings, calculate a price per share for Penstamen stock.

c. Which of the prices calculated in parts **a** and **b** would be more relevant to an investor considering the purchase of Penstamen shares? Why?

d. Penstamen currently is priced at $32.00 per share. Would you characterize the stock as undervalued, fairly valued, or overvalued?

18–2 **Using P/E ratios from published sources** After checking *Value Line* and several brokerage reports, Sam Greyson has come up with a consensus forward earnings estimate for Minkler Hose Corp. of $5.40 per share. Price/earnings ratios for other companies in the industry range from 12 to 15.

a. Estimate a range of possible prices for Minkler Hose on the basis of the range of P/E ratios for other companies in the industry.

b. If Minkler Hose stock is now priced at $72.00 per share, what price/earnings ratio is implied for it? Would you say that the stock is undervalued, fairly valued, or overvalued? What P/E assumption did you make to support your answer?

c. What further research would Sam need to do in order to refine his investment decision?

18–3 **Earnings estimates from published sources** Karen Brown has gathered the following estimates of next year's earnings for Bacon Computer, Inc., a maker of industrial robotics.

Brokerage report	$5.10
Value Line	4.95
IBES	5.00
First Call	4.90

Karen decided to use the P/E of a close competitor, 36, as a benchmark for estimating a price for Bacon.

a. Using the earnings estimates that Karen found for next year, put together a range of possible prices for Bacon.

b. One of the published sources that Karen used (IBES) represents a consensus of analysts' earnings estimates. Use it to come up with a price for Bacon.

c. What factors specific to Bacon might cause Karen to change the P/E that she used to make her estimate?

d. If Bacon currently is priced at $190.00 per share, would it be a good investment for Karen? Why?

  18–4 Revenue multiples and value Lorek.com is an online retailer of books and music. In business for 4 years, it has seen phenomenal growth in revenues but has yet to show positive net income. Oneida Daws is considering an investment in Lorek shares. Because she can't use earnings-based valuation models but wants to factor in the growth that the company has experienced, she decides to use the revenue multiple approach. From *Value Line,* Oneida learns that Lorek's trailing sales per share is $6.85. *Value Line's* estimate for the coming year's sales per share is $15.70. Looking at the figures for similar online retailers, Oneida learns that an appropriate revenue multiple is about 4 or 5.

a. Use Lorek's reported sales per share for the last year and the multiples that Oneida found to estimate a price range for Lorek shares.

b. Use *Value Line's* estimate of Lorek's forward sales per share and the multiples to estimate a price range for the shares.

c. Given that Lorek is smaller and younger than other companies in its industry group, how might Oneida decide what revenue multiple to use?

d. In this case, is it more appropriate to use trailing or forward sales per share? Why?

18–5 Valuation and price-to-book ratios Sy's Fries, Inc. has had a bad couple of years. Although the company once was profitable, trends in fast food have passed it by, and earnings have suffered. So has the company's stock price, currently $21.00. The one thing that the company does have going for it is 103 wholly owned restaurant locations in prime spots across 8 midwestern states. Dave Benning believes that these great properties make Sy's Fries a potential takeover candidate. Because the restaurant holdings are the basis of his interest, he decides to use a price-to-book method to value the stock.

a. Use the following data that Dave gathered to estimate a share value:

Book value per share:	$4.23
Price-to-book for competitors	11

b. What factors in the Sy's Fries situation would cause its stock to sell at a significant discount to the price calculated in part **a**?

  18–6 Initial public offering Margie Wright wanted very much to invest in the initial public offering (IPO) of Kitchen.com, an Internet provider of cooking supplies and gourmet foods. Unfortunately, her brokerage house could not get the shares for her. Still eager to purchase shares, Margie entered a buy order to purchase 100 shares at market on the day that the shares came public.

The IPO price of the shares was $50.00. By the time Margie's market order was placed, she bought them for $96.00 apiece. During the IPO day, the shares traded as high as $118.00 per share before settling back to $87.00 per share at the close. Margie kept her shares for 6 months, during which time she received no dividends, and sold them for $105.00 each.

a. Calculate Margie's holding period return on the basis of her purchase price of $96 and her selling price of $105.

  b. Calculate Margie's return if she had bought the shares at the high for the opening day's trading.

  c. Calculate her return if she had been able to buy at the IPO price of $50.

  d. Calculate the one-day return for investors who bought the shares at $50 and kept them through the close at $87.

18–7   **Using the indexes**   Jake Keller was given 100 shares of Blue Standard, Inc., a small insurance company traded on the Nasdaq. The day he received the stock, the Dow Jones Industrial Average went up 67 points, but his stock did not change in price. He is wondering whether there is something wrong with Blue Standard or whether there is a better way to track how his stock should be performing. Help him out.

  a. Explain what the DJIA is, what it measures, and why it may not be a good indicator of how Jake's stock will perform.

  b. Explain the Nasdaq Composite: what it is, what it measures, and why it may be a better indicator of how his stock will perform.

  c. Explain Nasdaq sector indexes to Jake and point out the Nasdaq Insurance Index. Use Figure 18.4 to show him how to find it in the *Wall Street Journal*.

18–8   **Individual stock price quotations**   On Friday, January 28, 2000, the following quotation for Abbot Labs common stock was published in the *Wall Street Journal*.

52week		stock	sym	div	yld %	p/e	vol 100's	hi	lo	close	net change
hi	lo										
53³⁄₁₆	29⅜	AbbotLab	ABT	.68	2.2	20	71789	31³⁄₁₆	29⅝	31¹⁄₁₆	+1¼

  a. What day's trading is represented by this quote?

  b. List in dollars and cents the highest and lowest prices at which this stock has traded in the last 52 weeks.

  c. What ticker symbol does Abbot Labs go by?

  d. How is the dividend yield of 2.2% calculated?

  e. On the basis of the P/E and the closing price, what was Abbot's most recent earnings per share?

  f. How many shares of Abbot Labs' common stock traded during the trading day reported?

  g. On the basis of the closing price and the net change, what did the stock close at on the prior trading day?

18–9   **Investing directly in the indexes**   On February 4, 2000, the Dow Jones Industrial Average closed at 10963.80 and the S&P 500 closed at 1424.37.

  a. If Dan Smith wished to invest in a single measure of large, well-established companies, what index-based security could he purchase?

  b. What would Dan have paid for the investment described in part **a** at the market close on February 4, 2000?

  c. If Dan wanted a broader representative of the market, what index based security could he purchase?

  d. What would he have paid for the security described in part **c** at the market close on February 4, 2000?

  e. Give at least two other ways in which Dan could invest in various composite indexes.

  f. How are dividends paid by these securities?

18–10   Market efficiency   Art Phillips is a self-proclaimed "technical analyst," one who bases all investment decisions solely on charts of historical stock price movements and trading volume. He can point to a few remarkably successful investments and is given to talking about the need to "fine-tune his system" when his investments are less than successful.

a. If Art's investments are consistently more successful than those of the average investor, what form of efficiency has been refuted?

b. What do studies suggest about Art's overall potential for generating abnormal risk-adjusted profits?

c. Explain what "abnormal risk-adjusted profits" are.

 18–11   Inefficiencies and effects   Howard Capito is about to graduate with a degree in electrical engineering. He already has his first job lined up at a salary he never dreamed he could be making. The College of Engineering put on an investments seminar for seniors to help them decide how to invest some of their newfound prosperity. Howard took notes during the seminar and thought he understood everything, but now he is confused, especially about market effects.

a. Howard's notes say it is better to sell stock on Friday afternoon than on Monday morning. Explain to him the effect behind that piece of advice and what studies have shown about it.

b. His notes say that it may be a good idea to purchase stocks late in December instead of waiting until January. Explain the effect behind that advice and what types of stocks may be especially vulnerable to this effect.

c. Howard has a mysterious (to him) note that says to buy low-P/E stocks. Explain what a P/E is and what studies have shown about the performance of low-P/E stocks.

  18–12   Taxes and commissions   Ingrid Rossi has a trading account with a well-known online brokerage firm. She watches the market closely in order to take advantage of opportunities to buy or sell stocks when their prices are to her advantage. Listed below is a compilation of Ingrid's trades during the last calendar year.

Item	Bought	Per share Cost	Sold	Per share Proceeds
100 sh Mack	Jan 2	$20	July 28	$18
200 sh Xero	Jan 16	10	May 2	23
150 sh Teton	Mar 10	35	May 2	41
100 sh Mills	May 2	107	Nov 21	132
50 sh Anwen	July 28	36	Dec 23	27

a. Without considering commissions or taxes, calculate Ingrid's costs and proceeds per trade and the total dollar amount of her net profits/losses for the year.

b. Assuming that each trade (each buy and each sell) costs Ingrid a $10 commission, recalculate her costs and proceeds and her net profits/losses for the year, after commissions.

c. Ingrid is taxed at a 28% marginal rate. Because short-term gains are taxed as ordinary income and short-term losses can be used to offset short-term gains, what is the after-commissions and after-tax total of her net profits/losses for the year?

web exercises

Search

Go to web site www.fool.com. Click on Quotes/Data.
1. What are the current values of the following indexes?

Index	Value	Change
DJIA		
Nasdaq		
S&P 500		
Russell 2000		

Enter **T** into the ticker symbol space and click **Go**.
2. What is the stock's current price? What is its change in dollars? What is its change in percentage?
Click on **Snapshot**.
3. Which company uses the symbol T?
4. What are the following for this stock?

52-week high	Price/sales
52-week low	Price/book
Beta	Price/cash flow
EPS	Dividend yield %
P/E	Annual dividend $

Click on **Financials**.
5. Find the following growth rates for this company's stock for 1 year, 3 years, and 5 years.
Sales%
EPS%
Dividend%
Click on **Estimates**.
6. What is the consensus estimate for this year? How much change is this from last year?
7. What is the range of estimates (high and low)?
8. What is the estimated long-term growth percentage?

For additional practice with concepts from this chapter, visit
http://www.awl.com/gitman_madura

Chapter

19

Investing in Bonds

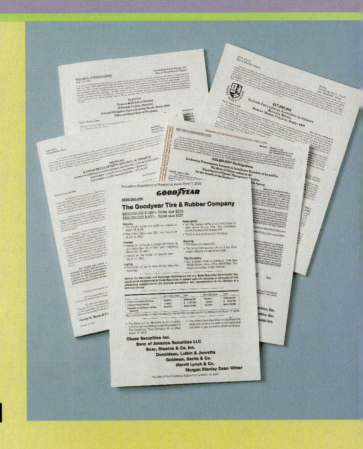

LEARNING GOALS

LG1 List the different types of bonds.

LG2 Explain how investors use bond quotations.

LG3 Describe how yields and returns are measured for bonds.

LG4 Describe the risks from investing in bonds.

LG5 Identify the factors that affect bond prices over time.

LG6 Describe the strategies commonly used for investing in bonds.

Background on Bonds

Bonds represent long-term debt securities that are issued by government agencies or corporations. The issuer of a bond is obligated to pay interest (*coupon*) payments periodically (such as annually or semiannually) and the par value (*principal*) at maturity. Most bonds have maturities of between 10 and 30 years. Bonds are classified by the ownership structure as either bearer bonds or registered bonds. **Bearer bonds** require the owner to clip coupons attached to the bonds and send them to the issuer to receive coupon interest payments. **Registered bonds** require the issuer to maintain records of who owns the bond and automatically send coupon interest payments to the owners.

Recall from Chapter 7 that a bond can be valued as the present value of its future cash flows. Thus, the value of a bond is affected by any conditions that influence the expected coupon payments. A bond's value is also affected if the return required by investors changes as a result of a change in the risk-free interest rate or in the risk premium.

Because many bonds are subject to default risk, investors commonly monitor the risk ratings that bond-rating agencies assign to bonds. As noted in Chapter 3, high ratings are assigned to bonds with low risk. If the rating agency believes that a firm's financial condition has weakened, it may reduce its rating. This normally causes investors to require a higher rate of return on this bond. The present value of the bond's future cash flows is reduced, which results in a lower bond price. An upgrade in bond ratings would have the opposite effect.

In general, bonds are not as risky as stocks because their future cash flows (coupon interest payments) are known. For this reason, bonds normally offer lower returns than the return expected on stocks of a given issuer.

Recall from Chapters 2 and 3 that bonds are distinguished by the type of issuer. Here we briefly review the different types of bonds.

Treasury Bonds

Treasury bonds are issued by the federal government and are perceived to be free from default risk. Some Treasury bonds are **stripped,** which means that the bonds have been partitioned into two separate securities. One security is the coupon interest payment, which was stripped from the Treasury bond. The other security is the principal. Thus, investors who are interested in purchasing a security that provides a fixed income without a principal payment at maturity can purchase the U.S. Treasury strips representing coupon interest payments. Conversely, investors who do not want to receive periodic income can purchase a strip that provides one lump-sum principal payment at maturity.

A special type of Treasury bond, called an **inflation-indexed Treasury bond,** is available for investors who wish to hedge against inflation. The coupon rate on inflation-indexed Treasury bonds is lower than that on traditional Treasury bonds, but the principal value changes semiannually in response to the changes in inflation (as measured by the consumer price index).

Municipal Bonds

Municipal bonds are issued by state and local government agencies. They are especially attractive because the income earned on them is exempt from federal

bearer bonds
Bonds that require the owner to clip coupons attached to the bond and send them to the issuer to receive coupon interest payments.

registered bonds
Bonds that require the issuer to maintain records of who owns the bond and send coupon interest payments to the owners automatically.

Treasury bonds
Bonds issued by the federal government, perceived to be free from default risk.

stripped bonds
Treasury bonds that have been partitioned into two separate securities, one consisting of the coupon payment and the other of the principal.

inflation-indexed Treasury bonds
Treasury bonds whose coupon rate is lower than that of traditional bonds but whose principal value changes semiannually in response to changes in the inflation rate.

municipal bonds
Bonds issued by state and local government agencies; income earned on "munis" is exempt from federal taxes.

*News*Line   **AN INTERNET FIRST**

Unlike the stock market, the bond market has been slow to use the Internet for bond sales and trading. However, more bond issuers and investment banks are expected to follow the lead of the Federal Home Loan Mortgage Association, which was a pioneer in offering its bonds to the public online.

Freddie Mac last week [January 2000] made what was billed as the first taxable bond offering on the Internet, pricing $6 billion worth of five-year debt that many customers actually bought over the Web.

The offering, led by Merrill Lynch & Co., Warburg Dillon Read, and the Salomon Smith Barney unit of Citigroup Inc., was exceptionally successful, according to officials involved. A Merrill spokesman said the Internet aspect created a buzz.... The notes were priced to yield 6.941%, or 51 basis points above comparable Treasuries....

Some said the deal signals the dawn of bond and debt security trading on the Internet. One official involved said Internet-based systems "will almost be the price of admission" by the second half of the year. As more such transactions move to the Internet, firms that fail to make the transition could face a tremendous disadvantage, the official said.

But this time around only some of the sales actually involved the Internet. Salomon and Merrill Lynch accepted orders only through traditional channels. Only Warburg

Dillon Read accepted orders over the Web, through a new Internet sales entity, DebtWeb.... Warburg's online ordering process was like buying or selling an item on eBay, the online trading and auction Web site, the spokesman said. Customers submitted orders through DebtWeb during a two-week period; once the price was set, Warburg allocated the securities to customers and notified them how much of each order it could fill. The firm...expects DebtWeb to become part of every deal.

Though Merrill did not accept Internet orders, as a test it input the orders received into a Web-based system it has been developing for years, the Merrill spokesman said. The test was "very successful," he said. "In the future, most if not all [Merrill] deals will use this system."

Thomas O'Donnell, an analyst at Salomon Smith Barney, credited Freddie Mac with an "innovative approach" in using the Internet to reduce costs....

Source: Robert Julavits, "An Internet First, $6B Freddie Sale with Web Connection," American Banker, *January 11, 2000, downloaded from www.americanbanker.com.*

income taxes. For municipal bonds, there are different risk classes that reflect the default risk of the issuer. Municipal bonds with a lower quality rating have a higher expected return.

Federal Agency Bonds

federal agency bonds
Bonds issued by federal agencies but not guaranteed by the U.S. Treasury.

Federal agency bonds are issued by federal agencies. The Government National Mortgage Association (called Ginnie Mae) issues bonds and uses the proceeds to purchase mortgages that are insured by the Federal Housing Administration (FHA) and by the Veteran's Administration (VA). Ginnie Mae bonds are secured by the mortgages that are purchased with the proceeds and are also backed by the federal government.

The Federal Home Loan Mortgage Association (called Freddie Mac) issues bonds and uses the proceeds to purchase conventional mortgages. Freddie Mac bonds are not backed by the federal government, but they have a very low default risk.

The Federal National Mortgage Association (called Fannie Mae) is federally chartered but is actually a corporation owned by individual investors. It issues bonds and uses the proceeds to purchase residential mortgages. Fannie Mae bonds are not backed by the federal government, but they have a very low degree of default risk because the agency's investments have relatively low risk.

Corporate Bonds

corporate bonds
Long-term debt securities issued by large firms.

Corporate bonds are issued by large firms. Because a corporate bond may be classified in one of several risk categories, investors have a wide selection of corporate bonds from which they can choose to match their return and risk preferences. At one extreme, the most creditworthy corporations can issue bonds at an annualized yield that is slightly higher than a Treasury bond with a similar maturity.

junk bonds
Corporate bonds that are below investment grade and are perceived to have a high degree of default risk but that pay higher returns than better-quality corporate debt.

Investors who are willing to tolerate more risk have the opportunity to purchase bonds with a much higher expected return. In particular, they may consider **junk bonds,** which are corporate bonds that are below investment grade and are perceived to exhibit a high degree of default risk. Junk bonds received much attention in the mid-1980s, because they offered investors a relatively high rate of return and had limited defaults. Many risky firms capitalized on the popularity of junk bonds by issuing them to investors to finance their acquisitions of other companies or repurchases of their own stock. The default risk premium on junk bonds was only a few percentage points above that of high-quality bonds, which enabled risky firms to use large amounts of debt to fund their operations. In fact, junk bonds were very popular with individual investors who were trying to earn a high return on bonds. Some institutional investors, such as savings institutions and bond mutual funds, were also major investors in junk bonds.

In the late 1980s and early 1990s, U.S. economic growth slowed. Several firms that had issued junk bonds failed, and the popularity of junk bonds subsided. Investors began to realize that the low default rate on junk bonds in the mid-1980s was partially attributable to the strong economy and that the default rate would be higher once economic conditions deteriorated. During the late 1980s, many savings institutions failed, partly because of their excessive holdings of junk bonds. The surviving savings institutions were then forced by regulators to phase out their holdings of junk bonds. This caused a major decline in the aggregate demand for junk bonds, because it eliminated some of the key investors. Consequently, the risk premium required on junk bonds rose, and many firms reduced their funding with junk bonds because there was not as much demand for them.

In the middle and late 1990s, junk bonds became popular again. They continue to offer a way for relatively risky firms to obtain debt financing to support their growth. They also provide a means in which individual and institutional investors can invest funds in a fixed-income instrument and earn a potentially high return. However, investors are now more aware of the potential risk of junk bonds than they were in the 1980s.

International Bonds

international bonds
Bonds issued by international governments or corporations to obtain long-term funding.

International bonds are bonds issued by international governments or corporations to obtain long-term funding. U.S. investors may consider purchasing these bonds when the expected return is higher than that available on U.S. bonds. U.S. institutional investors such as commercial banks, insurance companies, pension funds, and bond mutual funds often invest in international bonds. International bonds are commonly denominated in a foreign currency. Thus the coupon or principal payments received by a U.S. investor must be converted into dollars.

There are three motives for U.S. investors to consider investing in international bonds rather than domestic bonds. First, the annualized yields on some international bonds are higher than those on U.S. bonds. Second, if the interest rate of the currency in which the bond is denominated decreases, investors holding the bond will be able to sell it for a higher price. Third, if the currency in which the bond is denominated appreciates against the investor's home currency, this change will provide higher coupon or principal payments to the investor.

Risk from Investing in International Bonds

International bonds, like all bonds, are exposed to risk. Like U.S. corporate bonds, international bonds issued by corporations are subject to default risk. Thus, investors must assess economic conditions in foreign countries so that they can anticipate how the bond issuer's financial condition may be affected. Also like domestic bonds, international bonds are subject to price risk, because the bond prices decline if interest rates in the currency in which the bond denominated increase over the holding period. For this reason, investors in international bonds attempt to assess any economic conditions of the foreign country (such as inflation) that would affect the interest rates in that country.

In addition, international bonds are also subject to exchange rate risk, because the depreciation of a currency against the investor's local currency will reduce the return to the investor. For this reason, investors attempt to monitor any international economic factors (such as international trade or capital flows) that could affect exchange rates of the currencies in which bonds that they may purchase are denominated.

? Review Question

19–1   Why would some investors consider investing in junk bonds? In international bonds?

LG2   Bond Quotations

Bond quotations are used by investors to monitor the prices of the bonds over time. In this way, investors can measure their return as of that point in time. Quotations are available for some individual bonds, as well as for groups of bonds that fall in a specific category.

Quotations for Individual Bonds

Investors who invest in individual bonds can monitor the price of those bonds by reviewing bond price quotations.

Treasury Bond Quotations

An example of the Treasury bond quotations provided in the *Wall Street Journal* is shown in Figure 19.1. Those Treasury bonds that are closer to maturity are

FIGURE 19.1 **Treasury Bond Quotations**

Recent quotations on Treasury bonds, reported by the *Wall Street Journal.*

Source: Wall Street Journal, January 20, 2000, p. C24.

TREASURY BONDS, NOTES & BILLS

Wednesday, January 19, 2000

Representative Over-the Counter quotations based on transactions of 1$ million or more.

Treasury bond, note and bill quotes are as of mid-afternoon. Colons in bid-and-asked quotes represent 32nds; 101:01 means 101 1/32. Net changes in 32nds. n-Treasury notes. Treasury bill quotes in hundredths, quoted on terms of a rate of discount. Days to maturity calculated from settlement date. All yields are to maturity and based on the asked quote. Latest 13-week and 26-week bills are boldfaced. For bonds callable prior to maturity, yields are computed to the earliest call date for issues quoted above par and to the maturity date for issues below par. ‘-When issued.

Source: Telerate/Cantor Fitzgerald

U.S. Treasury strips as of 3 p.m. Eastern time, also based on transactions of $1 million or more. Colons in bid-and-asked quotes represent 32nds; 99:01 means 99 1/32. Net changes in 32nds. Yields calculated on the asked quotation. ci-stripped coupon interest. bp-Treasury bond, stripped principal. np-Treasury note, stripped principal. For bonds callable prior to maturity, yields are computed to the earliest call date for issues quoted above par and to the maturity date for issues below par.

Source: Bear, Stearns & Co. via Street Software Technology Inc.

GOVT. BONDS & NOTES

Rate	Maturity Mo/Yr	Bid	Asked	Chg.	Ask Yld.
5⅜	Jan 00n	99:30	100:00	....	5.24
7¾	Jan 00n	100:01	100:03	....	4.45
5⅞	Feb 00n	99:31	100:01	....	5.30
8½	Feb 00n	100:05	100:07	−1	5.20
5½	Feb 00n	99:30	100:00	−1	5.38
7⅛	Feb 00n	100:04	100:06	−1	5.26
5½	Mar 00n	99:30	100:00	−1	5.41
6⅞	Mar 00n	100:06	100:08	−11	5.46
5½	Apr 00n	99:29	99:31	−1	5.55
5⅝	Apr 00n	99:29	99:31	−1	5.67
6¾	Apr 00n	100:07	100:09	−1	5.64
6⅜	May 00n	100:04	100:06	−2	5.71
8⅞	May 00n	101:00	101:02	−1	5.40
5½	May 00n	99:27	99:29	−1	5.72
6¼	May 00n	100:03	100:05	−1	5.76
5⅜	Jun 00n	99:24	99:26	−1	5.79
5⅞	Jun 00n	99:31	100:01	−1	5.78
5⅜	Jul 00n	99:21	99:23	−1	5.92
6⅛	Jul 00n	100:01	100:03	−2	5.94
6	Aug 00n	99:31	100:01	−1	5.93
8¾	Aug 00n	101:17	101:19	−1	5.87
5⅛	Aug 00n	99:13	99:15	−1	6.01
6¼	Aug 00n	100:02	100:04	−1	6.02
4½	Sep 00n	98:27	98:29	−1	6.12
6⅛	Sep 00n	99:30	100:00	−1	6.11
4	Oct 00n	98:11	98:13	....	6.12
5¾	Oct 00n	99:21	99:23	....	6.11

GOVT. BONDS & NOTES

Rate	Maturity Mo/Yr	Bid	Asked	Chg.	Ask Yld.
5¾	Nov 00n	99:20	99:22	....	6.13
8½	Nov 00n	101:26	101:28	−1	6.10
4⅝	Nov 00n	98:21	98:23	....	6.17
5⅝	Nov 00n	99:16	99:18	....	6.14
4⅝	Dec 00n	98:17	98:19	+ 1	6.18
5½	Dec 00n	99:10	99:12	+ 1	6.19
4½	Jan 01n	98:08	98:10	+ 1	6.21
5¼	Jan 01n	99:10	99:03	+ 1	6.17
5⅜	Nov 00n	99:20	99:22	....	6.13
8½	Nov 00n	101:26	101:28	−1	6.10
4⅝	Nov 00n	98:21	98:23	....	6.17
5⅝	Nov 00n	99:16	99:18	....	6.14
4⅝	Dec 00n	98:17	98:19	+ 1	6.18
5½	Dec 00n	99:10	99:12	+ 1	6.19
4½	Jan 01n	98:08	98:10	+ 1	6.21
5¼	Jan 01n	99:01	99:03	+ 1	6.17
5⅜	Feb 01n	99:02	99:04	+ 1	6.23
7¾	Feb 01n	101:16	101:18	+ 1	6.22
11¾	Feb 01	105:19	105:21	....	6.21
5	Feb 01n	98:20	98:22	+ 1	6.24
5⅝	Feb 01n	99:09	99:11	....	6.24
4⅞	Mar 01n	98:11	98:13	+ 1	6.27
6⅜	Mar 01n	100:01	100:03	+ 1	6.28
5	Apr 01n	98:12	98:14	+ 1	6.28
6¼	Apr 01n	99:28	99:30	....	6.29
5⅝	May 01n	99:02	99:04	+ 1	6.32
8	May01n	102:01	102:03	+ 1	6.31
13⅛	May 01	108:13	108:15	+ 1	6.31

listed first, followed by those with longer terms to maturity. The first column lists the coupon interest rate of the bond, and the second column discloses the *maturity date.* The *bid price* (the highest price at which a bond dealer will pay for a bond) is in the third column, and the *asked price* (the lowest price at which a dealer is willing to sell a bond) is listed in the fourth column. The bid and asked prices are quoted with fractions in thirty-seconds. For example, a bid price of 100:16 has a fraction 16/32, or .50. Thus a bid price of 100:16 means that the dealer is willing to pay an investor $100.50 for every $100 of par value.

The change in the bond price (in thirty-seconds) is shown in the fifth column, and the bond's *yield to maturity* (based on the asked price) is shown in the sixth column. This table can be used to plot the term structure of interest rates, because it shows the yield to maturity for bonds with various maturity dates.

FIGURE 19.2 **Municipal Bond Price Quotations**

Prices on tax-exempt bonds, reported by the *Wall Street Journal.*

Source: Wall Street Journal, January 20, 2000, p. B18.

TAX-EXEMPT BONDS

Representative prices for several active tax-exempt revenue and refunding bonds, based on institutional trades. Changes rounded to the nearest one-eighth. Yield is to maturity. n-New. Source: The Bond Buyer.

ISSUE	COUPON	MAT	PRICE	CHG	BID YLD
Atl Ga Wtr&Wstwtr 99A	5.000	11-01-38	79¾	– ¼	6.43
CA State genl oblig	5.750	12-01-29	95¼	– ⅛	6.09
CA State genl oblig	5.750	12-01-24	96	....	6.06
CAHlthFinAuth	6.125	12-01-30	94⅜	+ ⅛	6.55
ClarkCoNV arpt	6.000	07-01-29	97⅛	....	6.21
Del River Prt Auth	5.750	01-01-26	95¾	+ ¼	6.07
Del River Prt Auth	5.750	01-01-22	96	....	6.07
Det MI sewage disp	6.000	07-01-29	97	– ¼	6.22
EmpireStdevCpNY	6.000	01-01-29	97⅜	+ ⅛	6.19
Farmington NM	5.125	04-01-29	84	+ ⅛	6.32
FL Pts Fin Comm99	5.500	10-01-29	90	+ ⅛	6.24
FLStBdEd	5.750	06-01-29	95⅝	....	6.07
HarrisCoHlthFacTex	5.375	07-01-29	85⅞	– ⅛	6.44
IL Hth FacAuth99	6.250	11-15-29	93	....	6.79
Lousvill&Jeffers Metro	5.750	05-15-33	94⅛	– ⅛	6.17
MA Wtr Poll Tr	5.750	08-01-29	94	– ⅛	6.19
Maa Tpk Auth	5.000	01-01-39	79½	– ⅜	6.44
MDHlth HigherEd	6.000	07-01-39	96⅝	....	6.23
Mesa IndDev AZ	5.625	01-01-29	91⅞	....	6.23
MI StHosp	6.125	11-15-26	94⅝	....	6.55

ISSUE	COUPON	MAT	PRICE	CHG	BID YLD
Miami-Dade Co Educ	5.750	04-01-29	95½	....	6.08
Miss Dev Bk Ser99A	5.000	07-01-24	83½	....	6.32
Mmphs-Shlby Airpt	6.000	03-01-24	97⅛	+ ⅛	6.23
MontyBMC Spc Care	5.000	11-15-29	80¾	....	6.45
NJ Hlth Fac Fin Auth	4.750	07-01-28	78½	....	6.39
NYC Genl Obl Bds	5.000	03-15-29	80½	....	6.49
NYC TSASC tobacco	6.250	07-15-34	94¾	– ⅛	6.64
NYC TSASC tobacco	6.375	07-15-39	95¾	+ ¼	6.68
NYS Dorm Auth	6.000	05-15-39		+ ⅛	6.36
NYS Dorm Auth	5.950	05-15-29	97	....	6.17
Ohio Air Qty Dev	5.150	05-01-26	85⅛	– ⅛	6.31
OK Indus Auth hlth	5.750	08-15-29	92	....	6.35
Phila Sch Dist PA	5.750	03-01-29	94⅜	....	6.17
San Diego Pub Fac Ca	5.000	05-15-29	83¼	....	6.25
Tampa FL Water	5.750	10-01-29	95½	....	6.07
Univ IL Bd Trustees	6.000	04-01-30	97	– ⅛	6.22
VirginIsl PubFinAuth	6.125	10-01-29	96	+ ⅛	6.42
Wash Co Auth PA	6.150	12-01-29	98⅝	+ ⅛	6.25
Washoe NV ltd cnv	6.400	07-01-29	99	....	6.48
Wichita KS hosp	6.250	11-15-24	94⅞	....	6.67

Municipal Bond Quotations

Prices of some municipal bonds are quoted in financial newspapers. For example, Figure 19.2 shows a listing of municipal bond quotations from the *Wall Street Journal.* The coupon rate, maturity, market price, change in the market price from the previous day, and yield to maturity are disclosed.

Federal Agency Bond Quotations

Quotations of bonds issued by federal agencies are provided in financial newspapers. An example of quotations provided on bonds issued by a variety of federal agencies are shown in Figure 19.3. The coupon rate is shown in the first column, the maturity date in the second column. The bid and asked prices are provided in the next two columns, followed by the yield to maturity. The yields that are shown here correspond closely with the yields on Treasury bonds with similar terms to maturity.

Corporate Bond Quotations

Figure 19.4 includes an excerpt from the New York Stock Exchange (NYSE) bond quotations reported in the January 21, 2000, *Wall Street Journal* for transactions through the close of trading on January 20, 2000. Review the highlighted corporate bond quotation for one of IBM's bonds. The numbers following the company name represent the bond's *coupon interest rate* that is applied to the

FIGURE 19.3 Government Agency Bond Quotations

Prices on government agency and similar issues, reported by the *Wall Street Journal*.

Source: *Wall Street Journal*, January 20, 2000, p. C26.

GOVERNMENT AGENCY & SIMILAR ISSUES

Wednesday, January 19, 2000

Over-the-Counter mid-afternoon quotations based on large transactions, usually $1 million or more. Colons in bid-and-asked quotes represent 32nds; 101:01 means 101 1/32.

All yields are calculated to maturity, and based on the asked quote. *-Callable issue, maturity date shown. For issues callable prior to maturity, yields are computed to the earliest call date for issues quoted above par, or 100, and to the maturity date for issues below par.

Source: Bear, Stearns & Co. via Street Software Technology Inc.

Fannie Mae Issues

Rate	Mat.	Bid	Asked	Yld.
5.63	3-01	98:31	99:01	6.51
4.63	10-01	96:22	96:24	6.64
6.63	1-02	99:26	99:28	6.69
5.38	3-02	97:08	97:10	6.73
6.25	11-02	98:17	98:20	6.79
5.25	1-03	95:24	95:27	6.82
5.75	4-03	96:20	96:23	6.90
4.75	11-03	92:18	92:21	6.98
5.13	2-04	93:10	93:13	7.02
5.88	4-04*	95:09	95:12	7.15
5.63	5-04	94:24	94:27	7.03
6.50	8-04	97:26	97:29	7.04
7.10	10-04*	98:14	98:17	7.47
5.75	6-05	94:04	94:07	7.05
5.75	2-08	90:26	90:30	7.25
6.00	5-08	92:03	92:07	7.26
5.25	1-09	86:19	86:23	7.29
6.50	4-09*	92:18	92:22	7.61
6.40	5-09*	92:08	92:12	7.55
6.38	6-09	93:22	93:26	7.29
6.63	9-09	95:09	95:13	7.30
7.25	1-10	99:18	99:22	7.29
6.25	5-29	86:11	86:15	7.38

Freddie Mac

Rate	Mat.	Bid	Asked	Yld.
4.98	4-00	99:20	99:22	6.09
5.00	2-01	98:17	98:19	6.38
5.38	3-01*	99:14	99:16	5.84
5.75	6-01	98:28	98:30	6.56
4.75	12-01	96:18	96:20	6.66
5.50	5-02	97:08	97:10	6.77
5.75	7-03	96:10	96:13	6.93
5.58	12-03*	99:22	99:25	5.64
5.00	1-04	93:00	93:03	7.01
6.00	6-04*	94:28	94:31	7.35
6.25	7-04	96:30	97:01	7.04
7.09	11-06*	93:12	93:15	8.36

Rate	Mat.	Bid	Asked	Yld.
6.70	1-07	96:14	96:17	7.34
7.10	4-07	98:22	98:25	7.32
6.22	3-08*	99:26	99:30	6.23
5.75	4-08	90:18	90:22	7.27
5.13	10-08	86:02	86:06	7.29
5.75	3-09	89:20	89:24	7.30
0.00	11-14	32:23	32:27	7.64
0.00	11-19	24:14	24:18	7.20
0.00	12-25	16:10	16:14	7.10

Farm Credit Fin. Asst. Corp.

Rate	Mat.	Bid	Asked	Yld.
9.38	7-03	107:04	107:07	7.01
8.80	6-05	107:02	107:05	7.17
9.20	9-05*	101:24	101:27	6.35

Federal Farm Credit Bank

Rate	Mat.	Bid	Asked	Yld.
6.28	6-01	99:15	99:17	6.63
6.10	9-01	103:10	103:12	4.00
5.70	6-03	95:20	95:23	7.14
6.75	6-07	97:06	97:09	7.23
5.75	12-28	80:24	80:28	7.36

Federal Home Loan Bank

Rate	Mat.	Bid	Asked	Yld.
5.53	2-00	99:30	100:00	5.39
4.49	11-00	98:02	98:04	6.97
4.98	11-00	98:22	98:24	6.54
5.62	1-01	99:06	99:08	6.44
5.20	9-01	99:30	100:00	5.20
4.86	10-01	96:26	96:28	6.82
4.63	10-01	96:08	96:10	6.95
4.66	10-01	96:15	96:17	6.81
4.95	11-01	100:00	100:02	4.91
6.18	12-01	98:22	98:24	6.89
4.99	12-01	96:18	96:20	6.88
5.01	2-02	96:22	96:24	6.73
4.64	10-02	94:02	94:04	7.04

Rate	Mat.	Bid	Asked	Yld.
4.68	10-02	94:04	94:06	7.05
6.18	10-02	97:14	97:16	7.19
5.66	1-03	96:06	96:09	7.07
5.37	1-03	95:09	95:12	7.12
5.42	1-03	96:02	96:05	6.85
6.03	5-03*	96:12	96:15	7.24
5.76	6-03	96:00	96:03	7.06
5.57	9-03	94:22	94:25	7.24
5.63	9-03	95:11	95:14	7.08
5.13	9-03	94:00	94:03	6.98
4.78	10-03	91:26	91:29	7.29
5.06	10-03*	99:27	99:30	5.08
5.28	12-03`	93:10	93:13	7.25
9.50	2-04	109:22	109:25	6.72
7.00	7-07*	94:22	94:25	7.93
7.00	8-07*	95:11	95:14	7.81
5.80	9-08	90:18	90:22	7.27

Financing Corporation

Rate	Mat.	Bid	Asked	Yld.
10.70	10-17	128:00	128:04	7.75
9.80	11-17	126:10	126:14	7.15
9.40	2-18	115:28	116:00	7.74
9.80	4-18	123:12	123:16	7.42
10.00	5-18	124:31	125:03	7.46
10.35	8-18	128:08	128:12	7.49
9.65	11-18	122:04	122:08	7.43
9.90	12-18	124:07	124:11	7.47
9.60	12-18	121:08	121:12	7.47
9.65	3-19	121:30	122:02	7.46
9.70	4-19	122:08	122:12	7.48
9.00	6-19	114:19	114:23	7.54
8.60	9-19	110:26	110:30	7.52

GNMA Mtge. Issues

Rate	Mat.	Bid	Asked	Yld.
5.50	30Yr	86:02	86:04	7.67
6.00	30Yr	89:13	89:15	7.66
6.50	30Yr	92:14	92:16	7.76
7.00	30Yr	95:13	95:15	7.83
7.50	30Yr	97:30	98:00	7.94
8.00	30Yr	100:11	100:13	8.00
8.50	30Yr	102:16	102:18	7.97
9.00	30Yr	104:06	104:08	7.89
9.50	30Yr	105:20	105:22	7.98

Inter-Amer. Devel. Bank

Rate	Mat.	Bid	Asked	Yld.
6.13	3-06	94:27	94:30	7.16
6.63	3-07	96:20	96:23	7.22

Rate	Mat.	Bid	Asked	Yld.
12.25	12-08	129:13	129:17	7.62
8.88	6-09	108:12	108:16	7.59
8.40	9-09	105:24	105:28	7.53
8.50	3-11	105:29	106:01	7.68
7.13	3-23*	88:26	88:30	8.20
7.00	6-25	96:13	96:17	7.30
6.80	10-25	94:06	94:10	7.29

Resolution Funding Corp.

Rate	Mat.	Bid	Asked	Yld.
8.13	10-19	109:03	109:07	7.24
8.88	7-20	117:15	117:19	7.22
9.38	10-20	119:10	119:14	7.51
8.63	1-21	114:27	114:31	7.23
8.63	1-30	110:19	110:23	7.70
8.88	4-30	123:14	123:18	6.99

Student Loan Marketing

Rate	Mat.	Bid	Asked	Yld.
4.84	2-00	99:30	100:00	4.74
7.50	3-00	100:04	100:06	5.77
6.05	9-00	99:22	99:24	6.41
7.00	12-02	99:16	99:19	7.16
7.30	8-12	96:26	96:30	7.69
0.00	10-22	17:25	17:29	7.72

Tennessee Valley Authority

Rate	Mat.	Bid	Asked	Yld.
6.00	11-00	99:04	99:06	7.10
6.50	8-01	99:13	99:15	6.86
6.38	6-05	96:09	96:12	7.20
3.38	1-07	93:00	93:03	4.54
6.75	11-25	93:02	93:06	7.34
8.25	4-42`	104:30	105:02	7.84
7.25	7-43`	93:15	93:19	7.77
6.88	12-43`	90:05	90:09	7.65

World Bank Bonds

Rate	Mat.	Bid	Asked	Yld.
8.13	3-01	101:15	101:17	6.66
6.38	5-01	99:12	99:14	6.81
6.75	1-02	99:06	99:08	7.17
12.38	10-02	111:20	111:22	7.55
5.25	9-03	94:22	94:25	6.88
6.38	7-05	96:20	96:23	7.11
6.63	8-06	97:07	97:10	7.14
8.25	9-16	109:22	109:26	7.23
8.63	10-16	113:06	113:10	7.24
9.25	7-17	115:10	115:14	7.64
7.63	1-23	102:26	102:30	7.36
8.88	3-26	114:03	114:07	7.61

par value to determine the annual coupon payments. For this IBM bond, it is 7 1/2%. The maturity date follows, and in this case it is the year 2013. This information allows investors to differentiate between the various bonds issued by the corporation. (On the day of this quote IBM had five bonds listed.) The next column gives the bond's *current yield*, which is found by dividing its annual coupon (7.5%) by its closing price (99). In this case the current yield rounds to 7.6 percent. The "Net Chg" in the last column indicates the change in the price of bonds since the previous day.

FIGURE 19.4

Corporate Bond Quotations

Selected Bond Quotations, reported by the *Wall Street Journal.*

Source: Wall Street Journal, January 21, 2000, p. C6.

Bonds	Cur Yld.	Vol.	Close		Net Chg.
Hollgnr 9¼07	9.6	90	96¼	−	½
Hollgnr 9¼06	9.5	9	97¼	+	⅛
Honywll zr01	...	35	89⅛	+	¾
Honywll zr09	...	15	45½	−	1/14
Huntply 11¾04	11.9	5	98½	+	1/12
IBM 6⅜00	6.4	32	99 9/16	−	¼
IBM 7¼02	7.2	24	100⅜	+	¼
IBM 7½13	7.6	160	99	+	¼
IBM 8⅜19	7.9	21	106½	+	¼
IBM 6½28	7.5	55	86¾	+	1
KCS En 8⅞08f	...	69	35¼	+	3⅛
KaufB 9⅜03	9.5	16	99		...
KaufB 7¾04	8.1	35	95¼	+	¾
KaufB 9⅝06	9.4	6	102⅞	+	1⅝
KentE 4½04	cv	25	81½	−	1
KerrM 7½14	cv	9	95	−	½
LibPrp 8s01	cv	40	120½	+	1¼
Loews 3⅛07	cv	12	82⅛	+	⅛
LglsLt 8.2s23	8.4	1	98		...
LouN 2⅞03	3.3	86	87	−	3
Lucent 6.9s01	6.9	115	100½	+	½
MBNA 8.28s26	9.4	10	88¼	+	½
MSC Sf 7⅞04	cv	75	87	−	1⅞
Mascotch 03	cv	100	75	−	½
McDnl 8 11	8.1	20	110	−	1
Medtrst 7½01	cv	80	90	+	3⅛
Mpac 4¼05	5.2	3	82	−	1⅛
Moran 8¾08f	cv	51	94	−	1

The final two columns include price information: the closing price and the net change in closing price from the prior day. *All bonds are quoted as a percentage of par.* This means that a $1,000-par-value bond quoted at 92 5/8 is priced at $926.25 (92.625% × $1,000). Corporate bonds trade in fractions of 1/8, which for $1,000-par-value bonds represents 1.25 *dollars.* Note that fractions are reduced to their lowest common denominator—2/8, 4/8, and 6/8 are expressed as 1/4, 1/2, and 3/4, respectively. Thus IBM's closing price of 99 for the day was $990 (99% × $1,000). Because a net change of +1/4 is given in the final column, the bond must have closed at 98 3/4, or $987.50 (98.75% × 1,000), on the prior day. Its price increased by 1/4, or $2.50 (1/4% × $1,000), on January 20, 2000. Additional information may be included in a bond quotation, but these are the basic elements.

Bond Index Quotations

There are various bond indexes that can be used as benchmarks for comparison purposes. The wide variety of bond indexes allows investors to assess the performance of a specific type of bond that they own, within a specific risk class, and within a specific maturity range. Some of the more well-known bond indexes are described here.

Corporate Bond Indexes

The securities firms First Boston, Lehman Brothers, Merrill Lynch, and Salomon Brothers have created bond indexes to reflect prices of corporate bonds. There is a corporate bond index for each rating (risk classification). There are indexes for the high-yield (junk-bond) category. There are even bond indexes that separate

FIGURE 19.5

Data on the bond market, reported by the *Wall Street Journal*.

Source: *Wall Street Journal*, January 21, 2000, p. B10.

BOND MARKET DATA BANK   3/6/00

BOND YIELDS

MATURITY	COUPON	PRICE	YIELD	Aaa YIELD	TAX EQUIV.	MUNI/TREAS YIELD RATIO	52-WEEK RATIO HIGH	LOW
12/31/01	6.125	99.12	6.470	4.48	6.49	69.2	73.7	63.4
05/15/02	6.500	97.00	6.594	4.55	6.59	69.0	75.4	64.4
11/15/04	5.875	96.26	6.657	4.83	7.00	72.6	81.6	68.5
08/15/09	6.000	94.19	6.776	5.23	7.58	77.2	88.2	76.5
8/15/29	6.125	92.08	6.732	6.10	8.84	90.6	98.3	87.2

The first four columns are under ───TREASURY ISSUES*───; the next two (Aaa YIELD, TAX EQUIV.) and the following under ───MUNICIPAL ISSUES †(Comparable Maturities)───

'Most recent auctions.   †From Delphis Hanover. Tax equiv. Based on 31% bracket.

MAJOR INDEXES

HIGH	LOW	(12 MOS)	CLOSE	NET	CHG	% CHG	12-MO CHG	% CHG	FROM 12/31	% CHG
U.S. TREASURY SECURITIES (Lehman Brothers indexes)										
5680.14	5529.99	Intermediate	5669.73	−	5.00	− 0.09	+ 107.74	+ 1.94	+ 30.59	+ 0.54
8503.22	7817.09	Long-term	8288.64	+	12.50	+ 0.15	− 4.76	− 0.06	+ 367.14	+ 4.64
1659.12	1446.80	Long-term(price)	1519.26	−	3.16	− 0.21	− 107.92	− 6.63	+ 49.02	+ 3.33
6251.84	6042.87	Composite	6232.44	−	6.79	− 0.11	+ 81.86	+ 1.33	+ 112.62	+ 1.84
U.S. CORPORATE DEBT ISSUES (Merrill Lynch)										
1023.88	976.88	Corporate Master	1001.90	−	1.36	− 0.14	− 1.56	− 0.16	+ 3.93	+ 0.39
733.62	710.98	1-10 Yr Maturities	729.23	−	0.67	− 0.09	+ 9.80	+ 1.36	+ 2.27	+ 0.31
816.60	754.03	10+ Yr Maturities	773.14	−	1.79	− 0.23	− 24.18	− 3.03	+ 4.39	+ 0.57
514.50	498.85	High Yield	506.37	+	0.44	+ 0.09	+ 6.52	+ 1.30	− 1.74	− 0.34
737.36	707.08	Yankee Bonds	730.33	−	0.69	− 0.09	+ 8.57	+ 1.19	+ 4.52	+ 0.62
TAX-EXEMPT SECURITIES (Bond Buyer Muni Index, from Dec. 22, 1999)										
106-24	91-04	Bond Buyer 6% Muni	93-01	−	0-01	− 0.03	− 12-19	− 11.92	+ 0.25	+ 0.85
146.78	141.73	7-12 yr G.O.	144.72	+	0.04	+ 0.03	− 0.83	− 0.57	+ 0.78	+ 0.54
153.73	143.11	12-22 yr G.O.	148.43	+	0.06	+ 0.04	− 3.78	− 2.48	+ 2.93	+ 2.01
147.89	132.49	22+yr Revenue	137.18	+	0.07	+ 0.05	− 9.29	− 6.34	+ 2.82	+ 2.10
MORTGAGE-BACKED SECURITIES (current coupon; Merrill Lynch: Dec. 31, 1986 = 100)										
318.99	302.87	Ginnie Mae(GNMA)	318.33	−	0.66	− 0.21	+ 6.86	+ 2.20	+ 2.36	+ 0.75
314.29	299.59	Fannie Mae(FNMA)	312.78	−	0.40	− 0.13	+ 5.42	+ 1.76	+ 1.00	+ 0.32
191.88	181.90	Freddie Mac(FHLMC)	191.61	−	0.27	− 0.14	+ 4.75	+ 2.54	+ 2.08	+ 1.10
BROAD MARKET (Merrill Lynch)										
832,75	804.30	Domestic Master	829.78	−	1.30	− 00.16	+ 10.15	+ 1.24	+ 8.42	+ 1.03
930.00	896.97	Corporate/Government	921.90	−	1.38	− 0.15	+ 7.93	+ 0.87	+ 11.16	+ 1.23

bonds for a given rating into long-term versus intermediate-term maturities. The Bond Market Data Bank published every day in the *Wall Street Journal* provides information on various types of bonds. For example, it provides corporate bond index levels for bonds with less than 10 years to maturity, more than ten years to maturity, and junk (high-yield) bonds, as shown in Figure 19.5.

Treasury Bond Indexes

Lehman Brothers, Merrill Lynch, and Salomon Brothers have created bond indexes to reflect prices of long-term Treasury bonds. These Treasury bond indexes are useful for investors who wish to track the general price movements of

FIGURE 19.6

International Bond Index Quotations

Rates of return on international bonds, reported by the *Wall Street Journal.*

Source: Wall Street Journal, January 21, 2000, p. B10.

Total Rates of Return of International Bonds

In percent, based on J.P. Morgan Government Bond Index, Dec. 31, 1987 = 100

	LOCAL CURRENCY ITEMS					U.S. DOLLAR TERMS				
	INDEX VALUE	1 DAY	1 MO	3 MOS	SINCE 12/31	INDEX VALUE	1 DAY	1 MO	3 MOS	SINCE 12/31
Japan	199.98	− 0.12	0.00	+ 0.56	− 0.41	229.55	+ 0.16	− 2.55	+ 0.99	− 3.33
Britain	332.35	− 0.28	− 2.44	+ 1.03	− 1.63	290.46	+ 0.20	+ 0.20	− 0.11	+ 0.60
Germany	220.07	− 0.03	− 0.88	+ 0.73	− 0.73	178.21	− 0.06	− 0.77	− 5.63	− 0.01
France	291.64	− 0.04	− 1.15	+ 0.72	− 0.88	238.67	− 0.08	− 1.04	− 5.64	− 0.16
Canada	303.62	− 0.14	− 1.08	+ 0.25	− 1.08	272.87	+ 0.20	+ 1.28	+ 3.18	− 0.73
Netherlands	233.21	− 0.03	− 0.91	+ 0.88	− 0.79	188.55	− 0.06	− 0.80	− 5.50	− 0.07
Euro	268.12	+ 0.01	+ 0.35	+ 1.04	+ 0.21	227.67	− 0.02	+ 0.46	− 5.35	+ 0.93
Global-a	260.59	− 0.08	− 0.70	+ 0.60	− 0.66	235.85	+ 0.01	− 0.94	− 1.80	− 0.87
EMBI + -b	173.02	− 0.03	+ 0.70	+ 10.81	− 0.90	173.02	− 0.03	+ 0.70	+ 10.81	− 0.90

a-18 int'l gov. markets   b-external-currency emerging mkt. debt, Dec. 31, 1993 = 100.

Treasury bonds over time. The *Wall Street Journal* discloses index levels for Treasury bonds with intermediate and long-term maturities in its Bond Market Data Bank, as shown in Figure 19.5.

Federal Agency Bond Indexes

Merrill Lynch has created a bond index for federal agency bonds. The index level for bonds issued by each type of federal agency is disclosed in the *Wall Street Journal* Bond Market Data Bank (see "Mortgage-Backed Securities"), as shown in Figure 19.5.

Global Bond Indexes

Lehman Brothers, J.P. Morgan, Merrill Lynch, and Salomon Brothers have created indexes for global bonds. There are bond indexes for individual countries, as well as composite indexes for all countries combined. Figure 19.6 shows the bond index levels of bonds issued by federal governments in various countries. The change in the index level is also shown for various investment periods, along with the change in the index level from a U.S. investor's perspective over those same periods.

Review Question

19–2   When a bond with a par value of $1,000 is priced at 102 1/2%, what is the market price of this bond?

Bond Yields and Returns

Issuers of bonds and investors who purchase bonds typically focus on the yields paid or received on bonds. They use two measures, the yield to maturity and the holding period return.

Yield to Maturity

yield to maturity
The annual rate of interest that is paid by the issuer to the bondholder over the life of a bond.

The bondholder's return is commonly measured by the **yield to maturity,** which was initially introduced in Chapter 7 and represents the annualized return that is earned by the bondholder over the remaining life of the bond. The yield to maturity is the annualized discount rate that equates the future coupon interest and principal payments to the price initially paid for the bond. The yield to maturity does not include transaction costs associated with issuing the bond.

Holding Period Return

holding period return
The return from investment in a bond that is held for a period of time less than the life of the bond.

An investor who invests in a bond when it is issued and holds it until maturity will earn the yield to maturity. However, many investors do not hold the bond to maturity, and so they focus on the **holding period return,** or the return from their investment over a particular holding period.

Estimating the Holding Period Return for Short Holding Periods

If investors hold a bond for a very short time (such as less than 1 year), they may estimate their holding period return as the sum of coupon interest payments plus the difference between the selling price and the purchase price of the bond, as a percentage of the purchase price. The return earned on a bond over a short holding period is commonly measured by redefining the terms in Equation 6.1 presented earlier:

$$HPR_t = \frac{Coup + P_t - P_{t-1}}{P_{t-1}} \qquad (19.1)$$

where

HPR_t = return on the bond during period t
$Coup$ = coupon payments received during the time period from the end of period $t-1$ to the end of period t
P_t = price of the bond at the end of period t
P_{t-1} = price of the bond at the end of period $t-1$

This measurement is similar to that used to estimate the return from investing in a stock, except that coupon payments are used here instead of dividend payments.

Example ▼ Six months ago Pat Bacavis purchased corporate bonds in the secondary market that have a $1,000,000 par value and a 7% coupon rate. She received $35,000 in coupon payments over the last 6 months. She paid $990,000 for the bonds and just sold them for $970,000. The return to Pat from investing in these bonds is

$$HPR_t = \frac{Coup + P_t - P_{t-1}}{P_{t-1}}$$

$$= \frac{\$35,000 + \$970,000 - \$990,000}{\$990,000}$$

$$= \underline{0.0152}, \text{ or } 1.52\%$$

FIGURE 19.7

Annualized Bond Returns Over Time

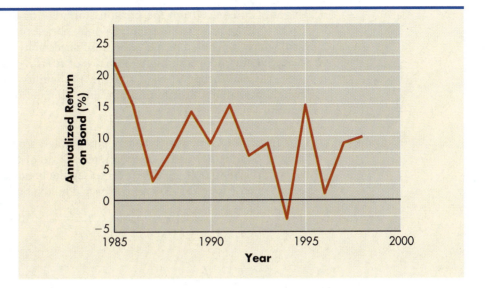

This percentage is for the 6-month investment horizon. The percentage could be annualized by dividing the return by the number of years in the investment horizon. In this example, the horizon was 6 months (0.5 year), so the annualized return is

$$\text{Annualized } HPR = \frac{0.0152}{.5}$$

$$= 0.0304, \text{ or } 3.04\%$$

The actual annual holding period return on all bonds from 1985 through 1999 is shown in Figure 19.7. This return differs from the yield to maturity in that it assumes the bonds were bought at the beginning of each year and sold at the end of each year. Note that the annualized return has been very volatile in recent years, which is attributed primarily to changes in general interest rate levels. The unusually high return on bonds occurs when there is a high coupon interest rate offered on bonds at the beginning of the year and then a substantial decline in interest rates causes bond prices to increase by the end of the year.

Bond returns can be negative during a period even when coupon interest payments are made on a timely basis. For example, in 1994 interest rates increased, causing bond prices to decline by more than the coupon interest payments that they paid. Thus, most investors who purchased bonds at the beginning of 1994 and held them for just that year earned a negative return.

Estimating the Expected Return

expected holding period return

A projected value for the return on a bond over a particular holding period.

The **expected holding period return** on bonds, denoted as $E(HPR)$ is the projected value for the return on a bond over a particular holding period. It can be estimated by forecasting the price at which the bonds will be sold at the end of the holding period. If the holding period is a short period, one year or less, the estimated selling price can be inserted into the formula for the holding period return:

$$E(HPR) = \frac{Coup + E(P_t) - P_{t-1}}{P_{t-1}} \tag{19.2}$$

The only difference from the previous formula for the holding period return is that the selling price is uncertain, so an expected price at the time of the sale is used, which is denoted as $E(P_t)$. Because uncertainty surrounds the selling price, some investors derive multiple estimates of $E(HPR)$ based on alternative conditions that may occur. If they attach a probability to each scenario, they can create a probability distribution of the holding period return over the period of concern.

Example ▼   Lenz Insurance Company considers purchasing corporate bonds that have a par value of $1,000,000 and a coupon interest rate of 8%. The prevailing price of the bonds is $980,000. Lenz expects to sell the bonds in the secondary market 1 year from now for $995,000. The expected holding period return on the bonds is

$$E(HPR) = \frac{Coup + E(P_t) - P_{t-1}}{P_{t-1}}$$

$$= \frac{\$80,000 + \$995,000 - \$980,000}{\$980,000}$$

$$= 0.0969, \text{ or } 9.69\%$$

Lenz recognizes that there is uncertainty surrounding the selling price of the bonds and therefore re-estimates the holding period return under two alternative scenarios that could occur. An alternative scenario is that interest rates decline substantially, in which case the selling price of the bonds will be $1,010,000. In this case, the holding period return will be

$$E(HPR) = \frac{\$80,000 + \$1,010,000 - \$980,000}{\$980,000}$$

$$= 0.1122, \text{ or } 11.22\%$$

Another scenario is that interest rates rise, in which the selling price of bonds will be $970,000. For this scenario, the holding period return will be:

$$E(HPR) = \frac{\$80,000 + \$970,000 - \$980,000}{\$980,000}$$

$$= 0.0714, \text{ or } 7.14\%$$

Assume that Lenz attaches a 50% probability to its first scenario, a 20% probability to the second scenario, and a 30% probability to the third scenario. This results in a probability distribution of holding period returns, as shown in Figure 19.8. The probability distribution illustrates the variation in holding period returns that could exist as a result of possible interest rate movements during the holding period. ▲

Impact of Exchange Rate Fluctuations on Holding Period Returns

The holding period return on international bonds must account for the exchange rate fluctuations over the holding period. U.S. investors can estimate the expected holding period return by forecasting the exchange rate at the time of each coupon interest payment and the exchange rate at the time the bond is to be sold.

FIGURE 19.8

Probability Distribution of Expected Holding Period Returns on Bonds for Lenz Insurance Company

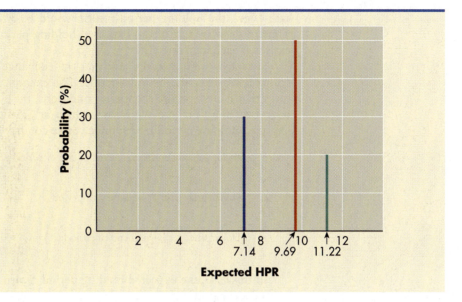

Example ▼ Stetson Bank of the United States considers investing in Canadian Treasury bonds because the yield to maturity offered on those bonds exceeds that of U.S. Treasury bonds. The prevailing price of the bonds is C$100,000, and the coupon interest rate is 9%, the interest of $9,000 ($.09 \times \$100,000$) to be paid at the end of the year. Stetson plans to hold the bonds for 1 year and expects that the selling price of the bonds will be C$100,000. Stetson also expects to benefit from an appreciation in the Canadian dollar. The Canadian dollar is presently worth $.60, but Stetson expects it to appreciate to $.66 by the end of the year. To determine its expected holding period return, Stetson must estimate the dollar price paid for the Canadian bonds, the dollar value of the coupon interest payment, and the dollar value of the price received for the bonds at the end of the 1-year holding period.

$$\text{Dollar value of coupon received at end of period (Coup)} = \text{C\$9,000} \times \$.66$$
$$= \$5,940$$

$$\text{Dollar price paid at beginning of period } (P_{t-1}) = \text{C\$100,000} \times \$.60$$
$$= \$60,000$$

$$\text{Dollar price received at end of period } (P_t) = \text{C\$100,000} \times \$.66$$
$$= \$66,000$$

The expected holding period return on the Canadian bond from Stetson's perspective is

$$E(HPR) = \frac{Coup + E(P_t) - P_{t-1}}{P_{t-1}}$$

$$= \frac{\$5,940 + \$66,000 - \$60,000}{\$60,000}$$

$$= 0.1990, \text{ or } 19.9\%$$

Note that the selling price in Canadian dollars is expected to be the same as the purchase price in Canadian dollars. Therefore, if we ignored the exchange rate effect, the holding period return would be 9% (the coupon interest rate). Thus more than half of the expected holding period return is attributed to the expected exchange rate effect.

Stetson is subject to the risk that the exchange rate of the Canadian dollar will weaken over the holding period. For example, assume that Stetson recognizes that under specific economic conditions, the Canadian dollar would depreciate over the year and would be valued at $.56 by the end of the year. The expected holding period return under these conditions is

$$\text{Dollar value of coupon received at end of period (Coup)} = \text{C\$9,000} \times \$.56$$
$$= \$5,040$$

$$\text{Dollar price paid at beginning of period } (P_{t-1}) = \text{C\$100,000} \times \$.60$$
$$= \$60,000$$

$$\text{Dollar price received at end of period } (P_t) = \text{C\$100,000} \times \$.56$$
$$= \$56,000$$

In this case, the expected holding period return on the Canadian bond from Stetson's perspective is

$$= \frac{\$5,040 + \$56,000 - \$60,000}{\$60,000}$$

$$= 0.0173, \text{ or } 1.73\%$$

The holding period return would be reduced substantially under this scenario, because Stetson would convert the proceeds from selling the bonds at a lower exchange rate than the exchange rate at which it obtained the Canadian dollars to buy the Canadian bonds.

Estimating the Holding Period Return for Long Holding Periods

For relatively long holding periods, a better approximation of the holding period return is the annualized discount rate that equates the payments received to the initial investment. Because the selling price to be received by investors is uncertain if they do not hold the bond to maturity, their holding period return is uncertain at the time they purchase the bond. Consequently, an investment in bonds is subject to the risk that the holding period return will be less than what is expected.

? Review Question

19–3 A U.S. investor just purchased a bond priced at par value with a 10-year maturity and denominated in a foreign currency. He could have purchased a U.S. bond with these same terms, the same risk, and the same coupon interest rate. Why might the U.S. investor prefer the foreign bond?

 Bond Risk

Bonds are subject to various types of risk, which are summarized in Table 19.1. Of all the types of risk, price risk is perhaps the most closely monitored on a day-

TABLE 19.1	Exposure of Bonds to Various Types of Risk
Type of Risk	**Description**
Price risk	The risk that the bond's price will decline. The primary force behind a decline in bond prices is an increase in interest rates. Thus, this type of risk is also referred to as *interest rate risk*.
Default risk	The risk that investors will not recieve the remaining coupon interest and principal payments that they are due. The default risk is related to the issuer's financial condition.
Reinvestment rate risk	Reflects the uncertainty surrounding the return that investors can earn when reinvesting the coupon interest payments or principal they receive from investing in bonds.
Purchasing power risk	The risk that the purchasing power of the steady stream of income provided over time through fixed coupon interest payments will be eroded by inflation. In the late 1990s, purchasing power actually increased, because inflation remained very low. However, given the long-term maturities of bonds, investors should recognize that purchasing power can weaken over time.
Call risk (prepayment risk)	The risk that a bond with a call feature will be called before maturity. Issuers commonly call their bonds when interest rates have declined and new bonds can be reissued with a lower coupon interest rate. When bonds are called, investors do not benefit from the decline in interest rates as much as if they were able to retain the bonds or sell them in the secondary market.
Liquidity risk	The risk that a bond may not be easily sold at their current price in the secondary market. The bonds issued by well-known firms tend to have less liquidity risk. Bonds issued by firms that are not well known do not always have an active secondary market, and investors may have to sell these bonds at a lower price to attract investors.

price risk
The risk that a bond's price will decline.

default risk
The risk that investors will not receive the remaining coupon and principal payments.

reinvestment rate risk
Uncertainty surrounding the return that investors can earn when reinvesting coupon payments or bond principal.

purchasing power risk
The risk that the purchasing power of the stream of income provided through fixed coupon payments will be eroded by inflation.

call risk (prepayment risk)
The risk that a bond with a call feature will be called before maturity.

liquidity risk
The risk that a bond may not be marketable in the secondary market.

to-day basis, because the values of bonds continuously change in response to interest rate movements.

The prices of bonds traded in the secondary market change in response to changes in the required rate of return. The main force behind a change in the required rate of return on bonds is a change in the risk-free interest rate. Although the prices of *all* bonds are inversely related to interest rate movements, the prices of some bonds are more sensitive to interest rate movements than others. Investors try to avoid investing in bonds whose prices are very sensitive to interest rate movements when they expect that interest rates will rise. As demonstrated in Chapter 7, the sensitivity of a bond's price to interest rate movements is primarily influenced by the time remaining until it matures and its coupon interest payments.

How Maturity Affects Bond Price Sensitivity

As the risk-free interest rate declines, the return that investors can earn with certainty declines. Under these circumstances, investors are willing to pay more for an existing bond that has fixed coupon interest payments, because they are now willing to accept a lower return. Consider a bond that has only one month left until maturity and will pay the par value of $1,000 at that time. If interest rates suddenly decreased, investors would not benefit much from investing in this bond, because there is only one more payment (the final interest payment plus repayment of the principal) by this bond. They could benefit more from an another bond that has, say, 20 more years until maturity, because that bond will still offer its fixed coupon interest payments over those years, even though interest rates just declined. Thus, in response to the decline in the risk-free interest rate, investors would increase their demand for the longer-maturity type of bond, which would cause that bond to increase much more than the bond with one month to maturity.

However, if interest rates suddenly increased, investors would be more adversely affected by the long-term bond, because they would be subject to the relatively low coupon payments for a long-term period. They would not be affected much by a bond with one month remaining until maturity because that bond would mature soon anyway, and the investors could use the proceeds at that time to invest in another similar-risk bond that offers a higher yield. Therefore, the prices of bonds with short time periods to maturity are less sensitive to interest rate movements than the prices of bonds with long time periods to maturity.

Given the different degrees of sensitivity, investors may prefer one type of bond maturity over another. Investors are more willing to invest in long-term bonds when they anticipate that interest rates will decline in the future. Conversely, they tend to prefer bonds with short time periods to maturity (or may prefer to buy no bonds at all) when they expect interest rates to increase in the future.

How the Coupon Interest Rate Affects Bond Price Sensitivity

To illustrate why a bond's coupon interest rate can affect its price sensitivity to interest rate movements, consider two Treasury bonds: a 9 percent coupon bond and a zero-coupon bond (which pays no coupon interest payments). Assume that each of the bonds has a 20-year maturity and that the 20-year risk-free rate is presently 9%. Under these conditions, the 9 percent coupon bond will be priced at its par value, because its coupon interest payments will provide the 9 percent annualized return that investors require.

If the risk-free rate suddenly increases to 10 percent, both types of bonds are adversely affected. The bond with the coupon interest payments is affected less, however, because the investors are receiving part of their compensation through coupon interest payments every year and can reinvest those funds at the prevailing interest rate. Conversely, the zero-coupon bond does not offer any coupon interest payments. Its entire compensation to be paid to investors is the principal, and that payment is 20 years away. Thus the entire amount of compensation is discounted 20 years back at the new (higher) required rate of return to determine the present value and therefore the proper market price to earn the 10 percent return.

? Review Question

19–4   Is a 30-year Treasury bond exposed to more or less risk than a 10-year Treasury bond? Why?

LG5 Factors That Affect Bond Prices Over Time

The existence of an active secondary market for bonds allows investors to revise their bond portfolios easily whenever they anticipate changes in the prices of these bonds. Investors in bonds need to understand the factors that affect bond prices, so that they can monitor these factors when they consider purchasing more bonds or selling some of their bond holdings. Recall from Chapter 7 (Equation 7.3) that the value of a bond can be written as

$$B_0 = I \times \left[\sum_{t=1}^{n} \frac{1}{(1 + k_d)^t} \right] + M \times \left[\frac{1}{(1 + k_d)^n} \right] \tag{19.3}$$

$$= I \times (PVIFA_{k_d, n}) + M \times (PVIF_{k_d, n}) \tag{19.3a}$$

where

B_0 = value of the bond at time zero
I = *annual* interest paid in dollars
n = number of years to maturity
M = par value in dollars
k_d = required return on a bond

This equation shows that the value of a bond is determined by the coupon interest payments offered by the issuer and the rate of return required by investors. Once a bond is issued, its coupon interest payments do not change. Therefore, the value of a bond changes over time in response to changes in the return required by investors. Specifically, the value of a bond is inversely related to changes in the rate of return required by investors. The required return on bonds is primarily composed of the risk-free interest rate and the default risk premium. Thus any factors that can affect the risk-free rate or the default risk premium can affect the required rate of return on bonds and therefore the values of bonds.

Factors That Affect the Risk-Free Interest Rate

An increase in the risk-free rate of interest results in a higher required rate of return on bonds and therefore reduces the value of bonds. Conversely, a reduction in the risk-free rate of interest results in a lower required rate of return on bonds and therefore increases the value of bonds. Recall from Chapter 4 that interest rates change in response to changes in the supply of funds and the demand for funds. The following factors tend to affect the supply or demand for funds in the financial system and therefore can affect interest rates and bond values.

The Fed's Monetary Policy

The supply of funds in the financial system is influenced by shifts in the Fed's monetary policy. When the Fed increases money supply growth, it increases the supply of funds and therefore places downward pressure on the risk-free interest rate. Conversely, a decrease in money supply growth places upward pressure on the risk-free interest rate.

Impact of Inflation

Inflation tends to discourage savers from saving, because savers prefer to purchase products now before prices increase further. Inflation also encourages households and firms to borrow more funds now to finance large expenditures that they prefer to make today before prices increase further. Both of these forces place upward pressure on interest rates.

Impact of Economic Growth

When economic growth increases, it encourages firms to expand, which requires that they borrow more funds to support the expansion. It may also encourage households to borrow more funds to finance large expenditures (such as buying a new home), because they are more confident that they will have an adequate stable income in the future that can be used to repay loans. In general, an increase in economic growth places upward pressure on the aggregate demand for funds and therefore places upward pressure on interest rates.

Factors That Affect the Default Risk Premium

The default risk premium is the premium that investors require above the risk-free rate as compensation for the possibility of default. When investors believe that a particular firm's default risk has increased, they increase the rate of return that they require to purchase bonds issued by that firm. A firm's default risk premium can change in response to economic conditions or to a change in the firm's financial condition, as explained next.

Change in Economic Conditions

An increase in economic growth can improve a firm's expected cash flows and therefore reduce the probability that the firm will default on its debt. In response to increased economic growth, investors may reduce the default premium that they require when purchasing bonds. Conversely, a reduction in economic growth may result in a higher default risk premium for bonds in general.

Figure 19.9 shows the yields offered on long-term corporate bonds and long-term Treasury bonds over time. The difference between the yields on the two types of bonds is attributable primarily to the default risk premium. Note that this difference is larger in some periods than others. In particular, the difference was large during the early 1980s, when the United States experienced a major recession, and in early 1991, when the economy was relatively weak.

Although the impact of economic growth on the default risk premium is clear, the impact of economic growth on the required rate of return on bonds is not, because the effects of economic growth on the risk-free rate must be considered along with the default risk premium. Because higher economic growth tends to increase the risk-free rate, any positive impact of economic growth on the default risk premium may be overwhelmed. That is, the increase in the risk-free rate can more than offset the reduction in the default risk premium, thereby increasing the required rate of return. This relationship is not perfect, but investors should attempt to separate the effects of economic growth on the risk-free rate and the default risk premium when determining how the required rate of return on bonds is affected.

FIGURE 19.9

Comparison of Corporate and Treasury (Risk-Free) Bond Yields

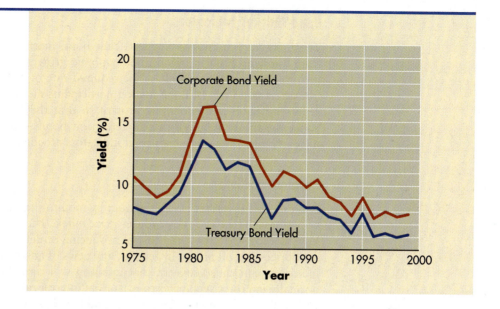

Change in the Firm's Financial Condition

The restructuring of a firm could increase the required rate of return and therefore reduce the price of its bonds. For example, when a firm revamps its capital structure to use more debt and less equity, it increases the risk that the firm will be unable to cover payments on its existing bonds. Thus, the prices of these bonds decline, because investors are willing to purchase these bonds in the secondary market only if they are priced low enough to offer a high yield. Those investors who had been holding the bonds at the time of the firm's restructuring are adversely affected.

Example ▼ A classic example of how restructuring can affect bond prices is the leveraged buyout (LBO) of RJR Nabisco Inc. by Kohlberg, Kravis, Roberts (KKR) in 1988. RJR Nabisco's capital structure contained more equity than debt before the LBO. When KKR acquired RJR Nabisco for $24.7 billion, it used an equity investment of $1.4 billion, or 5.7% of the total market value of RJR Nabisco. The remainder of the funds represented a mixture of short-term and long-term debt. The long-term debt by itself was more than 12 times the amount of the equity investment. The creditors that financed the LBO recognized the high degree of financial leverage and required a high premium to compensate for the risk. However, the investors who held bonds issued by RJR Nabisco before the LBO were not able to require such a risk premium, because those bonds were already issued. Thus they paid more for the bonds when they were issued than the price at which they could sell the bonds after the buyout. ▲

A change in a firm's investment policies can also affect its default risk. For example, firms that attempt to expand into noncore businesses may increase their risk if there is a question about whether they can properly manage these businesses. Additionally, the noncore businesses into which they expand may by their nature have greater business risk than the firm's core businesses.

Bond Market Indicators

The preceding discussion suggests that bond market investors would benefit from knowing how inflation and economic growth will change in the future, because these factors can affect the required rate of return on bonds and therefore affect bond prices. Bond market participants monitor several indicators that reflect inflation and economic growth so that they can develop expectations about the future required rate of return on bonds—and therefore about bond prices. Some of the more important indicators are identified here.

Indicators of Inflation

Bond market investors assess inflation by monitoring indicators such as the consumer price index and the producer price index. They also monitor the prices of key resources that affect the cost of producing or delivering some goods, such as steel prices and oil prices. In general, any news of an unexpected increase in these indicators can cause concern that inflation will rise. Bond market participants normally interpret such news to mean that interest rates will rise and bond prices will decline. Some bond investors respond to such news by selling bonds immediately. The abrupt increase in the supply of bonds for sale in the market tends to cause an immediate decline in bond prices. Thus bond prices can change abruptly in response to expectations, even if those expectations do not come true.

An unexpected decrease in any of the aforementioned inflation indicators is typically interpreted to signal a decline in inflation, which triggers an abrupt increase in the demand for bonds and places immediate upward pressure on bond prices.

Indicators of Economic Growth

Bond market investors assess economic growth by monitoring indicators such as the personal income level, the consumer spending level, the employment level, and various production indexes. In general, news of an unexpected increase in these economic growth indexes signals an increase in economic growth, which creates expectations of higher interest rates and therefore lower bond prices.

Many investors who trade bonds have a schedule of when all the inflation and economic growth indicators will be announced during the course of a month. They stand ready to buy or sell bonds immediately in response to a particular inflation or economic growth indicator. A common headline is "Bond Prices Fall in Response to Increased Employment Level," which illustrates how favorable news for the economy has an unfavorable effect on bond prices because of the potential rise in interest rates.

Indicators of a Firm's Financial Condition

Bond market investors assess not only such macroeconomic conditions as inflation and economic growth but also the financial condition of firms. They recognize that a change in a firm's financial condition can affect its default risk, and so they may buy or sell the firm's bonds in response. Some of the more commonly monitored indicators of default risk are measures of *financial leverage*, such as a firm's debt ratio or its times-interest-earned ratio. In addition, bond market participants may assess the sensitivity of the firm's performance to economic condi-

IT'S TIME TO SHED LIGHT ON BOND PRICES

No central bond exchange reports bond bids and offers, which makes it hard for investors to get good bond price information. As more bond trading and reporting move to the Internet, the number of serious bond investors could rise.

The $13 trillion U.S. bond market is the world's largest financial market. But just try to find out at what price a bond is trading. Unlike stocks, bonds don't have a central exchange or required reporting of bids and offers. So fixed-income investors, big and small, don't know how much dealers are marking up bonds. As a result, they don't know whether they're getting a good price.

More than likely, they're not. University of Notre Dame finance professor Paul Schultz found that for big institutions such as bond mutual funds, the average trading spread for corporate debt was 26 basis points. That means the fund is paying $2.60 above dealers' costs to buy and sell a bond. This depresses the yield and total return to investors. . . .

The Bond Market Association, the industry trade group, will soon implement a voluntary system reporting end-of-day prices for some 150 corporate issues on its Web site (**www.investinginbonds.com**). The plan is limited, at best, since only 15 firms expect to participate. The Bond Market

Association already lists previous-day municipal debt prices for the most actively traded issues. Piecemeal price data are available from other sources as well. . . .

Price reporting is also reaching the Internet. E*Trade Group (**www.etrade.com**) and Morgan Stanley Dean Witter's Discover Brokerage Direct (**www.discoverbrokerage.com**) now list real-time quotes for Treasuries and munis from its inventory. But more must be done. There's no reason why the technology that enables any investor to check stock prices from a computer can't work for bonds. . . .

Giving investors more price information may cost bond brokers their huge markups. But they would likely regain their losses quickly if lower trading costs attracted more investors to bonds and created a truly public market out of the current private club.

Source: Toddi Gutner, "It's Time to Shed Light on Bond Prices," Business Week, *June 7, 1999, p. 143.*

tions, industry conditions, and global conditions. Those firms whose performance levels are very sensitive to such conditions are more likely to experience changes in their bond values quickly and significantly. Bond ratings from agencies such as Moody's and Standard & Poor's provide professional assessments of a firm's risk. Bond market participants typically monitor all of the factors listed here so that they can revise their positions in bonds whenever new information becomes available to the market.

 Review Questions

19–5   Why do bond prices change in response to changes in the Fed's monetary policy?

19–6   How might a firm's bond price change in response to news that the firm is experiencing financial problems?

Bond Investment Strategies

Many investors follow a specific strategy for investing in bonds. Some individual investors purchase specific bonds, whereas others purchase bond mutual funds and rely on the expertise of a bond portfolio manager. Most bond portfolio managers who are employed by financial institutions follow one or more strategies for managing a bond portfolio. Some of the more common strategies are described here.

Passive Strategy

passive strategy
Strategy in which investors establish a diversified portfolio of bonds and maintain the portfolio for a long period of time.

A **passive strategy** is to invest in a diversified portfolio of bonds and maintain the portfolio for a long period of time. A passive bond portfolio may have limited exposure to default risk if the bonds are diversified across industries or even countries. There are different degrees of risk tolerance among investors who use a passive strategy to invest in bonds. Some investors may be less willing to incur risk, and they therefore focus most of their investment in Treasury bonds or other types of bonds that have a very high credit rating. Other investors may include some bonds with a higher degree of default risk in order to increase the expected return on the bond portfolio. Thus, a passive strategy does not necessarily represent an ultra-conservative strategy.

The use of a passive strategy can reduce trading costs (such as commissions) because the amount of trading is very limited. In general, a passive strategy may achieve a long-term return similar to that of a bond index that reflects the interest rate risk and default risk of the portfolio. Investors who use a passive strategy generally believe that it is not worth the time, effort, or expense to try to outperform a diversified bond index with frequent trading. Portfolio managers of financial institutions rarely use a passive strategy, because they are paid to try to manage the portfolio in such a way as to outperform passive strategies.

Matching Strategy

matching strategy
Strategy in which investors estimate future cash outflows and choose bonds whose coupon or principal payments will cover the projected cash outflows.

Investors who anticipate specific future expenses may invest in a bond portfolio that provides income matched to the expenses. This **matching strategy** involves estimating future cash outflows and then choosing bonds whose coupon or principal payments will be sufficient to cover those cash outflows. For example, an investor may invest in a bond portfolio that will provide sufficient income to cover a child's future college tuition expenses.

Laddered Strategy

laddered strategy
Strategy in which investors evenly allocate funds invested in bonds in each of several different maturity classes, to minimize interest rate sensitivity.

A **laddered strategy** represents an even allocation of funds invested in bonds in each of several different maturity classes. For example, an institutional investor may allocate funds evenly among bonds that have maturities of 10 years, 11 years, 12 years, and so on, up to 20 years. The laddered strategy is intended to diversify maturities, so that the sensitivities of the bonds to interest rate risk vary. This strategy reduces the adverse effects that rising interest rates would have on the bonds.

Barbell Strategy

barbell strategy
Strategy in which investors allocate funds into bonds with short-term and long-term, but few or no intermediate-term, maturities.

The **barbell strategy** represents the allocation of funds into bonds with two distinct maturities: short-term and long-term. The portfolio contains few or no intermediate-term bonds. When investors using the barbell strategy need cash, they can sell some bonds with the short term to maturity. Conversely, they rely on the bonds with the long term to maturity to provide a higher yield (although the long-term bonds are more exposed to interest rate risk). The barbell strategy essentially balances long-term investments, made to achieve a relatively high return, with short-term investments, included to cover liquidity needs.

Interest Rate Strategy

interest rate strategy
Strategy in which investors allocate funds to capitalize on interest rate forecasts and revise their portfolios in response to changes in interest rate expectations.

The **interest rate strategy** allocates funds in a manner that capitalizes on interest rate forecasts. Investors frequently revise their bond portfolios in response to interest rate expectations. The forecast of a recession may cause bond portfolio managers to anticipate lower interest rates and therefore to invest in longer-term bonds (whose prices would increase more in response to lower interest rates). Conversely, the expectation of higher inflation may cause bond portfolio mangers to expect higher interest rates and therefore to shift to bonds with shorter terms to maturity.

Because the interest rate strategy allocates funds according to interest rate forecasts, it has the potential to generate higher returns than other bond strategies. However, it can also result in relatively poor performance when the interest rate forecasts of portfolio managers are wrong.

? Review Question

19–7   What is the difference between a laddered strategy and a barbell strategy for investing in bonds?

TYING IT ALL TOGETHER

This chapter provided a background on bonds, including the types of bonds, the use of bond quotations, the measurement of bond yields, risk factors that affect bond prices, and bond investment strategies. The roles of managers, financial markets, and investors in the bond valuation process are summarized in the Integrative Table that follows.

INTEGRATIVE TABLE

Valuing Bonds and Executing Bond Transactions

Role of **Financial Managers**	*Role of* **Financial Markets**	*Role of* **Investors**
Financial managers make decisions that affect the expected future cash flows of the firm—and that therefore affect the value of the firm. They also can attempt to obtain additional funds by issuing more bonds. Their financial decisions affect the risk of the firm, which affects the price at which the firm can issue bonds.	The financial markets establish a market price for each bond that is traded. When investors use their own assessment of an issuer's risk and of future interest rate movements, they may derive a value that differs from the prevailing market price of the bond. Investors commonly purchase the bonds that they perceive as undervalued by the market.	Investors monitor the decisions made by a firm's financial managers, along with other conditions, when valuing a firm's bonds. Any decisions that affect a firm's default risk may affect the firm's bond prices. Investors also change their required rate of return on bonds in response to changes in the risk-free interest rate.

LG1 **List the different types of bonds.** Bonds are distinguished by the type of issuer. They are issued by the U.S. Treasury, municipalities, federal agencies, and corporations. There are also international bonds that are issued by government agencies or corporations in other countries.

LG2 **Explain how investors use bond quotations.** Investors use bond quotations to monitor the prices of individual bonds or of particular types of bonds. Quotations are provided by financial newspapers on individual corporate bonds, Treasury bonds, municipal bonds, and federal agency bonds. In addition, quotations are provided for indexes representing corporate bonds, Treasury bonds, federal agency bonds, municipal bonds, and global bonds with various maturities.

LG3 **Describe how yields and returns are measured for bonds.** A bond's yield to maturity represents the annualized return that is earned by the bondholder over the remaining life of the bond. The yield to maturity does not include transaction costs associated with issuing the bond. For investors who hold the bond until maturity, the yield to maturity represents their annualized yield. Investors who do not anticipate holding the bonds until maturity normally estimate the holding period yield that they will earn on the basis of the expected selling price of the bond at a future point in time.

LG4 **Describe the risks from investing in bonds.** Bonds can expose investors to a wide variety of risks such as price risk, default risk, reinvestment rate risk, purchasing power risk, call (prepayment) risk, and liquidity risk. Investors focus on price risk when monitoring day-to-day changes in the values of bonds, because bond prices are very sensitive to interest rate movements. The degree of a bond's sensitivity to interest rate movements is dependent on the bond's coupon rate and its remaining time to maturity. Bonds with higher coupon payments and shorter remaining times to maturity are less sensitive to interest rate movements.

LG5 **Identify the factors that affect bond prices over time.** Bond prices are inversely related to interest rate movements. Economic growth affects bond prices by influencing the default risk of the bonds and also by influencing interest rates. Inflation affects bond prices by influencing interest rates.

LG6 **Describe the strategies commonly used for investing in bonds.** Investors can use a variety of strategies to invest in bonds. The passive strategy represents the investment in a diversified portfolio of bonds on a long-term basis, without frequent changes in the investment positions. The matching strategy is intended to generate, from the investments, cash inflows to cover expected cash outflows. The laddered strategy allocates investments across bonds with different maturities. The barbell strategy divides an investment between bonds with short time periods remaining until maturity (for liquidity purposes) and long-term bonds (where the expected return is higher). The interest rate strategy is to allocate bonds to capitalize on interest rate expectations. When interest rates are expected to increase, the allocation would focus on bonds with a short term to maturity to reduce exposure to interest rate risk. When interest rates are expected to decrease, the allocation would focus on bonds with a long term to maturity that would benefit the most from a reduction in interest rates.

SELF-TEST EXERCISES

(Solutions in Appendix B)

LG2 **ST 19–1** **Understanding bond quotations**   Corporate bond quotations in the *Wall Street Journal* give a surprising amount of information. Examine this one and then answer the questions that follow. Assume that par value is $1,000.

Bonds	Cur. Yld.	Vol.	Close	Net Chg.
ATT 8⅜s31	8.3	124	103½	+½

a. Calculate the coupon payment per bond per year.
b. What is the price per bond in dollars and cents?
c. Demonstrate how this bond's current yield was calculated.
d. How many bonds were traded on the day reported?
e. At what price did the bond close at the previous day?

LG3 ST 19–2 Calculating holding period return   Six months ago, Paul Aguilara purchased corporate bonds with a par value of $400,000 and a 6% coupon rate. During the time that he held the bonds, he received $12,000 in coupon payments. He paid $408,000 for the bonds and has just sold them for $400,000.
a. What is his holding period return (HPR) on the investment?
b. What is his annualized HPR?
c. What would his HPR be if he had sold the bonds for $420,000?
d. What would that HPR be annualized?

EXERCISES

LG1 19–1 Bond value and changing conditions   Indicate the probable reaction of a bond's market value to the following events:
a. The risk-free rate of return increases.
b. Moody's changes the bond's rating from A to AA.
c. The market return on bonds decreases.
d. Moody's changes the bond's rating from BBB to BB.
e. General economic conditions are deteriorating.

LG1 19–2 Housing bonds   Government National Mortgage Association (GNMA), Federal Home Loan Marketing Association (FHLMA), and Federal National Mortgage Association (FNMA) all issue bonds and use the proceeds to purchase mortgages.
a. Explain the differences among the types of mortgages purchased by each of these entities.
b. Describe the default risk involved with each of these entities, and explain why it differs from one to another.

LG1 19–3 Municipal bonds   Bonds issued by state and local government agencies pay a lower coupon rate than comparable federally issued bonds.
a. Explain why a lower coupon rate on a municipal bond might still be more attractive to an investor than a higher rate on one issued by a federal agency.
b. What are some of the factors that might result in a lower-quality rating for a municipal bond?

LG1 19–4 Risk premium and bond type   Assume that all of the bonds listed below are of equal maturity. Arrange the types of bonds from lowest to highest by the probable size of their risk premiums. Justify the position you have assigned to each.
a. Investment-grade corporate bond

 b. FHLMA bond

 c. U.S. Treasury bond

 d. GNMA bond

 e. Corporate junk bond

19–5 Values of international bonds Classify each of the following events in terms of its probable effect on the market value of an international bond for a U.S. investor.

 a. The bond's currency of denomination appreciates against the U.S. dollar.

 b. Market rates of interest in the issuer's country increase.

 c. The U.S. dollar appreciates against the currency of denomination.

 d. The economy of the issuer's country is headed into recession.

19–6 Treasury bond quotations The following quotation was published in the *Wall Street Journal*:

Rate	Maturity Mo/Yr	Bid	Asked	Chg.	Ask Yld.
6¾	Aug 26	105:10	105:12	−29	6.33

 a. How much interest does this bond pay per $100 par value per year?

 b. On the basis of the bid price, how much would a selling investor receive per $100 par value for this bond? (Carry your answer out to hundredths of a cent.)

 c. On the basis of the asked price, how much would an investor pay per $100 of par value for this bond? (Carry the answer out to hundredths of a cent.)

 d. Assuming that the change is based on the ask price per bond, what price would an investor have paid at the close of the previous trading day per $100 of par value? (Carry the answer out to hundredths of a cent.)

 e. Explain what the asking yield for this bond represents and what cash flows it takes into account.

19–7 Corporate bond quotations A Lucent Technologies bond was quoted in the *Wall Street Journal* on February 24, 2000, as follows:

Bonds	Cur. Yld.	Vol.	Close	Net Chg.
Lucent7¼06	7.3	45	99⅝	−¼

 a. On the basis of this bond's coupon interest rate, how much interest does it pay per $100 par value per year?

 b. How many years does it have until it matures, if you assume that it will mature on December 31 of its maturity year?

 c. How many bonds traded on the reported day?

 d. How is current yield computed? Demonstrate with this bond quotation.

 e. At what price per $100 par value did the bond close?

 f. At what price per $100 par value did the bond close in the previous session?

19–8 **Bond return**   Eighteen months ago Bill Kelly purchased U.S. Treasury bonds with a par value of $50,000 and an 8% coupon rate. He paid $48,500 for the bonds and has just sold them for $50,200.

    a. Assuming that the interest on these bonds is paid semiannually, how much would Bill have received in 18 months?

    b. Given the increase in market value of the bonds during the time that Bill held them, in what direction did interest rates move during that time?

    c. What is Bill's holding period return on the bonds?

    d. What is his annualized return on the bonds?

19–9 **Estimated holding period return**   Martha Kirkley is considering the purchase of bonds for her company's pension plan. She has chosen corporate bonds with a par value of $1,500,000 and a 10% coupon, which are priced at $1,460,00. She plans to keep the bonds for 1 year, and then sell them. She has estimated a range of possible selling prices and has assigned probabilities to each estimate as follows:

Condition	Selling price	Probability
Interest rates increase	$1,400,000	10%
Interest rates unchanged	1,460,000	15
Interest rates fall some	1,500,000	60
Interest rates fall more	1,520,000	15

    a. For each possible return, calculate the holding period return.

    b. Combine the holding period returns with their assigned probabilities, and illustrate the resulting probability distribution as is done in Figure 19.8.

19–10 **Exchange rate fluctuations and bond returns**   Kenneth Jamison manages the investment portfolio for a large not-for-profit foundation. He is considering a 1-year investment in British Treasury securities for their superior yield and low default risk. He would like to purchase bonds with a par value of $100,000 and a 12% coupon rate that pay interest at the end of the year. The current exchange rate is $1.65 US per British pound. It is important to estimate the effect of exchange rate fluctuations on holding period return. Assuming that both purchase and sale are done at par value, calculate the holding period given the following range of possible exchange rates in 1 year.

U.S. Currency per British Pound
$1.70
$1.67
$1.65
$1.63
$1.60

19–11   Identifying sources of bond risk   Match the following situations to the risk source found in Table 19.1 that best fits.

a. Anna purchased $5,000 U.S. Treasury notes with a coupon of 5% and a 3-year maturity. During the time that she held the bonds, consumer prices increased at a 6.5% annual rate.

b. Tim purchased $25,000 par value of corporate bonds issued by an automobile company. During the next 6 months, the automaker suffered a major labor strike, and Moody's downgraded the bonds from A to BBB.

c. Mike purchased $30,000 par value of 10% coupon corporate bonds with 6 years until maturity. He planned to sell them in 2 years. Interest rates increased to 12.5% by the end of his planned 2-year holding period.

d. Sarah purchased $15,000 par value of 10% coupon callable corporate bonds with a maturity of 8 years. The bonds were called at par value when interest rates fell to 8%.

e. Hank purchased bonds issued by a small corporation that operated in his region of the country. When he tried to sell the bonds prior to their maturity, he had a hard time finding a buyer and ended up selling them at a deep discount.

 19–12   Bond price sensitivity to changes in interest rates   Interest rates are expected to fall dramatically in the next 6 to 9 months. Ed Hale wants to build a bond portfolio to take maximum advantage of the move in rates. Examine the U.S. Treasury issues listed below and rate them from 1 to 5 from the most sensitive to the least sensitive. For each, state why you ranked it as you did.

Maturity	Coupon rate
6 months	5%
7 years	8
10 years	6
8 years	10
17 years	10

19–13   Factors affecting risk-free rates and default premiums   Each of the situations that follow will affect either the risk-free rate of return or the default premium of an issuer. For each, state whether interest rates (risk premium) will increase or decrease, and explain why.

a. The Federal Reserve has announced that it will allow the money supply to grow at a 6% annual rate rather than the previously targeted 4.5% rate of growth.

b. The rate of growth in the economy has been negative for the last two reported quarters.

c. The general level of prices for goods and services is rising rapidly.

d. Jackson Rakes, Inc. has paid down its debt from 60% of assets to 40% of assets and has gained several large, long-term contracts with major new customers.

e. Massey, Inc. has been through a leveraged buyout and now has debt equivalent to 80% of its assets.

f. Nancy Jo, Inc., a well-known maker of cakes and baked goods, has announced a decision to branch out into producing pesticides.

LG5   **19–14**   **Economic indicators and bond prices**   Indicate the probable response of bond prices to each of the following unexpected economic events.

a. The producer price index rises by a surprising 0.4%.

b. Employment levels are reported to have been unusually strong during the last quarter.

c. Consumer spending drops to an unexpectedly low level.

d. Personal income has risen more than expected in the last month.

LG6   **19–15**   **Building a bond portfolio**   You have been given $1,000,000 to build a U.S. Treasury bond portfolio. Choose from the following list of bonds to create your portfolio using the strategy indicated.

U.S. Treasury Bonds	
Maturity	Coupon
11 years	6.00%
12 years	6.10
13 years	6.20
14 years	6.30
15 years	6.40
16 years	6.50
17 years	6.60
18 years	6.70
19 years	6.75
20 years	6.80

a. Use a laddered strategy.

b. Use a matching strategy with planned expenditures of $250,000 in 12 years and $750,000 in 18 years.

c. Use a barbell strategy.

d. Use an interest rate strategy with a forecast for recession.

Go to web site **www.investinginbonds.com**. Click on Information for Investors. Click on Investor's Guides Municipal Bonds. Click on The Tax Exempt Municipal Bond Market—How Big and Who Buys?

1. What is the value of Municipal Bonds outstanding? Who owns them?

Click on Arrow pointing to Left (←).

2 Where can you buy or sell Municipal Bonds?

3. What is the minimum denomination of most municipal bonds?

4. Where can you find the listed prices of municipal bonds?

Under Bond Prices, click on MUNICIPAL BONDS. Select Connecticut as the state and sort by CREDIT RATING. Click on SEARCH.

5. What is the range of YTMs on this chart?

6. How many dollars of bonds were traded?

Go to web site **www.cbs.marketwatch.com**. Click on Market Data. Under Bonds click on Corporates.

7. What is the range of YTM/Cs for the AAA Corporate Bonds?

8. What is the range of YTM/Cs for the BAA Corporate Bonds?

Using the BACK function on your browser toolbar, go back to the previous page. Click on Treasuries.

9. Give the yield for the various terms of U.S. Treasuries:

TERM	YIELD	TERM	YIELD
3 mo.		3 yr.	
6 mo.		5 yr.	
1 yr.		10 yr.	
2 yr.		30 yr.	

For additional practice with concepts from this chapter, visit
http://www.awl.com/gitman_madura

Chapter

20

Mutual Funds and Asset Allocation

L E A R N I N G   G O A L S

LG1 Describe the operations of stock mutual funds, and explain how these funds are used by investors.

LG2 Describe the operations of bond mutual funds, and explain how these funds are used by investors.

LG3 Describe the operations of money market mutual funds, and explain how these funds are used by investors.

LG4 Explain the meaning of asset allocation and the factors that influence a particular investor's asset allocation decision.

613

Stock Mutual Funds

stock mutual fund
Investment company that sells shares to individuals and pools the proceeds to invest in stocks.

Stock **mutual funds** sell shares to individuals and pool the proceeds to invest in stocks. The mutual fund is essentially investing the investor's funds, and the return on this investment is channeled back to the investors. When stock mutual funds invest in shares of stock that are offered through an initial public offering (the primary market), they are channeling funds from investors to finance new investment by firms. They can also invest in stocks in the secondary market, thereby transferring ownership among investors.

Stock mutual funds have become very popular because they enable individual investors to hold diversified portfolios of stocks with a small investment. In addition, they do not require any portfolio management by investors; they are managed by the fund's portfolio managers, who specialize in making investment decisions. There are now more than 3,500 stock mutual funds. The aggregate market value of all stock mutual funds exceeds $3 trillion, which is more than 10 times their aggregate value in 1990.

How Stock Mutual Funds Operate

Some of the key operations of stock mutual funds involve managing the portfolio, distributing gains to shareholders, deciding whether to function as open-end or closed-end fund, assessing sales charges (if any) and annual fees, and making marketing decisions. These operational issues are discussed next.

Fund Portfolio Management

Because mutual funds typically have billions of dollars to invest in securities, they use substantial resources to make their investment decisions. In particular, each mutual fund is managed by one or more portfolio managers who are trained to select securities for the fund's portfolio. These managers are armed with information about the firms represented by the securities in which they can invest.

Mutual funds commonly sell securities that they had previously purchased. However, given their large investment in a particular security, they may attempt to improve the performance of the security rather than sell it. For example, a given mutual fund may hold more than a million shares of a particular stock that has performed poorly. Rather than selling the stock, the mutual fund may try to influence the management of the firm to boost the performance of the firm, which may have a favorable effect on the firm's stock price.

Distribution of Gains to Shareholders

net asset value (NAV)
The current market value per share of the assets in a stock mutual fund; calculated as the market value of all assets in the fund divided by the number of fund shares outstanding.

At the end of each day, the market value of all the assets (stocks plus cash) of a stock mutual fund is determined. Any interest or dividends earned by the fund are added to the market value of the assets, and any liabilities of the fund and any dividends distributed are deducted from the market value of the assets. This amount is then divided by the number of shares outstanding to determine the so-called **net asset value** (NAV). When the prices of stocks in a mutual fund rise, so does the net asset value. Thus, gains to investors result from an increase in the net asset value.

Mutual fund investors can also experience gains from two other sources. They can earn a return from a distribution of dividends provided by the companies in which the fund has invested. Gains to investors may also be attributed to capital gains the mutual fund generated by selling stocks that it had previously purchased. Mutual funds are required to distribute these gains by the end of the year, and the gains are taxable as ordinary income in that year. Shareholders may choose to receive dividends and capital gain distributions in cash, or they may receive the distribution in the form of additional shares. For example, if the net asset value is presently $10 per share and an investor is owed $1,200, he or she could either receive a check from the fund or be awarded an additional 120 shares (which has a value of $1,200, based on the net asset value of $10 per share).

Open-End versus Closed-End Funds

open-end mutual fund
Mutual fund that sells shares upon demand to investors and purchases shares back from investors who wish to sell the shares.

Mutual funds can be classified in terms of how their shares are purchased or sold by investors. **Open-end funds** sell shares upon demand to investors and purchase shares back from investors who wish to sell the shares. In periods when withdrawals of money from a mutual fund exceed purchases of shares, an open-end fund may need to sell some of its stock holdings to obtain the money it needs to pay its shareholders. For no-load funds, the price per share at which open-end funds sell shares or buy back shares is the net asset value per share. For load funds, the price at which you can buy shares is above the price at which you can sell shares at a given point in time.

closed-end fund
Mutual fund that sells shares through an initial public offering and is then closed after that initial offering, although existing shares may be traded on a stock exchange when investors want to sell the shares they own.

Closed-end funds sell their shares through an initial public offering and are then closed after that offering. After the initial public offering, shares of a closed-end fund are traded only when investors wish to sell the shares they own. These shares are traded on a stock exchange just like common stock that was previously issued by a firm. Closed-end funds do not purchase the shares they originally sold. The distinction between open-end funds and closed-end funds is illustrated in Figure 20.1. The market price of shares of a closed-end fund is determined by the forces of demand and supply, just like the price of shares of stock.

Pricing Closed-End Funds   The market price per share of a closed-end fund tends to change in response to changes in its net asset value. Even so, it sometimes deviates from its net asset value per share. When its market price per share is less than the net asset value per share, the closed-end fund is priced at a discount. When its market price per share is more than the net asset value per share, the closed-end fund is priced at a premium.

Some research has documented high returns from investing in closed-end funds when they are priced at a large discount from their net asset value, which suggests that closed-end funds with large discounts in price are undervalued. The results from applying this strategy will not always generate high risk-adjusted returns, however, because some closed-end funds with large discounts experience a reduction in the market price over time.

Sales Charges

load fund
Mutual fund that charges a fee to investors when shares of the fund are purchased.

Some mutual funds charge sales commissions; others do not. A **load fund** charges a fee to investors who invest in the fund. An investor who wants to invest $3,000 in a load fund that has a sales charge of 8 percent incurs a load (fee) of $240.

616 PART 4 Investment Management

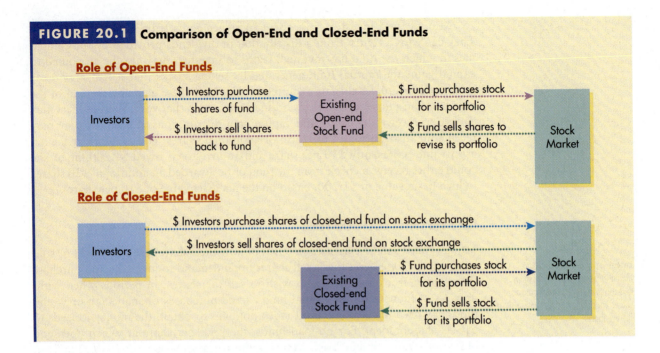

FIGURE 20.1 **Comparison of Open-End and Closed-End Funds**

Role of Open-End Funds

Investors — $ Investors purchase shares of fund → Existing Open-end Stock Fund — $ Fund purchases stock for its portfolio → Stock Market

Investors ← $ Investors sell shares back to fund — Existing Open-end Stock Fund ← $ Fund sells shares to revise its portfolio — Stock Market

Role of Closed-End Funds

Investors — $ Investors purchase shares of closed-end fund on stock exchange → Stock Market

Investors ← $ Investors sell shares of closed-end fund on stock exchange — Stock Market

Existing Closed-end Stock Fund — $ Fund purchases stock for its portfolio → Stock Market

Existing Closed-end Stock Fund ← $ Fund sells stock for its portfolio — Stock Market

no-load fund
Mutual fund that does not charge a fee to investors for investing in the fund.

A **no-load fund** does not charge a fee to investors for investing. Because no-load mutual funds normally do not rely on brokerage firms for promotional purposes, they typically sell directly to investors.

Some no-load mutual funds charge a 12b-1 fee that covers some of their marketing and distribution costs. More than half of all mutual funds charge a 12b-1 fee. The SEC limits the amount of the fee to 0.25 percent for mutual funds that are designated as no-load funds.

There is no evidence that load funds outperform no-load funds. Thus, most investors who are willing to make investment decisions without the services of a brokerage firm select no-load funds so that they can avoid paying sales charges.

Annual Expenses

expense ratio
A measure of the expenses of a mutual fund, calculated as the annual expenses divided by the net asset value of the fund.

Every mutual fund incurs expenses, including administrative expenses, portfolio management fees and trading commissions. These expenses are implicitly passed on to the investors, because the net asset value of the fund accounts for any expenses incurred. These expenses vary substantially among mutual funds, and investors should review the annual expenses of any fund before making an investment. Expenses can be compared among mutual funds by measuring the **expense ratio,** which is equal to the annual expenses divided by the net asset value of the fund. An expense ratio of 2 percent in a given year means that shareholders incur expenses that reflect 2 percent of the value of the fund. The higher this expense ratio, the lower the return for a given level of portfolio performance. Mutual funds that incur more expenses are worthwhile only if they offer a high enough return to offset the extra expenses.

Much research has been conducted to determine why some mutual funds perform better than others, and the one factor consistently identified is expenses. Mutual funds that have lower expense ratios tend to outperform others that have a similar investment objective. That is, the funds that have higher expenses are generally unable to generate higher returns that could offset their higher expenses.

Emphasis on Marketing

The mutual fund industry has shifted its focus from managing funds to marketing the funds. As the size of a mutual fund increases, it can retain its expense ratio and generate more fees. Many mutual funds use a large portion of the extra fees to do more advertising in order to attract more investors. However, this focus on marketing does not necessarily enable a mutual fund to achieve high performance relative to the market or other mutual funds. In fact, the marketing expenses increase the expenses incurred, which are passed on to shareholders who invest in mutual funds.

Fund Investment Objectives

Each mutual fund has a specific investment objective. Because there are many different investment objectives, there may be several mutual funds within a specific "family" of funds that cover most or all of the investment objectives. For example, Fidelity, Merrill Lynch, Vanguard, and other financial institutions offer a set (family) of open-end mutual funds that satisfy a wide variety of investment objectives. Some of the more popular investment objective categories are identified here.

Growth Funds

Growth funds contain stocks of companies that have not matured and have high potential for growth. These stocks do not provide steady income in the form of dividends, because the companies tend to reinvest more of their earnings to support their growth rather than pay dividends. But they offer the potential for a high increase in value of the stock.

Capital Appreciation Funds

Capital appreciation funds contain stocks that have high potential for growth. These stocks are normally less mature than growth stocks and are unproven. They tend to have a high degree of uncertainty but also offer the potential for a very high return.

Internet Funds

Internet funds focus their investment on Internet companies. These funds have performed extremely well recently because of the surge in stock prices of Internet companies. Investors who want to invest in technology but do not have any insight about specific companies commonly invest in these mutual funds.

Income Funds

Income funds contain stocks (and may include bonds) that offer a steady stream of income. The stocks that are contained in an income fund usually pay high dividends.

NewsLine   CHASING FUND RETURNS CAN BE DANGEROUS

Investors who choose mutual funds because they have a high current return many find themselves losing in the long run. The best strategy is to look for steady performers and benefit from compound growth.

Is it time to jump into one of the highflying Internet funds?

Chasing the hot fund of the moment is a tricky business. Many funds that soar off the charts have been pumped up by high expectations for the stocks in the fund, even though many of them may have little or no current earnings. It is the potential for astronomical earnings in years to come that keeps investors interested in these stocks. Unless your tolerance for risk over the long term is extremely high, it's best to limit your exposure to these funds to 10% to 15% of your investment portfolio.

Hot funds, such as today's Internet funds, may well turn out to be a solid investment idea, and an investor who holds one of these funds through its inevitable ups and downs could emerge with a tidy sum after 20 to 40 years. The problem is that no one really knows which of these funds will make it big and which will crash and burn.

Chasing the fund with the highest current return is not the way to ensure you are in a fund that will be successful over the long term. These funds often attract what is known as hot money. As the stocks in the fund move up and the fund gains media attention, investors pour more and more cash into the fund. This in turn provides fund managers more money to put into those same stocks. This frenzied buying, however, reflects the market's obsession with a few stocks. It does not mean the manager has picked the best possible stocks for the future.

Another problem with chasing returns is that investors often buy a fund after it has achieved spectacular gains, which is usually the time it is about to take a breather. When the fund declines, investors become disappointed and sell their holdings so they can hunt the next hot fund....

"Historically, chasing last year's hot performer has been a good way for investors to separate themselves from their money," said Scott Schoelzel, manager of $33.9 billion Janus Twenty Fund.... "Earning consistent returns of 15% to 20% year after year is a far better way to build wealth than chasing the fund with 200% returns one year and nothing the next."

Source: Peter McKenna, "Chasing Fund Returns Can Be a Dangerous Pursuit," Investor's Business Daily, *December 10, 1999, downloaded from www.investors.com/stories/IF/1999/Dec/10/53.html.*

International Stock Funds and Global Stock Funds

International stock funds contain stocks from foreign countries. Individual investors are limited when they invest in foreign stocks because they lack information about foreign companies. Thus they commonly choose to invest in international stock funds rather than investing the money themselves, so that they can rely on the portfolio managers of the international stock funds to make the investment decisions. In addition, investors may be able to reduce their transactions costs by investing in international mutual funds, because these funds can reduce their expenses by conducting large transactions. However, the expenses incurred by international mutual funds are typically higher than those incurred by other stock mutual funds, and these expenses are passed on to shareholders.

Global stock funds are distinguished from international stock funds in that they contain foreign and U.S. stocks. These funds may be more appropriate for investors who want such a diversified portfolio. Investors in international mutual funds may already have a sufficient investment in U.S. stocks and prefer that the fund focus completely on foreign stocks.

Index Funds

A *stock index fund* is a mutual fund that is intended to mirror movements in a particular stock index. Stock index funds have become very popular in recent years, in response to strong evidence that index funds outperform managed mutual funds (in which the portfolio is not intended to mirror an index). The high performance of index funds may be explained by the following reasons. First, the transactions costs incurred by the fund are low because the fund is not actively managed. That is, any changes in the funds portfolio are made simply to track a particular index.

Second, the index fund does not require the use of several analysts and portfolio managers, because it does not require active portfolio management other than to attempt to track an existing stock index closely. The lower transactions costs and management expenses allow index funds to charge lower fees to their respective shareholders than the traditional mutual funds. This may save shareholders 1 percent or more per year.

Not only are the lower fees important to shareholders, but a comparison between index funds and managed mutual funds also suggests that most managed funds do not outperform the index funds even when the higher expenses of managed funds are ignored. This implies that managed portfolio funds do not beat the market. That is, mutual funds do not outperform the index that represents a weighted average of all stocks that qualify for a particular investment objective.

Given the strong evidence in favor of index funds, many investors have shifted their investments into index funds in recent years. Many investment companies have created index funds in response to investors demand for them. For example, Vanguard has created several index funds, including a growth stock index fund, a mid-capitalization ("mid-cap") index fund (focusing on medium-size stocks), a small-capitalization ("small-cap") index fund (focusing on small stocks), and an S&P 500 index fund. Other mutual funds also have an S&P 500 index fund. There is now more than $600 billion invested in S&P 500 index funds alone.

Each index fund attracts investors with a particular investment objective. The growth stock index fund attempts to mirror a growth stock index, which means that it is composed of growth stocks whose returns tend to be highly correlated with returns of the index. But the index fund does *not* contain the complete set of growth stocks that make up the index. (This would be too costly.)

There are also international stock index funds that attempt to mirror the movements in the stock index of a particular country or region. For example, Vanguard offers a European index fund, which attempts to mirror the European stock index that contains stocks of 15 European countries, and a Pacific index fund, which attempts to mirror an index that contains stocks of 6 countries in the Pacific Basin.

Stock Fund Quotations

Investors monitor the price movements of open-end and closed-end mutual funds by reviewing quotations reported in financial newspapers.

Price Quotations of Open-End Mutual Funds

An example of open-end mutual fund quotations as disclosed in the *Wall Street Journal* is provided in Figure 20.2. The fund family is listed in bold print. The various stock and bond mutual funds that are offered within that family are identified below the family name. A given fund family may include several different

Open-End Mutual Fund Quotations

Prices on open-end mutual funds, reported by the *Wall Street Journal.*

Source: Wall Street Journal, January 21, 2000, p. C20.

Name	NAV	Net Chg	YTD %ret	Name	NAV	Net Chg	YTD %ret
AAL Mutual A:				ShtIntFx	11.81	...	− 0.2
Balance p	12.46	−0.08	−1.1	SmMidCp	27.88	+0.04	+ 1.8
Bond p	9.32	−0.01	−0.7	Value	20.15	−0.35	− 2.7
CGrowth p	38.96	−0.43	−1.6	**Accessor Inv:**			
EqInc p	14.03	−0.14	−1.8	GrowthInv p	34.16	−0.12	− 1.9
HiYBdA	7.76	+0.01	−1.0	IntlEqInv p	20.13	+0.11	− 5.6
Intl p	14.53	+0.09	−2.7	MortSecIn p	11.88	−0.02	− 0.8
MidCap p	15.74	−0.01	+0.7	SmMidInv p	27.64	+0.04	+ 1.8
MuniBd p	10.26	−0.01	−0.8	Value	20.14	−0.35	NA
SmCap p	13.68	+0.09	+2.6	**Achievement Fds:**			
AAL Mutual B:				BalTr	14.16	−0.09	− 2.4
Balance t	12.41	−0.08	−1.2	EqTr	18.93	−0.16	− 2.7
Cgrowth p 38.12	−0.42	− 1.7		IDmuBdTr	9.83	...	− 0.7
EqInc p	14.01	−0.14	−1.9	IntTBdTr	9.91	−0.01	− 0.7
HiYbdB p	7.76	+0.01	− 1.0	MuniBd	9.22	−0.01	− 1.1
Intl p	14.25	+0.09	− 2.8	STBdTr	9.80	...	0.0
MidCap	15.29	− 0.01	+0.7	**Acorn Funds:**			
SmCap p	13.38	+0.08	+2.5	AcornInt	36.08	−0.32	+ 2.1
AARP Invst:				Acorn40	20.01	+0.09	+ 0.4
BalS&B	19.45	− 0.02	− 0.4	AcornF	18.90	+0.05	+ 2.0
BdInc	13.78	−0.01	− 1.0	Acorn20	13.89	+0.05	+ 1.4
CaGr	71.97	−0.56	− 0.8	AcornUS	17.04	+0.07	+ 1.7
DivGr	18.67	−0.07	− 1.2	**Activa:**			
DivInc	15.68	−0.03	− 1.0	Growth	11.26	−0.11	− 1.1
GiniM	14.21	−0.02	− 1.0	IntmdBd	9.75x	−0.04	− 0.9
GlblGr	21.19	+0.09	− 1.1	Intratnl	13.32	+0.10	− 6.2
GthInc	50.09	−0.09	+ 0.2	Value p	6.56	−0.06	− 0.8
HQSTBd	15.62	...	0.0	**AdsnCa p**	24.71	−0.24	− 3.1
IntIG&I	22.70	+0.13	− 4.2	**Advance Capital 1:**			
SMCoStk	17.70	−0.04	− 1.6	Balanc p	17.06	−0.06	+ 0.3
TxFbd	17.27	−0.02	− 0.7	Bond p	9.45	−0.02	− 1.1
USStkI	27.49	−0.19	− 1.5	Corner p	13.49	−0.08	− 0.4
ABN AMRO Funds:				Equity p	28.00	+0.17	+ 5.9
AsiaTCm	10.89	+0.13	− 0.3	RetInc p	9.50	−0.03	− 0.9
Bal Cm	11.81	−0.08	− 1.3	**Advantus Fds:**			
FixIncCm	9.49	−0.01	− 0.8	BondA	9.39	−0.01	− 1.1
Gwth Cm	17.14	−0.22	− 1.7	BondB p	9.42	−0.01	− 1.1
IntlEqCm	23.47	+0.08	− 6.4	CStoneA	15.37	−0.10	− 1.3
IntlFICm	9.55	+0.01	− 1.1	CStoneB p	15.19	−0.09	− 1.4
LatinAm	13.96	−0.20	− 0.1	EnterpA	22.57	+0.63	+ 6.2
SmCpGrCm	14.43	...	+ 1.9	EnterB p	21.46	+0.60	+ 6.1
TE FICm	9.78	−0.01	− 0.6	HorznA	31.15	−0.05	− 1.3
ValueCm	12.35	−0.23	− 3.1	HorznB	29.48	−0.05	− 1.4
AFBA Five Star Funds:				Idx500A p	19.17	−0.14	− 1.6
Balanced 10.76	+0.04	+ 2.3		Idx500B p	18.99	−0.14	− 1.6
Equity	13.27	+0.15	+ 2.2	IntBalA	11.97	−0.04	− 1.0
USA Gbl	15.32	−0.18	+ 5.2	IntBalB p	11.81	−0.03	− 1.0
AHA Funds:				MtgSecA	10.03	−0.01	− 0.6
Balan	12.66	−0.01	− 0.5	MtgSecB p	10.05	−0.01	− 0.6
DivrEq	21.43	−0.02	− 0.5	SpectmA	19.26	−0.02	− 0.9
Full	9.51	−0.01	− 0.7	SpectmB p	19.15	−0.02	− 1.0
Lim	10.10	...	+ 0.1	VentureA	10.69	+0.03	+ 0.1

types of mutual funds, including a growth fund, an income fund, an international stock fund, and various bond funds.

For each fund identified in the first column, the net asset value (NAV) is reported in the second column, the net change in the NAV from the previous trading day (Net Chg) is reported in the third column, and the year-to-date return (YTD %ret) is reported in the fourth column.

Price Quotations of Closed-End Funds

Price quotations of closed-end funds are listed along with those of individual stocks under the specific exchange in which they are traded. In addition, they are

FIGURE 20.3 **Closed-End Fund Quotations**

Prices on closed-end funds, reported by the *Wall Street Journal.*

Source: Wall Street Journal, January 24, 2000, p. C22.

CLOSED-END FUNDS

Friday, January 21, 2000

Closed-end funds sell a limited number of shares and invest the proceeds in securities. Unlike open-end funds, closed-ends generally do not buy their shares back from investors who wish to cash in their holdings. Instead, fund shares trade on a stock exchange. The following list, provided by Lipper, shows the ticker symbol and exchange where each fund trades. (A: American; C: Chicago; N: NYSE; O: Nasdaq; T: Toronto; z: does not trade on the exchange). The data also include the fund's most recent net asset value, share price and the percentage difference between the market price and the NAV (often called the premium or discount). For equity funds, the final column provides 52-week returns based on market prices plus dividends. For bond funds, the final column shows the past 12 months' income distributions as a percentage of the current market price. Footnotes appear after a fund's name. a: the NAV and market price are ex dividend. b: the NAV is fully diluted. c: NAV is as of Thursday's close. d: NAV is as of Wednesday's close. e: NAV assumes rights offering is fully subscribed. v: NAV is converted at the commercial Rand rate. w: Convertible Note-NAV (not market) conversion value. y: NAV and market price are in Canadian dollars. All other footnotes refer to unusual circumstances; explanations for those that appear can be found at the bottom of this list. N/A signifies that the information is not available or not applicable.

Fund Name (Symbol)	Stock Exch	NAV	Market Price	Prem /Disc	52 week Market Return
General Equity Funds					
Adams Express (ADX)	♣N	40.00	33 13/16	−15.5	38.4
Alliance All-Mkt (AMO)	N	46.99	40 11/16	−13.4	8.8
Avalon Capital (MIST)	0	17.22	17	− 1.3	3.0
Bergstrom Cap (BEM)	A	289.17	253	−12.5	55.9
Blue Chip Value Fd (BLU)	♣N	8.68	8 3/4	+ 0.8	4.3
Boulder Tot Rtn (BTF)	♣N	12.66	9 9/16	−24.5	−14.2
Brantley Capital Corp (BBDC)	0	NA	9 3/8	NA	12.8
Central Secs (CET)	A	36.55	29	−20.7	26.4
Corp Renaissance (CREN)-c	0	13.14	11 3/8	−13.4	61.1
Engex (EGX)	A	45.19	48	+ 6.2	460.6
Equus II (EQS)	♣N	15.38	10 1/16	−34.6	−11.9
Gabelli Equity Tr (GAB)	N	12.89	12 5/8	− 2.0	24.5
General American (GAM)-a	♣N	41.17	37 1/2	− 8.9	37.4
Librty AllStr Eq (USA)	♣N	13.90	11 1/16	−20.4	−1.9
Librty AllStr Gr (ASG)	♣	13.40	11	−17.9	9.9
MFS Special Value (MFV)	N	13.99	13 15/16	− 0.4	4.7
Morgan Funshares (MFUN)-c	0	7.68	6 31/32	− 9.2	−8.6
Morgan Gr Sm Cap (MGC)	♣N	16.63	14 3/16	−14.7	44.6
NAIC Growth (GRF)-c	C	13.09	NA	NA	NA
Royal Focus Trust (FUND)	0	6.01	5	−16.8	17.6
Royce Micro-Cap Tr (OTCM)	0	11.57	9 21/32	16.5	20.4
Royce Value Trust (RVT)	N	16.39	13 11/16	−16.5	10.0
Salomon SBF (SBF)	N	19.24	18 3/4	− 2.6	25.7
Source Capital (SOR)	N	50.63	49	− 3.2	13.7
Tri-Continental (TY)	♣N	31.89	26 9/16	−16.7	8.2
Zweig (ZF)	♣N	11.68	10	−14.4	3.9
Specialized Equity Funds					
ASA Limited (ASA)-c	N	24.11	18 1/4	−24.3	10.9
C&S Realty (RIF)	♣A	6.68	7 1/8	+ 6.7	−13.7
Centrl Fd Canada (CEF)-cl	♣	3.87	3 9/16	− 8.0	− 9.3
Cohen&Steers TotRet (RFI)	♣	10.96	11 5/16	+ 3.2	−10.8
Duff&Ph Util Inc (DNP)	N	9.13	8 7/8	− 2.7	−13.1
Dundee Prec Mtls (DPM.A)-cv	T	13.79	8 19/32	−37.6	− 7.0
First Financial (FF)	N	8.71	7 15/16	− 8.8	−18.3
Gabelli Gl MltiMed (GGT)	N	20.35	19 1/8	− 6.0	104.5
Gabelli Utility (GUT)	N	7.70	7 11/16	− 0.1	NS
H&Q Health Inv (HQH)	♣N	34.02	27	−20.6	91.3
H&Q Life Sci Inv (HQL)	♣	28.34	23	−18.8	92.9
INVESCO GloblHlth (GHS)	♣N	20.39	16 3/16	−20.6	2.4
J Han Bank (BTO)	♣N	8.26	7 1/4	−12.2	−19.0
LCM Internet Growth (FND)	A	14.27	12 1/2	−12.4	NS
Petroleum & Res (PEO)	♣N	41.54	34 1/2	−17.0	19.0
Seligman New tech (N/A)	z	40.20	NA	NA	NS
SthEastrn Thrift (STBF	♣0	16.93	14 1/2	−14.4	−17.2
Thermo Opprtunty (TNF)	A	10.94	9	−17.7	38.5
Income & Preferred Stock Funds					
Chartwell Div&Inc (CWF)	♣N	12.96	10 1/2	−19.0	−12.2
Delaware Gr Div (DDF)	N	12.85	11 7/16	−11.0	−25.4
Delaware Grp Gl (DGF)	N	13.98	11 11/16	−16.4	−14.0
J Han Pat Globl (PGD)	♣N	12.52	9 15/16	−20.6	−18.1
J Han Pat Pref (PPF)	♣N	11.79	10 3/16	−13.6	− 8.4
J Han Pat Prm (PDF)	♣N	9.44	7 11/16	−18.5	−15.9
J Han Pat Prm II (PDT)-a	♣N	11.28	8 15/16	−20.7	−16.0
J Han Pat Sel (DIV)	♣N	14.36	12 1/8	−15.5	−13.7
Preferred Inc Op (PFO)-a	♣N	10.69	9 5/8	− 9.9	− 7.7
Preferred Income (PFD)-a	♣N	13.57	11 15/16	−12.0	− 9.1
Putnam Divd Inc (PDI)-a	N	10.80	9 1/4	−14.4	− 6.6
Convertible Sec's. Funds					
Bancroft Conv (BCV)	♣A	26.87	21 1/4	−20.9	9.0
Castle Conv (CVF)	A	27.28	20 11/16	−24.2	0.3
Ellsworth Conv (ECF)	♣A	11.46	9	−21.5	9.7
Gabelli Conv Sec (GCV)	N	11.34	10 5/16	− 9.1	− 2.5
Lincoln Conv (LNV)-c	♣N	22.90	16 11/16	−27.1	18.5
Putnam Conv Opp (PCV)-a	N	23.93	19 1/2	−18.5	− 5.1
Putnam Hi Inc Cv (PCF)-a	N	8.30	6 15/16	−16.4	−15.8
Ren Cap G&I III (RENN)	0	12.99	10 1/8	−22.0	76.7
TCW Conv Secs (CVT)	♣N	12.12	10 9/16	−12.9	24.2
VK Conv Sec (VXS)	N	36.12	27 3/8	−24.2	37.7
World Equity Funds					
Argentina (AF)	N	16.52	12 1/8	−26.6	55.5
Asia Pacific (APB)	N	13.96	10 1/2	−24.8	65.3
Asia Tigers (GRR)	N	13.58	10 1/16	−25.9	58.9
Austria (OST)	♣N	15.54	11 15/16	−23.2	37.9
Brazil (BZF)	N	23.85	18 1/4	−23.5	100.8
Brazilian Equity (BZL)	♣N	7.77	5 15/16	−23.6	63.9
Cdn Genl Inv (CGI)-y	♣T	17.60	12	−31.8	− 4.2
Cdn Wrld Fd Ltd (CWF)-cy	♣T	7.93	5 5/16	−33.2	9.3
Central Eur Eqty (CEE)	♣N	20.88	16 5/16	−21.9	20.8

sometimes shown separately in financial newspapers. An example of quotations of closed-end funds as reported in the *Wall Street Journal* is shown in Figure 20.3. The fund name is listed in the first column, and the stock exchange on which it is listed is given in the second column. The net asset value (NAV) is in the third column, the price per share in the fourth. Note that the price differs from the net asset value. Some funds are priced at a premium above net asset value, whereas others are priced at a discount. The fifth column shows the premium or discount in the price as a percent of NAV. A fund may have a premium at one point in time (when it was subject to heavy demand by investors), and a discount at another point in time. The sixth column reports the return over the last 52 weeks.

Review Question

20–1 Explain how prices of closed-end funds are determined.

Bond Mutual Funds

bond mutual fund
Investment company that sells shares to individuals and uses the proceeds to invest in bonds.

Bond mutual funds sell shares to individuals and use the proceeds to invest in bonds. The mutual fund is essentially investing the investor's funds, and the return on this investment is channeled back to the investors. When mutual funds invest in new bonds offered in the primary market, they channel funds from investors to finance new investment by firms. They also invest in bonds by purchasing bonds that are traded in the secondary market.

Bond mutual funds enable small investors to hold diversified portfolios of bonds by pooling their small investments. In addition, they do not require any portfolio management by investors.

How Bond Mutual Funds Operate

Bond mutual funds generate interest income and attempt to achieve appreciation in the fund's net asset value. The gains to investors may also be attributed to capital gains that the mutual fund generates when selling bonds that it had previously purchased.

Bond funds incur expenses for administrative and portfolio management tasks, and those expenses are deducted from the net asset value. Thus, the expenses are passed on to the shareholders. The expense ratio (expenses divided by net asset value) is generally less for bond funds than for stock funds, because the portfolio management of bond funds requires fewer resources.

Sales Charges

Like stock funds, bond funds can be classified in terms of whether they charge a load. Load bond funds charge a commission to investors who purchase shares; no-load funds do not. Bond funds are also classified in terms of the manner in which their shares are traded. Open-end bond funds sell shares directly to investors and purchase the shares back from investors who wish to sell them. Closed-end bond funds initially sell their shares through an offering of shares, but they do not purchase back shares from investors. The shares are traded in the secondary market through a stock exchange, and their prices are determined by the forces of demand and supply.

Bond Fund Investment Objectives

Bond funds attempt to represent a particular investment objective. Investors in bonds are primarily concerned about interest rate risk, default risk, and tax implications. Thus, most bond funds can be classified according to the maturities of the bonds (which affect interest rate risk) and the type of bond issuers (which affects default risk and taxes incurred).

Maturity Classifications

Intermediate-Term Bond Funds   *Intermediate-term bond funds* invest in bonds with 5 to 10 years remaining until maturity. They are exposed to interest rate risk.

Long-Term Bond Funds   *Long-term bond funds* typically contain bonds with 15 to 30 years until maturity. The bonds in these funds normally have a higher yield to maturity than the bonds contained in intermediate-term bond funds, and they are more sensitive to interest rate movements.

Type-of-Issuer Classifications

Treasury Bond Funds   *Treasury bond funds* invest in Treasury bonds and therefore are attractive to investors who prefer to avoid default risk. However, these bonds are subject to interest rate risk.

GNMA Funds   *GNMA funds* invest in bonds issued by the Government National Mortgage Association (GNMA). There is a low degree of default risk.

Corporate Bond Funds   *Corporate bond funds* normally invest in bonds issued by corporations that are perceived to be of high quality (low default risk). Even so, the quality of the corporations can vary among corporate bond funds.

High-Yield Bond Funds *High-yield bond funds* typically invest in low-rated bonds (junk bonds) issued by corporations. These bonds tend to offer high yields and have a relatively high degree of default risk.

Municipal Bond Funds   *Municipal bond funds* invest in municipal bonds. These bond funds are attractive to investors in high tax brackets because their interest income is exempt from federal taxation.

International Bond Funds and Global Bond Funds   *International bond funds* contain bonds from foreign countries. Individual investors may not be comfortable forecasting the future direction of interest rates in the currencies in which international bonds are denominated, so they choose to rely on the expertise of the portfolio managers of international bond funds. In addition, investors may be able to reduce their transactions costs by investing in the international bond funds, because these funds can limit their expenses by executing large transactions. However, the expenses incurred by international bond funds are typically higher than expenses incurred by other bond mutual funds, and these expenses are passed on to the fund's shareholders in the form of annual expenses charged against the net asset value.

FIGURE 20.4

Mutual Fund Performance Review

Performance yardsticks on mutual funds, reported by the *Wall Street Journal*.

Source: *Wall Street Journal*, January 21, 2000, p. C23.

Performance Yardsticks

How Fund Categories Stack Up

INVESTMENT OBJECTIVE	YEAR-TO-DATE	──────ON A TOTAL RETURN BASIS──────			
		FOUR WEEKS	ONE YEAR	3 YRS (annualized)	5 YRS (annualized)
Large-Cap Growth	+ 0.59%	+ 2.31%	+ 34.13%	+ 31.66%	+ 30.36%
Large-Cap Core	− 0.84	+ 0.35	+ 18.90	+ 23.17	+ 25.08
Large-Cap Value	− 1.47	− 0.55	+ 8.62	+ 17.08	+ 22.02
Mid-Cap Growth	+ 6.35	+ 10.19	+ 80.60	+ 31.98	+ 28.93
Mid-Cap Core	+ 4.36	+ 8.03	+ 43.73	+ 21.32	+ 21.68
Mid-Cap Value	+ 0.08	+ 2.94	+ 9.85	+ 10.73	+ 15.77
Multi-Cap Growth	+ 3.21	+ 6.47	+ 55.50	+ 31.63	+ 29.49
Multi-Cap Core	− 0.17	+ 1.88	+ 20.23	+ 20.61	+ 23.26
Multi-Cap Value	− 1.52	+ 0.16	+ 4.27	+ 11.55	+ 17.63
Small-Cap Growth	+ 5.79	+ 10.39	+ 68.71	+ 25.60	+ 24.79
Small-Cap Core	+ 3.71	+ 7.95	+ 33.45	+ 13.77	+ 17.88
Small-Cap Value	+ 1.12	+ 4.79	+ 7.11	+ 7.26	+ 14.26
Equity Income	− 1.64	− 0.63	+ 2.29	+ 11.22	+ 16.83
International (non U.S.)	− 2.82	+ 0.46	+ 35.12	+ 17.37	+ 15.48
Global (includes U.S.)	− 0.61	+ 2.46	+ 33.52	+ 18.70	+ 18.80
European Region	+ 0.26	+ 2.23	+ 24.08	+ 21.15	+ 20.52
Emerging Markets	+ 3.86	+ 8.36	+ 77.37	+ 3.74	+ 6.91
Science & Technology	+ 4.14	+ 7.18	+ 106.40	+ 51.83	+ 40.55
Utility	+ 2.42	+ 3.25	+ 16.25	+ 18.89	+ 19.11
Health & Biotech	+ 10.65	+ 13.09	+ 30.07	+ 19.82	+ 23.00
Balanced	− 0.90	+ 0.03	+ 6.96	+ 12.88	+ 15.93
Short Term Bond	− 0.19	− 0.10	+ 1.93	+ 5.20	+ 5.99
Intmdt US Govt	− 0.75	− 0.69	− 2.32	+ 4.60	+ 6.14
Intmdt Inv Grade	− 0.79	− 0.72	− 1.91	+ 4.88	+ 6.69
Mortgage	− 0.71	− 0.68	+ 0.25	+ 4.78	+ 6.55
Long Term Bond	− 0.90	− 0.78	− 2.83	+ 4.46	+ 7.11
Long Term US Funds	− 0.95	− 0.88	− 4.31	+ 4.57	+ 6.57
General US Taxable	− 0.55	− 0.40	+ 1.57	+ 4.17	+ 8.02
High Yield Taxable	− 0.57	− 0.38	+ 2.07	+ 4.79	+ 8.79
General Muni Debt	− 0.81	− 0.74	− 5.64	+ 3.08	+ 5.35
Single State Muni Debt	− 0.77	− 0.66	− 5.19	+ 3.14	+ 5.34
Intmdt Muni Debt	− 0.47	− 0.30	− 2.32	+ 3.66	+ 5.32

Global bond funds differ from international bond funds in that they contain foreign and U.S. bonds. These funds are attractive to investors who want a fund that includes both U.S. bonds and global diversification.

Combinations   Investors can use bond funds to satisfy a variety of investment goals by purchasing a combination of bond funds features. For example, investors who are concerned about interest rate risk and default risk may invest in bond funds that focus on Treasury bonds with intermediate terms to maturity. Investors who expect interest rates to decline but are concerned about default risk may invest in a long-term Treasury bond fund. Investors who expect interest rates to decline and are not concerned with default risk may invest in high-yield bond funds. Investors who wish to avoid federal taxes on interest income and are concerned about interest rate risk may consider short-term municipal bond funds. They may even invest in some hybrid mutual funds that contain the type of bonds they prefer, along with stocks.

Mutual Fund Performance

The mean performance levels for several categories of bond mutual funds and stock mutual funds are regularly reported in the *Wall Street Journal,* as shown in Figure 20.4. The performance is measured in terms of return for various holding periods. Note that the performance levels vary substantially across investment objectives. Also note that those categories that experienced relatively high performance in the most recent four-week period did not necessarily perform well over the long-term period. Clearly, the performance level for any category can change over time.

Review Question

20–2   Explain the difference between the potential return and risk characteristics of a Treasury bond fund and those of a high-yield bond fund.

 ## Money Market Mutual Funds

money market mutual fund (money market fund)
Investment company that sells shares to individuals and pools the proceeds to invest in money market securities.

Money market mutual funds (also called **money market funds**) sell shares to individuals and pool the proceeds to invest in money market securities. They invest their shareholders' funds, and the return on this investment is channeled back to the investors. Shareholders can sell the shares purchased from a money market fund back to the fund.

Money market funds are not given as much attention as stock mutual funds or bond mutual funds, because they tend to generate relatively low returns. They are important to investors, however, because they provide liquidity. Most money market funds allow a limited number of checks to be written against the account.

Investment Objectives

Because money market funds invest in money market securities, their return and risk characteristics are similar to those of money market securities. All money market funds offer a high degree of liquidity, but they can vary in their potential return and risk. In general, investors distinguish among money market funds according to their maturity (which affects the interest rate risk of the fund) and the type of issuer of securities purchased by the fund (which affects the default risk and tax status of the fund).

Maturity Classifications

The short-term maturity of the assets in a money market fund limits the fund's exposure to interest rate risk, but some money market securities have less exposure to interest rate risk than others. A money market fund whose securities have

FIGURE 20.5   Money Market Fund Quotations

Yields on money market funds, reported by the *Wall Street Journal*.

Source: *Wall Street Journal*, January 20, 2000, p. C25.

MONEY MARKET MUTUAL FUNDS

The following quotations, collected by the National Association of Securities Dealers Inc., represent the average of annualized yields and dollar-weighted portfolio maturities ending Wednesday, January 19, 2000. Yields don't include capital gains or losses.

Fund	Avg. Mat.	7 Day Yield	Assets
Money Funds			
AALMny	44	5.23	355
AARP HQ	17	5.14	411
AadMileP	42	4.97	440
AadvGovP	13	4.84	75
AAdvMMPlat	42	5.06	884
ABN AMROGovl	48	4.93	96
ABN AMRO Gvt	48	5.25	443
ABN AMROInv	37	5.10	262
ABN AMRO MM	37	5.46	1067
ABN AMRO Trs	40	4.90	322
AFD ExRsv A	35	4.94	210
AFD ExResB	35	4.44	242
AFD ExResC p	35	4.69	54
AIM MMCshRes	18	4.73	926
ARKGvtA	45	5.05	153
ARK GvIn II	45	5.21	110
ARK MMIn	45	5.47	292
ARKMM A	45	5.54	538
ARKMM A	45	5.31	267
ARKUSG A	45	5.27	1
ARKUST A	82	4.81	310
ARKUST A	82	4.58	18
ARKUST C	82	4.74	125
AXPCshMgdB p	36	4.71	276
AXPCshMgtY	36	5.48	146
AXPCashMgtA	36	5.47	5511
AZMunCTins	21	2.68	80
AccUSGov	49	5.11	367
ActivaMM	62	5.35	111
ActAsGv	60	5.10	1004
ActAsMny	69	5.49	19674
AetnaAdvs	41	5.66	185
AetnaBrokCsh	41	5.21	327
Aetna Sel	41	5.66	276
59WallStTreas	52	4.76	195
59WallStMM	52	5.36	1376
FInvTrUSGvt	31	5.40	264
FInvTrUSTrs	41	5.13	73
FinSqFed	40	5.49	5067
FinSqGov	28	5.53	3069
FinSq POF	32	5.76	10437
FinSqTrsv	50	5.14	530
FinSq TOF	26	5.25	3642
FinSq MMF	36	5.74	10899
FITPrMonMktl	38	5.66	143
FinSq PMMF	5	5.69	385
FstAMGvObD	43	5.09	437
FstAmGvObY	43	5.24	814
FstAmTrObD	46	4.86	3645
FstAmGvObA p	43	4.94	447
FstAmPrObA	40	5.12	4407
FstAmPrObY	40	5.49	7268
FstAmPrObD	40	5.34	499
FstAmTrObA p	46	4.76	31
FstAmTrObY	46	5.01	1793

Fund	Avg. Mat.	7 Day Yield	Assets
FirstCshRsvIII	46	5.47	85
FtInvCs	50	5.19	162
First Muni	34	3.03	51
FstOmahaGv	48	5.35	246
First USGv	41	5.28	102
First USTrs	1	5.02	8
FirstUSTrsyIII	1	4.64	2
FrsInstMn	41	5.48	2294
FirstrMM	34	5.15	167
FsrStelTreasY	50	4.82	2193
FirstUSGov	12	4.68	169
FirstarUST	56	4.51	99
FlexInst	48	5.65	944
FlexFd	48	5.42	277
NatnsTrRstrust	43	5.23	578
NatnsTrRsDly	43	4.73	851
NatnsTrRsLiq f	43	5.18	379
NatnsTrInvA	39	4.78	974
NatnsPrInvA	39	5.23	628
NatInvCshMMkt	54	5.25	787
NatInvCshUSGov	72	5.09	641
NatnsCRL f	40	5.60	1865
NatnsCRM f	40	5.30	2544
NatnsGMM	19	4.94	15
NatnsGInB	19	5.03	71
NatnsGRMt	35	5.18	386
NatnsGRC	35	5.62	423
NatnsPrPrB	39	5.33	8
NatnsTRMt f	43	4.88	1470
NatnsTrPrB	39	4.88	14
NatwMM	23	5.30	1356
NeubCsh	29	5.11	1135
NeubGvt	66	4.60	454
NewEngCMTY	47	4.95	173
NewEngCMTB	47	5.07	24
NewEngCMTA	47	5.07	632
Newpoint Gv	50	4.96	188
Nicholas	...	5.55	145
NorthInstGovSel	22	5.40	2151
Northern	36	5.40	5680
NorthernGvSl	20	5.09	848
NorthInstDivAst	32	5.57	7172
NorthInstGovt	34	5.27	2040
NorthernUSGv	30	5.07	513
OCC CashGov	48	4.67	85
OCC CashPr	45	5.05	2534
OLDE MM	53	5.16	530
OLDE PrPl	55	5.67	2556
OLDE Prem	55	5.35	369
OneGrGov	43	5.41	3554
OneGrinstPrime	57	5.81	2999
OneGrTreCshl	22	5.00	150
OneGrUST A	53	4.61	1834
OneGrUSTSc	53	4.86	5153
OneGrTresOn	52	5.22	950
ARKTaxFr A	38	2.88	70

Fund	Avg. Mat.	7 Day Yield	Assets
AXP TaxFr	31	2.70	211
ActAsCal	34	2.12	810
ActAstTx	32	2.72	2646
AlMuni	60	2.84	218
AlxB TF	37	2.63	1303
AllMuNJ	47	2.11	238
AllMunCal	34	1.65	866
AllMuCT	43	2.16	174
AlliMuFL	23	2.23	239
AlliMMass	29	2.11	109
AllianMuVA	32	2.19	131
AllMuNY	38	2.08	669
AllianMun	32	2.25	1339
AmAAdMuM	17	2.67	25
AmC CAMu	36	2.33	230
AmC CATF	43	2.18	610
AmC FLMu	82	2.73	99
AmC TF	66	2.87	243
AmSouthTEA	55	2.74	31
AmSouthTET	55	2.84	63
ArmadaOHI	44	2.81	128
ArmadaPAA p	53	2.84	47
ArmadaPA Txl	53	2.99	74
AtlasCA	45	2.26	38
BT InvNY	37	2.36	82
BT InvTxFr	39	2.56	131
BdfdTxFr	43	2.37	135
BRMuInst	30	2.80	281
BRMuSv	30	2.50	169
BR NC	36	2.91	97
BRNJSv	61	2.57	37
BROHInstl	62	2.89	60
BROHSv	62	2.59	10
BRPASv	21	2.47	77
BRVAInst	27	2.99	57
BR PA Instl	21	2.77	488
BR PA Invest	21	2.31	154
Boston1784 TaxFr	38	2.91	1070
Bradfd Muni	45	2.58	157
CMA AZMuni	40	2.61	228
CNICATxExA p	40	1.82	552
RepNY TF Cl A	33	2.55	127
ResrvCA II	35	1.44	70
ResrvFL	19	1.77	34
ResrvMA	37	2.05	12
ResrvNJ	44	2.12	39
RsrvConn	47	2.05	68
Resrvint	34	2.12	286
ResrvNY	29	2.05	202
RshFTx	76	2.43	17
SEI InTFA	48	2.98	925
SEIInsTxFB	48	2.68	52
SEI PA A	29	2.94	31
SEI TECA A	11	2.29	13
SEITxFrA	50	2.85	802
SGCowenStTE	29	2.79	161
SSgATFA	27	2.66	310
STITxFreeTr	31	2.67	307
SAFC TF	41	2.53	77
Salomon NY	18	2.67	179
ShwbCAValu	66	2.39	1580
SchwFLMuni	60	2.76	797

Fund	Avg. Mat.	7 Day Yield	Assets
SchwNJMuni	72	2.55	223
ShwbNYValu	68	2.79	308
SchwPAMuni	52	2.65	173
SchwabNY	68	2.55	633
ShwbTE	44	2.55	6316
SchwabTxEx	44	2.76	2442
Schwb CA	66	2.19	3617
Scout TxE	16	2.71	116
ScudTFMMinst	5	3.08	158
ScudTFMMMgd	5	2.76	142
ScudCal	21	2.12	69
ScudNY	20	2.70	79
ScudTxF c	29	2.88	215
SmBarCalMM	49	2.08	2428
SmBarInstMA	47	3.09	171
SmBarMuni	42	2.60	7197
SmBarNY	42	2.47	1511
StrngMu	29	3.36	2413
TRowSumMu	45	2.86	197
TrowCA c	37	2.12	105
TRowNY c	58	2.69	113
TrowTE c	50	2.78	686
TaxFrOb SS	39	2.76	996
TxExCA	17	2.02	548
TEMony	38	3.32	276
TaxFrInstSS	43	2.74	299
TaxFrInstIv	43	2.59	1766
TnmuniSS	34	2.73	20
TSR FD TE	28	2.68	184
USAA Cal	53	2.45	424
USAA FITxF	15	2.73	123
USAATxEx	31	2.87	1878
USAA VA	26	2.76	156
VAMuniCshSS	39	2.79	235
ValLinTxE	57	2.36	14
VanKmpTF	46	2.40	33
VangNJ	64	2.86	1285
VangCA	58	2.56	2389
VangOH	63	3.07	479
VangPA	39	2.98	2032
VangNY	59	2.97	847
VangTxEx	62	3.10	7188
VictoryNY	43	2.27	71
VictoryOH	48	2.46	1039
Victory TF	45	2.52	787
VAMuniCshIS	39	2.94	55
VisnNYTF	40	2.58	184
WMCalA	51	1.83	35
WMTxEMMA A	48	3.02	30
WPG TX	43	2.76	144
WachTF	34	2.90	249
WachTFInv	34	2.50	156
WarburgP NY	50	2.71	186
WaterhsMuni	41	2.66	514
WellsFargo CA	50	2.15	2500
WFNatInstMM	46	3.00	23
WellsFargoNatl I	46	2.85	1090
WellsFargoNTFA	35	2.47	177
WilmTaxEx	27	2.81	444
ZurichMM	28	3.12	774
ZurichYWMuni	32	3.57	163

an average term to maturity of 20 days is less exposed to interest rate risk than a money market fund whose securities have an average term to maturity of 100 days. However, the money market fund with shorter-term securities is typically expected to generate a lower return.

Type-of-Issuer Classifications

Each money market fund has its own name, but most can be classified into one of three categories by type of issuer of the securities purchased by the fund.

Treasury Money Market Funds   *Treasury money market funds* invest in Treasury securities with a short term to maturity (1 year or less). Because Treasury securities are backed by the federal government, Treasury money market funds are very safe.

Municipal Money Market Funds   *Municipal money market funds* invest in municipal bonds that have a short term remaining until maturity (generally 1 year or less). These funds are attractive to investors in high tax brackets because the income they generate is exempt from federal taxes. Their before-tax return is lower than that of other money market funds, but their after-tax return may be relatively high from the perspective of an investor in a high tax bracket.

Municipal money market funds are normally viewed as safe, although it is not unheard of for municipalities to default on debt. These funds have diversified portfolios, but any defaults on the financial assets contained within the portfolios would reduce the returns to investors who purchased shares of the funds.

Other Types of Money Market Funds   Other money market funds specialize in securities not issued by the federal or municipal governments. They tend to invest in money market securities such as certificates of deposit, commercial paper, and banker's acceptances. These money market funds offer a slightly higher return than the Treasury money market funds, because they invest in securities that have a slight degree of default risk. If some of the securities in this type of money market fund default, the return generated by the fund would probably be lower than the return provided by a Treasury money market fund.

Quotations of Money Market Funds

An example of money market fund quotations as reported by the *Wall Street Journal* is shown in Figure 20.5. The name of the money market fund is given in the first column, and the average maturity of securities held by each money market fund is shown in the second column. Note how short the average maturity of securities held is for each fund. The annualized yield over the last seven days is disclosed in the third column, and the size of the fund (measured by total assets in millions of dollars) is listed in the fourth column.

Review Question

20–3   A municipal money market fund generated a before-tax return of 4 percent, compared with 5 percent for a Treasury money market fund. In spite of these returns, why would some investors prefer the results of the municipal money market fund?

Asset Allocation

asset allocation
The decision of how to divide investment funds across various classes of financial assets.

The previous two chapters discussed investing in stocks and bonds. In this chapter, investing in mutual funds has been explained. Investors must decide which of these types of investments (and other types, such as money market securities) best meet their objectives. They must also decide what *proportion* of their funds to invest in each type of financial asset. The decision of how to divide investment funds across financial assets is called **asset allocation.** Deciding how to allocate one's assets is just as important as deciding which specific instruments to purchase within any particular financial asset class.

Allocating funds across a diversified portfolio of securities within one type of financial asset class has limited benefits. The prices of most stocks are driven by general stock market conditions, so if market conditions are poor, even a very diversified portfolio of stocks will be adversely affected. The prices of bonds typically decline in response to an increase in interest rates, so even a diversified portfolio of bonds and bond funds is very susceptible to substantial losses if interest rates increase. By diversifying funds among classes of financial assets, however, investors can reduce their exposure to any one force (such as stock market conditions or interest rates).

Asset allocation is influenced by the investor's profile and by the investor's expectations.

Impact of Investor's Profile on Asset Allocation

Asset allocation is influenced by where investors are in the life cycle, as well as by the individual investor's risk tolerance.

Impact of Investor's Stage in Life

Individual investors who expect to need funds in the near future tend to allocate most of their funds to relatively safe and liquid financial assets, such as money market securities. Individual investors who are early in their career path and will not need their funds in the near future may diversify among individual stocks, individual bonds, stock mutual funds, and bond mutual funds.

Many individual investors who expect to be working for many more years invest in financial assets that have a high potential for growth, including stocks of smaller firms and mutual funds that specialize in growth stocks. Conversely, those individual investors who are retired tend to allocate much of their funds to financial assets that will generate fixed income, such as individual bonds, stock mutual funds containing high-dividend stocks, and bond mutual funds.

Impact of Investor's Degree of Risk Tolerance

Investors also vary in their degree of risk tolerance. Some investors are very conservative. They tend to invest in stocks of very large and stable firms, or in stock mutual funds that focus on these types of firms and in bond mutual funds that focus on Treasury bonds or high-grade corporate bonds. Other investors are willing to tolerate a high degree of risk and invest in small stocks, junk bonds, and derivative securities. The low level of interest rates and the high returns in the stock market during the 1996–1999 period encouraged many investors to shift their funds into various stock mutual funds. This shift reflected an increase in the degree of risk investors are willing to tolerate in order to strive for higher returns.

Impact of Investor's Expectations

The prices of each type of financial asset are driven by particular factors. Investors assess these factors when attempting to forecast the future performance of each type of financial asset. They allocate a relatively large proportion of funds to those financial assets that are expected to achieve high performance, while maintaining some level of diversification. Recall that stock prices are driven by economic growth, whereas bond prices are driven by interest rate movements. Investors who expect interest rates to rise will normally reduce or eliminate their allocation to bonds or bond mutual funds and increase their allocation to stocks or stock mutual funds.

Investors who believe that stock prices are overvalued tend to reduce their allocation to stocks. Investors who believe that stocks are overvalued and that interest rates will rise may consider reducing their allocation to stocks and bonds. They may shift most of their funds into money market securities until conditions in the stock or bond markets are more favorable.

Portfolio managers who manage mutual funds or pension funds, or work for other financial institutions also adjust their asset allocation in response to their expectations. Even though portfolio managers are assigned to manage a portfolio of just one particular type of financial asset (such as stocks or bonds), they can shift a portion of their funds to money market securities when they are expecting lower prices for the type of financial asset that they manage. In addition, the financial institution for which they work may adjust the constraints it imposes on the investment of funds by different portfolio managers.

Example ▼ Utah Insurance Company maintains a stock portfolio and a bond portfolio. Recently, the stock portfolio had a value of $100 million and the bond portfolio a value of $200 million. The company normally allocates two-thirds (67%) of its investment in financial assets to bonds, and one-third (33%) to stocks. It employs several stock portfolio managers to manage the stock portfolio and several bond portfolio managers to manage the bond portfolio. Once a week, all of the portfolio managers in the company meet to discuss general expectations in the stock market and the bond market.

During the most recent meeting, most of the portfolio managers voiced their concerns that interest rates will rise over the next year. Consequently, they decided to shift their overall asset allocation to reflect a higher proportion of stocks and a lower proportion of bonds. Thus the bond portfolio managers agreed to sell $20 million of the bond holdings and transfer the proceeds to the stock portfolio managers, who will invest the proceeds in stocks. The total assets are still $300 million, but $20 million has been shifted from the bond portfolio to the stock portfolio. Thus the bond portfolio will make up 60% of the total financial assets and the stock portfolio represents 40% of the total financial assets.

 **WHO NEEDS ASSET ALLOCATION?**

Jim Jubak, a columnist on MSN MoneyCentral, discusses how he makes asset allocation decisions for his Jubak's Picks portfolio. The rest of the article explains his system in greater detail, including how he adjusts for the risk that his forecasts may be inaccurate.

I know that I'm supposed to diversify my portfolio, but after last year, why would anyone want to buy anything other than a technology stock?

I mean just look at the numbers, America Online (AOL) was up 128% for the year as of December 14, Nokia (NOK) climbed 167%, Broadcom (BRCM) was up 239%.

I should balance my portfolio by adding Coca-Cola (KO), down 7%, Gillette (G), down 11%, Pfizer (PFE), down 19%?

And that performance difference gets even worse if I'm willing to take on more risk and buy names such as BroadVision (BVSN), up 1,053% for the year to date, or JDS Uniphase (JDSU), up 534%.

So what's the point?

That's exactly what I'm asking myself as I try to figure out what to sell...to make room for Puma Technology (PUMA) and National Semiconductor (NSM)....Even before I added those two companies, technology stocks accounted for 17 out of 24 picks—a tad more than 70% of the portfolio....

In my opinion that's too much, not because it violates any eternal formula for how to build a portfolio, and certainly

not because concentrating a portfolio is in itself a bad idea....I think technology stocks will outperform all other market sectors next year, but I could be wrong. So I'd like to hedge my bets a bit.

I don't have much use for orthodox theories of asset allocation....But I do think asset allocation has a place in investment strategy. I think of it as an insurance policy against my own fallibility. Let me show you how I apply that idea of asset allocation as insurance to a portfolio like Jubak's Picks.

In principle, deciding which stock to add and which to delete from a fully loaded portfolio is simple. I calculate a target price for the new candidate and the potential return from owning that stock. Then I compare the result to the potential return from owning every other stock in my portfolio. If it's higher than the potential return on a stock I already hold, it goes in. The stock with the lowest potential return gets sold....

Source: Jim Jubak, "Who Needs Asset Allocation?" MSN MoneyCentral, December 17, 1999, downloaded from http://moneycentral.msn.com/articles/invest/jubak/4932.asp?ID=4932.

The same asset allocation principles that apply to institutional investors who manage large portfolios also apply to the smaller portfolios of individual investors.

 Review Question

20–4 In the late 1990s, stocks performed extremely well, yet some investors shifted their asset allocations after this period by increasing their investment in bonds and reducing their investment in stocks. Explain this behavior.

TYING IT ALL TOGETHER

This chapter provided a background on mutual funds, including the operations of stock funds, bond funds, and money market funds. It also explained the factors that affect asset allocation among different types of investments. The roles of financial managers, financial markets, and investors in the asset allocation process are summarized in the Integrative Table that follows.

INTEGRATIVE TABLE

Allocating Assets to Various Investments

Role of Financial Managers	*Role of* Financial Markets	*Role of* Investors
Many of the securities that are purchased by investors are issued by firms. The asset allocation decision by investors is partially dependent on the types of securities that firms make available.	For each type of financial asset, there is a market that facilitates trading between investors. Therefore, investors can easily adjust their asset allocation by selling one type of financial asset in its market and using the proceeds to purchase another type of financial asset in its market.	Investors must decide how to distribute the money they wish to invest across individual stocks, individual bonds, stock mutual funds, bond mutual funds, and other financial assets.

LG 1 **Describe the operations of stock mutual funds, and explain how these funds are used by investors.** Stock mutual funds sell shares to investors and use the proceeds to invest in stocks for those investors. Stock mutual funds allow investors to invest in a diversified stock portfolio even if they have only a small amount of money to invest, and investors in such funds can rely on the professional expertise of stock portfolio managers. Open-end mutual funds stand ready to issue new shares upon demand by investors, and they repurchase shares that investors sell. By contrast, closed-end funds are closed to new investors, and shares held by investors can be sold on an exchange. Load mutual funds charge an initial fee to investors for investing in the fund, whereas no-load funds do not charge a fee. All funds incur administrative and management expenses that they pass on to shareholders, but some funds incur much higher expenses than others. Each stock mutual fund attempts to satisfy a particular investment objective, such as income, growth, Internet emphasis, or investment in international stocks.

LG 2 **Describe the operations of bond mutual funds, and explain how these funds are used by investors.** Bond mutual funds sell shares to investors and use the proceeds to invest in bonds for those investors. They enable even small investors to invest in a diversified bond portfolio, and they offer the professional expertise of bond portfolio managers. Like stock mutual funds, bond mutual funds are classified according to whether

there is an initial fee (load versus no-load) and are also distinguished as either open-end or closed-end. Each bond mutual fund attempts to satisfy a particular investment objective that reflects the degree of interest rate risk and the degree of default risk that investors are willing to tolerate.

LG 3 **Describe the operations of money market mutual funds, and explain how these funds are used by investors.** Money market mutual funds sell shares to investors and use the proceeds to invest in money market securities. Although money market funds provide relatively low returns (compared to stock and bond mutual funds), they offer liquidity. Thus, most investors maintain a money market fund for liquidity while investing additional money in other investments. Money market funds are distinguished by the average maturity of their securities holdings (which affects interest rate risk) and by the type of issuer of the securities they purchased (which affects the default risk of the fund's portfolio).

LG 4 **Explain the meaning of asset allocation and the factors that influence a particular investor's asset allocation decision.** An investor's asset allocation decision involves determining what proportion of funds should be invested in each type of financial asset. This decision is affected by the investor's profile (stage in life and willingness to tolerate risk) and by the investor's expectations of future performance of different types of financial assets.

(Solutions in Appendix B)

SELF-TEST EXERCISES

  ST 20–1   **Mutual fund pricing and performance**   Tom Davis has just seen an advertisement for Triplett Fund, a mutual fund he purchased 1 year ago. The ad cites 1-year total return on the fund as 52.49%. At the time that Tom bought the shares, he paid NAV of $11.225 plus a front-end sales load of 4%. During the year, he received dividends of $.986 per share. The fund's NAV as of the ad date was $16.131.

a. How much per share did Tom pay for shares of Triplett Fund?
b. On the basis of his purchase price, what is his 1-year total return on the investment?
c. Calculate the fund's 1-year total return on the basis of its net asset value.
d. Explain to Tom why his return differs from the fund's advertised return.

  ST 20–2   **Asset allocation in changing conditions**   The Investment Management Commission for a large western state's Employee Pension Fund meets with its investment managers once a month. At that meeting, investment results are reviewed, the outlook for interest rates and the economy is discussed, and investment policy decisions are made. Investment policy decisions are reflected in the overall asset allocations for the pension fund. For the last year the allocation has been 70% stock, 30% bonds. The monthly meeting is set for this morning.

a. At the meeting, several of the fund advisers express concern that economic expansion in the United States is slowing. One even states the conviction that a recession (two quarters of negative economic growth and rising unemployment) is possible before the end of the year. What implications would these views have for the current asset allocation?
b. At that same meeting, data is presented that supports a conclusion that interest rates are likely to fall in the coming months. What implications would this have for the current asset allocation?
c. What asset allocation do you think the commission should adopt? Support your recommendation on the basis of your answers to parts **a** and **b**.

EXERCISES

20–1   **Net asset value and price for open-ended funds**   Hexagon Fund, a stock mutual fund, gathered the following information on fund performance on Monday, May 12. During the day the fund received dividends totaling $38,400.00 from stocks held. The market value of stocks held at the end of the day was $7,890,000. The fund had margin debt of $2,520,000. It paid out dividends of $1,354,000. At the end of the day there were 1,764,233 shares.

a. Calculate the NAV per share.
b. If the fund charges a 4% front-end load based on the net asset value of the shares, at what price per share did it end the day?
c. If an investor were to have liquidated (sold back) shares of this front-end-load fund on May 12, what price would have been received for them?

20–2   **Price versus NAV for closed-end funds**   Figure 20.3 shows quotes for a number of closed-end mutual funds. Scan the premium/discount column for those selling at a premium to NAV. Then check out the 52-week market return for those funds.

a. Do the majority of funds sell at a discount, at a premium, or at a value equal to their NAV?

b. Judging solely on the basis of the 52-week market returns found in Figure 20.3, what is your assessment of the potential for market return of a fund selling at a premium to its NAV?

c. What were the worst and the best 52-week market returns listed? What premium or discount to NAV was listed for these funds?

d. Judging solely on the basis of the information found in Figure 20.3, does there seem to be a clear connection between premium or discount to NAV and 52-week market return?

e. What has research suggested about the potential for returns of an investment in closed-end funds priced at a discount to NAV?

  20–3   **Front-end-load funds**   Valerie Rickert purchased $4,000 of Geo Fund, a global stock fund with a 5% front-end load, on May 3, 2000. On that day the fund closed at a net asset value of $11.8975 per share.

a. What price per share did Valerie pay?

b. Assuming that she will purchase full and fractional shares, how many shares did Valerie purchase?

c. What is the total of her sales load? What is that as a percent of the total funds she invested?

20–4   **Stock index funds and performance**   Index funds are popular ways to invest, because they offer the potential of tracking index performance when many non-index funds do not perform as well as the indexes. However, even the best index funds often are a percentage point or two below the performance of the index they seek to mirror. Give two different reasons why this might be true.

 20–5   **Fund price and performance quotes**   Use Figure 20.2 to locate as many funds with " growth" in the title as you can. Note that growth is abbreviated "gr" in some of the listings.

a. Describe what characteristics make a fund a growth fund as opposed to an income fund or a capital appreciation fund.

b. List the names, prices, and year-to-date percentage return for several of the funds that you found. How would you evaluate the performance of these funds if these quotes were published at the end of January? How would you evaluate them if these were quotes published in August?

c. If you ignore differences in the talent or luck of the fund managers, how else might you explain why the performance varies among the funds that you listed in part **b**?

20–6   **Investor concerns and bond fund objectives**   Bond funds generally are designed to generate interest income, though gains are possible if bonds can be sold for more than they were purchased for. The combination of the two (interest and gains) provides the yield for investors.

a. What types of bond funds might be chosen by an investor who wishes to maximize yield without regard to risk factors?

b. If an investor wished to balance yield against a concern for interest rate risk, what limiting factor might she or he use in choosing among funds? Explain why.

c. If an investor wished to balance yield against a concern for default risk, what types of funds might be eliminated? What types of funds might be good choices?

d. What type of bond fund is attractive to investors in high tax brackets?

LG2 20–7 Global and international bond funds Geographic diversification appeals to bond investors, but many are not comfortable investing in foreign bonds on their own. Instead, they invest in international and global bond funds.

a. Explain the difference between international and global bond funds.

b. How are the expense ratios of these bond funds different from expense ratios for other bond funds?

c. Besides interest rate risk, default risk, and taxation factors, what additional risk factor may play a bigger part in these funds than in other types of bond funds?

LG1 LG2 20–8 Mutual fund performance Use Figure 20.4 to answer the following:

a. List the best performer in each time category.

b. List the worst performer in each time category.

c. Use the figures listed for European Region funds to figure out what a $10,000 investment would now be worth if invested (1) at the beginning of the year, (2) 4 weeks ago, (3) 1 year ago, (4) 3 years ago, and (5) 5 years ago. Note that the returns for the 3-year and 5-year time categories are annualized.

LG3 20–9 Money market yields and taxation The interest income of municipal money market funds is not taxed by the federal government. Interest on other types of money market funds is taxed. Given an interest yield of 4.5% on a municipal money market fund and one of 5.5% on a taxable money market fund, figure the after-tax yield on each for investors in the following marginal income tax brackets:

a. 15%

b. 28%

c. 31%

d. 36%

LG3 20–10 Money market mutual funds Using data from Figure 20.5 (at least 30 quotes), make up a graph of "term structure of money market interest rates" (7-day yield vs. average maturity), putting the yield on the vertical axis and maturity on the horizontal.

a. What visible relationship is illustrated by the general direction of the overall plotted pairs of maturity and yield?

b. How could the plots that do not fit the general pattern be explained? What factors would cause a money market fund to have an unusually high or low yield for its maturity?

LG4 20–11 Asset allocation and life stage For each of the following investors, recommend appropriate asset allocations. Explain why your recommendations are appropriate.

a. Amy Meyer is a 20-year-old senior at her state university. She has just received a financial grant of $6,000 to be used for tuition and books for the year. She will not need to spend it for another 3 months.

b. Chad Goings is 66 years old. He retired from his long-time accounting position last year. He and his wife are entirely dependent on Social Security and his retirement savings to cover their living expenses.

c. Anne and David Smith, 30-year-old professionals, have started college savings funds for their two young children and are wondering how to allocate the money in them.

20–12   **Risk tolerance, expectations and asset allocation**   Describe likely asset allocation for the following investors. Explain why you chose those allocations. Ignore
life stage considerations for the purposes of this exercise.

    a. Greg Johnson has very high risk tolerance. He expects interest rates to fall
significantly in the next year, and he is confident that the economy will continue to grow.

    b. Sally Jennings has moderate to low risk tolerance. She expects continued eco-
nomic growth but believes that interest rates are likely to rise in the next
year.

    c. Bob Kilpatrick has moderate to high risk tolerance. He expects economic
growth to slow in the coming year and believes that interest rates will fall.

 20–13   **Asset allocation**   Marian Collins inherited $600,000 from her great aunt. She
has little experience in constructing a portfolio, so she has come to you for
advice. On the basis of the following profile, evaluate her life stage, risk tolerance, and expectations. Recommend an asset allocation for her and explain it to
her.

    Marian is a 43-year-old single mother, employed as a teacher in the public
schools. She expects to continue working until she is 60. She has three
children, ages 16, 12, and 10, whom she would like to help with college
expenses (she has no previous college savings). Other than that, she has
no immediate income needs but would not mind having a little extra cash.
She would like to save toward what she calls a "glorious retirement." Her
risk tolerance is moderate. Marian is not sophisticated about economic
matters, so she defers to your opinion on interest rates and economic
growth. You think that interest rates probably will not change much in
the coming year and that the economy will exhibit strong growth.

web exercises   [Search]

Go to web site **www.vanguard.com**. Click on **Education, Planning, & Advice**. Under **Vanguard
University**, click on **Course 2...Introduction to Mutual Funds**.
1. Under the Lesson Directory, according to Vanguard what are the four types of mutual
funds?
Click **Benefits and Drawbacks of Mutual Funds**.
2. According to Vanguard, what are the benefits of owning mutual funds? What are the drawbacks?
Click **Back** on your browser tool bar. Click on **Defining Mutual Fund Costs**.
3. What are the three types of loads? Define each and specify the percentage cost of each.

web exercises | Search

MORNINGSTAR.com

Go to web site www.morningstar.com. Enter **FUND**, which is the stock symbol for Royce Focus, a general equity fund.

1. In its ratings, how many stars does Morningstar give this fund? In which of Morningstar's categories is it?

2. What is this fund's market return for YTD?

3. How are the assets allocated in this fund? What are the Top 3 Stock Sectors and their percentages?

4. What are the Top 5 Holdings of this fund, and what is each holding's percentage of the net assets?

5. Repeat Questions 1 through 4 using **PDI**, the symbol for the Putnam Dividend Income fund.

6. Compare the two funds. Does it make sense to compare the funds?

For additional practice with concepts from this chapter, visit
http://www.awl.com/gitman_madura

Derivative Securities

LEARNING GOALS

LG1 Explain how call options are used by investors.

LG2 Explain how put options are used by investors.

LG3 Explain how financial futures are used by investors.

Background

derivative securities
Securities that are neither debt nor equity and whose values are derived from the values of other, related securities.

In recent years, derivative securities such as stock options and financial futures contracts have become very popular with investors. **Derivative securities** are securities whose values are derived from the values of other, related securities. Derivatives are neither debt nor equity but derive their characteristics from underlying financial assets. They are used by investors to capitalize on expected changes in the values of underlying financial assets.

options
Contracts that give their holders the opportunity to purchase or sell specified assets (typically stock) under specified conditions.

Two of the most popular types of derivative securities are options and financial futures. Options are discussed next, and financial futures are discussed later in this chapter. **Options** are contracts that give their holders the opportunity to purchase or sell stock a specified asset (typically stock) under specified conditions. They are classified as call options and put options, which are described in detail shortly. Options are traded at exchanges, such as the Chicago Board of Options Exchange. Each exchange facilitates the trading of options by ensuring that buyers and sellers of options fulfill their obligations, but it does not take positions in options. Contracts on financial futures, discussed later in this chapter, are agreements between two parties for one to sell, and the other to buy, a specified financial instrument on a specified future date.

Call Options

call option (on stock)
A contract that provides the right to purchase a specified number of shares of stock (typically 100) at a specified price by a specified date.

A **call option** on a stock provides the right to purchase 100 shares of a specified stock at a specified price, called the **exercise price** or **strike price,** by a specified date (the *expiration date*). The owner of a call option can "exercise" the option by buying the specified stock at the exercise price. The option holder does not *have to* exercise the option but can let it expire instead if the price of the underlying stock remains below the exercise price.

exercise (strike) price
The price at which the holder of an option can exercise the option.

Executing Call Option Transactions

option premium
The price of an option.

Investors purchase call options in a manner similar to purchasing stocks. They call their brokers or communicate through an online brokerage service to place an order. The order is then communicated to a trading floor, where option floor traders on an exchange execute the order. The price of the call option is called an **option premium,** and it is determined by the number of participants who wish to buy or sell the particular call option. Once the order is executed on the trading floor of the exchange, the brokerage firm informs the investor. The brokerage firm charges the investor a commission for executing the transaction.

American-Style versus European-Style Options

American-style call options
Call options that can be exercised any time prior to the expiration date.

European-style options
Call options that can be exercised only on the expiration date.

American-style call options allow for exercise throughout the life of the option, which enables investors to exercise the option any time prior to the expiration date. Conversely, **European-style call options** can be exercised only on the expiration date. Investors can obtain American-style or European-style call options from U.S. exchanges, although American-style options are more popular.

FIGURE 21.1

Stock Option Quotations

Data on stock options, reported by the *Wall Street Journal.*

Source: Wall Street Journal, January 21, 2000, p. C13.

Option	Strike	Exp.	—Call— Vol.	—Call— Last	—Put— Vol.	—Put— Last
FordMot	55	Mar	657	1½	10	4¾
51⅞	55	Jun	547	3	30	6
Fox Ent	20	Jan	1050	3	...	...
23	20	Apr	1050	4⅛	...	...
FGoldmn	7½	Feb	1038	1 5/16	100	¾
FruitL	5	May	501	5/16	40	2 15/16
G T E	70	Jan	640	⅜	289	1
Galileo	30	Jan	1370	1/16	...	...
Gap	45	Feb	15	3⅞	450	2 3/16
Gateway	55	Feb	2143	8⅝	62	2⅛
62 11/16	60	Jan	2449	2 9/16	1936	1 7/16
62 11/16	65	Jan	1788	¾	1400	4¼
62 11/16	70	Jan	818	5/16	147	7¼
62 11/16	70	Feb	268	2 1/16	1086	9¼
62 11/16	90	Jan	...	...	1001	26¾
Gen El	135	Jan	182	12	1085	1/16
146	140	Jan	1001	7	833	⅛
146	140	Mar	62	12¾	621	4⅞
146	145	Jan	1947	2½	1791	⅝
146	145	Feb	619	7¼	285	5
146	150	Jan	4396	5/16	1034	3½
146	155	Jan	552	1/16	42	10
146	155	Feb	2642	2⅞	60	10⅛
146	170	Mar	836	1⅝	...	...
GMagic	5	Feb	762	2½	85	9/16
6 15/16	7½	Feb	545	1	280	1 11/16
GenMotr	80	Feb	589	5⅛	108	2¾
GaPcGP	45	Feb	1010	1 7/16	...	...
42⅞	45	Jul	3	4⅜	3025	5⅝
Gillet	35	Feb	67	4⅛	1071	11/16
38 11/16	40	Jan	401	⅛	3549	1¼
38 11/16	40	Feb	133	1 7/16	5604	2½
38 11/16	40	Mar	862	2 1/16	52	3

Quotations of Options

An example of stock option quotations as reported in the *Wall Street Journal* is shown in Figure 21.1. The underlying stock is identified in bold print. The strike (exercise) price is in the second column, and the expiration date is listed in the third column. For call option contracts with that exercise price and expiration date, the volume of contracts is reported in the fourth column, and the latest ("last") price (or premium) of the option is shown in the fifth column. Information on put options is reported in the last two columns.

There are normally several different options for a particular stock, providing investors with a variety of exercise prices and expiration dates. Some investors may prefer call options with high exercise prices, because they can purchase them at a relatively low premium. However, these options are cheap because their underlying stocks are priced much lower than the exercise price, and hence they are less likely to be exercised.

in-the-money
Situation in which the prevailing stock price a call option's exercise price (or the prevailing stock price below a put option's exercise price).

at-the-money
Situation in which the prevailing stock price is equal to an option's exercise price.

out-of-the money
Situation in which the prevailing stock price exceeds a call option's exercise price (or the prevailing stock price is below a put option's exercise price).

Classifying Call Options

A call option is known as **in-the-money** when the prevailing stock price is above the exercise price, which means the price is at a level where the option may possibly be exercised. A call option is **at-the-money** when the prevailing stock price is equal to the option's exercise price. A call option is **out-of-the-money** when the prevailing stock price is below the option's exercise price.

TABLE 21.1   Classifying a Call Option

Call Option	Exercise Price	As of September 1, When the Stock Price Is $85	As of November 13, When the Stock Price Is $88
1	$85	At-the-money	In-the-money
2	88	Out-of-the-money	At-the-money
3	90	Out-of-the-money	Out-of-the-money

Example ▼   Consider three call options that exist for Starship stock, which differ only in their exercise price. Table 21.1 classifies the three call options in terms of their exercise price relative to the prevailing stock price. Note that the classification can change over time in response to a change in the stock price. **▲**

Just as there are call options with various exercise prices for a given stock, there are also call options with various expiration dates. For example, a call option may be available for four different expiration dates over the next year, and for each expiration date there may be options for five different exercise prices available. In this case, investors can choose among 20 different call options for a single firm, so they can select the exercise price and expiration date that they prefer.

Speculating with Call Options

Call options are purchased by investors who expect the price of the underlying stock to rise. An investor in the call option on a specific stock pays the option premium to purchase it. That investor then becomes the owner of a call option and can purchase the stock represented by the option for the exercise price at any time up until the expiration date. The benefit of owning a call option is that the investor has locked in the price to be paid for the stock even if the stock price rises. Investors can then sell the stock in the secondary market at the prevailing market price.

Example ▼   Bill Warden purchased a call option on Flight stock for $4 per share, with an exercise price of $60 per share. He plans to exercise his call option at the expiration date if the stock price at that time is above $60. He plans to sell immediately the stock he receives from exercising his call option. Bill wants to determine what his profit per share would be under various possible outcomes for the price of Flight stock. He first lists the possible price outcomes (as shown in the first column of Table 21.2) and then determines the net profit associated with each outcome.

This analysis can be extended by creating a so-called contingency graph that shows the profit per share for numerous possible outcomes for the price of Flight stock. A contingency graph is provided in Figure 21.2 for the call option that Bill purchased. As shown in the figure, the most money that Bill can lose is $4 per share (or $400 for 100 shares), which is the premium paid for the option. This result will occur if the stock price remains below $60.

TABLE 21.2	Possible Outcomes of Investing in a Call Option		
Possible Price of Flight Stock at Expiration Date	Premium Paid	Amount Received from Exercising Option	Profit Share from Investing in Call Option
$54	$4	Option not exercised	−$4
61	4	$ 1	−3
64	4	4	0
66	4	6	2
70	4	10	6

At any price above $60 but below $64 per share, Bill will exercise the call option but will incur a loss. For example, at the price of $61, Bill can exercise the option by purchasing the stock at $60 and then selling the stock at $61. But taking into account both this gain of $1 per share and the premium Bill paid of $4 per share, Bill will lose $3 per share on his investment.

At a price of $64, Bill will break even. The gain from selling the stock at $4 above the exercise price offsets the premium paid for the call option. At any price above $64, Bill will earn a profit from the call option.

Return from Speculating with Call Options

When we assess the potential profits or losses on a per-share basis, it may appear that call options have low potential return and risk. However, when we consider the small investment (the premium) to purchase call options, the gains or losses as a percentage of the investment can be very large. The return from investing in

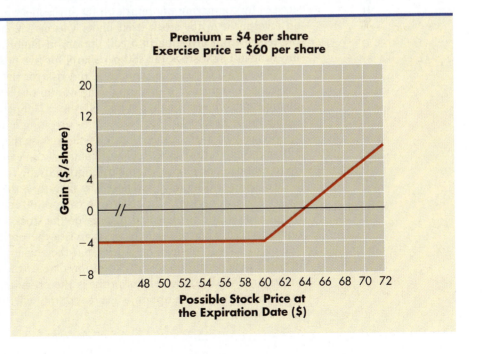

FIGURE 21.2

Contingency Graph for Purchase of a Call Option on Flight Stock

TABLE 21.3	Comparison of Returns from Investing in a Call Option with Returns from Investing in the Underlying Stock

Possible Price of Flight Stock at Expiration Date	Return from Investing in the Call Option	Return from Investing in the Stock Itself
$54	−100%	−10%
61	−75%	1.67%
64	0%	6.67%
66	50%	10%
70	150%	16.67%

a call option can be measured as the dollar amount of profit (after subtracting the premium paid) divided by the initial investment (which is equal to the premium paid). Assuming that Bill exercises his call option and then sells his newly purchased Flight stock for $66, the return on his option can be calculated as follows:

$$\text{Return on option} = \frac{\text{Profit from option}}{\text{Premium paid}} \tag{21.1}$$

$$= \frac{\$2}{\$4}$$

$$= 50\%$$

Investment in a call option can result in a much higher return than investing in the underlying stock, but it can also result in a larger percentage loss. This can be seen by comparing the return on the investment in a call option with that on an investment in the stock itself under various scenarios. Table 21.3 compares the return from investing in a call option on Flight stock with the return from investing in Flight stock (at $60 per share) for five possible price outcomes.

Note the difference in the return and risk for the two methods of investing. The range of returns for investing in an option of Flight stock (based on the five possible outcomes of Flight's stock) is from −100 percent to +150%, compared with a range from −10% to 16.67% for investing in the stock itself.

So far, we have assumed that Bill will exercise the call option (if he does so at all) on the expiration date. Recognize that Bill can exercise the option at any time up to that date, or he can sell the call option itself.

For every call option purchased by investors, there is a seller (also called a *writer* of a call option). The seller of a call option receives the premium paid by the purchaser and is obligated to provide the stock to the purchaser of the call option if and when the purchaser exercises the option. Investors are typically willing to sell call options on stocks that they believe are unlikely to appreciate over the time period up to the expiration date. If the option is not exercised by the expiration date, the seller's profit is the premium received from selling the call option. Even if the option is exercised, the seller of the call option may still earn a profit.

TABLE 21.4	Possible Outcomes for a Seller of a Call Option		
Possible Price of Flight Stock at Expiration Date	Premium Received by Seller of Option	Difference Between Amount Received and Amount Paid for Stock When Call Option Is Exercised	Profit
$54	$4	Option not exercised	$ 4
61	4	− $1	3
64	4	− 4	0
66	4	− 6	−2
70	4	− 10	−6

Example ▼ Assume that the call option purchased by Bill Warden was written (sold) by Alice Dawning. Alice plans to purchase the stock in the market if and when the call option is exercised. The profits to Alice under the five possible stock-price outcomes that were assessed for Bill are shown in Table 21.4.

This analysis can be extended by creating a contingency graph that shows Alice's profit per share for various stock-price outcomes, as shown in Figure 21.3. Ignoring the commissions paid, the profit to Alice from selling the call option is equal to Bill's loss from purchasing the call option, and any loss to Alice is equal to Bill's profit. ▲

FIGURE 21.3

Contingency Graph for Sale of a Call Option on Flight Stock

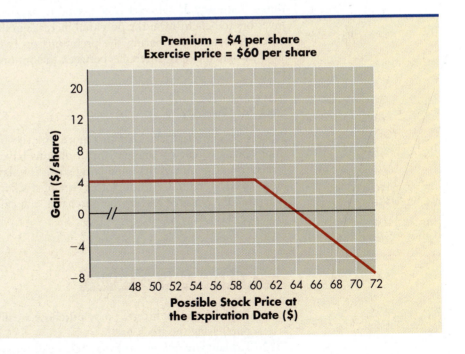

Premium = $4 per share
Exercise price = $60 per share

Gain ($/share)

Possible Stock Price at the Expiration Date ($)

Factors That Affect the Call Option Premium

The premium of a call option is influenced by the number of participants who are willing to purchase the option relative to the number of participants who are willing to sell the call option (demand and supply). The premium is primarily influenced by three factors, which we will discuss next.

Stock Price Relative to Exercise Price

The higher the stock price relative to the exercise price specified in the call option, the more desirable the call option. A lower stock price decreases the likelihood that the stock option will be exercised and makes the stock option less desirable. This relationship can be confirmed by reviewing call option premiums quoted for the same firm and the same expiration date, but for different exercise prices.

The level of the stock price relative to the exercise price is the most important factor in explaining why the premium of a particular call option changes over time. Because the exercise price of a call option does not change, the main force that causes a change in the premium of a particular call option is the change in the price of the underlying stock. As the stock price rises relative to the exercise price specified in the option, the call option becomes more desirable. Thus, demand for the option increases, which forces the option premium to increase. Conversely, a lower stock price makes the stock option less desirable. The demand for the call option decreases and forces the option's premium to decrease.

Time to Expiration

Call options with longer time periods to expiration have higher premiums, other things being equal. A longer time period to expiration allows more time for the investors to benefit from the potential increase in the price of the stock. This can be confirmed by comparing the premiums on two stock options on the same stock, where the only difference between the options is the time period to expiration.

Stock Price Volatility

Stock options on stocks that are more volatile have higher premiums, other things being equal. Purchasers of call options have more potential to earn high returns on an option if the underlying stock is volatile, because such a stock has more upside potential. Although this type of stock may also have much downside potential, the possible loss by the purchaser of a call option is limited to the premium paid for the option.

? Review Questions

21-1 Explain why an investor may purchase a call option on a stock instead of purchasing the stock itself.
21-2 Explain why an investor may sell a call option on a stock.

 **Put Options**

put option (on stock)
A contract that provides the right to sell a specified number of shares of a stock (typically 100) at a specified price by a specified date.

A **put option** on a stock provides the right to sell 100 shares of a specified stock at a specified price (called the *exercise* or *strike price*) by a specified date (*expiration date*). Like call options, put options can be purchased on an exchange and can be sold or exercised any time up to the expiration date.

Quotations of Put Options

Put option quotations are disclosed on the same table as call option quotations in the financial news, as shown in the option quotations from the *Wall Street Journal* in Figure 21.1. The sixth column provides the volume of option contracts traded, and the seventh column reports the closing ("last") premium for a put option.

There are normally several different options for a particular stock, providing investors with a variety of exercise prices. Some investors may prefer put options with low exercise prices, because they can purchase them at a relatively low premium. However, these options are cheap because their underlying stocks are priced much higher than the exercise price, and hence they are less likely to be exercised.

Classifying Put Options

A put option is *in-the-money* when the prevailing stock price is below the exercise price, which means the price is at a level where the option may possibly be exercised. A put option is *at-the-money* when the prevailing stock price is equal to the put option's exercise price. A put option is *out-of-the-money* when the prevailing stock price is above the option's exercise price.

Example ▼ Consider three put options that exist for Laser stock, which differ only in their exercise price. Table 21.5 classifies the three put options in terms of their exercise price relative to the prevailing stock price. Note that the classification can change over time in response to a change in the stock price.
▲

Just as there are put options with various exercise prices for a given stock, there are also put options with various expiration dates. Thus, investors who wish to purchase a put option on a stock typically have several different choices and can select an option that fits their desired exercise price and expiration date.

TABLE 21.5	**Classifying Put Options**		
Put Option	Exercise Price	As of February 5, When the Stock Price is $49	As of April 22, When the Stock Price is $45
1	$45	Out-of-the-money	At-the-money
2	48	Out-of-the-money	In-the-money
3	50	In-the-money	In-the-money

NewsLine   THE MARKET TURNS MY GREAT INVESTMENT TO TOAST

Investing in put options is a risky business, as this investment columnist for *Kiplinger's Personal Finance* magazine learned. (Let it be said, however, that investing in options doesn't always turn out this way. If it did, the market for options would soon dry up.)

It's December [1998]. Stocks are resuming their upward move into record bull territory but I'm not cheering on the stampede. In fact, I want the entire stock market to crater.

This is because three years back I decided the market was due for a fall. Standard & Poor's index of 500 blue-chip stocks stood at nearly 640—about a 40% hike in little more than a year. I couldn't see the market sustaining that kind of pace for much longer.

So what did I do? Being the hip, savvy, cutting-edge investor that I am, I bought puts, the options investors buy when they think a stock is headed down. Rather than a single stock, though, I bet on the S&P 500 index. I'd make oodles while the stocks dropped like a set of loose false teeth.

The options cost me $4,000 plus an $81 commission. They were written to make me money if the S&P 500 fell below 650—and they were good through 1998. I was confident something awful would happen to stocks by then.

Tick-Tock   The stock market disagrees with me, and the higher the market climbs, the less my puts are worth. By December of the first year, 1996, the bull market is knock-

ing my $4,000 puts down to $2,375. I do not sell. Contrarians like me shouldn't panic and get shaken out.

Nevertheless, something is clearly wrong. In February 1997, with the bulls in charge on Wall Street, my put options are worth $2,000....By last May they have settled into a $125 rut....My put options are by now an embarrassment....

In late November I capitulate. The S&P 500 stands at a record 1188. It would have to almost break in half in December for my 650s to be in the money.

Humbled, I call my discount brokerage to discuss selling the puts....Don't sell the options, he cautions....Avoid a commission; let the options expire at year-end.

Aside from the disappointment of losing the whole $4,000, the only thing I have learned from put index options is that it's no fun to root against the whole stock market....From here, puts look like a mostly no-win proposition. All I'll get for mine is a tax write-off.

Source: William Giese, "The Market Turns My Great Investment to Toast," Kiplinger's Personal Finance, *February 1999.*

Speculating with Put Options

Put options are purchased by investors who expect the underlying stock price to decrease. The benefit of owning a put option is that the investor has locked in the price at which the stock can be sold even if the stock price declines. Purchasers of a put option who do not own the underlying stock represented by a put option purchase the stock just before they exercise the option.

Example ▼   Emma Rivers purchased a put option on Zector stock for $3 per share, with an exercise price of $40 per share. She plans to exercise her put option at the expiration date if the stock price at that time is below $40. She plans to purchase the stock just before exercising her put option. Emma wants to determine what her profit per share would be under various possible outcomes for the price of Zector stock. She first lists the possible price outcomes (as shown in the first column of Table 21.6) and then determines the net profit associated with each outcome.

This analysis can be extended by creating a contingency graph that shows the profit per share for numerous possible outcomes for the price of Zector stock, as shown in Figure 21.4. The contingency graph shows that the most money Emma can lose is $3 per share (or $300 for 100 shares), which is the premium she paid for the put option. This result will occur if the stock price remains above $40.

TABLE 21.6	Possible Outcomes of Investing in a Put Option		
Possible Price of Zector Stock at Expiration Date	Premium Paid	Amount Received from Exercising Put Option	Profit Share from Investing in Put Option
$32	$3	$8	$5
34	3	6	3
36	3	4	1
39	3	1	−2
45	3	Option not exercised	−3

At any price below $40 but above $37 per share, Emma will exercise the put option but will incur a loss. For example, at a price of $39, Emma can purchase the stock at $39 and exercise the option by selling the stock at $40. But taking into account both this gain of $1 per share and the premium Emma paid of $3 per share, Emma will lose $2 per share on her investment.

At a price of $37, Emma will break even. The gain from buying the stock at $3 below the exercise price offsets the premium paid for the call option. At any price below $37, Emma will earn a profit from the put option.

For every put option purchased by investors, there is a seller (the *writer* of the put option). The writer of a put option receives the premium paid by the purchaser and is obligated to receive the stock from the purchaser of the put option if and when the purchaser exercises the option. Investors are typically willing to sell put options on stocks that they believe are unlikely to weaken over the term

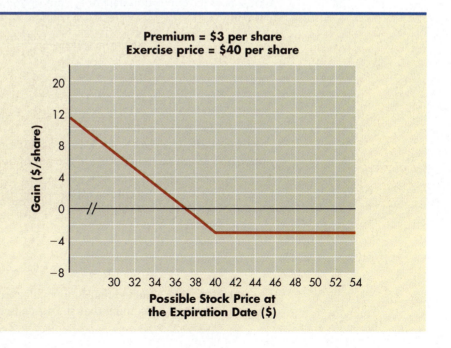

FIGURE 21.4

Contingency Graph for Put Option on Zector Stock

Premium = $3 per share
Exercise price = $40 per share

Gain ($/share)

Possible Stock Price at the Expiration Date ($)

TABLE 21.7	Possible Outcomes of Selling a Put Option		
Possible Price of Zector Stock at Expiration Date	Premium Received from Selling Put Option	Excess Amount Paid If Put Option Is Exercised	Profit Share from Selling a Put Option
$32	$3	$8	−$5
34	3	6	−3
36	3	4	−1
39	3	1	2
45	3	Option not exercised	3

up to the expiration date. If the option is not exercised by the expiration date, the seller's profit is the premium received from selling the put option. Even if the option is exercised, the seller of the put option may still earn a profit.

Example ▼

Assume that the put option on Zector stock purchased by Emma Rivers was written (sold) by Julie Souder. Julie plans to sell the stock in the market if and when the put option is exercised. The profits to Julie under the five possible stock-price outcomes that were assessed for Emma are shown in Table 21.7.

Note that the profit to Julie from selling the put option is equal to Emma's loss from purchasing the put option, and any loss to Julie is equal to Emma's profit. **▲**

Return from Speculating with Put Options

The return from investing in a put option can be determined in the same manner as the return from investing in a call option. For example, if Zector's stock price is $34 as of the expiration date of the put option, the return from investing in the put option is

$$\text{Return on option} = \frac{\text{Profit from option}}{\text{Premium paid}}$$

$$= \frac{\$6}{\$3}$$

$$= 2.0, \text{ or } 200\%$$

Conversely, if Zector's stock price is $39 at the expiration date of the put option, the return from investing in the put option is

$$\text{Return on option} = \frac{\text{Profit from option}}{\text{Premium paid}}$$

$$= \frac{-\$2}{\$3}$$

$$= -0.67, \text{ or } -67\%$$

So far, we have assumed that Emma will exercise put call option (if at all) on the expiration date. Assuming that she purchased an American-style put option, she could exercise the option at any time up to that date. Alternatively, she could sell the put option that she owns, and she could profit from this sale if the premium at the time she sells it is higher than the premium when she purchased the put option.

Factors That Affect the Put Option Premium

The premium of a put option is influenced by the number of participants who are willing to purchase the option relative to the number of participants who are willing to sell the option. The premium is primarily influenced by three factors, which we will discuss next.

Stock Price Relative to Exercise Price

The lower the stock price relative to the exercise price specified in the put option, the more desirable the put option. A lower stock price increases the likelihood that the stock option will be exercised and makes the stock option more desirable. This relationship can be confirmed by reviewing option premiums quoted for the same firm and the same expiration date, but for different exercise prices. This factor is the most important in explaining why the premium of a particular put option changes over time. Because the exercise price of a put option does not change, the main force that causes a change in the premium of a particular put option is the change in the price of the underlying stock.

Time to Expiration

As with call options, put options with longer terms to expiration have higher premiums, other things being equal. A longer term to expiration allows more time for the investors to benefit from the potential decrease in the price of the stock. This relationship can be confirmed by comparing the premiums on two put options on the same stock, where the only difference between the options is the term to expiration.

Stock Price Volatility

As with call options, put options on stocks that are more volatile have higher premiums, other things being equal. Purchasers of put options have more potential to earn high returns on an option if the underlying stock is volatile, because such a stock has more downside potential. Although this type of stock may also have much upside potential (which would create losses for the purchaser of a put option), the possible loss by the purchaser of a put option is limited to the premium paid for the option.

? Review Questions

21–3 Explain why an investor may purchase a put option on a stock.

21–4 Explain the relationship between a put option's price (premium) and the volatility of the underlying stock.

ⓛⓖ3 **Financial Futures**

financial futures contract
A contract in which one party agrees to deliver a specified amount of a specified financial instrument to the other party at a specified price and date.

Another type of derivative security is the **financial futures contract,** which is an agreement between two parties in which one party agrees to deliver a stated amount of a specified financial instrument to the other party at a specified price and date (called the **settlement date**). The buyer of a financial futures contract receives the financial instrument on the settlement date, and the seller delivers the financial instrument and receives payment at that time. Financial futures contracts are distinguished by the type of financial instrument. For example, there are financial futures contracts on Treasury bills, Treasury bonds, foreign currencies, and stock indexes. For each type of financial futures contract, there are certain settlement dates. Most financial futures contracts have settlement dates in March, June, September, and December.

settlement date
The date by which delivery must be made in a financial futures contract.

Financial Futures Transactions

Financial futures contracts are traded on exchanges such as the Chicago Mercantile Exchange and the Chicago Board of Trade. The exchanges facilitate the transaction between a willing buyer and seller of the same financial futures contract, but they do not take a position in any financial futures contract.

The specified price of the financial instrument that is quoted in a financial futures contract is based on the demand for (by buyers) and supply of (by sellers) that type of futures contract. The price of the contract normally moves in tandem with the price of the financial instrument.

Investors communicate their orders to a brokerage firm by phone or through an online network. The brokerage firm in turn communicates the order to a so-called **floor broker** who executes financial futures transactions on an exchange. Confirmation of the order is received by the brokerage firm and then communicated to the investors.

floor broker
A securities exchange member who executes trades on the trading floor.

Brokerage firms require that the investors maintain a deposit to cover any loss that might result from the futures position. Investors must provide an initial deposit with the brokerage firm at the time they take a position in financial futures. This amount is referred to as an **initial margin.** Brokerage firms also require additional deposits over time, if the value of the futures position declines, to ensure that there are sufficient funds to cover a loss.

initial margin
A sum of money put on deposit with a brokerage firm by an investor who makes an investment, to cover any loss the investor might incur.

Buyers of financial futures contracts can "close out" their positions by selling an identical contract before the settlement date. Sellers of financial futures contracts can close out their positions by buying an identical contract before the settlement date. The profit or loss from a futures position is based on the difference between the specified price for the financial instrument when the contract was bought and the specified price when it was sold.

Price Quotations of Financial Futures Contracts

An example of financial futures quotations as provided in the *Wall Street Journal* is shown in Figure 21.5. The first column lists the type of financial futures contract in bold print, with the settlement dates below it. For each contract with a

FIGURE 21.5

Financial Futures Quotations

Data on financial futures, reported by the *Wall Street Journal.*

Source: Wall Street Journal, January 20, 2000, p. C22.

FUTURES PRICES

INTEREST RATE

TREASURY BONDS (CBT)-$100,000; pts. 32nds of 100%

	Open	High	Low	Settle	Change	Lifetime High	Lifetime Low	Open Interest
Mar	89-18	89-22	89-10	89-17	+ 10	101-07	89-00	604,826
June	89-04	89-10	89-00	89-06	+ 10	99-15	88-22	45,528
Sept	....	....	....	88-29	+ 10	93-28	88-19	623

Est vol 280,000; vol Tue 278,006; open int 651,018, +7,884.

TREASURY BONDS (MCE)-$50,000; pts. 32nds OF 100%

	Open	High	Low	Settle	Change	High	Low	Open Interest
Mar	89-14	89-22	89-10	89-17	+ 9	96-01	89-00	8,481

Est vol 2,6000; vol Tue 4,081; open int 8,492, −223.

TREASURY NOTES (CBT)-$100,000; pts. 32nds of 100%

	Open	High	Low	Settle	Change	High	Low	Open Interest
Mar	94-11	94-15	94-08	94-11	+ 7	100-11	93-32	580,830
June	94-00	94-04	93-30	94-01	+ 7	96-10	93-22	26,119

Est vol 160,000; vol Tue 164,705; open int 606,949, +17,034.

5 YR TREASURY NOTES (CBT)-$100,000; pts. 32nds of 100%

	Open	High	Low	Settle	Change	High	Low	Open Interest
Mar	97-075	97-105	97-055	97-075	+ 4.0	00-055	97-00	387,303

Est vol 55,000; vol Tue 64,589; open int 397,250, +8,705.

2 YR TREAS NOTES (CBT)-$200,000; pts. 32nds OF 100%

	Open	High	Low	Settle	Change	High	Low	Open Interest
Mar	98-30	98-31	98-29	98-305	+ 1.7	00-035	98-267	33,760

Est vol 2, 100; vol Tue 2,328; open int 33, 760, +1,258.

30-DAY FEDERAL FUNDS (CBT)-$5 million; pts. of 100%

	Open	High	Low	Settle	Change	High	Low	Open Interest
Jan	94.540	94.550	94.535	94.540	− .005	95.260	94.400	8,626
Feb	94.22	94.23	94.22	94.22	+ .01	94.75	94.17	8,167
Mar	94.14	94.15	94.14	94.14	+ .01	94.50	94.10	3,646
Apr	94.02	94.03	94.02	94.02	+ .02	94.45	93.98	1,902
May	93.93	93.93	93.93	93.93	+ .02	94.20	93.91	482

Est vol 2,000; vol Tue 2,109; open int 33,760, +1,258.

MUNI BOND INDEX (CBT)-$1,000; times Bond Buyer MBI

	Open	High	Low	Settle	Change	High	Low	Open Interest
Mar	90-23	90-26	90-16	90-18	...	97-00	90-16	21,360

Est vol 1,900; vol Tue 1,535; open int 21,448, +130.

Index: Close 91-07; Yield 6.69

TREASURY BILLS (CME)-$1 mil.; pts. of 100%

	Open	High	Low	Settle	Chg	Discount Settle	Chg	Open Interest
Mar	94.43	94.45	94.43	94.44	+ .01	5.56	− .01	2,411

Est vol 34; vol Tue 0; open int 2,411, +0.

LIBOR-1MO. (CME)-$3,000,000; points of 100%

	Open	High	Low	Settle	Chg	Discount Settle	Chg	Open Interest
Feb	94.05	94.05	94.05	94.05	+ .01	5.95	− .01	14,530
Mar	93.91	93.94	93.91	93.93	+ .01	6.07	− .01	4,765
Apr	93.84	93.86	93.84	93.86	+ .01	6.14	− .01	1,317
May	93.75	93.75	93.75	93.74	....	6.26	....	208
June	....	....	....	93.57	+ .01	6.43	− .01	138
July	....	....	....	93.48	+ .01	6.52	− .01	447
Aug	....	....	....	93.41	+ .01	6.59	− .01	334
Sept	....	....	....	93.34	+ .01	6.66	− .01	450
Oct	....	....	....	93.25	+ .01	6.75	− .01	475
Nov	....	....	....	93.19	+ .01	6.81	− .01	400

Est vol 1,546; vol Tue 5,398; open int 38,467, +3,881.

particular settlement date, the daily open, high, low, and *settle* (latest) prices are disclosed, along with the high and low prices over the life of the contract and *open interest* (the number of contracts outstanding).

Speculating with Treasury Bond Futures

Investors take positions in Treasury bond futures contracts to speculate on the expected change in the price of Treasury bonds. The price specified in a Treasury bond futures contract tends to move in tandem with Treasury bond prices. Investors consider purchasing Treasury bond futures when they expect Treasury bond prices to rise.

Example ▼ As of October 10, Rita Richards expects that the price of Treasury bonds will rise over the next month. She can presently purchase a Treasury bond futures contract with a December settlement date for 101. The futures contract represents Treasury bonds with a par value of $100,000 that pay an 8% coupon rate and will have 15 years to maturity. The price of 101 implies that $101 will be paid for every $100 of par value, so the total price to be paid by Rita on the settlement date is $101,000. Over the next month, Treasury bond prices rise (as Rita expected), and the price specified in a Treasury bond futures contract with a December settlement date as of November 10 is 103. Rita sells a Treasury bond futures contract with a December settlement date at this time for 103. She will receive $103,000 as of the settlement date as a result of this contract. Rita now has one contract to buy Treasury bonds on the settlement date and another contract to sell Treasury bonds on the settlement date. The contracts offset each other. However, the amount she receives from selling Treasury bonds exceeds the amount she paid by $2,000. Therefore, Rita's gain is

Amount to be received from selling Treasury bonds, due to sale of Treasury bond futures = $103,000

Amount to be paid for Treasury bonds, due to purchase of Treasury bond futures = $101,000

Gain = $103,000 − $101,000
    = $2,000

The risk Rita takes in making this investment is that bond prices will decline after she purchases the Treasury bond contract. If Treasury bond prices had declined over the month, so that the Treasury bonds were priced at 98, Rita would have received $98,000 as of the settlement date. Combining this with the Treasury bond futures contract she purchased for 101 (i.e., $101,000), she would have experienced a loss of $3,000. She does not have to sell a Treasury bond futures contract at this time. However, it is possible that Treasury bond prices will decrease further before the settlement date, which would result in larger losses.

▲ The advantage of speculating with a futures contract instead of buying the Treasury bonds directly is that Rita only needs to maintain a margin to back her investment, which requires less funds than if she purchased the bonds.

Speculating with Stock Index Futures

A **stock index futures** contract specifies a stock index level that can be purchased or sold at a specified settlement date. The value of a stock index futures contract changes over time, because it normally moves in tandem with the actual index level. Thus, investors who speculate with stock index futures attempt to purchase stock index futures at a time when the index specified is relatively low. If they expect that the stock index will rise, they consider purchasing an index futures contract now and selling the same type of contract at a future date before the settlement date once the index has risen. If investors expect that the stock index will decline, they consider selling the stock index futures now and purchasing the same index at a future date when the index specified is relatively low.

NewsLine   CLICK HERE FOR INDEX FUTURES

Individual investors can now participate in financial futures trading. The Chicago Mercantile Exchange and the Chicago Board of Trade offer smaller futures contracts based on the S&P 500 and the Dow Jones Industrial Average, respectively.

Growing numbers of investors are using their PCs to get into the listed derivative markets. They're drawn by better trading sites, reams of free financial data, and plummeting commissions. Until recently, most of the online action focused on stock and stock-index options....But online futures trading is now taking off, thanks in part to the advent of smaller contracts aimed at retail investors.

The most popular is the "E-mini," introduced by the Chicago Mercantile Exchange in 1997 as a pint-sized version of the S&P 500 contract. The E-mini is valued at one-fifth of the larger S&P contract...and requires a margin payment of as little as $3,400 (versus over $16,000 for its big brother). The E-mini trades on Globex2, the Merc's 24-hour electronic network. That means an order placed from a Web site can get executed in seconds....

The Chicago Board of Trade is making a similar pitch to small investors with the Dow Jones contract....The Dow Jones contract is worth 10 times the value of the average ... and requires a down payment of $4,800....

The E-mini and Dow Jones contracts are simple directional plays, meaning they follow the market when it goes up or down. That differs from index options, which reflect market volatility and don't always mirror the underlying indexes. Transaction fees on futures are also typically less than alternatives....

[F]utures trading, particularly without a broker, is as risky a way to play the market as you can find. Futures contracts are leveraged, with margin requirements as low as 5%....The most you can lose buying stocks or put and call options on the S&P 500 is your investment. With futures, you're obligated to honor a contract. If the market moves against you, you have to ante up more cash to maintain your position, making your downside unlimited.

Because of the high risks involved in futures, the Commodity Futures Trading Commission requires brokers to check whether futures trading is a suitable activity for a client....

Source: Andrew Osterland, "Click Here for Index Futures," Business Week, January 25, 1999, p. 112.

Example ▼

short position
Created by the sale of a futures contract whose underlying instrument is not presently owned by the seller.

On July 8, Al Barnett notices that the DJIA futures contract with a September settlement date specifies an index level of 10,000, which is similar to the existing index today. Al expects stock prices to decline, so he anticipates that the price specified in the DJIA futures contract will decline in the future. Therefore, he sells a futures contract today. The sale of a financial futures contract creates a so-called **short position,** in which the underlying instrument that will be sold is not presently owned by the seller.

By August 24, stock prices have declined, and the DJIA futures contract with a September settlement date specifies an index level of 9,400. Al does not expect stock prices to decline further, so he purchases the DJIA index futures to offset his short position. The dollar value of the DJIA index specified in the futures contract is $10 times the index level. Thus, Al's gain is

Dollar value of stock index futures when a futures contract was sold = $10,000 \times \$10 = \$100,000$

Dollar value of stock index futures when a futures contract was purchased = $9,400 \times \$10 = \$94,000$

Gain = $\$100,000 - \$94,000 = \underline{\$6,000}$

If the stock index had risen over this period from July 8 to August 24, the stock index futures price as of August 24 would have been higher than the futures price specified on July 8. Therefore, Al would have incurred a loss from his initial position in DJIA futures. ▲

Hedging with Financial Futures

Many investors use financial futures to **hedge** an existing investment position. In general, this involves taking a position in financial futures contracts that will incur a gain to offset a loss in their existing investment portfolio.

Example ▼
Stanford Mutual Fund manages a large portfolio of stocks. The portfolio managers of this stock mutual fund anticipate that the prices of stocks will decline over the next month but will rebound after that time. They would like to hedge their portfolio against a loss over the next month. A stock index futures contract with one month to settlement date is available on the Dow Jones Industrial Average stock index at an index level of 10,000. Stanford decides to sell a futures contract on this index, because it believes that this index is highly correlated with its existing stock portfolio. In one month, at the settlement date, Stanford will purchase the same contract. If stock prices decline over this period, the index will decline as well, and so will the futures contract on the index. Stanford will gain on its futures position, because the price it paid for the index at the settlement date will be less than the future price at which it sold the index.

After one month passes, the market declined as expected, and the futures price of the DJIA is at an index level of 9,000. DJIA futures contracts are valued at $10 times the DJIA index, so Stanford's positions are as follows:

Sold DJIA futures for 10,000; receives 10,000 times $10 = $100,000

Purchased DJIA futures for 9,000; owes 9,000 times $10 = $90,000

Gain = $100,000 − $90,000
  = $10,000

Thus, Stanford gained from selling a DJIA futures contract. It benefited from a general decline in the market, which can partially offset the loss on its stock portfolio.

In reality, this one contract would not be sufficient to hedge a large stock portfolio. In fact, if Stanford wanted to hedge its entire portfolio, it would create a short position that had a value equal to the size of its stock portfolio (assuming that the index and its own stock portfolio change by the same magnitude). Thus, if Stanford's portfolio was worth $200 million, it would need 2,000 futures contracts (2,000 × $100,000) to create a short position that fully offset its stock portfolio position. If Stanford sold 2,000 futures contracts as explained in the previous example, its gain would have been $10,000 per contract for a total gain of $10,000 × 2,000 = $20,000,000.

What would have happened if the prices of stocks that make up the DJIA had increased rather than declined over this one-month period? Stanford would have experienced a loss on its DJIA index futures contracts. Under these conditions, however, it would have experienced a gain on its existing stock portfolio. Thus, the hedge would have had an offsetting effect. But if Stanford had expected stock prices to rise, it would have been better off not selling the DJIA futures contracts.

21–5   Explain why an investor would purchase a stock index futures contract.
21–6   Explain why an investor would sell a stock index futures contract.

TYING IT ALL TOGETHER

This chapter explained how investors can use call options, put options, and financial futures to speculate or to hedge their existing investment positions. These derivative securities are used to help investors attempt to capitalize on changes in the values of the underlying financial assets. The roles of managers, financial markets, and investors in using derivative securities are summarized in the Integrative Table that follows.

INTEGRATIVE TABLE
Buying and Selling Derivative Securities

Role of Financial Managers	Role of Financial Markets	Role of Investors
Financial managers commonly take positions in derivative securities to offset their exposure to interest rate movements or other market conditions.	For each type of derivative security, there is a market that facilitates trading between investors. Thus, investors have easy access to purchase of derivative securities such as stock options and financial futures. They can also sell these derivative securities easily in the financial markets.	Investors take positions in derivative securities to speculate on expected movement in the value of the underlying instrument. They may also take positions to offset the exposure of their existing securities holdings to market conditions.

LG1 **Explain how call options are used by investors.** Call options are commonly used by investors to capitalize on expectations of an increase in the price of the underlying stock. Investors pay a premium for the right to buy the stock at a specified exercise price. They consider purchasing a call option if they expect that the price of the stock will exceed the exercise price by an amount that more than covers the premium paid. Some investors who expect the stock price to remain stable or to decline consider selling call options.

LG2 **Explain how put options are used by investors.** Put options are commonly used by investors to capitalize on expectations of a decrease in the price of the underlying stock. Investors pay a premium for the right to sell the stock at a specified exercise price. They consider purchasing a put option if they expect that the price of the stock will be lower than the exercise price by an amount that more than covers the premium paid. Some investors who expect the stock price to remain stable or to increase consider selling call options.

 Explain how financial futures are used by investors. Buying a financial futures contract locks in the price at which one can purchase a specified instrument (such as Treasury bonds or a stock index) as of the future settlement date. Thus, investors consider purchasing financial futures contracts that represent securities or indexes whose values they expect to rise. Selling a financial futures contract locks in the price at which one can sell a specified instrument as of the future settlement date. Thus, investors consider selling financial futures contracts that represent securities or indexes whose values are expected to decline.

SELF-TEST EXERCISES   (Solutions in Appendix B)

ST 21–1   Laura Egan purchased a call option on Perspective stock for $3.50 per share, with an exercise price of $40 per share. She plans to exercise her call option at the expiration date if the stock price at that time is above $40. She plans to sell immediately the stock received from exercising her call option. She has prepared a spreadsheet to evaluate her profit per share under various possible outcomes for the price of Perspective stock.

a. Use her spreadsheet format to figure the profit on the sale of shares received from exercising the option and an overall profit considering the premium she paid for the option in the first place.

Possible price of Perspective at expiration date	Premium paid	Received from exercising option	Profit from investing in call option
$38	3.50		
$40	3.50		
$42	3.50		
$44	3.50		
$46	3.50		
$48	3.50		

b. At what price per share would Laura break even on the option investment?
c. What is Laura's percentage return on the option investment if Perspective stock is selling for $42 at the expiration date?
d. What is Laura's percentage return on the option investment if Perspective stock is selling for $46 at the expiration date?

 ST 21–2   Speculating with Treasury bond futures   As of April 3, Steve Mosey expects the price of Treasury bonds to fall over the next month. He can sell a Treasury bond futures contract with a June settlement date for 102. The futures contract represents Treasury bonds with a par value of $100,000 that pay an 8% coupon rate and have a 15-year maturity.

a. What is the total value of a Treasury bond futures contract on April 3?

b. Assume that Steve sold the contract on April 3. By May 25, Treasury bond prices have declined, and Steve purchases an offsetting contract with a settlement of 99. What did the offsetting contract cost Steve?

c. What profit or loss did Steve make as a result of his transactions?

d. What would have been Steve's outcome if, instead of declining, Treasury bonds had increased in price and he had purchased an offsetting contract on May 25 at 105?

EXERCISES

 21–1   In-the-money versus out-of-the-money   There are three call options currently being traded for Jerico, Inc. Compare each of the exercise (strike) prices listed to the price of Jerico stock as of April 1 and June 1. Classify the call options as in-the-money, at-the-money, or out-of-the-money as of those dates.

Call option	Exercise price	Stock price April 1 = $47	Stock price June 1 = $50
1	$45		
2	50		
3	55		

 21–2   American- and European-style options   Sally Trotter bought a call option with a June expiration date on Henley stock for $5.00 per share. The strike price of the option was $120.00 per share. In mid-April, Henley stock was selling for a high of $136.00 per share. By the June expiration date, Henley stock had settled back down to $124.00 per share.

a. If this was a European-style option, what is the most profit that Sally could have made by exercising it?

b. If this was an American-style option, what is the most profit that Sally could have made by exercising it?

  21–3   Writing a call option   Phillip Foster owns shares of Mills Co. common stock currently priced at $24. He decides to sell (write) call options on his stock with a strike price of $25 per share and an expiration date 2 months from today. He receives a premium of $3.00 per share for the calls. For each of the following price and option exercise possibilities, and on the basis of the current share price of $24, calculate profit (loss) and overall return (1) if the options are sold as described above, and (2) what he would have experienced if he had not written the option contracts. Ignore commissions.

a. Mills Co. common stock falls to $20 per share by the time the option expires unexercised.

b. Mills Co. stock remains at $24 per share throughout the option period, and the option is not exercised.

c. Mills Co. stock rises to $28 per share, and the option is exercised.

d. Mills Co. stock rises to $35 per share, and the option is exercised.

LG1 **21–4 Factors that affect call option premiums** Indicate what effect each of the following factors would have on the premium value of a call option (increase/decrease/no effect).

a. The price of the underlying stock increases.
b. The time to expiration has decreased to 1 week.
c. The price of the underlying stock does not change much in day-to-day trading.
d. The stock price has become very volatile in day-to-day trading.
e. The price of the stock has decreased.
f. The time to expiration is several months.

LG1 LG2 **21–5 Reading option quotes** Refer to the discussion of Figure 21.1 as you examine the option quotations presented below. Assume that you are reading these on March 1.

			—Call—		—Put—	
Option/strike		Exp.	Vol.	Last	Vol.	Last
Daisy	27½	Jul	—	—	550	⅞
34⅛	30	Apr	535	4¾	24	⅞
34⅛	32½	Apr	7166	3	30	1 7/16
34⅛	35	Apr	372	1⅝	15	2⅜
34⅛	42½	Jul	501	1 5/16	—	—

a. Identify the most active call option and the most active put options. For each, list the strike price, expiration, volume, and premium.
b. Locate the April call option with a strike price of 35. Is it in- or out-of-the-money? By how much?
c. Locate the April put option with a strike price of 35. Is it in- or out-of-the-money? By how much?
d. Compare the in-the-money or out-of-the-money amounts for the April 35 call and put options to their premiums. What factors may explain the difference between the amounts?
e. Compare the premiums for the April 32½ call option and the April 35 call option. Because both expire at the same time, what factors may be responsible for the difference in premium?
f. Explain why the premiums for the call options decline and the premiums for the put options increase as the strike price increases.
g. Explain why premiums for call options increase and the premiums for put options decrease as the price of the stock increases.

LG2 **21–6 In-, at-, and out-of-the-money puts** Consider four put options for Guion Corp. that differ only in strike price. Evaluate them as in-the-money, at-the-money, or out-of-the-money as of the dates and stock prices given.

Put option	Exercise price	As of July 10 Stock price of $89	As of Sept. 10 Stock price of $95
A	$90		
B	93		
C	95		
D	98		

21–7 Speculating with put options   Carole Jenkins purchased a put option on Flyer Corp. stock for $2.50 per share with an exercise price of $35 per share. She plans to exercise the option if the price of Flyer shares is less than $35 at the time of expiration. She plans to purchase the stock just prior to exercising the put options. She wishes to estimate her outcome using various possible prices for Flyer at expiration.

    a. Use the following possible prices for Flyer stock at expiration and the format of Table 21.6 to explore a range of possible investment outcomes. Possible prices at expiration: $39, $37, $35, $33, $31, $29.

    b. Use the information that you developed in part **a** to plot a contingency graph similar to that in Figure 21.4.

21–8 Speculating with put options   Juan Carillo purchased a put option on Woolford Corp. common stock for $4 with an exercise price of $80. Juan plans to sell (instead of exercising) the option if it has value at its expiration. Because there is no remaining time, any value for the option at expiration would be equal to the amount that it is in-the-money.

    a. Fill in the following table to create a distribution of possible outcomes from the investment.

Price at expiration	Premium paid	Premium at expiration	Net $ return	% return
$83	$4			
80	4			
77	4			
75	4			
73	4			

    b. Use the information developed in part **a** to create a contingency graph similar to that in Figure 21.4.

  21–9 Writing a put option   Vicky Evans has written a put option on Tecnic, Inc. stock with an exercise price of $72.50 and a premium of $3.00. The current price of the stock is $76. If the option is exercised, Vicky plans to sell the put stock immediately at market.

    a. Fill in the blanks of the following table to develop a range of possible outcomes from the investment.

Price at expiration	Premium received	Price paid for put stock	Profit (Loss)
$78	$4		
76	4		
74	4		
72	4		
70	4		
68	4		
66	4		

b. Use the information developed in part **a** to create a contingency graph of the possible outcomes.

  21–10 **Speculating with Treasury note futures**   As of March 4, Joe Haughey expects that the price of Treasury notes will fall in the near future. He can sell a Treasury note futures contract with a June settlement date for 95-22. The futures contract represents Treasury notes with a par value of $100,000. Remember that Treasury securities are priced in points and 32nds of points.
   a. How much would Joe receive per $100 par value if he sold?
   b. What total price would Joe be paid for one Treasury note contract if he sold?
   c. Assuming that he sold in March at 95-22 and then purchased the offsetting Treasury note contract at 92-10 as of May 12, how much would he pay for the offsetting contract?
   d. What profit or loss would Joe have made from the sale and purchase of the Treasury note contract?

 21–11 **Speculating with index futures**   As of October 10, Judy Sollazo expects blue-chip stocks to do very well in the near future. She purchases a December DJIA contract with a settlement of 12,180. By November 13, the DJIA has risen and the December DJIA futures contract has a settlement of 12,350. Judy decides to sell an offsetting contract that day.
   a. Explain the pricing of a DJIA futures contract.
   b. What is the dollar value of the December DJIA contract that Judy purchased on October 10?
   c. What sale proceeds would she have received from the sale of the December DJIA contract on November 13?
   d. What profit or loss did Judy make on this investment?

 21–12 **Speculating with index futures**   On July 10, Michael Griffin wishes to profit from what he sees as a strong possibility that stocks in the broader market will decline in the next few months. He is interested in the S&P 500 futures contract, but its pricing makes him realize that the risk exposure is greater than he is comfortable with. As a result, he chooses to sell a contract called the Mini S&P 500 with a September expiration and a settlement of 140,000.
   a. Explain the difference in pricing between the regular S&P 500 Index futures contract and the Mini S&P 500 contract.
   b. What is the dollar value of the contract that Michael sold on July 10?
   c. If the S&P 500 does decline and on August 24 the Mini S&P 500 futures contract has a settlement of 137,500, what would Michael have to pay to purchase the offsetting contract?

d. What would his profit or loss be as a result of the transactions on July 10 and August 24?

e. If Michael does not purchase on August 24, but waits, and the market turns upward so that by September 10 the Mini S&P 500 has a settlement of 143,260, what would Michael have to pay to purchase an offsetting futures contract?

f. What profit or loss would result from his actions based on the information in part e?

g. What difference would there be if Michael had been using the regular S&P 500 futures contract instead of the Mini?

 21–13   Hedging with Treasury bond futures   Nancy Holt has a portfolio of Treasury bonds with a par value of $500,000. She is concerned that interest rates will rise, resulting in a decrease in the value of her portfolio. She wishes to take a position in Treasury bond futures that would make a profit if rates increase, and thereby offset the decline in the value of her bond portfolio.

a. Refer for help to the text description of Treasury bond futures contract specifications. If Nancy wants to sell Treasury bond futures contracts that represent a par value equal to the par value of her portfolio, how many contracts must she sell?

b. Nancy decided to sell Treasury bond futures contracts with a September settlement date and a settlement price of 98. What is the value of the contracts that she sold?

c. If Nancy does nothing more, what will happen at the settlement date?

d. If 1 month after her sale at 98, Nancy purchases offsetting September Treasury bond futures contracts at a settlement of 94, what will they cost her?

e. What profit or loss will she have from the futures contract transactions?

f. What will have happened to the value of her Treasury bond portfolio during the month that she had the hedge (sale of futures contracts) in place?

web exercises   [Search]

Go to web site **www.adtrading.com**. In the Regular Articles section, click on **Beginners' Corner: The ADT Guide**. Then click on **1. Futures**.

1. What are financial futures?
2. Where are they traded? Who can trade there?
3. What are the types of contracts available?
Click **Back** on your browser. Then click on **4. Options 1 - An Introduction**.
4. What is an option? What are the benefits of buying an option?

Go to web site **www.cboe.com**. Click on **Education**.

1. What are the five benefits of buying options?

2. What are LEAPS?

Click on **Quotes**. Enter the stock symbol **ABT** for Abbot Laboratories into the symbol space.

Click on **List near term at-the-money options**, and then click **Submit**.

3. About how many options are listed for ABT? What is the time frame for these options (year, months, etc.)?

Go to web site **www.pacificex.com**. Click **Options**. Click **Glossary**. Scroll down to the **Options Trading Terms** section.

4. What are the classes of options?

For additional practice with concepts from this chapter, visit
http://www.awl.com/gitman_madura

exam-ace.net

Investor assessment of exam-ace.com's business

Dan Atkinson is approached by Tom Turner (owner of exam-ace.net) to support the newly proposed project for exam-ace.net. Recall that Dan already has an $80,000 equity investment in the company. Also recall that Tom Turner has decided to pursue the development of similar practice tests for accountants who take a special exam to become certified.

Although Dan liked Tom's initial business idea, to provide practice exams for college students, he strongly dislikes Tom's idea of providing practice exams for accountants. Dan is aware of many firms that already offer preparation materials for the accounting exam, and does not think that exam-ace.net should pursue this type of project. Not only is Dan unwilling to invest more of his funds in the new project, but he is also afraid that this new project will generate losses, which may cause exam-ace.net to fail. This concerns Dan, who will lose his original equity investment of $80,000 if exam-ace.net fails. Tom tries to convince Dan that the project would be feasible by providing the following information:

- The economy is expected to strengthen in the near future, so Tom anticipates that sales generated by this project would benefit from the strong economy.
- Tom expects the inflation rate to remain low, which he has learned is generally favorable for many types of firms.
- Although there are some competitors who help accounting students prepare for this special accrediting exam, Tom's industry analysis did not turn up any firm that was using the Internet in this way to provide practice exams. The competitors offer various tutorial aids, including some practice exams, but are not yet making these materials available over the Internet.

Questions

CC4–1 Do you think Tom's arguments might change Dan's mind about the feasibility of this project?

CC4–2 In the second year of business, exam-ace.net experiences positive earnings. Tom Turner has noticed that many Internet companies have engaged in initial public offerings (IPOs), in which they obtained millions of dollars in funding. He has noticed that these shares were commonly priced at more than 50 times the firm's recent annual earnings per share. In comparison, the stock of other firms that are publicly traded is normally priced at about 15 times recent annual earnings per share. Tom began to plan a major expansion so that he might someday engage in an IPO. He thought that he could offer practice testing for many other professionals (such as real estate brokers, attorneys, and insurance brokers) who take exams to obtain professional licenses. While he knew that several competitors already provided practice exams, he believed that his company's use of the Internet to provide practice exams would distinguish exam-ace.net from the other firms. Tom realized that he needed someone to organize this plan in more detail so that he could entice investors to buy shares during an IPO some day, and therefore he decided to hire consultants for a fee of $10,000 per month to help develop an expansion plan. He needed funding to pay the consultant.

Once again, he approached Dan Atkinson and proposed that Dan invest in some shares now, which he argued would be a better deal for Dan than if Dan waited for the eventual IPO to buy shares. Tom also suggested that he might attempt to obtain funds from the financial institution that previously provided a loan until the IPO occurs. Dan was furious when he heard of Tom's plan. He believed that an IPO should be considered only after a firm proved that it needed funds to support its expansion. He believed that Tom's goal was simply to engage in an IPO and that Tom was reaching for ideas that could justify the IPO. He believed that if Tom were able to engage in an IPO, he would not use the funds wisely. He also questioned Tom's general expansion idea, because the existing competitors could easily copy Tom's ideas and sell some of their testing services online. Dan was more concerned than ever that Tom's decisions would cause exam-ace.net to fail.

Do you think that Tom's idea makes sense? Explain.

Dan could avoid investing more funds in exam-ace.net and let Tom find some other investor to provide funding for now. Tom tried to convince Dan that the investment in this business would be safe because if there were any financial problems, the business would be backed by earnings generated from the original business. Why would Dan get so upset about Tom's plan regarding the future direction of exam-ace.net?

CC4–3 Communication
Tom asks for your opinion on his ambitious plan to expand. Write a memo to Tom with your recommendation.

CC4–4 Teamwork
Create a team of three students, in which one student plays the role of Tom, one student plays the role of the investor, and one student plays the role of the lender. The student who plays the role of Tom must determine how to try to get support form the investor and the lender. The student who plays the role of the investor must determine how to discourage Tom from pursuing his plan.

CC4–5 Ethics
If Tom does not obtain sufficient funding for this new project, he is considering the use of future earnings from his existing business to invest in the new business. When he started the business, his plan was to invest funds to pursue his business of practice tests for college students. However, Tom sincerely believes that the equity investor and the creditor will benefit more if he uses some funds to focus on practice tests for accounting licenses. Is it ethical for Tom to shift the funds toward a different type of business from what Tom originally proposed when he obtained the funds to start his business?

How Investors Monitor and Control a Firm's Managers

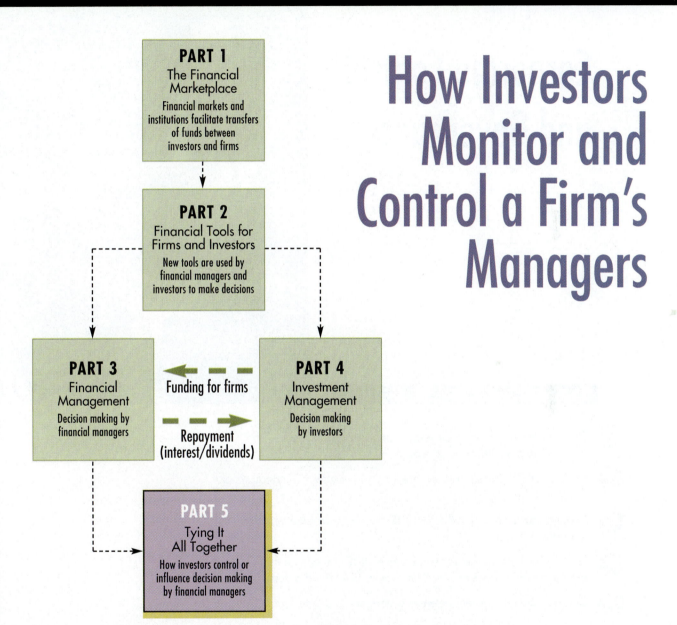

PART 1
The Financial Marketplace
Financial markets and institutions facilitate transfers of funds between investors and firms

PART 2
Financial Tools for Firms and Investors
New tools are used by financial managers and investors to make decisions

PART 3
Financial Management
Decision making by financial managers

Funding for firms

Repayment (interest/dividends)

PART 4
Investment Management
Decision making by investors

PART 5
Tying It All Together
How investors control or influence decision making by financial managers

Part 5 integrates the three components of the financial environment by illustrating how the decisions of financial managers are monitored by investors and how financial markets facilitate corporate control.

665

Corporate Control and Governance

LEARNING GOALS

LG1 Describe the relationship between managers and investors, and explain the potential conflict in goals.

LG2 Explain how a firm's board of directors can control the managers of the firm.

LG3 Explain how investors in the firm's stock can control the managers of the firm.

LG4 Explain how the market for corporate control can ensure that managers of firms serve their firms' respective shareholders.

LG5 Describe the relationship between managers and creditors.

LG6 Describe the relationship between mutual fund management and investors.

(LG1) Relationship Between a Firm's Managers and Its Investors

Institutional and individual investors who invest in the stock of any particular firm become the shareholders of the firm. As shareholders, these investors own the firm, whereas the firm's managers control its operations. Managers serve as agents for a firm's shareholders. They make decisions that are supposed to maximize the value of the firm and therefore maximize the value of the firm's stock price. Thus, investors who invest in the firm's stock rely on the managers to generate attractive returns from their investment in the firm.

The relationship between the investors who become shareholders and the managers of a firm is illustrated in Figure 22.1. Managerial investment and financing decisions affect the performance of the firm, which affects the dividend payments. These decisions also affect the stock price and therefore the size of capital gains realized by shareholders when they sell the firm's stock.

Ownership versus Control

agency problems
Conflicts of interest between a firm's managers and its owners.

The separation between ownership and control introduces conflicts, which lead to **agency problems.** Financial managers may be tempted to make decisions that are in their own self-interest rather than in the interest of shareholders. For example, they may want to expand specific operations that might lead to the creation, within the firm, of high-level positions for which they may qualify. Such expansion may be intended to serve their own interests rather than those of shareholders.

The separation between the ownership and the control of a firm encourages shareholders to monitor the firm's managers to ensure that they are serving shareholder interests. However, the ownership of a typical corporation is usually spread among many shareholders, such that no single shareholder holds a large proportion of the firm's shares. Thus, many shareholders are unwilling to monitor the firm's management style, because they would receive only a small proportion of any increase in the firm's value generated by their monitoring efforts. All

FIGURE 22.1

Relationship Between Investors and Managers

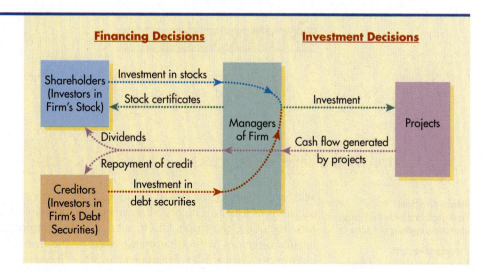

other shareholders would also "free-ride" off those shareholders who make the effort to keep managerial goals aligned with shareholder goals.

Asymmetric Information

In addition, there is the problem of *asymmetric information*. The firm's managers have information about the firm that is not available to shareholders. This further complicates any attempt of shareholders to monitor the firm, even if they are willing to use their time to monitor the firm.

Although firms are required to inform investors by providing financial statements, some firms use accounting procedures that may mislead investors. Thus, financial statements do not necessarily reduce the degree of asymmetric information. For example, Sunbeam reported high earnings for 1998, which hid the financial problems it was experiencing at that time. The financial statements provided by Sunbeam may have made it appear that managers were trying to serve the interests of shareholders. It was later determined that Sunbeam's performance was worse than reported.

Because it is difficult to determine whether a particular management decision will enhance shareholder wealth over time, shareholders cannot always identify managers who make decisions that are inconsistent with shareholder interests. Thus, shareholders commonly use stock-price performance as an initial indicator. If the stock-price performance of a firm is very poor relative to the market overall and to other firms in the industry, shareholders begin to question whether the managers are attempting to maximize shareholder wealth.

Many firms, including General Motors and IBM, suffered severe declines in their stock prices because managers were not focused on maximizing shareholder wealth. Ultimately, many of these firms restructured their operations, which led to a major improvement in efficiency, profitability, and stock-price performance. Even so, the changes commonly occurred several years after the problems began, which suggests a lag before necessary restructuring is enacted. There are several methods that are used to ensure that managers make decisions that are aligned with the interests of investors who purchase shares of the firm's stock. These methods are described in the following sections.

? Review Question

22–1 Explain how asymmetric information affects the relationship between owners and managers.

LG2 Control by the Board of Directors

inside directors
Those members of a board of directors who are also employed by the firm.

outside directors
Those members of a board of directors who are not employed by the firm.

Shareholders elect the board of directors, which oversees the key management decisions of a firm. The board members may include some so-called **inside directors** (including the firm's CEO), who are also employed by the firm, and some **outside directors,** who are not employed by the firm. The outside members may be employed as high-level managers at other firms, or they may be retired from a high-level management position. Alternatively, they may be portfolio managers with expertise in valuing businesses within a specific industry. A typical term of a director is 3 years, but the director may be re-elected for subsequent terms.

Duties of the Board

The board of directors appoints the high-level managers of the firm, including the chief executive officer (CEO). It also monitors the high-level managers to ensure that they are serving the interests of the shareholders. It is responsible for firing high-level managers who do not fulfill their responsibilities. Board members attend board meetings scheduled by the firm, in which they discuss issues such as the firm's recent performance, the firm's plans for future growth, and the compensation of the firm's high-level managers. In recent years, board members have tended to have a greater impact on firms than before. Firms typically schedule between five and ten board meetings a year.

Compensation for Board Members

Outside directors are normally paid for their service on the board. They commonly receive between $15,000 and $25,000 annually for serving on boards of relatively small publicly traded firms; they receive greater amounts for serving on boards of very large firms. In 1998, the mean level of compensation (including cash and stock options) for outside directors of the 200 largest firms was about $112,000. In particular, outside directors of the large technology and financial firms received relatively high compensation levels. Outside directors of large technology firms received an average of about $186,000 in compensation for the year, whereas outside directors of large financial firms received about $142,000. The relatively high compensation levels for outside directors of large firms was partially attributable to the strong stock price performance of the firms. The compensation for many outside directors is in the form of stock options, and therefore is tied to the firm's stock-price performance.

Impact of Board Characteristics on Its Degree of Control

The composition and compensation of the board of directors affects its motivation to ensure that the firm's managers serve shareholder interests. Some of the more important characteristics are discussed next.

Impact of Outside Directors

In general, outside directors are expected to be more effective than inside directors at enacting changes that improve the firm's stock price. Outside directors are independent of the firm and therefore may be more willing to identify problems. They can be more critical without concern of retaliation by the firm's CEO. In addition, their independence from the firm means that their compensation from their employer and their career path should not be affected by their input as a board member. Their independence gives them the flexibility to serve in the best interests of shareholders, even if their actions do not serve the interests of the firm's managers.

Inside directors, by contrast, may be less willing to identify problems of the firm for which they may be accountable. Furthermore, inside directors are less likely to enact changes that could adversely affect their fellow high-level managers. They are also less likely to enact changes that could adversely affect the firm's CEO, who has some influence over their future compensation and career path.

Example ▼

Consider a board that is composed of ten members, eight of whom are insiders (including the CEO). One of the outside board members raises an issue about the amount of compensation received by the CEO. The CEO's compensation is 20% more than the average received by the CEOs of other firms in the same industry and in the same size class. Most of the inside directors are concerned that if they support the criticism that the CEO's compensation is excessive, they will be penalized by the CEO in the future. Specifically, their future pay raises may be smaller, or they may not be promoted to a higher-level position within the firm. Consequently, they decide not to support the criticism of the CEO, and the discussion of the CEO's excessive compensation is quickly terminated. ▲

Given that outside directors may be more willing to enact changes to serve shareholder interests, boards of directors that have a higher proportion of outsiders are usually viewed more favorably by shareholders. There is evidence that boards dominated by outside board members are more likely to fire the CEO of a firm. This supports the notion that boards dominated by outside board members may be more willing to take necessary actions that serve shareholder interests.

Impact of an Outside Director as Board Chair

The chair of the board normally organizes the agenda for board meetings and oversees the process by which the board's decisions are made. Because one of the key issues for a board is the hiring, assessment, firing (if necessary), and compensation of the CEO, there is an obvious conflict of interest when the CEO is chair of the board. A board that has the CEO as its chair is less likely to enact changes that may serve shareholder interests. If a CEO runs the board meeting, other board members may be less capable of focusing on any problems of the firm for which the CEO is accountable. A board with an outside director as chair is more likely to represent shareholder interests.

Impact of Stock Ownership by Board Members

If board members invest in the stock of the firm, their efforts to maximize the value of the firm are rewarded. Thus, they may be more willing to enact changes that serve shareholder interests when they are shareholders. Outside board members are independent of the firm, but they may not necessarily be sufficiently motivated to enact change unless they are directly rewarded for any changes that improve shareholder wealth. Board members who are also shareholders may be more motivated. Some firms compensate their board members by granting them stock options to buy shares of the firm's stock at the prevailing stock price. If the stock price rises over time, the stock options become more valuable. Thus, the compensation of the board members is tied to how well they satisfy shareholders.

*News*Line   THE CHAMP OF BAD BOARDS

Boards of directors must oversee a firm's top managers. However, they do not always do this job well. In 1998, *Fortune* magazine began naming America's worst boards of directors in its *Fortune* 500 issue.

A company where all directors are elected for one-year terms, where at least two-thirds of the directors must meet a stringent test of independence, where no director may be elected after age 72, where outside directors meet alone at least once a year, where there's an independent lead director—this outfit sounds like a model of good governance. What's it doing on a list of companies with the worst boards? As usual at Occidental, there's more here than meets the eye. Turns out those governance measures were adopted just weeks ago, virtually at gunpoint. Whether they're for real remains to be seen.

Oxy is a legend among corporate-governance experts, many of whom consider it the all-time champ at shareholder abuse going back to the days of founder Armand Hammer. Best recent example: In 1997 the board bought out the remaining seven years of CEO Ray Irani's contract for $95 million; then, having in effect paid him for the next seven years at the stunning rate of more than $13 million a year, they gave him a new contract that guarantees him $1.2 mil-

lion a year. Some shareholders, including the Teachers' Retirement System of Louisiana, finally decided not to take it anymore and sued, charging corporate waste, breach of fiduciary duty, and unjust enrichment, among other things. Under the settlement, approved in February, Oxy agreed to a massive overhaul of its governance arrangements.

Anyone who follows Oxy will remain suspicious of these reforms until they're reflected in results, which remain dismal. Even in the context of a tough business, petroleum production, the company has been a terrible performer, though of course it paints a different picture....

The faint ray of hope is that the governance reforms really will make directors more accountable to shareholders, leading to improved performance or perhaps even the sale of the company at a reasonable price. In theory, that's what ought to happen. It will be fascinating to see whether it does—or whether there's yet more here than meets the eye.

Source: Geoffrey Colvin, "Bad Boards, Bad Boards—Whatcha Gonna Do?" Fortune, *April 26, 1999, pp. 411–420.*

On the other hand, stock ownership by board members may not necessarily motivate board members to maximize shareholder wealth. Many outside directors of a board are presently high-level managers of other firms, where their compensation exceeds $1 million per year. When they are granted options for a small amount of stock representing the firm for which they are outside board members, they may view the potential compensation for enacting major changes to be insignificant. Thus, some board members may believe that advocating major changes is not worth the effort, and they may focus their efforts on managing the firms where they are employed.

Impact of the Size of the Board

The board's size may affect its ability to ensure that the firm's managers serve shareholders. The ideal board size varies, but a board of 8 or 10 directors is normally preferred to a board of 20 or more directors. A relatively large board of directors tends to be less effective for the following reasons. First, there may be less communication among board members in firms with numerous directors. Second, the directors may not believe that their input will be as valuable within a large board because there are so many other members. A related reason is that views about the firm's management are more likely to diverge when there are many directors so it may be more difficult to reach a consensus when attempting to enact changes.

How the Board Aligns Manager and Investor Interests

Although the control of a firm (by managers) and the ownership of the firm (by investors) are separated, various methods can be used to align the interests of managers with the interests of the investors who own the firm's stock. Three common methods that can be implemented by a firm's board of directors to align the interests of managers and investors of a firm are (1) reducing free cash flow, (2) forcing stock ownership by high-level managers, and (3) aligning compensation and stock-price performance.

Reducing Free Cash Flow

If a firm's board is concerned that its managers are spending funds in ways that do not serve shareholder interests, they can enact restructuring that will constrain managers. In particular, boards of directors are concerned with how managers use the firm's *free cash flow*—extra cash available to managers that is not designated for a specific purpose. If managers have extra cash beyond what they need to support projects that will enhance the firm's value, they may be tempted to spend it on perquisites for themselves or on other projects.

When managers have access to a substantial amount of free cash flow, they commonly use the funds to acquire other firms. If managers are perceived to be making an acquisition because they happen to have excess cash available, rather than because it advances a strategic business plan, they will typically be penalized by the market as a result. In particular, some investors immediately respond to a firm's acquisitions of unrelated businesses by selling their holdings of the firm's stock, which results in a lower stock price of the firm. There is evidence that such firms tend to experience poor performance, on average, over several years following their acquisitions of unrelated businesses.

Of course, any firm is subject to potential agency problems in which managers make some expenditures that do not serve shareholder interests, but those firms with excess cash are more susceptible. The cash is already available, so managers may not have to justify their expenditures in order to obtain funding.

When a board of directors senses that the firm has excess free cash flow, it may consider initiating a *stock repurchase* to remove the free cash flow from managers. As a firm repurchases some of its existing stock that was owned by investors, it reduces the amount of its shares that are owned by investors. Thus any future wealth of the firm that is generated is allocated to a smaller number of shareholders. Assuming that the firm can support its business with less equity, it can achieve a higher return on the remaining equity investment provided by shareholders. A stock repurchase may also signal the confidence of managers and directors in their firm's value, because a firm would not repurchase its shares if it expected its stock price to decline.

Forcing Stock Ownership by High-Level Managers

A board of directors may force the firm's CEO and other high-level managers to invest in the stock of the firm they manage. As partial owners, the CEO and high-level managers may be encouraged to make decisions that maximize the stock price. By owning some of the firm's stock, they can benefit directly from their decisions. If they make poor decisions that cause the stock price of the firm to decline, their wealth will be reduced.

Aligning Compensation and Stock-Price Performance

High-level managers (including the CEO) may be more motivated to achieve high stock-price performance of the firm (the goal of shareholders) if their compensation is tied to the firm's stock-price performance level. Thus, many firms have created compensation plans that align pay with performance. This strategy is separate from that of requiring high-level managers to invest in the stock of the firm, but it is related in that it aligns their future wealth with the degree to which the managers increase the wealth of their shareholders.

Potential Distortions When Aligning Compensation with Stock-Price Performance   Although most shareholders and managers agree that CEO compensation should be related to a firm's stock-price performance, there is some concern about abuses that may occur when compensation is aligned with stock price performance. For example, some firms offer their high-level managers stock or stock options without requiring them to meet any performance goals. Advanced Micro Devices (AMD), for example, created a compensation scheme that offered AMD stock options to the CEO in specific periods as compensation for meeting various performance levels. However, these stock options were granted eventually anyway, even if the performance levels were not achieved. Thus, the incentive to achieve high performance was very limited.

A second type of abuse occurs when managers use creative accounting procedures to boost earnings temporarily. Such distortion of the firm's performance may boost expected future cash flows and therefore its stock price. To the extent that managers can manipulate earnings in a manner that temporarily increases the stock price, they may temporarily boost their compensation. Sunbeam's CEO was accused of this practice in 1999.

A third type of distortion can result from using absolute measures of performance. Consider the 1996–1998 period, in which the prices of many stocks doubled. If a firm's stock price increased by 40 percent during this period, and the stock prices of all of the firm's competitors increased by 120% over the same period, does the firm's CEO deserve extra compensation? Many compensation plans for CEOs were based on a specified measure of the return to shareholders (such as 40 percent). Under that arrangement, many CEOs benefited from the bullish stock market in the 1996–1998 period even though their firm's stock performance was worse than that of their competitors.

Because performance may be more properly measured on a relative basis than on an absolute basis, more recently devised compensation plans base extra compensation on how a firm performs relative to its competitors. This method controls for specific industry effects that could influence the stock-price performance of firms.

Example ▼   The board of directors of Z-Plus Inc. was attempting to determine how to compensate a CEO whom the firm was about to hire. The directors planned to provide a salary of $2,000,000 for each of the next 3 years, with additional compensation that would be based on the performance of the firm. They considered the following performance measures for determining the CEO's compensation:

- The firm's earnings per share
- The firm's stock return (including dividends paid and the appreciation of the stock price)

- The firm's excess earnings per share relative to the mean earnings per share of competitors
- The firm's excess stock return relative to the mean stock-price performance of competitors

They wanted the compensation to be tied to how well the CEO performed, but they struggled with the proper measure of the CEO's performance. They agreed that the CEO does not have much control over industry sales. Thus the CEO's compensation should not be dictated by the overall performance of the industry. They also agreed that the CEO does not have control of general stock market trends, and thus the CEO's compensation should not be dictated by general stock market conditions. They believed that the main objective of the CEO was to help the firm achieve relatively high performance compared with other firms in the industry. And they decided that the CEO has more control over the firm's performance within the industry relative to its competitors. Therefore, one way to align compensation with performance would be to measure the percentage by which the firm's earnings or stock performance exceeded the respective average of all the competitor firms. However, they were uncomfortable with the earnings measure because a firm can boost its earnings over a given period by merely applying specific accounting procedures. They decided to use the firm's excess stock return relative to the mean stock return of the firm's competitors. They also decided to impose maximum limits on the compensation that could be earned by the high-level managers who would be participating in the plan.

Examples of Actual Compensation Levels   The compensation levels of CEOs of some large well-known U.S. firms during 1998 are shown in Table 22.1. Note that this table includes long-term compensation, which includes the sale of stock options that were granted. The long-term compensation typically exceeds the annual salary and bonus. There may also be forms of long-term compensation that were granted, but were not exercised until after the year ended, and are therefore not shown in the table.

The fifth column shows the total compensation to the CEO over the 1996–1998 period, and the sixth column shows the dollar return to shareholders who invested in that firm over the same 3-year period. In particular, Michael Eisner's (Disney) 1998 compensation of about $570 million stands out. If compensation were aligned with stock performance, there should be a relationship between these two variables. In fact, there *is* some evidence that compensation of CEOs and stock performance levels across firms are positively related, but there are many exceptions. For example, note in Table 22.1 that the compensation for Cendant's CEO over a 3-year period is about $98 million, yet the dollar return is $85 per $100 invested (this reflects a 15 percent loss to shareholders over the period).

Revisions in Option Compensation Plans   When a firm's stock price declines substantially, the stock options owned by the high-level managers are usually far below the option's exercise price (they are "deep out-of-the-money"). Under these circumstances, the board of directors may consider adjusting the option's exercise price so that it is more achievable. In fact, more than 200 firms allowed this type of adjustment in 1998. Such an adjustment may motivate the managers who hold options, making them more likely to benefit if the firm improves.

TABLE 22.1	Examples of Executive Compensation				
Firm	Name of CEO	1998 Salary and Bonus	1998 Long-Term Compensation	1996–1998 Total Compensation	1996–1998 Dollar Return to Shareholders per $100 Invested
Boeing	P.M. Condit	$ 999,000	$ 2,027,000	$10,829,000	$ 86
Motorola	C.B. Galvin	1,813,000	0	7,382,000	110
Starbucks	H.D. Schultz	1,175,000	17,036,000	21,134,000	267
Kellogg	A.G. Langbo	1,028,000	1,856,000	10,424,000	95
Cisco Systems	J.T. Chambers	891,000	0	34,661,000	560
Cendant	H.R. Silverman	2,818,000	61,063,000	98,635,000	85
Maytag	L.A. Hadley	1,770,000	3,863,000	9,859,000	328
Disney	M.D. Eisner	5,764,000*	569,828,000	594,892,000	156

*Salary and bonus were waived.
Source: Business Week, April, 19, 1999.

Shareholders are generally against this adjustment, because it reduces the discipline necessary to prevent poor performance by managers. A large decline in stock price normally is the result of poor performance by the firm, so adjusting the stock options as explained above essentially eliminates the penalty for poor performance. And, if those firms rebound just to their original levels, the managers can receive substantial compensation from the options alone. Therefore, shareholders argue that managerial compensation via options should be strictly aligned with the stock-price performance.

? Review Questions

22–2   Explain why a board of directors may prefer to implement a stock repurchase rather than allow managers to use funds for expansion.

22–3   Explain why a board of directors may require that the CEO and high-level managers own stock of the firm.

LG3 Control by Investors

If the firm's board of directors does not effectively ensure that the firm's managers will serve shareholders interests, the investors may need to perform this task themselves.

 **PUTTING ON THE PRESSURE**

Institution-led shareholder activism has evolved over the past 10 years as institutional investors have demanded change—and gotten results.

Institutional investors are growing less shy about wielding their shareholder power. Activist shareholders have prompted Waste Management to fire its top management team and Marriott to reverse the spin-off of some operations....

Calpers, the massive California Public Employees Retirement System, voted its 11 million Bank of America shares against management on several issues this past spring [1999]....Nothing personal, Bank of America. It's just how Calpers operates. Part of its credo: "Calpers also strongly believes that 'good' governance requires the attention and dedication not only of a company's officers and directors, but also of its owners. Calpers is not simply a passive holder of stock. We are a 'shareowner,' and take seriously the responsibility that comes with company ownership."

Institution-led shareholder activism has evolved over the past 10 years or so, said Nell Minow, a principal with Lens, a well-known activist money manager from Portland, Maine....Minow's group has a standard operating procedure for nudging change out of managers. "We start by being nice and cooperative," Minow said. "We write a letter to the CEO: 'We couldn't help noticing that everyone else seems to be doing better than you.'" If managers ignore the letter, Minow tries to arrange a visit with the CEO....If Minow isn't satisfied with the meeting, the next step is another letter, sometimes copied to a Web posting, with specific suggestions. The company can take the suggestions, come up with a better idea, show how Lens' facts are wrong, or prepare for the next step: a proxy contest, often accompanied by as much publicity as Minow can generate.

But it's hard to argue with...results. A Wilshire Associates study examined the performance of 62 companies targeted by Calpers. In the five-year period before Calpers acted, the stock of these companies trailed the Standard & Poor's 500 index by 89 percent. In the five years after Calpers acted the same stocks outperformed the index by 23 percent, adding approximately $150 million annually in returns to the fund.

Source: Clifford Glickman, "Putting on the Pressure," The Charlotte (NC) Observer, December 6, 1999, downloaded from www.charlotte.com/ observer/business/bizmon/1206invest.htm.

Investors' Characteristics That Affect Their Degree of Control

The degree of control that investors have over managers is influenced by the following factors.

Number of Shareholders

A firm that has a small number of investors who own the majority of shares is subject to much control. Any one of those investors who owns a substantial portion of the firm will be recognized by the board and the management. Conversely, a firm that is owned by thousands of shareholders, each of whom owns a tiny percentage of the shares, is subject to very little control. No single investor has enough of the shares to receive much attention from the firm's board and from management.

Proportion of Institutional Ownership

A firm whose shares are owned largely by institutional investors is subject to a higher degree of control. First, institutional investors commonly invest a great deal of money when buying a firm's stock. Many financial institutions own millions of shares of a single firm, although this amount may represent a small percentage of the firm's total shares outstanding. Given the large dollar amount, they can benefit from exerting some effort to control the firm's operations.

Second, institutional investors assess firms on a daily basis and have expertise in monitoring firms. Thus, they have more resources than individual investors to monitor firms. They commonly communicate with some of the firm's high-level managers and have opportunities to voice their concerns about the firm's operations. The financial managers of firms may be willing to consider the changes suggested by large institutional investors, because they do not want those investors to sell their holdings of the firm's stock.

Institutional investors also have the resources to attempt to influence the firm's board. They may hire employees who spend much of their time assessing the performance of the firms in which they own shares, communicating with the board, and even initiating lawsuits against the board if it is not performing its duties for shareholders. Some institutional investors have become much more involved in monitoring the management of firms; they realize they can enhance the value of their security portfolios by ensuring that the firms in which they invest are properly managed.

Shareholder Activism

Shareholders who are displeased with the way the firm's managers are managing the firm have three general choices. The first is to do nothing, but to retain the shares in the hope that management behavior will ultimately lead to strong stock-price performance. A second choice is to sell the stock. This choice is common among investors who do not believe they can effect change in the firm's management or do not wish to spend time and money doing so. A third choice is to engage in shareholder activism.

Some of the more common forms of shareholder activism are described here.

Communication with the Firm

Investors can attempt to communicate their concerns to other investors in order to place more pressure on the firm's managers, or on its board members, to enact change. For example, shareholders may voice concerns about a firm that expands outside its core businesses, attempts to acquire other companies at excessive prices, or defends against a takeover that the shareholders believe would be beneficial.

Example ▼   One large institutional investor that commonly communicates its concerns to firms is the California Public Employees' Retirement System (CALPERS), which manages the pension fund of employees of the state of California. It manages more than $100 billion of securities and commonly maintains large stock positions in some firms. When CALPERS believes that these firms are not being managed properly, it communicates its concerns and sometimes proposes solutions. Some of the firms adjust their management to accommodate CALPERS. Others do not. CALPERS periodically announces a list of firms that it believes have serious agency problems. These firms may have been unwilling to respond to CALPERS concerns about their management style.

Another large institutional investor that commonly communicates its concerns to firms is the Teachers Insurance & Annuity Association/College Retirement Equities Fund (TIAA-CREF). It is the world's largest pension fund, with $255 billion invested in securities. TIAA-CREF has hired two former chief executive officers of firms to communicate its concerns to specific firms. It has also hired an expert in assessing a firm's governance characteristics (such as the number of outside directors on the board) that reflect the degree of each firm's allegiance to its shareholders. These specialists review the characteristics of many firms whose stocks are in TIAA-CREF's investment portfolios. If they believe that a firm's prevailing governance characteristics are inadequate, they send the firm a letter or try to meet with the firm's management or board. For example, they convinced AMD to include more outside directors on its board. They also convinced Disney to replace two of its inside directors with outside directors.

Proxy Contest

proxy
The assignment of voting power to a specified party during a corporate annual meeting.

A **proxy** transfers a shareholder's voting power to a another party who will attend the firm's annual meeting and vote the shares. Many shareholders commonly assign their votes to managers. However, when shareholders are dissatisfied with managers, they may also engage in proxy contests in an attempt to reorganize the composition of the board.

Shareholder Lawsuits or Other Actions

Investors may sue the board if they believe that the board is not fulfilling its responsibilities to shareholders. This action is intended to force the board to make decisions that are aligned with the wealth maximization goal of shareholders. For example, TIAA-CREF met with the CEO of Heinz to express its concern that a majority of Heinz's directors were insiders and friends of the CEO. The CEO of Heinz did not respond to this concern, so TIAA-CREF filed a shareholder resolution with the Securities and Exchange Commission (SEC). The pension fund recently withdrew the filing, because Heinz finally responded by restructuring its board to include more outside directors.

Review Questions

22–4 Explain why a firm that is owned by a larger proportion of institutional owners may have fewer agency problems than a firm owned by numerous individual investors.

22–5 Explain how shareholder activism may affect the value of the firm.

Market for Corporate Control

To the extent that a firm's managers do not act in the best interests of shareholders, the stock price of the firm will be less than what it would have been if the managers focused on maximizing shareholder wealth. However, an underperforming firm *is* subject to the "market for corporate control," because it is subject to a takeover by another firm.

Example ▼

Weak Inc. is a firm based in Long Beach, California, whose managers have been subject to very little monitoring. The high-level managers of the firm have used much of the firm's excess cash to expand their own departments, even when expansion was not warranted. The board is largely made up of these same managers.

Strong Inc. is in the same industry as Weak Inc. It recognizes that Weak's stock price is relatively low (because of poor performance) and believes that the firm could operate much more efficiently if it were managed properly. Strong Inc. has been considering expansion in the western United States and could achieve this objective by acquiring a firm like Weak Inc. The stock price of Weak Inc. is presently $20. Because Weak has 30 million shares of stock outstanding, its market value is $600 million. Strong Inc. believes that Weak's stock price would be about $40 if it were managed properly. Thus it decides to attempt to acquire Weak Inc. It plans to meet with Weak to discuss the acquisition, but if Weak is not willing to be acquired, Strong will attempt to buy enough of Weak's shares in the stock market to gain control of the firm. Strong expects that it will have to pay about $26 per share to acquire Weak Inc., but this is still substantially below the value the stock will assume if Weak's operations are properly managed. Once it gains control, Strong Inc. plans to reorganize the firm, which will result in the firing of Weak's high-level managers.

▲

This example illustrates how the market for corporate control works. If a firm's managers do not serve the interests of shareholders, the stock price may decline to a level at which some other firm decides to acquire it cheaply. Once the firm is acquired, the managers who did not serve the interests of shareholders may lose their jobs. Thus, the market for corporate control can impose a penalty on managers who do not serve shareholder interests. If the managers had served shareholder interests, the firm's stock price would be higher and the firm would not be a takeover target because it would be too expensive to acquire. Alternatively, even if it were acquired, the managers might be retained by the acquiring firm if they had been serving shareholder interests.

There is some disagreement about whether the market for corporate control has had favorable or unfavorable effects on firms. Some critics claim that acquisitions of inefficient firms typically lead to layoffs; therefore, they adversely affect economic conditions and are unfair to employees. The counterargument is that without the market for corporate control, firms would be allowed to be inefficient, which is unfair to the shareholders who invested in them.

Barriers to Corporate Control

The power of corporate control to eliminate agency problems at firms is limited by barriers that can make it more costly for a potential acquiring firm to acquire another firm. We will discuss some of the more common barriers to corporate control.

Anti-Takeover Amendments

anti-takeover amendments
Revisions to a corporate charter that attempt to prevent hostile takeovers.

Some firms have enacted **anti-takeover amendments** to their corporate charter, which are revisions to the charter that attempt to prevent hostile takeovers.

There are various types of anti-takeover amendments. For example, an amendment may require that at least two-thirds of the shareholder votes approve a takeover before the firm can be acquired. Anti-takeover amendments are supposedly enacted to protect shareholders from an acquisition that will ultimately reduce the value of their investment in the firm. However, it may be argued that shareholders are adversely affected by the anti-takeover amendments.

Recall the previous example in which Strong Inc. planned to acquire Weak Inc. because Weak's relatively low stock price made it a cheap takeover target. However, assume that Weak Inc. enacted an anti-takeover amendment before Strong initiated its takeover attempt. Strong Inc. might no longer be willing to pursue the acquisition because it would be more difficult to acquire Weak Inc. Consequently, Weak Inc. may continue its poor performance. The market for corporate control would not have worked effectively to discipline Weak Inc. for its poor performance.

Example ▼

AMP is a producer of electrical connectors. It experienced weak performance in the mid-1990s. Allied Signal contacted AMP to propose a takeover of AMP. When it received no response, Allied Signal publicized its desire to acquire AMP. The prevailing stock price of AMP was about $26 per share before Allied Signal announced its desire to purchase AMP's shares for $44.50 per share. The majority of AMP's shareholders approved the acquisition, but AMP's board initiated a court battle to delay responding to Allied Signal's acquisition attempt. Allied Signal withdrew its acquisition offer. AMP's shareholders ultimately got their wish when AMP was acquired (by Tyco International) on November 30, 1998. ▲

Poison Pills

poison pills
Special rights, awarded to shareholders or specific managers if specified events occur, which make it more expensive or more difficult for a potential acquiring firm to acquire the target.

Poison pills are special rights that are to be awarded to shareholders or specific managers if specified events occur. They can be enacted by a firm's board without the approval of shareholders. An example of a poison pill is the right of all shareholders to be allocated an additional 30 percent of shares (based on their existing share holdings) without cost whenever a potential acquirer attempts to acquire the firm. These poison pills make it more expensive and more difficult for a potential acquiring firm to acquire the target.

Example ▼

On March 3, 1999, Chubb Corporation enacted a shareholder rights plan that protected against the market for corporate control. The negative share-price response to this action, shown in Figure 22.2, reflects the potential adverse effects of Chubb's actions from the perspective of potential investors.

Similarly, on April 13, 1999, Lilian Vernon Company adopted a poison pill. The initial negative share-price response to this announcement is shown in Figure 22.2. The poison pill was perceived to protect Lilian Vernon from the market for corporate control. ▲

Golden Parachutes

golden parachute
An agreement that specifies compensation to managers in the event of the loss of their jobs or a change in the control of the firm.

A **golden parachute** specifies compensation to managers in the event of the loss of their jobs or a change in the control of the firm. An example is the right of all managers to receive 100,000 shares of the firm's stock whenever the firm is acquired. It may be argued that a golden parachute provides managers with secu-

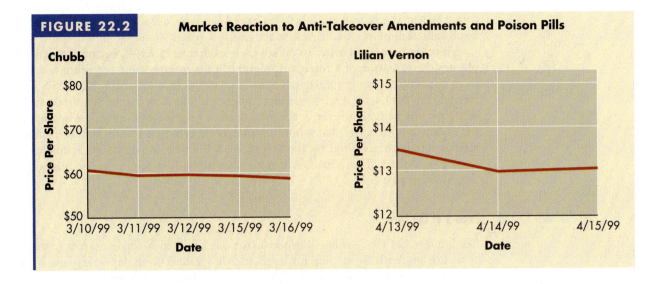

FIGURE 22.2   **Market Reaction to Anti-Takeover Amendments and Poison Pills**

rity so that they can make decisions that will improve the long-term performance of the firm. That is, if they are protected by a golden parachute, managers may be more willing to make decisions intended to enhance shareholder wealth over the long run even if these decisions adversely affect the stock price in the short run. The counterargument is that a golden parachute allows managers to serve their own interests rather than shareholder interests, because they receive large compensation even if they are fired.

Golden parachutes can discourage takeover attempts by increasing the cost of the acquisition. A potential acquiring firm recognizes that it will incur the expense associated with the golden parachute if it acquires a particular target that has enacted golden parachutes prior to the takeover attempt. To the extent that this (or any) defense against takeovers is effective, it disrupts the market for corporate control by allowing managers of some firms to be protected while serving their own interests rather than shareholder interests.

Global Market for Corporate Control

Just as U.S. firms may attempt to acquire local firms whose stock prices are low, they may also acquire foreign firms. Thus, the global market for corporate control may motivate managers of firms in foreign countries to serve shareholder interests, so long as those firms are subject to the possibility of a takeover.

However, the laws pertaining to the foreign countries may impose various restrictions on the acquiring firm, which may make the acquisition more costly. For example, a multinational corporation that acquires a firm in Europe may be prevented by European government agencies from firing any of the firm's employees, even if it can be shown that there are excessive numbers of them. In general, the laws in Europe have been more favorable to employees than to shareholders, and this is one reason why many investors who live in Europe do not invest in the stocks of firms. However, as European countries become more integrated, European government agencies are beginning to recognize that local firms must be efficient in order to survive competition from other European firms. Hence, the barriers to takeovers have been reduced, which has resulted in a substantial number of takeovers in the last few years.

Another potential barrier to takeovers is exchange rate risk, because it complicates the valuation of a foreign firm and can discourage some acquiring firms from pursuing targets in foreign countries. For example, a U.S. firm may detect a foreign firm that is not serving its shareholders and therefore can be acquired at a relatively low price. However, if the local currency is expected to weaken against the dollar, any earnings that would ultimately be remitted by the foreign firm, after it has been acquired by the U.S. firm, would be converted to a smaller number of dollars. Thus, the U.S. firm may not pursue the acquisition because of the exchange rate risk.

Impact of the Euro

On January, 2, 1999, eleven European nations adopted a single currency, the *euro*. It is presently being used for large financial transactions; day-to-day use by consumers will be phased in by 2002. The conversion of currencies in several European countries to the euro has improved the market for corporate control. Now that a single currency is used, it is easier for an acquiring firm to determine how one target firm's value compares with other European firms in the same industry.

The euro also encourages more cross-border takeovers. In the past, a firm may have appeared to be weaker than others in the industry but may not have become a takeover target because of concerns about exchange rate risk. Since the adoption of the euro, a firm may be acquired by another firm in Europe without concerns about exchange rate risk. Thus, European firms are more willing to acquire the weaker firms that have low stock prices and have potential for improvement.

? Review Questions

22–6   Explain in general terms how the market for corporate control can reduce agency problems of firms.

22–7   Explain why anti-takeover amendments may increase agency problems of firms.

Monitoring and Control by Creditors

Like shareholders, creditors must monitor a firm's management. However, creditors are more concerned with the firm's ability and willingness to repay its debt to them than with the firm's stock price. Therefore, they monitor a firm's management in a different manner than do shareholders.

How Management Decisions Can Affect Creditors

One of the main concerns of creditors is that managers will make decisions that benefit themselves and shareholders at the creditors' expense. For example, consider managers whose compensation is aligned with the stock price. Managers may consider issuing an excessive amount of debt and using the proceeds to repurchase stock in order to boost the firm's stock price. The existing creditors may be concerned that such a strategy will increase the risk that the firm will be unable to cover its debt payments. This large increase in financial leverage may temporarily increase the potential return to the existing shareholders, but it could reduce the value of the debt securities held by creditors.

If the creditors attempt to sell their holdings of these debt securities, they may receive a lower price as a result of the financial strategy used by the firm's managers. This example illustrates how managers may enact a strategy that is acceptable to shareholders but adversely affects the firm's creditors. In the long run, such strategies would even adversely affect shareholders, because the firm would not be able to obtain debt financing at a reasonable cost if it lost the trust of creditors.

How Creditors Control Managers

As noted in Chapter 3, creditors commonly include restrictive protective covenants in loan or bond indentures to safeguard themselves against managerial actions that might adversely affect the value of the debt securities they purchase. For example, a bond indenture may specify that a firm's debt ratio may not exceed some maximum percentage. This type of restriction can prevent managers from adjusting the capital structure in a manner that will increase the risk to creditors.

? Review Question

22–8   Why do creditors monitor a firm's performance in a different manner than stockholders?

Conflict Between Managers and Mutual Fund Investors

Just as investors monitor their investment in shares of firms, they monitor their investment in shares issued by mutual funds. Mutual funds accumulate investments from individual investors and invest these funds for individuals. Like firms, they utilize funds provided by investors to invest in assets. However, whereas firms focus their investment on real assets (such as buildings or machinery), mutual funds focus their investment on financial assets (securities).

Mutual Fund Agency Problems

Just as a firm's managers may sometimes be tempted to deviate from the objective of serving the firm's respective shareholders, a mutual fund's managers may be tempted as well. There are many examples in which a mutual fund's management does not necessarily serve the interests of the shareholders. Let's look at two such examples.

Managing Tax Liabilities for Shareholders

Mutual funds have some flexibility as to the accounting method (such as last-in–first-out) that they use to determine the capital gains on their stock transactions. The means by which mutual funds account for their stock transactions can affect the taxes ultimately paid by the shareholders of the fund. However, many mutual funds do not account for the transactions in a manner that is most beneficial to their shareholders.

Managerial Expenses Charged to Shareholders

A second example of a mutual fund agency problem pertains to the expenses that are charged to the shareholders. Consider a mutual fund that had a net asset value 1 year ago equal to $100 million and charged its shareholders $1 million in annual management and administrative fees. This reflects an expense ratio of 1 percent. Assume that over the last year, the amount invested in the fund remained the same but the net asset value of the fund increased to $140 million, simply because favorable stock market conditions caused the net asset value of the fund to rise by 40 percent. In this example, the expense of managing the portfolio should not have changed much, if at all. If the fund charges $1 million in annual expenses, the expense ratio is now about 0.71 percent, but if the mutual fund retains its expense ratio at 1 percent, it will collect annual charges from shareholders of $1.4 million (1% × $140 million). Over the last several years, many mutual funds have maintained a somewhat stable expense ratio as their stock portfolios have appreciated. Many investors do not realize that they are being charged higher expenses when the expense ratio remains stable while the fund's value increases.

Mutual Fund Boards of Directors

Each mutual fund has a board of directors that oversees the management of the fund. The board is responsible for ensuring that the fund's management is serving the interests of the shareholders. Directors can prevent abuses such as those just mentioned. They can ensure that proper accounting is used (within the accepted accounting guidelines) to minimize taxes paid by shareholders. In addition, they should not approve of an increase in annual expenses proposed by the mutual fund management unless there are obvious benefits that shareholders will receive as a result of being charged higher expenses.

Directors of mutual funds do not always protect the shareholders from the abuses described above. Investors in mutual funds do not have much power to influence the management of mutual funds. Because investors are usually individual (rather than institutional), they do not have the resources to influence the mutual fund management. In addition, there is no market for corporate control similar to the one for firms. Thus, a mutual fund's management is not threatened with takeover of its portfolio just because it charges excessive management and administrative fees.

Given that some mutual fund boards do not ensure that a fund's management serves shareholder interests, and given the very limited influence of investors, the agency problem in the mutual fund industry is pronounced. The agency problem would be reduced if mutual funds were forced to disclose information about their expenses in simple terms. Although the Securities and Exchange Commission (SEC) has been trying to mandate simple, standardized disclosure of expenses charged by mutual funds, it has not yet been successful in doing so.

? Review Question

22–9   Explain how a mutual fund might experience agency problems.

TYING IT ALL TOGETHER

This chapter described the potential conflicts between managers and investors. It explained how the firm's board of directors can exert control over a firm's managers and how investors can do so. It also described the market for corporate control, as reflected in the threat of takeover of underperforming firms. The roles of managers, financial markets, and investors in corporate control and governance are summarized in the Integrative Table that follows.

INTEGRATIVE TABLE

Managing and Monitoring a Firm to Ensure That Shareholder Interests Are Served

Role of **Financial Managers**	*Role of* **Financial Markets**	*Role of* **Investors**
Financial managers are expected to make investment and financing decisions that maximize the value of the firm. They are tempted to serve their own interests rather than shareholder interests, which would cause the firm's stock price to be lower than its potential price.	When financial managers make decisions that do not serve shareholder interests, the firm's stock price is less than its potential price. The firm may become a target for a takeover by other firms because it may be undervalued in the market. Thus the market for corporate control encourages managers to serve shareholder interests in order to prevent a takeover.	The firm's board of directors represents shareholders and is expected to oversee the decisions of the firm's managers. In addition, shareholders monitor the decisions made by managers and can initiate shareholder activism if they are not satisfied with those decisions.

LG1 **Describe the relationship between managers and investors, and explain the potential conflict in goals.** Managers serve as agents of the firm by managing the firm in a manner that is supposed to maximize the value of the firm's stock. However, managers may themselves benefit more directly by making decisions that are intended to serve their own interests rather than the interests of shareholders.

LG2 **Explain how a firm's board of directors can control the managers of the firm.** A board is normally expected to be more effective in exerting control over managers if it is dominated by outside directors, allows an outside director to serve as chair of the board, compensates the directors with stock instead of cash payments, and has a relatively small number of directors. The board may initiate restructuring that is better aligned with shareholder interests. It may alter the compensation of the CEO and other high-level managers to ensure that managerial decisions are aligned with shareholder interests. It also has the power to fire a CEO who does not attempt to serve shareholder interests.

LG3 **Explain how investors in the firm's stock can control the managers of the firm.** Investors can sell the firm's stock if the firm's managers do not serve shareholder interests. Alternatively, they may be able to communicate to the firm's board of directors that they are displeased with the firm's management. They can also attempt to sue the board of directors if it is not living up to its responsibility of serving shareholder interests.

LG4 **Explain how the market for corporate control can ensure that managers of firms serve their firms' respective shareholders.** If managers of a firm do not serve shareholder interests, the stock price will be lower than the price that would exist if shareholder interests were served.

This firm may become a takeover target because its stock can be purchased at a relatively low price. Other firms could acquire this firm at a low price and restructure it so that the business can be more efficiently managed as it is merged with the acquiring firm's existing business.

LG5 **Describe the relationship between managers and creditors.** If managers make specific decisions that temporarily maximize the value of the stock by increasing the potential return, they may increase the perceived risk of the firm. This could adversely affect the value of existing debt securities held by creditors. To prevent such actions, creditors normally demand restrictive covenants in the loan or bond indenture.

LG6 **Describe the relationship between mutual fund management and investors.** Mutual fund management is supposed to serve the interests of shareholders. However, the management may sometimes make decisions that do not serve their shareholders' interests. For example, some mutual funds charge a relatively high level of expenses that cannot be justified given their operations. Each mutual fund has a board of directors that is responsible for monitoring the management, but some boards do not effectively force mutual fund managers to act in the interests of shareholders.

SELF-TEST EXERCISES   (Solutions in Appendix B)

LG2 **ST 22–1   Control by the board of directors**   Fenstock Inc. has a board of directors that contains five inside directors, including the firm's CEO, and six outside directors, one of whom is the chairman of the board. The chairman reserves her vote for those situations in which a tie must be broken. Fenstock has received from one of its competitors a tender offer that would result in a merged company with greater efficiencies of scale and broader market share. Fenstock's shareholders have been offered the equivalent of two times the market value of their shares prior to the tender offer. It is apparent that Fenstock's CEO and much of the company's upper management may lose their jobs if the merger goes through. All of the members of the board of directors own significant amounts of stock in Fenstock Inc.

   a. What possible conflicts of interest do the five inside directors have in this situation? What do they stand to lose? What do they stand to gain?

   b. What qualities might the outside directors bring to this situation that will help to clarify the decision?

c. Assuming that the price offered is more than fair compensation for Fenstock shares, what action would be in the best interests of the shareholders?

d. If the board vote ends up tied, how would you vote if you were the chairman? Explain your vote.

LG4 ST 22–2   The market for corporate control   The descendants of William Polk control 45% of the voting shares of Artemesia, Inc., a commercial horticulture company he founded in 1890. At present, four of his great-grandchildren work in various management positions in the corporation. Family members sit in six of the ten directors positions on the company's board. Much of the firm's free cash flow has been invested in the development of new plant strains for which there is much scientific recognition but little commercial market. The share value has languished between $12 and $15 for several years. Dianthus, Inc., a rival seed company, believes that it could run Artemesia much more efficiently and at a greater profit, resulting in a share price of $32. After careful consideration, Dianthus has decided to make an offer to acquire Artemesia for $23 per share. The offer is opposed by a majority of Artemesia's board of directors.

a. What shareholder vote is likely if Dianthus pursues the offer over the objection of Artemesia's board of directors?

b. How have Artemesia's apparent management goals conflicted with the best interests of its shareholders?

c. What changes would Dianthus be likely to make in order to bring Artemesia's operations up to their potential efficiency and profitability?

d. What impact on the acquisition would result from the presence of "golden parachute" provisions in the contracts of Artemesia's current managers?

EXERCISES

LG1   22–1   Relationship between managers and investors   John Caskey is chief executive officer of Dallas Corp., a shareholder-owned firm. Recently he has become aware that the firm has an opportunity to make a strategic alliance with one of its competitors that would enhance the profitability of both companies. However, the alliance would take Dallas Corp. into an area about wherein Caskey has little knowledge or skill. That would have a negative impact on his ability to continue as CEO of Dallas Corp. John likes his job very much.

a. What recommendations or actions would be in John Caskey's best interests?

b. What recommendations or actions would be in the best interests of the Dallas Corp. shareholders?

c. Discuss the implications of withholding significant information from investors. How do those considerations apply to this situation?

LG1   22–2   Accounting information   For the last 12 years, Lorry Trailers, Inc. has used the last-in, first-out (LIFO) method for determining inventory costs. This year, increased raw materials prices have cut significantly into profitability. Lorry's CFO realizes that executive compensation will be based on the level of profitability. She is thinking about ways to present the financial statements in such a way as to maximize net earnings and cash flow. (Refer to earlier chapters on financial statement analysis and capital budgeting.)

a. If the firm were to switch inventory methods to first-in, first-out (FIFO), what effect would that change have on net income? Explain why.

b. If the firm were to replace some existing fully depreciated equipment with new machines to be depreciated using an accelerated method, what effect might that have on its net income? Explain why.

c. If executive bonuses were to be deferred from year-end into the first month of the next year, what effect would that change have on net income for the year just finished?

22–3   The chairman and the board   Yancey Clifton has been CEO and chairman of the board at House Industries, Inc. for the last 7 years. Prior to that, he spent 12 years as the company's chief financial officer (CFO) and another 3 years as its CEO before adding the title of board chairman. Yancey has strong ideas about the direction the company should move in and is known for his "one-man-show" approach to management.

a. What are the basic duties of a board chairman?

b. What are the duties of a member of the board of directors?

c. If the board were made up of six inside directors and four outside directors, what factors would affect presentation of shareholder issues and the action taken on those issues?

d. If the board were made up of eight outside directors and three inside directors, how would your answer to part **c** change? What influence would Yancey Clifton still have as chairman?

e. Make up a list of the pros and cons involved in having Yancey Clifton as an inside director and chairman of the board.

f. What information about Yancey Clifton and about House Industries would help you evaluate this situation?

22–4   Outside director compensation   Whopper Industries has six outside directors on its board. Each of them is a high-level manager of another corporation. Whopper has decided to enact board compensation that will encourage the board members to maximize shareholder wealth. Whopper is a small, publicly traded company. Its shares have a current value of $15. The plan under consideration is to compensate board members with 50 shares per meeting for each of the 10 meetings during the year.

a. How does the proposed compensation compare to normal board member compensation among small firms?

b. Is this compensation plan likely to motivate board members to maximize shareholder wealth? Why or why not?

c. What effect would an increase in the price of Whopper shares to $25 each have on board member compensation?

22–5   Free cash flow   For most purposes, the term *cash flow* can be defined as net income plus any noncash expenses. In most firms, the big noncash expense is depreciation, so one commonly accepted short definition of operating cash flow is net income plus depreciation. Firms use cash flow plus funds raised externally to finance projects and acquisitions. A measure of a firm's success is the amount of economic value that such projects and acquisitions add to the wealth of its shareholders.

a. Define the term *free cash flow*.

b. Why might free cash flow be considered negative for the value of a firm's shares?

c. How can a firm use a stock repurchase to reduce free cash flow?

d. What implications does a stock repurchase have for future earnings per share? Explain how a stock repurchase affects share value.

LG2   **22–6   Aligning compensation with performance**   Beeson Inc. is considering several ways to align the compensation of its management team with the performance of the company's common stock. Examine the options listed below. State the pros and cons associated with each one.

Plan	Basis for performance compensation
A	Compensation for performance levels met will be paid in the form of stock or stock options, regardless of the definition of performance.
B	Performance is to be measured in terms of price appreciation in the stock over a single reporting period.
C	Performance is to be measured in terms of the level of the stock price relative to the level of stock prices among competing firms.

LG3   **22–7   Investor control over managers**   Investment research services such as *Value Line Investment Survey* track and publish the percentage of institutional ownership of stock in a particular company, as well as the percentage ownership of stock by corporate insiders (managers and members of the board).

a. Why would an investor be interested in knowing whether insiders owned a significant amount of stock in a company?

b. What benefits could there be in institutional ownership of significant amounts of stock in a company?

LG4   **22–8   Shareholder interests versus local and employee interests**   Leading Edge Steel, Inc. has made an offer to acquire Old Forge Iron Works, Inc., an employee-owned company. Prior to the takeover offer, Old Forge's stock was valued in the market at $22 per share. Leading Edge is offering $35 per share and plans to move Old Forge's operations from Pennsylvania to Tennessee. It has offered to hire employees who are willing to relocate, though position, seniority, and compensation are subject to negotiation.

a. Explain the dilemma that the shareholder–employees of Old Forge face.

b. What attempts to influence the outcome of the merger might be made by the local community in Pennsylvania?

c. What sort of action might Old Forge's board of directors take to block the takeover even if a majority of the stockholders vote in favor of it?

LG4   **22–9   Anti-takeover measures**   High Country Timber, Inc. has an anti-takeover provision in its corporate charter that requires a 70% favorable share vote in order to pass an acquisition offer. Two months ago an offer from another forest products company was defeated in spite of a favorable vote by 60% of the stockholders. As a result of management inefficiencies in recent years, the firm's current share price is about 40% below its potential value. The board is considering enacting a "poison pill."

a. What is a poison pill? When does it go into effect?

b. What control do the shareholders have over the enactment of the poison pill?

c. What actions could shareholders take to register their opinions with regard to the poison pill?

d. What would be the impact on the firm's share price probably be if a poison pill were enacted?

22–10   Impact of management actions on bondholders   Magna Insurance Corp. purchased $100,000 worth of value of 8% coupon, 5-year-maturity Bosley Corp. bonds 2 years ago at par. At the time of purchase, the bonds were rated A by Moody's. Since then, Bosley has issued a substantial amount of new debt, using the proceeds to repurchase its own common stock. Last week Moody's lowered Bosley's bond rating from A to BBB, in recognition of its increased debt load and high debt/equity ratio. As a result, the bonds that Magna owns now sell at a yield-to-maturity of 10%.

a. Use the bond valuation method that appears earlier in this text to calculate the value of the bonds that Magna owns.

b. If Magna sold the bonds today, what would its loss be?

c. What is the probable short-term consequence of Bosley's actions in repurchasing its shares?

d. What may be the longer-term consequences, for Bosley's stockholders, of the firm's significantly increased debt load?

e. What restrictive covenant could have been placed in the bond indenture that would have prevented or limited Bosley's subsequent sale of debt in order to repurchase its own shares?

 22–11   Mutual fund reporting of taxable gains   The Wonder Fund began investing in Broaddus Scientific in the late 1980s and continued to invest additional amounts in the early 1990s. The end result was a fund position of 156,000 shares at original per-share costs ranging from $12 to $82. (A detailed schedule of the purchases appears below.) Early this year, Wonder Fund's managers decided to take some profits from their investment in Broaddus Scientific and sold 36,000 shares at $94 per share.

Wonder Fund Purchases of Broaddus Scientific Shares

Date	Number of shares purchased	Price per share
4/23/88	10,000	$12.00
7/12/89	5,000	15.50
2/01/90	20,000	16.25
5/08/90	20,000	22.75
6/24/92	25,000	38.00
11/12/93	30,000	63.25
1/15/94	26,000	68.50
3/26/95	20,000	82.00

a. If the fund calculates cost basis by using a first-in, first-out (FIFO) method, what will it report as the cost basis for the shares it sold? What will be the total amount of the taxable gain?

b. If the fund calculates cost basis by using a last-in, first-out (LIFO) method, what will it report as the cost basis for the shares it sold? What will be the total amount of the taxable gain?

c. If the fund calculates cost basis by using an average-cost method, what will it report as the cost basis for the shares it sold? What will be the amount of the taxable gain?

d. What cost basis policy should the board of directors be pursuing on behalf of the shareholders?

22–12 Mutual fund management and administration expenses   Paisley Equities Fund is proud that its management and administration expense fee is charged at 0.8% of net asset value, among the lowest in the business. The fund's literature boasts that by sticking with a flat percent-of-assets charge, management is rewarded for good performance and penalized for poor performance. Last year, the fund's NAV increased 14% from $9.85 to $11.23. At the same time, the S&P 500 increased 27%.

a. If the S&P 500 is a fair benchmark for fund performance, how would you judge the performance of Paisley Equities Fund? Use the following formula to compare Paisley's performance to the S&P 500:

$$\frac{(\% \text{ change in Paisley NAV}) - (\% \text{ change in S\&P 500})}{\% \text{ change in S\&P 500}} = \% \text{ difference in performance}$$

b. What could happen in a year in which the S&P 500 was down significantly and Paisley was down as well, but by a much smaller amount? In such a case, how would you rate the performance of Paisley's managers?

c. If you believe that management performance should be rewarded, but that the level of that reward should be separated from general market movements, what sort of performance measurement would result in fair compensation?

d. Say you believe that management should be compensated at a fair amount that is not tied to performance. What sort of compensation plan would you recommend that Paisley Equities Fund adopt?

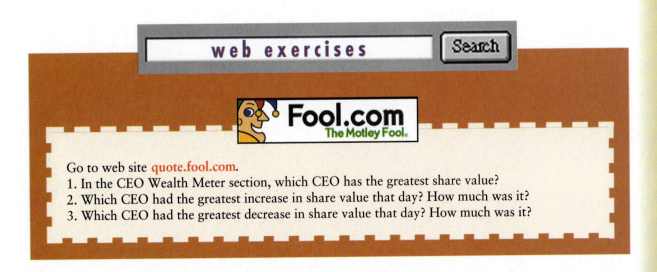

web exercises   Search

Fool.com
The Motley Fool.

Go to web site quote.fool.com.
1. In the CEO Wealth Meter section, which CEO has the greatest share value?
2. Which CEO had the greatest increase in share value that day? How much was it?
3. Which CEO had the greatest decrease in share value that day? How much was it?

web exercises   Search

![YAHOO!]

Go to web site **www.yahoo.com**. Click on **Business & Economy**. Click on **Y!Finance**. Enter **ABT**, the symbol for Abbot Laboratories, into the **Get Quotes** space. Click on **Get Quotes**. Under the **More Info** bar, click on **Insider**.

4. During the last year, how many insider transactions occurred? How many shares were involved in these transactions?

5. What were the different types of actions taken in these transactions?

In the **Action** column, click on **any letter that is in parentheses**.

6. What is a Form 3? A Form 4? A Form 5?

Go to web site **www.insidertrader.com**.

7. What is the Daily Table of Shame?

Under the **Daily Table of Shame**, click on **Today's Late Filers**.

8. How many late filings were there that day?

9. Who was the latest filer, and how many days were there between the day of transaction and the day of filing?

For additional practice with concepts from this chapter, visit
http://www.awl.com/gitman_madura

5

Investor–Manager Conflict at exam-ace.net

Recall that Tom Turner, owner of exam-ace.net, recently decided to provide testing services over the Internet to accountants and that he also plans to provide similar services for brokers, attorneys, and several other types of professionals who need to take a certification exam.

Over the last year, the venture for accountants has not performed well. The idea of online practice testing seemed to work much better for college students who were cramming for an exam (and therefore willing to buy a practice test online) than for accountants who had been studying for their certification exam for several months and had already purchased several study guides for this exam. Cash inflows were low, and the business recently experienced large cash outflows as a result of setting up the system to provide practice exams in accounting. The business is also still incurring expenses from a consultant who was hired to develop a plan in anticipation of an initial public offering someday. Given the recent poor performance of the accounting practice exams business, the entire expansion idea was questionable, because it was based on the same concept as the accounting practice exams. If exam-ace.net did not improve its performance in the near future, it would not even have sufficient funds to cover its debt payments and would fail. However, Tom Turner remained optimistic about the accounting practice exams and his ideas for expansion.

Dan Atkinson, who had originally invested $80,000, is upset that exam-ace.net has changed its business direction. exam-ace.net still provides a service to college students who are taking business classes, and the performance of that part of the business is still strong. However, there is no longer much money available to advertise that service, because funds are needed to cover the expenses associated with expansion.

Dan decided to appeal to Tom's board of directors, but the board was composed simply of Tom and a few of Tom's friends who did not have any experience in running a business. (Dan would have considered appealing to other investors in the business, but the only shareholder other than himself is Tom Turner.) Dan decided to have a formal meeting with Tom, in which he would suggest that Tom discontinue his expansion plans and focus on growing the one type of business that had proved profitable—the original practice testing business for college students.

In their meeting, Tom responded that Dan simply could not recognize the potential value in the new businesses that Tom was pursuing. In fact, Tom maintained that the college exam business had the least potential, because revenues from that business had declined recently (although Dan believed this decline occurred because the advertising was discontinued for lack of funds). Tom was even considering discontinuing that business so that he could focus completely on his expansion ideas.

In summary, the situation as it now stands is that Tom needs funding to expand his new business ideas, whereas Dan believes that the original business should be expanded and that the other, new businesses should be discontinued. Tom is not likely to get funding from anyone else because of the recent performance of the business. Dan is not forced to provide more funds, but he realizes that he will lose his existing investment in exam-ace.net if the business does not receive more funding and consequently fails. Dan wants to find a way to

- find funding for Tom's expansion ideas
- benefit from his belief in the potential of the original business
- avoid involvement in the equity ownership of those new businesses that he believes are likely to fail.

Questions

CC5-1 Offer your recommendation for how Dan could achieve his objectives.

CC5-2 Communication Playing the role of Dan, prepare an e-mail message in which you attempt to convince Tom of the solution you created for the previous question.

CC5-3 Teamwork Create a team of three students, in which one student plays the role of Tom, one student plays the role of Dan, and one student plays the role of the lender. Each student should describe the way he or she could gain from a possible buyout of exam-ace.net by Dan Atkinson.

CC5-4 Ethics If Dan were to offer to purchase the original business from Tom, would Dan, as an equity investor in Tom's original business, be acting ethically?

Appendix A

Financial Tables

TABLE A-1   Future Value Interest Factors for One Dollar Compounded at i Percent for n Periods:

$$FVIF_{i,n} = (1 + i)^n$$

TABLE A-2   Present Value Interest Factors for One Dollar Discounted at i Percent for n Periods:

$$PVIF_{i,n} = \frac{1}{(1 + i)^n}$$

TABLE A-3   Future Value Interest Factors for a One-Dollar Annuity Compounded at i Percent for n Periods:

$$FVIFA_{i,n} = \sum_{t=1}^{n} (1 + i)^{t-1}$$

TABLE A-4   Present Value Interest Factors for a One-Dollar Annuity Discounted at i Percent for n Periods:

$$PVIFA_{i,n} = \sum_{t=1}^{n} \frac{1}{(1 + i)^t}$$

TABLE A-1 Future Value Interest Factors for One Dollar Compounded at i Percent for n Periods: $FVIF_{i,n} = (1 + i)^n$

Period	1%	2%	3%	4%	5%	6%	7%	8%	9%	10%	11%	12%	13%	14%	15%	16%	17%	18%	19%	20%
1	1.010	1.020	1.030	1.040	1.050	1.060	1.070	1.080	1.090	1.100	1.110	1.120	1.130	1.140	1.150	1.160	1.170	1.180	1.190	1.200
2	1.020	1.040	1.061	1.082	1.102	1.124	1.145	1.166	1.188	1.210	1.232	1.254	1.277	1.300	1.322	1.346	1.369	1.392	1.416	1.440
3	1.030	1.061	1.093	1.125	1.158	1.191	1.225	1.260	1.295	1.331	1.368	1.405	1.443	1.482	1.521	1.561	1.602	1.643	1.685	1.728
4	1.041	1.082	1.126	1.170	1.216	1.262	1.311	1.360	1.412	1.464	1.518	1.574	1.630	1.689	1.749	1.811	1.874	1.939	2.005	2.074
5	1.051	1.104	1.159	1.217	1.276	1.338	1.403	1.469	1.539	1.611	1.685	1.762	1.842	1.925	2.011	2.100	2.192	2.288	2.386	2.488
6	1.062	1.126	1.194	1.265	1.340	1.419	1.501	1.587	1.677	1.772	1.870	1.974	2.082	2.195	2.313	2.436	2.565	2.700	2.840	2.986
7	1.072	1.149	1.230	1.316	1.407	1.504	1.606	1.714	1.828	1.949	2.076	2.211	2.353	2.502	2.660	2.826	3.001	3.185	3.379	3.583
8	1.083	1.172	1.267	1.369	1.477	1.594	1.718	1.851	1.993	2.144	2.305	2.476	2.658	2.853	3.059	3.278	3.511	3.759	4.021	4.300
9	1.094	1.195	1.305	1.423	1.551	1.689	1.838	1.999	2.172	2.358	2.558	2.773	3.004	3.252	3.518	3.803	4.108	4.435	4.785	5.160
10	1.105	1.219	1.344	1.480	1.629	1.791	1.967	2.159	2.367	2.594	2.839	3.106	3.395	3.707	4.046	4.411	4.807	5.234	5.695	6.192
11	1.116	1.243	1.384	1.539	1.710	1.898	2.105	2.332	2.580	2.853	3.152	3.479	3.836	4.226	4.652	5.117	5.624	6.176	6.777	7.430
12	1.127	1.268	1.426	1.601	1.796	2.012	2.252	2.518	2.813	3.138	3.498	3.896	4.334	4.818	5.350	5.936	6.580	7.288	8.064	8.916
13	1.138	1.294	1.469	1.665	1.886	2.133	2.410	2.720	3.066	3.452	3.883	4.363	4.898	5.492	6.153	6.886	7.699	8.599	9.596	10.699
14	1.149	1.319	1.513	1.732	1.980	2.261	2.579	2.937	3.342	3.797	4.310	4.887	5.535	6.261	7.076	7.987	9.007	10.147	11.420	12.839
15	1.161	1.346	1.558	1.801	2.079	2.397	2.759	3.172	3.642	4.177	4.785	5.474	6.254	7.138	8.137	9.265	10.539	11.974	13.589	15.407
16	1.173	1.373	1.605	1.873	2.183	2.540	2.952	3.426	3.970	4.595	5.311	6.130	7.067	8.137	9.358	10.748	12.330	14.129	16.171	18.488
17	1.184	1.400	1.653	1.948	2.292	2.693	3.159	3.700	4.328	5.054	5.895	6.866	7.986	9.276	10.761	12.468	14.426	16.672	19.244	22.186
18	1.196	1.428	1.702	2.026	2.407	2.854	3.380	3.996	4.717	5.560	6.543	7.690	9.024	10.575	12.375	14.462	16.879	19.673	22.900	26.623
19	1.208	1.457	1.753	2.107	2.527	3.026	3.616	4.316	5.142	6.116	7.263	8.613	10.197	12.055	14.232	16.776	19.748	23.214	27.251	31.948
20	1.220	1.486	1.806	2.191	2.653	3.207	3.870	4.661	5.604	6.727	8.062	9.646	11.523	13.743	16.366	19.461	23.105	27.393	32.429	38.337
21	1.232	1.516	1.860	2.279	2.786	3.399	4.140	5.034	6.109	7.400	8.949	10.804	13.021	15.667	18.821	22.574	27.033	32.323	38.591	46.005
22	1.245	1.546	1.916	2.370	2.925	3.603	4.430	5.436	6.658	8.140	9.933	12.100	14.713	17.861	21.644	26.186	31.629	38.141	45.923	55.205
23	1.257	1.577	1.974	2.465	3.071	3.820	4.740	5.871	7.258	8.954	11.026	13.552	16.626	20.361	24.891	30.376	37.005	45.007	54.648	66.247
24	1.270	1.608	2.033	2.563	3.225	4.049	5.072	6.341	7.911	9.850	12.239	15.178	18.788	23.212	28.625	35.236	43.296	53.108	65.031	79.496
25	1.282	1.641	2.094	2.666	3.386	4.292	5.427	6.848	8.623	10.834	13.585	17.000	21.230	26.461	32.918	40.874	50.656	62.667	77.387	95.395
30	1.348	1.811	2.427	3.243	4.322	5.743	7.612	10.062	13.267	17.449	22.892	29.960	39.115	50.949	66.210	85.849	111.061	143.367	184.672	237.373
35	1.417	2.000	2.814	3.946	5.516	7.686	10.676	14.785	20.413	28.102	38.574	52.799	72.066	98.097	133.172	180.311	243.495	327.988	440.691	590.657
40	1.489	2.208	3.262	4.801	7.040	10.285	14.974	21.724	31.408	45.258	64.999	93.049	132.776	188.876	267.856	378.715	533.846	750.353	1051.642	1469.740
45	1.565	2.438	3.781	5.841	8.985	13.764	21.002	31.920	48.325	72.888	109.527	163.985	244.629	363.662	538.752	795.429	1170.425	1716.619	2509.583	3657.176
50	1.645	2.691	4.384	7.106	11.467	18.419	29.456	46.900	74.354	117.386	184.559	288.996	450.711	700.197	1083.619	1670.669	2566.080	3927.189	5988.730	9100.191

USING THE CALCULATOR TO COMPUTE THE FUTURE VALUE OF A SINGLE AMOUNT

Before you begin, be certain to clear the memory, ensure that you are in the *end mode* and that your calculator is set for *one payment per year,* and set the number of decimal places that you want (usually two for dollar-related accuracy).

SAMPLE PROBLEM

You place $800 in a savings account at 6% compounded annually. What is your account balance at the end of 5 years?

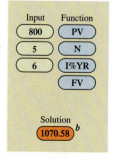

Input	Function
800	PV
5	N
6	I%YR
	FV

Solution
1070.58 [b]

---

[a]For the 12C, you would use the n key instead of the N key and use the i key instead of the I%YR key.
[b]The minus sign that precedes the output should be ignored.

TABLE A-1 (Continued)

Period	21%	22%	23%	24%	25%	26%	27%	28%	29%	30%	31%	32%	33%	34%	35%	40%	45%	50%
1	1.210	1.220	1.230	1.240	1.250	1.260	1.270	1.280	1.290	1.300	1.310	1.320	1.330	1.340	1.350	1.400	1.450	1.500
2	1.464	1.488	1.513	1.538	1.562	1.588	1.613	1.638	1.664	1.690	1.716	1.742	1.769	1.796	1.822	1.960	2.102	2.250
3	1.772	1.816	1.861	1.907	1.953	2.000	2.048	2.097	2.147	2.197	2.248	2.300	2.353	2.406	2.460	2.744	3.049	3.375
4	2.144	2.215	2.289	2.364	2.441	2.520	2.601	2.684	2.769	2.856	2.945	3.036	3.129	3.224	3.321	3.842	4.421	5.063
5	2.594	2.703	2.815	2.932	3.052	3.176	3.304	3.436	3.572	3.713	3.858	4.007	4.162	4.320	4.484	5.378	6.410	7.594
6	3.138	3.297	3.463	3.635	3.815	4.001	4.196	4.398	4.608	4.827	5.054	5.290	5.535	5.789	6.053	7.530	9.294	11.391
7	3.797	4.023	4.259	4.508	4.768	5.042	5.329	5.629	5.945	6.275	6.621	6.983	7.361	7.758	8.172	10.541	13.476	17.086
8	4.595	4.908	5.239	5.589	5.960	6.353	6.767	7.206	7.669	8.157	8.673	9.217	9.791	10.395	11.032	14.758	19.541	25.629
9	5.560	5.987	6.444	6.931	7.451	8.004	8.595	9.223	9.893	10.604	11.362	12.166	13.022	13.930	14.894	20.661	28.334	38.443
10	6.727	7.305	7.926	8.594	9.313	10.086	10.915	11.806	12.761	13.786	14.884	16.060	17.319	18.666	20.106	28.925	41.085	57.665
11	8.140	8.912	9.749	10.657	11.642	12.708	13.862	15.112	16.462	17.921	19.498	21.199	23.034	25.012	27.144	40.495	59.573	86.498
12	9.850	10.872	11.991	13.215	14.552	16.012	17.605	19.343	21.236	23.298	25.542	27.982	30.635	33.516	36.644	56.694	86.380	129.746
13	11.918	13.264	14.749	16.386	18.190	20.175	22.359	24.759	27.395	30.287	33.460	36.937	40.745	44.912	49.469	79.371	125.251	194.620
14	14.421	16.182	18.141	20.319	22.737	25.420	28.395	31.691	35.339	39.373	43.832	48.756	54.190	60.181	66.784	111.119	181.614	291.929
15	17.449	19.742	22.314	25.195	28.422	32.030	36.062	40.565	45.587	51.185	57.420	64.358	72.073	80.643	90.158	155.567	263.341	437.894
16	21.113	24.085	27.446	31.242	35.527	40.357	45.799	51.923	58.808	66.541	75.220	84.953	95.857	108.061	121.713	217.793	381.844	656.841
17	25.547	29.384	33.758	38.740	44.409	50.850	58.165	66.461	75.862	86.503	98.539	112.138	127.490	144.802	164.312	304.911	553.674	985.261
18	30.912	35.848	41.523	48.038	55.511	64.071	73.869	85.070	97.862	112.454	129.086	148.022	169.561	194.035	221.822	426.875	802.826	1477.892
19	37.404	43.735	51.073	59.567	69.389	80.730	93.813	108.890	126.242	146.190	169.102	195.389	225.517	260.006	299.459	597.625	1164.098	2216.838
20	45.258	53.357	62.820	73.863	86.736	101.720	119.143	139.379	162.852	190.047	221.523	257.913	299.937	348.408	404.270	836.674	1687.942	3325.257
21	54.762	65.095	77.268	91.591	108.420	128.167	151.312	178.405	210.079	247.061	290.196	340.446	398.916	466.867	545.764	1171.343	2447.515	4987.883
22	66.262	79.416	95.040	113.572	135.525	161.490	192.165	228.358	271.002	321.178	380.156	449.388	530.558	625.601	736.781	1639.878	3548.896	7481.824
23	80.178	96.887	116.899	140.829	169.407	203.477	244.050	292.298	349.592	417.531	498.004	593.192	705.642	838.305	994.653	2295.829	5145.898	11222.738
24	97.015	118.203	143.786	174.628	211.758	256.381	309.943	374.141	450.974	542.791	652.385	783.013	938.504	1123.328	1342.781	3214.158	7461.547	16834.109
25	117.388	144.207	176.857	216.539	264.698	323.040	393.628	478.901	581.756	705.627	854.623	1033.577	1248.210	1505.258	1812.754	4499.816	10819.242	25251.164
30	304.471	389.748	497.904	634.810	807.793	1025.904	1300.477	1645.488	2078.208	2619.936	3297.081	4142.008	5194.516	6503.285	8128.426	24201.043	69348.375	191751.000
35	789.716	1053.370	1401.749	1861.020	2465.189	3258.053	4296.547	5653.840	7423.988	9727.598	12719.918	16598.906	21617.363	28096.695	36448.051	130158.687	*	*
40	2048.309	2846.941	3946.340	5455.797	7523.156	10346.879	14195.051	19426.418	26520.723	36117.754	49072.621	66519.313	89962.188	121388.437	163433.875	700022.688	*	*
45	5312.758	7694.418	11110.121	15994.316	22958.844	32859.457	46897.973	66748.500	94739.937	134102.187	*	*	*	*	*	*	*	*
50	13779.844	20795.680	31278.301	46889.207	70064.812	104354.562	154942.687	229345.875	338440.000	497910.125	*	*	*	*	*	*	*	*

*Not shown because of space limitations.

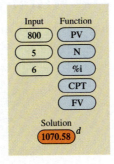

cFor the Texas Instruments BAII, you would use the `2nd` key instead of the `CPT` key; for the Texas Instruments BAII Plus, you would use the `I/Y` key instead of the `%i` key.
dIf a minus sign precedes the output, it should be ignored.

TABLE A-2 Present Value Interest Factors for One Dollar Discounted at i Percent for n Periods:

$$PVIF_{i,n} = \frac{1}{(1+i)^n}$$

Period	1%	2%	3%	4%	5%	6%	7%	8%	9%	10%	11%	12%	13%	14%	15%	16%	17%	18%	19%	20%
1	.990	.980	.971	.962	.952	.943	.935	.926	.917	.909	.901	.893	.885	.877	.870	.862	.855	.847	.840	.833
2	.980	.961	.943	.925	.907	.890	.873	.857	.842	.826	.812	.797	.783	.769	.756	.743	.731	.718	.706	.694
3	.971	.942	.915	.889	.864	.840	.816	.794	.772	.751	.731	.712	.693	.675	.658	.641	.624	.609	.593	.579
4	.961	.924	.888	.855	.823	.792	.763	.735	.708	.683	.659	.636	.613	.592	.572	.552	.534	.516	.499	.482
5	.951	.906	.863	.822	.784	.747	.713	.681	.650	.621	.593	.567	.543	.519	.497	.476	.456	.437	.419	.402
6	.942	.888	.837	.790	.746	.705	.666	.630	.596	.564	.535	.507	.480	.456	.432	.410	.390	.370	.352	.335
7	.933	.871	.813	.760	.711	.665	.623	.583	.547	.513	.482	.452	.425	.400	.376	.354	.333	.314	.296	.279
8	.923	.853	.789	.731	.677	.627	.582	.540	.502	.467	.434	.404	.376	.351	.327	.305	.285	.266	.249	.233
9	.914	.837	.766	.703	.645	.592	.544	.500	.460	.424	.391	.361	.333	.308	.284	.263	.243	.225	.209	.194
10	.905	.820	.744	.676	.614	.558	.508	.463	.422	.386	.352	.322	.295	.270	.247	.227	.208	.191	.176	.162
11	.896	.804	.722	.650	.585	.527	.475	.429	.388	.350	.317	.287	.261	.237	.215	.195	.178	.162	.148	.135
12	.887	.789	.701	.625	.557	.497	.444	.397	.356	.319	.286	.257	.231	.208	.187	.168	.152	.137	.124	.112
13	.879	.773	.681	.601	.530	.469	.415	.368	.326	.290	.258	.229	.204	.182	.163	.145	.130	.116	.104	.093
14	.870	.758	.661	.577	.505	.442	.388	.340	.299	.263	.232	.205	.181	.160	.141	.125	.111	.099	.088	.078
15	.861	.743	.642	.555	.481	.417	.362	.315	.275	.239	.209	.183	.160	.140	.123	.108	.095	.084	.074	.065
16	.853	.728	.623	.534	.458	.394	.339	.292	.252	.218	.188	.163	.141	.123	.107	.093	.081	.071	.062	.054
17	.844	.714	.605	.513	.436	.371	.317	.270	.231	.198	.170	.146	.125	.108	.093	.080	.069	.060	.052	.045
18	.836	.700	.587	.494	.416	.350	.296	.250	.212	.180	.153	.130	.111	.095	.081	.069	.059	.051	.044	.038
19	.828	.686	.570	.475	.396	.331	.277	.232	.194	.164	.138	.116	.098	.083	.070	.060	.051	.043	.037	.031
20	.820	.673	.554	.456	.377	.312	.258	.215	.178	.149	.124	.104	.087	.073	.061	.051	.043	.037	.031	.026
21	.811	.660	.538	.439	.359	.294	.242	.199	.164	.135	.112	.093	.077	.064	.053	.044	.037	.031	.026	.022
22	.803	.647	.522	.422	.342	.278	.226	.184	.150	.123	.101	.083	.068	.056	.046	.038	.032	.026	.022	.018
23	.795	.634	.507	.406	.326	.262	.211	.170	.138	.112	.091	.074	.060	.049	.040	.033	.027	.022	.018	.015
24	.788	.622	.492	.390	.310	.247	.197	.158	.126	.102	.082	.066	.053	.043	.035	.028	.023	.019	.015	.013
25	.780	.610	.478	.375	.295	.233	.184	.146	.116	.092	.074	.059	.047	.038	.030	.024	.020	.016	.013	.010
30	.742	.552	.412	.308	.231	.174	.131	.099	.075	.057	.044	.033	.026	.020	.015	.012	.009	.007	.005	.004
35	.706	.500	.355	.253	.181	.130	.094	.068	.049	.036	.026	.019	.014	.010	.008	.006	.004	.003	.002	.002
40	.672	.453	.307	.208	.142	.097	.067	.046	.032	.022	.015	.011	.008	.005	.004	.003	.002	.001	.001	.001
45	.639	.410	.264	.171	.111	.073	.048	.031	.021	.014	.009	.006	.004	.003	.002	.001	.001	.001	*	*
50	.608	.372	.228	.141	.087	.054	.034	.021	.013	.009	.005	.003	.002	.001	.001	.001	*	*	*	*

*PVIF is zero to three decimal places.

USING THE CALCULATOR TO COMPUTE THE PRESENT VALUE OF A SINGLE AMOUNT

Before you begin, be certain to clear the memory, ensure that you are in the *end mode* and that your calculator is set for *one payment per year,* and set the number of decimal places that you want (usually two for dollar-related accuracy).

SAMPLE PROBLEM

You want to know the present value of $1,700 to be received at the end of 8 years, assuming an 8% discount rate.

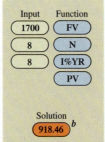

Input	Function
1700	FV
8	N
8	I%YR
	PV

Solution
918.46 [b]

---

[a]For the 12C, you would use the n key instead of the N key and use the i key instead of the I%YR key.
[b]The minus sign that precedes the output should be ignored.

TABLE A-2   (Continued)

Period	21%	22%	23%	24%	25%	26%	27%	28%	29%	30%	31%	32%	33%	34%	35%	40%	45%	50%
1	.826	.820	.813	.806	.800	.794	.787	.781	.775	.769	.763	.758	.752	.746	.741	.714	.690	.667
2	.683	.672	.661	.650	.640	.630	.620	.610	.601	.592	.583	.574	.565	.557	.549	.510	.476	.444
3	.564	.551	.537	.524	.512	.500	.488	.477	.466	.455	.445	.435	.425	.416	.406	.364	.328	.296
4	.467	.451	.437	.423	.410	.397	.384	.373	.361	.350	.340	.329	.320	.310	.301	.260	.226	.198
5	.386	.370	.355	.341	.328	.315	.303	.291	.280	.269	.259	.250	.240	.231	.223	.186	.156	.132
6	.319	.303	.289	.275	.262	.250	.238	.227	.217	.207	.198	.189	.181	.173	.165	.133	.108	.088
7	.263	.249	.235	.222	.210	.198	.188	.178	.168	.159	.151	.143	.136	.129	.122	.095	.074	.059
8	.218	.204	.191	.179	.168	.157	.148	.139	.130	.123	.115	.108	.102	.096	.091	.068	.051	.039
9	.180	.167	.155	.144	.134	.125	.116	.108	.101	.094	.088	.082	.077	.072	.067	.048	.035	.026
10	.149	.137	.126	.116	.107	.099	.092	.085	.078	.073	.067	.062	.058	.054	.050	.035	.024	.017
11	.123	.112	.103	.094	.086	.079	.072	.066	.061	.056	.051	.047	.043	.040	.037	.025	.017	.012
12	.102	.092	.083	.076	.069	.062	.057	.052	.047	.043	.039	.036	.033	.030	.027	.018	.012	.008
13	.084	.075	.068	.061	.055	.050	.045	.040	.037	.033	.030	.027	.025	.022	.020	.013	.008	.005
14	.069	.062	.055	.049	.044	.039	.035	.032	.028	.025	.023	.021	.018	.017	.015	.009	.006	.003
15	.057	.051	.045	.040	.035	.031	.028	.025	.022	.020	.017	.016	.014	.012	.011	.006	.004	.002
16	.047	.042	.036	.032	.028	.025	.022	.019	.017	.015	.013	.012	.010	.009	.008	.005	.003	.002
17	.039	.034	.030	.026	.023	.020	.017	.015	.013	.012	.010	.009	.008	.007	.006	.003	.002	.001
18	.032	.028	.024	.021	.018	.016	.014	.012	.010	.009	.008	.007	.006	.005	.005	.002	.001	.001
19	.027	.023	.020	.017	.014	.012	.011	.009	.008	.007	.006	.005	.004	.004	.003	.002	.001	*
20	.022	.019	.016	.014	.012	.010	.008	.007	.006	.005	.005	.004	.003	.003	.002	.001	.001	*
21	.018	.015	.013	.011	.009	.008	.007	.006	.005	.004	.003	.003	.003	.002	.002	.001	*	*
22	.015	.013	.011	.009	.007	.006	.005	.004	.004	.003	.003	.002	.002	.002	.001	.001	*	*
23	.012	.010	.009	.007	.006	.005	.004	.003	.003	.002	.002	.002	.001	.001	.001	*	*	*
24	.010	.008	.007	.006	.005	.004	.003	.003	.002	.002	.002	.001	.001	.001	.001	*	*	*
25	.009	.007	.006	.005	.004	.003	.003	.002	.002	.001	.001	.001	.001	.001	.001	*	*	*
30	.003	.003	.002	.002	.001	.001	.001	.001	*	*	*	*	*	*	*	*	*	*
35	.001	.001	.001	.001	*	*	*	*	*	*	*	*	*	*	*	*	*	*
40	*	*	*	*	*	*	*	*	*	*	*	*	*	*	*	*	*	*
45	*	*	*	*	*	*	*	*	*	*	*	*	*	*	*	*	*	*
50	*	*	*	*	*	*	*	*	*	*	*	*	*	*	*	*	*	*

*PVIF is zero to three decimal places.

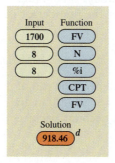

Input	Function
1700	FV
8	N
8	%i
	CPT
	FV

Solution
918.46 d

ᶜFor the Texas Instruments BAII, you would use the 2nd key instead of the CPT key; for the Texas Instruments BAII Plus, you would use the I/Y key instead of the %i key.
ᵈIf a minus sign precedes the output, it should be ignored.

TABLE A-3 Future Value Interest Factors for a One-Dollar Annuity Compounded at *i* Percent for *n* Periods: $FVIFA_{i,n} = \sum_{t=1}^{n} (1+i)^{t-1}$

Period	1%	2%	3%	4%	5%	6%	7%	8%	9%	10%	11%	12%	13%	14%	15%	16%	17%	18%	19%	20%
1	1.000	1.000	1.000	1.000	1.000	1.000	1.000	1.000	1.000	1.000	1.000	1.000	1.000	1.000	1.000	1.000	1.000	1.000	1.000	1.000
2	2.010	2.020	2.030	2.040	2.050	2.060	2.070	2.080	2.090	2.100	2.110	2.120	2.130	2.140	2.150	2.160	2.170	2.180	2.190	2.200
3	3.030	3.060	3.091	3.122	3.152	3.184	3.215	3.246	3.278	3.310	3.342	3.374	3.407	3.440	3.472	3.506	3.539	3.572	3.606	3.640
4	4.060	4.122	4.184	4.246	4.310	4.375	4.440	4.506	4.573	4.641	4.710	4.779	4.850	4.921	4.993	5.066	5.141	5.215	5.291	5.368
5	5.101	5.204	5.309	5.416	5.526	5.637	5.751	5.867	5.985	6.105	6.228	6.353	6.480	6.610	6.742	6.877	7.014	7.154	7.297	7.442
6	6.152	6.308	6.468	6.633	6.802	6.975	7.153	7.336	7.523	7.716	7.913	8.115	8.323	8.535	8.754	8.977	9.207	9.442	9.683	9.930
7	7.214	7.434	7.662	7.898	8.142	8.394	8.654	8.923	9.200	9.487	9.783	10.089	10.405	10.730	11.067	11.414	11.772	12.141	12.523	12.916
8	8.286	8.583	8.892	9.214	9.549	9.897	10.260	10.637	11.028	11.436	11.859	12.300	12.757	13.233	13.727	14.240	14.773	15.327	15.902	16.499
9	9.368	9.755	10.159	10.583	11.027	11.491	11.978	12.488	13.021	13.579	14.164	14.776	15.416	16.085	16.786	17.518	18.285	19.086	19.923	20.799
10	10.462	10.950	11.464	12.006	12.578	13.181	13.816	14.487	15.193	15.937	16.722	17.549	18.420	19.337	20.304	21.321	22.393	23.521	24.709	25.959
11	11.567	12.169	12.808	13.486	14.207	14.972	15.784	16.645	17.560	18.531	19.561	20.655	21.814	23.044	24.349	25.733	27.200	28.755	30.403	32.150
12	12.682	13.412	14.192	15.026	15.917	16.870	17.888	18.977	20.141	21.384	22.713	24.133	25.650	27.271	29.001	30.850	32.824	34.931	37.180	39.580
13	13.809	14.680	15.618	16.627	17.713	18.882	20.141	21.495	22.953	24.523	26.211	28.029	29.984	32.088	34.352	36.786	39.404	42.218	45.244	48.496
14	14.947	15.974	17.086	18.292	19.598	21.015	22.550	24.215	26.019	27.975	30.095	32.392	34.882	37.581	40.504	43.672	47.102	50.818	54.841	59.196
15	16.097	17.293	18.599	20.023	21.578	23.276	25.129	27.152	29.361	31.772	34.405	37.280	40.417	43.842	47.580	51.659	56.109	60.965	66.260	72.035
16	17.258	18.639	20.157	21.824	23.657	25.672	27.888	30.324	33.003	35.949	39.190	42.753	46.671	50.980	55.717	60.925	66.648	72.938	79.850	87.442
17	18.430	20.012	21.761	23.697	25.840	28.213	30.840	33.750	36.973	40.544	44.500	48.883	53.738	59.117	65.075	71.673	78.978	87.067	96.021	105.930
18	19.614	21.412	23.414	25.645	28.132	30.905	33.999	37.450	41.301	45.599	50.396	55.749	61.724	68.393	75.836	84.140	93.404	103.739	115.265	128.116
19	20.811	22.840	25.117	27.671	30.539	33.760	37.379	41.446	46.018	51.158	56.939	63.439	70.748	78.968	88.211	98.603	110.283	123.412	138.165	154.739
20	22.019	24.297	26.870	29.778	33.066	36.785	40.995	45.762	51.159	57.274	64.202	72.052	80.946	91.024	102.443	115.379	130.031	146.626	165.417	186.687
21	23.239	25.783	28.676	31.969	35.719	39.992	44.865	50.422	56.764	64.002	72.264	81.698	92.468	104.767	118.809	134.840	153.136	174.019	197.846	225.024
22	24.471	27.299	30.536	34.248	38.505	43.392	49.005	55.456	62.872	71.402	81.213	92.502	105.489	120.434	137.630	157.414	180.169	206.342	236.436	271.028
23	25.716	28.845	32.452	36.618	41.430	46.995	53.435	60.893	69.531	79.542	91.147	104.602	120.203	138.295	159.274	183.600	211.798	244.483	282.359	326.234
24	26.973	30.421	34.426	39.082	44.501	50.815	58.176	66.764	76.789	88.496	102.173	118.154	136.829	158.656	184.166	213.976	248.803	289.490	337.007	392.480
25	28.243	32.030	36.459	41.645	47.726	54.864	63.248	73.105	84.699	98.346	114.412	133.333	155.616	181.867	212.790	249.212	292.099	342.598	402.038	471.976
30	34.784	40.567	47.575	56.084	66.438	79.057	94.459	113.282	136.305	164.491	199.018	241.330	293.192	356.778	434.738	530.306	647.423	790.932	966.698	1181.865
35	41.659	49.994	60.461	73.651	90.318	111.432	138.234	172.314	215.705	271.018	341.583	431.658	546.663	693.552	881.152	1120.699	1426.448	1816.607	2314.173	2948.294
40	48.885	60.401	75.400	95.024	120.797	154.758	199.630	259.052	337.872	442.580	581.812	767.080	1013.667	1341.979	1779.048	2360.724	3134.412	4163.094	5529.711	7343.715
45	56.479	71.891	92.718	121.027	159.695	212.737	285.741	386.497	525.840	718.881	986.613	1358.208	1874.086	2590.464	3585.031	4965.191	6879.008	9531.258	13203.105	18280.914
50	64.461	84.577	112.794	152.664	209.341	290.325	406.516	573.756	815.051	1163.865	1668.723	2399.975	3459.344	4994.301	7217.488	10435.449	15088.805	21812.273	31514.492	45496.094

USING THE CALCULATOR TO COMPUTE THE FUTURE VALUE OF AN ANNUITY

Before you begin, be certain to clear the memory, ensure that you are in the *end mode* and that your calculator is set for *one payment per year,* and set the number of decimal places that you want (usually two for dollar-related accuracy).

SAMPLE PROBLEM

You want to know what the future value will be at the end of 5 years if you place five end-of-year deposits of $1,000 in an account paying 7% annually. What is your account balance at the end of 5 years?

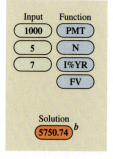

---

[a]For the 12C, you would use the n key instead of the N key and use the i key instead of the I%YR key.
[b]The minus sign that precedes the output should be ignored.

TABLE A-3   (Continued)

Period	21%	22%	23%	24%	25%	26%	27%	28%	29%	30%	31%	32%	33%	34%	35%	40%	45%	50%
1	1.000	1.000	1.000	1.000	1.000	1.000	1.000	1.000	1.000	1.000	1.000	1.000	1.000	1.000	1.000	1.000	1.000	1.000
2	2.210	2.220	2.230	2.240	2.250	2.260	2.270	2.280	2.290	2.300	2.310	2.320	2.330	2.340	2.350	2.400	2.450	2.500
3	3.674	3.708	3.743	3.778	3.813	3.848	3.883	3.918	3.954	3.990	4.026	4.062	4.099	4.136	4.172	4.360	4.552	4.750
4	5.446	5.524	5.604	5.684	5.766	5.848	5.931	6.016	6.101	6.187	6.274	6.362	6.452	6.542	6.633	7.104	7.601	8.125
5	7.589	7.740	7.893	8.048	8.207	8.368	8.533	8.700	8.870	9.043	9.219	9.398	9.581	9.766	9.954	10.946	12.022	13.188
6	10.183	10.442	10.708	10.980	11.259	11.544	11.837	12.136	12.442	12.756	13.077	13.406	13.742	14.086	14.438	16.324	18.431	20.781
7	13.321	13.740	14.171	14.615	15.073	15.546	16.032	16.534	17.051	17.583	18.131	18.696	19.277	19.876	20.492	23.853	27.725	32.172
8	17.119	17.762	18.430	19.123	19.842	20.588	21.361	22.163	22.995	23.858	24.752	25.678	26.638	27.633	28.664	34.395	41.202	49.258
9	21.714	22.670	23.669	24.712	25.802	26.940	28.129	29.369	30.664	32.015	33.425	34.895	36.429	38.028	39.696	49.152	60.743	74.887
10	27.274	28.657	30.113	31.643	33.253	34.945	36.723	38.592	40.556	42.619	44.786	47.062	49.451	51.958	54.590	69.813	89.077	113.330
11	34.001	35.962	38.039	40.238	42.566	45.030	47.639	50.398	53.318	56.405	59.670	63.121	66.769	70.624	74.696	98.739	130.161	170.995
12	42.141	44.873	47.787	50.895	54.208	57.738	61.501	65.510	69.780	74.326	79.167	84.320	89.803	95.636	101.840	139.234	189.734	257.493
13	51.991	55.745	59.778	64.109	68.760	73.750	79.106	84.853	91.016	97.624	104.709	112.302	120.438	129.152	138.484	195.928	276.114	387.239
14	63.909	69.009	74.528	80.496	86.949	93.925	101.465	109.611	118.411	127.912	138.169	149.239	161.183	174.063	187.953	275.299	401.365	581.858
15	78.330	85.191	92.669	100.815	109.687	119.346	129.860	141.302	153.750	167.285	182.001	197.996	215.373	234.245	254.737	386.418	582.980	873.788
16	95.779	104.933	114.983	126.010	138.109	151.375	165.922	181.867	199.337	218.470	239.421	262.354	287.446	314.888	344.895	541.985	846.321	1311.681
17	116.892	129.019	142.428	157.252	173.636	191.733	211.721	233.790	258.145	285.011	314.642	347.307	383.303	422.949	466.608	759.778	1228.165	1968.522
18	142.439	158.403	176.187	195.993	218.045	242.583	269.885	300.250	334.006	371.514	413.180	459.445	510.792	567.751	630.920	1064.689	1781.838	2953.783
19	173.351	194.251	217.710	244.031	273.556	306.654	343.754	385.321	431.868	483.968	542.266	607.467	680.354	761.786	852.741	1491.563	2584.665	4431.672
20	210.755	237.986	268.783	303.598	342.945	387.384	437.568	494.210	558.110	630.157	711.368	802.856	905.870	1021.792	1152.200	2089.188	3748.763	6648.508
21	256.013	291.343	331.603	377.461	429.681	489.104	556.710	633.589	720.962	820.204	932.891	1060.769	1205.807	1370.201	1556.470	2925.862	5436.703	9973.762
22	310.775	356.438	408.871	469.052	538.101	617.270	708.022	811.993	931.040	1067.265	1223.087	1401.215	1604.724	1837.068	2102.234	4097.203	7884.215	14961.645
23	377.038	435.854	503.911	582.624	673.626	778.760	900.187	1040.351	1202.042	1388.443	1603.243	1850.603	2135.282	2462.669	2839.014	5737.078	11433.109	22443.469
24	457.215	532.741	620.810	723.453	843.032	982.237	1144.237	1332.649	1551.634	1805.975	2101.247	2443.795	2840.924	3300.974	3833.667	8032.906	16579.008	33666.207
25	554.230	650.944	764.596	898.082	1054.791	1238.617	1454.180	1706.790	2002.608	2348.765	2753.631	3226.808	3779.428	4424.301	5176.445	11247.062	24040.555	50500.316
30	1445.111	1767.044	2160.459	2640.881	3227.172	3941.953	4812.891	5873.172	7162.785	8729.805	10632.543	12940.672	15737.945	19124.434	23221.258	60500.207	154105.313	383500.000
35	3755.814	4783.520	6090.227	7750.094	9856.746	12527.160	15909.480	20188.742	25596.512	32422.090	41028.887	51868.563	65504.199	82634.625	104134.500	325394.688	*	*
40	9749.141	12936.141	17153.691	22728.367	30088.621	39791.957	52570.707	69376.562	91447.375	120389.375	*	*	*	*	*	*	*	*
45	25294.223	34970.230	48300.660	66638.937	91831.312	126378.937	173692.875	238384.312	326686.375	447005.062	*	*	*	*	*	*	*	*

*Not shown because of space limitations.

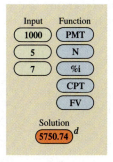

cFor the Texas Instruments BAII, you would use the [2nd] key instead of the [CPT] key; for the Texas Instruments BAII Plus, you would use the [I/Y] key instead of the [%i] key.
dIf a minus sign precedes the output, it should be ignored.

TABLE A-4   Present Value Interest Factors for a One-Dollar Annuity Discounted at *i* Percent for *n*

$$\text{Periods: } PVIFA_{i,n} = \sum_{t=1}^{n} \frac{1}{(1+i)^t}$$

Period	1%	2%	3%	4%	5%	6%	7%	8%	9%	10%	11%	12%	13%	14%	15%	16%	17%	18%	19%	20%
1	.990	.980	.971	.962	.952	.943	.935	.926	.917	.909	.901	.893	.885	.877	.870	.862	.855	.847	.840	.833
2	1.970	1.942	1.913	1.886	1.859	1.833	1.808	1.783	1.759	1.736	1.713	1.690	1.668	1.647	1.626	1.605	1.585	1.566	1.547	1.528
3	2.941	2.884	2.829	2.775	2.723	2.673	2.624	2.577	2.531	2.487	2.444	2.402	2.361	2.322	2.283	2.246	2.210	2.174	2.140	2.106
4	3.902	3.808	3.717	3.630	3.546	3.465	3.387	3.312	3.240	3.170	3.102	3.037	2.974	2.914	2.855	2.798	2.743	2.690	2.639	2.589
5	4.853	4.713	4.580	4.452	4.329	4.212	4.100	3.993	3.890	3.791	3.696	3.605	3.517	3.433	3.352	3.274	3.199	3.127	3.058	2.991
6	5.795	5.601	5.417	5.242	5.076	4.917	4.767	4.623	4.486	4.355	4.231	4.111	3.998	3.889	3.784	3.685	3.589	3.498	3.410	3.326
7	6.728	6.472	6.230	6.002	5.786	5.582	5.389	5.206	5.033	4.868	4.712	4.564	4.423	4.288	4.160	4.039	3.922	3.812	3.706	3.605
8	7.652	7.326	7.020	6.733	6.463	6.210	5.971	5.747	5.535	5.335	5.146	4.968	4.799	4.639	4.487	4.344	4.207	4.078	3.954	3.837
9	8.566	8.162	7.786	7.435	7.108	6.802	6.515	6.247	5.995	5.759	5.537	5.328	5.132	4.946	4.772	4.607	4.451	4.303	4.163	4.031
10	9.471	8.983	8.530	8.111	7.722	7.360	7.024	6.710	6.418	6.145	5.889	5.650	5.426	5.216	5.019	4.833	4.659	4.494	4.339	4.192
11	10.368	9.787	9.253	8.760	8.306	7.887	7.499	7.139	6.805	6.495	6.207	5.938	5.687	5.453	5.234	5.029	4.836	4.656	4.486	4.327
12	11.255	10.575	9.954	9.385	8.863	8.384	7.943	7.536	7.161	6.814	6.492	6.194	5.918	5.660	5.421	5.197	4.988	4.793	4.611	4.439
13	12.134	11.348	10.635	9.986	9.394	8.853	8.358	7.904	7.487	7.013	6.750	6.424	6.122	5.842	5.583	5.342	5.118	4.910	4.715	4.533
14	13.004	12.106	11.296	10.563	9.899	9.295	8.745	8.244	7.786	7.367	6.982	6.628	6.302	6.002	5.724	5.468	5.229	5.008	4.802	4.611
15	13.865	12.849	11.938	11.118	10.380	9.712	9.108	8.560	8.061	7.606	7.191	6.811	6.462	6.142	5.847	5.575	5.324	5.092	4.876	4.675
16	14.718	13.578	12.561	11.652	10.838	10.106	9.447	8.851	8.313	7.824	7.379	6.974	6.604	6.265	5.954	5.668	5.405	5.162	4.938	4.730
17	15.562	14.292	13.166	12.166	11.274	10.477	9.763	9.122	8.544	8.022	7.549	7.120	6.729	6.373	6.047	5.749	5.475	5.222	4.990	4.775
18	16.398	14.992	13.754	12.659	11.690	10.828	10.059	9.372	8.756	8.201	7.702	7.250	6.840	6.467	6.128	5.818	5.534	5.273	5.033	4.812
19	17.226	15.679	14.324	13.134	12.085	11.158	10.336	9.604	8.950	8.365	7.839	7.366	6.938	6.550	6.198	5.877	5.584	5.316	5.070	4.843
20	18.046	16.352	14.878	13.590	12.462	11.470	10.594	9.818	9.129	8.514	7.963	7.469	7.025	6.623	6.259	5.929	5.628	5.353	5.101	4.870
21	18.857	17.011	15.415	14.029	12.821	11.764	10.836	10.017	9.292	8.649	8.075	7.562	7.102	6.687	6.312	5.973	5.665	5.384	5.127	4.891
22	19.661	17.658	15.937	14.451	13.163	12.042	11.061	10.201	9.442	8.772	8.176	7.645	7.170	6.743	6.359	6.011	5.696	5.410	5.149	4.909
23	20.456	18.292	16.444	14.857	13.489	12.303	11.272	10.371	9.580	8.883	8.266	7.718	7.230	6.792	6.399	6.044	5.723	5.432	5.167	4.925
24	21.244	18.914	16.936	15.247	13.799	12.550	11.469	10.529	9.707	8.985	8.348	7.784	7.283	6.835	6.434	6.073	5.746	5.451	5.182	4.937
25	22.023	19.524	17.413	15.622	14.094	12.783	11.654	10.675	9.823	9.077	8.422	7.843	7.330	6.873	6.464	6.097	5.766	5.467	5.195	4.948
30	25.808	22.396	19.601	17.292	15.373	13.765	12.409	11.258	10.274	9.427	8.694	8.055	7.496	7.003	6.566	6.177	5.829	5.517	5.235	4.979
35	29.409	24.999	21.487	18.665	16.374	14.498	12.948	11.655	10.567	9.644	8.855	8.176	7.586	7.070	6.617	6.215	5.858	5.539	5.251	4.992
40	32.835	27.356	23.115	19.793	17.159	15.046	13.332	11.925	10.757	9.779	8.951	8.244	7.634	7.105	6.642	6.233	5.871	5.548	5.258	4.997
45	36.095	29.490	24.519	20.720	17.774	15.456	13.606	12.108	10.881	9.863	9.008	8.283	7.661	7.123	6.654	6.242	5.877	5.552	5.261	4.999
50	39.196	31.424	25.730	21.482	18.256	15.762	13.801	12.233	10.962	9.915	9.042	8.304	7.675	7.133	6.661	6.246	5.880	5.554	5.262	4.999

USING THE CALCULATOR TO COMPUTE THE PRESENT VALUE OF AN ANNUITY

Before you begin, be certain to clear the memory, ensure that you are in the *end mode* and that your calculator is set for *one payment per year,* and set the number of decimal places that you want (usually two for dollar-related accuracy).

SAMPLE PROBLEM

You want to know what the present value will be of an annuity of $700 per year at the end of each year for 5 years, given a discount rate of 8%.

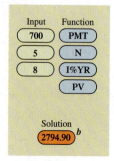

Input	Function
700	PMT
5	N
8	I%YR
	PV

Solution
2794.90 [b]

---

[a]For the 12C, you would use the n key instead of the N key and use the i key instead of the I%YR key.
[b]The minus sign that precedes the output should be ignored.

TABLE A-4 (Continued)

Period	21%	22%	23%	24%	25%	26%	27%	28%	29%	30%	31%	32%	33%	34%	35%	40%	45%	50%
1	.826	.820	.813	.806	.800	.794	.787	.781	.775	.769	.763	.758	.752	.746	.741	.714	.690	.667
2	1.509	1.492	1.474	1.457	1.440	1.424	1.407	1.392	1.376	1.361	1.346	1.331	1.317	1.303	1.289	1.224	1.165	1.111
3	2.074	2.042	2.011	1.981	1.952	1.923	1.896	1.868	1.842	1.816	1.791	1.766	1.742	1.719	1.696	1.589	1.493	1.407
4	2.540	2.494	2.448	2.404	2.362	2.320	2.280	2.241	2.203	2.166	2.130	2.096	2.062	2.029	1.997	1.849	1.720	1.605
5	2.926	2.864	2.803	2.745	2.689	2.635	2.583	2.532	2.483	2.436	2.390	2.345	2.302	2.260	2.220	2.035	1.876	1.737
6	3.245	3.167	3.092	3.020	2.951	2.885	2.821	2.759	2.700	2.643	2.588	2.534	2.483	2.433	2.385	2.168	1.983	1.824
7	3.508	3.416	3.327	3.242	3.161	3.083	3.009	2.937	2.868	2.802	2.739	2.677	2.619	2.562	2.508	2.263	2.057	1.883
8	3.726	3.619	3.518	3.421	3.329	3.241	3.156	3.076	2.999	2.925	2.854	2.786	2.721	2.658	2.598	2.331	2.109	1.922
9	3.905	3.786	3.673	3.566	3.463	3.366	3.273	3.184	3.100	3.019	2.942	2.868	2.798	2.730	2.665	2.379	2.144	1.948
10	4.054	3.923	3.799	3.682	3.570	3.465	3.364	3.269	3.178	3.092	3.009	2.930	2.855	2.784	2.715	2.414	2.168	1.965
11	4.177	4.035	3.902	3.776	3.656	3.544	3.437	3.335	3.239	3.147	3.060	2.978	2.899	2.824	2.752	2.438	2.185	1.977
12	4.278	4.127	3.985	3.851	3.725	3.606	3.493	3.387	3.286	3.190	3.100	3.013	2.931	2.853	2.779	2.456	2.196	1.985
13	4.362	4.203	4.053	3.912	3.780	3.656	3.538	3.427	3.322	3.223	3.129	3.040	2.956	2.876	2.799	2.469	2.204	1.990
14	4.432	4.265	4.108	3.962	3.824	3.695	3.573	3.459	3.351	3.249	3.152	3.061	2.974	2.892	2.814	2.478	2.210	1.993
15	4.489	4.315	4.153	4.001	3.859	3.726	3.601	3.483	3.373	3.268	3.170	3.076	2.988	2.905	2.825	2.484	2.214	1.995
16	4.536	4.357	4.189	4.033	3.887	3.751	3.623	3.503	3.390	3.283	3.183	3.088	2.999	2.914	2.834	2.489	2.216	1.997
17	4.576	4.391	4.219	4.059	3.910	3.771	3.640	3.518	3.403	3.295	3.193	3.097	3.007	2.921	2.840	2.492	2.218	1.998
18	4.608	4.419	4.243	4.080	3.928	3.786	3.654	3.529	3.413	3.304	3.201	3.104	3.012	2.926	2.844	2.494	2.219	1.999
19	4.635	4.442	4.263	4.097	3.942	3.799	3.664	3.539	3.421	3.311	3.207	3.109	3.017	2.930	2.848	2.496	2.220	1.999
20	4.657	4.460	4.279	4.110	3.954	3.808	3.673	3.546	3.427	3.316	3.211	3.113	3.020	2.933	2.850	2.497	2.221	1.999
21	4.675	4.476	4.292	4.121	3.963	3.816	3.679	3.551	3.432	3.320	3.215	3.116	3.023	2.935	2.852	2.498	2.221	2.000
22	4.690	4.488	4.302	4.130	3.970	3.822	3.684	3.556	3.436	3.323	3.217	3.118	3.025	2.936	2.853	2.498	2.222	2.000
23	4.703	4.499	4.311	4.137	3.976	3.827	3.689	3.559	3.438	3.325	3.219	3.120	3.026	2.938	2.854	2.499	2.222	2.000
24	4.713	4.507	4.318	4.143	3.981	3.831	3.692	3.562	3.441	3.327	3.221	3.121	3.027	2.939	2.855	2.499	2.222	2.000
25	4.721	4.514	4.323	4.147	3.985	3.834	3.694	3.564	3.442	3.329	3.222	3.122	3.028	2.939	2.856	2.499	2.222	2.000
30	4.746	4.534	4.339	4.160	3.995	3.842	3.701	3.569	3.447	3.332	3.225	3.124	3.030	2.941	2.857	2.500	2.222	2.000
35	4.756	4.541	4.345	4.164	3.998	3.845	3.703	3.571	3.448	3.333	3.226	3.125	3.030	2.941	2.857	2.500	2.222	2.000
40	4.760	4.544	4.347	4.166	3.999	3.846	3.703	3.571	3.448	3.333	3.226	3.125	3.030	2.941	2.857	2.500	2.222	2.000
45	4.761	4.545	4.347	4.166	4.000	3.846	3.704	3.571	3.448	3.333	3.226	3.125	3.030	2.941	2.857	2.500	2.222	2.000
50	4.762	4.545	4.348	4.167	4.000	3.846	3.704	3.571	3.448	3.333	3.226	3.125	3.030	2.941	2.857	2.500	2.222	2.000

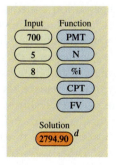

For the Texas Instruments BAII, you would use the 2nd key instead of the CPT key; for the Texas Instruments BAII Plus, you would use the I/Y key instead of the %i key.
[d]If a minus sign precedes the output, it should be ignored.

Appendix B

Answers and Solutions to Self-Test Exercises

Chapter 1

ST 1–1　The financial environment is composed of three components: (1) financial managers, (2) investors, and (3) financial markets. The financial manager is responsible for obtaining funds needed for the firm's existing operation and future expansions, deciding on the sources of funding, and evaluating future investment opportunities for the firm. If these responsibilities are carried out successfully, investors will put a high value on the firm and consequently will be willing to supply funds to purchase the securities issued by the firm. The financial market facilitates the process by which funds flow from investors to firms that need financing.

ST 1–2　First, investors will sell shares of firms that are not performing up to their expectations, thereby reducing the price of the shares and thus hurting managers whose compensation is tied to the firm's share price. Second, shareholders who own large blocks of shares can use their voting powers to replace the firm's management or board. Third, other investors (which may include the firm's competitors) or interested groups of shareholders may collectively buy enough of the firm's stock to gain controlling interest in the company and (typically) replace the board and management. It is then expected that the new leadership will achieve performance that is more consistent with shareholder wealth maximization, thereby justifying the drastic action. In many instances, the threat of a takeover is enough to keep managers on their toes. Other ways to align management's interest with that of shareholders' include designing reward schemes (such as stock options and profit sharing) that tie managerial compensation to the performance of the firm and the right to sue board members for failing in their duties to act in shareholders' interest.

Chapter 2

ST 2–1   Financial institutions collect funds from individuals and use these aggregate funds to provide loans or purchase debt securities issued by firms. For example, commercial banks accumulate deposits from individual accounts and use the deposited funds to provide credit and loans to firms or to purchase debt securities. Mutual funds use the proceeds from the sale of shares to individuals as their source of funds. Likewise, insurance companies invest the premiums they collect, and pension funds use the combined contributions of employers and employees to invest. With the exception of commercial banks, institutions also invest in equity securities issued by the firm.

ST 2–2

a. $\text{Annualized return} = \dfrac{(\$100,000 - 96,800) \times 365}{96,800 \times 180}$

$= 0.0670, \text{ or } 6.70\%$

b. $\text{Annualized return} = \dfrac{(\$98,100 - 96,800) \times 365}{96,800 \times 90}$

$= 0.0545, \text{ or } 5.45\%$

c. Let the value of the T-bill be V. Then

$(\dfrac{V - 96,800) \times 365}{96,800 \times 90} = 0.0670$

$V - 96,800 = \dfrac{0.0670 \times 96,800 \times 90}{365}$

$= 1599.19$

$V = 1599.19 + 96,800$

$= \$98,399$

Chapter 3

ST 3–1   Bonds are a form of debt capital. They represent long-term borrowing incurred by the firm. Most bonds are issued with maturities of 10 to 30 years with a par value or face value of $1,000. The payment, interest, to bondholders is fixed and is a tax deduction for the issuing firm.

   Common and preferred stock are forms of equity capital. Common stock is the most basic form of ownership under which owners receive what is left after all other claims are satisfied. Preferred stock has certain privileges that make it senior to common stock. Most importantly, they receive their fixed dividend before the common stockholders receive their funds. Unlike common stock, preferred stock and bonds typically receive their dividends. Unlike common stock, preferred stock and bonds typically receive no voting rights in the election of directors and on special issues. Both common and preferred dividends are not tax deductions for the firm. They are paid out of after-tax income.

ST 3–2   An investment banker acts as an intermediary between the issuer (the firm) and the buyers (investors) of new security issues. It purchases securities from corporate (and government) issuers and resells them to the general public, which includes both individual and institutional investors. For its role in assuming the risk of sale as well as advising the issuer, the investment banker profits from the discount, commonly called the spread, that it receives from the planned resale price.

Chapter 4

ST 4–1   **a.** After 1 year, Debbie will have $10,700 from her investment in the certificate of deposit from the 7% interest. The furniture will have cost $10,700 because of a 7% increase in price. So, buying the furniture 1 year later with the money from her investment leaves her with nothing. Hence she can expect no benefit from her investment.

b. After 1 year, Debbie will have $11,000 from her investment in the certificate of deposit. The furniture will have cost $10,700 leaving her with $300. That is, her real rate of return would be 3%; the $300 leftover divided by the $10,000 investment.

c. The real rate of return is the "true" return one expects after adjusting for inflation in the risk-free rate or nominal rate. It represents the expected increase in the buying power of one's money over the period of the investment.

ST 4–2   **a.** Premium due to maturity $= 7.10 - 6.60 = 0.50\%$

b. Real rate of return on money market securities is the difference between the 30-day T-bill rate and the expected inflation given by the expected change in the CPI. Real rate of return $= 6.60 - 3.10 = 3.50\%$

c. Risk premium on highest grade bond
$= $ Yield on 10-year Aaa corporate $-$ Yield on 10-year T-bond
$= 8.00 - 7.10 = 0.90\%$

Risk premium on lowest grade bond
$= $ Yield on 10-year B Corporate $-$ Yield on 10-year T-bond
$= 10.04 - 7.10 = 2.94\%$

d. The lowest-grade bond allowed for investment is the 30-year Baa corporate bond—that is, 8.55%. This represents the highest return for the financial institution.

Chapter 5

ST 5-1   **a.** *Bank A:*

$$FV_3 = \$10,000 \times FVIF_{4\%/3yrs} = \$10,000 \times 1.125 = \underline{\$11,250}$$
$$\text{(Calculator solution} = \$11,248.64)$$

Bank B:

$$FV_3 = \$10,000 \times FVIF_{4\%/2,2 \times 3yrs} = \$10,000 \times FVIF_{2\%,6yrs}$$
$$= \$10,000 \times 1.126 = \underline{\$11,260}$$
$$\text{(Calculator solution} = \$11,261.62)$$

Bank C:

$$FV_3 = \$10,000 \times FVIF_{4\%/4,4 \times 3yrs} = \$10,000 \times FVIF_{1\%,12yrs}$$
$$= \$10,000 \times 1.127 = \underline{\$11,270}$$

(Calculator solution = $11,268.25)

b. *Bank A:*

$$EAR = (1 + 4\%/1)^1 - 1 = (1 + 0.04)^1 - 1 = 1.04 - 1 = 0.04 = \underline{\underline{4\%}}$$

Bank B:

$$EAR = (1 + 4\%/2)^2 - 1 = (1 + 0.02)^2 - 1 = 1.0404 - 1 = 0.0404 = \underline{\underline{4.04\%}}$$

Bank C:

$$EAR = (1 + 4\%/4)^4 - 1 = (1 + 0.01)^4 - 1 = 1.0406 - 1 = 0.0406 = \underline{\underline{4.06\%}}$$

c. Ms. Martinez should deal with Bank C: The quarterly compounding of interest at the given 4% rate results in the highest future value as a result of the corresponding highest effective annual rate.

d. *Bank D:*

$$FV_3 = \$10,000 \times FVIF_{4\%,3yrs} \text{ (continuous compounding)}$$
$$= \$10,000 \times e^{.04 \times 3} = \$10,000 \times e^{.12}$$
$$= \$10,000 \times 1.127497$$
$$= \underline{\$11,274.97}$$

This alternative is better than Bank C. It results in a higher future value because of the use of continuous compounding, which with otherwise identical cash flows always results in a highest future value than any compounding period.

ST 5-2 **a.** On a purely subjective basis, annuity Y looks more attractive than annuity X because it provides $1,000 more each year than does annuity X. Of course, the fact that X is an annuity due means that the $9,000 would be received at the beginning of the first year rather than the $10,000 at the end of the year which makes annuity X awfully tempting.

b. *Annuity X:*

$$FVA_6 = \$9,000 \times FVIFA_{15\%,6yrs} \times (1 + 0.15)$$
$$= \$9,000 \times 8.754 \times 1.15 = \underline{\$90,603.90}$$

(Calculator solution = $90,601.19)

Annuity Y:

$$FVA_6 = \$10,000 \times FVIFA_{15\%,6yrs}$$
$$= \$10,000 \times 8.754 = \underline{\$87,540.00}$$

(Calculator solution = $87,537.38)

c. Annuity X is more attractive, because its future value at the end of year 6, FVA_6, of $90,603.90 is greater than annuity Y's end-of-year-6 future value, FVA_6, of $87,540.00. The subjective assessment in (a) was incorrect. The benefit of receiving annuity X's cash inflows at the beginning of each year appears to have outweighed the fact that annuity Y's annual cash inflow, which occurs at the end of each year is $1,000 larger ($10,000 vs. $9,000) than annuity X's.

ST 5-3 *Alternative A:*

Cash flow stream:

$$PVA_5 = \$700 \times PVIFA_{9\%,5\text{yrs}}$$
$$= \$700 \times 3.890 = \underline{\$2{,}723}$$

(Calculator solution = $2,722.76)

Lump sum: $\underline{\$2{,}825}$

Alternative B:

Cash flow stream:

Year (n)	Cash flow (1)	$FVIF_{9\%,n}$ (2)	Present value [(1) × (2)] (3)
1	$1,100	0.917	$1,088.70
2	900	0.842	757.80
3	700	0.772	540.40
4	500	0.708	354.00
5	300	0.650	195.00
		Present value	$2,855.90

(Calculator solution = $2,856.41)

Lump-sum: $\underline{\$2{,}800}$

Conclusion: Alternative B in the form of a cash flow stream is preferred because its present value of $2,855,90 is greater than the other three values.

ST 5-4 $FVA_5 = \$8{,}000$; $FVIFA_{7\%,5\text{yrs}} = 5.751$; $PMT = ?$
$FVA_n = PMT \times (FVIFA_{i,n})$ [Equation 5.14 or 5.23]
$\$8{,}000 = PMT \times 5.751$
$PMT = \$8{,}000/5.751 = \underline{\$1{,}391.06}$
(Calculator solution = $1,391.13)

Judy should deposit $1,391.06 at the end of each of the 5 years to meet her goal of accumulating $8,000 at the end of the fifth year.

Chapter 6

ST 6-1 **a.** Expected return, $\bar{k} = \dfrac{\Sigma \text{Returns}}{3}$ (*Equation 6.2a in footnote on p. 154*)

$$\bar{k}_A = \frac{12\% + 14\% + 16\%}{3} = \frac{42\%}{3} = \underline{14\%}$$

$$\bar{k}_B = \frac{16\% + 14\% + 12\%}{3} = \frac{42\%}{3} = \underline{14\%}$$

$$\bar{k}_C = \frac{12\% + 14\% + 16\%}{3} = \frac{42\%}{3} = \underline{\underline{14\%}}$$

b. Standard deviation, $\sigma_k = \sqrt{\dfrac{\sum_{j=1}^{n}(k_j - \bar{k})^2}{n-1}}$ *(Equation 6.3a in footnote 2 on p. 155)*

$$\sigma_{k_A} = \sqrt{\frac{(12\% - 14\%)^2 + (14\% - 14\%)^2 + (16\% - 14\%)^2}{3-1}}$$

$$= \sqrt{\frac{4\% + 0\% + 4\%}{2}} = \sqrt{\frac{8\%}{2}} = \underline{\underline{2\%}}$$

$$\sigma_{k_B} = \sqrt{\frac{(16\% - 14\%)^2 + (14\% - 14\%)^2 + (12\% - 14\%)^2}{3-1}}$$

$$= \sqrt{\frac{4\% + 0\% + 4\%}{2}} = \sqrt{\frac{8\%}{2}} = \underline{\underline{2\%}}$$

$$\sigma_{k_C} = \sqrt{\frac{(12\% - 14\%)^2 + (14\% - 14\%)^2 + (16\% - 14\%)^2}{3-1}}$$

$$= \sqrt{\frac{4\% + 0\% + 4\%}{2}} = \sqrt{\frac{8\%}{2}} = \underline{\underline{2\%}}$$

c.

	Annual expected returns	
Year	Portfolio AB	Portfolio AC
2002	$(0.50 \times 12\%) + (0.50 \times 16\%) = 14\%$	$(0.50 \times 12\%) + (0.50 \times 12\%) = 12\%$
2003	$(0.50 \times 14\%) + (0.50 \times 14\%) = 14\%$	$(0.50 \times 14\%) + (0.50 \times 14\%) = 14\%$
2004	$(0.50 \times 16\%) + (0.50 \times 12\%) = 14\%$	$(0.50 \times 16\%) + (0.50 \times 16\%) = 16\%$

Over the 3-year period:

$$\bar{k}_{AB} = \frac{14\% + 14\% + 14\%}{3} = \frac{42\%}{3} = \underline{\underline{14\%}}$$

$$\bar{k}_{AC} = \frac{12\% + 14\% + 16\%}{3} = \frac{42\%}{3} = \underline{\underline{14\%}}$$

d. AB is perfectly negatively correlated.

AC is perfectly positively correlated.

e. Standard deviation of the portfolios:

$$\sigma_{k_{AB}} = \sqrt{\frac{(14\% - 14\%)^2 + (14\% - 14\%)^2 + (14\% - 14\%)^2}{3-1}}$$

$$= \sqrt{\frac{0\% + 0\% + 0\%}{2}} = \sqrt{\frac{0\%}{2}} = \underline{\underline{0\%}}$$

$$\sigma_{k_{AC}} = \sqrt{\frac{(12\% - 14\%)^2 + (14\% - 14\%)^2 + (16\% - 14\%)^2}{3 - 1}}$$

$$= \sqrt{\frac{4\% + 0\% + 4\%}{2}} = \sqrt{\frac{8\%}{2}} = \underline{\underline{2\%}}$$

f. Portfolio AB is preferred, because it provides the same return (14%) as AC but with less risk [$(\sigma_{k_{AB}} = 0\%) < (\sigma_{k_{AC}} = 2\%)$].

ST 6-2 a. When the market return increases by 10%, the project's required return would be expected to increase by 15% (1.50 × 10%). When the market return decreases by 10%, the project's required return would be expected to decrease by 15% [1.50 × (−10%)].

b. $k_j = R_F + [b_j \times (k_m - R_F)]$
$= 7\% + [1.50 \times (10\% - 7\%)]$
$= 7\% + 4.5\% = \underline{11.5\%}$

c. No, the project should be rejected, because its *expected* return of 11% is less than the 11.5% return *required* from the project.

d. $k_j = 7\% + [1.50 \times (9\% - 7\%)]$
$= 7\% + 3\% = \underline{10\%}$

The project would now be acceptable, because its *expected* return of 11% is now in excess of the *required* return, which has declined to 10% as a result of investors in the marketplace becoming less risk-averse.

Chapter 7

ST 7-1 a. $B_0 = I \times (PVIFA_{k_d,n}) + M \times (PVIF_{k_d,n})$
$I = .08 \times \$1,000 = \$80$
$M = \$1,000$
$n = 12$ yrs
(1) $k_d = 7\%$
$B_0 = \$80 \times (PVIFA_{7\%,12yrs}) + \$1,000 \times (PVIF_{7\%,12yrs})$
$= (\$80 \times 7.943) + (\$1,000 \times .444)$
$= \$635.44 + \$444.00 = \underline{\$1,079.44}$
(Calculator solution = \$1,079.43)
(2) $k_d = 8\%$
$B_0 = \$80 \times (PVIFA_{8\%,12yrs}) + \$1,000 \times (PVIF_{8\%,12yrs})$
$= (\$80 \times 7.536) + (\$1,000 \times .397)$
$= \$602.88 + \$397.00 = \underline{\$999.88}$
(Calculator solution = \$1,000)
(3) $k_d = 10\%$
$B_0 = \$80 \times (PVIFA_{10\%,12yrs}) + \$1,000 \times (PVIF_{10\%,12yrs})$
$= (\$80 \times 6.814) + (\$1,000 \times .319)$

$$= \$545.12 + \$319.00 = \underline{\$864.12}$$
$$(\text{Calculator solution} = \$863.73)$$

b. (1) $k_d = 7\%$, $B_0 = \$1,079.44$; sells at a *premium*
   (2) $k_d = 8\%$, $B_0 = \$999.88 \approx \$1,000.00$; sells at its *par value*
   (3) $k_d = 10\%$, $B_0 = \$864.12$; sells at a *discount*

c. $B_0 = \dfrac{I}{2} \times (PVIFA_{k_{d}/2,2n}) + M \times (PVIF_{k_{d}/2,2n})$

$$= \frac{\$80}{2} \times (PVIFA_{10\%/2,2\times12\text{periods}}) + \$1,000 \times (PVIF_{10\%/2,2\times12\text{periods}})$$

$$= \$40 \times (PVIFA_{5\%,24\text{periods}}) + \$1,000 \times (PVIF_{5\%,24\text{periods}})$$
$$= (\$40 \times 13.799) + (\$1,000 \times .310)$$
$$= \$551.96 + \$310.00 = \underline{\$861.96}$$
$$(\text{Calculator solution} = \$862.01)$$

ST 7-2 **a.** $B_0 = \$1,150$
   $I = .11 \times \$1,000 = \$110$
   $M = \$1,000$
   $n = 18$ yrs
   $\$1,150 = \$110 \times (PVIFA_{k_d,18\text{yrs}}) + \$1,000 \times (PVIF_{k_d,18\text{yrs}})$
   Because if $k_d = 11\%$, $B_0 = \$1,000 = M$, try $k_d = 10\%$.
   $B_0 = \$110 \times (PVIFA_{10\%,18\text{yrs}}) + \$1,000 \times (PVIF_{10\%,18\text{yrs}})$
   $\quad = (\$110 \times 8.201) + (\$1,000 \times .180)$
   $\quad = \$902.11 + \$180.00 = \$1,082.11$
   Because $\$1,082.11 < \$1,150$, try $k_d = 9\%$.
   $B_0 = \$110 \times (PVIFA_{9\%,18\text{yrs}}) + \$1,000 \times (PVIF_{9\%,18\text{yrs}})$
   $\quad = (\$110 \times 8.756) + (\$1,000 \times .212)$
   $\quad = \$963.16 + \$212.00 = \$1,175.16$

Because the $\$1,175.16$ value at 9% is higher than $\$1,150$, and the $\$1,082.11$ value at 10% rate is lower than $\$1,150$, the bond's yield to maturity must be between 9% and 10%. Because the $\$1,175.16$ value is closer to $\$1,150$, rounding to the nearest whole percent, the YTM is 9%. (By using interpolation, we can determine that the more precise YTM value is 9.27%.)

(Calculator solution = 9.26%)

b. The calculated YTM of 9+% is below the bond's 11% coupon interest rate, because the bond's market value of $\$1,150$ is above its $\$1,000$ par value. Whenever a bond's market value is above its par value (it sells at a *premium*), its YTM will be below its coupon interest rate; when a bond sells at *par*, the YTM will equal its coupon interest rate; and when the bond sells for less than par (at a *discount*), its YTM will be greater than its coupon interest rate.

ST 7-3 $D_0 = \$1.80/\text{share}$
$k_s = 12\%$

a. *Zero growth:*

$$P_0 = \frac{D_1}{k_s} = \frac{D_1 = D_0 = \$1.80}{.12} = \underline{\underline{\$15/\text{share}}}$$

b. *Constant growth, g = 5%:*
$D_1 = D_0 \times (1 + g) = \$1.80 \times (1 + .05) = \$1.89/\text{share}$

$$P_0 = \frac{D_1}{k_s - g} = \frac{\$1.89}{.12 - .05} = \frac{\$1.89}{.07} = \underline{\underline{\$27/\text{share}}}$$

c. *Variable growth, N = 3, g_1 = 5% for years 1 to 3 and g_2 = 4% for years 4 to ∞:*
$D_1 = D_0 \times (1 + g_1)^1 = \$1.80 \times (1 + 0.005)^1 = \$1.89/\text{share}$
$D_2 = D_0 \times (1 + g_1)^2 = \$1.80 \times (1 + 0.005)^2 = \$1.98/\text{share}$
$D_3 = D_0 \times (1 + g_1)^3 = \$1.80 \times (1 + 0.005)^3 = \$12.08/\text{share}$
$D_4 = D_3 \times (1 + g_2) = \$1.80 \times (1 + 0.004) = \$2.16/\text{share}$

$$P_0 = \sum_{t=1}^{N} \frac{D_0 \times (1 + g_1)^1}{(1 + k_s)t} + \left(\frac{1}{(1 + k_s)^N} \times \frac{D_N + 1}{k_s - g_2} \right)$$

$$\sum_{t=1}^{N} \frac{D_0 \times (1 + g_1)^1}{(1 + k_s)t} = \frac{\$1.89}{(1 + .12)^1} + \frac{\$1.98}{(1 + .12)^2} + \frac{\$2.08}{(1 + .12)^3}$$

$$= [\$1.89 \times (PVIF_{12\%,1yr})] + [\$1.98 \times (PVIF_{12\%,2yrs})]$$
$$+ [\$2.08 \times (PVIF_{12\%,3yrs})]$$

$$= (\$1.89 \times 0.893) + (\$1.98 \times 0.797) + (\$2.08 \times 0.712)$$
$$= \$1.69 \times \$1.58 + \$1.48 = \$4.75$$

$$\left[\frac{1}{(1 + k_s)^N} \times \frac{D_N + 1}{k_s - g_2} \right] = \frac{1}{(1 + 0.12)^3} \times D_4 = \frac{\$2.16}{0.12 - 0.04}$$

$$= (PVIF_{12\%,3yrs})] \times \frac{\$2.16}{0.08}$$

$$= 0.712 \times \$27.00 = \$19.22$$

$$P_0 = \sum_{t=1}^{N} \frac{D_0 \times (1 + g_1)^1}{(1 + k_s)t} + \left[\frac{1}{(1 + k_s)^N} \times \frac{D_N + 1}{k_s - g_2} \right] = \$5.75 + \$19.22$$

$$= \underline{\underline{\$23.97/\text{share}}}$$

Chapter 8   **ST 8-1**

Ratio	Too high	Too low
Current ratio = current assets/current liabilities	May indicate that the firm is holding excessive cash, accounts receivable, or inventory.	May indicate poor ability to satisfy short-term obligations.
Inventory turnover = CGS/inventory	May indicate lower level of inventory, which may cause stockouts and lost sales.	May indicate poor inventory management, excessive inventory, or obsolete inventory.
Times interest earned = earnings before interest and taxes/interest	✕	May indicate poor ability to pay contractual interest payments.
Gross profit margin = gross profits/sales	Indicates the low cost of merchandise sold relative to the sales price; may indicate noncompetitive pricing and potential lost sales.	Indicates the high cost of the merchandise sold relative to the sales price; may indicate either a low sales price or a high cost of goods sold.
Return on total assets = net profits after taxes/total assets	✕	Indicates ineffective management in generating profits with the available assets.

ST 8-2

Balance Sheet
Orphan Industries
December 31, 2001

Cash	$ 30,000	Accounts payable	$ 120,000
Marketable securities	25,000	Notes payable	160,000^e
Accounts receivable	200,000^a	Accruals	20,000
Inventories	225,000^b	Total current	
Total current assets	$ 480,000	liabilities	$ 300,000^d
Net fixed assets	$1,020,000^c	Long-term debt	$ 600,000^f
Total assets	$1,500,000	Stockholders' equity	$ 600,000
		Total liabilities and	
		stockholders' equity	$1,500,000

^{a}Average collection period (ACP) = 40 days
ACP = accounts receivable/average sales per day
40 = accounts receivable/($1,800,000/360)
40 = accounts receivable/$5,000
$200,000 = accounts receivable

^{b}Inventory turnover = 6.0
Inventory turnover = cost of goods sold/inventory
6.0 = [sales × (1 − gross profit margin)]/inventory
6.0 = [$1,800,000 × (1 − 0.25)]/inventory
$225,000 = inventory

^{c}Total asset turnover = 1.20
Total asset turnover = sales/total assets
1.20 = $1,800,000/total assets
$1,500,000 = total assets
Total assets = current assets + net fixed assets
$1,500,000 = $480,000 + net fixed assets
$1,020,000 = net fixed assets

^{d}Current ratio = 1.60
Current ratio = current assets/current liabilities
1.60 = $480,000/current liabilities
$300,000 = current liabilities

^{e}Notes payable = total current liabilities − accounts payable − accruals
= $300,000 − $120,000 − $20,000
= $160,000

^{f}Debt ratio = 0.60
Debt ratio = total liabilities/total assets
0.60 = total liabilities/$1,500,000
$900,000 = total liabilities

Total liabilities = current liabilities + long-term debt
$900,000 = $300,000 + long-term debt
$600,000 = long-term debt

Chapter 9

ST 9-1 **a.** Capital gains = $180,000 sale price − $150,000 original purchase price = $30,000

b. Total taxable income = $280,000 operating earnings + $30,000 capital gain = $310,000

c. Firm's tax liability:
Using Table 9.2:
Total taxes due = $22,250 + [0.39 × ($310,000 − $100,000)]
= $22,250 + (0.39 × $210,000) = $22,250 + $81,900
= $104,150

d. Average tax rate = $\frac{\$104,150}{\$310,000}$ = 33.6%

Marginal tax rate = 39%

ST 9-2 **a.** Depreciation Schedule

Year	Cost[a] (1)	Percentages (from Table 9.5) (2)	Depreciation [(1) × (2)] (3)
1	$150,000	20%	$ 30,000
2	150,000	32	48,000
3	150,000	19	28,500
4	150,000	12	18,000
5	150,000	12	18,000
6	150,000	5	7,500
	Totals	100%	$150,000

[a]$140,000 asset cost + $10,000 installation cost.

b. Cash flow schedule

Year	EBDT (1)	Deprec. (2)	Net profits before taxes [(1) − (2)] (3)	Taxes [0.4 × (3)] (4)	Net profits after taxes [(3) − (4)] (5)	Operating cash flows [(2) + (5)] (6)
1	$160,000	$30,000	$130,000	$52,000	$78,000	$108,000
2	160,000	48,000	112,000	44,800	67,200	115,200
3	160,000	28,500	131,500	52,600	78,900	107,400
4	160,000	18,000	142,000	56,800	85,200	103,200
5	160,000	18,000	142,000	56,800	85,200	103,200
6	160,000	7,500	152,500	61,000	91,500	99,000

c. The purchase of the asset allows the firm to deduct depreciation—a noncash charge—for tax purposes. This results in lower taxable income and therefore lower tax payments. As a result, the firm's operating cash flows (in column 6 of the preceding table) exceed its net profits after taxes (in column 5 of the table).

Chapter 10

ST 10-1 **a.** Book value = installed cost − accumulated depreciation
Installed cost = \$50,000
Accumulated depreciation = \$50,000 × (0.20 + 0.32 + 0.19 + 0.12)
= \$50,000 × 0.83 = \$41,500
Book value = \$50,000 − \$41,500 = $\underline{\$8,500}$

b. Taxes on sale of old equipment:
Capital gain = sale price − initial purchase price
= \$55,000 − \$50,000 = \$5,000
Recaptured depreciation = initial purchase price − book value
= \$50,000 − \$8,500 = \$41,500
Taxes = (0.40 × \$5,000) + (0.40 × \$41,500)
= \$2,000 + \$16,600 = $\underline{\$18,600}$

c. Initial investment:

Installed cost of new equipment		
Cost of new equipment	\$ 75,000	
+ Installation costs	5,000	
Total installed cost—new		\$ 80,000
− After-tax proceeds from sale of old equipment		
Proceeds from sale of old equipment	\$ 55,000	
− Taxes on sale of old equipment	18,600	
Total after-tax proceeds—old		36,400
+ Change in net working capital		15,000
Initial investment		\$ 58,600

ST 10-2 **a.** Initial investment:

Installed cost of new machine		
Cost of new machine	\$140,000	
+ Installation costs	10,000	
Total installed cost—new (depreciable value)		\$150,000
− After-tax proceeds from sale of old machine		
Proceeds from sale of old machine	\$ 42,000	
− Taxes on sale of old machine[1]	9,120	
Total after-tax proceeds—old		32,880
+ Change in net working capital [2]		20,000
Initial investment		\$137,120

---

[1]Book value of old machine = \$40,000 − [(0.20 + 0.32) × \$40,000]
= \$40,000 − (0.52 × \$40,000)
= \$40,000 − \$20,800 = \$19,200
Capital gain = \$42,000 − \$40,000 = \$2,000
Recaptured depreciation = \$40,000 − \$19,200 = \$20,800
Taxes = (0.40 × \$2,000) + (0.40 × \$20,800) = \$800 + \$8,320 = $\underline{\$9,120}$

[2]Change in net working capital = +\$10,000 + \$25,000 − \$15,000
= \$35,000 − \$15,000 = $\underline{\$20,000}$

b. Incremental operating cash inflows:

Calculation of Depreciation Expense for New Machine

Year	Cost (1)	Applicable MACRS depreciation percentages (from Table 9.5) (2)	Depreciation [(1) × (2)] (3)
With new machine			
1	$150,000	33%	$ 49,500
2	150,000	45	67,500
3	150,000	15	22,500
4	150,000	7	10,500
Totals		100%	$150,000

Calculation of Depreciation Expense for Old Machine

Year	Cost (1)	Applicable MACRS depreciation percentages (from Table 9.5) (2)	Depreciation [(1) × (2)] (3)
With old machine			
1	$40,000	19% (year-3 depreciation)	$ 7,600
2	40,000	12 (year-4 depreciation)	4,800
3	40,000	12 (year-5 depreciation)	4,800
4	40,000	5 (year-6 depreciation)	2,000
Total			$19,200[a]

[a]The total of $19,200 represents the book value of the old machine at the end of the second year, which was calculated in part **a.**

Calculation of Operating Cash Inflows

	Year			
	1	2	3	4
With new machine				
Profits before depr. and taxes[a]	$120,000	$130,000	$130,000	$ 0
− Depreciation[b]	49,500	67,500	22,500	10,500
Net profits before taxes	$ 70,500	$ 62,500	$107,500	−$10,500
− Taxes (rate = 40%)	28,200	25,000	43,000	− 4,200
Net profits after taxes	$ 42,300	$ 37,500	$ 64,500	− 6,300
+ Depreciation[b]	49,500	67,500	22,500	10,500
Operating cash inflows	$ 91,800	$105,000	$ 87,000	$ 4,200
With old machine				
Profits before depr. and taxes[a]	$ 70,000	$ 70,000	$ 70,000	$ 0
− Depreciation[c]	7,600	4,800	4,800	2,000
Net profits before taxes	$ 62,400	$ 65,200	$ 65,200	−$ 2,000
− Taxes (rate = 40%)	24,960	26,080	26,080	− 800
Net profits after taxes	$ 37,440	$ 39,120	$ 39,120	−$ 1,200
+ Depreciation	7,600	4,800	4,800	2,000
Operating cash inflows	$ 45,040	$ 43,920	$ 43,920	$ 800

[a]Given in the problem.
[b]From column 3 of the first table.
[c]From column 3 of the preceding table.

Calculation of Incremental Operating Cash Inflows

	Operating cash inflows		
Year	New machine[a] (1)	Old machine[a] (2)	Incremental (relevant) [(1) − (2)] (3)
1	$ 91,800	$45,040	$46,760
2	105,000	43,920	61,080
3	87,000	43,920	43,080
4	4,200	800	3,400

[a]From final row for respective machine in the preceding table.

c. Terminal cash flow (end of year 3):

After-tax proceeds from sale of new machine		
Proceeds from sale of new machine	$35,000	
− Tax on sale of new machine[1]	9,800	
Total after-tax proceeds—new		$25,200
− After-tax proceeds from sale of old machine		
Proceeds from sale of old machine	$ 0	
− Tax on sale of old machine[2]	− 800	
Total after-tax proceeds—old		800
+ Change in net working capital		20,000
Terminal cash flow		$44,400

d.

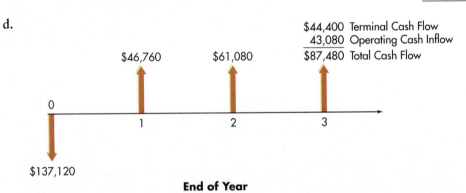

$44,400	Terminal Cash Flow
43,080	Operating Cash Inflow
$87,480	Total Cash Flow

End of Year

Note: The year-4 incremental operating cash inflow of $3,400 is not directly included; it is instead reflected in the book values used to calculate the taxes on sale of the machines at the end of year 3 and is therefore part of the terminal cash flow.

Chapter 11

ST 11-1   a. Payback period:

$$\text{Project M: } \frac{\$28,500}{\$10,000} = \underline{\underline{2.85 \text{ years}}}$$

---

[1]Book value of new machine at end of year 3
= $150,000 − [(.33 + .45 + .15) × $150,000] = $150,000 − (.93 × $150,000)
= $150,000 − $139,500 = $10,500
Tax on sale = 0.40 × ($35,000 sale price − $10,500 book value)
= 0.40 × $24,500 = $9,800

[2]Book value of old machine at end of year 3
= $40,000 − [(0.20 + 0.32 + 0.19 + 0.12 + 0.12) × $40,000] = $40,000 − (0.95 × $40,000)
= $40,000 − $38,000 = $2,000
Tax on sale = 0.40 × ($0 sale price − $2,000 book value)
= 0.40 × (− $2,000) = −$800 (i.e., $800 tax saving)

Project N:

Year *(t)*	Cash inflows *(CF_t)*	Cumulative cash inflows
1	$11,000	$11,000
2	10,000	21,000
3	9,000	30,000 ←
4	8,000	38,000

$$2 + \frac{\$27,000 - \$21,000}{\$9,000} \text{ years}$$

$$2 + \frac{\$6,000}{\$9,000} \text{ years} = \underline{2.67 \text{ years}}$$

b. Net present value (NPV):

Project M: NPV $= (\$10,000 \times PVIFA_{14\%,4yrs}) - \$28,500$
$= (\$10,000 \times 2.914) - \$28,500$
$= \$29,140 - \$28,500 = \underline{\$640}$
(Calculator solution $= \$637.12$)

Project N:

Year *(t)*	Cash inflows *(CF_t)* (1)	$PVIF_{14\%,t}$ (2)	Present value at 14% [(1) × (2)] (3)
1	$11,000	0.877	$ 9,647
2	10,000	0.769	7,690
3	9,000	0.675	6,075
4	8,000	0.592	4,736
	Present value of cash inflows		$28,148
	− Initial investment		27,000
	Net present value (NPV)		$ 1,148

(Calculator solution $= \$1,155.18$)

c. Internal rate of return (IRR):

Project M: $\dfrac{\$28,500}{\$10,000} = 2.850$

$PVIFA_{IRR,4yrs} = 2.850$
From Table A-4:
$PVIFA_{15\%,4yrs} = 2.855$
$PVIFA_{16\%,4yrs} = 2.798$
IRR $= \underline{15\%}$ (2.850 is closest to 2.855)
(Calculator solution $= 15.09\%$)

Project N: Average annual cash inflow $= \dfrac{\$11,000 + \$10,000 + \$9,000 + \$8,000}{4}$

$$= \dfrac{\$38,000}{4} = \$9,500$$

$PVIFA_{k,4\text{yrs}} = \dfrac{\$27,000}{\$9,500} = 2.842$

$k \approx 15\%$

Try 16%, because there are more cash inflows in early years.

Year (t)	CF_t (1)	$PVIF_{16\%,t}$ (2)	Present value at 16% [(1) × (2)] (3)	$PVIF_{17\%,t}$ (4)	Present value at 17% [(1) × (4)] (5)
1	$11,000	.862	$ 9,482	0.855	$ 9,405
2	10,000	.743	7,430	0.731	7,310
3	9,000	.641	5,769	0.624	5,616
4	8,000	.552	4,416	0.534	4,272
		Present value of cash inflows	$27,097		$26,603
	−	Initial investment	27,000		27,000
		NPV	$ 97		−$ 397

IRR = 16% (rounding to nearest whole percent)
(Calculator solution = 16.19%)

d.

	Project	
	M	N
Payback period	2.85 years	2.67 years[a]
NPV	$640	$1,148[a]
IRR	15%	16%[a]

[a]Preferred project.

Project N is recommended, because it has the shorter payback period and the higher NPV, which is greater than zero, and the larger IRR, which is greater than the 14% cost of capital.

e. Net present value profiles:

Data		
	NPV	
Discount rate	Project M	Project N
0%	$11,500[a]	$11,000[b]
14	640	1,148
15	0	—
16	—	0

[a]($10,000 + $10,000 + $10,000 + $10,000)
− $28,500 = $40,000 − $28,500 = $11,500

[b]($11,000 + $10,000 + $9,000 + $8,000)
− $27,000 = $38,000 − $27,000 = $11,000

From the NPV profile that follows, it can be seen that if the firm has a cost of capital below approximately 6% (exact value is 5.75%), conflicting rankings of the projects would exist using the NPV and IRR decision techniques. Because the firm's cost of capital is 14%, it can be seen in part **d** that no conflict exists.

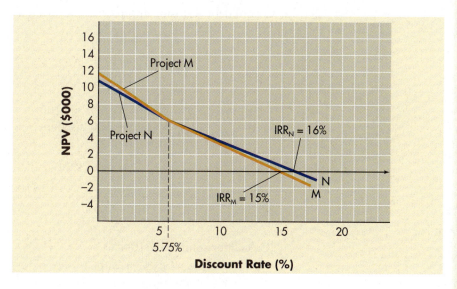

ST 11-2   **a.** $NPV_A = (\$7,000 \times PVIFA_{10\%,3yrs}) - \$15,000$
   $= (\$7,000 \times 2.487) - \$15,000$
   $= \$17,409 - \$15,000 = \underline{\$2,409}$
   (Calculator solution = $2,407.96)

$NPV_B = (\$10,000 \times PVIFA_{10\%,3yrs}) - \$20,000$
   $= (\$10,000 - 2.487) - \$20,000$
   $= \$24,870 - \$20,000 = \underline{\$4,870}*$
   (Calculator solution = $4,868.52)

*Preferred project, because higher NPV.

b. From the CAPM-type relationship, the risk-adjusted discount rate for project A, which has a risk index of 0.4, is 9%; for project B, with a risk index of 1.8, the risk-adjusted discount rate is 16%.

$$NPV_A = (\$7,000 \times PVIFA_{9\%,3yrs}) - \$15,000$$
$$= (\$7,000 \times 2.531) - \$15,000$$
$$= \$17,717 - \$15,000 = \underline{\$2,717}^*$$
(Calculator solution $= \$2,719.06$)

$$NPV_B = (\$10,000 \times PVIFA_{16\%,3yrs}) - \$20,000$$
$$= (\$10,000 \times 2.246) - \$20,000$$
$$= \$22,460 - \$20,000 = \underline{\$2,460}$$
(Calculator solution $= \$2,458.90$)

*Preferred project, because higher NPV.

c. When the differences in risk were ignored in **a,** project B is preferred over project A; but when the higher risk of project B is incorporated in the analysis using either certainty equivalents (**b**) or risk-adjusted discount rates (**c**), *project A is preferred over project B.* Clearly, project A should be implemented.

Chapter 12

ST 12-1   a. Cost of debt, k_i (using approximation formula)

$$k_d = \frac{I + \dfrac{\$1,000 - N_d}{n}}{\dfrac{N_d + \$1,000}{2}}$$

$$I = 0.10 \times \$1,000 = \$100$$
$$N_d = \$1,000 - \$30 \text{ discount} - \$20 \text{ flotation cost} = \$950$$
$$n = 10 \text{ years}$$

$$k_d = \frac{\$100 + \dfrac{\$1,000 - \$950}{10}}{\dfrac{\$950 + \$1,000}{2}} = \frac{\$100 + \$5}{\$975} = 10.8\%$$

(Calculator solution $= 10.8\%$)

$$k_i = k_d \times (1 - T)$$
$$T = 0.40$$
$$k_i = 10.8\% \times (1 - .40) = \underline{6.5\%}$$

Cost of preferred stock, k_p

$$k_p = \frac{D_p}{N_p}$$

$$D_p = 0.11 \times \$100 = \$11$$
$$N_p = \$100 - \$4 \text{ flotation cost} = \$96$$

$$k_p = \frac{\$11}{\$96} = \underline{11.5\%}$$

Cost of retained earnings, k_r

$$k_r = k_s = \frac{D_1}{P_0} + g$$

$$= \frac{\$6}{\$80} + 6.0\% = 7.5\% + 6.0\% = \underline{\underline{13.5\%}}$$

Cost of new common stock, k_n

$$k_n = \frac{D_1}{N_n} + g$$

$$D_1 = \$6$$
$$N_n = \$80 - \$4 \text{ underpricing} - \$4 \text{ flotation cost} = \$72$$
$$g = 6.0\%$$

$$k_n = \frac{\$6}{\$72} + 6.0\% = 8.3\% + 6.0\% = \underline{\underline{14.3\%}}$$

b. (1) Breaking point, *BP*

$$BP_{\text{common equity}} = \frac{AF_{\text{common equity}}}{w_{\text{common equity}}}$$

$$AF_{\text{common equity}} = \$225,000$$
$$w_{\text{common equity}} = 45\%$$

$$BP_{\text{common equity}} = \frac{\$225,000}{0.45} = \$500,000$$

(2) WACC for total new financing $< \$500,000$

Source of capital	Weight (1)	Cost (2)	Weighted cost [(1) × (2)] (3)
Long-term debt	0.40	6.5%	2.6%
Preferred stock	0.15	11.5	1.7
Common stock equity	0.45	13.5	6.1
Totals	1.00		10.4%

Weighted average cost of capital = 10.4%

(3) WACC for total new financing $> \$500,000$

Source of capital	Weight (1)	Cost (2)	Weighted cost [(1) × (2)] (3)
Long-term debt	0.40	6.5%	2.6%
Preferred stock	0.15	11.5	1.7
Common stock equity	0.45	14.3	6.4
Totals	1.00		10.7%

Weighted average cost of capital = 10.7%

c. IOS data for graph

Investment opportunity	Internal rate of return (IRR)	Initial investment	Cumulative investment
D	16.5%	$200,000	$ 200,000
C	12.9	150,000	350,000
E	11.8	450,000	800,000
A	11.2	100,000	900,000
G	10.5	300,000	1,200,000
F	10.1	600,000	1,800,000
B	9.7	500,000	2,300,000

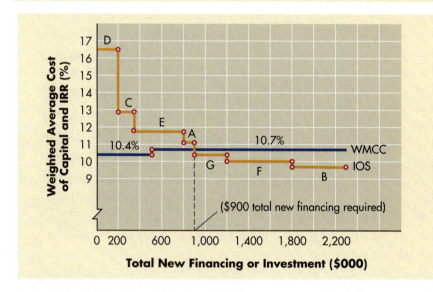

d. Projects D, C, E, and A should be accepted because their respective IRRs exceed the WMCC. They will require $900,000 of total new financing.

Chapter 13

ST 13-1

Data summary for alternative plans		
Source of capital	Plan A (bond)	Plan B (stock)
Long-term debt	$60,000 at 12% annual interest	$50,000 at 12% annual interest
Annual interest =	0.12 × $60,000 = $7,200	0.12 × $50,000 = $6,000
Common stock	10,000 shares	11,000 shares

a.

	Plan A (bond)		Plan B (stock)	
EBIT[a]	$30,000	$40,000	$30,000	$40,000
Less: Interest	7,200	7,200	6,000	6,000
Net profits before taxes	$22,800	$32,800	$24,000	$34,000
Less: Taxes ($T = .40$)	9,120	13,120	9,600	13,600
Net profits after taxes	$13,680	$19,680	$14,400	$20,400
EPS (10,000 shares)	$1.37	$1.97		
(11,000 shares)			$1.31	$1.85

[a]Values were arbitrarily selected; other values could have been utilized.

	Coordinates	
	EBIT	
	$30,000	$40,000
Financing plan	**Earnings per share (EPS)**	
A (Bond)	$1.37	$1.97
B (Stock)	1.31	1.85

b.

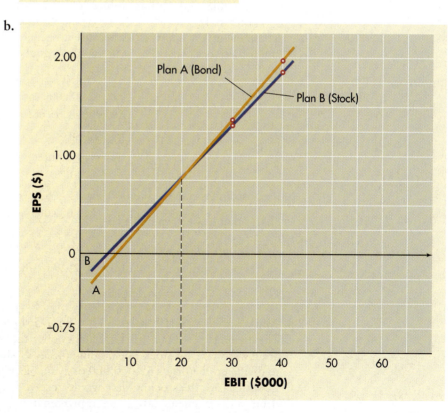

c. The bond plan (Plan A) becomes superior to the stock plan (Plan B) at *around $20,000* of EBIT, as represented by the dashed vertical line in the figure in **b.** (*Note:* The actual point is $19,200, which was determined algebraically by using a technique described in more advanced texts.)

ST 13-2 **a.**

Capital structure debt ratio	Expected EPS (1)	Required return, k_s (2)	Estimated share value [(1) ÷ (2)] (3)
0%	$3.12	0.13	$24.00
10	3.90	0.15	26.00
20	4.80	0.16	30.00
30	5.44	0.17	32.00
40	5.51	0.19	29.00
50	5.00	0.20	25.00
60	4.40	0.22	20.00

b. Using the table in **a:**
  (1) Maximization of EPS: *40% debt ratio,* EPS = $5.51/share (see column 1).
  (2) Maximization of share value: *30% debt ratio,* share value = $32.00 (see column 3).
c. Recommend *30% debt ratio,* because it results in the maximum share value and is therefore consistent with the firm's goal of owner wealth maximization.

ST 13-3 **a.** Earnings per share (EPS) $= \dfrac{\$2,000,000 \text{ earnings available}}{500,000 \text{ shares of common outstanding}}$

$\qquad\qquad = \underline{\$4.00/\text{share}}$

Price/earnings (P/E) ratio $= \dfrac{\$60 \text{ market price}}{\$4.00 \text{ EPS}} = \underline{\underline{15}}$

b. Proposed dividends = 500,000 shares × $2 per share = $1,000,000

Shares that can be repurchased $= \dfrac{\$1,000,000}{\$62} = \underline{16,129 \text{ shares}}$

c. *After proposed repurchase:*
Shares outstanding = 500,000 − 16,129 = 483,871

EPS $= \dfrac{\$2,000,000}{483,871} = \underline{\$4.13/\text{share}}$

d. Market price = $4.13/share × 15 = $\underline{\$61.95/\text{share}}$
e. The earnings per share (EPS) are higher after the repurchase, because there are fewer shares of stock outstanding (483,871 shares versus 500,000 shares) to divide up the firm's $2,000,000 of available earnings.
f. In both cases, the stockholders would receive $2 per share—a $2 cash dividend in the dividend case or an approximately $2 increase in share price ($60.00 per share to $61.95 per share) in the repurchase case. [*Note:* The $.05 per share ($2.00 − $1.95) difference is due to rounding.]

Chapter 14

ST 14-1   a.

	February	March	April	May	June	July	August
Cash Budget Caldera Company April–June						**Accounts receivable at end of June**	
Forecast sales	$500	$600	$400	$ 200	$200		
Cash sales (.30)	$150	$180	$120	$ 60	$ 60		
Collections of A/R							
Lagged 1 month [(.7 × .7) = .49]		245	294	196	98	$ 98	
Lagged 2 months [(.3 × .7) = .21]			105	126	84	42	$42
						$140 +	$42 = $182
Total cash receipts			$519	$ 382	$242		
Less: Total cash disbursements			600	500	200		
Net cash flow			$ (81)	$(118)	$ 42		
Add: Beginning cash			115	34	(84)		
Ending cash			$ 34	$ (84)	$ (42)		
Less: Minimum cash balance			25	25	25		
Required total financing (notes payable)			—	$ 109	$ 67		
Excess cash balance (marketable securities)			$ 9	—	—		

b. Caldera Company would need a maximum of $109 in financing over the 3-month period.

c.

Account	Amount	Source of amount
Cash	$ 25	Minimum cash balance—June
Notes payable	67	Required total financing—June
Marketable securities	0	Excess cash balance—June
Accounts receivable	182	Calculation at right of cash budget statement

ST 14-2   a.

Pro Forma Income Statement Digital Designs, Inc., for the year ended December 31, 2002	
Sales revenue (given)	$3,900,000
Less: Cost of goods sold (0.55)[a]	2,145,000
Gross profits	$1,755,000
Less: Operating expenses (0.12)[b]	468,000
Operating profits	$1,287,000
Less: Interest expense (given)	325,000
Net profits before taxes	$ 962,000
Less: Taxes (0.40 × $962,000)	384,800
Net profits after taxes	$ 577,200
Less: Cash dividends (given)	320,000
To retained earnings	$ 257,200

[a]From 2001: CGS/Sales = $1,925,000/$3,500,000 = 0.55.
[b]From 2001: Oper. Exp./Sales = $420,000/$3,500,000 = 0.12.

b. The percent-of-sales method may underestimate actual 2002 pro forma income by assuming that all costs are variable. If the firm has fixed costs, which by definition would not increase with increasing sales, the 2002 pro forma income would probably be underestimated.

Chapter 15

ST 15-1

Basic data		
Time component	Current	Proposed
Average payment period (APP)	10 days	30 days
Average collection period (ACP)	30 days	30 days
Average age of inventory (AAI)	40 days	40 days

Cash conversion cycle (CCC) = AAI + ACP − APP

$$CCC_{current} = 40 \text{ days} + 30 \text{ days} - 10 \text{ days} = 60 \text{ days}$$
$$CCC_{proposed} = 40 \text{ days} + 30 \text{ days} - 30 \text{ days} = \underline{40 \text{ days}}$$

Reduction in CCC $\underline{20 \text{ days}}$

Annual operating cycle investment = $18,000,000

Daily expenditure = $18,000,000 ÷ 360 = $50,000
Reduction in financing = $50,000 × 20 days = $1,000,000
Annual profit increase = 0.12 × $1,000,000 = $\underline{\$120,000}$

ST 15-2 **a.** *Data:*

S = 60,000 gallons
O = $200 per order
C = $1 per gallon per year

Calculation:

$$EOQ = \sqrt{\frac{2 \times S \times O}{C}} = \sqrt{\frac{2 \times 60,000 \times \$200}{\$1}} = \sqrt{24,000,000} = \underline{4,899 \text{ gallons}}$$

b. *Data:*

Lead time = 20 days
Daily usage = 60,000 gallons/360 days
         = 166.67 gallons/day

Calculation:

Reorder point = lead time in days × daily usage
         = 20 days × 166.67 gallons/day
         = 3,333.4 gallons

ST 15-3 Tabular Calculation of the Effects of Relaxing Credit Standards on Zoldan Rug Repair Company:

Additional profit contribution from sales		
[4,000 rugs × ($32 avg. sale price − $28 var. cost)]		$16,000
Cost of marginal investment in accounts receivable		
Average investment under proposed plan:		
$\frac{(\$28 \times 76,000 \text{ rugs})}{360/48} = \frac{\$2,128,000}{7.5}$	$283,733	
Average investment under present plan:		
$\frac{(\$28 \times 72,000 \text{ rugs})}{360/40} = \frac{\$2,016,000}{9}$	224,000	
Marginal investment in A/R	$ 59,733	
Cost of marginal investment in		
A/R (.14 × $59,733)		($ 8,363)
Cost of marginal bad debts		
Bad debts under proposed plan		
(0.015 × $32 × 76,000 rugs)	$ 36,480	
Bad debts under present plan		
(0.010 × $32 × 72,000 rugs)	23,040	
Cost of marginal bad debts		($13,440)
Net loss from implementation of proposed plan		($ 5,803)

Recommendation: Because a net loss of $5,803 is expected to result from relaxing credit standards, *the proposed plan should not be implemented.*

ST 15-4   **a.**

Supplier	Approximate cost of giving up cash discount
X	$1\% \times [360/(55 - 10)] = 1\% \times 360/45 = 1\% \times 8 = \underline{\underline{8\%}}$
Y	$2\% \times [360/(30 - 10)] = 2\% \times 360/20 = 2\% \times 18 = \underline{\underline{36\%}}$
Z	$2\% \times [360/(60 - 20)] = 2\% \times 360/40 = 2\% \times 9 = \underline{\underline{18\%}}$

b.

Supplier	Recommendation
X	8% cost of not taking discount < 15% interest cost from bank; therefore, *do not take discount.*
Y	36% cost of not taking discount > 15% interest cost from bank; therefore, *take discount and borrow from bank.*
Z	18% cost of not taking discount > 15% interest cost from bank; therefore, *take discount and borrow from bank.*

Chapter 16

ST 16-1   **a.** In a cash investment, there is no loan repayment. When Mike sells the shares, 100% of the proceeds come to him. He simply measures them against the original investment amount to figure his return. Using formula 16.1:

Sale at $30	Sale at $18
SP = $3,000	$1,800
II = 2,200	2,200
D = 0	0
LP = 0	0

Sale at $30:

$$R = \frac{(\$3,000 - 2,200)}{2,200} = \frac{\$800}{2,200} = 0.3636, \text{ or } 36.36\%$$

Sale at $18:

$$R = \frac{(\$1,800 - 2,200)}{2,200} = \frac{-\$400}{2,200} = -0.182 \text{ or } -18.2\%$$

b. When Mike borrows, the sale proceeds will have to cover repayment of the loan plus any interest due. Borrowing allows him to tie up less of his own money in the transaction. Margining should result in an enhanced return if the shares are sold at a gain, but it will result in a larger loss if they are sold for less than the purchase price. Again, using formula 16.1:

Sale at $30	Sale at $18
SP = $3,000	$1,800
II = 1,540	1,540
D = 0	0
LP = 712.80	712.80

Note that the LP (loan payment) portion of the formula includes the $660 borrowed and interest at 8% ($660 × 0.08) = $52.80.

Sale at $30:

$$R = \frac{(\$3,000 - \$1,540 + 0 - \$712.80)}{1,540}$$

$$= \frac{\$747.20}{1,540} = 0.4852, \text{ or } 48.52\%$$

Sale at $18:

$$R = \frac{(\$1,800 - \$1,540 + 0 - \$712.80)}{1,540}$$

$$= \frac{-\$452.80}{1,540} = -0.2940, \text{ or } -29.4\%$$

c. In this case, Mike is borrowing half of the cost of the stock. His increased borrowing should result in greater enhancement to his return if he sells the stock at a gain but, also, in greater loss if he sells the shares at a price below the original purchase price. Using formula 16.1:

Sale at $30	**Sale at $18**
SP = $3,000	$1,800
II = 1,100	1,100
D = 0	0
LP = 1,188	1,188

Again, note that the LP includes 8% interest, this time on a loan of $1,100.

Sale at $30:

$$R = \frac{(\$3,000 - \$1,100 + 0 - \$1,188)}{1,100}$$

$$= \frac{\$712}{1,100} = 0.6473, \text{ or } 64.73\%$$

Sale at $18:

$$R = \frac{(\$1,800 - \$1,100 + 0 - \$1,188)}{1,100}$$

$$= \frac{-\$488}{1,100} = -0.4436, \text{ or } -44.36\%$$

ST 16–2

a. The market order would have filled at $21.50 for a total of $2,150. The limit at $20 would have filled for a total of $2,000. The limit at $19 would not have filled because the stock did not trade that low. Two hundred shares would have been bought for ($2,150 + $2,000) = $4,150.00.

b. The market order would have filled at $20 for a total of $2,000. The limit order at $20 also would have filled at $20 for a total of $2,000. The limit order at $19 would have filled at $19 for a total of $1,900. Three hundred shares would have been bought for ($2,000 + $2,000 + $1,900) = $5,900.

c. The market order would have filled at $22 for a total of $2,200. Neither of the limit orders would have filled because the stock never traded below $22.

d. One obvious disadvantage that the club accepted when it decided to do the experiment is that three orders will carry a higher total commission cost than one order for the total of the shares. However, the club hoped to make up for the extra commissions with cost-per-share savings.

   a. The use of limit orders saved club members $150 on the 100 shares bought at $20 over the 100 shares bought at $21.50. However, the use of a low price limit on the $19 order shut them out of the opportunity to buy the third round lot.

   b. The use of limit orders saved the club $100 on the $19 limit order over the 200 shares bought at $20 on the $20 limit and the market orders.

   c. The use of limit orders may have cost club members the opportunity to buy more than 100 shares of this stock at a time when its price is rising. There is the possibility that they will not see prices this low again.

Chapter 17

ST 17–1 a. With a rise in interest rates the consumer demand for homes and cars will decline. This will cause a decline in the demand for Savannah's carpets for homes and cars. It is less clear what will happen to the demand for carpets for businesses and airplanes, as well as the demand for industrial upholstery.

   b. Savannah's suppliers would include manufacturers of industrial fibers, threads, backings, fabric treatments, dyes, adhesives, and other components of carpeting and upholstery. Also affected would be manufacturers of the tubes that fabric is wrapped around and of shipping cartons, as well as trucking and rail firms that carried the product to market and the utilities that supplied the power to Savannah's operation.

   c. Any firm that made component parts for vehicles or supplies for home building would be in a situation similar to Savannah's.

ST 17–2 a. At an exchange rate of $0.01 US per yen, the Japanese watch costs $(32,000 \times 0.01) = \$320.00$ US. A retail price of $450 represents a $[(\$450/320) - 1] = 40.63\%$ mark-up.

   b. At an exchange rate of $.012 US per yen, the Japanese watch would cost $(32,000 \times 0.012) = \$384.00$ each. If Allman's maintains its mark-up, it will price the watch at $[\$384.00 \times (1 + 0.4063)] = \$540.02$.

    c. At an exchange rate of $1.00 US per euro, the Swiss watch costs $320, the same as the Japanese watch in part **a.** A retail price of $450.00 represents a 40.63% mark-up.

    d. At an exchange rate of $.98 US per euro, the Swiss watch would cost $(320 \times 0.98) = \$313.60$. If Allman's maintains its mark-up, it will price the watch at $[\$313.60 \times (1 + 0.4063)] = \$441.02$.

    e. Allman's would change prices frequently if it maintained strict adherence to its mark-up. That probably would upset customers and undermine the credibility of the store. The consequences of maintaining a $450 price for both watches are a significantly lower margin on the Japanese watch and a somewhat higher margin on the Swiss watch. Overall, if it sold equal amounts of both watches, Allman's profit margin would be decreased.

Chapter 18

ST 18–1   **a.** With reported earnings per share of $2.45 and Jen's researched P/E ratio of 21, an estimate of price per share is calculated by multiplying the trailing earnings by the P/E.

$$(\$2.45) \times (21) = \$51.45$$

    b. If earnings per share grow at 40%, then next year's earnings per share will be $(\$2.45) \times (1 + 0.40) = \$3.43$. A price estimate based on these forward earnings per share is calculated by multiplying them by the P/E ratio that Jen's research came up with, 21.

$$\$3.43) \times (21) = \$\$72.03$$

    c. Most investment professionals would agree that the value of a share of stock is tied to its future dividend and price appreciation potential and that these are tied to its earnings potential. Because investing is a forward-looking enterprise, it makes sense to use the price estimate based on forward earnings per share, $72.03.

    d. The stock currently is selling for $75.00 per share, above the price estimate based on forward earnings per share. At this point, it is not a good buy for Jen. However, she may wish to keep an eye on it for any dips below her estimated fair market value of $72.03. At that point, it would be a good buy.

ST 18–2   **a.** Using the assumptions of 8% sales growth, no change in interest expense, and taxation at 30%, a percent- of-sales method would adjust the cost of goods sold and operating expenses to be the same proportion of sales in the coming year as they were in the year already reported.

Pro-forma income statement for Atkinson, Inc. (000's)	
Sales (10,000) × (1 + 0.08) =	$10,800
less:	
cost of goods sold (10,800) × (0.60)	6,480
gross profit	4,320
less:	
operating expenses (10,800) × (0.28)	3,024
operating earnings	1,296
less:	
interest expense (unchanged)	250
earnings before tax	1,046
less:	
taxes @ 30%	313.80
net income	$ 732.20

b. The trailing earnings per share based on reported net income of $665,000 is as follows:

($665,000 / 150,000) = $4.43 per share

c. Forward earnings per share is based on the estimated net income of $732,200 and 150,000 shares.

($732,200 / 150,000) = $4.881

d. Trailing price per share = ($4.43) × (10) = $44.30
Forward price per share = ($4.881) × (10)
= $48.81

Chapter 19

ST 19–1 a. The coupon payment is the product of the coupon interest rate and the bond's par value.

(0.08625) × ($1,000) = $86.25 per bond per year

b. The market price of this bond is its listed quotation as a percent of its par value.

(1.035) × ($1,000) = $1,035.00 per bond

c. The current yield of a bond is its coupon payment per bond per year divided by its current price.

($86.25)/($1035) = 0.0833 which rounds to 8.3%

d. The quotation's listing of 124 indicates that 124 bonds, or a total of $124,000 par value, traded on the day reported.

e. The net change is +½, indicating that the bond price is (0.005) × ($1,000) = $5.00 higher than the previous day. It closed the previous day at $1,030.00.

ST 19–2 a. Refer to formula 19.1 for the basic layout of this calculation. The bonds were purchased for $408,000 ($P_t$). They were sold for $400,000 ($P_t + 1$), and the coupon interest received was one semi-annual payment $(0.06) \times (\$4000,000) \times (0.5) = \$12,000$.

$$\text{HPR} = \frac{\$400,000 - \$408,000 + \$12,000}{\$408,000} = 0.0098, \text{ or } .98\%$$

b. Annualizing this calculation is accomplished by dividing the holding period return by the number of years held, in this case 0.5 year.

$(0.0098)/(0.5) = 0.0196$, or 1.96%

c. In this case, P_t changes to \$420,000, but the other variables stay as they were in part **a.**

$$\text{HPR} = \frac{\$420,000 - \$408,000 + \$12,000}{\$408,000} = 0.0588, \text{ or } 5.88\%$$

d. Annualizing follows the same process as in part **b.**

$(0.0588)/(0.5) = 0.1176$, or 11.76%

Chapter 20

ST 20–1 **a.** Tom's investment per share is the NAV plus the sales charge.

$(\$11.225) + (\$11.225 \times 0.04) = \$11.674$

b. Tom's return for the year is

$$\frac{\$16.131 - \$11.674 + \$0.986}{\$11.674} = \frac{5.443}{11.674} = .4662$$

c. The fund's total return for the year based on NAV is

$$\frac{\$16.131 - \$11.225 + \$0.986}{\$11.225} = \frac{5.892}{11.225}$$

d. The performance figures reported in advertisements are based on net asset value, whereas his performance needs to account for the sales load that he paid. Over time, his performance figures will come closer to the advertised figures because the sales load will average out over longer periods of time. However, he will never be able to equal the advertised performance exactly.

ST 20–2 **a.** A slowing or reversal in economic growth has negative implications for the stock market. The fund's heavy allocation to stock would suffer if the economy were to slow or go into recession.

b. As interest rates fall, bond prices rise. This would be good for the bond portion of the fund.

c. A variety of recommendations are acceptable here as long as they reflect the general reasoning of the one that follows as to a decrease in stocks and an increase in bonds: "A recommendation to decrease the proportion of the fund in stocks and increase the proportion in bonds is justified by the anticipated changes in economic conditions and interest rates. Because not all of the advisors are expressing concern for the economy, it may be wise to implement the shift gradually rather than taking drastic action at this time. Therefore, I recommend 60% stock and 40% bonds, subject to regular review at our monthly meetings."

Chapter 21

ST 21–1 **a.** Laura's spread sheet contingency graph illustrates the cash flows of her call option investment under various possible price outcomes for Perspective stock.

Possible price of perspective at expiration date	Received from premium paid	Profit from exercising option	Investing in call option
$38	$3.50	—	−$3.50
$40	$3.50	0	−$3.50
$42	$3.50	$2.00	−$1.50
$44	$3.50	$4.00	+$ .50
$46	$3.50	$6.00	+$2.50
$48	$3.50	$8.00	+$4.50

b. Laura would break even at a price that would be equal to the exercise price plus the premium paid for the call option: [$40.00 + $3.50] = $43.50. At that price, the profit from investing in the call option is zero.

c. The return on exercise and sale at $42.00 per share is calculated by dividing the profit from investing in the call option, −$1.50, by the premium paid, $3.50.

$$-\$1.50/\$3.50 = -0.4286, \text{ or } -42.86\%$$

d. The return on exercise and sale at $46.00 per share is calculated by dividing the profit from investing in the call option, $2.50, by the premium paid, $3.50.

$$\$2.50/\$3.50 = 0.7143, \text{ or } 71.43\%$$

ST 21–2 **a.** With a settlement of 102, the Treasury Bond futures contract would be worth $(100,000) \times (1.02) = \$102,000.00$ on April 3. Settlement price can be viewed as the price per $100 par value or as a percent of the total par value.

b. To purchase an offsetting contract with a settlement of 99, Steve would have to pay $(100,000) \times (0.99) = \$99,000$.

c. Steve made a profit of [$102,000 − $99,000] = $3,000.
If the offsetting Treasury Bond futures contract had to be purchased at 105, Steve's transactions would have resulted in a loss of [$102,000 − $105,000] = −$3,000.

Chapter 22

ST 22–1 **a.** The conflicts of the five inside directors stem from their status as employees of the firm. Their decisions will be colored by concern for their own welfare and also for the welfare of colleagues and lower-level employees. Upper management would stand to lose more than compensation from employment; a job loss could translate to a loss of status and perquisites. The search for a comparable job could be time-consuming and expensive. New employment almost certainly would involve uprooting the family and moving to a new home. On the other hand, the inside board members, as owners of significant amounts of Fenstock shares, stand to profit from the sale of the company.

b. The quality that the outside directors most obviously would bring to the table is objectivity. Because they do not have the conflicts of interest that the inside directors have, they can evaluate the offer without personal baggage. Most outside directors are highly successful people with skills and experience that can prove valuable in negotiating the future of the corporation.

c. The action that would be in the best interests of Fenstock's shareholders is the one that will maximize their wealth over the long term. If the price offered for the company represents a maximization of shareholder wealth, then the correct action is to sell it. If Fenstock has opportunities and abilities that will result in a better outcome for shareholders over time, then the better action is to refuse the acquisition offer or to negotiate a sale price that fully reflects the value that the board sees in the firm.

d. The chairman of the board has a responsibility first to the shareholders. Therefore, she must take the action that, in her judgment, results in serving their best interests. Her reasoning will follow that outlined in part **c** of this exercise. Although she reserves her vote to break ties, she can influence the direction of board discussions and votes by her setting of meeting agendas and her moderating of discussions.

ST 22–2 a. It is hard to predict with certainty the outcome of a shareholder vote in this situation. Although the family controls 45% of the shares, there is no guarantee that all of them will follow the board's recommendation to vote against the acquisition. However, the board may be able to attract enough other votes against a takeover. The recommendation of the board carries a lot of weight with some stockholders. All things considered, a shareholder vote would probably be in favor of an acquisition.

b. It appears that Artemesia has pursued horticultural excellence for its own sake and sacrificed profitability for recognition in its field.

c. Dianthus is likely to replace most of Artemesia's management with its own people. Research would be cut back or redirected toward the production of commercially viable plant strains. It may be that the combined companies can benefit from marketing that emphasizes Artemesia's long record of scientific excellence, while promoting products that have broader market appeal.

d. Golden parachutes are special compensation packages that take effect if members of management are terminated as a result of a merger. Generally they involve bonus payments, stock options, and/or continuing perquisites. They make the process of changing management considerably more expensive but generally do not stand in the way of eventual management changes by the acquirer.

Appendix **C**

Fantasy Stock Market Game Web Exercise

In this web exercise, you will be competing with classmates in your own Fantasy Stock Market League. You and your fellow students will each be given $100,000 of Fantasy money to trade any of the more than 25,000 stocks and mutual funds listed on the New York, NASDAQ, American, and other U.S. stock exchanges. Fantasy Stock Market will keep track of each student's portfolio and rank the players in your League. You may trade as often or as little as you choose, but note that there is a trading charge of $19.95 every time you buy or sell stock.

Student Instructions

As the first step, you need to become a member of Fantasy Stock Market and choose to play in the Fantasy Stock Market League. Your instructor will provide you with a *League Name* and *League Password*. Once you are accepted as a member, you are ready to play the game.

To become a member:

Go to **www.fantasystockmarket.com** and click on **Sign Up to Play**. You will now have to enter the following information: e-mail address, password, name, address, telephone numbers, and fax number. Click on **Sign me up now**.

To play the game:

Go to **www.fantasystockmarket.com** and click on **League Play.** Click on **League member Log In.** Enter your e-mail address as your *Fantasy Login Name* and your *Password*. Remember that your password is case-sensitive. You will also be required to enter the *League Name* and *League Password* exactly as your instructor gave them to you. Click on **Enter your League.**

This is your account status page. To make a trade, Click on **Place a Trade** in the marginal menu. To buy or sell, you are required to enter the stock's *Ticker symbol,* the *number of shares* you want to trade, and whether you want to *buy* or *sell.* Once you make your selections, click **Submit Order.** After checking that the trade data is correct, click **Confirm Order.**

Researching the Market

Because this is a competitive game, before trading you may want to research the issue you are thinking about trading. Individual stock information can be obtained at www.stockfantasy.com. This site identifies, for game players, the most popular stocks, gives charts for stock performance, and lists stocks to watch. In addition, if you click on Stock Listings, you can obtain a list of various popular industry sectors. Click on the Industry Sector you prefer in order to access a list of companies in this particular sector. Click on Research for the company for which you want additional information. This page provides brokerage recommendations and earnings estimates. It also gives you an opportunity to select the firm's Balance Sheet, Income Statement, EPS Surprises, and For More Stock Information about your firm. Or click on Chart, which will give you the stock's price history.

Before making a decision, you may examine which sector of the U.S. economy you think will grow more rapidly than other sectors. To do this Go to www.hoovers.com and then click Site Map. Under the Companies & Industry portion of the index, you will find Industry Sectors and Industry Snapshots. Industry Sectors consists of 28 sectors that encompass more than 300 industries. It has related descriptions, analyses, news, industries, snapshot, and company lists. Industry Group Snapshots gives in-depth overviews of 45 various industry groups chosen on the basis of revenue and/or popularity.

The Hoover's sector analysis may suggest certain companies to you. To get more company-specific data, Go to quote.yahoo.com. Enter your company's symbol into the Quote box and click GO. Then click on Research. This site will give you brokerage recommendations; estimates of earnings per share; and earnings growth information for the firm, industry, and S&P 500. If you go back to the original quote page for your firm, you can get stock price charts for the following time periods: 1 day, 5 days, 3 months, 1 year, 2 years, and 5 years.

Good Luck!

Monthly Report to Instructor

After playing the game for a month, please submit to your instructor a report in which you respond to the following questions.

1. Summarize your transactions over the past month.
2. Calculate P/E ratios for each of the issues you purchased during the month.
3. Create a summary of your portfolio's performance in which you annualize the monthly return.
4. What are the three main factors that influenced the value of your portfolio?
5. In retrospect, what did you do well and what did you do poorly in your investments over the past month?
6. How is your portfolio performing compared to those of your classmates? What factors contribute to your classmates' returns being better, worse, or the same as yours?
7. What changes are you going to make in your investment strategy next month?

Credits

Index

Page numbers in *italics* indicate figures; page numbers followed by *n* indicate footnotes; page numbers followed by *t* indicate tables; marginal terms are **bold**.

743